The Holocaust Encyclopedia

The HOLOCAUST *Encyclopedia*

Walter Laqueur, *Editor*

Judith Tydor Baumel, *Associate Editor*

Yale University Press   New Haven and London

Set in Ehrhardt Roman types by The Composing Room of Michigan, Inc., Grand Rapids, Michigan. Printed in the United States of America by R.R. Donnelley & Sons, Willard, Ohio.

Maps by William L. Nelson.

Library of Congress catalog card number: 00–106567.
ISBN 0–300–08432–3.

A catalogue record for this book is available from the British Library.

The paper in this book meets the guidelines for permanence and durability of the Committee on Production Guidelines for Book Longevity of the Council on Library Resources.

10 9 8 7 6 5 4 3 2 1

Yale University Press gratefully acknowledges the generous financial support provided for this publication by The Righteous Persons Foundation, The Skirball Foundation, The Guinzburg Fund, The Scherman Foundation, the Daniel and Joanna S. Rose Fund, The Rodgers Family Foundation, the Ira and Leonore Gershwin Philanthropic Fund, the Lucius N. Littauer Foundation, Oscar and Marion Dystel, The "1939" Club—A Holocaust Survivor Organization, an anonymous donor, and another anonymous donor in memory of the Welt, Kohn, and Eisen family members who perished.

Advisory Board

Project Staff

Executive Editor	Jonathan Brent
Managing Editors	Richard Miller
	Robert T. Flynn
Development	Edward E. Anthony
Production Editor	Susan Laity
Assistant Editors	Manushag N. Powell
	Brooke Conti
Editorial Assistant	Aileen Novick
Illustrations Coordinator	Susan Smits
Illustrations Assistants	Nicholas Raposo
	Leonora Gibson
Production Manager	Paul Royster
Production Controller	Maureen Noonan
Designer	James J. Johnson

· · ·

The editors wish to express their gratitude to Wesley Fischer, Josef Michman, Sybil Milton, the late George Mosse, Dina Porat, Walter Reich, Joseph Spieler, John Thornton, and Eli Tzur for their advice on a variety of points connected with the work on this encyclopedia. They would also like to thank Sherry Foehr, Aileen Kent, the late Janet Langmaid, and Howard Sargent for editorial assistance and translations, and David Augustyn, Anne Beale, Larissa Dinsmore, James Lambert, Ada Muellner, Jennifer Quasdorff, Daniel Silverman, Piebe Teeboom, Jeff Thomas, and Will Young for research and secretarial assistance.

Yale University Press would like to thank Michael Berenbaum, Richard Breitman, and Lawrence L. Langer for their exceptional generosity in giving unstinting advice, assistance, and wise counsel throughout the duration of this project.

Contents

In Place of a Preface

There have been massacres of hundreds of thousands, even millions of people before and since World War II. Throughout history millions have died in various periods as the result of war, forced starvation, expulsion, and deportation. The present work limits itself to one period, the Third Reich. It concentrates on one group of persecutors, Nazi Germany and its collaborators, and, in the main, one set of victims, the Jews. For the Nazis, antisemitism leading to the physical elimination of the Jews was a central issue, and it is the central topic of this book.

The term *holocaust* is unfortunate because it means a religious sacrifice, usually made by burning. (Its origin is in the Greek word *holokauston,* "burnt whole.") Whatever the cause and the significance of the mass murder of Jews and others by the Nazi regime, it was not a sacrifice. In Europe the term appears less and less; *genocide* or the Hebrew *shoah* (the preferred term in Israel) are used instead. But in the English-speaking world the word is so deeply rooted that it is impractical to deviate from it.

Is it possible now, more than 50 years after the Holocaust, to write about it with authority? Many new facts became known during the last decade of the twentieth century, especially in the former Soviet Union and the countries of Eastern Europe, including the former East Germany. Not all archives have been opened or will be accessible in the foreseeable future, certainly not many of those of the KGB and the GRU (Soviet civil and military intelligence), which would enable us to know what was known in Moscow at the time about the situation in the occupied territories. The same is true, by and large, with regard to the archives of most secret services, including the British, and of the Vatican. Some of the relevant materials may have been destroyed. Even some of the Jewish archives have become available only recently, including the papers of Nathan Schwalb, who played a leading role among the Zionist emissaries in Switzerland. It is most unlikely, however, that any future revelations will necessitate a radical revision of the present picture. They may confirm what we now know, or may do away with certain dubious theories, but basic reappraisals seem unlikely. Thus it is doubtful that a written order by Adolf Hitler concerning the extermination of European Jewry will ever be found; there is no reason to assume that such an order ever existed in writing. The greater the crime, the less the likelihood that written evidence will be found at the highest level of government.

It seems equally improbable that the exact number of victims will ever be established. This will come as a surprise only to those unfamiliar with the limits of statistical accuracy in the twentieth century, especially in wartime. The German authorities to this day do not know the number of German wartime casualties, civilian and military, despite the fact that German statistics were more complete and reliable than those of other countries. Existing records were destroyed during the last phase of the war; of those hundreds of thousands of German soldiers listed as missing in action, many may have deserted or surrendered; others may have survived battle but died in captivity, or they may have returned to Germany after the war without having been registered. There is no possible way to know the exact number of victims of the Allied bombing of Dresden in 1945 because we do not know the number of residents at the time; many Dresdeners may have fled the town, and many refugees in transit from the East may have been trapped there. If this is true with regard to the vanquished, it is equally true concerning the victors: there are considerable discrepancies in the U.S. statistics concerning American losses in World War II.

As to the Jews of Central Europe, there is a fairly accurate accounting of how many were deported to the East in 1942 and 1943. But the great concentrations of European Jews were in Poland, the Baltic countries, and the former Soviet Union. As for Russia and Ukraine, only estimates exist; with regard to other Eastern European countries the statistics were often out of date and incomplete. Nor can the reports of the agencies engaged in the murder of Jews be implicitly trusted. Some of the records were destroyed; others were inaccurate in the first place. The assignment, after all, was to kill a maximum number of people in a minimum amount of time, rather than to submit accurate figures. And yet, in the final analysis, the margin of error cannot be more than 10–15 percent, and it might well be less. Thus the fact that emerged in the late 1980s that fewer Jews were killed in Auschwitz than earlier thought is not a matter of great overall significance affecting the total number of victims. It is now accepted that the number of those who died of starvation or froze to death was considerably higher than previously thought, so that the difference in the overall death toll may have been small. During the Third Reich between 5 million and 6 million Jews were killed.

If there are major differences among scholars, they concern interpretation rather than fact. Did the Nazis kill Jews for ideological reasons or, as a few argue, did the German leadership merely want to create open space for German settlers in Eastern Europe? When—if possible, on what date—was the decision taken to liquidate European Jewry? Was there a deliberate and consistent policy, or was the genocide accidental in the sense that general ideas led willy-nilly to engagement in mass murder which, once begun, the Nazi leaders had no alternative but to continue to the end? These and similar questions have been endlessly discussed. Once the spadework had been done, historians and social scientists tended to engage in reinterpretation and revision, usually with diminishing returns.

No concept or theory, however far-fetched, should be dismissed out of hand if it is buttressed by solid facts. But it is pointless to consider all of them of equal importance, to look for the historical truth somewhere in the middle, and to pursue these debates forever. Some historians will always come forward with new interpretations irrespective of the subject, sometimes for ideological reasons but, equally often, simply in order to say something new. Nor is there any purpose in engaging in lengthy debates with antisemites, who are beyond rational persuasion; as soon as one set of their arguments concerning the Holocaust is refuted, they will submit a new one. Furthermore, the differences between bona fide experts are often minute. The issue in these debates is not, for instance, whether a decision was made to exterminate European Jewry. The mass murder began with the invasion of the Soviet Union in June 1941, and as the

Einsatzgruppen (mobile killing units) were established at least two months earlier, this decision must have been made before April 1941. The question thus comes down to which month the decision was made.

Study of the Holocaust is a comparatively recent phenomenon. In the first years after the war hardly anyone engaged in the systematic collection of evidence on the mass murder, and no one was building museums or establishing memorials. The survivors had to recover physically and mentally from years of deprivation and suffering and to create a new existence for themselves outside of the displaced-persons camps in which they found themselves as the war ended. For the Allied governments the disaster was merely a footnote to the war; they were preoccupied with the problems of recovery and reconstruction.

In the Nuremberg war crimes trial and its successor trials, an enormous amount of material was amassed in thousands of files; this was the first serious attempt to sift through the evidence. But in the verdict the mass murder of the Jews did not play a central role. Those who had conceived the trial and were responsible for the way it was run did not have time, nor perhaps always the inclination, to familiarize themselves with the mountains of evidence that their research assistants had collected. For many years the Nuremberg files remained the main source for historians of the Holocaust, but to a wider public this material was largely unknown. The German public certainly failed to understand the enormity of the crimes. When four years after the end of the war some of the worst criminals—the commanders of the Einsatzgruppen, each of whom had been responsible for the murder of tens of thousands of persons—were sentenced to death at Landshut, there was a storm of indignation. Leaders of the churches called for clemency. In contrast, the Nuremberg trial and verdict hardly provoked any protests. It was widely believed that the defendants at Landshut had been soldiers who had merely done their duty and were now being harshly dealt with by a vindictive Allied justice. The fact that these men (and many others) had committed crimes unprecedented in modern times in the civilized world simply did not register.

For a variety of reasons the Allied governments had no interest in publicizing the cases of those of their subjects who had cooperated with the Nazis. In the Soviet Union initially there had been a great deal of cooperation with the German occupation forces, particularly in Ukraine. Although leading collaborators were punished, especially if they had been instrumental in the denunciation and murder of Communists, many others further down the line were treated with leniency. Those who had benefited by stealing property that had belonged to the Jews were usually not punished, nor did they have to return what had been looted. In Britain the administrators and the police in the Channel Islands (the only part of the United Kingdom occupied by the Germans) who had helped with the deportation of Jews continued to work in their old positions, and some of them even received the Order of the British Empire for the bravery they had shown in the war years.

On the Continent some governments (those of the Netherlands and Norway, for example) dealt harshly with collaborators; elsewhere (such as Austria and Italy) the purge was erratic or even farcical. In Germany under the Allied military administration, before 1953 war criminals were not brought to trial because the German authorities were not as yet empowered to do so; the issue hardly figured in the media and public consciousness. Elsewhere a few survivors of the camps wrote their memoirs, but there was little interest. The case of Primo Levi is typical. His first book was rejected by most Italian publishers; it was eventually brought out by a small publishing house, but of the 2,000 copies printed, half were not sold for a decade. *The Diary of Anne Frank* was published in the 1950s and became a huge success in the large American market almost from the beginning; eventually it was made into a Broadway play and a movie. But the diary was not a book about the Holocaust; rather it recorded the impressions and moods of a 13-year-old girl confined to a little room in Amsterdam. Only two major studies concerning the so-called Final Solution were published in the first 15 years after the war: Gerald Reitlinger's *Final Solution: The Attempt to Exterminate the Jews of Europe, 1939–45* (1953) and Léon Poliakov's *Bréviaire de la Haine* (1951; Harvest of Hate, 1954).

In the first years after World War II the Jewish community in Palestine was immersed in a political and military struggle for independence and, after the declaration of the state of Israel in 1948, in economic and social tasks including the absorption of the majority of the survivors of the Holocaust. Jews in the United States and Great Britain were preoccupied, like the rest of American and British society, with the transition from a war economy to a peacetime existence and the gradual return to a normal life. In the Soviet Union and the Communist countries of Eastern Europe the Jews found themselves the target of a new wave of antisemitism. Under such circumstances the publication of articles and books about the persecution and extermination of Jews during the war was unthinkable. There was in the immediate postwar era a coalescence of factors that contributed toward maintaining silence about the genocide: the beginning of the Cold War, the need to rebuild an economically and physically devastated continent, a bad conscience among those who had been involved in the execution of the Final Solution or had stood by and done nothing to save lives.

Even those who had actively resisted nazism inside Europe often tended to ignore the suffering of the Jews. As they saw it, the Jews had not been active fighters against nazism but were persecuted merely because of their race. Even the surviving Jews of Europe had other priorities than confronting the Holocaust. Their families, homes, and communities destroyed, they were faced with finding a place to live and a means—psychological as well as economic—of living. They were inclined to suppress memories of the horrors of the camps and ghettos and to focus on the future. The birth of the state of Israel, and the immediate threat to that country's continued existence from its Arab neighbors, also helped to deflect attention from the past.

Greater interest in the fate of European Jewry developed only in the 1960s, beginning with the trial of Adolf Eichmann in Jerusalem in 1961. Still, the hundreds of correspondents who streamed to Israel to cover the trial focused mainly on the dramatic circumstances of Eichmann's capture and on the spectacle in court. Although Yad Vashem, the memorial institution on Mount Herzl in Jerusalem, had been founded ten years earlier, few people paid much attention to it during the first decade of its existence, nor did the Holocaust figure prominently in Israeli textbooks.

German courts began to put war criminals on trial in the late 1950s, but it soon appeared that prosecutors were neither able nor, in many instances, willing to pursue those cases vigorously. Judges had to be found who were not implicated in the dispensations of Nazi justice, and a central coordination and research office had to be established in order to create the precondition for a successful prosecution. The great trials against those who had committed atrocities as part of Einsatzgruppen and in Auschwitz, Majdanek, and other camps got under way after 1960. Gradually public awareness was growing in Germany that during

World War II an extraordinary horror had taken place that was not yet common knowledge. But the public and the parliamentarians were by no means convinced that these cases had to be pursued, and on three occasions between 1965 and 1979 the West German parliament (*Bundestag*) debated whether there should be an amnesty. The accused were now old men; the witnesses had died, or their memories could no longer be trusted. In the end the amnesty was not passed, mainly because of the discovery of new evidence confirming the guilt of those under indictment. Even more decisive (although few mentioned it) was the showing of the television miniseries *Holocaust* (1979), which, though riddled with inaccuracies, personalized the tragedy and triggered public and private discussions of events that had earlier been ignored.

The West German trials dragged on for many years, and after the initial excitement they ceased to be a media event. It was obvious, furthermore, that the punishment could not possibly be commensurate with the crime; it was calculated that in some cases the murder of one person resulted in three minutes of imprisonment. And yet the overwhelming details of atrocities committed by the defendants made a lasting impression and helped a wider public to understand the enormity of Nazi crimes. This new willingness to confront a horrible past manifested itself in the erection of monuments and museums as well as in organized trips to Poland to visit the sites of ghettos and extermination camps, especially in the late 1980s and early 1990s.

Whereas in the immediate postwar periods very little had been done to document and commemorate the Holocaust, by the 1970s the field was becoming quite crowded. Some argued that the new initiatives would lead to a burial of memory rather than a revival of it and a true confrontation with the past; but these fears seemed to be misplaced, at least in the short run. Claude Lanzmann's nine-hour documentary *Shoah*, released in 1985, had a much greater impact on public consciousness throughout the West than had any earlier work. During the 1970s and 1980s much research was done on the Holocaust era, and important scholarly works as well as fictional treatments were published. Chairs in the field of Holocaust studies were established in several countries, and research institutes were founded that collected source material and launched oral history programs based on interviews with survivors.

This upsurge of interest was by no means universal but was confined to Western Europe and North America. In the Third World there was no interest in the fate of the Jews, a subject remote from the Asian and African experiences. In the Soviet Union and its Eastern European satellites commemorations of the Holocaust were not permitted; on the contrary, according to the Communist party line, the rich Jews and the Zionists were at least in part responsible for the tragedy. After the collapse of the Soviet empire the Jews who had lived within it were at liberty to talk and write about the Holocaust and to erect monuments in commemoration of the dead. But the interest of the non-Jewish population remained limited, be it because sections of the local population had collaborated with the Nazis, or because Eastern Europeans had also suffered grievously during the war, or because Russia and Eastern Europe in the 1990s faced a situation similar to that of Western Europe after 1945—a near-total preoccupation with reconstruction and survival. The neo-Nazis and their sympathizers claimed that the mass murders had never taken place, or that in any case no more than a handful of people had been killed.

In Western Europe too there was for decades considerable resistance to confronting the reality of the Final Solution. Neither the Roman Catholic nor the Protestant churches, nor even the International Red

Cross, thought that they had been guilty of major sins of commission or omission as far as the murder of Jews was concerned. There was hesitation to punish the guilty and to reward those who had helped the victims. Thus it took more than 50 years for the rehabilitation of a police officer in Sankt Gallen, Switzerland, who had lost his job because he had saved a few Jews. If the French leaders François Mittérrand and Jacques Chirac and President Franz Vranitzky of Austria made declarations expressing regret for the misdeeds of some of their countrymen in World War II, these were the exception rather than the rule. If there were from time to time complaints among Jews and non-Jews alike against an excessive preoccupation with the Holocaust, these admonitions, justified or not, could not possibly be directed against the overwhelming majority of humankind, which had never heard of the Holocaust and had no interest in the subject.

In those countries in which the Holocaust continues to be a major issue, it was probably inevitable that several decades were needed for a full confrontation with the past. Distance in time, moreover, often helps in reaching a balanced judgment, though whether this maxim applies to crimes of such magnitude is less certain. True, shock and pain may lead to exaggeration, but how much can one exaggerate the horrors of Auschwitz? Even if it is not true that soap was made out of Jewish corpses, as was sometimes claimed during the war, the victims were still murdered in ghastly circumstances.

As time passes, all kinds of innovative theories about the cause of the genocide are launched on the market of ideas. Hitler's pathological fear of bolshevism, or the German bureaucracy and social planners, or the modern scientific and technological age, is made responsible, rather than nazism. This is the price we are paying for the growing distance in time. Such theories would have been unthinkable immediately after the events they purport to account for, just as no one would have been taken seriously had they told those just liberated from the camps that their experience had been joyous and that they had merely imagined the horrors they had been through.

At a distance of more than half a century, a great deal of empathy and imagination is needed on the part of new generations even to begin to understand what happened to the Jews of Europe during World War II. Documents cannot possibly tell the full story; they do not smell, they do not starve or freeze, they are not afraid. It is only natural to ask why so few people saw the coming disaster, why more people did not try to escape in time, why there was not more resistance. These are rightful questions on the part of a younger generation that grew up in civilized and relatively free societies, and an enormous effort is needed to understand a world remote in time and distance. Today Hitler and nazism are known, at least in general outline, even to high school students. But in early 1938 the greatest scholars and statesmen did not predict the massacre of millions. Many Jews left Germany and Austria mainly because they faced economic ruin and social ostracism, because they were treated as pariahs. But they were not aware that they were escaping certain death. And even had they been aware, there was no country in the world willing—or, in the case of Palestine, granted the permission—to give them shelter. Even during the early stages of the war there was no valid reason to fear gassing and the death camps. Up to 1941 emigration continued from Nazi-occupied Europe, albeit on a small scale; and although the Jews were starved and mistreated, few as yet had been killed, and there had been no systematic massacres.

But why did the Jews not put up more resistance? The bulk of the Jewish population did not consist of able-bodied men and women who had received military training. Even young people were decimated by starvation and disease; not a few froze to death in the harsh winters, as they were allowed neither warm clothing nor heating. Millions of Russian soldiers had been taken prisoner and were later killed by the Germans; these were fighting men, and yet most of them offered no resistance. To expect that the Jews would have acted any differently shows a lack of imagination as well as a lack of understanding concerning the hostile conditions that made such resistance nearly impossible. This is not to say that Jews were right to serve as police in the ghettos or that no members of the Jewish councils (*Judenräte*) were traitors. But it is ahistorical, if not unethical and indecent, to pass judgment on the behavior of persons in the most extreme peril for their lives and the lives of their families in the 1940s from the vantage point of the present and with the benefit of hindsight.

These are just a few of the hurdles that the contemporary student of the Holocaust has to overcome in trying to understand the plight of people who were living and dying in conditions unprecedented in human history. I hope that the present work, which focuses on issues rather than personalities and the geography of the mass murder, will make a contribution to such an understanding, even though there are questions and problems to which we may never have answers.

This encyclopedia is the collective work of more than 100 authors from 11 countries. They include Jews and non-Jews, academics and eyewitnesses, young men and women who grew up in peace and relative security well after the events described in these pages, and older people who went through the inferno but, owing to good fortune, survived to see the stars again.

I dedicate this work to the memory of my parents, who were deported from Germany in June 1942 and were murdered that same month at Izbica Lubelska, a camp in Poland, and to the memory of all the other parents and children who perished.

Walter Laqueur

Chronology

1933

30 January: Adolf Hitler sworn in as chancellor of the German Republic.

1 February: President Paul von Hindenburg dissolves the Reichstag (the German parliament) and calls new elections.

27 February: **REICHSTAG FIRE**: When arson claims the parliament building in Berlin, Hitler issues an emergency order suspending civil rights and allowing a wave of terror and arrests throughout Germany.

5 March: The Nazi party wins 44 percent of the vote in parliamentary elections and is forced to form a coalition with the German National People's party (DNVP).

11 March: Storm troopers (Sturmabteilung, or SA) attack Jewish-owned department stores, beginning a wave of violence against Jews throughout Germany.

20 March: The first concentration camp in Germany, **DACHAU**, is established near Munich. Two days later the first prisoners, mainly German Communists and Socialists, arrive at the camp.

23 March: First working session of the new Reichstag. Hitler's government is granted the power to enact emergency decrees for a four-year period.

26 March: Hitler calls for a boycott of all Jewish businesses.

27 March: Mass rally of American Jews in Madison Square Garden, New York, calling for a counterboycott of German goods.

1 April: **NAZI BOYCOTT** of Jewish-owned businesses in Germany begins.

4 April: Robert Weltsch's article "Wear the Yellow Badge with Pride" appears in the German Jewish newspaper *Jüdische Rundschau.*

7 April: Laws enacted ordering the dismissal of non-Aryan civil servants and teachers and prohibiting the admission of non-Aryan lawyers to the bar.

13 April: Establishment of the Zentralausschuss für Hilfe und Aufbau (Central Committee of German Jews for Relief and Rehabilitation).

21 April: Prohibition of Jewish ritual slaughter.

25 April: Introduction of a quota system limiting the number of non-Aryan students in German schools and universities.

26 April: Establishment of the **GESTAPO** (Secret State Police) under Nazi control.

6 May: The Reichsbund Jüdischer Frontsoldaten (Union of Jewish Veterans) sends a letter to Hitler pledging its loyalty to Germany.

10 May: Nazis burn thousands of books that oppose nazism, that are written by Jews, or that are considered degenerate.

3 June–25 August: **TRANSFER (HAAVARA) AGREEMENT** negotiated between the German Finance Ministry and the Zionistische Vereinigung für Deutschland (German Zionist Federation), allowing Jews emigrating to Palestine to deposit their assets in Germany and receive pounds sterling upon arrival.

27 June: British Jewry holds anti-Nazi rally in London.

14 July: Nazi party declared the only legal political organization in Germany.

20 July: German government signs **REICH CONCORDAT** with the Vatican.

28 July: Martin Buber publishes an article in the *Journal of the Mannheim Jewish Study Institute* calling on Jews to return to an education based on Jewish learning as a way of preparing themselves for the coming trials.

7 August: German army officers prohibited from marrying non-Aryan women.

20 August: American Jewish Congress declares a boycott of German goods.

17 September: Establishment of the **REICHSVERTRETUNG DER DEUTSCHEN JUDEN** (Reich Representation of German Jews) under the leadership of Rabbi Leo Baeck. The Reichsvertretung calls on German Jews to demonstrate "unity and honor." It seeks to assure Jewish existence under an antisemitic regime, with activities covering all aspects of Jewish life and all sectors of the Jewish community, including education, occupational training, social welfare, and emigration assistance.

4 October: Propaganda Minister Joseph Goebbels issues a decree ordering the removal of non-Aryan editors from German newspapers.

14 October: Germany walks out of disarmament talks at the League of Nations.

19 October: Germany leaves the League of Nations.

1934

1 January: Zentralausschuss directs Jewish elementary schools to cover both Jewish and German subjects while also promoting Palestine, teaching Hebrew, and developing physical fitness.

26 January: Germany and Poland sign a 10-year non-aggression pact.

5 February: Non-Aryan medical students prohibited from taking state licensing examinations.

6 June: Nazi party intelligence services transferred to the Sicherheitsdienst (SD), leaving no other intelligence agencies in Germany.

30 June: **NIGHT OF THE LONG KNIVES**: Hitler orders Himmler to purge the SA leadership. Commander Ernst Röhm and other storm troopers murdered.

July: Beginning of illegal emigration from Central and Eastern Europe. Organized by Hehalutz and the Revisionist Zionist movements as a protest against British Palestinian immigration policy, it helped save thousands of Jews.

25 July: Chancellor Engelbert Dollfuss of Austria killed in an unsuccessful coup attempt by Austrian Nazis.

2 August: German president Hindenburg dies.

20 August: German officials and soldiers required to take an oath of personal loyalty and obedience to Adolf Hitler.

11 September: At Nazi party rally Hitler appears before 100,000 members of the SS and SA and justifies the purge of the SA, claiming that Röhm had planned a second revolution.

12 December: Bavarian justice minister Hans Frank appointed to Hitler's cabinet as minister without portfolio, charged with bringing German law into line with Nazi ideology.

1935

7 January: Italian fascist dictator Benito Mussolini and French foreign minister Pierre Laval sign an agreement between Italy and France, paving the way for cooperation in the event of action by Germany.

13 January: Following a plebiscite held under the auspices of the League of Nations, France returns the Saar region to Germany.

1 March: Germany takes possession of the Saar region. Almost all Jews in the region apply for French or Belgian citizenship.

16 March: Conscription reinstated in Germany in violation of the Treaty of Versailles.

21 May: Defense Law prohibits non-Aryans from enlisting in the German armed forces.

18 August: Civil marriages between Aryans and non-Aryans forbidden.

15 September: **NUREMBERG LAWS**: Reich Law of Citizenship and Law for the Protection of German Blood and Honor decreed at Nazi party rally in Nuremberg. They provide that only persons of "pure German blood" can be citizens, and prohibit marriage and extramarital relations between Jews and Germans.

3 October: Italy invades Ethiopia.

10 October: Rabbi Leo Baeck issues a prayer to be read on Yom Kippur pleading for divine mercy for the Jewish community and emphasizing the spiritual greatness of the Jews. The Gestapo bans the prayer and arrests Baeck.

1936

4 February: David Frankfurter assassinates the leader of the German Nazi organization in Switzerland, Wilhelm Gustloff, in protest against the persecution of Jews in Germany.

7 March: **INVASION OF THE RHINELAND**: German forces enter the Rhineland in violation of the Pact of Locarno and without any significant reaction by the major powers.

9 March: Pogrom against the Jews of Przytyk, Poland.

17 March: Demonstration of Jews and leftist Poles against the pogroms in Poland.

19 April: Outbreak of Arab Revolt (1936–39) in Palestine, leading to a substantial cut in Jewish immigration quotas.

5 May: Fall of Ethiopia to Italy.

17 June: Heinrich Himmler appointed chief of German police.

30 June: General strike of Polish Jewry in protest of antisemitism.

July: Intervention of Germany and Italy in Spain.

16 July: Outbreak of Spanish civil war (1936–39).

25 October: Rome-Berlin Axis agreement is signed.

25 November: Signing of Anti-Comintern Pact between Germany and Japan against the Soviet Union.

1937

30 January: Hitler associates Jews with Bolshevism.

16–22 February: Hermann Göring's visit to Poland results in closer relations between Poland and Germany.

15 March: Mass anti-Nazi rally in New York organized by the Joint Boycott Council.

21 March: Pope Pius XI issues a statement against racism and extreme nationalism.

16 July: **BUCHENWALD** concentration camp opens.

August: Some 350 attacks on Jews in Poland.

20 October: Anti-Jewish violence in Danzig.

25 November: Germany and Japan sign a military and political agreement.

28 December: Antisemitic government led by Prime Minister Octavian Goga installed in Romania.

1938

21 January: Romania nullifies minority rights of Jews and revokes citizenship of many Jews.

10 February: Following the enactment of antisemitic laws, King Carol II of Romania deposes Prime Minister Goga.

13 March: **THE ANSCHLUSS**: Germany incorporates Austria into the Reich.

28 March: Jewish community organizations no longer recognized as legal entities by the government.

26 April: **DECREE REGARDING THE REPORTING OF JEWISH PROPERTY** is issued in preparation for the confiscation of Jewish property in Germany.

16 May: The first group of Jews begins forced labor in **MAUTHAUSEN** concentration camp.

15 June: 1,500 German Jews imprisoned in concentration camps.

25 June: German Jewish doctors forbidden to treat Aryan patients.

6–15 July: **THE EVIAN CONFERENCE**, an international conference to discuss the refugee problem, is convened at Evian, France, but little is accomplished.

8 July: Great Synagogue in Munich demolished.

17 August: Jewish men in Germany required to add "Israel" to their name; Jewish women required to add "Sarah."

26 August: **ZENTRALSTELLE FÜR JÜDISCHE AUSWANDERUNG** (Central Office for Jewish Emigration) established in Vienna under Adolf Eichmann.

27 September: Jews prohibited from practicing law in Germany.

29 September: **MUNICH AGREEMENT**: England and France allow the annexation of parts of Czechoslovakia by Germany.

5 October: Passports of German Jews marked with the letter "J" for *Jude.*

6 October: **SUDETENLAND ANNEXED** by Germany. Czechoslovak Republic established, with autonomy for Slovakia.

8 October: Hlinka Guard established in Slovakia.

28 October: 15,000 Polish-born Jews expelled from Germany to Poland; most are interned in Zbaszyn.

7 November: In response to the 28 October expulsion, Herschel Grynszpan, a Polish-Jewish student, shoots Ernst vom Rath, a third secretary in the German embassy in Paris. Rath dies two days later.

9–10 November: **KRISTALLNACHT**: in retaliation for vom Rath's assassination, Goebbels instigates pogroms in Germany and Austria. In one night 267 synagogues are destroyed, 7,500 stores are looted, and 30,000 Jews are sent to concentration camps. Ninety-one Jews are killed.

10 November: Antisemitic racial laws issued in Italy.

12 November: German Jewry fined 1 billion Reichsmarks in the wake of Kristallnacht.

15 November: Jewish children prohibited from attending German schools.

December: Establishment of the **MOSSAD FOR ALIYAH B** (illegal immigration) to Palestine.

3 December: Göring issues **DECREE ON ELIMINATING THE JEWS FROM GERMAN ECONOMIC LIFE**.

1939

January: Beginning of illegal immigration to Palestine from Germany. By the end of 1940, 27,000 German Jews will have immigrated.

24 January: Göring creates the **REICHSZENTRALE FÜR JÜDISCHE AUSWANDERUNG** (Reich Central Office for Jewish Emigration). Heydrich is appointed head of the office.

30 January: In a Reichstag speech Hitler threatens to exterminate the Jewish race in Europe if world war should once again break out.

21 February: Ordinance issued calling for the confiscation of gold and other valuables belonging to Jews.

2 March: Pius XII assumes the papacy.

4 March: **DECREE REGARDING EMPLOYMENT OF JEWS** provides for the forced labor of Jews in Germany.

13 March: Hitler summons Slovak nationalist leaders Father Jozef Tiso and Ferdinand Durcansky and orders them to declare Slovak independence. The following day the new state of Slovakia is declared, to be ruled by a pro-Nazi puppet government.

15 March: **OCCUPATION OF PRAGUE** by German forces begins. Bohemia and Moravia are declared a protectorate, in which ethnic Germans become German citizens and Czech inhabitants are defined as protectorate nationals.

16 March: German racial laws are applied to the Protectorate of Bohemia and Moravia.

22 March: Germany annexes the autonomous region of Memel in Lithuania.

28 March: The Nationalists, led by Gen. Francisco Franco, march into Madrid, marking the victory of the fascist forces in the Spanish Civil War.

7 April: Italy invades Albania.

27 April: Conscription in Britain.

Hitler declares the nullification of the 1935 naval pact with Britain.

28 April: Germany cancels nonbelligerence pact with Poland.

30 April: Legislation enacted allowing for the eviction of Jews by German landlords.

3 May: Jews in Hungary are prohibited from becoming judges, lawyers, teachers, or members of parliament.

5 May: The Second Anti-Jewish Law in Hungary defines who is a Jew and restricts Jewish participation in the economy.

15 May: Establishment of the **RAVENSBRÜCK** concentration camp for women.

17 May: British government issues the **MACDONALD WHITE PAPER,** restricting Jewish immigration to Palestine.

21 June: German citizenship laws of 1935 are applied to the protectorate of Bohemia and Moravia.

4 July: Official foundation of the **REICHSVEREINIGUNG DER JUDEN IN DEUTSCHLAND** (Reich Association of Jews in Germany) under Nazi law. The Reichsvereinigung is charged with the administration of Jewish schools and financial support of poor Jews.

22 July: Reich Central Office for Jewish Immigration establishes an office in Prague with Adolf Eichmann as its director.

23 August: **NAZI-SOVIET NONAGGRESSION PACT**: German foreign minister Joachim von Ribbentrop and Soviet foreign minister Vyacheslav Molotov sign an agreement, scheduled to be in force for 10 years, according to which Poland is to be partitioned between Germany and the Soviet Union.

1 September: Invasion of Poland by Germany. Two million Jews come under Nazi rule; 100,000 Jews serve in the Polish army fighting the Germans.

2 September: The Danzig region comes under Nazi rule. **STUTTHOF** camp established east of Danzig.

3 September: Britain and France declare war on Germany.

5 September: The United States declares its neutrality in the war.

6 September: Occupation of Kraków. SS Einsatzgruppen begin mass shootings of Jews.

7 September: Warsaw city government flees to Lublin.

8 September: Occupation of Lodz, Radom, and Tarnow.

9 September: The Gestapo decrees that Polish Jews in Germany are to be deported to Dachau.

11 September: Polish supreme commander declares that Warsaw is to be defended to the last drop of blood. Thousands of residents flee the city.

12 September: German Luftwaffe (air force) commences bombing of Warsaw.

13 September: Jewish quarter of Warsaw heavily bombed on eve of Rosh Hashanah (Jewish New Year).

15 September: Jews in Germany ordered off the streets after 8:00 p.m.

17 September: Red Army invades Poland.

18 September: Occupation of Lublin. Jews are seized for forced labor, and Jewish property is confiscated. Jews ordered to wear the yellow star. Synagogue services are outlawed and several synagogues destroyed.

19 September: Red Army occupies Vilna, home of 55,000 Jews.

21 September: Heydrich orders that Jews living in the parts of Poland to be annexed to Germany are to be expelled eastward and concentrated in communities of at least 500 near railroad tracks. Large communities are ordered to appoint a Jewish council (Judenrat) to be responsible for resettled Jews.

25 September: Heavy artillery bombardment of Jewish neighborhoods of Warsaw on Yom Kippur.

27 September: **REICHSSICHERHEITSHAUPTAMT** (Reich Security Main Office) established.

28 September: Warsaw surrenders.

29 September: **PARTITION OF POLAND** between Germany and the Soviet Union; Germany occupies Warsaw. Jews are attacked in the streets, seized for forced labor, and removed from food lines. Jewish schools are closed. Nazis murder thousands of mental patients in Reich-incorporated Poland as part of its so-called euthanasia program.

1 October: Polish government-in-exile established in Paris.

4 October: **WARSAW JUDENRAT ESTABLISHED** by Adam Czerniakow under orders from the Germans.

5 October: Poland surrenders.

6 October: Eichmann instructed to arrange for the "resettlement" of 80,000 Jews from Upper Silesia within the area which would become the Generalgouvernement.

7 October: Eichmann prepares the deportation of Vienna's Jewish community to the Lublin district.

8 October: **FIRST JEWISH GHETTO ESTABLISHED**, in Piotrkow Trybunalski. Large areas of western Poland are incorporated into the Third Reich.

10 October: Soviet Union transfers Vilna and the Vilna district to Lithuania.

13 October: Mordechai Chaim Rumkowski ordered to establish a Jewish council in Lodz.

20 October: Jews deported from Vienna and Katowice to the Lublin district as part of the Nisko Plan to form a Lublin agricultural reserve for Jewish laborers.

26 October: **GENERALGOUVERNEMENT ESTABLISHED**: the civil administration for those parts of Poland not incorporated in the Reich. Hans Frank is appointed governor-general and decrees that all Jews aged 14 to 60 must serve two years of forced labor.

29 October: Under Nazi orders the Warsaw Judenrat conducts a census of the city's Jewish population.

4 November: The United States allows the shipment of weapons to Britain in return for cash.

9 November: Lodz incorporated into the German Reich.

15–17 November: Destruction of all synagogues in Lodz.

20 November: Orders issued to arrest all Gypsies in Germany and deport them to concentration camps.

23 November: Frank orders all Jews in the Generalgouvernement to wear yellow stars and to mark Jewish businesses with yellow stars.

29 November: Himmler orders that Jews refusing deportation be put to death.

30 November: Soviet Union invades Finland.

2 December: Nazis begin using gas vans to murder mental patients.

14 December: League of Nations expels the Soviet Union.

Unemployed Jewish teachers in Warsaw organize to teach small groups of children in their homes.

18 December: Nazis cut food rations for Jews in Germany.

1940

January–February: Start of underground activities by Jewish youth movements in Poland.

1 January: Ovens and crematoriums installed at Buchenwald concentration camp.

5 January: Jews in the Generalgouvernement prohibited from changing their residence or leaving their homes between 9:00 p.m. and 5:00 a.m.

20 January: Judenrat established in Lublin.

24 January: Frank orders the registration of Jewish property in the Generalgouvernement.

26 January: Warsaw Judenrat ordered to pay a fine of 100,000 zloty for the beating of an ethnic German in Warsaw or face the execution of 100 Jews.

Continued deportations of Lodz community; 20,000 deported by 31 January.

2 February: Tax placed on Jews emigrating from Germany to finance Jewish emigration, Jewish schools, and Jewish relief.

8 February: **LODZ GHETTO ESTABLISHED.**

11 March: Order that the letter "J" be stamped on food ration cards held by Jews.

12 March: Soviet Union and Finland sign a peace treaty.

20 March: Transports arrive at **SACHSENHAUSEN** from Dachau and Flossenburg.

31 March: Polish youth beat up Jews and deface Jewish property. Nazis observe and take pictures.

9 April: **INVASION OF DENMARK AND NORWAY** by Germany.

12 April: Frank orders that Kraków be made *Judenrein* (free of Jews) by November.

25 April: Slovak parliament passes law calling for the confiscation of Jewish property.

27 April: **AUSCHWITZ ESTABLISHED**: Himmler orders the establishment of a large new concentration camp near the Polish town of Oswiecim to be known by its German name.

30 April: **LODZ GHETTO SEALED**, enclosing 164,000 Jews within 4 square kilometers.

Jews in the Generalgouvernement prohibited from using railroads.

May: Appearance of the Jewish underground periodicals *Dror*, published by Poale Zion, and *Bulletin*, published by the Bund.

4 May: Rudolf Höss appointed commandant of Auschwitz.

10 May: Germany invades Belgium, Luxembourg, and the Netherlands.

Neville Chamberlain resigns as prime minister of Great Britain and is replaced by Winston Churchill.

15 May: Nazis begin deporting Gypsies to ghettos in Poland.

The Netherlands surrenders.

17 May: **GERMANY INVADES FRANCE.**

25 May: Himmler recommends to Hitler that Polish Jewry be deported to Africa.

26 May: Evacuation of 338,226 Allied troops from Dunkirk begins.

28 May: Belgium surrenders.

9 June: Norway surrenders.

10 June: At the Topf works in Erfurt a model of an oven for incinerating human corpses is made.

Italy enters the war on the side of Germany.

14 June: Germany occupies Paris.

15 June: Soviet Union annexes the Baltic states.

16 June: **VICHY GOVERNMENT ESTABLISHED**: Marshal Philippe Pétain forms a collaborationist French government in Vichy.

17 June: Vichy government sets up forced labor camps in Morocco for European Jewish refugees.

22 June: France signs an armistice agreement with Germany.

24 June: France signs an armistice agreement with Italy.

28 June: Soviet Union annexes parts of Romania.

July: Rescue of 4,000 Polish Jews through Lithuania, the Soviet Union, and Japan begins.

1 July: Nazis begin gassing Jewish mental patients in Brandenburg.

12 July: Pierre Laval appointed prime minister of France.

16 July: Germany begins deporting the Jews of Alsace-Lorraine to southern France.

19 July: Telephones confiscated from Jews in Germany.

28 July: Jozef Tiso appointed president of autonomous National Socialist regime set up in Slovakia.

1 August: Frank issues a decree extending Nazi racial laws to the Generalgouvernement.

8 August: Beginning of the Battle of Britain. Four hundred German aircraft attack southern England.

15 August: **MADAGASCAR PLAN**: Eichmann dicloses plan to deport all European Jews to the island of Madagascar.

17 August: Mass demonstration staged by the starving inmates in the Lodz ghetto.

30 August: Hungary annexes northern Transylvania from Romania.

6 September: King Carol II flees Romania, and a new government is formed under Ion Antonescu. Fascist Iron Guard is the only legal party.

17 September: Confiscation of Jewish property in German-occupied Poland.

27 September: Signing of the **TRIPARTITE (AXIS) PACT** between Germany, Italy, and Japan.

3 October: First anti-Jewish laws enacted in Vichy France.

5 October: Law enacted calling for the confiscation of Jewish property in Romania.

12 October: **WARSAW GHETTO ESTABLISHED**: on Yom Kippur the Germans inform the Jews of Warsaw that a ghetto is to be established in the Jewish section.

16 October: Construction of the walls around the Warsaw ghetto begins.

18 October: Registration of Jewish property and businesses in occupied France.

22 October: Registration of Jewish businesses in the occupied Netherlands. Deportation of the Jews of Saarland, the Palatinate, and Baden to the Gurs transit camp in Vichy France.

28 October: Registration of Jewish property in occupied Belgium.

Italy invades Greece.

31 October: Anti-Jewish Vichy laws extended to Vichy-controlled Morocco.

4 November: Jewish civil servants in the Netherlands are dismissed by the Nazi occupation authorities.

15 November: **WARSAW GHETTO SEALED**, enclosing 450,000 Jews within 2.4 percent of the area of the city.

20 November: Hungary joins the Tripartite (Axis) Pact.

23 November: Romania joins the Tripartite Pact.

24 November: Slovakia joins the Tripartite Pact.

25 November: **SINKING OF THE *PATRIA*** in Haifa harbor. Some 250 illegal immigrants drown.

December: Emanuel Ringelblum establishes the underground archive **ONEG SHABBOS**, documenting Jewish life in the Warsaw ghetto.

9 December: Illegal immigrants from three ships on their way to Palestine deported to Mauritius.

1941

January: Two thousand die of starvation in the Warsaw ghetto.

4 January: Greek army advances into Albania, driving Italian forces from the border. Britain sends troops to Greece.

5 January: British forces occupy Bardia in Libya. Italian troops retreat to Tobruk.

6 January: President Franklin Roosevelt asks Congress to end the U.S. policy of nonintervention and to adopt the lend-lease program to anti-Axis countries.

Prisoner chamber orchestra plays for the first time at Auschwitz, accompanying departure and return of labor squads.

10 January: All Jews in the occupied Netherlands ordered to register.

11 January: Establishment of Coordination Committee in the Lodz ghetto between Socialists, Communists, and the Bund.

21 January: Attempted coup by the Iron Guard in Romania begins, accompanied by riots and massacres of Jews.

22 January: British forces occupy Tobruk.

1 February: Nazis begin deporting Jews to Warsaw ghetto.

5 February: Law for the Protection of the State in Romania makes Jews subject to double punishments.

17 February: Jews assigned racial definition in Bulgaria and their economic rights restricted.

Antonescu abolishes Romanian government and establishes a military dictatorship.

22 February: Nazis begin arresting Jewish males in Amsterdam and deporting them to Buchenwald.

25 February: Anti-Nazi strike in Amsterdam.

1 March: Himmler orders the construction of **BIRKE-NAU** camp at Auschwitz.

Bulgaria joins the Tripartite Pact.

2 March: German troops enter Bulgaria.

3 March: **KRAKÓW GHETTO ESTABLISHED**: some 20,000 Jews required to enter the ghetto by 20 March, when it is sealed.

Hitler issues the so-called Commissar Order to the Supreme Command, calling for liquidation of commissars and exempting German soldiers from the provisions of international law in the coming war against the Soviet Union.

11 March: U.S. Congress approves the **LEND-LEASE ACT** providing assistance for anti-Axis countries.

12 March: Confiscation of Jewish property in the Netherlands.

23 March: Himmler writes to Hitler, "I hope to see the very concept of Jewry completely obliterated."

25 March: Yugoslavia joins the Tripartite Pact.

27 March: Anti-Nazi coup by Yugoslav army officers, who repudiate the Tripartite Pact. Hitler decides to subdue Greece and Yugoslavia before invading the Soviet Union.

1 April: Jews in the Warsaw ghetto rounded up for forced labor.

6 April: Germany invades Greece and Yugoslavia.

7 April: Thirty thousand Jews of Radom placed in two ghettos.

9 April: Germany occupies Salonika (Thessaloníki), home to 50,000 Jews.

10 April: Zagreb occupied. Germany establishes a Croatian state with a fascist government. Anti-Jewish riots in Antwerp.

17 April: Yugoslavia surrenders.

20 April: First concentration camp in Yugoslavia established with 5,000 prisoners, including 500 Jews.

24 April: **LUBLIN GHETTO SEALED.**

15 May: Vichy France declares policy of collaboration with Nazi Germany.

Himmler approves use of Dachau prisoners in medical experiments.

Jews in Romania drafted for forced labor.

20 May: Circular issued to Gestapo prohibiting Jewish emigration from the Reich.

3 June: U.S. State Department institutes procedures discouraging refugees from German-occupied lands.

8 June: British forces, including the Palmach (commando unit of the Haganah in Palestine), invade Vichy Syria.

18 June: Turkey and Germany sign friendship treaty.

22 June: **OPERATION BARBAROSSA**: Germany invades the Soviet Union. Romania and Italy declare war on the Soviet Union.

Croatian Jews sent to concentration camps.

23 June: **EINSATZGRUPPEN** begin killings in the Soviet Union. Daily reports are submitted to Himmler.

24 June: Vilna and Kovno occupied by the German army. Within 48 hours the killing of Jews by Einsatzgruppen and local Lithuanians begins.

25 June: At Jassy 15,000 Jews murdered by the Romanian Iron Guard.

27 June: Einsatzgruppe C shoots 2,000 Jews at Lutsk with the help of local Ukrainians.

Hungary declares war on the Soviet Union.

28 June: Germans occupy Minsk.

30 June: Germans occupy Lvov. By 3 July, 4,000 Jews are killed.

July: Beginning of killings at Ponary outside Vilna. By July 1944 some 100,000 Jews will be murdered.

1 July: Germans occupy Riga. By the end of July 18,000 Jews are arrested and executed.

Einsatzgruppe D begins operations in Bessarabia. By the end of August at least 150,000 Jews are killed.

4 July: Vilna Judenrat established. In July 5,000 Jews are killed.

7 July: Seven thousand Jews shot at Lvov.

9 July: Germans occupy Zhitomir.

10 July: Vichy France surrenders in Syria.

17 July: Hitler gives Himmler full authority for mass murder in the German-occupied portions of the Soviet Union.

20 July: Ghetto established in Minsk to intern 100,000 Jews.

24 July: Ghetto established in Kishinev. Ten thousand Jews already killed.

25 July: Local Ukrainians launch pogrom against the Jews in Lvov and kill 2,000 in three days.

26 July: Jewish community of Vilna ordered to hand over 2 million rubles or the Judenrat will be shot. Only one-third of the money is raised, and two members of the council are shot.

31 July: Göring instructs Heydrich to prepare a plan for the so-called Final Solution of the Jewish problem.

1 August: Ghetto established at Bialystok. Fifty thousand Jews confined there.

2 August: Hungarian government promulgates racial laws prohibiting Jews from marrying non-Jews.

4 August: KOVNO GHETTO SEALED: 29,760 Jews live in the ghetto, enclosed by barbed wire.

5 August: Siege of Odessa. Eight thousand residents, mostly Jews, are shot.

6 August: Killing operations begin in Pinsk. Some 10,000 Jews are killed in three days.

14 August: President Roosevelt and Prime Minister Churchill sign the Atlantic Charter, expressing common interests and principles for the postwar period.

16 August: Bishop Bridges, the Catholic bishop of Kovno, forbids the clergy of Lithuania to aid Jews.

24 August: JEWISH ANTIFASCIST COMMITTEE ESTABLISHED in the Soviet Union.

27–28 August: KAMENETS-PODOLSK MASSACRE: 23,600 Jews are murdered; at least 14,000 of them had been deported from Hungary.

31 August: Completion of killing operation in Bessarabia. Between 150,000 and 200,000 Jews were murdered.

1 September: Nazi "euthanasia" program officially ends but continues unofficially. More than 70,000 persons are put to death in total.

Jews in Germany and Austria required to wear armbands with the Star of David.

Einsatzgruppen begin shooting Gypsies in Croatia.

3 September: First experimental gassings carried out at Auschwitz on Soviet prisoners of war.

3–5 September: VILNA GHETTOS ESTABLISHED: Two ghettos established and sealed off in Vilna.

8 September: SIEGE OF LENINGRAD begins.

12 September: Hitler orders that Leningrad be starved into submission.

15 September: Some 150,000 Jews deported from Bessarabia and Bukovina to Transnistria, where 90,000 will perish.

19 September: LIQUIDATION OF THE ZHITOMIR GHETTO: 10,000 Jews are killed.

German forces occupy Kiev.

27 September: Heydrich appointed governor of the Protectorate of Bohemia and Moravia.

29–30 September: BABI YAR MASSACRE: 33,771 Jews from Kiev killed at Babi Yar.

1 October: On Yom Kippur 3,000 Jews killed in Vilna.

2 October: German attack on Moscow begins.

4 October: Thousands of Jews without work permits removed from Kovno and killed at nearby "Ninth Fort."

8 October: Vitebsk ghetto liquidated. More than 16,000 Jews are killed. Construction begins on the Birkenau extermination camp at Auschwitz.

10 October: First conference on the "Solution of the Jewish Problem" convened at Prague. Heydrich and Eichmann are among those present.

11 October: Romanian authorities establish ghetto for 50,000 Jews in Cernauti.

12 October: German forces reach the outskirts of Moscow.

15 October: MASS DEPORTATIONS OF GERMAN JEWS BEGIN: German and Austrian Jews deported to Kovno, Lodz, Minsk, and Riga ghettos.

16 October: German forces occupy Odessa.

Deportations from Germany are extended to Warsaw and Lublin ghettos.

19 October: First deportations of Jews from Luxembourg to Lodz ghetto.

23 October: Nineteen thousand Jews killed at Odessa.

24 October: Romanian soldiers transport 20,000 Jews to Dalnik. Most are shot, and the rest are herded into warehouses, which are set on fire.

Eichmann approves plan to kill deported Jews in mobile gas vans on arrival in ghettos.

25 October: Armed Jewish resistance in the Smolensk district.

30 October: Germans begin deportation of the Jews of Bratislava.

1 November: Construction of the **BELZEC** extermination camp begins.

7 November: Einsatzgruppe C kills 21,000 Jews at Rovno.

7–9 November: Einsatzgruppe A kills 3,000 Jews in Latvia.

7–20 November: Einsatzgruppe B kills 19,000 Jews in Minsk.

10 November: First Jews from Hamburg arrive in Minsk ghetto.

20 November: **RUMBULA FOREST MASSACRE** begins outside Riga. Fifty thousand Jews will be killed.

24 November: Heydrich establishes **THERESIENSTADT** in Czechoslovakia as a "model camp."

25–29 November: Operation against German Jews in Kovno. In five days 4,934 Jews are killed.

Nazis establish the Association of Jews in Belgium to assist them in their treatment of the Jewish community. As a countermove, the underground Committee of Jewish Defense is established.

30 November–1 December: In Riga 10,000–15,000 Jews arrested and shot.

First transports arrive at **MAJDANEK** extermination camp.

6 December: Soviets begin Moscow counteroffensive.

7 December: **JAPANESE ATTACK PEARL HARBOR.**

Hitler issues **NIGHT AND FOG DECREE** to suppress resistance in Western Europe. Persons found to be endangering German security are to disappear without trace.

8 December: United States declares war on Japan.

First use of mobile gas vans at **CHELMNO** extermination camp.

11 December: Germany and Italy declare war on the United States.

13 December: Bulgaria and Hungary declare war on the United States.

21 December: More than 40,000 Jews shot at **BOG-DANOVKA** camp in Transnistria. By the end of December only 200 Jews remain alive at Bogdanovka.

22 December: Of the 57,000 Jews of Vilna, 33,500 have been killed, 12,000 with work permits remain in the ghetto, and 8,000 remain in hiding. The fate of the rest is unknown.

31 December: First partisan manifesto in Vilna declares that armed resistance is the proper response to the Germans.

1942

2 January: Western Crimea now declared *Judenrein.*

5 January: Jews in Germany required to hand in their winter clothing for the German war effort on the eastern front.

14 January: Deportation of Dutch Jews from Amsterdam begins.

16 January: Deportation of more than 10,000 Jews from Lodz to Chelmno. All will be gassed by 29 January.

20 January: **WANNSEE CONFERENCE:** Germans convene a conference at Wannsee outside Berlin to coordinate the so-called Final Solution of the Jewish problem.

21 January: United Partisan Organization established by 150 Zionists meeting in Vilna.

31 January: Einsatzgruppe A reports that to date 70,000 Latvian Jews have been killed; only 3,750 laborers remain alive.

8 February: First transport of Jews from Salonika to Auschwitz.

23 February: **SINKING OF THE *STRUMA*:** the refugee boat *Struma,* having been refused entry to Palestine or Turkey, is sunk off the Turkish coast by a Soviet submarine. All but one of the 768 Romanian Jews on board perish.

24 February: More than 30,000 Jews deported from Lodz ghetto to Chelmno. All will be gassed by 2 April.

1 March: Construction begins on Sobibor extermination camp in Poland.

13 March: S. B. Jacobson, a representative of the **JOINT DISTRIBUTION COMMITTEE** in Eastern Europe, reports at a New York press conference that the Germans have already killed 240,000 Jews in Ukraine alone.

14 March: *New York Times* publishes Jacobson's story on page 7.

17 March: Opening of the **BELZEC** extermination camp. Transports begin arriving within a few days carrying 30,000 from Lublin, 15,000 from Lvov, and 35,000 from elsewhere in the Lublin district.

20 March: Gas chambers operational in a farmhouse at **BIRKENAU** extermination camp.

26 March: Beginning of deportations of 60,000 Slovakian Jews.

28 March: First transport of French Jews to Auschwitz.

8 April: According to Einsatzgruppen reports, there are no longer any Jews in the Crimea.

29 April: Jews of the Netherlands are required to wear the yellow star.

30 April: Twenty thousand Jews of Pinsk required to establish a ghetto within 24 hours.

4 May: First **"SELECTION"** for gassing takes place at Auschwitz-Birkenau.

7 May: Opening of **SOBIBOR** extermination camp. By the end of the war, 250,000 Jews will be killed there.

18 May: *New York Times* publishes a report from Lisbon that more than 200,000 Jews have been shot by Germans in occupied Soviet territory.

27 May: Heydrich shot and fatally wounded in Prague.

Jews in occupied France and Belgium ordered to wear a yellow star.

2 June: British Broadcasting Corporation (BBC) reports that 700,000 Jews have been killed in occupied Poland. The *New York Times* carries the BBC report on 2 July.

4 June: Heydrich dies.

20 June: Germans begin deporting Jews from Vienna to Theresienstadt.

21 June: Germans take Tobruk from the British.

22 June: First transports from **DRANCY** camp in France to Auschwitz.

11 July: Nine thousand Greek Jews are drafted for forced labor.

16 July: Germans begin rounding up Jews in Paris.

19 July: Himmler orders the elimination of all Jews in the Generalgouvernement by the end of 1942.

20 July: Armed Jewish uprising at Nezvizh in Belarus.

21 July: **MADISON SQUARE GARDEN PROTEST**: a mass rally held in New York to protest the massacre of Jews in Poland.

22 July: **TREBLINKA** extermination camp completed. Beginning of mass deportations of Jews from Warsaw ghetto to Treblinka. More than 250,000 will be gassed by 12 September.

23 July: Adam Czerniakow, chairman of the Warsaw Judenrat, commits suicide rather than assist the Germans in deportations.

28 July: **JEWISH FIGHTING ORGANIZATION** (ZOB) formed in Warsaw.

4 August: Janusz Korczak and the children in his orphanage deported from the Warsaw ghetto to Treblinka, where all are gassed.

10 August: Deportations from Lvov ghetto to Belzec, where 50,000 Jews will be gassed by 23 August.

Jewish partisan brigade in Belarus under Yeheskel Atlas attacks a German garrison.

11 August: **RIEGNER TELEGRAM**: Gerhart Riegner of the World Jewish Congress sends news through the U.S. State Department for Rabbi Stephen Wise of German plans to annihilate Jews, but the department delays transmission until 28 August.

3 September: Armed Jewish resistance during liquidation of Lachva ghetto in Belarus.

Last deportations of Belgian nationals to **MALINES** camp in anticipation of transport to the East.

12 September: Battle of Stalingrad begins.

23 September: British counteroffensive at El Alamein begins.

24 September: Uprising during liquidation of Tuchin ghetto. Most Jews escape but are later caught and killed.

9 October: Italian racial laws enforced in Libya.

16 October: Jews of Rome arrested and deported to Auschwitz.

28 October: First deportations from Theresienstadt to Auschwitz.

29 October: Almost all Jews of Pinsk murdered.

1 November: First deportations from Bialystok to Treblinka.

2 November: British take El Alamein.

8 November: British and American forces invade North Africa.

9 November: Germany occupies Tunisia.

11 November: Germany occupies southern France.

19 November: Soviet counterattack near Stalingrad.

20 November: Deportation of 980 Jews from Munich to Riga.

25 November: First deportations of Jews from Norway to Auschwitz.

4 December: Council of Aid to Jews established in Poland.

6 December: Jews drafted for forced labor in Tunisia.

10 December: First transports of Jews from Germany to Auschwitz.

17 December: Allies condemn German policy of extermination.

23 December: Jewish Fighting Organization attacks German forces in Kraków.

1943

1 January: Dutch Jews prohibited from having private bank accounts.

9 January: Himmler tours the Warsaw ghetto, orders the deportation of another 8,000 Jews.

10 January: Jewish Fighting Organization and Zionist youth movements prepare for armed resistance in the Warsaw ghetto.

14 January: Roosevelt and Churchill meet at Casablanca, declare the unconditional surrender of Germany as the aim of the war.

18 January: Another round of deportations begins in the Warsaw ghetto. Jews led by Mordechai Anielewicz resist with pistol fire; most are killed by the Germans.

2 February: German 6th Army surrenders at Stalingrad.

5–12 February: Jews offer armed resistance to liquidation of the Bialystok ghetto. Germans deport 10,000 Jews from the ghetto to Treblinka, where they are gassed. Another 2,000 Jews are killed in the ghetto.

24 February: Ghetto established in Salonika.

26 February: First transport of Gypsies arrives in Auschwitz.

4 March: Jews of Thrace deported to Treblinka.

20 March: First deportations from Salonika to Auschwitz.

19 April: **BERMUDA CONFERENCE**: British and American representatives meet in Bermuda to propose means to rescue victims of the Nazis in Germany but arrive at no significant conclusions.

19 April–16 May: **WARSAW GHETTO UPRISING**: on Passover eve the Germans begin the liquidation of the Warsaw ghetto and meet with heavy armed resistance. Many Jews hide in underground bunkers. During the uprising more than 50,000 Jews are killed, and only a few survive in hiding.

20 April: First group of partisans escapes from Vilna ghetto into the forests.

7 May: Seven thousand Jews shot in Novogrudok ghetto.

8 May: Warsaw ghetto command bunker at Mila 18 falls.

13 May: Tunisia liberated.

18 May: Warsaw declared *Judenrein*.

24 May: Bulgarian government refuses to collaborate in the deportation of the Jews of Sofia and instead disperses them to the provinces.

1 June: **LIQUIDATION OF THE LVOV GHETTO** begins.

2 June: Nazis begin burning corpses in order to obliterate evidence of mass murder.

11 June: Himmler orders the liquidation of all ghettos in Poland.

21 June: Himmler orders the liquidation of all ghettos in the German-occupied Soviet Union.

28 June: All five crematoriums at Auschwitz-Birkenau completed by this date; 4,756 corpses can be burned in 24 hours.

5 July: Sobibor extermination camp converted into a concentration camp.

9 July: Allies invade Sicily.

25 July: Mussolini falls from power in Italy. Pietro Badoglio forms new government.

1 August: Germans begin final liquidation of ghettos in the Zaglembia region (Bedzin and Sosnowiec). Most of the Jews will be deported to Auschwitz. Jewish youth movements offer armed resistance.

2 August: **TREBLINKA UPRISING**: prisoners in Treblinka camp revolt against the guards. Most prisoners are shot; only 70 survive the rebellion.

15 August: Germans order the evacuation of the Bialystok ghetto.

16 August: As the Jews of Bialystok are reporting for deportation, the underground rises in rebellion.

18 August: Last of more than 43,000 Jews deported from Salonika arrive in Auschwitz.

20 August: Rebellion in Bialystok crushed by the Germans.

21 August: Deportation from Bialystok to Treblinka and Majdanek completed.

1 September: Unsuccessful attempt to rebel by Vilna underground.

5 September: Germans begin arresting Belgian Jews for deportation to Auschwitz.

Allies invade southern Italy.

8 September: Germans occupy Athens.

New Italian government signs an armistice agreement with the Allies.

Five organized groups leave the Vilna ghetto and join the partisans.

10 September: Germans occupy Rome.

11 September: Final liquidation of the Minsk ghetto begins.

23 September: **VILNA GHETTO LIQUIDATED.**

29 September: Prisoners of the Sonderkommando ordered to exhume 100,000 bodies at Babi Yar and burn them in order to hide all traces of mass murder.

1 October: **RESCUE OF DANISH JEWS**: in Denmark the Germans begin rounding up Jews for deportation. Many Danes, including King Christian, protest the action. The Danes organize the rescue of the Jews by sea to safety in Sweden. Altogether 7,220 out of 7,800 Danish Jews are saved.

3 October: Germans form a Sonderkommando in the area of Minsk to obliterate all traces of the murder of more than 40,000 Jews in the area.

8 October: On Yom Kippur several thousand Jews sent to the gas chambers at Birkenau.

Jewish partisan unit commanded by Josef Glazman in Vilna wiped out by the Germans.

9 October: Germans begin rounding up Jews in Trieste for deportation to Auschwitz.

13 October: Italy declares war on Germany.

14 October: **SOBIBOR UPRISING**: prisoners revolt at Sobibor extermination camp.

16 October: Germans arrest Jews in Rome.

18 October: More than 1,000 Jews deported from Rome to Auschwitz.

20 October: **UNITED NATIONS WAR CRIMES COMMISSION ESTABLISHED.**

25 October: Liberation of Dnepropetrovsk in Ukraine. From a prewar population of 80,000 Jews, only 15 remain.

3 November: Following the uprising at Sobibor, the Germans launch **OPERATION HARVEST FESTIVAL** to liquidate Poniatowa and Trawniki labor camps and Majdanek extermination camp. More than 40,000 Jews are killed, including 18,000 in one day at Majdanek.

6 November: Jews arrested in Florence, Milan, and Venice for deportation to Auschwitz.

Liberation of Kiev.

17 November: Jewish partisan unit liberates Jewish prisoners at Borshchev in Galicia.

28 November–1 December: **TEHRAN CONFERENCE**: Churchill, Roosevelt, and Josef Stalin meet at Tehran to discuss opening a second front against Germany and the future of Europe after the German defeat.

1 December: Italian **POLICE ORDER NO. 5** mandates that all Italian Jews be sent to concentration camps.

1944

16 January: U.S. Treasury Department official Josiah Dubois reports to the White House on the State Department's attempt to suppress information on the Final Solution.

Gen. Dwight D. Eisenhower appointed commander of Allied forces in Europe.

26 January: Roosevelt establishes the **WAR REFUGEE BOARD** (WRB), charged with "taking all measures within its power to rescue the victims of enemy oppression who are in imminent danger of death."

2 February: The WRB proposes that the United States urge Spain to relax its border restrictions in order to receive refugees. The U.S. ambassador to Spain refuses to implement the plan.

25 February: Deportations of remnant of Amsterdam Jewish community to Auschwitz.

27 February: Siege of Leningrad comes to an end.

9 March: Himmler agrees to Göring's request to use concentration camp inmates as slave laborers in the German war effort.

22 March: Germans establish a new government in Hungary under Döme Sztojay.

24 March: Roosevelt warns Hungarian government against taking harsh measures against the Jews.

5 April: Hungarian Jews required to wear a yellow Star of David.

7 April: **AUSCHWITZ PROTOCOLS**: two Jewish prisoners escape from Auschwitz and pass on to the papal representative in Slovakia a detailed report on the killings in the camp.

14 April: Allied air reconnaissance photographs industrial plants at Auschwitz in order to plan the bombing of German industry, but no photographs are taken of the extermination facilities at Birkenau.

16 April: Hungarian government orders the registration of all Jews and the confiscation of their property.

25 April: **"BLOOD FOR TRUCKS"**: Eichmann negotiates with Joel Brand of the Jewish Relief and Rescue Committee of Budapest for the release of Hungarian Jews in exchange for 10,000 trucks. The proposal is soon abandoned.

28 April: First Hungarian Jewish prisoners sent to Auschwitz.

3 May: Jews of northern Transylvania are deported to ghettos.

4 May: Plans made at a conference in Vienna for the total deportation of Hungarian Jewry.

15 May: Germans begin mass deportations of Hungarian Jewry. By 9 July, 454,551 will have been deported in 147 trains; most will be gassed at Auschwitz-Birkenau.

16 May: German attempt to liquidate the Gypsies at Auschwitz fails owing to Gypsy resistance.

4 June: American forces occupy Rome.

6 June: **D-DAY**: Allied forces land in Normandy, France.

9 June: Arrest of Palestinian paratrooper Hannah Szenes in Hungary.

17 June: Jews of Budapest confined to specially marked "Jewish buildings."

19 June: Jewish Agency representative in Hungary, Moshe Krausz, sends a shortened version of the Auschwitz Protocols to Western embassies in Switzerland.

23 June: Red Cross representatives inspect Theresienstadt and declare that the Jewish inmates are being treated humanely. Over the previous months, in preparation for the visit, the Nazis had cleaned up the camp, built false storefronts, and rehearsed interviews with inmates.

26 June: Allied air reconnaissance photos of Auschwitz reveal the whole camp, including gas chambers and crematoriums.

29 June: U.S. War Department rejects request to bomb extermination facilities at Auschwitz, on the grounds that it would be a diversion from the war effort.

5 July: Liberation of Minsk. Only a few Jews remain out of the prewar community of 80,000.

7 July: In response to international pressure the Hungarian government temporarily halts deportations to Auschwitz.

8 July: **KOVNO GHETTO LIQUIDATED.**

9 July: Swedish diplomat Raoul Wallenberg arrives in Budapest on mission to aid Jews.

15 July: **LIBERATION OF VILNA**: Jewish partisans in Rudninkai Forest take part in the battles. Out of 37,000 Jews in Vilna in June 1941 only 2,500 remain alive.

19 July: Eichmann has 1,450 Jews deported to Auschwitz against the will of the Hungarian regent Miklós Horthy.

20 July: **JULY PLOT**: German army officers attempt unsuccessfully to assassinate Hitler, take over the government, and sue for peace.

Two thousand Jews deported from the island of Rhodes to Auschwitz.

24 July: **LIBERATION OF MAJDANEK**: the Red Army liberates the extermination camp and finds masses of corpses.

Liberation of Lublin.

27 July: Liberation of Lvov. No Jews are found alive in the city, which had a prewar Jewish population of 110,000.

31 July: American forces break through German lines at Avranche in France.

1 August: Beginning of Polish uprising in Warsaw.

Liberation of Kovno. Only 90 Jews remain alive in the city.

7–30 August: **LIQUIDATION OF THE LODZ GHETTO** and deportation of 74,000 Jews to Auschwitz.

14 August: U.S. War Department insists that it cannot bomb Auschwitz without the diversion of considerable air forces. At the same time, German industrial installations eight kilometers from Auschwitz are bombed.

25 August: **LIBERATION OF PARIS.**

U.S. air reconnaissance takes photographs of industrial installations at Auschwitz. The pictures also show prisoners being marched to the gas chambers.

28 August: Beginning of the Slovak national uprising.

3 September: Liberation of Brussels. More than 27,000 Jews remain alive, many in hiding.

4 September: Liberation of Antwerp. Only a small number of Jews left alive out of a prewar population of 50,000.

3 October: Polish uprising in Warsaw crushed.

7 October: **SONDERKOMMANDO UPRISING AT AUSCHWITZ:** Crematorium IV is burned.

13 October: Liberation of Riga.

20 October: Liberation of Belgrade.

1 November: Jewish Brigade of British Army leaves for Italian front.

2 November: Germans discontinue gassings at Auschwitz and begin to hide signs of mass murder.

4 November: Meeting between Jewish, Nazi, and Allied leaders in Switzerland concerning rescue of Hungarian Jews.

7 November: Hannah Szenes executed in Budapest.

8 November: Deportations from Budapest resume with death march to Austrian border. Wallenberg secures release of those with a Swedish protective pass (*Schutzpass*).

12 November: Jews in Budapest with protective passes are assigned to special "protected houses."

13 November: Ghetto established in Budapest for unprotected Jews.

25–26 November: Germans dismantle Crematorium II at Auschwitz in an attempt to erase signs of mass murder.

15 December: Most inmates from Theresienstadt by now deported to Auschwitz. Jews from Slovakia are sent to Theresienstadt.

16 December: German forces launch a counteroffensive, the **BATTLE OF THE BULGE**, in southern Belgium with the aim of retaking the port of Antwerp.

1945

1 January: Otto Komoly, Zionist leader of the Hungarian Relief and Rescue Committee, murdered by the terror arm of the Hungarian fascist Arrow Cross party.

4 January: In Budapest the International Ghetto ordered to merge with the Central Ghetto.

5 January: **LAST TRANSPORT TO AUSCHWITZ:** five Jews arrive in Auschwitz from Berlin.

7 January: In Budapest, Wallenberg trades food to prevent the transfer of more Jews with foreign passports from the International Ghetto to the Central Ghetto.

9 January: Rudolf Kasztner, Zionist member of the Relief and Rescue Committee, meets in Vienna with a Nazi representative in an attempt to save Jewish survivors in the concentration camps.

10 January: Carl Burckhardt, the president of the International Red Cross, asks Jozef Tiso, the president of Slovakia, to halt the deportation of Jews. The latter answers that he does not have the power.

11 January: Arrow Cross gangs massacre staff and patients in a Jewish hospital in Budapest. Only the intervention of Wallenberg stops them from blowing up the Central Ghetto.

16 January: **INTERNATIONAL GHETTO IN BUDAPEST LIBERATED** by the Red Army. Wallenberg negotiates for the proper care of the inmates.

17 January: The Soviets, suspicious of Wallenberg's intentions, have the diplomat arrested. He is not seen again in the West.

LIBERATION OF WARSAW by the Red Army. Only a few Jews remain out of a population of 450,000 in 1942.

18 January: **EVACUATION OF AUSCHWITZ** begins. The Nazis begin the death march of 66,000 prisoners toward Germany. SS officers shoot prisoners too sick to participate in the death march. Soviets liberate Kraków.

19 January: **LIBERATION OF THE LODZ GHETTO** by the Red Army.

26–29 January: **KÖNIGSBERG DEATH MARCH** and **PALMNICKEN MASSACRE:** 7,000 inmates of Stutthof concentration camp are forced by German troops to march from the town of Königsberg to Palmnicken, in the Soviet Union. Some 3,000 die en route; the survivors are forced to flee into the icy Baltic Sea, where they are cut down by automatic weapons. Only a few survive; the Soviets later hide all traces of the massacre, which is not revealed until 1998.

27 January: **LIBERATION OF AUSCHWITZ** by the Red Army. The few remaining inmates are freed.

February–April: **DEATH MARCHES:** thousands of prisoners arrive at Bergen-Belsen at the end of a death march during which many thousands died or were killed.

1 February: Forty thousand prisoners forced to march from Gross-Rosen concentration camp to the German interior. Thousands die en route.

4 February: **YALTA CONFERENCE:** Churchill, Roosevelt, and Stalin meet at Yalta to discuss the political division of the postwar world.

13 February: Red Army completes liberation of Budapest. More than half of its prewar Jewish population remains alive either in the ghetto, with diplomatic protection, or in hiding.

7 March: American forces cross the Rhine.

16 March: Himmler prohibits murder or acts of atrocity against Jewish concentration camp prisoners.

19 March: Hitler orders the demolition of the German infrastructure so it will not fall into the victor's hands.

23 March: British forces cross the Rhine.

3 April: **LAST PRISONER ROLL CALL AT BUCHENWALD.** Over the next several days, prisoners are evacuated by forced march, and thousands perish.

11 April: **LIBERATION OF BUCHENWALD** by American troops. Most of the camp's SS guards have fled.

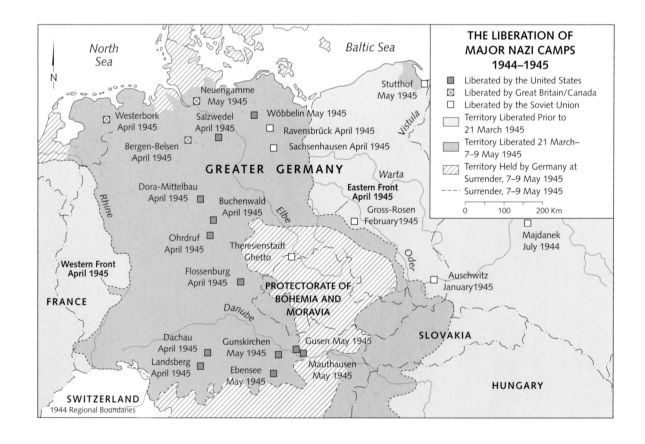

12 April: U.S. president Franklin Roosevelt dies. Vice-President Harry Truman becomes president.

13 April: Liberation of Vienna. Only 5,800 Jews remain out of a prewar population of 50,000.

15 April: **LIBERATION OF BERGEN-BELSEN** by British army. There are 58,000 survivors, most of them Jewish and in extremely poor health. In the coming weeks nearly 30,000 die from infectious diseases and the effects of chronic malnutrition.

20 April: American troops enter Nuremberg.

23 April: Soviet troops reach the outskirts of Berlin.

25 April: American and Soviet troops meet on the Elbe River.

26 April: Seven thousand prisoners at Dachau are force-marched south.

28 April: **FINAL GASSING AT MAUTHAUSEN.**

Mussolini shot by Italian partisans.

29 April: **LIBERATION OF DACHAU** by the Americans.

LIBERATION OF RAVENSBRÜCK by the Red Army.

30 April: Hitler and Eva Braun commit suicide. Adm. Karl Dönitz assumes command of German forces.

2 May: Soviet forces occupy Berlin.

3 May: Germans hand over Theresienstadt to the Red Cross.

5 May: **LIBERATION OF MAUTHAUSEN** by the Americans.

7 May: **GERMANY SURRENDERS** to the Allies. Eisenhower accepts unconditional surrender of Gen. Alfred Jodl.

8 May: **LIBERATION OF THERESIENSTADT** by the Red Army.

Rinat-ya Gorodnzik Robinson

Abbreviations and Acronyms

ACIP	Jewish Consistory of Paris	EDES	Ellenikes Dimokratikos Ethnikos Stratos (National Republican Greek Army)
AEG	Allgemeine Elektrizitätsgesellschaft		
AJ	Armée Juive	EIF	Eclaireurs Israélites de France (French-Jewish Scouts)
AJB	Association des Juifs de Belgique		
AK	Armia Krajowa (Home Army, Poland)	EJPD	Eidgenössisches Justiz- und Polizeidepartement (Confederal Justice and Police Department, Switzerland)
BBC	British Broadcasting Corporation		
B.C.E.	before the Christian era		
BOD	Board of Deputies (Great Britain)	ELAS	Ellenikos Laikos Apeletherotikos Stratos (Greek Popular Liberation Army)
BUF	British Union of Fascists		
CAR	Comité d'Aide aux Réfugiés (Refugee Aid Committee)	EPD	Eidgenössisches Politisches Departement (Confederal Political Department, Switzerland)
CBF	Central British Fund for the Relief of German Jewry		
		FI	Front d'Indépendance (National Front of Belgian Independence)
CCOJA	Commission Centrale des Organisations Juives d'Assistance		
		FPO	Fareynegte Partizaner Organizatsye (United Partisan Organization, Lithuania)
CDJ	Comité de Défense des Juifs (Jewish Defense Committee)		
		FS	Freiwillige Schutzstaffel (Slovakia)
C.E.	Christian era	FSJ(F)	Fédération des Sociétés Juives (Federation of Jewish Societies [of France])
CGD	Comité Général de Défense (General Defense Committee)		
		FTP	Francs-Tireurs Partisans
CIMADE	Commission Inter-mouvements auprès des Evacués	HASAG	Hugo Schneider Aktiengesellschaft
		HG	Hlinka Guard (Slovakia)
CKZP	Centralny Komitet Zydow w Polsce (Central Committee of Jews in Poland)	HIAS	Hebrew Sheltering and Immigrant Aid Society (New York)
CNR	Conseil National de la Résistance (National Resistance Council)	HICEM	Umbrella organization composed of HIAS, ICA, and Emigdirekt (Berlin aid society)
COMASEBIT	Comitato Assistenza Ebrei in Italia (Italian Jewish Aid Committee)	HO	Home Office (Great Britain)
		HSLS	Hlinkova Slovenska Ludova Strana (Andrej Hlinka's Slovak People's party)
CRIF	Conseil Représentatif des Israélites de France (Representative Council of French Jews)	HSSPF	Höhere SS- und Polizeiführer (Higher SS and Police Leader / Leaders)
CV	Centralverein	HUTA	Hoch und Tiefbau Aktiengesellschaft
DAP	Deutsche Arbeiterpartei (German Workers' Party)	ICA	Jewish Colonization Association (Paris)
		ICRC	International Committee of the Red Cross
		IGC	Inter-Governmental Committee on Refugees
DAW	Deutsche Ausrüstungswerke (German Armaments Work)	IKG	Israelitische Kultusgemeinde Wien
		IKL	Patriotic People's Movement (Finland)
DELASEM	Delegazione Assistenza Emigranti Ebrei (Aid Commission for Jewish Refugees)	IMT	International Military Tribunal
		IRO	International Refugee Organization
DNSAP	Danish National Socialist (Nazi) party	ISLD	Inter-Service Liaison Department (Great Britain)
DP	Displaced person		
EAM	Ethnikon Apeletherotikon Metopon (National Liberation Front)	IZL	Irgun Zvai Leumi

JAC	Jewish Antifacist Committee
JDC	(American Jewish) Joint Distribution Committee
JFC	Joint Foreign Committee
JJWB	Jung-Jüdischer Wanderbund
JNF	Jewish National Fund
JRSO	Jewish Restitution Successor Organization
JSS	Jüdische Soziale Selbsthilfe
JUS	Jüdische Unterstützungstelle
KdF	Kanzlei des Führers (Chancellery of the Führer)
KPD	Kommunistische Partei Deutschlands (German Communist Party)
LICA	International League against Antisemitism
MBF	Militärbefehlshaber in Frankreich (military command in France)
MIT	Munich Jewish Theater
MOI	Main d'Oeuvre Immigrée (Immigrant Workers Organization)
MP	Military Police
MUR	Mouvements Unis de la Résistance (United Resistance Movements)
NATO	North Atlantic Treaty Organization
NKVD	Narodnyi komissariat vnutrennikh del (People's Commissariat of Internal Affairs)
NSB	National Socialist Movement (Netherlands)
NSDAP	Nationalsozialistische Deutsche Arbeiterpartei (National Socialist German Workers' [Nazi] party)
NSZ	Narodowe Sily Zbrojne (National Armed Forces, Poland)
NZO	New Zionist Organization
OJC	Jewish Fighters Organization (France)
OMGUS	U.S. Office of the Military Government for Germany
ONE	National Committee for the Child (Belgium)
ORT	Institution for Vocational Guidance and Training
OSE	Oeuvre de Secours aux Enfants (Children's Aid)
OSI	Office of Special Investigations
OSS	Office of Strategic Services
OUN	Organization of Ukrainian Nationalists
POW	prisoner of war
PPF	Parti Populaire Français
PPR	Polish Communist Party
PPS	Polska Partia Socjalistyczna (Polish Socialist party)
RAB	Reichsautobahn
RAF	Royal Air Force (Great Britain)

RCM	Refugee Children's Movement
RJF	Reichsbund Jüdischer Frontsoldaten (Jewish war veterans' union)
RLIN	Research Libraries Information Network
RNP	Rassemblement National Populaire
RPZ	Relief Council for Jews (Poland)
RSHA	Reichssicherheitshauptamt (Reich Security Main Office)
RSI	Repubblica Sociale Italiana (the Fascist state after 1943)
SA	Sturmabteilung (storm troopers)
SD	Sicherheitsdienst (security police)
SIG	Schweizerischer Israelitischer Gemeindebund (Swiss Israelite Community Association)
SKIF	Socialist Children's Association (Poland)
SNP	Swedish National Socialist party
SOE	Special Operations Executive (Great Britain)
SS	Schutzstaffel (Nazi protection squads)
UGIF	Union Générale des Israélites de France (General Union of French Jews)
UHU	Ustredny Hospodarsky Urad (Central Economic Office, Slovakia)
UJRE	Union des Juifs pour la Résistance et l'Entraide
UN	United Nations
UNRRA	United Nations Relief and Rehabilitation Administration
UPA	Ukrainian Insurgent Army
VEDAG	Vereinigte Dachpappenfabriken Aktiengesellschaft
VNV	Flemish National Movement
WJC	World Jewish Congress
WJRO	World Jewish Restitution Organization
WRB	War Refugee Board (U.S.)
WVHA	Wirtschafts- und Verwaltungshauptamt (Economic and Administrative Main Office)
ZO	Zionist Organization
ZOB	Zydowska Organizacja Bojowa (Jewish Fighting Organization)
ZS	Zentrale Stelle der Landesjustizverwaltungen zur Aufklärung Nationalsozialistischer Gewaltverbrechen (Central Office for the Prosecution of National Socialist Crimes)
ZTOS	Zydowski Towarzystwo Opieki Spolecznej (Jewish Mutual Aid Society, Poland)
ZVfD	Zionistische Vereinigung für Deutschland (German Zionist Federation)
ZZB	Zydowski Zwiazek Wojskowy (Jewish Military Union, Poland)

A

Agudat Israel [Society of Israel] Anti-Zionist movement, founded in 1912, which functioned as a political party of Orthodox Jewry in Poland and elsewhere in Europe. See ORTHODOX RELIGIOUS THOUGHT

Albania Nation on the western edge of the Balkan peninsula, home to a very small Jewish community (200 in 1930) before the Italian invasion on 7 April 1939. The Italian forces deported some Jews to Italy, but they and the Albanian population generally treated the Jews well, and many Jews from Germany and Yugoslavia sought refuge in Albania. After the German conquest of the other Balkan countries in 1941, the provinces of Kosovo and Cameria were separated from Yugoslavia and Greece, respectively, and annexed to Albania, thus placing ethnic Albanians under the control of Italy. At the behest of Germany, Italy deported the Jewish refugees held in the Pristina prison in Kosovo to Belgrade, where they were executed. Germany took control of the ethnic Albanian sector after the Italian surrender in 1943 and in 1944 transported about 400 Jews from Pristina to Bergen-Belsen, where approximately 300 died. A somewhat greater number, as well as a few hundred refugees, hid with the assistance of the local population and survived.

Algeria See NORTH AFRICA

Aliyah B (Bet) Organized, clandestine immigration of European Jews to Palestine, in order to circumvent British mandatory restrictions on Jewish immigration. See ILLEGAL IMMIGRATION

Althammer Satellite camp of Auschwitz, established in September 1944 near Katowice to supply slave labor in the construction of a power station. Most of the 500 Jewish prisoners died during a death march in January 1945 when the camp was evacuated.

American Jewish Committee Jewish organization founded in 1906. See AMERICAN JEWRY

American Jewish Congress Jewish organization founded in 1918. See AMERICAN JEWRY

American Jewry The reactions of American Jewry to the plight of European Jews under the Nazis were made known to the administration of President Franklin Roosevelt primarily through 300 national Jewish organizations, each one representing a particular constituency and ideology. Most suggestions for the rescue of European Jews from Nazi Germany and from German-occupied lands could be implemented only with government approval and through government action. Though linked, the response of the American Jewry should not be mistaken for the response of the reluctant American government, through which it had to act. American Jews possessed insufficient political power to change national priorities. In the 1930s, because of the Depression, maintaining restrictive barriers against mass immigration was a high priority of the U.S. government; later, winning the war in Europe in and the Pacific quickly, with as few casualties as possible, was the uppermost national goal. Saving the Jews of Europe remained a minor issue throughout those years.

When Hitler came to power in 1933, there were about 4.7 million Jews in the United States. Some 15 percent were foreign-born, mostly from Eastern Europe. About one quarter lived in the New York metropolitan area, which served as the cultural hub of American Jewry. On the eve of the Holocaust, the sons and daughters of East European Jewish immigrants were gaining a foothold in the American middle class and assuming leadership roles in the major American Jewish organizations. Jews had established a prominent place in the garment, jewelry, and motion-picture industries as well as a wide range of small businesses that formed a specialized ethnic economy. As more and more colleges and universities opened their doors to Jewish students, the number of Jewish doctors, lawyers, teachers, and social workers grew out of proportion to the representation of other ethnic groups in the professions.

The Jewish ethnic economy also served as the incubator of the Jewish labor movement, which was composed of a newspaper, *The Forward*; an umbrella organization for the locals, the United Hebrew Trades; and a fraternal order, the Workmen's Circle. The only sector of American society where Jews exercised real power, if only over other Jews, was in their labor unions. The Jewish labor movement was strengthened by the Roosevelt administration's friendly attitude toward organized labor. In 1934 the International Ladies Garment Workers and the Amalgamated Clothing Workers of America established the Jewish Labor Committee for the specific purpose of rescuing European labor leaders. Rescue agencies were also established by the Agudat branch of Orthodox Jewry and by those concerned about the fate of European artists, writers, and musicians.

During the Depression thousands of Jewish businesses failed, and for a time the Jewish unemployment rate outpaced that of the general U.S. population. Support from organized Jewish philanthropy, which had experienced rapid growth during the 1920s, also declined precipitously. The growing number of unemployed Jews were compelled to turn to the federal government for relief. That sudden change of fortune had a strong bearing on the American Jewish response to the crises faced by European Jewry. American Jews were hard pressed to extend financial aid to their European brethren. Local Jewish communities, many of whom were now saddled with heavy mortgages after a synagogue-building spree in the 1920s, did not welcome the arrival of dependent refugees. Hence the strategy of "ransoming" German and Austrian Jewry, entertained in Berlin, London, and Washington after the Anschluss of 1938 and shortly before the outbreak of war in 1939, was never realizable.

The Depression also affected American Jews' sense of security. Social and racial tensions at home and financial help from abroad fueled an antisemitism of unusual virulence. By 1936, 120 professional antisemitic organizations were active in every region of the country. This renewed antisemitism limited employment

opportunities for young Jews, especially in basic industries such as the railroads and public utilities. Bolstered, after 1938, by the radio broadcasts of a Catholic priest, Father Charles Coughlin, organized antisemitism appeared to be gaining sufficient influence to place a "Jewish question" on the American political agenda, as it already had in Germany, Poland, and Romania. The dread that what was happening to Jews in Europe could happen in the United States drove the American Jewish response.

Though outsiders viewed American Jewry as a single religious and ethnic community, it had in fact become extremely diverse. Its heterogeneity was advanced by the different terms and pace of acculturation of German-speaking Jewish immigrants from Central Europe, who came to America in the mid-nineteenth century, and Yiddish-speaking Eastern European immigrants, who began to settle in great numbers after 1870. The religious practices of Eastern European Jews were conservative and traditional, and therefore not easily adapted to fit the Protestant Christian culture of America. Aside from the different ways they came to terms with their religion, hostility toward the earlier immigrants from Germany and central Europe was fueled by differences in class and culture. The terms *uptown* for German Jews and *downtown* for Eastern European Jews are a shorthand way to state these differences. The primary difference is that "downtown" Jews continued to view themselves as a distinct and separate people and were more inclined to accept Zionism, which is based on the idea of a Jewish peoplehood. Also within each group there were numerous divisions based on political ideology. The only common ground among these groups was their commitment to the New Deal and their political support for the Roosevelt administration. American Jewish voters became the Democrats' most loyal constituency. After 1936, the Jewish electorate consistently gave Roosevelt around 90 percent of its votes.

The crisis in Europe, rather than drawing Jews together, seemed to bring these latent divisions to the surface. The assumption that during the Holocaust there existed an American Jewish community able to speak to national leaders with one voice was far removed from reality. American Jewry was a community in name only.

The proliferation of Jewish organizations could easily be mistaken for a sign of communal cohesion. The multiplicity of organizations reflected the many conflicting ideological positions and interests among American Jews. Each faction—whether Zionist or socialist, whether Reform, Conservative, or Orthodox—maintained a full panoply of organizations to serve the social, economic, and cultural needs of its adherents. The American Jewish Committee, for example, represented the views of a much-diminished Reform, non-Zionist constituency, while the more militant American Jewish Congress acted as the secular pro-Zionist voice of the descendants of the "downtown" Jews of Eastern Europe.

Conflict arose over how best to respond to the Nazi threat. Some argued that the crisis required the immediate establishment of a Jewish political commonwealth in Palestine. There was conflict over the anti-Nazi boycott and the notion of a Jewish army. In 1938 Jewish organizations could not agree on whether to accept the terms of the Rublee-Wohlthat plan, in which American Jews would have paid ransom money to Nazi Germany to allow Jews to emigrate. And in 1944, at the height of the extermination, the American Jewish community was riven by the SS ransom proposal to exchange Hungarian Jews for 10,000 trucks.

There were, for example, differences between religious and secular Jews regarding the saving of Jewish lives through illegal means like ransoming. Usually religious Jews bound only by religious law were more willing to disregard secular law such as trading with the enemy in order to rescue lives. Agencies like the World Jewish Congress and the Jewish Agency for Palestine, both dominated by the ideology of Labor Zionism, tended to favor their own. The Jewish Agency was solely responsible for the distribution of life-saving Palestine Certificates which allowed refugees to find haven in Palestine. Vaad Hahatzala, which represented anti-Zionist Orthodox Jews, complained that their clients were being discriminated against in the distribution of the certificates. The World Jewish Congress and the non-partisan American Jewish Joint Distribution Committee (JDC), both involved in the spiriting of Jewish children across the Pyrenees to safety in Portugal and Spain, came into conflict about who should receive credit for the handful that were brought out. It disrupted the operation. The urgent need for unity between the organizations was difficult to achieve.

Between 1939 and 1944 the major national organizations (the American Jewish Committee, the American Jewish Congress, and B'nai B'rith, later joined by the Anti-Defamation League, the American Jewish War Veterans, and the Jewish Labor Committee) mounted four attempts to create a united front. But each time the organizations were reluctant to surrender their sovereignty, and the ideological differences could not be bridged. The final and most serious effort at achieving unity came in 1943, when B'nai B'rith convened the American Jewish Conference. But when the delegates supported a Zionist-sponsored resolution to form a Jewish commonwealth in Palestine, the anti-Zionist American Jewish Committee and Jewish Labor Committee withdrew.

Disunity also compromised the community's political effectiveness. In 1928, in support of the presidential candidacy of Al Smith, a Catholic, many Jewish voters switched their allegiance from the Republican to the Democratic party. Franklin Roosevelt, Smith's successor as governor of New York State, retained Smith's practice of welcoming Jewish talent into his inner circle. But in the antisemitic atmosphere of the 1930s, that strategy of inclusion earned the Roosevelt administration's New Deal the derisive name "Jew Deal." Roosevelt's reaction to being labeled a philosemite may account for his later reluctance to support risky and costly rescue plans that could be made to appear to show that the war was being fought to save the Jews. In September 1941 the aviator and folk hero Charles Lindbergh warned in a nationwide address delivered in Des Moines, Iowa, that Jews were the major group advocating intervention in the war in Europe. The so-called Jewish love affair with Roosevelt may also have indirectly affected Jewish political leverage on rescue activity. Unable to threaten Roosevelt with the removal of the Jewish vote, Jewish leaders were compelled to rely on less certain rewards for loyalty.

Nevertheless, Jewish loyalty to Roosevelt persisted throughout the crisis. Even the Jewish labor movement sought a vehicle to support Roosevelt without compromising its socialist principles. The American Labor party was founded in 1935 in New York State for that purpose. In the election of 1936, 250,000 Jewish votes were cast for Roosevelt on the American Labor ticket. The American Labor party thus broke the socialist hold on the left wing of the Jewish electorate and gave the liberal Jewish voter access to mainstream American politics.

One might expect that the Jews in Roosevelt's inner

circle—Isador Lubin, Benjamin Cohen, Felix Frank-furter, Sam Rosenman, Henry Morgenthau, Jr., Sidney Hillman, and others—would have appealed directly to Roosevelt on behalf of Jewish causes. But with the exception of Treasury secretary Morgenthau, none lobbied the president to support rescue operations. These officials considered themselves Americans who happened to be Jews—sometimes unhappily so. For different reasons, the 10 members of the Jewish congressional delegation, three of whom chaired committees that were in a position to aid in rescue—Foreign Affairs (Rep. Sol Bloom), Immigration and Naturalization (Rep. Samuel Dickstein), and Judiciary (Rep. Emanuel Celler)—were also loath to press the issue of liberalizing the immigration laws. Aware that public opinion opposed the admission of refugees, they were convinced that championing the admission of Jewish refugees would boomerang to produce even more restrictive legislation.

The earliest American Jewish reaction to Nazi anti-Jewish actions was the organization of a boycott of the sale of German goods. First proposed by the Jewish War Veterans and soon joined by other organizations, under the leadership of Samuel Untermeyer the boycott had become a worldwide movement by 1934. But from the outset it led to inordinate communal bickering. Some believed that the very idea of mobilizing purchasing power might appear to confirm an antisemitic stereotype of an all-powerful Jewish commercial conspiracy. Acknowledging that a key to the Roosevelt administration's economic recovery program was the promotion of free trade by reciprocal tariff agree-

Protestors in New York City's Madison Square demonstrating against Adolf Hitler's anti-Jewish activities in Germany. 10 May 1933(?)

ments, the leaders of the American Jewish Committee also opposed the boycott. They argued that it made no sense to enter a trade war with Germany, which was one of the biggest customers for American products and therefore had to be a partner in the economic recovery of the United States.

The boycott movement also placed the Zionist organizations in a quandary. It threatened the lucrative commerce that had developed as a result of the transfer agreements permitting the Jewish community in Palestine (the Yishuv) to import German capital goods, purchased with money from the blocked accounts of Jewish "capitalists" anxious to get some of their wealth out of Germany. Behind the contretemps over the boycott was a historic argument between Zionists and anti-Zionists regarding the viability of Jewish life in the Diaspora. In proposing to rebuild a Jewish state in Palestine, Zionists were rejecting the idea that civil and political equality was possible for Jews in the modern secular state. For Eastern European Jews, the deterioration of Jewish life served as confirmation of this pessimistic vision, but for Jews in the parliamentary democracies of the West, hope for full integration prevailed. American Jews especially remained convinced that the promise of full citizenship rights was realizable, at least in their country. At the turn of the century, the major sectors of the American Jewry—the Orthodox and the Reform branches of the religious community and the socialist-oriented political community—were either indifferent or opposed to Zionism. Germany was generally believed to be an enlightened nation of the West, where Jewish integration had been successfully completed under the Weimar constitution (1919).

The continual differences over Zionist nation-building aspirations did not magically disappear during the Holocaust. Rather, the conflict took a new form: Should the goal of rescue be separated from the commonwealth goal? If that were done, argued non-Zionists, communal support, especially the pioneering experience of the Zionist movement, could be mobilized to support Roosevelt's resettlement schemes outside Palestine.

In 1943 a small group of Jewish leaders organized the Council for American Judaism to oppose the establishment of a Jewish state. But increasingly that passionate antinationalist posture became the position of a dissident minority. As early as 1935, when the Nuremberg Laws expelled Jews from the German *pays légal*, American Jews began to accept the Zionist reading of the Jewish condition, at least as far as the refugees were concerned. It was apparent that what was required to resettle the refugees, when no nation offered haven, was a territory in which Jews were sovereign. The new consensus made possible the passage of the first commonwealth resolution by an Extraordinary Zionist Conference convened at the Biltmore Hotel in New York in May 1942.

Yet even after its rapid increase in membership and influence, the American Zionist movement remained riven. Its organizations represented the Jewish political spectrum from left-wing socialism to liberal capitalism and everything in between. After the Nazi invasion of Poland in September 1939, a group of Zionists affiliated with the militant right-wing Revisionist movement Irgun Zvai Leumi, led by Hillel Kook, alias Peter Bergson, founded an organization advocating the recruitment of a Jewish army to be composed of stateless and Palestinian Jews. For American Jews who wanted to strike back at the Nazis, and particularly for Zionists who recalled the Jewish mule corps of World War I, the idea of a Jewish army was very attractive. Capitalizing on an image of activism and militancy, the Bergson "boys" were catapulted into prominence. But from the outset the idea of a Jewish army was chimerical because the training and arming of such a Jewish militia was adamantly opposed by the Arab world. The British Foreign and Colonial Office therefore rejected the proposal. Not until 1942, when it appeared that Rommel's Africa Corps might occupy Palestine, did the British agree to train a brigade of 15,000 Palestinian Jews.

Having no rescue apparatus of its own, the Bergson group was limited in its activities to undertaking public relations and to prodding the mainline organizations. Unencumbered by formal and extensive membership branches, this small group was able to react quickly and sometimes imaginatively to the developing crisis in Europe. Acting as self-appointed community spokespersons, the Bergson group raised hackles, especially in the Zionist-oriented American Jewish Congress, whose president was Rabbi Stephen Wise. Decades earlier, the congress had, in the name of democracy, challenged the leadership of the oligarchic American Jewish Committee. The Bergson group seemed unaware that they were at odds with a movement that had placed democratic governance as its highest ideal.

Yet despite the fact that Bergson and his followers were viewed as outsiders unwilling to accept the discipline of the established leadership, their talent and energy in making the United States aware of what was happening to European Jewry was undeniable. Particularly successful were the numerous broadsides written by Ben Hecht which appeared in leading newspapers and the theatrical pageant "We Will Never Die," directed by Moss Hart and starring Paul Muni and Edward G. Robinson. During the spring of 1943 the pageant was viewed by thousands all over the nation. Unless the American public could be rallied in support of rescue actions, little could be expected from a reluctant administration. Predictably, the Bergson group's publicity activities aroused bitter conflict, not only within American Jewry generally but especially within the Zionist camp, where strife between Revisionist and mainline Zionism was constant. Whether the Bergson group saw the danger earlier than others and better understood what had to be done, as their supporters claim, or whether they intensified communal discord, as their detractors assert, is an open question.

The government and Jewish response falls naturally into two parts. In the first phase, from Hitler's ascension to power in 1933 through 1941, the central question was whether the Jews of Europe could be saved by resettling them outside the Nazi-occupied area. The second phase, beginning with the U.S. entry into the war in December 1941 and the Wannsee Conference of January 1942 and lasting until the German surrender in May 1945, is marked by the systematic implementation of the Final Solution—the extermination of the Jews of Europe. Although sporadic attempts to help Jews escape from German-occupied Europe continue, the primary efforts are aimed at halting deportations to the death camps and stopping the genocide.

American Jews' advocacy of a more open U.S. policy toward refugees during the first phase met with scarcely any success. President Roosevelt's refusal to support the Wagner-Rodgers bill of 1939, which would have admitted 20,000 Jewish refugee children outside the quota, doomed the legislation. And although a high proportion of the clergy, artists, scientists, and labor leaders from Germany and occupied lands who were granted special visas was Jewish, the number of these "special care" visas, probably less than 10,000, was small in comparison with the millions who needed to be rescued. Refugee admission procedures actually became more difficult after the outbreak of war. In June 1941 U.S. regulations were changed in order to deny visas to all those who had "close relatives" living under German occupa-

tion. The dismal record of relief efforts in the first phase presaged continued frustration in the second.

The almost total exclusion of refugees after Pearl Harbor lasted until 1944, when pressure by Jewish refugee advocates, together with the support of Henry Morgenthau, Jr., helped circumvent the immigration laws. The high point of the refugee phase was Roosevelt's convening of a conference at Evian in July 1938 for the Western nations, particularly the United States and Great Britain, to address the refugee problem. The conference raised hopes among American Jews that the thousands of German and Austrian Jews seeking to escape from Nazi persecution would be saved. But the failure of Evian to produce concrete results made Jewish leaders who attended the conference realize that no Western country intended to be a haven for the Jews of Germany and Austria, no matter how dire the conditions became for Jews in Nazi-controlled territories. Many foresaw and bemoaned the imminent destruction of Europe's rich Jewish culture, but genocide remained beyond the imagination. When news of the systematic killing of Jews leaked out of Switzerland in 1942, American Jews found the stories too gruesome to believe and hence were slow to urge the U.S. government to take action to stop Nazi implementation of the Final Solution.

In May 1939 the British issued a white paper that called for limiting Jewish immigration to Palestine. Many Zionists advocated resisting the white paper by all means. They opposed alternatives to resettlement in Palestine, such as proposals to establish British Guiana or the Dominican Republic as the primary destination of Jewish refugees, for those plans would drain scarce resources away from the resettlement effort in Palestine and would help the British to undermine the Yishuv. The position taken by the Zionists in Palestine divided the American Jewish community. The nonpartisan Joint Distribution Committee, which supported many individual projects in Palestine, cooperated with the State Department in the search for alternative resettlement areas and subsidized the settlement of Jewish refugees in Sosua, near Puerto Plata, on the northern coast of the Dominican Republic. American Zionist leaders spoke out against the Dominican Resettlement Association and the dozens of other resettlement projects proposed by the President's Advisory Committee on Political Refugees.

In the first months following the German invasion of the Soviet Union in June 1941, events moved too fast for the refugee-oriented Jewish rescue effort to confront the new and deadly threat to Eastern European Jews. Not until March 1943 did the Jewish organizations propose a unified rescue plan. The bombing of the rail lines and gas chambers, which today some see as the most practical response, was not included in the program in 1943.

Rescue advocacy became more insistent after the German defeat at Stalingrad in February 1943, but it never was able to convince the Roosevelt administration to include the rescue of the Jews in the labor and extermination camps as one of its war priorities. The official policy was that the way to save the Jews was to win the war as quickly as possible, and that nothing should be done that might interfere with that goal. Almost every proposal by rescue advocates, from sending food parcels to designating camp inmates as prisoners of war, from threats of retribution to the bombing of rail lines and gas chambers, was rejected on that basis. But the largely Jewish community of rescue advocates did have small victories, such as the removal of Breckinridge Long, the assistant secretary of state most responsible for blocking U.S. rescue efforts, from the position of power over the Roosevelt administration's rescue policy. After Long was identified as the principal roadblock during congressional hearings in November 1943, the rescue initiative within the administration shifted to the Treasury Department, where three of Secretary Morgenthau's assistants compiled a report detailing the State Department's sabotage of the rescue effort.

Four factors ultimately led to a breakthrough on the rescue front: the turn of tide in the war toward the Allies in mid-1943; the intense pressure of an aroused, albeit still divided, Jewish community; the mobilization of Henry Morgenthau, Jr., the most prominent Jew in the Roosevelt administration; and the election campaign of 1944, when Roosevelt sought a fourth term as president. In January 1944, Roosevelt issued Federal Order 9417, which established the War Refugee Board. Some of its key administrators were drawn from the Jewish community, and most of the funding came from the Joint Distribution Committee. No sooner had the agency been established than John Pehle, its director, was faced with the crisis in Hungary, the only Jewish community in Central Europe that remained relatively unscathed.

The War Refugee Board undertook an imaginative effort to save Hungarian Jewry. Embassies of neutral countries were alerted to the plight of the Jews, agents such as Raoul Wallenberg were recruited to help the Hungarian Jews emigrate, and stern warnings of retribution were issued. But although those efforts did manage to save thousands of people, between April and July 1944 more than 2,000 of the Jews of Hungary were deported to extermination camps and slaughtered, within full view of an alerted world.

It took almost four years for American Jewry to mobilize sufficient pressure on the Roosevelt administration to act to save European Jews. But although the Allied governments could influence Axis satellites or cobelligerents such as the Horthy regime in Hungary, such efforts had little influence on decisions in Berlin, where solving the so-called Jewish problem was the centerpiece of Nazi racial cosmology. Nazi atrocities against Jews were never more than a minor concern among the American people and their government. American Jewry never succeeded in convincing the American people that genocide warranted decisive action. By April 1945, photographs and stories published in the newspapers provided the American public with gruesome confirmation of the work of the extermination camps. But a year later it still took constant pressure from Jewish groups to get the Truman administration to separate Jewish displaced persons from their tormentors, Ukrainians and others, who ended up in the same displaced-persons camps.

The political influence of American Jews in the 1930s and during World War II was insufficient for the task history and kinship had assigned it. That conclusion remains valid even if we acknowledge that some of American Jewry's resources were dissipated by internal bickering among Jewish organizations. In the first phase of the crisis, it is certain that many thousands of German and Austrian Jews could have been saved had American Jews wielded enough political clout to effect changes in U.S. immigration policy. It is less clear, however, whether any action in the second phase—even bombing of the gas chambers and rail lines—could have severely hampered the extermination of the Jews in Eastern Europe. Nevertheless, no effort should have been spared to thwart a catastrophe of such awesome dimensions. *Henry L. Feingold*

American Policy The U.S. government was slow to take action in response to the Nazi persecution and mass murder of European Jews. In a simplified Holocaust world divided into perpetrators, victims, rescuers, and bystanders, the U.S. government was, until 1944, generally a bystander.

In spite of Franklin D. Roosevelt's reputation as a great liberal president, the atmosphere in the United States during his terms in office, from 1933 to 1945, was unfavorable for American humanitarian initiatives. The Great Depression had sharply reduced Americans' willingness and ability to involve their country in foreign problems. Polls consistently showed that many Americans thought that Jews had too much power: even in June 1945, after news of the Holocaust had been confirmed, 58 percent held that view. So the constraints of democracy may have imposed serious limits on the efforts that the Roosevelt administration devoted to the cause of Jewish refugees.

The response of the American government to Nazi persecution of Jews varied according to the political climate in Washington. During the first phase of American policy, from 1933 until the start of World War II, there were no centrally organized mass killings of German Jews—only a set of escalating Nazi policies to isolate, expropriate, and terrorize them. In these years the Roosevelt administration took a series of small steps to accommodate German Jewish refugees. The second phase, from late 1939 to late 1943, coincided with the period when most Nazi killings of Jews occurred. Paradoxically, in this phase the United States did remarkably little to save Jews and even reversed some earlier positive moves. The third, active phase of American refugee policy began in January 1944 and continued to the end of the war.

American immigration laws established an annual quota of immigrants from each nation outside the Western Hemisphere based on the share of that nation's population within the United States in 1890. Had all quotas been filled, total annual immigration to the United States would have been 153,800, but in no year from 1933 to 1945 did the number of immigrants approach that figure. The biggest barrier to German Jewish immigration during the early and mid-1930s was not the German quota limit of 25,957 but State Department policy. In 1930 the department had instructed American consuls, who interviewed applicants for immigration visas, to adopt a harsh interpretation of a regulation barring the immigration of persons who were likely to become a public charge. Previously the regulation had been applied mainly against the aged, infirm, or those without economic prospect, but now, as domestic unemployment contin-

ued to rise, it was used to prevent entry of any prospective immigrants who would need to work to support themselves.

In the face of Nazi legislation against Jews, the early (temporary) Nazi boycott of Jewish businesses and other confiscatory measures, and sporadic acts of anti-Jewish violence, some American Christian liberals and American Jewish leaders sought an active refugee policy to take in victims of Nazi persecution. After internal debates and occasional signs of interest from President Roosevelt, the State Department relaxed its immigration regulations and made possible a significant expansion of immigration from Germany during the mid-1930s. In late 1936, progressives within the State Department, bolstered by President Roosevelt's easy reelection, effected a quiet change in the interpretation of the public-charge regulation. American consuls in Europe were advised that, in evaluating immigration applications from German Jews, the test should be whether an applicant would *probably* become a public charge, not whether he or she could *possibly* become one. Consuls were to take into consideration the level of education and job skills of applicants as well as affidavits of support from American relatives. The number of immigration visas granted nearly doubled within a year, from less than 7,000 in fiscal 1936 to about 12,500 in fiscal 1937.

Shortly after the German annexation of Austria (the Anschluss) in March 1938, President Roosevelt suggested further liberalization of immigration procedures—as well as combination of the German and Austrian quotas, giving Austrian Jews a better chance at obtaining immigration visas. Soon the German quota was in full use. Roosevelt also created a President's Advisory Committee on Political Refugees to coordinate efforts among government, private agencies concerned with immigration, and a new international organization still to be created. This committee lobbied State Department officials to ease immigration regulations; it also drew up lists of talented and noteworthy victims of Nazi persecution whose admission to the United States would be in the national interest. In creating this committee, President Roosevelt avoided use of the term *Jewish refugees*, or even *religious and racial refugees*, in favor of the broader and less controversial *political refugees*, showing a politician's awareness of the unpopularity of Jews.

Immediately after Kristallnacht in November 1938, and upon the prompting of Secretary of Labor Frances

Perkins, Roosevelt also announced that he was extending the visitor's visas of 12,000–15,000 German Jews already in the United States by at least six months. Largely through administrative measures the government increased the flow of German refugees (primarily German Jewish refugees) from fewer than 2,000 in 1933 to more than 30,000 in fiscal 1939. Even so, the German quota could not accommodate anything like the number of Jews desperate to leave Nazi Germany. By early 1939 more than 300,000 Germans, perhaps 90 percent of them Jews, had applied for visas to immigrate to the United States.

By the late 1930s German ships carrying Jewish refugees with inadequate assurances of admission to the United States were arriving at South American and Central American ports. This practice provoked some countries in the Western Hemisphere to tighten immigration restrictions. The most publicized example of this development was the unfortunate voyage of the *St. Louis,* a ship of the Hamburg-American Line, in May 1939.

The *St. Louis* carried 933 passengers, virtually all of them Jewish refugees seeking temporary asylum in Havana, Cuba, where there was already a colony of about 2,500 Jewish refugees. Some of the passengers had applied for American immigration visas and had secured affidavits of support from Americans, but Nazi authorities were using force and intimidation to ship them out immediately. In effect, the refugees were hoping to wait in Havana for their turn to enter the United States under the quota system, a practice that was legal under American regulations.

Shortly before the *St. Louis* had set sail from Hamburg, however, Cuba's president Laredo Blu tightened immigration regulations and increased the entry fees for aliens. He also made shipping lines responsible for complying with the new requirements or returning passengers to Europe. When the *St. Louis* arrived in Havana, Cuban authorities refused to allow most of the refugees to disembark. The passengers sent a telegram to President Roosevelt asking for help. While negotiations with Cuba dragged on, the ship was forced to leave Havana harbor, and it maneuvered along the coast of Florida. A U.S. Coast Guard cutter followed it, with orders to prevent anyone from trying to swim ashore. State Department officials were opposed to putting strong pressure on the Cuban government and even more opposed to taking the refugees into the United States. President Roosevelt declined to intervene.

Eventually the ship headed back to Germany, where its passengers feared they would be sent to concentration camps. At the last minute, officials of the American Jewish Joint Distribution Committee, by offering large financial guarantees, succeeded in persuading Britain, France, Belgium, and the Netherlands to take in the desperate passengers

Given the opposition to increased immigration in Congress and among the public, the Roosevelt administration shied away from efforts to increase or circumvent the immigration quotas. In early 1939 New York senator Robert F. Wagner pushed a bill to admit 20,000 German Jewish children to the United States outside the regular immigration quota. But the hope of wide public support for sheltering refugee children proved to be vain: two-thirds of Americans, according to one poll, opposed the Wagner-Rogers bill. The Senate Immigration Committee amended the bill to give the 20,000 children preference within the German quota, leaving only 7,370 visas for German adults. The House Immigration Committee never reported the bill out.

Because of the restrictions of the American quota system, international diplomacy and resettlement outside the United States seemed to offer the only hope of haven for most German and Austrian Jewish refugees.

In a 1938 article in the journal *Foreign Affairs,* Dorothy Thompson had proposed the establishment of a new international organization to deal with the refugee problem. The plan appealed to President Roosevelt, because it promised that responsibility for resettling refugees would be shared among many nations and would not fall exclusively on the United States. And if the organization were funded privately, primarily with money donated by Jewish groups, Roosevelt could avoid having to ask for congressional approval.

State Department officials were eager to avoid the impression that holding a conference on refugee resettlement and establishing a new international refugee organization were purely American initiatives. Some of them doubted the wisdom of calling attention to the refugee question at a time when Europe was already in crisis and was heading directly toward war. Although strongly critical of the Nazi regime, Assistant Secretary of State George S. Messersmith feared that Nazi Germany might seek to use the refugee problem to extract economic concessions and create other dilemmas for the Western democracies. Secretary of the Treasury Henry Morgenthau, Jr., who was Jewish, personally championed the refugee initiative, but the Treasury Department took no official position. So the international conference that convened in the French resort town of Evian, near Lake Geneva, in July 1938 lacked American leadership.

Myron Taylor, a retired executive of U.S. Steel, headed the American delegation to the conference. Taylor urged the official representatives of 32 nations to cooperate in establishing a special refugee organization for Germans and Austrians. Following the existing line of U.S. government policy, Taylor described American laws and practices as liberal, and he indicated that the full annual German quota of 27,370 would be used. But if the United States was not willing to change its laws, most other countries present saw no reason why they should be expected to do so either. Although some officials expressed concern about persecution and hope for the eventual resettlement of refugees, many did not even identify the country creating the refugee problem; virtually no country offered to accept more refugees, and some nations explicitly declared that Jewish refugees could not be assimilated in their lands. The Evian Conference did, however, establish an Intergovernmental Committee on Refugees, headquartered in London, which was given a mandate to negotiate with Germany about the fate of those wishing to emigrate.

The situation in Berlin was clouded. Hjalmar Schacht, president of the Reichsbank, and Hermann Göring, minister of the economy, were interested in allowing some German Jews to leave for places of settlement abroad in return for economic benefits to Germany: seizure of Jewish property in Germany, the financing of resettlement by "world Jewry," and stimulation of German exports. But other Nazi officials were opposed to negotiations with the Intergovernmental Committee on Refugees as well as any regulated Jewish emigration. No one could fathom where Adolf Hitler stood, and Hitler's approval was essential for any bargain. For some time the director of the Intergovernmental Committee on Refugees, the American lawyer George Rublee, could not even get an invitation to Berlin.

Eventually, Rublee and Helmut Wohlthat of the German Economics Ministry did exchange memorandums of understanding in February 1939. Without signing a formal agreement, the two sides consented to an arrangement that would have provided Germany with economic benefits from refugee resettlement financed by Jewish money from outside Germany. But

the SS and police authorities ignored the arrangement, continuing to force Jewish emigration through intimidation and illegal means. American Jewish leaders and organizations were reluctant to take part in anything that might benefit Germany economically and sanction the confiscation of German Jewish assets. The deal smacked of ransom for Jewish hostages.

What was the alternative? In December 1938 the American consul general in Berlin, Raymond Geist, had warned Assistant Secretary of State Messersmith that the Jews in Germany were being condemned to death, and he urged measures to rescue them. In May 1939 Geist sent a clear warning to Washington: if resettlement opportunities did not open up soon, the Jews of Germany would be doomed. At a meeting that month with a small group of prominent American Jews and officials of refugee organizations, Roosevelt insisted that haste was essential: it was "not so much a question of the money as it was of actual lives"; the warnings from the American embassy in Berlin were "sound and not exaggerated." But the outbreak of war was only a few months away, and all the negotiating efforts went for naught.

Some critics of American policy have argued that if the United States had sponsored the large-scale resettlement of German and Austrian Jews, Hitler's march toward the destruction of European Jewry would have been halted. This argument overlooks both the limits on Nazi Germany's willingness to negotiate and the breadth of Hitler's ambition. Even under the Rublee-Wohlthat arrangement, hundreds of thousands of German Jews would have had to remain in Germany as hostages. Moreover, Hitler was obsessed not just with German Jews but with "world Jewry." Not hundreds of thousands, but the millions of Jews in Eastern Europe, France, and the Balkans would have had to be removed from Nazi reach to have averted mass extermination. Still, a stronger American role might have saved some lives in 1938 and 1939.

The outbreak of war and the shockingly rapid German military victories in 1939 and 1940 brought about a major shift in American policy toward Jewish refugees. The U.S. government not only shied away from steps to alleviate Nazi persecution of Jews; a new and tougher stance toward foreigners pervaded Washington and spread throughout the country. Previous measures to enable more German Jews and other German refugees to enter the United States in accordance with the American immigration quota were swiftly overridden by new restrictions on immigration in response to concerns about possible espionage by foreign nationals on American soil.

The American public and government officials became preoccupied with the dangers of fascism, communism, and internal subversion. German Jews who had relatives remaining in Germany were thought to be vulnerable to Nazi extortion, as President Roosevelt himself warned at a press conference in 1940. As early as November 1939, State Department officials had told American consuls to issue fewer visas and in June 1940 they were instructed not to issue a visa if there was any doubt about the applicant's qualifications for a visa.

The one official most directly in charge of the cutback in immigration was Assistant Secretary of State Breckinridge Long, head of the Special War Problems Division. A scion of two Southern aristocratic families, Long was a political appointee with personal ties to the president. Long held to some negative stereotypes about Jews, but he was more xenophobic than antisemitic. Long was one of many government officials in the State Department, the War Department, and the Federal Bureau of Investigation whose single-minded focus on protecting the United States from foreign subversion during the war led to excessive suspicion of refugees.

In June 1941 Congress passed the Bloom–Van Nuys Act, which authorized consuls to withhold any type of visa if they had reason to believe that the applicant might endanger public safety. New and more extensive application and screening procedures added delays and provided opportunities for further denials of visas. For the rest of the war only a small fraction of the German quota and some other European quotas were filled, although Jewish refugees in some neutral countries continued to apply for visas under the quotas of their countries of origin.

As the Nazi regime shifted in 1941 toward a policy of murdering as many Jews as possible, the U.S. government was preoccupied with military and political dangers created by the prospect of German conquest of Europe. Even after America entered the war in December 1941, the military situation was so critical for the Allies that there was little disposition to assist civilians in enemy territory. All governmental efforts were concentrated on winning the war as quickly as possible.

Reports about specific massacres of civilians by the Nazis were published in the Western press during late 1941, although the major American newspapers tended to understate the facts so as to attenuate the horror. Some intelligence reports of Nazi mass shootings of Jews during 1941 and early 1942 reached Washington through various sources, including Jewish officials and American diplomats in neutral countries and the Polish underground.

Unfortunately, many Americans likened reports of Nazi treatment of Jews to stories about German atrocities in occupied Belgium and northern France during World War I, claims that turned out to have been invented by Allied propagandists. Another factor in the slow public reaction to Nazi atrocities against Jews was that all citizens of German-occupied Europe were suffering under brutal Nazi occupation, and it was not always easy to see that the Nazis had different policies for different peoples. Pressure from American Jewish groups to recognize the growing tragedy overtaking the Jews of Europe was sometimes perceived as a request for special favors from the Allies. Those who were unsympathetic to these pleas believed that attempts to complicate the war effort and negotiate with Germany or its satellites regarding the release of Jews might delay a complete military victory. But the most important barrier to support for intervention to save European Jews was psychological: the calculated murder of millions of civilians was not only illogical and unprecedented, it was literally inconceivable.

The U.S. government was interested in broadcasting atrocity reports only if they helped to mobilize the public and the outside world to win the war. Foreign Jews were not among the most popular groups in the United States. Nazi radio propaganda and other media outlets daily broadcast the view that the Allies were fighting the war on behalf of the Jews—a false charge that Allied governments did not want to seem to support.

To overcome the political and psychological forces behind denial or even suppression of information about the mass killings, one needed hard evidence of the Nazi plan, including details of how and where the Final Solution was being carried out. Until the second half of 1942 the outside world knew little about the gas chambers and the extermination camps. One person to succeed in getting out word of the Final Solution was the German industrialist Eduard Schulte, who passed the information to Isidor Koppelmann, Benjamin Sagalowitz, and Gerhart Riegner of the World Jewish Congress in Switzerland. Riegner sent a telegram to Rabbi Stephen Wise, president of the American Jewish Congress, via American diplomatic channels in Switzerland in August 1942. One State Department official wrote off the message as a "wild rumor inspired by Jewish fears." Elbridge Durbrow of the European Division wrote in an internal memorandum, "It does not appear advisable in view of the . . . fantastic nature of the allegation, and the impossibility of our being of any assistance if such action were taken, to transmit the information to Dr. Stephen Wise as suggested." State Department officials criticized the American Legation in Switzerland for agreeing to pass unsubstantiated information to third parties. Shortly after the State Department had blocked the telegram, President Roosevelt announced at a press conference, "Our Government has constantly received additional information from dependable sources, and it welcomes reports from any trustworthy source which would assist in keeping our Government—our growing fund of information and evidence—up to date and reliable. In other words, we want news—from any source that is reliable—of the continuation of atrocities." The State Department bureaucracy was not exactly following the president's lead.

Wise eventually received Riegner's telegram through the World Jewish Congress in London. He rushed to see Sumner Welles, the second in command at the State Department. Welles argued that it would make no sense for the Nazis to kill large numbers of Jews when they needed laborers. He urged Wise to refrain from releasing the telegram to the press until further investigation confirmed or refuted the story. Wise met with representatives of the major Jewish organizations, including the Agudat Israel World Organization, which had received its own reports from Switzerland of the killing of Jews. Wise also got in touch with some other sympathetic government officials. Then he and other Jewish leaders carried on their campaign to arouse public attention to Nazi brutalities and mass murder, but without using the specific information from Riegner about the Final Solution.

By late November 1942 the State Department had gathered enough information from other sources to convince Welles of the veracity of the Riegner telegram. He summoned Wise to Washington and told him that his deepest fears were confirmed. Wise then arranged for press conferences in Washington and New York and made public what he knew. The Associated Press carried the story, which appeared in the *New York Herald Tribune* under the headline "Wise Says Hitler Has Ordered 4,000,000 Jews Slain in 1942."

Rabbi Stephen Wise delivering an address at an anti-Nazi protest at Madison Square Garden, New York City. 14 March 1937

With considerable difficulty, Rabbi Wise obtained a White House meeting for himself and four other Jewish leaders. On 8 December they gave President Roosevelt a memorandum entitled "Blue Print for Extermination," which included a section on Hitler's direct order to annihilate the Jews. Wise appealed to Roosevelt to bring the extermination program to the attention of the world and to try to stop it. Roosevelt said that the government was familiar with most of the facts, but it was hard to find a suitable course of action. He agreed to release another statement denouncing mass killings. From London, Samuel Zygielbojm of the Polish National Council and the Jewish Bund sent a cable to the White House in which he estimated that the Nazis had already slaughtered 2.25 million Jews in Poland. Zygielbojm pleaded for Allied action to prevent further killings. The pressure brought to bear in London and Washington, and the fact that Prime Minister Churchill took a personal interest in the matter, helped to overcome bureaucratic resistance in the British Foreign Office and the U.S. State Department to any kind of Allied statement. On 17 December the United States, Great Britain, and 10 Allied governments-in-exile issued a joint declaration denouncing Nazi implementation of "Hitler's oft-repeated intention to exterminate the Jewish people in Europe." The statement omitted any reference to extermination camps and the use of poison gas, although that information was available to Western governments. It also avoided any pledge of rescue efforts. Nonetheless, the declaration represented a turning point in at least official recognition of the reality of the Final Solution.

The period between December 1942 and January 1944, marked by steady Allied military gains, was one of missed American and British opportunities to respond to the Holocaust. British public opinion, led by the archbishop of Canterbury, become more openly critical of government inaction, while in the United States a range of Jewish organizations, labor unions, some liberal Christian groups, and other humanitarian activists sought to rally public opinion with mass meetings, marches, demonstrations, and articles and advertisements in the press. They were, however, fighting against the general current, as polls showed a rise in antisemitic sentiment.

Given the growing criticism of government inaction and the cross-currents in public opinion, something had to be done. So the United States and Britain sent representatives to a bilateral conference on refugee problems, to be held on the island of Bermuda in April 1943. In closed session, both sides in effect agreed not to tread on sensitive areas: the British did not want to take action that might inflame Arab opinion in the Middle East or might involve negotiations with Germany for the release of Jews or might require shipping food through the Allied blockade of Nazi-occupied Europe. The United States did not want to commit to any plan that would compromise its tight immigration policy. The restrictions left only limited options, such as establishing small refugee camps in North Africa and informing neutral countries of the American and British concern for refugees. The results of the deliberations were so meager that they were kept confidential.

The official American view began to change in July 1943. The American and British invasion of Italy and Soviet successes on the eastern front were likely one factor. Roosevelt also may have been influenced by a dramatic firsthand account of the organized murder of Jews given to him on 28 July by the Polish underground courier Jan Karski. At any rate, Roosevelt di-

rected the Treasury Department to take responsibility for possible relief and evacuation measures for Jews in Romania and France.

Treasury Secretary Morgenthau was the president's neighbor and a political confidant. Morgenthau had encouraged Roosevelt to pursue refugee initiatives in 1938 and 1939, but he did not stress the issue once the war began. Like many Americans, Morgenthau apparently believed the official line that the quickest way to end everyone's suffering was to win the war as soon as possible. Under the influence of information from Rabbi Wise about the Final Solution and private meetings with the Jewish activist Peter Bergson (Hillel Kook), Morgenthau began to shift his view. Then his own subordinates took up the cause.

Key officials in the Treasury Department—John Pehle, Randolph Paul, and Josiah DuBois (none of them Jewish)—not only discovered that certain State Department officials were obstructing the proposals for Jewish relief in Romania and France; they also turned up evidence of earlier State Department efforts to shut off the flow of information from Switzerland about the Final Solution. In a separate development, Assistant Secretary of State Long was found to have given to a congressional committee inaccurate and inflated estimates of the numbers of refugees who had entered the United States since 1933. Armed with this evidence, Morgenthau aggressively backed a plan drafted by Oscar Cox, head of the Lend-Lease Administration, for a special refugee commission that would remove jurisdiction over refugee matters from the State Department.

Josiah DuBois spent Christmas Day, 1943, drafting a document entitled "Report to the Secretary on the Acquiescence of This Government in the Murder of the Jews." He charged State Department officials not only with gross procrastination and failure to act, but also with attempts to prevent action by others to rescue Jews. He warned that a response was imperative, and he privately threatened to resign unless the president took initiative. Morgenthau retitled the document "Personal Report to the President," and he probably did not pass along DuBois's threat to resign, but he did warn Roosevelt of the danger of a scandal unless the White House acted swiftly.

On 22 January 1944 the president issued an executive order creating a War Refugee Board headed by the secretary of the treasury, the secretary of state, and the secretary of war. Key officials from the Treasury Department moved over to staff the board, and John

Pehle became the first director. Roosevelt gave the board $1 million from his emergency fund, and the War Refugee Board was authorized to accept funding from private persons and organizations. In the end, government money covered staffing and administrative expenses, and Jewish organizations financed most of the board's operations in Europe. No one was eager to ask for an appropriation from Congress.

The board received an official mandate to take all measures within U.S. policy to rescue victims of enemy oppression in imminent danger of death and to "provide relief and assistance consistent with the successful prosecution of the war." What that language meant in practice was to be determined through the interaction of various government agencies. State Department and War Department officials, as well as officials in the Office of War Information, remained concerned about any action that might complicate the task of winning the war, and some sought to frustrate the board at each opportunity. Some British officials saw the board as part of an election-year maneuver by the president that would, in the end, put pressure on them to take more Jews into Palestine. Even the Intergovernmental Committee on Refugees, which had shown little energy during the war, complained that the War Refugee Board would encroach on its mission. On the other hand, key officials in the Office of Strategic Services (OSS, the forerunner of the Central Intelligence Agency) supported the board in part out of self-interest: persons rescued from Nazi-controlled territories might provide a great deal of valuable intelligence. One OSS official in neutral Sweden, Iver Olson, was permitted to serve simultaneously as the local representative of the War Refugee Board.

In one area, not much changed. Pehle and DuBois hoped to dramatize the shift in American policy by admitting into the United States, on a temporary basis, substantial numbers of refugees who had found safe haven in neutral countries. By doing so, the United States would create space and resources in countries on Germany's borders for new escapees from territories controlled by Germany or its allies. But Secretary of War Henry Stimson, a defender of immigration restrictions, fought this proposal within the War Refugee Board, and in the end the president decided to admit only about 1,000 refugees in southern Italy as a special measure. To avoid immigration regulations, these refugees were interned in a camp at Oswego, New York.

The War Refugee Board was nonetheless able to effect a fundamental change in American government policy. The board raised American recognition that Nazi Germany had marked Jews for complete extermination, and that victory in the war might come too late to save virtually all of Europe's Jews. The president was persuaded to issue a statement describing the wholesale systematic murder of European Jews as one of the blackest crimes in history. Those who took part in deportations of Jews were threatened with postwar punishment.

Beginning in mid-1944, certain subordinate Nazi officials who claimed to be able to halt the killings or protect particular groups of Jews—or Jewish emissaries from these Nazi officials—contacted representatives of the War Refugee Board in Sweden and Switzerland and elsewhere. Precluded from any political discussions by the Allied policy of unconditional surrender and unable to deliver the Nazis any financial benefits for the release of Jews, board representatives Iver Olson in Sweden and Roswell McClelland in Switzerland nevertheless dangled potential benefits before Nazi officials and challenged them to show good faith. Once Heinrich Himmler became attracted by the prospect of using these negotiations as a channel for separate peace negotiations with the West, he authorized the release of several groups of thousands of Jews to Switzerland and Sweden.

During 1944 the War Refugee Board had considerable impact upon developments in countries allied with Germany and upon neutral countries. The show of strong American interest in the fate of European Jews provoked second thoughts among some governments and individuals previously cooperating to enforce Nazi policies. Neutral countries received reassurance that, if they took in larger numbers of Jewish refugees, the United States would provide assistance.

Hungary, where approximately 800,000 Jews became vulnerable to deportation to extermination camps after the German occupation in March 1944, was of particular concern to the board. After the board received reports of the first deportations of Jews from Hungary, it sent out requests to all neutral governments, asking that they obtain as much information as possible about developments in Hungary and that they expand their diplomatic representation in that country. The board asked the Red Cross and Pope Pius XII to use their influence to intercede on the part of the Hungarian Jews. On 27 May 1944 President Roosevelt warned publicly, "Hungary's fate will not be like that of any other civilized nation . . . unless the deportations are stopped."

In late May, Iver Olson asked the Swedish Foreign Office to cooperate in this effort to block the deportation of Jews from Hungary. A parallel effort by the Swedish government was already under way. In June 1944 Olson asked Kalman Lauer, a Hungarian Jew and the owner of an export-import firm in Sweden, to help him find a Swede to go to Budapest in order to rescue Jews. Lauer introduced Olson to one of his employees, Raoul Wallenberg, who was a member of a prominent Swedish business family.

With the assent of Washington and Stockholm, Wallenberg was appointed secretary of legation in the Swedish mission in Budapest. Olson arrived in Budapest on 9 July and began to use American funds and Swedish documents to protect Jews. For a time the Hungarian government responded to outside pressure by halting the deportations, but more German pressure and a change in government brought a resumption in October. Swedish and Swiss diplomats had by then set up a special protected ghetto for 33,000 Jews in Budapest, and Wallenberg continued to confront Nazi officials and extract other Jews from the death machinery. In the last days of the German occupation Wallenberg is said to have persuaded an SS general not to carry out a massacre of up to 70,000 Jews in the central ghetto in Budapest. Although the great majority of Hungary's Jews died, some 120,000 in Budapest managed to survive until the Soviets liberated the city. Aware of Wallenberg's connection with the American board—and American intelligence—through Iver Olson, the Soviets arrested him as a spy. He apparently died in a Soviet prison some years after the end of the war.

The failure to disrupt the killings at Auschwitz-Birkenau by bombing the rail lines to Auschwitz or the gas chambers and crematoriums is often cited as the central demonstration of the American government's indifference toward the fate of the Jews during the Holocaust. The War Refugee Board investigated the possibility of bombing the rail lines, only to learn that, even if successful, such action would cause but a temporary disruption. Moreover, in January 1944 the War Department had ruled out Allied military operations to rescue victims of Nazi persecution. In the face of some Jewish requests for bombing the gas chambers and crematoriums, on several occasions from June to November 1944 the board passed along the proposal to the War Department, which rejected it out of hand, claiming that air support would have to be diverted from military operations. In actuality, the I. G. Farben complex at nearby Monowitz was being bombed, and aerial reconnaissance photographs of Birkenau were available.

Historians and military experts continue to debate the American rationale for not bombing the gas chambers and crematoriums. The studies of precision bombing suggest that there would not have been a high likelihood of a successful mission. On the other hand, there is little documentary evidence that the logistical difficulties were the reason why the War Department rejected the proposal. A humanitarian operation that consumed military resources would have violated the War Department's basic premise of focusing all efforts on bringing the war to a speedy conclusion, and Assistant Secretary of War John J. McCloy, as well as many subordinate War Department officials, showed little interest in even examining the feasibility of such bombing.

Bombing the gas chambers would have been a potent symbol of American concern for European Jews. But it could not have been accomplished until the second half of 1944, and even a successful bombing of Auschwitz-Birkenau would only have reduced the efficiency of the killing machinery. The Nazi regime murdered more than 1 million Jews by shooting, and it continued to carry out death marches from various camps until the final days of the war. Moreover, one cannot entirely dismiss the humanitarian argument against diverting military resources; if the war had ended even a few days later, thousands of malnourished and sick Jews and other inmates in concentration and work camps would not have survived to be liberated.

Notwithstanding the limited action that the War Refugee Board was able to undertake, it is clear that the presence of a small government agency committed to humanitarian measures on behalf of Jews and others threatened by Nazi persecution managed to turn a negative policy into a positive one. Even tens of thousands of lives saved do not seem "enough" in view of the magnitude of the slaughter. Still, American refugee policy during the war at least closed with definite achievements.

Over the 12 years of the Third Reich, the shifts in U.S. government policy regarding Jewish refugees and the Final Solution preclude any simple and single characterization of the American attitude. One lesson is clear—and it has been reinforced by events since 1945 in such places as Bosnia and Rwanda. American politicians and government officials do not instinctively rush to save the lives of foreigners by risking those of American soldiers and civilians. If they are willing to act at all, they must first be convinced that humanitarian initiatives will work and that their constituents are willing to make necessary sacrifices, including potential loss of American lives. Elected officials normally pursue what they regard as national and political interests, not humanitarian ideals. Yet if public attitudes and sentiment in Congress imposed constraints on the Roosevelt administration, they were not so strict as to preclude all rescue and relief efforts, as the example of the War Refugee Board shows. A War Refugee Board created in 1942 or even earlier could have saved, if not millions, certainly thousands of lives.

Richard Breitman

Amsterdam Capital of the Netherlands and home of more than half (75,000 in 1940) of all Dutch Jews. See NETHERLANDS

Anielewicz, Mordechai (1919–43) Leader of the Hashomer Hatzair underground movement and of the Warsaw ghetto uprising in April 1943, in which he perished.

Antisemitism The term *antisemitism* was launched in 1879 by the German journalist Wilhelm Marr to define the terms on which the conflict between Jews and their neighbors was to be conducted in a secularized Europe. It assumed that under modern conditions race and nationality were the main agents of political identity, and proclaimed that the differences between Jews and non-Jews were therefore irreconcilable and would culminate in the victory of the one and the defeat of the other. Thus formulated, hostility to Jews was to move center stage in the political arena and to affect all those political, economic, and civic rights that Jews had acquired in most of Europe outside the Russian empire in the preceding 100 years.

The word was new, but the concepts it articulated were not. Conflicts between Jews and their neighbors are recorded for more than 2,000 years. An analysis of the origins of modern anti-Jewish movements and sentiments must ask whether they share features with older forms of Jew-hatred, or whether modern antisemitism and its culmination in the Shoah is a distinctive phenomenon.

The Ancient and Medieval Worlds

There is no reason to suppose that in the multiethnic, polytheistic Roman Empire there was systematic hostility toward Jews. It is doubtful that the occasional outbreaks of violence against them, especially in Alexandria, were qualitatively different from manifestations of other interethnic or political rivalries. In contrast with other populations in the Roman Empire, however, Jews maintained their internal cohesion through a monotheistic religion, thus highlighting their separateness and on occasion calling into question their loyalty to the emperor. Their self-chosen exclusiveness was a characteristic that they were to carry with them throughout their diasporas and that was to become an invitation to discrimination in Christian Europe.

Christian Europe had greater problems coexisting with the Jews than did pagan Rome. As Christianity sought to separate from Judaism, it held Jews in contempt for refusing to recognize Jesus as the Messiah and blamed them for Jesus' crucifixion. The declaration, in 392 by the emperor Constantine, of Christianity as the official religion of the Roman Empire turned the church into a political force. When, over the course of several centuries, the pagan religions of Europe gave way to Christianity, Judaism remained as the only vital non-Christian religion on the continent.

Although Christianity had its roots in Judaism and embraced the Hebrew Bible, which it called the Old Testament, as part of Holy Scripture, once it ceased to be a Jewish sect its apologists needed to emphasize the distinction between themselves and the residual Jewish community. At first Jewish nonbelief was attributed merely to spiritual blindness, but in time the persistence of Judaism was ascribed to wickedness. The resulting Christian intolerance was founded, ironically, on Christian tolerance. Though the universal truth of Christianity made the conversion of all mankind imperative, Jews were not to be forcibly converted. Saint Augustine taught that Jews were to be preserved as a witness to the truth of Christianity. Pope Gregory I explicitly decreed that Jews "ought to suffer no injury in those things that have been granted to them." In this way Christian doctrine ensured the survival of Jews, even if under unfavorable conditions.

Thus by the early Middle Ages, the Jews had become an outgroup, in theory under the protection of the state but in practice subject to intermittent abuse. Some of the greatest mistreatment came at the instigation of early church fathers. Both Tertullian and Origen accused Jews of having incited the Roman persecutions of Christians. In 388 Bishop Ambrose of Milan reproved the emperor Theodosius for disciplining a

SA men with signs that read, "Germans! Defend yourselves against Jewish atrocity propaganda! Buy only at German shops!"

bishop whose flock had burned down a synagogue. John Chrysostom, bishop of Antioch, denounced Jews in his sermons of 587 in the most extreme terms as "wild beasts who murder their own offspring . . . and worship the avenging devils who are the foes of our life."

The most draconian anti-Jewish measures were enacted in the Visigothic kingdoms of Spain and southern France, including prohibitions on intermarriage, of public office holding, Sunday work, and proselytization. Isidore, bishop of Seville in the seventh century, warned against indiscriminate conversion, since the converts, given the known obstinacy of Jews, could not be expected to keep to the faith. These accusations summarize a number of themes that were to become common: Jews as the authors of Christian misfortunes; Jews as devotees of an illegitimate religion; Jews as perjurers; and Jews as a people who are not full members of the human race. In the early Christian period, per-

secution based on these premises was unsystematic, and discriminatory measures were often ignored. Especially in northern Europe, where the Roman Empire had not reached and there was no tradition of theological dispute, social and political relations between Jews and Christians were mainly peaceful. By the eleventh century, the Roman church had established doctrinal uniformity, and a trans-European Christian consciousness had emerged. At the same time, Christian Europe was threatened by pagan invasions from the east, by Islam, and by heresy within. The church needed to counterattack and had the means to do so, a course of action of which the Jews were, more often than not, the incidental rather than the intended victims.

The First Crusade (1096) was accompanied by massacres of Jews and attempts at forced conversion in the Rhineland: it seemed logical to combat the enemies of Christ at home as well as abroad. Within the church there was a growing emphasis on Christ's sacrifice, as evidenced by the adoption of the doctrine of transubstantiation as dogma in 1215, the institution of the feast of Corpus Christi in 1264, and the increasing prominence of the cross as a unifying symbol. These trends made it easier for popular beliefs to arise about Jews as mockers of sacrament. The first accusation of "ritual murder"—that Jews required the blood of a Christian child for ritual purposes, especially for the baking of matzo at Passover—arose in Norwich, England, in 1150; a century later, 19 Jews were executed on the basis of a similar accusation in York. From there the accusation spread to continental Europe, to be followed by accusations of ritual crucifixions, ritual cannibalism, and profanation of the Host—accusations and rumors that frequently led to riots and murder. By the time of the Black Death in the 1340s, well poisoning had been added to the list of charges.

Although the church lent no official support to these superstitions, it took other steps that facilitated their acceptance. The Fourth Lateran Council of 1215 instituted the Inquisition—not primarily directed against Jews, but incidentally making them its victims—and decreed distinctive clothing for Jews, which led to the widespread adoption of the "Jew badge." The stricter the segregation between Jews and Christians, the greater the ignorance among Christians about the real lives of Jews, and the easier it became to harbor fantastic beliefs about a Jewish threat to Christianity. After the eleventh century, increased enforcement of the prohibition against Christians' engaging in usury, or interest taking, along with the growth of artisan and merchant guilds, which tended to exclude Jews from membership, narrowed the range of professions open to Jews and forced them into disdained occupations such as moneylending.

Between the middle of the twelfth and the middle of the fourteenth centuries, the place of the Jew in Christian society underwent a revaluation. The Jew was now fixed as the symbol of hidden menaces, evoking deep hostility, and was stripped of humanity and therefore made exempt from the normal restraints of civilized conduct. Popular outbreaks of violence, almost all in northern Europe, became common. Although popes and bishops generally sought to protect Jews from the worst excesses of the mob, their teachings established a degraded and dehumanized stereotype of the Jew within the European Christian mentality. Although religious beliefs continued to define the antagonists, increasingly the conflicts between Jews and Christians were caused by social and economic tensions.

Once the status of Jews as semi-outlaws was established, secular rulers could engage in persecutions with impunity. Jews were expelled from England in 1290, from France in 1394, from Prague in 1400, and from Vienna in 1421. The completion of the Christian reconquest of Iberia in 1492 was crowned by the expulsion from Spain (and, in 1497, from Portugal) of all Jews and Moslems who refused to convert. Where they were not expelled, they were compulsorily segregated, beginning in 1516 in Venice, which established the first Jewish ghetto, named after the unused foundry near which the Jews were required to settle.

Renaissance, Reformation, and Counter-Reformation

By the end of the fifteenth century the physical and economic segregation of the Jews of Europe was nearing completion and irrational popular beliefs about them were widespread. The intellectual upheavals of the sixteenth century associated with Renaissance humanism and the Reformation at first promised some relief, but on balance the situation of the Jews deteriorated further as a result of them.

The humanists placed the study of man in this world in the center of their thought and condemned religious dogmatism. Some, like the German Johannes Reuchlin, showed a sympathetic interest in Jewish theology, following in the footsteps of Giovanni Pico della Mirandola; others, like Erasmus of Rotterdam, were prominent in their denunciation of bigotry. But many humanists shared the prevalent image of Jews as backward and fanatical, in this way anticipating the views held by many luminaries of the eighteenth-century Enlightenment.

In the Lutheran Reformation, with its reverence for the Old Testament and its hostility toward Rome, Jews also saw prospects of relief. But, disappointed in the Jews' failure to convert to his new doctrine, Luther published *Concerning the Jews and Their Lies* (1543), which not only repeated all medieval libels against Jews but went further than his predecessors in explicitly preaching violence: "We are at fault in not slaying them," Luther wrote. In two respects, however, the Reformation eased the burden of hatred. Because Protestant churches rejected the doctrine of transubstantiation, accusations of ritual murder became rare in Protestant Europe. Calvinism, with its even stronger roots in the Old Testament, was in the main better disposed toward Jews. Spanish and Portuguese Jews found a haven in Amsterdam, and Oliver Cromwell invited Jews back to Reformation England in 1655. In both places they lived under conditions that were, though short of equality, benign by the standards of the day.

The Catholic Counter-Reformation, with its emphasis on the reaffirmation of doctrinal orthodoxy, was predictably hostile to Jews. The Jesuit order was founded in 1534 to spearhead the defense of the Roman Catholic church, and in 1542 Pope Paul III revived the Inquisition. Following the reconquest of Spain, the church turned its attention toward the supposed danger from *marranos*, Jews who had converted to Christianity but continued—or were suspected of continuing—to be faithful to Judaism. Hence the Jesuits instituted the "purity of blood" test, restricting membership in their order to those of proven Christian parentage.

One further element exacerbated Catholic-Jewish relations. In the course of the Middle Ages, knowledge of the Babylonian Talmud, completed around 600 C.E., spread to Western Europe, where it was perceived as a challenge to the church's claim to doctrinal monopoly. From 1240 onward, disputations between Christian theologians and Jewish scholars were staged with the aim of discrediting the Talmud. In 1555 Pope Paul IV tried to prohibit all talmudic study. Jewish pressure led to a compromise, but thenceforth the church claimed the right to censor not only Christian but also Jewish teaching.

In addition, the sixteenth century saw an intensification of popular anti-Jewish discourse, which the new technology of printing helped to spread. The coarse anti-Jewish carvings that had begun to appear on late medieval churches now gained wide circulation through woodcuts. One of the commonest of these images was the "Jew sow," which showed Jews in various obscene or humiliating positions with a pig. One legend, the origin of which is obscure but which gained popularity in print from the beginning of the seventeenth century, was that of Ahasuerus, the Wandering Jew, condemned to live forever for having demanded the crucifixion of Christ. Ballads and caricatures, cheaply reproduced, completed the repertoire.

The two centuries following the Counter-Reformation marked the nadir of Jewish existence in Christian Europe. The more efficient administration of the absolutist state meant that discriminatory ordinances were strictly enforced. In much of Europe, Jews were now confined to ghettos under conditions of increasing overcrowding. They were restricted to commercial occupations, which in most cases meant peddling.

They were frequently expelled from cities or states, and plundered by mobs. Segregated and impoverished, the Jews of Europe were the object of almost universal contempt. Even those who rose to wealth as court bankers led dangerous lives. Joseph Süss Oppenheimer, banker to Duke Karl Alexander of Württemberg, was tried on trumped-up charges after his protector's death, and his execution in 1738 was the occasion for a gruesome festival.

Literary antisemitism did not abate in this period. Its most ambitious product was Johann Andreas Eisenmenger's *Entdecktes Judentum* (Judaism Revealed, 1710), a compendium of medieval and later theological arguments against Judaism and its adherents, which was frequently plundered by later propagandists. But Eisenmenger's book also marked the end of an epoch, in that it restricted its arguments to the religious level. From the second half of the eighteenth century on, rationalism and enlightenment dominated the public debate. Though the outcome of rationalism was Jewish emancipation, the new learning was not an unmixed blessing for Jews.

Enlightenment and Emancipation

A central enterprise of the Enlightenment was a critique of religion. Though the primary object of scrutiny was Christianity, Judaism was not spared attention. Immanuel Kant criticized the alleged primitiveness and intellectual stagnation of Judaism, Baron d'Holbach tarred Judaism as the precursor of Christianity, and Voltaire denounced Jews in traditional terms for their parasitic and decadent lifestyle.

Advocates of toleration and emancipation, of whom the most influential was the Prussian civil servant Christian Wilhelm Dohm (*Über die Bürgerliche Verbesserung der Juden,* On Civic Improvement of the Jews, 1781–82), differed from their contemporaries in believing that human beings, including Jews, were capable of reform. Their starting point, however, was usually the supposed squalid condition of Jewry; they thereby helped unintentionally to perpetuate the traditional unfavorable image of the Jew. When in 1791 Jews were granted full civil rights in revolutionary France, Count Stanislas Clermont-Tonnerre declared, "Everything for the Jews as individuals, nothing for the Jews as a nation." Similar propositions appeared in Wilhelm von Humboldt's memorandum (1810) in favor of Jewish emancipation in Prussia. There emerged what became known as the Emancipation contract: Jews, in exchange for civil liberties, were to cease to be "a state within the state" and were to assimilate to general society. This development added two new dimensions to antisemitism. On the one hand, it consisted of those who resented the emergence of Jews from the ghetto. On the other, there were those who complained that emancipated Jews had failed to fulfill their part of the contract. Combined with the inherited prejudices, these new dimensions defined the agenda of post-Emancipation antisemitism.

Postrevolutionary Antisemitism

Whereas the effect of prerevolutionary antipathy toward Judaism was to emphasize the otherness of Jews, post-Emancipation antisemitism was a response to the Jewish attempt to enter general society and to the demand for equality—and hence access to power—in place of mere toleration. Before 1791 there had been a consensus concerning the inferiority of Jews but no systematic campaign against them. After 1791, the prejudice turned into an ideology, and slogans became policy. This evolution was possible because the new fear of Jews did not replace the old contempt; indeed, the firmly implanted consensus on Jewish inferiority taught that Jews were unfit for equal status.

This reaction to Jewish aspirations to equality spread from west to east in Europe. The earliest evidence of it appeared in France; it was formulated by the Abbé Auguste Barruel, who, having first blamed the French Revolution on freemasonry, in 1820 proclaimed that the Masons were dominated by Jews. Barruel's thesis served as the wellspring of belief in a Jewish world conspiracy. Also in France there appeared the first systematic antisemitic literature, stimulated by the rise of such banking houses as Rothschild, Pereire, and Fould and their close links with the French government. The hostile propaganda came on from antirevolutionary Catholic conservatives (such as Vicomte de Bonald), but even more from anticapitalist radicals like Pierre-Joseph Proudhon, Charles Fourier, and Fourier's disciple Alphonse Toussenel. Toussenel's *Les Juifs, Rois de l'Epoque* (1847) launched a slogan that has been a mainstay of antisemites worldwide: "Death to parasitism! War on the Jews!" French antisemitic literature of this type, which combined elements of the antiliberal right with those of the anticapitalist left, reached its apogee with Edouard Drumont's antisemitic best-seller *La France Juive* (1886) and his newspaper, *La Libre Parole*.

Further east, in German-speaking Europe, organized antisemitism developed later, in accordance with the later emergence of a public political sphere. Whereas in France it was directed against an Emancipation already achieved, elsewhere it was directed against an anticipated one. As in France, antisemitism was based both on inherited, prerevolutionary stereotypes and on a fear of the economic and political power that free and equal Jews might wield. Moreover, the notion of Jewish Emancipation challenged the Christian-Germanic ideology of cultural and even racial exclusiveness; it became tarnished by an association with French revolutionary ideas, as some of the most prominent political radicals of the first half of the nineteenth century—Karl Marx, Heinrich Heine, and Ludwig Börne, among others—were of Jewish parentage.

The outbreak of the revolutions of 1848 made antisemitism a pan-European phenomenon. Jewish Emancipation was one of the objectives of the liberals and radicals who led the revolutions. Many of the leading revolutionaries were Jews, thus reinforcing the equation of Jews with democracy and subversion. Above all, the large number of Jewish journalists gave rise to the right-wing denunciation of a so-called Judenpresse (Jewish press).

The nationalist element in the revolutions of 1848 opened another potential source of Jewish-Gentile conflict. Where would the allegiances of Jews lie in the new Europe of ethnic identities? Some of the new nationalist movements, such as the Hungarian, were eager to recruit Jews to their cause; others, like those of the Slav nationalities, resented the Jews' traditional economic roles and viewed them as allies of the dominant nation-states—as agents of German, Hungarian, or Russian power. In the years 1848–49 throughout Europe the so-called Jewish question became part of the public political agenda. Four themes dominated the debate: Jewish political radicalism, Jewish control of the media, the threat of Jewish economic dominance, and the question of whether the political and cultural gulf between Jews and non-Jews could be bridged.

Antisemitism as Mass Politics

Organized antisemitism, a phenomenon of the age of mass politics, emerged in the second half of the nineteenth century. Its ideological components were in place by the time of the 1848 revolutions, but their distribution and popularity varied from country to country. At one extreme, anti-Jewish sentiment amounted to little more than social snobbery directed at newly wealthy Jews, though such attitudes created serious obstacles to Jewish entry into elite institutions and professions. As a mass phenomenon, modern antisemitism represented two elements of unease in a changing world: the challenge that the growth of a money economy posed to the traditional occupations of peasants and artisans; and the insecure political identities of young nation-states. Organized antisemitism could take the form of specifically antisemitic political parties or of movements that included antisemitic paragraphs in more general programs.

The antisemitism of economic resentment first took organized political form in Germany and Austria-Hungary. In Germany, it was at the heart of the Christian Social party, launched in 1879 by the court preacher Adolf Stoecker, and of the more radical par-

ties, led by Otto Böckel and Hermann Ahlwardt, that displaced it in the early 1890s. In Austria, economic antisemitism appeared in the early 1880s in the artisan defense movement of the Österreichischer Reformverein (Austrian Reform Association) and achieved political success in 1895 when Karl Lueger, leader of the Christian Social party, was elected mayor of Vienna. These movements did not restrict themselves to economic resentment; both the Lutheran Stoecker and the Austrian Catholic journalist Karl Freiherr von Vogelsang, the chief intellectual supporter of the antisemitic movement, blamed Jews for the decline in traditional moral values.

Austria, a multinational polity torn by ethnic strife, also saw the rise of the antisemitism of national exclusiveness, pioneered by Georg von Schönerer, who sought to deny the aspirations of most educated and prosperous Austrian Jews to identify with German

Photographic propaganda in the Vienna "Eternal Jew" exhibition. 2 August 1940

culture. Doubts about Jewish loyalty to national causes, and indignation at their commercial role, also arose among other national movements in the Habsburg monarchy and beyond, especially among the Czechs; but, except in Poland, which was under Russian domination, nationalist antisemitic political parties were ephemeral and uninfluential. The antisemitism of nationalist exclusiveness was strongest among students in Central Europe. The younger generation felt most strongly the frustrations of the unfulfilled promise of nationhood that attended the creation of the German empire in 1871 and the adoption of the liberal constitution of the Austro-Hungarian monarchy of 1867. In both countries, student corporations progressively excluded Jews from membership, those of Austria resolving in 1896 to ban duels with Jews. In Germany, the antisemitic Verein Deutscher Studenten (German Students' Association), founded in 1881, derived its inspiration from the unsuccessful anti-Emancipation petition of 1880 and the series of articles published in 1879 by the historian Heinrich von Treitschke, which concluded with the cry, "The Jews are our misfortune!"

The decades before the First World War saw the further spread of organized antisemitism. The antisemitic revival in France, associated with Drumont, was a response to the liberalism of the Third Republic, founded in 1875. Its apparent failure to respond adequately to the 1870 defeat by Prussia fed a revanchist movement of all-embracing nationalism that was catalyzed by the Dreyfus affair, in which Alfred Dreyfus, a captain in the French army and a Jew, was falsely accused of espionage. The affair fed the antisemitic nationalism of Maurice Barrès and the reactionary monarchism of the Action Française under Charles Maurras (1868–1952). Antisemitism also spread to North America, where it was fostered by the same mixture of economic resentment and nationalist insecurity. Anti-Jewish overtones appeared in some populist propaganda but were especially prominent in mixture with the anti-immigrant and anti–African American rhetoric of nativist groups such as the Ku Klux Klan, to name the most extreme. The lynching of a Jewish factory-owner's nephew, Leo Frank, in Georgia in 1915, was dramatic evidence of this antisemitic reaction.

In this period, manifestations of antisemitism were most frequent and appalling in tsarist Russia. A series of pogroms broke out following the assassination of Tsar Alexander III in 1881 and again between 1903 and 1906. These mob actions, in which Jews were assaulted and their homes and businesses destroyed, occurred with the connivance or at least the tacit tolerance of the authorities. They were inspired by the familiar mixture of anticapitalism and the identification of Jews with revolutionary politics, though most of the victims of the random violence were neither rich nor revolutionary. The intensity with which conservative Russians feared Jews was shown by the publication in 1905 of the *Protocols of the Elders of Zion,* a plagiarism of an earlier French satire of the emperor Napoleon III, which purported to expose a conspiracy for Jewish world domination.

Any politically effective antisemitic movement before 1914 had to be ideologically eclectic, combining populist anticapitalism with exclusive nationalism and, at times, religious prejudice. *Der Talmudjude,* by the Catholic theologian August Rohling, rehashed Eisenmenger's denunciation of the Talmud; it went through a number of editions after initial publication in 1871. Accusations of ritual murder reappeared, first in Tisza-Eszlár in Hungary in 1882; there followed a series of incidents in Germany, Bohemia, and Poland, culminating in the trial (and acquittal) of Mendel Beilis in Kiev in 1913.

An ideological innovation of this reaction against Jewish emancipation was the resort to arguments based on race, as, for instance, in Houston Stewart Chamberlain's *The Foundations of the Nineteenth Century* (1899). Many anthropologists and other students of "race science" asserted that Jewish inferiority was immutably determined by nature and could not therefore be remedied by legislation. This mixture of antimodernist and modernist arguments demonstrates that antisemitism at the beginning of the twentieth century did not form one coherent ideology but could, whether out of fanaticism or opportunism, be modeled to appeal to different clienteles in different places at different times.

The High Tide of Antisemitism, 1918–45

Antisemitic movements were, with few exceptions, fringe phenomena before 1914. No government that had granted emancipation seriously thought of rescinding it. Only in tsarist Russia were Jews physically threatened by bodies like the League of the Russian People (the Black Hundreds). The ideological arsenal of antisemitism that was assembled in those years helped propel antisemitic activity after the First World War.

A march against antisemitism.

The causes of this escalation were manifold: the economic distress and social dislocation caused by the war; the intensified nationalism of the newly independent states of Europe; the fear of the spread of communism after the Bolshevik revolution in Russia; and opposition to the introduction of parliamentary democracy in the wake of revolutionary upheavals in Central Europe at the end of the war. Russian émigrés to the West brought with them the *Protocols of the Elders of Zion,* which now enjoyed widespread circulation, even after they were proved to be a crude fraud.

The strongest antisemitic outbursts after the war were in the defeated imperial states—Germany, Austria, and Hungary—and the newly created states—Poland, Romania, Lithuania, and Latvia—whose fragile national identity and underdeveloped economies seemed threatened by large Jewish populations. The multiple resentments in Germany led to a proliferation of organizations of the radical right, which recruited heavily among ex-servicemen and which engaged in violence against Jews and political opponents. The biggest of these was the Deutschvölkischer Schutz- und Trutzbund (Racist Protection and Defiance League), which was responsible for a number of political assassinations, including that of the Jewish foreign minister Walther Rathenau in 1922. The vandalization of synagogues and Jewish cemeteries and calls to boycott Jewish businesses persisted throughout the time of the Weimar republic.

The most extreme of the many radical-right bodies was the National Socialist German Workers' (Nazi) party, led from 1920 by Adolf Hitler. Although it outdid its rivals in the virulence of its propaganda, it invented no new arguments. It differed from the rest of the radical right only in its ability to assemble a mass following after the onset of the 1929 economic depression. Whether the Nazis' electoral victories were attributable primarily to antisemitism is difficult to es-

Four SA pickets sing in front of the F. W. Woolworth department store on the Alexanderplatz in Berlin. The Nazis assumed that the international chain was owned by Jews and included this store in their boycott of Jewish businesses. New York officials of the company later denied this claim.

tablish, but it seems to have been no obstacle. National Socialism also grew in Austria, where violence against Jews was even more widespread than in Germany. In both states, the various factions of the radical right found common ground in their denunciations of the newly democratic "Jew Republics."

In Eastern Europe, ultranationalism and anticommunism led to direct discrimination against Jews. Explicitly antisemitic movements were influential in Poland (National Democrats, or Endecija), Hungary (Arrow Cross), Romania (League of Saint Michael, or Iron Guard), and Slovakia (Hlinka Guards). In both Hungary and Poland, discriminatory measures were implemented, imposing quotas on university entry and participation in certain trades and professions, especially the state service.

Under the impact of post-1918 uncertainties and, after 1933, the example of Nazi Germany, antisemitism also spread in the liberal West. In France a number of radical-right movements appeared, in addition to Action Française, fanned by the scandal involving the financier Serge Stavisky. In Britain, the principal antisemitic forces were Sir Oswald Mosley's British Union of Fascists and the more extreme Imperial Fascist League. In the United States, antisemitism was vigorously propagated by Henry Ford's newspaper, the *Dearborn Independent*, and the Union party of the radio priest, Father Charles E. Coughlin, which contested the 1936 presidential election. But where liberal institutions were firmly implanted, antisemitism was politically containable; it was restricted to social attitudes and to literature, such as the works of Hilaire Belloc and G. K. Chesterton in Britain and of Louis-Ferdinand Céline, Pierre Drieu la Rochelle, and Robert Brasillach in France.

Antisemitism became an object of public policy most notably in Germany, where the Nazi party gained power in January 1933. There its implementation took three principal forms. The first was the exclusion of Jews from public life and government service, the deprivation of citizenship on the basis of descent (not religious affiliation) through the Nuremberg Laws of 1935, and the step-by-step expulsion from professions and commercial life that was virtually complete by 1938. Jewish property was either confiscated or forcibly bought up at depressed prices. The second form was publicly licensed violence, as in the boycott of Jewish shops and the book burnings of 1933 and the destruction of synagogues on Kristallnacht in November 1938. The third was the arbitrary detention and ill-treatment of Jews—and, indeed, many non-Jews—in concentration camps. These policies were extended to areas annexed or occupied by Nazi Germany, beginning with Austria in March 1938 and followed by the Sudetenland and then the rest of Bohemia and Moravia in 1938 and 1939.

The culmination of applied antisemitism came after the outbreak of the Second World War, with the deportation of the Jews of Europe to ghettos in Eastern Europe and then their murder in extermination camps. Although the Nazi leadership was responsible for initiating this policy, its implementation was possible only through the aid of collaborators in the occupied countries of Western and Eastern Europe. It is inconceivable that the thousands of individuals—from SS officers to captains of industry to average citizens who reported Jews in hiding—who willfully participated in the Shoah could have acted as they did had they not inherited prejudices that developed over two millennia, the effect of which was to dehumanize Jews and create a consensus that they were not entitled to equal civil rights.

Antisemitism after 1945

The Shoah discredited antisemitism, at least as it was openly practiced before 1945. This does not mean that antisemitism disappeared from Europe and North America, the regions where it had been most widespread. But overt discrimination, even in private institutions, was gradually outlawed, and public expression of antisemitism has come to be considered shameful. It is no longer possible to base a mainstream political career on an explicit antisemitic program.

There are, however, some developments that have aided a revival of antisemitism. The increasingly nationalist tone of Soviet politics under Stalin and his successors led to denunciations of "rootless cosmopolitanism" and, under the rule of Nikita Khrushchev (1953–64), to targeting Jews as scapegoats for economic shortcomings. The establishment of a Jewish state in Israel in 1948 led to the reintroduction of traditional antisemitic themes into anti-Zionist polemics, including the emphasis on Jewish financial power or influence in the media. Themes borrowed from European antisemitism have found their way into Arab or Islamic anti-Zionist discourse. The emergence of extreme nationalist movements and the social dislocation that followed the collapse of communism in the late

1980s have also helped to revive some of the cruder propaganda of the 1930s in Eastern Europe. At the turn of the twenty-first century, while in many of the old heartlands of antisemitism, particularly Central Europe and North America, an effective countervailing culture has been established, in more credulous regions, such as parts of the former Soviet Union or of the Arab-Muslim world, older beliefs have enjoyed a new life, buttressed in some cases by a resuscitation of the *Protocols of the Elders of Zion*. *Peter Pulzer*

Antonescu, Ion (1880–46) Pro-Nazi dictator of Romania (1940–44), responsible for the deportation and murder of more than 250,000 Jews. Antonescu was executed in 1946 as a war criminal. See ROMANIA

Armia Krajowa See HOME ARMY

Arrow Cross Hungarian fascist movement and pro-Nazi political party, founded by Ferenc Szalasi in 1937. During its brief time in power from October 1944 to January 1945 the Arrow Cross party sent 80,000 Jews on a death march to the Austrian border. See HUNGARY

Art When World War II ended in Europe in May 1945 and the concentration camps were liberated, the Allied nations were suddenly confronted with the reality of Nazi criminality. Despite the desperate situation of the survivors after liberation, they began almost immediately to collect documents, eyewitness testimonies, artifacts, and memorabilia that would show the horrors that they had experienced and witnessed. One aspect of this endeavor was the retrieval of art produced by professionally trained painters and sculptors in the ghettos, transit camps, and concentration camps between 1939 and 1945. Thus, the Czech artist Leo Haas (1901–83) returned to Terezin (Theresienstadt) after liberation to find 400 clandestine drawings that he had hidden inside the barracks' walls that he subsequently donated to the Terezin Memorial and the State Jewish Museum in Prague. Art made during the Holocaust was also discovered by accident: the U.S. Army medical officer Marcus Smith, for example, received several drawings made by Zoran Music, who had been a political prisoner in Dachau. Art often remained in the possession of the creators or their families. Not all Holocaust art, however, could be recovered, even when the locations where they were hidden were known. Thus, Esther Lurie was not able to retrieve 200 sketches buried in pottery jugs under the rubble of her sister's house in the former Kovno ghetto.

Despite the availability of this substantial but fragmentary record of Holocaust art in 1945, the immediate postwar period was not propitious for a broader reception and appreciation of art produced by victims. Unknown and underutilized for many decades, and overshadowed by the immense written record about the mass murder of European Jews and other groups, their works were initially considered a historical and aesthetic curiosity. The value of art and creative literature as a form of Holocaust documentation was not understood until the basic history of the Holocaust was written. Furthermore, historians and political scientists, untrained in evaluating visual sources of historical evidence, were uncomfortable with the nuances and symbolic language of the artistic record.

A number of factors led to the resurgence of interest in Holocaust art during the 1960s and 1970s. The rise of a new generation unfamiliar with the history of the Holocaust contributed to the demand for images that would provide explanations, immediacy, and authenticity. Hollywood had already discovered the Holocaust in such dramatic films as *The Diary of Anne Frank* (1959), *Exodus* (1960), and *Judgment at Nuremberg* (1961). Coincidentally, the television coverage of the Eichmann trial in Jerusalem was widely seen in the United States. Moreover, serious academic literature such as Raul Hilberg's classic *Destruction of the European Jews* (1961) and Isaiah Trunk's *Judenrat* (1972) became available. This context led museums and scholars after the mid-1970s to discover the subject of Holocaust art.

Until the 1970s the American public had perceived the Holocaust as an uncomfortable foreign experience whose primary impact was felt in Israel and Europe. The NBC television film *Holocaust*, which aired in 1979–80, marked a decisive shift by making the Holocaust a household term with more flexible meanings. Ironically, the film depicted the story of a persecuted artist and was based loosely on the life of Leo Haas. A new distinction arose between two parallel and overlapping phenomena: Holocaust art and art about the Holocaust.

The term *Holocaust art* refers to those works created in situ in Europe between 1933 and 1945 by artists who were simultaneously victims of Nazi persecution. It is not limited to a single school or style of art and reflects works produced by several different generations of artists trapped in Nazi Germany and occupied Europe.

It refers to works produced mostly by professionals, but also by amateurs and sometimes by children, in certain distinctive physical settings: in prisons, transit camps, concentration camps, labor camps, ghettos, hiding places, and the resistance. The artist and victim were one and the same person, not social critics or political artists like Daumier and Goya, who worked remote from actual events. The affected artists could not work openly; nor could they exhibit in museums or galleries if they were proscribed as racial or political opponents of the Nazi regime. The victim as artist served as his or her own chronicler, historian, archivist, and audience, having to improvise the materials needed for clandestine work, utilizing the backs of SS circulars, wrapping paper, medical forms, and even paper recycled from SS target practice for drawings. Color came from charcoal, rust, ink, food, and vegetable dyes. Unlike artists working in normal conditions, whose reputations derived from a careful selection of the finished products of their creative labors, the victim-artists of the Holocaust are usually evaluated through preliminary sketches and studies for works that often were never completed. Sometimes the surviving works of art were unsigned, and the artists' identities consequently remained unknown.

The second category, art about the Holocaust, or the Holocaust in art, refers to works whose subject matter concerns the Holocaust. It includes works created both during and after the war by survivors, refugees, and artists not directly involved in the events of 1933–45. Despite substantial differences in individual styles and in genres, art about the Holocaust has a cosmopolitan character, whereas Holocaust art created in situ is more self-contained. The iconography and motifs of art about the Holocaust are frequently derived from the broader symbolic vocabulary associated with art against war and oppression. Art about the Holocaust also includes postwar monuments, public sculpture, and memorials. These works are clearly more polished than the sketches, paintings, and small sculp-

Jozef Szajna, "Drang nach Osten—Drang nach Westen." 1987

Drawing by Bertalan Göndor. 29 April 1944

ture created under conditions of captivity. Individual stylistic preference, aesthetic judgments, and the skill and personality of the artist are obvious determinants of the character of the artistic product. Postperiod art about the Holocaust—that is, works created after 1945—involves a transformation and extension of the strictly historical usage of the term *Holocaust*, thereby testifying to the impact of the subject on the present-day imagination. What unites the art created during and after the Holocaust is that such art satisfies the need to give meaning to human suffering through creative expressions in art and literature.

The transition between Holocaust art and art about the Holocaust is reflected in the life of Alfred Kantor (born 1923, Prague). As a survivor of Theresienstadt, Schwarzheide, and Auschwitz, he had destroyed many of the in situ drawings he had completed in concentration camps and ghettos, fearing reprisals by the Nazis. His art was a mnemonic device used to imprint his experiences as documentary evidence. After the war he

wrote, "My commitment to drawing came out of a deep instinct for self-preservation and undoubtedly helped me to deny the unimaginable horrors of life at that time. By taking on the role of observer, I could at least for a few moments detach myself from what was going on in Auschwitz and was therefore better able to hold the threads of sanity."

An artist's detachment and aesthetic decision, stepping back to judge spatial relationships and composition, enabled victim-artists temporarily to transcend the brutal realities of life as prisoners in concentration camps. After liberation Kantor noted, "I packed my drawings and my sketches and joined a group of ex-prisoners who were going to a displaced persons' camp in Deggendorf, Germany. And it was here that I immediately began to work. Within a matter of days I went to look for a bookbinder. A week later a book of blank pages was ready and I proceeded to fill them, to record what I had seen and observed."

The art created in situ between 1933 and 1945 reflects what Jean Améry called "a spiritual frame of reference in the widest sense." The extant Holocaust art consists of approximately 30,000 drawings, paintings, and several sculptures. The number of works is probably even higher, if art by racial and political opponents and refugees between 1933 and 1939 is included. Extrapolating from known statistics and the thousands of localities containing concentration camps, it would be reasonable to estimate that the original corpus of the clandestine works may have exceeded 100,000 paintings, drawings, sculptures, and other objects, such as dolls and puppets. This figure is based on the assumption that, at best, only one out of 10 works survived. Zoran Music made 200 drawings in Dachau between 1943 and 1945; only 36 works survived. Of the 200 sketches that Esther Lurie buried in pottery jugs in the Kovno ghetto, only 11 were found in 1945. Almost none of the works that Max Linger completed between 1939 and late 1940 survived, because the artist had been unable to arrange secure hiding places while he was being transferred to a succession of internment camps in southern France. A collection of drawings done by Sachsenhausen prisoners was destroyed during the death march from Sachsenhausen to Buchenwald. Aleksander Kulisiewicz, a Polish political prisoner and musicologist safeguarding more than 50 works, awoke one morning to discover his fellow prisoners burning his collection as fuel for a bonfire so that they would not freeze to death in subzero weather.

It is not surprising that so small a proportion of Holocaust art survived, for the conditions that threatened human life also endangered the preservation of art. Many works fell prey to Nazi confiscations, vandalism, Allied bombings, vulnerable hiding places, the artists' deaths, repeated deportations, and the inherent fragility of the materials the artists had been able to acquire for their work. We do not even know the locations of all works that did manage to survive. Works were often traded for food and clothing; occasionally they were smuggled out of the camps by friends, fellow inmates, and members of the resistance, their destinations untraced. Some works were extorted from artist-victims by corrupt camp guards; others were given voluntarily as gifts to relief workers and Red Cross volunteers who had tried to ameliorate conditions in camps like Gurs in southern France. The Polish prisoner artist Karol Konieczny wrote of losing works that he had completed in a Gestapo prison in Vienna: "I did eight pieces of a small album in postcard size. I offered these to my cellmates; the rest were taken by a friendly Viennese guard who promised to hold them for me until the end of the war. He also transferred one album illegally to my mother. After the war, I learned that he had been caught carrying prisoners' letters, and was court-martialed and beheaded in Vienna in May 1944."

Artists also destroyed their own works because of "menacing SS surveillance." Alfred Kantor destroyed the works he made nightly from July 1944 to April 1945 in the Schwarzheide camp near Dresden. Janina Tollik and Halina Olomucki told of works they had voluntarily destroyed in Auschwitz-Birkenau for fear of discovery and subsequent torture. It is thus impossible to reconstruct the full range of art produced during the Holocaust. Nevertheless, the surviving works from hundreds of artists in various concentration camps and ghettos provide a representative cross-section of individual styles and common themes.

It is even more difficult to establish the absolute number and identities of the murdered artists. Deportation lists by profession rarely exist, and concentration camp registers and arrest records are incomplete. Many artists hid their profession, believing that physical strength and job skills rather than artistic imagination would lead to survival. The German Jewish Communist artist Herbert Sandberg, for example, survived the deportation of most Jews from Buchenwald to Auschwitz-Birkenau because he had become a skilled bricklayer and stonemason at Buchenwald. Moreover, the precariousness of Holocaust art in the face of virulent and destructive events is clear from the comparatively large number of works that were not signed so that they could not be traced back to specific prisoners if discovered by SS camp guards. In other instances, lists bearing names of artists survive, but their artworks have vanished. Several Jewish painters and sculptors, whose names were listed in an August 1943 report on the extermination of Polish Jews, were deported from the Warsaw ghetto to Treblinka in September 1942, but their ghetto artworks were never found.

Clandestine Holocaust art was preserved by a combination of conscious planning and fortuitous accident. The victim-artists were conscious of their role as witnesses and instinctively tried to preserve their diaries and artworks as historical evidence. When the artists hid their works in secret caches and smuggled them to the relative safety of the outside world, they assured that their probable deaths would not be compounded by silence and the loss of their documentary art.

Artists contributed to the well-established efforts at documentation in most ghettos. Emmanuel Ringelblum's secret archives hidden below the rubble of the Warsaw ghetto, code-named Oneg Shabbos (Hebrew for "enjoyment of the Sabbath"), included the diary and several portraits by Gela Seksztein. The Kovno ghetto archives included the works of several artists. In Theresienstadt artists hid their works in metal cases that were bricked and plastered into the walls of ghetto buildings. Other works were buried in the ground or hidden in attic lofts. Zoran Music chose a particularly ironic hiding place, storing them in a hollowed-out copy of Hitler's *Mein Kampf* shelved in the Dachau concentration camp library. Aldo Carpi secreted his works in a wall of a Gusen munitions factory that functioned as a satellite camp of Mauthausen. Other works survived because they were smuggled out of the ghettos and concentration camps. The artist Bruno Apitz smuggled his works out of Buchenwald with the help of a friendly Kapo; they were hidden with a family in a nearby village and retrieved after the war.

In addition to concealment and smuggling, some art was sent through the censored postal system. Bertalan Göndör openly mailed eight postcards, postmarked between March and May 1944 and stamped with censorship cachets, from the labor camps at Bereg in eastern Hungary to his wife in Budapest. Similar mailing opportunities existed in many other camps and ghettos; even in Auschwitz, some inmates were permitted to write at least one reassuring letter to their families. Obviously all mail by prisoners from concentration camps and ghettos was censored and limited in frequency, content, and format; only small amounts of art of relatively small size, usually decorating the margins of postcards or short letters and seemingly innocuous in content, were able to reach safety via the postal route.

Even works of art that had been carefully hidden from 1939 to 1945 were not all recoverable after the war. The survival of art followed the pattern of the survival of most Nazi and Jewish records. Much of it was barely intact even in 1945. Some of the works of Holocaust art were damaged during Allied bombing raids; other works were destroyed by moisture and mold in improvised storage locations. Loose paper was looted as souvenirs by soldiers and noncombatants alike, and documents as well as artworks were also used as fuel and toilet paper. Some art was found immediately in the displaced persons camps. This postwar recovery of

Holocaust art began immediately upon the liberation of camps and the end of the war in 1945 and continues today.

Holocaust art can be divided into five main categories: portraits and self-portraits, inanimate objects (including landscapes and still lifes), evidentiary art, caricatures, and abstract or nonrepresentational art.

The largest single group of Holocaust art is portraits and self-portraits, representing almost 25 percent of surviving drawings and sculptures. This overwhelming number of portraits is not an accident, as diaries and documents indicate that this was the most common genre. Portraits had a magical meaning in the setting of the concentration camps, as they do in many native and folk art forms. They gave the subject a sense of permanent presence among the living, extremely important when temporal physical presence was so fragile and tenuous. The German Jewish artist Felix Nussbaum, for example, conveyed his own plight in self-portraits. Occasionally portraits were also commissioned by Nazis for use as gifts to superiors and even as documentation of medical experiments: Josef

Self-portrait of Felix Nussbaum (1904–44) holding Judenpass. 1943

Mengele commissioned a Czech Jewish artist, Dinah Gottliebova, to do portraits of Gypsies as illustrations for a book he hoped to publish about his medical experiments.

The second largest category in the extant works of Holocaust art, representing about 20 percent of the surviving works, consists of drawings of inanimate objects, landscapes, and still lifes. These were especially numerous in the art of the Theresienstadt ghetto, where attics were crammed with confiscated and involuntarily abandoned Jewish property. Art produced in the ghettos, prisons, transit camps, and concentration camps reveal certain common architectural features that expressed the impact of incarceration—barbed wire, guard towers, closed gates, ghetto walls, prison bars, railroad tracks, and corpses or mannequins with blank faces. Imprisoned artists also depicted the bucolic landscapes outside the camps—especially at Theresienstadt—in vivid contrast to the interior landscape within the barracks.

The third type of Holocaust art was evidentiary. Thus, Karl Schwesig's miniatures show the daily life of internees in Gurs and Noé. Other drawings portrayed conditions in camps whose history is less well known, such as Compiègne in occupied northern France and Fossoli in northern Italy. Evidentiary art ranged from generic pictures of camp life (roll calls, selections, torture, food distribution, and forced labor) to specific images of skeletal corpses with their prisoner identification numbers, as for example in the work of Léon Delarbre in Buchenwald or Zoran Music in Dachau. This category accounts for about 20 percent of the surviving Holocaust artwork.

Holocaust art was also sometimes used as evidence in postwar trials. Thus, seven sketches about the crematoriums and gas chambers at Auschwitz-Birkenau by the Czech Jewish survivor Yehuda Bacon and 19 drawings made between 1943 and 1945 by the Polish Jewish prisoner Zofja Rosenstock were entered into evidence at the Eichmann trial in Jerusalem.

Caricatures (20 percent) and abstract nonrepresentational art (20 percent) show the artists' ability to distance themselves from their surroundings and even to mock their tragic situation or to transform actual daily terrors into nonobjective symbols. Most of these works were relatively small in size (usually 15 × 23 centimeters or less) and drawn in pencil, ink, and sometimes in primary ink colors. Bertalan Göndör drew cartoon sketches in pencil on the reverse side of censored postcards in Jewish labor camps in eastern Hungary, and the Czech artist Cisar filled a small notebook with satirical sketches in blue ink of daily life in Dachau. Hans Reichel produced 42 abstract works in watercolor in his notebook (later published under the title *Cahiers de Gurs*) during the summer of 1942. The diary accompanying these sketches relates conditions to color selections and the abstractions of flora and fauna.

Other Holocaust artwork included stage sets for cabaret and theater performances in the Theresienstadt ghetto, and illustrations were drawn in song books at Buchenwald, Sachsenhausen, and the Moor camps. Sculpture exists in very few concentration camp settings, primarily Buchenwald, Hinzert, and Majdanek. Many surviving artists extended their camp drawings in larger postwar cycles of paintings. In *Nous ne Sommes pas les Derniers,* for example, Zoran Music combined images of atomic annihilation with themes from Dachau reflecting death and torture.

Illegal art as well as officially commissioned art even came to the attention of the Auschwitz camp commandant Rudolf Höss, who complained in his Order No. 24 of 8 July 1942 that "prisoners are to be used for useful labor, art leads to an irresponsible and wasteful use of materials that are difficult to get." Such compulsory art was technically excellent as the interned artists' fate depended on compliance with SS orders and whims. This official art was not as significant as the artists' clandestine, self-motivated work.

Clearly, Holocaust art forms the beginning of a continuum between past and present. Although Jean-Paul Sartre, Theodor Adorno, and Elie Wiesel have theorized that artistic works and horror are incompatible, artist-survivors like Karol Konieczny and Jozef Szajna continued to paint to remind the world of their own haunted memories and the legacy of the Holocaust. A few of the survivor artists, such as Zoran Music and Boris Taslitzky, moved from specific camp-related themes to more general contemporary scenes of inhumanity after 1945. Others, like Leo Haas, Max Lingner, Halina Olomucki, and Yehuda Bacon have continued to draw on their Holocaust experiences and incorporate them in their postwar work. Mauricio Lasansky (born 1914), who trained in Argentina and emigrated to the United States in 1943, indicted the Nazi regime in a cycle of pencil and red-wash works first exhibited at the Philadelphia Museum of Art in 1967 under the title *The Nazi Drawings*. The Holo-

Karl Schwesig, ink-drawn postage stamps illustrating Liberty, Equality, Brotherhood, and Flight from the Gurs transit camp. 1941

caust has persisted as a theme of contemporary art in the works of Christian Boltanski, Jochen Gerz, R. B. Kitaj, George Segal, and many younger artists in Europe, Israel, and the United States. The haunting legacy and imagery of the Holocaust has enlarged our understanding of the role of memory of this tragic past.   *Sybil Milton*

Aryan Paragraph Clause, originating in the nineteenth century, that was inserted into the bylaws of certain clubs, associations, and political parties to exclude Jews from membership. The Aryan Paragraph served as the basis for many of the anti-Jewish racial laws in the early years of the Nazi regime.

Athens Capital of Greece, with a Jewish population of 3,500 in 1941. See GREECE

Auschwitz Auschwitz was founded as a German concentration camp in southwestern occupied Poland, about 60 kilometers west of the city of Kraków. Before the war the compound, located near the town of Oswiecim, served as a Polish artillery base. On 27 April 1940 the German army transferred the compound to the SS Inspectorate of Concentration Camps. Later this inspectorate was incorporated into the SS Economic and Administrative Main Office without change of function.

At first Auschwitz was to become a transit center (termed a "quarantine" center) for 10,000 hostile Poles who were to be sent on to Germany as forced laborers. Before long that purpose was reformulated to make the

Interior view of a barracks at Auschwitz-Birkenau. Circa 1944

Construction of Crematorium II at Birkenau. 1942–43

site an ordinary concentration camp. The original buildings were one- and two-story red brick structures that could not hold a sizable inmate population. Accordingly a second floor was added to the low buildings, and new houses were erected. Each of these structures was called a *Block* and given a number.

The man chosen to head the camp, Hauptsturmführer (SS captain) Rudolf Höss, did not hold a rank commensurate with a position of importance. He did have the distinction of having been the youngest sergeant in the German army during World War I and of having acquired Nazi credentials when the movement was still young. With experience of some years in the Dachau and Sachsenhausen concentration camps, his background, competence, and trustworthiness qualified him for command of a small camp in conquered territory. As Auschwitz grew, he was promoted to Obersturmbannführer (SS lieutenant colonel).

During the first half of 1941 the chemical concern I. G. Farben was looking for an appropriate location to produce synthetic rubber and fuel. Attracted by tax advantages, the presence of raw materials, and a railway junction, officials selected a place just east of Auschwitz. Inmates assigned to the company could be transported to work by train. For the SS construction chief Hans Kammler, this development was a signal for expansion. On 17 June 1941 he ordered the capacity of the camp to be enlarged to hold 18,000 inmates by the end of the year. At that moment the principal source of labor was newly arrested Poles from prisons, who were shipped to Auschwitz in daily batches ranging from a few to a few hundred. After the invasion of the Soviet Union on 22 June 1941 and the capture of several million Red Army men during the following months, an opportunity was glimpsed to obtain a much larger number of prisoners. When the German army agreed to hand over several hundred thousand of its captives, the Auschwitz complex was widened to include an expanse about three kilometers to the west, the SS prisoner-of-war camp Birkenau. Although that tract was partially a swamp, the SS planners believed that 125,000 inmates could be quartered there.

Beginning in 1941 construction on a major scale was a daily feature of Auschwitz. Locally three organizations were continually drawing up plans: the SS Zentralbauleitung (Central Construction Directorate), the construction office of the German railways, and the I. G. Farben construction staff. The Zentralbauleitung was responsible for roads, lights, water, guard towers, wire, and buildings, including the barracks in Auschwitz-Birkenau and two industrial halls near the Auschwitz main camp built initially for the Krupp company. The personnel of the Zentralbauleitung, under Karl Bischoff, consisted of barely a hundred architects, engineers, draftsmen, and clerks. Several SS enterprises and about 200 private firms delivered supplies and participated in the actual construction. Inmates were used for much of the manual labor. For all the projects, permission had to be obtained—from the Armaments Ministry to acquire materials, from the railways for the allocation of freight cars, from the

labor offices to station German employees in the area. The railroads in turn laid down track and added facilities for increased traffic. To eliminate daily commuting of prisoners, I. G. Farben built barracks for them adjacent to its rising plant. Opened at the end of October 1942, the company's camp, known as Monowitz, was administratively a part of Auschwitz.

Soviet prisoners began to arrive on foot at the end of 1941 from the nearby prisoner-of-war camp Lamsdorf. Soon the flow was stopped. Three thousand had been sent in to be executed, and the attrition among 12,000 who were intended for labor was so rapid that at the end of February 1942 fewer than 1,000 men were still alive. Yet given the ongoing investments in construction projects, the clock could not be turned back. One other major group now came into view: the Jews. Their destiny, however, was to be shaped by an overriding consideration. They were to disappear as a matter of principle, and Auschwitz was to play a major role in that operation.

Höss notes in his memoir that in mid-1941 he was

Prisoners at forced labor constructing the Krupp factory at Auschwitz. 1942–43

Hungarian Jews upon their arrival at Auschwitz-Birkenau. May 1944

called to Berlin by Reichsführer-SS Heinrich Himmler, who told him that Hitler had decided to annihilate the European Jews and that Auschwitz, by virtue of its location and railway communications, would be a camp for their destruction. The details, said Himmler, would be given to Höss by Adolf Eichmann, the specialist in Jewish affairs in the Reich Security Main Office (RSHA). Höss could not remember a precise date of his meeting with Himmler, and Himmler's appointment calendar, in which the pages for 25 June through 12 August 1941 are missing, contains no reference to Höss. Eichmann confirmed at his trial in Jerusalem that he had visited Auschwitz, but he recalled no date either.

During the summer of 1941, shooting was still the only method for active mass killing, and camps for pure annihilation were not yet on the drawing board. Höss did not know how many Jews would be sent to him or when, and he had no idea of how he would kill a great many people efficiently. One day, when Höss was absent, his deputy, Karl Fritzsch, poisoned a group of Soviet prisoners with hydrogen cyanide, a potent gas that was in stock for fumigation. Another gassing took place, with Höss present, in Block 11. It took two days to air the building. The experiment was repeated, this time in the mortuary of the crematorium. The prisoners tried to break out, but the door remained bolted shut. A camp physician assured Höss that they had suffered no agony, and Höss concluded that this bloodless method would not burden his own men. The cyanide, under the trade name Zyklon B, became the standard lethal agent in the gas chambers of Auschwitz.

The first gassing of Jewish deportees in the mortuary took place in mid-February 1942, when a transport assembled in the Silesian city of Beuthen arrived. In those early days a practice was instituted to deceive the incoming victims. An SS-man would make a speech to them about their having to take a shower before being assigned for work. Without their clothes they walked, unsuspecting, into the chamber. The ruse was so successful that it was used over and over for years.

The improvised facility was in operation at various times in 1942, but the capacity of its two ovens was limited. A new capability was created when two farm houses just outside the electrified fence of Birkenau were converted into gassing buildings with windows walled up and heavy airtight doors installed. One of the structures was ready in March, the other in June, 1942. They were designated Bunkers 1 and 2. Next to each of them, barracks were set up for undressing. The corpses were moved several hundred yards to excavated pits in forested terrain.

Jewish transports were now coming in not only from Upper Silesia but also from Slovakia, the Netherlands, Belgium, France, and Croatia and from other Polish regions. The prisoners were taken from the unloading ramp to the bunkers by truck, men separately from women and children. In the chambers the hydrogen cyanide gas produced death in minutes, but when the chamber doors were opened, some of the bodies were found covered with vomit, excrement, or blood. Himmler, when touring Birkenau during his visit to Auschwitz on 17–18 July 1942, watched without offering any comment as the living stepped out from a train and the dead were dragged from Bunker 2. Afterward he said to Höss that there would be a surge of transports and that Jews not capable of work would have to be annihilated.

As the pits at Birkenau were filled, they became a source of pollution, and between the end of summer and November 1942 they were opened to burn 107,000 maggot-covered bodies. In the meantime other camps, more primitive than Auschwitz and without industrial annexes, were operating on a much larger scale with slower-working carbon monoxide gas. Kulmhof (known as Chelmno in Polish), Belzec, and Sobibor were killing Jews from western and southern Poland, and Treblinka obliterated the Jews of Warsaw and Radom. Auschwitz did not maintain such a pace. As of 31 December 1942 it had received barely 175,000 Jews, while its competitors had already gassed more than 1.4 million.

Body disposal was always a problem in Auschwitz because of the high death rate of the inmates. On 27 February 1942 the SS construction chief Kammler came to Auschwitz to discuss a second crematorium, which at that point was to have two furnaces, each with three retorts. Kammler decided that the number of

furnaces should be increased to five. But that was not the only alteration. In the course of the next few months several other changes were made in the blueprints. A chute for dropping bodies to the morgues in the basement was eliminated, and a staircase that people would use to step down into it was inserted instead. One of the two morgues became an undressing room, and the other was to be equipped with drainage and ventilation systems. The redesigned structure, listed as Bauwerk 30 among the projects of the Zentralbauleitung, had evolved into a combination gas chamber and crematorium unit. It was designated Crematorium II and placed on a site in Birkenau, where its construction was begun on 2 July 1942.

Three additional crematoriums were on the list: 30a, 30b, and 30c. Bauwerk 30a became a twin of 30. Each of the other two, without a cellar, was to have its gas chamber and a double furnace fitted with eight retorts on the ground floor. The numeration was extended from Crematorium II to III, IV, and V, but some time after the original crematorium in the main camp was shut down, the combination units in Birkenau were renumbered I–IV.

The four crematoriums came on line between 31 March and 26 June 1943. It took nine months to finish the two with the underground chambers and about five months to construct the smaller one-floor models. For the ovens and gas chamber design the firm J. A. Topf and Sons of Erfurt was engaged. Its representative, Kurt Prüfer, was a regular visitor in Auschwitz. For the foundations, walls, roofs, smokestacks, plumbing, drainage, ventilation, and electricity, a dozen private contractors were brought in. The doors were assigned to an SS company specializing in carpentry.

The prolongation of the work was due to shortages, disputes, and the delays inherent in approval procedures. Thus the Allgemeine Elektrizitätsgesellschaft (AEG), which was responsible for the power station, told the SS that used parts in the crematoriums would render simultaneous gassing and incineration impossible. The German inmate in charge of prisoner work crews at the crematoriums was consulted to settle an argument about a faulty chimney. In the midst of interrupted deliveries at the end of January 1943 Bischoff wrote to Kammler that Hitler himself had ordered the accelerated completion of the camp. The highest priority, said Bischoff, was to be given to the "special measures" in Birkenau.

To the Zentralbauleitung the actual, albeit belated,

View of a construction site in Auschwitz III (Monowitz). 1942–43

commissioning of the gassing installations was a triumph. The maximum theoretical daily capacity for incineration in the five crematoriums of Auschwitz-Birkenau could now be projected at 4,756. To be sure, this estimate did not take into account repeated malfunctions, particularly in the new Crematorium IV (later designated III), which was one of the troublesome double-oven facilities. Still, Auschwitz had come into its own at last.

The year 1943, however, did not resemble 1942. Polish Jewry had already been reduced to remnants, and heavy inroads had been made into the Jewish communities of Germany, Slovakia, and the Western countries. Romania and Bulgaria refused to surrender Jews from their prewar territories, and Hungary was a holdout. During the first three months of 1943 Auschwitz received about 105,000 Jews. In the next 12 months the figure was 160,000, making a daily rate of less than a tenth of the calculated capacity for cremation. At the same time inmate labor for industrial production was becoming more important. Older Jewish men and women, as well as Jewish children, could be gassed,

but able-bodied individuals were to be selected for labor. In 1943 the total inmate population rose from 25,000 to 85,000. On average more than half were Jews.

The industrialization of Auschwitz spread to outlying areas, where satellite camps came into existence. Eventually this network comprised three dozen locations. The allocation of inmates to a company was fixed by a contract specifying their number and the wages, payable to the SS. The labor was inexpensive, but there was some anxiety among industrial negotiators that skilled prisoners or even the entire rented labor force might suddenly be "withdrawn" for political reasons. The officer in charge of labor in Auschwitz, Hauptsturmführer Heinrich Schwarz, had to reassure a questioner at a Krupp conference that such a contingency was unlikely.

The largest employer of inmate laborers was the SS itself, which used them for construction projects, camp administration, and its own industrial and agricultural enterprises. In second place was the I. G. Farben plant in Monowitz, by far the biggest industrial complex of Auschwitz under construction. I. G. Farben, not relying on inmate labor alone, made use of Poles hired in the free market as well as British prisoners of war. The third-largest user was Oberschlesische Hydrierwerke (Upper Silesian Hydrogenation Works) at Blechhammer. Krupp, also a major employer, was replaced by the firm Weichsel Metall-Union, which took over the Krupp work halls.

The labor force did not grow exponentially, because its turnover was considerable. Many weakened inmates died, and those who did not recover quickly in an infirmary would be killed, either by injections of phenol or in a gas chamber. Other deaths were the result of a typhus epidemic, starvation, overwork, exhaustion, accidents, and often enough injuries willfully inflicted by SS and inmate overseers. Because of high mortality rates two of the outlying camps, Blechhammer and a construction site of the Erdöl-Raffinerie company at Trzebinia, had their own small crematoriums. Even in times of perceived labor shortages the general attitude of camp personnel, passed down to inmate functionaries, was that prisoners were disposable and replaceable.

The SS physicians, headed by Eduard Wirths, who was stationed in Auschwitz because of a heart ailment, performed a variety of tasks. One was the quarantining during the typhus epidemic of almost all uniformed and civilian personnel from July 1942 to April 1943. Temporary quarantines were also imposed on incoming transports if typhus was suspected. Another activity was the selection of people at the ramp and in the sick bays, separating those who were to live from those who were to die. These decisions were made rapidly, with just a glance at an individual. A third was the utilization, mostly of healthy inmates, for medical experiments ranging from the testing by Dr. Hellmuth Vetter of anti-typhus medication, prepared by the pharmaceutical division of I. G. Farben, to sterilization techniques developed by Dr. Carl Clauberg, to studies of twins and dwarfs by Dr. Josef Mengele. Over the years the experiments multiplied alongside the industrial expansion. They too swallowed thousands of inmates.

In the course of these developments, construction of institutional buildings and barracks for inmates continued. The SS budget for these projects was rising, as the replacement of aging watchtowers, which were without amenities, was considered, or when a kennel building and a kitchen with refrigeration was

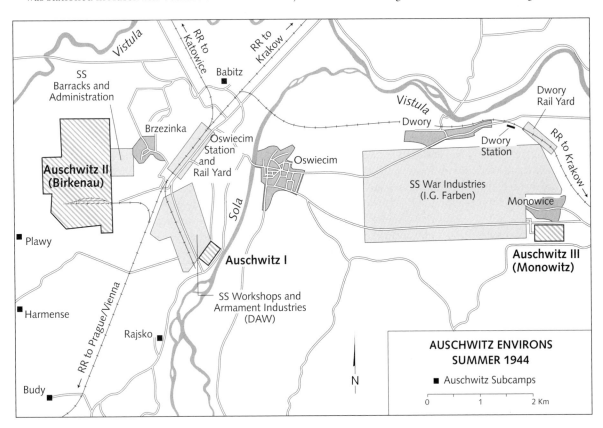

View of the prisoners' latrines in Auschwitz. 1943–44

proposed for the 250 dogs of the canine guard company. Savings were possible by cramming the inmates into so-called horse stable barracks *(Pferdestallbaracken)*, which were prefabricated and comparatively inexpensive. They were placed on bare earth or provided with a thin concrete floor. The same barracks were erected for latrines and washrooms. Space in the latrines was limited, and their use by inmates was timed.

One item of unfinished business was the rail spur for transports bringing deportees. For a long time a temporary ramp close to but outside of Birkenau was used. The SS wanted tracks to be laid through the gate of the Birkenau guard building so that the Jewish transports could be unloaded near the new gas chambers. With such an arrangement fewer guards would be needed, and potential problems would be lessened. There would also be a smaller chance that a train would be held back during times of congestion—a single horse stable barrack was carried by five freight cars. The desired spur, however, was classified as "private" because it would not be open to general traffic. The SS would have to finance the project and obtain the per-

mits for required materials. After many months the firm Richard Reckmann of Cottbus was given the contract, and on 19 April 1944 railroad inspectors approved the spur for use by locomotives.

The period from the completion of the gas chambers to the early spring of 1944 was one of solidification and reorganization. At the beginning of November 1943 Höss was transferred to a post in the Economic and Administrative Main Office, and his replacement, Obersturmbannführer Arthur Liebenschel, divided the camp into three autonomous sections: the main camp *(Stammlager)*, now designated Auschwitz I; Birkenau, no longer a prisoner-of-war camp but Auschwitz II; and Monowitz with the satellites, now Auschwitz III. Each of the camps had a commander: Liebenschel himself took over I, Sturmbannführer Fritz Hartjenstein reigned in II, and Schwarz in III. That month the SS garrison comprised one staff company and four guard companies in Auschwitz I; one staff company, three guard companies (one of which was filled with Ukrainian collaborators), and the guard dog company in II; and two guard companies in III. A substantial number of SS men were on rotation from or to combat units, and a growing portion of the Auschwitz force was made up of ethnic Germans from occupied countries and states allied with Germany. By April 1944 the combined strength of the SS companies and military personnel guarding satellite camps was nearing 3,000.

Augmenting the guards were inmates put in charge of barracks and work parties. The ranks of those in the barracks were camp elder *(Lagerältester)*, block elder *(Blockältester)*, and room orderly *(Stubendienst)*. The rank order in work parties was senior overseer *(Oberkapo)*, overseer *(Kapo)*, and foreman *(Vorarbeiter)*. In the early years of the camp the top positions in this hierarchy were given to German "habitual criminals." Later these men were afforded a chance to "redeem themselves" in a disciplinary unit of the SS. They were replaced by political prisoners, under whom the hardships of the ordinary inmate were somewhat attenuated. Jews had no access to the higher positions, but they could be assigned to indoor work as physicians in the dispensaries or clerks *(Schreiber)* in barracks. These people also held some power, and they had a better-than-average chance to survive.

Work parties *(Arbeitskommandos)* were clothed in striped pajama-style uniforms to frustrate escapes. Colored patches were used throughout the camp area

Prisoners at forced labor in Auschwitz.

to distinguish types of prisoners: red for political opponents, violet for Jehovah's Witnesses, green for criminals, yellow for Jews, black for "asocials" *(Asoziale)*, brown for Gypsies, pink for homosexuals. All inmates—other than Jews and Gypsies sent to a gas chamber on arrival or anyone quarantined or in transit—were given a number. In later years the low numbers were a sign of longevity and carried a certain prestige. The numbers were tattooed on the arms of virtually all except the German prisoners from the beginning of 1943 to late 1944.

Inmates recall that their principal respite was sleep, usually shared with one or two fellow prisoners on straw mattresses in a bunk, and that in the morning they would awake to a daily nightmare. The routine began with a lengthy roll call *(Appell)*. Those in work parties would leave for their stations accompanied by music played by an inmate orchestra. The outdoor workday usually lasted 11 hours, including a half hour allotted to lunch. Inmates performed heavy labor knee-deep in water, or in the mines, or in rain and snow. The corpses of those who died during the day had to be car-

ried back to the compound. Advantaged were men in workshops or women sorting the clothes of the gassed in a Birkenau section called *Kanada* (Canada). For most inmates, hunger never abated; their staples consisted of a meager ration of bread, a coffee substitute, and a soup with cabbage, turnips, carrots, and potatoes. The long day was not finished until after another roll call in the evening.

A special work party was the Jewish *Sonderkommando,* which ushered the doomed into the gas chambers and dragged out the bodies to burn them. Several inmates referred to as "dentists" tore gold fillings and inlays from the mouths of the dead, to be melted into bars in the camp and shipped with confiscated jewelry to Berlin. Severe punishments for minor infractions were part of the routine. Inmates were flogged, or were placed four men at a time into small dark rooms known as standing cells *(Stehzellen)* with no space to sit down, or were hanged. Several thousand prisoners, in the main Poles, were shot between Blocks 10 and 11 in the main camp, at a wall specially cushioned to absorb bullets. In this group were hostages who forfeited their lives when resistance activities took place in occupied Poland.

Jews were in a worse position than non-Jews to survive the camp ordeal for long, and Jews from Greece and Italy, who knew no German or Yiddish and could not understand commands, were more endangered than other Jews. Still, those inmates who were resourceful, tenacious, and circumspect had a chance of surviving the dangers and deprivations. They would eat anything and make themselves as inconspicuous as possible. If they were in an especially oppressive work party, they looked for a transfer to a safer post. But many inmates were bewildered and helpless. Some of them gave up any hope of survival. Recognizable because of their listlessness, they were called *Muselmänner* (Muslims). They would stop eating entirely or approach the electrified fence to be shot.

A sea change occurred in Auschwitz in the early spring of 1944. In little more than six months, more than 600,000 people, about 95 percent of them Jews, poured into the camp. The irreversible German retreat on the eastern front and the growing specter of a German defeat precipitated a determination in Berlin to root out the remaining Jews in its sphere of power. After German troops invaded Hungary on 19 March 1944 to forestall its surrender to the Allies, feverish preparations were launched to deport the 750,000

Hungarian Jews upon their arrival at Auschwitz-Birkenau. The man in the center wearing glasses is Sigmund Bruck, a mechanical engineer from Tab, Hungary. Bruck was denounced as a Communist, arrested, and deported to Nagy Kamizsa. He was sent to Auschwitz-Birkenau and then on to Gleiwitz, where he was killed by a guard during an escape attempt. May 1944

Arrival at Auschwitz.

Hungarian Jews. About 440,000 were moved out, all except the Hungarian Jewish labor companies and the Jewish population of Budapest. When a revolt broke out in the satellite state of Slovakia, Jews still living in that country were seized. The largest work ghetto, in Lodz, was emptied out as Soviet forces advanced into eastern Poland. Throughout that time, transports of Jews continued to depart from the Netherlands, Belgium, France, Italy, and Greece, from labor camps in Poland, and finally from the "Old People's" Ghetto of Theresienstadt. Except for Auschwitz and a briefly reopened Kulmhof, the death camps inside Poland had been closed down before 1944. Auschwitz was the remaining center for mass killing, the receiving station where the gas chambers and crematoriums were still in operation.

Höss returned to Auschwitz from Berlin on 8 May 1944, replacing Liebehenschel, and stayed until 29 July. After his departure Sturmbannführer Richard Baer, an adjutant to the chief of the Economic and Administrative Main Office, took over the camp, and in Birkenau Hauptsturmführer Josef Kramer, who had served in several concentration camps, followed Hartjenstein. Auschwitz remained in reliable hands.

At a much lower level SS sergeant Otto Moll, a widower who had acquired a reputation as a consummate sadist, was appointed on 9 May 1944 as chief of the crematoriums in Birkenau, a position he had held a year earlier. The Jewish Sonderkommando was enlarged until, by 29 August 1944, it contained 874 men. The gas supply had to be increased substantially, despite difficulties in gas production and distribution. Since the furnaces could no longer handle daily multiple transports arriving from Hungary with 3,000 Jews each, Bunker 2 had to be put back into operation for a short time as Facility 5. Meanwhile pits were dug under Moll's meticulous guidance to burn bodies en masse in the open.

The inundation of deportees brought with it an unprecedented wave of gassing coupled with a rising inmate count. For the Auschwitz command the higher numbers raised new concerns about security. Notwithstanding precautions to give no hint to newcomers about the fate awaiting them and to contain the inmates in their barracks and work places, a major breakout was considered a distinct possibility. By early April 1944 the highest-ranking SS officer in Upper Silesia, Ernst Schmauser, concluded an agreement with his army counterpart, Gen. Rudolf Koch-Erpach,

that in the event of a mass escape troops would man a line on an outer defense perimeter.

A resistance movement, in which political prisoners were predominant, had been in existence for some time. Its members collected information, and by August 1943 they prepared a detailed report with statistics and names that was smuggled out of the camp and transmitted to the Polish General Staff in London in January 1944. Copies were passed on to the U.S. Office of Strategic Services and to Military Intelligence at the War Department in Washington. Another copy was sent to the U.S. delegate to the United Nations War Crimes Commission. From London the Polish radio station Swit broadcast the gist of the report. These revelations produced no action.

When a young Jewish inmate from Slovakia, Rudolf Vrba (then Walter Rosenberg), who was a clerk in the camp, heard that the rail spur to the large Birkenau gas chambers was nearing completion, he assumed that the deportation of the Hungarian Jews was imminent. Aided by the underground, he and another Slovak Jewish inmate, Alfred Wetzler, escaped on 10 April 1944 and, walking at night, reached Slovakia. They were met there by a delegation of the remnant Jewish leadership on 25 April. Two days later a Slovak text was prepared, and then the 40-page document, emphasizing that Auschwitz was a death camp, had to be translated into Hungarian for church dignitaries, selected officials, and Jewish leaders in Budapest. The report was also brought in excerpt and in full to the Czechoslovak envoy in Switzerland, who received it in early June. Again nothing happened.

On 4 April 1944 an aircraft of the Mediterranean Allied Photo Reconnaissance Wing flew over Auschwitz. The mission was prompted by a desire to find out whether the construction of the I. G. Farben plant was still in progress. It was. After more photographs were taken in June and July, four raids were launched between 20 August and 26 December 1944. Altogether 367 planes dropped 3,394 bombs, but Birkenau was not targeted. Jewish requests for bombing the gas chambers were turned down in both Washington and London.

In Auschwitz gassing continued without interruption until 1 November 1944. Incidents at the portals of the chambers were few. The deportees were aware that large segments of European Jewry had vanished. Many had heard rumors about Auschwitz and gas, but they knew nothing about the layout of the camp, and they were caught in the unloading, selection, and undressing procedure before they could be certain that this was the end. Those who were led to the barracks for labor could not grasp that their next of kin were already dead. They were novices, locked into the routines of the camp. Among the experienced prisoners, Jews hoped for bombing raids that would demolish the crematoriums, but for non-Jewish inmates, explosions in or near the tightly packed barracks could only be another danger.

Most desperate was the situation of the men in the Jewish Sonderkommando. When word came from the underground on 7 October 1944 that the SS planned a large reduction of the work party, the crew of Crematorium IV (renumbered III) discussed open resistance. During their deliberations the Jewish prisoners were surprised by a German inmate informant, and they immediately killed him. When SS men approached, the crew attacked the guards with hammers, axes, stones, and secreted grenades and set the building on fire. In Crematorium II (renumbered I) members of the Sonderkommando mistakenly believed that the flames were a signal for a general insurrection, and they too struck. The SS trained its machine guns on the Jews escaping from IV and encircled a party that had broken out from II. Three SS men and 250 inmates were killed.

During the climactic period of 1944 an acute labor shortage in German industry led to a decision to transfer a substantial number of inmates from Auschwitz to other camps. Poles were placed at the head of the line, because they were considered a special security risk. Jews were included in the shift, and young Jewish women from Hungary made up a large contingent of this human cargo. On 12 January 1945 the Red Army launched an offensive in the direction of Auschwitz, and on 17 January the SS held the final roll call. There were still 67,000 inmates in the Auschwitz complex, and orders were given that day to march them out. Left behind were 1,000 corpses and more than 8,000 prisoners who were ill or in hiding. Soviet troops captured Auschwitz on 27 January.

According to calculations by Danuta Czech and Franciszek Piper, 1.3 million people had been deported to Auschwitz, close to 1.1 million of them Jews. The death toll was 1.1 million: almost 1 million Jews, nearly 75,000 Poles, more than 20,000 Gypsies, 15,000 Soviet prisoners of war, and more than 10,000 members of other nationalities. For the 200,000 inmates

who survived Auschwitz, the travail was not over. Thousands died of exhaustion or were shot to death during the marches to the railheads, still others perished in open coal cars of the trains, and many more succumbed to privation in Bergen-Belsen, Stutthof, Mauthausen, Buchenwald, Dachau, Flossenburg, Sachsenhausen, Neuengamme, and other destinations.   *Raul Hilberg*

Auschwitz Protocols Detailed information about Auschwitz transmitted to the West in April and May 1944 by two Jewish inmates, Rudolf Vrba and Alfred Wetzler, who had escaped from the camp. See AUSCHWITZ

Austria Following defeat in the First World War, Austria, with a population of 6.5 million, was left as a mere rump after the dissolution of the Habsburg empire. The political parties generally regarded the state, cut off from its sources of raw material and its industrial centers, as inviable; they tended to favor union with Germany, which still held a dominant position in Central Europe despite having lost the war. Political alliance with Germany (then socialist) in 1919 and an attempt in 1931 to form a Customs Union were foiled by the victorious Allied powers. Vienna first displayed a nationalist tendency in March 1933, when Chancellor Engelbert Dollfuss, imitating Hitler, dissolved parliament: in February 1934 he crushed the socialists in a bloody civil war and, with assistance from Italy, introduced a one-party system, the Fatherland Front (Vaterländische Front). The murder of Dollfuss during an attempted Nazi coup in July 1934 and Mussolini's closer relations with Hitler following his foray in Abyssinia deprived Austria of support. Consequently, in July 1936 the successor to Dollfuss, Kurt Schuschnigg, was forced to come to an agreement with Berlin that would constitute a preliminary to the Anschluss (union with Germany) of 13 March 1938.

The Jews in Austria had gained equality of status and residential rights in 1867: the monarchy encouraged their immigration, since Jews as a group were perceived as promoting industry. The Jewish population of Vienna increased from 6,217 in 1857 to a peak of 201,513, or 10.8 percent of the city's population, in 1910. Virulent antisemitism and the economic crisis caused a flood of emigration: at the beginning of 1938, 169,978 Jews were living in Vienna and 16,050 in the provinces.

The leader of the middle-class antisemitic Christ-

Austrian Nazis and local residents look on as Jews are forced to scrub pro-Schuschnigg government slogans off the pavement. Circa March 1938

ian Social party was Karl Lueger, mayor of Vienna from 1897 to 1910. The party represented the interests of large estate owners and backed a return to guilds and fraternities. Under the leadership of Otto Bauer, Jews had played an important role in the socialist development of the "Red Fortress of Vienna" between 1919 and 1934, and this further heightened the contrast with the Austrian *Länder* (federal states). During 1932–36, dissolution of the socialist trade unions and the dismissal of Jewish doctors from the hospitals led to increased burdens on the social department of the Israelitische Kultusgemeinde Wien (IKG), the Jewish community association in Vienna. The work load grew from 11,000 cases (relating to 44,000 recipients of welfare) to 23,000 cases (with 60,000 receiving assistance).

In 1935, out of 47,782 Jewish taxpayers, 25,000 were traders and manufacturers, 15,000 were employees and workers in the private sector, 4,500 were professionals; only 600 were state employees and only 150 worked in local government. The city of Vienna granted no federal subsidy to either the Jewish religious community or the Rothschild Infirmary; destitute Jews who were not entitled to permanent residence in Vienna were not accepted in the hospitals or nursing homes.

Antisemitism was an issue in Austrian universities. Although before the First World War the possibility of an academic career depended largely on the fact of baptism, after 1918 almost no Jews were appointed to professorships. In 1897 the Waidhofen Decree declared that Jews were "devoid of honor," so that no "satisfaction" was owed to Jewish students. The German-nationalist Reichstag deputy Georg von Schönerer incited student fraternities and athletic clubs to adopt racist principles. In 1930 Graf Wenzel Gleispach, the rector of Vienna University, and in

1932 Emmerich Czermak, the minister of education, attempted to introduce the so-called Aryan Paragraph, a regulation that limited the right of Jews to a university education. In September 1934, by Czermak's secret order, special classes for Jewish children were set up in primary schools. The Zionists, who in 1932 had replaced the liberal Union Österreichischer Juden in the community leadership, responded by founding a Jewish primary school, alongside the Chajes Realgymnasium and two religious schools. Jewish dueling fraternities such as Kadimah in Vienna and Caritas in Graz were formed to counter student terrorism at the universities. External pressure intensified social introversion. In 1937, out of 444 Jewish organizations in Vienna, there were 120 welfare societies, 88 synagogue groups, and 82 Zionist organizations. In the provinces, there were 181 associations; 72 of them, mostly religious, were in Burgenland (which in 1921 had opted to leave West Hungary to join Austria).

The Emigrant Welfare organization (Wanderfürsorge), founded in 1930, decided in 1937 to provide support for emigrants as far as the port of departure. An amalgamation of Jewish religious communities, initiated in 1935, did not receive government approval until 1936.

From the Anschluss to the November Pogrom

In the first few weeks after the Anschluss, thousands of Jewish homes were looted and the resident Jews ousted. Persecution and eviction of Jews satisfied the immediate economic and social needs of large parts of the Austrian populace and were a substitute for the social welfare assistance promised by the Nazis. On 18 March 1935 the Reichsführer SS and Gestapo chief Heinrich Himmler was empowered to enforce new ordinances, including measures "even beyond the usually appointed legal limits," and to establish Gestapo centers in provincial capitals. And so the prerequisites for legalized violence were put in place.

On the same day, the IKG was closed down and its board and the leaders of other Jewish organizations were arrested. Jewish-owned factories and businesses were seized. Elderly Jews were forced to clean roadways with toothbrushes and caustic soda (the Reibaktion, or Scouring Operation) and to join in the desecration of the main synagogue in Vienna. During March 1938, 220 Jews committed suicide. In two transports, on 1 and 15 April, 110 Jews were among 160 prisoners sent to the Dachau concentration camp. Under the rule of Gau-

A crowd of Viennese children looks on as a Jewish youth is forced by Austrian Nazis to paint the word *Jude* on his father's store. March 1938

leiter Joseph Bürckel, the Reichskommissar for the Reunion of Austria with the German Reich, Austria became the training ground for anti-Jewish practices.

When the IKG was reopened on 3 May, the first "compensatory payment" was exacted from Josef Löwenherz, the community office manager. The pretext was that contribution lists, which had fallen into the hands of the Gestapo, showed that 850,000 schillings had been paid "for the election of an independent Austria," whereas the money had really been smuggled out of the community box by social workers and used to relieve local poverty.

On Passover night, gangs of civilian marauders marched through the streets, attacking and beating Jews along the way. Orthodox Jewish women were forced to burn their wigs in public. From 24 to 27 May, 2,000 intellectuals were arrested and taken in four transports to Dachau; this action preceded the arrest of 1,500 "asocial" Jews in Germany on 15 June.

The Jews of Burgenland were the first to suffer eviction. Under the pretext that they were dangerously close to the frontier, they were forced to go to Vienna or hounded across the borders into Hungary and Czechoslovakia and left penniless; two groups were loaded onto barges and launched on the Danube. By February 1939, 1,900 Burgenland citizens had been forced across the frontier and 1,500 had been transferred to Vienna, where the Jewish community had to care for their needs.

On 26 March 1938 Hermann Göring, as head of the Four Year Plan for war preparation, signaled the "relentless" aryanization of business and economic life. The Jews were paid a miserable compensation, the "aryanizer" was lent money to cover a fairly high purchase price, and the benefit of the true value was pocketed by the Vermögensverkehrsstelle (Property Trading Authority). Out of 146,000 firms in Vienna, 36,000 were owned by Jews: Jewish capital assets amounted to 300 million Reichsmarks out of a total of 800 million. Twenty-five thousand businesses were taken over by non-Jewish commissars, in most cases without formal authority.

During a blackout rehearsal in September 1938, Jews were attacked and thrown in front of trams. Families were evicted from communal buildings and lodged in rundown military barracks. On the night of 4–5 October, the eve of Yom Kippur, the holiest day in the Jewish calendar, plainclothes SA-men seized Jews living in bourgeois areas, took their keys, and sent them away to Poland or Palestine. The perpetrators expected support in the form of spontaneous demonstrations by ordinary citizens. On 6 October Jews in the outer districts of Vienna suffered raids. This operation, initi-

Before the Anschluss, Kaffee Deutschland in Vienna was the Splendide, a Jewish-owned café.

ated by Odilo Globocnik, the party leader in Vienna, took Bürckel by surprise, and he managed to call it to a halt—but it would soon serve as a model for the November Pogrom. Throughout October, vandalizing attacks on Jewish businesses and schools and the burning of synagogues were everyday occurrences: in Vienna the events of 9 November seemed no more than an intensification of these "cold" pogroms.

The victims of these persecutions sought any means of escaping the country. At the Evian Conference concerning refugees held in early July, Löwenherz managed to have Austrian and German refugees amalgamated for the purposes of the U.S. immigration quota. The Youth Aliyah center in Berlin, which provided agricultural training for teenagers and furthered their emigration to Palestine, waived its claim to the summer schedule of 600 young people in favor of Vienna. The Revisionist Zionists organized illegal sea passage to Palestine via the Danube through Yugoslavia. In 1938 the few opportunities for emigration between May and the November Pogrom were publicized in just one newspaper, the *Zionistische Rundschau*.

To save would-be emigrants from having to wait in line all night outside public offices and police stations, during which time they were at risk of violent attack, Löwenherz and Alois Rothenberg, the head of the Palestine Office, proposed an advisory center, which was opened at the beginning of July as the Zentralstelle für Jüdische Auswanderung (Central Office for Jewish Emigration). Adolf Eichmann, head of the Jewish Section, laid out the departments so that Jews would be "processed on an assembly line." After being deprived of all property and assets, each Jewish applicant would leave the Central Office with a paper enabling him or her to emigrate. Eichmann's success prompted the establishment of a Reichszentrale in Berlin and a branch office in Prague. Emigration was rendered even more difficult by the introduction of the mandatory forenames Israel and Sarah and the red J stamped in passports—at the request of the president of the Swiss police, Heinrich Rothmund, to prevent Jews from slipping unnoticed across the border.

The Council for German Jewry in London and the American Jewish Joint Distribution Committee were responsible for providing the foreign currency needed for travel, embarkation, and proof of financial means. In return Eichmann unblocked equivalent funds arising from the levy on emigrants (to the value of 100 percent of anything taken abroad) and from the confisca-

tion of Jewish community property. Löwenherz also raised money by selling certificates for entry into Palestine for higher sums.

Jewish children were crammed together in unheated classrooms holding 70 to 80 pupils and were allowed to go to school only until age 14. Apart from those in the last year of studies, Jews were barred from universities. A successful three-month summer course on Judaism and Zionism for children aged 11 to 15 established the model for the Youth Aliyah school.

From the November Pogrom to the Deportations

On 9–10 November 1938, 42 synagogues, prayer halls, and funeral homes in Vienna were pillaged, 27 Jews killed, and 88 badly injured. In provincial communities, too, places of worship were destroyed and Jews arrested. Worst of all were the attacks in Innsbruck, where virtually all Jews were maltreated; two leading community members were murdered (one was stoned to death), and another man was fatally stabbed. Of 6,547 persons arrested in Austria, 3,700 were sent to Dachau and set free only when they had obtained emigration documents.

On 12 November the Viennese minister of trade, Hans Fischböck, drew up a plan for the final despoliation of the Jews and the seizure of their assets—houses, land, stocks, and businesses. Fischböck's ideas were enthusiastically received by Göring and put into practice. In consequence, whereas in 1938 three out of every four emigrants could themselves bear the cost of leaving the country, at the beginning of 1939 the same proportion, 75 percent, had to be subsidized. The number of daily soup kitchens, which also offered heated shelter, increased from five to 23. In September 1939, 35,000 people received food and 31,364 were helped in secret.

Between December 1938 and August 1939, the Jewish community organized 43 children's transports. Out of 2,844 children, 2,262 were accepted by Britain, 78 by Sweden, and five by Switzerland. Holland, Belgium, and France took in 375 children, but most of them were later captured during the German occupation.

On a wider scale, the community established retraining and vocational courses in preparation for emigration and qualification for employment in a trade. By 27 June 1939, 24,025 persons had been retrained and 1,601 courses offered, so that in a single year Vienna had caught up with Germany, where similar work had been in progress for six years.

The number of emigrants up to the outbreak of war totaled 106,690, but the process was too slow for the Nazis, who required 70,000 dwellings. By the end of 1938 some 44,000 had been "aryanized." In order to obtain the remaining 26,000, the Jews were first of all concentrated within a quasi-ghetto in the Leopold-stadt district. A plan to transfer Jews to two labor camps near Vienna was rendered obsolete by the outbreak of war in September 1939.

At that time Vienna's Jewish population consisted of 66,000 "Jews by religion," 39,000 "Jews by race," and 13,000 foreign and stateless Jews. At the beginning of October 1939, 1,048 Polish and stateless Jews were transported to the Buchenwald concentration camp. Not one of them survived. In the same month two transports carrying 1,584 people, in parallel with two transports from Mährisch Ostrau (Ostrova), were sent to Nisko on the San, ostensibly to build living quarters for the resettlement of Jews from Galicia. They were herded by gunfire over the frontier into Russia: 198 of them returned to Vienna.

Because of technical difficulties, Himmler ordered the transports to be suspended, thus allowing a chance for further emigration. Often, however, emigration at that time meant that men had to leave their wives, parents, and children behind.

The Jewish Cultural Office organized afternoon concerts with music by Jewish composers. In 1939 and 1940 Jewish calendars were printed. For the Jewish holiday Sukkot in fall 1940, Löwenherz received 150 *lulavim* (ceremonial plant sprigs and fruit); 75 of these were passed on to Poland. The Youth Aliyah school, headed by Aron Menczer, mounted a Zionist exhibition in September 1940, but in May 1941 the Palestine Office and Youth Aliyah were dissolved and the Zionist youth leaders sent to labor camps.

Deportation and the End of the Community

In February and March 1941, five transports carrying 5,005 persons left for Kielce in Poland. Löwenherz was forced into collaboration, since he had to provide replacements for doctors and important community officials scheduled for deportation. For a time, because of the German invasion of the Soviet Union in June, the transports again came to a halt.

The introduction of the yellow star on 21 Septem-ber 1941 foreshadowed the end of the community. From 15 October to 2 November 1941, five transports carrying 5,995 Jews departed for Lodz, followed shortly thereafter by four transports to Riga with 5,183 people, and by 11 more taking 10,478 people to Minsk, where they were marched to open trenches and shot. Six thousand Jews loaded onto six trains destined for Izbica were gassed at Belzec and Sobibor.

Four detention camps held Jews waiting for the next transport in intolerable conditions, many lying on stretchers or suffering high fevers. Once they had signed over all their property to the Reich, they were allowed to have baggage weighing 50 kilograms. The transport organizer, Alois Brunner (known as Brunner I)—who currently lives in Damascus under Syrian government protection—because of his efficiency and ruthlessness in Vienna was later employed by the Nazis as a transport specialist in Paris, Berlin, Bratislava, and Salonika.

In June 1942 came the first deportations of the elderly, ex-officers, and disabled war veterans to Theresienstadt, which by February 1945 had taken in 15,433 deportees. On 23 September 1942 a so-called notables transport was dispatched there, carrying Aron Menczer and other youth leaders. Desider Friedmann, who until 1938 had been community president, and Robert Stricker, vice-president of the Jewish community, had been reserved by Eichmann as hostages to guarantee a smooth-running organization of Jewish emigration but were now sent with the other deportees to Auschwitz. Since the IKG no longer served as an essential means of blackmail, it was dissolved on 1 November 1942, reemerging as the Council of Elders of the Jews in Vienna.

It is estimated that 48,504 Austrian Jews were deported to the East. Of 125,490 emigrants, about 15,000 were recaptured and deported during the German occupation of Europe. By August 1939 deportations to concentration camps numbered some 8,000, with 4,000 being released before the outbreak of war. In the winter of 1945, 2,142 survivors were known to be in Vienna. In all, 65,459 Austrian Jews, 35.19 percent of the pre-Anschluss Jewish population of Austria, met their deaths. For map, see under GERMAN JEWRY.

Herbert Rosenkranz

B

Babi Yar Ravine northwest of Kiev (in Ukraine), where 33,000 Jews were murdered on 29–30 September 1941. In reprisal for an explosion set off by Soviet partisans in the German command center in Kiev, SS units gathered the Jews of the city and marched them to Babi Yar. There they were ordered to hand over their valuables, strip, and approach the ravine's edge. As they did so, the SS *Sonderkommandos* (special killing squads) fired on them with automatic weapons, and the force of the shots cast their bodies into the ravine. Between 1941 and 1943 tens of thousands of Jews, Communists, and Soviet prisoners of war were executed by SS squads in this way. In August and September 1943 the Germans exhumed and burned many of the bodies to conceal their atrocities before the advancing Red Army forced them to retreat. Yevgeni Yevtushenko helped bring Babi Yar to world attention with the publication in 1961 of his poem "Babi Yar."

Bach-Zelewski, Erich von dem (1899–1972) SS general prominently involved in the murder of Eastern European Jews, including atrocities in Estonia, Minsk, and Mogilev and the suppression of the Warsaw ghetto uprising. Bach-Zelewski was not prosecuted for his actions against the Jews because he testified against some of the accused at the Nuremberg war crimes trials. In 1951, however, a Munich denazification court condemned him to a form of house arrest for 10 years, and in 1962 he was convicted of multiple murders committed in 1933–34 and was sentenced to life imprisonment.

Baeck, Leo (1873–1956) Berlin rabbi and spiritual leader of German Jews, survivor of Theresienstadt. In 1933 Baeck became president of the Reichsvertretung der Duetschen Juden and in 1939 chairman of the Reichsvereinigung der Juden in Deutschland. After his fifth arrest he was sent in 1943 to Theresienstadt,

Leo Baeck. 1948

where he was a member of the Jewish Council of Elders and helped to keep up morale. Baeck wrote parts of *The People Israel: The Meaning of Jewish Existence* (1955) while interned. See REICHSVERTRETUNG DER DEUTSCHEN JUDEN

Baltic Countries The three small states on the eastern rim of the Baltic Sea—Estonia, Latvia, and Lithuania—are conventionally termed the Baltic countries. At the beginning of World War II, these countries had a combined population of nearly 6 million, including 350,000 Jews—250,000 in Lithuania

German soldiers move through the main street in Kovno following the German invasion of Lithuania. 26 June 1941

(including war refugees from Poland), 95,000 in Latvia, and 4,500 in Estonia. Nearly all the Jews lived in cities and small towns and engaged in trade, industry, crafts, and the liberal professions. In the early 1920s the Jews received full civil rights and were granted a great deal of cultural autonomy. In Lithuania there was even a special minister for Jewish affairs, whose task it was to guard the Jews' civil rights against infringement by the government. In Estonia this autonomy lasted until the outbreak of World War II.

Beginning in the mid-1930s, the Jews' economic circumstances deteriorated because of intense competition from the majority Christians and an official policy of de facto discrimination. Nearly all Lithuanians are Roman Catholic; most Estonians and Latvians are Lutheran. Manifestations of antisemitism and physical assault mounted. Nevertheless, Jews continued to lead a vibrant cultural life and sustained their values by maintaining a network of cultural and educational institutions in Hebrew and Yiddish, a lively and diverse daily press, and yeshivas (religious schools) renowned

throughout the Jewish world. Jewry in these countries also underwent an awakening of Zionist activity conducted by a welter of political parties and youth movements—chiefly Hehalutz—which trained young Jews for resettlement in Palestine. The Maccabi and Hakoah sports associations, to name only two, were active in almost every city and town. In all of these countries, Jews were also active in the Communist parties, although the weight of these parties in Jewish society was minimal.

This constellation of Jewish community activity met its demise in the summer of 1940, when the Soviet Union forcibly annexed the Baltic states. The Soviet Communist regime, unlike the previous Baltic governments, allowed Jews to work in the civil service and lifted restrictions on admission to academic institutions. Nevertheless, it caused the Jews much suffering by nationalizing large industrial and commercial enterprises, abolishing Hebrew education, banning Zionist organizations, and hindering the observance of religious precepts such as the observance of the Sabbath as a day of rest. A national and Zionist underground began to form which attempted to keep the Hebrew language and culture alive and to facilitate emigration to Palestine.

When the Soviet security authorities perpetrated a mass expulsion to Siberia, on the night of 13–14 June 1941, of what they called "socially and politically dangerous elements," more than 12,000 Jews were swept up and removed from Baltic territories. Although the Jewish exiles vastly outnumbered the non-Jews, this traumatic event aggravated the Christian population's hostility toward the Jews, whom they blamed for the Sovietization of their countries. Additional stimuli to antisemitism were national underground organizations (such as the Lithuanian Activist Front, Perkonkrust in Latvia, and Omakaitse in Estonia), which, from their headquarters in Germany, flooded the Baltic states with incendiary leaflets preaching vengeance against the Jews.

The Jews understood the message clearly and feared for the future. In June 1941, when the armed forces of Germany invaded the Soviet Union, including the Baltic states, masses of Jews attempted to flee in the wake of the retreating Soviet troops. Because of heavy German aerial bombardment and vicious attacks by armed gangs of local nationalists, only 25,000 of them reached the Soviet interior. About 10,000 of those

refugees were inducted into the Lithuanian, Latvian, and Estonian divisions of the Red Army; the rest, mainly the elderly, women, and children, found jobs of various kinds or enrolled in school.

It took the Wehrmacht only a few weeks to overrun the Baltic. By the time the German troops reached various localities, the Jews had been subjected to murder, rape, and robbery at the hands of their Christian neighbors, who were led and encouraged by members of the local establishment such as army and police officers, teachers, and even members of the clergy. Although these crimes were usually committed on the pretext of settling scores with Communist and other activists who had sovietized their country and helped arrest national patriots, nearly all the victims had not only been uninvolved in sovietization but also had suffered under Soviet rule for ideological reasons—for being Zionist activists or for participating in wars of independence. Rabbis in particular were targeted for retribution. In many cases, they were tied to a horse's tail or bound to a cart and forced to sing the praises of Stalin before crowds that had turned out for the spectacle.

The calculated mass murder of most Jews in Ostland—the administrative entity that the Nazis created in the Baltic—began in the autumn of 1941. The Final Solution in this area was entrusted to a mobile killing

Jewish women leave a ghetto through a side gate on their way to forced labor in the Ozinski mill. 1943

unit called Einsatzgruppe A. This formation and its subunits, the *Einsatzkommandos*, were led by a small number of German officers, but most of the murders in the cities and towns were committed mainly by Lithuanians, Latvians, and Estonians. By the end of 1941, all the Estonian Jews had been annihilated. About 50,000 Jews were allowed to remain alive in Latvia and Lithuania in order to serve the German war effort. The majority of them were quarantined in ghettos and Lithuania (Vilna, Kovno, and Siauliai); smaller numbers remained in Latvia (Riga, Daugavpils, and Liepaja), and several hundred were taken to various labor camps.

In the ghettos, Jews were allowed a certain degree of freedom to conduct their religious and personal lives as they saw fit, as long as they met the labor quotas. The Jewish leadership in the ghetto made efforts to enforce the quotas, believing that the Nazis' need for cheap labor could keep the ghetto and its residents alive. Nevertheless, Jews were routinely executed for various "offenses," such as spending time outside the ghetto, smuggling food into the ghetto, and failing to wear the yellow patch. Even in this atmosphere of terror, however, the ghetto inhabitants managed to develop cultural, mutual-assistance, and anti-Nazi underground organizations. They managed to sabotage German army facilities, to stockpile arms, and to arrange the clandestine flight of nearly 1,800 men and women to the forests, where nearly all were admitted to the ranks of the anti-Nazi partisans.

On several occasions, tens of thousands of Jewish families were brought to Kovno (Kaunas) and Riga from Germany and other countries for ostensible resettlement in the ghettos. Most of them, however, were taken to the Ninth Fort in Kovno and the Bikernieki and Rumbula forests in the Riga vicinity, where they were murdered. In the autumn of 1943, when the Germans urgently needed to mobilize a labor force in Estonia—which had already been "cleansed" of Jews—thousands of Jews were transported there, mainly from the ghettos of Kovno and Vilna, and forced to perform grueling labor under the harshest conditions. The Vilna ghetto was liquidated at this time, and the remaining ghettos became labor camps, where many Jews died under the brutal regimen. In the summer of 1944, when the Germans were forced to retreat from the Baltic countries under pressure of the Red Army, they transferred the few remaining Jews to concentration camps in Germany. In the wake of epidemics, star-

Lithuanian nationalists use a hose to revive Jews after they were beaten during the Kovno pogrom. This photo belonged to a German officer of the 290th German division who was killed near Pustobrodovo. 27 June 1941

vation, lethal beatings, and systematic murder, only several thousand Jews were able to greet the Allied forces that liberated the camps in 1945.

After the war, most of the survivors chose to remain in displaced-persons camps in Germany until they were able to emigrate to Palestine or other countries overseas. A minority returned to their countries of origin, once again under Soviet rule, joining some of the partisans and Jews who had survived with the help of non-Jews in places of concealment. Eventually, some of the Jews who had survived service in the Red Army's Baltic divisions, and the refugees and exiles who had spent the war years in the Soviet Union, also returned. In all, only 20,000 Jews from the Baltic countries, 6 percent of the prewar Jewish population, were alive when the war ended.

Very few of the murderers of Jews were prosecuted in the postwar tribunals in Nuremberg, Riga, Tallinn,

Tanchum Peis (Theodor Pais), a Jewish policeman, guards the bundles that remained after a deportation action of Kovno Jews to Estonia. The bundles were to be taken later by the Jewish council and distributed among the needy. 26 October 1943

and Vilna. Many of them fled to Germany, North and South America, and Australia, where they usually succeeded in concealing their crimes. After the Baltic countries became independent in 1991, murderers of Jews there, too, were awarded legal rehabilitation, monetary grants, and gestures of honor, over the protests of the world media and Jewish organizations.

Dov Levin

Barbarossa, Operation German code name for the invasion of the Soviet Union, launched on 22 June 1941. See FINAL SOLUTION: PREPARATION AND IMPLEMENTATION

Barbie, Klaus (1913–91) German war criminal in Lyons, France, who was brought to justice in 1987. See FRANCE; WAR CRIMES

Bartoszewski, Wladyslaw (1922–) Roman Catholic member of Polish Home Army, survivor of Auschwitz (interned 1941–42), and Polish foreign minister in the 1990s. Bartoszewski assisted in the creation of the Council for Aid to Jews (Zegota) and was named one of the Righteous Among the Nations by Yad Vashem.

Becher, Kurt (1909–) SS commander who in 1944, on order of Adolf Eichmann, negotiated with Jewish leaders (primarily Rudolf Kasztner) in Hungary for the "rescue train," which took 1,685 Jews to safety in Switzerland in exchange for goods worth millions of Swiss francs. In 1945 Heinrich Himmler named Becher special Reich commissioner for all concentration camps. Becher testified for the prosecution at the Nuremberg war crimes trials and escaped prosecution partly because of the evidence of Kasztner.

Beit Lohamei Haghetaot (Ghetto Fighters' House) Museum and educational institute, created to perpetuate the memory of the ghetto fighters and Jewish resistance. Founded in 1949 by Holocaust survivors and resistance fighters in Kibbutz Lohamei Haghetaot near Nahariya, Israel, it offers workshops and seminars and collects materials related to the resistance and the Holocaust.

Belgium During the German occupation of Belgium, from May 1940 to September 1944, the persecution of the Belgian Jews proceeded from policies designed at

Klaus Barbie. This is the only known photograph of Barbie in uniform.

istration, warned against the imposition of unnecessary measures against the Jews that might decrease the willingness of the Belgian elites to cooperate with the Germans. Despite these reservations, at the end of October 1940 the Military Administration published the first anti-Jewish decrees on orders from Berlin. These included a proclamation prohibiting ritual slaughter and the basic statute governing the ensuing persecution, the Judenverordnung of 1940. The Judenverordnung instituted the 1935 Nuremberg definitions of who was to be considered Jewish, required the registration of Jews with Belgian authorities, and decreed the special marking of Jewish identity cards. It also ordered the registration of Jewish businesses and the identification of hotels and restaurants owned by Jews. A separate decree stipulated the suspension or dismissal of Jewish government officials, including schoolteachers and professors. Jews were prohibited from practicing law or from working as journalists. The segregation of the Jewish population had begun.

At the end of May 1941 Jews were required to register their property. Disposal was made subject to German approval, and proceeds from sales were placed in blocked accounts. The Germans had to create a special organization, the Treuhandgesellschaft, for the registration and disposal of Jewish property, since Belgian government agencies refused to participate in this operation. At the same time Jews were banned from supervisory or management positions in business, and they were required to hand in their radio sets. In late August 1941 a curfew from 8:00 p.m. to 7:00 a.m. was instituted, and at the end of the year Jewish students were excluded from Belgian educational institutions at all levels.

In November 1941, after a number of false starts, the Germans set up a Jewish organization called the Association des Juifs en Belgique (AJB), almost 10 months after the establishment of the Joodsche Raad (Jewish council) in Amsterdam. Like other Jewish councils in Europe, the AJB was designed in the first place as an instrument in the hands of the German police to implement the forthcoming deportations. In the second place, the organization was assigned the task of supervising Jewish civic and charitable organizations, with the exception of religious congregations. The association was headed by the grand rabbi of Belgium, Salomon Ullmann, and consisted largely of prominent Jews who had been active in community life. But in contrast to that of the Amsterdam council, its author-

the highest level of Reich authority and implemented from Berlin by Adolf Eichmann's office within the RSHA (Reich Security Main Office). Locally, measures against the Jews were modulated by the character and overall priorities of the Military Administration, by the scope and limits of cooperation of Belgian authorities and civilians, and by the responses of the Jewish people themselves.

At the beginning of the occupation, the German authorities claimed that no special measures against the Jews were planned. In fact, the Military Administration was opposed to the persecution of the Jews, for fear of negative public reaction. In his internal report to Berlin, Gen. Eggert Reeder, the head of the admin-

Belgian firefighters and civilians in the street outside of a synagogue in Antwerp during its destruction by Belgian antisemites. This incident was part of what has come to be known as the "Antwerp pogrom," an action instigated by German occupation authorities that resulted in the destruction of two synagogues and the home of Rabbi Marcus Rottenberg. 1 April 1941

ity was limited and vigorously contested within the Jewish community.

During the first few months of 1942 the Germans completed the job of isolating the Jews and depriving them of their livelihood. Physicians were prohibited from treating non-Jews, the pressure was stepped up to sell property, and Jews were squeezed out of economic life. In May Jews were required to wear a yellow star in public.

Concrete plans for the deportation of Jews from Western Europe were drawn up in a conference held in Berlin on 11 June 1942. At that time Eichmann assigned to Belgium a quota: 10,000 Jews were to be deported from the country. The quota was increased to 20,000 in August. During a visit to Berlin, Reeder sought a post-

ponement of or release from the order, but the only concession he could secure was the exemption of Jews of Belgian nationality "for the time being."

A week after the establishment of an office for the labor draft within the AJB on 15 July, the German police had the AJB distribute approximately 5,000 notices summoning Jews to report to an assembly point, the Caserne Dossin in Malines. These first notices did not include children or the elderly, in order to preserve the pretext of labor service.

After initial compliance in late July and early August, fewer and fewer people reported "voluntarily" in Malines, despite an appeal by the AJB on 1 August urging Jews to comply and threatening retaliation against families and the entire Jewish community. In an attempt to meet Eichmann's quota, the German police increased their raids on Jewish residences and in public places. In four major raids in Brussels and Antwerp between 15 August and 12 September, the Germans captured more than 4,000 victims of all ages. In a final effort at Antwerp the German police raided rationing offices and schools. These actions aroused so many protests that Reeder ordered the German police to abandon this method in order to prevent further public disturbances. Despite these obstacles, by the end of October the German police had succeeded in arresting and sending east about 17,000 people—approximately two-thirds of the number of Jews deported during the entire Nazi occupation of Belgium, but 3,000 short of Eichmann's target.

In June 1942 the Germans began to implement a plan to draft more than 2,000 unemployed Jewish men to build fortifications in northern France under the auspices of the German military construction company Organisation Todt. This project was initiated by the Military Administration (rather than the police) and was carried out by the Belgian Labor Offices, which identified prospective recruits and sent out draft notices. At first these assignments were thought to provide protection against deportation to the East, but toward the end of October the contingent was taken to Malines and deported from there to Auschwitz. More than 10 percent of the original draftees managed to escape from the labor camps or from the deportation trains.

During the last stage of the persecution, from October 1942 to the end of the occupation, the German police attempted to catch Jews wherever they could find them. The Germans paid a bounty for denunciations of Jews in hiding. Approximately 8,000 Jews were captured during this period.

In the summer of 1943 Himmler decided to deport Jews of Belgian nationality. Reeder's efforts to secure a reversal of the decision failed, and the German police began to arrest Belgian Jews after receiving approval from the military commander, Gen. Alexander von Falkenhausen. However, on 3–4 September they once more staged a series of mass raids in Brussels and Antwerp, netting approximately 1,000 persons.

The German officer in charge in Antwerp, Erich Holm, employed a particularly devious deception in this round-up. On the pretext of transacting business, he arranged to meet with his intended victims; then he arrested them when they showed up. When one group of these arrestees arrived at Malines in a moving van, it was discovered that nine had died of suffocation and 80 were unconscious. This incident created such a flurry of protest by Belgian dignitaries that no further large-scale actions took place for the balance of the occupation.

After October 1943 there remained in Belgium a group of approximately 4,000 "protected" Jews, in addition to the much larger number of Jews in hiding. The protected Jews included AJB members, as well as children and the elderly placed in residential facilities managed by the AJB. The German police had the addresses of these persons on file and therefore were in a position to arrest and deport them when conditions were right. That moment occurred when the Military Administration was replaced in July 1944 by a civilian administration headed by a gauleiter, and the police force was given the independence it had long sought. But preparations for the arrest and deportation of protected Jews came to naught because of the German withdrawal in the face of the Allied advance. A final deportation train dispatched at the end of August never left the country.

The reaction of the Christian population of Belgium to the persecution of the Jews was mixed. In general, the collaborationist parties supported measures against the Jews, especially in the publications of the Flemish National Movement (VNV) and the Flemish SS. The latter furnished manpower for raids on the Jews. The organs of Rex, a mostly francophone proto-fascist movement headed by Léon Degrelle, also endorsed anti-Jewish policies. These were fringe groups, however, and antisemitism was uncommon except in Antwerp, where many Jewish immigrants from Eastern Europe lived.

Belgian government agencies, led by the secretaries-general, the highest authorities left after the departure of the government, steered a careful course, claiming that the scope of action they might take against Jews was limited by the Belgian constitution and by Belgian law. This position, in principle, left much of the enforcement of anti-Jewish measures to the Germans themselves. In practice, however, the policy was sometimes more honored in the breach than in the observance. For instance, the dismissal of Jewish government servants in 1940 was carried out by Belgian agencies, and so was the registration of the Jews in 1941 and the summons to compulsory labor service in 1942. On the other hand, Belgian agencies refused to carry out the sequestration of Jewish property, and

Belgian police were not used in the round-up of the Jews, except in one (unauthorized) instance in Antwerp, where measures against the Jews often were taken to an extreme. The unavailability of Belgian police frequently left the SS strapped for manpower.

Thousands of ordinary Belgians participated in the rescue of Jews. Aid came largely (though not exclusively) from two groups: the clergy and laity of the Roman Catholic church and, even more important, Jewish and non-Jewish working men and women, who frequently belonged to Communist and socialist organizations.

The Roman Catholic church pursued a somewhat ambiguous course in support of the Jews. On the one hand, Cardinal J. E. van Roey—the archbishop of Malines and primate of the church in Belgium—never issued a public protest against the persecution of the Jews, nor did he advocate aid to the Jews in public announcements. However, he protested privately to the Military Administration against the persecution, and he authorized and encouraged clerics under his authority to assist Jews. The bishop of Liège worked with local contacts to help Jews and instructed officials in his diocese to make Catholic retreat facilities available to Jewish children. Many other clerics and officials of Catholic institutions provided shelter to perhaps as many as 2,500 Jewish children. This action was especially effective because it employed existing Catholic institutions, where the risk of betrayal was smaller than in newly founded resistance organizations.

The Jewish response to persecution was divided. Middle- and upper-class Jews of Belgian nationality and recent German immigrants were prepared to implement German orders by serving on the AJB, always in hopes of aiding the Jewish community and softening the blows, as well as saving themselves and their families. But the authority of the AJB remained quite limited in scope and duration, because its legitimacy was contested by groups of recent East European immigrants who succeeded in creating an alternative underground community outside of the structures of the AJB.

At the beginning of the summer of 1942 the AJB played the part assigned to it by the German police. It established a file on Jews and their residences, and transmitted the notices of convocation prepared by the German police. On 1 August the AJB urged people assigned to deportation to obey the German summons, repeating German assurances that the deportees would be put to work in the East. As fewer and fewer Jews turned up at the assembly point, and the German police began to rely on mass raids, the role of the AJB diminished. In July 1942 a Communist Jewish resistance group set AJB files on fire, partially destroying the registry, and at the end of August a Communist team "liquidated" the head of the AJB's Labor Draft Office. When in response to the assassination the AJB temporarily suspended its cooperation with the German police, the Germans arrested six AJB leaders, including its head, Rabbi Ullmann. These dignitaries were released a week later, after the intervention of the queen mother, Elisabeth; the archbishop of Malines; and the secretary-general of justice. From this point on, however, the AJB no longer played a major part in implementing deportations, but it continued to supply services to prospective deportees and to operate institutions for children temporarily exempted from deportation.

Whereas the effectiveness of the AJB waned with time, the scope of the resistance to deportation, emanating from the Jewish working class, increased during the summer of 1942 and beyond. This growing effectiveness arose from the close affiliation of many working-class Jews with the Communist party and other left-wing organizations, including the Front de l'Indépendance, a resistance organization largely directed by Communists. In an effort to provide a focus for the rescue of the Jews, associates of the Front de l'Indépendance founded the Comité de Défense des Juifs (CDJ) in the summer of 1942. Thenceforth the CDJ became the principal organization concerned with the rescue of the Jews. It attacked the legitimacy of the AJB, branding it a tool of the German police. Jewish underground groups and clandestine publications appealed to Jews to disregard deportation orders and to go into hiding instead. They made it possible for Jews to remain underground by providing shelter, false identity cards, and rationing books.

The Germans were only moderately successful in deporting the Jewish population of Belgium, particularly in comparison to the more substantial results in the neighboring Netherlands. Of the 56,186 Jews caught up in the registration of 1941 (apart from Jews in mixed marriages, who were not targeted for deportation), 25,124 were deported from Belgium. Only 1,323 of these deportees survived in the camps. Therefore, 23,801, or approximately 42 percent of the Jews registered in 1941, perished; a majority survived, mostly in hiding. These figures do not include Jews who had fled to France in 1940, many of whom were also deported to the East.

A number of factors contributed to the limited success of the Germans in Belgium. One was the nature of the German regime and the priorities of its leaders. The Germans governed Belgium through a military command structure (until July 1944) with clearly defined and closely pursued goals: to preserve internal and external security and to exploit Belgium economically in support of the German war effort. The military commander, General von Falkenhausen, while sharing the traditional antisemitic prejudices of his class, thought little of the racial theories that animated national socialism. Eggert Reeder, the head of the Military Administration (actually the civilian branch of the command area, primarily concerned with economic and political issues), was a career Prussian civil servant. His policy priority was to produce in Belgium a maximum economic contribution to the German war effort through the cooperation of the existing administrative and business elites, and through the acquiescence of the general population. Whatever his personal attitude toward Jews may have been, he did what he could to make sure that German measures against them would not interfere with his main goal by compromising the collaboration of those elements of society whose cooperation was needed. Therefore he sought to control the activities of the German police and SS to the extent he could. The restraints placed on the police by the Military Administration limited the effectiveness of the SS.

The second major factor in the outcome of the persecution was the makeup of the Jewish population. Ninety-two percent of the Jewish population of Belgium were noncitizens, most of them fairly recent immigrants from Poland. Many belonged to Communist or socialist organizations. Some were left-wing Zionists and most had preserved a good part of the culture of the shtetl, including the close social networks characteristic of village and small-town society. The Communist and other left-wing associations had made these people predisposed toward illegal and underground action, since their organizations had been subject to persecution in Eastern Europe. Both socialism and Zionism provided ideological bases for active opposition to Nazi persecution. Therefore these immigrants were less inclined than middle-class assimilated Jews to submit passively to persecution.

The third major factor was the character of Belgian society and governmental structures, and the historical experience of German rule in World War I and of the Belgian resistance it had engendered. Having lived under foreign rule for hundreds of years before independence in 1831, and, at least in the francophone sections of the country, partaking of a Latin tradition of distrust of government, many Belgian citizens were more likely than their "law-abiding" Dutch neighbors to disregard the injunctions of the occupying power. Belgian government agencies, mindful of experiences under the previous occupation, were more predisposed toward setting limits to their cooperation with such undertakings as the deportation of the Jews than were their Dutch or French counterparts. The combination of the priorities of the German military regime, the character of the Jewish community, and the historical experience of Belgian society and government allowed more than half the Jews living in the country in 1940 to survive the German campaign of annihilation.

Werner Warmbrunn

Belorussia Jews have been living on Belorussian territory, from the Bug and Nieman rivers to the Dnieper and Pripet, for almost 700 years. The first written record of Belorussian Jews dates from the fourteenth century. The granting of certain privileges and freedoms to the Jewish communities of Grodno (1388) and Brest (1389) by the Lithuanian prince Vytautas the Great demonstrates that Jews actively participated in the social and economic life of the state. The broad rights of self-government that the Jewish communities enjoyed were preserved when as a result of the Union of Lublin (1569) the Belorussian Jews became subjects of the Polish-Lithuanian Commonwealth (Rzeczpospolita).

At the end of the eighteenth century, after three partitions of the Commonwealth, the Belorussian Jews found themselves under Russian imperial sovereignty. Catherine the Great decreed that the Jews "be left where they live and as they live." At the turn of the twentieth century the Jews of Belorussia made up one of the largest Jewish communities in the Diaspora. In the 1897 Russian census they numbered about 725,000, or 14 percent of the population of Belorussia.

Belorussia was a center of Jewish learning, culture, and spiritual life. Yeshivas in Minsk, Volozhin, Ivje, Mir, Slutsk, and other cities produced many distinguished rabbis and scholars renowned throughout the Jewish world.

All Belorussian districts fell within the Pale of Settlement, that section of the Russian empire where Jews were allowed to reside. Some 650 laws and statutes restricted the rights of the Jewish population. In Belorussia, as throughout the empire, antisemitism was a constituent part of state policy. The February 1917 revolution in Russia and the end of tsarist rule eliminated all legal restrictions on Jews within Russian territory. The Bolshevik coup in October did not meet with unanimous approval from the Belorussian Jews, but the majority supported the new government.

In the Belorussian Soviet Socialist Republic, which was proclaimed in 1919 and brought into the Soviet Union in 1922, Jewish economic, social, and cultural life proceeded in accordance with the ideological prescriptions of the ruling Communists. The authorities continually reaffirmed the equal status of all nationalities within the new country, including the Jews, while at the same time they aimed to assimilate the Jews into the "Soviet people." In the late 1930s all Jewish educational and scientific institutions were closed, and most newspapers and magazines were shut down. Many Jewish cultural figures were arrested. The war on antisemitism came to a halt.

The situation worsened in 1939 when the Soviet Union and Germany concluded a nonaggression pact, including an agreement on borders and various secret protocols. A massive Soviet disinformation campaign suppressed the truth about Germany's treatment of Jews and its belligerent German foreign policy. Nothing was revealed about Adolf Hitler's open threats regarding the future of the Jews, about their persecution in countries annexed or occupied by the Germans, or about the ghettos in Lodz, Warsaw, and other Polish cities. For the Belorussian Jews, the consequences of this silence were fatal.

In September 1939, in accordance with the terms of their pact, Germany and the Soviet Union divided the territory of the Polish state between themselves. The annexation of western Belorussia doubled the population of the Belorussian Soviet republic and more than doubled the number of Jews within its borders. By June 1941, when Hitler broke the nonaggression pact and invaded the Soviet Union, some 670,000 Jews lived in western Belorussia, compared to 405,000 in the eastern section of the republic.

Hitler saw the war in the East not only as a struggle with the Soviet dictator Josef Stalin, who had similar aspirations to world dominance, but also as a war against the Jews. From 1941 to 1945 Belorussia was one of the centers for the implementation of the Nazi plan to eradicate the Jews of Eastern Europe.

On 22 June 1941 the Wehrmacht crossed into Soviet territory. Belorussia was in the strike path of Army Group Center as it drove toward Moscow. The Soviet forces, caught off guard by the German attack, immediately abandoned Brest. Over the next seven weeks every major city in Belorussia fell to the Germans: Grodno (23 June), Baranovichi (27 June), Minsk (28 June), Borisov (2 July), Vitebsk (11 July), Mogilev (26 July), and Gomel (11 August). By the end of August the republic was completely occupied. The front moved so swiftly that those who tried to flee east ahead of the advancing German troops were unsuccessful. On 24 June the leaders of the Belorussian republic slipped out of Minsk without having made any announcement of an evacuation. As a result very few managed to save themselves. Even in eastern Belorussia, which had more time to prepare than did the central and western regions, only one-third to one-half of the urban Jewish population—even fewer in the countryside—were able to be evacuated. For the most part the Jews remained unaware of the threat that Hitler posed to them. Lacking reliable information about the situation at the front, they presumed that the initial defeats were temporary setbacks and that the enemy would be stopped. The vast majority of Belorussian Jews—more than 800,000—were deserted by the authorities and left behind in occupied territory.

In preparing for war with the Soviet Union, the German authorities worked out a plan for the total annihilation of Jews as "carriers of Bolshevism." Responsibility for its implementation lay with Reichsführer SS Heinrich Himmler and Gestapo chief Reinhard Heydrich. By agreement with the Wehrmacht high command, four special terror squadrons, the SS *Einsatzgruppen*, were formed. Einsatzgruppe B, commanded by Gen. Arthur Nebe and composed of Sonderkommando 7a and 7b and Einsatzkommando 8 and 9, was assigned to Belorussia. Latvian, Lithuanian, and Ukrainian SD battalions, as well as local police units, took an active part in the war crimes of German squadrons.

From the first days of the occupation Einsatzgruppe B began executing innocent people solely on account of their Jewish ancestry. In Brest, where 26,000 Jews lived, the SS murdered 5,000 (mostly men) on 28–29 June. In Minsk at the beginning of July they rounded up, under the pretense of labor conscription, 3,000 scholars, teachers, students, engineers, and attorneys and shot them the same day. In Pinsk on 5–7 August the Germans killed 4,500 Jews. The military governor of Slonim, Gerd Erren, reported that upon his arrival there were 16,000 Jews in the city, more than two-thirds of the entire population. "It was almost impossible to seal the ghetto," he wrote, "as there was no barbed wire and insufficient security. . . . The SD action of 13 November freed me from useless spongers: the 7,000 Jews remaining in Slonim have been included in the process of production." The other 9,000 Jews of Slonim had been tortured and shot by the SD.

A cruel occupation regime settled in throughout Belorussia. Cities and towns were covered by a network of military garrisons and police departments. Until September 1941 the territory of the republic had been subject to German military administration, and much of eastern Belorussia remained under that authority thereafter. Bialystok and Grodno comprised a separate administrative unit. The southern regions of Polesye were placed under the direction of the Reichskommissariat Ukraine. The remaining territory was organized into the Belorussian district of the Reichskommissariat Ostland.

After the first wave of terror, those Jews who were still alive were isolated from the rest of the population. Unspeakable outrages and assaults were committed against them, including the theft of all Jewish property. Jews were ordered to hand over all gold, silver, and precious stones in their possession. In Minsk alone the Germans confiscated and then sent to Berlin 5,875 gold rubles issued by the tsarist mint, 10 kilograms of gold objects, 112.7 kilograms of silver coins, and 351 kilograms of various silver objects. All Jews were forced to wear a yellow badge as a distinguishing mark. Jews were forbidden to change their residence without official permission or to have commerce with non-Jews. In effect the Jews of Belorussia lived outside the law and at the whim of the authorities. With unprecedented cruelty the SS strove to humiliate the Jews, to destroy any feeling of self-worth they might cling to, and to strangle all attempts at self-defense.

Some 200 ghettos were created on Belorussian territory. The largest was in Minsk, where 100,000 Jews were concentrated. Living conditions in the ghetto were intolerable. The Germans forced most of the healthy adults to work 12–14 hours a day for no pay and only starvation rations. Children and the elderly who did not work received nothing. The mortality rate soared. In Pruzhin one-third of the 18,000 ghetto inmates died of hunger, hard labor, and beatings during the winter of 1941–42. Gauleiter Wilhelm Kube, whom Hitler had put in charge of Belorussia on 17 July 1941, thought that the so-called Jewish problem had to be solved "by a single blow, once and for all." By his order units of Einsatzgruppe B undertook the systematic, cold-blooded murder of the Jewish population. In eastern Belorussia all the ghettos, except in Minsk, were liquidated by the end of 1941. In Bobrujsk the Nazis killed 25,000 Jews, in Mogilev 20,000, in Vitebsk also around 20,000, in Slutsk 18,000, in Mozyr and the nearby towns more than 10,000, in Gomel 6,365, and in Bychov 4,679. In Rakov, where more than 900 Jews lived, the SS drove them into a synagogue and set it on fire; they were burned alive. In Klimovichi, Logojsk, Narovlja, Chausy, Chechersk, and many other towns the Jewish population was wiped out.

In the Minsk ghetto every day brought new round-ups and executions. The Einsatzgruppe B report of 9 October 1941 noted the liquidation of 30,064 Jews. In connection with the imminent deportation of Jews from Western and Central Europe, in November 1941 Himmler and Adolf Eichmann, the SS officer in charge of planning and administering the Final Solution, personally inspected the Minsk ghetto. They found the pace of removal of the inhabitants to be unsatisfactory and ordered that a technical innovation in mass murder be used for the first time: gassing vans. In the course of pogroms on 7, 8, and 20 November, the Germans sealed Jews into the backs of vans and flooded them with toxic fumes from the engine exhaust. Then they drove the vans to the village of Maly Trostinets, where the corpses were burned in a specially built crematorium. Approximately 27,000 persons were killed over those three days. Jews from Greater Germany as well as occupied countries were soon transported to Minsk to replenish the vacant ghetto. In November 1941 and from May to October 1942 the Nazis brought to Minsk 6,428 Jews from the Altreich (Germany within its pre-1938 borders), 10,476 from Austria, and about 7,000 from the Protectorate of Bohemia and Moravia. The majority went straight from the trains to Maly Trostinets, where they were killed; the rest were incarcerated in the ghetto.

On 20 January 1942, at the Wannsee Conference to plan the implementation of the Final Solution to exterminate European Jewry, Heydrich put the number

Jews performing forced labor in Bialystok. 28 June 1941

of Jews in occupied Belorussia at 446,484, not including an estimated 400,000 in the Bialystok-Grodno region.

In the second half of 1942 the Nazis put into motion the annihilation of the western Belorussian ghettos. On 15–18 October they liquidated the Brest ghetto, which had housed more than 30,000 Jews. On 27 October Himmler himself gave the order "to liquidate the Pinsk ghetto immediately, without any consideration of economics." Two days later a large SS contingent arrived in Pinsk and murdered 15,000 Jews. In Lida the Germans butchered 16,000 Jews, in Baranovichi 15,000, in and near Slonim 22,000, in Volkovysk 10,000, in the two ghettos of Novogrudok 10,000, in Vilejka 6,972, and in Stolbtsy 3,500.

When the ghettos were organized, the inhabitants viewed the Nazis' interest in forming Jewish councils (*Judenräte*) for self-governance as a sign that loyal be-

havior and hard work would somehow save them. But Hitler's policy of genocide scattered those illusions. Forcibly herded behind the barbed wire along the ghetto's perimeter and doomed to total destruction, the Jews courageously sought and found the means to resist German oppression. Jewish resistance appeared in the very first days of the occupation. In many ghettos underground organizations and fighting units formed. In the Minsk ghetto the anti-Nazi movement was headed by Mikhail Gebelev. More than 300 people participated in 22 underground groups. They carried out acts of sabotage against industry and railways, destroyed systems of communication, and smuggled thousands of other Jews out of the ghetto to join the partisans in the forests.

Well before the famous April 1943 uprising in the Warsaw ghetto, Jews revolted in many of the ghettos of Belorussia, including Nesvizh (20 July 1942), Kletsk

(22 July), Derechin (24 July), and Lachva (3 September). The Jews of the Bialystok ghetto took up arms on 16 August 1943 and, led by Mordechai Tenenbaum, fought valiantly for five days. Most were killed in action. Those who remained alive escaped to a nearby wood and formed the Vpered (Forward) partisan unit. In the Glubokoye ghetto on 19 August 1943 the Germans had to bring up tanks and artillery to quash a spirited uprising by the Jewish underground.

Similarly desperate armed revolts by Jews against the Nazis and their collaborators occurred in Slonim, Druja, Sharkovshchina, Braslav, Volozhin, Kaldychev, and Lenino (Pinsk district). Inmates succeeded in daring escapes from a series of ghettos—300 people from Mir, 233 from Novogrudok, 100 from Kobrin, about 80 from Miory, and 208 from the concentration camp in Novy Serzhen. In the town of Radun in May 1943, 180 Jews who had been rounded up for execution suddenly threw themselves at the SS guards. Although the Germans were armed, the prisoners managed to gain the advantage. Twenty died in the struggle, but the rest got away.

The leadership of the Minsk ghetto underground was unable to launch the uprising it had been preparing but did succeed in conveying some 10,000 Jews into the nearby forests. The majority of those who escaped attached themselves to partisan fighting units. Yitzhak Arad (born Yitzhak Rudnicki) was 16 years old when he joined the Belorussian forest partisans. The experience determined his future calling as longtime director of the Israeli Holocaust memorial and museum Yad Vashem. "People must know," said Arad. "We did not go to our deaths quietly and submissively. We battled as best we could—often with our bare hands and always without help from anyone else." Among the organizers of the partisan movement in Belorussia were several Jews—Samuel Sverdlov (Rogachev district), Wolf Israilit (Mekhov district), Solomon Geller (Osveisk district), Zus Chernoglaz (Elsk district), Ruvim Goland (Osipovichi district), Chaim Vargavtik (Petrikov district), and Chaim Shkliar (Chechersk district).

The core of the first partisan detachments in the Belorussian forests consisted of escaped ghetto inmates and Red Army soldiers. Jews from the Minsk ghetto made up a significant portion of nine partisan detachments (the Kutuzov, Budenny, Frunze, Lazo, Parkhomenko, Shchors, 25th Anniversary of the Belorussian Republic, No. 106, and No. 406) and the first

battalion of the 208th independent partisan regiment. Jews were active in many other partisan groups as well. In the Lenin brigade (Baranovichi district) 202 of the 695 fighters and commanders were Jews, in Vpered 106 of 579, in Chkalov 239 of 1,140, and in Novatory 48 of 126. Jews composed more than one-third of the partisans in the detachments that fought in the Lid partisan zone. In the Naliboki wood 3,000 of the 20,000 partisans were Jews, many of them in positions of command. Incomplete data record that some 150 Jews were commanders, chiefs of staff, and commissars of partisan brigades and detachments.

The partisan movement was particularly large and widespread in Belorussia. Much of the territory was forests and marshlands, which provided extremely favorable cover for partisan groups. According to official Soviet statistics, 370,000 partisans and underground fighters took part in the movement. Among them were 30,000 Jews, who were driven by a desire for revenge against the Nazis for the murder of their loved ones and who fought with no less selflessness than did their Christian brothers in arms.

On 31 July 1942 Governor Kube reported to Hinrich Lohse, the Reichskommissar of Ostland: "In all armed skirmishes with the partisans in Belorussia it has become clear that Jewry . . . is the main inspiration of the partisan movement." Kube himself was killed in his residence in Minsk on 22 September 1943. The operation was led by a Jew, David Keimakh.

It was not at all easy for a Jew fleeing the ghetto to become a partisan. Gentile units accepted Jews unwillingly, even when they brought along arms. In early November 1942 the chief of the central staff of the partisan movement, Panteleimon Ponomarenko, ordered his brigade commanders to reject individuals and small groups of people who had by some miracle escaped from the ghettos—namely, Jews. The pretext could not have been more transparent: among them, said Ponomarenko, there might be "agents sent by the Germans."

The Kremlin demonstrated complete indifference to the fate of the Jews in the ghettos. On 5 September 1942 Stalin, in his role as people's commissar of defense, published Decree No. 189, "On the Problems of the Partisan Movement." It contained not a word about helping the Jews, who had been condemned to death. Only one commander, Pavel Proniagin of the Shchors detachment, took it upon himself to rescue ghetto inmates when in June 1942 he organized the escape of 170 Jews from Slonim. In August his partisans routed the German garrison in Kosovo and freed 200 more ghetto Jews, who in turn joined the detachment.

The central staff of the partisan movement did everything it could to hinder the creation of independent Jewish partisan detachments, and in a number of cases such units were disbanded. The most important role in saving people who had fled the ghettos was played by partisan detachments of Jewish families. The idea of founding the family detachments came from Tuvia Bielski, who in the spring of 1942, together with his three brothers, Asael, Zusia, and Archik, engineered an escape from the Novogrudok ghetto and created a detachment in the Naliboki wood. In all, 1,230 Jews from the ghettos of Novogrudok, Lida, and Minsk took refuge with the Bielski partisans. Another Jewish family detachment, organized by Sholom Zorin, numbered 600 persons, and Yeheskel Atlas established a large family detachment in the Lipchansky wood, where Jews fleeing many towns in the Prinemansk region took refuge. There were similar detachments in the Miadel district by Lake Naroch, the Lukoml district at Vitebshchino, and in Polesye. The Israeli historian Leonid Smilovitsky put the number of persons in Jewish family detachments in Belorussia at 5,000.

In 1943 the pace of Nazi implementation of the Final Solution in Belorussia quickened. On 21 June, Himmler ordered the liquidation of all remaining ghettos. In August 30,000 Jews were killed when the Bialystok ghetto was eliminated, and on 18 September the Jews of the Lida ghetto were transported to the extermination camp at Majdanek. The final victims of the Holocaust in Belorussia were the inmates of the Minsk ghetto. On 21 October the SS loaded 4,000 Jews into gassing vans in Minsk and drove them to Maly Trostinets.

The Jews of Belorussia suffered irrecoverable losses. Approximately 800,000, one-quarter of them children, were tortured and killed. Hundreds of Jewish villages ceased to exist. The spiritual and material world of the Belorussian Jews, which had flowered over the course of centuries, was consumed in the flames of the Holocaust. Belorussia was also the last stop before their murder for 55,000 Jews from Germany, Austria, the Protectorate of Bohemia and Moravia, Poland, France, the Netherlands, Belgium, and other countries.

Kurt von Gottberg, who had become the new gauleiter on 25 September, informed Berlin that Belorussia was now *Judenfrei*, free of Jews. This observation was not, however, altogether accurate. Jews

Posed portrait of Jewish forced laborers in Belzec. Circa 1942

continued to fight the enemy in partisan units, played an active role in the "rail war," and participated in battles to drive the German occupation forces out of Belorussia.

After World War II the long-suffering Belorussian Jews had to withstand a new set of trials. In 1949 the Soviet authorities launched an antisemitic campaign throughout the country, including the Belorussian republic, aimed at combating manifestations of Jewish "bourgeois nationalism" and "stateless cosmopolitanism." It reached its peak in January 1953, with the arrest of Jewish doctors in Moscow on trumped-up charges of medical assassination, but subsided after Stalin's death two months later. Antisemitism remained, however, a covert element of Soviet state policy. Jews faced restrictions on university admissions and career advancement, and obstacles were placed in the way of the practice of Judaism. In the mid-1980s some of these restrictions were loosened during the period of perestroika under Soviet president Mikhail Gorbachev, and Jewish cultural life in Belorussia underwent a revival.

In 1991, upon the disintegration of the Soviet Union, the independent republic of Belarus was established. Under President Aleksandr Lukashenko, elected in 1994, antisemitism was again allowed to flourish. The proliferation of Judophobic publications, without interference or reaction from the government, fanned the flames of interethnic strife and racial hatred. The threat of pogroms was one of the main reasons for a mass exodus of Belorussian Jews to Israel, the United States, and other countries. According to Soviet census figures, 157,000 Jews lived in the Belorussian republic in 1979. By the middle of 1999, in Belarus, only 17,000 remained, a decline that signals the end of a Jewish community that had prospered on Belorussian soil for seven centuries. For map see UKRAINE.   *David Meltser*

Belzec   Second camp to function solely as a killing center and the first camp to have permanent gas chambers. Belzec was established in March 1942 in southwestern Poland, on the Bug River east of the Lublin district. Approximately 600,000 Jews were killed there. The exterminations at Belzec ended in November 1942. See EXTERMINATION CAMPS

Ben-Gurion, David (1886–1973)   Chairman of the Jewish Agency Executive for Palestine (1935–48) and leader of Mapai, the Israeli Workers party. Born David Gruen in Poland, Ben-Gurion settled in Palestine in

David Ben-Gurion, chairman of the Jewish Agency executive, speaks to displaced persons during a visit to Zeilsheim. 1946

1906. In 1939 he orchestrated the response of the Jewish community (Yishuv) to the British white paper that restricted immigration to Palestine. Ben-Gurion called for Jews to assist Great Britain in the war effort against Nazi Germany and at the same time promoted illegal immigration to Palestine. He was the first prime minister (1948–53; 1955–63) and the first defense minister (1948–53; 1955–63) of the state of Israel. See RESCUE; YISHUV

Berdichev   City in northwest Ukraine with a prewar population of approximately 65,000, including 30,000 Jews. After the Germans occupied Berdichev in July 1941, it became the site of a Nazi extermination camp. On 15 September 1941, 18,600 of the 20,000 Jews who remained in the city were shot and thrown into pits. When Berdichev was liberated on 15 January 1944, only 15 Jews were found alive.

Bergen-Belsen Concentration camp near Celle in northwest Germany. Originally designed as a prisoner-of-war and transit camp to house 10,000 prisoners, by the last weeks of the war Bergen-Belsen held 41,000. Some 35,000 to 40,000 inmates died of starvation, overcrowding, hard labor, and disease or were killed on the orders of the commandant, Josef Kramer. Anne Frank died at Bergen-Belsen in March 1945. On 15 April 1945 Bergen-Belsen was the first camp to be liberated by the Western Allied forces.

Berlin Berlin, the German capital, was the largest and most important Jewish community in the German state from its founding until the total destruction of German Jewry. Jews resided in Berlin already in the thirteenth century. They were subject to periodic expulsion and readmission by the Brandenburg princes.

The expulsion of 1571 remained in force for a century until 1671, when 50 wealthy Jewish families who had been expelled from Vienna were allowed to resettle in Brandenburg as part of the princes' regional economic policy. Seven of these families were brought to Berlin, and their arrival marks the inception of Berlin's modern Jewish community. The community experienced rapid growth, as the civil authorities continued to issue "letters of protection" to its members. According to the population census of 1700, 70 "protected" Jewish families with permits resided in Berlin; another 47 families who were without permits also lived in the city. In addition, the census noted the presence there of approximately 1,000 Jewish peddlers and beggars. The vast majority of Berlin's Jews were involved in commerce. The systematic monetary exploitation of the Jews, a policy implemented after the accession of

Burning the last hut at the Bergen-Belsen camp. June 1945

the elector of Brandenburg, Frederick, to the Prussian throne in 1701, reached new heights in the mid-eighteenth century under his son, Frederick the Great. Several Berlin Jews who had profited greatly during the Seven Years' War as purveyors to the army now had their privileges broadened. In 1791 full citizenship was granted to entire Jewish families. Nonetheless, the king continued to exploit the tax apparatus to the fullest, issuing the notorious "porcelain decree," which forced Jews to purchase fixed quantities of porcelain from the government factory.

In the late eighteenth century came the emergence of the Haskalah movement, which called for cultural integration with the surrounding Gentile society. The first Jewish school where German was the language of instruction, the Jüdische Freischule (Hinukh Nearim), was founded in 1778. Scholars congregated at the home of the philosopher Moses Mendelssohn, and the salons of Henriette Herz and Rahel Varnhagen became meeting places for Berlin's high society, both Christian and Jewish. But the granting of equal civil rights lagged behind this development. Only after Prussia's defeat by Napoleon in 1809 were Jews granted citizenship in the city of Berlin, and some restrictions remained in force for decades thereafter. In 1812 the Jews were awarded Prussian citizenship, and the remaining restrictions and special taxes were revoked. In 1837, the existing arrangements for internal Jewish administration were canceled. From that point on, an elected board of seven, with three alternates, presided over the Jewish community.

After the grant of full citizenship in 1860, the Jews of Berlin became more active in the life of the city. They played a prominent role in its press—the editors and publishers of Berlin's two most important liberal newspapers, *Berliner Tageblatt* and *Vossische Zeitung*, were Jews—and in theater and music. This state of affairs was seized upon by the antisemitic movement, whose Berlin constituency grew following the establishment of the German state in 1871, when it also began to absorb racist ideas. Jews took an active part in the city's economic life as bankers, entrepreneurs (founders of department stores), and textile manufacturers. They also entered the universities and the professions, mainly law and medicine, but they played only a minor role in public and government services.

Berlin's Jewish population experienced rapid growth: from 12,000 in 1852 to 108,000 in 1890 and 173,000 in 1925, when they made up 4.3 percent of the city's population and 30.6 percent of the total German Jewish population. By 1933 their numbers had declined to 160,000, in part owing to intermarriage and renunciation of Judaism: between 1911 and 1932 there was an average of 1,500 intermarriages and 750 conversions annually. This decline was offset, however, by immigration from eastern Germany and Poland. The influx from the east further sparked antisemitic agitation. Unlike other German Jewish communities, Berlin granted citizenship rights to its new residents, in effect reinforcing those elements in the Jewish community that still identified strongly with Judaism and the *kehillah* (Jewish community).

Religious and Community Life

The Haskalah, beginning in the mid-nineteenth century, propelled a modification of the liturgy and religious rites in the synagogue. Changes were introduced, albeit moderate, even within those circles that still adhered strictly to halakhah (rabbinic law). The radical reformers, led by Samuel Holdheim, went so far as to transfer Sabbath observance to Sunday. The "Reform Congregation" did not, however, take root in Berlin; it was the more moderate reform element, later called liberal, united under the aegis of the Vereinigung für das liberale Judentum, which comprised the mainstream in the Berlin kehillah. Tensions erupted in 1866 after the dedication of the elaborate New Synagogue on Oranienburgerstrasse: the synagogue was fitted with an organ—Jewish tradition had prohibited musical instruments from houses of worship—and its congregation introduced radical liturgical revisions. Nevertheless, liberal and Orthodox elements did collaborate in the kehillah administration. Among Berlin Orthodoxy, however, there were breakaway elements. In 1869, Berlin followers of Rabbi Samson Raphael Hirsch founded an independent kehillah, Adass Yisroel. Led by Rabbi Azriel Hildesheimer, in 1885 it received official recognition as an autonomous corporation in accordance with the German law of Austrittsgesetz (1876). By the 1930s, the Berlin Jewish community maintained 16 synagogues: seven Orthodox, one Reform, and the rest Liberal. In addition it supported some 50 religious congregations, primarily made up of Eastern European Jews.

Berlin became the headquarters for the majority of the German Jewish national movements founded in the late nineteenth and early twentieth centuries: the Deutsch-Israelitischer Gemeindebund (1869), Ver-

Offices at Central-Verein Deutscher Staatsbürger Jüdischen Glaubens. Berlin, 1934

band der Deutschen Juden (1904), the Order of B'nai B'rith (1883), Central-Verein Deutscher Staatsbürger Jüdischen Glaubens (1893), Hilfsverein Deutscher Juden (Ezra Society, 1901), Zentralwohlfahrtsstelle der Deutschen Juden (1917), Zionistische Vereinigung für Deutschland (1897), and others. Berlin also boasted two institutes of higher learning in Jewish studies: the liberal Hochschule für die Wissenschaft des Judentums (1872) and the Rabbinerseminar für das Orthodoxe Judentum, founded by Adass Yisroel (1873).

In 1922 Berlin's Jewish community helped form a union of the Prussian Jewish kehillot, the Preussischer Landesverband Jüdischer Gemeinden. This union embraced some 600 communities; with Berlin it encompassed approximately two-thirds of German Jewry. The Berlin kehillah assumed the obligation of providing aid to the region's smaller, poorer communities; concurrently, Berlin acquired preeminent status within the overall structure of the German-Jewish communities.

Berlin also served as headquarters for various Jewish youth movements: Blau Weiss; Hehalutz and its religious counterpart, Brit Halutzim Datiim (Bahad), as well as other Hehalutz affiliates; and Kameraden, whose offshoots in the early 1930s included the Zionist Werkleute movement, the religious Ezra movement, and the Bund Deutsch-Jüdischer Jugend, among others.

Following World War I, the Zionists joined the communal political establishment. In 1920, the Zionist vehicle for communal involvement, the Jüdische Volkspartei (1919)—an alignment of the Zionist Federation, the Mizrahi, and the Union of Eastern European Jewish Organizations—won four places on a council numbering 21 representatives; in addition, a representative of Poale Zion was elected. Four years later, a coalition of the Volkspartei and several small parties achieved a tiny majority. Georg Kareski, the Zionist representative, served as president of the community for two years. In 1932, however, the liberals regained the upper hand. Wilhelm Kleeman was appointed president, to be followed by Heinrich Stahl in May 1933.

Intrinsic differences of opinion regarding the role of the community divided the liberals and the Zionists. While the liberals saw its function as restricted to providing for religious needs, the Zionists wanted to transform it into a popular body, the bearer of sociocultural autonomy—a *Volksgemeinde*. The Zionists viewed the Jewish school as the primary tool for

achieving this end. Jewish students who attended public schools received religious instruction; moreover, the community put Hebrew schools at the public schools' disposal. There were three educational institutions for adults: the Freie Jüdische Volkshochschule, the Schule der Jüdischen Jugend, and the Lehranstalt (communal Hebrew college).

Nonetheless, the liberals did not interpret the term *religious community* narrowly, and they established many institutions for the communal good. The kehillah operated a central library whose 54,000 volumes circulated from eight branches; its art collection formed the core of the city's Jewish Museum; and its newsletter, which had a distribution of 79,000 in 1932, appeared monthly until 1934, then weekly. The community maintained hospitals, health services, a home for the aged, schools for the blind and the deaf, two orphanages, day-care centers, and dormitories for needy young people. It also sent hundreds of children to summer camps each year. A community-sponsored playing field was completed in the early 1930s. In addition, the community operated an employment office and a vocational counseling service.

The period between the two world wars saw the intensification of antisemitic propaganda in Berlin and an increased incidence of physical assault on Jews. In 1923 residents of Grenadierstrasse, located in a quarter of Eastern European immigrants, were attacked. Antisemitic agitation further intensified with Joseph Goebbels's appointment as gauleiter of Berlin. In 1931 Jews on their way home from synagogue were assaulted by storm troopers on the Kurfürstendamm in western Berlin. By and large, however, as residents of the Third Reich's capital, Berlin's Jews experienced fewer such assaults under the Nazi regime than Jews in provincial cities did.

Hostile demonstrations against Jews accompanied the Nazi rise to power on 30 January 1933. The attacks peaked with a general boycott of all Jewish-owned shops and professional offices on 1 April 1933. As the initial shock wore off, the leaders of the Jewish community quickly took steps to deal with the new state of affairs. Their first priority was to find jobs for persons fired as a result of anti-Jewish legislation or whose businesses had been appropriated in accordance with the Nazi party's aryanization policy. It also became necessary to absorb pupils who had been expelled from the public schools or whose parents had removed them because of the prevailing hostility, as well as to find new vocations for youths whose traditional paths had been blocked. Moreover, assistance had to be provided to the many Jews who wished to emigrate.

The Berlin Central Office for Jewish Economic Assistance (Zentralstelle für Jüdische Wirtschaftshilfe), founded in early April, granted loans to Jews whose businesses had been damaged or dissolved, provided legal counseling, gave housing advice, and took steps aimed at sustaining existing enterprises and at initiating alternative ventures. It provided vocational retraining and matched youths with job-training opportunities. The communal employment office also stepped up its activities and attempted to find jobs for the unemployed in Jewish businesses.

New members began to stream to the youth movements, the Zionist ones especially. The Berlin Hehalutz branch alone grew from a few hundred members to 2,200 in November 1933. Synagogues were once again well attended. The Jewish newspapers increased their circulation, particularly the Zionist paper *Jüdische Rundschau;* on Boycott Day (1 April 1933), it ran an editorial by Robert Weltsch that declared: "Wear the Yellow Badge with Pride," a slogan that resonated with many German Jews. In the fall of 1933 the Jüdischer Kulturbund Berlin was founded in order to provide employment for performers barred from the public stage; soon, however, the Kulturbund came to sponsor theatrical performances for the Jewish community, as both legal measures and public hostility deterred Jews from attending public events. In 1935, when the Cultural Society of German Jews (Kulturbund Deutscher Juden) was established, the Berlin society served as its core.

By April 1933, the official opening of the school year, the kehillah had founded eight new elementary schools. Existing educational establishments also underwent rapid expansion. In 1937 a new high school was established. As early as 1932, Recha Freier had founded the Jüdische Jugendhilfe, which later developed into Youth Aliyah and supported Jewish settlement in Palestine. The Berlin kehillah itself did not encourage emigration. Even two years after the Nazi rise to power, we find in the communal newsletter: "We shall not cease to see Germany as the land of our fathers and our children." This statement notwithstanding, the community did provide assistance to emigrants, whose affairs were handled by the Jewish Agency's Palestine Office and the German Jewish Hilfsverein.

The Berlin Jewish community gave its backing to the Central Committee for Aid and Construction (Zentralausschuss für Hilfe und Aufbau), founded in April as a centralized economic body. Under its umbrella, all the major political organizations were united for the first time. The kehillah displayed a more ambivalent attitude toward the new political representation, the Reichsvertretung der Deutschen Juden, founded in September 1933.

As early as 1932, a nationwide representation for the German Jewish communities had been formed under the aegis of the Prussian Union (Preussischer Landesverband) and the Berlin kehillah, but it was soon revealed as lacking in initiative. In the summer of 1933, representatives of the unions of the Jewish communities in southern and western Germany began consultations with an eye to creating a new representative body, whose leadership was to be chosen along the lines of the Central Committee (Zentralausschuss), with Rabbi Leo Baeck of Berlin as president and Otto Hirsch of Stuttgart as managing director. In this they were motivated by the longstanding rivalry between the Berlin community and the kehillot in western and southern Germany, and they sought by these means to forestall Berlin's attempts to monopolize the institutional framework. These complex negotiations reached a successful conclusion, and on 17 September the formation of a national representation was announced in Berlin by the president of the Berlin Jewish community, Heinrich Stahl. Nonetheless, the Berlin kehillah never truly accepted this state of affairs and made unceasing attempts to turn the clock back to the time when it dominated the national body.

In this struggle, Stahl cooperated with Georg Kareski, leader of the Zionist faction. In April 1933 Kareski was expelled from the Zionist Federation following a violent Betar (a right-wing Zionist group) demonstration in front of the communal welfare office. Only in 1936 was unity again achieved within the Berlin Zionist faction. In that year, the Zionist demand for parity in the kehillah administration was attained without elections, the result of a Gestapo order that fixed the number of kehillah board members at seven, in compliance with the 1847 constitution. Accordingly, three liberal representatives were forced to resign.

Jewish businesses in Berlin were adversely affected by the creeping aryanization, by threats from Nazi party members and its dependents, and by open calls for a boycott. In 1934–35 the department store owners

Tietz and Wertheim were forced to turn over their businesses or sell them for a price far below their real value. In 1935 direct welfare payments made up 35 percent of the Berlin kehillah's budget. Toward the end of that year, the Jews were expelled from the public winter welfare program (Winterhilfswerk), but the community quickly organized its own project, which was renewed yearly. With the passage of the Nuremberg Laws in 1936 the process of aryanization was stepped up. In 1938 the last private Jewish banks, textile mills, and clothing plants were seized. In Berlin alone, from April 1938 until Kristallnacht, 1,000 requests for aryanization were tendered. Concurrently, the liquidation of the smaller kehillot proceeded apace, and many of their former members moved to Berlin, which now housed half of the German Jewish population.

In August 1938, a directive was issued ordering the Jews to add Israel or Sarah to their names. Previously, on 28 March 1938, the Berlin Jewish community, along with all the other German kehillot, had been deprived of its status as a recognized public corporate body and thereby denied the right to collect taxes. As most of the Jewish communities were no longer self-supporting, there was a pressing need for effective organization on the local, regional, and national level. Following prolonged and difficult negotiations, an agreement was reached to found a National Union (Reichsverband); within this framework the Prussian Union was to comprise the communal division. However, because of Kristallnacht, this program was never implemented.

During the night of 9–10 November 1938, Berlin's synagogues were torched, as were synagogues throughout the country. Offices and businesses were broken into and ransacked. While community leaders strove to prevent a recurrence of the disturbances, mass arrests were being carried out. The detainees were deported to the Sachsenhausen concentration camp. Kristallnacht resulted in break-ins at dozens of Jewish institutions and the expropriation of Jewish property, including the libraries of the Hochschule für die Wissenschaft des Judentums and the Rabbinerseminar, as well as the communal library and museum, among others.

The following day Hermann Göring, in his role as minister of the economy, announced that Jews were now excluded from the German economy. The last remaining means of earning a living were expropriated.

Göring imposed a billion-mark fine, which the Jews of Berlin managed to remit in large part.

The authorities now took steps to set up new measures governing the Jewish community. To this end they entered into negotiations with representatives of the Reichsvertretung. The SS was represented in these talks by the Reich Central Office for Jewish Emigration (Reichszentrale für Jüdische Auswanderung), established in Berlin in early 1939, which later formed the basis for Eichmann's department. At the time the SS perceived its task primarily as one of accelerating Jewish emigration. In the course of these contacts Stahl, the community president, presented a memorandum to the Gestapo with the recommendation that the Berlin kehillah machinery be adopted as the new national organization's administration. The Gestapo ignored the proposal. Shortly thereafter Stahl resigned and was replaced by Moritz Henschel. These talks culminated with the creation of the Reich Union of Jews in Germany (Reichsvereinigung der Juden in Deutschland), in which membership was compulsory for every Jew defined as such by the Nuremberg Laws. The kehillot comprised its branches. The union, which was subject to close Gestapo supervision, absorbed all existing Jewish organizations, with the exception of the Cultural Association. The larger Jewish communities continued to maintain a modicum of independence; over time, however, they were incorporated as well.

The last kehillah to be deprived of its autonomy was Berlin's. This occurred on 29 January 1943, when barely 30,000 Jews remained in the city. Yet even earlier, members of the Reich Union had become directly involved in the running of the kehillah administration. The Jewish papers had ceased publication, with the exception of the *Jüdisches Nachrichtenblatt*, which continued to appear in two editions, one for Berlin and the other for Vienna. A *Judenbann* was imposed—Jews were barred from Berlin's central squares and main streets—and unless the conditions of their employment dictated otherwise, they found themselves confined to their residential areas. Evictions from certain neighborhoods also began, in order to provide housing for non-Jewish Berliners whose residences had been appropriated as part of Albert Speer's overall building plan for Berlin.

Anyone who could do so now applied for emigration, and the remaining organizations, the kehillah and the Reich Union, did their utmost to provide assis-

Ruins of the Fasanenstrasse synagogue in Berlin-Charlottenburg, which was destroyed during the Kristallnacht pogrom. After 9 November 1938

tance. But as conditions worsened, the number of options diminished. At the outbreak of war, in September 1939, 75,344 Jews remained in Berlin.

Anti-Jewish measures were now issued with ever-increasing frequency. Jews who still possessed funds were forced to deposit them in a closed account, from which only a fixed amount could be withdrawn. Hard upon the confiscation of automobiles came the confiscation of radios, bicycles, typewriters, furs, and even pets. Telephones were disconnected. With the introduction of rationing, Jewish coupons bore a special stamp, and the rations were reduced from the level allowed the rest of the population. Certain commodities were simply not available to them, particularly items of high nutritional value—meat (from a certain date), eggs, and milk. The number of stores open to Jews was restricted, and shopping was limited to one hour a day.

In September 1941 Jews were required to wear the Jewish star—the *Judenstern*. Use of public transportation required a special permit. Moreover, a process of ghettoization began, as Jews were crowded into designated apartment houses. In June 1942, at the height of the deportations, the Jewish schools were closed. At that time, 10 synagogues were still functioning.

Compulsory labor was introduced in two stages: first there was a labor draft (*Arbeitseinsatz*) for welfare cases; then, from 1941, universal compulsory labor was instituted, particularly in the armaments industry and in public works. Wages were extremely low, and the treatment was generally harsh. All social benefits were canceled.

Deportations commenced in October 1941. Concurrently, the last trickle of emigration was terminated. On the Day of Atonement in 1941, the president of the Jewish community and his deputies were summoned to the Gestapo, only to be informed of the inauguration of a resettlement program (*Umsiedlung*). The Jewish community was now required to invite several thousand candidates to fill out questionnaires, from among whom the Gestapo would at intervals choose 1,000 for transport. The Levetzow Street synagogue became an assembly point for the deportees. The Gestapo acceded to the Berlin community leaders' request that the Reich Union be informed of these measures, and following joint consultations a decision was reached to cooperate with the deportations in order to avert potentially greater evil. The first transport of 1,082 Jews left Berlin's Grunewald station on 16 October 1941 for the Polish city of Lodz. Three additional transports had Lodz as their destination. On 24 October transports to Minsk, in Belorussia, began; some deportees were destined for the ghetto, while others were sent straight to the killing ground at Maly Trostinets. This was the case for the transports to Riga, Latvia, as well: some Jews were executed on the spot, while others were sent to the ghetto, whose former residents had recently been exterminated. Transports from Berlin also reached Kovno and went directly to the so-called Ninth Fort, a killing ground. In the spring of 1942 transports were sent to Lublin. In June, the first direct transport to Theresienstadt, mainly of the elderly, took place as part of the SS disinformation campaign. The elderly, who lived in appalling conditions in the Berlin ghetto, were ostensibly sold beds in a nursing home. In July 1942 the first direct transport to Auschwitz left Berlin, and from November 1942 Auschwitz replaced the other ghettos and killing grounds in the east as the destination for Berlin's Jews.

In May 1942 a largely Communist-Jewish underground group attempted to firebomb an anti-Soviet propaganda exhibition. Most of the group's members were caught and executed. In reprisal the Gestapo arrested 500 Berlin Jews; half of them were shot on the spot and the remainder were then deported to Sachsenhausen.

In the winter of 1942 Adolf Eichmann's deputy, Alois Brunner, was brought from Vienna to Berlin to accelerate the deportations. Brunner exercised his duties with extreme brutality. In December 1942, when the stipulated number of Jews failed to report for deportation, others who happened to be in the Jewish community offices were seized to fill the quota and im-

mediately sent to the deportation train. On 27–28 February 1943, munitions workers, until then exempt from the transports, were rounded up at their workplace and taken straight to the assembly points. Also arrested on that occasion, in contradiction of Gestapo directives, were the Jewish husbands of non-Jewish women. Following a public demonstration by their wives, the Gestapo was forced to release them. Some 25,500 Jews now remained in Berlin, but their numbers dropped drastically with the spring and summer deportations to Auschwitz.

As long as the Berlin kehillah remained functional, its workers did everything in their power to ameliorate the lot of the deportees by providing food, clothing, and other essentials for their purported stay in labor camps. Nonetheless, Berlin was the only German city where members of the kehillah and the Reich Union were drafted to remove Jews from their homes by force and to prevent them from evading deportation. They were also charged with forestalling suicides, which, much to the displeasure of the SS, increased during deportations.

On 19 June 1942 the first deportation of Reich Union employees took place. Fifty workers who arrived late to work were taken, along with another 50 specified individuals, including senior officials. On 26–27 January 1943 Rabbi Leo Baeck, who refused overtures that he escape individually and insisted on staying with the community, Reich Union president Paul Eppstein (successor to Otto Hirsch, who died in a concentration camp), Heinrich Stahl, and Philip Kotzover, another senior official, were deported to Theresienstadt. In June, Moritz Henschel was deported. On 10 June 1943 the Jewish community was declared officially closed. Some 5,400 Jews remained in Berlin at that juncture, mostly of mixed parentage or partners in mixed marriages. The Reich Union was never officially disbanded. Based in the Jewish hospital, where several dozen protected Jews resided, it continued to function under Dr. Walter Lustig, former head of the union's health division.

A total of 63 transports to the east left Berlin, carrying 35,738 deportees, and 117 transports were sent to Theresienstadt, with 14,797 deportees. Thus a total of 50,535 Jews were deported from Berlin.

In Berlin chances for survival underground were slim. Persons of mixed parentage with non-Jewish relatives and those who received organized help had the best chance. The precise number of "illegals" is impossible to determine; the records indicate that when the Russians occupied Berlin in May 1945, 1,024 people emerged from hiding. Estimates place the number of Jews in hiding as high as 5,000, but of these only a minority survived. Among them were members of a Zionist youth group, the Halutz circle. Led by Yitzhak Schwersenz, this group engaged in dynamic Jewish and Zionist activity while in hiding. Some of its members were caught, but others succeeded in escaping to Switzerland.   *Yehoyakim Cochavi*

Bermuda Conference   The second international conference on refugees from Germany and German-controlled territories took place in April 1943, almost five years after the first conference on the issue, which was held at Evian in July 1938. With German invasion of Poland in September 1939 and of France in June 1940, millions of refugees from Eastern and Western Europe joined the hundreds of thousands that had already left Germany, Austria, and Czechoslovakia (Greater Germany). In most cases inhabitants of German-occupied territory could not longer make their way legally to Allied countries. After the United States entered the war in December 1941, that haven too was closed to many, if not most, refugees.

News of the Final Solution, which reached the free world in mid-1942, again brought the refugee issue to the fore. Public pressure was exerted on both the American and the British governments to take concrete steps toward rescuing European Jewry. To temper the public outcry in Great Britain, the British Foreign Office had sent a memorandum to the U.S. State Department proposing an informal conference of the United Nations (the Allies) to consider the rescue issue with particular regard to refugees who had already reached neutral European counties. It was emphasized, however, that the refugee question could not be handled as a Jewish problem, because not all refugees were Jewish and criticism would result if preference were shown to rescuing Jews. Furthermore, it was feared that antisemitism would be stimulated in areas where large numbers of foreign Jews were settled. A third concern was that the Germans and their allies would flood Western countries with refugees and thereby force the Allies to siphon resources from the war effort to resettlement.

The reply from Washington was delayed by several weeks as Undersecretary of State Breckinridge Long considered how to respond to the British initiative. In the end the American reply sidestepped the issue. It stated that the best approach would be to work through the already existing Inter-Governmental Committee on Refugees (IGC), which had been founded as a result of the Evian Conference, and suggested holding an Anglo-American meeting in Ottawa, Canada, to explore ways to strengthen the IGC. In one respect the American answer suited the British: both countries agreed that the refugee problem must not be considered a Jewish issue and that deliberations should not be confined to persons of a particular religion or ethnicity.

During the early spring of 1943, as word of the conference spread to the public, it was decided to hold the deliberations in Bermuda. The secluded location help shield the participants from public opinion. Moreover, the press and delegations from Jewish organizations would be unable to attend because of the wartime restrictions on access to the island. Originally it had been thought that Myron Taylor, the central figure at the Evian Conference who had been associated with the IGC since its formation, would act as chairman of the American delegation. But Taylor declined, saying that he was heavily involved in postwar planning. In truth, it appears that Taylor believed that the conference would achieve nothing and so found an excuse to bow out. Only a week before the conference opened, Harold W. Dodds, the president of Princeton University and a person with no international experience, agreed to serve as chairman. Dodds was accompanied by two members of Congress, Senator Scott Lucas of Illinois and Representative Sol Bloom of New York. In contrast to the American delegation, the British delegates were experienced, high-level Cabinet officials: Richard Law, the son of a former prime minister and the parliamentary undersecretary of state for foreign affairs; Osbert Peake of the Home Office; and George Hall from the Admiralty.

On 19 April 1943, as the Warsaw ghetto uprising was breaking out in Poland, the two groups began their deliberations at the Horizons Oceanside resort in Bermuda. For 12 days the diplomats, assisted by a bevy of secretaries and technical experts, examined the refugee issue from various perspectives. During this period their meetings were covered for the wire services by only five correspondents—the number allowed to travel to the island by the American government. The delegates had three main objectives: to devise steps to encourage neutral European nations to accept more escaped refugees; to seek temporary havens in territories of the Allied nations in Europe and Africa and to locate transport to them; and to call an early meeting of the IGC to implement the decisions reached in Bermuda.

As the conference neared adjournment, the delegations prepared a joint report for the American and British governments. They recommended that no approach be made to Hitler for the release of potential refugees, proposed that the two governments act immediately to obtain neutral shipping to transport refugees, requested that the British consider admitting refugees to Cyrenaica (in North Africa), suggested moving refugees out of Spain, proposed a joint Allied declaration on the postwar repatriation of refugees, and made plans to reorganize the IGC. It appears that the paucity of tangible results caused the conference members to keep their report a secret and to release only a one-page bulletin to the press, which stated in general terms that they were submitting a "number of concrete recommendations" to their governments, and that as these recommendations involved other governmental and military considerations, they would have to remain confidential.

American press coverage of the Bermuda Conference was negligible, owing to lack of interest and to close governmental control of information. The general feeling, which Chairman Dodds stressed even before the conference began, was that the true and long-lasting solution to the refugee problem was for the Allies to win the war. Time and again the delegation members emphasized that they saw little chance of immediate help for refugees. The Bermuda Conference, called a hoax and a mockery by a number of its critics, was denounced publicly by American Jewish leaders, organizations, and publications. But Jews were not alone in their distress over the Bermuda Conference. Frank Kingdon, a prominent Christian educator, denounced the deliberations and the results as "a shame and a disgrace." Among the protestors were the Socialist party leader Norman Thomas and a group of distinguished Christian churchmen led by Reinhold Niebuhr and Daniel Poling.

The practical results of the Bermuda Conference were indeed negligible. One small camp for Jewish refugees was established in North Africa. The real objective of the diplomacy at Bermuda was not, however, to rescue European Jewry but, in the words of one historian, "to dampen the growing pressures for rescue."

In this the delegations at Bermuda appeared to have succeeded. The Anglo-American demonstration of callousness smashed any hope among the refugee organizations and made their continuing efforts seem futile. *Judith Tydor Baumel*

Bessarabia Region in Eastern Europe lying within Moldova and Ukraine, bounded by the Prut and the Dniester rivers and the Black Sea. Bessarabia was ruled by Romania from 1920 to 1940, when it ceded under duress to the Soviet Union. After the German invasion of the Soviet Union in June 1941 it was reclaimed and occupied by Romania. Ion Antonescu, the Romanian dictator, ordered the killing of most of the 250,000 Jews in the region and deported the remainder of the population to Transnistria. Bessarabia was seized by the Red Army in 1944 and reincorporated into the Soviet Union. See ROMANIA; TRANSNISTRIA

Bialystok Town in northeastern Poland. More than 50 percent of Bialystok's prewar population of 100,000 was Jewish. The Germans captured the city in Sep-

Severely beaten Jewish women in a Bessarabian village. September 1941

Round-up of Jewish men in the Bialystok ghetto. 1940–42

tember 1939 but gave it over to the Soviets that same month, as part of the Ribbentrop-Molotov pact. In June 1941 the Germans reoccupied the city, and the Jews were placed in a ghetto in August 1941. Approximately 10,000 Jews were sent to Treblinka in February 1943. In August 1943 the ghetto was liquidated after a failed uprising, and approximately 30,000 Jews were sent to Treblinka and to Majdanek. See RESISTANCE IN EASTERN EUROPE

Birkenau Extermination camp, also known as Auschwitz II, one of the three main camps in the Auschwitz complex. Opened in October 1941, Birkenau had four gas chambers designed to kill up to 6,000 people a day. Between 1.1 and 1.3 million people died at Birkenau, 90 percent of them Jews. See AUSCHWITZ

Blechhammer Labor camp in Poland, near Gliwice, built in April 1942 to intern Jews from Upper Silesia. Blechhammer was infamous for its death rate from disease and starvation. After April 1944 it was placed under the authority of Auschwitz and called Auschwitz IV. Blechhammer held approximately 52,000 prisoners in the course of the war. On 21 January 1945

the camp was liquidated and 4,000 inmates were sent on a forced march to Buchenwald.

Blobel, Paul (1894–1951) Head of the *Sonderkommando* (special killing squad) in Ukraine responsible for the massacre at Babi Yar in September 1941. Blobel later was put in charge of Aktion 1005, whose purpose was to hide or destroy the evidence of mass murders in Eastern Europe. He was convicted of war crimes in 1948 and executed in 1951.

Bohemia and Moravia, Protectorate of In Munich on 19 September 1938, Adolf Hitler, Benito Mussolini, Neville Chamberlain, and Edouard Daladier signed the agreement that caused a total remodeling of the first Czechoslovak Republic. The state split into three autonomous entities: Bohemia and Moravia, Slovakia, and Ruthenia. It ceded territories to Germany, Hungary, and Poland.

According to the 1930 census, 117,551 Jews lived in Bohemia and Moravia, the Czech-speaking regions of Czechoslovakia; nearly one-quarter (27,073) resided in the territories ceded to Germany (the so-called Sudetenland). Between 1930 and 1938 changes had taken place in the Jewish population. Perhaps 35,000 Jews had emigrated, while thousands more from Germany and Austria had sought asylum in Czechoslovakia. Some 4,200 Jews from Slovakia lived in the Czech-speaking lands, and Jewish expatriates from other countries made Bohemia-Moravia their home. On 15 March 1939 a census determined that there were 118,310 Jews living in the territory. This number was disputed and can only be taken as an estimate. Including those people categorized as Jewish or partly Jewish (*Mischlinge*) under the Nuremberg Laws adds several thousand to this total. It can be assumed, therefore, that the total number of Jews living in the Czech lands on the eve of the Nazi destruction of Czechoslovakia was somewhere between 115,000 and 125,000. Of these, about 78,000 perished, some 14,000 survived, and approximately 26,000 emigrated. Thousands remain unaccounted for.

The first victims of the situation in Czechoslovakia were the Jews of the Sudetenland. With the arrival of German troops in the region on 1 October 1938, most Jews tried to escape; others were forced to emigrate. Some of the few who stayed on were arrested. During the Kristallnacht pogrom in November 1938 several dozen Jews were taken to concentration camps. The rest were to be rounded up in the years to come and sent to their deaths.

Once the Sudetenland had been annexed to Germany, Reich legislation, including the Nuremberg racial laws, became valid. The Germans set fire to several synagogues, and most of the rest were destroyed during Kristallnacht. The Jews of the Sudetenland lost their property, regardless of whether they fled or stayed. Those who fled were also exposed to hostile treatment in Czechoslovakia. The Czech population and administration considered them part of the hated Sudeten Germans, because of their German-based culture. Even the Czech Jews were not hospitable, for they feared that the sudden influx of Jewish refugees would cause an antisemitic backlash from Czech Gentiles. As the Germans were pushing the Jews across the border, the Czech authorities were trying to force them back. German troops prevented their reentry, and the victims were left at the border in no-man's-land. Eventually, international pressure obliged the Czechs to accept the victims and made the Germans stop the evacuation. Many of the Jews of the Sudetenland were able to emigrate abroad; because of their

tragic situation they were accorded preferential treatment.

The condition of Czech-speaking Jewry was also deteriorating. The new government, acting under enormous German pressure and out of anxiety to please the Berlin government, sought to ostracize the Czech Jews. Prague's task was not an easy one: Czechoslovakia was still a law-abiding, liberal country, and its citizens were loathe to commit arbitrary acts. Although the Czechs were becoming increasingly antisemitic, whether owing to Nazi and local fascist instigation or to the spontaneous release of dormant hatreds, they still were not willing to accept unqualified persecution. Antisemitic demonstrations and brutal treatment of Jews were still rare. Several middle-class groups were the pioneers of formal anti-Jewish discrimination: students, lawyers, merchants, and farmers who wanted to exploit the new conditions to eliminate economic competitors. Czech nationalists and German groups under Nazi influence incited the Czech public against the Jews. Under student pressure the last Jewish teachers at the German university in Prague lost their jobs.

The Czechoslovak government refused to be outmaneuvered. In spite of the anti-Jewish feelings of some ministers, the politicians were afraid that actions against Jews would result in a rapid outflow of capital, damage to the economic life of the country, and the disapproval of the British and French governments. Britain and France had promised loans but did not approve of the antisemitic trend they observed in Prague and the surrounding region.

In the mid-1930s there was an expansion of the Zionist movement in Czechoslovakia, undoubtedly spurred by the hope of emigrating to Palestine. The Anschluss (annexation) of Austria to Germany in March 1938 and the Munich Pact six months later provided an added impetus. Jews searched frantically for a country that would allow them to immigrate. Great Britain, which contributed considerable funds to easing the plight of the people displaced from the Sudetenland, led in absorbing the victims. Thousands, in particular orphaned children, left for Britain. London also accepted 2,500 Czechoslovak Jews into England but kept the gates of Palestine closed. Thousands of Jews tried to enter Palestine illegally in boats hired by Zionists or private entrepreneurs. Many perished on the way or suffered enormous hardship before reaching their destination.

Others sought refuge in South American or Asian countries—anywhere willing to let them in.

The Jews under the Protectorate

In spite of Hitler's promise in Munich to refrain from further demands on rump Czechoslovakia, in mid-March 1939 he completed the destruction of the state. After making Slovakia nominally independent and permitting Hungary to occupy Ruthenia, he invited the Czechoslovak president, Emil Hacha, to Berlin and forced him to sign a document establishing the Reich Protectorate of Bohemia and Moravia. On 16 March German troops occupied the protectorate, and Hitler went to Prague to view the new acquisition. A Czech president and government remained in office but with quite limited powers. The new ruler was the Reich protector, and Hitler hand-picked Konstantin von Neurath for the post. While the Reich protector could legislate without consulting the Czech administration, the local Czech government was at the mercy

After the annexation of Czechoslovakia by Germany, a policeman hangs a sign reading "Adolf Hitler Square" in the former Square of Liberty in Bruenn, Moravia. 23 March 1939

of the German authorities. The Jews were among the first to sense, and suffer from, these double standards. Whereas the Czechs had procrastinated in promulgating anti-Jewish laws, the Germans acted swiftly. If Germans and Czechs proclaimed contradictory or parallel legislation, German laws prevailed.

A typical example of this duplication was the so-called aryanization of Jewish property. Aryanization was expropriation without compensation, the legalized theft of Jewish assets. On 21 June 1939 Neurath issued a decree transferring Jewish property directly to German hands, thus barring Czech enrichment. Consequently the Czechs lost interest in the economic persecution of Jews. A side effect of aryanization was to evoke Czech sympathy for the harassed Jews.

The German banking and industrial establishments were set to swallow up the considerable number of major businesses held by a few Jewish families. The property was mostly given away by the Jewish owners, who managed to escape to the West with a fraction of their assets. They were able to do so because of their close relations with Western industrial leaders.

Forced Emigration and Persecution

The Nazi aim was to make the protectorate *Judenrein* (cleansed of Jews)—and eventually free of Czechs too. The Zentralstelle für Jüdische Auswanderung (Central Agency for Jewish Emigration), founded in June 1939, executed the task. It expropriated the Jewish property and transferred it to the Auswanderungsfond (Emigration Fund), the tool for processing the emigrants' property, which in turn transferred the property to the Germans. The Zentralstelle and the Auswanderungsfond, both of them SS bureaus, were originally responsible for greater Prague but later extended their activity to the entire protectorate.

The Zentralstelle forced Jews to emigrate—or rather to play a game akin to emigration. Jews were ordered to visit the office, where any property they still owned was taken from them; they were forced to pay exorbitant taxes. By the time they left, they had no possessions, but they did have permission to emigrate. Jews from the countryside were made to come to Prague and so had to take rooms in hotels, an additional burden.

Unfortunately, no country was willing to accept the Czech Jews. Boats filled with emigrants were still trying to reach Palestine illegally, and the free port of

Toppled headstones in a Jewish cemetery. July 1942

Shanghai was another destination. Attempts to reach the United States, Cuba, and South American countries had very limited success. Until the outbreak of war Poland, and to a degree Slovakia, served as a transfer station from which Jews could attempt to move further. German-authorized emigration lasted until September 1941. Officially 26,111 Jews emigrated from the protectorate.

Throughout the period of emigration, the persecution of Jews within Bohemia and Moravia spiraled. During the first weeks of the German occupation, except for the hunt for refugees, most Jews were left relatively unmolested. The entry of German troops was immediately followed by Aktion Gitter (Operation behind Bars), in the course of which Czech public figures, known leftists, and individual Jews were detained. Jews were arrested in the countryside under various pretexts. A few synagogues were set on fire, and Czech fascists attacked Jews in the streets. The Germans were still concerned about world opinion and were also afraid of violent outbursts within the country. Demonstrations by Czech students in the fall of 1939 led to the severe oppression of Gentiles and an end to the milder treatment of Jews.

Within certain segments of the population happy to be rid of Jewish competition, Nazi propaganda fell on fertile ground. On 21 June 1939 a decree issued by Reich Protector Neurath eliminated Jews from economic life and ordered them to register with the authorities. Segregation of Jews from the rest of the population advanced rapidly. Jews had to leave certain city quarters and streets; they were prohibited from visiting public places or using public transportation, communication, or services. Gentiles were forbidden to associate with Jews or to provide them with any assistance. Jewish food rations were reduced, and Jews were banned from shopping during most of the day and from buying many commodities. The authorities expelled Jewish children from schools and forbade the hiring of private teachers. Jews had to hand in all valuables, including certain clothes and foodstuffs. Jewish employees were summarily dismissed, and Jews were not entitled to collect social benefits. A special agency within the community assigned unemployed Jews to a limited number of jobs. Members of Jewish youth movements who sought work with peasants were shamelessly exploited and were threatened by the Gestapo. Jewish professionals, except for a small number serving Jews only, were forced out of their offices and clinics. Heavy taxes were imposed. On 15 September 1941 the Germans ordered Jews to wear the yellow star, which marked them as Jews when they appeared in public. Thus daily life for Jews was made extraordinarily harsh, and their existence—hungry, unemployed, and loitering in the streets—constituted a public problem.

The Final Solution

In September 1941 Hitler dismissed Neurath as Reich protector and appointed in his stead Reinhard Heydrich, a high-ranking SS officer and a chief lieutenant of Heinrich Himmler. It was Heydrich who brought the Final Solution to the protectorate. On 10 October Heydrich called a meeting of leading officials to discuss the so-called Jewish question. It was decided to concentrate Czech Jews in the city of Terezin (Theresienstadt) as an interim measure until the "final goal" was achieved.

To manipulate the Jewish institutions for Nazi purposes, on 26 July 1939 the Germans established in Prague the Zentralstelle für die Regelung der Judenfrage in Böhmen und Mähren (Central Agency for the Regulation of the Jewish Question in Bohemia and Moravia). (Within a few weeks the name was changed to the Zentralamt or Central Office.) It cooperated with the Zentralstelle für Jüdische Auswanderung as well as with the Prague Religious Congregation. This body, the Congregation Bureau, aimed to take care of local Jews, but the Nazis soon saddled it with the task of serving the entire Jewish population of the protectorate. On 27 March 1942 all Jewish congregations were subjected to the authority of the Zentralamt der Jüdischen Kultusgemeinde (Central Office of the Jewish Congregation), which on 2 February 1943 was transformed into the Ältestenrat der Juden (Council of Jewish Elders). The Jewish leadership underwent frequent alterations and was composed of non-Zionists and Zionists.

The numerous branches of the Council of Jewish Elders included a welfare department (which had to sustain thousands of destitute Jews), a labor exchange,

a statistical department, and (after 24 November 1939) the editorial board of the weekly *Jüdisches Nachrichtenblatt / Zidovske Listy* (Jewish News). The Congregation Bureau's saddest assignment was the preparation of lists of Jews to be deported to the East or to Terezin.

The first mass deportation occurred in late October 1939. On Himmler's order an "agricultural reservation" was planned in occupied eastern Poland, near the city of Nisko, close to the Soviet border. Two transports carrying a total of 1,291 Jewish men from Moravia were dispatched, but impossible living and working conditions forced the Germans to abandon the undertaking. The 469 survivors returned in April 1940.

Heydrich's first initiative was to dispatch 5,000 Jews to the Lodz ghetto in Poland between 16 October and 3 November 1941. Only 253 of them survived the war. Shortly afterward 1,000 Jews were sent to Minsk in Belorussia. All but seven perished at the hands of the Nazis.

In the meantime the concentration of the Czech Jews in Terezin began. The project, which began in November 1941, was a part of the Final Solution discussed at the Wannsee Conference on 20 January 1942. Terezin was earmarked as a showplace. Jews in Terezin were allowed to engage in some cultural and intellectual activities, and the living conditions of certain parts of the population (for example, the children) were preferable, but Terezin actually served as a transfer station before their deportation to extermination camps. Eventually, most of the inmates were shipped to Auschwitz. Jewish Mischlinge (who were considered under German law to be Jews) in the protectorate were also gathered in more than 70 locations, the largest being Ceska Lipa and Hagibor Square in Prague.

The Congregation Bureau carried out the deportations. They took place mostly at night, to prevent the Gentile population from watching. Those Jews named on the deportation lists were made to assemble in the trade fair grounds and were sent off from the nearby railway station. Initially the Jewish leadership preferred that Jews remain in Czech territory instead of being transported to an unknown destination abroad, believing that productivity through employment would make the Jews valuable in German eyes. Debates over whether they should go to Terezin ensued in the Zionist youth movements. The majority decided to go, but one small movement, Hashomer

Hatzair, did not trust the Germans and decided against this course. The first unit, composed of volunteers, moved to Terezin to prepare the grounds. Between 24 November 1941 and 20 April 1945, 75,661 Czech Jews were deported to Terezin. About 3,000 survived the war.

On 27 May 1942 two Czechoslovak parachutists succeeded in assassinating Heydrich. In the fierce reprisals that followed, Jews were among the primary victims. Many of the 13,119 persons detained were Jews; most of these were executed and the rest sent to camps. A transport of 1,000 Jews was sent on 10 July 1942 to the Majdanek extermination camp; one man survived. According to Adolf Eichmann, 500 more Jews were apprehended; half of them were shot and the rest sent to camps.

Throughout the time of the protectorate Jews, persons who had sheltered Jews, and Jewish members of the Communist and non-Communist undergrounds were arrested, interrogated, and frequently executed. Jews from Poland, Ruthenia, and Slovakia were also living in the protectorate, and when they were rounded up, they too were sent to Terezin.

Resistance

The main activities of the anti-Nazi underground included spying, terrorism, and propaganda. For Jews such work carried a double danger—as Jews and as members of the resistance. Nevertheless, Jews were among the founders of the pro-Western underground, and several Jews were leading members of the Communist resistance and publishers of its press. This resulted in Jewish casualties, whether in action, during interrogation, or by execution. The Communists provided shelter for the members of Hashomer Hatzair who refused to go to Terezin. Some of them were killed by the Germans.

Overall, the ethnic Czech population had a mixed record. Hating the Germans and their collaborators, Czechs were willing to express solidarity with Jews and occasionally assisted them. But Czechs lived under oppressive terror, which caused fear and apathy. Support for the persecuted often meant death. Bravery and civil courage were not commonly seen during this period, whereas denunciations were frequent. Gentiles were content to keep Jewish property or to loot neighboring apartments belonging to deportees. The Czech government included zealous individuals eager to cooperate with the Nazis for personal benefit

or out of a belief that they were serving the best interests of their country. Most non-Jewish spouses, however, were faithful to their partners, provided food and security, and lived unmolested by their neighbors. During the last weeks of the Reich so-called death marches of Jews evacuated from camps in the East under German guard crossed Czech territory, and there are reports of kind and supportive treatment of the prisoners by Czech civilians. After liberation, camp inmates, particularly those in Terezin, suffered from hunger, cold, and sickness and were quickly given assistance.   *Yeshayahu A. Jelinek*

Bormann, Martin (1900–1945?) Press officer in Thuringia, Nazi party delegate to the Reichstag, and chief of staff to Rudolf Hess. After his appointment as head of the Führer Chancellery in May 1941, Bormann had control over Adolf Hitler's schedule, and the confidence that Hitler placed in him gave him considerable power. Bormann signed orders to deport Jews to the East, to consolidate control of the Jews under the SS, and to conceal Nazi atrocities. He disappeared after the war, was tried in absentia and found

Martin Bormann.

guilty of war crimes, and sentenced to death in 1946. In 1973 the West German government accepted the report of a forensic expert that a skeleton unearthed the previous year in West Berlin was Bormann's and officially declared him dead.

Brack, Viktor (1904–48)   SS colonel, coordinator of the so-called euthanasia program, and key figure in the murder of the disabled, political prisoners, and Jews. Brack was convicted on war crimes charges and sentenced to death in 1947. He was hanged in 1948. See EUTHANASIA

Brand, Joel (1907–64)   Hungarian Jewish activist chosen by Adolf Eichmann for a mission to Turkey in 1944. A member of the Relief and Rescue Committee of Budapest, Brand helped smuggle Jews into Hungary until that country was invaded by the Germans in 1944. Eichmann sent him to Istanbul to transmit to the Allies the "blood for trucks" proposal, in which the Germans proposed the release of 1 million Jews in return for supplies. The British rejected the plan. Brand was im-

prisoned by the British in Cairo and debriefed for some months. Upon his release in October 1944 he went to Palestine. See KASZTNER, RUDOLF

Brest-Litovsk (Brzesc nad Bugiem)   Town in eastern Poland, home to a large Jewish community (21,400 in 1931). Brest-Litovsk passed from Polish to German to Soviet control in September 1939. On 23 June 1941 the Germans regained control of Brest-Litovsk and in November interned 30,000 Jews in the ghetto. In 1942 an underground of approximately 80 people, led by Aryeh Scheinmann, attempted resistance actions that were largely ineffective because non-Jewish armed groups disarmed and killed the Jewish fighters when they fled to the forest. On 15 October 1942 the Germans began the final liquidation of the Brest-Litovsk ghetto. All but 200 Jews were shot or deported.

British Jewry   The behavior of British Jews during the Nazi era is a matter of some controversy. Initially it was assumed that, since the British government enforced a niggardly policy toward Jewish refugees from Hitler's

Jews assembled in Brest-Litovsk (Brzesc nad Bugiem) for deportation. Circa October 1942

Germany and seemed intent on blocking relief and rescue measures during the war, British Jews could have achieved little by calling public attention to the plight of Jews in Nazi-occupied territory. During the 1980s, however, the awareness that governmental intransigence had not prevented groups of American Jews from protesting the fate of Jews in the Third Reich provoked deeper inquiry into the case of Britain.

Early accounts of British Jewish responses to news of the Final Solution dwelt on the practical impediments to constructive action: the negative influence of British civil servants and the overpowering geostrategic expedients deployed by officials to justify the minimum of initiatives. Another explanation was psychological: the gap between knowing and believing, and the debilitating effect of powerlessness. More recently, scholars have drawn attention to the way ideology and "mentalities" constricted Jewish freedom of action.

In 1933, the Jewish population of Great Britain stood at about 350,000, less than 1 percent of all inhabitants. Roughly two-thirds lived in the London area. The other large communities, none exceeding 30,000, were in Manchester, Leeds, and Glasgow. In the 1930s, British Jews were going through a period of deep and painful social transition. The small but venerable Sephardic community had lost its dominance. Leadership roles were taken over by a wealthy elite of Ashkenazi families. They presided over the highly centralized agencies representing British Jews. The Board of Deputies (BOD) was the chief representative organ, consisting mainly of delegates from synagogues. Business relating to Jews abroad was conducted by the Anglo-Jewish Association (AJA) in cooperation with the BOD through a Joint Foreign Committee (JFC). The Jewish Friendly Societies, numbering around 40,000 members, and Jewish trade unions upheld the interests of Jewish working people but had limited representation on the BOD. They, along with the Zionist movement and the British Section of the World Jewish Congress (WJC, established in 1936), provided the power base for a new generation of leaders with quite different social origins from those of the old elite.

British Jews were divided along lines of origin, generation, geography, class, and ideology. Eastern European immigrants resented the paternalism of the anglicized elite and suspected their commitment to Jewish traditions. Young, mainly working-class, British-born Jews were estranged from the culture of their immigrant parents but were hardly integrated into the Anglo-Jewish middle-class mainstream. Simultaneously, antisemitism alienated them from British society. Economic recession had badly hit the Jews residing in the first areas of settlement in British cities, such as London's East End. By contrast, Jews who had moved to the suburbs enjoyed considerable material comfort. They were also insulated from the harassment and violence spread by the British Union of Fascists in the 1930s. Working-class inner-city Jews tended to embrace left-wing movements, while middle-class suburban Jews favored Zionism. Under this banner, a new professional and entrepreneurial elite was challenging the old families for control of communal institutions.

In 1933, the BOD elected a new president, Neville Laski, who ostensibly exemplified this rising middle class. Laski was a 43-year-old barrister from a pro-Zionist Manchester family, but he shared the attitudes of the old Anglo-Jewish families. He worked harmoniously with the anti-Zionist Leonard G. Montefiore, the president of the AJA. Both subscribed to the notion that relations between the Jews, on the one hand, and the state and society, on the other, were governed by a tacit "Emancipation contract" under which Jews had been granted civic equality in 1858. It defined Jewish identity as denominational, prescribed conformity to cultural norms, and required the effacement of a particularistic ethnic identity or agenda.

News of violence against German Jews in the wake of Hitler's accession to power provoked outrage among British Jews. In London's East End a spontaneous boycott of German goods and services developed. On 23 March 1933, East Enders marched in protest to the German embassy. However, Laski and Montefiore rejected calls for an "official" boycott. They argued that a boycott would only incite the Nazis, who, they believed, would otherwise be reined in by conservatives in the German government. This stance did not placate East Enders. A protest committee was set up to orchestrate the boycott. The committee held an anti-Nazi rally in July 1933, in Hyde Park, attended by an estimated 30,000 Jews. In lieu of BOD leadership, a Jewish Representative Council was set up to run the boycott. It claimed to represent more than 350 Jewish organizations, with about 170,000 members.

The boycott movement lost momentum in 1934–35. It was weakened by the Haavara agreement (negotiated by the Zionist movement to enable German Jews emigrating to Palestine to take with them some of their capital in the form of German goods) and by opposi-

Thousands march in a procession from the East End to Hyde Park as protest against the persecution of Jews in Germany. 20 July 1933

London policemen escort protestors carrying an effigy of Hitler as a hangman. 11 April 1933

tion from the BOD. Zionists had played a salient part at its inception, but several leading figures felt obliged to resign owing to the agreement. Henry Mond, the second Lord Melchett, left after pressure from Laski and Zionist colleagues. The boycott movement was also unable to broaden its support beyond the Jewish community or to dent the government's commitment to fostering Anglo-German trade.

The BOD confined itself to organizing a public protest in London's Queen's Hall on 27 June 1933, at which the speakers were predominantly non-Jews. Leaders of the BOD believed that it was impolitic for Jews to campaign for their German co-religionists, since this smacked of supranational allegiances and disloyalty toward the British government, which had adopted a policy of appeasing Germany. Laski and Montefiore were also opposed by temperament to noisy mass demonstrations and believed, with some justice, that backstairs diplomacy was more effective. On 21 March 1933 the Foreign Office advised Laski and Montefiore that demonstrations would be counterproductive. However, Laski's requests for the Foreign Office to intervene, via the League of Nations, on behalf of German Jews were unsuccessful. Two Jews prominent in British politics, Viscount Herbert Samuel and Lord Reading, made equally ineffectual private visits to the German ambassador in London to express the concern of British Jewry and to ask for the improved treatment of Germany's Jews.

British Jews responded quickly to the plight of German Jews who were fleeing the Third Reich or were forced into exile after losing their jobs in the April 1933 purges. Otto Schiff, the head of the Jews' Temporary Shelter, which was responsible for aiding Jewish refugees, established a Jewish Refugee Committee in March 1933 (later called the German Jewish Aid Committee). Schiff was a 58-year-old merchant banker. Born in Germany, he had settled in Britain and achieved distinction in refugee work during the First World War. The chairman of the Jews' Temporary Shelter since 1922, he had a close working relationship with officials in the Home Office Aliens Department, which handled refugee and immigration matters.

In late March 1933, Schiff, Laski, and Montefiore offered the Home Office (HO) a guarantee that no refugee admitted to Britain would become a financial burden on the state. They also requested a concomitant liberalization of the country's strict immigration rules. On 7 April 1933, the Cabinet rejected any changes to the rules: permission to enter Britain would be restricted to those with capital or work permits, or to transmigrants. However, the Cabinet saw the guarantee as a useful backstop. It was also ready to use Jewish agencies to screen potential immigrants, thus relieving government officials of the burden. Jews in Britain thereby became responsible for selecting German migrants and funding them once they arrived. The guarantee, made without wider consultation, later placed British Jews in an invidious position.

In 1933, it was envisaged that only a few thousand Jews would depart from Germany. The Central British Fund for the Relief of German Jewry (CBF) launched an appeal in May 1933 to finance such limited resettlement and to assist the German Jewish community. Fundraising for resettlement was potentially divisive: British Zionists commanded the allegiance of many of the Jewish nouveaux riches, but the old non-Zionist or anti-Zionist families were still influential. So the CBF reached an agreement with the Zionist movement that pro-Palestine fundraising would be suspended in favor of a fixed allocation from the monies raised for German Jewry. The CBF money was itself distributed by an allocations committee with equal representation of Zionists and non-Zionists. The Zionists were constantly dissatisfied with these arrangements. Chaim Weizmann, who sat on the allocations committee from 1933 to 1934, refused to serve for the 1935 appeal because non-Zionists resisted the allocation of money to resettle German Jews in Palestine.

These conflicts occurred behind the scenes. In public Anglo-Jewry was united and raised millions of pounds to aid German Jews. The Jewish Refugee Committee vetted applications for admission to Britain, provided hospitality for new arrivals, supported refugees, and supplied training to facilitate their reemigration. Britain was not perceived as a place of large scale permanent settlement. By the end of 1937, only about 11,000 German Jews had made new homes there. In 1936, a few months after the Nuremberg Laws signified the end of a viable Jewish life in Germany, the CBF transmuted into the Council for German Jewry, an Anglo-American combined effort to resettle every German Jew. The council saw its task as spread over many years, but events accelerated.

After the annexation of Austria, steady emigration turned into panic flight. The pledge of March 1933 was now revealed as a hostage to fortune. British Jewish relief agencies could neither process the crowds of

Jews seeking admission to Britain nor provide them with a guarantee. Schiff warned the HO that British Jews could no longer underwrite refugees entering the country and persuaded the government to impose visa requirements on would-be migrants to prevent unvetted Jews from gaining admission and claiming maintenance. By contrast, after the Evian Conference the government modified its policy and made it slightly easier for Jewish refugee bodies to bring over young women who could find work in domestic service.

In October 1938, Schiff warned the HO that the German Jewish Aid Committee was collapsing under the administrative and financial strain and requested a temporary halt to the admission of refugees. Following Kristallnacht, however, the government actually relaxed its immigration policy and permitted the temporary admission of unaccompanied minors and young men classified as "transmigrants." Under these liberal arrangements, about 40,000 Jewish refugees entered Britain in the year before the war. The change in government policy resulted from the wave of sympathy for Jews that had been aroused by Kristallnacht. The BOD contributed with a public protest, spearheaded by non-Jews, at the Royal Albert Hall on 1 December 1938.

On 21 November 1938, the government announced that it would allow the entry of an unlimited number of unaccompanied minors, provided they could be guaranteed (at a cost of £50 each). This measure followed a deputation to the prime minister, Neville Chamberlain, by Zionists and non-Zionists acting in unison. The Refugee Children's Movement (RCM) was set up to handle this underage exodus. The RCM was swamped by applications, but too few Jewish families offered to foster the Jewish children who were brought over. Consequently, many were placed with Christian families motivated by proselytization. Some Jewish families took in and then exploited teenage girls as domestic servants. It also proved hard for the RCM to raise funds; in December 1938 it was saved from disaster only by the allocation of money from the nonsectarian Lord Baldwin Fund for refugees.

The work of the RCM was marred by intracommunal conflict. The scheme's managers played down the religious identity of the children in order to win broad support. They horrified Orthodox rabbis by their readiness to place Jewish children with non-Jews as the price of rapid evacuation. The Zionist Youth Aliyah movement raised substantial sums but only dis-

A gathering outside an office in London's East End. Spectators view a display of photographs showing Jewish persecution under the Nazis. 23 November 1938

bursed them to youths being trained for emigration to Palestine. At the end of August 1939, the RCM ran out of money and imposed a freeze on the acceptance of more children.

Although British Jews responded generously to appeals for money and volunteers, to many of them the refugees appeared burdensome. They feared that the refugees would aggravate antisemitism. Opposition to the "refuJews" by professional bodies, sections of the press, and the resurgent British Fascist movement substantiated this apprehension. Rather than assert asylum as a human right, the BOD issued apologetic leaflets justifying the presence of the refugees. The refugees themselves were given reading material advising them not to speak German in public, to avoid complaining, never to compare Britain unfavorably to Germany, to dress conservatively, and to display loyalty to their new domicile at every opportunity.

Personal prejudice affected the treatment of refu-gees. Instead of understanding the shock with which middle-class German Jews encountered certain aspects of British life, Laski told Schiff in December 1938 that "the refugees are pestilential in the matter of derogatory remarks about various things in this country." Schiff regarded Austrian Jews as "largely of the shopkeeper and small trader class," deeming them harder to assimilate into British life or to reemigrate. Similar prejudices restricted the chances that Orthodox Jews would be selected as potential entrants to Britain. Consequently, the Orthodox rabbi Solomon Schonfeld mounted a private initiative to rescue Orthodox children during 1938–39. With the backing of Chief Rabbi Hertz and his Religious Emergency Committee, Schonfeld brought over around 300 Viennese Jewish children.

British Jews made great sacrifices for the refugees and achieved much, but they were hampered by considerable, and not unjustified, insecurity about their standing in British society as well as the tyranny of received ideas and prejudices. Most British Jews were of Eastern European origin and manifested a reverse snobbery toward German Jews. This may account for the shabby treatment of some refugee domestics. Yet British Jews were not generally wealthy, and the discomfort of domestics may be attributable to the precariousness of their employers' incomes. These modest economic circumstances could also explain why British Jews, numbering about 350,000 souls, were unable to find homes for 8,000 Jewish children.

At the outbreak of hostilities, all aliens in the country were classified by Aliens Tribunals to determine their fate in the event of a national emergency. The bulk of the 78,000 foreigners were categorized as harmless refugees, but after the fall of France Winston Churchill, the new prime minister, ordered the mass internment of all aliens on the basis that they might harbor a fifth column. By early June 1940, around 27,000 refugees had been detained, of whom 5,000 were deported to Canada and Australia. Mass internment was halted only when one of the deportation ships was torpedoed, with the loss of 650 innocent Germans and Italians. Initially, British Jews passively accepted the mass internment of Jewish refugees, some of whom had previously been incarcerated in Dachau and Buchenwald. The policy was even endorsed by the opinion-forming newspaper the *Jewish Chronicle* on 17 May 1940.

Contrary to the conviction, widely held after 1945,

that little was known during the war about the fate of Europe's Jews, research has shown that British Jewry had plenty of sound information. The *Jewish Chronicle* obtained precise reports on the terrible situation of Jews in Warsaw and other Polish cities during 1939–41. The paper had greater difficulty in tracking and comprehending the operations of mobile killing units (*Einsatzgruppen*) on Soviet territory after June 1941. Although much of the information it disseminated was accurate, its coverage was fragmented, and the unreliability of the sources was signaled by the sparsity of editorial comment.

The full dimensions of the Final Solution emerged fitfully. On 19 June 1942, the *Jewish Chronicle* announced: "News is filtering through of recent ghastly massacres of Jews in Nazi Europe. Some 85,000 men, women, and children are mentioned in the reports to hand." This front-page story concerned massacres only in Lithuania. On 3 July 1942, it carried the Bund report that 700,000 Polish Jews had been exterminated. Throughout the summer of 1942, it printed reports of deportations from occupied Europe "to the East." On 2 October 1942, the paper published a version of Gerhart Riegner's telegram to Rabbi Stephen Wise describing the Nazi extermination plans—albeit on page 6. On 27 November 1942, it led with the story that 250,000 Polish Jews had died in the previous six months at Sobibor, Treblinka, and Belzec. Following the confirmation that a Europe-wide campaign of genocide was under way, the 11 December 1942 issue of the *Jewish Chronicle* was dressed with a black border signifying mourning. Throughout 1943, the volume and quality of information remained high, including detailed reports of the Warsaw ghetto uprising. The deportation of Jews on Hungarian soil, from March to July 1944, was fully covered.

Despite these appalling reports, until October 1942 there were no official public expressions of concern by the leadership of British Jewry and no spontaneous protests. Circumstances appeared unpropitious for British Jews to focus on the suffering of their coreligionists, and they feared that to do so risked incurring a backlash. During the "blitz" in 1940–41, British civilians were subjected to terrible aerial bombardment by the Luftwaffe. Britain was fighting for survival and enduring catastrophic defeats. Insofar as Nazi massacres were considered, it was believed that supporting the war effort was the best reply.

The BOD associated itself with the St. James's Palace Declaration of Allied Governments-in-Exile on war crimes on 12 January 1942. Otherwise, it restricted itself to vain requests that legal immigration to Palestine be enlarged, and to protests at the fate of ships that came to grief while carrying illegal immigrants. The revelations during mid-1942 finally led the BOD to organize a protest rally in the Albert Hall on 29 October 1942. Sidney Silverman, a Labour MP and WJC activist who on 10 August 1942 had received a copy of the Riegner telegram, spearheaded a WJC deputation to the Foreign Office to seek a government response. On 3 December 1942, the JFC held an emergency meeting to discuss the crisis. The chief rabbi announced a day of fasting, on 13 December 1942, which would inaugurate a week of mourning. On 17 December 1942, the women's Zionist movement held a mass meeting in the Wigmore Hall, London. The BOD held a major public meeting on 20 December 1942, addressed by three members of Parliament, and the WJC convened a similar gathering at the House of Commons. A delegation that represented the spectrum of British Jewry saw the foreign secretary, Anthony Eden, on 22 December 1942. Ten days later, Selig Brodetsky, the BOD president, met Foreign Office officials to seek concessions regarding refugee immigration.

Suggestions at the JFC meeting for a mass rally in Trafalger Square or street marches were deemed discordant with the popular mood. But even among London's Jews, the day of fasting was honored more in the breach. Most British Jews seemed to have kept an emotional distance from the reality of the events in Europe.

The limited protests did have some effect. The BBC broadcast warnings to occupied Europe and allotted air time to Jewish speakers. In addition to the Allied statement on war crimes on 17 December 1942, the British government felt compelled by public opinion to make a helpful gesture. After consulting with the Roosevelt administration in the United States, it announced a conference on the "refugee problem" to be held at Bermuda on 19 April 1943. The conference served to parry and wear down continuing pleas for rescue action. Brodetsky again visited the Foreign Office, on 29 January 1943. The marchioness of Reading wrote personally to Churchill on 16 January 1943, while Lord Samuel used a debate in the House of Lords on 23 March 1943 to condemn the lack of positive initiatives.

British Jews were deeply disillusioned by the out-

Young Jews and sympathizers march in protest through the West End of London. 13 November 1938.

come of the Bermuda meeting. For the next year, however, concern about Europe's Jews faded. Energies became focused on the struggle for power between Zionists and anti-Zionists at the BOD, conflicts over how best to obtain a distinctive military contribution by Jews to the war effort, and anxiety about the high level of domestic antisemitism.

The German occupation of Hungary provoked a second phase of sustained protest. On 21 March 1944, the BOD convened an emergency conference and dispatched a deputation to the Foreign Office demanding that the BBC broadcast threats of retaliation, suggesting negotiations with Josef Stalin and Josip Tito to provide assistance for Hungarian Jews, and exploring the transfer of funds to buy Jewish lives. In April 1944, Chaim Weizmann wrote directly to Churchill and on

18 June broke precedent by addressing a plenary session of the BOD, where he excoriated the performance of British Jews. He also participated in a deputation to Eden on 30 June 1944, at which proposals were put forward for bombing Auschwitz-Birkenau or the railway lines leading to the camp. The government rejected almost all proposals for intervention. The WJC and BOD continued to make representations after the deportations had ended, and tried to persuade the Foreign Office to involve the Russians in rescue work when the Arrow Cross takeover in Budapest boded disaster for the surviving Hungarian Jews.

In the last weeks of the war, British Jews were involved in various rescue schemes and sent relief workers, somewhat tardily, to Bergen-Belsen concentration camp. Their efforts might have succeeded earlier if the

British had not opposed the dispatch of a specifically Jewish aid team to work with just the Jewish survivors. Official opposition to "particularistic" demands persisted into peacetime, even after the full truth of the German assault on the Jews was revealed.

The response of British Jewry to the fate of Europe's Jews was at best erratic. Most British Jews passively accepted the official line that only victory would save the Jews of Europe. Throughout 1941, early 1942, and most of 1943, there was official and popular silence. Yet great efforts were made in the winter of 1942–43 and in mid-1944 to achieve immediate rescue measures. This episodic and limited reaction can be explained, first, in terms of Anglo-Jewish ideology. British Jews felt barred from acting as an ethnic lobby, least of all at a time of national emergency. They placed their faith in liberalism to deliver the Jews in the long run and failed to see that optimistic notions of progress had no relevance to actual events. Mainstream Zionists were no less prey to illusions, believing that positioning for the postwar era was an appropriate response. In the face of official policy and geostrategic realities, the campaign for immigration to Palestine, like the demand for a Jewish fighting force, was no more than therapy. But both approaches further divided and weakened British Jewry.

There were exceptions. Intellectuals like the Jewish historian Cecil Roth and the socialist thinker Harold Laski perceived the scale of the disaster before most other Jews did. Over December 1942, the left-wing publisher Victor Gollancz wrote a burning pamphlet, "Let My People Go," containing ideas for rescue measures. It sold 150,000 copies in a few weeks. Sidney Silverman, a member of Parliament, was a tireless campaigner on behalf of the WJC. Solomon Schonfeld, the Orthodox maverick, organized an Early Day Motion that attracted the signatures of more than 270 MPs in the first months of 1943, despite opposition from BOD leaders who objected to the omission of increased immigration to Palestine from the list of rescue options it set out. Zionist Revisionists also took a more vociferous approach to rescue work and were more critical of the government. These exceptions indicate the crippling effect of mainstream Anglo-Jewish political culture.

Secondly, the poverty of the response can be attributed to the unsympathetic British context. The government refused to accept the plight of the Jews as unique and therefore as requiring a targeted response.

It subordinated rescue to ultimate victory, a strategy that made sense and played on British Jewish convictions about the exigencies of their hard-won and, they believed, tenuously held citizenship. Everyone was making sacrifices for the war effort. Apart from seeming selfish, British Jews feared that to "privilege" Jewish suffering would have violated the liberal universalist outlook of government and society. It was part of Anglo-Jewish ideology to understand antisemitism as in some way the fault of the Jews, which was certainly how government officials treated it. They warned that even minor concessions on the refugee issue would arouse antagonism. British Jews thus had scant room for political maneuver. As they were disempowered and demoralized, psychic survival precluded constant attention to the doom of European Jewry. Energies were poured into futile and divisive secondary causes, which decades later left a damning impression of disorganization, waste, and pettiness.

David Cesarani

British Policy   From the outbreak of war in September 1939, news of German atrocities in Europe was transmitted to Britain by underground and resistance movements (especially the Polish resistance) and by journalists (especially American) who remained in Europe. Ostensibly, the reaction of the British government was swift. In late October the government issued a white paper on German atrocities in Europe—but only after having been goaded into doing so by German accusations about British concentration camps during the Boer War. However, the white paper referred only to the prewar period. The pamphlet sold well but was judged to be a propaganda failure.

Thereafter the government decided to avoid "atrocity propaganda" as far as possible. On 25 July 1941 the Ministry of Information's planning committee reached the conclusion that it should use only a limited amount of "horror" in home propaganda, and only in reference to "indisputably innocent people"—not "violent political opponents," and not Jews. The government feared that any specific reference to the persecution of Jews might backfire, since the public might believe that people thus singled out were probably a "bad lot" anyway. Finally, the Jews were considered to be "not entirely reliable witnesses" concerning the incidents reported.

A major source of information regarding events in Europe were reports obtained by the British intelligence services. Messages in the German administrative code Enigma (broken and deciphered by the British in December 1940) provided details of atrocities being committed in Russia by the German Ordnungspolizei (Order Police) and the SS beginning in June 1941, when Germany invaded the Soviet Union. From 1942 onward, the heavy traffic of Jews being transported to the concentration and extermination camps was monitored by British intelligence.

The British press, too, had access to information about Nazi policies in occupied Europe and kept the public well informed. In June 1942 the first prominent article on the massacre of Jews appeared in a major British newspaper, when the London *Daily Telegraph* published a report by the Jewish Labor Bund of Warsaw on mass shootings in the ghettos, the liquidation of ghettos, and execution by gassing at Chelmno. The article stated that 700,000 Polish Jews had already been killed and that the Nazis planned to eliminate all the Jews of Europe. This report and others from Poland received wide press coverage in Britain during the summer of 1942, but they had a limited impact on public opinion. They created the impression that widespread atrocities, rather than planned exterminations, were being committed, but against Polish Jews only.

News of the Holocaust peaked in Britain during the winter of 1942–43. Although considerable detail was available afterward, neither the government nor the media gave it much publicity. During the spring and summer of 1944 the open deportation and extermination of Hungarian Jewry elicited little public interest in Britain. Some even claimed that the public had become bored by atrocity stories.

Anti-Alienism and Antisemitism in England

Another explanation of British apathy toward the fate of the European Jews concerns anti-alien and antisemitic trends in Britain. The conflict with Nazi Germany strengthened English nativism and fostered an emphasis on exclusive nationalism, which regarded Englishness and Jewishness as incompatible. Government circles feared that Jewish immigrants, especially those from Eastern Europe, would cause an upsurge of antisemitism in Britain. In 1939 Britain effectively closed its doors to Jewish refugees by canceling all visas previously granted to enemy nationals. It was assumed that any refugee who left German-controlled Europe had German permission and was therefore automatically suspect. During 1940 the Germans did in fact help to organize the movement of Jews out of Europe, mainly to Palestine. The British assumed that, apart from ideological and financial motives, the Germans must be exploiting this traffic in order to infiltrate their agents into the Middle East. However, no Jewish enemy agents were ever uncovered.

During the summer of 1940, following the collapse of France and owing to fears of a German invasion, a panic over a possible fifth column swept Britain. Consequently, nearly one-third of the refugees from Nazism were interned in special camps. The government later issued a hollow justification for its actions, stating that during the months when Europe was collapsing under Nazi attack, the refugees had needed protection from the native population.

The internment policy was implemented by a Cabinet committee headed by Lord Swinton, whose activities were not subject to public scrutiny. Furthermore, several committee members were deeply hostile to refugees. Other influential but publicly unaccountable bodies, such as MI5 (British intelligence) and the cabinet's Joint Intelligence Committee, who also distrusted Jewish exiles, played key roles in the decision to incarcerate aliens. Many aliens were deported to British colonies. On the voyages the deportees were subjected to abuse and robbery by British troops; the captain of one ship, the *Dunera*, described the Jews as "subversive, liars, demanding, and arrogant"; hundreds were drowned when another ship was torpedoed. After 1940, however, anti-alienism based on security concerns waned as fear of a German invasion declined. And with the resumption of full employment in Britain, even economic opposition to aliens began to evaporate.

Government Policy on the Rescue of Jews

In addition to its policy toward aliens, the British government also had to address the issue of the rescue of Jews from Nazi-occupied Europe. Winston Churchill, who became prime minister in May 1940, delegated responsibility for creating a rescue policy to the Foreign Office. Early on in the war, the Foreign Office established three policy principles regarding the Jews trapped in Nazi-occupied Europe: (1) no aid to the Jews that might involve breaking the economic blockade that Britain had imposed upon the Continent; (2) no negotiations with the Germans on anything that might be represented as leading to a separate peace or to peace on terms other than the unconditional surrender of Germany; (3) no large-scale movement of Jews out of Europe—either to Palestine or to Britain and its colonies. By 1943, it was also being claimed that the main escape routes passed through areas where Allied military interests were vital and must therefore take precedence.

Thus the Foreign Office determined not to single out the Jews of Europe for any special rescue measures—even though they had been singled out by Hitler in Europe and had been singled out in 1940 by the British government as potential enemies of the state. The argument that the government put forward was that the greatest relief to Europe's Jews would come from total victory over Hitler's Germany, which had to be the first priority. The Jews were to be treated like all other nationals of Nazi-occupied Europe. As one Foreign Office official put it, "We cannot give any assurance that we propose to collaborate in the German policy of a *Judenrein* Europe."

The Foreign Office conceded that the Jews had suffered enormously from Hitler's policy of genocide. It insisted, however, that to single out the Jews from among the many ethnic and religious groups that suffered under the Nazis would be to play into the hands of the antisemites. In July 1943 the chairman of the Cabinet's Joint Intelligence Committee, Victor Cavendish-Bentinck, alleged that "the Poles, and to a far greater extent the Jews, tended to exaggerate German atrocities, 'in order to stoke us up.'"

The Holocaust and Palestine

The British government also feared that if rescue efforts were successful, they would lead to an overwhelming influx of Jews either at home or in Palestine. With regard to Palestine, the government determined that there must be no retreat from the 1939 white paper, which had limited all further immigration into that region to 75,000 until March 1944. After that date Jewish immigration would be contingent upon Arab consent.

In February 1944 Charles Baxter, head of the Eastern Department at the Foreign Office, insisted that "the outstanding balance of 27,500 places for Jewish immigrants must if possible be made to last for the whole of the remaining period of the war against Germany." In fact, the immigration quota was not exhausted until December 1945. Another department official warned that Britain must not allow an "avalanche" or even a "trickle" of Jews ("complete rabble")

into Palestine, for they might upset relations with the Arabs. Consequently, for reasons of ideology, pragmatism, and realpolitik, the government assumed that there was no possibility of large-scale rescue of Jews from Europe, and it warned against unreal expectations.

The December 1942 Declaration

In August 1942 the first authenticated news of the Final Solution was transmitted to the West by Gerhart Riegner, the director of the office of the World Jewish Congress in Geneva. During the fall and winter of 1942 pressure grew for an allied declaration condemning Hitler's plan, calling for an end to the mass murders, warning of punishment for the perpetrators, and promising refuge for those who could escape. The British government was reluctant to make the declaration and relented only under pressure from the Polish government-in-exile; the Poles believed that the Jews' suffering would arouse more concern in the West than did that of the Poles. By the time the declaration was finally issued, on 17 December 1942, most of the Jews of Poland had been killed. The mass deportation of the Jews of Western Europe had been under way for almost six months.

With the declaration, for the first and only time in the war the special fate of the Jews under the Nazis was highlighted. Foreign Secretary Anthony Eden, who on behalf of the government issued the declaration in the House of Commons, deplored the Germans' "bestial policy of cold-blooded extermination" toward the Jews of Europe and affirmed the "solemn resolution" of the United Nations to exact retribution against all those involved. On 31 December 1942, following the unexpectedly widespread public response to the declaration, the Foreign Office set up a secret Cabinet Committee on the Reception and Accommodation of Jewish Refugees. But the initial euphoria in some Jewish circles was soon transformed into bitter disillusionment and accusations of betrayal.

The British government's immigration policy was first tested seriously in February 1943, when the Romanian government offered to transfer 70,000 Jews to any refuge selected by the Allies, indicating that Palestine appeared to be the most convenient location. The Foreign Office rejected the offer outright, on the grounds that it flouted two central principles of British war policy—no deals with the enemy and no diversion of military resources for "Jewish causes." There were some pangs of conscience at the Foreign

Office. One official remonstrated: "How can we say that we have every sympathy and willingness to play our part when we refuse to take any positive steps of our own to help these wretched creatures? Why should anyone else do anything if we refuse?" The consensus, however, was that the Romanian offer was "clearly a piece of blackmail which, if successful, would open up an endless process on the part of Germany and her satellites in southeastern Europe of unloading, at a given price, all their unwanted nationals on overseas countries." On 27 February 1943, in a telegram to the British embassy in Washington, the Foreign Office forwarded its conclusions on the project: "The blunt truth is that the whole complex of human problems raised by the present German domination of Europe . . . can only be dealt with completely by an Allied victory, and any step calculated to prejudice this is not in the interest of the Jews in Europe."

In April 1943 the remnants of the Jewish ghetto in Warsaw revolted against the Nazis, who had mounted a callous military operation to liquidate the ghetto. The Jews' pleas for arms and supplies from the Polish underground and the Allies went largely unheeded. It became apparent to the survivors of the Warsaw ghetto uprising that the encouragement held out by British government broadcasts following the December declaration was as ethereal as the radio waves over which they had been transmitted. On 12 May Samuel Zygielbojm, a Jewish Bundist deputy to the Polish National Council in London, who in December 1942 had appealed to Churchill for aid, committed suicide in protest against Allied inaction and hypocrisy.

The National Committee for Rescue from Nazi Terror

In March 1943, in the wake of the general disillusionment with the British government, a group headed by Eleanor Rathbone, a non-Jewish member of Parliament, formed the National Committee for Rescue from Nazi Terror. The group denounced the lack of change in government policy since the December declaration and urged public demonstrations against the British position. Rathbone became something of a bête noire for Foreign Office officials, who were aggravated by her "misguided, even if well-meaning illusions" about the Jewish predicament in Europe. The Foreign Office referred to her as an "impatient idealist" who was trying to monopolize the time of ministers who, in her view, were "too busy or too indifferent" to deal with practical problems.

On 19 May, following the universal disappointment on both sides of the Atlantic that greeted the results of the Bermuda Conference, the government felt obliged to hold a debate on its refugee policy. It even mobilized some of its supporters to speak, so as to prevent its critics from monopolizing the debate and to ensure "a more balanced point of view." Even so, only four speakers supported government policy.

But the National Committee's momentum was soon lost, and by summer it had relapsed into a sense of "fatalism and despair," in part because of the government's delaying tactics and its constant warnings of the dangers of stimulating antisemitism at home. In addition, the committee suffered from a lack of funds and from the death and illness of some of its leaders. The public debate in Britain now focused on averting racial friction at home owing to the influx of Jewish refugees and shifted away from rescue efforts abroad. As the war turned in favor of the Allies, government officials gave their attention to securing the departure of refugees from Britain after the war, in effect abandoning wartime efforts to save the European Jews.

The Crisis in Hungary

In 1944 the British government policy was tested repeatedly and severely, following the Nazi occupation of Hungary and the start of the mass deportation of Hungarian Jews to Auschwitz. On 19 May Joel Brand, a member of the Hungarian Zionist Relief and Rescue Committee, brought British authorities in the Middle East a proposal from Adolf Eichmann, the SS officer in charge of implementing the Final Solution. Eichmann offered to release all of the surviving Hungarian Jews, and possibly some Jews from neighboring countries, in return for 10,000 trucks (to be used only on the Eastern front) and provisions (soap, coffee, tea, and cocoa). The offer, which originated apparently with the head of the SS, Heinrich Himmler, was regarded by the Allies as a desperate attempt by the Germans, on the eve of defeat, to seek a separate peace with England, France, and the United States, thereby splitting them from the Soviets. (Indeed the Soviets, fearing that the Atlantic allies might make a separate peace, would on 11 June make clear their opposition to the German offer.) It was also considered to be a dangerous precedent that would lead to the extortion of money in exchange for the lives of European victims of the Nazis. The British in particular feared that large numbers of the rescued Jews would want to migrate to

Palestine and thereby would undermine the British position in the Middle East.

On 31 May 1944 the Cabinet Committee on Refugees decided against any dealings with the Nazis or any bargaining for refugees' lives in exchange for matériel. However, the British had to be circumspect, lest the proposal find favor in certain circles in Washington. At the end of June, Foreign Secretary Eden told the committee that the proposal was "worded in such a mixture of terrorist threats and blackmail" that the government would be justified in rejecting it out of hand.

But the committee still did not reject the Brand scheme immediately, possibly at the urging of Prime Minister Churchill, who had just been supplied with further information by the Jewish Agency for Palestine on the operation of the gas chambers in the Nazi death camps. Also, the Foreign Office feared that in an election year the Roosevelt administration would be anxious to show that it had neglected no steps that might save Jews. So at the beginning of July Eden telegraphed Washington to inquire whether the Americans were prepared to negotiate directly. And indeed on 9 July the Americans did propose allowing Brand to return to Budapest to tell the Germans that the Allies would convey their response through a Protecting Power.

But the Brand mission suffered a fatal blow when British intelligence reported that Brand's companion, Bundy Grosz, was a double agent who also worked for the SS. Finally, Churchill himself was adamantly opposed to negotiations of any kind with the Germans on the release of Hungarian Jews. On 11 July he dismissed Eichmann's proposal as "nondescript" and unworthy of serious consideration. Churchill's views were endorsed by the Cabinet committee two days later. The British press was unanimous in its support of the government's contemptuous rejection of the ransom offer.

The Horthy Offer

On 18 July 1944 the Foreign Office learned that Adm. Miklós Horthy, the Hungarian regent, had on 7 July ordered a halt to the deportations of Hungarian Jews. The largest Jewish community in Hungary, that of Budapest, was still largely intact. The Hungarian government informed Swiss diplomats in Budapest that all Hungarian Jews in possession of entry visas for other countries, including Palestine, would be allowed to leave Hungary. It was also reported that the Germans would grant transit visas for such emigrants to cross territories occupied by their forces.

Although this new plan for the rescue of Jews did not include ransom demands, the British government feared that the Germans were behind Horthy's offer and hoped to flood Palestine with Jewish refugees. At a meeting of the British Cabinet in early August, the colonial secretary warned that any "sudden influx" of Jews into Palestine would precipitate "a most critical situation" in the Middle East. The high commissioner in Palestine warned that he had room for a maximum of 4,000 immigrants from Hungary.

Under American pressure, on 16 August the British joined the Americans in a statement accepting the Horthy offer and promising that "temporary havens of refuge" would be found for Jews leaving Hungary. In private, however, the British government received American assurances that the flow of refugees into British-controlled territories would be "limited."

Ultimately, no Hungarian Jews ever benefited from Horthy's offer or from the Allied declaration. The German government vetoed the emigration of any Hungarian Jews. At Eichmann's initiative the Germans did agree "in principle" to the emigration of some 7,400 Hungarian Jews, but this gesture was predicated on the conditions that no Jews be allowed to go to Palestine—for fear of impairing German relations with the Muslim world—and that shipments of the remainder of Hungarian Jewry to Auschwitz be resumed. In mid-October the Horthy regime was overthrown and a pro-German puppet regime established. Eichmann returned to Budapest and resumed his activities against the remaining Jews in the city.

The Proposal to Bomb Auschwitz

In July 1944 Jewish Agency representatives asked the British government to bomb the extermination camp at Auschwitz and the railway lines leading to it. By this time, the grim facts about the killings at Auschwitz were public knowledge: on 8 July *The Times* of London had published data received from Polish intelligence concerning the number of persons killed at the camp. On 15 May agents had counted 62 railway cars entering Auschwitz, each filled with children under eight years of age.

Foreign Secretary Eden brought the Jewish Agency's plea to the attention of Prime Minister Churchill. Calling the Final Solution "the greatest and most horrible single crime ever committed in the whole history of the world," Churchill instructed Eden to "get what he could out of the RAF [Royal Air Force]." It has been claimed that Churchill alone among the high British officials seems to have comprehended the unique historical significance of the Holocaust. No evidence has yet been presented, however, to indicate that Churchill made any further effort to promote the plan to bomb Auschwitz or to prevent government bureaucrats from sabotaging it. Moreover, in a speech before the House of Commons on 1 August 1946, Churchill even claimed that until the liberation of the death camps in 1945, he had had no idea that millions of Jews had been massacred.

The British Foreign Office and Air Ministry continued to debate the bombing project until early in September 1944, when they finally rejected it, alleging insuperable technical and logistical obstacles. But it has since been established that, contrary to what the Jews were told at the time, Allied air forces did possess the logistical and technical capacity to bomb at least some of the death camps. The Allies did in fact bomb the I. G. Farben petrochemical plants in the Auschwitz industrial zone, just a few kilometers from the camp. Indeed, quite by accident a few bombs fell on the camp itself. Further, in August 1944 fleets of RAF aircraft, flying the largely futile mission of dropping supplies to the abortive rising against the Germans by the Polish Home Army in Warsaw, flew almost directly over the Auschwitz death camp on the much longer route from their bases in northern Italy.

It has also been claimed that the British decision was political rather than military, resulting from Admiral Horthy's order to stop the deportation of Hungarian Jews to Auschwitz. Yet even if Horthy's decision were taken to mean the salvation of the remainder of the Hungarian Jewish community, the Auschwitz death machine continued to kill Jews from other European countries—up to 60,000 a day—until the liberation of the camp by the Red Army in January 1945. Moreover, when the Foreign Office asked the Jewish Agency whether, after Horthy's order, they still wanted Auschwitz to be bombed, the reply was an emphatic yes. Ivor Linton, the agency's representative in London, added that, given the Germans' dwindling war capacity, there was now greater hope that if the Auschwitz installations were destroyed, the Germans would find it difficult to reconstruct them.

Over the past 20 years the historical debate over the Allies' failure to respond adequately to the Holocaust

has fluctuated between two extremes. On one side are those like David Wyman (*The Abandonment of the Jews,* 1984) who are certain that meaningful rescue efforts and military operations should and could have been mounted; on the other are those like William D. Rubinstein (*The Myth of Rescue,* 1997) who make the claim that no Jew who perished during the Nazi Holocaust could have been saved by any action which the Allies could have taken at the time. Wyman's "estimates" of how many Jews could have been saved are as impossible to substantiate as Rubinstein's claim is untenable.

Much of Rubinstein's case against the bombing of Auschwitz rests on articles by U.S. military historians such as James H. Kitchens III (*The Journal of Military History,* 1994) and Richard Foregger (*Holocaust and Genocide Studies,* 1990), whose major conclusion is that Allied air forces did not possess the technology for pinpoint bombing, and that many inmates of the camp would have therefore perished. But we do know now, from the testimony of survivors, that the inmates of Auschwitz, seeing Allied planes flying overhead, yearned for them to bomb their own hell on earth, if only to show that they had not been forgotten by those making war on Hitler. It is also argued that only the Americans had the aircraft to carry out daytime raids; but by August 1944, when the Jewish Agency's request to bomb Auschwitz was still under discussion, Allied air forces had secured complete control of European skies.

But all the "technical" arguments miss the central point—that during World War II the Holocaust never achieved a high-enough priority among the Allied decision-making elites to warrant action. In August 1944, in a vain effort to ensure that Poland remained in the Western camp after the war, Churchill sent hundreds of British planes on a far longer journey, from Italy to Warsaw, to drop supplies to the futile rising of the Polish Home Army in that city. Not only was the Auschwitz project still being shunted like an orphan between the British Foreign Office and Air Ministry at that very time, but the RAF aircraft virtually overflew Auschwitz on their way to their destination.

The British government refused to consider the Jews' sufferings sui generis, for to have done so might have strengthened the Zionists' claim that they were a nation deserving of their own state. The British (and the Americans) insisted that the Jews wait their turn, along with all the other peoples suffering under Nazi

Main gate of Buchenwald concentration camp.

occupation, and that the best way to help them all would be to win the war as rapidly as possible. Nothing should be done to divert military resources from this single, supreme goal—though this policy did not hold when it came to the Polish Home Army or, indeed, when the Allies mounted several missions to rescue their own prisoners of war.

The Allies did not reject the project to bomb Auschwitz because their air forces did not have the technical capability of doing so but because they had other, higher priorities, not all of which contributed to the quicker ending of the war. The lives of Allied pilots *were* placed at risk on missions not strictly connected with the aim of defeating Hitler. But none was placed in harm's way for the sake of stopping the heinous work of Hitler's death camps.

No one can now ascertain how effective such bombing raids would have been in saving Jews from the gas chambers. Neither can it be determined how many more Jewish refugees might have escaped Nazi-occupied Europe had the British been less concerned about provoking antisemitism at home or the hostility of the Arab world if they allowed more Jews into Palestine. Of course, there were intimidating technical and logistical problems. But there was also a critical lack of political will and, at times, sheer prejudice and antisemitic sentiment in the hearts and minds of those officials and ministers who drafted and took the decisions. *Michael Cohen*

Brunner, Alois (1912–92?) SS official who worked for Adolf Eichmann in Austria, Germany, Greece, and France. Brunner organized the deportation of Jews in the cities of Vienna, Salonika, and Nice and the regions of Thrace, Macedonia, and Slovakia. After the war he fled to Syria and went into hiding. In 1954 a Paris court tried Brunner in absentia and sentenced him to death. He eventually was granted asylum by Syria.

Brussels Capital of Belgium, with a Jewish population of approximately 33,000 in 1940. See BELGIUM

Bucharest Capital of Romania, with a Jewish population of approximately 100,000 in 1940. See ROMANIA

Buchenwald Concentration camp near Weimar, established in 1937, where over the years approximately 239,000 Germans and foreigners, including many political prisoners, were interned. Although the Germans installed no extermination facilities at Buchenwald, disease, malnutrition, exhaustion, ill-treatment,

View of the now liberated camp at Buchenwald. 1945

and physical abuse killed approximately 43,000 inmates. Karl Otto Koch and his sadistic wife, Ilse, ran the camp between 1937 and 1941. Inmates were used in pseudo-scientific experiments in which they were injected with infectious diseases or equally deadly vaccines. Resistance cells began operating in 1938, aided by the political prisoners who handled most of the camp administration. On 11 April, after most of the SS personnel had fled, the prisoners seized control of Buchenwald from the remaining guards.

Budapest Capital of Hungary, with a Jewish community of about 200,000 in 1940. See HUNGARY

Bukovina (Bukowina) Territory comprising part of the northeastern Carpathian mountains and their plain that had a Jewish population of approximately 184,000 in 1941. Bukovina was ruled by Austria-Hungary prior to 1918, by Romania between the two world wars, and by the Soviet Union from 1939 to 1941. Romania controlled the territory between 1941 and 1944. It was divided between the Soviet Union and Romania after World War II. Most Jews in Bukovina were deported during the war and perished in Nazi concentration and extermination camps. See ROMANIA

Bulgaria The survival of Bulgarian Jewry—despite Bulgaria's pro-Nazi regime and the physical presence of German troops on Bulgarian soil—represents a unique chapter in European Jewish history during the World War II era. At the start of the war Bulgaria's

Jewish population numbered approximately 48,000, with some 60 percent residing in the capital, Sofia. Mainly Sefardim, the Jews constituted less than 1 percent of the total population. Generally speaking, the attitude of Bulgarians toward Jews was tolerant, even friendly, and Jews enjoyed equal rights anchored in the constitution promulgated with the state's founding in 1878. Against this background the Jews of Bulgaria achieved economic, social, and cultural integration in the life of the state over several decades. Concurrently, Bulgarian Jewry was recognized as an autonomous national entity with its own independent communal administration.

The majority of Bulgarian Jews were employed as small businessmen, artisans, clerks, and laborers. Although Jewish representation in the free professions was on the rise, it did not account for more than 5 percent of the total number of wage earners. The Jewish moneyed class was limited to a handful of industrialists, bankers, and exporters who made a significant contribution to the development of Bulgarian industry and commerce.

The Zionist movement comprised the prime public force, and its representatives controlled communal organizations on both the local and the national level. It democratized the conduct of communal affairs, laid the foundation for Hebrew education, promoted Zionist youth groups, encouraged aliyah (emigration to Palestine), and fortified the link with the Jews in Palestine and the Diaspora.

In short, Bulgaria's Jewish community possessed many outstanding characteristics: an extensive system of Hebrew education; communal autonomy; close economic, cultural, and social ties to Bulgarian society; and an active communal life of a secular Zionist nature, which was clearly reflected in the Jewish press.

Internal political developments, the growing power of fascist organizations, and the prevailing pro-Nazi trends within Bulgarian governmental policy shattered this peaceful existence. One of the government's

Under the direction of Romanian soldiers, Jews are deported from Bessarabia and Bukovina to Transnistria. Two German soldiers are visible to the left. July 1941–June 1942

first anti-Jewish measures, enacted in September 1939, was the swift expulsion of 4,000 Jews who were foreign nationals. Barred from entering neighboring countries, those expelled were forced to seek refuge elsewhere. The majority sailed to Palestine as illegal immigrants, reaching its shores in barely seaworthy vessels.

The penetration of race theory and Nazi ideology created fertile ground for anti-Jewish legislation and for a campaign aimed at delegitimating Jews in Bulgarian eyes. Anti-Jewish legislation was ratified by parliament at the initiative of the Bulgarian cabinet and King Boris III even before Bulgaria's enlistment in the Axis Powers on 1 March 1941.

This legislation, the Law for the Protection of the Nation, which went into effect on 23 January 1941, stripped the Jews of their basic individual and communal rights. Jews, Jewish homes, and Jewish businesses had to be marked with the Star of David, which made them a visible target. The Commissariat for Jewish Questions (Komisarstvo za Evreiskite Vuprosi), which was responsible for overseeing all Jewish affairs and for implementing the Bulgarian government's anti-Jewish policy, was established in 1942. Its head, Aleksander Belev, maintained direct contact with the German regime via the SD (security police). Jews were issued special identity cards and required to change any "non-Jewish-sounding" names. Furthermore, they were stripped of the right to belong to unions, to hold public office, and to attend institutions of higher learning.

Jews were barred from private employment as well as from serving in any public, municipal, or governmental capacity. All Jewish organizations, schools, theaters, cinemas, publishing houses, restaurants, and hotels had to be disbanded. Shopping was restricted to special stores. Intermarriage with non-Jews was outlawed, as was Jewish employment of Bulgarian workers. The Jews were confined to their residential areas and could not move without police permission. They were also required to declare their property, and their financial holdings were placed in sealed accounts. Released from army service, all Jewish males between the ages of 20 and 40 were sent to forced labor camps, where they paved roads and built bridges under harsh conditions and heavy guard, and without pay. These labor conscripts were released every winter and drafted again each spring.

Jews were denied access to a long list of professions, and a *numerus clausus* (quota) was instituted, limiting Jewish participation in all areas of the economy to their proportional representation in the general population. All others had to liquidate their businesses. As Jews were concentrated in certain sectors of the economy, this decree deprived thousands of breadwinners of their jobs without providing alternative means of gainful employment.

The Law for the Protection of the Nation divested the Jews of their property, livelihood, civil rights, and personal security. It also damaged their standing in the eyes of the Bulgarian population: Jews were characterized as enemies of the state and its national values, as manipulators bent on destroying its economy. The law was an attempt to undermine the foundations of the Bulgarian Jewish presence among a people to whom these Jews had demonstrated their loyalty during peacetime and wartime alike. Several factors contributed to the enactment of this anti-Jewish law: the Bulgarian leadership's antisemitic views, political advantage to be gained from a preferential relationship with Nazi Germany, and economic profit from divesting the Jews of their property and jobs.

The government's anti-Jewish policy and measures triggered manifestations of sympathy for the Jewish plight and protests against the antisemitic propaganda that cast aspersion on Jewish loyalty to the state. A variety of organizations, institutions, and individuals registered their opposition. The antifascist underground distributed leaflets denouncing the government's anti-Jewish policy, and its radio station exhorted the nation to oppose the discriminatory legislation and to support the Jews. Associations of workers, clerks, and artisans addressed telegrams of protest to parliament. Important professional associations, including the bar and the medical societies, issued strongly worded protests against the anti-Jewish legislation. Statesmen and public figures, like Khristo Punev and Dimo Kazasov, published pointed letters opposing the government's antisemitic campaign. Parliamentarians, in particular Petko Stainov and Nikola Mushanov, courageously struggled to block the passage of anti-Jewish legislation. The metropolitans of the Bulgarian Orthodox church openly condemned the anti-Jewish legislation. Retired generals spoke out against the aspersions cast on Jews who had fought under their command, calling attention to the several hundred Bulgarian Jewish soldiers and officers who had lost their lives in the Balkan campaigns and World War I. Especially compelling was the public protest by 21 leading writers calling for public opinion to militate against the contemptible anti-Jewish policy that dishonored Bulgaria.

Advocates of the government's policy launched their own campaign urging the government to persevere, even to accelerate its anti-Jewish program forthwith. Government backers aired their views in the press, in manifestos, at meetings, and through telegrams endorsing the government's policy. They also inflicted physical harm on Jews and Jewish communal property, especially synagogues. The opponents of the anti-Jewish measures marshaled legal, moral, national, religious, educational, and historical rationales in support of their arguments. They contended that the government's policy was immoral on humanitarian grounds, contravened the constitution, and was politically and economically damaging as well. They argued further that it ran counter to the national tradition of tolerance toward minorities and represented capitulation to German pressure.

The impressive number of manifestos, essays, letters, telegrams, and memorandums addressed to the king, the prime minister, and the speaker of parliament by individuals and associations throughout Bulgaria almost certainly had a cumulative effect. Nonetheless, the likelihood that these protests and condemnations of the government's anti-Jewish policy would either halt its intention to enact the legislation or even mitigate its provisions was slight. Indeed, the government's parliamentary majority approved the anti-Jewish legislation. The deciding factor was the Bulgarian government's unyielding determination to pass the Law for the Protection of the Nation even before signing a treaty with Nazi Germany.

Within the Bulgarian Jewish community, power was concentrated in the hands of two groups: the Jewish Consistory (Zentralna Konsistoria), the officially recognized representative Jewish body, which also provided for individual and communal needs in the national, educational, religious, and social spheres; and the Zionist movement, the leading force among Bulgarian Jewry, whose members controlled local Jewish institutions as well as the nationwide Consistory. The speed with which the Bulgarian government adopted Nazi policy toward the Jews took the Jewish community and its leadership by surprise and undermined its feeling of security. Fear of impending events now became a feature of Jewish lives.

The rapidly deteriorating situation in 1939 and 1940 generated an intense debate in the Jewish community concerning the question of what the future held for Bulgarian Jewry and the preparatory steps that should be taken. Three distinct responses emerged:

Faith and hope. Those who relied on the traditional Bulgarian toleration of Jews believed that reason, justice, and morality would triumph over hatred, injustice, and discrimination. Faith and hope that evil would dissipate like a passing cloud provided a temporary refuge from the gathering storm. The Consistory adopted a cautious policy aimed at preventing panic within the Jewish community. The communal institutions continued to function, thereby ensuring the continuity of Jewish life, Hebrew education, and assistance to the stream of Central European refugees passing through Bulgaria en route to Palestine. At the same time the Consistory directed its main efforts to the struggle against the growing tide of antisemitism and the regime's anti-Jewish policy.

Aliyah and rescue. Supporters of this option argued that, given the steadily worsening conditions and the threat of ultimate destruction in light of the collective fate of European Jewry, it was essential to press for the organization of mass emigration to Palestine, even by illegal means. Bulgarian Jewry, with its long-standing Zionist affinities, was ripe for mass aliyah, they contended. Time was running out; a defensive posture in response to the regime's policy was inadequate. Rather, the organization of wholesale rescue was now the supreme priority.

The struggle against fascism. Some believed that Jews should join forces with Bulgarian antifascists, as equal participants in the momentous struggle that in their opinion overrode Jewish national aspirations. This argument was voiced by young Jewish Communists, as well as by graduates of the Zionist Hashomer Hatzair, Maccabi, and Betar youth groups who had despaired of ever reaching Palestine. Several hundred Jewish youths joined the ranks of the Bulgarian underground, primarily on an individual basis; a minority formed Jewish underground cells. They distributed leaflets and carried out acts of sabotage. Dozens of these young Jews fought in the ranks of the Bulgarian partisans.

The Jewish leadership was charged with formulating a clear-cut policy. Was the time ripe to set mass emigration to Palestine in motion, or was there a chance that Jewish life could continue on Bulgarian soil? The leaders faced a serious dilemma: in the absence of an assured means of mass escape from Bulgaria, was it preferable to issue a public warning of the danger, thereby sowing despair, or was it perhaps more politic to continue unobtrusive efforts to combat the anti-Jewish decrees, suppressing their own apprehensions in the hope that circumstances would improve?

Despite the setbacks suffered in 1939 and 1940, the majority of the Consistory's members continued to adhere to the belief that a stance of circumspection on their part, coupled with the help of Bulgarian sympathizers, would suffice to check the regime's anti-Jewish policy. The Jewish leadership's campaign among the Bulgarian people was intended to provided a convincing answer to the antisemitic crusade in the press, to maintain Jewish pride, and to strengthen the Jews' allies among the Bulgarian public. Jews contributed to the Jewish and Bulgarian press, and influential Bulgarians who detested the wave of antisemitism spoke out in their defense. Nonetheless, as vigorous as this propaganda campaign was, it did not succeed in stemming the rising tide of government-supported antisemitism.

In addition to these activities aimed at the populace, the Jewish leadership launched a broad-based campaign directed mainly at the Bulgarian regime—the king, the cabinet, and the parliament—and at influential public figures, with an eye to soliciting their backing. Consistory members, together with Zionist leaders, contacted politicians, church officials, and institutional and organizational executives, as well as influential personal friends, apprising them of the dangers facing Bulgarian Jewry.

Consistory-prepared memorandums were forwarded to cabinet ministers and members of parliament during the course of the parliamentary debate on the anti-Jewish legislation. These documents, with their extensive historical, statistical, legal, and economic data, buttressed the stance of the many Bulgarians who sympathized with the Jews and objected to the regime's anti-Jewish policy. But the anti-Jewish legislation could not be blocked. The Consistory's efforts were a last-ditch attempt to forestall a worsening of the Jewish status.

On the other hand, by mid-1940 the heads of the Zionist Federation had come to the realization that they had to support a concerted effort to organize mass aliyah. Nonetheless, their insistent demands to the Jewish Agency in Palestine for additional permits over and above their set quota of certificates were ignored, and their plans to initiate illegal mass emigration failed as well.

The only members of the Jewish communal leadership who consistently adhered to the idea of mass aliyah were the youth movements. Efforts to obtain certificates having failed, in 1939 and 1940 hundreds of youth movement members entered Palestine illegally. This illegal immigration was held up as an exemplar that constituted the only available means of implementing the Zionist ideal.

The Jews' growing sense of fear and vulnerability in the face of events enhanced Jewish aspirations to leave Bulgaria for Palestine by all and any means—legally, in possession of a certificate, or illegally, conveyed by means of unseaworthy vessels. But the Jewish leadership was unable to guarantee even illegal immigration, known as Aliyah B. The sole project promoting Aliyah B, a private initiative by Baruch Confino, came under criticism from the Zionist Federation for its failure to ensure the immigrants' safety.

Owing to the force of changing circumstances, as well as the escalating number of applicants, it now became clear that aliyah was the primary item on the Bulgarian Jewish community's agenda. In November 1940 a tripartite program was instituted, which provided for assistance to Jewish immigrants passing through Bulgaria en route to Palestine, prevention of extortion of excessive fees from immigrants by private entrepreneurs for aliyah, and the establishment of a communal framework for the implementation of mass aliyah. The Bulgarian Zionist Federation was compelled to abandon its long-standing policy of selective aliyah, which had given precedence to veteran Zionists and youth group members with prior training. Because of the situation the federation was now forced to endorse mass immigration even though it was viewed as less compatible with the needs of the Yishuv (the Jewish community in Palestine).

Events unfolded rapidly, leaving the Jewish community little time for extended deliberations. In December 1940 the chairman of the federation, Albert Romano, relayed to the Jewish Agency in Jerusalem reports on two disasters that had befallen Bulgarian Jewry: the death of 230 Jews on board the *Salvador* when the ship sank in a storm and the passage of the Law for the Protection of the Nation. Romano then inquired, "What about certificates?" and concluded on a note of despair: "You know what must be done, and deliverance is the Lord's."

Political events put an end to the attempts to organize mass aliyah. Several hundred Jews managed to board the *Dorian 2* at the eleventh hour on 1 March

1941, the very day that German troops entered Bulgaria. Shortly thereafter the ports were closed, and emigration ceased almost entirely.

The shift from a policy of faith and hope to one of aliyah and rescue, which occurred just as the Bulgarian borders were being sealed, raises doubts regarding the Jewish leadership's ability to gauge the situation accurately. Evidently, the call for mass aliyah and Aliyah B escalated precisely at a time when the practical opportunities for their implementation were nearly exhausted.

Bulgaria's enlistment in the Axis Powers on 1 March 1941 precipitated a radical change in the Jewish status. The Bulgarian government's pro-Nazi policy, coupled with German pressure to "solve the Jewish question" within its borders, completely undermined Bulgarian Jewry's social, economic, and legal standing.

If from 1939 to 1941 the Bulgarian regime's strategy was to deprive Jews of their statutory rights, after March 1941 its objective was their physical removal from Bulgaria's borders to German jurisdiction. On 25 June 1942 parliament enacted a law "authorizing the government to formulate and implement a solution to the Jewish problem." This task devolved on the Commissariat for Jewish Questions, established in August 1942, which was chaired by the antisemite Aleksander Belev. Charged with enforcing the Law for the Protection of the Nation and with overseeing all Jewish affairs, this agency also carried out secret negotiations with Germany to transport Bulgarian Jews to Polish death camps.

The official rationale for deportation was primarily grounded in realpolitik. The expulsion of Bulgarian Jewry was portrayed as congruent with the political-ideological line that would further enhance Bulgaria's relations with Nazi Germany, thereby enabling its full integration into the constellation of Axis Powers. In addition, opportunistic motives played a role. Certain circles supported the anti-Jewish policy in hopes of benefiting economically from the appropriation of Jewish property, homes, and bank accounts.

In February 1943 Bulgaria and Germany signed an agreement stipulating the deportation of Bulgarian Jewry to camps in Poland. Initially Bulgaria was to deliver 20,000 Jews to the Germans. The plan's first step called for the "purification" of the Bulgarian-occupied territories of Thrace and Macedonia (awarded to Bulgaria for its participation in the German attack on Yugoslavia and Greece in April 1941). As the number of Jews in Thrace and Macedonia fell short of the projected total, the difference was to be offset by the deportation of 9,000 Bulgarian Jews. In March 1943 Bulgarian police rounded up the Jews of Thrace and Macedonia at night and placed them in detention camps under extremely harsh conditions. Their property and their houses were confiscated prior to their deportation in the later part of the month. Sealed trains transported 11,384 Jews, mainly via the Danube River, to death camps, from which almost none returned.

On 9 March the round-up began within Bulgaria itself of the 9,000 Jews slated for deportation to Polish camps. Although planned to the last detail, the final implementation of this operation was delayed when the deportees were already partly concentrated at schools and train stations. The suspension followed an intense struggle involving Jews and Bulgarians alike.

News of the fate of Thracian and Macedonian Jewry, along with rumors of the impending deportation of Bulgarian Jewry and Jewish pleas to their Bulgarian friends, sparked a vigorous public reaction. A delegation of Bulgarian and Macedonian officials from the town of Kyustendil, with the collaboration of the deputy speaker of parliament, Dimitur Peshev, and 43 coalition and opposition parliamentarians, presented a strongly worded protest to the government demanding that the order be rescinded. Thanks to the lobbying by parliamentary representatives, the intervention of public figures with influence on the regime, and the unequivocal opposition of the Bulgarian Orthodox church, the deportation order was canceled, on the very day of its planned execution.

Germany and its Bulgarian backers continued to press for the implementation of the Final Solution in Bulgaria. The Bulgarian regime enacted punitive measures, including the harsh internment of the Bulgarian Jewish leadership in the Somivit concentration camp in May 1943.

In late May and early June 1943 Sofia's 25,000 Jews were given three days' notice to pack bags (up to a 20-kilogram limit) and to abandon their homes, property, and jobs, in preparation for exile. They were resettled in the provinces under humiliatingly impoverished conditions. Despite their own difficulties, the small provincial Jewish communities absorbed the exiles and tried to provide for their needs. Hebrew schools continued to function, soup kitchens were opened, and local Jews housed the refugees. Food and jobs were proffered by the local Bulgarian population, both urban and rural, in defiance of regulations.

The Jewish situation took a further turn for the worse in the latter half of 1943, when complete ghettoization was imposed in conjunction with an almost total curfew. Free contact with the Bulgarian population was restricted, food supplies were reduced, and employment opportunities dried up.

The attempt to deport Bulgarian Jewry to concentration camps in Poland aroused such strong opposition on the part of influential circles in Bulgaria that the proposed consignment of Bulgarian Jews to extermination camps was halted. What can explain this phenomenon, given the minimal effect of public opinion on government policy? There was no free press in Bulgaria, and all printed matter was strictly censored. Political organization was outlawed, and life proceeded under close police scrutiny. The regime was highly centralized, fully endorsed by the king, and unencumbered by parliament, which lacked authority. In such a political climate extra-establishment protests exercise minimal influence on government decisions.

Of all the organizations that protested against and took steps to prevent the deportation of Bulgarian Jewry in 1943, only two succeeded in directly exerting their influence on the king and the government. One was a group of parliamentarians led by Deputy Speaker Peshev, which created a storm of protest in the house; in turn parliament pressured and threatened the interior minister into canceling the deportation order. The other was the Holy Synod, the supreme body of the Bulgarian Orthodox church. Using its power base among the faithful to exert its influence on the king and his advisers, the synod courageously intervened at crucial moments, thereby preventing the deportation of Bulgarian Jewry.

This observation is in no way meant to detract from other individual, group, and organizational efforts to prevent the persecution and expulsion of Bulgarian Jewry. Nonetheless, the political reality in Bulgaria from 1939 to 1943 dictated the restriction of effective intervention to such persons as parliamentarians and church leaders, who exercised direct influence on the king and the government.

Overt expressions of protest by Bulgarian citizens against the government's anti-Jewish policies contributed substantially to the resilience of the Bulgarian Jews. Although their lives were threatened by the regime, Bulgarian Jews drew strength from the support of outstanding figures, prestigious organizations, and ordinary citizens. The majority of the Bulgarian people accepted neither the fate of their Jewish citizens nor the government's damaging policy with equanimity. The Bulgarian public reaction was a major factor in the survival of Bulgarian Jewry.

The pro-German Bulgarian regime was ousted on 9 September 1944. A coalition government dominated by the Communist Fatherland Front took over the reins of power, declared war on Germany, and began to safeguard the new regime. This change instilled fresh hope in the Jews, as the government canceled all discriminatory legislation and made promises to restore Jewish property, homes, and businesses to their owners. Sofia's Jews were allowed to return to the capital. Their impoverishment and impaired status notwithstanding, the Bulgarian Jews had nonetheless escaped total destruction.

Immediately after the ouster of the old regime, intensive steps were taken to renew Jewish communal life. The Jewish Communists now administered communal institutions and Hebrew schools, dispossessing the Zionists, who had been in control for decades. Nevertheless, the various Zionist trends and youth movements did not refrain from reestablishing their organizations or from engaging in broad educational and ideological activity.

Aliyah became a practical issue for Zionists and anti-Zionists alike. The question of whether Bulgarian Jews should direct their energies toward Zionism and immigration to Palestine or toward rehabilitation in Bulgaria demanded an unequivocal answer.

The Jewish Communist camp made every effort to suppress Zionist activity and to discourage mass aliyah. Still, the inclination toward aliyah remained strong. With the reversal of the Soviet Union's attitude toward the founding of a Jewish state, government-approved mass aliyah from Bulgaria became practical, regardless of the opposition by Jewish Communists.

On 9 September 1944 approximately 50,000 Jews remained in Bulgaria. By 1952 some 45,000 had emigrated to Israel. Was this exodus a mass flight or an expulsion? It appears that Bulgarian Jewry chose aliyah of its own volition, not owing to lack of an alternative. The fact that almost the entire Bulgarian Jewish community emigrated to Palestine/Israel, and that this movement took place both before and after the declaration of a Jewish state in 1948, serves to pinpoint the nature of this aliyah. It was motivated neither by the desire to flee an inhospitable country, nor by the yearning for an idealized land flowing with milk and honey. Rather, its driving force was the ideal of aliyah itself.

Did the course of events during World War II predispose Bulgarian Jewry to make aliyah as a group? Although some of the factors that determined Bulgarian Jewry's almost total commitment to aliyah are rooted in long-term historical processes and the community's long-standing Zionist orientation and accomplishments, others are intrinsically related to its early postwar experiences. Some have to do with the nature of the new Communist regime and to its failure to effect the rapid economic rehabilitation of the Jewish community. Others lie in the Zionist sympathies of European Jewry as a whole in the wake of wartime atrocities, and in the impact of the struggle to promote aliyah and settlement and to establish a Jewish state in Palestine.

Significant weight must also be given to factors specifically related to wartime experiences. The wholesale extermination of European Jewry, and the traumatic deportation of Thracian and Macedonian Jewry to death camps in particular, undermined the Bulgarian Jews' sense of security and their belief in the possibility of a continued Jewish existence in Bulgaria. The expulsion of Sofia's 25,000 Jews to the provinces also had a lasting negative effect. Upon their return to the capital after 15 months of physical uncertainty and economic deprivation, they no longer comprised an economically strong and confident community, having been stripped of their property, housing, permanent jobs, household goods, and even clothing. Efforts by the Jewish Communist leadership at rapid rehabilitation (with the generous assistance of international Jewish organizations) met with only minimal success, and in the perception of many Jews a firm basis for the reconstitution of Jewish life in the capital was lacking. When aliyah became a possibility, the overwhelming response was immediate readiness to move. What is more, during the postwar period there was an increase in overt expressions of antisemitism and social tensions between Bulgarians and Jews against the background of competition for jobs, failure to restore Jewish property, and exclusion of Jews from public office. The replacement of the pro-Nazi regime by a Communist one failed to bring improvement, a development that profoundly disappointed the Jews and intensified their desire to immigrate to Palestine in order to begin a new life among Jews.

Shlomo Shealtiel

Bund The General Jewish Workers Union of Lithuania, Poland, and Russia, known as the Bund, was founded in 1897 in Vilna, Lithuania, which was then part of tsarist Russia. A Marxist party that believed in overthrowing the capitalist order and establishing a democratic socialist society, the Bund also fought for Jewish "national autonomy"—that is, the right of the Jews to have their own administrative and cultural institutions in their own language, Yiddish, spoken at that time by the vast majority of Eastern European Jews. Thus the Bund considered itself at one and the same time an "internationalist" and a specifically Jewish party. It combated Zionism, which it saw as a utopian fantasy aimed at diverting the millions of Jews from struggling for their rights in situ together with the other oppressed subjects of the tsarist regime.

After World War I the Bund, like all non-Bolshevik parties, was banned by the Soviet government. A small minority of Bundists joined the Third International, and the Bund reconstituted itself in independent Poland. It promoted a wide number of activities, established numerous cultural institutions, dominated the Jewish trade unions movement, and gained many loyal supporters, although it remained essentially a sectarian party.

In the early 1930s the position of the Bund drastically changed. Indeed, within a few years the Bund could rightly consider itself the strongest Jewish political party in Poland. Between 1934 and 1939 the number of its registered members tripled. It scored impressive victories in the elections to the Jewish communities (*kehillot*) in 1936 and 1937 and even improved its showing in the general municipal elections of 1938 and 1939. In Warsaw alone the Bund won 17 of the 20 Jewish seats, and in Lodz it took 11 out of 17. In 15 other towns the Bund outdistanced other Jewish parties and, together with the Polish Socialist party (Polska Partia Socjalistyczna, PPS), brought about socialist majorities in the towns' ruling bodies.

Prominent Bundists, such as Henryk Erlich, cautioned party comrades that many of those who voted for the Bund did not necessarily subscribe to its ideology. It was also true that the Bund had become a staunch defender of the interests of the "Jewish masses," including the right to practice ritual slaughter and to keep the Sabbath, even though such practices ran counter to the Bund's resolutely secular Marxist orientation. At the end of the 1930s, the Bund even began to induct hasidic workers into its militia units, which were formed to protect Jewish street vendors.

Open-air meeting of Bund, in Warsaw. Early 1930s

The Bund's large constituency, its cooperation with the PPS, and its ties with social democrats in other countries (it had joined the Second International in 1930) all proved useful under German occupation. Yet neither these factors nor the past experience of underground activity in tsarist Russia were of much avail against a power bent on the total destruction of Poland's Jewry. Within a few days after the German invasion in September 1939, thousands of Jews, including several leaders of the Bund, fled to the east, partly to save themselves from the rapidly advancing German armies, partly in response to the appeal of the Polish

government that all men capable of bearing arms head eastward, where new front lines were to be established.

As the memoirs of many Bundists attest, the decision to leave was heart-rending, as it was felt to be an abandonment of their fellow Jews. Three years later, after most of Poland's Jews had been killed, the representative of the Bund's Central Committee in Warsaw, Leon Feiner, commiserated with his comrades in the West: "We realize how difficult it is for you," he wrote in a letter sent by a courier, "to be so far from one's own people, from those near and dear to you . . . at a time more extraordinary than any our people have ever lived through. In a sense, our situation is considerably better than yours." Some of the Bundist leaders made their way back to Poland after the Soviet troops crossed Poland's eastern frontier in mid-September 1939. Others, under threat of arrest and deportation by the Soviet secret police (NKVD), began heading south or northeast, toward the Baltic countries. Many were apprehended by the Soviet "liberators." Two internationally celebrated leaders, Henryk Erlich and Victor Alter, were imprisoned as "British intelligence agents," released after the German invasion of the Soviet Union in June 1941, and then rearrested in December 1941. They disappeared into the cellars of the Lubyanka, secret police headquarters in Moscow. The Soviet government, despite protests and pressures from the West, remained silent about their fate until May 1943, when it announced that the Bund leaders had been executed for engaging in "pro-Nazi propaganda." This was of course a canard, but the information about the execution was also false: Alter was shot in 1943, and Henryk Erlich, as archives of the Soviet security police (KGB) have now revealed, had committed suicide a year earlier.

In addition to Bundist leaders who remained in Poland and those on Soviet territory, a number of Bundists, including members of the Central Committee, managed to elude both the Nazis and the Soviets and in 1940–41 fled to New York. There they established the U.S. "representation" of the Bund in Poland, with its own publishing house, a monthly magazine called *Undzer Tsayt* (Our Time), and, eventually, a seat in the Polish National Council in London, Poland's parliament-in-exile.

In Poland the scope and nature of the Bund's activities during the war varied, depending on location, on the size of the party organization, on the party's relations with other left-wing groups, both Jewish (such as Poale Zion and Hehalutz) and Polish (PPS and the Communists), and on the policies pursued by the Nazis.

In Lodz, which housed the second-largest Bund organization after Warsaw, a wide net of activities developed, despite depletions within Bund leadership. Conditions in Lodz were monstrous. The prewar structures of Jewish life had been destroyed almost overnight, and the Jews of Lodz were at the mercy of local German factory owners or were deported for work in Germany. On 1 May 1940 the ghetto was formally established, with 157,000 Jews being herded into

an area measuring four square kilometers and containing about 31,000 small flats; only 725 had running water, and few had electricity. A few months later, with tens of thousands of Jews brought from surrounding towns and villages, the number of inhabitants grew to more than 200,000.

The head of the *Judenrat* (Jewish council), Mordechai Chaim Rumkowski, allowed the formation—under his control—of industrial branch committees consisting of both workers and former employers. The workers, largely under the direction of the Bund, staged several protest meetings and strikes, forcing Rumkowski to yield to their demands, in the first place to provide the starving population with soup kitchens. When the unrest continued, Rumkowski organized special squads of underworld bullies who, together with the Jewish police, beat up protesters and tossed them into jail. In consequence the tension between Rumkowski and the Bund intensified. After the Bund's underground paper published a highly unflattering cartoon of the Judenrat chairman, he expelled Bundists from their places of employment and closed down Bundist-run institutions.

In December 1941 the deportations from Lodz to Chelmno and Auschwitz began. Although the Bund remained active until August 1944, the Lodz Jewish community was decimated—of the 68,000 left in the ghetto, all but 1,000 were deported. As late as 1 May 1944 the Bund managed to hold several small celebrations in private apartments and to warn against Rumkowski's odious ruse that Jews were merely being sent away to "work," and his demand that a certain number of children be turned over to the Jewish police lest the whole ghetto be erased by the Germans. The Bund also tried to organize protests jointly with the Communist group, one of the more active in the ghetto, and with the left-wing Poale Zion, its traditional ally. Poale Zion, along with other Zionist organizations, maintained that drastic action against the Judenrat would spell the demise of the whole Jewish population in Lodz, whereas the Communists, convinced that the Red Army was making rapid headway, preferred to concentrate on pro-Soviet propaganda.

Similar illusions stymied the attempts of the Bund (with nearly 1,000 members on the eve of the final deportation) to organize an armed uprising. The other Jewish parties were convinced that the chances of success were nil, and most of the Jews thought that with the war about to end, the Nazis would cease the slaughter. The PPS, the Bund's single Polish prewar ally, did not succeed even in establishing its own armed group. With Lodz having been incorporated into the Third Reich, the party had virtually no contact with any other PPS organizations or with the Polish Home Army (Armia Krajowa, AK), which in Warsaw constituted the main source of weapons. Thus the ghetto and the Bund in Lodz came to an end.

In Czestochowa the Bund had a large following, but, unlike in Lodz, the socialist-Zionist groups, as well as the Communists, had also been active before the war. To put pressure on the local Judenrat, the left-wing parties formed a united trade union. Discussions about armed resistance against the Nazis began in 1941, but efforts to obtain weapons led nowhere, primarily owing to the hostile attitude of the Home Army, which was convinced that "Communists" were behind the plan. On 22 September 1942 the German, Latvian, and Ukrainian forces launched an "action" (*Aktion*) designed to liquidate the Czestochowa ghetto. Within five weeks 40,000 Jews were shipped off to Treblinka and Auschwitz, and 6,000 were herded into a minuscule area to work in local factories.

Until the action the Bund carried on its work. It maintained two Yiddish schools, oversaw the activities of Tsukunft (Future, the Bund's youth organization) and SKIF (Socialist Children's Association), transferred—slowly and painstakingly—the archives of the party to a safe hiding place, and ran its library, the Medem Bibliotek, out of the apartment of one woman, to which most the volumes had been transferred.

After the deportations such activities were impossible. New plans for armed resistance began to be hatched, but the underground split: the Bund and the left-wing Poale Zion were in favor of defending the ghetto, while the Communists, Hashomer Hatzair, and others advocated a partisan struggle in the woods. An attempt to resolve the differences came to naught when, in June 1943, a Jewish policeman betrayed the plans to the Germans. Within a few days the ghetto was destroyed, and so was the hope of Jewish resistance.

Vilna was in many respects distinctive. The city's 60,000 Jews (out of a total population of 200,000) represented the usual kaleidoscope of political parties, believers and secularists, Yiddishists and Hebraists, hasidim and mitnaggedim, the few rich and the many poor. But certain features were common to this heterogeneous group: virtually the whole population spoke Yiddish; Communists, however bitterly opposed, were accepted as legitimate political rivals, as were the Zionist "Revisionists"; and creativity, organization, and discipline were regarded as supreme values.

Because the Bund had been born in Vilna, it had developed deep roots and strong traditions in that city—traditions that had continued to thrive in independent Poland. Some of its leaders—Arcadi and Pati Kremer, Anna Rosental, Yankev Zheleznikov, and others—played outstanding roles in the Bund and in the social and cultural life of the city before and after 1917. This pattern continued in German-occupied Vilna. The first Judenrat was formed in July and consisted of 25 members, three of them Bundists. It was dissolved by the Germans just before the ghetto was established—initially comprising two parts, later combined into one—in early September 1941. Some of its members were taken to Ponary, the wooded area not far from Vilna that became the graveyard of 70,000 Jews. A new five-man Judenrat was then formed, two of whose members were Bundists.

Grigori Jaszunski, a Bundist who came to Vilna from Warsaw, became the most prominent member of the Judenrat. At various times he headed the Education and Cultural Department, and he was active in other departments as well. A Yiddishist, he waged a struggle against those teachers, mostly from Zionist and religious groups, who wanted the schools (organized shortly after the formation of the ghetto) to put greater emphasis on Hebrew language and literature and on Bible studies. The language of instruction of all schools, however, was Yiddish. In April 1943 Jacob Gens, whom less than a year earlier the Germans had appointed "Ghetto representative" and who was a right-wing Zionist by conviction, removed Jaszunski and appointed a General Zionist teacher, Leo Bernstein, as head of the Education Department.

The Bund played a decisive role in areas such as the Judenrat's Committee for Social Help (Gezelshaftlekher Hilf Komitet). While some of its members opposed any contact with the Judenrat after Gens became virtual dictator, most Bundists, like members of other political groups, felt that contacts with Gens were necessary and justified. In this respect, the relations between the Judenrat and the underground in Vilna were radically different from those in such ghettos as Lodz and Warsaw.

The story of the United Partisan Organization (FPO) inside and outside Vilna ghetto is told elsewhere in this book. The Bund, after some hesitation, joined the FPO after it was created by several socialist-Zionist groups and the Betar, and remained a loyal constituent part of the organization until its end.

Warsaw was the center of the Bund's activities before the war, and continued to be so both before and after November 1940, when the ghetto was established. The Bund published more newspapers and journals in Yiddish and Polish than any other underground group, and was astonishingly well-informed on local and international events. It ran a teachers' seminary and a children's theater school, and reopened the Medem Sanatorium for children near Warsaw that had been closed on the eve of the war. (In the summer of 1942 the sanatorium's 160 children and staff were deported to Treblinka.) Some activities, such as the workshops of cobblers, tailors, and other craftsmen, were nominally under the aegis of the Judenrat, but in fact were run by the Bund and other organizations, such as Poale Zion, Hashomer Hatzair, and Dror.

The Bund in Warsaw, and for that matter in other towns, was organized along strictly conspiratorial lines, with basic units consisting of five people sworn to secrecy and ignorant of the identity of other units. The highest party organ was the Central Committee, with a number of other bodies subordinated to it. In addition, there was also a Red Cross committee, and committees on financial, economic, and archival affairs.

Unlike in Vilna, where the Bund participated in the Judenrat, the Bund in Warsaw by and large refused to have anything to do with the Jewish council. The council's chairman, Adam Czerniakow, was considered an essentially good but weak man, and his suicide in July 1942 was condemned by the Bund, as it was by socialist-Zionists and the Communists: they felt that he should have used his death to warn the Jews about the impending catastrophe and to call on them to resist. (The suicide of the Bund's representative in the London-based Polish National Council, Samuel [Szmul] Zygielbojm, in May 1943, was meant to alert the world to the fate of the Jews in Europe.)

It is doubtful whether an appeal would have made any difference. The Jews in Warsaw, unlike those in Vilna, did indeed come to support the Jewish Fighting Organization, ZOB (Zydowska Organizacja Bojowa), in April–May 1943, but this was after the Germans had deported nearly 350,000 Jews to Treblinka, and the remaining Jews had realized that there was nothing left but to resist.

The story of the ZOB has been told many times. One point, however, deserves special comment—namely, the Bund's stubborn rejection of a common bloc with the other left-wing groups. Yet while the Bund's traditional hostility to Zionism played an important part in this attitude, the Zionist-socialist parties, too, displayed the same behavior, the relatively insignificant differences among them notwithstanding. Keeping one's party organizationally and doctrinally uncontaminated was a hallmark of Jewish political life before the war, and it continued to be so in the underground.

The differences were eventually resolved by the creation of a united fighting organization, which was composed of all political groups except the Betar, and also two umbrella bodies: the Jewish National Committee, which embraced all groups except the Bund; and the Coordination Committee, the overall political body representing both the Bund and the National Committee. Many fighting units were composed of men and women from the same party, on the theory that personal ties would help to forge a better esprit de corps. Within a matter of days, however, doctrinal differences no longer mattered, as Bundists, Zionists, and Communists fought and died side by side. The panoply of the umbrella organizations, too, disintegrated in the ghetto in the course of the uprising.

By 9 May, when the insurrection was coming to an end, a number of fighters had succeeded in escaping through the sewers to the Aryan side, where their comrades helped them find shelter among a generally hostile Polish population. Others, trapped in a bunker by the Germans, committed suicide. As late as September, the sewers were still yielding survivors of the Warsaw ghetto. In August 1944, when the Warsaw uprising broke out, many of the surviving Bundists and others joined the struggle, but under the aegis of the Communist-led People's Army. The People's Army was relatively hospitable to Jews; the Home Army was not.

For the surviving Bundists, fervent internationalists all, the poisonous antisemitism in Poland, which in fact had intensified during the war, was a particularly bitter pill to swallow. The memoirs of Bundist leaders such as Vladka Mead (Miedzyrzecki) and Bernard Goldstein detail the magnitude of anti-Jewish hatred that pervaded all segments of Polish society. During the 1944 Warsaw uprising, writes Bernard Goldstein in his *Five Years in the Warsaw Ghetto* (1962), anyone recognized as a Jew was "refused food and shelter," and after the Nazi defeat "the overwhelming number of Poles regarded the

Jews with loathing and hostility. . . . Wherever you went you could hear 'still so many Jews!'"

In May 1944 the Bund's representative in the Polish parliament in London, Emanuel Sherer—who took over the position left vacant by Samuel Zygielbojm's suicide—reported the "shattering" impression he received when he visited the Polish army barracks in Scotland earlier in the year. The walls, he said, were covered with slogans reading "Beat the Jews," the Polish army daily carried antisemitic cartoons "à la Streicher," and Jewish soldiers related to him daily incidents of derision and humiliation. When Sherer complained to the head of the army and minister of defense, he was told that these were just "sporadic phenomena."

Due in no small part to its ties with the outside world, the Bund was the first to send abroad detailed reports about the Nazi carnage, in May 1942 and again in June 1943. It was the Bund's representative on the Aryan side of Warsaw, Leon Feiner, together with the Poale Zionist Adolf Berman, who in August 1942 entrusted the AK courier Jan Karski with the task of alerting world public opinion and in particular Western leaders to the horrors taking place in Poland, and to plead for immediate help. His mission, which he carried out with singular dedication, had few results.

In sum, then, the Bund largely pursued policies forged during the prewar period, though subject to local circumstances. A genuine political party with years of experience among Jews and non-Jews, its range of activities was considerably wider than that of most Zionist-socialist youth groups. Moreover, while other groups, such as Hashomer Hatzair, were loath to give up their illusions about the Soviet Union, the Bund's anticommunism, already strong before the Holocaust, deepened during the war years, mainly because of the Erlich and Alter case.

After the war the Zionist parties resolutely championed leaving Poland. The Bund, however, remained ideologically consistent, faithful to the concept of *doikayt,* which held that the Jews must solve their problems in situ. Despite the wave of bestial antisemitism that raged in Poland after the war, leading tens of thousands of Jews to leave the country, the Bund decided to resuscitate the party, or what was left of it, in 1945. Three years later, like other non-Communist groups, the Bund was disbanded: this was its coup de grâce. *Abraham Brumberg*

C

Catholic Church, Roman For many centuries the Roman Catholic church maintained a deliberate and systematic doctrinal antagonism against Judaism. The need to validate Christian claims and to discredit the Jewish adversary was coupled with a consistent opposition to Jewish "unbelief" and led to an easily transferable prejudice reinforcing a variety of widely differing social and economic sources of intolerance. Even though several popes issued edicts against indiscriminate persecution of individual Jews, the continuity of widespread antipathy against Judaism and Jews in general cannot be doubted. The theological presuppositions of this anti-Judaism were never challenged.

With the rise in the nineteenth century of antisemitism based on racial ideas, these long-held theological prejudices became interwoven with more rabid expressions of anti-Jewish hatred. Many Catholics, particularly in Central and Eastern Europe, became susceptible to the conflation of nationalist, racist, and religious stereotypes, despite open acknowledgment by racial ideologues of their anti-Christian as well as anti-Jewish bias. Although Catholic anti-Judaism was not a necessary precondition for the Holocaust, it was clearly a contributing factor to Nazi antisemitism.

In 1933 the majority of German Catholics enthusiastically greeted the rise to power of the Nazis, seeing in Hitler's regime a desirable restoration of authoritarian government and their best defense against the danger of communism. The signing of the Concordat between the Holy See and the German Reich in July 1933 seemed to safeguard the position of the Catholic church in the new state and to remove the reproach that Catholics were not fully integrated into the German nation. Thereafter the Catholic bishops stressed their adherence to the national community and, despite growing alarm at the Nazis' totalitarian ambitions, never revoked their pledge of allegiance to the established government. Nor were they willing to challenge the Nazi party's campaign against the Jewish people but instead agreed with the alleged need to curtail the supposed overrepresentation of Jews in leading positions in German society. The Nuremberg Laws of 1935 were accepted by the Catholic population without large-scale objection. Catholic silence at the time of the notorious Kristallnacht pogroms of November 1938 was complete. Apart from measures to assist individual Jews who had converted to Catholicism to emigrate, and representations against Nazi plans for compulsory divorce between Catholics and Jews in mixed marriages, no vigorous protests or outrage against the persecution of the Jews were ever voiced. The predominant attitude among Catholics was to protect their own subculture and institutions. Their leaders believed they had no mandate to intervene on behalf of outside groups such as the Jews.

Catholics in Germany sought to portray themselves as loyal followers of the regime. They gave unqualified support to Hitler's expansionist foreign policies and participated willingly in his aggressive wars, especially against the much-feared Soviet Union. Only when Catholic organizations and institutions came under direct Nazi attack, or when—as in the so-called euthanasia program—Catholic lives were being ruthlessly terminated, did protests occur. But they were clearly designed to protect those persons regarded as falling within the Catholic "circle of obligation." The Jews in general were not included. Moreover, such Catholic remonstrances were directed not against the regime as such but against specific policies believed to be instigated by overzealous underlings. This reluctance was reinforced not only by the pressures of wartime patriotism but also by the overcautious attitude of the presiding bishop, Cardinal Adolf Bertram of Breslau, who consistently followed a path of accom-

The signing of the Concordat between the German Reich and the Holy See in the chancellery of the Vatican. The man second from left (1) is Franz von Papen, vice-chancellor of the Reich. At the head of the table (2) is Eugenio Pacelli, cardinal, Vatican secretary of state, and, eventually, Pope Pius XII, chief architect of the Concordat. 1933

modation rather than of outright resistance even to the Gestapo's most flagrant breaches of the Concordat. At no time were German Catholics taught to recognize the demonic nature of the Nazi regime or warned against the dynamic force of the Nazi determination to remodel society along totalitarian and racial lines. Only in the aftermath did German Catholics begin to claim that they too were the victims of Nazi ferocity, but without belatedly recognizing how far their previous silence and readiness to collaborate had contributed to the fate of the Nazis' primary victims, the Jews. A further factor militating against the mobilization of Catholic opposition was the widespread conviction that the initiative for protests, whether against the infringements of the Concordat or on wider issues, such as the persecution of the Jews, should come from the highest level of Catholic authority, that is, from the Holy See in the Vatican.

Debate about the "failure" of the Vatican during the Holocaust has continued for several decades and was prompted particularly in the early 1960s by polemical attacks upon the so-called silence of Pope Pius XII. The Vatican's response was to arrange for the unprecedented publication of 11 large volumes of documents from the war years, including the telegrams, memorandums, and correspondence between the Holy See and its staff of papal nuncios and apostolic delegates around the world. These volumes were edited by a small team of Jesuit scholars and were necessarily a selection from such a vast corpus. But the fact that the originals are still not open to all scholars has been a point of criticism. Half of these documents deal with the papal efforts to maintain peace or to limit the spread of hostilities, while the others describe the manifold but largely unsuccessful attempts to mitigate the plight of war victims, including Jews. Had this evidence appeared earlier, the heated debates about Pope Pius XII's conduct of Vatican diplomacy might have been conducted with more insight, and a more realistic assessment might have been made of what was done and what was left undone on behalf of the persecuted Jewish community.

Critics of papal policy, including some of the Curia's own officials, such as the French cardinal Eugène Tisserant and members of the Polish hierarchy in exile, have at the time or since have taken issue with the overly diplomatic approach adopted by Pius XII, believing that fearless public protests against Nazi crimes would not only have enhanced the moral position of the church throughout the world but would also have deterred Hitler from implementing his policies of terrorism and extermination. The failure, it is claimed, to mobilize the moral resources of the papacy by openly defending human rights and freedoms, especially with regard to the Jews, made the church an accomplice in the most terrible crimes of the twentieth century.

Such criticisms are often accompanied by speculations as to what could or should have been done to relieve the plight of the Jews had a different and less cautious pope reigned in the Holy See.

These strongly felt expressions of moral outrage, however, tend to ignore the realities of the political context in which the pope and his advisers had to operate, and the theological presuppositions that guided the Curia's attitudes toward Judaism. The critics often overestimate papal authority in political as well as religious matters, and they are unwilling to recognize that the pope's power was not nearly as effective as they suppose. The cumulative evidence over the past decades has sharply demonstrated the limited scope of influence and action available to the Vatican during the traumatic years of the Holocaust.

The reign of Pius XII began in March 1939 inauspiciously enough, with his first few months being devoted to resolute but abortive attempts to prevent war. As far as the Jews of Central Europe were concerned, the events of 1938—the failure of the Evian Conference to produce new offers of asylum, the evidence from Kristallnacht of the Nazis' envenomed brutality, and Mussolini's introduction of new racial laws in Italy—produced an entirely unfavorable climate for Vatican initiatives.

The outbreak of war in September 1939, the conclusion of the unsavory Nazi–Soviet pact, and the rapid conquest of staunchly Catholic Poland were blows to the Vatican's efforts to preserve the framework of European civilization. Pius XII nevertheless maintained his resolve to seek to limit the spread of hostilities, attempted to persuade the Italian government not to join in, placed his hopes in the peaceful policy of the United States, and even began secret negotiations with representatives of the German opposition to achieve this goal. But the events of 1940 and 1941 proved disillusioning. The Vatican was soon overwhelmed by thousands of individual appeals for help, which only revealed the lack of effective machinery to mount any worldwide relief campaign. All the combatant governments frustrated the Vatican's humanitarian moves. The numerous remonstrances, for instance, delivered by the nuncio in Berlin to the German government were insolently ignored or sidetracked. Efforts to secure entry visas for Jews from the Catholic states in Latin America, or to urge the United States to increase its quota for European refugees, were rejected, as was the offer of a papal relief team for Poland. In short, the pope's influence was far too slight to overcome the universal failure to rescue Europe's increasingly victimized Jews. The Vatican was forced to recognize that only in the smaller satellite states of Eastern Europe could interventions have some hope of success.

From the end of 1941 the situation grew darker. Reports reached Rome of forcible deportations of Jews to unknown destinations in the east. Conditions for the Jews in Poland and Ukraine were known to be disastrous. In Slovakia, in March 1942, the apostolic delegate reported that President Jozef Tiso, a Catholic priest, was proposing to deport some 80,000 Jews, the great majority to certain death. The Vatican immediately protested against this move, which was endorsed by the Slovakian parliament, including its clerical representatives. As a high Vatican official bitterly commented: "It is a great misfortune that the president of Slovakia is a priest. Everyone knows that the Holy See cannot bring Hitler to heel. But who will understand that we can't even control a priest?" The most that could be achieved were some temporary mitigations and exemptions from the deportation order.

This pattern was repeated in other countries, such as Romania and Bulgaria. In Hungary, which came under Nazi control in March 1944, the papal nuncio sought mitigation of decrees passed against the Jews, issued rescue certificates, and set up safe houses. But such measures found little support even from the conservative and nationalist Hungarian Catholic hierarchy. It took a personal open appeal by the pope to the Hungarian regent, Adm. Miklós Horthy, to reinforce the latter's decision to suspend the deportation of Jews. In Croatia the Ustashi regime, strongly supported by the Catholic church and spurred on by German demands, insisted on mass expulsions of Jews, only a minority of whom were able to find safety in Italian-occupied areas. The Ustasha's vicious excesses against the Jews, and its equally murderous vendetta against the Orthodox peasantry, were never condemned by any specific papal pronouncement and left an enduring legacy.

In Holland the Catholic bishops took a more forceful line. In 1942 they issued a pastoral letter protesting against injustice and mistreatment of the Jews by the German occupiers. But the result was an immediate intensification of countermeasures by the Gestapo, including the forcible capture of converted Jews in monasteries and convents and their deportation to Auschwitz. This news was profoundly disturbing to Vatican officials, revealing as it did the costliness of such high-minded protests and the limits of the church's ability to prevent worse disasters.

In France and Italy the Catholic hierarchies were deeply divided, for both theological and political reasons, in their attitudes toward Jews, especially refugees. The establishment of the Vichy regime, with its explicit affirmation of Catholic values, had been seen by many churchmen as a welcome restoration of national pride. Its willing subordination to German pressures, especially over the expulsion of foreigners and refugees, including Jews, was therefore not opposed. On the other hand, several congregations and church leaders, such as Cardinals Jules Saliège of Toulouse and Pierre Gerlier of Lyons, were appalled by the inhumane treatment of Jews and other minorities and in secret took vigorous measures to provide partial relief and to circulate clandestine journals, such as *Le Témoignage Chrétien,* which sharply attacked the Vichy regime's complicity in such crimes. In Italy the established harmony between the church and the fascist state hindered any direct confrontation, though numerous religious communities were prepared to hide or shelter Jews from the waves of persecution.

With hindsight, many observers believed that had the fate of the Jews been more widely proclaimed and more positive resistance called for, many more lives could have been saved. But to suggest that the moral power of the churches was sufficient to produce a significantly different situation is to exaggerate their potential influence and to ignore the virulence of the ideological hatreds of an inflamed nationalism strengthened by centuries of antipathy. In fact, as the pope's letters to the German bishops make clear, Pius was continually assailed by doubt as to the results of a more defiant or prophetic stance and was well aware of the danger that his words would be exploited for propaganda purposes by one side or the other. For these reasons, and despite strong and continued urgings from the Polish bishops in exile, Pius turned down their suggestions for more forceful protests on behalf of the Jews of Europe. The Vatican had been forced to realize that Hitler's intentions could not be altered by entreaties from Rome, however vigorous or frequent. On the contrary, there was evidence enough to fear that retaliation would fall not only on the Catholic church but also on the victims for whom it was pleading. The diminution of papal influence during the years of war and terror was incontrovertible. The silence imposed by this situation was only deepened in the claustrophobic atmosphere in 1943, when German troops surrounded the Vatican following Mussolini's downfall.

How much did the Vatican know? How much could it believe of the reports of the terrible persecutions proceeding in Poland and elsewhere? No one now defends the view that the Vatican was ignorant of the existence of concentration camps or the killing of Jews on an unprecedented scale. Information supplied by Jewish sources was confirmed in reports from the nuncios in Eastern Europe and by church leaders in Ukraine and Lithuania. But the difficulties of distinguishing between sure fact and unsubstantiated rumor continued. The full extent of the horror was never acknowledged.

There is no evidence to suggest that Vatican officials at the time were more percipient than other church bodies, such as the World Council of Churches in Geneva, or even the Jewish organizations outside the Nazi sphere of control, in realizing the deliberate intent of the Nazi genocide of European Jewry, let alone the implications for Christianity and the Roman Catholic church that the Holocaust brought with it. On the contrary, there is evidence that even if the Vatican had adopted a more courageous and risky stance on behalf of the Jews, the majority of European Catholics would have hesitated to follow its lead. (The numerous, if belated, efforts by Catholics on behalf of individual Jews should not, however, be overlooked.) The desire to protect the Roman Catholic church's own institutional autonomy, when it was being so brutally attacked, undoubtedly contributed to the seemingly halfhearted willingness to include Jews within the "circle of obligation" for whom more vigorous defensive measures were required. How far this stance was dictated by individual hesitation, or by institutional apathy, or by the failure to take more timely measures to counteract the indoctrinated "teaching of contempt" for Jews, remains a matter of controversy. Only long after the Holocaust, beginning under Pope John XXIII, has the church, led by the Vatican, begun to take radical steps to alter its theological stance toward Judaism, to condemn antisemitism, and to support the conviction of the Polish pope, John Paul II, that such catastrophies must never be allowed to occur again.   *John S. Conway*

Cernauti (Czernowitz) Capital of Bukovina, with a Jewish population of approximately 50,000 at the beginning of World War II. See ROMANIA

Chelmno (Kulmhof) First camp built solely for the purpose of extermination, established in December 1941 at a site 60 kilometers from Lodz. Approximately 300,000 Jews were killed at Chelmno, primarily by firing squad and by asphyxiation in mobile gas vans. The Nazis destroyed Chelmno in late 1944. See EXTERMINATION CAMPS

Children Among the 6 million Jews who died in the Holocaust, a million and a half were children, most of them under the age of 15. Almost from the onset of the Nazi regime Jewish children were deprived of basic rights, including the right to attend state schools. This law was applied to Jewish children in Germany as early as April 1933 and was later put into effect in all annexed and occupied countries. With the invasion of Poland in September 1939, the law was also applied to Jewish children in the east and, after the takeover of Western Europe in 1940, to those living in the west.

On 8 October 1939 the first ghetto was established in the Generalgouvernement in Pioterkow Trybunalski, the sector of Poland under direct German administration. Children in particular suffered there from overcrowding, lack of proper sanitation and medical care, malnutrition, and emotional stress. Many children were forced to take to the narrow streets in search of food and activity. The social welfare organizations that tried to help the Jewish inhabitants paid special attention the children: they opened children's kitchens as well as children's libraries called "children corners." But in a large ghetto like that in Warsaw only a few thousand children could enjoy those facilities; tens of thousands remained out of reach. In the densely populated and ill-supplied ghettos, many children became their families' providers. They would smuggle in food, particularly in those ghettos that had contact with the Aryan side of town. In the Warsaw ghetto, for example, many children smuggled bread and potatoes to keep their families alive. Often the smugglers were caught by the Polish or the Jewish police; in some cases they were shot. Disease and starvation also took their toll among Jewish children, costing thousands their lives in 1940–41.

Education

In many ghettos the leadership encouraged and sometimes even sponsored educational activities for children. Jacob Gens in Vilna and Mordechai Chaim Rumkowski in Lodz took advantage of their special relations with the German authorities and were proud to

Fence at the Lodz ghetto.

show off their efforts on behalf of ghetto children. Nevertheless, in October 1942 Rumkowski did not hesitate to ask the mothers in the Lodz ghetto to send their children to the transport, and thus to their deaths, in order to save the working population of the ghetto. The women tried to hide their children, but most of those under 10 years of age were kidnapped by the Jewish police and deported to Auschwitz.

In spite of the Nazi order prohibiting educational activities, underground schools were sponsored by various organizations. One example was the high schools, founded by the Zionist youth movement Dror, in Warsaw and in other ghettos. The best teachers tried to teach history, literature, mathematics, and science even as students stood guard at the doors, ready to warn if Nazis approached. This school was the base of the first underground activities of the Dror youth movement. The children were active in posting underground announcements and newspapers on the ghetto walls. Later, some of them became active in the preparations for the Warsaw uprising.

One legendary ghetto educator was Dr. Janusz Korczak (Henryk Goldszmit), a Jewish doctor who began working with Jewish and non-Jewish orphans in 1911. In the ghetto he cared for hundreds of children, fighting with the authorities to provide them with food and other basic needs. At the same time he tried to educate the children in humanistic values and to give them a sense of responsibility and human dignity. When the time came for the ghetto orphans to be evacuated and taken to the Umschlagplatz, Korczak and his deputy, Stephania Wilcinska, dressed the children in their best clothes, gave each of them a small sack, and told them that they were going on a trip. Korczak, holding a baby in his arms, led the children in song as they marched to join the rest of the Jews. The Germans offered to allow Korczak to remain in the ghetto, but he refused and accompanied the children to Treblinka, where he died with them.

Theresienstadt

In the Protectorate of Bohemia and Moravia, Jewish children were forbidden to attend non-Jewish schools. There was only one Jewish school in Prague, which belonged to Youth Aliyah and which prepared young Zionists for immigration to Palestine. During the German occupation the school was opened to other children, but it could not accommodate all the Jewish children of Prague. The leadership of the Jewish community, headed by the Zionist Jakob Edelstein, tried to address this dire situation. The Zionist youth movements were recruited to do the educational work, and many classes were soon established in private apartments. Teachers, students, and other members of the movements went from place to place giving lessons to the young. The youth movements organized afternoon activities for the children in places designated by German and Jewish authorities. Children played games, learned songs, even in Hebrew, and played sports.

The decision to establish a ghetto in the Protectorate was taken in October 1941. At a time when hundreds of thousands of Jews had already been shot in the occupied Soviet territories, the Jewish community in the Protectorate felt fortunate to stay in the borders of Bohemia and be transferred to Theresienstadt rather than being sent to camps in Poland. Theresienstadt was unique among the destinations to which the Germans sent Jews in that it functioned both as a concentration camp and as a ghetto. The inmates were allowed to establish a sort of self-government, including a special department for young people and children. A whole educational system was developed in the barracks. The idea was to separate the children from the overcrowded adults, who had no privacy and lived in the worst physical conditions. In the summer of 1942, after the last Czech inhabitant had left the town, the Nazis agreed to allow the children to live in separate housing.

Children's homes were established for older boys and girls (10–15), and later on other homes and also kindergartens were opened for younger children (5–10). By the beginning of 1943, most children had left the barracks and moved to the children's homes and lived separately from their parents. Life there was regulated as in ordinary boarding schools. Classes were held in the mornings, at first clandestinely, as they were forbidden by the Nazi authorities. In the afternoons children joined in social activities, and many even participated in youth movements. Each room—called a *heim* (home)—was a separate social unit that had an instructor in residence. The children were responsible for cleaning the room and bringing food rations from the central kitchen; they created their own rules and even had their own "court of justice" to punish those who broke the community guidelines.

Some homes published their own weekly magazines, in which they expressed their opinions and ideas and shared their experiences with friends. The children were fortunate to have some of the best intellectuals and artists of the ghetto as their teachers, including the famous Bauhaus painter Friedl Dicker-Brandeis, who was brought to Theresienstadt from Germany. She encouraged the children to draw pictures, through which she was able to learn about their inner lives and their problems. The children's paintings were saved and now serve as crucial documentation of life in the ghetto.

The main idea of this educational system was to keep the children away from the miseries of the ghetto, in particular from the distressing human reactions to ghetto conditions. They were not, however, entirely cut off from their families, being obliged to visit their parents at least once a week. One of the educational projects encouraged by the leaders of the youth movement was the Helping Hand, in which the children volunteered to visit lonely and neglected elderly people. They helped the elderly change their bedding, brought them food from the central kitchen, read for them, prepared small gifts for them, and sometimes even entertained them with music. In this way the children were taught not to be self-centered but to have compassion for those who had even less than themselves.

The children had to work several hours a day, part of which was spent cultivating the gardens surrounding the ghetto walls. This gave the children an opportunity to enjoy fresh air for a few hours a day. But when the time came and the transports from Theresienstadt began, the children left their friends in the homes to join their families according to the transport lists and were taken east to Auschwitz-Birkenau.

The Final Solution

Young children were particularly targeted by the Nazis to be murdered. Unlike adolescents and healthy adults, they had little value as slave laborers. Moreover, they posed a particular threat to the Nazis' plan to annihilate the Jewish people, because were they to survive they would grow up to parent a new generation of Jews.

On the way to the concentration and extermination camps, many children suffocated in the crowded cattle cars. At Majdanek and Auschwitz-Birkenau, when the train stopped, those who remained alive were immediately separated from the adults and taken directly to the gas chambers. When an anguished mother protested the separation, she was told to join the child,

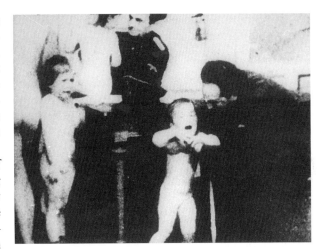

Polish children undergo racial inspection by SS men. 1941–43

and they went together to their deaths. In the other death camps—Treblinka, Sobibor, and Belzec—there was no selection; the children were rushed to their deaths along with their whole family.

At Majdanek and Auschwitz-Birkenau, many of the larger and taller children lied about their age in order to survive the first selection. Boys were sent to the camp barracks together with the adult men; girls joined the adult women. Some parents even managed to hide their children after helping them to pass the selection. Still other children, twins in particular, were chosen to remain alive at Auschwitz by Dr. Josef Mengele, who selected them for so-called medical experimentation. Those picked by Mengele were usually taken to a special hut, where they received better nourishment than the rest of the inmates. Ultimately, however, most of them suffered miserable deaths from infection and other complications of the gruesome experiments. German officers at the camps also sometimes chose boys as their personal servants. Such children were often sexually abused and in camp parlance were called "Piepels," meaning personal boys.

In Auschwitz-Birkenau, special barracks in the women's section B2a housed the children who were subjected to Mengele's experiments. The children were taken to the special barracks during the experiments, and then returned to the regular ones afterward. One of the adult inmates working in the camp painted pictures on the walls to entertain the children.

In general, adult inmates did their best to help the children, often sharing their own scanty food ration.

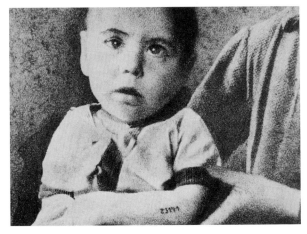

A child inmate with the number 23141 tattooed on his arm.

In their bond with the children, adults found an emotional reason to fight to remain alive. Sometimes a mother and daughter, or father and son, could look after each other, and their mutual mission helped them survive until liberation.

Mainly for propaganda purposes, the transports from Theresienstadt were brought to a special section of Auschwitz-Birkenau. From the fall of 1943, people in these transports were taken to section B2b. Unlike the other prisoners, they did not have to pass through selection and have their heads shaved, and men, women, and children were not separated. Freddy Hirsch, a famous educator in Prague and Theresienstadt, was assigned as the kapo in this annex. He received the camp commandant's consent to open a *Kinderblock* (children's barrack) in one of the empty huts in B2b.

This was a unique phenomenon in the appalling death camp of Auschwitz-Birkenau: hundreds of children going every morning to school, where they sat on the floor in small groups with instructors who told them stories, played games with them, sang and danced with them, and organized parties and plays—all this while the crematoriums were burning the bodies of thousands of other Jews daily. Amid the stench emanating from the crematoriums' chimneys, they celebrated Passover and sang the chorus "Ode to Joy" from Beethoven's Ninth Symphony. Mengele himself came to listen to the children of an "inferior race" sing the verse "All men are brothers."

Section B2b in Auschwitz-Birkenau was dissolved in summer 1944, when most of the families were sent to the gas chambers; some adults were chosen for forced labor, and 96 children aged 15 and 16 were sent to the men's section. Out of 15,000 children from Theresienstadt, only 150 under the age of 16 survived the Holocaust. Most of them died in Auschwitz-Birkenau.

Starving Kozara children in Stara Gradiska concentration camp. Circa 1942

Children in Hiding

When Jewish families realized that they were in mortal danger, many tried to find hiding places, at least for the children. It was easier to find refuge for younger children who were not aware of their Jewishness, especially girls (as boys were circumcised), although few non-Jews were ready to endanger themselves by taking Jewish children into their homes. Other hiding places included religious institutions, such as convents, and boarding schools. The effort to hide Jewish children depended for its successes on the generous humanitarian assistance of non-Jewish underground organizations as well as individuals. In much of Nazi-occupied Europe resistance cells considered the rescue of children to be as important as sabotage activities.

Some children were hidden together with a brother or sister; others had to be separated from siblings in order to find hiding places for all. In France an entire village of 5,000 inhabitants, Le Chambon-sur-Lignon, volunteered to hide a group of children who had escaped from their Jewish children's home just before the Nazis came to deport them.

In Poland—especially in Warsaw—the Polish organization Zegota helped Jewish children to find refuge with families outside the ghetto in the city or in the countryside, especially after the uprising of April 1943. Similar situations arose in Belgium and Holland. The rescuers greatly endangered themselves: whole families faced the death penalty, and sometimes punishment was meted out to the whole block, street, or village. In many cases local collaborators informed on such families, who would then be shot in front of their neighbors as a warning.

After the war, some of the children who had survived in hiding were fortunate enough to be reunited with their parents, or at least with one parent; but in most cases the children were the only survivors in their families. Children rescued by religious institutions had in some cases converted to Christianity. Many children hidden in Christian families were unaware of their Jewish heritage and remained with their foster parents. Sometimes children became so close to their foster parents that they did not want to leave to rejoin their other surviving family members. Several Jewish organizations, especially the Jewish Agency, dedicated themselves to finding hidden Jewish children and restoring them to their birth relatives or delivering them to Jewish orphanages. Youth Aliyah was in charge of children in displaced-persons camps and helped them emigrate to Palestine. More than 50 years after the liberation of Europe, there were still adults who were only just discovering their Jewish origins and being reunited with living relatives.

Nili Keren

Chisinau See KISHINEV

Churchill, Winston Spencer (1874–1965) British prime minister, 1940–45 and 1951–55. See BRITISH POLICY

Cinema and Television In a small way the cinema foretold the Holocaust. Hans Karl Breslauer's silent feature *Die Stadt ohne Juden* (City without Jews), which opened in Vienna in July 1924, proposed a satiric fantasy about contemporary society. Devastated by inflation and incited by the antisemitic "Pan-Germans" in its parliament, the city of Utopia decides to blame and then to banish its Jews. All Jews, even those who have been baptized or who were born of mixed marriages, are sent by rail to Zion—never exactly identified, but shown to be full of Jews, palm trees, and people in Arab headdress. In Jew-free Utopia, things change only for the worse. Unemployment and inflation grow; for lack of customers the fashionable shops, cafés, theaters, and brothels fail. So when the young Jewish hero, disguised behind a moustache as a rich Frenchman, sneaks back with a plan to save Utopia's economy and also his romance with a non-Jewish girlfriend, it proves not so difficult to frustrate the Pan-Germans, turn parliament around, and open a now-grateful Utopia to its returning Jews.

But along with the urbane comedy of *Die Stadt ohne Juden* come an ease with antisemitism and the imposition of racial/religious law, and an image of deportation that should chill any current audience. The trains loading their unwilling passengers might fit a documentary showing transports 20 years later, while the notion of ridding a society of its Jews resonates through the Holocaust and the decades after it.

Questions of whom to get rid of occupied Nazi cinema during the mid-1930s. Educational films depicted the mentally ill, the retarded, and the congenitally deformed, and argued at least for compulsory sterilization. By the late 1930s, when retarded children and adults were being killed, a movie called *Existence without Life* (now in fragments, presented in Joanne Mack's television documentary *Selling Murder: The*

Killing Films of the Third Reich) proposed "deliverance through death" to justify efforts at mass murder. The best-known of these films, Wolfgang Liebeneiner's 1941 *Ich Klage An!* (I Accuse!), remains problematic. Presented as the trial of a doctor accused of the mercy killing of his young wife, who asks to die as relief from incurable sclerosis, the movie questions certain laws. But it is considered far from doctrinaire. The audience is left with a problem, not a solution. And perhaps significantly, its August 1941 release coincided with a temporary suspension of the Nazi euthanasia program.

In 1939 and 1940 there appeared a concentration of antisemitic films, the major examples being Veit Harlan's *Jud Süss* and Fritz Hippler's *Der Ewige Jude* (The Eternal Jew, both released in 1940). Hippler headed the Propaganda Ministry's film division at the time he made his 45-minute "documentary" exposing Jews as vermin, easily recognized in the East but hidden be-hind a veneer of civilization in Germany. Some of Hippler's footage, staged in Polish ghettos, has found its way into later Holocaust cinema, but his film has otherwise passed into obscurity.

Jud Süss, an adaptation (with antisemitic script additions by Joseph Goebbels) of a 1925 Lion Feuchtwanger historical novel about a powerful eighteenth-century German Jew who works his own destruction, received wide distribution. By late 1940 it was playing in more than 60 Berlin theaters. As *Le Juif Süss* it broke box-office records in Vichy France. Heinrich Himmler made it compulsory viewing for German troops, and where death camps were to be located it was shown so as to foster antisemitic sentiment in the local population. As late as the 1960s Arabic-dubbed versions were reported in the Middle East. After the war, to answer for his movie, Harlan stood trial for crimes against humanity. Lack of conclusive proof acquitted him, and he resumed a film career in the 1950s.

To confront Nazi policies, the cinema offered very little. The Soviet film *Professor Mamlock* (1938), directed by Adolph Minkin and Herbert Rappoport, in which a Jewish medical-school professor is forced from his position but remains a loyal German until machine-gunned to death, equates the Nazi treatment of Jews and Communists. That equation became unpopular after the German-Soviet Nonaggression Pact, and *Professor Mamlock* was for a time withdrawn from service. (There is a 1961 East German remake by Konrad Wolf.)

Political considerations of a different sort troubled the release of Charlie Chaplin's *The Great Dictator* (1940). In his 1964 *My Autobiography* Chaplin recounted problems, including President Franklin Roosevelt's worry over possible repercussions in Argentina. Chaplin claimed that when he made the movie he had no idea of the extent of Jewish suffering under the Nazis. But in the United States of 1940 there was still concern not to offend Germany.

Thirteen years after the advent of sound, *The Great Dictator* was Chaplin's first talking picture. As script model he chose the speeches of Adolf Hitler, raised to a maniacal babble in the ravings of Adenoid Hynkel, who, behind his Charlie Chaplin moustache and with his sidekicks Herring and Garbitsch, rules Tomania, dreams of world conquest, and persecutes Jews. In the ghetto lives a modest barber, also played by Chaplin, whose uncanny resemblance to the dictator launches the plot. Chaplin's ghetto is a sentimental simplifica-

Poster for the film *Der Ewige Jude* (The Eternal Jew), a documentary about world Jewry, produced by Fritz Hippler. 1940

tion. But his Hynkel is comic inspiration, and if the movie fails as a plea for peace and tolerance, it succeeds as unequaled political satire.

Because it belongs to the same era as *The Great Dictator,* because it also pits comedy against events overwhelming the world, and because in the context of American brink-of-war cinema it is a masterpiece, Ernst Lubitsch's *To Be or Not to Be* (1942) deserves mention. A Jack Benny comedy set in occupied Warsaw, it was notorious in its day for its bad-taste gags about the camps: "We do the concentrating; the Poles do the camping!" chortles the bug-eyed Nazi colonel "Concentration Camp" Ehrhardt. This is not so much a Holocaust movie (its one identifiable Jew puts the SS down with a bit of Shylock) as a movie that challenges the preconditions for the Holocaust with an excess of theatrical intelligence and civilized style. Thus begins a practice that seems to influence the best of Holocaust film drama, down to and including *Schindler's List.*

Except for a few film clips, some infamous Nazi documentation, and the heart-breaking albums of still photographs that have become the stock images of almost every treatment of the period, the cinema of the Holocaust begins with the work of military film crews—Soviet, American, and British—at the liberation of the camps.

It was the British, under the producer Sidney Bernstein, then with the Ministry of Information, who in April 1945 started filming at Bergen-Belsen three days after the Allies entered the camp. They recorded the most terrible scenes of starvation, bodies stacked in mass graves, crematorium ovens bearing their Topf and Sons manufacturer's name plate, camp personnel forced to drag the dead to burial. The film made of this was never released as planned; the cooling of East-West relations after the war's end again made it expedient not to offend Germans. But there is a print, *Memory of the Camps,* narrated by Trevor Howard, that includes substantial material. More useful, the 1985 British television documentary, *A Painful Reminder,* offers this material along with interviews in Berlin with Bernstein and others who shot the film. Bernstein says it was his friend Alfred Hitchcock who had the material filmed and edited in unusually long takes, typically with a panning camera, so that the Germans and their victims should be seen together and so that viewers would know that the horrors and the juxtapositions were not faked. Hitchcock also included shots of the tranquil, untouched countryside around Bergen-Belsen and created montages of human hair, false teeth, and eyeglasses removed before the killings and preserved by the executioners.

In the decades since the liberation virtually every aspect of the Holocaust that can have been documented on film or videotape has been so recorded. From the very important—such as Alain Resnais's *Night and Fog* (1955) or Claude Lanzmann's *Shoah* (1985)—to the relatively minor, hundreds of such records exist. There has grown up a cottage industry of young filmmakers' returning their parents or grandparents to the ghettos or campsites, or to the farmhouses where they were hidden. Sometimes there is little to say and, often, nothing to see.

But there are substantial ghetto chronicles as well. Alan Adelson and Kathryn Taverna's haunting and original *Lodz Ghetto* (1989) contains unique archival footage and a segment in which Jerzy Kosinski reads the words of Mordechai Chaim Rumkowski, the much-reviled ghetto elder. About the camps themselves, Mike Rossiter's *Nazi Designs of Death* (1994) explores their architecture and construction. Laurence Jarvik discloses the inaction of the U.S. government, and of some prominent American Jews, in *Who Shall Live and Who Shall Die?* (1981). *Escape to the Rising Sun,* another documentary, recalls how Sempo Sugihara, Japan's vice-consul in Kovno, virtually smuggled Jews to Shanghai and Canada by way of Kobe. From Danish television comes *The Power of Conscience* (1994), about the largely successful efforts, perhaps with the tacit approval of German occupation forces, to ferry Jews from Denmark to safety in Sweden. The students of the White Rose, the theologian Dietrich Bonhoeffer, and the officers who plotted against Hitler are all examined in Hava Kohav Beller's *The Restless Conscience: Resistance to Hitler within Germany, 1933–1945.* Jon Blair's *Oskar Schindler,* made for British television, is no match for *Schindler's List* (or for Blair's own later *Anne Frank Remembered*), but it has wonderful interviews with some elderly Jewish women who still find Schindler irresistible, and with the former mistress of the Plaszow camp commandant Amon Goeth, who protests that her lover was no monster because he didn't kill Jews "just for the fun of it." Among the oddest and most appealing of the survivor-interview tapes is *Holocaust Survivors Remember* (1994), from Maine Public Television, in which an uncommonly articulate group of survivors, now long-time New Englanders, seem as involved with the memoirs they are writing as they are with their memories.

But memory remains central to Holocaust documentary, and putting memory on record is the urgent effort of Steven Spielberg's *Survivors of the Holocaust,* an ongoing videotaped oral history project. The key image in all this is the talking head—interviewed survivors and their families—as it has been in most Holocaust documentaries since the 1960s, when the authoritative unseen voice-over narrator faded from the documentary sound track. But the talking head, whether subject of interview or cross-examination, is a more problematic figure than much Holocaust documentary seems to allow.

A curious case in point might be Hans-Jürgen Syberberg's *The Confessions of Winifred Wagner* (1978), in which Richard Wagner's daughter-in-law does not so much "confess" as positively bask in the memory of Adolf Hitler's visits for the annual Bayreuth Festival. By no means a wholly unsympathetic figure (there remain questions of Syberberg's own sympathies here and in his later gigantic studies of Nazi history and mythology), she has of course been set up by her interviewer. But the setup becomes a principal editorial device of the ambitious Holocaust documentarian. By the nature of his project he will be able to film no events, only memories or evasions—and sometimes the drama simply of getting the interview.

The three huge documentaries of Marcel Ophuls, *The Sorrow and the Pity* (1970), *The Memory of Justice* (1976), and *Hotel Terminus: The Life and Times of Klaus Barbie* (1988), all deal with crimes of World War II: French collaboration, the Nuremberg trials, the murder and deportation of French Jews. Each of these films has a second agenda: typically to expose a pattern of guilt running from the past to the present. Either old crimes have gone unpunished, or those who meted out the punishment have gone on to commit equal crimes of their own. For Ophuls, the perpetrators of the Holocaust and American forces in Vietnam fall pretty much into the same compartment.

All the Ophuls documentaries touch on the Holocaust, but *Hotel Terminus* deals with one figure extensively. It is long—more than four hours—ambitious, relentless in pursuing the career, the flight, and finally the trial of Klaus Barbie, the Gestapo chief of Lyons. Never Barbie himself, but everyone around him is questioned—his childhood friends, wartime victims and colleagues, postwar American intelligence contacts, business associates in Bolivia, and finally his lawyer, who declares the conviction a sad day for justice. This is virtuoso filmmaking in its sophistication

and range—and also in its intimacy. Ophuls gets close to his subjects, shares the camera frame with them, probes, cajoles, attempting to construct a continuity between past and present that must not be lost if only because the pain and the guilt remain.

The culmination of all this so far—and maybe for all time, given the ages of Holocaust survivors and their torturers—is Claude Lanzmann's *Shoah.* Nine and a half hours long, it is twice the length of any Marcel Ophuls marathon, and probably twice the length it ought to be. But clearly it means to exhaust its audience. The camera visits Sobibor, Auschwitz, Chelmno, and Treblinka many times; but there is no use of archival footage. Sometimes in these visits, given the destruction of the camps, there will be almost nothing to see. Unlike Ophuls, who tends to uncover the relation of past to present as potential conspiracy, Lanzmann uncovers loss. *Shoah* is the one major documentary to understand the Holocaust as a dreadful, perhaps unfathomable void.

Nevertheless it loads us with information. From Raul Hilberg, interviewed in New England, we learn the economics of transport: group rates on the trains, children under 10 at half fare; the Jews paid. From a former camp guard (recorded surreptitiously; as in a crime melodrama, we enter the surveillance van) we learn that there was a Treblinka marching song—"Franz wrote the words; the melody came from Buchenwald"—and much camp spirit. A survivor details Nazi methods of calming those about to enter gas chambers. Some Poles on a main street say that the Jews had never been a comfortable fit, that they helped bring on their own troubles. An old correspondence informs us that trial and error taught how best to construct a gassing van. The manufacturer was Saurer. A truck passes carrying the Saurer logo. They are still in business.

Lanzmann's interview technique is sometimes devious, as with the Poles, or with a Dr. Grassler, a Nazi deputy in the Warsaw ghetto who now remembers nothing. Sometimes it is straightforward, as with Hilberg and several Israeli survivors who remember everything. And sometimes it is insistent, slightly bullying, as with other survivors, who would rather forget. Lanzmann insists they must remember. Why? Many of the Holocaust documentaries lead to tears—hardly surprising given the subject. But *Shoah* sometimes actively promotes tears, not for sympathy, but as the price to be paid for completing the project.

Completion comes, but slowly, after so many trips to

the gate at Auschwitz, the rail siding at Sobibor, the killing site at Treblinka that is now only a field of monumental stones. By design and by neglect, that is what remains of the Holocaust's places. But such emptiness is also the Holocaust's most eloquent expression. People in the movie experience the Holocaust as a coming of silence: for a former Nazi guard, when there is no more noise from the back of a gas van; for a camp survivor, when the tumult of arrivals at the unloading platform translates within a few hours into silence. The Nazis who conveniently can't remember, the Jews who would rather not remember, fit into a pattern against which the film struggles but to which it must lose. Near the end Lanzmann interviews the former Polish courier Jan Karski, who begged for an Allied response to the Holocaust during the war and who now sits in a handsome apartment, himself reduced to weeping for all he didn't accomplish, and for his memory of the Warsaw ghetto, a world full of people who were only dying. Then comes a last interview, with an Israeli survivor who returned to the ghetto just after the uprising to find the lingering smell of burned flesh, a woman's voice crying somewhere in the rubble, but no visible people. He felt, he said, as if he were the last Jew. With that, and with another shot of a passing train, the film ends.

At another extreme, Alain Resnais's *Night and Fog* is one of the first and, at 31 minutes, one of the shortest films to contemplate the Holocaust. There are no interviews—just a narration written and read by Jean Cayrol, himself a camp survivor. Calmly the film compares the camp sites as they appear in 1955—peaceful, pastoral, empty, shown in soft colors—with the camps at their liberation, the old black-and-white footage, not so familiar in 1955, edited into images of a terrifying beauty.

The film is informative, with an account of the camps and their history. But throughout his career Resnais has been one of cinema's great poets of time. To this particular remembrance of things past, only 10 years past when *Night and Fog* was made, he brings special insight. Where Lanzmann struggles with the process of forgetting, Resnais incorporates forgetting into the structure of his film. Everything of the Holocaust that has been made to disappear now belongs to film, to orders of seeing that can mediate between a dreadful history and a too peaceful present. Unlike *Shoah*, nothing is invisible to *Night and Fog*. But like *Shoah*, its reason for seeing is to stare into the abyss.

It might be argued that fiction film has no business approaching anything so catastrophic as the Holocaust. It might as reasonably be argued that the Holocaust as subject has brought the movies very little besides embarrassment and grief. Any historical theater—stage or screen—prospers most where it can unearth ambivalence: Shakespeare's histories, the John Ford westerns, Alfred Hitchcock's spy films of the Cold War. The Holocaust, whatever drama hovers at its edges, has emerged as such an absolute that the only themes appropriate to it have seemed annihilation, endurance, and escape.

Marvin Chomsky's miniseries *Holocaust: The Story of the Family Weiss* runs for almost eight hours without commercials—though it had commercials when it played on television in 1978. It had a lot else besides. A veritable display case of Holocaust vignettes, it exposes its Berlin Jewish doctor's family to book burnings, Kristallnacht, euthanasia, deportation, Theresienstadt, Auschwitz, Babi Yar, Himmler, Heydrich, Eichmann, the Warsaw ghetto uprising, the escape from Sobibor, the death marches, the gas chambers, and on . . . It is all genuinely earnest and profoundly inauthentic. For good reason, serious critics dismiss it. But it was the broadest education about the Holocaust a generation of Americans might have had, and it told no major lies. Commercial film and television confronting the unspeakable remain commercial film and television. Higher ambitions have not always been more successful.

Stanley Kramer's *Judgment at Nuremberg* (1961) and George Stevens's *The Diary of Anne Frank* (1959) represent higher ambitions with a vengeance. Kramer argues issues of Holocaust responsibility. Stevens, essentially filming a prestigious Broadway play, presents its pathos. *The Diary* was remade, for television, in 1980. But the best treatment of that story, and the best theater, came years later in Jon Blair's *Anne Frank Remembered* (1996), a documentary containing interviews, reading from the diary, and a bit of amateur film showing Anne at an apartment house balcony before the family went into hiding. The heart of the movie is its collection of snapshots of Frank, showing an irrepressible face the camera loves—as surely as the girl must have loved the camera. Next to her, the actress in Stevens's movie, an ethereal Millie Perkins, hasn't a chance. On film the real Anne Frank achieves a posthumous artistic triumph that helps justify the industry of remembrance that has been created in her name.

Sidney Lumet's *The Pawnbroker* (1965) and Alan Pakula's *Sophie's Choice* (1982) carry the memory of the camps into densely overwritten drama of postwar New York City anguish. Daniel Mann's television drama *Playing for Time* (1980), the Holocaust story of the café singer Fania Fénélon, treats its camp as a madhouse where the keepers are all insane. Dr. Josef Mengele especially, with his simpering tender sadism, is casting for a grade-B horror film.

The post-Holocaust adventure films do better. Franklin Schaffner's *The Boys from Brazil* (1978) and John Schlesinger's *Marathon Man* (1976) both make melodrama with the afterlife of Dr. Mengele (fictionalized into a dentist for *Marathon Man*), and both generate an energy from their inventive nonsense, in contrast to the public soul-searching of a Kramer, a Lumet, or a Daniel Mann, that actually feels like the movies.

At least one of the old films gets a curious boost from the passage of time. Stuart Rosenberg's *The Voyage of the Damned* (1976) dramatizes the 1939 voyage of the liner *St. Louis*, which carried well-to-do Jews from Hamburg to Havana and then off into the inhospitable seas of cowardly international diplomacy. The story is well known, and it has been the subject of a documentary. When Rosenberg's movie opened, it received its share of derision—for its inappropriate opulence, its naive narrative, not least for its walk-on celebrity cast of dozens. But cinema recedes in time, and much that had seemed blatant takes on a subtlety not entirely its own. For example, the corrupt Cuban government that refuses landing to the *St. Louis* passengers appears for just a few sequences on screen. But it includes James Mason, Orson Welles, Fernando Rey, and José Ferrer—extraordinary power for Cuba or this movie. Now all those stars have died, though not their performances. We find ourselves experiencing a double history. Hollywood and the Holocaust share the same universe.

In East Germany the Holocaust emerges as a subject just after the war in Wolfgang Staudte's *The Murderers Are among Us* (1946), opposing a former camp commandant and a principled doctor in the ruins of Berlin. Frank Beyer's *Jakob the Liar* (1974) is a rueful fairy story, detailing the loves of some ghetto Jews right up until their deportation. But in a late East German work, Siegfried Kühn's *The Actress* (1988), the fable is both more probable and more fabulous. The background is the Berlin theater, beginning near the close of the 1930s. The actress, a rising star and potentially a Nazi favorite, isn't Jewish; her actor husband is. So she stages her own suicide, darkens her hair, assumes a Jewish identity, and, as an actress, prepares to share in her husband's destruction. This is wildly romantic material, and also rather beautiful. It ends when will and movement end, when there is no more space for performance, no more theater.

Polish cinema has used the Holocaust to study relations between Gentiles and Jews. Andrzej Munk's unfinished *Passenger* (1963) has two women, one an Auschwitz survivor, the other a former guard, who encounter each other on an ocean liner after the war. In Agnieszka Holland's *Angry Harvest* (1985, produced in Germany) a Jewish woman is kept hidden by an initially antagonistic non-Jewish farmer; while the young Jewish hero of Holland's *Europa, Europa* (1990, a French/German co-production) survives among Germans by posing as Aryan, part of the time in the Hitler Youth. And during the Warsaw ghetto uprising, the Jewish heroine of Andrzej Wajda's *Holy Week* (1995) seeks safety with a university friend in a family of intellectuals living almost normally on the Aryan side of the wall.

Probably the most influential Western European film to consider the Holocaust remains Vittorio de Sica's *The Garden of the Finzi-Continis* (1971), in which an aristocratic, very blond, slightly decadent Jewish family experiences isolation and then deportation from Ferrara upon the Nazi occupation in 1943. We see this story in the light of the Holocaust, but the film itself scarcely acknowledges it. The splendid garden, where the young people must play tennis since they have been excluded from the country club, is more than just a symbol for fatal inattention. Along with Nicol, the beautiful, enigmatic daughter of the Finzi-Continis, it is really the film's subject. And with such a langorously beguiling surface the depths must be elsewhere, in everything that has been left out.

In France, the Holocaust figures as deportation, or disguise, or both. Joseph Losey's *Mr. Klein* (1976) is about a Parisian non-Jew with an unfortunate name, who finds himself drawn into the orbit of another—Jewish—Klein, until finally he takes a place in the round-up of Jews at the Vélodrome d'Hiver. That infamous July 1942 event is also the subject of Michel Mitrani's *Black Thursday* (1974), which, like *Mr. Klein*, finds its villains to be the French delivering over their own countrymen. On the other hand, the nine-year-

The German liner *St. Louis* returns to Antwerp after a double Atlantic crossing. The 907 Jewish refugees on board were refused landing in Cuba. This event was dramatized in Stuart Rosenberg's film *The Voyage of the Damned* (1976). 17 June 1939

old hero of Claude Berri's *The Two of Us* (1966) survives the occupation on the farm of an old antisemite who never does learn that the boy he has come to love is Jewish. But the young Jewish students of Louis Malle's more serious *Au Revoir, les Enfants* (1987) will not survive, and neither will the headmaster of their boarding school, a Catholic priest, who tries to protect them. Malle's is the best of this cinema: spare, minimally emotional, truly earning its right to present the Holocaust as a departure rather than as terror.

Michel Drach cast his wife, the actress Marie-Josée Nat, and his young son, as his mother and himself in *Les Violons du Bal* (1973), an autobiographical occupation melodrama about a rather fashionably managed flight from Paris and deportation. Despite an intrusive

framing device—an account of filming and peddling this project in the current French film industry—the actual escape, across France to Switzerland, succeeds in portraying one of the few kinds of victory the occupation allowed.

Another kind of victory, much deeper, motivates *The Last Metro* (1980), one of François Truffaut's last great works. His heroine, a Parisian actress-manager, both keeps her theater open and her Jewish producer-director husband hidden in a room beneath the stage throughout the occupation. As for responses to the Nazis, the film compares a range, from collaboration, to fear, to indifference, to resistance with bombs and bullets. But the key to everything is the theater and its craft. In this, as in many details, Truffaut takes Lu-

bitsch as his model. As in *To Be or Not to Be,* the play-
ers of *The Last Metro* succeed partly just because they
are in a movie and on stage. They can deceive, compromise, play tricks, dazzle—combat bad theater with
good. If all the cinema could do with the Holocaust
were to record or remember, then it would indeed be
helpless. But if the evil might be trapped within a theater not of its own choosing, it might be made to suffer
at least the illusion of defeat. Illusion, not just documentation, is what the movies have to give.

The two most important fiction films confronting
the Holocaust make ample use of theater while keeping
remarkably close to fact. Movies more different than
Heinz Schirk's *The Wannsee Conference* (1984) and
Steven Spielberg's *Schindler's List* (1993) would be
hard to imagine. *Schindler's List* is long, eventful, astonishing in its theatricality. *The Wannsee Conference* is
short (90 minutes, the reported time of the actual con-

Still from the movie *Schindler's List,* 1993.

ference), limited to one event, but also astonishing in
its theatricality. There is no complete transcript of the
Wannsee Conference. According to the film, Reinhard
Heydrich saw to that. But we know who was there, and
why—to implement the Final Solution as of January
1942. In the film, Heydrich, assisted by Adolf Eichmann, controls what is not so much a conference as a
dissemination of plans already made. Of course, questions are raised: logistics, record-keeping, financial responsibility. An SS officer approves the Final Solution's "elegance" with perhaps too much gusto. One
official actually tries to protect mixed marriages and
their offspring. But with tact, good humor, authority,
and charm, Heydrich disposes of everything—and
even manages a public flirtation with an attractive
young secretary. Schirk's camera attends the conference in rapid pans and tracking shots, moving us
through and out almost before we know it. Things
could hardly have been more agreeable. There is good
brandy and a light meal at the end. There is no moral-
izing or editorial distancing, or even too great a shock
at such cheerful efficiency. Anything we might feel
about perhaps the worst 90 minutes in human history
we shall not be pushed to feel. The film stands to one
side of its dreadful knowledge. For knowing about the
Holocaust, as the cinema can know it, this is in one way
exactly right.

Another way, in *Schindler's List,* has provided the
most authoritative movie-making yet about the Holocaust. Of Oskar Schindler and his Jews much is known,
though the motives for his goodness remain obscure.
Except for one sentimental misstep near the end, when
Schindler breaks into tears because he had done too
little to help save Jews, the film has the sense to leave
his motives that way. Schindler is a closely observed
enigma, as is the grandly sadistic commandant of the
Plaszow camp, Amon Goeth. They are as much cre-
ations of the cinema as figures in history—complex
presences, but of no analyzable psychological depth
at all.

Schindler's List is in one sense an utter anomaly: a
Holocaust movie with a happy ending. There may have
been only one such story in the Holocaust, this story.
And choosing it may owe as much to a genius for show-
manship as to a passion for telling the world some
truth. For all its fervor, its extraordinary educational
fulfillment, this is a Steven Spielberg movie. And like
The Wannsee Conference, it too sees in the Holocaust a
chance for theater. The great set pieces—the sacking

of the Kraków ghetto, the selections and the escape to the Plaszow latrines, the human target practice of Goeth; Schindler's kiss; the typing of the list; the women's shower at Auschwitz that turns out to be . . . a shower; the postscript in Israel, in color, with cast members leading Schindler's Jews, now grown old, to the real Oskar Schindler's grave—these extraordinary demonstrations are also cunning devices, coups de théâtre that happen wonderfully to be true.

With some exceptions, the Holocaust has not inspired a major cinema. By its nature it has tended to use the movies for testimonial, even in the fiction film. The Holocaust both confounds the imagination and stifles it. Given that history, what mere movie could be important enough? As a result, few movies have been important enough; some of the best have discovered strategies for skirting the subject, avoiding "importance." Some of the very best have taken the subject head on and then transformed it into cinema. That may require the meeting of a Schindler and a Spielberg—not too likely again in the near term. Yet the faces, the photographs that look out to us from the books and the museum walls deserve something besides promises never to forget. Forgetting is inevitable anyway. No coming generation will know the Holocaust except as history, increasingly remote. If there can be a vital integration of that past with any future present, it will be by way of art. Film is a uniquely time-bound art: compare the experience of old movies with the experience of equally old paintings or books. But it is exactly cinema's fragility that may suggest a common space. This was the first great human catastrophe to have so many pictures taken of it. Moving pictures ought not to be far behind.

Roger Greenspun

Clauberg, Carl (1898–1957) SS official, physician, leading figure in the so-called medical experiments conducted at Auschwitz. Clauberg was sentenced to 25 years in prison in the Soviet Union after the war but was released in 1955. He died in a German hospital shortly before a new trial against him was to begin. See MEDICAL EXPERIMENTATION

Collaboration *Collaboration* became a political term with moral implications after the conquest of France by Germany in 1940. At least initially, the term was used by the parties who cooperated with the Germans. At the meeting between Adolf Hitler and the head of the Vichy regime, Marshal Philippe Pétain, in Montoire (24 October 1940), the French leader spoke about "collaboration in principle." Pétain's appearance on the radio after the meeting placed collaboration in the collective awareness. As the German occupation continued and the steps taken by the German forces alienated a growing part of the French population, the term took on an increasingly negative hue. Soon it was adopted throughout German-occupied Europe to denote active cooperation with the enemy. In 1944, after the liberation of France, *collaboration* received legal definition. After about 50,000 persons had been accused of collaborating with the Germans, the French courts discovered that this particular crime did not figure in the legal codex. Therefore in October 1944 a parallel judicial system was set up to deal with collaboration, with the High Court of Justice as its apex. Three levels of collaboration were defined: (1) sharing of intelligence with the enemy, or acts damaging the external security of the state; (2) actions revealing the intention of aiding the enemy; and (3) acts of national unworthiness—*indignité nationale*—such as aid to Germans and damage to the unity of the nation, the liberty of the French people, or equality among them. This set of definitions covered pro-Nazi heads of state as well as petty informers.

The complex nature of Hitler's war policy created a distinction between typical forms of treason and the phenomenon of collaboration. For Hitler the war served ideological and national aims as well as providing for territorial expansion. Hence it was possible for someone to collaborate with the Germans on the economic level and yet to see himself or herself as a patriot. Another distinction between traditional treason and collaboration is that treason is conceived as individual acts, whereas the essence of collaboration is its institutional character.

There were four main types of collaboration: accommodation, administrative collaboration, economic cooperation, and ideological collaboration. Accommodation was a psychological attitude, adopted mainly by the elite in Western Europe during the first period after a national army's defeat, of accepting German political and military hegemony and willingly seeking a modus operandi with the victors. The attitude was based on the presumption of the totality and immutability of German domination. If psychologically it stemmed from the trauma of the defeat, its theoreticians endeavored to base it on long-range developments. In a book published in 1942 Dirk Jan de Geer, the former Dutch prime minister who had tried to mediate a peace between Great Britain and Germany after the fall of France, presented accommodation as a natural continuation of the prewar mood of appeasement, "the spirit of Munich." The progenitors of accommodation viewed their attitude as a convergence between the traditional political institutions of the West and the new totalitarian system and tended to abandon democratic institutions. The Western accommodationists expressed their tendencies in mass organizations, which combined accommodation with radical anticommunism, social conservatism, and traditional nationalism. In the Netherlands the Nederlandse Unie was the largest mass movement in Dutch history until it was prohibited by the German authorities in December 1941. In defeated France the political conservatives supported the Vichy government because of similar views and sentiments. The spirit of accommodation was widespread among the parliamentary right wing, which feared the left, was scornful of "democratic corruption," and believed in the fascist future. This did not prevent the Germans from being contemptuous of their French adherents. This combination did not exist in Eastern Europe. The right wing there, deeply religious and extremely nationalistic, could not accommodate the antireligious policies of the Nazis and the German denigration of their countries. Unlike in the West, where the conquered population preserved some vestiges of autonomy, in the East the Germans demanded total and unconditional servitude and hence left no scope for willing accommodation.

Administrative collaboration was the most usual and natural form of collaboration, for it was accepted by the population as an instrument of German rule and as the last resort of self-government. The boundaries between those two aspects of the administrative collaboration were blurry and depended on local German policies. In 1941 Werner Best, the chief legal adviser to the SS, defined the relations between Germany and the conquered states of Europe: "The hegemonic state [i.e., Germany] limits itself . . . to the establishment of a supervisory administration . . . for watching over the entire administration of the state." His memorandum differentiates between allied administrations, supervised administrations, governmental administrations, and colonial administration in the East.

The idea of administrative collaboration predated the war, for as early as 1937 the Belgian government published guidelines for civil-service behavior in the case of war, in which civil servants were required to stay on their posts for the good of their compatriots. They should resign only if their continued service would conflict with their patriotic duty. In the Netherlands the defeated nation's escaping cabinet transferred its powers to the Council of Secretaries-General, a body of senior civil servants that had existed (in a different form) since 1902. This institution, initially headed by the Dutch commander in chief, Gen. Henri Gerard Winkelman, but later acting under the auspices of the German authorities, worked under the provision of not damaging Dutch national interests. The existence of the codex of rules that enabled the smooth administrative transition from an independent state to the occupied provinces of the Nazi empire, coupled with moral limits, however vague, presents a major obstacle to defining the boundaries of unlawful collaboration.

The four categories in Best's administrative topology were defined according to the German interest in exploiting Europe at the lowest price and with the least resistance. Denmark, the model protectorate, kept all its symbols and institutions of national independence until the summer of 1943, when it became another occupied part of the German *Grossraum*. Those who continued their cooperation after this date were described as collaborators. A similar transformation occurred in Hungary in March 1944 and in Slovakia in the summer of the same year. In Vichy France, even before that state lost its partial independence in November 1942, the police cooperated with SS emissaries in deporting Jews to the death camps; indeed, the Vichy governments on their own had inaugurated anti-Jewish actions before there were any German demands. The Vichy authorities also shipped Spanish republican fugitives to Germany, whence they were transported to Auschwitz.

In those occupied states under German administration, the occupying forces sought to increase the scope of cooperation by promoting to the leading posts those nationals who were totally committed to Nazi Germany. The local police forces assisted in mass deportations of Jews and politically undesirable elements. Despite this collaboration the degree of self-management decreased over the course of the war, so that by war's end it was a mockery. The governmental administration prevented any self-rule: native officials who remained in their posts became cogs of occupying administration. The Polish administration functioned only in rural areas, where its members had to prove personal allegiance to the Nazis. In the Soviet and Serbian territories the local population was persecuted by civilian, military, and SS authorities. The purpose, beyond the economic exploitation and prevention of resistance, was also the decimation of the local population, leaving no place for local administrators. Although differing in the depth of the German intervention, in the long range the four types of administrative collaboration served the same purpose: to promote German rule based on Nazi ideology and race. That purpose was interpreted differently by various German agencies, which activated other segments of the local administration. Throughout Nazi-dominated Europe the SS and SD used the local police forces, and the German civil and military garrison administration exploited the local officialdom, fighting each other in the process. The conflict over ways to achieve the long-range Nazi aims, and the inner struggle for influence in the ruling group, were carried out directly in the East and indirectly in the West through various institutions of the local administration, molding the power hierarchy in this entity and terrorizing the population.

Economic exploitation, vital for the German war effort and for the continuing support of the German masses for the Nazi leaders, was often disguised as economic cooperation. The term *economic cooperation* describes only those economic relations based on a negotiation according to the rules of the free market. Cooperation was also necessary for the survival of the subjugated population, but the captains of industry in the occupied countries were not above profiting from it. They claimed that without cooperation to maintain the health of the German economy, the occupied nations would be exposed to famine, as happened to the Dutch population during the general strike in September 1944. They also claimed that economic cooperation helped prevent German industry from taking over and dismantling local businesses. Even if those claims were true, the scope of industrial cooperation went far beyond the limits of exigency. French industrialists signed an agreement with the Germans to supply raw materials necessary for aircraft production. Eventually French industry became the largest partner, among the occupied nations, in the German war effort: half of all French production went to Germany. Similarly, by 1944 about half of Dutch industrial pro-

duction was designated for German customers. About 80 percent of Belgium's coal production was shipped to Germany, as was most of the Danish agricultural production—much more than the quotas stipulated in German agreements with those countries. Western European industry not only hoped to supply the German military market but also to join the Germans in their exploitation of the East. In December 1941 Danish ventures were founded for the promotion of "initiatives in Eastern and Southeastern Europe." The Danish eagerness was thwarted by the Germans, who refused to take partners in their planned exploitation of Eastern Europe.

The European labor force also tried to exploit the new employment opportunities. The military mobilization of millions of German workers created a strong labor market in the occupied nations, which had suffered high unemployment in the 1930s. Although the Germans filled the void with prisoners of war, slave labor, and conscript workers, a large demand remained, especially for professionals. Many workers in the occupied countries, having to choose between unemployment at home and well-paid jobs in Germany, preferred the latter. Among 2.1 million non-German workers who volunteered to work in Germany, there were 1 million Poles, 59,000 French, 122,000 Belgians, and 93,000 Dutch. Besides those who were employed in Germany, the Germans hired many workers in the occupied countries for Organisation Todt, established to build military infrastructure and fortifications. In Belgium alone Organisation Todt employed 82,000 workers. The German railway hired thousands of foreign workers to operate military transports and the trains that carried Jews and other persecuted peoples to the extermination camps. On the eastern front, menial workers, called Hiwis, toiled in the compounds of the combat units. The Hiwis, recruited from among Soviet prisoners of war or the local population, did not work for wages; they also served the Germans as a recruiting pool for the local police and for jobs in the concentration camps. Appearing in the first months of the German-Soviet war, according to the German estimates in July 1943 they numbered more than 1 million persons. Economic collaboration, both by industrialists and by workers, was an outcome not only of the wish for personal survival but also of the desire to enjoy the economic fruits of the new German empire.

The term *collaboration* also has ideological and political dimensions. The eclectic features of Nazi ideology made it possible for some political organizations in occupied countries to establish relations with the Nazi party while remaining opposed to the main tenets of Nazism. Among such collaborators were nationalists who, while opposing German rule in every possible way, accepted German activity in a particular field. A segment of the Polish underground army (the NSZ), while fighting the German forces, took an active part in the Nazi extermination of the Jews in Poland. Similarly, an authoritarian nationalist wing cooperated with the Germans in order to fulfill national inspirations; they planned to found their states on an authoritarian base, following the Nazi model, to ensure internal stability and order. This group of "patriotic traitors" included the conservative nationalists in Eastern Europe, such as Miklós Horthy in Hungary or Ion Antonescu in Romania, as well as Vichy supporters and conservative politicians in smaller Western states. These respected politicians discovered too late the gap between their national inspiration and German aims, for they were disposed of by their German masters after they outlived their utility. Another group of right-wing politicians welcomed the defeat of their national armies as a chance for national reconstruction. In the wake of the French defeat, Vichy's foreign minister, Paul Baudouin, declared in an interview, "Twenty years of uncertainty, discontent . . . paved the way for total revolution." The general attitude of this group was to revitalize their national institutions along Nazi lines, in order to establish a national regime as successful as the Nazis' in Germany. The exemplar of this way of thinking was the Norwegian politician Vidkun Quisling. Upon the German invasion of Norway in April 1940, Quisling, leader of the National Union party, proclaimed a new, Nazi-style government that would maintain friendly relations with Germany but not be subordinated to it. Quisling presumed that his government would establish relations with Germany similar to those of fascist Italy, but he underestimated Norwegian popular resistance to his regime and misunderstood the German structure of subjugation and exploitation. Within a week, the Quisling government was replaced by an administrative council under the direction of a German commissioner. Political collaborators in the occupied countries also played down the implications of Nazi racial theory. Vichy France, for example, could not long remain partners with Germany, for the Nazi ideology held the French to be racially inferior. The Germans willingly let the illu-sions of partnership flower in the short term, while Germany was establishing hegemony over Europe.

The most extreme group of collaborators were those political leaders who were nominated to their posts by the occupying forces and hence depended on German support for their political and personal survival. Some of the collaborators began as genuine nationalists, believing that the Germans would help them fulfill their aspirations to national independence. But as these hopes ran counter to the interests of the states who prosecuted the war against Germany, the nationalists were pushed into the German embrace: they became unconditional instruments of Nazi policy, with no room for autonomous action. This fate was shared by Ukrainian nationalists, such as Stepan Bandera and Andry Melnyk, commanders in the anti-Soviet Russian army of Gen. Andrei Vlasov, and some of the leaders of national minorities in Soviet-occupied territories.

Whereas these leaders were victims of a political trap they dug for themselves, the local fascist movements that collaborated with the Germans were fully aware of the implications of their choice. Yet despite the willing cooperation of the fascist movements, the German occupying forces tended to ignore them, preferring to deal with the right-wing conservative parties that enjoyed broader popular support. After the German experience with Quisling, a Norwegian fascist who disagreed with the German plans for his country, Hitler never again promoted fascist leaders in the West to positions of real power. In spite of their total collaboration with the Germans, the Dutch fascist leader Anton Mussert, the Danish Fritz Clausen, Léon Degrelle in Belgium, and Jacques Doriot in France never gained real power in their countries, which remained solidly in German hands. The fascist movements in Eastern Europe, such as the Arrow Cross in Hungary, became political powers only on the eve of the German collapse. The only fascist movement in power throughout the war, the Ustasha in Croatia, achieved this status because Croatia was a buffer state. All the variations of collaboration were based on the conjunction between German interests and the collaborators' illusory hopes to use their countries' defeat to advance their ideological programs.

An agenda for collaboration was nonexistent for the Jews in occupied Europe. By physically segregating them from the Christian population, the Nazis removed the Jews from European economic and legal systems without granting them autonomy. The Nazi ideology that demonized the Jews prevented collaboration in any accepted sense of that term. Still, in the early stages of the war, when the overt Nazi policy was to encourage Jewish emigration from Europe and before the Nazi program of extermination was in place, some degree of Jewish cooperation with German directives was possible. Throughout the existence of the ghettos, the Germans conveyed to the Jews the understanding that their aim was to make the Jewish community more "productive." The goals of emigration and productivity were accepted, even striven for, by some Jews, who believed that cooperation in their attainment would forestall more severe anti-Jewish measures. Recognition of this context is necessary for any discussion of purported Jewish collaboration.

Accommodation in Jewish society differed from collaboration among other Europeans in that the Jews could not presume to establish conditions for long-term coexistence with Nazi rule. Once all avenues of emigration were closed, they hoped to find the means to outlive the Nazis—*iberleben,* as it was called in Yiddish. Jewish accommodation was a way of surviving until an outside power would, in the near future, restore civilization.

From the onset of the Nazi regime in Germany in 1933 until the early stages of the war in 1939–40, the German Jewish self-governing institutions and the Nazi administrative organs colluded to achieve the same goal—Jewish emigration from Germany. Although almost all Jewish organizations were committed to encouraging emigration from Germany, the right-wing State Zionists organization demanded total and immediate evacuation to Palestine. In order to achieve its goal, its leader, Georg Kareski, not only turned to the German organs (especially the Gestapo) for support but also used in his correspondence quasi-Nazi terminology, becoming the best-connected Jewish leader in the country. In spite of his efforts and Nazi support, he failed, and the onus of organizing Jewish emigration to Palestine fell to another group, the Jewish youth organization Hehalutz. Eventually 235,000 German Jews emigrated, mainly to Palestine. In Austria, after the Anschluss, the Jewish community—especially the Palestinian Office, which was also responsible for Hehalutz—cooperated with the SS-organized Central Bureau for Jewish Emigration, led by Adolf Eichmann. The Central Bureau, which later became an instrument for deportation to Poland, not only enjoyed Jewish cooperation but was even suggested by the Jewish leadership. From the Jewish point of view this cooperation with the SS was justified, as the number of German and Austrian Jews who emigrated to Palestine and elsewhere was higher than in any other part of Nazi-occupied Europe. This achievement was emulated elsewhere. In the wake of the conquest of Poland, both the Zionist leaders and prominent hasidim turned to the SS commanders to allow Jewish emigration. But as the Nazi Jewish policy changed and support for Jewish emigration from Europe ended, the German government in Poland ignored these appeals. Even after implementation of mass extermination had begun, Jews in occupied lands pleaded for emigration. In Slovakia, during the late summer of 1942, after the deportation of two-thirds of the native Jews, a "working group" led by Rabbi Michael Dov Ber Weissmandel and his cousin, the Zionist activist Gisi Fleischmann, contacted the SS officer Dieter Wisliceny with a proposal to collect money from world Jewry to buy freedom for the remaining Slovakian Jews. After the Warsaw ghetto uprising some prominent Jews accepted German promises of free emigration and left their hideouts for the Vittel camp in France, only to be sent to their deaths in Auschwitz. In spite of these failures, the further evidence of this method occurred in Hungary in 1944, in the midst of the extermination of Hungarian Jews. While hundreds of thousands were sent to Auschwitz, two leaders in different countries—the Hungarian Zionist leader Rudolf Kasztner and the Swiss politician Jean-Marie Musy on behalf of the Orthodox rescue committee—negotiated with high-ranking Nazis for the release of several trainloads of Hungarian Jews to be transported to Switzerland. Those limited successes only emphasize the general failure after 1939 of the policy of accommodation.

Whereas accommodation translated a general mood into organized political activity, administrative collaboration was an act of deliberate political decision. Unlike the occupied nations of Europe, which had civil administrations in place at the time of the German takeover, the Jews had no state. Hence Jewish administrative bodies had to be created by the Germans to serve their own needs. Such bodies in Germany and Austria were supposed to pave the way for emigration from Europe, while the organs of Jewish administration in Poland—the *Judenräte*—were established to carry out whatever directives the Germans might issue. In this restricted sense the Judenräte may be considered an embodiment of administrative collaboration.

The Judenräte fulfilled two contradictory roles: their activities were indispensable for the survival of the ghetto dwellers, as without them the inhabitants would have died soon after building the ghetto walls, but at the same time they served as a necessary tool for the Germans. In the first months after their establishment, there was often little contradiction between the two roles. From mid-1941, when many labor camps were established, to mid-1942, when the Final Solution began to be carried out in the Generalgouvernement, the Judenräte helped to preserve social quiet and a feeling of normalcy—even as the mass exterminations were being planned on the basis of data gathered by the Judenräte. The existence of the Judenräte insulated life in the ghetto from most contact with the German ghetto administration, which restricted its communication with Jews in the ghettos to announcements of death sentences and other penalties.

The complicated character of the Judenräte is almost entirely absent with regard to the ghetto police. Although founded to be an executive arm of the Judenräte, its double subordination to the ghetto administration and to the SS organs, as well as its age, social composition, and inbred cult of might, caused it to be a more compliant instrument in the ghetto's liquidation. The Jewish police collected deportees for the death camps, assisted the Germans at the train depots, and fought Jewish opposition. In many ghettos, where during the mass deportations the traumatized Judenräte collapsed, the police became the sole site of power, in some cases usurping authority even before the deportations began. Police actions reflected not only the power struggle inside the ghetto, in which the institution committed to deeper collaboration was destined to win, but also the infighting among their German superiors, where the winners were the more extreme and dedicated elements, usually from the SS ranks. The relations between the SS masters and their Jewish servants were contradictory and unstable. In the majority of cases the SS defended the policemen and their families until the last stages of the ghetto's existence. But in the Vilna ghetto, in December 1941, the SD executed its Jewish staff as proof to its competitors from the ghetto German administration that it was possible to operate with smaller Jewish staffs. The three levels of administrative collaborators—Judenrat officials, the police, and Gestapo operatives—symbolized the tragedy of the ghettos, the inevitability of their destruction, and the power games of the Nazi establishment dedicated to the extermination of the Jews.

Economic cooperation was viewed in a different light by the Germans and the Jews. For the Germans, the two main economic values, capital and property on one hand and labor on the other, were entities to be transferred from the Jews to the Germans automatically and unconditionally. Since 1939 the Nazi laws of Jewish property (the so-called aryanization laws) made many types of Jewish ownership illegal and demanded the transfer of property to non-Jews. At the same time Jews in Germany with outside support endeavored to make this transfer negotiable and thereby ease the path of emigration. The Nazi regime was compelled to endow its overt policy of encouraging emigration with a cloak of legality. This guise, preserved to some extent in the West, was disposed of in the East, where a policy of total expropriation of Jewish property without any compensation was firm, and the only limitation was personal unauthorized acquisition. Thus economic collaboration between the Jewish communities and the Nazis is an illustration of the relations between the robbed and the robbers.

To the Nazis, the Jews in the ghettos were just one part of a forced-labor system that included prisoners of war, concentration camp inmates, and other conscripts transferred from occupied Europe to Germany or put to work in their home countries. Toward the end of the war, forced labor in Germany accounted for 9 million workers—20 percent of the labor force. The Germans used Jewish labor in several ways. After the conquest of Poland, Jews were rounded up on the streets and conscripted for menial jobs in army installations. In an effort to alleviate the terror of these random conscriptions, the Judenräte offered to supply the Germans with Jewish workers, who were then sent to labor camps operated by the army. The Jews in the East included many artisans with skills not widely represented in the general population, and the Germans decided to take advantage of this concentration of talent by establishing factories in the ghetto. These modes of employment were a compromise between the needs of the German war economy and the Nazi ideological aim to exterminate the Jews. The outcome was the result of a struggle for power between the Wehrmacht and the economic establishment on one hand and the SS on the other.

The Judenräte were largely unaware of this power struggle and the decision to annihilate European Jews. They believed in the economic rationalism of the Ger-

CONCENTRATION CAMPS

mans and in their ability to convince their masters of the necessity of ghetto industry. They equated their ability to contribute to the German war effort with survival, and they endeavored to convey this view to both the German administration and the ghetto population. The famous example of the Lodz ghetto, which survived into the summer of 1944, and of the ghetto's leader, Mordechai Chaim Rumkowski, emphasizes this attitude. In his speech of February 1941 Rumkowski, a leading proponent of the slogan "Survival through labor," proclaimed: "My cry is to give work to as many people as possible." The Judenräte's leaders hoped to convince the Germans to enlarge the ghettos' industries; they saw their actions as normal commercial negotiations, and the ruthless exploitation of the ghetto as economic cooperation. The last stage of ghetto existence was the transformation of the ghetto into a labor camp centered around a factory, but even this move did not save its inmates from extermination.

Whereas in occupied Europe some groups and individuals tied their fortunes to those of the Nazis, either out of a belief in German invincibility or because of fascist leanings, among the Jews ideological collaboration with a power that swore their extermination was very rare. In spite of this obvious attitude, there were three circumstances of activities that belong in this category. First, after the Nazis gained power in Germany, the Zionist Revisionist party tried to approach the Nazis in order to organize a mass Jewish evacuation from Germany by using fascist terminology and dwelling on an ideological affinity between the two parties. Second, because during World War I the German army had allowed unrestrained cultural and political activity among the Jews in Poland and Russia, some Polish Jews viewed all Germans, including the Nazis, in a favorable light, and after the German invasion of September 1939 they went to work for them, whether openly or clandestinely. One of the most notorious of these was Alfred Nossig, who spied for the Gestapo in the Warsaw ghetto and was executed for his activities by the Jewish Fighting Organization in 1943. The most famous, largest, and best-documented case of ideological collaboration was the Gestapo network in the Warsaw ghetto, the so-called Thirteen (from its headquarters on Leszno Street), led by Abraham Gancwajch. The network operated a number of economic and cultural organizations, and its core was composed of refugees from outside Warsaw. Its ideology was based on Nazi publications from the prewar period, which presented the establishment of the ghetto as an opportunity to create a pure, uncontaminated Jewish culture and as the preamble to a mass evacuation of the Jews from Europe. The Thirteen counted on German victory, propagating anti-Soviet and anti-Slavic attitudes. Supported by the SD, it often was at loggerheads with the Judenrat and the police. After the Warsaw uprising it disappeared without a trace.

After the expulsion of the Wehrmacht from occupied Europe, the liberated nations began to hunt down and try those suspected of collaboration with the Germans. The definition of collaboration and the numbers of those accused reflected the power relations in a given area, the events of the immediate past, and the patterns for future politics. England executed the broadcaster of Radio Berlin, the infamous "Lord Haw-Haw," but absolved from the crime of collaboration the officials of the Channel Islands, which had been occupied by the Germans. The French government detained thousands of women who had consorted with the Germans but closed their eyes to the acts of Vichy leaders. In Eastern Europe all the non-Communists were suspected of collaboration and prosecuted. After the establishment of the state of Israel in 1948, the Knesset adopted a law allowing the prosecution of Nazi war criminals as well as those who collaborated with the Nazis in their crimes. Under this law John Demjanjuk was extradited from the United States and put on trial as "Ivan the terrible," a Ukrainian collaborator who served as a guard in the Treblinka extermination camp. (The Israeli Supreme Court later overturned his 1988 conviction on the ground of evidence that Demjanjuk may not have been Ivan.) Also, close to forty Jews were convicted of "assisting the Nazis" and sentenced to imprisonment. In the West and in Israel such trials served as a method of national catharsis, whereas in Eastern Europe they became a tool for legitimizing the new Communist regimes.

Eli Tzur

Concentration Camps Shortly after the Nazis came to power in 1933, they developed a new tool of political persecution—the concentration camp system. The first of these camps, Dachau, opened in early March 1933, when the prisons became overcrowded with political and ideological opponents of the regime. The first prisoners were primarily Communists, Social Democrats, and other political enemies of nazism who were seen as being in need of political reeducation.

A section of Bergen–Belsen concentration camp. After 15 April 1945

Former prisoners of the "little camp" in Buchenwald stare out from the wooden bunks. Elie Wiesel is pictured in the second row of bunks, seventh from the left, next to the vertical beam. 16 April 1945

Women suffering from typhus and dysentery at the now liberated camp of Bergen-Belsen. 28 April 1945

Within one year the Nazi SS had become the dominant force in running the concentration camps, having pushed the regular police out of its supervisory role and set up detention centers separate from prisons. In 1934 SS chief Heinrich Himmler gained control of the camps and established a uniform system regarding the admission and supervision of prisoners. The SS gave the camp commandants supreme authority over the meting out of punishments, including the death penalty.

Between 1936 and 1941 new economic objectives and new categories of prisoners led to a considerable rise in the number of inmates, from approximately 7,000 at the beginning of 1937 to almost 25,000 at the beginning of the war and close to 75,000 by the middle of 1941. During this period camp conditions deteriorated rapidly, primarily where the prisoners worked at forced labor, mainly in quarries and the construction of camps, including Buchenwald and Mauthausen. With the outbreak of war the mobilization of labor in these camps in the hope of a speedy victory led to the deaths of thousands of prisoners, particularly those considered racially inferior, such as Jews and Poles.

From 1938 on, large groups of Jewish prisoners had been brought to concentration camps, particularly after the November pogroms (Kristallnacht). As the camp population changed from "asocials" and "criminals" to Jews, the camps took on new functions, and living conditions became subhuman. A change in the orientation of the camps occurred only after 1942, when economic considerations prevailed and the labor potential of the camps became integrated into the private sector of the economy. An increasing number of prisoners were now engaged at skilled labor in a central production sector. Major corporations operating factories in or near the camps sometimes took over the feeding and housing of the prisoners and therefore shared in the responsibility for their fate. Meanwhile, with the expulsion of Jews from the Reich, those in concentration camps were removed to Poland, primarily to extermination and labor centers.

During the final period of the war the concentration camps were spread over the entire area of the Reich and the occupied territories. By 1944 the number of inmates had risen to 600,000 and included numerous nationalities, with Soviet prisoners forming the target group. Toward the end of the war, as the Nazi infrastructure was breaking down and when some of the camps were being dissolved, the SS attempted to maintain the concentration camp system and even tried to set up a new camp in late 1944. Thus we see how political persecution, economic manipulation, and ideological extermination came together in what more than one prisoner termed the concentration camp universe. *Judith Tydor Baumel*

Cracow See KRAKÓW

Croatia See YUGOSLAVIA

Czechoslovakia See BOHEMIA AND MORAVIA, PROTECTORATE OF

Czerniakow, Adam (1880–1942) Head of the Warsaw *Judenrat* (Jewish council), which was responsible for the feeding, health care, housing, sanitation, and economic activity of the Jews in the Warsaw ghetto. Czerniakow tried to prevent the Germans from controlling the day-to-day activities in the ghetto, but his close contact with the authorities led to accusations of collaboration. When the Germans ordered Czerniakow to assist in the round-up of all Jews—including children—for deportation, he committed suicide rather than comply. His diary was discovered in the 1960s.

Czernowitz See CERNAUTI

D

Dachau Town north of Munich, site of the first major concentration camp, which became the model for later camps. Established in March 1933 to intern political prisoners (although by the end of the war about one-third of the inmates were Jews) and liberated in April 1945. Prisoners functioned as slave laborers at armament factories. Of the approximately 200,000 prisoners interned throughout Dachau's 12 years at least 32,000 died of starvation and disease, including the 1945 typhus epidemic. Others were killed in experiments or transported to extermination camps. See Medical Experimentation

Daluege, Kurt (1897–1946) SS general, chief of German police, deputy head of occupation administration in the Protectorate of Bohemia and Moravia, and Reichsprotektor during the 1942 Lidice massacre, in which the Czech town was destroyed and all the inhabitants killed or deported. Executed as a war criminal in 1946.

Dannecker, Theodor (1913–45) Senior SS official in charge of deportation of Jews from France, Bulgaria, and Italy to the extermination camps in Poland. Committed suicide in an American prison in December 1945. See France; Italy

Death Marches As the Soviet army approached the death camps, the surviving inmates were evacuated and forced to walk to the west. Thousands were shot because they were too weak or ill to walk; others died of starvation, disease, and exposure. Of 66,000 evacuated from Auschwitz about 15,000 died. Death marches also took place from other camps, such as Dachau, Mauthausen, Ravensbrück, and Neuengamme and from cities such as Budapest. Prisoners from Stutthof, Gross-Rosen, Buchenwald, Sachsenhausen, and Magdeburg and from the region of Bessarabia were simi-

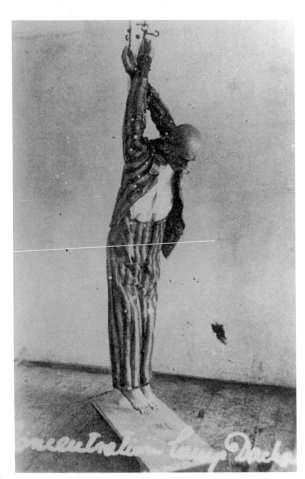

A prisoner in Dachau being tortured by the SS.

larly evacuated. In the last two months of the war 250,000 prisoners were sent on such marches. See Auschwitz

Death Toll Although the number of persons killed in the Holocaust has been a subject of discussion since

Survivors of a death march from Buchenwald to Laufen, near Munich. From a group of 1,500 prisoners only these few survived. The donor, Sam Shear (originally from Bedzin, Poland), is pictured in the bottom row, second from the right. April 1945

Prisoners on a death march from Dachau move south along Noerdliche Muenchner street in Gruenwald. German civilians secretly photographed several death marches from the Dachau concentration camp as the prisoners moved slowly through the Bavarian towns of Gruenwald, Wolfrathshausen, and Herbertshausen. Few civilians gave aid to the prisoners on the death marches. 29 April 1945

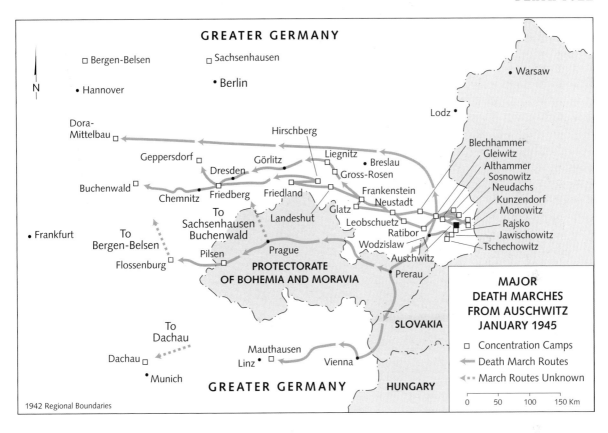

the end of World War II, the round figure of 6 million admits of no serious doubt. An interest in minimizing the estimate of the number of victims ranges from radical right-wing apologists for national socialism to self-described Holocaust revisionists who deny that the mass murders took place. The revisionist thesis cannot withstand scrutiny but persists merely to serve political interests and bolster neo-Nazi ideology.

It is difficult to determine the precise number of Holocaust victims. The Nazi regime shrouded the genocide by the euphemism "the Final Solution" and located death camps in remote places. Evidence of many of the mass murders of Jews is not found in any document, either because no such document ever existed or because it was destroyed by the perpetrators toward the end of the war. People who were shipped to such camps as Auschwitz and Treblinka and were not selected for slave labor were not recorded on a list or given any prisoner number but were sent straight to their deaths in the gas chambers; the same is true of shooting victims in Belorussia, Ukraine, Latvia, Estonia, Lithuania, and Yugoslavia.

These complications have been exploited by persons seeking to belittle or deny the Holocaust. Yet it was from the mouths of the murderers themselves that the facts first emerged, in conversations between co-workers and comrades of Adolf Eichmann, head of the deportation and extermination department in the Reich Security Main Office (Reichssicherheitshauptamt, RSHA). For historians, these were the earliest pointers to the magnitude of the crime. On 26 November 1946 at the Nuremberg war crimes trials Dr. Wilhelm Hoettl, a former SS Sturmbannführer and department head for Southeastern Europe in the RSHA's Amt IV (Foreign Reports Service), swore to a conversation in Budapest at the end of August 1944. He declared that in the summer of 1944 Eichmann had prepared a report for SS chief Heinrich Himmler, who wanted to know the exact number of Jews who had been killed. From his own information Eichmann had concluded that in the various extermination camps some 4 million Jews had been killed, and that another 2 million had perished by other means—the great majority shot during the Russian campaign by the

Graveyard of the Hadamar Insane Asylum, Germany. As many as 44 victims are buried in a single grave. 16 November 1945

security police *Einsatzgruppen* (mobile killing units). Himmler was not convinced by this report, since in his opinion the number of Jews destroyed must have been greater than 6 million.

On 3 January 1946 a close associate of Eichmann's, Dieter Wisliceny—formerly in charge of the mass deportations of Jews from Slovakia, Greece, and Hungary—was asked by the Nuremberg tribunal how many Jews had been murdered. He testified in a deposition that Eichmann had always spoken of at least 4 million and that "sometimes he even mentioned a figure of 5 million." At his trial in Jerusalem in 1961 Eichmann did not deny these conversations or figures.

One of the most important statistical sources on the death toll is still extant: the 19 April 1943 report of Richard Korherr, who was attached to the SS as inspector for statistics. By 31 March 1943, the report

states, Nazi policy concerning the Jews of Europe had already cost more than 2.5 million lives. Korherr cautioned that "Jewish population figures are in general to be taken as lowest figures only." He also made the general observation that Jewish population statistics should "always be taken with some reserve" because "partly from expedience, partly through the extensive correlation between Jewish race and Jewish faith, partly through confusion in nineteenth-century denominational thinking, the Jews are in the last resort thought of, not according to their race, but according to their religious adherence."

The Korherr report offers essential clues for statistical methodology in calculating the total number of Jews murdered. In addition, historical research has at its disposal the Einsatzgruppen reports on the destruction of Jews, primarily in the Soviet Union. Hel-

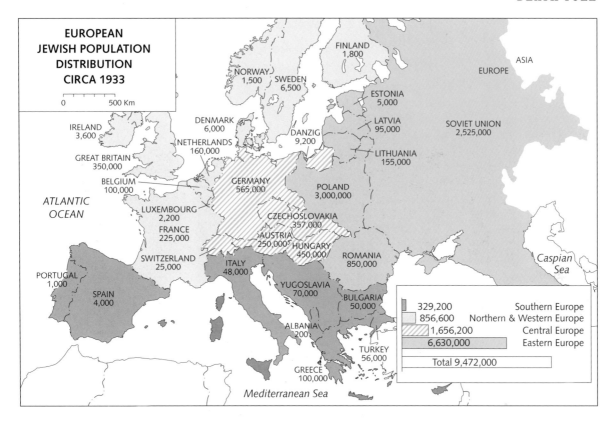

EUROPEAN JEWISH POPULATION DISTRIBUTION CIRCA 1933

0   500 Km

IRELAND 3,600
GREAT BRITAIN 350,000
BELGIUM 100,000
LUXEMBOURG 2,200
FRANCE 225,000
SWITZERLAND 25,000
PORTUGAL 1,000
SPAIN 4,000
NORWAY 1,500
SWEDEN 6,500
DENMARK 6,000
NETHERLANDS 160,000
DANZIG 9,200
GERMANY 565,000
ITALY 48,000
FINLAND 1,800
ESTONIA 5,000
LATVIA 95,000
LITHUANIA 155,000
POLAND 3,000,000
CZECHOSLOVAKIA 357,000
AUSTRIA 250,000
HUNGARY 450,000
ROMANIA 850,000
YUGOSLAVIA 70,000
BULGARIA 50,000
ALBANIA 200
TURKEY 56,000
GREECE 100,000
SOVIET UNION 2,525,000

ATLANTIC OCEAN

ASIA
EUROPE
Caspian Sea
Mediterranean Sea

329,200	Southern Europe
856,600	Northern & Western Europe
1,656,200	Central Europe
6,630,000	Eastern Europe
Total 9,472,000	

mut Krausnick and Hans-Heinrich Wilhelm have made full use of this material in their pioneering study, in which Krausnick confronted the general question of the Einsatzgruppen and their relationship to the Wehrmacht, while Wilhelm concentrated on Einsatzgruppe A and attempted an overall balance sheet for the extermination of Jews in the Soviet Union.

The murder of at least 535,000 Jews is documented in 194 surviving "incident reports USSR" (out of a total of 195) made by the heads of the security police and the SD covering the period 23 June 1941 to 24 April 1942, in 55 "reports from the occupied Eastern territories" by the heads of the security police and the SD command staff (1 May 1942 to 21 May 1943), and in 11 comprehensive "activity and situation reports by the Security Police and SD Einsatzgruppen in the USSR." From available source materials relating to further extermination operations, pogroms, and massacres it is apparent that a minimum of 700,000 to 750,000 Jews were murdered in the first nine months alone of Nazi occupation in Soviet territory.

One of the earliest investigations into victim num-

bers, undertaken to counter revisionist claims, was presented in mid-1951 by the Institute of Jewish Affairs in New York. The report compared the European Jewish population in 1939 (9.5 million) with the 1945 population (3.1 million), and after allowing for some 600,000 emigrants, concluded that on the order of 5.8 million European Jews had perished during that six-year period. In 1959 the population statistician Jacob Lestschinsky, basing his calculations on the 1939 statistics as well as on data indicating that 2.75 million European Jews remained alive in 1950, estimated the number of Jewish victims of Nazi genocide to be more than 6 million. An investigation carried out by Léon Poliakov on behalf of the Centre de Documentation Juive Contemporaine in Paris put the figure at more than 5.5 million. Poliakov followed Lestschinsky in establishing the number of victims of the SS Einsatzgruppen at 1.5 million; he also used the assessment by the Polish Commission for Research into War Crimes that 1.85 million Jews died by gassing in the extermination camps of Belzec, Sobibor, Treblinka, and Chelmno. Similarly, he accepted the figure of 200,000 dead at Majdanek. Rudolf

Höss, the commandant at Auschwitz, had said that 2.5 million human beings were gassed at Auschwitz, but Poliakov thought that a closer estimate would be 2 million. These early estimates of the number of Jews murdered in the extermination and concentration camps depend on sources that are not as reliable as those which have since come to light.

In 1953 Gerald Reitlinger, in the first large-scale comprehensive depiction of genocide, researched the fate of Jewry in all the nations of Europe and also presented a statistical overview of the Final Solution. He trained a critical eye on the information known or reported at that time, starting from the figure of 5,721,800 contained in the November 1945 war crimes indictment at Nuremberg. Reitlinger's guiding rule was to arrive at an indisputable minimum figure, and accordingly he selected evidence with the utmost care. Reitlinger estimated the number of deaths at Auschwitz to be no more than 750,000, far below the figures cited by Höss at the Nuremberg trials. Similarly, in doubtful cases he refused to rely even on official Nazi sources. Reitlinger's final assessment of the number of Jews murdered by the Nazis was a minimum of 4,194,200 and a maximum of 4,581,200. His object in favoring lower estimates was that under no circumstances should the forces of antisemitism be given any opportunity "to discredit the whole horrific chronicle and the lessons drawn from it."

Reitlinger doubted the round figure of 6 million dead, which had been regarded as certain since the Nuremberg trials, and took as his starting point the basis of Robert Jackson's charge of 21 November 1945 in Nuremberg. Jackson, Chief of Counsel for the United States at the Nuremberg trials, had declared, "5.7 million Jews are missing from the countries in which they formerly lived and over 4.5 million cannot be accounted for by the normal death-rate nor by immigration; nor are they included among the displaced persons." The indictment itself contains the passage, "Of the 9 million Jews who lived in the parts of Europe under Nazi domination, it is conservatively estimated that 5.7 million have disappeared, most of them deliberately put to death by the Nazi conspirators." Reitlinger traces the difference between the 6 million figure and his own maximum of 4.6 million to "the highly conjectural estimates of the losses in territory at present controlled by the Soviet Union and in Romania, where figures have been adduced that have no relationship with the facts as known."

The extensive preparations for prosecutions of former Nazis on war crimes charges held in the Federal Republic of Germany in the 1960s and 1970s contributed reliable statistical evidence concerning the victims of the Holocaust. Lawyers and historians collaborated in ascertaining that in the extermination camps on Polish territory nearly 3 million Jews were murdered: 152,000 in Chelmno (late 1941–May 1942 and September 1942–March 1943), 600,000 in Belzec (March 1942–early 1943), 250,000 in Sobibor (May–June 1941, October–December 1942, March–August 1943), 1 million in Auschwitz-Birkenau (September 1941, January 1942–November 1944), 900,000 in Treblinka (July 1942–August 1943), and 60,000–80,000 in Majdanek.

The enumeration of victims in Auschwitz has given rise to misunderstandings and to revisionist speculation. In April 1946, with reference to Eichmann, Rudolf Höss stated at the Nuremberg trials that 2.5 million Jews had been gassed in Auschwitz; later, speaking from memory, he amended this number to 1.135 million. In 1945 investigation commissions appointed by the Polish and Soviet authorities came to the conclusion that about 4 million persons had been murdered in Auschwitz. This figure relied on the testimony of surviving prisoners, on a calculation of the capacity of the gas chambers and crematoriums, and on the length of time that the extermination apparatus had been in use. A round figure of 3–4 million victims in Auschwitz alone has been widely mentioned in the literature (by Jan Sehn, Eugen Kogon, and others); in the Auschwitz Museum this figure was regarded as official and unchallengeable up to early 1990, and it appeared on information and memorial notices and in publications until that date.

The correction of this figure after public debate in the Israeli, German, and American press was celebrated by the revisionists as a victory and deemed "proof" that the number of victims in Auschwitz was much lower even than the 1 million established by recent research—a figure that has been accepted as indisputable by standard Holocaust literature. But the number of persons killed in Auschwitz has been a perennial political issue: many Holocaust survivors reject any downward amendment of figures as a mockery of the victims; similarly, former officials of the socialist regime find in it a relativization of Nazi crimes. The most recent calculation of the Auschwitz death toll—undertaken on behalf of the Auschwitz Museum in

1993 by Franciszek Piper, who relied on the evidence of all available sources, coupled with the advantage of nearly 50 years of scholarly research—is that around 1 million Jews perished in Auschwitz, the largest of the extermination camps.

What are the fundamental difficulties in ascertaining the total number of Jewish victims of Nazi genocide? Two means of calculation are possible, and a combination of both should theoretically be successful. The direct means is to add together evidence from the documentary sources (deportation lists, transport notifications, lists of arrivals in the camps, death books, firing squad dispatches, and so on). Such evidence cannot be totally satisfactory, however, since the Nazis for the most part destroyed the records and removed other traces of the murders. Witnesses' testimony, judges' verdicts, and survivors' reports cannot entirely fill the gaps left by the perpetrators. A further problem

is that a careful count of the Jews murdered in the gas chambers or by mass executions in the Soviet Union and Southeastern Europe was often not made. Historians are therefore obliged to fall back on estimates. For the countries of Western and Central Europe it is possible to compare deportation lists with names of survivors, provided they claimed restitution after the defeat of Germany or came under official notice as displaced persons or emigrants. For Eastern Europe this possibility is severely limited by the anonymity of the murder victims.

The second means of ascertaining the death toll relies on the evaluation of population statistics before and after the Holocaust. This method quickly reaches its limits, on account of the lack of useful statistics, particularly in the Eastern and Southeastern European countries. For example, population surveys in the Soviet Union are insufficiently broken down into eth-

American troops with the 82nd Airborne Division look on as Germans exhume corpses from a mass grave. 6 May 1945

nic and religious categories, and the numerous boundary shifts in Eastern and Southeastern Europe mean that what statistics are available lack a complete basis of comparison.

Further limitations exist. A particular problem is posed by the emigration movement promoted by the Nazis. The deportation lists and losses recorded for France and the Netherlands, for example, frequently show Austrian and German Jews who emigrated to those countries between 1933 and 1940—an obvious source of duplication of names that appear in both the French and the German lists.

Boundary changes during and immediately before World War II create further complications. Many areas, such as the Baltic states and eastern Poland, Bukovina, and Bessarabia, changed nationality several times. In the region of Transnistria, officially administered by Romania and Germany, Holocaust victims were by nationality Romanian, but the territory in which they met their death was considered Ukrainian. Similar difficulties arise for Hungary and Czechoslovakia, as well as for Greece, Bulgaria, and Yugoslavia. The Bulgarian Jews are said to have survived because the government in Sofia refused to allow genocide on old Bulgarian territory; nevertheless, more than 11,000 Jews were deported from the Bulgarian-occupied territories of Thrace and Macedonia and were murdered. The loss of the Macedonian and Thracian Jewries could be added to the Greek account as logically as to the Bulgarian account. Even when dealing with Jews inside the German Reich, there are boundary problems. Most Jews within the Czech regions an-

Woman attempts to identify bodies under the supervision of U.S. Army officials.

nexed in 1938 (the Sudetenland) escaped to other areas of Czechoslovakia and shared the fate of Czechoslovakian Jewry: similarly, the majority of Jewish inhabitants of Memel, which in March 1939 was declared to be part of the German Reich, fled to Lithuania, but in the summer of 1941 they perished as Lithuanians at the hands of the firing squads.

The best estimate of the death toll of European Jews in the Holocaust, on the basis of the latest research, is that at least 6 million persons were murdered by gas or shootings or died of starvation and physical abuse. The figures by country are as follows: Germany, 144,000; Austria, 48,767; Luxembourg, 720; France (including people of other nationalities), 76,000; Belgium (including people of other nationalities), 28,000; the Netherlands, 102,000; Denmark, 116; Norway, 758; Italy, 5,596; Albania, 591; Greece, 58,443; Bulgaria, 7,335; Yugoslavia, 51,400; Hungary, 559,250; Czechoslovakia, 143,000; Romania, 120,919; Poland, 2,700,000; the Soviet Union, 2,100,000.

Wolfgang Benz

Delegatura The underground representatives of the Polish government-in-exile living inside Poland during the German occupation. In 1943 it established a branch specifically to deal with the Jewish question and to maintain contact with the Jewish population. See POLISH GOVERNMENT-IN-EXILE

Denmark On the night of 2 October 1943 the Germans tried to initiate the Final Solution in Denmark. The operation failed. Only 485 Jews were captured and deported to Theresienstadt. A large-scale Danish rescue effort succeeded in conveying between 7,000 and 8,000 Jews across the Øresund to safety in Sweden.

The rescue of the Danish Jews is one of the great heroic events in the history of the German occupation of Europe. Yet the sentimentalization and idealization of the Danish effort have often obstructed a deeper understanding of how and why such a comprehensive rescue was possible in Denmark but not in other occupied nations.

One decisive factor is the system of governance that the Germans allowed in Denmark. After the country was occupied on 9 April 1940, the Germans declared that they would continue to respect its sovereignty and neutrality. This meant that the Danish agents of state—the king, the parliament, the administrative bodies, the armed forces, and the police—all continued to function. The occupation could therefore be supervised by

diplomats from the German foreign office, which pursued a rational and moderate policy toward the Danes and excluded the SS and the Gestapo, if only for egotistic and bureaucratic reasons. The German plenipotentiary (*Reichsbevollmächtigte*) had no executive authority nor any right to issue decrees: thus all German demands, irrespective of the real power structure, in principle had to be negotiated on the diplomatic level. A political collaboration was established, based on common Danish-German interests in preserving law and order and in maintaining trade and production. The arrangement of 9 April 1940 lasted until 29 August 1943, when the resistance movement, supported by a large portion of the Danish public, rose against the system of collaboration. The occupying authorities countered by declaring martial law, and the government resigned.

The date of 29 August 1943 is the great dividing line of the Danish occupation. It marks the transition from a pro-German policy of neutrality, directed by the Danish establishment, to a resistance-led alliance with the Western powers. No new parliamentary government was formed after that date, and cooperation with the Danish police was reduced to a minimum. Instead, the Gestapo came into Denmark and set up a system of police terror that included antisabotage operations, deportations, and political murders. Nevertheless, Danish collaboration with the occupying forces continued, though it was now the heads of government departments who worked with the Germans.

The question of collaboration divided the Danish nation during the war and has since become a subject of intense dispute. Collaboration helped to bring Denmark through the war with less damage than any other occupied country. At the same time, however, it implied moral, political, and especially economic support for Hitler. It is against this background that the myths surrounding the rescue of the Danish Jews should be viewed.

Until 29 August 1943 Danish Jews were protected by the system of political collaboration, and the government threatened to resign if the Germans introduced anti-Jewish measures. At the Wannsee Conference of January 1942 implementation of the Final Solution in Denmark was postponed, on the grounds that it might create great unrest. The Gestapo in Berlin raised the question forcefully at the end of that year but was prevented from taking action by the new Reich plenipotentiary, Werner Best.

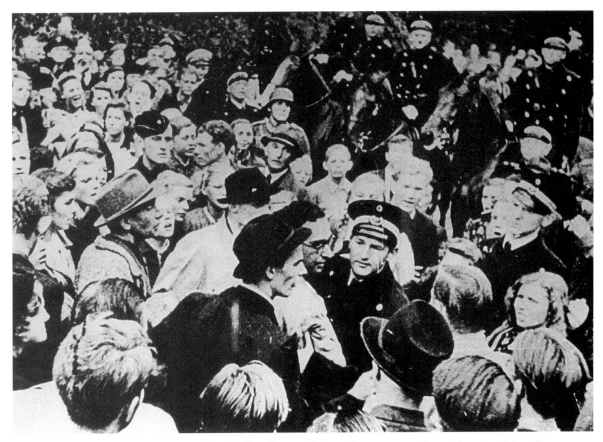

A Danish Nazi, center, in black raincoat and hat, has just discovered a Jew. The angry crowd forces him to hand the prisoner over to the Danish police, who later helped him to escape. October 1943

Best had been deputy head of the Gestapo and also deputy to Reinhard Heydrich in the Reich Security Main Office (RSHA). He was a *völkisch* antisemite and had been deeply involved in the Third Reich's anti-Jewish policy. As a high official in the military bureaucracy in France, he had organized deportations to Auschwitz beginning in 1942. Yet after arriving in Denmark he behaved quite pragmatically, blocking implementation of the Final Solution because, as he pointed out, the great advantages of collaboration outweighed the marginal importance of the Jewish question. After 29 August 1943, however, the Danish government was no longer taken into consideration, and the way was thus paved for extending the persecution of the Jews to Denmark.

Antisemitism in Denmark, unlike in many other European countries, was not widespread. The small and relatively homogeneous Danish society was without deep class distinctions and so had no need to focus on the Jew as a scapegoat. The fact that the Jewish population was not large also contributed to the rarity of antisemitism. By the constitution of 1849 Jews had been declared equal citizens. They had played, and continued to play, an important role in political, economic, and cultural life and were regarded both by themselves and by others as Danes. Hence practically the entire population of Denmark was outraged when in 1943 the Jews were segregated and attacked.

Most Jews in Denmark were from assimilated "old Danish" families. A small group of more Zionist-oriented Eastern Europeans had immigrated to Denmark around the turn of the century. Twelve hundred German Jews, including the so-called Aliyah children and agricultural trainees from Hehalutz, had fled to Denmark after 1933. Their number was limited by the restrictive refugee policy of the 1930s, which the Danes imposed out of fear of provoking the big neighbor to the south and in an attempt to preserve jobs for Danish citizens during the Depression.

The Danish Nazi party (DNSAP) was a marginal movement. Even in the general election of 1943, with Wehrmacht soldiers in control of the country, the DNSAP obtained only 2.1 percent of the vote. The occupation did of course provide opportunities for anti-semitic attacks against Jews and Jewish property. Nevertheless, the Germans did not bring the DNSAP into power, as they did the Nasjonal Samling in Norway.

The leaders of the Jewish community kept a low profile in order not to incite the Germans to intervene, and they continually warned younger members against engaging in underground activities or taking refuge in Sweden. It was with their full concurrence that the Danish government practiced a mild form of discrimination: it prohibited the appointment of Jews to high office and prohibited Jews from making public appearances. The legalistic mind-set of the community leaders prevented them from preparing any plan for evacuation, and up to the last the government persuaded them that the Jews would not be targeted for deportation or extermination.

On 8 September 1943 Best unleashed the Final Solution in Denmark by sending a telegram requesting that Berlin carry out the operation while martial law was still in force, so as to suppress any possible rebellion. This recommendation was passed on to Hitler, who gave authority for implementation on 17 September. However, Best then began to obstruct the action. First he attempted to have it canceled; when that move failed, he leaked the operational date to the Danes on 28 September through a member of his staff, Georg Ferdinand Duckwitz. As a result, when the Germans arrived on the night of 2 October, most Jews had already left their homes—a circumstance that was a primary reason for the meager result of the round-up.

Historians still argue about Best's motives, and the fragmentary nature of the sources allows scope for speculation. Some maintain that he was not playing a lone hand, and that the warning to the Jews was issued in accordance with Himmler's plans. The SS did not have the capacity (so the argument goes) to capture and deport the Danish Jews, so a more ingenious solution was chosen, that of terrifying them into taking refuge in Sweden. Thus Denmark could be declared "free of Jews" and the action seen, not as a fiasco, but as a complete German success. It must be said, however,

that this theory bears the mark of subsequent rationalization and is not consistent with the source material.

Best himself maintained, during his 1948 trial in Denmark for war crimes, that it was Hitler who took the initiative and that the telegram of 8 September was an indirect attempt to check the operation by stressing the domestic problems that it would cause. But the documentation in Berlin severely damages such a defense, for it unambiguously shows that the first move came from Copenhagen. Nevertheless, this does not rule out the possibility that Best, with his Gestapo past and his intimate knowledge of the SS murder machine, recognized the near certainty that, once government collaboration had collapsed and the Final Solution had been completed in the other occupied countries, Denmark was next in line for deportation of the Jews. By taking a lead, he could consolidate his reputation in Berlin, where it had had sunk to the lowest point when his policy of cooperation had failed on 29 August. At the same time, he might hope for a measure of personal control and the possibility of restraining the operation, in order that the Danes might experience the least possible provocation. The most important concern was to avert resignations in protest by the new partners in collaboration, the heads of departments. His chicanery succeeded: the link with the department heads held, and there was no uprising. Cleverly, on the day of the operation Best prohibited the Gestapo from breaking into Jewish homes. After a few hours he declared the hunt to be over, and in the following weeks, while the escape to Sweden was taking place, he held back his force of 1,800 military police. The Jews embarked for Sweden more or less openly, often haphazardly, and would have made easy prey if the police had struck. Such arrests as did take place seemed to be random. Moreover, an order forbidding help to the Jews was prepared but never issued.

A similar passivity characterized the German military authorities. The army took part reluctantly and sporadically, and only after having been whipped into line by Berlin. As to patrolling the Øresund between Denmark and Sweden, the German navy had been completely dependent on collaboration with the Danish navy, which had been dissolved on 29 August and its sailors interned. Not until November did the Germans have sufficient capacity to patrol the sound, and by then all the Jews had crossed into Sweden. Not one ship carrying refugees was intercepted by the Germans at sea.

Another factor in the success of the rescue was the attitude of Sweden. In the first years of the war the Swedes had pursued a policy of neutrality that tended to assist the Germans. But when the tide turned to favor the Allies in 1943, humanitarian help to the victims of nazism became a means of ensuring goodwill toward Sweden. On 2 October 1943 the Swedish government informed Germany that it was willing to take in and intern all Danish Jews. This offer was refused, but on the same night Swedish radio announced that all Jews would be received, even though the country had formerly rejected Danish refugees. The opening of this frontier across a slim body of water engendered an optimism and confidence in the rescue operations that can hardly be overestimated.

On the evening of 1 October, when rumors of an imminent action had become absolutely compelling, the department heads tried to persuade Best to allow the Danish authorities to intern the Jews themselves and to detain them in camps in Denmark until the war was over. This was a desperate plan, obviously intended to avert the worst outcome, death in the eastern camps. Best refused, thus ending any possibility of a diplomatic rescue, and others now had to take the initiative.

A vast number of people, institutions, and organizations protested the deportations publicly: the king, the universities, students, bishops, the supreme court, trade unions, the Danish employers' confederation, farmers' and traders' organizations, ministerial heads, and politicians. Moreover, Denmark was the only country in Hitler's Europe where the Germans had not looked to the national police to assist in the capture of Jews. The Germans judged correctly, for the Danish police, particularly the coast guard, took a key role in protecting the embarkation of Jews to Sweden. Judges and prison authorities allowed arrested Jews to disappear down the corridors of bureaucracy. The newly established umbrella organization of the resistance movement, the Danish Freedom Council, urged every citizen to help and threatened postwar punishment for anyone who sided with the Germans. Resistance members arranged internal transport and established contact with the fishermen on the Øresund and Kattegat shores. Within a bare two weeks they had brought the fugitives to Sweden in large and small vessels, making 600 to 700 voyages. The fishermen had a key function in the rescue operations and demanded a high payment for the risk they had to run—an unpleasantly realistic note in the traditional story and a blemish on the humanitarian Danish effort.

Most helpers were not attached to the resistance organizations and returned to obscurity when the rescue was over. Among them were many doctors in Copenhagen hospitals, which were used as hiding places and transit centers for Jews on the way to Sweden. Assistance from ordinary people was spontaneous and overwhelming. They provided flats and summer houses for the Jews to occupy and gave them food, clothes, and money. There were only a few examples of refusal or betrayal.

Throughout 1943 dissension concerning the Danish government's policy of collaboration had torn the nation apart. Now that the government had fallen, everyone could join in a task where political and moral questions were easy to answer, amounting simply to whether one was for or against a crime. Many helpers felt uplifted, even purified, when after the humiliating collaboration they could assist their compatriots in their time of need. These feelings were no doubt a driving force in the work of rescue. Today it is recognized that the helpers ran only a small risk, but this was by no means obvious in the first phase of the rescue operation, when the majority of Jews crossed the sound.

The 485 Jews who were deported were given a privileged position in Theresienstadt. By agreement with Eichmann, Best ensured that they were not sent to Auschwitz, and they were able to receive gift parcels from Denmark. These advantages meant that only 51 Danish Jews died in the camp, mostly the old or sick. In June 1944 a Danish delegation obtained permission to visit Theresienstadt, and to hoodwink the delegates the Germans gave the camp a temporary face lift. In March 1945 Himmler released the Danish Jews and allowed them to be transported to Sweden by the Bernadotte action, a rescue operation organized by the vice president of the Swedish Red Cross, Count Folke Bernadotte. *Hans Kirchhoff*

Deportations The first deportations of Jews from Germany took place even before the outbreak of the war. In October 1938, 17,000 Polish Jews were deported to the no-man's-land between the German and Polish borders. In Poland, Jews were deported from small towns, cities, villages, and hamlets, to larger towns, where they were placed in ghettos. The major deportations were euphemistically called "resettlement in the East" by the Nazis. This liquidation of the ghettos began systematically in 1942 with the opening of the major death camps. Further small deportations took place from southwest Germany to France in 1940,

Kovno ghetto residents are boarded onto trucks for deportation to Estonia. 26 October 1942

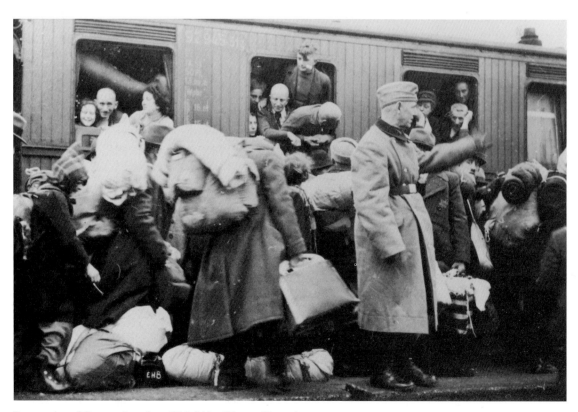

Deportation of German Jews from Bielefeld to Riga, 13 December 1941.

but systematic deportations to the extermination camps in Eastern Europe on a massive scale began only after the German invasion of the Soviet Union in June 1941. Participating in these deportations were German police, special police, and also volunteers from various Eastern European countries. In the deportations from Western and Southern Europe, local police units were involved. Large deportations took place in Austria, Belgium, Croatia, France, northern Greece, Hungary, the Netherlands, Romania, and Slovakia. See AUSTRIA; BELGIUM; DENMARK; FINAL SOLUTION: PREPARATION AND IMPLEMENTATION; FINAL SOLUTION: PUBLIC KNOWLEDGE; FINLAND; FRANCE (MAP); GREECE; HUNGARY; ITALY; NETHERLANDS; ROMANIA; SLOVAKIA; TRANSNISTRIA; YUGOSLAVIA

Dirlewanger, Oskar (1895–1945) Senior SS officer, commander of a special unit (Brigade Dirlewanger) that consisted mainly of common criminals, and commandant of a slave labor camp in Dzikow. Dirlewanger's unit was exceptionally brutal and was responsible for the mass murder of civilians. Dirlewanger participated in the massacre of Jews in Eastern Europe and in campaigns against the partisans. He combated the Warsaw uprising as well as the Slovak uprising in 1944. He died in Altshausen, a French prison camp.

Displaced Persons At the end of World War II there were about seven to eight million displaced persons (DPs) in Germany and the territories of its former allies. The DPs included former concentration camp inmates, prisoners of war, and East European nationals who had fled from Communist rule to Hitler's Germany. Most DPs were repatriated soon after the end of the war in May 1945: by July 4.2 million had returned to their home countries, and by September the number had risen to 6 million. In that period Jews consti-

A mother and child rest on a wooden bunk in the courtyard of the displaced persons' shelter at the Rothschild Infirmary in Vienna. They are among the hundreds of recently arrived Jewish DPs from Poland who have made their way westward with the Bricha. Circa July–September 1946

Arrival of Polish displaced persons in Vienna. They will be sheltered at the Rothschild Infirmary DP camp. 1946

tuted only a small minority of DPs. Approximately 50,000 Jews, mostly from Eastern Europe, who had survived the camps and the death marches, were liberated within German and Austrian territory. Many of them died after liberation as a result of malnutrition, disease, and exhaustion. The survivors, who referred to themselves as *she'erit hapletah* (the surviving remnant, a biblical term from Ezra 9:14 and 1 Chron. 4:43), wished to leave what they regarded as the cursed soil of Germany as soon as possible. But the doors of Palestine and other destinations remained closed, and in many cases their physical and psychological condition made any immediate move impossible.

Just one year after the end of Nazi rule, Germany and the territories of its former allies became the major destinations of Jewish refugees who fled violent antisemitism in Poland and other countries of Eastern Europe. The flight of Polish Jewry culminated after the Kielce pogrom of July 1946, when about 700 Jews a day left the country. By the end of 1946 a quarter of a million Jews lived in Germany, Austria, and Italy, with the vast majority in the American occupation zone of Germany, which was considered by the survivors a stepping stone for emigration to Palestine or the United States. During their stay, between 1946 and 1950, DP camps such as Feldafing, Föhrenwald, Landsberg, and Pocking—located near small towns that had never hosted a Jewish community—for a short time became centers of a vibrant Jewish cultural and religious life.

Initial Assistance

Among the first persons to assist the survivors were two groups of Jews who had arrived in Europe in 1945 in the uniforms of the Allied armies. Soldiers of the Jewish Brigade, which had been set up in Palestine as a separate unit in the British army in September 1944, reached Germany via Italy in May 1945. The other Jews in uniform, who played a major role in the first step of restoration of Jewish life in freedom, were

American Jewish military chaplains. Individual chaplains, first and foremost Rabbi Abraham Klausner, were often crucial figures in advocating the interests of the survivors to the American military administration.

Most important in the actual welfare operations were international organizations, such as the United Nations Relief and Rehabilitation Administration (UNRRA), the International Refugee Organization (IRO), and especially the American Jewish Joint Distribution Committee, which provided education and prepared the Jewish survivors for emigration. In the British occupation zone, a Jewish Relief Unit representing British Jewry performed similar tasks. Other Jewish organizations to assist the survivors included the Jewish vocational education organization ORT, the United HIAS Service, and Jewish youth movements. The Jewish Agency established a mission in Munich in December 1945, headed by Chaim Hoffmann (Yahil).

Political Representation

In many DP camps the liberated Jews elected representatives almost immediately after liberation. In Bergen-Belsen they formed a representative committee as early as 18 April 1945, until the first Congress of Liberated Jews in the British zone convened in September of that year. In the American zone, the Committee of Liberated Jews in Bavaria (later expanded to the Committee of Liberated Jews in the American Zone) was constituted at a meeting on 1 July 1945 in the DP camp of Feldafing. The small community of Jewish DPs in the French zone elected a similar central committee in December 1947. The two major political leaders elected by the DPs in 1945 were, in the British zone, Josef Rosensaft, a businessman from the Polish town of Bedzin, and, in the American zone, Zalman Grinberg, a physician from the Lithuanian city of Kovno. Most of the prewar Jewish parties of Eastern Europe participated in the elections, including the socialist Bundists and the Orthodox Agudat Israel. Unlike in prewar Europe, however, Zionists of all shades now clearly dominated the political spectrum. The official line of all organizations representing the she'erit hapletah was Zionist. They repeatedly called on the British government to open emigration to Palestine, and David Ben-Gurion's visit to the DP camps in October 1945 helped to amplify enthusiasm for the Zionist cause.

Plans to create a united organization in all Allied occupation zones of Germany failed, partly owing to the unavoidable loss of influence that the committee in the British zone would have suffered had Jewish DPs there been lumped together with their more numerous counterparts in the American zone. Demographic and political differences added to the distinct developments of Jewish organizations in the two zones. In the British zone, the majority of all Jewish DPs lived in the camp of Hohne-Belsen, which was a few miles outside the main camp of Bergen-Belsen. In the American zone they were spread among numerous smaller camps or lived outside any camp among the German population. The gap in numbers between the American and British zones widened in 1946 as a result of the stream of immigration from Eastern Europe. In February of that year, there were 46,000 Jewish DPs in the American zone as compared to 17,000 in the British zone. In the summer of 1947 the American zone had 157,000 Jews, the British zone only 15,000. The numbers of Jews in the French zone had risen in the same period from 1,600 to about 10,000. In Austria there were an additional 44,000 Jewish DPs in 1947, and in Italy about 19,000. In November 1946 more than 70 percent of all Jews in the American zone were Polish nationals, 6 percent were from Hungary, 4 percent from Czechoslovakia, and the rest came from other countries of Eastern and Central Europe.

The Harrison Report and Its Consequences

The growing differences between the American and British zones were based on the disparate political interests of the two Western powers. The British, who still controlled Palestine, were anxious to limit the number of Jewish refugees and refused to recognize Jews as a separate nationality, because such a step would have meant a justification for the establishment of a Jewish state. In the American zone a similar policy was pursued during the first months after liberation. A turning point was reached, however, after the publication in September 1945 of a Report by an investigative committee set up by President Harry Truman and led by Earl G. Harrison, dean of the faculty of law at the University of Pennsylvania. The Harrison Report stated in the most dramatic terms that "as matters now stand, we appear to be treating the Jews as the Nazis treated them except that we do not exterminate them.

European refugees at Fort Ontario, a former military complex in Oswego, New York. Visitors and relatives communicated with the refugees through the fence, as seen here. 1944

They are in concentration camps in large numbers under our military guard instead of SS troops. One is led to wonder whether the German people, seeing this, are not supposing that we are following or at least condoning Nazi policy."

One of the most important results of the Harrison Report was the recognition of the Jewish DPs as a separate national category, followed by the appointment of an "Adviser of Jewish Affairs." The United States, however, did not follow Harrison's urgent advice to receive some of the DPs. When in June 1948, after long deliberations, Congress finally passed the Displaced Persons Act, it seemed like a mockery to the Jewish survivors. It made only those DPs eligible for admission who had arrived in Germany, Austria, and Italy before 22 December 1945, thereby excluding most of the Eastern European Jewish refugees. In addition, it explicitly preferred ethnic German refugees (*Volksdeutsche*) over Jewish survivors. Thus, only around 20 percent of the 400,000 DPs who entered the United States between 1945 and 1952 were Jewish. Similarly, the recommendation of an Anglo-Jewish Commission of Inquiry, which visited the DP camps in February 1946, to open the doors of Palestine immediately to 100,000 Jewish DPs from Germany, was rejected by the British government.

Still in 1945, exclusively Jewish DP camps were created in the American zone, mostly in Bavaria, Württemberg, and Northern Hesse, as a response to the Jewish DPs' refusal to share the same camp with those DPs who had collaborated with the Germans. While some of the Jewish camps were relatively comfortable and located in hospitals or hotels, others differed little in their outward appearance from the barracks of the concentration camps. Most camps were either former military barracks or emptied apartment complexes. In many respects the life in DP camps was based on the traumatic experiences of the war years spent in German concentration camps. The return to "normal life" was extremely difficult after years of physical deprivation and psychological hardship. The camp administration had to restore a feeling of responsibility for their own lives and a sense of self-respect among a population that had been deeply humiliated. Cleanliness in the DP camps was a major issue during the first months, as was the possibility to return to interim occupations in or outside the camps. What rendered many of those attempts futile was the continued lack of freedom. "We were liberated, but we are not free," was a line often found in the statements of Jewish DPs. Most of the DP camps had barbed wire around them, all had armed guards, and survivors were often forbidden to leave the camp even to search for surviving family members.

Cultural Life

The aftermath of the Holocaust witnessed for a few years a flourishing of Jewish life on German soil unknown in Imperial and Weimar Germany. The survivors created secular and religious forms of culture in Jewish languages—Yiddish and Hebrew—as opposed to German, which had been the language of the prewar German-Jewish culture and religion. They published close to 100 Jewish newspapers in Europe during the immediate postwar years. Initially, the mostly Yiddish papers had to be printed in Latin characters owing to the lack of Hebrew printing presses. The first Yiddish newspaper, *Tehiat Hametim* (Resurrection of the Dead), in Buchenwald, appeared even before the war had ended, on 4 May 1945. The most significant Yiddish newspaper in postwar Germany was *Unzer Veg* (Our Way), which appeared in Munich between 1945 and 1950 as the official organ of the Central Committee of the Liberated Jews in Bavaria. Among the newspapers produced in the camps, the *Landsberger Lager Cajtung* (after 1946 *Jidisze Cajtung*) in the American zone and *Unzer Sztyme* in the British zone received the most attention. Besides news, the newspapers and journals published lists of survivors, recollections of concentration camp experiences, and literary supplements. An especially important historical source, the journal *Fun letztn hurban* (From the Last Destruction) was published by the Central Historical Commission of the Central Committee of Liberated Jews in the American Zone and contained numerous testimonies of survivors, pictures of the horror in the camps, and songs composed by the inmates. In 1947 there existed 59 local historical commissions recording 1,022 testimonies and preserving numerous documents and artifacts from the time of persecution.

The larger camps had their own theater troupes, the best known of which was the Munich Jewish Theater (MIT). Often the traumatic experiences of the previous years were reenacted on stage. The MIT troupe performed plays with such telling titles as *Kiddush Hashem* (Sanctification of the Holy Name, which in Jewish tradition means martyrdom) or *Yizkor,* the name of the prayer for the dead. The leading spirit of MIT, the director and actor Israel Becker, was the major force behind the first feature film on the Holocaust,

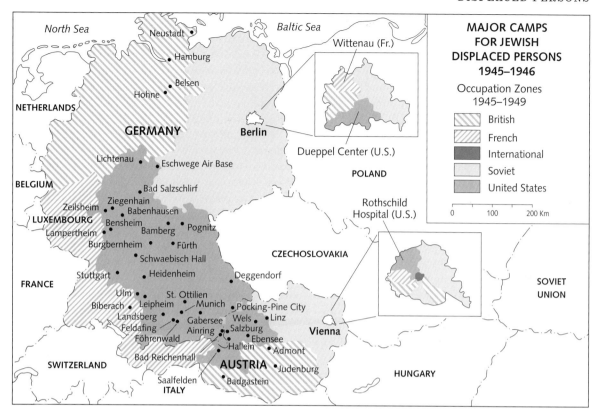

MAJOR CAMPS
FOR JEWISH
DISPLACED PERSONS
1945–1946

Occupation Zones
1945–1949

British
French
International
Soviet
United States

Lang ist der Weg (Long Is the Road, 1948), which depicted the fate of a Jewish mother and her son during their life in prewar Poland and in postwar DP camps in Germany.

Schools were established both for the few surviving children and for adults eager to acquire language skills and to prepare for new occupations. Many camps had their own yeshivas, often led by famous rabbinical authorities. Rabbis Samuel Abba Snieg and Samuel Jacob Ros prepared a complete reprint of the Babylonian Talmud, which appeared in Heidelberg in 1949 with a remarkable cover illustration showing the barbed wire of the concentration camps as contrasted with freedom in a Jewish state. Almost each camp had its own sports club, and Jewish soccer teams played each other in several regional leagues.

Most survivors had lost their entire families, and one of the most vivid expressions of their recovered will to live was to found new ones. Weddings were a regular scene in the larger DP camps, and the extremely high birth rate among Jewish survivors stood in blatant contrast to the birth rate among the German population. Thus in 1945 there were 14 births per 1,000 Jewish DPs in Bavaria but only five births per 1,000 among the non-Jewish population. The high number of births was also related to the atypical age structure among the survivors, most of whom were in their twenties and thirties.

DPs and German Jews

The Jewish DPs were not the only Jewish survivors. Approximately 12,000 German Jews had survived in hiding or had returned from concentration camps or from exile immediately after the end of the war. In contrast to the DPs, these German Jews had been closely related to their German environment. Most of them were able to survive only because they were children or partners in mixed marriages. With few exceptions, they had been little or not at all involved in the activities of the Jewish communities before the war. Tensions between the German and East European Jews, a common phenomenon in the prewar Jewish communities of Germany, resumed soon after the war. Many East European Jews despised German Jews for speaking the language of the murderers and for expressing their willingness to stay in Germany. German Jews, meanwhile, were afraid of losing control over the affairs of the reestablished Jewish communities, in which they were now a minority. In some cities they severely restricted the right of DPs to be elected to the representative bodies of the Jewish communities. In Hannover, as a continuation of a prewar tradition, non-German citizens were not even allowed to become members of the Jewish community. In Augsburg the DPs who decided to stay fought until the mid-1950s for membership in the Jewish community. As a result of these tensions, and also of different interests and concepts of Judaism and Jewishness, in many cities there existed side by side a German-Jewish *Gemeinde* (community) and an East European Jewish Committee. However, other communities saw a more harmonious cooperation between the two groups of survivors, and the leadership in the Central Committee of Liberated Jews in the British Zone was shared between the Polish-born Josef Rosensaft and the German-born Norbert Wollheim.

DPs and the German Population

In the eyes of the German population, the distinction between German Jewish survivors and East European DPs went much further. The Bavarian minister of agriculture received consenting laughter as a response from his audience, members of the Christian Social Union, when he exclaimed in 1947: "Without the Jews and particularly the Jewish businessmen in the United States and the rest of the world we will never manage. We need them for the resumption of our world trade relations. As regards the many *Ostjuden* here in Bavaria, I am of a different opinion, gentlemen. I was unfortunately compelled to take part in the Jewish congress in Reichenhall. The one pleasing thing at the meeting for me was the resolution that was unanimously adopted: Out of Germany!" The major argument against the presence of East European Jews was their involvement in black market activities. Those accusations were not unfounded. Indeed, the Möhlstrasse in Munich was the center of both local East European Jewish life and black market activities, and the situation in some other cities was similar. Even German Jews were often embarrassed to hear about the accusations against the DPs, and one German-Jewish woman declared: "If there is a God, why, after making us suffer so terribly in the past, has he punished us with the Möhlstrasse, which is a disgrace to us before the world and which must make every decent Jew blush with shame?" Those speakers often overlooked the specific circumstances of the DPs in postwar Germany. Whereas the German population, even in this time of turmoil, could draw on salaries, prewar property, personal savings, or agricultural resources of friends and relatives to survive those first years, the only source Jewish survivors could live on were care packages provided by Jewish relief organizations. These often contained goods unavailable on the German open market and therefore became a natural resource for the black market.

Black marketeering was the official explanation for German police raids in DP camps, which were otherwise under the supervision of allied forces. When German policemen in uniform and with German shepherd dogs raided a Stuttgart DP camp in March 1946, the residents associated them with their former tormentors and reacted furiously. In the ensuing shooting one Jewish survivor was killed. A month later, riots broke out in Landsberg after two Jewish DPs had disappeared. Only shortly before, some inmates had been beaten and two Jewish DPs elsewhere had been murdered. In response, some 700 Jews from Landsberg attacked Germans in the area, without, however, seriously hurting anyone. No acts of systematic revenge were reported from any group of survivors, with the exception of a failed attempt led by the Vilna ghetto fighter Abba Kovner to poison German prisoners of war in a camp near Nuremberg in April 1946.

Instead of physical revenge, survivors took rather to acts of symbolic revenge, stressing their survival on the ruins of a defeated Nazi Germany. Thus, after the conclusion of a DP conference in July 1945, Jewish DPs marched to the ill-famed Munich Bürgerbräukeller, associated with Hitler's rise to power, where they recited the kaddish prayer and sang *Hatikvah* (Israel's future national anthem). Another example of symbolic revenge was the establishment of Jewish institutions at former Nazi sites. Perhaps the most extreme case was the transformation of the former farm of the most radical Jew-baiter, Julius Streicher (the editor of *Der Stürmer*), into a kibbutz, where Jewish DPs prepared for the move to agricultural settlements in Israel. Kibbutzim featured prominently in the lives of the survivors. In early 1947 more than 16,000 members lived in 276 kibbutzim, among them "Kibbutz Buchenwald," in Hessian Geringshof, founded by former inmates of the Buchenwald concentration camp.

In the kibbutzim, contacts with Germans were reduced to a minimum. By contrast, the 40,000 Jews who remained outside the camps were often in close contact with the German population, living in the same houses and sharing their places of work. And it was certainly not without concrete cause that the Regensburg Yiddish paper, *Unzer Moment,* repeatedly reprimanded its readers on the title page: "The Germans murdered your father, your mother, your brothers and sisters. Eternal shame to those who marry German women! The Jewish public must expel those who have married Germans from the community!" More common than affairs and marriages between Germans and Jewish DPs, however, were complaints about antisemitic comments. In a few Bavarian towns, such as Memmingen and Bayreuth, Jews had to counter accusations of attempted ritual murder. The first spokesman of the Jewish survivors in Bavaria, Philipp Auerbach, complained in July 1947 that it was impossible for a Jew to ride a train in Germany without being cursed and spat on. One month later, the second Congress of Liberated Jews in the British zone issued the following statement: "In the last 26 months, not only have the great majority of Germans indicated that they have emerged from defeat without learning anything, but rather they prove every day that, on the Jewish question, they still adhere to the same point of view that was taught by Nazi ideology."

Allied Supervision

Relations with Allied guards and officers were less strained by historical events but were not necessarily harmonious. In the British zone the anti-Zionist policy had a deep impact on the relations between the camp administration and its inmates. In the American zone some of the camp commanders were Jews themselves, and others were often sympathetically inclined toward the survivors. Individual acts of antisemitism, however, were reported from many places. The most notorious was that of Gen. George S. Patton, the commander of the U.S. 3rd Army, under whose administration in Upper Bavaria most Jewish DPs lived in the months after liberation. His diary entries leave no doubt about his feelings toward those survivors. After a visit to a DP camp in September 1945 he noted: "We entered the synagogue which was packed with the greatest stinking bunch of humanity I have ever seen. . . . Either the Displaced Persons never had any sense of decency or else they lost it all during their period of internment by the Germans. My personal opinion is that no people could have sunk to the level of degradation these have reached in the short space of four years."

Although Patton's views were certainly not representative, they were not unique either. Many American officers were impressed by the rapid efforts of recon-struction among the German population but appalled by the apathy of the Jewish survivors. Often they overlooked the fact that the liberated Jews were naturally disinclined to help to rebuild the society that had produced the machinery of mass murder from which they had barely escaped. Any attempt at productive work on German soil was therefore rejected by the survivors, who waited for the first opportunity to leave. To join in establishing a Jewish state was now their primary goal. Even among those Jewish survivors who had been anti-Zionists before the war, most were now convinced of the necessity for a Jewish state. But while virtually all of them mentioned Israel as their primary destination, many chose to live elsewhere, such as the United States or European states, when it came time to make a decision.

Emigration

The opportunity to make a free decision did not arrive, however, until the establishment of the state of Israel in May 1948. Before then, a semi-clandestine Jewish organization, Briha (Hebrew for "flight"), brought Jews from Eastern Europe, often through German DP camps, to Palestine. Other survivors were caught by the British authorities and interned in Cyprus. The most dramatic case of a failed attempt at illegal immigration was that of the *Exodus 47,* which had 4,500 Jewish survivors on board when British warships forced it back from the shores of Palestine to Marseilles and ultimately to Hamburg in the summer of 1947. While this involuntary return to the land of their murderers was a nightmare to the passengers aboard the ship, the attention this incident received helped to demonstrate to the international community the need for a Jewish state.

About half the Jewish DPs in Germany, Austria, and Italy—about 120,000 between 1947 and 1950—emigrated to Palestine/Israel. A somewhat smaller number, estimated at 80,000–90,000, went to the United States. This number would have certainly been larger had the Americans opened their doors to emigration more widely. About 20,000 Jewish DPs established homes in Canada, and approximately 5,000 went to Australia and South America, respectively. Many other countries welcomed smaller numbers of Jewish DPs.

In April 1948, one month before the establishment of the state of Israel, there were still 165,000 Jewish DPs in Germany; five months later, their number had

Drancy transit camp

dwindled to 30,000. Displaced-persons publications and official statements by Jewish organizations around the world called on the last Jewish DPs to follow suit and leave Germany. Most of them did, but a considerable minority stayed behind, unable or unwilling to leave. A few thousand returned to Germany from Israel after their failure to settle in the Jewish state. In 1952, 12,000 Jewish DPs were still in Germany; most of them became active in the reconstruction of the Jewish communities there. The last DP camp, in Föhrenwald, closed in February 1957, thereby bringing to an end the chapter of displaced persons in postwar Europe.   *Michael Brenner*

Dora-Mittelbau   Concentration camp near Nordhausen in central Germany in which tens of thousands of captives (approximately 34,500 in March 1945), including many Jews, were forced to build an underground factory for the production of V2 missiles. The mortality rate was very high. At the time of the liberation the U.S. forces found only a few survivors.

Drancy   Transit camp in a Paris suburb with approximately 70,000 French Jews during the course of the war. The prisoners were held at Drancy, which was created from a converted apartment complex, prior to their deportation to extermination camps in Poland. The French police administered Drancy until July 1943, when the SS took over. See FRANCE

Duckwitz, Georg (1904–73)   Attaché at the German embassy in Copenhagen, who informed Danish friends in October 1943 about the impending plans to arrest all Danish Jews. Duckwitz went to Sweden to induce the Swedish authorities to give shelter to Jewish refugees from Denmark. He also worked for the Abwehr (German military intelligence). It is not certain to what extent he acted on his own initiative or whether his superiors in Copenhagen encouraged him to issue warnings. See DENMARK

E

Edelstein, Jakob (1903–44) Czech Zionist, president of the Theresienstadt Judenrat. Killed in Auschwitz. See THERESIENSTADT

Ehrenburg, Ilya (1891–1967) Russian Jewish journalist who wrote anti-German columns for *Red Star*, the Soviet Army newspaper. In 1943 Ehrenburg and journalist Vasily Grossman began documenting anti-Jewish atrocities by Nazis on Soviet territory for *The Black Book*, to be published by the Jewish Antifascist Committee. But Stalin banned publication and the book did not appear until 1980. See RUSSIA AND THE SOVIET UNION; JEWISH ANTIFASCIST COMMITTEE.

Eichmann, Adolf (1906–62) SS officer who directed the implementation of the Final Solution. Eichmann joined the SS in 1933, later became their expert on the Jewish question, and steadily advanced in that organization. He was made chief of the Gestapo's Jewish section in 1939. In 1939–40 Eichmann developed the method by which the deportations of Jews from Germany and the occupied countries were carried out. On the orders of Reinhard Heydrich he planned and wrote the protocols of the Wannsee Conference, at which the various department heads of the German government learned of the Final Solution and their role in its implementation. Eichmann's office, section IVb4 of the Gestapo, issued the orders to deport Jews to labor, concentration, and extermination camps. At the end of the war Eichmann escaped to South America. In 1960 the Israeli secret service captured him in Argentina and secretly removed him to Israel, where in 1961 he was tried by an Israeli court and convicted of crimes against the Jewish people and crimes against humanity. He was hanged in 1962. See FINAL SOLUTION: PREPARATION AND IMPLEMENTATION

Eichmann Trial On 23 May 1960 the prime minister of Israel, David Ben-Gurion, issued a brief statement in the Israel parliament, the Knesset: "Adolf Eichmann, who, together with the Nazi leaders, was responsible for what was known as the Final Solution of the Jewish Problem—in other words the annihilation of 6 million European Jews—is currently imprisoned in Israel and about to stand trial." This came as a thunderbolt to the country's population, one-third of whom were Holocaust survivors.

Although Adolf Eichmann had been apprehended by the Israeli security services and brought to Israel 10 days before the Knesset announcement, Ben-Gurion had had to verify the prisoner's identity before releasing the information to the nation. The affair continued intermittently for two years, culminating in Eichmann's execution. The first period ran from 23 May 1960 until 21 February 1961, when Israel's attorney general, Gideon Hausner, signed the indictment. The second episode was the trial, which lasted four months, from 11 April to 15 August 1961. The third and final stage began on 11 December 1961, when the verdict was read and the death sentence imposed. Eichmann's attorney presented an appeal to the Israeli Supreme Court on 22 March 1962; two months later, on 29 May, the court upheld the conviction and sentence. When Eichmann's plea for a pardon was rejected by Israeli president Yitzhak Ben-Zvi, the execution proceeded. Eichmann was hanged on the night of 31 May 1962.

In the first stage, the long and involved collection and preparation of evidence was handled by the Israeli Police Force Department 06, which was formed specifically for this purpose and was headed by Maj. Gen. Abraham Zelinger and Maj. Gen. Ephraim Hofstadter. The department gathered all the recorded material on the Holocaust, spread over a large geographical area, seeking in particular to establish proof of Eichmann's part in the Final Solution. That most of the re-

Defendant Adolf Eichmann listens as the court declares him guilty on all counts. 15 December 1961

searchers, however, knew little about the history of the Holocaust hampered the sorting and cataloging of the vast quantities of documents.

The researchers based their work on Gerald Reitlinger's book *The Final Solution*. Most of the recorded material came from Yad Vashem in Jerusalem, the Ghetto Fighters' House in the Western Galilee, Tuvia Friedman's Holocaust Research Institute in Haifa, and the archives of European countries willing to cooperate with the Israelis. The Soviet Union was exceptional in its refusal to share evidence with Israel, whereas East European countries supplied partial information, mainly via the Israeli embassies.

Once the investigative material had been handed over to the attorney general, Department 06 was disbanded, leaving only a small auxiliary department, which assisted Hausner throughout the trial. Hausner

was supported in the prosecution by a six-man team of legal advisers, some of whom cross-examined witnesses. Eichmann was defended by Dr. Robert Servatius, a German attorney from Cologne who had defended Nazi war criminals at the Nuremberg trials. He was assisted by a young lawyer from Munich, Dieter Wechtenbruch. Their fees were paid by the Israeli government. The trial took place in the National Hall of the Jerusalem District Court, which had been specially prepared for this purpose. Judge Moshe Landau of the Israeli Supreme Court presided, assisted by the president of the Jerusalem district court, Binyamin Halevi, and the Tel Aviv district court judge, Yitzhak Raveh. Eichmann was accused of four types of crime, according to the Nazi and Nazi Collaborators (Punishment) Law, 1950: (1) crimes against the Jewish nation, (2) crimes against humanity, (3) war crimes, and (4) membership in an enemy organization (mainly the SS and the Gestapo, which had been defined at Nuremberg as criminal organizations).

Holding the trial in Israel, before an Israeli court, symbolized for the Israelis the idea that Israel was the representative of the Jewish nation in all matters concerning the Holocaust. It was a claim that they had unsuccessfully asserted in the 1952 reparations agreement with Germany, when Israel wished to be considered the lawful heir of the millions of Holocaust dead. In 1953 the Knesset passed the Law of Holocaust Remembrance, Yad Vashem, which supposedly made the state of Israel responsible for preserving the memory of the Holocaust.

The trial opened with a three-point appeal by Servatius against the legality of the proceedings. He claimed that as the judges were Jewish, they would be unable to judge Eichmann fairly; that the accused had been brought to Israel illegally; and that the Law of Recrimination against Nazi War Criminals and Their Helpers transgressed accepted legal standards, because it applied retroactively and extraterritorially to events that had taken place prior to the existence of Israel as a state and outside its territorial borders. These claims were rejected by the court, which declared: "Even when presiding over a court, the judge does not cease to be a flesh-and-blood entity with feelings and desires. But he is required by law to overcome these feelings and desires, since otherwise he would never be a judge qualified to consider a nauseating criminal prosecution, such as treason, murder, or any other heinous crime." Regarding Eichmann's alleged kidnapping, the court coined a definition: "A criminal escaping from the family of nations." Such a person, who had committed crimes against humanity, could be brought to justice in any place, and any country was entitled to try him. Thus, the means by which Eichmann was brought to Israel were irrelevant. Finally, the judge ruled that the Law of Recrimination against Nazi War Criminals and Their Helpers was a legitimate tool for bringing to justice criminals whose illegal deeds Nazi Germany chose to disregard. Nor did the judge consider the case to be extraterritorial, since the Final Solution also included Jews who lived in Palestine at the time of the war. Furthermore, the state of Israel came into being in order to ensure that people who committed crimes against the Jewish nation be called to account for their actions.

It was determined from the beginning that the trial would have a wide scope and would serve to unfold the story of the Holocaust in general, not just Eichmann's role in the atrocities. The evidence combined documents (a total of 1,600, including those presented by the defense) and survivors' testimonies. A public furor was aroused by the 108 witnesses, each of whom represented a different country, town, or underground organization. Dr. Servatius based some of Eichmann's defense on the assertion that much of the testimony had no direct relevance to the defendant. The defense did not deny that the Holocaust had occurred; it merely contended that a firm link between Eichmann and the crimes the witnesses described had not been established. Most of the witnesses were not even cross-examined, and Eichmann was described as "a small cog in the well-oiled murder machine."

In their summary the judges concluded that Eichmann had not been a "small cog" who was merely following orders; on the contrary, the evidence clearly showed that he had been responsible for implementing the Final Solution with boundless efficiency. This determination was especially obvious with regard to the murder of Hungarian Jewry.

The subsequent death sentence created a public debate. Israel had abolished the death penalty in 1953, and several of the country's more outspoken intellectuals—including Gershom Scholem and Martin Buber—came out strongly against the sentence. The main fear was that executing Eichmann would make him a Nazi martyr, and Germany would be recast as a victim instead of a perpetrator of war crimes. Furthermore, the hanging might revive antisemitic imagery of the Jews crucifying a Gentile. These were rejected with the assertion that Eichmann had been found guilty, and must be sentenced according to the Nazi and Nazi Collaborators Law, and this meant the death penalty.

After the hanging, Eichmann's body was cremated and his ashes scattered over the Mediterranean Sea outside Israel's territorial waters. The Eichmann trial had a deep effect in Israel on public awareness of the Holocaust, especially among the younger generation, who had until then tended to view the victims of the Holocaust as sheep who willingly went to the slaughter. With its emotional and moral aspects, the trial clarified the complex situation of the Jews under Nazi rule as well as the meaning of Jewish resistance. It also had other effects: Israel's educational system began dealing more deeply with the issue of the Holocaust; an annual Remembrance Day, which was enacted in 1959, became a real day of national mourning, following Eichmann's capture and trial; and a large number of research projects on different aspects of the Holocaust were initiated in the country's universities. The Eichmann trial also served as an incentive to the German government to bring dozens of Nazi criminals to trial during the 1960s.

While in prison awaiting the court's verdict, Eichmann wrote an 1,100-page memoir detailing the Nazi machinery of deportation and mass murder. In it he acknowledged the extermination of European Jewry as "the most enormous crime in the history of mankind" but minimized his own role and responsibility, calling himself "one of the many horses pulling the wagon." For decades the Israeli government refused to release Eichmann's manuscript to the public, partly because of the assertion of copyright by Eichmann's son, Dieter, and partly out of concern that the memoir might become a rallying point for defenders of nazism. In February 2000 the Israeli government made the memoir public in order to allow lawyers for the American scholar Deborah Lipstadt to present it as evidence in her defense of a libel suit brought in London by David Irving, a controversial writer on Nazi affairs.

Hanna Yablonka

Eicke, Theodor (1892–1943) Commander of SS Death's Head units. Eicke reorganized Dachau in 1933, instituting methods of extreme brutality (including torture and execution) and requiring complete obedience from his subordinates. He brought these policies to the rest of the camps in 1934, when he was named chief inspector of German concentration camps. Closely associated with Himmler and Heydrich, Eicke took command of an SS unit in 1939 that fought on the eastern front and committed many war crimes, such as the murder of prisoners of war. He was killed on the eastern front during a reconnaissance mission.

Einsatzgruppen Six major units attached to the German armies after the invasion of the Soviet Union for the specific purpose of killing "hostile elements," above all, Jews. Organized by Reinhard Heydrich, Einsatzgruppen consisted of members of the Security Service (SD) of the SS as well as the German police and were subdivided into smaller units (*Einsatzkommandos*). Although mobilized during the Polish campaign of 1939, their main activity took place in 1941 and 1942. Instrumental in killing hundreds of thousands of Jews in Russia and Ukraine, Einsatzgruppen,

working together with local gendarmerie, order police, and native collaborators, were the primary agent of the Final Solution prior to the establishment of the extermination camps. In addition to Jews, they also murdered Gypsies and Communist party officials. Often assisted by local police, Einsatzgruppen gathered entire populations of fallen towns, shot them, and threw the bodies into pits. They also utilized gas vans—trucks sealed shut into which exhaust fumes were piped—to kill prisoners during transport. The Einsatzgruppen were disbanded in 1943, and efforts were made to conceal evidence of their work. The Einsatzgruppen leaders were tried at Nuremberg, where 22 out of 24 were sentenced to prison or death. See FINAL SOLUTION: PREPARATION AND IMPLEMENTATION

Einsatzstab Rosenberg A commission headed by the Nazi ideologist Alfred Rosenberg responsible among other things for plundering art and important cultural artifacts from the Jews. See ROSENBERG, ALFRED

Elkes, Elchanan (1879–1944) Chairman of the Kovno *Judenrat* (Jewish council) in Lithuania. A Zionist and physician, Elkes clandestinely supported the underground resistance. He died in Landsberg concentration camp.

Endlösung See FINAL SOLUTION: PREPARATION AND IMPLEMENTATION; FINAL SOLUTION: PUBLIC KNOWLEDGE

Eppstein, Paul (1901–44) Social worker, educator, leading figure in the Reichsvertretung, and chair of the Council of Jewish Elders at Theresienstadt from 1943 to 1944. Executed in 1944. See REICHSVERTRETUNG DER DEUTSCHEN JUDEN; THERESIENSTADT

Estonia Small country bordered by the Baltic Sea to the west, the Gulf of Finland to the north, Russia to the east, and Latvia to the south. Estonia had a Jewish population of approximately 4,500 in 1940, when it was annexed by the Soviet Union. In the German invasion during the summer of 1941 the entire Jewish population fled or was killed. In 1942 the Germans sent some 20,000 Jews from Eastern Europe to labor camps in Estonia. See BALTIC COUNTRIES

Europa Plan *Europa Plan* was the code name for a large-scale rescue operation devised by Slovak Jewish leaders, who hoped to bribe Nazis to cease implementation of the Final Solution. The scheme had its roots in the sudden cessation of deportations in Slovakia in October 1942, which the local Jewish Rescue Committee believed had come about because of bribes paid to Dieter Wisliceny, Adolf Eichmann's representative in Bratislava. Current scholarship has shown, however, that the pause was a result of decisions taken by the Slovak authorities rather than of any ransom deal with the SS. Various parties involved nevertheless maintained that since the first contacts with Wisliceny were initiated by Jewish rescue workers in Slovakia, the plan could have succeeded had Jewish and Zionist leaders abroad been ready to make use of it at the proper time.

The Suspension of Deportations from Slovakia

In August 1942 the Slovak Council of Ministers decided to stop deportations of Jews to death camps in Poland. By October, after two last transports had left for Auschwitz, the deportations from Slovakia came to an end. Available documents suggest a variety of reasons for the halt, but bribery of Wisliceny or high SS officials is not one of them.

A report of 22 August 1942, sent by the SD (German security police) section in Bratislava to the superior section in Vienna, described prevailing conditions in Slovakia. The number of Slovak Jews had indeed diminished by 67,000, but most of those deported were "humble people" without useful connections, whereas the rich and influential Jews were mostly still in Slovakia. This complaint contradicts the assertion by the rescue worker Rabbi Michael Dov Ber Weissmandel that bribes had persuaded the Germans to end the killings: the SD in Bratislava was well aware that Wisliceny remained a part of the killing mechanism under Adolf Eichmann and in fact was not the only person in charge of deporting the Jews of Slovakia.

The report offered other explanations for the suspension of deportations. Some Jews had converted to Roman Catholicism in order to enjoy the church's protection under the Catholic-Fascist coalition in Slovakia. Almost all had either a work permit or a certificate verifying that they were essential to the Slovak economy or a letter of amnesty issued by Slovak president Jozef Tiso. Since these Jews were free from the obligation to wear the yellow star, the report continued, the impression was given that the Jewish problem had been completely solved, whereas the Jews themselves were behaving "in a provocative and outrageous manner"—such as riding streetcars. The Bratislava SD went on to report efforts by Slovak interior minister Alexander Mach to renew the deportations, following a police operation that had uncovered a "Jewish center

for providing false papers." It also mentioned a letter of protest against deportations issued by the Protestant bishops of Slovakia, which had greatly annoyed the Catholic president. On 11 August 1942, said the report, a meeting of the Council of Ministers had "suddenly" been convened by Prime Minister Vojtech Tuka: both the economy minister and the secretary-general of the Industrial Union had told those present that the economy could not withstand continued deportations of Jews. Accordingly, the council had decided to halt deportations, proposing to resume them after the war. It was this, and not the bribing of Gestapo and SD henchmen, that temporarily saved the remaining Slovak Jews.

In fact, according to the same report, Tuka had informed the SS officials in the German mission in Bratislava—Wisliceny and his superior, an SS Major Grüninger—about the positions taken by the economy minister and the secretary-general but had said nothing about postponing deportations until after the war. He did affirm that deportations of Jews, in three stages, would continue until the end of the year. There would be exemptions, however: about 380 Jews were essential to industry, and 2,000 were needed by the economy minister.

Tuka was therefore maintaining two contradictory positions. In the Council of Ministers he favored a halt to deportations, while for the benefit of Grüninger and Wisliceny he accepted that most of the remaining Jews should be deported. It is clear that, since Wisliceny had a superior SS officer also directly involved in talks with the Slovaks, bribing him would have been of little avail. He seems, however, to have adopted a realistic view of the Slovak decision—which he, as *Judenberater* (Jewish adviser) in an ostensibly independent allied nation, had to tolerate—while the SD report rejected the attempt to cease deportation. Wisliceny agreed that the number of Jews who were to remain—exempted individuals plus families—amounted to some 14,000–15,000. The writer of the report commented that Wisliceny's estimate might be too high. He cited the leader of the Slovak grain producers as putting the number of "vital" Jews at about 500–600; and he figured that the average Jewish family had no more than four members, since the "Jewish intelligentsia" had few children. A six-person family, on the basis of which Wisliceny had reckoned, must include grandparents, cousins, and other relatives who should have been killed as a matter of course. The SD writer went on to make his own calculation: of 22,000 Jews remaining in Slovakia, 7,000–8,000 were available for deportation.

The writer of the SD report criticized the German mission because, "strangely enough," it was apathetic about deporting the remaining Jews and at first refused to bring any pressure to bear on the Slovaks. The mission had also discussed other matters related to the deportations, including a shortage of rail stock, but Wisliceny had declared that the railroad authority in Breslau (in charge of the Auschwitz line) had provided enough for him. Lastly, the SD report expressed higher hopes about President Tiso than about the German mission itself. On 16 August 1943 Tiso had publicly spoken in favor of continuing the deportations, a position that had isolated Tuka, eventually forcing him to limit the number of "essential" Jews and their families to 4,000–5,000. Wisliceny also summarized his favorable view of maintaining the deportations, adding that the mission should accept the German demands made in his summary and submit them to the prime minister, "so that continued deportations may be expected this year."

This view proved mistaken. Most Jews who had survived until August 1942 remained in Slovakia for two more years, but not because of bribes paid to SS Hauptsturmführer Wisliceny. What temporarily saved them was a complex of internal Slovak political and economic interests, bribes paid to key Slovak officials in charge of deportations, Vatican pressure, and SS priorities to implement the Final Solution elsewhere than Slovakia, where relatively few Jews remained. Their fate, however, was finally sealed in September 1944, following an anti-German uprising in Slovakia in the summer of that year, when most were sent to Auschwitz and gassed by the end of the month.

The Plan: November 1942–September 1943

Wisliceny, whose official job was to organize the deportations, did his best to continue them until the fall of 1942, when he was approached by a Jew who said he was acting for Rabbi Weissmandel and claimed to speak for JDC's Swiss representative. Following this contact Wisliceny promised that he would not press forward with deportations from Slovakia. The first bribe, about $20,000, may have been paid around that time, when Wisliceny knew that the Slovaks had stopped the deportations anyway. Shortly afterward, in October 1942, the same middleman paid a further

$20,000. Wisliceny informed Eichmann of this payment and wrote a report for Himmler. Since the deportations did indeed stop, the Rescue Committee assumed that this was a case of cause and effect. Himmler gave orders through Eichmann that Wisliceny should stay in touch with the Slovak rescue workers. Meanwhile, Weissmandel approached the JDC and Zionist representatives in Switzerland for more money, complaining bitterly of their slow response, which was in fact dictated by their meager resources, Allied economic warfare regulations, and real doubts about the whole affair. Wisliceny, nicknamed "Willy" by the Rescue Committee and sometimes given the title "Baron" by the Zionist rescue workers in Istanbul, seemed a suitable go-between for a much more ambitious scheme—the Europa Plan to effect a decisive cessation of the Final Solution in return for millions of dollars in bribes raised by world Jewry. Wisliceny told the rescue workers that his superiors were interested; he also notified them of deadlines and the sums of money required. The plan was adopted by the Zionist Rescue Mission in Istanbul, despite evident skepticism, and eventually by the leaders of the Yishuv (Jewish community in Palestine), which finally made funds available to the Bratislava Rescue Committee. In September 1943 Wisliceny told the committee that his superiors had tabled the idea but might return to it.

In this way Wisliceny appeared to have renewed the plan and, by means of a letter of recommendation from Weissmandel when the Nazis occupied Hungary in March 1944, convinced the Zionist Rescue Committee in Budapest that he was ready to resume ransom deals. The Zionists attempted to use his offer to gain time and involve the Western Allies in negotiations with the SS; their actions aroused Allied suspicions but had little influence on the Final Solution in Hungary itself.

The Negotiations: German Intentions

The Jewish rescue group had no idea that its plans were known to the Nazis. According to Wisliceny's postwar testimony, he never received any response from Himmler to the Europa Plan; he was allowed to maintain contact with the Jews but could promise nothing in exchange; and in September 1943 he was explicitly ordered to end the negotiations.

Ransoming of individual Jews in exchange for "large amounts of foreign currency" was authorized by Adolf Hitler at the end of 1942. Hence the offer made by the Bratislava Rescue Committee to Wisliceny, following their attempt to stop the deportations from Slovakia itself, could at best have fallen into the "individual Jew" category.

Himmler may have seen in such deals an opening for personal negotiation. Capitalizing on Hitler's limited permission to exchange a few human beings for a great deal of money, he might have used Jews for a genuine political approach to the West for a separate peace after the defeats at El Alamein and Stalingrad, as some scholars have asserted. Himmler may also have drawn back from Hitler's adamant adherence to the Final Solution. But the German surrender at Stalingrad, early in 1943, came months after the Europa Plan was proposed; moreover, in the summer of 1943 the Germans still hoped for major victories in the East. The Nazis later feared that the home front might yield to Allied pressure from all sides. Hence the Final Solution, relentlessly pursued everywhere except Slovakia during the Europa Plan negotiations, became an open secret. This was a means of galvanizing German resistance to the Allied threat. Extreme antisemitic propaganda beamed at the West in 1943 openly admitted the existence of the Final Solution, presenting it as a justified response to the "Jewish war" waged against Germany. Himmler might have used the Europa Plan negotiations to trick the Western public into believing that their governments gave preferential treatment to Jews, on whose behalf the genuine (non-Jewish) soldiers were fighting. If this were the case, Himmler would merely have been toying with negotiations; in fact no significant exchange deals were made.

Another reason for dismissing the Europa Plan concept was Wisliceny's relatively low rank and complete subordination to Eichmann, without any direct channel to Himmler. Though he had apparently become personally interested in a deal early in 1943, he might well have pocketed some of the money himself. Indeed Wisliceny's involvement in the plan and his bid to save Jews in the final stages of the war, when Eichmann's apparatus had practically disintegrated, were always regarded by some rescue workers with skepticism, in contrast to Weissmandel's complete faith in him and in the scheme. Furthermore, bribing the Germans was the only alternative to doing nothing—and doing nothing was rejected by Weissmandel as morally unacceptable. It was this combined approach that led Weissmandel to accuse the Jewish and Zionist establishments abroad of criminal negligence.

In the final phase of World War II even limited deals to rescue Jews—as probed into by the Western Allies—aroused Hitler's wrath. It was therefore extremely difficult to enter into negotiations with Himmler and his aides, despite their readiness in principle to make a deal.

The Subsequent Debate

The so-called rescue debate, in which Jews themselves were blamed for the Holocaust, began well before the war, when ultra-Orthodox groups condemned Zionists for selecting their own friends and fellow Zionists for migration to Palestine. This accusation was hypocritical, inasmuch as most Orthodox rabbis disapproved of emigration until it was too late. The Europa Plan affair, however, seemed to provide a much sounder case, especially since Weissmandel's view of Wisliceny's sincere intentions and his superiors' willingness to bargain (provided that serious amounts of money were forthcoming) was shared by other rescue workers, even if with less bitterness and crusading fervor. It has been asserted that a chance had been missed and that rescue could have been promoted if more money had been allocated by the "conventional" Jewish establishment. In fact, the Zionist leadership and JDC representatives in Europe invested much thought and energy in the plan and (despite grave doubts about its origins and purposes) made the requested advances—but, in the opinion of the Bratislava Rescue Committee, not quickly enough. For Weissmandel, the plan and its collapse became an emotional and religious preoccupation, and his accusations were published posthumously by ultra-Orthodox leaders in order to explain the Holocaust in their own terms, that is, as a result of Jewish secularization. This turn away from Orthodoxy, they believed, had led on the one hand to catastrophe for European Jewry, as a divine punishment, and on the other to the betrayal of righteous Jews by secular ones. *Shlomo Aronson*

Euthanasia *Euthanasia* was the euphemism used by the Nazi regime for the murder of the disabled, a group of human beings defamed as "life unworthy of life" (*lebensunwertes Leben*). Although Adolf Hitler and his associates talked about "mercy death" (*Gnadentod*), their aim was not to shorten the lives of persons with painful terminal diseases but to kill those they considered inferior, those whose physical and mental incapacities threatened the imagined perfection of the so-called Aryan race.

Mental patients described as "idiots!" This photo is from a filmstrip put out by the Reich Propaganda Office showing frightening images of mental patients that were intended to develop public sympathy for the T4 euthanasia program.

The idea that mentally and physically disabled human beings must be excluded from the gene pool was a staple argument of the international eugenics movement, in Germany known as racial hygiene, and had led to widespread sterilization of the congenitally disabled in various countries, including the United States. The Nazis incorporated the goals of the eugenicists into their racial worldview. On 14 July 1933, only four and a half months after Hitler became chancellor, the German government enacted the Law for the Prevention of Offspring with Hereditary Diseases (Gesetz zur Verhütung erbkranken Nachwuchses), the so-called sterilization law mandating the compulsory sterilization of the disabled. The law, which took effect on the first day of 1934, led to the sterilization of 300,000–400,000 persons, representing about 0.5 percent of the German population.

The pool of persons from which individuals were selected for sterilization did not only include those suffering from mental diseases like schizophrenia or manic-depressive psychosis. It also included those suffering from epilepsy, a favorite target of the eugenicists. Another targeted group was blind or deaf individuals, and those with a physical deformity. The largest group of persons sterilized was the "feeble-minded," who were selected on the basis of crude intelligence tests. Finally, the law provided for the inclusion "on a discretionary basis" of persons suffering from severe alcoholism.

The sterilization law was only the first of a large number of eugenic and racial laws. The Marriage Health Law (Ehegesundheitsgesetz) of 18 October 1935, enacted one month after the Nuremberg racial laws, prohibited a marriage if one of the partners suffered from any of the disabilities covered by the sterilization law. Thereafter, couples had to produce a Marriage Fitness Certificate to obtain a marriage license. The long-range aim of the enforcing bureaucracy, situated in the Reich Ministry of the Interior, was the creation of a national registry including information on the hereditary health of every German.

The attack on patients with disabilities in state hospitals and nursing homes (*Heil- und Pflegeanstalten*) during the 1930s had involved sterilizations and a reduced standard of care. But this was only the beginning. In 1935 Hitler had told Gerhard Wagner, the Reich physicians' leader, that once war began he would implement the killing of the disabled. As Nazi policy became more radical, it crossed the line separating traditional eugenic policies from killing operations. Although this radical decision had been initiated by the political leadership, the scientific and medical community did not oppose it, because the idea had circulated since at least 1920, the year the jurist Karl Binding and the psychiatrist Alfred Hoche published *Die Freigabe der Vernichtung Lebensunwerten Lebens* (Authorization for the Destruction of Life Unworthy of Life).

The perpetrators later justified the killings by arguing that they needed the scarce resources consumed through the institutional care for the disabled, and most postwar historians have accepted this interpretation of their motives. But the conservation of resources could not on its own have been a reason, although the perpetrators undoubtedly considered it a useful side effect. The effort expended was totally out of proportion to the anticipated economic benefits. Moreover, economic benefits could not balance the potential danger to the regime from negative public opinion. Unlike the process of making ordinary economic and military decisions, the decision-making process for killing operations did not include, as far as we can tell, analyses that balanced risks against benefits. Racial and eugenic ideology served as the motive for the murder of the disabled, just as it did soon thereafter for the murder of Jews and Gypsies.

The killings started with the murder of infants and young children born with mental or physical disabilities. Set in motion by an appeal to Hitler concerning the "Knauer baby," a severely disabled infant whose parents wanted the child dead, so-called children's euthanasia ran as a top-secret program. Hitler appointed

Karl Brandt, his escorting physician, and Philipp Bouhler, who headed the Chancellery of the Führer (Kanzlei des Führers), or KdF, to direct the killing operation.

Viktor Brack, chief of Office II in the KdF, was appointed by Bouhler to implement Hitler's order. Brack assigned two of his officials, Hans Hefelmann and Richard von Hegener, to direct the murder of disabled children. They assembled a group of physicians to plan the operation. Although the KdF directed the killing enterprise, it appeared only under the impressive-sounding name of the Reich Committee for the Scientific Registration of Severe Hereditary Ailments (Reichsausschuss zur Wissenschaftlichen Erfassung von Erb- und Anlagebedingten Schweren Leiden), a front organization without an independent existence. But as the Reich Committee had no power of enforcement, the Reich Ministry of Interior, represented by the physician Herbert Linden, issued all necessary directives.

Physicians, midwives, and hospitals reported disabled infants and children to the public health service, which transmitted the reporting forms to the Reich Committee, whose physicians selected children for the killing program. The children were transferred to children's wards for expert care at selected hospitals. Parents voluntarily surrendered their children, because they were deceived through promises that new medical procedures would lead to a cure. Against those who refused the ministry employed various forms of coercion.

The first children's ward was established near Berlin in the Brandenburg-Görden hospital headed by Hans Heinze. Others soon opened in Eglfing-Haar under Hermann Pfannmüller, Eichberg under Friedrich Mennecke, Kaufbeuren under Valentin Faltlhauser, and Vienna's Am Spiegelgrund under Erwin Jekelius and later Ernst Illing. Eventually more than 20 children's wards served the killing program. In these wards physicians and nurses murdered the children through the administration of common barbiturates, mostly morphine-scopolamine, luminal, and veronal, but at times also through starvation. In addition, the physicians experimented on the children before death and removed organs for study after death.

Even before the murder of the children had been fully implemented, Hitler ordered the killing of disabled adults. At first he gave the commission for this job to Leonardo Conti, the Reich physicians' leader who also served as state secretary in the Reich Ministry of the Interior, but almost immediately he transferred it to Brandt and Bouhler. They again charged Brack to oversee implementation. Duplicating the structure earlier established for children's euthanasia, Brack assembled a team of collaborators and housed them in a Berlin villa at Tiergarten Street Number 4, and the entire killing enterprise was thereafter known as Operation T4.

Although the KdF and its staff directed T4, in public its work was hidden behind the facade of several front organizations with fancy names, including the Reich Cooperative for State Hospitals and Nursing Homes, headed by Werner Heyde and later Paul Nitsche, the Charitable Foundation for Institutional Care, headed by Dietrich Allers, and the Charitable Foundation for the Transport of Patients, known as Gekrat (from *Gemeinnützige Kranken Transport*) and headed by Reinhold Vorberg. Teams of physicians, led by Heyde and Nitsche, collaborated with the KdF in the work of Operation T4.

The procedure employed to collect the victims followed the pattern set in the murder of disabled children. In the fall of 1939, the Reich Ministry of the Interior compiled data on all institutions that housed the disabled and thereafter requested that each institution complete a questionnaire for each patient. Operation T4 employed about 40 physicians, mostly psychiatrists, to review the questionnaires as junior experts. Without personally examining the patient or reading his or her medical file, these experts used only the questionnaires to select patients for inclusion in the killing operation. Paid by the piece, they processed large stacks of questionnaires in record time, reaching decisions on the life or death of a patient in just a few minutes. Thereafter the senior experts reviewed each case. But as only three men—Heyde, Nitsche, and Linden—served as senior experts, they could not possibly review all decisions.

To entice physicians to join T4 and to convince other government agencies to cooperate in the killing enterprise, the KdF needed official orders from the Führer. But as Hitler refused to issue a public euthanasia law, the KdF obtained only his authorization. Following a procedure later copied in Reinhard Heydrich's office to obtain Hermann Göring's letter of authorization for the Final Solution, the KdF drafted a letter filled with euphemisms for Hitler's signature; Hitler signed it in October but predated it to 1 September 1939, the day the Germans had invaded Poland.

The T4 physicians used medication to kill disabled children, but to kill the far larger number of adults with disabilities they had to devise a different method. For those victims, the T4 technicians invented killing centers where human beings were murdered in gas chambers. In December 1939 or January 1940, T4 arranged a demonstration at the old jail in Brandenburg. The demonstration was attended by the two plenipotentiaries Brandt and Brack, as well as by Conti and Linden from the Reich Ministry of the Interior, and by senior T4 physicians and supervisors, including the Stuttgart police detective Christian Wirth. Brandt and Conti personally killed several patients with injections; for comparison, two chemists from the Criminal Technical Institute of the security police, Albert Widmann and August Becker, administered gas to kill a group of patients in a newly constructed gas chamber. All agreed that gassing was the most efficient procedure. After Hitler approved this method, the killing program was implemented.

Operation T4 established killing centers at Brandenburg, Grafeneck, Hartheim, and Sonnenstein. Later in 1940, Brandenburg and Grafeneck were closed because their operation had become too public. They were replaced by Bernburg and Hadamar. Each center was headed by a physician-in-charge—Irmfried Eberl at Brandenburg and Bernburg (and later Treblinka), Horst Schumann in Grafeneck and Sonnenstein (later active in Auschwitz), and Rudolf Lonauer in Hartheim—assisted by one or two junior physicians. The physicians shared power with the nonmedical supervisors, almost always recruited from the police, such as Christian Wirth, Franz Reichleitner, and Franz Stangl at Hartheim.

All six killing centers were equipped with a gas chamber and a crematorium, as well as reception rooms and housing for the staff. But there were no facilities for disabled patients, because they were killed soon after arrival. First, the physician and his staff examined the victims to ensure that the paperwork had been correctly completed. Then the victims were photographed for a permanent record and were led to the gas chamber. Once they were locked in the chamber, the physician opened the valve of the carbon monoxide container located next to the chamber. The gas entered the chamber through a pipe while the physician observed the victims through a window. After one or two hours the chamber was ventilated, the physician pronounced the victims dead, and the stokers (*Brenner*) removed the bodies. Next, the staff looted the corpses—the stokers broke out all gold teeth and gold bridgework, and a physician removed organs for scientific research from a few selected victims. The stokers then cremated the corpses.

To hide this mass murder, T4 launched a vast obfuscation operation involving letters of condolence and fraudulent death certificates designed to fool relatives and guardians of victims. But these measures could not hide the true cause of the deaths. Widespread knowledge forced the closing of two killing centers; the anger of relatives at the murder of their kin sparked protests from the judiciary and the churches. Although the regime was able to pacify such official protests, public unrest led Hitler to order a cessation of the gassing in August 1941. By that time about 80,000 disabled persons had been murdered. But Hitler's order did not end the euthanasia, because gas was not the only means available. The murder of the children continued unabated. The killing of disabled adults also continued, but, like the murder of children, it was now confined to special hospitals and carried out by means of medication and starvation. Known as "wild" euthanasia, by the end of the war it had claimed even more victims than had gassing.

At first, disabled Jews were selected, transported, and killed together with non-Jewish patients. In April 1940, however, T4 changed the procedure. Following a census by the Reich Ministry of the Interior, T4 concentrated disabled Jewish patients at selected hospitals, including Buch in Berlin, Eglfing-Haar in Munich, Langenhorn in Hamburg, Wunstorf near Hannover, and Am Steinhof in Vienna. During the summer and fall of 1940 they were picked up by Gekrat, taken to one of the killing centers within the German Reich, and gassed without the usual medical evaluation. In the beginning of the operation, T4 simply wanted the disabled Jews to disappear, and thus if inquiries arose they replied that the Jews had been transferred to the Generalgouvernement in Poland. Later, T4 decided to collect additional fees from relatives, welfare agencies, and insurance companies, and therefore mailed death certificates from a purported hospital in Chelm—sometimes spelled Cholm—near Lublin. In fact, no such hospital existed; all Chelm documents were forged in Berlin. But the charade permitted T4 to collect per-diem maintenance fees for the period between the patient's murder and the date provided in the fraudulent death certificate.

Although Hitler had ordered a stop to the gassing of the disabled on German soil, the killing centers at Bernburg, Sonnenstein, and Hartheim continued to operate, because they were used for the murder of concentration camp prisoners. Although the number of prisoners in the camp system grew substantially during the first year of the war, the camps did not yet possess the facilities to kill large numbers of prisoners at one time. Operation T4 therefore placed its facilities at the disposal of the camps and, in early 1941, the murder of prisoners in T4 killing centers commenced. The T4 physicians selected the prisoners in the camps; those selected were transported to a T4 killing center and gassed there by T4 personnel. Known as Operation 14f13, the murder of concentration camp prisoners by T4 continued until 1943, when the expansion of the killing center at Auschwitz-Birkenau made T4's facilities superfluous. Bernburg and Sonnenstein closed, but Hartheim continued to operate until the end of 1944 as a killing facility for the nearby Mauthausen concentration camp.

After the invasion of the Soviet Union in June 1941, the SS *Einsatzgruppen* (mobile killing units) murdered disabled hospital patients alongside Jews and Gypsies. They followed the precedent set earlier in Poland. As soon as the war had started in September 1939, SS units had shot disabled German patients in Pomerania on the eastern border of the German Reich. The same method—mass execution—was used to kill the disabled in various parts of occupied Poland. In the annexed Warthegau, however, a special SS unit commanded by SS captain Herbert Lange murdered Polish disabled patients in gas vans, piping carbon monoxide from canisters into the interior of the van. The success of the Lange unit led in 1940 to its deployment at the camp of Soldau in East Prussia to murder disabled German patients from that province. The same unit later staffed the first killing center for Jews and Gypsies, which opened in the Warthegau at Chelmno (Kulmhof) in December 1941.

The SS leaders charged with implementing the Final Solution turned to T4 and its associates for assistance. The chemist Albert Widmann tested killing methods in Belorussia, including the use of exhaust gas from diesel engines; the chemist August Becker inspected and improved the gas vans used by the Einsatzgruppen; the T4 chemist Helmut Kallmeyer advised about gas chambers in both Riga and Lublin; and the stone mason Erwin Lambert, "the traveling construction boss of Operation T4," built gas chambers and crematoriums in the Lublin camps. Odilo Globocnik, the SS and police leader in Lublin charged with implementing Aktion Reinhard, negotiated with Philipp Bouhler for the use of T4's trained killing experts. The KdF delegated approximately 90 T4 operatives, led by Christian Wirth, to staff the extermination centers at Belzec, Sobibor, and Treblinka. After those camps closed in 1943, the men were transferred as a group to Trieste, where they operated a notorious camp for Jews and partisans at the Risiera di San Sabba.

The T4 managers, physicians, and supervisors, as well as the rank-and-file staff, were not forced to join the T4 killing operation. They willingly accepted an assignment they could have refused, as did one physician, an SS officer, who declined to head the Grafeneck killing center. They were haphazardly selected, and they joined from a variety of motives. Although they supported the ideological and racial goals of the Nazi regime, this alone does not explain their willingness to take direct part in the killings. Careerism was the guiding motive for the T4 managers, supervisors, and physicians, who expected rapid advancement for their service to the regime. For the junior staff the motive was financial gain and peer pressure. Furthermore, these jobs were attractive because they brought the benefit of wartime service far away from places where the enemy could shoot back.

Henry Friedlander

Evian Conference   The Anschluss (annexation) and occupation of Austria by Nazi Germany in March 1938 opened a new chapter in the history of the Holocaust. The takeover abruptly added 200,000 Jews to the ever rising flood of refugees, which by the spring of 1938 was finally being recognized as an international problem.

The United States was being pressured both internally, in particular by American Jewish organizations, and externally to make some sort of gesture toward finding a solution for the refugee crisis. In March 1938 President Franklin Roosevelt called on 30 European and Latin American countries to send representatives to an international conference to facilitate the emigration and resettlement of Jewish refugees from Germany and Austria. This call was the first American government initiative with respect to refugees from Nazi Germany.

Almost up to the date of the conference it was hoped that the United States, with its low population density, would offer a viable solution. These hopes, however, were illusory. By late spring 1938 the United States had abdicated all responsibility for the conference preparations and looked to representatives of various regions, notably Latin America, to sponsor rescue proposals on their own territory. Three and a half months after the invitations were issued, it appeared to all participants as if a stalemate had been reached.

Two of the main problems facing the organizers of the conference were the finances for resettlement and the prospect that the millions of Jews in such countries as Poland, Romania, and Hungary might also in the near future become refugees. It was becoming evident that it would be beyond the resources of private refugee organizations to finance emigration on a large scale. Furthermore, anti-Jewish measures were being intensified in Eastern Europe, and it was feared that any settlement schemes agreed to at Evian would act as an incentive to those governments to pressure their Jewish minorities to leave.

On the afternoon of 6 July 1938 some 200 delegates, members of the press, and observers from private organizations convened at the Hôtel Royal in Evian, France, overlooking Lake Geneva. Only Great Britain, the United States, and France sent special delegations; all other countries were represented by regular diplomats at the League of Nations or from nearby capitals. Two basic approaches to the refugee problem had crystallized: a conservative one, adopted by Great Britain, which feared that any helpful arrangement would encourage the German government to accelerate the expulsion of the Jews; and a liberal one, taken by the United States, which aimed at establishing a system for dealing with the current flow of refugees from Germany and Austria as well as any future migration from Eastern Europe.

Some delegates were apprehensive of American pressure to absorb refugees. These fears proved groundless, however, when at the first session Myron Taylor announced that the United States, in a magnanimous gesture toward the refugees, had taken steps to consolidate the German and former Austrian immigration quotas, thereby enabling a total of 27,370 immigrants to enter the United States in any one year. He urged that a permanent intergovernmental committee be established to continue the work of the conference. The delegates sat stunned that the Americans had assem-

Conference for refugees at Evian. American delegate Myron Taylor pleads for the establisment of an international committee to facilitate Jewish emigration. July 1938

Not all countries responded to the invitation with enthusiasm. Italy flatly refused to attend, and Romania, wishing to rid itself of a "surplus" Jewish population, asked to be categorized with Germany and Austria as a "refugee producer." Switzerland had been the Americans' first choice as a conference site, but the Swiss feared antagonizing Berlin and so requested that the conference not be held within their borders. The date ultimately selected for the conference was early July and the location chosen was Evian, France.

The weeks slipped by, and the United States still had not given any further indication of what Roosevelt had in mind and what the procedure and scope of the meeting should be. Shortly before the conference it was announced that Myron C. Taylor, a former president of United States Steel Corporation who had almost no experience in international affairs, was to be the conference chairman, with James G. McDonald, the former high commissioner for refugees from Germany, acting as his deputy.

bled the nations of the world to discuss the refugee problem when they had so little to offer by way of a solution.

And yet the speech was also received with a sense of relief. Whereas for the Jews of Europe, Taylor's speech was a cruel disappointment, for the nations represented at Evian it was a reprieve from having to take action. If the United States was only willing to fill a preexisting quota, no other nation could be expected to do more. The British delegate, carefully confining himself to his government's instructions, did not refer to Palestine by name but only mentioned overseas territories under British jurisdiction where "local political conditions hinder or prevent any considerable immigration." His silence on Palestine was strongly criticized by the Jewish organizations and the press, particularly in the United States. On the last day of the conference the British delegate returned to the subject, explaining the acute problems that had arisen in Palestine which necessitated a temporary restriction on Jewish immigration so as to maintain what he termed a "balance of population" in the area. He ended his speech with a clear warning that other countries should not concern themselves with the Palestine question, for which Britain bore sole responsibility.

Representatives of other countries followed suit. The delegates from France, Belgium, Switzerland, the Netherlands, and the Scandinavian countries emphasized the large numbers of refugees they had already admitted, and asserted their inability to absorb further refugees except for those in transit to countries overseas. The South American governments sympathized with the refugees but stated point-blank that their laws made it impossible to contemplate absorbing large numbers of immigrants. By the end of the conference no country aside from the Dominican Republic (which offered to host 10,000 Jewish refugees a year for a two-year period) proposed any solution to the refugee problem.

Following the plenary session the actual work of the conference took place in two subcommittees. The Technical Subcommittee heard statements concerning the immigration laws of individual nations and the immigration practices of particular governments, and noted the numbers of immigrants each would be willing to receive. It had little to do as countries rarely added to what they had already said in their formal statements to the plenary session. The Subcommittee for the Reception of Organizations Concerned with

the Relief of Political Refugees held confusing and repetitive sessions that irritated its members and disheartened the representatives of refugee organizations, which were dismayed at the lack of response to their anguished appeals.

The only tangible result of the nine days of deliberations at Evian was the unanimous resolution adopted at its closing session on 14 July: the formation in London of an intergovernmental committee to continue and develop the conference's refugee work. The committee, led by George S. Rublee, a 70-year-old American with extensive experience in international law, was directed to persuade countries to permit the entry of a greater number of immigrants and "to undertake negotiations to improve the present conditions of exodus and to replace them by conditions of orderly emigration." By limiting membership in the committee to government representatives, the nations precluded the participation of nongovernmental organizations that had been allowed to send representatives to the Evian Conference, such as the Jewish Agency in Palestine.

The Evian Conference was primarily an American exercise in public relations. Nevertheless, it was also the first time that the problem of Jewish refugees from Europe was recognized as an international issue affecting not only Jews. And yet as the events of 1938–39 unfolded—the Munich Pact, the takeover of the Sudetenland, Kristallnacht, the occupation of Czechoslovakia, and the German declaration of war on Poland—the gap between realization and action continued to widen. At the end of the conference more than one refugee had remarked wryly that "Evian" was merely "naive" spelled backward. For the thousands of Jewish refugees seeking asylum, the multitude of resolutions at Evian, combined with the absence of solutions, were not only naive, they were life-threatening.

Judith Tydor Baumel

Extermination Camps The six stationary killing centers established by the Nazis throughout occupied Poland between 1941 and mid-1942 were called extermination camps (or death camps). More than 3 million Jews lost their lives in these camps between the winter of 1941 and the fall of 1944. The series of killing centers was an integral part of Nazi Germany's governing system and was used as a tool for achieving its political aims. Two of the centers—Auschwitz-Birkenau and Majdanek—had originally been created as concentration and prisoner-of-war camps; the others—

Victims' shoes piled up in front of a camp warehouse. After 22 July 1944

Chelmno (or, by its German name, Kulmhof), Sobibor, Treblinka, and Belzec—were opened solely to serve as death factories. All six camps were part of the "SS State," headed by the Reichsführer SS, Heinrich Himmler, and three of them (Treblinka, Belzec, Sobibor) were established within the framework of Operation Reinhard (named for the assassinated SD chief, Reinhard Heydrich), the code-name for the liquidation of Eastern European Jewry and the Generalgouvernement's appropriation of the Jews' property and goods. The extermination camps were administered solely by the SS, who in some of them were assisted in their daily tasks by Ukrainian auxiliaries.

Although many thousands of Jews were killed by the Nazis in the first 21 months of World War II, the German invasion of the Soviet Union on 22 June 1941 is usually cited as the beginning of the Final Solution. Along with the advancing German army there proceeded four mobile killing squads, or *Einsatzgruppen,* whose specific task was to murder Jews, Communist party officials, political commissars in the Red Army, and Gypsies. With the assistance of local collaborators the Einsatzgruppen rounded up men, women, and children, took them to locations near their homes, and shot them. Where they existed, natural ravines and anti-tank ditches were used as mass graves. In other cases the Jews were ordered to dig large burial pits for themselves before they were murdered. The decision to establish stationary killing centers stemmed in part from the psychological and practical difficulties of carrying out mass murder by means of the Einsatzgruppen. A second factor pointing to the efficiency of stationary death camps was the experiments carried out as part of the so-called euthanasia program relating to murder by carbon monoxide. It was decided to locate these camps in occupied Poland principally because of the large concentration of Jews in Eastern Europe.

At the end of 1941 the leaders of Operation Reinhard initiated preparations for the extermination of Jews in the Generalgouvernement, the area of central Poland under German administration. But they did not foresee how many death camps would have to be constructed and operated for this purpose. As they had no model on which to base their plans, a number of guidelines for selecting sites were drawn up. The camps would have to be near the main areas of the Generalgouvernement, which were heavily populated by Jews. They would have to be near the main railways to facilitate transports and deportations. Furthermore, camps had to be located in desolate places, far from inhabited areas, to maintain secrecy and to keep the local population from knowing what was happening within them. The camps would also have to be in the vicinity of the German-occupied territories of the Soviet Union to encourage the belief that Jews who had disappeared had eventually reached labor camps in the East.

The extermination process required a great deal of streamlining. From experiments carried out at Belzec, the most efficient method of handling the transports of Jews from arrival to murder and from murder to disposal of the bodies was developed. The basic structure of the camps and the processes that the victims were forced to undergo as soon as they had left the train were intended to ensure that they would remain oblivious to the fact that they were to be exterminated until virtually the last minutes of their lives. The aim was to give the victims the impression that they had been sent to a labor or transit camp. In order to ensure this lack of comprehension, all activity had to be carried out with the utmost speed. Victims were made to run so that they would not have time to reflect on what they were going through. The deception took place in a time of shock in order to forestall any impulse to escape or resist. Furthermore, by speeding up the extermination process it was possible to increase the killing efficiency of the camps and to annihilate more Jews each day.

Thus the ultimate murder system used in almost all these camps was the same. In each camp a few hundred Jews were removed from the transports to carry out the physical labor involved in the extermination process. These special units, or *Sonderkommandos*, dealt with the live Jews on their arrival, with the possessions they brought with them (sorting and preparing clothing and valuables for reshipment to the Reich), and with disposal of the bodies of the murdered Jews. After a month or two of such work, most were sent to their deaths. An additional group of Jews—usually professional welders, locksmiths, electricians, and other skilled laborers—was selected to carry out service jobs in the camps. They were kept entirely separate from the Jews selected from transports on arrival and engaged in the extermination process. Nevertheless, the service workers too were ultimately sent to the gas chambers.

Auschwitz-Birkenau, officially called Konzentrationslager Auschwitz, covered 40 square kilometers

At Auschwitz–Birkenau, women prisoners are forced to dig gravel. This photograph was used as evidence against Rudolf Höss during his trial. 1942–43

and was located 60 kilometers west of Kraków. Eventually becoming a vast complex of several dozen sub-camps, Auschwitz was divided into three major camps, the second of which, officially known as Birkenau or Auschwitz II, was earmarked as an extermination center. In April 1940 the order to establish the concentration camp Auschwitz was issued. The first Polish prisoners were sent there on 14 June 1940. From the spring of 1942 onward, transports of Jews from all over Europe were sent to Auschwitz for extermination. The camp also retained a core of Jewish prisoners for labor purposes. Eventually the Auschwitz complex became both the largest of all camps and, with the addition of gas chambers, the largest installation for extermination. Until the early 1990s Polish statistics showed that 2.8–4 million persons perished in Auschwitz, at least 2.5 million of them Jews. But the estimations of Western and Israeli historians fluctuated between 1 and 1.5 million. After the research of Georges Wellers and Franciszek Piper had been published, scholars agreed that approximately 1–1.5 million persons, 90 percent of them Jews, lost their lives in the camp.

Majdanek, the second concentration and extermination complex, was established in a suburb of Lublin in eastern Poland. In July 1941, following the German invasion of the Soviet Union, Himmler inspected the Lublin area to find a site on which to build a new concentration camp large enough to hold 50,000 inmates. He anticipated setting up additional camps in the vicinity of the first camp when it filled. In September 1941 the SS designated Majdanek as a camp for prisoners of war and civilian internees. Construction began in October 1941; it was carried out by Polish Jews, Soviet prisoners of war, and peasants from nearby villages. Officially designated as a prisoner-of-war camp until February 1943, Majdanek was in practice a concentration camp and later an extermination center. The camp's national mix was varied, representing more than 50 nationalities, but the majority of the 300,000 inmates were Jews (about 120,000) and Poles (about 100,000). Of these, 235,000 perished in the camp.

Almost from its inception Majdanek functioned as both a concentration and an extermination center. Rather than focusing on one extermination process, the SS preferred to use several methods, sometimes simultaneously. During the first years of the camp's existence—1941 and 1942—the SS murdered Soviet prisoners of war by shooting, with mass executions often taking the lives of up to 1,000 soldiers and offi-cers. In addition, prisoners were killed by hanging, drowning (in the small camp reservoir), strangling, beating, and trampling. Many prisoners also died from disease and exhaustion that resulted from the living conditions in the camp.

The most common method of mass murder in Majdanek, as in most of the other extermination camps, took place in special gas chambers. In August–September 1942 two provisional gas chambers were used in Majdanek. Before being put to death, prisoners were driven by the guards supervising the process into buildings marked "showers." These were actually gas chambers, two of which were lighted so that the SS men could watch the gassing through peepholes. Gassing usually occurred at night, when the prisoners were asleep, and those who worked at the gas chambers were isolated from other prisoners. Thousands of Jews were brought to Majdanek, primarily between May and July 1943, from the Warsaw ghetto to be executed. From October 1942 Majdanek had three permanent chambers, in which prisoners were put to death by asphyxiation, using either carbon monoxide or Zyklon B. (Carbon monoxide kills by binding with hemoglobin in the bloodstream and displacing oxygen; the hydrocyanic acid in Zyklon B interferes with oxygen metabolism in the cells.)

The largest execution at Majdanek took place on 3 November 1943, when the SS shot 18,400 Jews in ditches near the crematorium. Forced to strip and lie facedown in the dirt, the Jews were machine-gunned by the SS until layers of corpses filled the ditches. Throughout the day of the massacre, songs were played over camp loudspeakers to muffle the sounds of the shooting and the cries of the dying. Following the operation prisoners were brought in to help eliminate all traces of the massacre by covering the graves and burning the corpses that could not fit in them. A special mill ground the remaining bone pieces to a powder, which was put into sacks and taken to the SS warehouses for use as fertilizer.

Body disposal was a major problem of most extermination camps. At Majdanek, as in many other camps, corpses at first were buried in mass graves. In June 1942 two small crematoriums were built, but they could not cope with the masses of bodies. Eventually corpses had to be burned in the open air on specially made pyres. Using a method perfected at the Treblinka extermination camp, iron chassis from old trucks were placed in a gratelike fashion over deep pits, and alternate layers of bodies and logs were piled on them. Squads then poured gasoline or methanol on the pyres and set them on fire. Eventually larger crematoriums were erected with a capacity of 1,000 bodies a day. By 1943 the only limits on extermination in Majdanek were machinery breakdown and railroad disruptions.

The Nazis began to evacuate Majdanek long before the Russians liberated the camp in July 1944, so that only approximately 1,000 prisoners remained to greet the advancing Soviet forces. But as the SS personnel had little time to destroy the camp installations, the Russian troops found gas chambers, crematoriums, dead bodies, and large warehouses spilling over with goods taken from the prisoners. In this respect Majdanek differed from the four remaining extermination centers, which were closed down by the Nazis long before the areas in which they were located were liberated.

Chelmno was the first of the four camps created solely for the purpose of extermination. Located 60 kilometers from Lodz in the Warthegau (the area of Poland annexed by Germany in the fall of 1939), Chelmno was the graveyard of 150,000–300,000 Jews, many of them from Lodz. Opening in December 1941, the killing center was originally meant to be used to clear the Warthegau of its 450,000 Jews. The establishment of the Chelmno extermination camp marked the beginning of a new phase in the Final Solution. As it was the first operable killing center, Chelmno borrowed both personnel and techniques from the killing squads in Russia and from the Nazis' euthanasia program, which was being carried out in Germany.

Chelmno was not a camp in a true sense of the word, as the Germans had no intention of accommodating prisoners for any length of time. By means of firing squads and, later, gas vans, the camp could "process" about 1,000 prisoners a day, unloading their bodies in a nearby wood, where a Sonderkommando threw the dead victims into mass graves after having removed their valuables. The major problem of body disposal was solved only in the fall of 1942, when vast pyres of iron rails and wooden sleepers were built in the form of underground furnaces. An additional enterprise begun at Chelmno was the salvaging of gold from the mouths of the dead; this eventually became a normal first step in body-salvage operations at all camps. Having eliminated most of the Jews in the Warthegau, Chelmno was originally closed down in April 1943 but reopened a year later to reduce the number of Jews re-

maining in the Lodz ghetto. In late 1944 the camp and the crematoriums were completely destroyed, and in January 1945 the last of the Jewish workers were executed as part of the camp's final liquidation. Two of them survived. Of the 150,000–300,000 Jews brought to the camp for extermination, fewer than 10 managed to escape.

Belzec, the second of the camps that functioned solely as extermination centers, was located in southwestern Poland beside the Bug River, east of Lublin. The first camp at Belzec was established at the beginning of 1940 as a labor camp for thousands of Jews from the Lublin district, who were sent there as slave laborers to build fortifications on the Soviet-German line of demarcation. This camp was liquidated in the fall of 1940. The extermination camp of the same name was opened in March 1942. It was separated from the war effort and had minimal industrial activity. As at the other single-purpose camps, at Belzec almost all the victims were Jews. Unlike Chelmno, which used mobile killing vans, Belzec was the first camp to be equipped with permanent gas chambers, which had the capacity to kill 15,000 persons a day. A total of 600,000 Jews were exterminated in Belzec; their bodies were burned in open mass graves. With the extermination of Galician Jewry, Belzec's killing days ended in late November 1942. Nevertheless, Jewish Sonderkommandos worked at destroying the mass graves until June 1943. To destroy evidence of their crimes ahead of the advancing Red Army, the Germans were forced to return to reopen the graves and burn the putrefying corpses; they then ground the bones to a fine powder and distributed it over neighboring fields. Only two inmates escaped from Belzec, and only one survived the war.

Opening its gates in May 1942, the Sobibor extermination camp in eastern Poland, located about a kilometer from the Bug River, claimed 200,000–250,000 lives during its 17 months of existence. Most of the victims were Jews from Poland and German-occupied territories of the Soviet Union; others arrived from Slovakia, the Protectorate of Bohemia and Moravia, Austria, France, the Netherlands, and other countries. Located in a swampy, wooded, and thinly populated area, the camp was originally built by a group of 80 Jews from nearby ghettos who were shot after completing their work. As in a few of the other extermination camps, a number of Jews arriving in subsequent transports were kept alive to care for the SS camp personnel, run the gas chambers, sort and ship the victims' possessions, bury the corpses, and eventually cremate the bodies. In October 1943 a revolt broke out among the 600 prisoners who were then at the camp. Led by a Soviet prisoner of war, Alexander Pecherski, the inmates first eliminated the SS officer group, then attacked the weapons arsenal and the guards, broke through the wire fence, and made for the woods. Four hundred of them succeeded in breaking out of the camp, but about half of those were killed by the land mines along the perimeter. Some were killed by the SS, police, and German troops; others were murdered by Polish fascists, gangs of thieves, bandits, and sometimes, in spite of the policy of the command, by the members of the underground Home Army (Armia Krajowa). About 100 prisoners reached freedom, and about 35 survived until the end of the war. Following the revolt Sobibor was razed to the ground by the Nazis, without leaving a trace.

The last of the extermination camps was Treblinka, which opened as a killing center on the Bug River in July 1942. The experience gained in the operation of Belzec and Sobibor was applied to Treblinka, and hence it became the most streamlined camp constructed within the framework of Operation Reinhard. Because of its location some 120 kilometers northeast of Warsaw, Treblinka's site was selected for the extermination of the Warsaw ghetto Jews. Between July 1942 and the fall of 1943 some 750,000–800,000 Jews from central Poland, Germany, Austria, Czechoslovakia, the Netherlands, Belgium, and Greece were killed by gassing at Treblinka, their bodies incinerated on massive funeral pyres.

In early 1943 a group of Treblinka prisoners formed a resistance committee, which attempted to procure weapons. Plans for revolt and escape went into high gear in the late spring of 1943, when the prisoners realized that the camp was soon to be liquidated. On 2 August 1943 the resident Jewish slave laborers staged an uprising. Tension among the prisoners had been high all that day. Many had secretly packed a bundle of clothing for the road and prepared to remove money and valuables from hiding places, where they had been kept in the hope of eventual escape. Later that day weapons were removed from the storeroom and preparations were made to set the camp on fire. At 4:00 p.m. the shot rang out that set the mechanism of revolt into motion. Several hundred prisoners reached the forest; probably no more than 60 of them survived the war. In November 1943 the Nazis blew up the camp and built a farmhouse on the site. The remaining Sonderkommandos were forced to level the area, clear it of its mass graves, and plant pines on the site. Hence at the Treblinka site, as at the sites of the other three single-purpose extermination camps, no trace of the mass murders remained at the time of liberation.

Today the sites of the extermination camps are all marked by monuments erected by the Polish government during the 1950s and 1960s. Majdanek and Auschwitz have become state museums, in which the former barracks house exhibitions about the history of the camps and artifacts from the killing operations. A massive square memorial block on columns stands on the clearing at Chelmno; a large stone monument was erected in Treblinka, surrounded by 17,000 granite shards brought to the site; the Sobibor camp is marked by a memorial statue and a huge circular mound erected over the area where the gas chambers stood; the camp at Belzec, claiming only one postwar survivor, is marked by a memorial wall with an inscription and a statue of two skeletal figures supporting each other in their torment.   *Judith Tydor Baumel*

F

Farben, I. G. See I. G. FARBEN

Fascism in Western Europe The fascist parties in Western Europe were generally small, weak, and lacking in political influence. Their political and ideological orientation was influenced more by Italian fascism than by German national socialism—with the exception of the tiny Scandinavian parties—and thus in the early phases were often not antisemitic. This, however, tended to change by the late 1930s under the influence of Nazi expansion. During World War II all the fascist parties in occupied Western Europe followed the German lead and practiced strong and categorical antisemitism.

The ideological roots of Western European fascism lay in late-nineteenth-century France, originating during the generation that followed France's defeat in the Franco-Prussian War of 1870–71. An extremist social nationalism was first espoused by Paul Déroulède's League of Patriots during the 1880s, though not all sectors of the league were at first fully xenophobic and antisemitic. French antisemitism reached its fullest expression during the notorious Dreyfus affair of 1898–1900, in which Alfred Dreyfus, the only Jewish officer on the French general staff, was unjustly convicted of treason. At that point, antisemitism was politically more active in France than anywhere else in Europe, with the exception of Russia. Its most voluble leader was Edouard Drumont, whose book *La France Juive* (Jewish France, 1886) sold a million copies and helped make him the most popular antisemitic writer in Europe. Drumont's Antisemitic League of France (1889–1902) gained 10,000 members and won several local elections in French Algeria. The winners in Algiers organized a pogrom in 1897 that killed several Jews and injured approximately 100, though the French government soon removed their local leader from office. The

league returned four deputies from Algeria in the national elections of 1898; in the following year Déroulède tried to incite a coup d'état and in consequence was banished from France. The victory of the Dreyfusards and the liberalization of the republic decisively defeated these forces, sending them into irreversible decline.

The first proponent of national socialism in France was a quixotic adventurer, the Marquis de Morès, a sometime ranch-owning neighbor of Theodore Roosevelt in the Dakota Territory of the United States in the 1880s. Returning to France, the marquis founded a radical circle known as Morès et Ses Amis (Morès and His Friends). This group attempted to combine extreme nationalism with limited economic socialism, racism, and direct action. It also organized a strong-arm group for street battle and attempted to employ racist antisemitism as a means of popular mobilization, but it met with little success. Somewhat the same program was adopted by the "socialist nationalism" preached by the noted writer Maurice Barrès in the elections of 1898, though Barrès later adopted a more moderate and conservative position.

The only fin-de-siècle French radical nationalist and antisemitic group to survive as a force into the twentieth century was the right-radical monarchist Action Française, founded in 1899. Though the German scholar Ernst Nolte has called it the "beginning of fascism," Action Française remained ultrarightist and never developed the popular revolutionary characteristics of a genuine fascist movement. It strongly emphasized antisemitism, but its influence was greater in certain literary and intellectual circles than in the broader political arena.

The direct imitation of Italian fascism in France was first attempted by Georges Valois, a young militant of Action Française who formed a group called Le Faisceau in 1925. It eschewed the extremes of German nazism—including antisemitism—and, like its Italian counterpart, was even willing to admit Jewish members. It soon went into decline and disappeared in 1928.

A more moderate right-wing authoritarian nationalism was far more popular in France than generic fascism, and the temporary growth of Le Faisceau was soon exceeded by that of a new authoritarian youth movement, the Jeunesses Patriotes (Patriot Youth) of Pierre Taittinger. This movement declared itself open to members of all French religious groups, including Jews. During these years the representatives of wealthy sectors of French Jewish society maintained relations with a number of authoritarian French nationalist groups, so long as they were not overtly fascistic, and Taittinger was closely associated financially with a Jewish banking firm. The Jeunesses welcomed Jewish support and by 1929 had a total membership of 102,000. Subsequently they went into decline, and by 1933 Taittinger took a more radical turn, calling for a dictatorship and beginning to equivocate somewhat on the issue of antisemitism.

As the Jeunesses dwindled, a more clearly right-radical league emerged in Solidarité Française, organized by the perfume magnate François Coty in 1933. It was overtly antisemitic and profascist and increasingly authoritarian in tone, but it soon began to fade.

The most popular of all the right-wing national groups in France was the Croix de Feu (Cross of Fire), organized in 1927 by a recently retired army officer, Lt. Col. François de la Rocque. Later reorganized as the Parti Social Français, it achieved a membership of several hundred thousand by the late 1930s. It was also the most moderate of all the new parties and movements, and it officially disavowed antisemitism.

Only one categorically fascist party emerged in France during this decade, the Francistes of Marcel Bucard, founded in 1933. It tried to copy Italian formulas, declaring that it was not antisemitic and rejecting German racism. After the formation of the Rome-Berlin Axis in 1936, however, Bucard switched positions on both issues, but he failed to gain significant support.

More important was the Parti Populaire Français (PPF), organized by Jacques Doriot in 1936. It moved steadily in the direction of social nationalism, corporatism, and extremism but acquired the characteristics of a clear-cut fascist movement only under the German occupation. Doriot was a former key leader of the French Communist party and tried to maintain a "progressive" posture, initially rejecting antisemitism. After a brief period of success, the PPF began to decline in 1938.

The most notable fascist-type movement in Belgium prior to World War II was the Verdinaso (an acronym standing for Federation of Low Countries National-Solidarists), founded in 1931. It adopted a style, structure, and ideology roughly analogous to Italian fascism and was hostile to Germany but was nonetheless antisemitic in doctrine. It never achieved more than 5,000 members. The main force of Flemish nationalism in these years, the Flemish National Movement (VNV), was a right-wing Catholic group that did not exhibit fascist characteristics and was not antisemitic. Ultimately the most important fascist movement in the country was Christus Rex, a Catholic nationalist movement founded among French-speakers in 1935. It became a genuine fascist-type movement only under the impact of German occupation in World War II, but was always antisemitic in orientation.

There were a number of fascist movements in the Netherlands, the only significant one being the National Socialist Movement (NSB), founded by Anton Mussert in 1931. It advocated a moderate Italian-style fascism, more appropriate to the tolerant and democratic Dutch society, and eschewed racism. Mussert declared that "every good Dutch Jew is welcome in our party." After gaining some initial success in 1935, the NSB went into decline and revived only under the German occupation.

There were a number of tiny right-radical and would-be fascist groups in Great Britain, but the only one to attract any attention was the British Union of Fascists (BUF), formed in 1932. The BUF was modeled on Italian fascism and was not originally anti-Jewish; indeed, some of its strong-arm squads were at first trained by the Jewish boxer "Kid" Lewis. By 1936, however, the BUF, seeking to arouse greater support, had moved to antisemitism as a corollary of extreme nationalism. In Britain it was not the Jews but the fascists who were destined for the ghetto, and after a few years of modest growth the BUF went into serious decline.

By contrast with many of the Western European fascist parties, the ones that developed in Scandinavia were more directly influenced by nazism and hence overtly antisemitic. This was the case with the Swedish National Socialist party (SNP), the Danish National Socialist Workers party (DNSAP), and the Icelandic

Nationalist Movement, as well as other even smaller groups. All these forces failed to rally support.

The most important Scandinavian proto-Nazi movement was Vidkun Quisling's Nasjonal Samling (National Unity) party in Norway. Quisling drew closer and closer to Nazi Germany, ideologically and politically, but in peacetime was never able to win more than 2 percent of the national vote.

The only sizable fascist-type organization to emerge in Europe west of Germany and Italy was the Spanish Falange Española, organized in 1933. There were only a handful of Jews in Spain, and the Falange did not emphasize antisemitism. The intellectual who introduced Italian fascist doctrines in Spain during the 1920s, Ernesto Giménez Caballero, strongly advocated Sephardic culture as an enduring aspect of a broader Spanish-language culture. Giménez Caballero made a trip across the Mediterranean to study Sephardic culture and devoted a special section of his leading avant-garde journal, *La Gaceta Literaria,* to it. The main leader of the Falange, José Antonio Primo de Rivera, on occasion silenced anti-Jewish cries at Falangist meetings, condemning negative slogans. There was nonetheless an antisemitic sector within the Spanish movement, and an occasional antisemitic article appeared in the Falangist press.

During the Spanish civil war the Falange was made the official state party of the conquering Franco regime, which dominated Spain in 1939. It was, however, merged with other Catholic groups, and its Italian-style fascism became somewhat diluted in the process. During the civil war Falangist publications expressed more of a tendency toward antisemitism, but this never became a major feature of its program, particularly in view of the paucity of Jews in Spain, and the Falange rejected Nazi-style racism as anti-Catholic.

The German conquest of most of western continental Europe in 1940 created a decisive new situation. It greatly stimulated the crystallization and expansion of fascistic movements in the occupied countries, and it also turned them strongly toward the Nazi model with its categorical antisemitism.

The most significant changes occurred in France, for the most important new regime to emerge in any of the countries defeated or occupied by Germany was the French regime in Vichy. Limited by the terms of the surrender to no more than central and southeastern France, the new regime—the only one in occupied Europe to retain a modicum of independence—under the 84-year-old Marshal Philippe Pétain, was legally voted power to govern by decree in the final meeting of the last democratically elected parliament of the Third Republic. It created no new political party but rested on a broad ad-hoc coalition of moderates, conservatives, and rightists. Its name was derived from the choice of the south-central resort town of Vichy as the seat of government.

Vichy immediately became a regime of moderate right-wing authoritarianism (though with increasing right-radical overtones) that generally rejected extremist revolutionary fascism. Genuine French fascists and protofascists mostly remained in the German northern occupation zone, whose center was Paris. Nonetheless, Pétain's government soon decided to align itself with German antisemitism, and the first anti-Jewish legislation was introduced in October 1940. This was followed by increasingly stringent measures, defined in family and racial rather than religious terms. During the next three years, the regular Vichy police did most of the work of the SS in organizing tens of thousands of Jews, beginning at first with refugee Jews from other countries but later including many French citizens, who were rounded up to be handed over to the administrators of the Final Solution. Though Vichy was not an uncompromisingly fascist regime, its Jewish policy was much more destructive than that of Italian fascism. By early 1943 incidents had developed near the boundary between the two regimes in southeastern France when Jews hunted by the Vichy police were protected by the Italians.

The regular French fascist parties played only a limited role in the arrest and deportation of Jews in France. Under the occupation, Marcel Bucard's very small Parti Franciste remained active. It repudiated the handful of Jewish members who had once joined it and became virulently antisemitic. Doriot's Parti Populaire Français completed its politico-ideological transformation into a completely fascist movement and became the largest of all French fascist parties, undergoing increasing nazification, including the adoption of racial antisemitism. The same might be said of a variety of tiny would-be French fascist parties. The most important of these was the so-called Mouvement Social Révolutionnaire of Eugène Deloncle, which formed small militia or police groups that engaged in terrorist acts, helped seize Jews, and fought the resistance. Other groups of the same nazified orientation were the Parti Français National Collectiviste, the

Parti National-Sociale Français, and the Croisade Français du National Socialisme.

The only partial exception among the French fascist groups was Marcel Déat's Rassemblement National Populaire (RNP), organized in 1941. Déat, a former socialist leader, developed the most "left fascist" of the French parties. The RNP was second in membership to the PPF. Déat directly invoked the heritage of the French Revolution and economic modernization, as well as a more moderate semi-internationalist position. He also took a more moderate antisemitic position than did his ultrafascist rivals, but his left fascism was tolerated, and even to some extent supported, by the German authorities as a ploy to draw part of the French left toward the Third Reich. Déat subsequently became labor minister of the Vichy government in March 1944 as Vichy took on more of a directly fascistic coloration in its final phase.

Puppet fascist parties also played a role in Nazi antisemitic policies in occupied northwestern Europe. Of these the most notorious was Quisling's Nasjonal Samling in Norway, which was eventually given administration of part of the government of occupied Norway in February 1942. It completely failed, however, in its effort to inculcate pro-Nazi and antisemitic attitudes among Norwegians.

In Holland, Mussert's Dutch National Socialist Movement had once been proportionately the largest fascist party in Western Europe but had dropped from 47,000 members in 1935 to 29,000 by the time of the German invasion. Mussert was at first denied any role under the occupation, partly because of his more moderate Italian-style fascism, with its earlier absence of antisemitism. The new Nazi-type Dutch parties under the occupation, the National Socialist party of Dutch Workers and the National Fascist Front, failed to generate support, however, and in December 1941 the NSB was recognized as the sole legal political party in Holland. During the remainder of the war the more radical, pro-Nazi, and extreme antisemitic sector of the party came to the fore and achieved some success in making the NSB a real force in Dutch life and in encouraging a greater degree of active collaboration than in the rest of occupied Western Europe.

There was distinctly less collaboration in Belgium, but there the Rexist movement of Léon Degrelle became transformed under the occupation from a right-wing Catholic nationalist movement to a radical and nazified party, racist and virulently antisemitic. Rex never had more than about 8,000 members, but it organized various small auxiliary formations, military, police, and others, which loyally served all the policies of the Third Reich. In the final phase of the war Rex went farther than most fascist parties in occupied Europe in trying to define a "Eurofascism" or "Euronazism" based on all the allegedly superior racial elements in Central and Western European countries, purified of Jews and other inferior elements.

Thus, though most Western European fascist parties (with the exception of the Scandinavians) had originally tended to follow the Italian model and did not espouse extreme racism or antisemitism, this state of affairs began to change with the expansion of Nazi influence during the mid-1930s. The effect of German occupation was to create a trend toward growing, if never complete, uniformity of Western European fascist parties under the German hegemony. This tendency prominently featured the adoption of racial doctrine and an incendiary antisemitism. Though the Western European fascist parties were rarely the authors, or even the primary executioners, of the policies that implemented the Holocaust, they all came to cooperate with and help to promote those policies.

Stanley Payne

Feiner, Leon (1888–1945) Leader of the Bund, member of the Warsaw ZOB (Jewish Fighting Organization) and of Zegota. Survived on the "Aryan side" when the ghetto was liquidated but died of illness shortly thereafter. See BUND

Filderman, Wilhelm (1882–1963) Leader of Romanian Jewry during World War II, negotiated with Antonescu and the Romanian authorities in an attempt to forestall deportations to Transnistria and the Polish death camps. See TRANSNISTRIA

Final Solution: Preparation and Implementation The circumstances and decisions that brought about the destruction of European Jewry continue to be the focus of intense research and debate. Documents relating to decisions are scarce. The Nazi system was secretive: many discussions were not recorded, and important orders were often given verbally. Such German documentation as did exist was largely destroyed at the end of World War II. Some of the surviving documents, especially those recovered by the Red Army in Eastern Europe and Berlin, ended up in archives that were closed to researchers until the end

A Polish survivor shows U.S. soldier John L. Lyndon the crematorium ovens used to burn corpses in Dora-Mittelbau. April 1945

of the Cold War. Many archives have yet to make all their documents available to scholars.

Yet despite the missing and dispersed documentation, there exists an enormous amount of written evidence on the decision-making process, the preparations for the Final Solution, and the mass murder itself. Such a gigantic crime could not be kept totally secret. Even while it was being perpetrated, several key persons, including Adolf Hitler, made public statements about the "fate of the Jews" that clearly betokened their complete destruction.

The various scholarly interpretations of the documents concerning the Final Solution are based on differing views of the Nazi phenomenon and are influenced by fundamental methodological differences. Since the 1960s the debate has been dominated by two trends: intentionalism and functionalism. The inten-

tionalists focus on Hitler's ideology, which in their view led Hitler early on to decide that Jews should be murdered en masse. Later events resulted from the tactics (or the different stages) of gaining power and the necessary means of achieving this preconceived end. The functionalists argue that the Third Reich was such a diffuse structure that events were driven by huge bureaucracies carrying officials on their backs. On first attaining power, the Nazis had no concrete plans for translating their ideology into practice, or no sense of how far that process should go. Hence, events were determined by the working of mechanisms which, although created by the Nazis, took on lives of their own. This process of "cumulative radicalization," caused by the necessities of practical events coupled with a lack of "positive solutions" and a consequent "selection of negative elements in the Nazi ideology," generated the conditions for mass murder, even though (the functionalists assert) no explicit order had been is-sued by Hitler.

The functionalist view appears to have been influ-enced by an understanding of twentieth-century na-tion-states, first proposed by Max Weber and adopted in the 1930s and 1940s by various social scientists and historians, as essentially bureaucratic. Later research and recent developments in the character of modern nation-states challenge such an interpretation and cast doubt on its historical validity in Nazi Germany, in which Hitler's role was unquestionably decisive. On the other hand, the intentionalist approach may have been influenced by the juridical approach and termi-nology adopted by the Nuremberg prosecutors, who attempted to show a Nazi conspiracy to commit crimes from the outset. There needs to be further investiga-tion of Hitler's direct involvement in the regime's "Jewish policy" and its step-by-step development into the Final Solution, as well as the role of SS figures such as Heinrich Himmler, Reinhard Heydrich, Hein-rich Müller, and Adolf Eichmann. However, an expla-nation focusing on individuals is incomplete unless their original intentions are interpreted within the his-torical framework that transformed those ideas into reality. In the 1990s historians started to reach beyond intentionalism and functionalism by trying to bring richness and complexity to the historical picture that had been executed in only a few bold strokes.

Attention has turned to a range of new questions that have bearing on the planning and implementation of the Final Solution. What was the relation between Nazi ideology and German politics at various points along the time line of the Third Reich? What is the place of the decision to annihilate the Jews within the broader Nazi scheme to create a German-dominated racial "new order" in Europe? Did the Nazis see the fate of the Jews as unique or central in comparison to the fates of other so-called inferior races? How did Nazi percep-tions of the behavior and actions of third parties such as Great Britain, the Soviet Union, and the United States affect the course of the Final Solution?

Other considerations must also enter into any new analysis. The Nazi regime's decisions relating to Jews should be linked to its preparation for worldwide "total warfare." The part played by the allies of Nazi Germany must also be brought into the larger picture. The inner structure and dynamics of the Nazi regime itself should be clarified, and Nazi perceptions of the German peo-ple's responses to the Reich's Jewish policy—that is, the effect of public opinion—should be studied.

The Road to the Final Solution, 1919–38

The idea of a Jewish world conspiracy dominated the Nazi perception of reality after World War I. The Nazis used antisemitic notions to explain almost every political development within or outside Germany. They promised (and believed) that once the country was liberated from the Jewish yoke, a complete change of Germany's political, cultural, social, and economic realities must follow. Moreover, they saw themselves primarily as political men whose main task was to trans-late ideology into action. Though not yet a concrete program of actual measures, Nazi doctrine harbored a commitment to radical antisemitic action.

Following their takeover of the German government in 1933, the Nazis launched their *Judenpolitik*, a series of anti-Jewish actions deriving from antisemitic ideol-ogy. Thus they created a new political dimension hith-erto unknown in Germany, or indeed internationally, with its own terminology, logic, and dynamics. The Jewish question was now introduced into the politics of a major European power as a factor overshadowing every aspect of national behavior. In practical terms, this meant the education and organization of the masses by means of indoctrination, terror, and dictato-rial rule. Within this framework the basic antisemitic, ideological intentions, and the political realities in which the Nazis made decisions (the functional di-mensions of their behavior), are to be regarded as two sides of the same coin.

The idea that the Jews should be removed from Germany can be discerned from the beginning as a prime Nazi intention. Hitler's early correspondence and speeches underlined his conviction that theoreti-cal racism and antisemitism must be translated into a program of action. In *Mein Kampf* Hitler used anti-semitism to bind together the disparate ideas and in-terests within the German radical right. Antisemitism was thus a major ideological postulate, and also a polit-ical power tool, to be used according to the historical circumstances of the *Kampfzeit* (time of struggle).

The first program of the Nazi party (NSDAP), in 1920, hinted at an end to Jewish emancipation in Ger-many, removal of the Jews from the civil service, and cessation of free immigration into Germany. These el-ements reflect a postwar antisemitic consensus, espe-cially in southern Germany. Much more radical tendencies could be detected in Hitler's speeches and in official and semiofficial publications, such as Julius Streicher's weekly *Der Stürmer* and Alfred Rosenberg's *Der Mythus des 20. Jahrhunderts*. At the same time Nazi propaganda raised the Jewish issue in different parts of Germany in various forms, according to the leaders' calculations of political effect. In the early 1930s, when the NSDAP became a mass party needing a larger consensus, the Jewish issue appears to have been deliberately played down, as emphasis was laid on foreign policy and domestic economic problems.

Between 1933 and 1938 the regime's Jewish policy gradually became radicalized. Each new phase was preceded by public acts of violence, was instigated by party radicals, and culminated in anti-Jewish legislation. The forces at work, the storm troopers and various regional organizations, created an atmosphere of crisis that called for intervention by Hitler, decisions that can now be regarded as acts of state. In this way a new, temporary antisemitic consensus emerged, which still left room for the next, more extreme interplay of activities from below and intervention from above.

Each wave of increasingly radical behavior was related to developments in domestic politics, the German economy, and foreign relations. In between, however, were periods of relative calm and ostensible stabilization of the previous stage. Yet by its nature the Nazi phenomenon was dynamic: no settled condition could be accepted for any length of time, since quiescence was perceived as a return to that past which the party considered due for radical change. Hence a policy aimed at establishing a status quo would have been regarded as an intolerable gain for surviving pre-Nazi forces and values, such as traditional Christianity, liberalism, and leftist ideologies. All these were perceived as Jewish-inspired. At the same time, each wave of antisemitic radicalization brought with it an expansion of Nazi power at the expense of traditional elites: new institutions were created to deal with the current issue, or alternatively the existing bureaucratic machinery was geared to furthering the regime's antisemitic plans.

The first period started in March 1933 with attacks against individual Jews and Jewish property. The new regime converted this sporadic violence into a general boycott, culminating in the anti-Jewish legislation of spring 1933. During this phase Jews were completely removed from German public life.

The next stage began in spring and summer 1935 with a series of mob actions against Jews in several German cities. The peak came with the Nuremberg anti-Jewish legislation, which for the first time implemented the principle of biological separation, thus making Jews second-class citizens, or rather subjects, of the Third Reich. Anti-Jewish economic legislation, demanded by the party radicals, was not adopted as yet. From 1937 onward, however, massive pressure was brought to bear on Jewish businesses.

The third phase opened with a series of antisemitic attacks immediately following the annexation of Austria (the Anschluss) in March 1938 and reached its climax in the pogroms of 9–11 November 1938, known as Kristallnacht. This unprecedented violence was followed by collective punitive measures and radical legislation aimed at the expropriation of all Jewish property and at forced emigration. The policy of forced emigration was institutionalized in January 1939, when a Gestapo Central Office for Emigration was created, following the establishment of a similar office in Vienna in summer 1938. This meant that handling of the so-called Jewish problem was increasingly transferred to the SS.

Nazi "Jewish Policies," 1939–40

Following the Munich Agreement of September 1938, which allowed the Germans to occupy the Sudetenland in Czechoslovakia, Nazi policy toward the Jews was more and more involved with preparation for a European war. Forced emigration schemes aimed at German and Austrian Jews, and later at Czech Jews, continued while the Germans were negotiating with Western governments and the Intergovernmental Committee on Refugees (established after the Evian Conference) on large-scale evacuation plans. The proposal was that Jews from Europe should be relocated with Western approval and Jewish finance, but nothing had been achieved when the Germans invaded Poland on 1 September 1939. The ensuing war, and the resulting failure of the evacuation plans, drove the Nazis to radicalize their Jewish policy still further: they introduced forced labor for German Jews and considered such measures as imprisonment in army camps. Moreover, the focus changed, so that the Nazis perceived the Jewish question as a pan-European issue, even beyond the German sphere of influence.

On 30 January 1939 Hitler had first raised the Jewish question in Europe publicly as an issue of life or death for the continent. "If the international Jewish financiers inside and outside Europe should again succeed in plunging the nations into a world war," he warned, "the result will be, not the Bolshevization of the earth and thus the victory of Jewry, but the annihilation of the Jewish race throughout Europe." This statement could have been perceived as a threat, directed toward the Jews in the free world and toward the West, that the Jews under his dominion would pay the highest price for any outside resistance to Hitler's hegemonic plans in Europe. During the Final Solution Hitler used to refer to this "prophecy," as he called it, and note that it was being realized. Hence the Final Solution was not a complete secret to his own people in this and other respects.

The occupation of Poland added two considerations to the previous Jewish policies of Nazi Germany. Two million Polish Jews were now under German control, and the character of the German invasion sanctioned massive atrocities against the Polish elite and Jews. And at the outset of World War II Hitler ordered a full-scale euthanasia program, aimed at the murder of tens of thousands of people defined as mentally ill or retarded. These circumstances promoted the devaluation of human life and gave the Nazis experience at murder by poison gas.

On 21 September 1939 Reinhard Heydrich, head of the Reich Main Security Office and the SD, discussed the Jewish question with his aides. Topics included removal of the German Jews to Poland and a possible evacuation of Polish Jews to Soviet-occupied Poland. Finally, Heydrich canvassed his SS subordinates in Poland concerning short- and long-term solutions of the Jewish question. He ordered the concentration of Polish Jews in ghettos so that they could be moved as efficiently as possible. Their final destination was not specified, but it is clear that Heydrich was aiming at a reservation (*Reservat*) in eastern occupied Poland.

The reservation was also intended to absorb all the Jews from greater Germany. Adolf Eichmann, the "resettlement" expert of the Reichssicherheitshauptamt (RSHA, the combined Gestapo and SD), decided to set up a transit camp for the deportees in Nisko on the River San in the eastern part of the Generalgouvernement. Following the arrival in Nisko in October 1939 of the first transports of Jews from Upper Silesia, the Czech Protectorate, and Vienna, this improvised experiment was quickly abandoned. It proved that without careful planning, mass deportations in winter would result in an enormous death toll—not the intention at that time, as the Germans obviously would bear direct responsibility.

After the collapse of the Nisko plan, however, leading Nazis did not give up the idea of deporting all Jews under German control to the Generalgouvernement or to a special reservation in the Lublin area. Remarks by some of the authorities in occupied Poland during the winter of 1939–40 show that such a reservation was also supposed to facilitate the forcing of Jews over the demarcation line into Soviet-occupied territory in Poland or, if that was not possible, to remove and decimate them by means obscure even to senior officials. Their statements betoken an intention to treat the deportees brutally even to the point of causing fatalities, but not (at this stage) to kill them all. Still, German territorial plans of 1939–40, including the idea of concentrating the Jews near Lublin, show a predisposition to murder, since the living conditions of the deportees were intolerable.

A Jewish reservation was also seen as a means of putting pressure on the Western powers. Similar plans were connected with wide-ranging notions of resettlement from German-annexed lands in western Poland. In fact, deportations of Poles and Jews from those areas began at the end of 1939 but were halted in view of the growing resistance of the Governor-General of Poland, Hans Frank, whose territory was expected to absorb the deportees.

Jews living in the Generalgouvernement were subjected to especially harsh treatment. Beginning in November 1939 they had to wear the yellow badge, and in December their freedom of movement in the country was limited. Soon thereafter they were flung into closed ghettos and conscripted into forced labor.

The swift victory over France in the summer of 1940 appeared to give the Germans an opportunity to expel all the Jews from Europe. Under the Madagascar Plan 4 million Jews were to be transported to the island of Madagascar, off the eastern coast of Africa. Such a solution, in Hitler's eyes, would further his plans for hegemony and combine with Western acceptance of Nazi Germany as the creator of the new order in Europe. The plan also contained an element of hostage-taking to keep the United States, with its politically active Jewish communities, in check. It envisaged Madagascar as an SS-controlled territory, so that the Jews on the island would remain at the mercy of the Nazis. The whole plan was at once rejected by the

British. The fantastic aspirations, the vast numbers, and the possible exploitation of the plan for a variety of purposes cast strong doubt on its viability and on the intentions behind it.

The Decisions That Led to the Final Solution

The decision to annihilate the whole of European Jewry was taken in response to the changed strategic and foreign policy situation of Nazi Germany from the end of 1940 to autumn 1941. Great Britain had mounted unexpectedly vigorous resistance to German air attacks and showed no sign of capitulation. American aid to the British was growing: the United States sold destroyers to Great Britain, President Franklin Roosevelt succeeded in moving the Lend-Lease Act through Congress, and the U.S. Navy intervened on the British side in the Battle of the Atlantic. As American neutrality seemed to evaporate, Hitler believed that the value of the European Jews as hostages was fast disappearing.

Germany used these American actions, which were regarded as dangerous and provocative, to argue that the conflict had been widened by the Jews (who, according to Nazi propaganda, dominated U.S. politics) and had now become a global "Jewish war." Similar arguments may have also provided ammunition for those Nazis who were seeking a radical solution to the Jewish question.

At the same time, plans for Operation Barbarossa—the invasion of the Soviet Union, thus depriving the British of a potential ally—encouraged the indulgence in utopian ideas of establishing an Aryan racial empire that would span Europe. The realization of such fantasies would justify and necessitate unprecedented measures: the destruction and enslavement of so-called inferior races. These aspects of yet another phase of radicalized Nazi behavior entailed the first truly murderous "settlement" of the Jewish question in the occupied Soviet Union.

The planning of some kind of solution to the Jewish question in Europe was increasingly dominated by preparations for Operation Barbarossa. Documents suggest that by the end of 1940 Hitler had ordered Heydrich to prepare a new plan for deporting the Jews from German-controlled Europe (except the Soviet areas). At this stage the route and destination of the victims was not clear. Yet once Hitler signed Directive 21 on 18 December, ordering preparations for Bar-

barossa, the future goal of deportation could easily be imagined: it must lie in Soviet territory, which the Nazis expected to occupy in the summer of 1941. This background explains Heydrich's order of January 1941 renewing deportations from German-occupied areas to the Generalgouvernement, which evidently was perceived as a transit area only. By March 1941, however, the transports (which included Jews from Vienna) were hampering military movements assigned to Operation Barbarossa and were therefore stopped.

This setback did not interfere with Heydrich's preparations for the deportation of European Jews. In March 1941, according to a document recently found in Moscow, Heydrich submitted to Hermann Göring a draft plan for the "Final Solution of the Jewish Question." The subsequent order was signed by Göring on 31 July 1941, following an agreement concerning the powers of Alfred Rosenberg's new Ministry for the Occupied Eastern Territories. The order gave Heydrich authority "to act so as to carry out all the necessary organizations, substantive and material preparations for an overall solution (*Gesamtlösung*) of the Jewish question in the German area of influence in Europe." The fact that Rosenberg's powers figured in the discussions shows where the "overall solution" was to take place: in occupied Soviet territory.

Apart from their activities in Russia, the Nazi authorities planned a campaign of annihilation against the elites of peoples in the occupied countries, especially Jews and Bolsheviks. This large-scale murder was carried out by special killing units (*Einsatzgruppen*), by SS and regular police units, and in a number of cases by regular Wehrmacht units. In addition, local, German-created auxiliary police forces frequently participated in such operations.

German anti-Jewish policy in the occupied Soviet territories developed in three stages. The first began at the outset of the war in the East, with pogroms and improvised executions. The definition of the target population was broad enough to allow mass executions in various areas, and in some places the entire male population of military age was liquidated. The second stage, beginning in August 1941, was much wider in scope and was aimed at whole families, including women and children. It is estimated that within two months about 50,000 people were shot, while from August to January 1942 about half a million perished. The third phase followed the initial conquest of certain areas by the

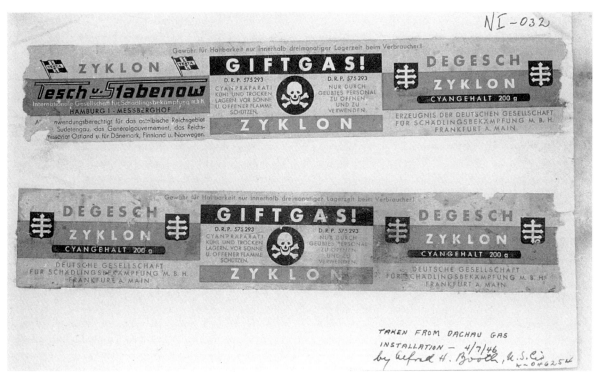

Labels taken from canisters of Zyklon B from the Dachau gas installation. The center panel reads, "Poison Gas!" "Cyanide Preparation! [skull and crossbones] To be opened and used only by trained personnel." 7 April 1946

Germans and the creation of permanent local occupation offices. It consisted of ghettoization and forced labor, together with continued mass shootings, and began in the western parts of the occupied territories in August 1941, spreading to the eastern areas in the fall. The policy relating to the slaughter of Jews in the Soviet Union had now become long-term and systematic.

The heads of the Nazi security police realized that only limited destruction of Soviet Jews could be achieved by firing squads. Rumors of mass shootings were becoming rampant, the approaching winter would make gravedigging by the victims themselves more difficult, and the executions were putting an emotional strain on soldiers who pulled the triggers. Accordingly, a search began for alternative methods of mass killing. By September–October 1941 the mass murder of Jews was also taking place outside the Soviet Union. Thus, the planned Final Solution of the Jewish question in Soviet territory following a swift German victory had already begun in another form even during the campaign. Later, it was widened step by step to become a program to destroy all the Jews of Europe.

Hitler's own words, as well as other documents,

demonstrate his obsession with Jews in general and his extreme approach toward the fate of the Jews under his control. At the same time, the technology of murder already used in the euthanasia program began to be transferred to the East. In September 1941 the head of Einsatzgruppe B, Arthur Nebe, ordered a lethal experiment on patients in a mental home in Mogilev (Belorussia), where engine exhaust containing carbon monoxide gas was fed into a sealed room. The success of this execution led the RSHA's Criminal Technical Institute to develop gas vans, in which the passengers in a sealed truck could be dispatched by the exhaust fumes as the vehicle moved along. The initial testing of these vans was carried out at the end of November 1941 in the Sachsenhausen concentration camp; 30 men were murdered in this way. Several of these vehicles were then built, and they were in operation by the end of the year in Chelmno and the East.

A larger group of euthanasia experts was sent in the fall of 1941 to Odilo Globocnik, the SS and police chief of the Lublin district. In October–November 1941 work began on constructing the killing center at Belzec, where mass murder by exhaust fumes was also planned. In October the creation of new ghettos anywhere in the Generalgouvernement was forbidden, and leaving a ghetto without permission was made punishable by death. There are indications that around this time Globocnik received a direct order from Himmler to murder the Jews of his district, which was scheduled to become a center of SS settlements. In the following year, 1942, these orders were broadened to include all the Jews in the Generalgouvernement.

At the same time, experiments on an alternative method of murder by gas were carried out in Auschwitz. In October 1941 preparations were under way for a large crematorium. Probably in December several hundred Soviet prisoners of war and political prisoners were murdered in an experiment with Zyklon B gas. Whether at this stage Auschwitz was envisaged as the center for the systematic destruction of Europe's Jews is still an open question. Here two phases can be discerned: between February and June 1942 approximately 25 transports of Jews arrived. The Jews from Upper Silesia were immediately murdered; the others, brought from Slovakia, France, and the Czech Protectorate, were sent to the concentration camp. After July, transports included Jews of other countries and arrived almost daily. It was in July that a system was introduced to select some of the deportees from each transport for forced labor; the rest were gassed immediately.

Adolf Eichmann told interrogators in Jerusalem in 1961 that two or three months after the beginning of the Soviet campaign Himmler had informed him that Hitler had ordered the physical destruction of the Jews to be carried out by the SS. Although this statement appears plausible, there are indications that the conversation took place several months later.

In September 1941 Hitler decided to deport all Jews eastward from Germany proper, possibly during that year, in preparation for transport still further east in the coming spring. Documents of that time show a flood of appeals made by Nazi officials to Hitler to deport the Jews from Germany (and also from other countries, including France). Among the reasons given were the increasing air offensive, the shortage of housing, and security considerations.

At first the deportation of 60,000 Jews to the Lodz ghetto was planned, but this number was reduced by more than half, to 25,000 (including 5,000 Gypsies), following vigorous representations by the local German civil administration. (The deportations were carried out between 15 October and 8 November.) In exchange for this concession, it appears that Gauleiter Arthur Greiser received permission from Himmler to liquidate about 100,000 Polish Jews in his area. As a consequence, the gas truck station Chelmno was established in November–December 1941.

Between November 1941 and January 1942 a second wave of deportations struck, carrying away approximately 50,000 Jews from Germany, Austria, and the Czech Protectorate to the ghettos of Minsk and Riga. The first five transports destined for Riga, however, were sent to Kovno instead, where 5,000 deportees were shot immediately. The remainder, crammed into the ghettos of Minsk, Riga, and Lodz, survived for a time. Hence it may be assumed that at the end of 1941 no general order had yet been issued to kill all the Jews of Central Europe.

In Serbia it was mostly Jewish men who were selected by the German army for murder, in retaliation for partisan actions against the Wehrmacht: 100 civilians were shot for every German soldier killed. Almost the whole Jewish male population of Serbia was destroyed within a few weeks by the same method of mass shootings employed in the occupied Soviet territories, although the initiative in Serbia was taken by the regular German army. The women and children were murdered between March and May 1942, following orders issued by the local SS security police.

In this way the Final Solution was extended over occupied Europe. Originally it was to have been a postwar action carried out in Soviet territory. But as the war in the East unexpectedly dragged on, a widening of the plan's scope and form occurred. The Wannsee Conference of 20 January 1942 was one of the peaks of this progression.

Such a process of radicalization could be explained by a number of factors within the framework of a limited war that the Nazis themselves were transforming into a world conflict. First, the creation and use of a multistage killing machine generated an inner logic of destruction related to the prolongation and brutalization of the war in Russia. Since orders were given to the killing units ahead of the campaign itself, it is clear that the brutality was preconceived. Second, given the inner structure of the Nazi regime and the permanent competition and rivalry among its leading representatives, any act of radical antisemitism was encouraged because it served personal and institutional ambitions. This radical antisemitism was cumulatively institu-

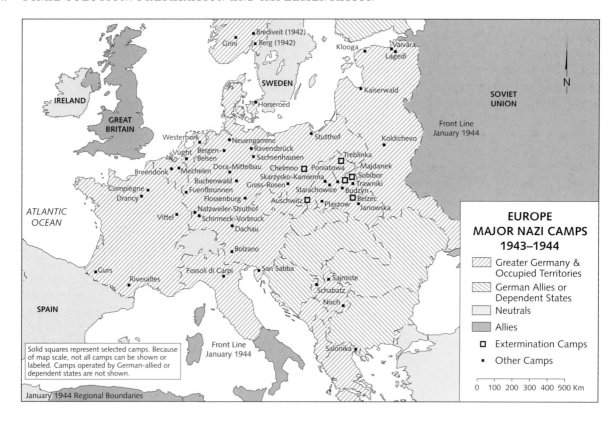

EUROPE
MAJOR NAZI CAMPS
1943–1944

Greater Germany &
Occupied Territories

German Allies or
Dependent States

Neutrals

Allies

□ Extermination Camps

▪ Other Camps

Solid squares represent selected camps. Because of map scale, not all camps can be shown or labeled. Camps operated by German-allied or dependent states are not shown.

January 1944 Regional Boundaries

0 100 200 300 400 500 Km

tionalized in an ongoing competition in evil. Third, the proclamations by top Nazis that the Jewish question would be solved during the war meant that radical elements in the party formed an expectation of murder as a solution. When the war was not won quickly, when the German home front was threatened by Allied air raids and aggrieved by losses at the front, those expectations were reinforced by a violent desire for revenge. During the second half of 1941 there was rivalry among some Gauleiters to be the first to rid their regions of Jews. Deportation of Jews was perceived as compensation for the war effort, not only ideologically and politically but also practically, since it reduced housing shortages, and allowed the "aryanization" of Jewish property all over Europe.

Fourth, the prospect of a grand military triumph beyond all imagination, extending from the Bay of Biscay to the Volga River, may have given the Nazis a feeling of omnipotence and spurred them on to outdo all previous deeds. Fifth, this sense of omnipotence may have been mixed with a wish to strike out against the United States for supporting the British and aiding the besieged Soviet Union. Hitler believed that U.S. anti-Nazi policies were dictated by American Jews, whom he held responsible for changing the limited conflict in Europe into a world war. Growing tensions between the United States and Japan in 1940 and 1941, culminating in the attack on Pearl Harbor, freed Hitler from any need to placate the Americans.

A further theory about the Final Solution considers destruction of European Jewry as merely a first step toward more universal Nazi goals. This "spearhead theory" assumes that the decision to exterminate the Jews legitimized far-reaching oppression and plans for the annihilation of other foreign peoples. A later version of this theory holds that the destruction of the Jews was part of a Nazi plan to enforce ethnic cleansing upon other countries and create a "pure German" area of settlement and economic modernization. Both theories try to universalize the Final Solution, thereby minimizing the centrality of antisemitism in Nazi doctrine and practice, while ignoring the continuation of the Final Solution until the very end of the Third Reich.

The Final Solution may also have offered a domestic political advantage. Perhaps the Nazis wished to create a sense of collective guilt, thereby binding the German people to the regime as accomplices in an unprecedented crime. Internal resistance against the Nazi regime might then be rejected by the West as insufficient to exculpate any German from responsibility in the mass murder.

The result of this radicalization process was the Wannsee Conference, when Heydrich informed the heads of the main German ministries about the further development of the Final Solution. According to him, the Jews throughout Europe were to be marched to work in the newly conquered territories of the East. The rigors of these forced marches would subject the deportees to "natural decimation." Survivors would receive appropriate "treatment"—that is, they would be murdered by other means. These statements still reflected the original RSHA plans to deport the Jews to a reservation in occupied Soviet territory: this scheme was in fact partially carried out by the deportations to Minsk and Riga up to November–December 1941. At the time of the Wannsee Conference RSHA had already begun to work out much larger deportation schemes for the spring or summer of 1942, intended to send European Jews to the killing centers in the East. The fact that Heydrich mentioned Jews beyond German control, such as those living in Great Britain, North Africa, and Turkey, reveals that the Final Solution was intended to last into the postwar period and to include all Jews in any future German sphere of influence.

It is clear that the move to implement the Final Solution was not taken at the Wannsee Conference, which was aimed at involving the heads of the German civil administration as accomplices and establishing the leading role of the SS in the process. Another purpose was to regulate the sensitive issue of mixed marriages and their offspring on the basis of a broader definition of Jewish identity, which would allow the SS the final verdict.

After the Wannsee Conference

To understand the complexities of the Final Solution, both the decision to undertake it and the various implementations of that decision must be scrutinized. The way in which it was fulfilled resulted from many interrelated actions taken by different authorities and coordinated over a long period of time. In many cases the phases of decision and implementation can hardly be separated, and sometimes operations began while the decision-making process was still evolving. Rather than a simple execution of a detailed, preconceived blueprint, the Final Solution was a general framework for genocide carried out in accordance with many different decisions under a variety of circumstances. There was no uniform process.

In occupied Soviet territory, mass shootings and the use of gas vans continued throughout 1942 and 1943. Those Jews who remained were imprisoned in ghettos and killed in preplanned operations, when the inhabitants were taken from some parts of each ghetto and shot nearby. Smaller communities, and Jews who had managed to escape into the countryside, were hunted down, mostly under the pretext of antipartisan action. Numerous German units were involved in these actions: agencies of the German and auxiliary local police, Wehrmacht and Waffen SS units, and other armed groups drawn from civilian bodies such as Organisation Todt, the forestry administration, and farming inspectors.

In Poland, in the spring of 1942, destruction of the Jews was extended from the Lublin district to the Generalgouvernement as a whole, according to the priorities set at the Wannsee Conference. After the assassination of Reinhard Heydrich in Prague in the late spring, the plan was code-named Operation Reinhard to commemorate the slain Nazi leader. Globocnik was put in charge, probably on verbal orders from Himmler. A special staff was created to plan and coordinate deportations from the ghettos, confiscation of property, and killings in the camps. Aside from Belzec, where systematic mass murder started in March 1942, two other death centers were built: Sobibor in the Lublin district and Treblinka, also in the eastern part of the Generalgouvernement, in the Warsaw district. All three camps were straightforward machines for immediate murder by carbon monoxide exhaust from diesel motors. In the region of Lublin another extermination camp was created—Majdanek.

Polish Jews from German-occupied territory were killed in other camps. Those from the Warthegau (the annexed territory of western Poland) were murdered in Chelmno—not at a camp, but at a gas truck station. The Jews of eastern Upper Silesia were deported to Auschwitz.

As in many parts of the occupied Soviet territory, Polish ghettos, sealed off by the Germans from the outside world, were used as transit stations on the way to systematic execution. Many died in the ghettos from hunger, disease, and random German brutality.

In 1942 the Germans began to liquidate the more than 600 Polish ghettos. In the smaller ones the inmates were murdered out of hand. The Germans depopulated the larger ghettos in stages, using their nominees on the Jewish councils (*Judenräte*) and the Jewish auxiliary police to gain a measure of cooperation in the deportations. After liquidation of the ghettos in the Generalgouvernement was completed in 1943, those Jews who had escaped the transports were tracked down and executed.

Not only was Poland's large Jewish community almost entirely destroyed, but the country became the graveyard of most European Jews. In the summer of 1942 the concentration camp at Auschwitz, where killing had begun at the end of 1941, became the largest death camp in Nazi-occupied Europe. Jews from throughout the continent were brought there. Upon arrival they underwent selection to determine those fit for work; the rest, mainly old people and children, were at once sent to the gas chambers. The forced laborers were worked to death or, after a short time, sent for selection and gassed.

Majdanek, located in the Lublin district and officially known as KZ Lublin, was a slave labor and extermination camp. Its gas chambers went into operation in the fall of 1942. As with many other camps in this region, almost all the inmates were shot on 3 November 1943 in the Erntefest action, which may have been a response to the revolt of Jewish inmates at Sobibor the previous month.

Majdanek and Auschwitz were administered by the SS Economic and Administrative Main Office (WVHA), but the order to carry out systematic mass killings in Auschwitz was, according to the commandant Rudolf Höss, given by Himmler personally. In Majdanek, Globocnik was instrumental in operating the system in conjunction with the WVHA.

Systematic deportations to the death centers began in the early spring of 1942. They were organized by the Jewish Section of the RSHA under Adolf Eichmann. Guards came from civilian police, and transport was supplied by the German Ministry of Transportation or directly through the German railway system. Many other civil authorities—including the judiciary, the finance administration, the Propaganda Ministry, and local governments—played an active part in preparing, organizing, and benefiting from the deportations.

In order to deport thousands of people from a town, the whole local police apparatus had to be mobilized; a large transit area, such as the local freight depot, was taken over and guarded. Tax officials made out lists of Jewish property and arranged for confiscation; labor department staff revoked work permits; housing office staff collected keys and arranged the transfer of empty dwellings to the new tenants. In Poland regular police units and personnel from the SS training camp at Trawniki frequently carried out the deportations.

The German Foreign Ministry was actively involved in the somewhat complicated implementation of the Final Solution in countries allied to Germany. Ministry representatives working with the RSHA—sometimes even competing with the SS—helped in establishing the necessary legal, administrative, and political mechanisms in countries friendly to Germany such as Slovakia, Romania, Croatia, northern (Fascist) Italy, and Hungary (after March 1944). They maintained contact with local ethnic-German groups, sometimes using them to put pressure on reluctant allies so that the Final Solution should be enforced or so that Jews would be transferred into German hands.

In Greater Germany (Germany, Austria, and the Czech Protectorate) individual deportations were carried out as early as the end of 1939. There followed a wave of mass deportations to ghettos in Eastern Europe between October 1941 and January 1942. Most Jews from Greater Germany were transferred to the killing centers between March 1942 and the summer of 1943.

A special role was given to the ghetto in Theresienstadt, near Prague, which was supposed to allow the survival of some privileged Jews, including veterans of World War I, spiritual leaders, and the aged. In fact, however, Theresienstadt served as camouflage for the Final Solution by creating the fiction of a Jewish "home for the elderly" and being used to deceive the International Red Cross. Most of its inmates were murdered in Auschwitz, however, later in 1944. A special role was foreseen for Bergen-Belsen as a hostage camp, in which the Nazis would hold Jews to be exchanged for German nationals or for Allied goods and money, or to be exploited as political capital. In the final stage of the Third Reich, Bergen-Belsen was overcrowded with thousands of the remaining Jewish slave laborers, many among whom did not survive.

The deportations from France, Holland, and Belgium, which started in the summer of 1942, were ordered and coordinated by Eichmann's staff but carried out by local police. Most deportees were sent to Auschwitz. In Holland the deportees were usually Dutch Jews, whereas in France most were foreigners, many of whom had lived in France for years. About half of Belgian Jewry was deported. In Norway there were two deportations, carried out by local police, in November 1942 and February 1943; they involved about half of the small Jewish community, who were murdered in Auschwitz. Denmark was an exception: a massive operation to save Danish Jewry, undertaken by the Danish underground in October 1943, was largely successful.

In Serbia the Germans did not bother to deport the Jews to camps outside the region but dealt with them on the spot. Almost the entire population of Serbian Jews had been killed by May 1942. Most of the Jews of Greece were deported to Auschwitz in the spring of 1943.

Following the occupation of Italy in the fall of 1943 the Germans established their own police apparatus, which arrested several thousand Jews and deported them to Auschwitz. In November the reestablished fascist government in the north ordered all Jews to be imprisoned in concentration camps. Between February and December 1944 many inmates of those camps were deported to Auschwitz and elsewhere, under orders from the SS security police. About one-fifth of the Italian Jews were deported.

After the invasion of the Soviet Union, the Final Solution was also carried out in territories occupied by the Romanian army and the Wehrmacht in Bessarabia, northern Bukovina, and Transnistria. It is possible that Hitler told the Romanian dictator, Ion Antonescu, about his initial plans in regard to the Jews in Soviet territory when they met in June 1941. It was on their own initiative, however, that the Romanians interned urban Jews in Bessarabia and Bukovina, and that Romanian police units killed the remaining Jews there. In the summer of 1941 all Jews in those areas are presumed to have been murdered by German and Romanian army units supported by SS killing groups from Einsatzgruppe D and by local auxiliary units made up of Romanians and Ukrainians. In the first phase of this action about 160,000 Jews were killed. In mid-September the Romanians ordered the deportation of the survivors to Transnistria, where most of them died. The Romanian army was also involved in the mass murder of Ukrainian and southern Bukovinian Jews.

At that time the Jews of Romania itself had not yet been deported, although those living elsewhere under German control were deprived of their citizenship and later killed by the Nazis. Germany urged Romania, both behind the scenes and even publicly in Bucharest, to deport the remaining 292,000 Jews to Belzec. This pressure failed, for various reasons: Hitler's inability to subdue the Soviet Union, national Romanian considerations concerning its neighbors, and Romania's own interests toward the Allies. In addition, the activities of the skillful Romanian Jewish leadership, Vatican intervention, and Romania's strategic location, with oil reserves vital to Germany, all prevented the implementation of the Final Solution in Romania proper. In 1944 several thousand survivors were even able to return from Transnistria. After Romania switched allegiance to the Allies in August 1944, it provided a refuge for several thousand Hungarian Jews.

Bulgaria was the only member of the Axis alliance that did not join in Operation Barbarossa. Nevertheless, it did acquire territory as a result of the German campaign against the Soviet Union. Some traditionally Bulgarian lands that had been in Soviet control, as well as Macedonia, Thrace, and eastern Serbia, were transferred by Germany to Bulgaria. In early 1943 about 12,000 Jews from those areas were delivered to the Germans, who had demanded 20,000. The shortfall—8,000 human beings—owed their preservation to the intervention of Bulgarian and Macedonian public figures, although the Jews in occupied Bulgarian territories were deported to Treblinka and murdered. Continuing German pressure on the Bulgarian government to deport the Jews of Bulgaria itself led to severe legal and other measures directed against the survivors, but the combined resistance of leading figures in Bulgarian society prevented the planned deportations, sometimes at the last moment.

The Final Solution in Hungary was carried out with the utmost speed following the German occupation in mid-March 1944. For this purpose Eichmann's Berlin staff came to Budapest as a *Sonderkommando* (special killing squad), and—with the help of the Hungarian Interior Ministry, the gendarmerie, and other bodies controlled by antisemites and pro-Germans—immediately started to identify and ghettoize provincial Jews, who then were deported to Auschwitz. Budapest remained untouched at this stage, since the Germans thought it best to preserve Hungarian national pride. Moreover, Adm. Miklós Horthy, who remained at least formally in power, hampered the exercise of direct Nazi control over the city against his wishes. Between 15 May and 9 July 1944 about 437,000 Jews were de-

Hungarian Jewish women and children awaiting selection on the ramp at Auschwitz-Birkenau death camp. Young children, their mothers, and the elderly were destined for an immediate death in the gas chamber.

ported to Auschwitz; most of them were summarily murdered. Others passed through Auschwitz to German concentration camps and their associated military factories, probably to offset the serious shortage of labor in the Nazi system at that late stage of the war. This may also have been the reason for the arrival (and subsequent survival) of about 21,000 Jews from the south of Hungary in Strasshof, near Vienna.

On 7 July Horthy rebelled against the German occupying power and ordered a halt to the deportations. Hitler tried personal negotiations with Horthy on the fate of the Budapest Jews, offering to release a few in exchange for the majority. On 15 October 1944, however, Horthy's regime was replaced by local fascists and their German-Hungarian allies. Eichmann, who had been forced to leave Hungary in July, returned, and the Final Solution was resumed by marching Budapest Jews to the frontier. Many were shot along the

route or died from the intolerable conditions of the march. Many more were killed by Hungarian fascists in Budapest itself, while the survivors were confined in a ghetto. Between December 1944 and February 1945, pressure by foreign governments, Red Cross intervention, humanitarian efforts by foreign envoys such as the Swedish diplomat Raoul Wallenberg, the arrival of the Red Army, and perhaps also rifts within the Nazi system itself allowed about 100,000 Hungarian Jews to survive, out of the 800,000 members of the original community.

Slovakia was an autonomous ally of Nazi Germany. Accordingly, at the beginning of 1942 its nationalist-Catholic government was ready to transfer most Slovak Jews to the Germans for "training and reeducation" in the East. The Slovaks even paid the Germans for these services. The gas chambers of Auschwitz and Majdanek received about 58,000 Slovak Jews between

March and October 1942, when deportations were suspended. Among the remaining Slovak Jews, about 10,000 managed to flee to neighboring Hungary, and some 20,000 survived in Slovakia until August 1944, when Jews joined a Slovak attempt at a general uprising against the Germans. Many were killed on the spot; others were murdered in Auschwitz. The suspension of the Final Solution in Slovakia from late 1942 until mid-1944 has been ascribed to a deal—the so-called Europa Plan—between the SS and local Jews, which it is said might have saved all survivors of the Final Solution had foreign currency been made available and enough attention paid to the Slovak case. There is no evidence for this assertion, and the decision to halt the Final Solution in Slovakia seems to have been made, against explicit SS wishes, by the Slovak government itself as a consequence of foreign intervention and domestic calculations.

In Croatia a pro-German government, which also controlled parts of Bosnia and Herzegovina, set up camps in late 1941 near Zagreb and elsewhere in Croatia. Most of the Jewish population was murdered in these camps, which were sometimes used as transit areas. The majority of the surviving prisoners were deported to Auschwitz between March and August 1942. The Final Solution in Croatia was largely a domestic action, though it was carried out within the overall German Final Solution and with the active support and local initiative of Nazi officials in Zagreb and Sarajevo.

The various events that brought about temporary lulls in the Final Solution in Slovakia and Hungary were sometimes ascribed by survivors to orders issued by Himmler to stop the Holocaust altogether, either because of their own rescue efforts or owing to those of others, such as the American War Refugee Board, or as a consequence of bribes, or simply because of Himmler's more pragmatic behavior after Stalingrad. In the fall of 1944 these efforts were thought successful, even though Eichmann and other subordinates undercut them by continuing the death marches in Hungary. The belief that rescue efforts were making headway appears to spring from Nazi propaganda aimed at splitting the Allies and sowing enmity among the Jews themselves. There may have been belated rescue initiatives by SS officers such as Kurt Andreas Becher, but Himmler was never ready to carry out any such action without Hitler's knowledge and consent, at least until the last days of the Third Reich. Thus in September 1944 many prisoners in Theresienstadt were deported to Auschwitz and murdered. Hitler remained a decisive factor in the complex catastrophe of the Holocaust.

The End of the Final Solution

From the fall of 1944, with the Russian advance on Budapest, and throughout the winter, the Nazi machine of destruction was falling apart. To some extent it survived independently, for example in Vienna, where Jews were used as slave laborers, and perhaps in Budapest itself. It may be that some SS officers, even on Eichmann's staff, tried to rescue Jews on their own initiative. Himmler gave them a chance to do this, without assuming responsibility, hoping to obtain Allied concessions and so persuade Hitler to change his course. This approach met with an outright rebuff from the German dictator.

Red Army advances compelled the abandonment and, if possible, the demolition of the killing centers in the East, in an attempt to cover up the Final Solution and enable Himmler to enter into negotiations with the West. As a result, concessions were granted to the remaining prisoners in Theresienstadt, and there was a meeting between Himmler and the representative of the World Jewish Congress, Norbert Masur. Such events may have been the reason for Hitler's decision to oust Himmler from all his offices and declare him a traitor. Often, the disintegrating mechanism of destruction continued to function on its own within the camps or by means of death marches up to the very end. Beginning in late 1944 the survivors were marched westward from the abandoned killing centers for purposes of forced labor, as hostages for Himmler's hypothetical negotiations, or to other camps. Few lived long enough to be liberated by the Allies, and of this remnant many would still die shortly after liberation from the legacy of their captivity: disease, malnutrition, and exhaustion.

The Final Solution was a process of genocide whose features and forms changed in response to a variety of circumstances. It follows that the period between 1942 and 1944 was not simply one of implementing a single decision taken at the Wannsee Conference of January 1942, but rather a time when numerous decisions were made and specific tools employed in killing more than 6 million Jews. Although research on the history of the destruction of European Jewry continues, a provisional list of factors allowing for implementation of the Final Solution can be made.

The first, and usually decisive, factor was the degree of Germany's control over and intentions for a given territory. In Poland, the Netherlands, and other countries that were to become part of a greater German empire, where German control was total, the Jewish population was almost completely annihilated. In countries allied with Germany, or in those that were occupied but retained a degree of autonomy, the attitude of the individual government and bureaucracy was also important. For example, the attitude of the Bulgarian elite was decisive in preventing the Final Solution altogether in most parts of that country, whereas in Slovakia and to some extent in Romania the German-allied governments were initiators and active collaborators. Nevertheless, they did prevent the complete destruction of their Jewish communities.

In cases where governments within the German sphere of influence refused to collaborate, the strategic location of the country and the significance of its resources for the German war machine were also material to the fate of the Jewish population. Hungary avoided the Final Solution altogether until the German occupation of March 1944. In Romania, on the other hand, strategic considerations and dependence on that country's oil fields prevented not only direct German occupation but also full implementation of the Final Solution in central Romania.

The geopolitical situation and the conditions immediately following occupation also had an effect. In central Poland and the Soviet Union the degree of German control was comparable; yet survival chances in occupied Russia were better, because Jews had been mobilized by the Red Army ahead of the Germans, were included in Soviet-organized evacuations, and had more opportunity to move eastward. The availability of personnel, transport, and other facilities is a further factor in explaining the degree of implementation of the Final Solution in particular localities.

Another explanation for the continuation of the operation, including the futile death marches, well into 1945, is that they were part of a calculated Nazi strategy to use the murder of the Jews, once it became public knowledge, to create a sense of collective guilt. This moral burden—or its corollary, ideological pride and an obligation laid on future generations—might prevent internal collapse and so prolong the war indefinitely. From the distorted perspective of the Nazis, the Final Solution was the result of a "Jewish war" imposed on Germany by the Allies in consequence of

Jewish ideas, interests, and real power in the West. By Nazi logic, then, the Final Solution could only be completed with the end of the Allied war against Germany. The Allies, obviously, did not accept this reasoning. They saw the destruction of the Jews of Europe as indissolubly linked to Nazi aspirations to European and world hegemony, and they therefore made the unconditional surrender of Nazi Germany a priority over the salvation of European Jewry. They feared that a rash identification with the Jewish victims might lend credibility to the notion of a Jewish war, thereby allowing the murderers to score a propaganda victory. Moreover, the Allies suspected that the Final Solution might somehow be a ploy to force substantial concessions to Nazi Germany. They also feared that direct action to halt the Holocaust would enable the Germans to drive a wedge between the Western powers and the Soviet ally—indeed a major point of German policy. Faced with the Nazi drive to murder and Allied hesitancy to intervene, the Jews of Europe were caught in a remorseless trap.

Shlomo Aronson and Peter Longerich

Final Solution: Public Knowledge The question of who knew what, and when they knew, about the Final Solution is vital to any understanding and interpretation of the Holocaust. It had been widely argued in the first decades after World War II, in Germany as well as other countries, that the secret of the plan to exterminate the Jews of Europe was so well kept that little or nothing could have been known until shortly before the end of the war, or even thereafter. The details of the Final Solution were indeed kept secret by Hitler and his closest associates. Only those who needed to know were made privy to the plan. It seems possible, for instance, that the Italian dictator Benito Mussolini and several top Nazi leaders and German government ministers received information only during the summer of 1942. On the other hand, a great many people both inside and outside Germany had to have been told, because without their cooperation the execution of the deportations and mass murder would have been impossible. Needless to say, a secret known to tens of thousands, even if not in all its details, is not a secret. From Gestapo reports about the mood of the population it emerges that the fate of the Jews was widely known. It was certainly not a state secret of great sensitivity, and there is no documented case of anyone's having being punished for divulging it.

Well before the attack on Poland in 1939, Hitler had announced that if there were a war, the Jewish race in Europe would be destroyed. So it came as no surprise when in 1942 articles began to appear declaring that the Jews of Germany and much of Eastern Europe had vanished. Hitler himself announced in 1942 that no longer was anyone laughing about his prophecy of 1939. Those who had to be informed of the details of the extermination plan included SS chief Heinrich Himmler; head of the Reich Main Security Office Reinhard Heydrich; the chief of the Jewish Office, Adolf Eichmann; government ministers such as Hermann Göring; senior civil servants and police officers; those in charge of German transport, in particular the railways; financial authorities; and bankers whose bank vaults were to receive the assets of the deported Jews.

Those aware of action against Jews included the postal services and the courts, as well as the thousands of citizens who saw Jews being marched or driven to the railway stations. At that time, most knew no more than that the Jews were disappearing. What exactly happened to them was known at that early stage only to those instrumental in their physical destruction—the *Einsatzgruppen* (mobile killing units) and the personnel of the death camps, as well as industrialists who had provided the gas ovens and other machinery for genocide. Most of the Jews were murdered in Eastern Europe, and although ordinary German citizens had no access to the killing fields, much was known from those who had inadvertently witnessed the scenes of mass murder. Some witnesses photographed these scenes, even though taking pictures was forbidden.

Most of the killing after the invasion of the Soviet Union did not take place in camps isolated from the outside world, but openly in Russian cities and villages or their immediate surroundings. Long before the first camps began to function, many hundreds of thousands had been exterminated. This information reached not only Germany but even Paris, where Ernst Juenger, a reserve officer and renowned writer, noted in his diary that the killing at Babi Yar, near Kiev, was widely discussed by German officers in their casinos.

The Soviet government was informed about these happenings in its territories under German occupation by its agents and told the Western Allies about them as early as 1941. The Polish government informed London by radio and by courier in October 1941 that many thousands of Jews had been killed in the Lomza region, Bialystok, Vilna, and other parts of eastern Po-

land. In January 1942 reports announced that virtually all the Jews in Lithuania had been murdered, and shortly thereafter it was confirmed that the whole Jewish population of Belorussia and Ukraine no longer existed. Most of this information came not from Jewish sources but from informants who by no means were always kindly disposed toward the Jews.

At that time Eastern Europe was not sealed off from the outside world. German officers and soldiers frequently went home on leave; military missions, journalists, various delegations, and Red Cross representatives toured Russia, Poland, and other countries. Citizens from neutral countries resided permanently in Eastern Europe, and at one stage the Swedish colony in Warsaw played an important role in relaying news abroad. From its ambassador in Bucharest the Swiss government knew within a few weeks that the Jewish population of Odessa had been exterminated. Very few massacres remained a secret, even though the time of transmission of the news varied—sometimes merely a week, other times five or six weeks. Furthermore, it was possible to send letters abroad from Poland, Romania, and other Eastern European countries, and even to use the telephone. In view of the censorship it was inadvisable to mention specific facts and figures in a letter, but a general picture of the situation could be conveyed. Yet another source of information, albeit a minor one, was German deserters who (as was established after the war) also reported details about massacres of Jews.

Thus the murder of hundreds of thousands of Jews, even before the Wannsee Conference of January 1942, was widely known. There was much less secrecy about the activity of the Einsatzgruppen than there was later about the existence of extermination camps. The German Foreign Ministry was officially informed in 1941 about the killings. Thousands of German officers and soldiers had witnessed the scenes and reported them to their families and friends; the same is true with regard to Italian, Hungarian, and Romanian military personnel on active duty on the eastern front. The massacres in Transnistria became known almost immediately. News of Chelmno, the first extermination camp, which opened on 8 December 1941, was received in Warsaw less than four weeks later and was published soon thereafter in the Polish underground press. The existence and function of Belzec and Treblinka were known in Warsaw among Jews and non-Jews soon after the gas chambers had started operat-

Dr. Philip Friedman (left) and other war crimes commission members examine a mobile killing van in which Jews were gassed while being transported to the crematoriums at Chelmno. Circa 1945

ing. News of the suicide on 23 July 1942 of Adam Czerniakow, head of the Warsaw *Judenrat* (Jewish council), reached the Jewish press within a very short time. The deportations from Warsaw in July and August 1942 were known in London within four days. There were, however, some exceptions. The true character of Auschwitz-Birkenau did not become known among Jews and Poles for several months after the camp had been turned into an extermination center. At the time it was generally (and correctly) believed that there were only two kinds of camps—labor and extermination. That Auschwitz-Birkenau combined the two caused confusion.

London, Washington, and the other Allied governments received their information from a great variety of sources. As far as the Western secret services were concerned, the fate of the Jews was not a top priority, but agents and wireless intercepts (including those emanating from German army and police communications) included news of the deportations and killings.

The most important single source remained the dispatches from Warsaw to the Polish government-in-exile in London. Although some of the material collected in Warsaw was not deemed of sufficient importance to transmit, and some transmitted reports were suppressed by the Polish evaluators in London and the

British Foreign Office staff, enough got through so as to provide a fairly detailed and accurate picture. Some material found its way into the Polish-language press in London, into press bulletins, and occasionally into the Jewish, British, and American press. The press in the neutral countries was in a more difficult situation, as Swiss and Swedish censors were afraid of offending the Germans. Newspapers were threatened with sanctions or actually punished for disregarding instructions concerning the dissemination of "atrocity stories." But some disregarded these orders, and news relating to the mass murder of Jews was published in Sweden and Switzerland as early as 1941.

Among those best informed was the Vatican. As early as October 1941 the papal nuncio in Slovakia informed Rome that all Jews, irrespective of age and gender, were being killed in the East. Similar reports followed from Hungary, Romania, and other countries where the Vatican had diplomatic representatives. In addition, information reached the office of the papal state secretary, Cardinal Luigi Maglione, from Catholic priests throughout Central and Eastern Europe. However, Pope Pius XII and leading clerics feared the ire of the Germans. They did not dare to publicize the fact that thousands of Polish priests had been imprisoned and that many had been killed; it was unthinkable that they would risk their relatively trouble-free relations with the Nazi regime because of the Jews. (The Vatican did intervene, halfheartedly and ineffectively, in Slovakia, where it had influence, and in Romania, where it had almost none.) In addition, there were millions of German Catholics, at least some of whom, being involved in the execution of mass murder, asked their priests for spiritual guidance. All in all, it is doubtful whether there was anyone in Europe better informed than Cardinal Maglione, and it is unlikely that he kept the pope wholly in the dark.

The evidence regarding the extent to which Jews in Nazi-occupied Europe, England, the United States, and Jewish Palestine knew of the Final Solution is inconclusive. It seems that the Jews of Europe should have been aware of the horrible truth about what was happening to them. The official German story, that the Jews were being resettled, did not make sense. Given the conditions of transport, it was clear that many of them would not reach their new destination alive. Since the deportations proceeded in stages, those who were left behind should have known that, but for a brief note received after their departure, those who had been deported were never heard from again. In addition, warnings through many channels reached those Jews who had not yet been deported that the journey east meant death. Commenting on one of the first deportations, on 21 November 1941, the Swiss consul general in Cologne reported to Bern that the transport of 1,000 Jews to Minsk had created panic in the community because all Jews were convinced that this meant their end. Many committed suicide on the eve of the deportation in Cologne, as elsewhere.

Yet there is evidence of ignorance and illusion throughout 1942 and in some places even as late as 1944. The Jews were not in a good position to receive reliable information: they were cut off from their surroundings, and their radios had been taken away early in the war. It is not even certain that the presence of radios made a decisive difference, as the Hungarian example shows. The great majority of Hungarian Jews seem to have been genuinely unaware of what was awaiting them in Auschwitz, whereas in neighboring Slovakia (and also in Romania) Jews had hardly any illusions about their fate. Furthermore, communication between Jewish communities in Poland had virtually ceased; they could not telephone or write letters to each other, couriers were few. In the Soviet Union Jewish communal life had been destroyed by the authorities and there was no cohesion or cooperation whatsoever.

Jewish institutions in London, New York, and Palestine heard about the massacres almost from the beginning. This information came through the Polish government-in-exile, among whose inner councils were several Jews, including Ignacy Schwarzbart and Samuel Zygielbojm, who were kept informed. Individual Jews continued to arrive in Palestine from Europe even during the war, as did letters from the Nazi-occupied territories. Groups of Palestinian citizens who had been caught in Europe by the outbreak of war were repatriated in exchange for German nationals resident in Palestine in December 1941, November 1942, February 1943, and on other occasions. These Palestinians arrived from various cities in Poland, Germany, Holland, Belgium, and Austria. Although they had no general idea of the extent of the catastrophe, they certainly knew what had happened to the Jews in their immediate vicinity. Thus in November 1942, from interviews of a group of 137 repatriates, a detailed picture emerged.

If there were any illusions left by early 1942 that the tragic events in Europe were no more than pogroms on a giant scale rather than a master plan to destroy European Jewry, these were dispelled by the July mission to Switzerland of the German industrialist Eduard Schulte. Schulte's information, transmitted to Swiss Jewish leaders and the World Jewish Congress in Geneva, and through them to London and Washington in the Riegner telegram, stated that the extermination of European Jewry had been decided upon in Hitler's headquarters and was being carried out. Emissaries of the Jewish Agency—and, to a lesser extent, of other Jewish organizations—were stationed in Istanbul, Geneva, Lisbon, and Stockholm, after the outbreak of war to maintain contact with Jews in Nazi-occupied countries. Their ability to help was strictly limited, but they learned a great deal about what happened under Nazi rule. Richard Lichtheim, a veteran Zionist diplomat stationed in Geneva, had no illusions whatsoever about the Nazis' plans for the Jews. In October 1941 he predicted that the remnants of the Jews of Central Europe would be destroyed before the war ended. His reports over the next several months were dire: "Their fate is now sealed" (November 1941). "The number of our dead after the war will have to be counted not in thousands or hundreds of thousands but in several millions" (February 1942). "Escape will be possible only in a few cases" (June 1942). "The process of annihilation is going on relentlessly. . . . Hitler has killed or is killing four million Jews in continental Europe and no more than two million have a chance of surviving" (August 1942).

True, Lichtheim's dispatches were at first thought by some of his colleagues in Jerusalem to be exaggerated and excessively pessimistic, but within a few months, during the summer of 1942, they accepted that he had been right. Lichtheim was not a spymaster of genius but merely an intelligent and experienced observer of world affairs. The information, received from various parts of Europe, on which he based his somber conclusions was accessible to many others. He merely put together the pieces. In retrospect, the evidence was so overwhelming that no particular political intelligence and experience were needed to recognize the pattern that emerged.

The great riddle is not how the Final Solution could have been kept secret for such a long time (it was not), but why there was such resistance on the part of Jews and non-Jews alike to acknowledge that systematic mass murder was taking place. Were able-bodied adults of normal intelligence, concerned about their own survival and that of their families, fooled by a clever deception? The existence of Auschwitz and the other extermination camps was never mentioned in the German press or on the radio. According to the official propaganda, the Jews were merely being "resettled." Yet German newspapers announced as early as November 1941 that the order of the Führer "is being carried out at this time. At the end of the war, Europe will be free of Jews." Whether this end was to be brought about by gassing or shooting or starving the Jews to death was merely a technical detail. It cannot be argued that the Nazi leaders tried very hard to keep the murdering a secret. Their lies were threadbare. Attempts to obliterate all trace of the extermination, by destroying the killing machinery and the remnants of the victims, were made only beginning in 1943, when the tide of the war had turned against Germany.

Why did many Jews in Eastern Europe disbelieve the information that reached them? Soviet Jews had been kept uninformed about the character of the Nazi regime and its practices. Polish Jews believed in 1941 that the massacres would be limited to the former Soviet territories. When the deportations from the Polish ghettos began in March 1942, it was still widely thought that the Jews would merely be transported to places further east. The scheme of total extermination was beyond human imagination, and most Jews considered the German authorities incapable of the murder of millions. Perhaps the Nazis did, after all, need a large part of the Jewish population as a labor force for the war economy; perhaps the war would soon be over; perhaps a miracle of some sort would happen. Only after the German invasion of the Soviet Union in June 1941 did there seem to be a valid reason to believe that large sections of European Jewry would not survive the war. Isolated rumors of mass executions in the east eventually turned to certainties. Any moderately well informed Jewish citizen of Warsaw should have drawn the correct conclusion by May 1942. But the time and place were not conducive to detached, objective analysis; the disintegration of rational intelligence is one of the recurrent themes of those who have written about that period on the basis of inside knowledge. The psychological pressures militated against clear thinking and created an atmosphere in which wishful illusions seemed to offer the only antidote to utter despair.

The Final Solution proceeded in stages, chronologically and geographically. Yet hard facts about the fate of the Eastern European Jews rarely penetrated to the Jewish communities in the rest of Europe. There were rumors of a high suicide rate among those ordered to report for deportation, but what firm conclusion could be drawn therefrom? Were the Jews of Europe a "foolish people, and without understanding; which have eyes, and see not; which have ears, and hear not"? The people saw and heard, but what they perceived was not always clear. And when the message was unambiguous, it left no room for hope and was therefore unacceptable. The reaction of Dutch or Hungarian Jews can be compared to that of people facing a flood or a fire who, in contradiction to all experience, believe that they will not be affected. Danish Jews could easily have escaped to Sweden long before the mass evacuation in late 1943; that they waited until the very last moment shows that they genuinely believed they would not be deported. Similarly, Jews living on the isle of Rhodes could have fled without difficulty to Turkey had they known the fate that awaited them in Auschwitz. But they did not know. Elsewhere Jewish communities were trapped, and hopelessness led them to resignation to fate. In other cases, however, the inactivity of Jews, both individuals and communities, was the result not of paralysis but of unwarranted optimism. This is true, for instance, of many German, Austrian, and Czech Jews. They had grown up in civilized countries where the idea that the authorities could commit mass murder was unthinkable. Many of them felt deportation to be a horrible fate but did not take it to mean certain death. The same considerations applied to Jewish leaders and the Jewish public in Great Britain, the United States, and Palestine, the great majority of whom found it exceedingly difficult to accept the ample evidence about the Final Solution and did so only after considerable delay. They thought in terms of persecution and pogroms at a time when a clear pattern of mass murder had already emerged. This failure of intelligence and imagination was caused, on the one hand, by a misjudgment of the murderous nature of nazism and, on the other, by false hopes. If the evidence of genocide was played down by the leadership, it was not out of a desire to keep the community in a state of ignorance but because they too found the evidence hard to believe.

In the case of Palestine, the immediate military danger confronting the Yishuv (Jewish community) in the summer of 1942 played an important role as Rommel's army seemed poised to cross the Nile and threaten Egypt and Palestine. Only when a group of Palestinian citizens repatriated from Europe in November 1942 bore witness to the killings in Poland did the leaders of the Jewish Agency, who had been reluctant to accept written evidence gathered by experienced observers, come to believe the truth about the Nazi genocide.

Millions of Germans knew by 1942 that the Jews had disappeared from their country. Rumors about their fate reached Germany through many channels, and there were clear indications in the speeches of the Nazi leaders and in the press that something more drastic than resettlement had happened. Knowledge about the exact manner in which the German Jews had been killed was restricted to a few. Although many Germans thought that the Jews were no longer alive, they did not necessarily draw the logical conclusion that they were dead, nor were they interested in finding out. It was simple for Germans to let the hardships of daily life, in a wartime economy and under threat of Allied bombardment, distract them from such unpleasant questions, and discussion of the fate of the Jews was officially discouraged. The assertion by many—perhaps most—Germans at the end of the war that they had not known about the Final Solution was therefore correct in part: the whole issue had been pushed out of consciousness for the duration.

The neutral states and the international organizations were relatively well informed about the fate of the Jews at an early date. They did not know the whole truth but knew enough to understand that few, if any, Jews in Europe would survive the war. The neutral diplomats who played down the extent of the mass murder did so not because they disbelieved the facts but because the fate of the Jews figured low on their list of priorities and because they thought themselves powerless to intervene. Their assignment, as they saw it, was to establish and maintain normal or good relations with the German government. To raise the issue of the fate of the Jews, even of individual cases, would have been an unwelcome distraction from their main task. It would at best have led to German suggestions that these countries offer Jews asylum, a move that would have been unpopular in most of those countries at least until well into 1943, by which time most European Jews had already perished.

Washington, London, and Moscow showed no interest in the fate of the Jews. They were well informed through their own government and intelligence channels, and Jewish organizations provided further information. The official Soviet line was not to permit mention in public of the fact that Soviet citizens of Jewish origin were treated differently from other Soviet citizens under the German occupation. Although many Soviet citizens, especially Communists, were persecuted and often killed, the great majority of the population survived, whereas the Jews were singled out for extinction. Until the period of glasnost in the 1980s, those who dared to assert this fact were denounced as Jewish nationalists and Zionists. On the other hand, the Soviet government publicized the massacres soon after they occurred, even though without much emphasis, at a time when some commentators in the West rejected such stories as Communist propaganda.

The facts about the Final Solution were known in London and Washington from an early date and reached the intelligence services and the foreign and defense ministries. But they were not considered to be of great interest or significance, and many officials either disbelieved the reports or thought them exaggerated. After all, during World War I all kinds of stories about German atrocities had surfaced that later proved to be false or exaggerated. The idea of genocide seemed far-fetched to most British and American officials who received the reports; the evil nature of nazism was beyond their comprehension. Barbaric fanaticism was unacceptable to people thinking along pragmatic lines, who believed that slave labor rather than annihilation was the fate of the Jews in Europe. For this reason the reports about the mass murder were not widely disseminated until fall 1942, and sometimes they were suppressed. Even when the facts about the Final Solution were accepted in London and Washington, stopping the deportations and murders still figured low among Allied priorities. In 1942, with the Germans and the Japanese still on the advance, U.S. and British strategists and bureaucrats were not to be deflected from the pursuit of victory by considerations they felt were not directly connected with the war effort. These officials harbored a certain amount of antisemitism, or at least a distrust of the Jews. Everyone was suffering under Nazi rule: why had the pushy Jews to be at the head of the line? And would prominence given to Jewish suffering not be damaging because it would appear to confirm Nazi allegations that the Allies were fighting a war on behalf of Jewish interests? Too much publicity about the mass murder was also undesirable because it was bound to generate demands to aid the Jews that would distract from the war effort. Even after 1943, when victory seemed assured, there was little willingness among the Allies to help. Winston Churchill showed more interest in the Jewish tragedy than Franklin Roosevelt did, and also more compassion, but even he was not willing to devote much thought to the subject. Everything was subordinated to victory, which would liberate the Jews as well as all Europe. For most Jews, alas, victory came too late.

Public opinion in Great Britain, the United States, and elsewhere in the West was kept informed by the press and other media about the progress of the Final Solution, but the impact of the news was small and short-lived. The fact that millions were killed was more or less meaningless. People could identify with the fate of a single individual or a family, but not with the fate of millions. The statistics of the murder were either disbelieved or dismissed from consciousness. Hence the surprise and shock at the end of the war when the reports from Bergen-Belsen came in. Yet Bergen-Belsen had been a mere transit camp, not a center of mass murder with gas ovens and other killing machinery. In summary, the Final Solution was not a secret in the sense that the atomic bomb and the German Enigma code were secrets. Information reached Germany, the Allies, the neutral countries, international organizations, and Jews through many channels, even though not all the details were known. Why, then, were the signals so frequently misunderstood and the message rejected for so long? The plan for total extermination of the Jews of Europe became known only in summer 1942. The information from Eastern Europe was not always widely disseminated, and on occasions it was deliberately held up. But above all, the news frequently was not accepted, and in many cases the full significance was not understood until after the end of the war. *Walter Laqueur*

Finland In the 1930s the Finnish public and authorities were aware of the Nazi persecution of Jews. The government, wishing to maintain good relations with Germany, was more circumspect than the public media in voicing criticisms. Beginning in 1938, several hundred foreign Jews, mainly from Austria and Germany, arrived in Finland; most were in transit to other countries, but some stayed.

The government at first had no consistent policy toward the refugees. The Finnish consul in Vienna generously granted provisional visas to Jewish applicants. On 13 August 1938 the 50 Jews on board the *Ariadne*, which sailed into Helsinki harbor from Stettin, were allowed into the country; but a week later, the same ship with 60 Jews on board was turned back. On 23 August the Finnish foreign ministry rebuked the consul in Vienna for his policy and ordered him to refuse to issue visas to Jews without return visas to German territory. Government policy tightened from fear of becoming the final destination of tens of thousands of Central European Jews and as a result of parliamentary pressure from the small but vocal fascist party, the Patriotic People's Movement (IKL). In 1942 between 150 and 200 foreign Jews who had been granted asylum were living in Finland; native Finnish Jews numbered approximately 2,000.

The fate of Finland's Jews depended on the extent to which the Helsinki government could maintain its freedom of action. Finland's autonomy was reduced by its increased dependence on Germany. In November 1939 the Soviet Union attacked Finland and annexed the eastern province of Karelia; the Finns, smarting from defeat and wishing to win back the lost territory—and gain additional real estate—joined Nazi Germany in June 1941 in attacking the Soviets. German pressure on the Finnish government could less easily be resisted when Finland was so dependent on Germany for its survival.

Fateful to Finland's Jews were the close relations between German authorities and Finnish officials in charge of refugees—notably, the Finnish interior minister Toivo Horelli, a known antisemite and germanophile, and the head of the Finnish secret police (Valpo), Arno Anthoni, who was friendly with Gestapo officials in Tallinn (Estonia) and Berlin. The two singled out the Jews, among the various foreigners who had taken refuge in Finland, for particularly harsh treatment, rounding them up for work in the Arctic region and later in Suursaari, an island near Estonia subject to Russian bombardment.

Although Jews in Finland represented an insignificant number, they were of interest to Berlin. In March 1941 the Gestapo-controlled Reichsvereinigung der Juden in Deutschland (Reich Union of Jews in Germany), under the guise of wishing to publish a statistical study of Jewry, tried to collect detailed information on every Jew in Finland. The Wannsee Conference in January 1942 listed Finland as having 2,300 Jews. Even though they were located in an allied, cobelligerent nation, they were targeted for annihilation.

In July 1942 the SS leader Heinrich Himmler visited Helsinki. Although the main purpose of this visit is in dispute, archival documents reveal that at least once during his visit he suggested that Finland rid itself of the foreign Jews and hand them over to Germany. There is no contemporary archival evidence to prove either that the Finnish government acquiesced or that it refused this proposal. Starting in August 1942 Anthoni, in several communications with Martin Sandberger, the Gestapo chief in Tallinn, indicated that he would hand over certain foreign Jews to German authorities. The total number slated to be deported is unclear, but between late August and early November 1942 he named at least 35 Jews.

In late October 1942 Valpo rounded up a group of foreign Jews with the intention of sending them to German-occupied Tallinn. The number who were supposed to be deported was variously estimated to be between 20 and 100. The dates of these deportations suggest that they were part of a larger Nazi plan in 1942 aimed at Jews in Scandinavia.

The group scheduled to be deported—and probably the remaining foreign Jews—would have been handed over if the veil of extreme secrecy surrounding the deportation plans had not been breached. One of the would-be deportees sent a postcard to Abraham Stiller, head of the Helsinki congregation. Stiller sought out cabinet members and asked them to stop the deportation, warning that if the refugees were handed over, they would certainly be killed. Word of the impending deportations leaked out: newspapers and members of parliament—especially the Socialists—protested the planned deportation. In the town of Pietersaari, 200 citizens signed a petition asking the government not to hand over the Jews. The official position was that those who were to be deported were criminals. The government of national unity, which included both Conservatives and Socialists, nearly broke up over the issue. The Conservatives backed their colleague Hormel's insistence that there should be no interference with his functions as interior minister, which included responsibility for refugee affairs; the Socialists, meanwhile, opposed the measure as a violation of humanitarian practices. Fewer Jews than originally listed were deported: on 6 November the *Hohenhörn* sailed out of Helsinki harbor to Tallinn with 27 deportees on board: eight Jews (including two children), 14 Estonians, four Russians, and one person listed as of "unclear citizenship." The Jews were transported to Auschwitz; only one, the Austrian-born Georg Kollmann, survived.

The scandal that had erupted in late October 1942 discouraged Finnish authorities from considering further deportations, and in fact they began to explore ways to prevent them. They entered into negotiations with the Swedish government to evacuate 150 Jews to Sweden if further German demands made it necessary. In January 1943 the German envoy in Helsinki suggested that Berlin stop pressing Finland on the refugee issue, as the October crisis had threatened Finno-German relations. But Martin Luther, head of the German Department in the Foreign Office, who had been present at the Wannsee Conference and was supposed to see its goals implemented at this ministry, sternly instructed the German legation to exert influence on the Finns regarding the need for "the ruthless destruction of Jewish political and economic power."

This directive presumably included Finnish Jews. It was a familiar pattern for the Nazis, after first pressing a local government to deliver its foreign Jews, they would then demand the native ones. When Himmler had visited Helsinki in July 1942, he had asked about Finland's Jews; during his stay Finnish intelligence officials searched his briefcase, where they found a copy of the Wannsee Conference and a list of Finnish Jews. There is indirect evidence that during the October crisis the cabinet discussed the issue of Finnish Jews, although the exact terms of the debate are unclear. And during the crisis, when confronted with demands by Finnish Jews to refrain from delivering up the refugees, Horelli menaced them with repercussions if they did not keep silent on the deportation of foreign Jews. While these may have been idle threats, they may also have been veiled warnings that the protesters would be handed over to Germany. Except for the eight foreign Jews deported 6 November, no more were handed over for the duration of the war. And Finnish Jews, though anxious about their fate, remained safe.

The best explanation for the survival of the refugees and the Finnish Jews was the changing war situation. By late 1942 German forces were in retreat in North Africa and under extreme pressure from the Russians at Stalingrad. On 3 February 1943 the Finnish government decided to find a way to leave the war. In March the pro-German foreign minister Rolf Witting and Interior Minister Horelli were dropped from the cabinet. There were far too few German soldiers in Finland, and the country was too remote, for Germany to round up the Jews. So they survived.

After the war, under pressure from the Armistice

Commission, Arno Anthoni, the head of Valpo, was arrested for having handed over refugees to the Germans. After a lengthy trial the court freed him but found him guilty of dereliction of duty—he had not followed the rules regarding the deportation of undesirable aliens—and of jeopardizing Finnish international relations by collaborating with Nazi Germany in this operation. Anthoni sued the government for compensation for what he claimed were three years of unwarranted incarceration; in 1950 a Finnish court granted him a payment of 1.3 million marks ($20,000).

The record of Finland's government during the war in facilitating the murder of Jews was less reprehensible than that of many governments. In the October crisis many Finns had worked hard to prevent the extraditions. If they did not completely succeed, they were at least able to reduce the number of refugees handed over. But the record was less heroic than popular myth would have it—though many Finns subscribed to it. The story is that the Jews of Finland were saved because of the resolute acts of the Finnish government, especially its strongman Marshal Mannerheim. No credible evidence to support this interpretation has been found. Luck and geography seem to be a better explanation.

William B. Cohen and Jürgen Svensson

First-Person Accounts Testimonies about the Holocaust by Jews and others who were persecuted by the Nazis provide a personal perspective on the events leading up to and culminating in genocide. Mass murder often turns the individual victim into a statistic among a welter of statistics. Eyewitness accounts testify to the unique fate of the narrator and his or her family members, friends, and community during the Nazi period. The victims and survivors have repeatedly stated that the main reason they make the effort to tell their stories, painful as that may be, is to remember the dead and to prevent others from ignoring or forgetting the tragedy of the Holocaust. As the Holocaust survivor and historian Philip Friedman asserted, through the use of accounts of victims and survivors Holocaust history can be written "from the inside."

Types

The main forms of first-person accounts are diaries, letters, testimony given at trials, memoirs, autobiographies, interviews, and oral histories. They may be preserved in writing or on audiotape and videotape. In ad-

dition to the victims and survivors of the Holocaust, many other people—foreign diplomats, journalists, relief workers, and liberators—have also provided first-person accounts of what they experienced and witnessed.

Throughout the period of the Third Reich (1933–45) some Jews kept diaries—often at great risk to themselves—in which they documented how their lives and those of their loved ones were affected by the Nazi reign of terror. Emmanuel Ringelblum, director of the Warsaw Underground Archives (code-named Oneg Shabbos), noted that everyone—from journalists and teachers to children—wrote. To encourage writing, Oneg Shabbos sponsored contests and issued cash prizes. In part, Ringelblum planned to use the vast amount of accumulated information as evidence in court against the Nazis. Some of the most noted works to survive the war are the first-person accounts written and collected by Oneg Shabbos's committee of 100 historians.

Many of the diaries, letters, and other testimonies were lost as the Jews were rounded up, deported, and killed. Others were undoubtedly destroyed by those who discovered them. Few such accounts remain in existence.

Various agencies in some of the neutral and Allied countries made efforts to collect accounts and records both before and during the war. Organizations such as Vaad Hatzala and the Jewish Agency in Israel, the World Jewish Congress in New York, the YIVO Institute for Jewish Research in New York City, and the Jewish Relief Committee in Geneva collected testimony from Jews and other witnesses who escaped the Nazis during the war period.

Even some of those assigned to Sonderkommandos, units of Jewish prisoners forced to work in the gas chambers and crematoriums, kept diaries. Such records were buried in the ashes at Auschwitz and were discovered after the liberation of the camps. Few first-person statements written in the death camps survived the war.

At the war's end, numerous institutes, commissions, and centers throughout Europe began to collect and produce documentation, including first-person accounts, about the Holocaust. While some were gathering first-person testimony specifically for the historical record, others were doing so in order to provide evidence against Nazi criminals. Historical commissions in Poland, Germany, Austria (Linz and Vienna), Italy (Rome), and France (Centre de Documentation,

Paris) were engaged in gathering material through interviews, eyewitness records, questionnaires, and other methods. Another early source of survivor testimony was the *Landsmannshaften* (associations of fellow countrymen), which collected accounts from all across Europe, including displaced persons camps.

In New York, YIVO conducted an autobiography contest for surviving Jewish children in Europe. The life histories of 161 children were assembled in this way, and by 1950 YIVO had collected more than 1,200 eyewitness records.

In the years immediately after the war there was an outpouring of memoirs by survivors. After tapering off to a trickle in the 1950s, the flow of narratives again became a flood in the early 1960s. The arrest, trial, and conviction of Adolf Eichmann galvanized concern among survivors who had not told their stories and who, with increasing age, had begun to feel an urgent need to leave a record of what they had experienced under the Nazis. As public interest in the Holocaust increased, numerous Holocaust resource and memorial centers were established, and a large part of their work includes the collection of first-person accounts by survivors. Some of these centers were established at colleges and universities, and as a result educators began to organize projects focusing on such evidence. Many early memoirs were tape recorded, and the proliferation of first-person records—primarily written and videotaped—continues to this day. Tens of thousands, and possibly several hundred thousand, first-person accounts of Holocaust survivors and other witnesses exist in English, German, Yiddish, Hebrew, and other languages. The Yad Vashem Archive in Jerusalem has alone amassed more than 50,000 accounts and continues to add about 500 a year.

The tribunals organized by the Allied Powers to try Nazi officials on charges of war crimes led to the collection of massive amounts of testimony by survivors and other witnesses. Later trials of Nazi war criminals, including Adolf Eichmann in Israel and Klaus Barbie in France, resulted in still more testimony. Eyewitnesses have also given testimony in proceedings for denaturalization, deportation, and extradition when the United States and other countries have taken action against former Nazis who illegally established residency and citizenship.

Although the maltreatment and murder of the Jews of Europe are well documented in personal testimonies, there is a dearth of accounts about the fate of other Holocaust victims, such as the mentally and physically handicapped, the Gypsies, and homosexuals. Not until the 1980s was a concerted effort made to collect first-person accounts from the Gypsy survivors. Now scholars are actively seeking out the remaining Gypsy survivors of the Holocaust to record their stories.

First-person accounts and statements by the perpetrators also exist. Many of these statements, made by camp commandants and guards and Nazi officials, are self-serving. Indeed, Lawrence Langer, the literary critic and Holocaust scholar, has noted that the testimony of Rudolf Höss (commandant at Auschwitz), Franz Stangl (commandant at Treblinka), and Adolf Eichmann are riddled with evasions, half-truths, denials, and lies.

Beginning in the early 1980s, an ever-increasing number of Holocaust organizations began to videotape the stories of survivors and other witnesses. One of the most active organizations in the United States has been the Fortunoff Video Archive for Holocaust Testimonies at Yale University, which has collected more than 1,000 testimonies. The archive grew out of the earlier efforts of the Holocaust Survivor Film Project, which was established in 1979 to videotape the accounts of survivors in an effort to offset what was felt to be the trivializing and falsifying tendencies of television productions such as the miniseries *Holocaust*. The onscreen presence of a human face and voice, as opposed to static words on the printed page, allows viewers a unique opportunity to see survivors and witnesses as real people. Videotape also allows one to experience the witnesses' unrehearsed words, emotions, and facial expressions as they relate their stories in whatever order they are recalled from memory. Lawrence Langer has argued that in the videotaped testimonies there takes place "a merging of the time senses," where the survivor speaks in the present but may seem to return momentarily to the period being recalled. For the viewer and listener, this move changes the dynamic of attempting to understand the story, for the speaker appears to be reliving, not simply retelling, the event he or she experienced.

In order to facilitate access to the testimonies, the Fortunoff Archive places catalog records, with written summaries of the testimonies, on the national computer database RLIN (Research Libraries Information Network). In addition to conducting interviews with survivors, the Fortunoff project is developing sets of accounts relating to the experiences of special groups (e.g., the deaf) and themes (e.g., the interaction of survivors with their children). The archive has also worked with Facing History and Ourselves, a national foundation, to produce excerpts for educational use in secondary schools.

The director and producer Steven Spielberg has also established a major videotaping project. The express purpose of the Survivors of the Shoah Visual History Foundation is to preserve videotaped accounts of the Holocaust by every living survivor. The foundation has conducted more than 50,000 interviews, in 57 countries and 32 languages, and has produced nearly 115,000 hours of videotape.

Some scholars are concerned about the accuracy of the information in videotapes made 50 or 60 years after the events described. They are also concerned that amateurs without deep historical knowledge of the period are conducting many of the interviews, thereby contributing to the proliferation of documentation lacking historical grounding and calling into question the authenticity of the reports.

Value

Among the most valuable first-person accounts are the diaries and the letters written while the events of 1933–45 were unfolding. These documents have the advantage of greater accuracy than accounts recorded many years or even decades later, when witnesses have to rely on distant memories that may be influenced by popular notions about what must have taken place. Those memoirs, oral histories, and interviews written or taped shortly after the war, before memories had time to fade, are also prized for the freshness and accuracy of their recollections. Eyewitness testimony during war crimes trials, though sometimes taken long after the atrocities were committed, are valued because they focus on specific individuals and events observed by the witnesses, eschewing secondhand information and hearsay, and are tested by cross-examination.

The weakest and least valuable accounts are those that are ghostwritten, use invented dialogue, or otherwise fictionalize or dramatize events. In all these cases, the authentic voice of the witness is lost and the testimony is distorted. In the interests of the story, vital incidents and details are often omitted or altered, and it is impossible to distinguish between imagination and fact.

Those scholars who question the value of firsthand accounts contend that they lack objectivity and are extremely difficult to test for reliability. Information presented as fact may be biased, founded on hearsay or faulty memory, or inaccurate for some other reason. The acclaimed novelist and essayist Elie Wiesel, himself a survivor of Auschwitz and Buchenwald, has asserted that "only those who were there will ever know, and those who were there can never tell." His point is that daily life and death in the Nazi camps were so horrifying and brutal, so far beyond the power of ordinary imagination, that it is nearly impossible to convey what they were truly like.

Conversely, many scholars prize first-person accounts as historical sources. They point out that eyewitness testimonies can provide a wealth of otherwise inaccessible information about little-known incidents, persons, and places. They include details and provide a personal perspective not found in other types of documentation such as official reports and dispatches. As to accuracy, it is often possible to corroborate the evidence of one account by comparing it to others. Personal statements can thus be used to create documentation where it did not previously exist. First-person accounts also provide material with which to counter the patently false arguments of Holocaust deniers, who rely on Nazi records that are ideologically tainted and deliberately designed to cover up the truth.

Brana Gurewitsch, an archivist at the Center for Holocaust Studies in New York, has argued that although the German military, civil, and economic records are fundamental to historical inquiry, the very way they were written, with intentional euphemisms and other linguistic subterfuges, disguises the reality of what was taking place. It is through oral history, she argues, that one discovers how Jews reacted and responded to the events in which they were engulfed.

Still, concern about the accuracy of memories in first-person accounts, most of which were recorded more than five years after the end of World War II, must be addressed forthrightly. As memory fades, general outlines as well as fine details may become garbled or irretrievably lost. Specific dates may be incorrectly reported, and even the chronology of major experiences and events might be mistaken. Certain perceptions may be influenced by later experiences or commonly accepted notions of what occurred. While some witnesses may confuse rumors with reality, others may inadvertently embellish certain details and then, over the years, accept them as facts. Still others may make historical generalizations that constitute misinformation. Survivors, who at the very least will be aware of bits and pieces of the historical background, may draw on personal experience to fit a particular interpretation of the events. That is, they may have trouble—particularly under the influence of disturbing emotions as they recall tragic events—in distinguishing between their own personal judgments and historical fact. The uninformed reader or listener may accept such distortions as true and perpetuate the misinformation. In order to stave off psychic pain, some survivors may shy away from the most horrific aspects of their experiences and thus dwell on less upsetting experiences.

There is also the possibility that some may apply self-censorship by not relating information that might show themselves, family members, or friends in a poor light. The actions so suppressed may range from the most innocuous collaboration with a persecutor to failure to assist family members, from stealing food from others to mistreating other victims.

Of course, individuals are only able to relate accurately what they have personally witnessed. Those incarcerated in huge ghettos, concentration camps, and death camps can tell but a fraction of what took place there. Experiences were also dictated by where a person lived, by the places of imprisonment, and even by the knowledge or lack of knowledge of certain languages. The information may suffer from a lack of impartiality and be affected by personal bias, exaggeration, and hyperbole. Researchers and others who use first-person accounts need to keep these factors in mind and to differentiate between direct and secondhand evidence.

In many cases it is difficult to verify the accuracy of the information in first-person accounts, and publishers, videotapes, and others often do not even make an attempt to do so. While it is fairly easy to find corroboration for the more general events in which large numbers of people were involved, it becomes much more problematic when testimonies concern little-known or isolated events involving as few as a single individual. Verification requires time-consuming checking and cross-checking of the information found in one account against others, and against information in official dispatches, reports, and other sources. In some cases, particularly those involving reports of isolated incidents by the sole survivors of a community, it is virtually impossible to confirm the details. Up to now, much greater emphasis has been placed on the collection of accounts than on the scrutiny of information for accuracy.

Another major limitation on the value of certain oral histories and video testimonies is posed by a lack of knowledge on the part of those who are collecting the accounts. An interviewer with only limited knowledge of the history of the period will be hard-pressed to ask probing initial or follow-up questions, particularly those that attempt to explore discrepancies in the speaker's story. In such cases the accounts collected lack the accuracy that would make them a valuable historical source. Moreover, just like some witnesses, some interviewers let their emotions override objectivity in their inquiry, and this too can interfere with, if not destroy, the objectivity of the statements they have recorded.

As long as there still are living survivors, first-person accounts will continue to be written, taped, and videotaped. At the same time, other information written down or taped years ago and long held in archives

Gisi Fleischmann. 1940–44

such as Yad Vashem will no doubt be unearthed and made available to scholars and educators. But it is also time for historians to begin actively to analyze, abstract, catalog, index, and annotate accounts in order to hunt down incorrect, unclear, or little-known information, including dates, times, locations, and names of people and organizations. All this needs to be done so that the testimony of those who lived through the Holocaust may be given full value as documents of factual history.   *Samuel Totten*

Fleischmann, Gisi (1897–1944) Slovak Jewish leader of the Working Group, which attempted to stall Jewish deportations in Slovakia. After her arrest and release by the Gestapo, Fleischmann continued her anti-deportation efforts until she was arrested again in 1944 and sent to the gas chambers of Auschwitz.

Forced Labor Forced labor was an integral part of the war economy of the Third Reich. The maltreatment and physical destruction of men and women compelled to work without pay and under appalling conditions are among the greatest crimes committed by Nazi Germany.

There were different categories of forced laborers: prisoners of war, foreign nationals conscripted for work in Germany (*Fremdarbeiter*); persons deported from the occupied Soviet territories (*Ostarbeiter*); concentration camp prisoners; and Jews. More than 8.4 million foreign workers were employed in Germany at the end of 1944. Among them were about 2 million prisoners of war, some 5.7 million so-called civilian workers, and 700,000 concentration camp prisoners. The largest national groups among the civilians were French (about 1.3 million), Poles (1.7 million), and Soviet citizens (2.8 million, half of them women).

Workers from Western Europe were better treated than those from the East, whom the Nazis considered racially inferior. Ostarbeiter were subject to a reign of terror, severely punished for the smallest offense, and not allowed to move outside a limited zone. Owing to these conditions, about 10 percent of the Polish workers perished. Even worse was the plight of the Russian and Ukrainian workers.

The hardest lot was reserved for the Jews. The treatment of the Jewish forced laborers was part of the Nazi policy of persecution leading to total physical destruction.

Immediately after the invasion of Poland, the Germans introduced large-scale round-ups of Jews, in the streets and from homes, for forced labor in Germany. Thousands of German soldiers, police, and SS men took part in these actions. Jews were tortured and even murdered at their place of work. Later, Jewish councils (*Judenräte*) were ordered to organize working parties for forced labor. Among the anti-Jewish laws promulgated was the order issued on 26 October 1939 by Governor General Hans Frank introducing compulsory work for all Jewish males aged 14 to 60. In due time forced labor orders were expanded to include women.

Forced labor was introduced in the ghettos established in occupied Poland during 1940 and early 1941. In addition, from the spring of 1940 onward large forced labor camps for Jews were set up in occupied Poland. Altogether 437 such camps were established on occupied Polish territory.

The first 10 camps were located near the Bug River,

Prisoners in Dachau hauling supplies for the camp. 24 May 1933

Prisoners in Dachau make strands of barbed-wire fencing, a relatively desirable task.

which became the new border between Germany and the Soviet Union. The largest of them was the Belzec concentration camp, which later became a death camp. Thousands of Jews built fortifications and constructed waterworks. During the summer of 1940 new camps were organized throughout the Lublin district and in the Radom and Kraków districts. Most prisoners, tortured by the German staff, starved and deprived of medical treatment, died after a short time in these camps. During 1940 and 1941 about 70 forced labor camps for Jews (known as the RAB, or Reichsautobahn, camps) were established in the Poznan region (part of the Warthegau). There about 12,000 Jews, most of them deported from the Lodz ghetto, were employed building the Berlin-Poznan highway. Only a handful of them survived.

In Silesia about 160 forced labor camps for Jews were organized under SS Oberführer Albrecht Schmelt; hence they were known as the Organisation Schmelt camps. The number of prisoners they held at the be-

ginning of 1943 exceeded 50,000. At the end of 1943 most of these camps were liquidated and the prisoners deported to Auschwitz. Some of the Organisation Schmelt camps were integrated into the subcamps of Auschwitz and Gross-Rosen.

Another network, comprising six forced labor camps for Jews, was run by the industrial company HASAG (Hugo Schneider Aktiengesellschaft) in the Radom district. These camps held more than 17,000 prisoners, most of whom perished.

After the invasion of the Soviet Union in June 1941, the cruel policy of forced labor was applied to all Jews who survived the first waves of pogroms and mass murder campaigns by the *Einsatzgruppen*. Forced labor camps for Jews were also organized by the satellite countries of Nazi Germany. In Slovakia, large forced labor camps for Jews were arranged in Novaky, Sered, and Vyhne. Forced labor was introduced in the Romanian-occupied territory of Transnistria. The Hungarian authorities also organized labor battalions for Jews, employing them in road building and fortifications for the Hungarian army in Ukraine and Serbia. About 42,000 Jews perished in these battalions.

At the beginning of 1942 a deliberate policy of physical destruction through work (*Vernichtung durch Arbeit*) was adopted as part of the Final Solution. It was decided that those Jews able to work would be temporarily spared from death in the gas chambers. Instead they were to be assigned to brutal labor, which they would survive for only a short period. This system was adopted as a result of an agreement between the SS and a number of German companies, which were interested in continuing the exploitation of cheap Jewish labor that had begun when the Nazis established Jewish ghettos and slave labor camps.

In September 1942 it was decided to expand the system of destruction through work to include certain non-Jewish concentration camp prisoners: Gypsies, Russians, and Ukrainians, Poles sentenced to more than three years' imprisonment, and Czechs and Germans with sentences of more than eight years. Those employed within the framework of the destruction-through-work principle became a special category of prisoners. Their plight, and their treatment by the Nazis, differed from that of other prisoners, forced laborers, prisoners of war, and persons deported for compulsory work in Germany.

The destruction-through-work system was implemented mainly, but not solely, in the hundreds of sub-

Prisoners working on a rifle production line in the SS-owned munitions factory at Dachau. 1943–44

camps of the major concentration camps, such as Auschwitz, Gross-Rosen, Buchenwald, Stutthof, and Mauthausen. Auschwitz had 45 subcamps, Buchenwald 130, Gross-Rosen 200 (including 42 for women), Stutthof 70, and Mauthausen 33. Some were subcamps for Jewish prisoners only; others were "mixed," interning both Jews and non-Jews. The management of forced labor in the concentration camps was entrusted to the Economic and Administrative Main Office (Wirtschafts- und Verwaltungshauptamt, or WVHA), a branch of the SS headed by SS Obergruppenführer Oswald Pohl.

In March 1943 a new SS economic enterprise, the Ostindustrie, better known as Osti, was organized within the framework of the WVHA. Osti assumed control over a number of forced labor camps for Jews in the Lublin and Radom districts of the Generalgouvernement. The largest of these, Poniatowa and Trawniki, were liquidated in November 1943, together with the Lublin-Lipowa camp for Jewish prisoners of war, during the *Erntefest* (Harvest festival) mass murder action, when 43,000 Jew-

ish forced laborers were shot. Another SS enterprise engaged in exploitation and destruction was the German Armaments Work (Deutsche Ausrüstungswerke, or DAW). Among the larger camps run by the DAW was the Lvov-Janowska camp, where many thousands of Jewish forced laborers were murdered. Also active in the exploitation of concentration camp forced laborers was Organisation Todt, founded by Fritz Todt and headed after his death by Albert Speer.

A number of large German firms engaged in heavy industry used concentration camp prisoners and contributed to the implementation of the destruction-through-work system. Among them were Heinkel Flugzeugwerk, Steyr-Daimler-Puch, Stahlwerke Braunschweig, Vacuum Oel, and Delta Flugzeughallen und Barackenbau.

In the last phase of the war, with the Red Army approaching from the east and American and British armies from the west, the Nazis evacuated the concentration camps and their subcamps. Tens of thousands of forced laborers, most of them Jews, were sent on what became known as the death marches. These were forced marches under heavy guard, over long distances and in intolerable conditions, during which the prisoners were brutally mistreated and often killed by their escorts. In many cases the Nazis murdered entire columns of prisoners. One of the first major death marches began on 28 July 1944, when the Gesia camp, established on the ruins of the former Warsaw ghetto, was evacuated. Some 3,600 Jewish forced laborers, most of them from Greece and Hungary, had to march to Kutno, a distance of 129 kilometers. About 1,000 prisoners perished on the march. When the remainder reached Kutno, they were put on a freight train, 90 persons to a wagon. Several hundred died on the train before reaching the final destination, the Dachau concentration camp.

On 18 January 1945 the Germans began evacuating Auschwitz and its subcamps. Around 66,000 forced laborers, mostly Jews, were marched to Wodzislaw (Loslau) and from there were transported by train to other concentration camps. At least 15,000 perished during the march.

At the same time, the evacuation of the Stutthof subcamps in the Königsberg area began. About 7,000 Jewish forced laborers, mostly women from the subcamps at Heiligenbeil, Schippenbeil, Jessau, Seerappen, and Königsberg, were forced to march. Except for a handful of survivors, all of them were murdered, most being shot on the night of 31 January–1 February 1945 by the seashore near the town of Palmnicken. Another 20,000 Jewish women were evacuated from the Stutthof subcamps in Pomerania at the end of January 1945. Ninety percent of them were murdered on the death marches following the evacuation, just a few days before the region was liberated.

The evacuation of Gross-Rosen and its subcamps began in early February 1945. Of the 20,000 Jewish prisoners employed as forced laborers in the Eulengebirge subcamps, nearly all were murdered, most of them just before the evacuation or during the death march.

On 6 April 1945 the evacuation of Buchenwald and its subcamps began, resulting in the murder of more than 20,000 forced laborers, mostly Jews. Rehmsdorf was the last of the Buchenwald subcamps to be evacuated. Of the 4,340 prisoners who left the camp on 13 April 1945, fewer than 500 survived.

A quarter of a million forced laborers in concentration camps died or were murdered on the death marches between the summer of 1944 and the surrender of Germany in May 1945. It is impossible to ascertain the total number of forced laborers who perished in Germany and Nazi-occupied and satellite countries. It is obvious, however, that the collapse of Nazi Germany saved tens of thousands of human beings.

The introduction of forced labor and the brutal treatment of the workers that led to their deaths were considered war crimes and crimes against humanity. After the war a number of persons responsible for the system and its atrocities were arrested on such charges. Two of the highest-ranking Nazis responsible for forced labor crimes were tried before the International Military Tribunal: Fritz Sauckel, plenipotentiary-general for labor mobilization, and Albert Speer, minister of armaments. Sauckel was sentenced to death and was hanged on 16 October 1946; Speer was sentenced to 20 years in prison.

Later, the U.S. Army organized 12 Nuremberg military trials, four of them explicitly concerned with crimes of forced labor. In the Pohl case (Trial 4) 18 leaders of the WVHA and Osti were tried. The main defendant, Oswald Pohl, and two others were sentenced to death. Friedrich Flick, a coal and steel producer, was accused (Trial 5) and sentenced to seven years' imprisonment. In the I. G. Farben case (Trial 6) 24 directors and engineers were convicted, but they received light sentences. The main defendants, Otto Ambros and Walter Dürrfeld, were sentenced to no more than eight years in prison. In the Krupp case (Trial 10) Alfred Krupp von Bohlen and 11 directors of his company were accused of implementing the Nazi policy of forced labor. Krupp was sentenced to 12 years' imprisonment, as were Erich Müller and Friedrich von Bülow. The others received lighter sentences. *Shmuel Krakowski*

France The introduction of anti-Jewish laws in wartime France began almost immediately after the country's sudden defeat and occupation by Nazi Germany in June 1940. Within a month of the armistice, the newly formed government at Vichy set up an investigative commission to review the status of all citizens naturalized since 1927. As a result, more than 15,000 individuals lost their citizenship, including some 6,000 Jews. In late August the Vichy government repealed the Marchandeau Law, passed in April 1939, that had prohibited racist propaganda. Other laws enacted in August and September limited the participation of for-

FRANCE , BELGIUM, AND THE NETHERLANDS

■ Concentration camps

0   50   100   150 Km

NORTH SEA

FRIESLAND

THE NETHERLANDS

Amsterdam
Leiden
The Hague
Rotterdam
Utrecht
Amersfoort
Ommen
Almelo
Westerbork

GREAT BRITAIN

Maas

Vught

Essen
Düsseldorf

GERMANY

Ostende   Bruges
Dunkirk
Calais
FLANDERS
Ghent
Lille

Antwerp
Breendonck
Brussels
Liège

Aachen
Cologne
Bonn

BELGIUM

Bastogne

Rhine

Frankfurt
Württemberg

ENGLISH CHANNEL

Somme

Amiens

ARDENNES

Moselle

Saar

Saarbrücken

Cherbourg

Le Havre
Rouen
Caen   NORMANDY
Compiègne-Royallieu
Suresnes   Drancy
Paris

Reims
Verdun
CHAMPAGNE

Metz

Nancy

Moselle

Strasbourg
Natzweiler-Struthof

Brest

BRITTANY

Seine

Le Mans

Orléans

Loire

Troyes

BURGUNDY

FRANCE

Besançon

Basel

Angers
Nantes

Tours

Bourges

Bern

SWITZERLAND

Poitiers

Vichy line of
demarcation

Vichy

Roanne

Lausanne

Geneva

ATLANTIC
OCEAN

Lyons

Bordeaux

Dordogne

Rhône

ITALY

AQUITAINE

Garonne

Avignon

Nice

Toulouse
Noé   Récébédou
Rieucros

PROVENCE
Les Milles   Aix-en-Provence

Gurs

LANGUEDOC

Marseilles

SPAIN

Rivesaltes
Perpignan
Argèles

MEDITERRANEAN SEA

1930 National Borders

N

French Legionnaires departing to fight in Russia. On the side of the train is scrawled "Death to the Jews." 29 January 1943

eigners in the legal and medical professions. Though Jews were not mentioned specifically in either law, it was well understood that they played a prominent role in both occupations.

How does one account for the flurry of antisemitic activity in the first months of the new regime? Recent historical scholarship has refuted the claims made by Vichy apologists after the war that the government's anti-Jewish legislation was a response to pressures from Nazi authorities. The disturbing truth is that long before any actions were taken by German officials in France, and without any direct orders from the Nazi regime, the Vichy regime had decided to take steps to solve the so-called Jewish question in areas under its control.

The roots of this commitment can be found in the turbulent interwar period and especially in the decade before the outbreak of World War II. The 1930s saw an explosion of antiforeigner sentiment in French society and the first significant public manifestations of violence against Jews since the Dreyfus affair. The devastating effects of the Depression led to a clamor for restrictions on the employment of foreigners and for the expulsion of "undesirables." In particular, French officials and journalists attacked immigrant Jews from Russia and Poland in the clothing and textile trades for

allegedly stealing jobs from native artisans and workers. Antisemitism in the 1930s was also fueled by fears of national decline and degeneration. Respected scholars and government advisers wrote menacingly about the threat of East European Jews in Paris ghettos, who were said to undermine French language and culture from within.

As the 1930s progressed, France's desire to avoid war at all costs bred hostility toward Jewish victims of nazism, who were viewed as warmongers. Hatred of Jews as subversives and fomenters of international conflict was reinforced by the accession to power of Léon Blum in June 1936. Attacking the Popular Front as a Judeo-Bolshevik scheme, extremist elements on the right denounced Blum as a Polish Jew whose allegiance lay with dark forces allied against the nation. Such attitudes climaxed in popular protests against the regime's involvement in the Spanish civil war and then later during the Munich crisis, which merged anti-Jewish hostility with concerns over the possibility of French military entanglement.

Popular fears of subversion from within and outside by Jews and other aliens swelled the ranks of fascist and extreme nationalist movements in France in the 1930s. Although not all right-wing groups were anti-Jewish, many of the newer, more dynamic movements regarded previous forms of French antisemitism as too passive and tame and called for the adoption of Nazi racial ideology and policy in France. Blending the disparate anti-Jewish sentiments in France during the period into an all-embracing ideology of antisemitism, such groups held world Jewry responsible for the international crisis, parliamentary indecision and corruption, the weakening of the national ideal, and the conformism and decadence of bourgeois culture. With little encouragement from the German government, some supporters of French fascism in the 1930s even went so far as to call for mass murder as a solution to the "Jewish problem" in France.

By far the most telling indication of the growth of antisemitism in France in the mid- and late 1930s was the appropriation of anti-Jewish language and attitudes by elites. Particularly vocal were professional groups, who in their eagerness to prevent competition from German Jewish doctors and lawyers openly called for the adoption of quotas on their admission into France. Throughout the interwar period all elements of the political spectrum freely adopted statements and statistics about Jews and other foreigners from ex-

treme right-wing newspapers with little or no attempt to verify them. Traditional moral arguments that rested on the image of France as an asylum for political refugees were drowned out by growing hysteria over the destructive impact of "aliens" upon the nation's economy and international standing.

Such sentiments were reinforced in the days that followed the Nazi occupation. The armistice had divided the country into an occupied zone controlled by the Germans that included northern France and the area bordering the entire Atlantic coastline, and an unoccupied zone administered by the newly formed Vichy regime comprising much of central and southern France. In attempting both to assert its authority in a divided France and to provide an explanation for the country's humiliating defeat, the Vichy government publicly announced its decision to root out foreign and especially Jewish influence from society. After issuing a series of ad hoc measures, in October it enacted its first comprehensive legislation dealing with the Jewish question. The so-called Statut des Juifs (Statute on Jews) of 3 October defined Jews in more radical racial terms than those applied by German authorities in the occupied zone. The law also excluded most Jews from public service, the officer corps of the army, journalism, teaching, theater, and film. Four days later, the regime extended its policies to the French empire by formally revoking the French citizenship of Algerian Jews. On 25 October the minister of war removed all Jewish enlisted men from the armed forces.

At the same time, the regime attempted to deal with the thousands of foreigners, including many Jews, who had fled to the unoccupied zone in the wake of the Nazi occupation of Belgium, Holland, and northern France. Vichy's goal was clearly to expel all "aliens" from France, but in the confused atmosphere of late 1940 and early 1941 there was simply nowhere to send them. As a temporary measure, foreign-born Jews and other refugees were assigned to live under police surveillance in remote villages in the south or were placed in forced labor detachments in France and North Africa. In an ominous foreshadowing of future policies, the government authorized prefects to place foreign Jews in "special camps" such as Gurs and Rivesaltes in the Pyrenees, which had been used previously for refugees from Franco's Spain. By the end of 1940,

French Jewish refugee children, Marseilles harbor.

some 40,000 aliens and refugees, 70 percent of whom were Jews, had been interned in unoccupied France.

In the first two years of the war the decision by the Vichy government to initiate its own action against Jews in the southern zone was met by stupefaction and anger on the part of Nazi officials. Indeed, the goals of the two administrations often seemed to be at cross-purposes, as thousands of Jews found themselves caught between attempts by the Vichy government to ship refugees back to their homelands and efforts by the invading German forces to expel Jews from areas under their military control. In general, German treatment of Jews in the occupied zone lagged behind the more enthusiastic efforts of Vichy officials. The one major ordinance in Nazi-occupied France dealing with Jews in the early period of the war, issued in September 1940, merely created a census and required special placards to be displayed in Jewish shops. The differences in the treatment of Jews in the two zones were so marked that many Jews from Paris who had fled southward after the Nazi invasion soon returned to the occupied north to avoid the effects of Vichy's discriminatory legislation.

It was not until the creation of a Commissariat Général aux Questions Juives (General Commission on the Jewish Question) in February 1941 that any serious effort was made to coordinate Jewish policy in the two zones. The decision to establish a central office to administer Jewish affairs was actually initiated by the German ambassador in Paris, Otto Abetz, but for the moment Nazi officials left responsibility for Jewish policy throughout France largely in the hands of Vichy officials. The commissariat's first minister, Xavier Vallat, sought primarily to expand on the policies of previous French governments, which had persecuted foreign Jews but generally had spared native-born citizens. Nevertheless, on 2 June 1941 the commissariat issued a new Statut des Juifs, which broadened the definition of who was Jewish and incorporated many persons born of mixed marriages who had previously been spared persecution. The new law also extended the list of occupations prohibited to Jews, allowed local officials to intern both French and foreign Jews, and established procedures for a census of all Jews in the unoccupied zone.

The independence of Vichy policymakers would not long survive, however. As the balance of power gradually shifted from Vichy to the Third Reich, and as German officials began to map out far-reaching plans for dealing with the Jewish question, Vallat's programs were soon outstripped by the more radical policies and actions of the occupying authorities. At the very inception of the commissariat, Nazi authorities had urged Vallat to begin arresting all the Jews in Paris. In response to these pressures, and with little protest, the Vichy regime rounded up thousands of foreign Jews in the French capital in May and again in August 1941. In December the first *rafles* (round-ups) of French-born Jews began. Arrests generally were carried out by French police under the watchful eyes of German authorities. In contrast to the early months of the occupation, Nazi officials now took the lead by initiating anti-Jewish policies in the north, which Vichy officials then rushed to apply in the southern zone. As a reflection of the growing coordination of policy between Nazi and French authorities, the Vichy regime passed a law in November 1941 creating the Union Générale des Israélites de France (General Union of French Jews), a national Jewish council with branches in both the occupied and unoccupied zones.

Within a few months of the convening of the Wannsee Conference in January 1942, German authorities began to carry out their program for the Final Solution in occupied France. A vast network of bureaucrats under the supervision of SS captain Theodor Dannecker, chief of the Gestapo's Jewish office in Paris, now set about implementing the new policy. Ultimately the Nazi regime wished to see the Final Solution carried out in all of France. As a result, it could no longer accept even the nominal independence of the Commissariat Général aux Questions Juives and its limited discriminatory legislation against foreign Jews. In April 1942, in the wake of broader measures passed to define and segregate Jews, German officials replaced Vallat with Louis Darquier de Pellepoix, a rabid antisemite who openly supported the Nazis' radical policies. In June it was decided that France would supply 100,000 Jews, to be taken from both zones, for extermination. In a desperate and cynical attempt to retain a modicum of French independence, Premier Pierre Laval, who had been appointed in April in response to Dannecker's demands for a more pliant Vichy administration, promised German officials the complete cooperation of the French police. Moreover, he offered to add to the

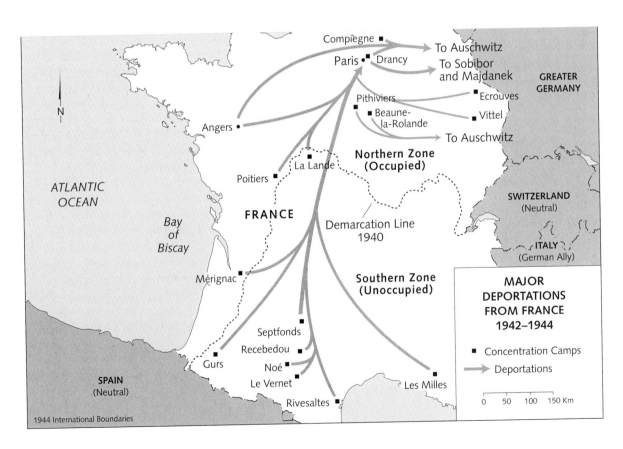

convoy children of foreign Jews under 16 in return for sparing French-born Jews. After numerous delays, on 16 July 1942 French policemen went from house to house in Paris and rounded up close to 13,000 foreign Jews, including 6,000 children.

Round-ups continued throughout July and August in the southern zone. By the end of the summer close to 11,000 Jews had been rounded up. Those arrested in the north were immediately sent to so-called transit camps. Some, like Pithiviers and Beaune-la-Rolande, which were situated south of Paris, originally had been used by German officials to intern French political prisoners in 1939 and 1940. Others, like Drancy, just north of Paris, were reserved expressly for Jewish deportees beginning in mid-1941. The occupation of the southern zone by German troops in late November 1942 merely formalized a reality that had become apparent for some time, namely the complete domination of France by the Third Reich. The unification of the two zones also meant that the implementation of the Final Solution could now proceed without interruption and without differentiation between foreign-born and French Jews.

The first deportations of foreign Jews in France to Auschwitz occurred on 27 March 1942. The deportation of a convoy of French Jews shortly thereafter occasioned no opposition from the Vichy government. Beginning in June 1942 the deportations were accelerated, and they continued almost without interruption throughout 1943. Most Jews were sent to Auschwitz. A small number were deported to other camps, including Natzweiler-Struthof near Strasbourg, which had been established largely for political prisoners. Even Jews who had fled to the safety of the Italian zone that had been created in November 1942 in southeastern France could not escape the Nazi onslaught. After the overthrow of Benito Mussolini in September 1943, the area was occupied by German troops. Deportations of Jews in Grenoble and Nice quickly followed.

Between March 1942 and July 1944, when the last train left French soil, 100 convoys containing between 80,000 and 90,000 Jews were sent to Auschwitz, primarily from Drancy. It is estimated that close to 80,000 Jews from France, the overwhelming majority of them immigrants and refugees, eventually met their death in extermination camps. Almost one-third of the victims were French citizens; nearly 2,000 were under the age of six, and more than 6,000 were under 13. The fact that three-quarters of the population of the prewar community of 300,000 was not deported can be attributed largely to the desperate effort by Vichy authorities, especially in the early period of deportations, to maintain a fragile independence by bartering foreigners for native-born Jews.

Another factor that explains the high rate of survival of Jews in France was the altruism of many Frenchmen, especially after 1942. There is little doubt that in the unoccupied zone, Vichy's plans for a revitalized France free of foreign elements was greeted enthusiastically by most citizens desperately seeking an explanation for their country's catastrophic defeat. As tens of thousands of residents of the German-controlled northern zone fled southward, newly arrived Jews were singled out and attacked for creating food shortages, engaging in black market activities, living ostentatiously, and disseminating anti-German propaganda. Antisemitism appears to have been especially strong in villages and towns in rural areas where Jews were relatively unknown before the war and where food rationing was most acute.

It is generally accepted that there was more opposition to anti-Jewish measures in the occupied zone, if only because they were imposed by a foreign power. In the first few years of the occupation, however, Vichy laws generally still applied in the north, and French Jews were not segregated from the larger society. Until 1942 German officials correctly assumed that as long as anti-Jewish activity was limited to legal measures, it would occasion little opposition from the majority of the French public. In the absence of any public statements of concern from their leaders, and in the face of their own suffering, most French men and women in the north probably paid little attention to the plight of refugees and foreigners.

A turning point in French public opinion seems to have come with the round-ups in the summer of 1942. It was one thing to persecute foreigners; it was quite another to harm innocent children and native-born citizens. For the first time in France, there were public outcries against anti-Jewish policies. Particularly vocal were Protestant leaders, who were fearful that discriminatory measures would soon be taken against other religious minorities, and left-wing Catholics, who used the opportunity to condemn the timidity of traditional church leadership. The fact that Vichy never officially prohibited emigration, even after the Nazi occupation of the south, meant that there were opportunities for the French to aid Jews to escape across the Pyrenees

A deportation action in the Marseilles region. Circa 1943

and the Swiss border. As the moving story of the Huguenot village of Le Chambon-sur-Lignon suggests, many French men and women hid Jews in their homes even at the risk of their own lives. Hundreds of young Jews whose parents had been deported were taken in by French families or found refuge in convents and monasteries.

On 17 August 1944 Nazi troops fleeing Paris filled a car on a train heading east with 51 special Jewish prisoners from Drancy. It was the last deportation from France. A week later, a brigade from Charles de Gaulle's Free French Forces liberated Paris. Yet de Gaulle realized soon after his accession to power in October that the troubling issue of French collaboration with German authorities during the war, and participation in the deportation of Jews in particular, could only divide the nation and hinder its chances of reconstruction. In addition, most French citizens showed little interest in undergoing a serious self-examination of their behavior during the occupation. The result was the gradual emergence of a national myth that viewed the overwhelming majority of French men and women during World War II as resisters to nazism, and portrayed the Vichy regime as an aberration whose traitorous deeds resulted from the venality and fanaticism of a crazed few.

Nowhere was the masking of Vichy more evident than in the treatment of French collaborators. Thousands of French citizens were summarily tried and in many cases executed by victorious resistance movements in the heated atmosphere of the liberation. With the restoration of government control, however, brutal purges soon gave way to a concerted effort to punish only the most egregious offenders. A series of show trials in 1945 and 1946 of the most visible leaders of Vichy reflected the government's reinterpretation of recent historical reality. Despite exhaustive efforts by the prosecution to secure the maximum sentence, no mention was made of the persecution and deportations of Jews. To do so would have compromised the central purpose of the trials, which was to portray Vichy as a betrayal of the shared ideals and values of the French.

In the end, the painful reality of the complicity of thousands of citizens in the execution of government-sponsored anti-Jewish measures during the occupation could not be easily incorporated into the postwar government's manichean view, which divided wartime French men and women into a mass of heroic resisters and a few cowardly collaborators.

As the events of the Holocaust in France faded from popular view, the number of trials of collaborators and Vichy officials decreased, and punishments became less severe. Many of those responsible for France's anti-Jewish policies who survived the war, such as Louis Darquier de Pellepoix; Jean Bousquet, chief of police under Vichy; and Paul Touvier, head of the Lyons branch and later regional chief of the Milice (a paramilitary force of fascist supporters), successfully avoided punishment by fleeing the country or simply disappearing into French society. A noteworthy exception was Klaus Barbie, a German officer who had been assigned to Lyons as chief of the second-largest Gestapo force in France. Captured in 1983, Barbie was by far the most important war criminal to be put on trial in France. Thirty-one years earlier, the most powerful SS official in occupied France, Karl-Albrecht Obert, had been tried and convicted by a military tribunal in Paris, but the French, preoccupied with what one writer called "more timely problems," seemed to have paid little attention to the courtroom proceedings. Barbie's case was potentially far more explosive, for aside from his participation in the deportation of Jews he was also implicated in the torture of Jean Moulin, de Gaulle's representative in France during the war.

Ultimately, however, the trial proved to be a major disappointment. After refusing to participate in the proceedings, Barbie finally agreed to cooperate in May 1987. After a summary trial that lasted less than two months, he was sentenced to life imprisonment. None of Barbie's victims who survived were able to confront him directly. Although pinpointing many of his actions against Jews, French prosecutors judiciously avoided any serious discussion of Barbie's relationship with French collaborators. In doing so, France missed yet another chance to come to grips with its past. As for Barbie, the former Gestapo leader was all but forgotten when he died in jail in September 1991.

Recent events in France suggest that despite popular acceptance of the myth of French resistance to nazism, the events of the Holocaust continue to haunt the national conscience. The deathbed revelations of President François Mitterrand concerning his indifference toward Vichy's anti-Jewish policies during the war and his close friendship with René Bousquet shocked most French men and women and pointed up the difficulties that even respected public leaders face in dealing with the tragedies of the Holocaust. And while some war criminals, such as Bousquet and Touvier, were finally indicted for war crimes in the 1980s (though Bousquet was assassinated by a deranged individual before he could be tried), others, like Maurice Papon, who organized the deportation of Jews from Bordeaux, continue successfully to avoid judgment.

In February 1993 the French government made a dramatic announcement declaring 16 July a national day of remembrance for Jewish and other racial victims of Vichy policies. The decree also called for monuments to be erected at sites throughout France where victims were concentrated or held before deportation. In addition, commemorative plaques were to be erected in every department in France.

It is too early to assess the implications of the government's action. On the one hand, the unprecedented decision marks an important departure from the tendency of postwar French governments to ignore the role of their country in the implementation of the Holocaust. The fact that the decree was announced in a period in which there had been a disturbing increase in the incidences of antisemitism and xenophobia in Europe makes it even more significant. Yet the French government's decision to confront the crimes of Vichy came only in response to ongoing protests by Jewish and resistance groups. Public pressure also seems to be behind the recent efforts by government officials to investigate bank accounts, insurance policies, and art works left by Jewish victims. Most disturbingly, little has been said so far about the need to teach the lessons of the Holocaust to the next generation through the incorporation of its history in school curricula.

Indeed, French educators and scholars have generally chosen to ignore the history of the Final Solution in their country. Yet the events surrounding the persecution and deportation of Jews under Vichy can serve as an important test case for students of the Holocaust. It is in France that one clearly sees the impact of deeply rooted antisemitism on the development of the genocidal policies of World War II. So, too, the collaboration of Vichy officials and the shifting attitudes of the French toward the plight of Jews reveal the complex behavior of men and women in occupied Europe in the face of the evil of nazism. Finally, postwar France's unsettled memory of the deportations points up the continuing significance of the Holocaust for contemporary consciousness. *David Weinberg*

Frank, Anne (1929–45) Anne Frank was a German-Dutch Jew whose diary of life in hiding from the Nazis in Amsterdam is the best-known personal document associated with the Holocaust and one of the most widely read books of modern times.

Born Anneliese Marie in Frankfurt am Main on 12 June 1929, she was the second daughter of Otto Heinrich Frank (1889–1980), a member of an assimilated, successful Frankfurt banking family that had suffered financial setbacks during the economic crises of the 1920s, and Edith Frank-Holländer (1890–1944), the daughter of a well-to-do manufacturer in Aachen. After the Nazis came to power in March 1933 and began to persecute the Jews, Otto Frank tried to protect his family and livelihood by moving to Amsterdam (a city he knew well), where he established an independent branch of Opekta Werk, a firm that made pectin, a fruit extract used in jams and jellies. His wife and children joined him in the winter of 1933–34 and the Franks moved to an apartment on Merwedeplein, a quiet neighborhood in the south of the city. In the late 1930s, Anne and her sister, Margot, lived the conventional lives of upper-middle-class Dutch children, attending a local Montessori school and socializing with a wide circle of friends; but after the Germans invaded Holland in May 1940 and began to restrict the economic and social activities of Jews, the girls were compelled to attend a segregated school (the Jewish Lyceum), and their father transferred overt control of Opekta and a subsidiary firm to Gentile co-workers. He also began to make preparations to go into hiding in a sealed-off set of rooms behind his office and warehouse at 263 Prinsengracht. In May 1942 Jews in Holland were ordered to wear yellow stars for instant identification, and on 29 June plans were announced to deport all Jews to labor camps in Germany. On 6 July, the morning after Margot received a call-up notice, the Frank family and three friends (Hermann, Auguste, and Peter van Pels), fearing deportation and worse, moved into what became known as the secret annex, or *het achterhuis* (the house behind). An acquaintance, the dentist Fritz Pfeffer, subsequently joined them there.

Earlier, on 12 June, Anne started keeping a diary in

Anne Frank in Amsterdam, 1942.

an album she had received as a gift from her parents for her thirteenth birthday, writing on the front page: "I hope I will be able to confide everything to you, as I have never been able to confide in anyone, and I hope that you will be a great source of comfort and support." The "you" was not only the diary itself but an imaginary friend, Kitty, to whom she described the daily lives of the incarcerated Jews and her own reactions to growing up in hiding. During the early months of confinement, Anne wrote vividly about domestic routines and tensions (notably quarrels with her mother), worries about friends, fear of discovery, longing for independence and freedom, and the stark accounts that reached her of the Nazi persecution of Jews in Amsterdam and elsewhere. As time passed, however, she also recorded with urgency, humor, and beauty an expanding awareness of herself as a sexual, moral, political, and philosophical being, and as a writer. In March 1944, in her twenty-first month in hiding, she heard a broadcast from London in which the education minister of the Dutch government in exile urged his fellow citizens to keep accounts of what they endured under German occupation, and she decided to rewrite and edit her diary for publication after the war. Recasting earlier passages, fictionalizing the names of the actual inhabitants, and sharpening her style, she produced an unfinished, but unfailingly interesting tale of fugitives in hiding, a bittersweet adolescent romance involving Peter, and a stirring psychological drama of a girl becoming a young woman. While sequestered, she also wrote a handful of short stories that were to appear in 1956 as *Tales of the Secret Annex*.

On 4 August 1944 German and Dutch security police (tipped off by an unidentified informer) raided the secret annex and arrested the eight Jews who had been sheltered there for 25 months. Anne's original and revised diaries, scattered on the floor, were recovered that afternoon by Miep Gies and Bep Voskuijl, two of the Dutch Christians who had courageously kept the occupants alive (the others were Victor Kugler, Johannes Kleiman, and Jan Gies). The Franks, van Pels, and Pfeffer were taken first to a local police station, then to the transit camp at Westerbork, and finally, in September, to the extermination camp at Auschwitz-Birkenau. Hermann van Pels and Edith Frank died there; Peter van Pels perished in Mauthausen, Fritz Pfeffer in Neuengamme, and August van Pels most probably in or near Theresienstadt. Anne and Margot were sent to Bergen-Belsen, where they died of typhus and starvation in March 1945, a few weeks before the liberation of the camps by the British and three months short of Anne's sixteenth birthday. Otto Frank, the only one of the group to survive, had been freed when Auschwitz was liberated by the Russian army in late January 1945.

After Otto Frank returned to Amsterdam in June 1945 and eventually learned that his daughters were dead, Miep Gies gave him Anne's diaries and exercise books. In the weeks that followed, he began copying out sections that might interest relatives and friends. Since parts of the diary existed in several versions, Frank served as editor as well as transcriber. When others read his selections, they were convinced of the manuscript's unusual value both as a document of the war and as an engrossing story of a lively young girl's maturation, and they urged Frank to seek a publisher. At first he thought the diary would attract little attention outside the immediate family, but he was persuaded to allow friends to make inquiries. In early April 1946 (after several Dutch firms turned it down) the Amsterdam newspaper *Het Parool* printed on its front page an eloquent article by the historian Jan Romein, praising the diary as a strikingly graphic account of daily life in wartime and a revelation of the "real hideousness of fascism," which had destroyed the life of a talented, endearing young girl. Uitgeverij Contact published *Het Achterhuis* in an edition of 1,500 in June 1947, and it received uniformly positive reviews.

Publishers in other countries were at first skeptical that there would be a market for what some saw as the mundane jottings of a little Dutch girl and a bleak reminder of the recently ended war, but French and German translations appeared in 1950. The turning point in the history of the diary was its remarkable reception in the United States in the summer of 1952. A brilliant review by the novelist Meyer Levin on the front page of the *New York Times Book Review* helped make *Anne Frank: Diary of a Young Girl* (which had been rejected by a dozen U.S. publishers before Doubleday agreed to issue it) an immediate best-seller. Adapted for the theater by Frances Goodrich and Albert Hackett in 1955, *The Diary of Anne Frank* brought tears to large audiences, many of whom felt as if one of the unknown Jewish dead in Europe had risen from a mass grave and taken on a distinctive identity. Honored with the Pulitzer Prize, the Tony Award, and the New York Drama Critics Award, the play was soon staged in many other countries. A film version by George Stevens in 1959 further popularized the heartrending, yet in these versions reassuring story of the child, her fate, and her book. Dozens of translations followed, and sales reached into the millions.

By the late 1950s, Anne Frank had become a legend: known around the world not only as the doomed author of a vivid, life-affirming book, but also as the prime symbol of the sufferings of innocent victims of Nazi genocide. "One voice speaks for 6 million," the Russian writer Ilya Ehrenburg wrote, "the voice not of a sage or a poet but of an ordinary little girl." Streets, schools, youth villages, and forests were soon named in her honor; paintings and statues perpetuated her image; poems and songs were composed in her memory; and—as Alvin H. Rosenfeld has observed—"public figures of every kind, from politicians to religious leaders, regularly invoke[d] her name and quote[d] lines from her book. In all of these ways, her name, face, and fate [were] kept constantly before us."

In 1957, Otto Frank had further memorialized his daughter by helping to establish the Anne Frank Stichting in Amsterdam, a foundation whose original aim was "to repair and renovate the property at 263 Prinsengracht and especially to maintain the building's back annex, as well as to propagate ideals left to the world in the diary of Anne Frank." In May 1960 the Anne Frank House opened as a museum, and the foundation supported youth conferences, lectures, and exhibitions designed to combat antisemitism and racism. Activities soon expanded. A specialized library brought together a collection of books, newspapers, and magazines about discrimination and threats to the rights of minorities; the educational department developed programs, courses, and teaching aids to be used in schools and other settings. In 1985 the traveling exhibition "Anne Frank in the World: 1929–1945" was organized by the foundation and has since been seen in hundreds of cities and towns across Europe, North and South America, and Asia. The number of visitors to the Anne Frank House has grown from about 9,000 in 1960 to more than 600,000 each year in the 1990s, making it something of a shrine, as well as one of the most popular museums in Europe. Anne Frank Centers were also established in New York and other cities, and one is planned for Berlin. In Basel, the Anne Frank-Fonds oversees matters related to copyrights and reprint permissions, and also supports educational and philanthropic projects. Such has been the phenomenal fame of Anne Frank's life and diary, and so often has she been invoked as *the* Holocaust martyr— symbol of the murdered, guiltless 6 million Jews— that critical reactions were and continue to be inevitable. As early as the late 1950s, neo-Nazis—in their efforts to prove that accounts of German genocide were exaggerated or even fabricated—claimed that the most famous Holocaust document, the diary itself, was a forgery. These frequently repeated charges led to several lawsuits and in the 1980s to an exhaustive scholarly and forensic study by the Netherlands State Institute for War Documentation to assess the authenticity of Anne Frank's writings. The result was the authoritative *The Diary of Anne Frank: The Critical Edition,* which proved beyond a doubt that the diary was genuine and that the neo-Nazi allegations were groundless. Published first in the Netherlands (1986) and then in Germany, France, Italy, and the United States, the *Critical Edition* is now recognized as the most reliable source for the text and history of Frank's writings.

Revised and expanded editions of the diary for general readers followed, and in this new form the book again became an international best-seller.

Other, more creditable critiques of the so-called "mythologizing of Anne Frank" were advanced in the 1970s and afterward. Although people continued to revere the girl and to treasure her book, commentators questioned the many, often bizarre uses to which her name and image had been put. Frequently quoting Hannah Arendt's 1962 remark that the adoration of Anne Frank was a form of "cheap sentimentality at the expense of great catastrophe," critics argued that an adolescent Dutch girl could not possibly be "the voice of the 6 million"; no single person could. Her diary, which ended before she had certain knowledge or direct experience of the German genocide, did not convey the horrific actuality or meaning of the unprecedented historical disaster. Her book could not and should not be described as the representative Holocaust text. To focus solely on Anne Frank as a symbol of the victims of the Holocaust is, critics argue, to turn an enormous calamity into a story of an assault on fugitives and innocent children rather than of a systematic effort to eradicate an entire people and culture.

Another aspect of the ongoing controversy about the Anne Frank legacy concerns the Jewish specificity of the diary. The best-known adaptations (the Goodrich and Hackett play and the George Stevens film) minimized the Jewish content in order to achieve a greater universality, and hence consolation and commercial success. For years after the premier of the play and film, the heroine was widely perceived not only as a symbol of the Holocaust but as a ubiquitous emblem of hope, a persecuted victim whose utterance "In spite of everything, I still believe that people are really good at heart" encapsulated her inspirational message to the entire world. That Anne Frank was Jewish, and was killed for that reason only, became less significant than the comforting image of her as the ardent child who, during a barbaric time, never lost faith in the basic goodness of human beings. In the diary itself, however, Anne writes powerfully of the suffering of the European Jews and ponders the reasons for their persecution. Also neglected in the Broadway and Hollywood accounts of the girl who kept faith is the fact that she wrote the much-quoted sentence before she was arrested and condemned to see mass murder, and before she herself died wretchedly in Bergen-Belsen. As Lawrence Langer has said, the sentence (taken out of context and used as the uplifting curtain line of the Goodrich and Hackett play) "floats over the audience like a benediction assuring grace after momentary gloom," and is "the least appropriate epitaph conceivable for the millions of victims and thousands of survivors of Nazi genocide."

Other controversies have swirled around the name Anne Frank, some of which provoked bitter quarrels and lawsuits. Meyer Levin, who helped popularize the diary in America, accused Otto Frank of blocking his right to adapt it for the Broadway stage, took him to court, and kept the dispute alive for 30 years. Otto Frank was also involved in litigation against the individuals and groups who charged that his daughter's diary was a forgery; and disputes have arisen between the Anne Frank Stichting in Amsterdam and the Anne Frank-Fonds in Basel over copyrights, the uses of money generated by the vast sales of the diary, and other matters related to ownership of the child's name, image, and book, and to the question of how her life and death should be memorialized. Survivors of the camps and others have also expressed indignation and sadness at what they see as the exploitation of an Anne Frank cult.

Persistent efforts, however, have also been made to counter the most sentimental and misleading aspects of the mystique of Anne Frank. Two school curricula were designed to place her story more accurately in context: Karen Shawn's *The End of Innocence: Anne Frank and the Holocaust* (New York, 1989, 1994) and Alex Grobman's *Anne Frank in Historical Perspective* (Los Angeles, 1995). Alvin H. Rosenfeld's valuable essay "Popularization and Memory: The Case of Anne Frank" appeared in *Lessons and Legacies* (Evanston, Ill., 1991); and Robert Alter has usefully warned of the false consolation involved in trying to clutch "eternal hope from the heart of hell." In 1995 Jon Blair produced a two-hour documentary film, *Anne Frank Remembered*, that tried to balance history and myth.

Yet despite some of the questionable uses to which the Anne Frank legend has been put, her book and legacy remain of permanent value. The diary itself is a profoundly moving testament to the fine observational powers and the swift growth of a quicksilver young girl, and to the pathos of her brutally abbreviated life. If read as the first (and not the only, the last, or the definitive) book about people persecuted by the Nazis, it can fairly serve as an unforgettable reminder of what Philip Roth once called "the millions of unlived years robbed from the murdered Jews."

Lawrence Graver

Frank, Hans (1900–1946), also known as Frank II Early member of the Nazi party and governor of the Generalgouvernement (Poland) during World War II. Frank ordered the execution of thousands of Poles and helped create the Polish ghettos. At Nuremberg after the war he was tried and convicted on charges of war crimes. In his prison memoirs he was one of the few Nazi leaders to express regret for the crimes he and the Nazi party had committed. He was hanged in 1946.

Frankfurt am Main City with the second-largest Jewish community in Germany prior to 1933 (more than 26,000). Deportations from Frankfurt to Lodz, Minsk, Riga, Theresienstadt, and other destinations began in October 1941. When American forces liberated Frankfurt in April 1945, only a handful of Jews were found.

Freudiger, Fülöp (1900–1976) Leader of the Budapest Jewish community and member of the Budapest *Judenrat* (Jewish council). Freudiger bribed the SD officer Dieter Wisliceny to release a few Orthodox Jews from Hungarian ghettos. Freudiger escaped to Romania in 1944 and eventually settled in Israel. In 1961 he appeared as a witness for the prosecution in the trial of Adolf Eichmann.

G

Gas Chambers Ever since the Holocaust the term *gas chambers* has been associated with the Final Solution—the genocide of the Jewish people—and with Nazi crimes against other peoples in occupied nations as well as against Germans targeted for "euthanasia" in Operation T4.

A gas chamber is a room or hall in a mobile or stationary structure in which people were suffocated by means of poison gas. Nazi authorities—medical agencies, the SS, or the Main Office of Reich Security (Reichssicherheitshauptamt, RSHA)—selected for extermination those persons they considered to be undeserving of life according Nazi racial ideology. The principal victims of murder in the gas chambers were physically handicapped Germans, the mentally ill, homosexuals, so-called asocials (*Asoziale*), Gypsies, and Jews. The gas chambers allowed the Germans to commit mass murder and genocide under a cloak of secrecy. This secrecy was needed to stanch resistance on the part of the victims and their families, to carry out the mission with a minimum of guards, and to deceive the victims until the last possible moment.

The introduction of gas chambers solved three problems the Nazis had encountered in the summer of 1941, when they resorted to shooting as the means of mass murder of civilians in the occupied territories of the Soviet Union. Mass shootings were time-consuming, costly (because of the expenditure of ammunition), and psychologically taxing on the executioners. In the gas chambers hundreds of persons could be killed in minutes by means of a relatively inexpensive poison. Most important of all, however, gassing helped the executioners to distance themselves from the direct consequences of their actions. SS men who rounded up the doomed civilians did not have to aim at women or children, pull a trigger, and watch them die.

Mass murder carried out through state-of-the-art industrial methods was a unique innovation of the Nazi regime. The magnitude of the crime helps to explain why it took people so long to acknowledge the existence of the gas chambers. Even when confronted with unequivocal firsthand evidence, and even after potential victims knew they might be put to death in this fashion, they resisted the horrific realization of the truth and dismissed the possibility that a civilized na-

A door to a gas chamber in Auschwitz. The note reads, "Poison gas! Entering endangers your life." February 1945

tion like Germany could commit such an abominable crime.

Poison Gas

Mass killing by gas was effected by means of two principal compounds: carbon monoxide and hydrogen cyanide (also known as hydrocyanic acid or prussic acid).

Carbon monoxide is a colorless, odorless gas, lighter than air and water soluble, that can be stored and transported in canisters under high pressure. It is expensive to manufacture in its pure form, but as a constituent of the exhaust fumes of poorly tuned diesel engines it was delivered in sufficient concentration to be effective for mass killing in large gas chambers, such as those in Treblinka and Belzec. It kills by bonding with hemoglobin in the blood more efficiently than oxygen. A victim of carbon monoxide poisoning suffocates because not enough oxygen is available to be delivered to the brain and other organs.

Hydrogen cyanide also kills by asphyxiation, though not by binding with hemoglobin; rather, it blocks the absorption of oxygenated hemoglobin by the tissues. It penetrates the bloodstream easily through the mucous membranes of the nose, mouth, esophagus, stomach, and lungs. Hydrogen cyanide had been in use as a fumigant since the 1920s. In 1923 the German firm Deutsche Gesellschaft für Schädlingsbekämpfung (known as Degesch) manufactured a stable form of the chemical absorbed in diatomite pellets that was marketed under the trade name Zyklon B. It was used, inter alia, as a disinfectant in the German army and navy. Because hydrogen cyanide becomes gaseous at approximately 25 degrees Celsius, a minimum temperature had to be maintained in the gas chambers. The body heat generated when the chambers were packed full of people helped maintain the temperature, but artificial heating systems were also employed. On rare occasions (in Natzweiler-Struthof and Sachsenhausen, for example) cyanide chlorides were dissolved in water to instigate a reaction that created hydrogen cyanide. This delivery system was called Zyklon A.

Persons who inhaled either hydrogen cyanide or carbon monoxide suffered grievously. But because carbon monoxide took longer to have an effect, it was the crueler method. Since the concentration of poison gas in the air decreased with every breath the victims took, the chambers could be ventilated rather quickly after each gassing.

Operation Euthanasia

To the best of our knowledge, the first instance of mass murder by gas occurred on 15 November 1939 at the Owinski psychiatric hospital near Poznan. The 1,100 victims, including 78 children, were Polish mental patients, and the gas used was carbon monoxide.

On 7 December, 1,201 patients at Tygenhof psychiatric hospital in Germany were gassed to death in an operation that marked the first use of gas vans. A *Sonderkommando* (special squad) led by SS captain Herbert Lange was put to work in this operation.

The Nazi regime adopted gassing systematically to eliminate undesirables in Operation Euthanasia, which began in January 1940. Early that year the gassing method was tested for the commanders of the operation at the former prison in Brandenburg-Havel. The victims were psychiatric patients. To demonstrate the advantages of gas, some of the victims were posted to a control group and given doses of medicines and drugs; the rest were gassed to death. At the end of the test, those who had been given medicine were also gassed because the pharmaceuticals had proven ineffective.

Following the trial run and Hitler's approval, the commanders of Operation Euthanasia—Philipp Bouhler (chief of the Führer Chancellery), Viktor Brack (a staff member in the office), Hans Calmeyer (a chemist), Leonardo Conti (the chief state physician), and Karl Brandt decided to make regular use of carbon monoxide, but only with close "medical supervision."

Beginning in January 1940, tens of thousands were murdered by gas at various Operation Euthanasia centers such as Hartheim, Brandenburg, Bernburg, Grafeneck, Sonnenstein, and Hadamar. The number of victims of Operation Euthanasia was at least 71,088, as we know from bookkeeping records of the operation's administration in Berlin, and may exceed 100,000.

A key figure in lethal gassing of psychiatric patients in the Reich and elsewhere was SS officer Christian Wirth, who made this activity his specialty and conducted the first experiments. In 1940 Wirth was appointed inspector of Operation Euthanasia facilities in the Greater Reich (Germany and annexed Austria and Czechoslovakia), and in 1941 in Lublin he established the first Operation Euthanasia center outside the Reich proper. Subsequently he was involved in the construction of extermination camps in Poland, where more than 2 million Jews would be gassed to death.

Viktor Brack took a special interest in the effects of gas on the victims and personally interviewed the members of the Operation Euthanasia medical staff. When the Final Solution was implemented, Brack shared the cumulative practical experience of the operation's actions with the SS leadership for application in the murder of Jews in the gas chambers of the extermination camps in Poland.

Murder at the Operation Euthanasia centers was committed in special rooms that had been converted into gas chambers and made to resemble shower facilities. Carbon monoxide gas was delivered in steel containers affixed to their exterior wall.

Although Operation Euthanasia was officially terminated in September 1941 (upon an order given on 24 August), it continued a rogue existence and claimed tens of thousands more lives—all in the eastern occupied areas—some by gas, others by the injection of poison. The list of Operation Euthanasia victims also includes prisoners from three concentration camps—Sachsenhausen, Auschwitz, and Mauthausen—who were taken to the Operation Euthanasia centers.

In April 1941 Operation Euthanasia was expanded to the large concentration camps in Germany. In this phase of the operation, encoded "14f13" by SS chief Heinrich Himmler, thousands of prisoners were put to death. The victims were people the Nazis wished to dispose of: the disabled, persons "unfit for labor," Jews, Soviet prisoners of war, and offspring of mixed marriages. The victims were selected by medical committees that visited the camps for this purpose. They were chosen on the basis of earlier reports by the camp commanders and perfunctory medical examinations of the prisoners on the lists. The condemned were removed from the camps and taken in groups to gassing facilities, foremost among them Bernburg and Hartheim, and to camps in which such facilities already existed.

On 27 April 1943 Himmler issued an order limiting Operation 14f13 to "mentally ill" persons selected by a medical committee. Other prisoners who were unfit for labor for reasons of illness or disability would not be included in the operation. In practice, however, the doctors continued to dispatch mentally sound prisoners to the gas chambers.

The second phase of the operation began on 11 April 1944, when the order to resume the killing of prisoners was given. This time the victims were se-lected not by medical committees but by the medical staff of the camps themselves. This phase, in which the killing was perpetrated at the Hartheim center (near Linz, Austria), continued until the facility was dismantled in December 1944.

The number of persons murdered in Operation 14f13 cannot be stated with precision because the documentation pertaining to it has not survived. At least 1,609 prisoners from the Mauthausen and Gusen camps were murdered at Hartheim in 1941–42. In contrast, the exact death toll in the second phase of the operation, from April to November (or December) 1944, is known: 3,328 prisoners were taken from Mauthausen and Gusen to Hartheim. We also know that approximately 5,000 prisoners from the two camps were murdered at Hartheim in the two phases of the operation. Additional prisoners were taken to Hartheim from Dachau—3,075 in the first phase and 150 in the second phase. The total number of victims at Hartheim exceeds 18,000. Prisoners from Ravensbrück and Buchenwald were taken to the Operation Euthanasia facilities for lethal gassing. Their exact numbers cannot be determined, but it is known that a transport bearing more than 400 internees from Buchenwald reached Bernburg sometime between 2 and 14 March 1942. On 28 July 1941, 575 prisoners from Auschwitz were delivered to the Sonnenstein facility.

The widespread use of gas chambers to kill thousands of "undesirables" in Operation Euthanasia created the psychological, technical, and administrative climate in which the same method could be implemented against the Jews. Moreover, the forced interruption of Operation Euthanasia, even if only partial, made the experienced team available for new duties in carrying out the so-called Final Solution of the Jewish Problem. A large majority of the SS men who were assigned to build the first extermination camps had participated in Operation Euthanasia. This was especially so in the extermination camps in Poland built under Operation Reinhard, where 92 "euthanasia experts" took part in the gassing of Jews.

The transformation of Nazi Germany into the world's strongest military power and the progression of events on the battlefield in World War II facilitated these crimes by concealing the authorities' actions from the view of any player who could frustrate or terminate the criminal murder of thousands of innocents. Public opinion in the free world, too, was no longer a factor of consequence. Thus the combination of practical experience, available manpower, general absence of public resistance in Germany (except for the Roman Catholic and Evangelical churches, which protested the actions sotto voce), and military and political developments set the stage for the extensive use of poison gas and gas chambers in the murder of Jews in occupied Europe.

Gas Vans

Vans serving as mobile gas chambers were introduced because the *Einsatzgruppen* (killing units) had long been dissatisfied with the use of gunfire in mass murder operations in the occupied Soviet territories. Einsatzgruppen members had been complaining to the RSHA about the psychological distress they suffered from having to shoot tens of thousands of women, children, and the ill face to face. The accumulation of such grievances prompted the Einsatzgruppen commanders to seek alternative murder methods.

The commander of Einsatzgruppe B, Arthur Nebe, who also directed Department V of the Criminal Police at the RSHA, experimented with the injection of exhaust fumes from a truck engine into a sealed room. The success of this experiment led to a decision by the RSHA to apply the method in the murder of targeted populations. Walter Rauff, director of the administrative division of the RSHA (Department IIb), was charged with the technical implementation of the new solution. After further testing in a garage to refine the method, Rauff oversaw the modification of vans so that engine exhaust, bearing carbon monoxide gas, would be piped into the trailer compartment, where the condemned were being held. Death from asphyxiation occurred within minutes.

The efficiency of the first gas vans was tested on Soviet prisoners of war at the Sachsenhausen concentration camp in September 1941. The SS chemists who witnessed the experiment recounted that the corpses that tumbled from the trucks after the gassing had the characteristic pinkish color of victims of carbon monoxide poisoning. By 23 June 1942 approximately 20 trucks had been outfitted for this use, and another 10 were being assembled.

The mobile gassing units consisted of trailer compartments mounted on large trucks. To prevent gas seepage, large doors with gaskets created a hermetic seal. Engine exhaust was pumped into the compartment through a hose connected to the regular exhaust

pipe of the truck. To keep the victims from preventing their own asphyxiation, German engineers installed a device that frustrated interference with the flow of gas. Two models of gas vans were used in occupied Soviet territory: the Diamond-Wagen, which had a capacity of 25–35 people, and the Saurer-Wagen, which could hold 50–60 people.

Every truck had a permanent driver who was in charge of its operation. (Some of the drivers gave testimony after the war.) The interior of the trailer compartment was illuminated, as we know from complaints to Berlin about damage caused to lighting fixtures as the victims attempted to break out. It took 15–20 minutes to asphyxiate a truckload of prisoners.

At the Chelmno camp, three Renault gas vans were used, one of them large. From the outside the vehicles resembled moving vans. The gas chamber was a sealed box, 4–5 meters in length, 2.2 meters in width, and 2 meters in height, with double doors in the back. The interior was lined with galvanized steel; the floor was made of wooden slats. Prisoners were led into the van over a gangplank. After they entered, the driver closed the doors and affixed a dangling lock. After the victims were asphyxiated, the driver unhooked the hose from the exhaust pipe and drove to a camp in the forest, where the corpses were unloaded and interred in mass graves. Later on, they were incinerated in crematoriums.

The first mobile killing vans were sent into action as early as November 1941. One was employed in the killing of Jews in Poltava that month and in Kharkov the next month. Between December 1941 and June 1942 three trucks were used in the murder of 97,000 Jews in Ukraine. In all, the Einsatzgruppen deployed some 15 gas vans in the sector of the Soviet Union that they occupied.

In May 1942, following complaints about frequent technical malfunctions, August Becker was sent from Berlin to inspect the trucks. His report emphasized the two common problems in the murder process: the frequent mechanical failures of the vans and the psychological hardship of unloading the corpses when the doors of the vans were opened.

Outside the occupied Soviet territory, gas vans operated in locations such as the Semlin (Sajmiste) concentration camp in Yugoslavia, where they were used to murder approximately 7,000 prisoners—mostly Jewish women and children. Vans were also used in Lublin in the murder of Jews and non-Jews. But this method of eliminating "undesirables" fell short of the Nazi authorities' expectations, largely because the trucks kept breaking down, so they replaced it with stationary gas chambers.

Gas vans operated in the following areas, among others: Belorussia, Estonia, Latvia, Minsk, and the Maly Trostenec extermination camp, the Crimea, and the southern Caucasus. In all, approximately 700,000 persons were murdered in the vans—roughly half on occupied Soviet soil and the remainder at the Chelmno extermination camp.

Extermination Camps

Chelmno. The first mass gassings of Jews took place in the Chelmno extermination camp, 60 kilometers west of Lodz. Chelmno was also the first site outside the German-occupied Soviet zone where large numbers of Jews were murdered as part of the Final Solution.

The gas chambers at Chelmno, unlike those at the other extermination camps, were mobile, comprising two or three Renault trucks. Initially those who were to be killed were gathered in the courtyard of a castle in the village of Chelmno, where, to soothe them, they were told that they needed to shower and be disinfected pending transport to a labor camp. Afterward they were led in groups of 50 to the ground floor of the castle, where they were ordered to undress and then were taken to the cellar. From there the victims were made to run up a gangplank, hidden from prying eyes on either side, to the loading gate of a gas van into which they were forced with much violence. As they seated themselves in the freight compartment of the truck, a hose was inserted to carry the exhaust fumes of the engine into the trailer. The driver then closed and locked the doors. The engine was gunned for about 10 minutes, during which time those inside the compartment suffocated from inhaling the carbon monoxide fumes. The exhaust hose was then disconnected, and the truck was driven to the disposal site—initially open pits dug by Jewish forced laborers in a nearby forest, later two incinerators for cremation. From the first transport to Chelmno (7 December 1941) until the last (14 July 1944) approximately 320,000 people, nearly all of them Jews, were murdered in the mobile gas chambers of the camp.

Belzec. In February 1942 gassings of Jews under Operation Reinhard began to take place in three extermination camps in Poland. The first was Belzec, located in the southeastern part of the Lublin district on the Lublin-Lvov railway. Initially three gas chambers were installed in a building with double walls filled with layer of sand for insulation. Each chamber measured 32 square meters in area. The floors and the lower half of the walls were lined in metal. The soundness and efficiency of the gas chambers in Belzec were tested in late February 1942 on Jews from the town of Lubycza Krolewska and other Jews who had been forced to build the camp. Mass murder there was inaugurated on 17 March. Carbon monoxide gas was delivered in metal canisters and injected into the chambers through hoses. In a later test a 250-horsepower diesel engine was installed to produce the gas and pump it into the chambers. From then on, the use of canisters was discontinued.

Victims were led to the chambers through a connecting vestibule. The chamber doors had rubber gaskets that permitted hermetic sealing. They closed from the outside and were constructed of a special lumber that resisted pressure applied from inside. Each chamber had a second door through with bodies were removed. In Belzec and the other extermination camps, as in Chelmno, Jewish prisoners were made to drag corpses out of the gas chambers and haul them to burial pits. Each of these details, which were known in Belzec (as in Auschwitz-Birkenau) as *Sonderkommandos,* would work for a few weeks and, once exhausted, be murdered in the same gas chambers in which they had toiled.

From the first day of the gassing process in Belzec, 12 March 1942, until December of that year about 600,000 Jews were murdered. With the exception of perhaps as many as several thousand Gypsies, all the victims were Jews. In Belzec, as in Chelmno and all other extermination camps, systematic deception was practiced. The Jews were told that they had come to a transit camp en route to labor camps, and that for reasons of hygiene they must bathe, be disinfected, and turn over any cash and valuables that they had brought. After women and children were separated from the men, the victims were ordered to undress and run, prodded by shouts and beatings, to the "showers." The chamber was sealed, the diesel engine was started, and carbon monoxide gas was pumped into the chamber. Within 20–30 minutes everyone inside was dead.

In July 1942 the original three gas chambers were dismantled and replaced with a brick and concrete structure holding six chambers, each 20 square meters in area. To enter the new chambers, victims passed through a vestibule to doors that opened to the inside. Bodies were removed through another opening, in the exterior wall of each chamber. The motor that delivered the gas was situated in a shed outside the building. The six chambers had the capacity to murder between 1,000 and 1,200 persons at a time.

Two sources provide detailed accounts of the gassings in Belzec: the testimony of Rudolf Reder, the only prisoner who escaped from Belzec and survived, and that of Kurt Gerstein, an SS officer who visited the camp in August 1942. Gerstein, the director of the Technical Disinfection Department under the SS Health Technical Division, was in charge of "toxic disinfection gases." He observed the gassing murder of a transport of Jews in Belzec and gave detailed written testimony while interned in France in May 1945.

At the time of the Wannsee Conference (20 January 1942) on implementation of the Final Solution, the Germans had not yet decided which technique of annihilation to employ. By then gas vans in Chelmno had been serving as mobile killing machines for six weeks, and stationary gas chambers were under construction at Belzec. An experiment in asphyxiation by Zyklon B gas had been performed in the cellar of Block 11 and the incinerator building of the main camp in Auschwitz in September 1941, and the first gas chamber in Birkenau, Bunker 1, was on the drawing boards. But the practical experience in lethal gassing that the Nazi regime had gained in Operation Euthanasia and in Chelmno was insufficient to dictate the optimal technology for murder on the scale necessary to annihilate the millions of European Jews.

Sobibor. The second extermination camp to be outfitted with permanent gas chambers was Sobibor. Gassing commenced there in May 1942, after trial runs in April. Three gas chambers were situated in a brick building. Each measured 16 square meters and could hold up to 180 persons. The chambers were entered from a front porch, and the corpses were removed through an exterior door. Carbon monoxide was generated by a 200-horsepower engine stationed in a shed near the chambers, and the gas was injected through a network of hoses. The gassings lasted 20–30 minutes.

The technique used in Belzec was duplicated in Sobibor, and the deceptive ruses were similar. In the first stage of mass murder in Sobibor, ending in July 1942, at least 77,000 Jews from the Lublin area in Poland and from Austria, Germany, and the Protectorate of Bohemia and Moravia (including Theresienstadt) were murdered, and by early November 1942 about 25,000 Jews from Slovakia were also killed. In all, approximately 100,000 Jews were gassed to death in Sobibor at that time. In late summer deportations to the camp were suspended for two months to allow work on the Lublin-Chelm railway. At the same time three more gas chambers were added, boosting the gassing capacity of the complex to 1,200 persons, in order to keep pace with the expected inrush of transports. When extermination actions resumed in early October 1942, Jews were brought there from towns in the Lublin district, from eastern Galicia, and from the Majdanek camp. By July 1943 another 70,000–80,000 Jews had been murdered in Sobibor. In addition to them, the roster of the annihilated in 1943 included 4,000 Jews from France (March), 35,000 from the Netherlands (March–July), and 14,000 from the ghettos of Vilna, Minsk, and Lida (second half of September). In all, approximately 250,000 Jews were gassed in Sobibor.

Treblinka. The Treblinka extermination camp was also equipped with permanent gas chambers. Gassings there began on 23 July 1942, with the first transports from the Warsaw ghetto. By 21 September, 254,000 Jews had been murdered in Treblinka, and by the time the camp was dismantled in August 1943, 738,000 Jews from the Generalgouvernement had been killed there. Another 107,000 Jews from the Bialystok district were murdered in the gas chambers of Treblinka between November 1942 and January 1943, as were Jews from countries other than Poland: Slovakia (7,000 in the summer and fall of 1942); Bohemia and Moravia (8,000 from Theresienstadt, 5–25 October 1942); Thrace, an area annexed to Bulgaria (more than 4,000 in the second half of March 1943); Yugoslav Macedonia, also annexed to Bulgaria (7,000 in late March and early April 1943); and Salonika (2,800 in late March 1943). Approximately 2,000 Gypsies were also murdered there. In all, at minimum 870,000 people were slaughtered in the gas chambers of Treblinka.

Initially Treblinka had three gas chambers, each 16 square meters in area, housed in a brick structure. A diesel engine in a nearby shed pumped toxic exhaust fumes into the chambers through a network of pipes that terminated in shower heads installed for purposes of deception. Each chamber had an entrance door and, across from it, a door through which the bodies were removed after the gassing. The extermination technique in Treblinka closely resembled that used in Belzec and Sobibor, but the deception that preceded the murder was much more refined. As the deportees exited the trains, they, like their counterparts elsewhere, were told that they had reached a transit camp en route to labor camps and had to shower and disinfect their clothing before they could move on. To reinforce the illusion, they were given receipts when they handed over their cash and valuables. The reception area was camouflaged as an ordinary railroad station. The gas chambers themselves were made to look like shower rooms, and flowerbeds were planted around the perimeter of the building. Even the entrance to the chambers was disguised; draped over the door was a curtain with the biblical inscription, from Psalm 118, "This is the gate of the Lord, into which the righteous shall enter."

The deportees were ordered to undress (men in the transport yard, women and children in a barracks) and, naked, were made to run directly to the gas chambers along a 90-meter path called the Tube (*Schlauch*). Once they were packed inside, the doors were sealed and the diesel engine was started. All the people died of suffocation within 20–25 minutes.

As it became clear that the existing gas chambers could not accommodate all the transports, the Treblinka authorities decided to build 10 more. The new chambers added a total of 320 square meters of killing space. Deportees were led to the chambers through a vestibule in the middle of the building. After the gassing, bodies were removed through other doors that opened from the outside. The commanders in Treblinka even made accommodations for members of incoming transports who lacked the strength to walk to the gas chambers. The Lazaretto was built for them— a facility where the ill and weak were shot and cremated.

Belzec, Sobibor, and Treblinka were all built under Operation Reinhard, the master plan for the extermination of Jews in the Generalgouvernement. It seems that only carbon monoxide was used to kill people in these three camps. The camps were not equipped with crematoriums. Initially, bodies were buried in massive pits; later on, they were incinerated in huge bonfires.

Majdanek. The only extermination camp where mass murder was committed by means of both carbon monoxide and hydrogen cyanide gas was Majdanek,

on the outskirts of Lublin. Carbon monoxide was piped into the chambers from storage canisters kept in a control room nearby. Zyklon B was dropped in through holes in the ceiling. (These openings, like the bluish tint on the walls caused by the gas that soaked into them, are still visible at Majdanek.) The camp headquarters urged the supplier of the gas, Tesch und Stabenow, to deliver ever-increasing quantities of Zyklon B for purposes of "disinfection." In all, the Majdanek authorities consumed 7,711 kilograms of Zyklon B.

Seven gas chambers of different sizes were built in Majdanek. In even the smallest of them, continual efforts were made to maximize capacity by forcing more and more people inside. Even the space between the ceiling and the heads of standing people was used. Unlike in Belzec, Sobibor, and Treblinka, murder victims were removed to crematoriums, the largest of which was built in September 1943. Some of the bodies were first subjected to "surgery" in search of hidden valuables.

Lethal gassings at Majdanek evidently began in October 1942 and were halted in the autumn of 1943. The source of information concerning the gassing murder of Jews in this camp is the Polish underground, which reported that up to 1,000 Jews a day were being suffocated in the gas chambers. In contrast to the other extermination camps, the precise number of gassing victims in Majdanek is difficult to determine because prisoners there were murdered in several different ways and without any systematic registration. In all, approximately 360,000 persons were put to death in Majdanek, 40 percent (144,000) through mass extermination methods (gas chambers and firing squads). Nearly half a million people from 28 countries passed through the camp. Most of the non-Jewish inmates were Polish and Soviet prisoners of war and prisoners from other concentration camps in Germany and Poland. The Jews in Majdanek came from Poland, Germany, Czechoslovakia, Belgium, the Netherlands, France, and Hungary. Jews accounted for at least one-third of the murder victims in Majdanek and a majority of those murdered by gas.

The new arrivals in Majdanek were duped in several ways. There, as in the other camps, they were told that they must be disinfected. Not only were the buildings housing the gas chambers camouflaged, but the victims were given real showers before they entered the chambers. The purpose of the showers may have been to further the deception and keep the victims calm; in addition, some of the perpetrators claimed that showering expedited the dispersal of the poison gas.

Auschwitz

On 3 September 1941, in the cellar of Block 11 in the Auschwitz main camp, 600 Soviet prisoners of war and 250 Polish inmates who had fallen ill were suffocated by means of hydrogen cyanide gas, which was released when pellets of Zyklon B, a common pesticide and disinfectant, came in contact with air. Satisfied with the result of this experiment, Rudolf Höss, the commandant of Auschwitz, selected Zyklon B poisoning as the primary method of mass murder in the camp. Zyklon B was superior to carbon monoxide poisoning via engine exhaust fumes because it was relatively cheap, it was easy to deliver—the pellets need only to be dropped into the killing chambers—and, most important, it took effect much faster than carbon monoxide.

The first permanent gas chamber in Auschwitz was created at the main camp, in the morgue of Crematorium I, the room where corpses had been stored pending incineration. The large and narrow hall—17 meters along one side—was converted to use for mass killing by sealing some of the doors and making several openings in the ceiling through which Zyklon B pellets could be thrown. During the gassing, trucks and motorcycles would gun their engines outside the building to cover the cries of the dying. Jewish and non-Jewish inmates, including Soviet prisoners of war, were murdered in this chamber between the fall of 1941 and October 1942. Jews in the first RSHA-organized transports also were put to death there. The last murders by gas in Crematorium I were in December 1942, when the Sonderkommando members who had disposed of the corpses of thousands of murder victims were themselves put to death in the chamber. Thereafter the gassing operations were moved to new facilities at Birkenau, although the ovens remained in use until July 1943.

By early 1942 the capacity of Crematorium I was severely taxed by the continuous arrival of thousands of Jewish deportees condemned to be murdered as well as by the mounting death toll among prisoners suffering from disease, starvation, exhaustion, and physical abuse, whose bodies needed to be disposed of. Some transports began to be redirected to the Birkenau camp. Murder in the new facility was perpetrated in two vil-

lage houses that had been spared when the Germans destroyed the Polish villages in the area. One of these buildings, called the Red House, was prepared for use as a gas chamber in mid-March 1942, and the other was outfitted for that purpose in late June. The prisoners who worked in these buildings called them Bunker 1 and Bunker 2; subsequently this terminology entered the SS lexicon.

Before entering the chambers, the condemned were made to undress in wooden barracks, two near Bunker 1 and three alongside Bunker 2. Both bunkers were more than twice as long as they were wide; Bunker 1 measured nearly 95 square meters, Bunker 2 more than 140 square meters. Zyklon B pellets were dropped into the six chambers—two in Bunker 1, four in Bunker 2—through small, hermetically sealed windows. After a gassing, the dead bodies were removed by the Jewish Sonderkommando prisoners via doors opposite the ones through which the living had entered. The bodies were dumped in large trenches dug in nearby fields and were incinerated. The Sonderkommandos then scrubbed out the chamber walls and floors in order to avert suspicions on the part of those arriving in subsequent transports.

Approximately 200 Slovak Jews were conscripted from the Birkenau barracks to work in Bunker 1. A group of about 50 Jews was put to work in Bunker 2. At first these gas chambers operated only at night, and after a gassing the Germans would air the room before making the Sonderkommandos enter it to clear out the bodies and debris. But when the killing operations were extended to the daytime, the Jewish conscripts, wearing gas masks, began to work inside the chambers as soon as the doors were opened. Detailed testimonies about Bunkers 1 and 2 have been left by surviving members of the Jewish Sonderkommandos (Sigismund Paul Bendel, Milton Buki, Shaul Chazan, Shlomo and Abraham Dragon, Eliezer Eisenschmidt, Andre Lettich, Filip Müller, Dov Paisikovic, Joseph Sackar, and Henryk Tauber), by Sonderkommando men who did not survive (including Salman Gradowski and Leib Langfuss), and by SS men who served at these facilities (Paul Johann Kremer, Oswald Kaduk, Pery Broad).

The first gassings in Birkenau took place around 20 March 1942; the victims were Jews from Upper Silesia and the Dabrowa region. Subsequent transports of Jews came from Slovakia, France, the Netherlands, Belgium, Yugoslavia, and the Theresienstadt ghetto.

As the RSHA stepped up the pace of the transports, it was decided to equip Birkenau with larger and more sophisticated murder facilities. The new complex of four buildings, unlike the bunkers it replaced, contained all the necessities for carrying out mass extermination and covering up its traces: undressing halls, gas chambers, incinerators, "treatment" rooms where the dead bodies were relieved of their fine hair and gold teeth, warehouses for storing furnace fuel and gas containers, and housing for SS and Sonderkommando personnel. By putting all phases of the murder operation under one roof, the Germans were able to cut the amount of time needed to kill a transport of prisoners and dispose of their bodies, and hence made the machinery of murder more efficient. Beginning in the spring of 1943, Jews from Greece, various parts of Poland, Germany, Luxembourg, Norway, and Hungary were taken to the new facilities for extermination. The gas chamber and ovens at Crematorium II (the first of the four combined facilities) were ready for operation on 31 March 1943, and Crematorium III was completed on 25 June. Crematoriums IV and V were put into service earlier: IV on 22 March and V on 4 April.

The main construction work on the new complex was awarded to four civilian companies, Topf und Söhne of Erfurt, W. Riedel und Söhne of Bielitz, Robert Koehler of Myslowitz, and Joseph Kluge of Alt-Gleiwitz. Topf manufactured the incinerators; the company executives and engineers who were involved in their design and manufacture were Ludwig Topf, Jr., Ernst-Wolfgang Topf, Martin Klettner, Wilhelm Koch, Kurt Prüfer, and Karl Schultze. Koehler built the chimneys, and Kluge constructed the brick and stone parts of the ovens in Crematoriums IV and V.

Several other companies, most of them from Upper Silesia, collaborated in building the four facilities. They included the Kattowitz (Katowice) branch of Hoch und Tiefbau Aktiengesellschaft (HUTA); Karl Falck of Gleiwitz; Vereinigte Dachpappenfabriken Aktiengesellschaft (VEDAG) of Breslau, which waterproofed the basements of Crematoriums II and III; Triton Bauunternehmung of Kattowitz; Konrad Segnitz-Baugeschäft, which supplied the materials for the ceilings and roofs; Karl Falck of Gleiwitz; Continentale Wasserwerks-Gesellschaft of Berlin, which installed the plumbing; Albert Bsolok of Beuthen, which inspected Segnitz's roof assembly plans; Industrie-Bau-AG of Bielitz, which installed the roof surfaces; and

Hermann Hirt Nachfolger of Beuthen, which along with other firms installed natural ventilation apertures in Crematorium IV (and perhaps V). Degesch of Frankfurt am Main manufactured the Zyklon B that was used in Birkenau; Tesch und Stabenow (Testa) of Hamburg, by agreement with Degesch, supplied the poison to the camp; Heerdt-Lingler GmbH of Frankfurt am Main, another retail agent, was also involved.

Several SS men kept in contact with these companies. Four who did so on behalf of the Central Construction Department of the Waffen SS were Karl Bischoff, Walter Dejaco, Fritz Ertl, and Hans Kirschnek. Those responsible on behalf of the Economic and Administrative Main Office (WVHA) of the SS were Oswald Pohl and Heinz Kammler.

The undressing halls and gas chambers of Crematoriums II and III were underground. The gas chambers there were quite large, 30 meters long and 7 meters wide. The facilities at the other two crematoriums, IV and V, were built at ground level. They included two small gas chambers, each approximately 43 square meters in area, and two nearly 100 square meters in area (95.3 and 98.5). In all, the gas chambers of these four buildings had the capacity to asphyxiate 6,000 people a day. The doors to the chambers in II and III had peepholes, fitted with rubber gaskets, from which observers could look into the chamber. Because the people trapped inside during gassings would break the glass in an effort to get fresh air to breathe, the peepholes were protected with metal covers. Each door was fastened shut with an iron bar and could be screwed into its frame to provide a tight seal. The chambers had electric lighting, and walls were painted white. Fake plumbing and shower heads, to aid the deception of prisoners begun in the dressing rooms, where signs pointed the way "To the Baths," hung from the ceilings.

In Crematoriums II and III, SS men in gas masks poured Zyklon B from metal canisters into the chambers through four openings in the ceiling and roof made to look like small chimneys when viewed from the outside. Each opening had a concrete lid with two wooden handles. A square chute made of metal mesh descended into the chamber to an elevation of only 15 centimeters from the floor. Its purpose was to facilitate the descent and immediate vaporization of the gas. The space between the chute and the floor was left so that remaining bits of gravel substrate (the diatomite pellets) could be cleaned away after the gassing. A different technique of gas injection was used in facilities IV and V: the contents of the containers were thrown in through small windows. The Zyklon B was supplied to the camps by Dessauerwerke für Zucker und Chemische Industrie AG, a vendor for Degesch headquartered in Friedberg-Hesse. These acts were observed and recorded by members of the Kanada work detail (Jewish prisoners who sorted through the victims' belongings), whose barracks were near the crematorium buildings. Each gassing lasted on average 10–25 minutes. Then the Germans opened the doors, and Jewish Sonderkommando men removed the bodies. To avert suspicion on the part of prisoners in the next transport, they flushed the chambers thoroughly after each gassing.

None of the four killing facilities in Birkenau was still standing when the camp was liberated by the Red Army. Crematorium IV was destroyed during the Sonderkommando revolt of 7 October 1944. Crematoria II and III were demolished in late December 1944 and early January 1945. Crematorium V, in which the bodies of dead prisoners were still being burned after the camp had been evacuated, was destroyed on 26 January 1945, the day before liberation.

Many acts of resistance and selflessness occurred in these gas chambers. On 23 October 1943 a Jewish woman inside the undressing room killed the SS officer Joseph Schillinger. Filip Müller, a Sonderkommando member, could not bear to see his fellow Czech Jews from the Theresienstadt "family camp" (Familienlager) put to death, and he decided to share their fate in the chamber. But some of the condemned women prevailed on him to spare himself a senseless death so that he might survive to bear witness to the mass murders—which he did, in his published memoirs and in an interview included in Claude Lanzmann's documentary film *Shoah*. Müller and other survivors of the Sonderkommandos have described the scene in the chambers when the doors were opened following a gassing. Heaps of interlocking, tangled corpses attested to a desperate struggle for life. It was apparent that as the poison gas wafted up from the floor, people had climbed on top of one another in the hope of finding good air near the ceiling. Family members tended to huddle together.

In Auschwitz, the largest of the concentration and extermination camps, industrialized mass killing by gas attained its greatest scale and efficiency. The number of people murdered in the Auschwitz gas chambers cannot be known for certain. No camp documents recording the exact number of persons sent directly from the transports to the crematoriums have been found. Nevertheless, it is possible to make a confident estimate of the number of the gassing victims on the basis of strong indirect evidence. In several countries records were kept of Jews who were sent to Auschwitz. Moreover, documents left behind at Auschwitz reveal the exact number of prisoners from each transport who were selected upon arrival as "fit to work" (arbeitsfähig) and hence were processed as inmates rather than sent to their immediate deaths; a calculation may then be made of the remainder, who were marched straight to the gas chambers. (Many transports, however, were gassed without any selection having been made and so have left behind no numerical data, and we cannot know how many persons recorded as Auschwitz prisoners were later sent to the gas chambers, after illness or malnutrition had sapped their strength and rendered them unfit for hard labor.) By such means, historians have established that between 1.1 million and 1.5 million people died by poison gas in Auschwitz, with the consensus favoring a figure of 1.25 million. Among non-Jews, the victims included some 90,000 Poles, 21,000 Gypsies, 15,000 Soviet prisoners of war, and 10,000–15,000 persons of other nationalities. The vast majority of those killed—around 90 percent—were Jews.

Other Camps

Mauthausen. The gas chamber in Mauthausen, a concentration camp east of Linz, Austria, was built in the fall of 1941 in a cellar that had served as a prison. The room was nearly square; each side was just under four meters long. The gas chamber, which was camouflaged as a shower hall, was equipped with a ventilation system to remove traces of gas after each operation. Sections of the walls were covered in ceramic tile, and its two doors could be hermetically sealed. Gas canisters were kept in a small adjacent room, whence the Zyklon B was injected into the chamber through an enamel-coated slit located so that it would be hard for the victims to see where the gas was emanating from.

The Mauthausen gas chamber, as well as the crematorium built nearby, was operated by a team of camp prisoners including Jews, three of whom managed to survive. The existence and operation of this gas chamber are confirmed in testimonies of SS men who served at the camp (including the doctor of the team, Eduard Krebsbach, and the pharmacist, Erich Wa-

Photograph taken immediately after the departure of the Germans from Auschwitz-Birkenau. Sacks of human hair packed for dispatch to Germany. January 1945

sitzky), which indicate that thousands of prisoners were murdered there. The commander of the crematorium, Martin Roth of the SS, testified that he had participated in the murder of 1,692 prisoners by means of Zyklon B between March 1942 and late April 1945. Further unequivocal evidence of the existence of the gas chamber at Mauthausen is provided by the 13 statistical "death registers" (*Totenbücher*) that the SS did not have time to destroy before the camp's liberation.

Details of the process of murder by gas came to light during Roth's trial. In Mauthausen, as elsewhere, the victims were deceived and misled in the phases of the process before they entered the chamber. SS men in doctors' garb "examined" them in the undressing room, but the real purpose of the procedure was to mark victims who had gold teeth in their mouths in order to have their corpses set aside after the gassing. The duration of gassing in the chamber at Mauthausen was roughly 15 minutes. Before the doors were opened, the chamber was checked with indicator pa-

per to make sure no gas residues remained inside that might endanger the German and Jewish members of the evacuation team.

After the gassing and before the bodies were cremated, the women's hair was shorn and gold teeth were pried from the victims' mouths. The supplier of gas in Mauthausen was Slupetzky, Ltd., which specialized in disinfectants. In 1944 the owner of the company, Anton Slupetzky, participated in a conference on hydrocyanic acid, in the course of which SS agents explained that various companies in the industry manufactured and distributed Zyklon B. Gassings of Jews and non-Jews in Mauthausen continued until shortly before the liberation in May 1945. Large groups of Czech prisoners were executed there (in retribution for the assassination of the RSHA chief Reinhard Heydrich), as were Austrian antifascists. Slovakians, Germans, Italians, Yugoslavs, and French were also murdered there. In all, approximately 3,500 persons were gassed in Mauthausen.

Decisive evidence also exists that inmates were killed in several gassing operations at Gusen, a subcamp of Mauthausen. In addition, somewhere between 900 and 2,800 inmates, including Soviet prisoners of war, were murdered in gas vans that shuttled the five kilometers between Mauthausen and Gusen.

Sachsenhausen. The murder facilities in Sachsenhausen, a concentration camp 35 kilometers northeast of Berlin, were separated and concealed from the rest of the camp by a high wall. Gas vans were tested there as a means of mass murder in the fall of 1941, but killing by gas, as well as other methods, did not begin in earnest until mid-March 1943, when the gas chamber was built. This chamber was used on special occasions only, by explicit orders from Berlin.

In Sachsenhausen, as elsewhere, the gas chamber was disguised as a shower room and was entered from an undressing room. An SS physician attended every gassing in order to confirm that the victims were dead. Two types of gas were used: Zyklon A capsules and Zyklon B pellets. The chamber was equipped with a device that automatically opened the gas canisters and a pressure-activated ventilator that delivered the gas into the room through a set of heated tubes. For this reason the SS men servicing the gas chamber at Sachsenhausen did not need gas masks, as their counterparts at other camps did.

Gassing continued even in the final weeks before liberation in February 1945, as several thousand ill and exhausted prisoners were murdered. There is inadequate historical evidence, however, to determine the total number of persons killed by poison gas in the two years that the Sachsenhausen chamber was in operation.

Ravensbrück. The Ravensbrück camp, about 90 kilometers north of Berlin on the Havel River, primarily interned women. Construction of a small concentration camp for men began nearby in April 1941.

The gas chamber in Ravensbrück, which could hold up to 150 persons, was activated in late January or early February 1945. It was situated about three meters from the undressing barracks and five meters from a crematorium that went into operation in April 1943. The SS doctor Percival Treite testified that he had broached the idea of building a gas chamber in order to avoid, to the extent possible, the brutal murder of women prisoners by gunfire and the incineration of live victims. The camp commander, Johann Schwarzhuber, ascribed the initiative to build the gas chamber to two other SS men, Otto Moll and an officer named Sauer.

The standard deception and camouflage measures were used. The chamber was concealed from the rest of the camp by a fence two meters high. The condemned were told that they were about to undergo disinfection. Sometimes they were also told that they were awaiting transport to a nonexistent "resort camp" called Mitwerda.

In Ravensbrück inmates were gassed and their bodies cremated only at night. An SS staff specially brought in from Auschwitz carried out these operations. Gassing of women in the camp continued until shortly before the liberation; the camp authorities went about this activity even as they turned over other women prisoners to the Swedish Red Cross. According to Schwarzhuber, 2,300–2,400 people were gassed to death in Ravensbrück by means of Zyklon B.

Neuengamme. The concentration camp at Neuengamme, near Hamburg, was the site of at least two large-scale gassings in 1942, with 193 victims in the first and 291 in the second. The operations took place in a bunker that had been used as a lockup. It had been refitted with gas-impervious doors and a set of heating ducts through which gas was injected and the chamber was ventilated. Only Zyklon B was used. The SS officer in charge of the gassings was Willi Bahr. Pursuant to the standard operating procedure, a physician (one Hans Bothmann) attended every gassing, as did the camp commander and other officials. All staff in attendance were required to wear gas masks.

Stutthof. In the Stutthof concentration camp, 32 kilometers east of Danzig at the mouth of the Wisla River, the gas chamber was a converted clothing-disinfection room 15 square meters in area. The Zyklon B used in Stutthof was dropped into the chamber through a small opening in the roof. To maximize the efficiency of the gas, the chamber was heated before each operation. The SS officer in charge of the gassings was Otto Karl Knott, who had been trained for that duty in an SS vocational course at the Oranienburg concentration camp.

There is incontrovertible evidence of several gassings in Stutthof. In one such operation, on 22 June 1944, approximately 100 Polish and Belorussian prisoners were murdered. Several prisoners attempted to flee on the way to the chamber and were shot to death; the others were forced into the chamber and asphyxiated. In the second gassing, on 26 July 1944, 12 members of the Polish underground were put to death. The victims of the third gassing were approximately 40 disabled Soviet prisoners of war condemned by order of the camp commander, Paul Werner Hoppe. Subsequent gassings in Stutthof, conducted between August and November 1944, claimed the lives of Jewish prisoners in the camp (mainly women, the elderly, and the ill), who had been informed that they would soon be transferred to a hospital or another camp.

A gassing is also known to have occurred in a railroad car on a siding that led to the camp. The car was hermetically sealed, and a small hole was created to admit the gas. The car was used in order to mislead the victims, who had been told that they would soon be transported elsewhere. To complete the deception, an SS man was dressed as a railroad conductor, and an ordinary railroad car was positioned next to the rolling gas chamber. It took 10–15 minutes to suffocate the victims, who, according to eyewitnesses, struggled so vigorously that the car rocked.

Additional victims of gassing in Stutthof were 300 Jewish women from Hungary, who were asphyxiated in the chambers in August 1944, and 600 prisoners who were killed in October. The latter group was composed largely of women; there was also a small group of men. Shortly before the gassings ceased in November 1944, another 250 women were taken to the chambers and murdered.

Natzweiler-Struthof. Surviving documents on the history of the Natzweiler-Struthof camp, 48 kilometers south of Strasbourg, provide one of the most explicit references to the existence of gas chambers in the Holocaust. A bill sent on 26 September 1943 by the construction department of the camp (controlled by the Waffen SS and the police) to the anatomy department of the University of Strasbourg specifies: "For order of equipment and performance of work under the guidelines of the Natzweiler concentration camp administration, and for construction of a gas chamber in Struthof." The people who wrote this bill evidently disregarded the vague terminology that Nazi officials ordinarily used in reference to their crimes. Construction of the gas chamber in Struthof cost 236.08 Reichsmarks. The chamber was built in part of the town hotel, about half a kilometer from the camp entrance. The room was small—3.5 meters by 2.4 meters. The door and frame were refitted to prevent gas seepage. An observation slot was installed, and two apertures covered by grills were installed in the ceiling.

The gas chamber in Natzweiler-Struthof was built for a unique purpose: to allow several Nazi doctors to perform medical experiments on the basis of the Nazi racial doctrine and ideology. One of the persons most interested in killing prisoners, in order to collect their skeletons, was the director of the anatomy department at the University of Strasbourg, Professor August Hirt, who chose the poisoning agent, Zyklon A, and himself delivered the capsules to the camp commander, Josef Kramer, in August 1943. Under Hirt's guidelines 130 prisoners, mostly Jews, were brought to Struthof from Auschwitz in the summer of 1943 and were put to death in the gas chambers there. Afterward their skeletons were turned over to the institute. Additional lethal gassings were perpetrated by request of Professor Otto Bickenbach, who investigated the effect of varying concentrations of phosgene, a poison gas used in World War I, on camp prisoners, in this case mostly Gypsies.

Theresienstadt. The testimony of survivors of the Theresienstadt ghetto, corroborated by other documents, shows that in early 1945 the few remaining inmates of Theresienstadt were to be gassed to death. Adolf Eichmann, head of the RSHA's Jewish Section responsible for implementing the Final Solution, made the decision in deliberations with his deputy Rolf Günther, the commanders of the Kleine Festung (Little Fortress) in Theresienstadt, Gestapo members in Prague, and his colleagues in Berlin. On the agenda were various methods of killing the Theresienstadt inmates before the liquidation of the ghetto; one of the options was gas. The *Judenältester* (Jewish elder) of the ghetto, Dr. Benjamin Murmelstein (appointed to the position after Dr. Paul Eppstein was murdered), recounted in his postwar interrogation that a gas chamber was built in Theresienstadt after Günther had visited the ghetto. Jewish engineers were conscripted to design and build the facility. After the liberation two of the engineers, Erich Kohn and a man named Kulisch, described the building in minute detail. According to their testimony, they sabotaged the construction work at several junctures. An airtight door was installed in the chamber. Under heavy pressure from the Jewish engineers and the ghetto inhabitants, Murmelstein asked the Theresienstadt commander, Karl Rahm, to divulge the truth about rumors that had spread through the ghetto and created much anxiety. Rahm denied the veracity of the rumors and threatened Kohn with death if he confirmed them. After this talk, however, Rahm evidently halted the construction of the gas chamber. A contributing factor in this decision seems to have been the Germans' panic in view of the turn of events against them in the war.

Dachau. The Germans built a gas chamber in the second crematorium building (Building X) of Dachau, about 15 kilometers northeast of Munich, in March 1942. Only one unequivocal testimony—that of Frantisek Blaha, a doctor who had served in the camp—asserts that the chamber had been used, under the instructions of the SS physician Sigmund Rascher, who conducted cruel medical experiments on inmates. According to Blaha, who testified at the Nuremberg trials and at the hearings that preceded them, several executions were carried out in the Dachau gas chamber. An American documentary film made on 3 May 1945 contains footage of the gas chamber and shows the inscription "Showers" on one of its doors. Four small disinfection rooms on the left side of the building bore the warning, "Attention! Gas! Danger of death. Do not open!" Because of the mantle of secrecy that cloaked the operation of the Building X—a facility located in the SS area of the camp—it is difficult to corroborate Blaha's statements and say with certainty whether the Dachau gas chamber was ever used for its designed purpose.

Demolition and Remains

Operation Euthanasia was officially terminated on 1 September 1941, after it had come under growing criticism, mainly among German church circles. In the practical sense, however, so-called euthanasia killings continued to occur in various medical institutions in Germany and elsewhere. Some of these venues are still standing. To the best of our knowledge, none of the gas vans deployed by the commanders of the operation has survived. The vans were decommissioned in late 1942, when the extermination camps went into full-scale operation.

In early September 1944 an operation to incinerate corpses and obfuscate evidence of mass murder began at Chelmno. The burial pits are still visible there, but the crematoriums have not survived.

In December 1942 mass killings in Belzec were terminated, and the commanders of Operation Reinhard decided to liquidate the camp. Between that time and the spring of 1943 the Germans disinterred the bodies, cremated them, and pulverized any bones that were not incinerated. The ashes and bone fragments were then reinterred in the original burial pits. The camp and all its facilities, including the gas chambers, were dismantled, leaving no trace of the crimes committed there.

After the prisoners' uprising in Sobibor on 14 October 1943, the Germans decided to liquidate the camp, and it shut down by the end of the year. The area was plowed and planted; the farm established at the site was turned over to a Ukrainian who had served at the camp. No trace of the Sobibor gas chambers remains.

Treblinka met a similar fate. After the rebellion on 2 August 1943, the Germans dismantled the buildings that survived the fire that broke out during the uprising, leaving no facility standing. To obfuscate all traces of their crimes, they plowed the camp under, planted field crops and trees, and created a farm, much as in Sobibor. There is no indication today of the presence of the Treblinka gas chambers.

Majdanek is an exception in the Nazis' efforts to conceal evidence of their crimes. Because the Germans underestimated the speed of the Red Army's progress toward the area, the camp commanders were unable to destroy some of the gas chambers and the prisoners' barracks. The large crematorium was torched, but the furnaces themselves survived. Consequently, a special Polish-Russian investigative committee was able to examine the events at the camp and prove that the alleged crimes had indeed been committed. Visitors to the Majdanek site today may enter the five surviving gas chamber facilities.

In Auschwitz-Birkenau some of the murder facilities were left standing, and traces of others survived. The gas chamber in the main camp (Crematorium I) remained intact although the present structure is incomplete and not exactly like the original. Visible in Birkenau today are the foundations of Bunker 2, the concrete perimeter of the two undressing halls, and the covered cremation and burial pits. Nothing remains of Bunker 1; a residential structure has been built on its site. All that remains of the four facilities that replaced the bunkers in 1943 are the ruins left behind after the buildings were demolished after the Sonderkommando rebellion and before the evacuation. The ruins of Crematoriums II and III include the underground shaft of the undressing hall and the gas chamber, a section of the furnace room, and remnants of the second floor. Relatively little remains of Crematorium IV, which was torched during the Sonderkommando uprising. Crematorium V is in much the same condition.

Sachsenhausen was liberated on 22 April 1945 by an

advance unit of the Red Army. The Ravensbrück camp was liberated by the Soviet army on the night of 29–30 April 1945. The main camp at Natzweiler-Struthof was dismantled in August–September 1944. Its sub-camps were evacuated in March 1945, and its prisoners were taken out in death marches. Stutthof and its subcamps were evacuated in January 1945; the prisoners were removed on death marches. Dachau was liberated on 29 April 1945 by the U.S. 7th Army. Its gas chamber remains standing.   *Gideon Greif*

Generalgouvernement   The part of Poland under direct German rule which was not incorporated into the Reich following the German military victory in 1939 nor ceded, temporarily, to the Soviet Union. The five districts of the Generalgouvernement—Warsaw, Lublin, Radom, Kraków, and Galicia—were home to approximately 1.8 million Jews before the war. In 1940, by order of the governor general, Hans Frank, all Jewish property was confiscated and the Jewish population interned in ghettos. Between 1942 and 1944 the ghettos were liquidated and all the Jews killed on the spot or deported. The area was liberated by the Soviet army in 1945.

Gens, Jacob (1903–43)   Head of the Vilna *Judenrat* (Jewish council). Gens believed that providing a valuable work force would save Jewish lives and urged Vilna Jews to work obediently for the Germans. At one point Gens decided to hand over 406 Jews who were too old or ill to labor, in order to save 1,500 women and children from deportation by the police. When liquidation of the ghetto began in 1943, he refused attempts by friends and relatives to help him escape and was shot by the Gestapo. See JUDENRAT; VILNA

German Jewry   In 1933, when Hitler was made chancellor of Germany, the Jews in Germany were organized in religious communities that enjoyed the status of corporations under public law. Despite several attempts at unification, starting from the middle of the nineteenth century, German Jewry failed to overcome internal ideological differences and religious fragmentation to create a single representative agency. Only in September 1933, in the face of the Nazi danger, did it manage to set up such an organization, the Reichsvertretung der Deutschen Juden (Reich Representation of German Jews), in 1935 renamed Reichsvertretung der Juden in Deutschland (Reich Representation of Jews in Germany). This was an umbrella organiza-

tion of the major Jewish agencies, communities, and unions of communities set up on a voluntary basis, which functioned until 1939. Even at this stage the Nationalist German Jews—a politically conservative, militantly assimilationist faction that manifested extreme devotion to and identification with German nationalism—and extreme Orthodox communities refused to join the Reichsvertretung.

In March 1938 the Nazi government changed the legal status of the Jewish communities from public corporations to private associations. The practical meaning of this step was the financial collapse of the individual communities. This and other factors led to increased negotiations to set up a single nationwide Jewish framework. As a result of the negotiations and of the Nazi ambition to impose a central organization for all Jews in order to speed up their emigration from Germany, a new body, the Reichsvereinigung der Juden in Deutschland (Reich Union of Jews in Germany), was established in February 1939 and confirmed by law in July 1939. The change of name clearly reflected the deteriorating condition of Jews in Germany. This new organization operated under the supervision of the Gestapo until June 1943, when it was closed by the Nazi authorities.

Hitler's appointment as German chancellor forced communal institutions, which had been marginal in Jewish life, to become central. The reversal of emancipation meant that Jews could not survive without the support of the Jewish establishment. Yet the fact that Jewish society was excluded from the process of creating uniformity (*Gleichschaltung*) enabled it to deepen its activities in all areas of Jewish life in Germany. Thus, at the same time as Jews were being expelled from German institutions and professions, there was a revival of Jewish culture, adult education, social work, vocational training, and other communal activities.

Between 1933 and 1945 the Jewish population in Germany was reduced from some 525,000 persons to an estimated 25,000. Nearly 300,000 emigrated from Germany before Jewish emigration was forbidden in October 1941. Age and socioeconomic status were among the factors that determined which Jews decided to emigrate as anti-Jewish actions proliferated and which chose to remain in Germany. In the cities the free professionals and former civil and state employees were the hardest hit by Nazi laws that cost them their livelihood. In addition, the difficulties in obtaining entry visas for the absorbing countries, as

Members of the Jewish Kulturbund performing Shakespeare in Berlin. 1937

Jewish sports club Bar Kochba in the Grunewald athletic field in Berlin. 1933

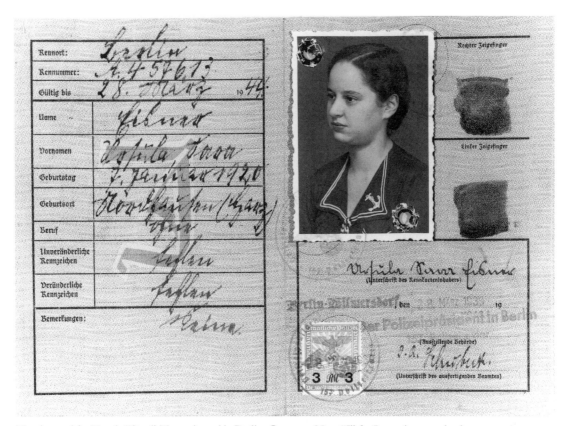

Identity card for Ursula "Sara" Eisner, issued in Berlin, Germany. Note "J" for Jew written on the document.

well as conditions abroad, affected emigration. This explains the fluctuations in the flow of emigrants. In some cases, emigrants were forced to return to Germany when the countries in which they sought refuge refused them entry.

That the degree of antisemitic violence can serve as a barometer of emigration is beyond question. In the years 1933–35, 20–25 percent of the Jewish population left Germany. What effect did the legal harassment, particularly the Nuremberg Laws, have on the will to leave? The answer is equivocal. The sources speak of various, sometimes contradictory reactions among different portions of the Jewish population and in different localities. In some cases, the desire to remain in Germany became stronger; in others, the wish to leave predominated. Data from the Central Committee for Aid and Reconstruction (Zentralausschuss für Hilfe und Aufbau) of the Reichsvertretung illustrate a significant increase in emigration following the

promulgation of the racial laws. Yet in some places the laws seem to have had the opposite effect. The desire to leave the country waned because Jews thought that the new legal framework would stop the physical attacks on Jews and Jewish property and permit continuation of normal life in Germany. Similarly, the large-scale vocational retraining programs for adults in the years 1936–37 point to the fact that many German Jews saw no future for themselves in Germany and were preparing to leave. On the other hand, the statistics show that fewer Jews left Germany in 1936 than in 1935, and in 1937 the emigration index fell to its lowest point. Only the unprecedented persecutions of 1938 reversed this trend.

The internal migration of Jews from towns and villages to the major cities began well before the rise of nazism. Nevertheless, the rise of the Third Reich accelerated urbanization. By 1937 the Reichsvertretung was reporting the scale and extent of the dissolution of small communities. Sixty percent of German Jewry was concentrated in six cities. All regional material substantiates the disappearance of rural Jewish life. Even the few traditional Jewish occupations, such as cattle trading, which had escaped the worst effects of the boycott, were abandoned. The pressure grew so intolerable that the Jewish cattle dealers were compelled to migrate to the larger cities or leave the country. It was natural for Jews to flock to the cities, where employment opportunities were greater and where better-organized communal services were available.

It is understandable that the only workable solution to the steady weakening and financial collapse of small communities was their amalgamation and the transfer of property to the Reichsvertretung. Rural Jews were the hardest hit, not because farmers were more antisemitic than city dwellers, but because of the more efficient administration of the boycott in those areas in which the Nazis could effectively supervise the implementation of anti-Jewish policy and severely punish those who violated it. In villages most Jews earned their living from the rural economy, so constant pressure from Nazi farmers' organizations made trading conditions in grain and cattle exceedingly difficult. But it was not only a matter of personal freedom or work possibilities. The fact that all communal services had gradually ceased to function also forced Jews to leave. This demographic trend helps explain the relatively stable number of Jewish residents in some cities, despite increased emigration. The new arrivals apparently took the place of emigrants, thereby decreasing the rate at which the major Jewish communities shrank.

The Jewish communities' educational and welfare activities, including economic aid and an employment service, were attempts to adjust to the new conditions. The sense of crisis sparked the communities to increase their self-help activities in all social and cultural fields. Vocational training in particular was geared toward the young who were preparing to emigrate.

Additional schools were established with curricula adapted to meet the pressing needs of the day. Concerted attempts were made to cultivate Jewish youth and reinforce self-awareness by instilling Jewish historical tradition. In September 1935 the minister of education issued a decree removing the Jews from the educational system. The law was imposed only in 1939, but Jews started organizing to expand their educational network independently of the measure. The distress of Jewish pupils, who suffered from popular antisemitism in the general educational system, contributed to the decision to establish Jewish schools. In many regions it became virtually impossible for Jewish children to attend German schools, and the suffering of Jewish pupils made them seek each other out. In establishing sports centers the Jewish communities also sought to provide alternatives for those youngsters who had ceased to attend general clubs. Adult education was also encouraged, and various activities were aimed at facilitating the adaptation of Jewish women to the new reality.

By 1938 welfare services were becoming crucial to many Jews. As Jews increasingly were evicted from economic life, they became extremely dependent on the community's institutions and organizations. Furthermore, the continuous internal migration drastically altered the communities' demographic balance, multiplying the number of people requiring assistance, particularly among the elderly.

Cultural activities were sponsored by the Jewish Kulturbund. This organization, established in July 1933, had twin objectives: to absorb Jewish artists and intellectuals who had lost their source of income because of the anti-Jewish laws, and to meet the cultural needs of the Jewish communities. The Kulturbund put on operas, plays, concerts, recitals, literary evenings, and lectures.

It is true that the Kulturbund confined the Jews to a social ghetto: the public, artists, and administration were all Jews, and the programs were advertised only in the Jewish press. A glimpse at the authors of the plays performed, however, shows that it was by no means a cultural ghetto. German Jews considered themselves the last bastion of the true heritage of European culture in Germany, long since abandoned by the surrounding society under the Nazis, and as such they strove to integrate in their artistic productions works by Mozart, Shakespeare, Ibsen, Offenbach, Pergolesi, Beethoven, Smetana, Molière, Pirandello, Verdi, Shaw, and others.

The fact that the major ideological and political movements of German Jewry preserved their basic principles in the Third Reich also accounts for the persistence of personal and factional power struggles in the Jewish communities. Three of those movements deserve special attention.

The Centralverein. A private association, founded in 1894, the Centralverein (CV) concentrated its efforts in fighting antisemitism and furthering a German Jewish identity. Fidelity to the Jewish liberal worldview and to the humanistic heritage abandoned by German society were key components of the CV's activities under the Nazis. By retaining their traditional values, liberal German Jews may have wished to escape reality, immersing themselves in a world of nostalgia. Equally strong, however, was their wish to demonstrate—to themselves and to the Nazi regime—that the Jews were not abandoning their German cultural heritage. The concerted influence of these efforts, the sense of attachment to the past and of self-perception as an inseparable link in the chain of Jewish history, acted as a barrier against despair, a compensation for the humiliation and degradation to which Germany was subjecting Jews.

As far as the interpretation of Nazi antisemitism was concerned, the CV drew on the fundamental conceptions of liberal German Jewry. Its declarations and tactics show that, at least in the early years of Nazi rule, Nazi antisemitism was seen as a policy to be opposed with conventional strategies. The different ways in which the CV protested against the Nazi challenge were based on decades of legal battles for Jewish rights, and its activists assumed that even in the Third Reich legal means could obstruct anti-Jewish measures. It might seem bizarre in retrospect that the CV persisted in waging an anachronistic legal struggle with the Nazi state. Given the CV's ideological premises, however, the new predicament in the Third Reich not only justified the continuation of its endeavors but indeed called for their intensification. If there had been a need to defend Jewish interests in the Second Reich and the Weimar Republic, then all the more so in the Third Reich, when a sword of Damocles hung over the Jews. The CV leaders thought that any concession in the battle for Jewish rights was apt to be interpreted by the regime as acquiescing to antisemitic policy and thus would eventually lead to further limitations, until Jews were totally removed from all aspects of civic life. Furthermore, they believed that even if traditional methods of dealing with the government would not change the situation, in utilizing them Jews would at least manifest their opposition to the Nazi policy. Moreover, through negotiations and intercession with various governmental offices, the CV sometimes succeeded in delaying, moderating, or even abrogating antisemitic steps. These achievements increased the hopes of stabilizing the Jews' status. This confidence also helps explain the CV's rejection of the total exo-

dus of German Jewry, although it favored the emigration of those Jews who had no livelihood in Germany. While it cooperated with and supported emigration endeavors, this was an ad hoc compromise, the acceptance of a necessary evil as a concession to the pressing needs of the Jewish masses.

The CV's literature and press in the early years of the Nazi regime show that it did not accept the verdict that Jews lived in a postemancipation era but rather took great pains to redefine German Jewish identity and the terms of emancipation. The CV did not abandon the principle of Jewish equality in German society but reinterpreted it as a new postemancipatory integration of the Jews as a group rather than as individuals. This new strategy of integration would also rehabilitate German Jews: whereas in the "old" emancipation Jews sought amalgamation with Germany through the internalization of values and behavioral patterns from the surrounding society, group integration would be achieved by retaining Jewish values.

The concrete steps taken to attain the so-called second emancipation included the creation of vocational training schools as one method that would reshape Jewish society and not just prepare future emigrants. Despite superficial similarities, these schools should not, however, be equated with the Zionist training camps. The Zionist camps were founded on an ideology of productivization necessary for the renaissance of the Jewish nation in its own land. In contrast, CV social planning, although backed by ideological rationalization, did not emanate from an all-inclusive worldview to transform the economic and social stratification of the Jews. It responded to the pressing needs of those who had lost their sources of income and was an attempt to find an original solution to the deplorable living conditions of German Jews.

The CV did achieve some temporary economic relief. It was convinced that the fate of German Jewry hinged on breaking the antisemitic principle in the economy. Here we see in embryo the line of reasoning of some of the Jewish councils during the war: the Jews would be protected so long as they could show their economic value to the Nazis. Some historians maintain that however noble the attempts of CV activists to ease the lot of the Jews, and however extraordinary their refusal to comply with the Nazi persecution, the courage manifested in the confrontations with the Nazi authorities was shortsighted. Because the CV was still attached to its old world, its temporary achievements

seduced it into believing that, once consolidated, the regime would moderate its antisemitic policy. Although some minor successes granted passing relief, they objectively blunted the sense of danger presented by the Nazi regime.

The Zionists. As a direct consequence of the Nazi ascension to power, there was a remarkable enlargement of the Zionist movement and increase in its influence in Jewish society. The Zionist movement had always given precedence to winning over the younger generation to the Jewish national idea. It now redoubled its efforts, concentrating on education aimed to reorient Jewish youth toward emigration to Palestine. One tangible result of these endeavors, testifying to their success, was the enormous expansion of the Hehalutz youth movement. Hehalutz had some 500 members in 1933; only two years later the number had risen to 15,000. The Zionist ideal ran counter to the traditional direction of German Jewry toward embracing European (especially German) identity and culture, and this nonconformity may even have been an advantage in attracting Jewish youth. And even if young people wanted to conform, they had few alternatives to emigration. Young Jews had no prospects: almost all professions in the civil service, municipal offices, journalism, theater, teaching, public health, and law were closed to them. Even in commerce and the private sector the public was discouraged from employing young Jews. With universities barred to them, many also dropped out of school, showing little interest in retraining for the meager prospects of a future life in Germany. Small wonder that the sense of frustration among the younger generation led to an ideological identification with a Jewish national ideal. The Zionists' rapid move from the margins of Jewish society to its center explains the deteriorating relations between them and the CV. The Centralverein not only was concerned that it was losing ground in community leadership, but also lamented the massive withdrawal of youth from CV institutions and rightly sensed that liberal Judaism was losing the younger generation. The Zionist organization's educational activities were not confined to the young, however, as shown by the establishment of vocational schools and Hebrew courses for adults and the founding of women's associations as well as other social and educational institutions.

Professor Martin Buber at a Jewish Youth Seminar in Berlin. 1935

Promoting emigration was the Zionists' most distinctive activity, but the necessity of realistically assessing the reluctance of most adult Jews to emigrate to Palestine led them to adopt a more affirmative position toward community work. Their efforts were aimed at national-cultural autonomy. In adult education the emphasis was placed on an active commitment to cultural renaissance and national consciousness, in an effort to restore the Jews' lost dignity and enhance their self-image. These developments explain the Gestapo's concern with Zionist activities and its ambivalent attitude toward Zionist success. The Nazi authorities welcomed Zionism when they believed it would increase Jewish emigration. Yet they felt that it infused new hopes and inner strength for coping with persecution and thereby reinforced the self-image and national foundations of Jewish society in the Third Reich.

The Reichsbund Jüdischer Frontsoldaten. From its inception in February 1919, the Jewish war veterans' union, the Reichsbund Jüdischer Frontsoldaten (RJF), avowed its desire for full integration into German society, blurring the differences generated by the historical antagonism between Jews and Germans. Its members wished to counteract the belief prevalent in Germany after World War I that, having avoided service or holding only office posts in the army, Jews did not share the war experience. The RJF reiterated that the Jews had fulfilled their duty to Germany and made the same sacrifices as their Gentile comrades, 12,000 Jewish soldiers having given their lives in the war. By 1933 the RJF comprised 30,000 members in 360 local branches. Its youth organization, Der Schild, included 90 clubs with sports fields, gymnastics halls, and rowing clubs that served 9,000 members.

When Hitler assumed power, the RJF decided to defend the interests of its rank and file, who had been shattered morally and economically by the antisemitic policy, and attempted to obtain preferential treatment for its members through intercession with President Paul von Hindenburg. From 1933 on, the RJF strove to achieve two objectives: as regards the state, to vindicate the rights of Jewish veterans and protect their interests by preventing the extension of the segregation policy; and within the Jewish community, to prove the validity of its ideals and reiterate its immutable German patriotism. This position was also adopted in the education of the 14,000 youngsters connected with the organization. This background clarifies the RJF's renunciation of its former political neutrality in internal

Group portrait of war veterans of Jewish descent. Circa 1937

Jewish affairs and its increasingly vehement opposition to Zionism. On practical issues with the Reichsvertretung, however, it was ready to cooperate with the Zionists.

After the racial legislation the RJF subordinated its principles to a more realistic practical unity, understanding that in the Nazi state a dogmatic response could not meet German Jews' demands. Consequently, while in principle it zealously pursued its own ideology, seeking valid ways of adapting itself to the regime, in practice it had to yield and support emigration. Thus from 1936 on, the RJF oscillated between two opposite attitudes: the urges to adjust to the Third Reich and to support emigration. It still dared to participate in a military memorial ceremony; strove stubbornly to connect itself with German officer unions; and expanded its sports activities for youth as a makeshift substitute for military service. It grudgingly consented, however, to moderate its negative attitude toward emigration, at least for those Jews who could no longer subsist in Germany. To this end the RJF entered into negotiations with the Jewish Colonization Association to find places in South America and cemented its ties with English war veterans in order to obtain visas for British colonies. The economic hardship inspired the organization, although it consistently opposed emigration, to organize its own agricultural training groups. By 1938, however, even the most stubborn and tenacious RJF leaders came to realize that only the complete destruction of Jewish life in Germany would satisfy the Nazis. By that time more than 60 percent of Jewish enterprises were "aryanized" and almost 80,000 Jews were receiving welfare from the Jewish community. It was at this point that emigration became the official policy of all factions in the Jewish community, because most Jews seem to have realized what Leo Baeck is alleged to have said in 1933: the 1,000 years of Jewish life in Germany had come to a close.

From 1939 on, all Jewish organizations and communities were incorporated into the new, centralized Reichsvereinigung, and all their activities had to be conducted with the consent of the Gestapo. Vocational training agencies were successively liquidated. The

Kulturbund was closed at the end of 1941, and Jewish schools ceased to exist in 1942. With the dissolution of the Reichsvereinigung on 10 June 1943, organized German Jewry officially ceased to exist.

David Bankier

Gerstein, Kurt (1905–45) SS officer who tried on several occasions to alert foreign diplomats and the papal nuncio in Berlin to the mass murder of Jews. Gerstein joined the SS to gather information after his sister was killed in the so-called euthanasia program. He became head of a department in the SS Institute of Hygiene in Berlin, in which position he purchased the gas used in the death chambers of Auschwitz. Gerstein committed suicide in a French prison after the war.

Gestapo (Geheime Staatspolizei) German political police established in April 1933 by Hermann Göring to suppress opposition to nazism. Commanded from 1934 by Reinhard Heydrich, the Gestapo was not subject to judicial scrutiny and had total freedom to spy on, arrest, interrogate, and deport Jews, intellectuals, Gypsies, Roman Catholics, homosexuals, and anyone else deemed an enemy of the Reich. From 1939 it functioned as Department IV of the RHSA (Reich Security Main Office) under Heinrich Müller, with representatives in both Germany and the occupied territories. Adolf Eichmann directed Section IVb4 of the Gestapo, which deported Jews to concentration and extermination camps.

Ghetto Cultural Life Varied and lively cultural and artistic activity was a prominent feature of life in the Jewish ghettos, particularly the largest ghettos—in Warsaw, Vilna, Lodz, and Theresienstadt. Under constant threat of death, what motivated this intense activity in music, theater, and other arts? How could cultural life proceed, in some cases even while deportations to the extermination camps were taking place? What benefits did it confer on performers and audiences?

For the performers, continued artistic activity meant the perpetuation of contact with the lives and identities they had established before incarceration in the ghettos. In the Riga ghetto, for example, veterans of the Berlin Jüdischer Kulturbund staged excerpts from plays that had originally been presented in Berlin.

Members of the administration of the Lodz ghetto pose with a sports team.

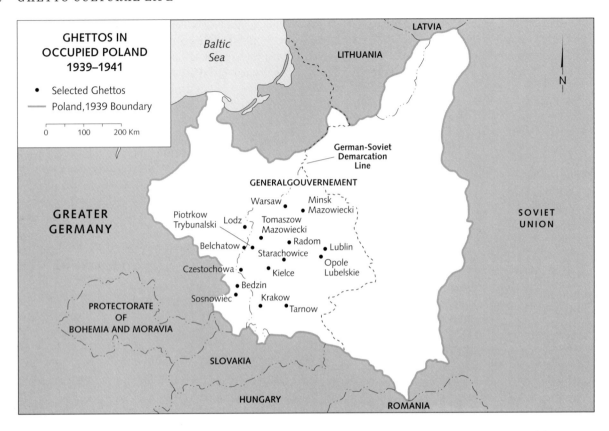

GHETTOS IN OCCUPIED POLAND 1939–1941

• Selected Ghettos
— Poland, 1939 Boundary

0   100   200 Km

Baltic Sea

LATVIA

LITHUANIA

German-Soviet Demarcation Line

GENERALGOUVERNEMENT

Warsaw
Minsk Mazowiecki

Piotrkow Trybunalski
Lodz
Tomaszow Mazowiecki

Belchatow
Radom
Lublin

Starachowice

Opole Lubelskie

Czestochowa
Kielce

Bedzin

Sosnowiec
Krakow

Tarnow

GREATER GERMANY

SOVIET UNION

PROTECTORATE OF BOHEMIA AND MORAVIA

SLOVAKIA

HUNGARY

ROMANIA

N

Such productions provided a forum for the artists to give vent to their feelings regarding the present. This perhaps explains why in Theresienstadt the number of participants in theatrical productions far exceeded the number of professional entertainers. The spectators, for their part, not only gained several hours of respite from the harsh reality of life but also took from the performances a measure of strength to deal with the emotional and moral challenges of that reality. As the ghetto historian Isaiah Trunk noted, the aim of these cultural activities was "spiritual resistance," to shield the Jewish consciousness of the ghetto inhabitants from the pernicious effects of the naked materialism of ghetto life, and at the same time to oppose the dehumanization and moral denigration of the Jews by the Nazis.

The Germans did not explicitly outlaw Jewish cultural activities. This tolerant attitude may have been indirectly motivated by a desire to lull the Jews into a false sense of security. Before 1938 the Gestapo viewed the activity of the Jüdischer Kulturbund with suspicion, as they believed it might create a complacency that would inhibit the desire for emigration. No such

rationale applied to the Polish ghettos. This was not only because emigration was no longer feasible. The Jews in the Polish ghettos were trapped; they could perhaps be deluded as to their eventual fate, or their final destination, but not as regards their present situation. In any event, the Jewish lack of power worked in favor of cultural tolerance. Whereas the Germans interfered with Polish cultural activities out of fear that they might provide cover for political organizing, they felt no such apprehension concerning the Jews. Nonetheless, German policy was not entirely consistent. In Warsaw, Lodz, and Vilna Jewish theaters were allowed to operate, whereas in the Czestochowa district the request to establish a theater was denied. Nor was the German policy toward the artistic repertoire uniform. In Warsaw the performance of "aryan" works was not outlawed until April 1942; when disregarded, this order led to a months-long cancellation of performances, which were never renewed owing to the deportations. In Vilna no restrictions were in effect; nevertheless, the majority of the repertoire was Jewish in origin. In Lodz, on the other hand, Beethoven and Schubert were popular. The theater company and orchestras in

Theresienstadt, which were afforded special treatment by the Germans, offered the best of the European repertoire, including selections from German works.

The initiative to organize cultural activities generally emanated from institutions and groups that had engaged in such activities before the war, most often from the performers themselves. The first performances were held in private homes or in front of select audiences. In Warsaw the many unemployed artists, who were now joined by their non-"aryan" Christian colleagues, performed in private circles and in the cafés that sprang up in the so-called Jewish quarter. They were patronized largely by parvenus, and the artistic level was correspondingly crude. With an eye to raising the performance standards and to expanding the areas of artistic endeavor, in the fall of 1940, shortly after the formation of the ghetto, a central programs commission was created at the initiative of the artists themselves in conjunction with the Jewish Mutual Aid Society (Zydowski Towarzystwo Opieki Spolecznej, or ZTOS). Over time, 267 stage performers and 150 musicians registered with this commission, and by October 1941 it had sponsored 1,814 performances. The profits from ticket sales generally were earmarked for welfare purposes.

In Vilna artists, writers, musicians, actors, and painters founded a joint association in February 1942, at the start of the "stable period" between deportations. This association sponsored a weekly artistic-literary meeting in one of the public soup kitchens. The program usually consisted of a lecture, literary readings, and songs in Yiddish and Hebrew. In Lodz the Jewish cultural society, which was founded as early as October 1942, started a library, a people's university, and Yiddish courses for adults. A choir and a symphony orchestra were organized as well. However, the chairman of the *Judenrat* (Jewish council), Mordechai Chaim Rumkowski, disbanded these independent associations in order to establish his jurisdiction, perhaps at the mandate of the German authorities. After February 1941 the Lodz Judenrat controlled all cultural activity. Regular public performances began in March, with the opening of the House of Culture, operated by the Judenrat's employment division.

In Theresienstadt artistic performances for the inmates took place in the barracks and for small gatherings immediately upon the arrival of transports from the Protectorate of Bohemia and Moravia. Study groups were formed, but only after the initiative was placed in the hands of a specific department by the ghetto council did this activity branch out significantly. The direction and nature of cultural activity in Theresienstadt was markedly affected by the desire of the SS to display the camp to the world as a model ghetto, "an autonomous Jewish city." Consequently, Theresienstadt had at its disposal cultural resources not available to the Jewish population in other locations.

The transfer of jurisdiction over cultural activity to the Judenräte was inevitable. Not only were the Jewish councils charged with authorizing public activities, but they also possessed the resources to promote and support them, as well as the power to block a performance when it did not meet with their approval. Moreover, the Judenräte viewed this control as a factor that enhanced their authority; hence they were unwilling to forgo it.

In Warsaw the Judenrat chairman, Adam Czerniakow, attempted to wrest control of cultural activity from the Mutual Aid Society by founding a Judenrat-sponsored committee. This committee first tried to merge with the already existing one in the hope of undermining its autonomy. When this step proved ineffective, the Judenrat attempted to disband the independent commission. These actions notwithstanding, the autonomous commission continued to function until the final deportation. Jacob Gens, chief of the ghetto police in Vilna, was the moving force behind the first theatrical performance there precisely at a time when the police were engaged in a struggle for supremacy in the ghetto administration.

In Lodz there is evidence for a constant close relationship between the ghetto theater and Judenrat chairman Rumkowski. Not only did Rumkowski attend nearly every performance in the House of Culture, but he often took advantage of the occasion to make a speech. Moreover, he was known to intervene if he felt circumstances warranted it, as when he interrupted the performance of a play on the grounds that he found it personally offensive. (The play revolved around the figure of an emperor, which was Rumkowski's ghetto nickname.) He also conveyed the distinct impression that the life of the famed ghetto poet Isaiah Spiegel would be in danger if a certain lullaby of his was again performed in the House of Culture. In the poem a mother says to her son, "Father did not go away on business"—the implication being that the Jews deported from the ghetto were no longer among the living. In Theresienstadt the Judenrat-appointed cultural department confined itself to the role of assisting and coordinating all cultural and artistic activities.

Theater. "Little theater" or "revues," as they were called, were the mainstay of ghetto theatrical life. Outside of Theresienstadt full-length productions of plays were rare. Skits, either well-known favorites or newly written pieces, generally comprised the core of a theatrical evening, along with poems and songs (some also composed expressly for the performance) and musical selections. The nature of this theatrical activity was largely determined by the prewar tradition in each locale, as was its Jewish content, which was especially pronounced in Vilna.

Ghetto conditions were conducive to productions based on Jewish themes. The treasures of Jewish culture were cherished even as secular culture continued to be cultivated. Emanual Ringelblum provides evidence that in Warsaw even assimilated Jews attended literary evenings of Jewish content. The study of Yiddish culture in Theresienstadt also bears witness to this trend. On the other hand, Polish culture was cultivated in circles distant from Judaism, in Warsaw especially, where a large number of Jewish converts to Christianity were now forced to live in the ghetto. This activity engendered a sense of temporary escape from the ghetto, just as the involvement in Jewish culture did for those rooted in its heritage. In this instance, however, there was an added dimension: the participants wished to distinguish themselves from the rest of the ghetto's inmates. For those involved in Yiddish culture, the opposite was true.

Before the war Warsaw was the center of Jewish theater in Poland. Upon the war's outbreak all theatrical activity ceased. Some actors moved on to Soviet-held territory and performed there; others remained behind and were unable to find an outlet for their skills. With the formation of the ghetto five professional theater troupes appeared, two performing in Yiddish and three in Polish. (Another source lists four troupes, only one performing in Polish.) The audiences were drawn mainly from the nouveaux riches, and the companies adjusted their programs accordingly, playing down to their taste. The Polish-language programs sometimes represented a higher level. The repertoire consisted mainly of comedies, usually musicals. Even when grounded in ghetto life and experience, they tended to be superficial, like the comedy about two young couples who clashed over housing problems. Nor was the opportunity to criticize the Judenrat overlooked. But old favorites like Jacob Gordin's *Mirele Efros* also had their place.

The Vilna ghetto was graced with a wide variety of high cultural activity. The influx of Polish intellectuals among the refugees enhanced Vilna's already rich cultural base at a time when the smaller communities were experiencing the loss of their intelligentsia to Poland's eastern regions. The varied cultural activities offered in the Vilna ghetto encompassed most of its residents.

Nonetheless, the first scheduled performances of Vilna's ghetto theater aroused objections, despite the fact that another "little theater" group was already appearing in a café. This occurred in January 1941, soon after some 50,000–60,000 Jews—more than two-thirds of the Jewish population in Vilna at the time of the German occupation—had been killed at Ponary. Placards on the ghetto walls proclaimed, "Theatrical performances should not be held in cemeteries," and in proletarian party circles there were discussions as to whether a disturbance should be created on opening night in addition to the planned boycott of the performance. The opening-night program was attended by the elite, mainly by members of the ghetto police. German and Lithuanian officials, among them individuals who had personally participated in the executions, attended a repeat performance, so there was no room for overt protests.

The composition of the programs in general displayed an understanding of and sympathy for the ghetto residents' emotional state. The initial performance opened with a poem by Hayyim Nahman Bialik, "S'glust zikh mir veynen" (I am moved to weep), and the seventh and final program, performed when the ghetto was being liquidated, was titled *Moyshe Halt Zikh* (Moyshe, Stand Fast). Opening night included excerpts from *Mirele Efros* and from Y. L. Peretz's *Di Goldene Keyt* (The Golden Chain), a Chopin piano concerto, and a cantorial rendition of "Eli, Eli, Lamah Azavtani" (My God, why have you forsaken me?).

The same spirit guided the programs that followed. Excerpts from Halpern Lieweck, Peretz, Sholom Aleichem, and Abraham Goldfaden were staged. Most of the programs were produced by Katriel Broide, including the fourth, which was titled *Vaytsene Yarn* (Years of Wheat), a play on the words "Vey tsu di yarn" (Alas, to my years). Broide's poem, the title piece of the final program, was intended to encourage the ghetto inmates at a time of renewed deportations:

"Remember we must leave here / Remember, we will leave here." Fondness for children, the intoxication of young love and springtime, mild criticism of the Jewish police, despair and hope—all these themes were profoundly felt. Many of the songs performed were later sung in the streets, and objections were no longer raised. Herman Kruk, who had sharply criticized the initial performances "in a graveyard," later wrote about them in his diary, "And yet life is stronger than anything else."

In addition to revues, several full-length plays were produced in Vilna, including Peretz Hirshbayn's *Grine Felder* (Green Fields—28 performances to a full house with a capacity of 450 seats), Otto Indy's *Der Mench untern Brik* (Man under a Bridge—46 performances), and David Pinski's *Der Oytser* (The Treasure). Preparations for Sholom Aleichem's *Tevya the Milkman* were suspended because of the deportations.

Vilna's Brit Ivrit (Hebrew Union) also sponsored a theatrical troupe, with the active participation of young people from the Zionist movements. The preparations for the first production, of Pinski's *Der Eybiger Id* (The Eternal Jew), highlight the prevailing spirit of the day. The group wanted to put on a play about the Jewish struggle for freedom in its land, but apart from an old Habima program there were no copies of Pinski's play in the ghetto. So the troupe reconstructed the play based on memory and the Habima program. Its performances met with an enthusiastic reception.

In the Lodz ghetto revues were also the principal theatrical productions. They were very popular, and obtaining tickets to performances often required connections. By late 1941 the first program had been performed 85 times and the second 45. In June 1942 a third program was mounted. Seventy thousand people attended performances in the House of Culture from its founding until late 1941.

The revues usually included musical selections or songs performed by individuals or troupes. Even jazz, which was outlawed in Germany, and satirical skits written especially for the show were permitted as long as they directed no insults at the Judenrat chairman. In Lodz the local talent was reinforced by newcomers deported from the west. Among the new ghetto inmates were 60 artists—actors, singers, musicians, and painters.

In Lodz, especially close ties existed between artistic performances and the production lines. With an eye to increasing productivity, special performances were held for workers in the so-called *Arbeitressorte* (labor departments) and their branches. Indeed, shortly thereafter all cultural activity took place only within the bounds of the workplace. After the deportations in 1942, the House of Culture was disbanded and the artists scattered. Nonetheless, cultural activity continued. In early 1943 "jubilee celebrations" were held in the workshops to mark the second or third anniversaries of their founding. Each shop prepared its own revue, and the final results ultimately reflected the number of workers, their talents, and the shop manager's ambition and connections. Some in the ghetto objected to this superficiality. Nevertheless, the ghetto chronicle made the following pronouncement: "The will to live should not be suppressed." Everything connected with the show—the preparations, the anticipation, the performance itself—"all renew the forces of life."

Performances were held either in the House of Culture (before it was dissolved) or in the factories. Especially popular was the performance of the Ordnungsdienst (regular police), which was praised for its high quality and its orderliness. Although most of the program was in Polish, the language of the playwright, there were three skits in Yiddish as well. The program included a satire, "Without Vaseline," according to the comment recorded in the ghetto chronicle. Directed by a refugee from Prague, this program was enacted several times during the first months of 1943, but in June the president of the Judenrat proscribed further "political revues." Perhaps the ban emerged from the conditions in the ghetto, which was then in the throes of deportations, or from fear that the skit "Without Vaseline" would spark resistance. The expropriation of musical instruments by the Germans in 1944 marked the end of cultural activity in Lodz, several months before the final liquidation of the ghetto.

The first underground performances in Theresienstadt, held before the barracks residents, rapidly gave way to an organized and multifaceted network under the aegis of the Judenrat's Freizeitgestaltung (Division for Leisure Time). In late December 1941 permission was granted for social evenings in the barracks. Possession of musical instruments was forbidden, but some instruments, mostly harmonicas, were successfully smuggled in.

The Freizeitgestaltung neither commissioned performances nor took a hand in their production. It encouraged public and private initiatives alike without inquiring too closely into specifics, as long as the programs remained within the bounds of permitted activities. It also provided a venue and equipment for each performance. The role of the Freizeitgestaltung, at first only a modest body merely tolerated by the SS, changed when the SS began implementing its plans to exhibit Theresienstadt to the world as a "normal" ghetto. When a "café" opened in December 1942, musical instruments and scores—property stolen from Jews in the Protectorate—were brought to Theresienstadt and distributed. It now became possible to replace the legless piano supported by boxes with the real article. For the performances attics, which until then had served as the venues, were replaced by actual halls. These improvements aroused great interest in the various productions, and tickets became scarce.

The theatrical repertoire included classics like Shakespeare and Molière as well as modern plays by G. B. Shaw and Ferenc Molnár, works by Theodor Herzl and Czech playwrights, productions of Y. L. Peretz in the original Yiddish, and plays written in the ghetto. Operas were in great demand and were performed frequently. Concert versions as well as full-scale productions, albeit with piano accompaniment, were mounted of works by Smetana, Mozart, Verdi, and other composers. The children's opera *Brundibar* was especially well received. Although it was composed in Prague, opening night was held in Theresienstadt. The child actors participated enthusiastically, even though the deportations to Auschwitz altered the composition of the group for each performance. The choral repertoire included oratorios by Haydn and Mendelssohn, and a performance of Verdi's *Requiem* aroused controversy.

Light entertainment was also quite popular. Cabarets provided an outlet for satirical criticism of the Judenrat. There were also productions of various operettas. The jazz band that performed in the café was known as "The Ghetto Swingers."

Concerts The Jewish Cultural Organization in the Warsaw ghetto sponsored performances by a symphony orchestra, a string quartet, and choirs—for folk songs and popular songs, as well as a children's choir, the Hebrew Shir (Song) choir, and the Great Synagogue choir (following the closing of the synagogue).

The Vilna ghetto supported a symphony orchestra, a chamber group, a jazz band, and a mandolin troupe. There were several choirs: a Yiddish one and a Hebrew one, each with 80 singers, and a religious one as well.

Even music school students took the opportunity on occasion to appear before an audience.

Cultural activity in Kovno at first met with public resistance. Plans for symphony concerts elicited such comments as, "How can we hold concerts on the graves of our holy martyrs?" Only after due consideration was a request for an orchestra tendered to the Germans, in the guise of a request for permission to form a small Jewish police band. Opponents of the concerts were countered with the following argument: "Music can express not only joy, but also pain and mourning." The first concert was held in August 1942, a year after the initial wave of killings, in the hall of the Slobodka yeshiva. The program opened with a rendition of the traditional version of *Kol Nidrei*, the solemn prayer that begins the Yom Kippur service, which brought the audience to tears. The orchestra, which had 35 musicians, performed both Jewish and non-Jewish works, but no German pieces were played. Its 80 performances were in great demand. In the words of a reliable eyewitness, the concerts "were a source of spiritual encouragement to the imprisoned ghetto inmates in their desperate struggle." Germans occasionally attended the concerts, and at times the orchestra was ordered to give special performances for the German staff. It also gave concerts in the nearby work camps.

In Lodz the orchestra played symphonic works by Beethoven, Schubert, Brahms, Liszt, and Mendelssohn, as well as Jewish tunes and songs. These programs were often performed for the workers in the various shops. Many piano, string, and vocal recitals were also held. In the early days of the ghetto the veteran Hazamir choir renewed its performances. The influx of deportees from the west gave this musical activity further impetus.

Organized concerts could in no way provide employment for all the musicians, and some were forced to perform in the street. Street performances were a common feature of ghetto life, and some of the witty epigrams coined by the entertainers, who took advantage of the license afforded to court jesters, became part of ghetto parlance.

Of all the ghetto concerts, the ones at Theresienstadt were most notable for their high artistic level. The musicians at the ghetto committee's disposal included some of the foremost performers of Czechoslovakia. The audience enjoyed extraordinary offerings; H. G. Adler wrote that "the performance of Beetho-

The Kovno ghetto orchestra: Stupel is the violin soloist, and S. Hofmekler conducts. Circa 1942

ven's sonata Opus 111 or Brahms's *Variations on a Theme by Handel,* represented the victory of pure morality over defiled reality, which was nearly unbearable." Nonetheless there were some bizarre incidents, as when Paul Eppstein, the Jewish elder (*Älteste*) appointed by the Germans, sent a dance band to play at the assembly point for deportees on the eve of Yom Kippur, 1943.

Social Gatherings and Study. The performances in the cultural halls by no means comprehended the full range of social gatherings. The various clubs, which became soup kitchens in the ghetto, served as meeting places for friends with common backgrounds, political or otherwise. For many who ate their only daily meal there, it was an opportunity to maintain links with the past. Meetings were dedicated to the memory of great figures on the anniversary of their deaths. Talks were given on academic issues that were debated as if the world were still whole. Holidays were also celebrated together.

In the summer of 1940, as in earlier times, the memory of Herzl and Bialik was honored in Warsaw's Zionist Soup Kitchen. Holidays commemorating the salvation of the Jews from their oppressors were celebrated with especial vigor. Regarding Hanukkah that year an eyewitness related, "Never before have there been so many Hanukkah parties as this year." A few months later the soup kitchen, described by the same observer as "a refuge for eating, for rest, for a little reading and a little theater," hosted a boisterous celebration of Purim.

Ringelblum noted a memorial meeting for Ber Borochov which he attended, as well as meetings devoted to the memory of Sholom Aleichem, Mendele Mokher Sefarim, and Y. L. Peretz. These literary gatherings, which featured lectures, literary readings, and songs, were popular in the ghetto, and although illegal, they continued to be held. In the words of the chronicler of the Warsaw ghetto, "Everything is forbidden, but we do it anyhow."

Intellectual programs for adults were rarer in the unstable atmosphere of the ghettos. Although a people's university was founded in the early days of the Lodz ghetto, there is no evidence of its continued activity. The Vilna Hebrew Society naturally concerned itself with study. We also know of the existence of academic study groups in mathematics, physics, chemistry, nature, linguistics, philosophy, and the social sciences.

In Theresienstadt the lecture series was outstanding both for the variety of subjects offered and the excellence of its lecturers, some of whom were thinkers and scholars of renown, such as Leo Baeck. Many of the study groups chose topics far removed from ghetto reality; at the same time, fixed seminars undertook a scientific examination of the ghetto's structure. The presence of eminent scholars gave different groups— Zionist and assimilationist, German and Czech Jews, and others—a chance to emphasize their identities and to forge links to their past.

It is not always possible to make a clear-cut distinction between general cultural activity and the intensive study undertaken in ghetto schools and youth movements. When the poet Itzhak Katzenelson staged Bible plays with his students from the underground Dror gymnasium in Warsaw; when members of the Vilna youth club or students in the Lodz schools appeared in front of audiences; when members of the Kovno school choir or dramatic society performed—those were always general ghetto events. Even the youth movement's underground seminars, attendance at which entailed the danger of crossing ghetto borders, as well as the festive gathering of Hashomer Hatsair in Warsaw in the winter of 1941, which was disguised as a literary event, must be considered events of public importance and integral parts of ghetto cultural activity.

Literature and Writers. Writers and poets continued to compose literary works in the ghetto, mostly in Yiddish. Their works are a central contribution to the enduring legacy of Jewish culture during the Holocaust.

The ghettos in which literary creativity was greatest were those that had been Jewish literary centers before the war—Warsaw, Bialystok, Vilna, Lodz, Kovno, and Kraków. Ghetto literary works do not represent a fictional escape from reality; rather, they reflect and deal with that reality, giving voice to the suffering, hopes, and fears of the ghetto's inmates. These works were disseminated in dozens of shows and literary evenings. For example, Abraham Sutzkever's works were recited in the Vilna ghetto, and Isaiah Spiegel's songs were sung at public performances in the Lodz Hall of Culture. Other works, like those of Itzhak Katzenelson in Warsaw, reached their audience via underground newspapers. Songs composed by ghetto poets such as Mordechai Gebirtig in Kraków became extremely popular; some, like Gebirtig's "S'brent" (It is burning), composed before the war, became a rallying cry

for rebellion. To this category must be added, from Vilna, Shmaryahu Kaczerginski's works and Hirsh Glick's "Song of the Partisans."

Ghetto songs were perhaps the literary vehicle most embraced by the masses. When religious Jews in the Warsaw ghetto sang "I Believe in the Coming of the Messiah," their faith was strengthened. The masses wept with Pesah Kaplan's "Rivkele Hashabatit" of Bialystok in mourning her lost lover, who disappeared the day the Germans occupied the city. With her they hoped that he still lived, and they shared her feeling that "the dark ghetto has existed for too long." Like S. Shenkar of the Kovno ghetto, they were sad because "today the sun did not shine," and through Kaczerginski's eyes they saw that the ghetto produced no flowers, only graves, yet they continued to hope for "the dawning light of liberation." More than any other form of artistic expression, the hundreds of songs composed in the ghetto bear the stamp of a folk genre.

Libraries. Books accompanied the Jews to the ghetto and served as a transient source of comfort and encouragement. Although the large public libraries were expropriated at the beginning of the war—the Tlomackie Street Synagogue Library in Warsaw was closed in 1939, and Vilna's Strashun and YIVO libraries were shut down in the winter of 1942—over time permission was granted to open bookstores and lending libraries. In Warsaw, moreover, the importation of books on Judaism from outside the ghetto was authorized. In January 1942 the Warsaw ghetto libraries were ordered closed; nonetheless, clandestine lending libraries continued to function, delivering books directly to readers' homes.

The popular Mefizei Haskalah Library in Vilna was founded immediately upon the ghetto's establishment. Here, too, books were transferred to the ghetto from outside. In 1943 the ghetto chief Jacob Gens ordered all books in private possession turned over to the library. Jews who worked outside the ghetto smuggled in books along with bread, and the Jews involved in cataloging the YIVO library for Einsatzstab Rosenzweig (the special staff of Nazi minister Alfred Rosenzweig, who collected Jewish treasures from throughout Europe) took grave risks by smuggling out books from this important collection.

In 1942 the public library in Vilna had almost 100,000 volumes, which it distributed among its 4,000 regular subscribers from the total ghetto population of 17,000.

The library also maintained reading rooms, which served 100–200 readers a day. A bookstore was also opened at the library's initiative.

Only one library remained in the Lodz ghetto; the rest were confiscated by the Germans. Small private lending libraries sprang up, and the political organizations maintained illegal libraries. Thirty thousand volumes that remained in Jewish homes after the deportations were collected at the initiative of the Judenrat, then sorted and cataloged. Some were transferred to mobile libraries that lent books to young people in various institutions.

The Theresienstadt library possessed an unusually fine collection of scholarly works, especially in the field of Judaica. It functioned mainly as a mobile library: selected books were lent to a barracks or youth dormitory. The imbalance in the makeup of the library is only partially attributable to the nature of the population deported to Theresienstadt. It was also partly a function of SS policy. Although the library played a smaller role than other cultural institutions in projecting "a positive image," the Gestapo transferred tens of thousands of volumes confiscated from Czech and German Jewish institutions to Theresienstadt. In addition, the Gestapo brought in many thousands of books to Theresienstadt as part of its plan to study Judaism. Cataloging this collection was a task delegated to the experts in the ghetto.　*Yehoyakim Cochavi*

Ghettos: Hunger and Disease

Hunger

In the initial stages of the destruction of European Jewry, the Germans confined the Jews to ghettos, removed them from their sources of income, and instigated a policy of planned, systematic starvation. Ghettoization was a method of indirect annihilation through the denial of elementary means of existence. In August 1942 Hans Frank, head of the General-gouvernement, which was established in the occupied

A child selling produce from his own garden in the Lodz ghetto.

Polish territories not annexed to the German Reich, declared: "Since we are discussing the starvation of 1.2 million Jews there's no need to waste words. It's very clear: if the Jews don't die of starvation, it will be necessary to implement anti-Jewish legislation."

The food supply to the inhabitants of the ghettos was severely limited. The official daily food ration was 1,100–1,400 calories per person. Some researchers claim, however, that in practice the ration was no more than 700–900 calories. Those not working received 46–58 percent of the minimum calories necessary for survival; while workers received about 66 percent of the minimum.

In the Warsaw ghetto, beginning in January 1941, the inhabitants received a daily food ration that provided only 219 calories, or 9 percent of the calories necessary for survival; in August the ration fell to 177 calories. In the Lodz ghetto the food rations distributed to the working population provided 65 percent of the minimum caloric requirement, and those distributed to the nonworking population provided even less. The caloric value of the daily ration in Lodz was estimated at 1,100 calories during the last ten days of May 1942, at 1,444 calories at the end of January 1943, and at 1,132 calories in the two weeks from 24 April to 7 May 1944. In the Kovno ghetto each inhabitant received a daily ration of 750 calories. In the Vilna ghetto the caloric value of the daily food ration was 500–600 calories per person. By comparison, the minimum daily caloric requirement for an average adult male, set by the United States in 1948, was 2,400 calories; the Canadian and British standards, set in 1950, were 2,480 and 2,250 calories, respectively. A daily food ration of less than 1,800 calories causes severe disruption to the human body, and will lead to death from starvation in a matter of months. A daily food ration of less than 1,000 calories will lead to death in a matter of weeks.

The general diet in the ghettos consisted of turnips, rotten potatoes, groats, moldy flour, a meager portion of bread, and a small monthly supplement of margarine and meat. In the Warsaw ghetto the starvation rations included 180 grams of dry bread per day and 220 grams of sugar per month. In the early period of the Vilna ghetto each inhabitant received 50 grams of bread per day and a similar amount of foods such as potatoes and horse meat. In the Lodz ghetto, on 2 June 1940, an announcement detailed the goods to be distributed weekly to each inhabitant: 250 grams of sugar

and rye flour, 500 grams of groats, 100 grams of salt, 30 grams of bicarbonate of soda and chicory, 100 grams of artificial honey, 50 grams of coffee substitute, 50 grams of preserved onions, 20 grams of oil, and five kilograms of coal. Children up to the age of three were given a daily supplement of one-quarter liter of milk, two eggs, 250 grams of semolina porridge, and a piece of soap.

With time, the physical debilitation of the inhabitants became more and more pronounced, and the mortality rate in the ghettos rose to extreme levels: during the period of the Warsaw ghetto (November 1940–May 1943), some 100,000 inhabitants died of starvation and disease. In the Lodz ghetto, from May 1940 to August 1944, some 40,000 people died of those causes.

Starvation was most severe among the weaker population groups in the ghettos—children, the elderly, the sick, and those not working. Malnutrition was widespread in all the ghettos. The principal means of individual action to counter the forced starvation were smuggling and bartering. The scale of food smuggling in a given ghetto depended on the nature of its administration. In the ghettos that were not sealed off—Warsaw, Vilna, Kovno, Bialystok, and others—work details were allowed to leave the ghetto, and non-Jewish clerks and laborers entered the ghetto to work. This provided a channel for the smuggling of food. The Lodz ghetto was exceptional in being completely sealed off. No one entered or left the ghetto, and virtually no smuggling took place. As a result, the effects of starvation were felt soon after the ghetto was established, and this led to angry riots in August 1940 (just three months after the ghetto had been established) and January 1941.

Smuggling food into the ghettos was extremely dangerous. Stationed at the entrance to each ghetto were guards—some Jewish and some Lithuanian (in Vilna), Polish (in Warsaw), or German (in Lodz). Each person entering the ghetto was searched thoroughly, and tools and clothes were closely examined. The discovery of smuggled food resulted in instant punishment, from beatings to imprisonment and murder. Great resourcefulness and inventiveness were required to conceal this illegal activity.

Smuggling was an important contributor to the Warsaw ghetto economy, and men, women, and children all took part in it. The trade in smuggled goods was maintained by a network of fences, vendors, and guards who took bribes. At its peak, about 80 percent of the food in the ghetto was smuggled. Goods entered the ghetto through buildings bordering on "Aryan" Warsaw, over the walls, through concealed gaps in the walls, and via underground tunnels. Children were especially useful because they could fit through such small passages and hide easily. They would stow away on a cable car to the Aryan part of the city and there purchase or steal food, cigarettes, and other goods. Some of these items would be sold in the ghetto, and some provided the sole source of nourishment for the children's starving families.

The Vilna ghetto also had an extensive smuggling network. Inhabitants would conceal valuables or food in deep inner pockets sewed into pants or corsets and would conceal pieces of wool and other fabric in bandages wrapped around their limbs. Those working outside the ghetto would fit false bottoms into tool buckets in order to smuggle goods in the hidden compartment. Jewels, watches, and other small valuables to exchange for food would be smuggled out of the ghettos in loaves of bread.

In addition to smuggling in small quantities of food to feed oneself and one's family, large-scale smuggling in bulk quantities also took place. In buildings bordering on the Aryan part of town, sacks of flour and other foodstuffs were smuggled into the ghetto through passageways leading through the walls, attics, and cellars. Christians outside the ghetto usually colluded with the smugglers in exchange for payments. Burial carts and garbage wagons were also used to smuggle goods into the ghetto.

In Vilna the main economic activity of the German authorities took place outside the ghetto, and members of Jewish work squadrons from the ghetto would smuggle and barter goods. During working hours individual Jews employed by German institutions would steal such items as drugs, bread, canned food, wire, and cigarettes. This activity was also considered an effective means of sabotaging the Nazi machine.

Another way of combating forced starvation was bartering, which from the outset was a significant part of the ghetto economy. As the months passed, however, the inhabitants became steadily more impoverished, eventually parting with all their valuables and articles of clothing, selling their last items of property for a crust of bread.

When the Jews were being concentrated in ghettos, some entrusted their property, furniture, and valuables to Christian acquaintances, often neighbors. When the effects of starvation began to be felt, many of those people sneaked out of the ghetto, despite the great danger, in the hope of collecting their assets and exchanging them for money with which to buy food. All too frequently, when they managed to elude the police and make their way to their destination, they discovered to their dismay that their Christian acquaintances would not return their property.

In the Lodz ghetto bartering became widespread after October 1941, when some 20,000 refugees arrived from Germany, Vienna, Prague, and Luxembourg, bringing with them large parcels of clothing. As these refugees had no work, they soon felt the effects of the forced starvation and began selling portable goods for food. Bartering was also widespread among those destined for deportation. Persons named in the lists of deportees sold property and goods for next to nothing in order to purchase food.

The scale of bartering in a given ghetto depended in no small degree on the attitude of the local Jewish council, or *Judenrat* (pl. *Judenräte*). In Lodz the president of the Judenrat, Mordechai Chaim Rumkowski, was utterly opposed to any illegal activity and even threatened to imprison anyone found bartering. In other ghettos, such as Bialystok, the Judenrat actually set up marketplaces for illegal trade. In some ghettos, among them Zamosc, Shavli, and Lachva, members of the Judenrat took part in the black market.

In the Warsaw ghetto bartering was usually conducted without the involvement of the Judenrat. Business was restricted to certain streets, and trade was mainly in clothes and bed linen, which were either sold or exchanged for food. Most of the Judenräte were tolerant of bartering because they knew that it was the only means of combating the progressive starvation of the inhabitants.

Not all the attempts to counter starvation were clandestine. Indeed, most were officially organized by the Judenräte, which were responsible for the collection of food, and this activity became one of their most important tasks. To this end they set up special agencies with departments having specific roles: to buy foodstuffs and essentials, to raise funds for purchasing goods, or to organize storage rooms, bakeries, and soup kitchens.

Aside from the Germans, the Judenrat was the only

authority in the ghetto permitted to purchase food, from either Polish food cooperatives or German food suppliers. The buying of food was strictly supervised by the Germans, and in practice the ghetto inhabitants often received less than their allotted rations. Sometimes, as a deliberate policy, the food supplied to them was of substandard quality and unfit for human consumption. In October 1940 the Germans distributed large quantities of rotten food to the Lodz ghetto, and in the winter of 1942 thousands of tons of decomposing vegetables were removed from the ghetto. In March 1943 the Warsaw ghetto Judenrat had to pay a sanitation contractor 100,000 zloty to get rid of 3,000 tons of rotting potatoes that had been delivered to the ghetto.

On the initiative of the Judenrat, factories were set up in some of the ghettos with the aim of supplementing the starvation rations. The factory in the Vilna ghetto produced flour and starch from dehydrated potato peelings, and saccharine, bicarbonate of soda, and candy from sugar crystals. Bar soap was manufactured from horse bones, soap powder from ashes, and syrup and candy from potatoes. Vitamin substitutes were also produced. In the Lodz ghetto "vegetable salad" was a nickname for vegetable refuse (rotten leaves), relatively unblemished pieces of potato, and moldy bread. Low-fat or sour milk was used to make curds and whey. These products, which were produced in quantities of thousands of kilograms, were distributed mainly to the working population. In the Lodz ghetto, 300 square meters of land were allocated to each school to enable the children to grow vegetables for enriching their diet.

The Judenräte opened shops in the ghettos for selling food products. In the Vilna ghetto, shops were set up for the sale of smuggled goods. At the end of 1941, there were 45 bread shops and general stores in the Lodz ghetto, 16 shops selling milk and milk products, 16 butchers, and four dietetic shops for the sick and for those with privileges.

In February 1941 the Warsaw ghetto had a network of 601 food distribution points, 273 soap distribution points, and 70 bakeries, all supervised by the ghetto supply agency. In some of the ghettos workshops were set up—the "resorts" in Lodz and the "shops" in Warsaw, for example—to produce goods for the German military and civilians. The leaders of the Judenrat hoped that the workshops would make the ghetto inhabitants economically productive and thus save them from deportation and extermination. If the opportunity arose, finished products from the workshops were stolen and sold on the black market outside the ghetto. The contribution of the ghetto factories and workshops to the income of the inhabitants was trifling, because the Germans paid hardly anything for the finished products.

Workers in the ghettos were given work cards, which proved to be lifesavers. Each cardholder was entitled to receive a daily food ration at the central kitchens of the ghetto, which were often located in the workshops. For some workers, this was their one meal of the day.

Central kitchens were set up by the Judenräte in the factories, workshops, and schools. Great importance was placed on children's nutrition, and for this reason special kitchens were established. Supplementary food rations were given to various groups in the ghettos, such as members of the Judenrat, guards, medical personnel, children and adolescents, and the sick. This privileged treatment created resentment among those not eligible to receive additional rations.

Starvation was not the only adverse result of the inadequate food rations. The illegal economic activity enabled a small number of people to make excessive profits, and some quickly became rich. Clandestine restaurants, cafés, and nightclubs opened only to these nouveaux riches, whose lifestyle was in sharp contrast to that of the starving majority.

Disease

The mass deportation of European Jews and their concentration at intolerable densities was a major cause of widespread disease in the ghettos. Of the 20,000 Jews deported from Central Europe to the Lodz ghetto in October 1941, 22.4 percent died owing to the unbearable nutritional and hygienic conditions, for which they were totally unprepared. Severe overcrowding in damp, ramshackle houses unfit for human habitation created appalling living conditions. In the Lodz ghetto most of the buildings were made of wood, and some 95 percent were without toilets or running water. Water pumped from wells and courtyards was regularly flooded with sewage. Similar conditions existed in the other ghettos.

Starvation rations and the bitter cold also contributed to disease. The imbalance and caloric deficiency of the ghetto diet, which consisted primarily of carbohydrates with a virtual absence of protein or fat, produced com-

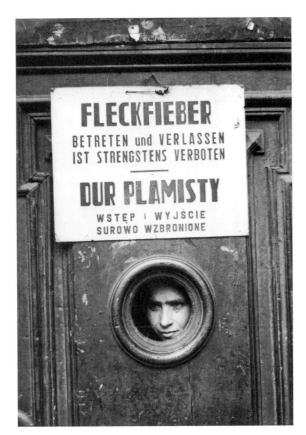

FLECKFIEBER
BETRETEN und VERLASSEN
IST STRENGSTENS VERBOTEN

DUR PLAMISTY
WSTĘP i WYJŚCIE
SUROWO WZBRONIONE

Sign in the Warsaw ghetto, reading, in German and Polish, "Typhus! It is strictly forbidden to enter or leave." 1941

binations of disorders unknown in normal circumstances: weakening of the bones (osteomalacia), tissue loss (necrosis), severe diarrhea, intestinal disorders, severe weight loss, and edema. The inhabitants of the ghettos were supplied with inadequate means of heating or with none at all. People burned furniture, fences, and floorboards to heat their houses. Many froze to death, especially babies and elderly people.

Another cause of disease was poor sanitation. The refuse in the courtyards between the buildings was often left uncollected for weeks at a time. There was a severe shortage of soap and clothing, and the inhabitants of the ghettos washed themselves and their clothes only infrequently. This led to infestations of lice and fleas that spread to every section of the ghetto.

Nearly all the ghettos suffered epidemics of typhoid fever, spotted fever, and dysentery. These were caused by poor sanitation, lack of vital nutrients, and the presence of human and animal corpses in the streets. It is estimated that in the Warsaw ghetto alone some

100,000 people contracted spotted fever. The German authorities threatened to destroy the ghettos and their inhabitants if the medical services failed to control these epidemics.

Vitamin deficiency (avitaminosis) resulted in a number of conditions: night blindness (vitamin A deficiency), pellagra (B2), anemia and neurological dysfunction (B12), scurvy (C), rickets and other bone diseases (D), particularly among children. Insufficient fat and protein in the diet led to urinary tract disorders.

About half of the inhabitants of the ghettos contracted tuberculosis. The disease reached epidemic proportions and had a high mortality rate, as the sufferers were already weakened by starvation and exhaustion. The lack of proper sanitation also caused skin diseases such as scabies, which spread rapidly owing to the severe overcrowding. The incidence of heart disease in the ghettos was unusually high and resulted in many deaths. The mortality rate can be attributed to living conditions in the ghettos, the lack of work, general weakness from starvation, the bitter cold, hormonal disorders, protein deficiency, and anxiety and fear, especially during deportation periods.

Amenorrhea affected 75–85 percent of premenopausal women in the ghettos. The causes were mainly psychological but also nutritional. There was also a relatively high rate of miscarriage among pregnant women.

Ghetto children were particularly vulnerable to disease. In addition to characteristic childhood illnesses, they suffered from all the other afflictions prevalent in the ghettos. The first victims of starvation were children, especially babies. Starvation caused the loss of up to 50 percent of body weight, retardation of physical and mental growth, skin disorders, edema, muscle weakness, damage to the internal organs, and psychological conditions such as depression.

Children and adolescents experienced a high incidence of tuberculosis, scrofula, and meningitis. Dysentery was also widespread, mainly among infants up to the age of one year. From June through December 1940 about 30 percent of the babies in the Lodz ghetto succumbed to a dysentery epidemic, 208 children died of scarlet fever, 401 of diphtheria, and 443 of whooping cough.

Another disease prevalent among children was goiter. Caused by lack of iodine in the diet, the disease reached epidemic proportions among the young. A particularly large number of children contracted the disease in the Vilna ghetto, where inhabitants subsisted for long periods on cabbage, which is rich in a goiter-inducing chemical (goitrin).

Although disease was rampant in the ghettos, the incidence of cancers was relatively low. A comprehensive explanation for this anomaly has yet to be proposed, but it has been suggested that protein and fat deficiencies were factors.

In most of the ghettos the Judenräte set up systems of medical services, in an attempt to deal with the widespread disease. The difficulties of this task, however, were overwhelming. When the Jews were deported to ghettos, they had been forced to leave behind medical equipment and drugs. Medical personnel and facilities were also in short supply, and the Germans interfered with efforts to deal with the shortages. Hospitals were organized in the ghettos, but many were located in unsuitable premises.

The Lodz ghetto established a health department with a medical director and an administrative director. In the summer of 1940 the department had a medical staff of 1,228, including 94 physicians, 464 nurses, 128 pharmacists and assistant pharmacists, 61 dentists, and 481 dental technicians. In 1940 a number of medical facilities were established: a maternity hospital, a hospital for infectious diseases, an eye hospital, a hospital for sexually transmitted diseases, a children's hospital, a psychiatric institution, a women's clinic, and a family health clinic that monitored infant development, administered vaccinations, and prepared a special milk substitute for babies. In addition, five outpatient clinics were set up, together with two preventive medicine clinics for children and adolescents, two first aid clinics, a dental clinic, a sterilization plant, a tuberculosis clinic, a radiology clinic, and a diabetes clinic. In March 1942 the ghetto had five hospitals, one of which contained some 500 beds and a number of hospital departments: internal medicine, gynecology, pediatrics, surgery, ophthalmology, and dermatology. In November 1942 the ghetto was divided into 40 districts, each of which had its own general physician responsible for some 2,500 people.

In the Lodz ghetto, in which schools operated until October 1941, medical facilities were organized on school premises. The children took an active part in promoting better hygiene by going from door to door to explain the importance of cleanliness both inside and outside the home. A sanitation unit was responsible for cleaning the streets and maintaining the drainage system. Laboratories conducted medical tests and manufactured drugs, which supplied the seven pharmacies in the ghetto. There was also a veterinary unit that supervised the slaughter of animals and the production of milk and meat products. The system of medical services operated until August 1943, when the Germans ordered the hospitals to be turned into workshops. Thereafter only the sanitation unit, three public baths, and a sterilization plant continued to function.

The Warsaw ghetto had six health centers staffed by hygiene and sanitation experts, two hospitals, three outpatient clinics, a sanitation committee, eight sterilization plants, four public baths, and three quarantine facilities. In August 1941 there were 19 pharmacies in the ghetto. The Jews were forbidden to purchase expensive drugs but in any case lacked the funds for such purchases. Drugs improvised from a variety of materials were therefore common. The pharmacists displayed great resourcefulness in producing drugs and vitamin substitutes, and the shortage of drugs was further reduced by the purchase or smuggling of medication from outside the ghetto.

A clandestine medical school, disguised as a teaching facility for "sanitation courses on the prevention of epidemics," was established in the Warsaw ghetto. The school operated from May 1941 to July 1942, training more than 500 students, all of whom were employed in the system of medical services. In the Lodz ghetto, a medical-scientific body was set up to oversee medical training, organize weekly lectures and discussions on medical issues, and conduct research in the fields of medicine and veterinary medicine. The health department of the Vilna ghetto operated a range of medical services and employed about 380 staff members. The department took measures to prevent epidemics and provided medical treatment to both the adult and child populations. There were two hygiene units and a vaccination clinic, as well as a sanitation unit and an epidemiology unit.

The Germans prohibited births in the ghettos, particularly the Vilna and Kraków ghettos, and in some ghettos pregnancy was punishable by death. Jewish physicians did not enforce this decree, however, and women gave birth in secret. Physicians and nurses delivered the babies in specially prepared hideouts.

The medical services organized in the large ghettos did not exist in the smaller ones, or existed only in very reduced form. The lack of facilities, medical equipment, medical personnel, and drugs was acute in those ghettos, preventing the establishment of a proper system of medical services. On more than one occasion, inhabitants were treated by physicians from the large ghettos. This happened only infrequently, however, since the large ghettos also suffered from a severe shortage of medical personnel.

Naomi Grossman

Globocnik, Odilo (1904–45) Senior SS officer who administered the Final Solution in Poland from 1941 to 1943. Globocnik directed that Jews be conscripted into slave labor and that their property be confiscated. More than 2 million Polish Jews were murdered on his orders. He committed suicide in May 1945 while awaiting trial for war crimes. See FINAL SOLUTION: PREPARATION AND IMPLEMENTATION

Goebbels, Joseph (1897–1945) Minister of propaganda and, prior to 1933, head of the Nazi organization in Berlin. Goebbels was an intimate associate and loyal follower of Adolf Hitler's. He effectively used the media to portray Jews as the enemy of Germany and to create the popular mythology of the Führer. Goebbels spearheaded efforts to clear Berlin of Jews. In November 1938 he helped to instigate the Kristallnacht pogroms. Goebbels was appointed Reich plenipotentiary for total war in 1944. He committed suicide, along with his wife and six children, in Berlin during the last week of the war.

Goeth, Amon (1906–48) SS official and commander in 1943–44 of the Plaszow camp near Kraków and other labor camps. Goeth was responsible for over-

Hermann Göring. 1941.

sight of the liquidation of the Polish ghettos and labor camps. After the war he was tried by the Polish supreme court for mass murder, convicted, and executed as a war criminal in Kraków.

Göring, Hermann (1893–1946) President of the Reichstag, prime minister of Prussia, commander-in-chief of the Luftwaffe, and commissioner in charge of the Four Year Plan for the war economy. An early recruit to nazism, Göring helped Adolf Hitler to attain dictatorial powers. He was put in charge of the Jewish question in 1938 and made nominally responsible for the execution of the Final Solution, though his influence waned during the latter years of the Nazi regime. Convicted of war crimes at the Nuremberg trials, Göring committed suicide the day he was scheduled to hang.

Grawitz, Ernst (1899–1945) Chief SS physician, prominently involved in the Final Solution, the medical experiments at Auschwitz, and the so-called euthanasia program. Grawitz advised Heinrich Himmler on plans for gas facilities and held an interest in almost all types of "experiments," including exposure to temperature and pressure extremes, infection, chemical warfare, and sterilization. He committed suicide in 1945. See MEDICAL EXPERIMENTATION

Greece The Holocaust (from the Greek word meaning "whole burnt offering") of Greek Jewry took place

Joseph Goebbels, German Propaganda Minister. 27 March 1933.

A group of elderly Jews, some of whom are Sephardic rabbis, in the Baron de Hirsch quarter of Salonika. September 1941

in two stages: spring–summer 1943, for the Sephardic Jews of Salonika (Thessaloníki) and Thrace, and spring–summer 1944, for the Greek-speaking Jews of Central, Western, and Southern Greece and the Italian-speaking Jews of Corfu and Rhodes. It resulted in the destruction of more than 85 percent of the prewar community of some 80,000 Jews, two-thirds of whom lived in Salonika. Some 10,000 Jews fled to the mountains, at least 650–1,000 to fight with the resistance, thousands more to serve the resistance as translators, doctors and nurses, and other ancillary personnel. Others brought urban and university skills to the mountain communities and assisted in the modernization process introduced by the resistance. The remainder hid, under the protection of the resistance or with the hospitality of the local villagers. Several thousand escaped with resistance aid, mainly in late 1943 and in 1944 to Egypt, Turkey, and Palestine.

The wartime story of Greece is complicated by the division of the country among the Axis partners, Germany, Italy, and Bulgaria. In each zone of occupation the Jews were subject to different political vicissitudes until the deportations. The Italian invasion of Greece on 28 October 1940 was halted and pushed back into Albania, where a stalemate ensued for the next six months. This success was recognized by the British as the first Allied victory of the war; Greek valor against the Italians, and later against the Germans during the Nazi invasion, was noted by Hitler in his May 1941 decree releasing all Greek prisoners of war. One of the heroes honored by Greece was Col. Mordechai (Mordocheos) Frizis, who lost his life in the successful November counterattack. Some 13,000 Jews served with the Greek forces in Albania and Thrace, sustaining such heavy casualties that they were officially honored by the Greek government. In April 1941 the Germans invaded and overran Yugoslavia and Greece; by the end of May 10 days of bloody fighting in Crete extinguished the country's independence; the king and his government retreated to Cairo, but the resistance continued in the mountains. In the subsequent partition Bulgaria realized its irredentist claims to Thrace and Macedonia, while Germany took Salonika and its environs, the stretch along the Turkish border separating the Bulgarians and Turks, and most of Crete. The remainder of mainland Greece and its islands, several already occupied before the war, were given to Italy.

During the first year of occupation in Salonika many of the wealthier Jewish factory-owners were subjected to expropriation, and the middle-class Jewish shopkeepers (ca. 1,800) in Salonika had their goods either seized or bought up with worthless notes. Jews in the Bulgarian zone were pressured to accept Bulgarian citizenship and participate in the bulgarization of Thrace; most refused. Young people were drafted for forced labor and the repair of roads. In the Italian zone Jews enjoyed the protection of the Italian occupying forces, and many of the wealthier Jews fled to Athens. Italian-speaking Jews from Rhodes also migrated to Athens, where business opportunities were somewhat better than on the islands.

In Salonika the community council was arrested. Many Christians and Jews were rounded up as hostages and later shot during German reprisals against acts of Greek resistance. A plaque at the U.S. consulate commemorates David Tiano, the chief Jewish clerk there. Chief rabbi Zvi Koretz was later arrested and jailed in Vienna; he left on the same plane with the Communist leader Nikos Zachariades, who spent the rest of the war in Dachau. Einsatzstab Rosenberg soon arrived in Salonika armed with detailed lists of Jews and Freemasons as well as addresses of synagogues, lodges, banks, and residences. These lists were used to arrest critics and enemies of the Reich, exploit the wealthy, and confiscate community treasures, archives, and libraries for the planned Nazi Museum. Several Jewish politicians and intellectuals had already fled the city with the retreating British in anticipation of arrest, among them the journalist Baruch Shibi, who was later active with EAM (Ethnikon Apeletherotikon Metopon, the National Liberation Front) in Athens and the Peloponnese. Working-class Jews and the poorer members of the Jewish community, however, did not at first experience any special persecution.

Jews in general suffered alongside the Greek population (especially during the winter famine of 1941–42), and no hint of the ensuing Holocaust was per-

ceived. Many refugees from Salonika returned to their homes during the first year of occupation and attempted to reestablish their lives in the occupied city; Greek Jews with Italian citizenship who had been interned during the fighting also returned. Some Greek Jews who had served with the Greek army in Thrace and Albania stayed in the mountains and joined the resistance bands, which were not yet fully organized. Also in the mountains, escaped prisoners of war and remnants of the Greek, British, and Yugoslav armies could be found. Records exist of a number of Palestinian Jews, volunteers with the British Expeditionary Force, who had escaped to the mountains after capture; most Palestinians, however, remained prisoners of the Germans and survived the war in prisoner-of-war camps. In brief, the occupation was mainly restricted to the cities and the food sources in the valleys, while the mountains remained free. The Germans and Italians occasionally sent punitive expeditions into the mountains; they usually committed atrocities against villagers in lieu of engaging the resistance bands and their British liaison officers, who had become active after November 1942.

In July 1942 male Jews of Salonika aged 18 to 45 were forcibly registered for labor to repair the damage incurred during the British retreat. Jews of foreign nationality, such as the many Spanish and Italian Jews, were exempt. The Swiss representative of the International Red Cross went beyond his brief to register the dead and injured victims of this process, which was violently carried out on Saturday, 11 July, and the following Monday, 13 July. Of the 9,000 Jews registered by the Germans, many were called in successive groups over the next few months to service roads and repair railroads and bridges: working conditions were appalling. A few men escaped to the mountains, but most stayed for fear of reprisals against the remaining Jews. Many died from dysentery, malaria, and malnutrition. Their female relatives made forceful protests to the new community council, which entered into negotiations with the German civilian authority, Dr. Max Merten, to buy the forced laborers out of their service. Merten demanded 3 billion drachmas, and the Jews, dying from malnutrition (as was the Greek population), raised some funds (largely owing to the efforts of Yomtob Yakoel, the community's lawyer) from their own declining reserves and from the Salonikan refugees in Athens. They negotiated a reduction of the amount by ceding the 500-year-old graveyard to the city of Salonika, which subsequently cleaned the site, recycled the stones for the repair of Italian bombed buildings including the Metropolitan Church of Saint Demetrios, built a swimming pool for the German army, paved roadways, and expanded the University of Thessaloníki on the site. The men returned home, save for 1,500 who continued to work until they were deported to Auschwitz in the summer of 1943.

The decision to deport the Jews of Salonika in all probability was handed down in late November 1942. Rabbi Koretz, who had returned from Vienna in December 1941 to serve the community, was made president of the *Judenrat* (Jewish council) in mid-December 1942. This act provoked much dissension in the community council, because it violated the autonomous constitution of the community recognized by the Greek government as a relic from the Ottoman period. This official Judenrat replaced the former collaborationist council, some of whose members (Vital Hasson, Edgar Chounio, L. Topaz, and J. Albala) had despoiled and persecuted the trapped community. Hitler had already indicated to his chief of staff in October 1941 that the Salonikan Jews could be deported at any convenient time; in November and December 1942 the defense of the Balkans was reorganized, thus sealing the fate of the Jews of Bulgarian- and German-controlled Macedonia and Thrace.

In February 1943 Adolf Eichmann's emissaries, Dieter Wisliceny and Alois Brunner, arrived in Salonika bearing unsigned decrees to introduce the Nuremberg Laws to mark, isolate, and ghettoize the Jews. The rapid issuing of decrees (eight in five weeks were signed by Wisliceny and Merten) confused an already exhausted community, so that it was totally unprepared when the order came for the first deportation in mid-March; a written protest by the International Red Cross representative led to his replacement (but not until June). The well-organized community, with an array of volunteer groups to feed and clothe the poor, now arranged for its own deportation, neighborhood by neighborhood, via the Baron Hirsch ghetto. In the space of two and a half months nearly all the Greek Jewish citizens of the German zone—approximately 48,000—were deported to Auschwitz, where 85–90 percent were gassed on arrival and cremated. Rabbi Koretz, having quickly made a protest against the deportations to the Greek government and church, was arrested and deported with his family. Along with the Judenrat and other prominent Jews, he spent two

years in a subcamp of Bergen-Belsen and died of typhus shortly after liberation. His role as head of the Judenrat is still controversial, although historians are beginning to reassess his actions in light of the general problem of the wartime Judenräte.

On 4 March 1943 the Jews of the Bulgarian zone (around 4,100) were rounded up in one night and deported to Treblinka, where all were gassed and cremated on arrival. These Jews of Thrace were part of a deal agreed to by the Bulgarian minister of internal affairs, Petur Gabrovski, to protect the Bulgarian-Jewish citizens from Nazi demands. At the beginning of May the Greek-Jewish citizens of the Turkish border zone (Didymotihon, Souflion, and Nea Orestias) were arrested and trucked to Salonika, where they joined one of the death trains. Out of some 48,000 Salonikan deportees perhaps 1,200 returned; of those from the border zone only a few dozen made it back. The only survivors from the Bulgarian zone were those men on forced labor at the time of the deportation or who had fled to the resistance, which was then at its inception.

By the summer of 1943 there were hundreds of young Jews fighting with ELAS (Ellenikos Laikos Apeletherotikos Stratos, the Greek Popular Liberation Army), the newly formed resistance group in Greece that controlled most of free Greece in the mountains of the Pindus and Olympus ranges. Attempts by ELAS to save other young Jews had failed because youths refused to abandon their parents or the older Spanish-speaking Jews who could not face the hard life in the mountains. Hundreds of Italian Jews escaped to Athens by train in a mass exodus organized by the journalist Sam Modiano with help from the Italian consulate. The Spanish Jews of Salonika and later Athens were deported to Bergen-Belsen, one group being repatriated to Spain, which passed them on, with the aid of the American Jewish Joint Distribution Committee, to North Africa, whence they eventually reached Palestine. Another group was en route to Spain when the war's end found them stranded on a train in France.

Italy surrendered on 8 September 1943 and relinquished its zone of occupation, in some cases after hard fighting, to German control. At the end of September Rabbi Eliahu Barzilai was ordered by the Nazis to surrender lists of the Athens Jews. They accepted that previous lists had been destroyed by antisemitic attacks the previous year, and he was sent home to prepare new ones. But with the aid of ELAS (which was prepared to kidnap, if not kill him) and Archbishop Damaskinos, he escaped to the mountains, where he issued propaganda statements on behalf of the resistance forces. The Athens community went underground, save for a handful of despondent Jews, and ignored the order to register that was published on 7 October by SS Gen. Jürgen Stroop. Laws were passed confiscating Jewish property. Toward Passover in 1944, the Germans announced that matzo would be distributed at the Athens synagogue, and the number registered reached 800.

All the Jews in the mainland communities of the former Italian zone were arrested on the first night of Passover, 24–25 March. Many in Thessaly had been warned by ELAS and were helped to escape by the Greek police and civil and religious authorities, such as those of Katerini, Larissa, Volos, Trikkala, and Karditsa. Macedonian and Epirote communities, however, were too isolated and suffered almost complete deportation. Scarcely any Jews (except four doctors) were to be found among the more conservative resistance group in Epirus, EDES (Ellenikos Dimokratikos Ethnikos Stratos, the National Republican Greek Army). Those young men who had gone to the mountains were recalled by their mothers at the insistence of Sabbetai Kabelli, the interim leader of the Ioannina community, even though he had been warned by the imprisoned president, Dr. Moses Konfinas, to advise them to escape. A number of Jewish refugees from Yugoslavia were also caught in the round-up. The Jews of Agrinion in southwest Greece—about 40 in all—had agreed beforehand to escape to the mountains: they suffered a year of deprivation but nonetheless survived. Most of the few Jews of Patras survived high in the central mountains of the Peloponnese, as did the Jews of Chalkis, the central point in the escape route to Turkey. The 270 Jews of Zakynthos escaped deportation partly because of the resistance of local Greek officials, the disinterest of the occupying force (a punishment battalion with an Austrian commander), and the absence of Anton Burger, the SS officer responsible for the deportation.

Most of the Jewish deportees from Athens were either Salonikan refugees or the starving poor trapped by the Nazi offer to distribute matzos. The remainder of the Athens Jews, with the help of Jews and Christians in EAM, went into hiding after the disappearance of Rabbi Barzilai. A few Jews were located by Jewish collaborators (the Rekanati brothers) or turned in by Greek blackmailers. But most of them survived in the city. They fled along the escape route organized by ELAS and the Haganah to Euboea and thence by caique to Turkey, whence they were taken to refugee camps in Gaza and Sinai, or they went into the mountains to hide or fight with ELAS. The church supplied some false baptismal certificates and hid Jewish children; the police issued fake identity cards. Most of the Athenian officials protested and actively resisted the deportations in Athens: Archbishop Damaskinos presented a petition signed by many of the civic and professional leaders. Freemasons too had a part in rescuing British soldiers and Jews.

Of the Jews deported to Poland, all the approximately 4,000 Thracian Jews sent to Treblinka were killed upon arrival at the extermination camp; of the 54,000 sent to Auschwitz, only some 12,000 were drafted for slave labor, and less than 2,000 of these survived the war. The largest losses from the 1944 deportations included most of the 1,860 Jews of Ioánnina and most of the 763 Jews of Kastoria. The 2,000 Jews of Corfu were arrested in June 1944; only some 200 returned. The 1,700 Jews of Rhodes were arrested in July, and less than 200 survived. The ship deporting the 260 Jews of Crete and Italian prisoners of war was probably torpedoed and sank with no survivors.

Greek Jews could be found in all the major camps and in many of the subcamps. They suffered all the vicissitudes of enslavement, including the sterilization experiments in Auschwitz, Majdanek, and Natzweiler. They helped in the cleanup of the Warsaw ghetto from September 1943 to July 1944; less than 300 survived the march to Dachau. The group left to dismantle the ghetto was able to join the fighting that broke out in the Warsaw revolt of August 1944; at least 27 of these were alive after the war. Greeks served in the Sonderkommando in Auschwitz and took part in the revolt of October 1944 under the leadership of the Greek military veteran Joseph Varouh; of these, an unknown number survived after chance inclusion in a transport to Mauthausen. Perhaps a dozen survived the later death marches and reached Dachau, where they were eventually liberated. A number of Greek women who had been in the sterilization experiments at Auschwitz were reassigned to blood serum experiments in the Institute of Hygiene in the Auschwitz subcamp of Rajsko and so survived the war; several gave testimony at the Uris-Dering libel trial in London. Thus the continued existence of a handful of Greeks was a matter of luck, pluck, and the unknown efforts of camp resistance activists. The solidarity of the multilingual Greeks (only a handful spoke German), necessary in the face of Yiddish-speaking Ashkenazi antagonism, was notorious in the camps, particularly Auschwitz and Stutthof.

At the war's end the survivors went to the nearest or most convenient havens—Sweden, France, Belgium, the United States, and South America. Less than 2,000 returned to Greece. Some 300 found their way to the displaced persons camp at Feldafing, where a small group organized a thriving black market for several years and intermarried with Hungarian and other survivors. The returnees to Salonika—many via Italy, where they were helped by DELASEM (Delegazione Assistenza Emigranti Ebrei, or Aid Commission for Jewish Refugees)—met with an inhospitable reception in their native city. Their homes and properties were occupied by the plethora of Greek refugees (more than 30,000) driven out of Thrace and Macedonia by the Bulgarians. The Jews who fought with ELAS were persecuted as Communists in the developing civil war that was to ravage Greece for the next five years. Thousands emigrated to Palestine with the help of the Haganah, and many were to fight with honor in the ensuing Israeli war of independence.

In the period 1945–55 nearly two-thirds of the 15,000 Greek Jews emigrated, most to Israel. Of the remainder, some 3,500 settled in Athens, about 1,200 in Salonika, 400 in Larissa, 90 each in Ioánnina and Chalkis, and a handful in other centers. There are no Jews left in Thrace. The Salonika community is burdened with the administration of the "heirless property" of the deported Jews, which was returned to the surviving Jewish communities in 1945, the first such restoration of confiscated property by a European country. In recent years the Athens community has supported a Jewish Museum to record the millennial symbiosis of Greeks and Jews, and a museum has been established in Thessaloníki to commemorate the fate of the Jews of northern Greece during the Holocaust. Greece was the only country to have wartime trials of Jewish collaborators, these having been demanded by the Jews themselves. One of the first surveys of an entire destroyed Jewry appeared in 1948, *In Memoriam*, by M. Molho and J. Nehama (in French, with subsequent Hebrew and Greek expanded editions). Recent studies have begun to examine in depth the role of the Greek Jews in the resistance, the social and economic history of wartime Greece, and the German and Italian armies. The materials from the former Soviet Union include lists from various camps, which should allow a more detailed tracking of Greek Jews. Some of the archives from Thessaloníki and other Greek communities have also come to light in this way; part of the Salonika archives is located in YIVO, in New York. The Soviet materials were photographed and are now being edited at the Diaspora Institute of Tel Aviv University. Wartime archives from the Bulgarian occupied zone were turned over to the Jewish Museum of Greece.

Steven B. Bowman

Grossman, Chaika (1919–96) Jewish leader of the resistance in the Bialystok ghetto. After the 1943 ghetto revolt Grossman joined a partisan unit. She settled in Palestine after the war and served in the Knesset (Israeli parliament) from 1961 to 1981 and in 1984. Grossman wrote *The Underground Army* (1987) about her Bialystok ghetto experiences.

Gross-Rosen Concentration and labor camp in lower Silesia. The number of inmates in 1944–45 was almost 100,000, some 40 percent of them Jews. During the last phase of the war many inmates were deported to camps in central Germany. Approximately 40,000 of the 125,000 prisoners who came to Gross-Rosen died there. See FORCED LABOR

Gruenbaum, Yitzhak (1879–1970) Zionist, leading figure among Polish Jewry, member of the Polish parliament. Gruenbaum moved to Palestine in 1933. He became a member of the Jewish Agency's Executive and head of the Rescue Committee (1943–44). See YISHUV

Grüninger, Paul (1891–1972) Senior police official in Sankt Gallen, Switzerland. Grüninger ignored instructions to refuse entry to refugees from Austria. As a result many hundreds of Jews entered Switzerland and were saved. Grüninger was dismissed for insubordination, was fined, lost his pension, and was denied access to employment. After a public campaign that lasted for decades, he was rehabilitated posthumously in 1996 by the Swiss government. The Israeli Holocaust memorial Yad Vashem named Grüninger one of the Righteous Among the Nations.

Grynszpan, Herschel (1921–43?) Polish Jewish refugee who immigrated to Paris in 1936. After learning that his family had been deported to Poland from Germany, on 7 November 1938 Grynszpan shot and

Paul Grüninger (left). 1 February 1934

Herschel Grynszpan. November 1938

killed Ernst vom Rath, a German diplomat stationed in Paris. Grynszpan quickly surrendered to the French police. The Nazis justified the Kristallnacht pogrom two days later as retribution for the assassination. The Vichy government handed Grynszpan over to the Germans in 1940, and he subsequently disappeared.

Gurs Major internment camp in France, near Oloron-Sainte-Marie and 80 kilometers from the Spanish border. Established in 1939 to absorb Republican refugees from Spain, Gurs served later as a concentration camp for Jews from France and refugees from other countries. While under the administration of Vichy France (1940–42) most non-Jewish prisoners were released and approximately 2,000 Jews were permitted to emigrate. In 1941 Gurs held some 15,000 prisoners. The camp was controlled by the Germans from 1942 to 1944, during which time several thousand inmates were deported to extermination camps in Poland. An unknown number succeeded in escaping and reaching Spain or hiding in southern France. Gurs was liberated in the summer of 1944.

Gypsies The Gypsies are an ancient people that originated in India and wandered into Europe during the fourteenth and fifteenth centuries. In some countries, Gypsies were welcome upon their arrival, in others tolerated for awhile, but in most they were repeatedly subjected to expulsion. For staying, they were hounded, flogged, condemned to the galleys, branded, or hanged. In some areas the local inhabitants were free to kill them. Spanish rulers attempted to assimilate and settle them forcibly. Romanian aristocrats and monasteries kept them as slaves until the middle of the nineteenth century. In other areas of the continent they moved in caravans, sustaining themselves as tinsmiths, musicians, and horse dealers or in seasonal agricultural work. At various times anyone who took to a nomadic life was called a Gypsy. By 1933, however, most Gypsies had become sedentary. They adhered to the religions of the societies in which they dwelled, keeping only their own Romani language and ancestral customs.

At the beginning of the twentieth century, Gypsies

View of the Gurs transit camp from a water tower.

were still regarded with suspicion. They were frequently described as dishonest, lazy, dirty, and ignorant. Considerable thought was given to their suppression. The leader in these efforts was Bavaria, where the Munich police created a Gypsy information office in 1899 to track Gypsy movements. The Bavarian authorities established a registry, which by 1905 contained the names of more than 3,000 Gypsies. In 1911 Bavaria introduced fingerprinting of Gypsies and two years later began to compile Gypsy births, name changes, marriages, and deaths. On 29 April 1929 the German Criminal Commission designated the Munich office as the Central Office for Combating Gypsies. That organization was renamed the Reich Center for Combating the Gypsy Plague in 1938 and moved to Berlin as a component of the German Criminal Police. At the beginning of 1938 it had records of 16,743 "racial" Gypsies, 4,502 racially doubtful cases, and 9,640 non-Gypsy nomads.

Although the Criminal Police was the primary agency concerned with Gypsy matters throughout the Reich,

it was not the only one. From 1935 to 1939 German municipal officials assigned decrepit squares or swampy land with poor hygienic facilities as "rest places" to Gypsy families living in carts. Some Gypsies were expelled from public housing or other quarters and given used-up furniture vans or dilapidated barracks. The enclosures for Gypsies appeared in several major cities, including Cologne, Berlin, Frankfurt am Main, Kiel, Gelsenkirchen, Essen, and Düsseldorf. In the Frankfurt encampment, movement to outside areas was allowed only for work, school, and shopping. Daily leave for other purposes was limited to one hour.

The Criminal Police and its companion agency, the State Police (Gestapo), sent Gypsies to concentration camps. Seizures by the Criminal Police were called "preventive arrest," whereas Gestapo round-ups, which occurred in 1938, were conducted under the rubric of "protective custody," which meant protection of the state. At first, arrests were made in small numbers, but in the late 1930s they were made by the hundreds. Two large groups comprised Austrian Gypsy men routed to Dachau and then transferred to Buchenwald, and Austrian Gypsy women, who in 1939 were sent to Ravensbrück.

The arrested Gypsies were considered "asocial." Among the asocials were persons with a record of minor but repeated infractions who, in the opinion of the police, did not live the kind of ordered life that was expected in Germany. This group included itinerant Gypsies. Also designated asocial were Gypsies and persons moving about like Gypsies, who "showed no will" to work regularly. Such individuals were labeled "work-shy asocials," a term that could be extended to cover the arrest of workers living under the restrictive conditions of a Gypsy urban camp. A special category of the asocials consisted of Gypsy female fortune tellers, whose "preventive arrest" was ordered by the Criminal Police on 20 November 1939, lest their prophecies disturb the equanimity of Germans in wartime.

From the middle of the 1930s a number of Gypsy men, women, and children were sterilized simply because they were "inferior." Officially, they gave their consent by declaring themselves "ready" for the procedure. Gypsy adults were to make such declarations for children in their care.

On 8 December 1938 Heinrich Himmler, as chief of the German police, issued an ordinance for the discovery of who was a Gypsy, or a so-called *Mischling* (mix) of Gypsy and German extraction, or a non-Gypsy roving from place to place in a Gypsy-like manner. The final determination was to be made in each case by the Criminal Police, based on an expert opinion obtained from the Race-Hygienic and Population Research Center of the Reich Health Office. The Criminal Police were to issue identity cards with fingerprints—brown for pure Gypsies, brown with light-blue diagonal stripes for the Mischlinge, and gray for roving non-Gypsies.

The Race-Hygienic Center was headed by Robert Ritter, who had already begun investigations in 1936.

Gypsies with belongings in tow at Halle. Circa 1940

With his assistant, Eva Justin, he examined records and people, noting physical and behavioral characteristics. In 1941 he announced a preliminary estimate of some 30,000 persons of Gypsy ancestry, 19,000 of them in the Old Reich and 11,000 in Austria and the Sudetenland. It had turned out, however, that less than 10 percent of that population were "pure" Gypsies. Inasmuch as the majority were Mischlinge, subclassifications of these part-Gypsies were needed. Despite the scarcity of adequate genealogical evidence, a system was set up under which those of predominantly Gypsy descent were labeled ZM+ and those with equal shares of German and Gypsy "blood" (such as offspring of half-Gypsies) ZM. If one parent was a pure Gypsy and the other a German, the designation ZM of the first degree was used. For one-quarter Gypsies it was ZM of the second degree, and for individuals predominantly German but with some Gypsy ancestry (such as one-eighth Gypsies) ZM-. A further distinction was made by Himmler in 1941 between Sinti, who were German Gypsies, and Roma, whose background was primarily Hungarian and who lived in the former Austrian province of Burgenland. By March 1942 the estimate was 35,000–40,000, but only 13,000 had been fully investigated.

On 13 March 1942 all full Gypsies and Gypsy Mischlinge, except for the category ZM+, were subjected to wage regulations applicable to Jews, and to the Social Equalization Tax payable by Poles and Jews. Gypsies were still serving in the armed forces, but under a regulation of 11 February 1941, anyone with a "conspicuously" Gypsy appearance was to be severed from active military service. On 10 July 1942, all Gypsies and Gypsy Mischlinge, regardless of wounds or decorations, were ruled "unsuitable." Because of the war, dismissals were slow, and some Gypsies remained in military units as late as 1943.

During the 1940s a catastrophe overtook the Gypsies, first in the Greater German Reich, then in several countries occupied by or allied with Germany. There is an expression in the Romani language that is comparable to the English *holocaust* and the Hebrew *shoah*. It is the word *porajmos*.

The first major blow was an order dated 27 April 1940, by Reinhard Heydrich, who was in charge of the Criminal Police and the Gestapo, to deport 2,500 Gypsies from a large region in western Germany to the Generalgouvernement, an area of Poland under a German civil administration. Gypsies in mixed marriages,

those with fathers or sons in the military, and a few other categories were exempt. The ostensible reason for the deportation was the danger posed by Gypsies in a war zone. The action, begun in May and ultimately affecting about 2,800 persons, brought the Gypsies as far east as the labor camps on the Polish Bug River. The deportees had to wear a white arm band with a Z. Eventually some of them were quartered in houses that had to be abandoned by Jews or in emptied ghettos. A Jewish survivor recalls that one of three blocks in the Siedlce ghetto was occupied by Gypsies. The attrition due to hardships among the deportees was heavy.

Some 4,000 Roma Gypsies of the Austrian Burgenland were concentrated in a camp at Lackenbach, where a typhus epidemic broke out at the beginning of 1942.

In November 1941, 5,007 Austrian Gypsies, including 2,000 from Lackenbach, were shipped to the ghetto of Lodz. Typhus claimed the lives of 613 by 1 January 1942. A munitions factory at Poznan received 120. All the rest were taken in early January to Kulmhof and killed in gas vans.

In October and December 1942 Himmler made some fundamental decisions. Pure Sinti were henceforth to be left in place under existing restrictions. They were to be allowed to pursue their special trades and to belong to the Reich Music Chamber. Nine Gypsy "speakers" were named in each of nine cities to be in charge of this privileged community, which in effect consisted of not many more than the extended families of the speakers. Most of the others, including the Roma and Mischlinge, were to be deported to a concentration camp. On 29 January 1943 Heydrich designated Auschwitz as that camp. The Gypsy barracks, which he referred to as the *Zigeunerlager*, were located in Birkenau, a part of the Auschwitz complex where the gas chambers were.

The contrasting treatment of pure Gypsies and Gypsy Mischlinge was the reverse of the policy with respect to Jews. Pure Jews were to be killed, whereas half- and quarter-Jews were generally spared. On the other hand, Gypsy Mischlinge were doomed, because Himmler and German criminologists were convinced that only members of a German underclass, such as footloose swindlers (*Jenische*) who spoke a special dialect mixed with Hebrew and Romani words, would marry Gypsies.

The Heydrich directive did contain provisions for excepting certain individuals from deportation, among

Gypsies being deported from Simmering, a district in Vienna, to the transit camp of Bruck on the Leithe River. Late 1938

them "good" Mischlinge (if acceptable to the pure Gypsies), intermarried Gypsies, soldiers, and Gypsies with permanent addresses and jobs. Heydrich also stated, however, that the remaining Gypsies, other than the pure ones and the "good" Mischlinge, were to be sterilized.

Heydrich's instructions did not apply to Austria and areas outside the Reich, but subsequently they were extended to Austria, Alsace-Lorraine, Luxembourg, Belgium, the Netherlands, and the Bialystok district, which was attached to East Prussia. From all these regions, plus the so-called Protectorate of Bohemia and Moravia, approximately 22,700 Gypsies were brought to Auschwitz. About half came from the Old Reich. Czech Gypsies from Bohemia and Moravia numbered at least 4,500, Polish Gypsies (mainly from the Bialystok district) more than 3,000, and Austrian Gypsies 2,800. A total of 351 Gypsies arrived from Belgium, 246 from the Netherlands, and smaller groups from other areas. The registered Gypsies, whose names are known, were 20,943.

There was no plan to kill the deportees outright, but

when a Bialystok transport arrived with 1,700 Gypsies in March 1943, all these people were gassed without registration a few days later, because of a suspicion of typhus. Again, in May of that year, more than 1,000 registered Gypsies, the large majority of them from Bialystok, were gassed for the same reason.

The Auschwitz Gypsies were detained for more than a year. During that time several transports left for other destinations. On 9 November 1943 several hundred young and healthy Gypsies were transported to the Natzweiler concentration camp. On 15 April 1944, 1,357 were transferred, the men to Buchenwald, the women to Ravensbrück. On 24 May 1944, 226 young Gypsies were taken to Flossenburg and Ravensbrück. On 2 August 1944, 1,408 went to Buchenwald, and that evening the 2,897 remaining inmates of the *Zigeunerlager* were gassed. Gypsies were not listed in Auschwitz after that date, but on 5 October about 800 were returned from Buchenwald; five days later they were gassed.

The available Auschwitz statistics do not explain such factors as the arrival of many more young girls than boys or account for every death by date, but it is apparent that most of the deportees died in Birkenau of privation and that most of those deaths occurred in 1943. There were many children, a few hundred of whom were born in the camp, and although the Gypsies had brought along some food and could stay together as families, their resources and stamina declined rapidly. Notwithstanding any SS indecision about them, their detention in Auschwitz was tantamount to annihilation.

In the Generalgouvernement, which comprised the districts of Warsaw, Radom, Kraków, Lublin, and Galicia, several thousand Gypsies were doomed. Between April and June 1942 nearly a thousand Gypsies from the Warsaw district, including some Sinti who were probably 1940 deportees from Hamburg, were sent to the Warsaw ghetto. They were swept up in the deportation of the Jews that summer and gassed in Treblinka. In other regions of the Generalgouvernement Gypsies were shot from time to time in small batches. In the southern areas alone, there were more than 900 victims.

East of the Generalgouvernement lay the Soviet Union, which was invaded on 22 June 1941. A large territory was occupied, but there were no uniform guidelines in Gypsy affairs for the whole of this expanse. On 10 October 1941 the military commander in Belorussia, Gustav Freiherr von Bechtolsheim, ordered that roving Gypsies should be shot because they were a danger to his troops. In southern Latvia no distinction was made between Gypsies, and they were concentrated in three camps. From the camp at Ludza a young Gypsy, Janis Petrovs, sent an appeal to the German civil administration on 11 November 1941, pointing out that the prisoners had committed no crime and that they had either lived in the area or were refugees from Riga. All 234 Gypsies in Ludza were nevertheless shot. Similarly, in Estonia 243 Gypsies incarcerated in the Harku camp were shot on 27 October 1942.

Army Group Center, which was advancing toward Moscow, distinguished between Gypsies moving through the countryside and those who could prove a fixed domicile for at least two years. The former were to be shot, and their carts were to be confiscated. In fact, military units together with mobile units dispatched by Heydrich wiped out small groups of Gypsies encountered in this area. To the south there was also sporadic killing, but in the Crimea Gypsies were shot systematically, with the result that about 2,000 or more died.

German agencies were not the only initiators of lethal measures against Gypsies. One country that acted on its own was Romania. In this respect, the Romanian record vis-à-vis Gypsies mirrors Romanian activities against Jews. In 1941, following Romanian territorial losses by cession to neighboring states, the Romanian army reconquered northern Bukovina and Bessarabia from the Soviet Union. In addition, Romania acquired control over Transnistria, a territory between the Dniester and the Ukrainian Bug rivers. A large number of Jews were deported to Transnistria in 1941; most of them died of sickness or bullets. In the summer of 1942 the Romanian government decided to deport 12,000 nomadic Gypsies and 12,000–14,000 "dangerous ones" from what had been truncated Romania to Transnistria. That number was a substantial segment of the Gypsy population. About 20,000 of the deportees were concentrated at Kovalevka near the Bug, where 6,000 died of typhus and from where another 11,500 were transported to the nearby Trikhaty railroad station to be shot by an SS unit. Also in Transnistria, a Jewish survivor of the camp at Vapniarka, who delivered bread to an adjacent Gypsy camp in December 1942, noted that the inmates were barefoot and starving. He heard later that almost all had succumbed to typhus.

Yugoslavia was another major scene of actions against Gypsies. Its territory was occupied by German, Italian, Hungarian, and Bulgarian troops. The Germans annexed part of Slovenia and held Serbia under a military administration; Bulgaria acquired the Macedonian region; Hungary obtained Batchka and the Italians parts of Slovenia, Dalmatia, Kosovo, and Montenegro. Croatia, which included Slavonia, Bosnia, and Herzegovina, became a satellite state with two zones, one occupied by Germany, the other by Italy. This division of Yugoslavia also delineated to some extent the treatment of the Gypsy population.

In the Yugoslav census of 1931, 70,425 inhabitants listed Romani as their native language. Most of the Gypsies were Muslims, the remainder Catholic and Serbian Orthodox. The Italians, Hungarians, and Bulgarians did not shoot Gypsies, although Macedonian Gypsies were sent to do forced labor in Bulgaria. Croatia was cautious in its handling of the Muslim minority in Bosnia, which it courted. It called Muslim Gypsies "white" and even tried to protect them in German-occupied Serbia. The situation of the other Yugoslav Gypsies, however, was more hazardous.

In Serbia on 30 May 1941 the German military commander issued a decree against Jews and Gypsies under which both groups were subject to compulsory labor, a curfew, and the wearing of yellow arm bands. Both had to register with Serbian offices, which had to construct lists. The regulation was amended on 11 July 1941 to exempt Gypsies with "respected" occupations who carried on an orderly life and could trace their family domicile in a locality to 1850. Following the loss of German lives at the hands of partisans in October 1941, Jews and Gypsies were selected to be shot in reprisal. Several hundred young Gyspy men were killed. In a local reprisal action on 13 October 1941 Gypsy men, women, and children became victims alongside Serbs in Kragujevac, when German army units engaged in indiscriminate shooting. Again, in subsequent years, smaller numbers of Serbian Gypsies were occasionally seized and shot.

Croatia arrested most of its Jews in 1941 and killed them in Croatian camps. Then, in 1942, the round-up of the Gypsies was ordered on 19 May, and in early June thousands of them were transported to the Jasenovac camp, where the large majority eventually perished.

Short of outright killing, measures against Gypsies were taken in other countries as well. Slovak Gypsies had to perform forced labor, and in France the Vichy regime interned nearly 3,000 nomadic Gypsies in camps, which also served as pools for involuntary labor and in which food rations were at times as low as 1,400 calories a day.

In sum, Gypsies were targeted for a variety of stated reasons. From country to country their victimization could depend on whether they were Mischlinge or pure Gypsies, nomadic or sedentary, Christian or Muslim. In the end, however, men, women, and children died as a result of hunger, disease, bullets, or gas because they were Gypsies. The census data and documents uncovered so far do not allow precise calculations of the final toll, but the sources at hand indicate that many Gypsies lost most members of their families and that entire Gypsy communities were wiped out altogether. *Raul Hilberg*

Haavara "Transfer agreement" between the German economic ministry, the Zionist Organization of Germany, and the Anglo-Palestine bank, concluded in August 1933, according to which Jewish emigrants from Germany could transfer part of their property to Palestine in the form of export of German goods. This agreement remained in force up to 1938.

Heydrich, Reinhard (1904–42) Chief of the RSHA (Reich Security Main Office). Heydrich played a pivotal role in planning the Final Solution. He ordered the concentration of Polish Jews in ghettos, planned the deportation of German Jews, and organized the *Einsatzgruppen* (mobile killing units). In January 1942 he convened the Wannsee Conference, a meeting of top Nazi officials to confirm a plan for the extermination of the Jews. Heydrich was assassinated by Czech parachutists in June 1942 while serving as deputy head of the German military administration in Prague. See Bohemia and Moravia, Protectorate of; Final Solution: Preparation and Implementation

Himmler, Heinrich (1900–1945) Head of the SS and German minister of the interior, during the war second only to Adolf Hitler in the Nazi hierarchy. Himmler was the main figure in the terror apparatus of the Third Reich and the Nazi leader more directly involved than any other in the Final Solution. He established Dachau, the first concentration camp in Germany, and the extermination camps of Eastern Europe. During the last phase of the war, he stopped the mass murders and advised that Germany surrender to Eisenhower, whereupon Hitler stripped him of power. Himmler was captured by the British at the end of the war but committed suicide before he could be brought to trial. See Final Solution: Preparation and Implementation

Hirsch, Otto (1885–1941) Chairman of the Reichsvertretung der Deutschen Juden (Reich Representative Council of German Jews). Killed in Mauthausen concentration camp. See Reichsvertretung der Deutschen Juden

Historiography The word *holocaust*, widely used in North America since the early 1970s to refer to the wartime persecution and murder of European Jewry, is itself the object of dispute. Most scholars have come to accept the term, which obtained legitimacy during the 1960s, having appeared extensively in the writings of the Nobel Prize laureate Elie Wiesel. Some continue to challenge this usage, however. Preferring the Hebrew word *shoah*—a biblical term denoting a terrible and unforeseen disaster—or even *Judeocide,* critics consider the original Greek meaning of *holocaust*—a sacrifice totally consumed by fire—as singularly inappropriate terminology for mass murder without any sacrificial meaning and having nothing necessarily to do with fire. A minority have also challenged the exclusive focus on Jews, arguing that the victimization the Sinti and Roma (Gypsies), for example, and the murderous assault on some Eastern European peoples should be considered part of a common process. Some would include in the Holocaust all victims of Nazi wartime atrocities, numbering about 11 million persons. Still others would apply the term *holocaust* only in a generic sense to denote any large-scale massacre, without any necessary reference to Nazis or Jews.

Despite the terminological imprecisions or inaccuracies associated with the word's origins, most English-speaking historians (and many others as well) accept that the term *Holocaust,* as a proper noun, signals a certain uniqueness in the motivation and the process of the Nazis' victimization of European Jewry. At the same time, historians commonly seek connections

Himmler inspects Dachau. 8 May 1936

with other victims of nazism and with other episodes of mass killing, both during the war and throughout history. They continue to disagree on the right balance, however, with some approaching the subject from the wider perspective of victimization and others concentrating more specifically on the Jews. Indeed, balance is the most important continuing challenge for Holocaust historians.

The historiography of the Holocaust parallels that of Nazi Germany in many respects. As with writing on the Third Reich, there is disagreement over beginnings, especially the place of antisemitism in the assessment of origins. To be sure, no one denies the great importance of Jew hatred in Hitler's personal ideology—to the point that many see it at the very core of his worldview. And few would dispute the importance of antisemitism within the Nazi leadership, in the policies of the regime, and in German and European society. The problem is one of emphasis. How important was opposition to the Jews in the Nazis' campaign for

power before 1933? What are the links between Hitler's own hatred of Jews, the antisemitism of the Nazis, and the attitude toward Jews of the German population as a whole? What role did calculation and ideology play in the campaign against the Jews of Germany from the moment Hitler became chancellor in 1933? By what process did antisemitic policies escalate to the ultimate anti-Jewish objective—pan-European mass murder? Historians have also tried to determine the place of anti-Jewish rhetoric and thought in evaluating the responses of the Jews themselves and of bystanders both inside Nazi-occupied Europe and elsewhere—particularly in North and South America—to the destruction of European Jewry.

Historians differ on the motivations behind anti-Jewish mobilization and on the degree to which Nazi anti-Jewish policies formed part of a coherent, predetermined program. Although few would dispute that Hitler had a key role in decisions concerning the Jews, historians differ on how closely he followed events, on the extent to which he directed Nazi Jewish policy, and on when he determined that comprehensive mass murder was the goal of Nazi policy toward the Jews. Debate over both the timing and the character of the decisions taken has been extensive, owing largely to a paucity of documentary evidence on the decision-making process. Since Hitler preferred to give orders on the subject orally, and since he often chose to inspire subordinates to act rather than to dictate a specific course of action, historians' assessments are often quite speculative.

Intentionalists, such as Lucy Dawidowicz, Gerald Fleming, or Richard Breitman, see both Hitler's ideas about the Jews and the Nazis' anti-Jewish program of the mid-1930s as pointing deliberately to the genocide. War, according to this perspective, simply gave Hitler a pretext to carry out a long-considered, murderous objective on a grand scale. Some intentionalists have investigated the roots of Nazi antisemitism in the German or European past. These writers have different points of emphasis: some look to Christian anti-Jewish motifs common to many European societies; some have explored the *völkisch* or racist ideology of late nineteenth-century Germany, and still others have sought to associate anti-Jewish thinking with some of the deepest currents of German culture. In a recent return to a viewpoint commonly expressed in the immediate postwar period, Daniel Goldhagen has argued that Germany was the home of a particularly virulent anti-Jewish commitment, which he terms "eliminationist antisemitism," that permeated the culture and required the removal of the Jews from German society. In Goldhagen's view, Hitler launched a murderous program that countless Germans truly desired.

To other historians, antisemitism is too limiting an ideological perspective in which to understand the genocidal ambitions of nazism. In light of the radicalization of Jewish policy during Operation Barbarossa against the Soviet Union in 1941, they understand the murder of European Jews in the context of the Nazis' unbounded ambitions for Eastern Europe—the creation of a *Lebensraum,* "living space," in which the German people would be regenerated—a transformation involving catastrophic consequences for indigenous peoples, especially Jews. In a study of Auschwitz, Debórah Dwork and Robert-Jan van Pelt situate the death camp within the framework of a centuries-long vision of German settlement in Eastern Europe. Located on the frontier of German colonization, the town

of Auschwitz stimulated the imagination of Nazi occupation officials to create a terrifying Utopia that required the uprooting of millions of local inhabitants, the creation of new cities and highways, the slave labor of hundreds of thousands, and of course the elimination of the Jews.

Functionalists, including Hans Mommsen, Uwe Dietrich Adam, Christopher Browning, and Philippe Burrin, stress the evolution of Nazi policy toward the Jews and contend that mass murder emerged as a realistic option only during the ideologically charged Barbarossa campaign. They see the Nazis as groping toward a "solution" of a "Jewish problem" that they themselves had defined. A comprehensive strategy of mass murder was adopted, they argue, only when other options were blocked and when, through trial and error, they had developed techniques by which an entire people could be destroyed. Several interpreters, notably Martin Broszat, point to the frustration of local decisionmakers with Berlin's inattention to Jewish policy in the early years of the war, and to the intense competition among such officials to reach an ideologically sound outcome, as pivotal factors in the move toward genocide. Their initiatives, it is claimed, launched and extended the killing process to the point that it became a pan-European program during the course of 1942. Christopher Browning, Saul Friedländer, and others have criticized the notion of local initiatives, even while agreeing with Broszat's picture of the confusion and rivalry within the Nazi administration. Instead they see the impulse for the Final Solution as coming rather from the center—from Hitler himself.

When were the principal decisions for pan-European killing actually taken? Most intentionalists look to the planning phase for the Barbarossa campaign, and some see a crucial shift in the direction of mass murder as early as March 1941. Among functionalists, some believe that Hitler decided on the Final Solution during the summer of 1941, in the midst of the first euphoric victories against the Soviet Union. Others identify the point when Nazi policy crossed the line to killing throughout Europe shortly thereafter, in the autumn, when Hitler realized that Germany would not achieve an early victory over the Soviets and lashed out at the Jews in anger and frustration. Christopher Browning contends that there were *two* decisions for mass murder. The first, in mid-July, called for the elimination of Soviet Jewry and is marked by Himmler's dispatch of vast numbers of Order Police to captured Soviet territory. The second, in early October, occurred when Hitler approved the deportation of Jews eastward from the Reich following Germany's spectacular military successes in Ukraine and during the Wehrmacht's seemingly unstoppable progress toward Moscow. These writers offer various interpretations of the motivation of decisionmakers: some see a leadership flushed with victory, whereas others see a vengeful, frustrated reaction prompted by the first taste of defeat.

Following Raul Hilberg's pathbreaking book *The Destruction of the European Jews* (1961), perhaps the most important single work ever written on the Holocaust, some scholars concentrated more on the "how" than the "why" of the subject. They explored the ways in which the Nazis mobilized the resources of the modern state for the purpose of murdering millions. Historians who investigate such questions are preoccupied with the vast scale and extent of the murderous enterprise, which was carried out across an entire continent and administered by large bureaucracies, with broad complicity throughout German and European society. In his magisterial synthesis Hilberg, influenced by his mentor at Columbia University, Franz Neumann, developed the notion of "the machinery of destruction." This image of a machine—suggesting powerful, impersonal forces operating independently of individual decisionmakers—reflects a widespread sense of the Nazi apparatus that turned against the Jews and its capacity to engage an ever-widening circle of perpetrators in the murderous task.

Historians following Hilberg have investigated various dimensions of the murder process, attempting to understand the Holocaust by looking in detail at parts of the machinery of destruction. Studies have appeared on various elements of the SS (by Helmut Krausnick and Hans-Heinrich Wilhelm, Robert Koehl, and Ruth Bettina Birn), on the Wehrmacht (by Jürgen Förster), on the purge of Jews from the German economy (by Helmut Genschel), on the Jewish section of the Foreign Office (by Christopher Browning), on German public opinion (by Ian Kershaw, Otto Dov Kulka, and Avraham Barkai), on German population policy (by Götz Aly), as well as on specific localities. This growing list of studies underscores the complexity of the process of killing throughout Europe, the varying degrees of involvement from country to country, and the need to understand sectors of society and government within their own particular contexts.

For scholars such as the sociologist Zygmunt Bau-

man, the key to understanding the Holocaust lies in the "modernity" of the Third Reich—the Nazis' freedom from the constraints of traditional society, their forward-looking goals, and their use of the most up-to-date bureaucratic, scientific, and technological methods. Clearly implied in this interpretation is the susceptibility of other modern societies to turn to mass killing and genocide as a way of solving problems—a point made many years ago by Richard Rubenstein in his writings on the Holocaust. Close examination of the killing process, however, may not bear out the contention that the murder of European Jewry was a quintessentially modern phenomenon. As several writers have insisted, popular understanding of the Holocaust has been distracted by an excessive focus on gas chambers and crematoriums, such as existed in the Birkenau death camp. But much of the murder of Jews in Eastern Europe, as Goldhagen in particular has reminded us, was conducted by firing squads—massacres that hardly benefited from the application of modern organizational methods or scientific technique—and many deaths resulted from beatings, disease, and starvation under the inhuman conditions imposed by the Nazis. Moreover, everything we have learned about the killing process in Auschwitz and the other death camps suggests that the murder machinery owed more to artisanal fabrication than to the kind of scientific and technological innovations that produced high-speed aircraft or the atomic bomb.

For other historians, what counts is less science than pseudo-science. The Nazi obsession with a racial utopia and with geopolitics, rooted in Darwinism and energized by thoughts of empire, extended far beyond a fixation with Jews. Michael Burleigh and Wolfgang Wippermann's *The Racial State: Germany 1933–1945* (1991) stresses the broadly gauged effort of national socialism to transform German society along racial lines—to create a hierarchical *Volksgemeinschaft*, or "national community," purged of unwanted elements and resplendent with biological and spiritual health. In his *Toward the Final Solution* (1995) Henry Friedlander carefully documents the way in which killing operations against the disabled, Gypsies, and Jews were linked by a pseudo-scientific belief in inequality and a determination to cleanse the German nation of so-called inferior biological traits.

In her reports on the 1961 trial of Adolf Eichmann (which first appeared in the *New Yorker* and then were published as a book, *Eichmann in Jerusalem*), Hannah

Hannah Arendt upon arrival in the United States.

Arendt popularized the notion of the "banality of evil" as a vehicle for understanding lower- and middle-ranking perpetrators. The theme was picked up in a study of mass murders committed by one police battalion from Hamburg in a book by Christopher Browning entitled, appropriately enough, *Ordinary Men* (1992). From Arendt's and Browning's vantage point the behavior of organizers, facilitators, and lower-echelon persecutors, as well as those involved more directly in killing, can be explained in large measure by the circumstances in which the perpetrators found themselves: persons of diverse backgrounds, acting together in groups, influenced by group loyalties, careerist ambitions, conformity, and the pressures of a repressive regime.

At issue in assessing the notion of the banality of evil is an understanding of not only those who did the actual killing but also the great army of "desk murderers" and other workers who took charge of transportation, scheduling, construction, and disposal of the Jews' property. In *Vordenker der Vernichtung* (Visionaries of Destruction, 1993) Götz Aly and Susanne Heim examine part of this process, focusing on middle-echelon German administrators—technocrats whose commitment to economic rationalization and modernization, they claim, pointed toward the elimination of the Jews within the Nazi empire, particularly in Poland. This understanding of the perpetrators contrasts with approaches that stress the high degree of ideological motivation and the often irrational decisionmaking involved in a policy of mass murder—not least the wasteful elimination of a highly skilled Jewish labor force.

One line of inquiry has focused on societies drawn into the orbit of the Third Reich—allies, collaborators, occupied populations, and neutrals. During the 1970s and 1980s studies began to appear examining the impact of the Holocaust in various European localities. Important works have been written on France (by Michael Marrus and Robert Paxton, Serge Klarsfeld, Asher Cohen, and André Kaspi), Belgium (by Maxime Steinberg; also a collection edited by Dan Michman), the Netherlands (by Jacob Presser, Louis de Jong, and Bob Moore), Denmark (by Leni Yahil and Hans Kirchhoff), Hungary (by Randolph Braham), and Romania (by Jean Ancel). An important common thread is that German officials, sorely stretched in terms of manpower and reluctant to bear the burden of anti-Jewish actions, preferred whenever possible that local authorities take responsibility for the persecution, round-up, and deportation of the local Jewish population. Collaborationist regimes and German allies, for the most part, did not disappoint. In Vichy France, which had a considerable degree of independence, the French authorities were much more enthusiastic in proceeding against foreign Jews than they were in the deportation of native French Jews. Whereas Robert Paxton and Michael Marrus have shown an important Vichy initiative in anti-Jewish persecutions in 1940 and 1941, they also note the mounting reluctance, as the war turned against Nazi Germany, to participate in a brutal and public process that involved sending Jews to near-certain deaths. Randolph Braham's *The Politics of Genocide* (1981) makes similar distinctions with respect to Hungarian policy: although the Hungarians energetically and on their own initiative persecuted the Jews during the first part of the war, the government in Budapest withheld Jews from deportation to extermination camps and yielded only after the Germans occupied the country in March 1944.

Denmark and Italy provide interesting exceptions. The Jews benefited from Denmark's position as the "model protectorate" within the German empire during the first years of the war. Then in 1943, with the intensified repression by the Germans and with the local population increasingly restive, there was an attempt to move against the small group of 7,000 Jews. What happened next remains a matter of some dispute. In October almost all the Jews escaped to a Swedish haven thanks to the Danish rescuers who ferried them across a narrow body of water to Sweden. Was this a rescue in which a heroic and democratically minded population outwitted the Germans? Or was the entire affair the result of a maneuver by the German occupation, headed by the SS police expert Werner Best, who, wanting at a stroke to rid Denmark of its Jewish presence, made sure that the Jews were warned? Leni Yahil's classic *The Rescue of the Danish Jewry* (1969), now supported by the Danish historian Hans Kirchhoff, takes the former position; other scholars, emphasizing one aspect or another of the complicated German decisionmaking process, take the latter.

Italian society responded differently from others to the German-initiated anti-Jewish campaign. Books by Renzo De Felice, Meir Michaelis, Susan Zuccotti, Jonathan Steinberg, and Daniel Carpi have indicated how unenthusiastic important segments of the Italian population were when it came to persecuting the Jews and deporting them to Eastern Europe. What accounts for this reluctance on the part of Italians both high and low to join their Axis partner? Historians have offered a variety of explanations: the absence of a powerful current of antisemitism in Italian society, because Jews were very few and were well integrated; the inability of the Fascist regime fully to control that society and to extinguish a historic pattern of civility; the Italians' distrust of Nazi-style racism that only thinly disguised German sentiments of superiority; and Italian war-weariness and resentment of German-imposed schemes.

Thanks to these studies of particular European countries, comparative analyses are now possible. A well-known example that uses sophisticated statistical techniques is Helen Fein's *Accounting for Genocide* (1979). The problem with such comparisons, of course, is that one is never quite comparing equal circumstances. Some countries, such as Poland and Hungary, had huge Jewish populations; others, such as Finland, Norway, and Denmark, had only a few thousand. The Germans considered countries like Poland to be in the heart of their European empire and sphere of interest, whereas they saw Bulgaria and other countries as being on the periphery. Inevitably, the outcome was shaped not only by the specific conditions for Jews in various countries but also by the shifting Nazi priorities, the play of local forces, and the changing circumstances of war.

The role of bystanders outside Nazi-occupied Europe has become an important theme of inquiry among historians of the Holocaust. One school, associated in particular with the earliest wave of writing on the subject, tends to condemn the democratic countries and their leaders for failure to take any significant steps (such as easing immigration quotas, facilitating the passage of Jews to neutral countries, or bombing the access routes to extermination camps or the camps themselves) on behalf of the Jews of Europe. The titles of these works declare their point of view: *While Six Million Died,* by Arthur Morse (1967); *The Jews Were Expendable,* by Monty Penkower (1983); and *The Abandonment of the Jews,* by David Wyman (1984). The emphasis in these works is plainly on what did *not* happen—information on the Holocaust was not digested, Jews were not admitted as refugees, Jewish communities outside Europe failed to unite, and proposals for rescue operations were rejected. Historians have called to account not only the policies of the Allies but also those of neutral countries, such as Sweden, Spain, and Switzerland (and the banks in that country), and international institutions, such as the Vatican and the International Committee of the Red Cross.

In recent years there has been some break in this highly critical writing on bystanders. Revisionist works seek to understand reactions in particular contexts—highlighting the onlookers' failure to grasp clearly what was happening to the Jews, their vulnerability, their fear of heightening antisemitism at home, the lack of precedent for dealing with a calamity of this character, the distraction of other issues, and the lack of resources available to construct viable alternatives to strict neutrality or to the Allies' focus on prosecuting the war. Richard Breitman, Alan Kraut, and Henry Feingold have written cogently on the United States in this vein. On the response of the Yishuv (the organized Jewish community in Palestine)—there have been several works, notably Dina Porat's *The Blue and Yellow Stars of David* (1990) and Dalia Ofer's *Escaping the Holocaust* (1990), a study of illegal immigration to Palestine. Both of these works consider the way in which the organized Jewish community came to terms with the Jewish catastrophe through the intellectual framework of Zionist ideology. Important new research suggests that, along with a deadly complicity and shameful abdication of responsibility, there was also ignorance, confusion, and distraction outside the Nazi orbit, along with the indifference, fear, and intimidation more common in occupied Europe. Judgments, in short, have gone from studies in black and white to those that include some shades of gray.

In a further departure from the earlier preoccupation with accusation, some historians have turned to the study of rescue—a theme popularized by the film *Schindler's List* (1994)—in an attempt to comprehend the historical dynamics of altruism. Research on circumstances as different as those in France and Poland, for example, has shown that assistance to Jews was considerable in Nazi-occupied Europe, and that tens of thousands of Europeans may have been involved in high-risk activity on behalf of their Jewish neighbors. Here too the challenge is to get the balance right. There have sometimes been heated disputes over the relative importance of rescue activity—whether it should be understood as a rare exception to a general pattern of hostility and indifference or as a sign that the Nazis' propaganda and intimidation failed to eliminate the basic decency of substantial numbers of Europeans. Pulling together some of the threads of rescue in a recent volume, *The Altruistic Personality* (1988), Samuel and Pearl Oliner have championed the study of rescue as a necessary accompaniment to historical inquiries into the motivations and activities of the killers.

Another focus of attention is the comportment of the Jews themselves. Prompted in part by passages in Arendt's *Eichmann in Jerusalem* and Hilberg's *Destruction of the European Jews*, some historians took up the charge, originally made by young Jewish resistance fighters in the ghettos of Eastern Europe, that European Jews went to their deaths "like sheep to the slaughter." Arendt's focus was really on the complicity of the leadership of the *Judenräte*, the Nazi-imposed Jewish councils set up across Europe. Hilberg's charge was that traditional patterns of Jewish behavior militated powerfully against open resistance. Since the 1960s historians interested in this issue—many of them from Israel, in particular Israel Gutman and Yehuda Bauer—have heavily criticized this point of view. We now have the magisterial work of Isaiah Trunk on the Judenräte of occupied Poland, which presents a far better informed and balanced view than that of Arendt, together with numerous monographic studies of particular ghettos under Nazi rule. Critics of the idea of Jewish passivity have underscored the limited resources that Jews had available to them. The Jews had few allies, were sometimes the target of the active hostility of the surrounding society, had at their disposal few sources of intelligence and supply, and consequently possessed the most meager capacity to strike out against the Germans or their allies. Comparative studies, in addition, have shown that Jewish reactions to extreme situations did not differ appreciably from those of other groups, notably Soviet prisoners of war, some 3.3 million of whom were murdered, out of a total of 5.7 million captured.

Researchers have discovered a variety of Jewish responses to the Germans, from automatic compliance to extraordinary efforts to buy time, in order to maintain individual and collective dignity, to survive, or to communicate an account of the Jewish ordeal to an outside world or a future generation. Using source material produced by the Jews themselves, historians have combed the surviving documentation from ghettos of Eastern Europe and have edited numerous diaries of Jews who experienced persecution, life underground, flight, deportation, and the camps. Israeli scholar Renée Poznanski's *Etre Juif en France pendant la Seconde Guerre Mondiale* (1994) is an outstanding book on the daily life of Jews in France during the war; studies in a similar vein are likely to appear for various countries and regions.

As part of this trend there has been substantial work on Jewish resistance—both in Western and Central Europe, where underground activity was mainly devoted to rescue, and in Eastern Europe, where, in addition to dangerous strategies to ameliorate the lot of stricken Jewish communities, there were several important ghetto revolts and even a few uprisings in camps. The Warsaw ghetto uprising has been highlighted in Israel Gutman's *The Jews of Warsaw* (1982) and occupies an important symbolic place in the history of Jewish reactions to the Holocaust. There is now a growing body of literature on such diverse matters as Jewish partisans in Eastern Europe, the Jewish underground in ghettos, and Jewish existence in concentration and death camps. *Michael R. Marrus*

Hitler, Adolf (1889–1945) Adolf Hitler was born on 20 April 1889 in Braunau am Inn, a small Austrian border town, where his father was a customs official. He spent five years in primary school, moved to Linz, then to Steyr, where he was a boarder, and finally to Vienna in 1907. There Hitler, who had artistic aspirations, sold some of his drawings and paintings of the city to tourists, produced posters for small traders, and tried, unsuccessfully, to gain entrance to the Academy of

Adolf Hitler. "Ein Volk—ein Reich—ein Führer" (One people—one nation—one leader)

Graphic Arts. Isolated, embittered, and with a loathing of the multinational Austro-Hungarian Empire, whose very existence was an insult to racists and a certain kind of German nationalist, the young man made his way to Munich in 1913. On the outbreak of war in August of the following year, he enlisted in the Bavarian army. Decorated twice and promoted to corporal in 1917, Hitler saw in that great conflict the camaraderie that united Germans against a common enemy, a unity that was in his view tragically absent from the divisive politics of postwar Germany. While in the hospital recovering from a mustard gas attack, Hitler first learned of his country's surrender—in the wake, as he thought, not so much of military defeat as of domestic revolution, which engulfed the Reich in the first two weeks of November 1918 and ushered in the democratic experiment that was the Weimar Republic.

When he left the hospital, Hitler moved to Munich, the Bavarian capital, where he became active in extremist right-wing politics while working as an informer for the military. He quickly established a reputation as an impressive speaker with one of the many racist and nationalist (*völkisch*) groups in the city, the German Workers' Party (Deutsche Arbeiterpartei, DAP), which was led by the locksmith Anton Drexler and combined antisemitism with a somewhat ill-defined social radicalism, especially in its hostility to big business. On 24 February 1920 the small group changed its name to the National Socialist German Workers' Party (Nationalsozialistische Deutsche Arbeiterpartei, NSDAP or Nazi party) and adopted a program calling not only for the revision of the Treaty of Versailles and the return of lost territories in France and Poland but also for the unification of all ethnic Germans in a single Reich and the exclusion of all Jews from citizenship. To these racist and nationalist demands, however, the program added certain economic aims, which included the expropriation of war profiteers, nationalization of industrial trusts, communalization of large department stores, and abolition of unearned incomes. Whether this radical social project ever meant much to Hitler is open to doubt, although his racism and nationalism are not. In any case, as his party sought to woo middle-class supporters in the late 1920s, this economic radicalism was explicitly disavowed by Hitler, who explained to one audience in 1928 that it was only Jewish property that would be confiscated by a Nazi state.

In Munich in the early 1920s Hitler met many of those who were later to play a major role in the Nazi movement before 1933 and the governance of the Third Reich thereafter: Hermann Göring, Ernst Röhm, Rudolf Hess, and Alfred Rosenberg. They shared his belief that Germany had been betrayed at the end of the war, that the country was confronted by the menace of Marxism, and that the nation had to be rid of Jews. Some of them became lifelong friends of Hitler, who possessed the ability to engender an intense personal loyalty. At that time the NSDAP was only one of many radical right-wing groups in the city. Together with some of those groups and the disaffected war hero Gen. Erich Ludendorff, the party became involved in a rather pathetic attempt to seize power, the so-called Beer Hall Putsch of 8 November 1923. In the wake of the putsch's failure the Nazi party was declared illegal, and Hitler was imprisoned in the Bavarian town of Landsberg am Lech, where he was to write *Mein Kampf.*

Mein Kampf, insofar as it possesses any structure at all, is partly an autobiography and partly an account of the early history of the NSDAP. On both counts it is highly unreliable, badly written, repetitious, crude in its argument, and blatant in its prejudices. Much of the book deals with the issue of propaganda: Hitler believed that the masses were swayed, not by logical argument or the presentation of detailed evidence, but by an appeal to their emotions and prejudices through the constant repetition of a few simple but vehemently expressed ideas. This premise helps to explain the intellectual deficiencies and stylistic inadequacies of *Mein Kampf.* The book was not intended as an elegant piece of prose but rather was meant to echo verbal propaganda, for Hitler believed the spoken to be more powerful than the written word. The most persistent and vitriolic part of *Mein Kampf* articulates Hitler's vicious antisemitism, founded in illegitimate logic and a scarcely digested pseudo-science. In the central chapter "People and Race" he asserts that humans can be divided into three races, between whom a state of constant and unavoidable warfare obtains: the creators of culture, invariably "Aryan" (a term abused and never defined); the bearers of culture, capable of imitation but not initiation of culture (also undefined and normally confused with military or political strength); and those who destroy culture—the Jews. Small groups of Aryans create civilizations through the subjugation of inferior peoples, but subsequent intermixing with these inferiors (the "sin against the blood") leads to inevitable decline and destruction. Hence Hitler came to believe that it was the state's foremost duty to maintain the purity of the Aryan race.

Bereft of the qualities that Hitler believed to be exclusive to Aryans (for him a term synonymous with "Nordic" or "Germanic"), namely the capacity for selfless labor, the fulfillment of public duty, and self-sacrifice for the communal good—the Jew (whose Jewishness is held to be genetically determined and not a question of religious belief) in this world view is the embodiment of duplicitous evil. The Nazi leader held that Jews were incapable of sacrificing themselves for a greater good. They were self-interested materialists seeking to control the world through an improbable conspiracy of international finance capital and international Marxism. Jews aimed to subvert real nations/races (words Hitler used interchangeably), not only through capitalist dominance and socialist subversion, but also through sexual intercourse with their Aryan superiors. Jews were parasites: they were rats, germs, a plague of bacilli, and they were responsible for Ger-

many's defeat in World War I, American intervention in that war, the Russian and German revolutions of 1917–18, the Treaty of Versailles, and even syphilis. The language used to describe Jews in this absurd malice was not without significance: the portrayal of a group as inhuman legitimates its treatment in an inhuman fashion. If Jews were vermin, then they should be treated as such and eliminated.

It is tempting to see these antisemitic rantings as the product of some kind of psychopathology, and volumes have been produced that attempt to identify Hitler as a madman. It is true that he had a somewhat obsessive nature, that he was a hypochondriac, and that he was extremely fastidious about his food—he became a vegetarian in the 1930s. He was preoccupied with personal cleanliness, possessed an incredible belief in his own destiny, found it difficult, if not impossible, to accept contradiction, and on occasion behaved publicly in an apparently manic way, as in the tantrums thrown in front of foreign diplomats or the hysteria that seems to inform film records of his public speeches. But to view Hitler as in the thrall of uncontrollable psychic processes is not wholly accurate. Hitler often behaved eccentrically for instrumental reasons: his speeches were carefully rehearsed, and even his gestures were practiced in front of mirrors. It is scarcely surprising that as the war ran on to its disastrous conclusion for the Führer, he lost touch with reality: by the spring of 1945 he was living in remote forests, dependent on drugs for the alleviation of illnesses real or imagined, and confronted by enormous military and political problems. Before the defeats of 1942, however, there is little sign of anything that could be described as madness in Hitler's behavior.

Mental illness was no necessary condition for virulent antisemitism. Hitler's hostility toward Jews, like his violent antipathy to socialism, was little different from the attitudes of many people in Eastern and Central Europe in the early twentieth century. Indeed, his views were relatively commonplace in Viennese café society. It is probably significant that Hitler came from Austria rather than the more western parts of Germany, where Jews were more integrated and far less numerous than in the east. In Eastern Europe, race achieved a political significance partly because national and ethnic boundaries did not overlap. Moreover, the growing self-awareness of other racial groups within the multinational Austro-Hungarian Empire generated a response among the dominant Germans, some of whom, such as Georg von Schönerer, the founder of Pan-Germanism, came to advocate the creation of a single German Reich to incorporate all ethnic Germans. The virulence of popular antisemitism in parts of Eastern Europe was also a response to the fact that the Jews were both more numerous there than in the German Reich and more visible, insofar as Jews in the East were less assimilated and far more likely to live in ghettos. (The Jews who made up less than 1 percent of the population of the Weimar Republic did not.)

A major problem concerns whether the brutal antisemitism that Hitler displayed in *Mein Kampf* constituted a blueprint for racial policies in the Third Reich and in particular for the Final Solution—the attempted annihilation of European Jewry. Many historians have seen a direct line from the vicious remarks of that book to the extermination camps. Others have cast doubt on this "intentionalist" explanation of the Holocaust, preferring to stress the chaos of governmental decision making, multiple pressures from competing organizations and "from below," and the apparent variations and vacillations in policy over time. Even if *Mein Kampf* and Hitler's antisemitic views did not elaborate a master plan for later policies, they did, in Ian Kershaw's words, constitute a "framework for action" for those who believed they were implementing the Führer's wishes. Without those views the Final Solution would have been inconceivable.

Apart from the central issue of antisemitism, *Mein Kampf* concerned itself with the proper foreign policy aims of the German state: the revocation of the Treaty of Versailles, the return to Germany of lands lost to Poland and France in that treaty, and the unification of all ethnic Germans in a single Reich (*ein Volk, ein Reich*). This last demand already took Hitler's territorial ambitions beyond the limits of the Second Reich; the same was true of his claim that the overcrowded German people should find "living space" (*Lebensraum*) elsewhere. It could not be found through colonial acquisitions, which might alienate Britain (the fatal mistake of German foreign policy before 1914) and were difficult to defend, but beckoned in the East—in particular in Russia, where a Jewish conspiracy had, according to Hitler, brought the Bolsheviks to power. Thus a war for *Lebensraum* in the East would also be a holy crusade against communism and Jewry.

Hitler was released from Landsberg jail at the end of 1924 and returned to *völkisch* politics in a strong position, for the trial had made him a hero at a time when the NSDAP was torn by internal divisions. When these rivalries began to look as if they might threaten his own position, Hitler engineered a party conference in Bamberg in 1926, at which he dispensed with his more radical and North German rivals. Henceforth his leadership of the Nazi movement was to be uncontested, and former critics such as Joseph Goebbels came over to the Hitler camp. In the next two years the party underwent a major reorganization, which equipped it for its later electoral successes and swallowed up virtually all the remaining far-right, racist groups. Hitler's successes within the Nazi movement were not yet mirrored in the wider world of German politics, however. In the Reichstag elections of 1928, for example, the NSDAP won just 2.6 percent of the total votes cast.

The rise of the Nazi party and of its leader, Adolf Hitler, to national prominence in the years after 1928 was as spectacular as it was rapid. In the Reichstag elections of 1930 the NSDAP won 18.3 percent of the vote, and by the first of two national elections in 1932 it had seen that figure rise to 37.4 percent. Hitler was now the leader of by far the largest political party in Weimar Germany, albeit one that still enjoyed no share in national government. The Nazi leader's importance for the party's electoral success cannot be doubted. It was he who held the rival factions within the movement together and invested it with a good deal of its dynamism. His power as a public speaker was acknowledged by many contemporaries who attended the party's political rallies. Yet that success also rested on the development of a unique propaganda machine within the NSDAP, the creation primarily of Joseph Goebbels. Not only did Goebbels's propaganda department play on the traditional themes of middle-class and conservative German politics—anticommunism, antisocialism, nationalism, and the revocation of the Treaty of Versailles—but it also had offices that issued specialized messages to different sections of the population. It promised small retailers protection against department stores, agricultural protection against foreign food imports, subsidies, and sharp reductions in taxation, and big business the demolition of Weimar labor legislation that was seen as giving too much power to the unions, the restoration of management's "right to manage," and reductions in taxation and insurance contributions. Perhaps even more important, the Nazi party made sure its propaganda reached the German provinces, which had been largely ignored by the established political organizations. Never implicated in government and with a relatively young and supposedly uncorrupted leadership, the NSDAP combined its nationalism and antisocialism with a more populist claim to speak for the small man and the previously disenfranchised—hence its success in winning the support of so many previous nonvoters.

Of course, the skill of Hitler and his fellow Nazi propagandists is only part of the story of his rise to power. Most obviously they were able to exploit the multiple problems that the Weimar Republic had to confront: military defeat and the humiliation of Versailles, widespread antidemocratic values among the German middle class, the loss of power and privilege of big business, agriculture, and the military to the representatives of labor and the trade unions, resulting in a sea change in industrial relations and the advent of direct taxation. Yet even this combination of Nazi skills and governmental difficulties does not tell the whole story. Why, after all, did those skills produce so little result before 1929? In fact there is some evidence to suggest that, at least in the early stages, the propaganda and electoral slogans of the NSDAP followed rather than caused the breakthrough at the polling booths. For example, up to 1928 the party devoted most of its efforts to winning votes among the working class of urban Germany. The failure of that strategy—indeed the first Nazi electoral gains in 1928 came in some of the rural areas of Protestant Germany, such as Lower Saxony and Schleswig-Holstein—led the Nazis to change the main thrust of their propaganda thereafter to the middle-class and agrarian districts.

Why, though, did Nazi electoral propaganda have so much greater an impact after 1929? One factor was the increasingly professional organization of the NSDAP, especially its propaganda wing, and the fact that the party switched to more promising electoral targets in 1928. Other factors, however, were far beyond party control. The onset of the world economic crisis in the wake of the Wall Street crash in October 1929 compounded the difficulties of an economy that was already fragile on account of its dependence on foreign loans and in which agriculture and heavy industry (coal, iron, and steel) were already experiencing problems of demand and foreign competition. The crisis now threw agriculture into a massive indebtedness, which made rural communities all the more aggrieved by taxation than they had been when agricultural prices were fairly high in 1918–22. Falling prices destroyed the profitability of big and especially small businesses, making aspects of the Weimar system (insurance contributions, welfare taxation, and the supposed power of the trade unions) infinitely less tolerable than they had been in the days of high profits in the immediate postwar period. At the same time organized labor, which had defended the republic against a right-wing coup—the so-called Kapp Putsch—in 1920, was hopelessly divided by the split between Social Democrats and Communists and by the consequences of mass unemployment in the Depression. The idea that the unemployed themselves turned to the Nazis is in the main untrue, at least as far as the blue-collar unemployed are concerned. They were far more likely to vote for the German Communist party (KPD). But the experience of joblessness set employed against unemployed, male against female, young against old, region against region. This combination of labor's impotence and the ever-deepening alienation of large numbers of Germans from the political system produced the situation in which Hitler and his followers not only mobilized their traditional supporters but also attracted protest voters, especially among the young and previous nonvoters, and in which the Nazi seizure of power could take place with relative ease.

Still, the NSDAP's electoral message was more successful with some groups of the German population than others. The most solid basis of Nazi support was in the peasantry of rural Protestant Germany and among the *Mittelstand* (the lower middle class, including independent artisans and small retailers) of urban Protestant Germany. In the main, Catholics continued to give their support to the Center party or the Bavarian People's party. Recent research has indicated, however, that significant numbers of upper-class Germans and many workers—in particular those in small-scale industry, the German provinces, and regions where political mobilization had previously been limited—also voted for Hitler. Yet this electoral support alone was not sufficient to bring the NSDAP and its leader to power. In the second Reichstag election of 1932, in November, the Nazis lost 2 million votes in comparison with July, and their party was gripped by an internal crisis. What made Hitler chancellor in early 1933, therefore, was not only the scale of his party's support at the polls but also political intrigues on the part of conservative elites, in particular the army and agriculture, which decided to make a deal with him. Thus the cabinet sworn in by President Paul von Hindenburg on 30 January 1933 contained only three Nazis, the remaining posts being occupied by Nationalists, who fondly believed that they would be able to manipulate Hitler for their own ends.

The policies pursued by Hitler once in power, first as chancellor and then as undisputed leader (*Führer*), included (in addition to antisemitism) the elimination of all opposition, the creation of a one-party state, the domination of all areas of private as well as public life by the NSDAP and its agencies, the revitalization of the German economy, rearmament, and preparation for war. In February 1933 Hitler persuaded his conservative allies to agree to fresh elections on the grounds that they would be the last for some time. Hostile political meetings and publications were banned, even before the Reichstag building was burned down on 27 February. That conflagration, however, was then used as an excuse to suspend the freedoms of press, speech, and association. Auxiliary police under Göring's control were deployed against social democratic and communist activities in the run-up to the elections of March 1933. And yet the Nazis still failed to win an absolute majority at the polls, gaining 44 percent of the vote. With a majority, in alliance with the Nationalists, Hitler was then able to pass the Enabling Act, which allowed him to govern Germany without parliamentary or presidential approval. The consolidation of Nazi power through constitutional channels at the political center was complemented at the local level by much violence, as Nazis wreaked vengeance on their political enemies, murdering some and throwing others into so-called wild (spontaneously and unofficially sanctioned) concentration camps. The power of the separate states (*Länder*) within the Reich was ended by a similar mixture of central government initiatives and direct action at a local level. Reich police commissars removed the old authorities in several states, and in April 1933 Reich governors—all 18 of whom were Nazis—took charge in every state.

Nazi control of state and society was further extended by purging the civil service of Jews and potential political opponents, and independent parties and pressure groups either dissolved themselves or were made illegal. Thus by the middle of 1933 Germany had already become a one-party state. The churches continued to enjoy a degree of independence, yet in this they were almost unique. The one nonparty institution to remain relatively immune from Nazi interference at this early stage of the seizure of power was the

army. Hitler had realized that interference here might prove fatal, especially while Hindenburg was still alive; and the position of the army was protected against the pretensions of the SA (Nazi storm troopers) when the leadership of that organization was murdered on the Night of the Long Knives on 30 June 1934. Thereafter, Hitler's personal position was almost impregnable, especially as the army swore an oath of personal allegiance to him after Hindenburg's death on 2 August 1934.

In the drive to eradicate all potential levers of collective and individual opposition after 1933, the media were censored and ultimately taken over by Goebbels's Ministry of Propaganda, which organized the public rallies and mass demonstrations of the Third Reich. The syllabuses of schools and universities were changed to reflect the racism and geopolitical aspirations of Hitler and the party faithful; and those independent organizations and pressure groups which had represented various economic and social interests, and had acted as a buffer between them and the state, were suppressed, dissolved, and replaced by specifically Nazi organizations. Thus the trade unions were destroyed, their assets sequestrated, and their role theoretically subsumed under a new organization, the German Labor Front, led by Robert Ley. This Labor Front was meant to reconcile the interests of employers and workers in a common purpose. In practice, though, it became a mechanism for controlling the work force. Strikes were made illegal, and the Labor Front played no part in the determination of wage levels. Other Nazi organizations sought to control private life and leisure, as well as the political and industrial arenas. Children were expected to join the Hitler Youth or the League of German Maidens; failure to do so could cause difficulties for the families involved. Another organization, Strength through Joy (*Kraft durch Freude*), brought virtually all sporting and leisure activities under its banner.

The abolition of organizations independent of the Nazi state or party robbed dissenters of a backbone and was a crucial weapon in the control of the German people between 1933 and 1945. Institutionalized terror compounded the difficulties and dangers of dissent. In the Third Reich, individuals were not protected by the courts against the actions of the NSDAP, the SA, the SS, the Labor Service, or the Wehrmacht. The process of law was subverted as civil liberties ceased to exist. Any sign of opposition was likely to be met with a beating and with arrest, imprisonment, or incarceration in a concentration camp. The first inmates at Dachau, which opened in 1933, only weeks after Hitler came to power, were the political opponents of the Nazis: Social Democrats and Communists. Later the camps came to intern all those who did not fit the Nazi image of a "normal" German citizen: the "work-shy," "asocials" (tramps, beggars, and alcoholics), homosexuals, Jehovah's Witnesses, and those considered racially inferior (the Gypsies and the Jews). In its treatment of real or imagined enemies, the Third Reich was brutally comprehensive and systematic. Between 1933 and 1939, 12,000 Germans were convicted of high treason, and a further 15,000 were sentenced to death during the war. The lowest number of persons held in concentration camps during the regime was 7,500 in the winter of 1936–37, a figure which does not include those imprisoned for political offenses. The persecution of German Communist party members, who numbered almost 330,000 in January 1933, was vicious: almost half of them experienced life in prisons or concentration camps, and around 32,000 were murdered.

It is not the case that Hitler's state survived only as a result of violent suppression. Many policies, such as anticommunism, removal of tramps and Gypsies from the streets, and the imprisonment of homosexuals, enjoyed a wide popularity, especially among the German middle class. Foreign policy successes before 1939—remilitarization of the Rhineland, union with Austria, and the annexation of Czechoslovakia—did even more to cement Hitler's position, especially as these gains were made without war. Yet to understand the relative absence of overt opposition to the regime, we need to take into account the violence and power of Nazi organizations between 1933 and 1945. The success of such repression was also the consequence of a massive apparatus of surveillance that invaded the workplace, the apartment block, leisure organizations, and even the family, where the Hitler Youth offered youngsters an alternative source of authority to teacher, priest, and parent. In fact the Gestapo was far too small in number to keep an eye on the whole population and relied for much of its information on ordinary Germans, who denounced their fellow citizens to the security forces. Most denunciations, however, arose less from ideological conviction than from a plethora of mundane concerns, such as the desire to be rid of unwanted spouses or neighbors, envy of property, and the settling of old personal scores.

The dictatorial state was founded on the *Führerprinzip*, in which the word of the leader was meant to be the sole source of authority. It might seem reasonable to believe that in such a state Hitler gave the orders, which were then transmitted downward to the various agencies of the state and party and then enacted by the relevant authorities. It is certainly true that no one carried out policies contrary to the wishes of the Führer; and it is equally clear that, in the area of foreign policy, virtually all initiatives stemmed directly from Hitler. In other areas, however, the nature of government in the Third Reich was much more complicated. In fact, it was often chaotic, confused, and contradictory, for between 1933 and 1945 there existed a plethora of state and Nazi organizations with no clearly defined boundaries or responsibilities, and often with overlapping jurisdictions and no bureaucratic hierarchy. Even in foreign affairs, there was rivalry between the diplomatic corps under Konstantin von Neurath and the party foreign policy office under Joachim von Ribbentrop. In matters of economic policy and rearmament, the Wehrmacht, the Economics Ministry, the gauleiters, and, increasingly, Göring's Office of the Four Year Plan were all involved in the formulation and implementation of policy, and these organizations competed with one another for power and influence. Göring's office typified another aspect of Hitler's rule, namely the creation of ad hoc organizations independent of the existing NSDAP and state bureaucracy. Among these was the Todt organization, established to deal with public works and later, under Albert Speer, armaments. These various bodies came to resemble private fiefdoms: Himmler's SS, Robert Ley's German Labor Front, Göring's Office of the Four Year Plan. Unfettered by rules or bureaucratic conventions, they vied for the spoils of conquest in Nazi-dominated Eastern Europe after 1939, and their leaders resembled the competing warlords of late Imperial China.

The consequence of this polycratic structure of government in the Third Reich was that decision making was often fragmented and uncoordinated, especially as Hitler increasingly dispensed with cabinet meetings: there were only six in 1937, and just one in the following year. The complexity of power relations within the Nazi regime was compounded by Hitler's personal style, for he was largely uninterested in the routine of domestic policymaking. After the death of Hindenburg, he would stay in bed until late morning, then read the newspapers in an unhurried fashion and perhaps

Reichsmarschall Hermann Göring, in the name of the army
and the German people, congratulates Hitler on his birthday.
1943

meet some senior Nazis—all this followed by a ride in
his limousine. Hitler disliked Berlin and spent a great
deal of time at his mountain retreat, Berchtesgaden, in
Bavaria. Thus the way was open for initiatives to be unleashed from the multiple rival agencies of party and
government. In fact, Hitler disliked making difficult
and potentially unpopular decisions and often vacil-
lated, as in the economic crisis of the winter of 1935–36
and on the question as to whether horse racing should
be allowed during the war.

Yet however much some policies originated "from
below," it is quite clear that the leaders of all party institutions saw their actions as conforming with, and
sometimes even anticipating, the wishes of the Führer,
who alone stood at the peak of the party, the SA, the
SS, the state bureaucracy, and the military. This un-
trammeled power was directed at resurrecting the
German economy, not simply to generate wealth and
eradicate unemployment, but with the ultimate aim of
preparing Germany for war. In the process, unemployment was finally eliminated by 1936, and the next two
years saw a shortage of skilled labor and raw materials
become a major headache for the regime. The shortfall

in the work force also meant real wage rises, though
primarily as a result of longer hours for German workers. This turnaround in the economic situation was not
the result of radically new economic policies. Much of
the decline in unemployment can be explained, at least
initially, by the removal of women from the labor market, conscription of men into the armed forces and the
Labor Service, and the governmental massaging of statistics. Also many of the policies that did create jobs
had been put in place by earlier chancellors, who had
already begun to witness an improvement in Germany's
economy in the second half of 1932. Budgets were not
allowed to become too unbalanced, savings were encouraged, and tax levels remained high. Furthermore,
most Nazi economic policies were not part of some
long-term strategy but were developed ad hoc. Some
of the jobs were created because of the proliferation of
bureaucratic posts in both state and party administration; others resulted from investment in public works,
most famously in the case of Autobahn construction.
The most significant factor, however, was arms production. Sustained levels of consumption and the relatively slow development of a "total war economy"
were far less the consequence of deliberate planning
than a function of inefficiencies in planning and policy
implementation, owing in part to the conflicting aims
of the numerous agencies involved in managing the
economy and a certain resistance to change on the part
of industrial interests.

Hitler had always intended the revocation of the
Treaty of Versailles and the creation of a greater German Reich. However much other politicians (often
foreign) contributed to the crisis in the Sudetenland in
1938 or the events that led to the invasion of Poland in
1939, it was Hitler who took the decisions that led to
war, as he did again in 1941 with the fatal invasion of
Russia. The war that was meant to create the "Thousand Year Reich," but ended with the destruction of
nazism and the division of Germany, made ever clearer
the essence of nazism: terrorism, governmental fragmentation, and brutal racism. The SS empire of Heinrich Himmler in 1944 numbered 40,000 concentration
camp guards, 100,000 police informers, 45,000 Gestapo officers, and 2.8 million policemen. It and the
other fiefdoms plundered the occupied territories as
their warlords competed with one another. The gauleiters gained more and more power at the expense of the
state bureaucrats; and the process of the subjugation of
law, already marked before the outbreak of war, reached

new depths. Power was unfettered, and decisions were often made and implemented through no formal process and without reference to convention or legality. Such was the case, for example, with the so-called euthanasia policy of the Third Reich. This barbarous action was set in motion when a father petitioned Hitler to have his badly deformed child "put to sleep." Hitler agreed and had his own physician carry out the task. Thereafter the Führer's Chancellery acted on this signal, at first treating similar children in the same way and later proceeding to adult cases. Thus began a program in which roughly 70,000 Germans were murdered and which was deliberately removed from the control of the Interior Ministry or the health authorities. No law was ever passed authorizing euthanasia, nor was any minister ever consulted about it. It began with a single case and without written authorization.

The maintenance of Aryan racial purity and the pursuit of an imagined eugenic ideal culminated most notoriously in a variety of antisemitic measures before 1939, and thereafter in the attempted extermination of European Jewry. The violence of the Nazi state against outsiders and its own people who were deemed unhealthy was not restricted to the persecution of Gypsies and Jews, however. It was also evident in the euthanasia program, abandoned in public in 1942 as a result of opposition, primarily from the Roman Catholic church, but continued in secret against those considered mentally defective, incurably ill, or in some other way "abnormal." Pro-natal policies, which encouraged women to return to the home and breed for the Fatherland, were restricted to "Aryans" and the "healthy." Women of Jewish and Gypsy origin, those reckoned to have a hereditary illness, alcoholics, and the "asocial" were subject to a program of compulsory sterilization; some 400,000 suffered as a result. Hitler's own racist pseudo-science constituted the backdrop to such intolerance, even if it did not invariably initiate it.

For Hitler the war, especially in the East, was a war against Marxism, Jews, and Slavs—almost, in his eyes, a holy war. He expected it to last but a few weeks, a miscalculation that spelled his downfall. Much as he might try to blame others, no longer could Hitler escape the charge that the responsibility for the disaster was his own. He became increasingly anxious and despondent, as he spent more and more time on his own, and progressively lost touch with reality. His intervention in military affairs, which was increasingly dysfunctional for the German war effort, became ever more intolerable to sections of the army. The assassination attempt against him in July 1944—a bomb plot that involved many senior officers—exacerbated his physical and mental illness. His increasingly arbitrary and infrequent interventions betokened depression and insecurity. Those who met him noted a dramatic deterioration in his health and an accelerated aging. Surrounded by the destruction of his dreams and faced with defeat on all fronts, Hitler committed suicide in the bunker of the Reich Chancellery on 30 April 1945. *Dick Geary*

Holocaust Denial Holocaust denial is a phenomenon at whose core lies the rejection of the historical fact that close to 6 million Jews were murdered by the Nazis during World War II. Alongside explicit repudiation of the Holocaust, denial includes the minimization, banalization, and relativization of the relevant facts and events, in order to cast doubt on the uniqueness or authenticity of what happened during the Shoah. This softer variant of Holocaust denial is designed to gain public acceptance for its viewpoint as the "other side" of a legitimate debate. According to the hard-line deniers or "revisionists" (as they like to describe themselves), the extermination of the Jews never actually took place: the German authorities never planned to kill the Jews of Europe and they never built or operated any death camps in which Jews were gassed. The revisionist accounts rarely put Jewish losses between 1939 and 1945 above 300,000 persons, and these deaths are usually blamed on wartime deprivations, hardship, and disease.

According to the deniers, the Nazi concept of a Final Solution always meant only the emigration of the Jews, not their annihilation. The Jews "missing" from Europe after 1945 are assumed to have resurfaced in the United States (as illegal immigrants), in Israel, or elsewhere. The massive documentation on the Holocaust—including official papers of the Third Reich, statements by Nazi criminals, eyewitness accounts by Jewish survivors, diaries, memoirs, and the mountains of evidence from court trials—is invariably dismissed by deniers as unreliable and fantastic or as an outright lie. For the deniers, no testimony by Jews is acceptable because it was the Jews who invented the Holocaust "myth" in the first place, to serve their own financial and political ends. In the same way, all the volumes of documentation assembled by the Allies at the Nuremberg war crimes tribunal in 1946 are rejected; they are seen as part of a vengeful act of injustice by the victors, who stand accused by the deniers of having mistreated the Germans. According to the dean of American revisionist historians, Harry Elmer Barnes, what Germans suffered at Allied hands—bombing of civilians in German cities, starvation, invasion, and the mass expulsions of ethnic Germans from Eastern Europe after 1945—was far "more brutal and painful than the alleged exterminations in the gas chambers." As for postwar Nazi testimony, the deniers allege that German defendants had no choice after 1945 but to confess guilt to false charges in the hope of receiving clemency. Confessions such as those of the Auschwitz commandant, Rudolf Höss, are routinely regarded by Holocaust deniers as having been extracted by torture and intimidation.

The propaganda of the deniers relies on a number of standard techniques. They like to focus relentlessly on any discrepancies in the testimonies of witnesses, any contradictions in documents or disagreements among scholars, in order to undermine the credibility of the Holocaust "story." They make much play of the fact that no explicit order from Hitler for a mass murder of the Jews has been found; that the Wannsee Conference of January 1942 did not refer to gassings in the present or future; and that Allied aerial reconnaissance of Auschwitz did not indicate gas chambers or crematoriums with constantly burning chimneys. The deniers also cynically exploit the ambiguity of Nazi euphemisms like *Sonderbehandlung* (special treatment) for the gassing of Jews, so as to suggest that this term actually meant "privileged" treatment. They provide similarly benign interpretations for the forced "evacuation" of Jews to the East.

The revisionists usually explain away the large number of crematoriums in the death camps as a means of dealing rapidly with the growing number of victims of typhus and other epidemics toward the end of the war. At the same time they suggest that most photographs of the Holocaust showing the liberation of survivors are nothing but fakes or else have been presented in a distorted way to exaggerate German barbarity. In any case the Allies themselves were to blame, for through their ruthless bombing they created the total breakdown in the supply of food and medicine that produced the epidemics and the emaciated victims of 1945, whose condition so shocked the eyes of a disbelieving world. Moreover, by juggling world Jewish population figures before and after World War II, the de-

niers generally maintain that Jewish losses in the camps remained in the hundreds of thousands rather than in the millions, as has been accepted since the end of the war. All these arguments and many more can be found in *The Six Million Swindle: Blackmailing the German People for Hard Marks with Fabricated Corpses* (1973), by Austin J. App, formerly a professor of English at La Salle College in Philadelphia. App, whose antisemitism was quite explicit, blamed Communists as well as Israel and world Jewry for inventing the myth of the gas chambers to divert attention from their own crimes.

Holocaust deniers have for some time focused special attention on the gas chambers, as the so-called myth or hoax that they believe can be most readily disproved by scientific or technical arguments. Thus the French revisionist and literary critic Robert Faurisson, extrapolating from American gas chamber executions of single prisoners and from evidence about the commercial use of Zyklon B as a disinfectant, deduced to his own satisfaction that mass gassings by means of Zyklon B were impossible in Auschwitz. This assertion was then "tested" by Fred Leuchter, a self-proclaimed expert on execution hardware, whose work was financed by revisionists. Leuchter took forensic samples in Auschwitz-Birkenau and Majdanek and could find no significant traces of hydrocyanic acid (the toxin in Zyklon B). His evidence was dismissed, however, at the 1988 trial in Toronto of Ernst Zündel, a German-Canadian neo-Nazi and revisionist, and his complete lack of expertise was summarily exposed. This did not stop the controversial British historian David Irving from publishing the Leuchter Report in 1989, declaring that it was "the end of the line" for the Auschwitz "myth." Leuchter's claims were decisively refuted by Jean-Claude Pressac in his *Auschwitz: Technique and Operation of the Gas Chambers* (1989), but this has not prevented them from taking on a life of their own in revisionist circles.

As far back as 1977, in his best-selling *Hitler's War*, Irving asserted that the mass murder of Jews had been carried on behind Hitler's back. In his published work, he has been a consistent apologist for the Nazis and a denigrator of Winston Churchill and Allied leaders; for many years he has maintained close links with the Deutsche Volksunion, an extreme-right group in Germany that has consistently deplored Nazi war crimes trials and has made no bones about its sympathy with the Hitler regime. Since the result of the Zündel trial, Irving has consistently stated (with one brief exception) that he has found "no document whatsoever indicating the Holocaust occurred." In May 1992 Irving was fined by a Munich court for claiming that the Auschwitz gas chambers were "fakes" built after the war to attract tourists to Poland. In April 2000, Irving lost his libel suit in a British court against American scholar Deborah Lipstadt for her characterization of him in her *Denying the Holocaust* (1993).

In the United States, Holocaust denial goes back to the works of Harry Elmer Barnes, a passionate opponent of America's entry into World War I and of its involvement in the war against Nazi Germany. Toward the end of his life Barnes became increasingly paranoid and obsessed with what he termed the "historical blackout," a "conspiracy" against publishing his isolationist views. By the mid-1960s he was also denying that Nazi Germany had committed mass murder. It was Barnes who encouraged a former Harvard student, David Hoggan, to go to a neo-Nazi publishing house with his *Der Erzwungene Krieg* (The Forced War, 1961)—a revisionist version of his dissertation about the origins of World War II, which presented the British as warmongers, the Poles as provocateurs, and Hitler as an angel of peace. Hoggan's book was warmly received by the German radical right. So too was the far more sophisticated if perverse revisionist work by the respected British historian A. J. P. Taylor, *The Origins of the Second World War* (1961), which denied that Hitler had ever planned a general war, presenting him as a normal statesman no worse than his contemporaries in Britain, France, or the United States. Taylor's sympathies were far removed from those of the radical right or the neo-Nazis or indeed from any intent to deny the Holocaust. But by spreading the blame for World War II and "normalizing" Hitler, his book proved to be grist to the revisionist mill.

David Hoggan gravitated to outright Holocaust denial with his short book *The Myth of the Six Million* (1969), which attacked all the existing eyewitness testimony about the murder of European Jewry while distorting, suppressing, and inventing sources in the classic revisionist manner. The book was published by Noontide Press, a subsidiary of Liberty Lobby, one of the best-organized and wealthiest antisemitic organizations in the United States. Willis Carto, head of Liberty Lobby, has for decades promoted the idea that international Jewish bankers were at the heart of a conspiracy that threatened the "racial heritage" of the white Western world. Carto, like many Holocaust

deniers, believed that in World War II the Western Allies had fought against the wrong enemy in Nazi Germany and instead should have allied with Hitler against communism. In 1966 Carto took control of the *American Mercury*, an antisemitic monthly that almost immediately began to feature major articles on Holocaust denial. The theme was also given considerable prominence in the Liberty Lobby's newspaper, *The Spotlight*, which could claim at its peak a circulation of around 300,000 copies. Carto has remained the éminence grise of Holocaust denial in the United States for about 30 years, and by creating the Institute of Historical Review in 1979 and its revisionist *Journal of Historical Review* (published a year later in Torrance, California) he succeeded in giving revisionism a more solid forum. The *Journal of Historical Review*, with its quasi-scholarly format, footnotes, and involvement in organizing revisionist international conventions, heralded the drive of Holocaust deniers in the 1980s toward obtaining academic legitimacy.

The earliest and most significant example of this new-style "critical" and "scientific" Holocaust revisionism can be found in *The Hoax of the Twentieth Century* (1976), by Arthur Butz, a professor of electrical engineering and computer science at Northwestern University in Evanston, Illinois. Butz adopted a more reasonable tone than some of his predecessors, claiming that "exterminationists" (historians who believe in the reality of the death camps) had either misinterpreted or deliberately distorted the evidence. In his view, there had never been any exterminations at Auschwitz, which was essentially a huge industrial plant and also a highly productive work camp; the chemical Zyklon B was nothing but insecticide for disinfecting workers' clothing; the gas chambers were in fact baths, saunas, and mortuaries; the stench from the camp was due to hydrogenation and other chemical processes, not the burning of dead bodies.

Like other deniers, Butz blamed the Holocaust "hoax" on Allied propaganda designed to justify the high economic and human costs of war; on Zionist machinations, which had successfully manipulated the Allied Powers, especially the United States; and on Communist self-interest in magnifying Nazi atrocities. But it was above all the Jewish and Zionist role in this world conspiracy that was central to Butz and other deniers because they think the Holocaust generated the popular sympathy necessary for creating the state of Israel. Like most revisionists, Butz also believed that the emotional grip of the Holocaust myth on the world is what enabled Israel to blackmail a prostrate postwar Germany for reparations and to extract enormous political dividends from a guilt-ridden America. Moreover, the Holocaust, by becoming a new "canon of faith in the Jewish Religion," strengthened the ties of the international Jewish community and made it more powerful than ever. Butz saw his task as debunking this "universe of lies" constructed by occult Zionist forces. The unemotional tone of his book, with its seemingly meticulous investigation of the facts, masks the underlying belief in a secret and sinister Jewish conspiracy controlling international events.

In Great Britain a role analogous to that of Butz's work was played by the booklet *Did Six Million Really Die? The Truth at Last* (1974), by "Richard Harwood," who claimed to be a student at the University of London. The author's real name was Richard Verrall, editor of the British National Front journal *Spearhead*. Verrall borrowed heavily from Hoggan's *Myth of the Six Million* and from the Frenchman Paul Rassinier, a founder of the revisionist school in Europe. Typically, Verrall rationalized Nazi antisemitism, describing it as a legitimate response to attacks by "international Jewry"; insisted that Hitler only wanted to transfer all Jews to Madagascar; asserted that Jewish population figures after the war proved their losses to have been minimal; and called the diary of Anne Frank a hoax.

This transparent piece of propaganda was the most widely quoted work of Holocaust denial before Butz. Its political significance, however, lay more in its relation to race problems in Britain. Harwood maintained that Anglo-Saxons could not speak out openly about the need for racial self-preservation because the Holocaust "lie" had placed the subject beyond the pale. Britain and other European countries faced the gravest danger from the presence of "alien races" in their midst (Africans, Asians, and Arabs, as well as Jews), which was leading to the destruction of their culture and of their national heritage. The Jews had allegedly poured millions into deliberately supporting "race-mixing," in the hope of securing their global domination by weakening other nationalist identities throughout the world. Self-defense against this peril had been sapped by the Holocaust, which had given nazism and all other forms of self-assertive racism a bad name. But if the Holocaust were nothing but a myth, then national socialism and movements like the National Front in Great Britain might once more become feasi-

ble options. This has clearly been a major consideration in the nearly universal adoption of Holocaust denial by extreme-right groups worldwide during the past twenty years.

It was, however, in France that Holocaust revisionism put down its firmest roots and attained a modest degree of academic respectability. Already in 1948 the prominent French fascist Maurice Bardèche had published his *Nuremberg ou la Terre Promise* (Nuremberg, or the Promised Land), which claimed that the Jews and the Allies had instigated the war, falsified facts at Nuremberg, and concocted the fiction of the gas chambers. But it was a former socialist, Paul Rassinier, himself a prisoner at Buchenwald and other concentration camps, who first gave revisionism a certain plausibility for true believers. Rassinier was partly motivated by a bitter hatred of communism, which gradually drove him to an apologia for nazism. Initially he did not deny the Holocaust, but he did dismiss survivor testimony about death camps as grossly exaggerated. After 1950 Rassinier began to attack Jewish historians and scholars as "falsifiers" and to bitterly denounce Israel and world Jewry for hugely magnifying the death toll to increase their "ill-gotten gains."

By the early 1960s Rassinier was adamant that the "genocide myth" had been invented by the "Zionist establishment." At the same time, in his writings, he transformed the Nazis from perpetrators into benefactors, insisted that there was no official German policy of extermination, and even managed to praise the "humane" behavior of the SS. Already in 1955 Rassinier's book *Le Mensonge d'Ulysse* (Ulysses' Lie, first edition 1950, with a preface by Albert Paraz, a neofascist friend of the fanatically antisemitic French writer Céline) had been published by an extreme-right firm. So were his book on the trial of Adolf Eichmann and *Le Drame des Juifs Européens* (The Drama of the European Jews, 1964), which categorically denied the existence of the gas chambers. By the mid-1960s Rassinier had become closely identified with the French far right. In 1964 he lost a libel case against Bernard Lecache (head of the International League against Antisemitism, or LICA), who had publicly accused him of making common cause with neo-Nazis in his revisionist writings.

Rassinier's most influential successor in France has been Robert Faurisson, formerly a professor of literature at the University of Lyons and a critic who claimed to be entirely apolitical while in practice whitewashing the Germans and consistently invoking the inordinate power of the Jews. In 1978 Faurisson first published a major article denying the existence of gas chambers. That same year Darquier de Pellepoix (former commissioner for Jewish questions in the Vichy government) created a scandal in France with his notorious remark "Only lice were gassed in Auschwitz." Two years later, on 17 December 1980, Faurisson declared on French radio, "The claim of the existence of gas chambers and the genocide of Jews by Hitler constitutes one and the same historical lie, which opened the way to a gigantic political and financial fraud of which the principal beneficiaries are the state of Israel and international Zionism, and the principal victims the Germans and the entire Palestinian people."

In 1981 Faurisson published his *Mémoire en Défense contre Ceux qui M'Accusent de Falsifier l'Histoire: La Question des Chambres de Gaz*, with a preface by the renowned American Jewish scholar and left-wing libertarian Noam Chomsky. Although Chomsky admitted that he was not exactly familiar with Faurisson's work, he deplored efforts to silence Faurisson, saying that he was the target of "a vicious campaign of harassment, intimidation, slander," and strongly supported his right to free speech. Chomsky quite misleadingly called Faurisson a liberal and praised his associate Serge Thion (a prolific leftist Holocaust denier) as a "libertarian socialist scholar." Amazingly, Chomsky even wrote that he could see "no hint of antisemitic implications in Faurisson's work" or in denial of the Holocaust as such. Nor did Chomsky, a savage critic of the United States and Israel, find anything antisemitic in the claim that the Holocaust "is being exploited, viciously so, by apologists for Israeli repression and violence."

Faurisson's writings have been distributed in France by both the extreme right, associated with the Parisian bookstore Ogmios, and the extreme-left publishing house La Vieille Taupe under the leadership of Pierre Guillaume. Nor surprisingly, Guillaume and Ogmios joined forces in 1987 to found a quarterly journal specializing in Holocaust denial, *Annales d'Histoire Révisionniste*. For the extreme left, it was not initially antisemitism, and even less identification with Nazi ideology or nostalgia for totalitarianism, that motivated their assault on the "myth" of the gas chambers. They began from a dogmatic revolutionary position that nazism was no worse than Western bourgeois capitalism and that both were equally guilty of crimes against the working class. By adopting first Rassinier and then Faurisson, the revisionist far left around Guillaume and Thion believed it could undermine the postwar antifascist consensus of the democratic world, which was based on the idea that nazism and fascism were unique evils. If there were no gas chambers, they argued, then there was nothing unique about Nazi oppression. Some eccentrics on the anarchist left even suggested that Soviet propaganda had concocted the "legend" of the gas chambers to cover up Stalinist crimes and make the Gulag (the Soviet prison camp system) seem less oppressive (J. G. Cohn-Bendit). Stalin in their eyes was no better than Hitler—a position widely shared on the far right.

Faurisson's attractiveness to the far left and even to some liberals in France was partly explicable by the court trials he underwent between 1979 and 1983, which in the eyes of naive civil libertarians made him into a victim of censorship and repression, not to mention a symbol of free speech. Like Butz in the United States, Faurisson shrewdly claimed to be challenging the "religious dogma" of the Shoah in the name of "enlightened" visions of science, progress, and a dispassionate search for the truth. Holocaust revisionism, in a grotesque parody of the Dreyfusard struggle for "revision" a century earlier, assumed the mantle of martyrdom for dissident views of a sect wrongly persecuted solely for its pursuit of truth and justice.

Another strategy adopted by Holocaust deniers (on both the left and the right) is to emphasize that there have been several holocausts in history and that the Jews cannot therefore claim a monopoly on suffering. The left-wing lawyer Jacques Verges, who defended the Nazi criminal Klaus Barbie in France in the late 1980s, consistently compared French colonial oppression in Algeria with the Holocaust precisely in order to relativize and neutralize its uniqueness. Although Verges stopped short of denying that the Holocaust actually happened, there were others who used such relativist arguments as part of a more wide-ranging effort to negate the Shoah. Thus Pierre Guillaume and his followers could find no difference between the Holocaust and American internment of Japanese-born U.S. citizens during World War II, between French official harassment of Spanish Republicans and anti-Nazis before 1939 and German concentration camps, or between what happened to millions of Russians, Poles, and Ukrainians who were shot or died in camps and the fate of the Jews.

Particularly striking in France has been the infiltration of the universities by so-called *négationnisme*—the French term for Holocaust denial. In 1985 Henri Rocques, who had been active in extreme-right movements since the war, received a doctorate in history with honors from the University of Nantes for a thesis that challenged the existence of gas chambers at Belzec, rejecting the eyewitness testimony of Kurt Gerstein on the subject. The judges for his dissertation included some distinguished academicians, who were mostly influenced by the ideas of the French New Right. In 1987 Bernard Notion, a professor of economics at the University of Lyons, writing in a prestigious journal, relied on Faurisson and Thion when calling into question the number of Jewish victims in World War II. There have been further instances since then where lecturers have been dismissed for espousing revisionist theses.

Moreover, negativist publications like *Révision* continue to exist in France despite the government's efforts to ban them. *Révision*'s editor, Alain Guionnet, is an anarchist on the far left, but his journal—much more radical than its predecessors in the 1970s—is closer to the New Right. Holocaust denial lies at its core, providing a link between its conspiracy theories about Jews and freemasons, its anticommunism, and virulent anti-Zionism.

Holocaust denial in France, as in some other European countries, is undoubtedly linked to efforts to rehabilitate Nazism and fascism. Its impact, while still limited, cannot ultimately be divorced from a climate in which since the early 1980s the ultranationalist Front National of Jean-Marie Le Pen has become solidly entrenched in the French political landscape, and the New Right has achieved considerable intellectual respectability. The Front National does not, it is true, officially circulate Holocaust denial propaganda, but it has a clear interest in minimizing and casting doubt on the Shoah. Yet beyond its attractions for neo-Nazis, racists, ultranationalists, and antisemites, negationism also appeals to some anarchists, dissident Marxists, and ex-Trotskyists, as well as to Catholic integrists and some misguided liberals.

In West Germany, as in France, the first efforts to repudiate the Holocaust began in the 1950s, and ever since then this has become a staple theme of the neo-Nazis, the German nationalist far right, and the *Deutsche National Zeitung.* But it was only in the 1970s that books published by Germans which openly denied the Holocaust began to attract some attention. In 1973 a former SS officer and neo-Nazi, Thies Christopherson (who had actually worked on the periphery of Auschwitz in 1944), published his scurrilous *Die Auschwitz Lüge* (The Auschwitz Lie). He was followed by the jurist Wilhelm Stäglich, whose book *Der Auschwitz-Mythos* (The Auschwitz Myth, 1979) led Göttingen University to deprive him of the title of doctor. Both authors were concerned to prove that the Holocaust was a propaganda hoax designed to stigmatize and shame the Germans into an unjustified sense of guilt. The aim of the deniers was to decriminalize German history by presenting a more favorable picture of Hitler and National Socialism, above all by denying the existence of gas chambers.

Since the late 1980s the emphasis in Germany has moved, however, more to scientific and technical arguments to prove the impossibility of mass murder in any of the death camps—hence the concern with the capacity of the crematoriums, the time needed to burn a body, and the properties of Zyklon B poison gas. In 1992 Germar Rudolf, a qualified chemist, wrote "Expert Opinion on the Formation and Verifiability of Cyanide Compounds in the 'Gas Chambers' of Auschwitz." Rudolf, who was dismissed from the prestigious Max Planck Institute for Solid State Research for circulating the report as if it were an official document of that institute, has had his work challenged and discredited by reputable scientists. The report was commissioned by one of Germany's veteran and best-known neo-Nazis, Otto Ernst Remer, a major-general in the Wehrmacht, who had suppressed the July plot of the German resistance to assassinate Hitler in 1944. In 1992 Remer stood trial for denying the genocide of the Jews, and the Rudolf Report (rejected by the court) was part of his defense. In an accompanying letter to the report Remer wrote that in an age of religious freedom, "all of us must oppose the 'holocaust religion' which the courts have forced upon us."

Also in 1992 the chairman of the right-wing extremist National-Democratic Party of Germany (Nationaldemokratische Partei Deutschlands), Günter Deckert, was fined and given a suspended sentence for inciting racism and insulting the victims of the Holocaust. In June 1994, in a judicial review of the case that rescinded the sentence, Deckert was described as a man of "strong character with a sense of responsibility," who was motivated by the understandable wish "to strengthen resistance among the German people to Jewish claims based on the Holocaust." The Karls-ruhe High Court's empathy extended to Deckert's bitter resentment of financial, moral, and political reparations 50 years after the war, and the judgment even considered his revisionism an extenuating circumstance. The judge's substantiation several times called Jews "parasites" who had misused their situation as survivors to place a heavy financial burden on the German people. This ruling aroused a storm of public indignation. It was denounced as a disgrace by Chancellor Helmut Kohl and condemned by the German justice minister. By December 1994 it had been reversed by the federal German court.

The Deckert case underlined the fact that in Germany Holocaust denial not only is an expression of extreme-right nationals and ignorant skinheads but also serves as a code for a new kind of antisemitism and as a bridge between the old and new Nazi generations. In December 1994 a law went into effect that permits sentences of up to five years in jail for denying the Holocaust. One of the first to be imprisoned under this act was Ewald Althans, a leading Munich-based neo-Nazi activist of the younger generation, who had openly spouted Holocaust denial propaganda in a documentary film *Profession: Neo-Nazi*, which subsequently was banned throughout most of Germany.

There is no doubt that the ideology behind the spread of Holocaust denial has been open or latent antisemitism—especially obvious in the all-pervasive notions of a world Jewish conspiracy and a secret Jewish power that invented the Shoah and relentlessly uses it against Germany. At the same time the revisionists play on understandable German desires to be released from shame and guilt, to normalize the Nazi past, and to assert a robust patriotism. Even notable scholars like the German historian Ernst Nolte turn to arguments in their writings that have clearly been taken from the revisionists. Thus Nolte has quite absurdly insisted that a statement by Chaim Weizmann (then president of the World Zionist Organization) in September 1939 that Jews would support Britain and the democracies amounted to a declaration of war on Germany, thereby justifying Hitler's treatment of them as hostages; moreover, he has constantly argued that the Holocaust (except for the technical detail of the gas chambers) was no different from any other massacre in the twentieth century. Even more provocatively, he has suggested that Nazi genocide was merely a pale copy of the Soviet Gulag, a Bolshevik extermination of the kulaks

and other class enemies; indeed, for Nolte it was essentially a preventive measure against "Asiatic" barbarism from the East. Hitler, in other words, imitated Lenin and Stalin (though there is no convincing evidence for this at all).

These relativizing arguments of Nolte gave rise to the well-known *Historikerstreit* in Germany in the mid-1980s, when they were sharply rejected by most responsible German historians. Nevertheless, Nolte has received considerable support from a younger generation of conservative and nationalist historians, scholars, and writers, who regard his claims as a liberating act. This is especially troubling, since in a book published in 1993 Nolte wrote that the "radical revisionists [i.e., Holocaust deniers] have presented research which, if one is familiar with the source material and the critique of the sources, is probably superior to that of the established historians in Germany."

By contrast, in the former Soviet Union, under Communist rule, there was no denial of the Holocaust with regard to the events themselves. But Soviet writings consistently masked the fact that Jews were murdered only because they were Jews, presenting them always as Russians, Ukrainians, and citizens of different European countries. Hence there was no monument to the overwhelmingly Jewish victims of the Babi Yar massacre on the outskirts of Kiev in September 1941 or at other Holocaust sites. The specificity of the Shoah was deliberately dissolved under the rubric of millions of Soviet victims of all nationalities who suffered under German fascism. More serious still, beginning in the mid-1970s a group of "anti-Zionist" publicists, sponsored by the Soviet government, began to propagate the slander that Zionist leaders had callously "collaborated" with the Nazis in the murder of their own people. This was part of an intensive antisemitic campaign by the Soviet Union and the Communist bloc to present the state of Israel, Zionists, and many diaspora Jews today as fascists who had manipulated the Holocaust for cynical ends, in order to cover up their own crimes. As a political line, such accusations were also widespread in Czechoslovakia and many Eastern European countries under Communist rule, where they helped to create an antisemitic climate of opinion.

Some of the more extreme anti-Zionists, like the Soviet publicist Lev Korneev, came close to outright Holocaust denial. In June 1982 Korneev wrote, "The Zionists' vile profiteering at the expense of the victims of Hitlerism places in doubt the number, which is current in the press, of 6 million Jews who were allegedly destroyed during World War II." For Korneev and his ilk, there were evidently no limits to Zionist perfidy. This was also a favorite theme of left-wing revisionists in the West like Lennie Brenner (an American Jewish Trotskyist), whose book *Zionism in the Age of the Dictators* (1983) was based on the premise that Zionism and nazism were essentially congruent and that Zionists had cynically profited from the Holocaust, even after their leaders had colluded in the genocide of Jews. This was not so much Holocaust denial as a delirious discourse, which, like Soviet propaganda, radically revised the tragic events of World War II in order to morally delegitimize Israel and Zionism.

With the end of the Cold War and the overthrow of Soviet communism, the trend toward Holocaust denial has grown in Russia and especially in Eastern Europe. The revolutions of 1989 restored free speech and thereby provided new openings for popular antisemitism and for prewar conspiracy theories like the *Protocols of the Elders of Zion* to be revived. Moreover, newly liberated countries like Croatia and Slovakia had compromised models on which to build their statehood: during World War II, as semi-independent allies of Nazi Germany, they had particularly grim Holocaust records. The recent efforts at rehabilitating Father Jozef Tiso in Slovakia or Ante Pavelić in Croatia usually involve excusing, denying, or sometimes justifying their genocidal actions. In 1989 Croatia's president, Franjo Tudjman, wrote a book entitled *Wastelands of Historical Reality,* which not only greatly minimized Jewish casualties during the Holocaust but also displaced the blame for Croat massacres of Serbs in World War II onto the Jews. In Slovakia, despite recent efforts to commemorate the murdered Jews and publicize the real story of the Holocaust, many Slovaks still regard Tiso as a national hero and martyr. To bolster this belief, they misleadingly claim that the Slovak rulers were forced by the Nazis to deport Jews, and that they did not know the true nature of the crimes committed against them in the East.

In Romania the drive to rehabilitate the wartime leader and ally of Hitler, Marshal Ion Antonescu, has also led to serious distortions of the Holocaust. Already under the dictator Nicolai Ceaucescu, the official Communist line was to pretend that the Romanian Holocaust did not happen, though the deportation of Jews to Auschwitz from Hungarian-controlled northern Transylvania was deliberately emphasized. Since 1990 right-wing politicians and media have harshly attacked President Ion Iliescu whenever he criticized the Antonescu regime or seemed sympathetic to Jewish efforts to have Romanian complicity in the Holocaust recognized. His attendance at the opening of the Holocaust Memorial Museum in Washington was characteristically denounced by Romanian nationalists as a "pitiable lack of dignity in front of the global Zionist trend of stigmatizing peoples and nations in order to control humankind unchallenged."

In Hungary, too, attempts to rehabilitate the wartime leader, Adm. Miklós Horthy, which coincided with his reburial amid much public fanfare in September 1993, led to distortions that ignored his complicity in the Jewish deportations from Hungary. On 5 October 1994, however, the Hungarian government officially apologized for its country's role in the Holocaust. Similar apologies have been forthcoming from the leaders of Poland, Ukraine, and the Baltic states. Nevertheless, attempts to minimize the role of Nazi collaborators and to whitewash the past, including that of native war criminals living in Eastern Europe or in the West, continue to be widespread. This is particularly true in the Baltic states, where Soviet atrocities and the part played by the Jews in the Communist apparatus are used to play down the extent of local collaboration in the Holocaust.

Holocaust revisionism enlists a wide variety of strategies and assumes many different forms adapted to the history and political cultures in which it operates. It has nonetheless developed into an international movement with its own networks, gatherings, public forums, propaganda, and pseudo-scientific journals. Since the mid-1970s, when it first began to crystallize in an organized way and achieve a certain cultural legitimacy, it has attracted considerable media attention and gathered momentum. It is no longer a marginal phenomenon, though it has yet to penetrate the broad mainstream of informed public opinion and serious scholarship in the United States or Europe. But by the mid-1990s it had become far more sophisticated in its drive to be accepted as a legitimate form of research or as an "alternative school" of history.

Today, high technology is being perverted as the Holocaust deniers, especially in the United States, use the Internet as a tool to disseminate their baseless theories. A pioneer in exploiting the World Wide Web has been the German-born Canadian Ernst Zündel, an inveterate showman who runs a mini-multimedia empire out of Toronto. For years Zündel has cast himself as a heroic warrior against "the lie of the century," seeking to vindicate Hitler and the Nazis while maligning the Jews. The Internet has provided him with a way to circumvent increasingly stringent European legislation, especially in Germany, designed to punish neo-Nazi propagandists and Holocaust deniers. Similarly, the Institute for Historical Review in California has its own Web sites to promote the notion that the Holocaust was a Zionist (or Stalinist) fiction. One of the institute's most active collaborators, Bradley Smith, has used the Web as an extension of his "Campus Project" to promote Holocaust revisionism at American colleges and universities. Above all, Smith wants to legitimize Holocaust denial as an authentic part of Holocaust study, exploiting the commitment of universities to open inquiry and academic freedom.

On American campuses the advertisements sponsored by Smith's deceptively named Committee for Open Debate on the Holocaust have indeed sparked an intensive debate on the limits of free speech. Through a misguided understanding of the First Amendment, some campuses have accepted his texts, despite their blatant falsification of history and gross insult to the memory of survivors. In such disinformation campaigns, deniers have learned to present themselves as martyrs for free speech, fearlessly challenging the "religious dogmas" and taboos of a so-called Holocaust establishment and its thought police.

The reality is, of course, very different, for the "truths" of the deniers are themselves fabrications, which dismiss a mass of evidence that runs counter to their conclusions. As part of their academic facade, they borrow freely from one another in a vicious merry-go-round of incestuous falsehoods, while seeking to maintain a misleading veneer of scientific objectivity. The revisionists are engaged not so much in rewriting the history of the Holocaust or of World War II as in expunging its memory and relativizing or minimizing Nazi crimes. For some, this exercise is primarily about rehabilitating nazism, fascism and racism, with Holocaust denial acting as the bridge between the generations and as their new ideological cement. Antisemitism almost inevitably plays a crucial role in this endeavor, since the Holocaust "hoax" is defined a priori as a Jewish or Zionist conspiracy. For others, anti-Zionism, allied to a dubious pro-Palestinian enthusiasm and a hostility to Israel, is a primary driving force

(on the extreme left as much as the far right). The desire to delegitimize the Jewish state undoubtedly accounts for the Arab and Islamic funding of Holocaust denial literature. There are also some dissident leftists, Third World ideologues, and even a few liberals who have been attracted to this trend by their eagerness to indict Western colonialism at any price and to highlight other massacres or injustices that they feel have been overshadowed by the Holocaust.

From a Jewish standpoint, Holocaust denial is more often seen as a particularly perverse form of incitement to hatred—the most up-to-date rationalization for hating Jews, thinly disguised under the mask of revising history. Not for nothing have the deniers been called assassins of memory, sectarians engaged in a kind of symbolic genocide against the Jewish people. Beyond the shameless assault on Jewish memory, however, there is an even more fundamental negation of the basic premises of a reasoned society, an implicit leveling of all values, and the implied destruction of historical reality.   *Robert S. Wistrich*

Holocaust Education in Europe How the subject of the Nazi genocide of Jews is taught in Europe depends on each country's particular experiences during the war; its postwar perceptions of those experiences; and its postwar political circumstances.

For nearly two decades after 1945, most European school systems paid little or no attention to Nazi Germany's persecution and extermination of the Jews. A common criticism of the German school system and its textbooks was that most or all aspects of the Nazi period were glossed over or ignored altogether, reflecting the general unease of German society, in the Federal Republic at least, about that recent past. Elsewhere in Europe the tendency was to focus primarily on the national history of each country during the war, with due emphasis on its people's suffering and resistance to German wartime occupation.

Today an entirely different situation prevails. Education on the Nazi genocide of the Jews seems well established at school and university levels in most European countries, albeit in varying depths. The change in attitude was prompted in part by the trial of Adolf Eichmann in Jerusalem in 1961 and the European transmission in 1979 and 1980 of the American television series *Holocaust*. Thereafter, a growing academic and public interest, bolstered by the widespread publicity accorded to the German "historians' debate" (*Histori-*

At the ANS Garrison Cinema, townspeople of the German village of Burgsteinfurt view a "horror film" produced by British government authorities showing footage shot on location at Bergen-Belsen and Buchenwald concentration camps. 7 June 1945

kerstreit) of the late 1980s, eventually ensured that some attention would be paid to Holocaust education.

These developments were helped forward by the convening of three international conferences in Europe devoted to the Holocaust. The first, primarily an academic conference on the dispute between the so-called functionalist and intentionalist historians of the Third Reich, was held at the Rathaus in Stuttgart, Germany, 3–5 May 1984. The second was held at the University of Oxford, 10–13 July 1988, under the title *Remembering for the Future.* Its successor, *Remembering for the Future II,* was held at the Humboldt University of Berlin, 13–17 March 1994.

In the unified Germany, since October 1990, the teaching of the Nazi period in all its aspects, including Nazi policy toward the Jews, is compulsory in all types of school and at all levels of education. Although education in Germany is the responsibility of the individual states (*Länder*), the directives issued by each state government concerning syllabus content and objec-

tives nevertheless accord with national guidelines issued by the states' Standing Conference of the Ministers of Education and Cultural Affairs. The syllabus directives from each of the state governments do not establish detailed lesson plans, but their determination of the topics to be covered and the teaching objectives—reinforced by the fact that it is they who approve school textbooks—means that throughout Germany there exists a certain amount of official coordination and agreement about the need to incorporate teaching of the Holocaust in the school history curriculum. Some individual states, such as Bavaria, also promote courses specifically on Jewish history and culture. Moreover, in 1985 the official German-Israeli textbook commission published the results of its inquiry into the treatment of Jewish life and history in Germany, including the Holocaust, and this too had considerable influence on the content of school textbooks in Germany.

Consequently, the teaching of the Holocaust at different grades as part of twentieth-century German and European history has been established in German schools. Moreover, students intending to go to college need to pass the *Abitur* examination, which requires at least two years' instruction in modern German history. Many history students in Germany, whatever their

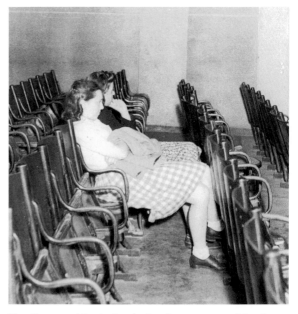

Two German girls who laughed as they came out of the cinema were ordered by British military authorities to see the Bergen-Belsen and Buchenwald "horror film" again. 7 June 1945

level, obtain further enlightenment about Germany's Nazi past by visiting museums established at the sites of concentration camps such as Bergen-Belsen, Buchenwald, Dachau, Flossenburg, and Sachsenhausen. In addition, Am Grossen Wannsee 56–58 in Berlin, site of the January 1942 conference at which implementation of the Final Solution was set in motion—is now open to the public as a museum, library, and study center. In Bavaria teachers are also encouraged to take their students to the Jüdisches Kulturmuseum (Museum of Jewish Culture) in Augsburg.

History teaching in Germany is intended—through official guidelines—to widen student horizons beyond the key facts of history to include an understanding of the dangers for their own society of those things that made the Nazi regime and the Holocaust possible, such as racial discrimination and intolerance toward minorities. Thus, as in the United Kingdom, schoolchildren in Germany also learn about the Holocaust in civics and current affairs courses, which emphasize that democratic societies may disintegrate through the destruction of government based on the rule of law, to the point where genocide becomes a key part of that society. The Holocaust is likewise examined in courses on religion and ethics, with particular reference to the intolerance of German society toward the Jews in the Nazi era. Such courses highlight, among other things, right-wing xenophobia in present-day Germany toward its Turkish population. Another relevant subject covered in courses on postwar German literature is the problem of "coming to terms" (*Vergangenheitsbewältigung*) with the Nazi era and the Holocaust.

Vergangenheitsbewältigung also has been an issue in education in Austria, which was annexed to the Third Reich in March 1938. Like Poland, Austria has had a reputation for antisemitism since the latter part of the nineteenth century. Today, however, the Holocaust is taught in history and social studies courses in all Austrian schools in the eighth grade. In addition, cross-curricular political education takes place at all grade levels and in all types of schools. The Austrian Ministry of Education and Cultural Affairs also supplies schools with explanatory materials on contemporary history, the Holocaust, national socialism, and present-day right-wing extremism, besides organizing and funding a program of regular visits to schools by persons persecuted under the Nazi regime.

Similar questions came to the fore in Poland only after the dissolution of communism in 1989. Before then any mention of the wartime position of Jews in Poland was always subject to contemporary political trends in the country. Under communist governments, the Polish experience in the war generally and references to Auschwitz-Birkenau in particular were treated almost exclusively as antifascist propaganda. It was only in 1990 that Polish historians publicly acknowledged that about 1.1–1.5 million people were killed in Auschwitz-Birkenau, of whom some 90 percent were Jews.

After 1989 the Polish educational system began to confront more openly and expansively the totality of the country's experience under Nazi occupation in the war, including that of Polish Jews and the relations between the Jewish and Gentile communities.

Today, as part of the Polish national curriculum, students in both primary and secondary schools must be taught about World War II and the Holocaust, with more attention being paid to these subjects at senior levels in the school system. This beginning has been reinforced by the production of school textbooks that deal in a more balanced and extensive manner with the wartime persecution of the Jews than was possible before 1989. That approach even includes facing up to the fact that some Poles contributed to the precarious situation of the Jews during the Nazi occupation.

As in Germany, students in Poland also learn about the Holocaust through literature, although as a strongly Catholic country there has been hardly any attempt to incorporate study of the Holocaust in religion courses. Polish students at every level are taken on educational visits to the sites of the former Nazi extermination camps. Increasing numbers of school students are also introduced to Polish-Jewish history and culture through visits to places like the Museum of Judaism in the Old Synagogue in Kraków. Already in 1986, three years before the dissolution of the communist regime, there was established at the Jagiellonian University in Kraków the Research Center on Jewish History and Culture. Educational initiatives are likewise supported by the Mordechai Anielewicz Center for the Study and Teaching of the History and Culture of Jews in Poland at the University of Warsaw.

Germany, Austria, and Poland are not the only European countries whose wartime experiences have had a decisive effect on how their educational systems have dealt with the history of World War II and the Nazi treatment of the Jews. Among those countries occupied by the Germans, France appears to have had the most trouble coming to terms with its role in the Holocaust. It has been convenient to assign all collaboration with the Nazis to the Vichy regime in southern France, and thereby to maintain the fictions that all French men and women outside the Vichy government supported the resistance.

Myths and taboos thus surround all discussion of France's behavior in World War II. Likewise, any public or educational discussion of the fate of the Jews under nazism was avoided, because of the large number of Jews deported from France to Auschwitz-Birkenau between 1942 and 1944. Most non-French observers believed that the Vichy regime of Philippe Pétain and Pierre Laval was closely implicated in the deportations, although scholars have shown that the full picture is much more complex.

Consequently, although some examination of the Second World War entered French primary education soon after 1945, it was several years before students at the secondary level were given the opportunity to study it. And it was not until the early 1970s, in the long wake of interest generated by the trial of Adolf Eichmann in Jerusalem in 1961, that the Nazi genocide of the Jews was officially introduced into the history curriculum of the *classes de troisième* for 14-year-olds. Beginning in 1983 the subject was added to the curriculum for more senior high school students. Students wishing to take the *baccalauréat* examination, a key to career advancement in France, are required to study in depth the period 1880–1945, including details of the Nazi persecution and extermination of the Jews. The subject is also now mandated to be covered in the final year of the primary school. Developments outside the classroom—most notably the 1987 trial of the former Gestapo officer Klaus Barbie, the so-called Butcher of Lyons, and the release that same year of Claude Lanzmann's documentary *Shoah*—have played a part in generating greater interest throughout France in the country's role in the persecution of Jews.

The problems surrounding Vergangenheitsbewältigung are less acute, though not entirely absent, in Belgium, Denmark, and the Netherlands, which were also occupied by Nazi Germany. The Netherlands had its own brand of National Socialists and collaborators during the war, and the proportion of Jews deported and killed from the Netherlands (75–80 percent) was among the highest in Europe. Moreover, some 8,000 of the 24,000 Dutch Jews who hid from the Nazis were betrayed to the occupiers. Twenty-eight thousand Bel-

gian Jews were murdered, but some 40,000 survived thanks to the help of their fellow citizens.

In Belgium, particularly after the approval in 1985 by the minister of education of a special paper on the war, the Nazi regime and the Holocaust have been a compulsory subject for all secondary school students. As in Germany, such education is intended to go beyond the historical facts to instill the positive values of democratic political systems. In Denmark, which has one of the best wartime reputations for having saved almost all Danish Jews by secretly transporting them to Sweden on the eve of deportation to Germany in October 1943, the Holocaust is dealt with in four main areas of study: history of World War II, history of the Danish resistance during the war, survivors' accounts of deportation and survival, and contemporary studies of ethnic and racial discrimination.

In the Netherlands, it was not until well after the 1960s that significant attention came to be paid in the school system to the war years, and only since around 1990 has Holocaust education in particular come into focus. For at least two decades after 1945, most study was concerned with the fate and resistance of the non-Jewish Dutch people under German occupation. Painful reflection on Dutch actions seemed to be deliberately avoided, even though much world attention centered in Amsterdam because of the Anne Frank House. The previous imbalance is now being corrected, as the Dutch school system has come to concentrate on "rehumanizing the victims of the Holocaust" by studying the wartime experience of individuals (be they Jews or non-Jews) and communities rather than governments in relation to the incarceration of Dutch Jews in the Westerbork camp and their ultimate deportation to Auschwitz-Birkenau.

In Great Britain, systematic study of the Nazi genocide of the Jews did not begin in the secondary schools until the subject of World War II was made a compulsory part of the history curriculum in the early 1990s. But before then, neither the war nor Nazi policy toward the Jews was entirely ignored in schools. Many history papers for the General Certificate of Education (GCE, usually taken at the age of 16 and now superseded by the General Certificate of Secondary Education, GCSE) or Advanced Level examinations (usually taken at the age of 18 to qualify for university admission) covered the history of the twentieth century, Nazi Germany, and World War II. At the initiative of individual teachers, reference would be made to Nazi policy toward the Jews. Throughout the 1980s, as one response to racism in the wake of growing immigration from former African, Asian, and Caribbean colonies, there was a discernible trend in many schools and some teacher-training colleges to discuss the subject of the Holocaust in civics and religion courses.

Today the Holocaust is a compulsory subject in the British national curriculum for history. School students between the ages of 11 and 14 must study the history of World War II, including the Holocaust. The latter becomes a focus of further study when 14- to 16-year-olds study for the GCSE exam. Likewise at A-level, 16- to 18-year-olds study the Holocaust in special papers on twentieth-century European history and totalitarian regimes, specifically Nazi Germany. A similar development has taken place in British universities, where there has been a trend toward offering courses on the Nazi genocide of the Jews and the history of modern antisemitism. Previously the subject was dealt with only as part of wider courses on the Third Reich—a situation that still prevails in many European universities and institutes of higher learning.

Throughout Europe, study of the Holocaust in schools and universities is now a firmly established fact—though the level of attention varies from country to country. Evidence of this focus is the prodigious amount of authoritative scholarly publications to have appeared since the 1980s, especially by German authors. That situation reflects positively on the intention in Europe to resist any resurgence of national socialism and other extremist movements based on racism. *John P. Fox*

Holocaust Education in the United States Since the mid-1970s education about the Holocaust in the United States has been directed by an eclectic group: individual teachers and professors, state departments of education, a variety of community-based and district-wide committees, nonprofit educational organizations, Holocaust resource centers, and specialized museums. Because U.S. public education is decentralized, it is not surprising that school districts and the states have taken the lead in Holocaust education and that federal involvement in establishing mandates or developing curricula has been minimal.

No systematic study has yet been undertaken to assess the extent and quality of Holocaust education in the United States. But thousands of teachers, from elementary school through college, are involved in teaching various facets of the Holocaust. The development of special Holocaust education programs (Facing History and Ourselves, for example, and the Teachers' Summer Seminar on Holocaust and Jewish Resistance), the establishment of two major Holocaust museums (the U.S. Holocaust Memorial Museum in Washington, D.C., and the Beit Hashoah Museum of Tolerance in Los Angeles), the support and assistance of scores of Holocaust resource centers and memorials across the United States, and various state recommendations and mandates to teach about the Holocaust have all contributed to a marked expansion in Holocaust awareness. Yet in a talk at the 1995 European Conference on Holocaust Education in London, Marcia Sabol, a Holocaust educator from the U.S. Holocaust Memorial Museum, asserted that "it is estimated that only about 65,000 of the 135,000 social studies/history teachers for grades 7–12 mention the Holocaust at all in their lessons. The overwhelming majority provide the information in three lessons or less."

When taught at all in secondary schools, the Holocaust is generally covered in such courses as World History, U.S. History, or English. Much more rarely an entire course on the Holocaust might be offered as an elective. A major problem, though, is that (according to the 1988 Bradley Commission report) up to half the students in elementary and secondary schools do not study world history or Western civilization. Thus despite strides in Holocaust curriculum development, teaching about the Holocaust in both public and private schools across the United States is still extremely limited, rudimentary, and shallow.

The Early Years, 1945–67

For many years following the end of World War II, there was little or no discussion of the Holocaust in most American public schools. The reasons were numerous: a lack of knowledge about and interest in the Holocaust on the part of teachers; a lack of attention to the Holocaust in school textbooks; the absence of any mention of the Holocaust in school, district, county, and state curriculum guidelines; and a dearth of curricular resources. If the Holocaust was taught at all, it was by the individual teacher who perceived the need to do so and had an interest in the subject.

From the mid-1950s on, if students were even introduced to the Holocaust, it was generally through *The Diary of Anne Frank*, most often in the form of an excerpt in a literature textbook. Frequently the diary, in which a Dutch Jewish teenager records her coming of age while in hiding with her family in Amsterdam, was the sole curricular resource on the Holocaust. Although reading the diary may have helped students to empathize with the plight of the Jews in occupied Europe, it hardly increased their knowledge of the ghettos, the deportations, the concentration and extermination camps, the selections, or the gas chambers.

The capture of Adolf Eichmann, the SS officer in charge of implementing the Final Solution, in Argentina in 1960 and his 1961 trial following his extradition to Israel focused a great deal of worldwide attention on the Holocaust. But although the trial sparked an intellectual debate over the nature of evil, a different event two years later seems to have had a more profound effect on Holocaust education: the 20th anniversary of the Warsaw ghetto uprising. Following a national conference on the uprising, held under the auspices of the National Council of Jewish Education in 1963, a flurry of educational activity about the Holocaust was undertaken by Jewish educators. Innovations included the development of curricular outlines, lessons, and units on various facets of the Holocaust.

At the same time, more and more Holocaust survivors began to speak out and tell their stories, thereby generating greater interest in the subject of the Holocaust. Throughout the 1960s those involved in Jewish education were more active in teaching about the Holocaust than were their counterparts in the public schools, where teaching about the Holocaust remained rare.

The Middle Years, 1967–93

A major factor in the early 1970s that roused even greater Jewish interest in the Holocaust, which in turn encouraged its exploration in the wider American culture, was the 1973 war in the Middle East. The very real fear that Israel might be annihilated by its Arab neighbors had the effect of inducing reflection about the Holocaust and its ramifications for modern society. As a result, Jewish organizations undertook a major effort to focus attention on the Holocaust and the need for Holocaust education. Roughly during the same period various school districts, including those in New York City and Baltimore, developed a Holocaust curriculum as part of a multicultural project to reduce prejudice.

In the 1970s, as increasing attention was focused in the United States and abroad on the deprivation of human rights across the globe, educators in the public schools began to focus on the issues of human rights, genocide, and the Holocaust. In the United States, at least in part, this concern arose from the ongoing efforts of civil rights activists. Also, both in the United States and internationally, a major catalyst of such concern was the pioneering efforts of Amnesty International, the international human rights organization that was awarded the Nobel Prize for Peace in 1977. There was also a tremendous rise in the publication of first-person accounts by survivors and other witnesses of the Holocaust, which prompted an increased interest in issues related to the Holocaust. As a result of all of the above, individual teachers in the public schools—particularly social studies and English teachers—began to undertake the teaching of this complex history. Various educational conferences, especially those devoted to teaching social studies, also began to include sessions on the Holocaust.

By the mid- to late 1970s there was an explosion of teaching activity in regard to the Holocaust. In 1972 one of the first formal Holocaust education programs in a public school district was implemented in Great Barrington, Massachusetts. In 1973 New Jersey became the first state to recommend the teaching of the Holocaust and genocide at the pre-college level. In 1975 a conference cosponsored by the Jewish Community Relations Committee and Temple University to examine the Holocaust and to explore the possibility of incorporating Holocaust studies into the Philadelphia school system resulted in the development of a curriculum for use in the Philadelphia secondary schools (grades 7–12). In 1976 in Brookline, Massachusetts, an 8–10-week unit entitled Facing History and Ourselves was initially developed for use with the social studies curriculum in the eighth grade and then was adapted for inclusion in art, English, and history classes at the high school level. In 1977 the New York City Board of Education mandated that a major curriculum entitled The Holocaust: A Study of Genocide be taught in its schools.

Another factor that generated great interest in the subject of the Holocaust in the United States in the late 1970s was the broadcast of the television miniseries *Holocaust*. Castigated by some survivors and scholars as inaccurate and a distortion of the real events, it had a tremendous impact on the general population in terms of informing them about the atrocities of the Holocaust and raising concern about it. The series spawned a wide array of curricula on various aspects of the Holocaust and stimulated even more teachers to instruct their students in the facts of the Holocaust.

In 1984 Vladka Meed, who was a courier for the Warsaw ghetto resistance, initiated the Teacher's Summer Seminar on Holocaust and Jewish Resistance, which is sponsored by the Educators' Chapter of the Jewish Labor Committee, the American Federation of Teachers, and the Education Committee of the American Gathering of Jewish Holocaust Survivors. The teachers' program involves three and a half weeks of intensive study in Poland—where participants visit Auschwitz-Birkenau, Majdanek, Treblinka, and the Warsaw Ghetto Memorial—and Israel, where the participants listen to lectures and take part in discussions at Yad Vashem and the Ghetto Fighters' House of Kibbutz Lohamei Haghetaot with such scholars as Yehuda Bauer, Martin Gilbert, and Israel Gutman, as well as various survivors and witnesses. More than 500 teachers from 45 states, the District of Columbia, and the Virgin Islands have participated in the seminars, and it is estimated that those teachers pass on their experiences to at least 100,000 students.

Throughout the 1970s and 1980s school boards across the United States endorsed the teaching of the Holocaust. Among them were Atlanta, Baltimore, Des Moines, Los Angeles, Milwaukee, Minneapolis, New York City, Philadelphia, and Pittsburgh. In some cases, however, teaching the Holocaust may have involved as little as a single day's lecture in a history or social studies course. In other cases the Holocaust may have been addressed through the study of a single book, such as *The Diary of Anne Frank* or Elie Wiesel's *Night,* and in still other cases it may have meant that teachers were encouraged to address Holocaust history in their courses when (and if) they deemed it appropriate to do so. Such leeway may have resulted in perfunctory coverage in some schools that left the students bereft of real knowledge regarding the antecedents leading up to and resulting in the Holocaust, let alone the facts about the Nazis' systematic destruction of the European Jews and their murder of millions of other persons, such as Gypsies, Slavs, Soviet prisoners of war, and political opponents. Other schools offered more in-depth instruction, devoting a unit—five or ten class days—to the study of the history of the Holocaust.

The Later Years (since 1993)

The trend toward incorporating the Holocaust in public school curricula continued into the 1990s. By 1995 five states—California, Florida, Illinois, New Jersey, and New York—had mandated the teaching of the Holocaust in their public schools. Ten other states—Connecticut, Georgia, Indiana, North Carolina, Ohio, Pennsylvania, South Carolina, Tennessee, Virginia, and Washington—either recommended or encouraged their public school personnel to teach about the Holocaust. In 1995 Nevada created a council to develop resources and teacher training programs on the Holocaust. California has developed state guidelines, and eight states (Connecticut, Florida, New Jersey, New York, Ohio, Pennsylvania, South Carolina, and Virginia) have established a curriculum on the Holocaust or genocide. Georgia has prepared a study guide and is working on a resource book for teachers. In the case of California, the subjects of the Holocaust, the Turkish genocide of Armenians in the early twentieth century, and the Khmer Rouge genocide of its own Cambodian people are included in the state's History–Social Science Framework, which begins in kindergarten and continues through grade 12. Tennessee has established a Holocaust Commission, whose charge is to commemorate the Holocaust through education.

Many of the state-sponsored curricula are better at describing the events that took place during the Holocaust period than they are at explaining why and how the Holocaust happened. Such programs typically skirt the long history of Christian antisemitism and its influence on the Nazis' racist state policy, as well as the fact that premeditated mass murder was an instrument of that policy.

To encourage or recommend, rather than mandate, that something be taught leaves the fate of any educational program to chance. If a teacher is not interested in teaching about the Holocaust, then he or she may choose not to do so. Thus when Connecticut, for example, encourages "local and regional boards of education to provide instruction concerning the Holocaust . . . and to include Holocaust education and awareness in school district in-service training programs," the state has little leverage.

Nonetheless, city- and state-sponsored programs have sanctioned the teaching of human rights violations and genocide, including the Holocaust. They have provided teachers with important institutional support to teach about the Holocaust and have paved the way for teachers to spend more classroom time on Holocaust history. Yet some critics decry any mandatory study of the Holocaust, claiming that such mandates endanger the quality of educational endeavors. Many educators, they point out, are not conversant with, let alone well versed in, the history of the Holocaust. Further, these and other critics assert that if someone who does not care about this history is forced to teach it, it could result in a pedagogically unsound program.

The development of curricula and teaching guides has proved valuable in filling a near vacuum in the standard textbooks. Social studies, government, and literature textbooks generally have a dearth of information on the Holocaust. At best, the history of the Holocaust is allotted two or three pages, including pictures and sidebars, which often include excerpts from books, newspapers, and first-person accounts. Still, many of the curricula and teacher guides—local as well as state—are wanting in clear rationales, well-developed objectives, age-appropriate readings, thought-provoking activities, and accurate content that avoids oversimplification and even outright errors. Many curricula also lack adequate depth on key topics and thus leave students with a sense that they "know" a subject or topic when in reality they know very little. Some curricula and teacher guides equate other genocides and human rights violations with the Holocaust, thus ignoring the Holocaust's uniqueness of scale, planning, and systematic implementation and thereby trivializing it.

Far too many curricula rely on questionable activities such as simulations and role-playing exercises that purport to provide students with a sense of what the victims experienced or to give them the opportunity to ascertain how they would have acted when confronted with the moral dilemmas—the many "choiceless choices," as Lawrence Langer, the literary critic and Holocaust scholar, put it—that arose for Jews in Nazi-controlled Europe. There is also a propensity to include simplistic learning exercises such as crossword and other puzzles that are of dubious educational value. It is, of course, one thing to recommend or even mandate that a topic be taught and another to actually teach it in a comprehensive and effective manner.

The opening of the United States Holocaust Memorial Museum in Washington, D.C. (1993), the establishment of the Beit Hashoah Museum of Tolerance in Los Angeles (1993), and the release of Steven Spielberg's motion picture *Schindler's List* (1993) resulted in a huge surge of interest in the Holocaust on the part of the general public, teachers, and students.

In 1978 President Jimmy Carter appointed the President's Commission on the Holocaust. In its report the commission recommended the establishment of a Holocaust memorial museum as an institution that would, among other things, help make the study of the Holocaust "a part of the curriculum in every school system throughout the country." Furthermore, the congressional mandate that formally established the museum required that it meet the needs of educators throughout the United States by providing them with services, including professional development opportunities and curricular and resource materials about the Holocaust.

The Holocaust Memorial Museum's permanent exhibit, which presents a comprehensive history of the Holocaust through artifacts, photographs, films, and eyewitness testimonies, has been visited by hundreds of thousands of students since it opened in 1993. The museum actively encourages visits by school groups; in certain cases, museum educators provide an on-site orientation regarding the focus of the permanent exhibit and lead the students in a discussion of their experience at the conclusion of the visit. Upon request the museum also gives teachers materials before the visit with which they can prepare their students for the experience.

Another integral part of the museum's effort to meet the needs of teachers is a resource center, which houses curricula and lesson plans developed by state departments of education, private organizations, and individual teachers. Included in the collection are key texts, bibliographies, filmographies, and other adjunct teaching materials. The museum also has a learning center, where students and teachers, as well as the general public, can explore the Holocaust in more depth at touchscreen or multimedia workstations, which allow access to historical photographs, interviews with Holocaust survivors, documentary footage, historical audio recordings, and maps.

As part of its educational outreach program the museum, together with educational consultants, has developed a series of teaching materials, including Guidelines for Teaching about the Holocaust, written by William S. Parsons and Samuel Totten with major input from historian Sybil Milton, an Artifact Poster Set (comprising colored posters with photographs of artifacts on display in the permanent exhibit), and an accompanying teacher's guide, an annotated bibliography, and an annotated filmography. The bibliography and filmography were specially prepared for use by educators at various levels of instruction, from elementary school through college. Tens of thousands of copies of the Guidelines have been distributed to educators. The museum also hosts and conducts numerous conferences, both on site and at various locations across the country, on teaching about the Holocaust.

The Beit Hashoah Museum of Tolerance, established under the auspices of the Simon Wiesenthal Center, features two major installations: one on the "American Experience" of prejudice, discrimination, and violence and the other on the Holocaust. The museum's express purpose is to reach out to young people and make them aware of the legacy of racial and religious intolerance. The section on the Holocaust chronicles the rise to power of national socialism in Germany in 1932–33, the escalating persecutions in the mid- and late 1930s of Jews and others deemed racially inferior by the Nazis, and, after the outbreak of World War II, the horrors of the round-ups, ghettoization, deportation, and mass murder. Multimedia installations include audio-visual exhibits, hands-on computer stations, interactive displays, graphics, and films. In order to place the Holocaust within the context of the American experience, the museum also explores other issues including the nature of prejudice, other twentieth-century genocides, and race riots in Los Angeles. It thus works to inculcate tolerance of all peoples within the framework of learning about the Holocaust.

The museum also houses a Multimedia Computer Learning Center on the subject of the Holocaust. The learning center's database consists of more than 50,000 photographs, almost 12 hours of videotape, and nearly 4,000 text files, maps, and documents. The learning center allows patrons to conduct research on the Holocaust, World War II, and antisemitism.

The Simon Wiesenthal Center complements the museum's exhibits with numerous resource materials for teachers, including films and teacher guides as well as a poster series featuring photographs and maps. Many of these materials are available at the Wiesenthal Center's site on the World Wide Web (http://www.wiesenthal.com).

As interest about the Holocaust has increased over the years, so has the number of Holocaust resource centers and museums. As of January 1999 there were approximately 50 Holocaust resource centers, 12 memorials, and 19 museums in the United States. The express function of many of the centers and museums is to conduct public outreach programs on various aspects of the Holocaust and to support the teaching of the Holocaust in local and regional school districts. Centers assist schools in developing curricula, provide staff-development programs to teachers in private and public schools, and assist teachers and students in locating speakers (including survivors and liberators), films, and adjunct materials. They have also developed their own curricula.

The Development of Unique Holocaust Education Programs

One of the earliest and most influential Holocaust education programs aimed at training teachers was the Facing History and Ourselves program. William S. Parsons and Margot Stern Strom, two public school teachers who founded the program in Massachusetts in 1976, specifically designed it to teach the universal themes of the history of the Holocaust through "a rigorous examination of its particularities." Purporting to use content and methodology that promote careful reflection and critical thinking, and eschew simplistic answers to complex issues, it sought to help teachers and students make connections between the study of history and its relationship to one's own life and society. Since its inception Facing History has gradually expanded from a local to a regional and then to a nationwide program.

A key component of Facing History's work is its professional development activities, wherein teachers learn how to challenge students to confront questions of prejudice, tolerance, and social and individual responsibility raised by the Holocaust. Facing History reports that the program reaches more than 30,000 educators, and that over 500,000 students a year are taught about the Holocaust in accordance with the program's philosophy and methodology.

Following a three-year period (1977–80) during which Facing History implemented, monitored, and evaluated its teacher training and dissemination programs in schools throughout New England, the U.S. Department of Education's National Diffusion Network granted the program its imprimatur. The Facing History program was placed on the prestigious National Diffusion Network and recognized as an "exemplary model program worthy to be replicated across the nation." Over the past 20 years both secondary schools and universities throughout the United States, Canada, and Europe have used this program.

Despite its resounding success as well as its wide acclaim by educators and historians, Facing History has faced some criticism and opposition. In 1986, while one senior department official in the U.S. Department of Education recommended it as a top priority for support and funding, various reviewers argued the program was anti-Christian and unfair to Nazis and the Ku Klux Klan. One reviewer who objected to the program said, "The program gives no evidence of balance or objectivity. The Nazi point of view, however unpopular, is still a point of view and is not presented nor is that of the Ku Klux Klan." Such criticism resulted in the rejection of federal funding of the program. Supporters of Facing History and Ourselves, including some members of Congress, vehemently protested such accusations; but despite the fact that the program underwent a second review and received a rating of 89.1 (out of 100), the department then denied funding by eliminating the overall funding category under which Facing History had applied, citing a lack of funds. For three years the department rejected requests for funding from the Facing History program. Finally, in September 1989, after its fourth review, the Education Department reversed itself and approved a four-year grant to Facing History.

Facing History and Ourselves has also received criticism from Holocaust scholars. Some maintain that by striving to be relevant to a wide range of interest groups, the curriculum—whether intentionally or not—encourages teachers to draw fallacious parallels that distort history. Some of these critiques come from members of the New Right who are critical of many current educational trends and practices, including multicultural education and social-responsibility educational initiatives (e.g., Lucy Dawidowicz) while other points come from those critics who claim that the Facing History and Ourselves approach undermines the uniqueness of the Holocaust (e.g., Deborah Lipstadt).

Another curricular program, A Holocaust Curriculum: Life Unworthy of Life, an 18-Lesson Instructional Unit, which was developed by the Center for the Study of the Child in Detroit, Michigan, is also part of the National Diffusion Network. Highly touted by many, including Lucy Dawidowicz, it addresses the Holocaust through the "stories of specific children [and] families" in order "to uncover the human dimension of such inhumanity."

Holocaust Education in American Colleges and Universities

As in secondary schools, since the mid-1970s there has been a proliferation of Holocaust teaching in colleges and universities. Such courses are taught in various disciplines, including history, political science, psychology, English, German, comparative literature, religion (including Judaic studies), philosophy, and sociology. Since 1990 endowed chairs in Holocaust studies

have been established at universities in California, Florida, Massachusetts, and New Jersey.

In a 1995 study of university-level courses on the Holocaust, the scholar Stephen Haynes surveyed 236 Holocaust educators at American institutions of higher learning. He found that almost all courses on the Holocaust were offered as electives and were not required for graduation; that teacher interest, not a mandate from the university or the state, was the main rationale for offering such courses; that "exactly half the respondents ranked 'perpetrators' as their primary focus, while the other half answered 'victims'"; that whereas virtually every course covered the rise of nazism and life in the camps only a minority paid attention to rescue and resistance, the role of bystanders (both individuals or nations), or Jewish life in Europe before the Third Reich. According to Haynes, such matters as Holocaust denial, gender issues, non–Jewish victims of Nazi persecution, and other genocides were treated in only 10–15 percent of course syllabi. In July 1999 the Research Institute of the U.S. Holocaust Memorial Museum completed a comprehensive survey of postsecondary Holocaust education.

Several college- and university-based programs are worthy of note. Yeshiva University established the first academic chair in Holocaust History in 1976. Clark University created the first full-time, fully endowed professorship specifically in Holocaust History in 1996 and followed this with a second in 1997. Clark also inaugurated a Ph.D. program in Holocaust History in 1998. In 1999 it concretized this program by establishing the Center for Holocaust Studies, directed by historian Debórah Dwork. Also in 1998, Richard Stockton College of New Jersey created what is believed to be the nation's first Masters of Art program in Holocaust and genocide studies, the core of Stockton's National Academy for Holocaust and Genocide Teachers Training, established in 1997.

Obstacles to Teaching the Holocaust

The growing interest among educators in teaching about the Holocaust has not been without its drawbacks. As the historian and Holocaust survivor Henry Friedlander warned in his groundbreaking essay, "Toward a Methodology of Teaching about the Holocaust" (1979), both the popularization and the proliferation of such pedagogical activity could prove to be detrimental, because a lack of focus and attention to detail, such as accurate content and sound teaching methodologies, might result in a shallow or facile understanding of the subject. In far too many cases this is exactly what has happened in American schools.

Developing and teaching lessons, units, and courses on the Holocaust present many difficulties. The subject matter is extremely complex and requires an inordinate amount of preparation time on the part of teachers—especially because textbooks typically discuss the Holocaust only in passing, if at all. The sheer bulk of information on the Holocaust that teachers and students face—from official documents as well as the testimony of survivors, perpetrators, collaborators, and bystanders—is formidable. On the other hand, lack of availability of accurate, detailed Holocaust resources can be just as serious an obstacle to course planning. Many school libraries and public libraries have poor collections of Holocaust-related materials.

Even those educators who are interested in teaching about the Holocaust are often unsure as to which of its many aspects and themes to stress or how to gauge the presentation of the horrifying and brutal events to reach students in various grades and at developmental levels. The curricular programs of most U.S. schools are already overloaded, so teachers are forced to wrestle with how they can fit a cogent unit on the Holocaust into a packed curriculum. In some communities, moreover, whether and how to teach about the Holocaust is controversial. Parents, particularly of younger students, may be concerned about exposing their children to such emotionally wrenching material, or may oppose any instruction on a topic about which they themselves harbor ambivalent feelings. And, because some school officials and community members may perceive the Holocaust as "ethnic history," teachers may worry that they lack the necessary political support to focus on the Holocaust in courses.

Reception and Effectiveness of Holocaust Curricula

The general reception of Holocaust curricula in the schools, as evidenced in the professional journals, has been positive. At the very least the curricula have provided teachers with a starting point from which to develop their own teaching strategies and learning activities in order to meet the developmental needs and interests of their students.

It is also true, however, that in those states that have mandated or recommended the teaching of the Holocaust, the response by individual teachers has been mixed. Some teachers have wholeheartedly embraced the subject matter, but others have not. Those who are unenthusiastic may provide only superficial coverage of key topics and issues. They may engage students in low-level cognitive activities, such as rote memorization of dates, places, people, and events, instead of challenging them to analyze and come to terms with the totality of the subject matter. Some teachers simply cannot see the relevance of the Holocaust, claiming that an event that took place more than half a century ago can have little or no meaning for their students.

Numerous educators and scholars have also noted that many of the curricula now available are not as strong as they could or should be. That is true in regard to both their content (including such issues as accuracy, comprehensiveness, and depth) and their suggested pedagogy (including such issues as the levels of thinking that are required and the types of learning activities that are included).

Despite the proliferation of Holocaust curricula, resources, programs, and conferences, there is a dearth of research on the effectiveness of current educational practices about the Holocaust. Until such studies are conducted, educators will continue to rely largely on their intuition and on state guidelines, which are often perfunctory and error-prone.

Many young scholars, however, are now conducting such research and publishing their findings. The topic that has been explored in the greatest detail is the coverage of the Holocaust in school textbooks, particularly social studies and history texts.

Most research on the efficacy of Holocaust education has focused on the Facing History and Ourselves program. Numerous case and ethnographic studies, qualitative studies of entries in student journals, and longitudinal studies of the impact of the program on students have been conducted. Marcus Lieberman, of Harvard University, found that students who had been taught about the Holocaust by means of the Facing History approach demonstrated both increased understanding of the history of the Holocaust and more complex thinking about moral issues. Mary Brabeck, of the Boston College School of Education, studied the impact of the Facing History program on eighth graders in the public schools and concluded that the program promoted in students an increase in complexity of moral reasoning, heightened social concern, and increased sensitivity to the plight of others.

More and more professional journals—including *Social Education*, the official journal of the National

Council for the Social Studies, *The Social Studies*, and *Dimensions: A Journal of Holcaust Studies*—are publishing articles and essays on Holocaust education on a fairly regular basis. As a result, an ever-increasing number of teachers are beginning to share their ideas, methods, and successes. There are several Internet list servers whose focus is teaching about the Holocaust, and these too provide an avenue for educators in the public schools, colleges, and universities to discuss both historical and pedagogical issues germane to Holocaust teaching, as well as to share information about resources. Along with these activities, and an increase in research into that which is most efficacious in teaching about the Holocaust, there is a real hope that the field of Holocaust studies will steadily become more sophisticated and pedagogically more sound.

Samuel Totten

Home Army (Armia Krajowa) Polish underground military organization and resistance movement. See POLES AND JEWS IN WORLD WAR II; POLISH JEWRY

Homosexuals Under national socialism, homosexuals were grouped with criminals, vagrants, the congenitally disabled, and the insane. All were bracketed as "asocial," and individuals who could not be restored to so-called normalcy and productivity were marked for destruction. The declared aim was to eradicate homosexuality. To achieve this end the Nazis played on two concerns: the fear of a decline in population and the anxieties of a state that saw itself as a *Männerbund*, or men's association, writ large. Many calls for action warned against the supposed menace that homosexuality posed to the health and survival of the "Aryan" race. Nazi racial policy encouraged the fear that this disease, as the Nazis saw, could destroy the race from within. The fear of a population decline was used to justify persecution and all measures directed against homosexual men. Some also called for the suppression of lesbians; but although women suspected of lesbianism were kept under observation, actual persecution was explicitly rejected. It was considered that the female psyche was so constructed that same-sex acts were bound to be temporary aberrations. Such a woman could still bear healthy children.

Prosecutions of homosexual men and other repressive measures began just a few weeks after the Nazis' seizure of power in early 1933. In subsequent years, pressure on them became more intense and severe, and Germany's various anti-homosexual measures escalated within the framework of a comprehensive system of manipulation. Some 20 relevant regulations, secret commands, and special rules were enacted, from which the proceedings of the Nazis against homosexuals can be understood.

Nazi measures against homosexuals fall into three periods. The first phase extends from the seizure of power to 1935. Institutions and associations that were active in the sexual reform movements of the Weimar Republic were eliminated, and the first campaign against homosexuals, including an immense propaganda effort in 1934 after the so-called Röhm coup, was launched. This phase was also marked by police and Gestapo terror tactics as well as other planned actions against homosexuals, their clubs, and their meeting places. Finally, the alteration of the criminal laws, in particular the reinforcement of Article 175, which outlawed male homosexual acts, signaled a definite break with the past.

The second phase covers the period from 1936 to the beginning of the war. It brought the establishment of a special administrative body, the Reich Office for the Combating of Homosexuality and Abortion, a drastic increase in the number of persons arrested under Article 175, and the second antihomosexual campaign of the Third Reich, the so-called Cloister Trials directed against Catholic clerics with eager and aggressive demagoguery. The third phase runs from the outbreak of the war in September 1939 up to the collapse of the regime in 1945. It involves the extension of physical terror and the formal legalization of deportations to concentration camps, the introduction of capital punishment in "especially serious cases," and increased efforts to legalize forced castration.

With the support of new legal definitions of crime, a tightly knit national police and security apparatus, and a public opinion manipulated by propaganda, the rate of prosecutions for homosexuality greatly increased after 1936. Whereas just 1,000 people were convicted in 1934, there were already 5,310 in 1936 and 8,562 two years later. Between 1933 and 1945 about 50,000 male homosexual adults and juveniles were sentenced by the Nazi criminal courts. About 5,000 of those sentenced were deported to concentration camps after serving their sentence.

In the camps homosexuals were the lowest caste. In comparison with other prisoners the stigma of being a homosexual gave them a dangerous status. They were isolated in many ways: from their friends, who did not dare write for fear of being registered as homosexuals themselves; from their families, which out of "shame"

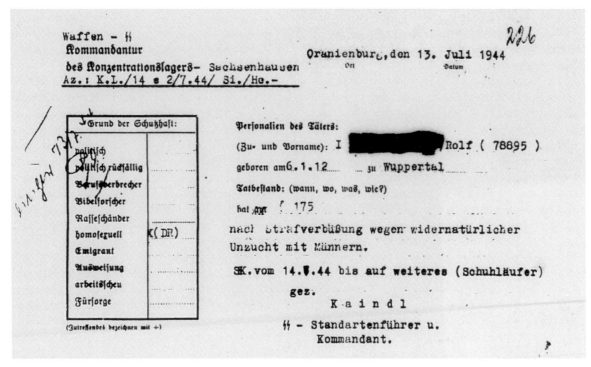

An official order, assigning Rolf (last name withheld) to Sachsenhausen concentration camp for a homosexuality offense. There he was attached to the Strafkompanie (penal commando) of "shoe runners." Their task was to test new shoes of different sizes on a specially constructed track with various surfaces. The daily allotted distance was circa 30 kilometers, carrying a weight of 10 kilograms. 13 July 1944

might disown father or son; and from other groups of prisoners, who avoided men with the pink triangle both to keep clear of suspicion and because they shared the widespread prejudices against "queers." No solidarity with the homosexuals was evident among political prisoners or Jehovah's Witnesses, and homosexuals had correspondingly little influence in the prisoners' structure of communication and authority. As a consequence only a few survived. Of those 5,000 who were deported to the camps about 3,000 were murdered or died.

This periodization might give the impression of a carefully thought-out, long-range strategy for a "final solution to the homosexual problem," comparable in some sense to the extermination of the Jews. But Nazi policy was directed against homosexuality, not necessarily against homosexuals as individuals. All the decrees, directives, orders, and prohibitions were designed to deter homosexuals from their sexual practices and to integrate them as heterosexuals into mainstream society or, failing that, to force them to forgo sex. The main tool was *Umerziehung,* or reeducation. At the same time, the criminal law threatened drasti-

cally increased punishment: reeducation through deterrence. Whoever did not respond to the treatment was liable to be deported to a concentration camp for reeducation through work. Psychology was also brought into service: reeducation through psychotherapy. And even "predisposed" homosexuals, for whom the Nazis held out no hope of improvement, could still be exploited as laborers for the "national community" provided they were first castrated. The crucial point for all activities against homosexual men was to find out that the subject had engaged in homosexual activity, and not just that he had homosexual inclinations. This was a further difference from the practice of antisemitic persecution, in which it was quite immaterial whether someone observed the rules of their faith in everyday life or had renounced the Jewish altogether. In other words, there was no distinction between Judaism and the individual Jew. The racial enemy belonged to a special category and had to be destroyed root and branch.

Although only some homosexuals were physical victims of Nazi persecution, the day-to-day life of every German homosexual during the Third Reich was deeply affected and influenced by the official repressive policies. Policymakers and the general public alike rejected homosexuality. Nowhere was there any particular group to protest against the rigorous policies.

Homosexuals were not expected to resist. They were not safe from denunciation from heterosexual associates. Moreover, unlike socialists, communists, and the Jews, they were not able to form a more or less coherent subculture within or outside the camps and were therefore left totally defenseless. Those who did not perish in the camps reacted by conforming to accepted patterns of public behavior.

After the war the main body of politicians in both parts of Germany refused to grant homosexuals a status analogous to that of other groups that had been persecuted under the Nazi regime. They declared that the Nazis acted out of military necessity, as well as in line with traditionally widespread sanctions against criminal behavior. This meant that homosexuals were not regarded as subject to "typical" Nazi injustice, an interpretation that evaded any necessity to prosecute the perpetrators. Neither the Nuremberg trials nor the trials of medical doctors invoked any crimes committed against homosexual men as such. The legal cornerstone of discrimination against homosexuals, Article 175, remained in effect in Germany until 1994.

Günter Grau

Horthy, Miklós (1868–1957) Last commander of the Austro-Hungarian navy, president (regent) of Hungary, 1919–44. Horthy authorized and implemented antisemitic legislation during his regime but resisted German pressure to ghettoize or deport Hungarian Jews or to force Jews to wear identifying badges. German occupying forces compelled his government into compliance in early 1944. Horthy ordered the halt of the deportation of Jews in July 1944. He was forced to abdicate and was arrested by the Germans in October 1944. See HUNGARY

Höss, Rudolf (1900–1947) Senior SS official employed in the administration of Dachau and assigned as first commandant of Auschwitz, 1940–43. Höss was hanged outside the gas chamber of Auschwitz I in April 1947. At his trial and in his autobiographical prison writings he provided detailed descriptions of the organization of the largest of the camps. See AUSCHWITZ

Hungary From the middle of the nineteenth century the modernization of Hungary was linked to the integration of the Jews into the Hungarian nation, then part of the multinational Austro-Hungarian (Habsburg) empire. After the signing of the Treaty of Trianon in 1920 Hungary became independent, losing two-thirds of its previous territories, and was transformed into a national state. The Jewish population, which had reached 911,000 in 1920, within the new borders shrank to 473,000 (6 percent), nearly half of whom lived in Budapest. In 1938–41, when northern Transylvania was reannexed from Romania, northeastern Hungary was reabsorbed from Czechoslovakia, and Bacska (Backa) was reincorporated from Yugoslavia, hundreds of thousands of Jews returned to Hungarian sovereignty. By 1941 the number of Jews in Hungary was 825,000, including some 100,000 Christians of Jewish origin.

Political turmoil at the end of World War I resulted in two leftist revolutions—led by Mihaly Karolyi in 1918 and Bela Kun in 1919. The excesses of Kun's Communist regime fueled a counterrevolution. Kun was driven from Budapest on 1 August, following the occupation of Budapest by the Romanian army. The counterrevolutionary government that came to power under Adm. Miklós Horthy unleashed an indiscriminate "White terror" against its political opponents. The principal victims were the Jews, for the participation of Communists of Jewish origin in the Kun regime was considered evidence of their lack of loyalty to Hungary and the failure of assimilationist policies.

In 1937 Ferenc Szalasi, an ex-army major, established the Hungarian National Socialist party, known as the Arrow Cross (Nyilaskeresztes). In 1939 it numbered close to 500,000 members and won 31 seats in parliamentary elections.

Two anti-Jewish laws, enacted in 1938 and 1939, created a legal distinction between Jewish and non-Jewish citizens. Jews were banned from regular army service and instead were recruited into special Labor Service (*munkaszolgalat*) units under army command. A third statute, in August 1941, forbade marriage and sexual relations between Jews and non-Jews. The new laws explicitly cited the "failure of assimilation," and the Hungarian definition of "Jew" closely followed the German version promulgated in the Nuremberg Laws of 1933, thus including about 100,000 Christians.

Nevertheless, most of the Jews of Hungary continued to ignore and deny the existence of a Jewish question and to believe in assimilation. The majority of the prominent Jewish personalities in cultural, artistic,

SILESIA

POLAND

SOVIET
UNION

Theresienstadt (Terezin) ■ Prague
Pilsen
Ostrava

Lvov
○ Vinnitsa

Bershad
○

Southern Bug
UKRAINE

BOHEMIA
Brno
MORAVIA

○ Kosice

Cernauti (Czernowitz)
RUTHENIA

TRANSNISTRIA

Vertugen
○

Domanievka
■

CZECHOSLOVAKIA

Miskolc
○

Dorohoi
○

BUKOVINA

BESSARABIA

Bogdanovka
■ ■

GERMANY

Danube
Vienna
Linz
○ Bratislava
■ Mauthausen
Salzburg

Debrecen
○

Jassy (Iasi)
○

Kishinev
(Chisinau)
○

Acmicetka
■ ■

Odessa
○

MOLDAVIA

Budapest
○

AUSTRIA

HUNGARY

TRANSYLVANIA

Innsbruck
○

Graz
○

Szeged
○

ROMANIA

Galati
○

SLAVONIA

Pecs
○

Bolzano
■

Lepoglava ■
Danica

Slavonska-Pozega
○

Bucharest
○

Constanta
○

Verona
○

Risiera di
San Sabba

Ljubljana
○

Zagreb ■
SLOVENIA Sisak

Loborgrad ■

Osijek
○

Novi Sad
○

Calarasi
○

BLACK
SEA

Po

Trieste
○
Venice
○

Jastrebarsko ■
ISTRIA Rijeka
Jadovno ■

Stara
Gradiska ■ Krapje

Dakova
○

Banjica
■

WALACHIA

Varna
○

Fossoli di Carpi
■
Genoa
○

Bologna
○

Jasenovac ■

Kruscica
■

Sava

Sajmiste-
Zemun ■

Belgrade
○

Kragujevac
○

Danube

Plven
○

Burgas
○

ITALY

Zadar
○

CROATIA

Banja
Luka
○

BOSNIA

Sarajevo
○

Morava

SERBIA

Nis
○

BULGARIA

Stara Zagora
○

Sofia
○

Florence
○

DALMATIA

Split
○
Slano
○
Dubrovnik
■

YUGOSLAVIA

Skopje
○

MACEDONIA

Plovdiv
○

Istanbul
○

THRACE

TURKEY

Rome
○

Tiber

Tirana
○

Salonika
(Thessaloníki)
○

Bari
○

ALBANIA

GREECE

Naples
○

Taranto
○

THESSALY

Patrai
○

Athens
○

RHODES

MEDITERRANEAN SEA

CRETE

SOUTHEASTERN EUROPE

■ Concentration camps
▬ National borders, 1930
⋯ National borders, 2000

0   100   200   300 Km

Arrow Cross members, who have been arrested in connection with the massacre at the Maros Street Hospital, are lined up in front of the victims of the massacre. 22 April 1945

economic, and political life were not active in Jewish affairs. A real political leadership of Hungarian Jewry did not and could not exist. There were, however, three Jewish communities. The largest and most important community (*kehillah*), constituting 65.5 percent of the Jews, was the Neolog (Conservative) National Bureau of the Jews of Hungary (Magyarorszagi Izraelitak Orszagos Irodaja). The Orthodox community (29.2 percent) was organized in the Central Bureau of the Autonomous Orthodox Jewish Community (Magyarorszagi Autonom Orthodox Izraelita Hitfelekezet Kozponti Irodaja). The remaining 5.3 percent of Hungarian Jews belonged to the Status Quo Ante kehillah, which had no national body. The Zionist Organization was the object of the open animosity of the kehillot and had no great influence.

Despite the new dissimilationist statutes, the situation of the Jews in Hungary was better than in many European countries. Still, there were further menac-ing signs. More than 16,000 "alien" Jews, mainly of Polish background, were expelled in August 1941. Most of them were shot by the SS and their Ukrainian hirelings near Kamenets-Podolsk in eastern Galicia. A few, however, managed to escape, and as a result of their report the interior minister, Ferenc Keresztes-Fischer, immediately ordered a stop to the action. When Hungary entered the war on 27 June 1941, more than 14,000 young Jews had been drafted into the La-bor Service. Early in 1942 a mass conscription took place, and 50,000 Jewish men were sent to the eastern front. Living conditions were atrocious, and more than 40,000 lost their lives. Also in early 1942 the govern-ment, headed by Laszlo Bardossy, launched a cam-paign of slaughter in the Backa around the city of Ujvidek (Novi Sad). The pretext was a police opera-tion against partisans, and the victims were 2,500 Serbs and 700 Jews. Early in March 1942 Horthy dismissed Bardossy and nominated Miklós Kallay as prime minister. It appeared, then, that Horthy was not ready to go beyond a certain limit in action against Jews, whose situation stabilized under Kallay's government. Yet at the same time that the Hungarian regime was taking steps to protect Jews, the Germans were planning the destruction of European Jewry at the Wannsee Conference in January 1942.

In April 1942 the beginning of deportations of Jews from Slovakia brought a wave of refugees to Hungary. The Jewish organizations that wished to help the refugees refused to adopt an illegal route, although that was the only one available. This predicament led to the establishment of the Relief and Rescue Committee led by Otto Komoly, Rudolf Kasztner, and Joel Brand.

In October 1942 for the first time the Reich Foreign Ministry asked Hungary to eliminate Jews from the cultural and economic life of the country, to require Jews to wear a yellow star on their clothing, and to begin deporting Jews eastward. The Hungarians unequivocally rejected the German requests. The fact that the Hungarian Jews survived relatively intact as late as 1944 was an undeniable result of the government's policy.

Meanwhile, reports from refugees from Slovakia and Poland into Budapest (and thence to Istanbul and Palestine) afforded the first opportunity to realize the full scale of the Final Solution.

On 19 March 1944 the German army swept into Hungary, and soon it set up a collaborationist government under Dome Sztojay, a fervent supporter of the Nazi policies. The new regime included four members of the previous government and no one from the Arrow Cross party. The Hungarian administrative machinery remained intact. Adolf Eichmann, who came to the country to direct the deportation, assembled the two Budapest kehillah leaders and ordered the establishment of a Jewish council (*Judenrat*), headed by Samu Stern, the president of the Neolog kehillah. The first reaction of shock was followed by a state of paralysis among the Jews and intensive legislation by the government. The law mandating that Jews wear the yellow badge was published on 29 March and went into effect on 5 April. Jews were removed from all liberal professions, their bank accounts were frozen, they were forbidden to engage non-Jews to do housework and were forbidden to travel or to own and use telephones, cars, and radios.

After the establishment of the government two well-known antisemites, Laszlo Baky and Laszlo Endre,

were nominated as state secretaries in the interior ministry, where the concentration of Hungarian Jews in ghettos was planned with the assistance of Eichmann's *Sonderkommando* (special squad). Jews in larger towns were to be moved into specially designated districts. In the rural communities they were to be rounded up temporarily in synagogues and community buildings and transferred to a ghetto in a neighboring town with adequate rail facilities for swift deportation.

These measures were first applied in Carpatho-Ruthenia and northern Transylvania. In the former, the round-up and the concentration of the Jews started on 16 April, the first day of Passover. The largest of the 15 major ghettos was in Munkacs (Mukacevo), where some 14,000 rural Jews were kept in a brickyard and approximately 15,000 Jews of the city were ordered into a ghetto. The leaders of the Jewish council in Budapest, who had learned some details about the horrors, approached Endre, who denied "all the horror stories."

The ghettoization of the 160,000 Jews of northern Transylvania began on 3 May and was completed within a week. The Jews were concentrated in 11 cities. The largest ghetto was in Hagyvarad (Oradea), which was divided into two: one for the city's 27,000 Jews and the other for the 8,000 Jews brought there from other communities.

The first deportations from the ghettos of northern Transylvania and Carpatho-Ruthenia occurred on 15 May. Thereafter four trains, each carrying about 3,000 persons crammed into freight cars, left daily for the Slovak border, where they were transferred to German authorities. By 7 June 289,000 Jews had been deported.

In northern Hungary, from Kassa (Kosice) to the German border, beginning on 5 June some 65,000 Jews were concentrated into 11 centers, and the deportations started five days later. Then it was the south's turn, including two major cities, Szeged and Debrecen. Ghettoization began on 16 June, deportations on 25 June, and within four days more than 40,000 persons had been removed in 14 trains. The 50,000 Jews of Transdanubia (Dunantul) were also deported before the end of June. There remained only the Jews of Budapest and the surrounding towns. Some 25,000 persons were deported from the suburbs in eight trains on 6–8 July. Others were taken from various internment camps, such as Kistarcsa, Horthyliget, and Sarvar. The Hungarian gendarmerie reported that between 15 May and 8 July, 434,351 Jews were deported in 147 trains.

Everywhere the operation was directed by the local mayors. The internal administration of the short-lived ghetto was entrusted to a local Jewish council consisting of the traditional leaders of the community, who had been isolated from the outside world. If they had contact with the Jewish council in Budapest, they received only false, calming messages. In some cases the Hehalutz youth movements sent emissaries to alert the communities and the local leadership of the dangers of deportation, with tragically meager results. Ghettoization was implemented smoothly, and the deportations were carried out by the Hungarian gendarmerie with great brutality, far beyond the demands of collaboration. The Nazi plan for deportation and annihilation would never have been possible without both the statutory base that a legally recognized Hungarian government provided and the administrative facilities of the state. What was unique about the implementation of the Final Solution in Hungary was that the national government and the local administrations were allowed a meaningful degree of sovereignty.

Because the German occupation of Hungary came late in the war, state authorities as well as prominent individuals in the Jewish communities certainly knew much about what was happening to the Jews in Eastern Europe. But the Jewish councils, created on German orders, displayed a tragic failure of leadership. This impotence was a nearly inevitable consequence of the contradictory interpretation given to assimilation during the interwar years. The course of events was determined by the character of Hungarian Jewry, by the specific ties that linked Hungarians and Jews, but also by the unprecedented swiftness of the deportations. In Poland Jews remained in ghettos for two or three years before it was decided to send them to the death camps. In Hungary, by contrast, the ghetto period was very short—just long enough to extort the money from the Jews and to arrange transport.

As the smaller cities were emptied of Jews, Budapest's Jews were crowded in special buildings whose facades were marked with yellow stars. In the first days of July, when the gendarmerie was brought to Budapest, a sudden and unexpected turnabout occurred, and on Horthy's order the deportations were halted.

In April the Relief and Rescue Committee of Budapest, which until 1944 had assisted only refugees, initiated a unique negotiation with some officers in Eichmann's Sonderkommando. The SS offered 600 certificates, which were available to the Palestine Of-fice in Budapest for admission to Palestine, as a basis for possible emigration. Eichmann himself presented his notorious "blood for trucks" proposal to free Jews in exchange for matériel. On this basis he sent Joel Brand to Istanbul on 17 May. At the same time the resistance of the *Halutz* youth movements was organized. It succeeded in smuggling a few thousand Jews into Romania and warned other Jews of the danger of deportation. The resistance maintained close contact with the Relief and Rescue Committee.

In mid-June, when the Jews of Budapest were concentrated and it became evident that Brand's mission would be rejected by the Allies, Kastner was authorized to prepare a first transport to leave Hungary. The number of Jews to be selected kept growing: from 600 to 700, then to 1,000 and to 1,500. The train that left Budapest on 30 June carried 1,685 persons. It was sent to the Bergen-Belsen concentration camp, where the Nazis maintained several special sections, including one for inmates scheduled to be exchanged. The first group of 518 people left Bergen-Belsen for Switzerland in August. The remainder followed in December. At the same time Eichmann made another gesture to Kasztner. Some 15,000 Jews were directed to the concentration camp at Strasshof, near Vienna, instead of Auschwitz; about 75 percent of them, including children and the elderly, survived the war.

In July, after the deportations were halted, the government allowed the emigration of 7,800 Jews at the request of the Swiss and the Swedes. The plan was sabotaged by the Germans, but a vital element remained— the authorization for neutral states to grant a protective pass (*Schutzpass*) to any Jew registered for emigration. The most comprehensive rescue operations were directed by Carl Lutz of the Swiss legation, who represented Great Britain's interests in Hungary, and Raoul Wallenberg, a Swedish official, who issued thousands of protective passes to Jews. Spain, Portugal, and the Vatican likewise began to issue protective passes, though in smaller quantities. The Spanish Red Cross offered to take in 500 children. Friedrich Born, the representative of the International Red Cross, named Otto Komoly, the president of the Zionist Organization, to direct Department A to prepare, among other things, the transfer of children to Spanish Tangiers.

On 15 October Horthy made a dramatic announcement: Hungary was laying down its arms and accepting a cease-fire. The illusion of salvation lasted less than a day. The Germans immediately installed the Ar-

Jews waiting in front of the Swiss Mission in Budapest.

row Cross party in power, with Ferenc Szalasi as head of the government. By removing Horthy, the Germans assured that Hungary would remain in the war when the front was already at its borders. The Hungarian army continued to fight, and the Hungarian civil administration continued to operate more or less normally; but immediately upon taking power, the Arrow Cross party sent out armed units to seize control of the streets of the capital. The first step of the new regime was to forbid Jews from leaving their homes. Then the forced march of men between the ages of 15 and 60 and women between the ages of 18 and 40 was initiated for the building of fortifications along the Hungarian-German border.

The new government ratified the power of the protective passes and the right of the International Red Cross to organize an emigration of children. In contrast to the situation during the first months of occupation, these legal frameworks could now be used for larger rescue activities by the Hehalutz resistance. Since only persons of working age had been deported, children were left without care. One of the most horrifying phenomena in the ghettos of Eastern Europe was the starvation of abandoned children. This did not occur in Budapest because of the short period of time under German domination, Komoly's activities within the framework of the International Red Cross, and the efforts of the resistance. Soon there were 50 children's homes, with 4,000–5,000 children under their direction. The resistance continued to produce forged documents, by which many Jews managed to survive, and began to create false protective passes. When the government realized that many more protective passes were in circulation than had been officially issued, it ordered all those who held such passes into "protected houses" (*vedett hazak*).

Beginning in November 1944 no more trains were available to transport the deportees westward. Until

Leaders of the National Council of the Arrow Cross after the Szalasi takeover. Pictured from left to right are an unidentified man, Jeno Szollosi, Bela Imredy, Josef Gera, and Ferenc Kassai-Schallmajer. October 1944

the Soviet encirclement of Budapest on 24 December, Jews were herded by the Arrow Cross, the police, and the gendarmerie on a forced march to the border town of Heyeshalom. Many died of exhaustion along the way or were murdered by their escorts, in broad daylight and on open roads. The route was about 220 kilometers, and the deportees covered it in seven or eight days without a supply of food and water, without rest or shelter, and without medical attention. Many "protected" Jews were also taken on the march, and this circumstance provided the representatives of neutral countries with the pretext to intervene. Members of the legations and of the Hehalutz resistance, as representatives of the Swiss legation or the International Red Cross, came to the highways with trucks to distribute food and sometimes succeeded in rescuing a few of the Jews. Even so, between October and December about 80,000 Jews had been deported to Germany.

By the end of November the sound of Soviet ar-

tillery could be clearly heard in the suburbs of Budapest, and the government began to evacuate westward both industrial enterprises and government institutions. The capital was left under the unlimited control of Arrow Cross men of third and fourth rank. A Jewish ghetto was set up at the beginning of December, and by 10 December it consisted of 70,000 people, mainly the sick, the elderly, children, and pregnant women. Anarchy reached its peak on Christmas Eve, when the Soviets besieged the city. When it was no longer possible to get Jews out, mass murders began on the banks of the Danube. Killing on the streets became a common occurrence. Thousands of Jews were taken night after night, and their bodies were tossed into the river. Wallenberg and armed resistance members disguised in SS or Arrow Cross uniforms were sometimes able to rescue a few of those who had been rounded up.

On 17 January 1945 liberation came to the Budapest ghetto, including the entire east bank of the Danube, where almost all the surviving Jews of Budapest were living in the so-called yellow-star houses and in hiding. There were many reasons for the survival of this large Jewish community—some independent of the Jews and some a direct consequence of their efforts. The period from October 1944 through January 1945 was marked by a combination of unique conditions: the weakening of the central authority allowed room for rescue activities, and new instruments created by locally based international bodies were efficiently used by the Hehalutz resistance. That the time of Arrow Cross rule was less than four months also contributed to the community's survival.

Hungarian Jewry within the 1941–44 borders lost approximately 564,000 persons; 64,000 of them were killed prior to the German occupation. Although the Jewish community in Hungary remained relatively intact till the final year of the war, its casualties by the end of the conflict were enormous.

With the liberation Jews emerged from the ghetto and from hiding and reappeared on the streets of Budapest. Soon some deportees and Labor Service men started to return. They had to adapt not only to the new situation in Hungary but above all to the fact that the majority of their kin had perished and that the Hungarian people bore much responsibility for the catastrophe. In March 1945 a new board of the kehillah was constituted, for the first time including a Zionist.

The attitude of ethnic Hungarians to the Jews was complex. Two pogroms marred the immediate postwar period—in May 1945 in Kunmadaras and in June 1946 in Miskolc. Before the Communist takeover of Hungary in early 1949 a large number of Jews had posts in the government ministries of the postwar regime. This Jewish involvement in the affairs of the country confirms that the remnant of Hungarian Jewry remained assimilated, felt strong ties with Hungarian culture, and held on to its Hungarian national identity. Although the number of immigrants to Palestine (later Israel) was nearly four times greater in the period 1944–51 than it had been during the previous twenty years, the choice of the overwhelming majority of the more than 100,000 Hungarian Jewish survivors was, for the time being, to stay in Hungary. Even today the largest Jewish community in Eastern Europe is in Hungary. *Asher Cohen*

I

I. G. Farben Leading German chemical company, created by the merger of several concerns, some of which had belonged to Jews. During World War II, I. G. Farben exploited the forced labor of thousands of Jews. It operated the Buna factory at Monowitz, part of the Auschwitz complex of camps. Degesch, an I. G. Farben subsidiary, supplied Zyklon B, the main poison used in the gas chambers of the extermination camps. See AUSCHWITZ

Illegal Immigration Because of restrictions on legal Jewish immigration to Palestine in the 1930s and 1940s under the British Mandate, tens of thousands of European Jews sought entry without official permits. This illegal immigration, known as Aliyah B, constituted a

Reichsführer SS Himmler visiting the Buna-Werke construction area, accompanied by Bauleiter Faust (first on the left), chief engineer for I. G. Farben. 17–18 July 1942

rejection of the British immigration policy. Because of the growing need in the 1930s for Jews living in Nazi Germany and under other antisemitic regimes (including Poland) to leave Europe, illegal immigration to Palestine became a primary means of finding a safe haven. By immigrating, Jews saved themselves from persecution at the same time as they promoted the political solution and goals of the Zionist movement: to establish a Jewish state in Palestine.

From 1934 until the establishment of the state of Israel in 1948, some 130,000 Jews entered Palestine illegally—almost one-quarter of the 530,000 Jewish immigrants to Palestine in that period. Of these, 104,000 arrived by sea, in 136 boats; the rest entered by various overland routes.

In 1939 illegal immigration was directed and organized by official bodies of the Zionist movement: Labor, which then headed the Zionist Organization (ZO), established Mosad Lealiyah (Immigration Foundation) with Saul Meirov as its director, and the Revisionists' New Zionist Organization (NZO) founded Merkaz Lealiyah (Immigration Center) in Paris. In 1938–39, when the Nazi policy of forced Jewish immigration reached its peak, a number of private entrepreneurs, most connected with the Zionist movement, such as Baruch Konfino of Bulgaria and Wilhelm Perl of Vienna, joined in the operation. Illegal immigration was initially a movement of individuals and groups, including Hehalutz and Betar youth movements. Emissaries such as Yehuda Braginsky, Pino Ginsburg, and Moshe Averbuch—all members of kibbutzim—were sent to Europe from Palestine to organize illegal immigration with the consent of the Jewish Agency leadership.

The Zionist political leadership attempted to control these activities in accordance with proclaimed political goals. This caused underlying tensions between the activists, whose sole goal was to bring immigrants secretly into Palestine, and the leadership, who viewed illegal immigration in the context of wider political considerations. Chaim Weizmann, president of the World Zionist Organization, and the American Zionist leader Rabbi Abba Hillel Silver both stated that an internationally recognized movement representing the Jewish people should not use unlawful means to achieve its goals. On the other hand, the Zionist Labor activist Berl Katznelson proclaimed that illegal immigration was the pillar of fire that would lead the Zionist movement toward the goal of Jewish statehood.

From 1934 until the beginning of World War II, 18,176 people reached Palestine illegally by boat. Of these, 17,240 arrived between January 1938 and August 1939. Illegal immigrants composed about half the total immigration to Palestine from January 1938 to August 1939, and 7.4 percent of all Jewish immigration from 1934 to 1939.

The extension of Nazi anti-Jewish policies to the territories overrun by the Germans in 1939–41 intensified the need for Jews to flee Europe. Opportunities to enter other countries, however, were limited. The closing of borders, a British ban on all immigration from enemy countries, and fear of the possible entry of enemy agents into Palestine restricted the chances for most European Jews to emigrate legally. The organizers of illegal immigration, meanwhile, were confronted with many new obstacles: exorbitant prices to hire ships and seamen, complications the crossing national borders to reach Mediterranean or Black Sea ports, and the absence of emissaries from Palestine, who were now viewed as enemy aliens and had to leave the countries under German rule.

In addition, political impediments increased. The British government did not ease restrictions on immigration to Palestine. They chose to interpret Nazi permission for Jews to emigrate after the beginning of the war as evidence of Germany's efforts to plant agents and a fifth column in Palestine. The British pressured Balkan governments to stop the movement of people, and they halted illegal boats, arresting their captains and crew. In the fall of 1940 they even adopted a policy of deporting illegal immigrants to the island of Mauritius.

Other obstacles originated in the changed attitude of Zionist policymakers toward illegal immigration. During 1939 illegal immigration was one of the main vehicles of resistance to the British white paper (May 1939) that intended to put an end to the development of Palestine as a Jewish national home. The Zionist leadership believed that illegal immigration, by forcing Great Britain to act against the helpless immigrants, would reveal the immorality of the Palestine policy and arouse world public opinion. But with the start of the war, Zionist policy shifted toward cooperation with Great Britain against Hitler, in the hope of establishing a Jewish army that would take part in the war. The leadership was thus faced with a dilemma: how to undercut British immigration policy and at the same time lend Great Britain active support in the war effort.

Following Italy's declaration of war against Great Britain and France in June 1940, sailing on the Mediterranean became dangerous, and fears for the safety of Jewish immigrants grew. This obstacle, along with other problems, weakened the incentive to organize illegal immigration and added to the ambivalence of the Zionist leadership toward it. In January 1940 Mosad Lealiyah managed the successful completion of the voyage of the *Hilda*, which carried 728 immigrants, and in March 1941 the *Darien* arrived in Haifa with 789 passengers. The voyage of the *Darien* followed a great debate between the Zionist political leadership and the Mosad Lealiyah activists, and internally among the activists themselves. The core of the controversy concerned the issue of whether the primary responsibility of Mosad Lealiyah was toward illegal immigrants or the political leadership, whose decisions seemed contrary to the immigrants' interest. The completion of the *Darien*'s voyage was proof that the activists were loyal to the immigrants, but it was the last act of illegal immigration organized by Mosad Lealiyah until 1943.

The Revisionists organized two ships during the war, the *Sakariya*, which reached Palestine in February 1940 with more than 2,000 immigrants, and the *Pencho*, which left Bratislava, Slovakia, in the summer of 1940 with 510 immigrants. The *Pencho* never reached Palestine, as it ran aground near the Dodecanese Islands. The passengers were rescued by an Italian warship and stayed in southern Italy throughout the war, immigrating legally to Palestine in 1944.

Baruch Konfino was active until December 1940, when the *Salvador* sank in the Sea of Marmara and some 220 people drowned. Konfino helped more than 1,600 immigrants during the first 15 months of the war, and he resumed his activities in 1945.

The largest individual operation was conducted by Berthold Storfer on behalf of the Viennese Jewish community, which was controlled by the Central Office of Jewish Emigration (Zentralstelle für Jüdische Auswanderung) established by Eichmann in August 1938. Between 1 and 24 November 1940 three ships, the *Pacific,* the *Milos,* and the *Atlantic,* arrived in Haifa harbor with some 3,500 passengers. The British decided to deport the immigrants to Mauritius, and they began to transfer passengers to the *Patria,* a more seaworthy vessel. In a desperate attempt to halt the deportation, the Haganah (the Jewish underground defense force) sabotaged the *Patria.* A miscalculation caused the boat to sink swiftly, and 267 people lost their lives. The survivors, however, were allowed to stay in Palestine. In December 1940, 1,600 immigrants on the *Atlantic* were deported to Mauritius; they returned to Palestine legally after the war.

The Revisionists in Romania were involved in the outfitting of the *Struma,* which left Constantsa in December 1941 with 769 passengers on board. On 23 February 1942, following 10 weeks of waiting at Istanbul harbor and after all negotiations and pleas to obtain entry visas to Palestine had failed, the Turks towed the *Struma* back out into the Black Sea, where the vessel was hit by a Soviet torpedo. Only one passenger, Jacob Stoliar, survived. This tragedy brought a halt to organized illegal immigration.

In 1943, as the extent of the catastrophe that had already befallen European Jewry was made known, the organization of illegal immigration resumed under the auspices of the Palestine Rescue Committee, which was established in Palestine in March 1943. Mosad Lealiyah emissaries, operating within the framework of the Palestine rescue delegation, were dispatched to Istanbul with the aim of bringing Jews out by way of Bulgaria and Romania. They hired non-Jewish travel agents, who chartered small freighters departing from Constantsa to bring the immigrants to Istanbul. From there the immigrants continued by land, after having received entry visas from the British.

In this phase the barriers and illegality came from Nazi authorities in the Balkans who opposed the release of Jews. Balkan governments, already aware that the war was reaching an end, were more agreeable to Jewish emigration. In Great Britain the presentation in Parliament in December 1942 of news about the Final Solution shook public opinion, and great pressure was exerted on the government to act on behalf of Eu-

ropean Jewry. In July 1943 the government decreed that every Jewish refugee who reached Turkey would receive an entry visa to Palestine. In Istanbul, Mosad Lealiyah agents were assisted by British intelligence agents, who were interested in obtaining information from the Jewish immigrants on the situation in the Balkans.

Between March and December 1944, 11 ships left Constantsa for Istanbul with more than 4,000 people, among them refugees from Poland and Romania and orphans from Transnistria. The ships did not meet safety standards and did not sail under the protection of the International Red Cross or a neutral country. They were thus in danger of hostile attacks from either side. On 5 August 1944 the *Mefkure* was sunk by a Soviet submarine; only five of the 379 immigrants on board were rescued. Despite the tragedy a decision was taken to continue illegal immigration.

After World War II illegal immigration became even more important for Zionist policy than it had been during the war, since the British did not change the white paper policy and the restrictions on Jewish immigration to Palestine despite the Holocaust. Illegal immigration demonstrated that the Zionist movement was committed to resolve the homelessness of the remaining Jews (*she'erit hapletah*). It provided survivors with the possibility of acting on their own behalf and promoting the goals of Zionism. It became a unifying force throughout the Jewish world and was supported by Zionists and non-Zionists alike. Illegal immigration embodied the central tenet of Zionism, that the only solution to the problems of the she'erit hapletah was free immigration to Palestine and the establishment of a Jewish state.

During the years 1945–48 the sole organizer of illegal immigration efforts was Mosad Lealiyah, still headed by Saul Meirov. The organization maintained offices in Italy, France, Romania, Bulgaria, and Greece. The ships were owned by Mosad Lealiyah and were run by volunteers—officers and crews—from Palestine (belonging to a section of the defense force named Palyam) and by Jewish volunteers from Western countries (including 200 volunteers from the United States). Properly trained crews dealt with communication at sea and the landings in Palestine. A well-coordinated organization of emissaries conducted the transfers from the various European countries to Mediterranean ports. In each immigration center in Europe the operations were adapted to the specific local political and social situation. During this period Mosad Lealiyah moved more than 70,000 people on 64 ships on a budget of more than $7 million.

In August 1946 the British decided to suppress illegal immigration by deporting the immigrants to Cyprus. Three large detention camps were established in Cyprus, and some 52,000 immigrants were held on the island. A large number of these immigrants remained in Cyprus until the establishment of the state of Israel.

Each of the illegal ships had its particular story and could illuminate some of the meaning of illegal immigration. But the *Exodus,* which sailed from Europe in July 1947 with some 5,000 people aboard and was forcibly returned with its passengers to Germany, epitomized the plight of all Jewish refugees. It illustrated the well-organized illegal immigration operation and the dedication of the passengers to Zionist goals. It galvanized public opinion against the British Palestine policy and, despite the plight of the passengers, served the Zionist cause well.   *Dalia Ofer*

Iraq Country in the Middle East, centered on the Tigris and Euphrates rivers. In 1940 more than 100,000 Jews lived in Iraq, most of them in the cities of Baghdad and Basra. One month after the pro-Axis rebellion headed by Rashid Ali in April 1941, a major anti-Jewish riot broke out in Baghdad among Nazi sympathizers in the local population. Some 200 Jewish men and women were killed and about 2,000 injured.

Iron Guard (Garda de Fier) Romanian fascist movement, founded in 1927 as the Legion of the Archangel Michael. In the elections of 1937 the Iron Guard emerged as the third-strongest party in Romania. It was instrumental in antisemitic propaganda and physical attacks against Jews. The Iron Guard was defeated by the Romanian army when it tried to challenge the government of Ion Antonescu in January 1941.

Istanbul Emissaries The sending of emissaries from the Jewish community (the Yishuv) in Palestine to promote Zionism and immigration or to carry out specific tasks was a central component of the policy of the Zionist movement between the two world wars. Emissaries had a special aura, which stemmed from the fact that they represented the Zionist movement and lived in Eretz Yisrael (the Land of Israel), often on kibbutzim—collective agricultural settlements, usually socialistic. They were regarded as persons of high moral stature who left home and family in order to

Horea Sima, the leader of the Iron Guard, salutes his supporters during a ceremony commemorating the deaths of Ion Mota and Vasile Marin, Iron Guardsmen who were killed in the Spanish civil war. 13 September 1940

serve the Zionist cause. At the same time, they represented specific parties and movements and maintained close contact with those organizations' leaders.

Being geographically close to both Palestine and the Balkans, Istanbul acted as a bridge between those areas and occupied Europe. As a neutral country, Turkey hosted the embassies and consulates of belligerent nations, offices of the International Red Cross and representatives of the Vatican, intelligence services of neutral and occupied countries and their governments-in-exile, agents and businessmen of many nationalities and loyalties. In short, Turkey became a center of espionage and political intrigue during World War II.

The Turkish authorities did not make it easy for those wishing to use it as a neutral base. The government banned political activities, forbade transactions of foreign currency unless exchanged with the Turkish official currency, and maintained an inefficient and suspicious bureaucracy. The emissaries, who could not obtain legal permission to stay and operate, had to move between rented apartments and cheap hotels and to pass themselves off as representatives of the press or commercial companies. Most of their activities, such as currency transactions, meetings with agents and couriers, and correspondence with occupied Europe, were therefore illegal.

A delegation from the Yishuv was gradually established in Istanbul by the Jewish Agency, the official organization overseeing the building of a Jewish home in Palestine, as the Yishuv and its leaders came to grips with the reality of the Holocaust. Istanbul first became the focus of rescue operations during the second half of 1940, when it became impossible to reach Palestine from Italy. At that time Chaim Barlas, head of the Immigration Department of the Jewish Agency, went to Turkey to organize the passage of refugees from Poland through a new route (from Lithuania via the Soviet Union, Turkey, and Syria), which was kept open almost until the German invasion of the Soviet Union in June 1941. Other emissaries, especially those dealing with illegal immigration to Palestine, stayed in Turkey from time to time.

Distressed by the return of its emissaries from Europe shortly after the outbreak of the war, the umbrella organization of the Zionist pioneering youth movements in Palestine was looking for ways to enhance the ties it continued to maintain with its members in occupied Europe. Despite pressure from the leaders of that organization, the Jewish Agency was not convinced that the time was ripe for the establishment of a permanent delegation in Istanbul, mainly because in 1940–41 the Yishuv did not imagine that an overall policy aimed at the extermination of the Jews of Europe existed. The ghettos in Poland were then considered the worst manifestation of Nazi policy, and the mass murders in the Soviet Union, which had begun in the summer of 1941, were as yet unknown. Only in August 1942 was a delegate, Eliezer Leder, sent to collect information on behalf of the Committee for Polish Jewry; and only in November, following the Jewish Agency's formal announcement that systematic mass murder was being carried out, did the members of its executive change their minds and did emissaries leave for Istanbul. During that month Leder and Barlas (together with Dr. Joseph Goldin, head of the Jewish Agency's Palestine Office before the war) were joined by Venia Pomerantz from Kibbutz Ramat-Rachel, and in January 1943 Menachem Bader of Kibbutz Mizra was also sent. Two

more emissaries dealing with illegal immigration, Ze'ev Shind and Moshe Averbuch (later Agami), and three from the Jewish Agency's Political Department— Eliyahu Eilat, Ehud Avriel, and Teddy Kollek—soon followed.

In Palestine, Istanbul was considered "the window to occupied Europe," and thus many parties exerted pressure to have their delegates placed in the delegation that was being formed. Eventually the group included (in addition to those already mentioned) Joseph Klarman of the Revisionist party, Yakov Griffel of the ultra-Orthodox Agudat Israel, David Zimend and Kalman Rozenblat of the General Zionists A and B, and Akiva Levinsky of Gordonia (later a treasurer of the Jewish Agency), who worked for Youth Aliyah (youth immigration). Complaining that only Polish Jews were being cared for, the associations of immigrants such as Bulgarian, Yugoslav, and Greek Jews added two more emissaries. The American Joint Distribution Committee (JDC) added Reuven Reznick in the summer of 1944; Eri Jabotinsky came to Istanbul on behalf of the U.S.-based Emergency Committee of the Etzel (National Military Organization, an offshoot of the Revisionist party); and the War Refugee Board was represented by its delegate to the Middle East, Ira Hirschman. By the end of 1944 there were at least 15, and sometimes closer to 25, Jewish emissaries and delegates in Istanbul.

Since the emissaries represented different organizations and various political affiliations, a central committee, subcommittees, and specific tasks were agreed on and from time to time renewed. Still, personal and political relations among them were not always smooth. Barlas, was the only emissary officially recognized by the Turkish government. Goldin and Leder were older and more cautious than younger emissaries such as Pomerantz and Kollek. Concern over the most delicate issue—which parties and movements would gain the right to be remembered as affiliated with the ghetto fighters—led to bitter debates among the delegates. The need to operate in clandestine conditions created a division between a small nucleus of members who knew more and those on the periphery who knew less. Operations were initiated by the delegation as a whole, but separate activities were undertaken by members who felt that they and their movements had been cut out.

Despite the many difficulties, the emissaries did accomplish aid and rescue work in a number of areas.

They transferred food parcels, medicines, and cash; they smuggled forged documents and passports over borders in Europe; they assisted in legal and illegal immigration to Palestine; and above all they maintained communication with occupied Europe. In addition to money and letters, a publication entitled "A Letter to Brothers in the Diaspora under Occupation" from the leaders of the Yishuv was dispatched from Istanbul in a number of languages. Before the war, immigration permits and budgets for education and training abroad and settlement in Palestine were divided according to a "party key," namely, the numerical strength of the various parties in the Zionist movement. The key was not officially abolished during the Holocaust, yet both the Jewish Agency and the emissaries decided to disregard it and to send aid to whomever they could find. Toward the end of 1943 it was also agreed that a symbolic common signature—*Moldati*, meaning "my homeland"—be put on all letters.

Establishing lines of communication was by far the most important service rendered by the delegation to Jews in occupied countries. These lines were first opened by delegates in Geneva, first and foremost Nathan Schwalb, who sent thousands of letters to occupied Europe. When the Istanbul emissaries started their work in the beginning of 1943, mail connections hardly existed, the murder operations were at their height, and the forced labor camps were operating at full capacity. The notion of an address lost its meaning in occupied Europe. Hence the emissaries had to rely on shady double and triple agents, though some anti-Nazi diplomats and businessmen offered their services free of charge. These channels of communication entailed numerous risks: some agents were mere thieves; others were caught by the German intelligence authorities, who were aware of their contacts. Adolf Eichmann, who was charged with organizing the Final Solution, generally freed those who were arrested so as to keep an eye on the contacts maintained by "world Jewry." The Jewish parties and organizations in Palestine indeed kept in touch through Geneva and Istanbul with Western Europe, the Reich, the Balkans, Hungary, Slovakia, and Poland. The first direct contact between Istanbul and Poland, however, was not made until the summer of 1943, when the tragedy of Polish Jewry had already been completed. No contact was established with areas beyond the Bug River or with the Baltic countries.

About 740,000 Palestine pounds sterling (approximately $17.8 million), collected mostly from the Yishuv but also from the JDC and from local loans, was transferred to Geneva and Istanbul in dollars, marks, gold coins, and diamonds. Poland received £85,000 for food and weapons, a third of which went to Warsaw; Greece received £3,275 for rescue, Romania £165,000 for rescue from jails and general needs, Bulgaria £17,000 for public kitchens and ransom from hard labor, Western Europe £160,000 for general needs, Hungary £135,000 for living costs of refugees. In addition, Transnistria received £30,000 for food and clothing, and Slovakia £100,000 for bribery and the maintenance of workshops.

About 100,000 food parcels were dispatched through non-Jewish companies that were paid and directed by the emissaries. In 1943 mail ceased to function, and the International Red Cross sent parcels to Theresienstadt and to ghettos in Poland, as well as to France. A five-kilogram parcel cost a quarter of an average monthly salary in Palestine. Toward the end of 1943, when the JDC officially joined the aid and rescue work, $1 million worth of parcels (225 metric tons) was planned for Transnistria, Poland, and Theresienstadt but was stopped after the shipment of five wagons because of the changing front lines and because of warnings from Jews that the Germans were deceiving the Red Cross and seizing the parcels.

Several Latin American consuls agreed to issue tens of thousands of passports for Jews, although their countries had not always authorized them. About 35,000 confirmations of family certificates were transferred via the representatives of the Vatican, the Swiss government, and the Red Cross. These organizations, assisted by the Swedish legate Raoul Wallenberg and the Swiss consul Carl Lutz in Hungary, and by the Yishuv emissaries in the four neutral countries (Spain, Sweden, Switzerland, and Turkey), also issued tens of thousands of protective documents.

The commendable deeds of the Istanbul emissaries still raise a number of questions. Were Zionist activists helped more than others? Why did the Yishuv leaders stay in Istanbul for short visits only and not dedicate themselves full-time to rescue work there? Was interparty dissent an obstacle to rescue work? Was the Istanbul delegation favored by Yishuv leaders more than the smaller delegations in Geneva, Madrid, and Stockholm because of its proximity to Palestine? Researchers are divided: some claim that the needs of Zionism dictated limited rescue work, while others argue that more could have been done. But it is doubtful that much more aid could have been delivered, as the emissaries and the Zionist leadership had few resources and very little political influence with the Allies to affect the conduct of the war or forestall the Final Solution. In any case, a greater share of the rescue effort was shouldered by the small Jewish community in Palestine than by any other community.

Dina Porat

Italy From the establishment of the unified national state in 1861 until the start of the "race campaign" in 1938, hatred for Jews did not figure prominently either as a popular phenomenon or as a factor in social and political life. The small number of Jews in the country—about one in 1,000 of the entire population—and their high degree of integration into local culture meant that the equality of civil rights which the Jews were granted in the second half of the nineteenth century mainly solemnized a long-established reality. The liberal state, which among other things arose out of a struggle against the temporal rule of the Roman Catholic church, formed a convenient framework for continuing this process, and it allowed Jews to become a part of social and economic life and in a few cases even to rise to senior positions in the national leadership.

Toward the end of the nineteenth and the beginning of the twentieth century, a new antisemitism with nationalist and racist overtones penetrated Italy from Germany, Austria-Hungary, and above all France. These modern antisemitic ideas found fertile ground in some Catholic circles, where the attempt was made to graft them onto the ancient trunk of Catholic anti-Jewishness. These ideas also influenced views in nationalist circles, which in 1910 organized themselves

A unit of Italian blackshirts stands at attention holding spades during a fascist demonstration. 12 April 1934

into a political movement. But in the main, the reach of such ideas was limited, and their effect on social and political reality was marginal.

The rise to power of the Fascist movement, led by Benito Mussolini, in 1922 and its merger with the Nationalist Association in 1923 opened up new horizons to the bearers of antisemitic thinking. They became a source of worry in Jewish (particularly Zionist) circles, as Mussolini was known to harbor an attitude of suspicion and intolerance toward Jews and Judaism. Mussolini firmly believed in the power of "international Jewry" and in its ability to orchestrate major political moves through control of international finance. In numerous articles in his newspaper *Il Popolo d'Italia* from 1918 to 1922, Mussolini expressed the greatest hostility toward the World Zionist Movement, since its political and nationalist aspirations were designed to be realized in a region, the Middle East, which in Mussolini's view was to provide living space (*spazio vitale*) for the new Fascist state.

And yet precisely because of this fantastical belief in the power of Jews internationally, during the early years of his regime Mussolini took care to avoid open confrontation. There were a few instances where he even considered using Jewish agencies and communities outside Italy, including the World Zionist Organization, to obtain loans from international institutions or to further Italian political or economic interests around the Mediterranean. At the same time, this activity did not restrain him from repeated denunciations of the very existence of the Zionist Federation in Italy, which in his view cast doubt on the sincerity of the patriotic sentiments and intentions of those Jews who belonged to it. This ambiguous policy, arising out of the conflict between his ideological hostility and considerations of realpolitik, did not survive for long.

The turning point took place between the end of 1936 and mid-1937. Several factors contributed to the introduction of an antisemitic political program: the racist policy and legislation adopted toward Ethiopians after the conquest of Ethiopia in May 1936; a strengthening of the pro-Arab orientation in Italian foreign policy; the rapprochement with Nazi Germany on both the ideological and governmental levels following the League of Nations resolution condemning the invasion of Ethiopia; and the myth of "the new European civilization," centered in Rome and based largely on racist principles, which Mussolini and some of his associates conjured up during that period.

In addition, Fascist propaganda claimed that the Italian government had taken offense at the hostile attitude adopted by the Jewish press and organizations in various countries, first and foremost in Palestine, toward the Fascist regime and its campaign in Ethiopia. The government regarded this attitude as further proof that international Jewry and the Zionist movement had aligned themselves openly with the front ranks of international antifascism.

The first indications of the change that was to take place came in a series of editorials published in September and October 1936 in *Il Regime Fascista*, the newspaper of Roberto Farinacci, leader of the radical wing (*ala intransigente*) in the Fascist party. In these articles the Italian Jews were accused of collusion with international Jewish organizations like the Zionist Federation and the World Jewish Congress. "It is true that the Duce [Mussolini] has not so far felt the need to make distinctions of race or religion in Italy," the columnist wrote on 24 October, "but there are certain Italian Jews who make a point of setting themselves apart from Italians of other faiths by participating in pro-Zionist campaigns and in meetings of the International Jewish Congress." They must understand, the writer concluded, that sooner or later they would have to bear the consequences of their actions.

Also in October, Quinto Mazzolini, one of the diplomats most closely identified with the Fascist party, was appointed consul-general in Jerusalem. He was not hostile to Jews as such (despite what has sometimes been stated), but he was a most aggressive opponent of the Zionist movement, particularly its colonizing operations in Palestine. At the same time Mussolini personally approved a massive grant of money and weapons to the Arab rebellion under the leadership of Haj Amin el Husseini against the British administration of Palestine and the Jewish community there. A few months later, in the spring of 1937, during a visit to Libya and in front of cheering crowds, Mussolini drew "the sword of Islam" and declared himself the defender of Islam in the countries of the Mediterranean.

In March 1937 the notorious book *Gli Ebrei in Italia*, by Paolo Orano, was published. Aside from making traditional antisemitic accusations, such as the alleged greed implanted in Jewish souls and the supposed innate Jewish tendency toward subversion, it denied the right of Italian Jews to preserve their individuality and express their affinity for Judaism anywhere beyond the bounds of religion in the narrowest sense. Orano directed his weightiest accusations against Zionism and the Italian Zionists, who he believed represented a danger to Fascist Italy in two spheres: internationally, through the ambition to establish a Jewish state in Palestine that would become a base for British imperialism in the Mediterranean, and domestically, because the Zionists were members of an international political organization that in Orano's view was totally incompatible with their citizenship in a totalitarian Fascist state. The echoes of these words throughout Italy, in the newspapers and over the radio, were initiated and well orchestrated by the Ministry of Popular Culture. The ministry's involvement demonstrates beyond doubt that the decision to pursue an official antisemitic policy had already been taken.

In the weekly *Israel*, the unofficial mouthpiece of the Italian Zionist Federation, and the Revisionist Zionist periodical *L'Idea Sionistica* the Zionists attempted to refute the accusations directed against them. In *Israel* Dante Lattes rejected the claims that Italian Zionists lacked loyalty toward their homeland, and he argued forcefully against the Committee of Jewish Fascists (Comitato degli Italiani di Religione Ebraica), who had no compunction about adding their voice to the chorus of denigration against Zionism and the Italian Zionists. In *L'Idea Sionistica,* Leone Carpi firmly denied the claim that Zionism was a servant of British imperialism. But these courageous voices could not block the imminent collapse of the situation. What is more, the protests coming from the Zionists were drowned in a flood of publications from above—articles, brochures, and pamphlets published between spring 1937 and fall 1938, in which the most virulent and absurd claims were directed against the Jews and Zionism.

Despite all these indicators, which everyone understood to have been directed from the top, the leaders of the regime for some time refrained from revealing their intentions toward Italian Jews, thus giving themselves time to prepare public opinion for the change of direction in their policy. In some cases they even attempted to dissociate themselves from responsibility both for the campaign of antisemitic incitement already in progress and for the conclusions to be drawn from it for the future. Thus when Nahum Goldman, who was acting as representative of the Zionist Federation to the League of Nations, was received on 4 May 1937 for an interview by Foreign Minister Galeazzo

Ciano, the minister, in his own name and the Duce's, declared that "the official position of the government in relation to the Jews of Italy and to Zionism had not changed and would not change." He added that "some of the recently published books and articles in the press express the opinions of individuals and do not represent the official position,"—a patent lie in the Italy of that time.

Informazione Diplomatica No. 14, a semi-official government announcement published in February 1938, still declared, "The Fascist government has never considered and is not considering the adoption of political, economic, or moral measures against the Jews as such," and went on to say, "The universal Jewish problem has to be solved in only one way—by the establishment of a Jewish state in some part of the world, not in Palestine." It is now known for certain that the document was written by Mussolini himself—except for the last words, "not in Palestine," which were added at the last moment by Ciano, according to him out of consideration for the Arabs.

In contrast to these declarations, the daily *Il Giornale d'Italia* on 14 July 1938 published an article entitled "Fascism and Racial Problems," later known as the Race Manifesto (*Il Manifesto della Razza*). This manifesto, published anonymously, was ascribed to a group of scholars from several Italian universities working "under the aegis of the Ministry of Popular Culture." In reality the document had been drawn up by a young anthropologist and university lecturer named Guido Landra. Landra had been presented to Mussolini at the beginning of 1938 by Dino Alfieri, the minister of popular culture, and had immediately received the order directly from the Duce to draw up the document. Mussolini later bragged that the document "had in fact been dictated" by himself. The manifesto's 10 clauses stated that different races exist; that they are unequal in their importance; that the concept of race is purely biological; that the Italian population is mostly of Aryan origin and that its civilization is mostly Aryan; that "a pure Italian race already exists"; that "the Jews do not belong to the Italian race" because "they are the only population that was never absorbed by the Italians, being composed of non-European racial elements totally differing from those elements that provided the origins of the Italians." A few days later, on 25 July, an announcement was published in the press, in the name of the secretary of the Fascist party, praising the work of the 10 "scholars" who supposedly had written the manifesto. The announcement stated that "fascism had in fact been pursuing a racial policy for 16 years" and that the principles of the manifesto were an original and authoritative expression of the Fascist racial concept. At the same time Mussolini wanted a promise of silent consent from the Vatican. He obtained it in the middle of August, after brief negotiations conducted by Ciano, apparently in return for vague assurances concerning freedom of action granted to Catholic organizations.

Finally, at a session of the Council of Ministers on 2 September 1938, the first two laws for the protection of the race were approved. The law dated 5 September (RDL No. 1390) prohibited studying and teaching by "members of the Jewish race" at all the governmental and public schools "of any rank and grade," and also forbade membership by Jewish academics in any cultural institution. The second law, dated 7 September 1938 (RDL No. 1381), prohibited the permanent residence in Italy of foreign Jews, retroactively annulled Italian citizenship granted to Jewish immigrants after 1 January 1919, and ordered all those who had arrived after that date to leave the country within six months. Yet another law was published on 5 September, relating to the establishment of the General Directorate for Demography and Race (*Direzione Generale per la Demografia e Razza*, RDL No. 1531). This department of the Interior Ministry, which had actually begun operation a few months earlier, was now granted extensive powers in anything that concerned the initiation and implementation of race policy. In the course of the next five years, the General Directorate was to be the central lever for directing and implementing the regime's race policies.

On the night of 6–7 October 1939 the Grand Council of Fascism was convened at the Palazzo Venezia to discuss—and of course approve—the Declaration on Race (*La Dichiarazione sulla Razza*), which Mussolini presented as the basic document of the regime's race policy. The Declaration on Race established the principles and main points of the legislation for the protection of the race that was to be published shortly. In fact, just as the Race Manifesto supposedly established the theoretical foundations for the biological racism of the Fascist party, so the Declaration on Race formed the foundation of political racism that the Fascist regime was intending to put into operation. Three members of the Grand Council—Italo Balbo, Luigi Federzoni, and Emilio De Bono—had asked that the

severity of the proposed decrees be moderated, and expressed their opposition to the approval of the declaration that had been brought before them. Achille Starace, Roberto Farinacci, Guido Buffarini-Guidi, and Giuseppe Bottai, on the other hand, were openly fanatical and uncompromising in their position. Bottai, who at that time was serving as minister of education, zealously defended the expulsion of Jewish pupils and teachers from schools. "If we allow them back," he argued, "they will hate us for expelling them and despise us for readmitting them."

Following the decision by the Grand Council of Fascism, the comprehensive and inclusive basic law for the protection of the Italian race (*I Provvedimenti per la Protezione della Razza Italiana*, RDL No. 1728) was published on 17 November 1938. The law prohibited marriages between Jews and "Italian citizens of the Aryan race." It defined those who "belong to the Jewish race" as persons born of two parents of the Jewish race, even if they themselves are not of the Jewish religion; persons born of one Jewish parent and a parent of foreign nationality; persons born of a Jewish mother and an unknown father; and persons born of parents of Italian nationality of whom only one is of the Jewish race, so long as the person's religion is Jewish or the person has expressed an affinity with Judaism.

Further, the law made it the duty of all "who belong to the Jewish race" to declare themselves and be recorded in the population register as Jews. It also mandated social and economic restrictions: Jews could not be members of the Fascist party or serve in the armed forces: they could not act as guardians of minors not of their own race; they could not own businesses, real estate, or houses whose value exceeded a given amount; they could not employ "Aryan" servants; they were forbidden to hold any office or function in a government or public institution, or in an establishment or business supported by the state; and they could not be employed by banks or insurance companies.

Unlike the German racial laws, however, the Italian basic law allowed some exceptions to the restrictions. The *provvedimenti* stipulated that the families of Jews who had fallen in Italian wars, as well as Jews who had been awarded military honors or were war invalids, would be allowed to apply to the Interior Ministry for recognition as persons eligible for favorable discrimination (*discriminati*). They would thus be exempt from the prohibitions on ownership of real estate and houses and on employment of Aryan servants, but would be subject to all the other restrictions. Jews who had registered with the Fascist party in the years 1919–22 or in the second half of 1924 (when the party was in disfavor following the assassination of the Socialist leader Giacomo Matteotti) were granted the same exemptions.

Subsequent laws increased the severity of these restrictions. The value of property that Jews were allowed to own was greatly reduced (RDL No. 126, 9 February 1939), and Jews were expelled from the liberal professions (RDL No. 1054, 29 June 1939). In addition, Jews were forbidden to stay in holiday resorts, own radio receivers, or publish in the press.

Mussolini betrayed his motives for conducting this policy in a restricted-circulation speech that he delivered on 25 October 1938 to the members of the National Council of the Fascist party. The Duce proudly recounted the steps he had recently taken in his struggles against the bourgeoisie: "The first blow was the introduction of the goose step (*paso romano*) . . . another little blow was the abolition of *Lei* [polite "you," formal address]. . . . Another tremendous belly-blow has been the racial question. . . . The racial question is of vital importance and its introduction into Italian history will have incalculable consequences."

The conversion of "race protection" into a declared policy of the regime, and its implementation in extensive legislation, hit the small Jewish community in Italy hard. Some 200 teachers, 400 government officials, 500 employees in public institutions, 150 regular army personnel, and 2,500 members of the professions were dismissed from their jobs overnight. Forced out to the edges of society, a daily target of accusations mingled with contempt and mockery from the trumpets of official propaganda, many Jews saw in the racial laws the collapse of their social world and the disintegration of cultural and patriotic ties to Italy that they had constructed over generations. The state of the assimilated Jews was particularly difficult: they had to labor hard to comprehend their own affinity to Judaism, of which they had known hardly anything and yet because of which they were now expelled from society. Some preferred to forgo this painful self-criticism and sought a mostly ineffectual asylum in conversion to Catholicism recorded by the Union of Jewish Communities (Unione delle Comunità Israelitiche Italiane). The emigration of 5,966 Italian Jews—apart from the thousands of foreign-born Jews who were expelled—after the summer of 1938 must be added to this painful

loss. The population of the small Jewish community in Italy dropped from 47,000 on the eve of publication of the race laws to 35,000 at the end of 1939 and 32,000 at the beginning of September 1943, just before the German takeover.

Nevertheless, after the initial period of confusion and perplexity, the Jews of Italy were on the whole able to meet the challenge and threat posed by the new laws honorably, remaining internally united and mustering impressive moral and organizational powers. Primary schools for Jewish pupils were opened in all communities, and in the larger ones, such as in Milan and Turin, there were also secondary schools staffed by Jewish teachers who had been expelled from the government school system. According to many people, these schools were among the best in the country at their levels.

Furthermore, thanks to the work of distinguished personalities like Rabbi Nathan Cassuto in Milan and Rabbi Riccardo Pacifici in Genoa (both of whom perished in the Holocaust), youth groups met after school to discuss subjects of general literary and historic interest as well as Jewish matters mostly connected with the Zionist movement and Jewish settlement in Palestine. Largely on the initiative of Zionist activists, institutions were established by the communities to assist refugees who were continuing to infiltrate into Italy despite the legal prohibitions.

The most important of these institutions were COMASEBIT (Comitato Assistenza Ebrei in Italia, or Jewish Aid Committee), which the authorities closed down in 1939, and DELASEM (Delegazione Assistenza Emigranti Ebrei, or Aid Commission for Jewish Refugees), established in its place in November 1939 with approval from the authorities and under the leadership of the lawyer Lelio Vittorio Valobra. During its first months of operation DELASEM was already assisting some 3,000 refugees who were living in Italy while awaiting a chance for emigration. With the rising stream of refugees in the middle of 1942, the organization gave aid to 3,500 refugees in detention camps, to 5,000 who had been "confined" (sent to small villages), and to 500 who remained free. Over the same period, from the beginning of 1939 to September 1943, it helped some 5,000 refugees emigrate, and during the German occupation from September 1943 to May 1945 it saved the lives of thousands of Jews through its valiant underground activities. Behind many of these operations was Raffaele Cantoni, a Zionist leader who because of his positions against fascism was prevented from openly holding public office. After the severe crises of 1938 and at the beginning of 1939, the Union of Jewish Communities under the leadership of Dante Almansi, who had been elected chairman in September 1939, adopted a course of action that was consistent, resolute, and honorable. It thereby acquired moral authority among the Jewish communities and also with Italian authorities, in particular the heads of the Directorate for Demography and Race.

This awakening of the Jewish community arose in large measure from the activities of the small band of Italian Zionists under the leadership of Dante Lattes and Alfonso Pacifici. Since the beginning of the century this group had made a decisive contribution to-ward preserving and reestablishing links with Jewish culture and Jewish tradition in the face of a broad trend among Italian Jews toward assimilation.

The vast majority of Italians stood by the persecuted Jews, both morally and socially. Two newspapers in the front rank of Italian culture came out against the race campaign: *La Critica,* led by the philosopher Benedetto Croce, and *Artecrazia,* owned by the father of Futurism, F. T. Marinetti. These were joined by the periodical *La Camicia Rossa,* edited by Ezio Garibaldi. Even some Italian Fascists openly voiced support for and solidarity with the Jews, and between the end of 1938 and July 1943 hundreds of them were expelled from the party for this misdeed. In fact, in the early

Jewish forced laborers working on the Tiber embankment in Rome. 1942

The desecrated interior of the synagogue in Trieste, which was used as a warehouse for confiscated property. 18 July 1942

1940s, apart from a few cases of physical violence and acts of vandalism perpetrated by gangs of Fascists against synagogues in Padua, Ferrara, and Trieste, the Jews felt no immediate danger to their lives and personal safety.

The outbreak of war in 1939 and the entry of Italy on the side of the Germans on 10 June 1940 did not immediately change the legal status of the Jews of Italy, though the economic and social troubles they faced became more and more difficult. On the eve of Italy's entry into the war thousands of foreign Jews—those who had disregarded the expulsion order of 1938 and some who had infiltrated into Italy from the countries under German occupation—were arrested, together with some 200 Italian Jews either suspected of subversive activities or known to oppose fascism. Men, women, and children were thrown into prison without trial and under hard conditions. A start was made on the con-

struction of internment camps: on 4 September 1940, at the time of publication of the Law of Internment for Citizens of Enemy Countries (RDL No. 239), 15 camps were already in existence. (Their number eventually rose to 40.)

Many of the Jews, both foreign and Italian, who had been arrested earlier were also brought to these camps by administrative order. Those not so transferred were confined to remote areas. Living conditions in the camps were at first quite hard—mainly because of overcrowding and shortages of equipment. But in the course of time there were great improvements: families lived together, schools were set up for the children, and, with the approval of the authorities and the assistance of Jewish organizations headed by DELASEM, there was extensive welfare and cultural activity. For the most part the internees' only tasks involved camp maintenance and service. The government paid them a fixed sum of money, which together with outside assistance was sufficient for their modest needs. The largest camp was at Ferramonti di Tarsia, near the town of Cosenza. A total of 3,823 Jews were detained there between June 1940 and August 1943; all but 141 of them were refugees. These were the first Jews on European soil to be liberated by the Allied Forces, among them Jewish soldiers in units from Palestine. On 14 September 1943, the day of their liberation, there were just over 1,500 Jews at the Ferramonti camp. Living conditions for the Jews who had been confined to remote villages were somewhat better, despite the oppressive isolation. Sometimes the local authorities allowed the "confined" persons to engage in their professions— or at least they turned a blind eye, particularly when doctors, who were scarce in such areas, continued to practice.

On 6 May 1942 the Ministry of the Interior announced that male and female Italian citizens between the ages of 18 and 55 "belonging to the Jewish race" would have to report for "obligatory labor." The reason given was that this work would substitute for military service, which was obligatory for "Aryan" citizens. The registration procedure, however, was so involved that by 25 July 1943, when the Fascist regime was overthrown, only 2,038 Jews had been sent to work out of the 15,517 to whom the order applied. For the most part those who had been recruited were employed on farms, in industrial plants, or paving roads, and they received a small wage.

Mussolini's downfall and the surrender of Italy to the Allies on 8 September 1943 were turning points in the fate of the Jews in Italy. When Gen. Dwight Eisenhower's headquarters in Algeria published the announcement of the surrender agreement, the Germans put into action their plan to take control of the country. King Victor Emmanuel III and a few government ministers fled to southern Italy; the army, meanwhile, disintegrated and surrendered its arms. Within a few days the country was divided in two: its southern districts had been liberated by the Allies, whereas the central and northern areas came under German rule. The Jewish refugees who had been held in concentration camps or confined to remote villages in the south were saved. On the other hand, the division had catastrophic consequences for Italian Jews, who for historical reasons were concentrated in Rome and the towns north of the city. In this area the Repubblica Sociale Italiana (RSI), the Fascist state under German protection, was established with Mussolini and the *intransigente* wing of the Fascist party at the helm. Many of these leaders had long promoted antisemitic ideas and were now ready to collaborate wholeheartedly in implementing German policies toward the Jews. In only 45 days the Jews of Italy thus passed from a regime of social and economic discrimination under the law, through an ephemeral period of liberty and hope for equality (25 July 1943–8 September 1943), to a time of terror as they fell into the net of the Final Solution.

In September SS Obergruppenführer Karl Wolff was appointed military governor in northern Italy. Wolff established his headquarters in Verona, and by the end of that month branches of the security services had been set up in all the occupied districts. At the same time Theo Dannecker, one of the most experienced officers in Department IVb4 (headed by Adolf Eichmann, who was in charge of implementing the Final Solution), was sent to Italy. Dannecker had run the operation to eliminate the Jews of France. It appears that he arrived in Italy in early October 1943, together with a small group of assistants, and began at once to organize the arrest of Jews in all the main communities.

Even before Dannecker's arrival, severe measures were being taken against Jews in German-occupied Italy. On 16 September, 25 Jews from the town of Merano were arrested and sent to Auschwitz, and between 15 and 24 September soldiers of the Adolf Hitler Leibstandarte division massacred some 40 Jews, most of them refugees from Salonika who had taken temporary refuge in Meina, Arona, and Baveno on the shore of Lake Maggiore. The SS commander in Rome, Herbert Kappler, ordered on 26 September that the Jews of the city deliver 50 kilograms of gold within 36 hours or 200 hostages would be shot. The gold was collected and delivered before the deadline, but this compliance did not prevent the Germans from bursting into the community on 29 September, plundering its rich library of ancient and rare books and confiscating other valuables.

Strange as it seems today, these initial acts did not open the eyes of most of Italy's Jews to the fate awaiting them. The reason may be that only a little of what was beginning to happen came to their knowledge, or that the hazy news concerning the fate of the Jews in the other occupied countries, especially in neighboring Yugoslavia, was considered unreliable—the preposterous exaggerations of people driven out of their minds by relentless persecution. Moreover, unlike in other occupied countries, in Italy the Germans refrained from preparatory steps against the Jews, such as the establishment of ghettos, the imposition of the obligation to wear the yellow star, and the appointment of Jewish councils (*Judenräte*), which would have aroused suspicion. One way and another, most of the Jews in Italy failed to search for the means of escape that were still available, such as hiding among the Christian population, crossing the front lines to the regions already liberated, or seeking asylum in neighboring Switzerland. All these options were dangerous and did not ensure salvation, but they would have been a wiser course than complacency and false hopes that they would not be murdered by the Nazis.

In the last three months of 1943, after Dannecker's arrival, the organized round-ups or actions (*Aktionen*) were carried out in all the main Jewish communities—in Trieste, Rome, Genoa, Florence, Milan, Venice, Ferrara, and elsewhere. In the course of these actions some 3,200 Jews were dragged from their homes; nearly all were sent to Auschwitz in five transports that set out between 18 October 1943 and 30 January 1944. Only 46 of these deportees returned after the liberation.

The way such operations were carried out is revealed in a report, addressed to Wolff and signed by Kappler but apparently drawn up by Dannecker; on the 16 October action in Rome:

> The operation against the Jews was today initiated and completed. All available forces of security and public-order police were employed. The participation of Italian police was not possible, given their unreliability. For this reason individual arrests in the 26 zones of the operation could not be effected rapidly. Blocking off entire streets was not practicable, considering the character of the Open City and also the insufficient aggregate of only 365 German police. Nevertheless, during the operation, which lasted from 5:30 a.m. to 2 p.m., 1,259 persons were arrested in Jewish apartments and brought to a central collection point at a military college here. After releasing the part-Jews, the foreigners (including one citizen of Vatican City), the members of mixed marriages (including their Jewish partners), the Aryan domestics and subtenants, 1,007 Jews remained in custody. Deportation set for Monday, 18 October, at 9 a.m. They are to be escorted by 30 men from the regular police. The behavior of the Italian population was total passive resistance, which in many individual cases amounted to active assistance. In one case, for example, the police came upon the apartment of a Fascist in a black shirt and with identity papers, who had certainly not been in the apartment for more than an hour. As the German police were breaking into some homes, attempts to hide Jews were observed, and it is believed that in many cases they were successful. The antisemitic section of the population was nowhere to be seen during the action, only a great mass of people who in some individual cases even tried to cut off the police from the Jews. In no case was there any need to use firearms.

The action in Rome, as in other cities, was carried out from street to street and from house to house, according to the detailed lists of names that the Germans had obtained from the district governors' offices. These lists had been drawn up on the basis of self-declarations by Italian Jews as mandated by the 1938 racial laws. The Italian forces did not as a rule participate in the actions. (An exception was in Venice, where the operation on the night of 5–6 December was carried out entirely by members of the Italian police.) In contrast, the Fascist militias that had organized themselves with the establishment of the RSI collaborated with the Germans in every case and without reservation. In Rome Jews married to non-Jews were released, perhaps out of special consideration for sensitivity of the Vatican to actions taking place "practically under its windows," according to a contemporary source. Elsewhere, however, everyone considered to be "of the Jewish race" was arrested.

The detained Jews were at first confined locally, in prisons, barracks, or schools. They were later brought to special concentration camps erected in northern Italy, the largest of which were at Fossoli di Carpi and Bolzano. From there transports left periodically for the extermination camps until the end of 1944. Only in Rome, where 1,030 Jews (including 200 children under 10 years of age) were arrested in the 16 October action, were the prisoners sent directly to Auschwitz without first going through the concentration camps in northern Italy. They reached their final destination on 23 October. On arrival 149 men and 47 women were selected for work; the remainder were immediately put to death in the gas chambers. Only 18 of the Jews deported from Rome survived the war.

The first wave of actions, when whole communities of Jews suffered mass arrest, ceased toward the end of 1943. The remaining Jews fled for their lives. Thousands crossed the border into Switzerland (and at times were returned to the Germans by the Swiss border police); others made their way south across the front line to the liberated regions or joined groups of partisans operating in the mountains. Most, however, preferred to hide among other Italians, as far as possible from their permanent place of residence, in the homes of "Aryan" friends, in Catholic institutions, and with farmers and villagers.

Thus began a new stage in the persecution of Italian Jewry, in the course of which individual Jews and Jewish families were hunted down. Dread of the raids (*razzie*) conducted by the German security forces and Fascist militia units, the danger of betrayal by Fascist neighbors, and the need to keep on the move to avoid discovery marked the life of Italian Jews in this fearful period, which continued until liberation. During this period, too, Jews became aware of the solidarity of many Italian people, who were quite often prepared to take serious risks in order to aid the persecuted.

At the beginning of 1944 SS Sturmbannführer Friedrich Bosshammer replaced Dannecker as the man in charge of implementing operations against the Jews. From then until the end of the war the German security forces and the Fascist militias succeeded in arresting at least 3,000 more Jews and deporting them to Auschwitz. The total number of Jews deported from Italy during the German occupation was 6,746, more than one-fifth of the 32,000 living there in September 1943. Only 830 deportees returned after the liberation. An additional 1,805 Jews were deported from the island of Rhodes, which belonged to Italy, and 183 of them returned. At least another 291 Jews met their deaths in massacres perpetrated within Italy—in Rome (Fosse Ardeatine), Pisa (the Pardo Roques house), the townships on the shore of Lake Maggiore, and elsewhere. About a hundred Jews fell in battle in the ranks of the partisans, among them 13-year-old Franco Cesana, the youngest partisan to be killed in Italy, and Rita Rosani, the only woman in Italy known to have died in battle.

One chapter that stands alone concerns the attitude of the Italian authorities to Jews outside Italy, in particular Jews living in enemy countries occupied by Italy. For more than three years, while the Italians were fighting in the war alongside the Germans, broad regions in a number of countries came under the control of the Italian army. These included parts of southeastern France, Dalmatia and the adjoining regions of Croatia and part of Slovenia, and most of Greece. Similarly, until November 1942 Tunisia was under Italian influence through a branch of the Italo-French Armistice Commission. While in authority—that is, from 10 June 1940 to 8 September 1943—the Italians extended their protection over the Jews who lived in those regions and over the numerous refugees who had joined them, for the time being preventing the Germans and local collaborators from implementing the Final Solution.

Within this period two distinct stages in the policy of Italian occupying forces can be discerned. During the first stage, to mid-1942, in regions that came under their direct rule, the Italian army did not publish discriminatory laws, and in Greece they prevented the local authorities from doing so. Since the Italian racial laws did not apply in the occupied territories, a strange situation prevailed, whereby from a legal point of view the status of Jews resident in these areas was preferable to that of Jews in Italy itself. At the same time, Italian consular and diplomatic representatives, on explicit orders from the Foreign Ministry, protected Jews with Italian nationality resident in the regions occupied by the Germans or subject to German influence. Particularly widespread and determined action was carried out in the German-occupied zone of France, in which there were 1,500 Jews of Italian nationality, most of them living in Paris; in Tunisia, where there were 5,500 Jewish Italian nationals, many of them holding important positions in the local society and economy; and in Salonika, where there lived several hundred Italian Jews of position and means. Thus the Italians protected their Jewish citizens not only as a matter of duty but also because it was in their own vital interest. The disappearance of these groups of Jews was liable to represent, and later did represent, a fatal blow to the Italian presence in the region. Moreover, at that time the Italians were still seeking to preserve equality with their German allies and were not prepared to condone discrimination against their own citizens of whatever race.

The second stage began in mid-1942 and continued until September 1943. The arrests, manhunts, and deportations of entire Jewish populations that the Italians had witnessed in Western Europe and Greece, the atrocities performed before their eyes in Croatia, and the rumors about events in Eastern Europe convinced many Italian soldiers and diplomats that it was their humane duty to assist the persecuted Jews regardless of their nationality. What was no less than a rescue operation was then mounted in the regions controlled by the Italian army in Dalmatia and Croatia, where 5,000 Jews from the remainder of Yugoslavia had found asylum; in southern France, where more than 25,000 Jews had gathered, mostly refugees from northern France; also in Athens and other parts of Greece in the Italian zone, where there were some 13,000 Jews. Altogether some 40,000 Jewish refugees from various countries found a safe haven in the areas of Italian occupation. (In addition, a few thousand refugees had been permitted to enter Italy itself and gained asylum there.)

Despite repeated protests, in no case did the Italians surrender the Jews to the Germans, the Croatian Ustasha, or the Vichy police. They maintained this position in the face of intense pressure, coupled with demands for extradition, exerted by the Germans at various diplomatic levels and even upon Mussolini himself. At least twice Mussolini succumbed to these pressures and gave orders to surrender the Jewish refugees in the Italian zone of Croatia, but the diplomats and high-ranking military officers around him joined forces to evade implementation of this criminal order. Among those who acquitted themselves honorably in this affair were Deputy Foreign Minister Giuseppe Bastianini and senior diplomats Luca Pietromanchi, Luigi Viau, and Roberto Ducci in Rome; diplomatic representatives Guelfo Zamboni, Giuseppe Castruccio, and Pellegrino Ghigi in Greece; the diplomats Vittorio Zoppi, Alberto Calisse, and Gustavo Orlandini in France; and Vittorio Castellani in Croatia. Among military personnel three generals, Giuseppe Pièche, Giuseppe Amico, and Mario Roatta, merit recognition. Other distinguished figures were Police Inspector Guido Lospinoso, who operated in southern France, where he was assisted by the Jewish banker Angelo Donati and the Capuchin friar Pierre-Marie Benoît. Unfortunately, some of the Jews who had found asylum in the Italian occupied zone were arrested by the Germans after 8 September 1943 and died in the Holocaust. *Daniel Carpi*

J

Japan Japan, Germany's ally in World War II, developed an antisemitic Jewish policy of its own, which changed over the course of the war from one which allowed mass immigration to one that enforced segregation of Jewish refugees in Shanghai, but stopped well short of mass extermination. The vast areas under Japanese occupation were home to several sizable Jewish communities which largely survived unharmed. In Shanghai, for example, tens of thousands of Jewish refugees were forced to live apart from the rest of the inhabitants of the city, but they survived the war largely unharmed.

The seeming contradictions in Japan's attitude toward and treatment of the Jews in this period have their roots in the history of the country's contacts with Jewish immigrants, merchants, and bankers and with international antisemitism of the late nineteenth and early twentieth centuries. Japan's first contact with Jewish immigration came in the mid-nineteenth century when Jewish merchants from Europe and the Middle East settled Kobe, Yokohama, and Nagasaki. In the 1860s Yokohama and Kobe were the main centers of Jewish life in Japan. The Jewish population increased as a result of immigration from Russia following the revolutions in 1905 and 1917. Most Russian Jews settled in Manchuria and northern China, but Jewish aid organizations had their headquarters in Japan and directed a stream of Jewish refugees to the United States and South America.

Early Jewish immigrants were not perceived as a group separate from other Westerners. They were seen as foreign business people; outwardly they appeared to be assimilated citizens of Western states who practiced their religion in private. It was the intervention of Jacob H. Schiff, originally from Germany but whose fortune was made as a New York banker, that first made Tokyo aware of Jewish influence in international politics. In 1904, when war between Russia and Japan seemed imminent, Schiff decided to give financial support to the Japanese government. Since Japan had lagged behind it in naval development, the loans attracted considerable attention. When Schiff openly explained that his involvement was the result of his disdain for the tsarist regime and Russia's history of bloody pogroms against Jews, Japanese elites first became aware of a rift between Jews and other Westerners.

An important episode in the shaping of Japanese attitudes toward the Jews was the country's involvement in the war between the Whites and Reds in Siberia during the Russian civil war (1918–22). For the first time Japanese officers came into direct contact with a large Jewish population and encountered standard antisemitic propaganda such as the *Protocols of the Elders of Zion.*

Antisemitic literature from German, English, French, and American sources influenced a small group of middle-echelon army and navy officers, who developed a theoretical and ideological antisemitism that became part of Japan's mainstream attitude toward world affairs. In contrast to the European situation, however, this theory-based antisemitism did not translate into a political movement or enter the platform of any important political party. In the 1920s and early 1930s Japan's military and foreign policy establishment focused on containing communism, which was perceived as the main threat to Japan's expansionist plans in Asia. Because of this keen interest in anti-Bolshevist theory, the so-called Jewish question was discussed in the editorials of foreign policy journals.

All Japan's foremost "experts" on Jewish issues were military officers: Col. Senko Yasue, Capt. Koreshige Inuzuka, and Col. Moto. Through serious publications and crude antisemitic stereotypes, they managed to spread both information and disinformation about Jews and Jewish issues, adapting Western clichés and knowledge for use in Japan's geopolitical situation. Moto, for example, studied Judaism in the years after World War I and even undertook a trip to Palestine, which he described in a book. His work highlighted many typical anti-Jewish attitudes, but he also painted an overwhelmingly positive picture of Jewish achievements in Palestine. In his many articles, however, he spread archetypal anti-Jewish prejudice, including the perennial stereotypes about the Jews' supposed love of money and power and their desire to control the world. In his view, Jews were responsible for World War I and the destruction of Germany, the Austro-Hungarian empire, and Russia, as well as the rise of Bolshevism, which in his words was as Jewish as capitalism.

Throughout the 1930s this type of antisemitic literature flourished in Japan. The emphasis was simultaneously on Jewish influence in world financial markets, and on Jewish authorship of communism and Bolshevism. But aside from these standard beliefs, Japanese antisemitism focused on what was seen as Jewish influence in the Far East and Japan. Japan, such articles typically emphasized, was being encircled by the Jews in the West through their control of the League of Nations, by their coreligionists in Asia, and through Communist infiltration in Japan, China (particularly Shanghai), and elsewhere. The same Jewish power groups who were said to be advancing the Communist cause were supposedly harming Japanese business interests in the financial markets. Even the Second Sino-Japanese War was considered a product of Jewish plotting.

These Japanese arguments fit well into Western antisemitic discourse. The recommendations made by Japanese antisemitic theoreticians, however, were different from those advanced by European, American, and German antisemites. Jewish power was to be watched, contained, and controlled but eventually put to use for Japan's own purposes. Japan should observe the Jews and be aware of their influence, these writers declared, but not become their outright enemy. In the end, not the removal or extermination of Jews but cooperation with powerful Jewish lobbies was the road Japan chose, at least in the first years of World War II.

Articles advancing such ideas were not mainstream reading but were written and read by small circles of interested intellectuals in the army and navy. Only after Japan made an alliance with Germany was the Japanese general public introduced to these concepts. Contact with Germany's antisemitic policy and a close alliance with that country helped to move the so-called Jewish question a little closer to the mainstream of Japanese political life. Even after the establishment of Nazi rule in Germany in 1933, however, there was little understanding in Japan of the practical consequences of Hitler's racist policies. On the contrary, Germany's use of racial classifications in political practice led to friction between the two countries. Japanese citizens in Germany were classified as "colored," and the outlawing of mixed marriages required frequent interventions by the Japanese ambassador in Berlin. Japanese newspapers gave lengthy accounts of Germany's segregationist laws and highlighted hatred of "non-Aryans" living in Germany. Before antisemitic articles were widely distributed, the practical consequences of racist policies were widely discussed in Japan. German racism did not find much favor among a people that perceived the world as being biased against it.

Several recent incidents had sensitized the Japanese public to racist or segregationist policies. In 1918 the Western nations had rejected Japan's appeal for a declaration of the equality of all races in the Treaty of Versailles. In 1924 the United States had put restrictions on Japanese immigration, and the memory of Kaiser Wilhelm's use of the term *yellow peril* was still fresh when Nazi Germany began implementing its racial policies. Japan, the dominant Asian power, still felt an outcast in international affairs. In its experience, industrial and military power was insufficient to gain international recognition.

German diplomats in Japan frequently appealed to the Berlin authorities to consider restraining anti-Japanese practices, allowing German-Japanese mixed couples and children to integrate into German society, and restricting the use of the terms *yellow* and *yellow peril* in the press. Even superficial measures such as these were beyond the powers of the foreign ministry, which was not a major player in the Berlin of the mid-1930s.

A new dilemma for German diplomats was presented by refugee German-Jewish artists who were trying to make a living in Japan. Nazi ideology demanded that such artists be openly declared Jews and thus decried as unable to represent German culture. But the embassy in Japan soon realized that it was impossible to exert pressure on the host country to prevent the exiles from representing German music or fine arts. Employing foreign artists, they were told, was a purely internal matter to be left to Japan. When Nazi party officials in Japan launched a campaign to smear German Jewish artists, conflict arose with the German embassy in Tokyo, which feared an outbreak of anti-German sentiment. In the end many German Jewish artists were able to continue their careers, as the Japanese regarded their work as none of Germany's business. The situation eased in 1935, when the Nuremberg Laws showed that German racial policy was directed against Jews, who were exclusively defined as "non-Aryans"; Asian nationals were not marked for discrimination.

The rising threat of a new world war led to a search in Japan for global explanations of the crisis. Shortly before the Japanese attack on Pearl Harbor, the German ambassador happily described mass meetings in Japan condemning Jews and their power over world events. As anti-Bolshevist sentiment receded and anti-Allied feelings grew, Jews were made responsible for preparations for war against Japan by their alleged domination of Allied policymaking. Jewish refugees and business people in Japan were targeted by the Japanese antisemitic press. Jews were characterized as rich and powerful and therefore undeserving of pity. They were accused of inventing Freemasonry and such immoral institutions as coffee shops and dance halls. The presence of about 3,000 Jewish refugees in Japan were seen as a danger, for they might exert a subversive influence. Even the government was affected by such writings and began to transfer to Shanghai a few hundred Jewish refugees from Poland and the Baltic states who had previously been granted permission to stay in Japan indefinitely. In September 1941 antisemitic demonstrators in Tokyo urged the Japanese people to study Jewish history in order to prepare for the necessity of an anti-Jewish policy.

The war in the Pacific strengthened antisemitic sentiments. In early 1943 a large exhibition opened that denounced the Jews and Freemasonry, "a Jewish secret society." One and a half million Japanese saw the exhibition, which was secretly sponsored by the German embassy. There were few consequences for Jews who remained in Japan, but those Jews living in Japanese-occupied Asia—in particular the large Jewish communities in Manchuria, northern China, and Shanghai—were more adversely affected.

Before the arrival of large numbers of Central European Jews, Jewish life in the Far East was concentrated in the northern Chinese cities of Harbin and Tianjin, as well as in Shanghai. In Harbin, Jews found business opportunities in the wake of the construction of the New East China Railway. After Japan occupied Manchuria in 1931 and exerted pressure on northern China, many Jews went south to Shanghai in search of new opportunities. In 1937, as Japan's aggressive territorial interests mounted, the Jewish population of China was increasingly caught up in the Japanese war policy, whose chief object was total control of all residents under its rule and the effective loyalty of all citizens. Harbin, home to 8,000 Jews (out of a total population of 500,000), came under Japanese occupation after 1937. Yasue was made liaison officer to the Jewish population and set up the National Council of Jewish Communities in the Far East. This organization reported to Yasue and was responsible for compliance with Japanese laws in the occupied areas. A proclamation by the first Congress of Jewish Communities in Harbin stated that "the Jewish people in the Far East condemn communism and declare their gratitude for the Japanese efforts to fight the Soviet Union, the enemy of the people. Since Japan and Manchuria guarantee the protection of the Jewish people, it will act in accordance with the interest of both peoples." Yasue, convinced that it would be counterproductive to make the Jews enemies of Japan, was satisfied with the resolution and its implementation. The Jews should be controlled and registered, Yasue maintained, and only if they violated their allegiance to Japan should they be punished.

Officially, the Jews were considered a national minority and were accorded all cultural rights under Manchurian and Japanese occupation laws. Because they cooperated, Japan could consider its nonconfrontational tactics a success. German diplomats were of course extremely unhappy with the Japanese policy, which the Nazis rationalized as resulting from Japan's wish once again to curry favor with Jewish business circles in New York and London. Even after the outbreak of war in Europe in 1939, Japanese attitudes toward the Jews changed only in minor ways. During the third and last Congress of Jewish Communities in the Far East, the policy of equal treatment of all races was officially reaffirmed.

A year later, the planned fourth congress was called off after German intervention. Yasue was removed from office. Japan's new partnership with Germany and Italy, the impressive success of the German army,

Ghoya, the Japanese commander of the "Ghetto," a closed area in the Hongkou district of Shanghai that served as a Japanese detention camp from 1943 until 1945, distributes transit passes to the Jews who earned their living outside the quarter. 1940s

and the looming conflict with the Western powers led Japan to comply with Germany's policy goals. This did not, however, include agreement with German extermination policies. Jews in northern China were now isolated and no longer a danger to Japan, whose long-term strategic goals and alliance with the Axis were more important than a few thousand Jews in no position to help or harm.

After Pearl Harbor, Japanese policymakers on the Jewish question shifted their attention to Shanghai, the new center of Jewish life in Asia. After Kristall-nacht, the city had become a haven for approximately 17,000 Jewish refugees from Germany, Austria, Poland, and Czechoslovakia because of its status as an international free port. Shanghai was neither a part of China nor a colony of the Western powers. In the Opium Wars of the mid-nineteenth century, China had been forced to cede certain extraterritorial rights in parts of the town later known as the International Settlement and the French Concession. Japan controlled entry to

Shanghai after its seizure of the noninternational area of the city during the early days of the Second Sino-Japanese War. The Japanese Imperial Navy, however, did nothing to discourage immigration, as it was hoped that benevolence toward Jewish immigrants from Germany would cause Jewish circles in London and New York to exert their influence on Japan's behalf.

Most of the immigrants had been unable to transfer any funds to the city and arrived virtually penniless. The large majority settled in Hongkou, part of the International Settlement but occupied by Japanese forces since 1937. The occupying power was not the army but the Imperial Navy. Before the summer of 1939 no visa was required to enter Shanghai, one of the few ports in the world still open to virtually any Westerner with a valid (and expensive) ship ticket. For many Jews in Germany and occupied Austria, and especially those already imprisoned in concentration camps and freed only on condition that they leave the country immediately, Shanghai was their last hope. Most refugees arrived on ships from Trieste, Genoa, and Hamburg with many of their movable possessions but without money.

In the spring of 1939, panic struck the immigration officials and the Shanghai Municipal Council. By then every third foreigner in Shanghai was a Jew from Central Europe. Nearly every foreign consulate lobbied the Japanese to halt immigration into Shanghai on the grounds that there were no funds for housing and feeding such a mass of people. Antisemitism and fear of losing their privileged position in Shanghai led even American and British officials to appeal for a stop to immigration. Japan remained aloof until the summer of 1939, when it became obvious that the problem had to be solved. Restrictive immigration laws, requiring prospective immigrants to bring a minimum amount of cash and to obtain an advance visa, were passed. The International Settlement and the French Concession followed suit. Still, Japanese policy did manage to keep the door to Shanghai open to Jewish immigration from Germany almost until the outbreak of war in Europe.

Plans to settle Jews elsewhere in China or move them elsewhere in the world failed. Most notable was a plan presented by the prominent German Jewish banker Jakob Berglas to create a Jewish settlement in Yunnan. Approved by parts of China's Guomindang regime, it nevertheless failed to attract support from European and American governments and was not realized for lack of funding.

Most European Jews had to carve out a niche for themselves in Shanghai, where they encountered economic recession, turmoil, a mass of Chinese refugees fleeing the Japanese advance, and discrimination from Shanghai's upper classes. Even Shanghai's long-standing Bagdhadi Jewish community, though active in aiding refugees, refused social contact with them. Shanghai's Russian Jews, themselves refugees from tsarist and Bolshevik persecution, were engaged in fierce economic competition with many of the newly arrived German speakers, whose economic situation was on the whole abominable. Only 20 percent managed to survive on their own, whereas the vast majority depended on daily handouts from the American Jewish Joint Distribution Committee and local aid institutions.

But after Japan occupied the International Concession in December 1941, any citizens of countries at war with Japan were interned in camps. Central European refugees, however, were considered stateless rather than enemy aliens. Russian Jews also escaped internment, as Japan was not at war with the Soviet Union until 1945. Some of the Sephardic Jews were British subjects and were interned. In early 1943 Japan published a declaration ordering all stateless refugees—German, Austrian, Czech, and Polish Jews—to move into a restricted area in Hong Kong that had already been settled by the majority of Central European Jews. This proclamation was meant to appease Germany, which insisted that something be done about this large group of Jews under Japanese rule. Nevertheless, Japanese authorities were quick to forbid the area's being called a camp or a ghetto and to emphasize that their policy was not racist. "The area designated in the proclamation is neither a ghetto nor a jail," a proclamation published in the *Shanghai Jewish Chronicle* of 9 May 1943 stated, "but an area which is full of hope for the refugees, in which they may build a haven for themselves where they may carry on peacefully with great advantage to themselves. All concerned should do their best with this view in mind."

The life of the refugees was now concentrated in this area, which they could leave only with Japanese consent. There were no walls, and there was little barbed wire. Jewish refugees were entirely dependent upon the Japanese, and for their livelihood they increasingly relied on dwindling aid from the Joint Distribution Committee. Conditions for the Jewish refugees in Shanghai were hard, but unlike in the European ghettos established by the Nazis, the Jews under Japanese authority did not suffer famine; and there were relatively few cases of Japanese brutality and random arrest. Moreover, despite persistent rumors to the contrary, there is little evidence that the Japanese were preparing to exterminate the Jews.

Shanghai's Jewish population was liberated in 1945, and many reemigrated to Palestine (after 1948, Israel), the United States, and Australia. Once the victory of the Communists in the Chinese civil war became inevitable, all but a few Communists and leftists and some elderly people prepared to leave the city. A sizable portion of the community returned to Germany and Austria, primarily owing to a lack of other options.

Japanese antisemitism, confined as it was to a small circle of zealots, nevertheless helped shape Japan's treatment of Jewish populations under its control. But antisemitic theories derived from Western models led to different conclusions in Japan: Jewish influence was to be used if possible and contained if necessary. This basic pragmatism formed the backdrop to such decisions as allowing thousands of Jewish immigrants into Shanghai and confining them to a closed area. Consequently, a large Jewish population was able to survive, albeit under difficult circumstances.

Matthias Krön

Jasenovac Croatian concentration and extermination camp about 115 kilometers south of Zagreb in which, under the Ustashi regime, many civilians were killed, mainly Serb nationals but also thousands of Jews. The estimates of the number of victims range between 100,000 and 700,000. See YUGOSLAVIA

Jassy (Iasi) Town in northern Romania, unofficial capital of the Iron Guard. About 8,000 to 10,000 Jews were killed in a major pogrom in Jassy in late June 1941; thousands more were deported to Transnistria.

Jeckeln, Friedrich (1895–1946) Senior SS commander who participated in the execution of the Final Solution in Ukraine. Units under his authority killed thousands of Jewish deportees in Ukraine and took part in the Babi Yar massacre. Jeckeln commanded the

Friedrich Jeckeln.

1941 extermination of the Jews in Riga. He was hanged in Riga as a war criminal in 1946.

Jehovah's Witnesses The Jehovah's Witnesses, also known as the International Bible Students Association, are an eschatological religious community of belief founded in the United States in the 1870s. Incorporated as the Watchtower Bible and Tract Society in Pennsylvania in 1884, they moved their headquarters in 1909 to Brooklyn, New York. The Witnesses actively proselytized for converts, and their missionaries in Germany after the 1890s registered steady increases in the numbers of followers. Although they were isolated and condemned as heretics by mainstream Protestant and Catholic churches, the tenets of their faith posed few problems for governments in times of peace and prosperity. Their beliefs were millenarian and comprehensive: they saw themselves as citizens of Jehovah's Kingdom and refused to swear allegiance to any secular government. Although they would not bear arms for any nation, the Witnesses were not pacifists, but believed themselves soldiers in Jehovah's army. This stance contributed to the growing hostility the Witnesses encountered in Germany throughout the 1920s and, in part, motivated their persecution and prohibition in Nazi Germany after 1933.

On 12 July 1921 the Watchtower Bible and Tract Society became legally registered in Germany as a corporation with headquarters in Magdeburg. At that time the Witnesses were known in Germany as *Ernste Bibelforscher* (serious Bible scholars). The German printing plants and property were chartered as a subsidiary of the American parent corporation, a status that later facilitated American diplomatic assistance in protecting Witness printing plants and property from immediate confiscation by Nazi German authorities during 1933 and 1934. The Witnesses' membership increased from about 4,000 followers in 1919 to about 20,000 by 1933, in part because of the traumatic economic and political conditions of the Weimar Republic. Their members were largely law-abiding lower-middle-class manual laborers, servants, pensioners, and other economically dependent members of society. Their Magdeburg printing plant had more than 200 employees, and they distributed German editions of their periodicals, *The Watchtower* and *The Golden Age*, as well as numerous biblical tracts.

Articles 135–137 of the Weimar constitution (1919) guaranteed the rights of Jehovah's Witnesses as a religious organization. Nevertheless, the Witnesses were repeatedly harassed and arrested by the police after 1925 for violating sales regulations by peddling their publications door-to-door and on street corners. Although most of these prosecutions were unsuccessful, the Witnesses were nevertheless occasionally compelled to pay fines. In 1924 and 1925 Jehovah's Witness publications charged the Protestant and Roman Catholic churches as "advocates of militarism and war."

Throughout the 1920s the Witnesses were frequently attacked as "Communists disguised in religious clothing" by German *völkisch* and ultranationalist circles as well as by the well-established Protestant and Roman Catholic churches. As early as 1923 the Nazi theorist Alfred Rosenberg attacked the Witnesses for acting on behalf of a "Jewish-communist international conspiracy," equating the role of "democracy and Marxism in politics to the role of the Witnesses in religious life." Early Nazis such as Dietrich Eckart attacked the Witnesses in his posthumously published 1924 brochure, *Bolshevism from Moses to Lenin: My Talks with Adolf Hitler,* as being financed by Jews and Freemasons. The growing number of antisemites in Weimar Germany hated the Witnesses for their respect for the Old Testament—exemplified by their emphasis on Jehovah, the divine name in the ancient scriptures—and their belief that Jews would return to the Holy Land at the Apocalypse. For Roman Catholics, such as Cardinal Michael von Faulhaber of Munich, the Jehovah's Witnesses practiced a "false religion" influenced by "American and Communist activities." By the early 1930s Nazi paramilitary organizations such as the SA (storm troopers) were breaking up Bible study meetings and beating individual Witnesses in many localities. This set the stage for persecution after 1933 of the essentially conservative and nonpolitical Jehovah's Witnesses for their alleged affinity with communism and Zionism.

After the Nazis came to power in January 1933, attacks on Jehovah's Witnesses escalated almost immediately because of their beliefs and their behavior, particularly their refusal to pay obeisance to the Nazi state or to join any subsidiary Nazi Party organization. The Witnesses' response was homogeneous and cohesive, in conformity with their comprehensive religious code. The Nazis misinterpreted such noncompliance as subversive: the Witnesses refused to raise their arms in the "Heil Hitler" salute, would not display the swastika flag, did not vote in Nazi elections or plebiscites, would not

join the German Labor Front or contribute to the Winter Welfare Fund, and would not permit their children to join the Hitler Youth. Jehovah's Witnesses were frequently detained and beaten, their offices searched and vandalized, their funds seized, their presses and publications censored and banned. Hundreds of Witnesses were interned in jails and concentration camps in so-called protective custody (*Schutzhaft*). In April 1933 Jehovah's Witness groups and publications were banned throughout the Reich. That same spring, many individual German states—Mecklenburg (10 April), Bavaria (13 April), Saxony (15 April), Thuringia (26 April), Baden (15 May), and Prussia (24 June)—banned all Witness activities. The politics of intimidation and reprisal expanded when Prussian police occupied the Witnesses' Magdeburg offices, confiscating their property and printing plants in late June 1933. In late August nearly 60 metric tons of Bibles and other

Helen Gotthold with her children Gerd and Gisela. Gotthold was a Jehovah's Witness arrested for her anti-Nazi views. She was convicted, condemned to death, and beheaded in the Ploetzensee Prison on 8 December 1944. Gerd and Gisela survived the war. 25 June 1936

Witness literature were burned in Magdeburg. Subsequent American diplomatic intercession led to the release of confiscated Witness property on the grounds that the seizure was a violation of the 1923 German-American Friendship Treaty: American diplomats in Berlin viewed Nazi behavior toward the American-incorporated Witnesses as a potential precedent for the "arbitrary seizure of other American investments in Germany." Although the Magdeburg properties were eventually released, the Witnesses liquidated their offices inside the Reich and moved their printing activities to Switzerland. Throughout 1934 German police noted that Jehovah's Witnesses smuggled illegal religious literature from abroad and had developed clandestine personal networks to continue their religious activities as reading circles.

On 25 June 1933, 7,000 Witnesses gathered at the Wilmersdorf Sports Hall in Berlin. They drafted a declaration that protested the violations of their religious worship and existence in Germany. The statement was printed in millions of copies and even sent to Adolf Hitler. Although the German Supreme Court and other state tribunals had upheld their rights under Article 137 of the Weimar constitution, police measures providing for protective arrest and detention were implemented against the Witnesses in Bavaria and other states, resulting in a growing number of arrests and the remand of prisoners from jails to indefinite detention in concentration camps.

On 7 October 1934 every Witness congregation in Germany sent the German government an official statement of principles in a spectacular affirmation of total resistance to the authority of the Nazi state: "During the past year, and contrary to God's law and in violation of our rights, you have forbidden us as Jehovah's Witnesses to meet together to study God's Word, and worship and serve Him. . . . Therefore this is to advise you that at any cost we will obey God's commandments, will meet together for the study of His Word, and will worship and serve Him as He has commanded. If your government or offices do violence to us because we are obeying God, then our blood will be upon you and you will answer to Almighty God. We have no interest in political affairs, but are wholly devoted to God's Kingdom under Christ His King. We will do no injury or harm to anyone. We would delight to dwell in peace and do good to all men as we have opportunity, but, since your government and its offices continue in your attempt to force us to disobey the highest law of the universe, we are compelled to now give you notice that we will, by His Grace, obey Jehovah God and fully trust him to deliver us from all oppression and oppressors." On 1 April 1935 the Reich and Prussian Ministry of Interior prohibited all Jehovah's Witness religious activity and publishing throughout the Reich.

During the first two years of Nazi rule Witnesses had lost their jobs as civil servants and as employees in private industry because of their refusal to join the Reich Labor Front, to use the "Heil Hitler" salute, or to vote in elections. On 23 January 1935 the Reich and Prussian Interior Ministry decreed that failure to use the German "Heil Hitler" greeting would result in employment termination in the civil service and private industry. On 2 February 1936 the Reich and Prussian Labor Ministry declared that all unemployment and pension benefits could be withheld from Witnesses. Moreover, their personal possessions and business property could be confiscated under the Law for the Confiscation of Subversive and Enemy Property, which was initially used to seize assets of proscribed and denaturalized political opponents. Witnesses also refused to obey the racial laws, for they believed that "all human beings are equal in the eyes of God." Their unemployment, welfare, and pension benefits were often denied, and with the introduction of compulsory military service in 1935 their refusal to be drafted or perform war-related work led to increased detention in prisons and concentration camps. In early 1935 Gestapo regulations mandating the arrest and protective custody of Jehovah's Witnesses became more systematic.

The children of Jehovah's Witnesses were subjected to an unending barrage of insults and propaganda in school and became sporadic targets of physical violence by classmates and teachers. The repressive apparatus of the Nazi state extended to the family life and child-care arrangements of Jehovah's Witnesses. The children, ostracized by noncompliance with the norms of Nazi education, were often declared juvenile delinquents and incarcerated in correctional institutions because of their unwillingness to enroll in the Hitler Youth. Parental custody was removed, in accordance with Paragraph 1666 of the German civil law code, on the pretext that Witness parents endangered their children's welfare by "alienating them from German ways in the spirit of National Socialism." By 1938 Witness children had been removed from more than 860 families to correctional institutions, reform schools, and Nazi homes. A circular decree from the Reich Interior Ministry to all youth offices and communal supervisory authorities issued on 27 December 1938 mandated the removal of children from "politically unreliable families" to Nazi households. Moreover, the Nazi state also denied payment of supplemental child bonuses to Jehovah's Witness parents.

Before 1939 Jehovah's Witnesses routinely followed their individual and collective consciences, defying Nazi surveillance and repression through noncompliance. They continued to print and distribute illegal religious literature and to meet in clandestine Bible study groups in private homes. By evasion and improvisation Witnesses maintained their cohesive nonconformist subculture, and an elaborate religious network of believers continued to distribute foreign editions of *The Watchtower* and other brochures. Although the Witnesses never seriously threatened the stability or consensus of Nazi rule, they were nevertheless arrested and often placed on trial. Their resistance was essentially over theological questions, and the question of assistance to Jews was peripheral. Mass trials of more than 400 Jehovah's Witnesses for printing and distributing illegal literature occurred in 1937 in Essen, Hamburg, and Leipzig. Most were sentenced to several years' imprisonment.

Between 1935 and 1939 Jehovah's Witnesses were often transferred from protective custody in prison to indefinite detention in concentration camps. The Witnesses constituted a substantial percentage of the growing population of concentration camp prisoners after 1935 and represented more than 10 percent of all concentration camp prisoners before the war. By 1939 nearly 7,000 Witnesses from Germany, incorporated Austria, and Czechoslovakia were detained inside concentration camps. In May 1938, 12 percent of all prisoners at Buchenwald were Witnesses; in 1938, at the Lichtenburg women's camp, there were 260 Jehovah's Witnesses, approximately 18 percent of the prisoners.

After 1940 the growing inmate population in all categories arriving from occupied Europe outnumbered the earlier prisoners from Germany and Austria and consequently decreased the proportion of Witnesses in all camps. Small numbers of Belgian, Czech, Dutch, Norwegian, and Polish Witnesses were added to the 10,000 German and Austrian Jehovah's Witnesses confined in the concentration camps in late 1940. The Witnesses were isolated in Dachau and as-

signed to forced labor in special punishment companies there and in Mauthausen, Sachsenburg, and Sachsenhausen. They were assigned to work in the crematorium at Flossenburg and to clean the latrines at Esterwegen. Witnesses were frequently required to work on Sundays in violation of their religious beliefs. Witnesses held at the women's camps of Moringen, Lichtenburg, and Ravensbrück were subjected to forced labor, undernourishment, exposure, corporal punishment, and isolation. Their "uncompromising spirit of opposition and martyrdom as no other group" received special notice in the reports of *Deutschland Berichte* distributed by émigré socialists during the 1930s. In one such report about Lichtenburg from October 1938, it is recorded that Jehovah's Witness prisoners had refused to listen to a speech by Hitler that had been broadcast throughout the camp. "The SS used water hoses against the Witnesses and beat them, forcing them to stand soaking wet for more than one hour while the Führer spoke. It was late October and bitterly cold. Afterwards, none of them received medical treatment, and food was withheld for two or three days."

After 1938 the Witnesses were given the opportunity to be released from concentration camps and prisons if they signed a statement recanting their faith and membership in the International Jehovah's Witness Association, promised to denounce coreligionists who contacted them, and agreed to perform military service. Few Witnesses signed such declarations, and their refusal resulted in the execution of more than 40 Witnesses in Sachsenhausen and brutal corporal punishments in Buchenwald in September 1939. Jehovah's Witnesses were also denied the privilege of receiving or sending mail in many concentration camps. Preprinted forms used after 1940 at Ravensbrück stated: "The prisoner continues to be a determined Jehovah's Witness and refuses to relinquish its false doctrine. For this reason, she has been refused the usual correspondence granted to prisoners." Contemptuously nicknamed Bible-bees, and Bible-worms by their SS tormentors, the Witnesses earned a reluctant and secret respect, which occasionally resulted in lighter work assignments as domestic servants in SS homes. Because of their beliefs Witnesses refused to escape or to resist, but their religious scrupulousness sometimes proved dangerous. The Witnesses' abhorrence of military service led to their refusal to tend rabbits, whose fur was used in military clothing, and resulted in the execution of several women prisoners for treason at Ravensbrück and Auschwitz. Eugen Kogon, whose classic study of life at Buchenwald was prepared for the Allies after liberation, commented that the SS "was never quite equal to the challenge offered them by the Witnesses." Even in the camps Witnesses, typically marked by an inverted purple triangle sewn on their prison jackets and trousers, continued to meet, pray, and make converts. In Buchenwald they had an underground printing press and secretly distributed religious tracts. About 2,500 of the 10,000 imprisoned Jehovah's Witnesses perished in the concentration camps.

The Witnesses' refusal to serve in the German military after 1938 led to more than 250 death sentences and executions for subversion of the armed forces (*Wehrkraftzersetzung*) in Germany and incorporated Austria. Jehovah's Witnesses were considered "obstinate ideological offenders" and sentenced to death by military tribunals under regulations promulgated in the special military criminal code of 26 August 1939. Their courage and defiance in the face of torture and death punctures the myth of a monolithic Nazi state ruling over docile and submissive subjects.

Sybil Milton

Jewish Agency   Executive arm of the World Zionist Organization charged with assisting Jews in the settlement of Palestine. Chief institution of the Jewish community in Palestine prior to the establishment of the state of Israel. See RESCUE; YISHUV

Jewish Antifascist Committee (JAC)   Two months after the German invasion of the Soviet Union, on 24 August 1941, a unique gathering of Soviet Jewish public figures took place in Moscow. Led by the renowned Yiddish theater director and actor Solomon Mikhoels, they appealed by radio to Jews throughout the world, particularly in the United States and England, to join the fight against Nazi aggression. Their speeches, filled with vivid descriptions of Jewish suffering and calls for Jewish unity, contradicted two decades of Soviet propaganda, which had long denied any connection between Soviet Jews and those of other countries. But with the Red Army reeling under the German offensive, Stalin saw the need to create a national committee of recognizable Jewish figures. This was the origin of the Jewish Antifascist Committee (JAC). Its history cannot be separated either from Hitler's Final Solution or from Stalin's own antisemitic paranoia.

Initially, members of the JAC, who included such

Nahum Goldman, president of the World Jewish Congress (center), and Rabbi Stephen Wise (right), president of the American Jewish Congress, shown with Solomon Mikhoels (left), chairman of the Jewish Antifascist Committee of the USSR, at an open-air reception in honor of Mikhoels and Itsik Feffer. 8 July 1943

important figures as Mikhoels, the writer Ilya Ehrenburg, such Yiddish poets and writers as Itsik Feffer, David Bergelson, Lev Kvitko, David Hofshteyn, and Peretz Markish, and scientists and military officers, all accepted the need to send anti-Nazi, pro-Soviet propaganda to the West. In the spring of 1943, Mikhoels and Feffer were even sent to North America and England for eight months in order to encourage support for the Red Army. Their trip took place just after the victory at Stalingrad, when Soviet prestige was at its height. Coming at a time when the Jews of Europe, including the Soviet Union, were threatened with annihilation, the presence of Mikhoels and Feffer stirred unprecedented emotion. In New York, nearly 50,000 people greeted them in the Polo Grounds on 8 July 1943.

As the Red Army advanced, it began to uncover evidence of Nazi crimes, including large-scale open-air massacres of Jews in cities and small towns throughout Belorussia, Ukraine, and the Baltic states. Members of the JAC could not ignore this suffering. They remained Soviet patriots, but they also identified with their fellow, martyred Jews, among whom were many close relatives. So they tried to expand the functions of the committee. Proposals were made to help resettle Jewish refugees, to reestablish Jewish collective farms, and to revive Jewish cultural life. The JAC also welcomed Jewish partisans to Moscow and often arranged meetings for them with large audiences. This broader activity provoked objections from Soviet officials.

One JAC project was particularly significant. Under the leadership of Ilya Ehrenburg, two dozen writers and journalists, Jewish and non-Jewish, collected documents and firsthand testimony of Nazi atrocities for a proposed publication, *The Black Book*. The writer Vasily Grossman visited the extermination camps of Majdanek and Treblinka soon after their liberation and was among the first to describe them. The poet Abraham Sutzkever prepared more than 200 pages on Nazi atrocities in Lithuania. Others gathered material in Ukraine, Latvia, and Belorussia. Ehrenburg's plan was to create—before it ended—a record of the greatest catastrophe to befall Soviet Jews: the murder of more than 1.5 million Jews by the *Einsatzgruppen*, four killing units that followed the Wehrmacht into Soviet territory. But after the war Stalin banned publication of *The Black Book*, and it did not appear in print until 1980, when it was published by Yad Vashem in Jerusalem.

Following the war, the JAC continued to function but under an increasing cloud of Soviet suspicion. The regime disbanded the organization in November 1948 and arrested many of its most active members. Fifteen were condemned at a secret trial in the spring and summer of 1952. Accused of treason, espionage, and bourgeois nationalism, 13 of the defendants were executed on 12 August 1952. Their heartfelt responses to the Holocaust, including *The Black Book* and poems and articles about Jewish suffering, were among the evidence cited to establish their guilt.

Joshua Rubenstein

Jewish Brigade Military unit of the British army established in 1944, after a prolonged diplomatic campaign. Chaim Weizmann, president of the World Zionist Organization, suggested early in the war that an armed unit of Jews be created. Plans to form a unit stalled in part because the British feared a negative Arab reaction. About 30,000 Jewish volunteers from Palestine joined throughout the war. Initially they were kept from the front lines, but a brigade of 5,000 was formed with Churchill's support in the fall of 1944. The unit saw action in Italy and Austria in 1945. It was demobilized with the rest of the British army in 1946.

Jewish Council See JUDENRAT

Jewish Religious Life It is impossible to comprehend how Jews coped with the catastrophe of the Holocaust without understanding the possibilities and expressions of Jewish religious life under Nazi rule.

Nazi antisemitism differed from former types of Jew-hatred and anti-Jewishness by its use of racial concepts. These concepts, although not applied systematically until the advent of the Third Reich, originated in the minds of racial and modern antisemitic theorists such as Richard Wagner, Eugen Dühring, Wilhelm Marr, Houston Stewart Chamberlain, and others during the second half of the nineteenth century. Judaism as a concept and phenomenon was perceived by them not as a religion but as an evil consisting of a will for world domination, capitalist exploitation, communism, stupefying materialism, cosmopolitanism, licentious permissiveness, and unrestricted freedom of the press. For them Judaism embodied all the negative features of modernism and modernization. Under the influence of racial and social-Darwinist theories, the Jewish people as a whole and Jews as individuals were perceived as a race of carriers of the vices of this Judaism. Consequently, conversion to Christianity—or any other solution on the level of religion—could not provide a real answer to the so-called Jewish problem. Quite the contrary, Jewish conversion would intensify the problem, as it would diminish alertness to the Jewish threat and lead to integration of this "sickness" into the national body.

Nazi antisemitism continued this line of thought. Hitler, in his first political writing (September 1919), stated that "Jewry is undoubtedly a race and not a religious association." Consequently, Nazi antisemitic policies, while intending to persecute the Jews and to eliminate Jewish influence, did not focus on the religious aspects of Judaism, even when religious symbols were attacked. Some anti-Jewish measures unwittingly supported Jewish religious objectives in various ways. For example, the first nationwide anti-Jewish action carried out by the Nazi party after Hitler's ascent to power was a one-day economic boycott of Jews—but it was held on a Sabbath, a day on which, according to their religion, Jews have to abstain from work anyway. The Nuremberg Laws of 15 September 1935 pro-

Women wearing yellow stars bearing the word *Jude* pray at an outdoor High Holiday service in the Lodz ghetto.

hibited intermarriage between Jews and Germans; whereas marriage between Jews and non-Jews is also opposed by Jewish law. In the 1930s in Germany and in the 1940s in the occupied countries of Western Europe, religious services and other activities in synagogues continued almost undisturbed. Hence the practice of Jewish religion was the least affected of all aspects of Jewish life.

In fact the National Socialist regime never developed clear-cut official policies on Jewish religious affairs, and no central government office for that area was ever established—even though there proliferated dozens of offices aimed at all aspects of Jewry and Judaism. Consequently, attitudes themselves diverged greatly, especially during World War II, when Germany occupied many countries. A wide range of new officials with varying educational backgrounds were appointed to influential positions all over Europe. In addition, relationships between the occupier and the local population, and former relations between Jews

and Gentiles in any location, played an important role. Consequently, the conditions for preserving Jewish religious life were, in general, harsher in Eastern than in Western Europe. At the beginning of the 1940s religious services in synagogues were prohibited in many localities in Poland; by contrast, the importation of the *arba'a minnim* (the "four species"—palm, willow, myrtle, and citron—required for celebrating Sukkot, the Feast of Tabernacles) to Austria and the Netherlands from outside German-occupied countries gained official approval. Limited religious activities were tolerated even in several concentration and labor camps.

Nevertheless, in many instances the Nazis attacked Jewish religious targets, the most notorious incident being the destruction of hundreds of synagogues during Kristallnacht (9–10 November 1938). All known cases may be explained, however, by a will to assault and desecrate objects not because of their religious significance but because they were perceived as symbols of Jewishness: the Jewish method of slaughtering animals stood for Jewish cruelty, and synagogues were looked upon as the convening places of the leaders of the Jews together with their flock.

Rabbis were generally regarded by the Nazi authorities as leaders of the Jews, even though in most European countries by that time the stature of rabbis in the Jewish communities had declined markedly, as a result of a century and a half of emancipation and secularization. Hence in the 1930s in Germany proper—when official policy toward the Jews was to isolate them, segregate them from German society, and drive them to emigrate—the authorities usually treated rabbis with respect. In the 1940s, however, when the escalation of anti-Jewish policies culminated in systematic mass murder, that attitude generally deteriorated. From the conquest of Poland onward, rabbis were often molested, especially by SS men, who often harbored the most extreme anti-Jewish views. Nevertheless, in the *Schnellbrief* (telegram) of 21 September 1939 to the commanders of the *Einsatzgruppen* (mobile killing units), Reinhard Heydrich emphasized that the *Judenräte* (Jewish councils) to be established in each Jewish community should be "composed of the remaining persons having authority, and rabbis." In fact the order was applied only in a limited number of Jewish councils, the result not of German intentions but of the diminished position of rabbis within Jewish society. Rabbis served as chairmen of Jewish councils (or their equivalent) only in a minority of cases—in Germany and Belgium, and in the cities of Bialystok and Salonika.

Rabbis played a special and sometimes tragic role in the Jewish communities during the Nazi period. They were called upon to supply Halakhic answers—that is, answers according to Jewish law and tradition—to a wide variety of problems resulting from unprecedented conditions: May one cook with lard if margarine or other kosher fats are not available? May one shave during the Three Weeks (a period of mourning over the destruction of the Temple in Jerusalem) in order not to be recognized as a Jew in the streets? In several cases they were even required by Jewish Councils to decide who would be on the deportation lists. The most important aspect of rabbinical activities during the period, however, was spiritual and social. Homiletics and social care—in many cases not only for religious Jews—were invaluable in encouraging those seeking spiritual assistance. Several sermons were written down and preserved, such as Rabbi Leo Baeck's sermon in the wake of the promulgation of the Nurem-

berg Laws (September 1935); the hasidic rebbe Kalonymous Kalman Shapira's weekly homilies in the Warsaw ghetto (collected and published after the Holocaust in his book *Esh Kodesh*, "Holy Fire"); and the circular by the chief rabbi of Rotterdam, A. B. N. David, which was handed out to deportees in 1942. On the other hand, some rabbis lost their own faith, while others left their communities and fled.

Daily Life

Not all religious Jews—the term is a generalization covering a wide range of religious practice—maintained strictly Orthodox observance of all the religious laws (*mitzvot*) and customs (*minhagim*). Consequently, individual religious Jews faced different levels of complexity in coping with the hardships they endured. Liberal Jews in Germany and Western Europe were able to adapt to the changing conditions more easily than the Orthodox, especially Eastern European Jews. Nevertheless, some basic problems faced all religious Jews: the supply of kosher meat after the Nazis prohibited the slaughter of animals without stunning (not permitted under Jewish law); the rapidly diminishing number of kosher articles in the 1940s as a result of rationing and the increasing use of nonkosher animal fats instead of vegetable or mineral oils; matrimonial problems in the wake of deportations (at first to labor camps) that separated spouses; efforts at escape that required shaving beards and sidelocks, using false baptismal certificates, and evading deportation orders, thereby causing other Jews to be arrested in their place. It is clear that cleaving to strictly traditional modes and precepts of Jewish religious life complicated the situation for religious Jews even more than for nonreligious Jews.

Jewish religion grants a central place to the synagogue, both as a place of worship and as the gathering place of the community. Testimonies concerning Jewish life in the Nazi period make it clear that the synagogue (or *shul*, as it was commonly called by Ashkenazi Jews) regained this role, which had suffered a constant decline through the nineteenth and early twentieth century as Jews assimilated and secularized. Under the Nazis, Jews came to the synagogue to commiserate with other Jews, to hear the latest news, and to find comfort in traditional liturgical melodies—but also to recover their faith. Consequently, synagogues became a favorite target for attacks, both by Nazis and by local non-German antisemites.

From the very beginning of the Third Reich, the Nazi regime provoked religious reactions. As the regime's power expanded and its methods of domination became ever more cruel, so the inner need to comprehend its deeper meaning within the divine scheme increased. Reflection on their condition led Jews to a broad variety of reactions within the sphere of faith: from the blunt heresy of abandoning belief in God, through the acceptance of God's existence but the ascription of evil intentions to God, to continuation of undisturbed faith, intensification of belief and religious feeling even to the point of ecstasy, and ultimately a return to faith among secular Jews. Probably the most amazing and unexpected reaction to the persecutions was a limited resurgence of Jewish proselytism in Germany in the mid-1930s and the Netherlands in the early 1940s.

Many believers expressed their feelings in special prayers and lamentations, of which only a tiny number have been recorded. Some wrote theological treatises under the impact of their experiences. Of major interest are the writings and sermons of Rabbi Leo Baeck from Germany; Rabbi Yissokhor Dov Teichthal, an ultra-Orthodox, anti-Zionist rabbi who fled from Slovakia to Hungary (he was murdered in a train carrying inmates evacuated from Auschwitz in January 1944) but managed to write a comprehensive rabbinical treatise supporting Zionism (*Em Habanim Smeha*, "The Mother of Many Children Will Rejoice"); and Rabbi Kalonymous Kalman Shapira of Warsaw, the "Piasecz-ner rebbe," who also died at the hands of the Nazis but whose homilies were published posthumously.

The Holocaust destroyed the traditional spiritual bastions and the strongest demographic centers both of European religious Liberalism and of organized Orthodoxy (hasidism, mitnaggedism, German neo-Orthodoxy, and the political parties and school systems allied to them). Thus the crucible in which these movements had been forged, the seat of the core spiritual leadership, had been obliterated. New centers of the various religious groups were formed in Israel and the United States, to which the remnants of European Jewry fled. The reconstruction process was carried out without the backing that had once existed and mostly by new leaders, in entirely different environments of both language and culture and with greatly reduced numbers of followers. The voice of Orthodoxy particularly suffered much from this situation, and its influence diminished during the first 30 years after the war.

The theological questions raised by the Holocaust—why God inflicted such a fate on his chosen people, including close to 1.5 million children—are tremendous. Several attempts to provide religious answers have been undertaken—some applying traditional Jewish concepts, others taking more revolutionary routes—but no single set of answers has been widely accepted. Nevertheless, Jewish religious life did revive after the Holocaust, and has even flourished, especially during the last quarter of the twentieth century. If the theological questions raised by the Holocaust have not been resolved, the prospering of Jewish religious life is by itself some answer of inner faith and conviction. *Dan Michman*

Jewish Women More than half of the Jewish victims of the Holocaust were women. Like the Jewish men, the women were shot and gassed simply because they were Jews. But the principle of sexual inequality evident in Nazi ideology was also expressed in policy toward Jews. No woman is known to have been appointed to a Jewish council (*Judenrat*). Inequality was the rule in labor, too. Under agreements between private employers and the SS for the "leasing" of camp inmates, male labor commanded a higher price than female labor. The Germans sometimes took into account women's physical limitations when assigning jobs but frequently gave them the most arduous tasks. In mixed concentration and labor camps women were not appointed to high-ranking positions in the internal administration (*Lagerverwaltung*) or the police.

Degradation with direct sexual implications, such as being forced to stand naked in front of SS guards, was routinely carried out on both male and female prisoners. Male guards often humiliated the women more than the men.

The fate of Jewish women highlights the total break of Nazi ideology with the morals and attitudes of Western bourgeois culture. The accepted concept of a woman as a symbol of motherhood, tenderness, beauty, and delicate feelings in need of male protection was destroyed by the Nazis. In their behavior toward Jewish women (and men) they sought to implant and reinforce in German minds the idea that the Jew was a subhuman element. This was the essence of the Nazi racial antisemitism that prepared the way for the Final Solution.

The higher death rate among Jewish women than Jewish men in Eastern Europe has to do with other fac-

A Dutch woman wears the handirons she had on when freed from the prison camp at Waldheim, Germany. 12 March 1945

tors than the slight prevalence of women in the ghettos. Men were more useful to Nazi goals—such as to meet the need for heavy physical labor—so their deaths were sometimes delayed. Most women with small children were immediately sent to the gas chambers, as the children were nearly useless to the Nazis, and the commotion that separating the women and children might have caused would have jeopardized the orderly killing process. Women were singled out for so-called medical experiments in contraception and fertility. In one of the more infamous experiments, newborn babies were taken away from nursing mothers to see how long the infants could survive without feeding. The suffering of women in traditional feminine roles was thus often prolonged before they were killed.

Women in the Ghettos

Jewish women played a crucial role in the maintenance of life in Eastern Europe immediately following the Nazi occupation and during the ghetto years. In the fall of 1939 women made up 52–56 percent of the total population in most large cities of Poland, including Warsaw, Lodz, Kraków, and Bialystok. When the Jews of Poland were confined to ghettos, from April 1940 to the spring of 1942, the proportion of women increased further. After the German invasion of Poland in September 1939 many men fled across the borders to the east and south to escape deportation to forced labor camps, which consisted mostly of men, very few of whom returned home alive. During the first months of the occupation in Poland, men were attacked more often than women, and more men were imprisoned. In July 1941, in the first wave of mass killings following the invasion of the Soviet Union, more men than women were killed. As a result many women were left to care for their families alone.

In normal times, middle-class and lower-middle-class Jewish women did not usually work outside the home; hence they had few marketable skills. The anti-Jewish laws further narrowed economic activities and employment opportunities, and the restrictions on Jewish independent businesses and on bank savings made the economic situation for Jews still harsher, even for the upper middle class. In these circumstances competition for any kind of job was fierce, and the chances that women would find employment were almost zero.

Personal testimonies and reports gleaned from ghetto archives disclose a variety of strategies that women used in their struggle to keep their families from hunger and disintegration. Women were inventive in cooking at home, in caring for their children, and, despite all the obstacles, in finding work. Those of the lower middle class who previously had worked at home, or had helped only to a small extent in their husbands' businesses, took over businesses when husbands were arrested or were forced to stay home because of the danger of being seized in the streets. Women joined in the smuggling industry in Warsaw, either acting on their own or working for larger operators.

Educated women were employed in public assistance projects maintained by the Jewish self-help organizations and by the Judenräte. Some managed public kitchens or worked as cooks and waitresses; others worked in orphanages or as nurses in hospitals. These women were able to preserve some semblance of a daily routine as well as acquire basic food supplies for themselves and their families. They were able to survive on their small wages and from savings. A frequent occupation of middle-class women to sustain their families was the sale of household articles such as china, furniture, and linen.

The wives of men appointed to the Jewish councils and employed in other public institutions had more stability in their lives than others did, and some were active in community volunteer organizations. In Warsaw, where house committees were established, women ran "children's corners" in their homes, endeavoring to replace the closed schools and to care for otherwise unattended children. Others cooked in their apartments and distributed food among the poor and the refugees. In Warsaw in 1942 women took over the leadership of the house committees. In some cases, however, the wives of Jewish council members and Jewish ghetto police officers, as well as women from wealthy families, showed indifference to the plight of other Jews and did not get involved in community service.

A small fraction of the population in the ghettos (1–2 percent in Warsaw) benefited from the new order. They cooperated with the Nazis, operated the large-scale smuggling enterprises in the ghetto, or handled other businesses that were important to the Germans. Some women from respectable families that had lost their means of financial support found shelter with these nouveau riche entrepreneurs, who often had histories of underworld and black-market activities. Their extravagant lifestyle in the midst of the terrible starvation and poverty that Nazi policies had created in the ghetto seemed shameful to most of their fellow Jewish inmates.

Working-class women constituted the great majority of the female population in the ghettos. Their husbands were more frequently deported than other Jewish men because they were unable to ransom themselves from forced labor. These women depended on the inadequate subsidy they received from the Jewish councils in return for their husbands' assignment. Often this allowance was discontinued after only a short period, and the women had to look for jobs to support their children and elderly parents. These families typically lacked savings or other resources—before the war about one-third of Polish Jewry was sustained by local aid and by relief supplied by the American Jewish Joint Distribution Committee—and they were among the first to be struck down by hunger and disease.

In ghettos such as Lodz, Vilna, and Bialystok, where industries were developed to serve German needs, many women found work washing and mending garments and preparing brushes and mattresses. The Lodz ghetto came to resemble a labor camp, and by the end of 1941 almost all women there worked. Still, as a general rule, men had priority in obtaining jobs. Those unfit to work received hardly any food supplies and were in constant danger of being deported.

To function as a wife and mother under these conditions was especially difficult and frustrating. All home routines were disrupted. The familiar physical environment—one's neighborhood, apartment, furniture—was destroyed when the Jews were forced to move into extremely cramped quarters in the ghettos. Schools were closed, and the preoccupation with acquiring the basic necessities of life deepened the gloom in the family. The inability of men to support their families, the growing Nazi terror, and the increasing uncertainties in everyday life exacerbated tensions between husbands and wives, parents and children, brothers and sisters. It was difficult to keep a family from disintegrating; children had to mature quickly, and norms of human behavior and interaction became almost impossible to maintain. Nevertheless, women's testimonies reveal that the challenges of keeping families together and of providing food and shelter for children and even husbands fired their determination not to give up. Despite all these hardships the family was an important source of encouragement and support. Once the family unit was broken by death, desertion, or deportation, the ability to persevere diminished sharply.

Single mothers who took on new roles suffered the most. As they were desperate for employment, they were among the first to be sent out of the ghetto to work. Although forced labor offered an opportunity to acquire food on the Aryan side, it also exposed Jewish women to the risk of molestation and abuse.

Many women worked in the garment industry. The hours were long—from sunrise to sunset—and the wages were negligible, even less than for men. Frequently the soup and bread they received at work were their only food for the day, and sometimes it replaced their pay. The very poor saved some of this food to take home to their children. Ghetto diaries describe the distress that mothers felt as they worked, knowing that their children were unattended at home or in the streets. Many had to shut their eyes to their children's dangerous smuggling activities in the endless effort to obtain food.

When deportations began, mothers were confronted with even greater dangers and moral dilemmas. As most of them were unemployed, they were the first to be targeted for deportation to the death camps, as were

Women's barracks, Auschwitz.

children. Mothers with babies and other children too young to control their crying had trouble finding hide-outs during round-ups. The chance to hide or escape sometimes depended on abandoning children, but most mothers were unable to do that. Whether through love or under compulsion by the police or the SS, they walked together with their children to the deportation areas. Survivors who recall having been forced to abandon their children report having suffered desperately from guilt.

Testimonies and ghetto diaries generally refer to women as having been more able than men to accommodate to ghetto life. Accounts of women giving their food rations to their children and spouses were more common than reports of men doing so. Recollections of men eating their weekly bread ration in a day are quite common. The records reveal that women were physically and mentally more capable of enduring hunger. Women of the middle and upper-middle classes, who had some reserves of money and property, were in the best position to stretch their resources to keep their

families fed and clothed and thus were best able to carry on until the final liquidation of the ghettos.

Hiding on the Aryan Side

Jewish women were more apt than Jewish men to try to save themselves by passing as or hiding among Gentiles. Jewish men could be easily identified because of circumcision, but women had a chance to pass if their physical features did not conform to the stereotype of Jewish "looks" or if they dyed their hair and dressed fashionably. They needed to acquire authentic identification papers or convincing forgeries and had to invent a simple and clear family history. More important, they had to speak the local dialect and be familiar with local manners and customs. Jewish girls possessed these advantages. Jewish boys were usually sent to religious schools (yeshivas), whereas girls, for whom a religious education was deemed less essential, often attended neighborhood schools together with Gentiles before the war.

In finding hiding places, women had no advantage

over men. Wealth and social contacts were needed, and men generally had more of both from business dealings with non-Jews. Among Jewish children, however, girls had a better chance than boys of finding a Gentile home or religious institution (such as a convent) that was willing to hide them. Girls were harder to identify than boys because of the boys' circumcision. Also, many survivors record that prospective families were more interested in sheltering girls because they could be helpful in home chores. Often couples or families hid together. Testimonies describe the extreme stress and anxiety for both sexes and tell of the varied strategies that Jews in hiding developed to overcome emotional breakdowns and remain in hiding.

Resistance

Resistance to Nazi policies encompasses a range of acts and behaviors that goes far beyond joining the forest partisans. By coping with the horrors of everyday life in the ghettos and by helping their families to endure under the siege conditions imposed by the Germans to break their wills, individual women offered stern and persistent resistance.

Women were also part of the organized resistance led by members of the Jewish youth movements and political parties. They were crucial in establishing communication among the isolated ghettos in Poland and Lithuania. Women couriers, passing as Aryans, moved from town to town to make contact with youth movement members. They devised many ruses to evade capture as they conveyed money, letters, papers, and information from ghetto to ghetto. They also acquired guns and ammunition from non-Jews for the resistance. Their visits to the isolated ghettos were a source of hope and encouragement, not only because the couriers brought news of the outside world but also because they demonstrated that the youth movements continued to function. More than once, the expression "motherly warmth and love" is used in testimonies to describe the friendship and solidarity of the women couriers. Many were caught by the German or local authorities and were killed. Some, such as Frumka Plotnitzka and Tema Schneiderman, became legends during the Holocaust years.

In the summer of 1941 information conveyed by couriers to the headquarters of the youth movements in Warsaw, Vilna, and other major centers made it clear that systematic murder was taking place in the East. In Warsaw, Chaika Grossman's account of the deporta-

tions and killings in Ponary, near Vilna, and in the Ninth Fort, near Kovno, and her report of Abba Kovner's call "not to go like sheep to the slaughter" added to previous knowledge of the mobile killing operations in eastern Poland and the gassings in Chelmno. Such information was crucial to the Jews' growing awareness of the Nazi policy of destruction.

Women took part in the small fighting units organized in Warsaw beginning in the late fall of 1942. Zivia Lubetkin led the Warsaw ghetto uprising alongside Mordechai Anielewicz. Young women were also found among partisan groups in the forests of Lithuania and Belorussia, but they did not usually participate in the actual fighting. Most of them reverted to traditional roles such as cooking, washing, and waiting on the men. Traditional male-female roles and conventions of behavior held true, so that age, attractiveness, and attachment to a particular man were important to a woman's status.

Women in the Camps

Men and women were separated, and families disbanded, in the death camps and in most forced labor camps. Although camp experience was essentially the same for all Jewish inmates, men and women devised certain survival strategies that differed according to sex. Owing in large measure to traditional gender behaviors inculcated in Jewish boys and girls before the war, the camps' lack of facilities for keeping clean distressed the women deeply—in particular during menstrual periods, which for many Jewish adolescent girls were a source of sharp embarrassment. The dreary surroundings were more depressing for women than for men. In Auschwitz-Birkenau the facilities in the women's section were far worse than those in the men's. Some camp routines, such as the shaving of hair, disinfection, and bodily examinations in which inmates were forced to stand naked in front of male SS guards, were particularly shameful for women. In addition, the strenuous outside work weighed more heavily on women than on men.

About half of the women worked in what could be defined as SS and camp services, which included the packinghouse, the mess, and the offices of the political and labor departments. These jobs were mostly indoor and provided safer working conditions than outdoor assignments did. The best types of work were tied to places where women could "organize" food, or items to be traded for food. For instance, women

Survivors at Bergen-Belsen concentration camp. 22 April 1945

who worked in the detail known as *Kanada* (Canada), which sorted articles brought by new arrivals, were able to steal goods for exchange. Often, however, the psychological stress of these tasks was overwhelming. In Kanada women found pictures, cards, and other personal items, sometimes belonging to friends and relatives, to whose deaths the evidence in their hands bore witness. Women working in the registry of Auschwitz saw crematorium lists and other information confirming the fate of husbands, parents, and other loved ones. These women were terrorized and bound to silence, for any leak of information would immediately cause them to be sent to the gas chambers.

A few hundred women worked in the armament factory union, which manufactured fuses for artillery shells. Others were employed in removing rubble, dredging and cleaning fish ponds, and picking crops and mowing hay, which was exceptionally strenuous. All the women who worked outside the camp had to walk several kilometers from Birkenau in the winter cold and in summer heat. Many women were unable to endure the physical and emotional assaults in the

camps, and the death toll was frightening. Of the 28,000 women imprisoned in Auschwitz in 1942, barely 5,400 remained alive at the end of the year. In 1943, 28,000 women prisoners died in Birkenau, 9,000 in the month of December alone. The frequent selections in Auschwitz-Birkenau decimated the population.

Memoirs and testimonies by inmates give a picture of the complex social and psychological realities of the camps. They show that warmth, affection, and camaraderie were vital for women's survival. A sense of solidarity and even of strong friendships formed between inmates, despite this most fragmented of societies. The words by which women survivors refer to their inmate friends—*sister, cousin, mother*—show the intensity of the bonds between them. Many have testified that the responsibility of caring for someone else—often a younger person—became a source of strength despite the risks it entailed. Small groups of women (typically two, three, or four) would get together after work to do such chores as mending clothes or fixing wooden clogs. They also cooked together when they were able to find potato peelings, cabbage, or anything edible.

From the end of 1943, when the Germans' need for labor grew and the number of Jewish males still alive to work had decreased considerably, more and more women were deported to forced labor and SS camps, such as Plaszow and Janowska, established near large ghettos by the SS authorities and administered by SS officials. They were also sent to factory camps (for example, Skarzysko-Kamienna and Starachowice) established by private German companies and administered by guards who reported directly to company management.

In all the SS camps, as in the concentration camps, men and women were housed separately. In factory camps, however, the men's and women's quarters were built in the same area without fences or partitions. In general, conditions were slightly better in the factory camps than they were in other camps. There was a chance to meet a husband, relative, or friend and to have some contact with Poles outside the camp.

In the final year of the war the forced labor camps in western Poland and in Germany were packed with Hungarian Jewish women. Many of them had passed through Auschwitz before reaching other destinations. They arrived in a state of shock from their sudden deportation, even as the Allied armies were forcing the Germans to retreat, and their appalling experiences in

Youth Aliyah group bound for Palestine from Berlin. 1936

Auschwitz after their more or less normal lives in Hungary. The survival rate among these women has yet to be established.   *Dalia Ofer*

Jewish Youth Movements In 1896, a 21-year-old student, Hermann Hoffmann, who served as a teacher at the high school in Steglitz, a section of Berlin, began to organize hikes for high school students in the countryside and forests outside the city. Through the deep camaraderie that emerged from these experiences they tried to create a "world of youth" free from adult conventions. Out of this nucleus developed the German youth movement, which declared at a rally at Hohe Meissner that "the free German youth want to shape their own lives according to their own decision, on their own responsibility, and guided by their own inner truth." As a result of the rally, three physicians, Gustav Franke, Erwin Von Hattinberg and Knud Ahlborn, drafted the Meissner Formula—the declaration of intentions of the German youth movements—on 13 October 1913.

When Adolf Hitler came to power in 1933, several Jewish youth movements, modeled on the German movement but specifically Jewish in content, already existed in Germany. Blau-Weiss (Blue-White), the first Jewish youth movement, had been established in 1912 as a result of the merger of several hiking groups, including the Wanderbund, which was founded in Breslau (Wroclaw) in 1907. Three more youth movements were founded during World War I: Jung-Jüdischer Wanderbund (JJWB), Esra, and Kameraden. One of Kameraden's factions, Der Kreis (The Circle), split off and became known as Werkleute (Working People). The Kadimah movement was created out of the remnants of Blau-Weiss when that group dissolved in 1926; and Habonim Hanoar Hahalutzi was established in 1933 when the JJWB and Brit Haolim merged with Kadimah. One year later, in 1934, the Jüdischer Pfadfinderbund in Deutschland (Jewish Scouts League in Germany) and Makkabi Hatzair merged to become Jüdischer Pfadfinderbund–Makkabi Hatzair. At about the same time German branches of both the Eastern European movements Hashomer Hatzair and Betar were also established.

In the first decades of the twentieth century, several Jewish youth movements formed in Germany. (Girls and young women were equal members of the Jewish youth movements, among them leaders of movements and groups within them.) Most members of the move-

ment belonged to the third generation since Jewish emancipation and had grown up as German citizens deeply rooted in German culture and thought. Nevertheless, full and harmonious social and cultural integration was not achieved. Jewish youth increasingly felt an inner conflict between their Jewishness and their German identity.

Brought together by the common experience of the search for self-identification, Jewish adolescents set up a variety of movements and organizations. With few exceptions, all these groups underwent a gradual process of returning to the sources of Judaism. In embarking on this course the young people were as a rule not concerned with politics, let alone political parties. The process was one of self-discovery by means of introspection in their striving for integrity. The Jewish youth movements accepted the aims, characteristics, symbols, and forms of the German youth movements but adapted them to the Jewish situation. The young peoples' emotional state of "being moved" and the experience, often their first, of life under the open skies, prompted them to reject "society," particularly Jewish society, with its conventions and its "unyouthful" and "unnatural" attitude to its own Jewishness. That rejection went hand in hand with a deep yearning for a "true" community, which, as the Jewish youth movement persuaded itself without too much rational discussion, could in the nature of things only be a Jewish community. Thus, these young Jews were driven to the primary sources of a pristine Judaism not yet corrupted by "society." Moreover, applying the Meissner Formula to their own situation, the Jewish youth activists were prepared to find and grasp the Judaic heritage within themselves by intuition, in the spirit of "inner truth."

A small number of German Jewish adolescents remained devoted to assimilation and prepared to adapt it to the aims and characteristics of the youth movements, such as the yearning for a "true community" and "inner truth." According to them, the inner truth need not be of Jewish certitude, nor need the real community lead to Judaism. Rather than interpret their ideologies in the light of political or party considerations, both the Zionist and assimilationist Jewish youth movements spoke in terms of ethics, sentiments, and beliefs, reflecting an attitude dictated by inner truth and thus worthy of young minds molded by the youth movements.

As economic conditions deteriorated in the 1920s

Group portrait of members of the revisionist Zionist youth group Betar in Kolbuszowa. The children hold portraits of Vladimir Jabotinsky, founder of Betar, and Theodor Herzl, founder of the modern Zionist movement. 1937

and antisemitism spread, the youth movements were gradually brought down to earth and forced to take practical action. The Socialist and Communist parties demanded unequivocal commitment to politics and political activity in the service of the proletariat. Hehalutz, the Zionist pioneer organization, wanted the Jewish youth movements to place their activities in the service of turning the Zionist ideology into reality, to proclaim the young generation's return to the Jewish people and Jewish thought, and to organize vocational training and other preparation (*hachsharah*), for emigration to Palestine. This demand was reinforced practically by the foundation of the German Hehalutz and Brit Hanoar organizations, which embraced the Halutzic ideal of turning the Jewish youth of Russia and Eastern Europe into Zionist workers who would go to Palestine to rebuild the land of Israel.

In Eastern Europe, too, several Jewish youth movements were established between the two world wars, and their membership reached about 60,000. Movements like Hashomer Hatzair, Dror, and Gordonia adapted a Zionist and socialist ideology; Hanoar Hatzioni and Akiva focused on Zionism and Hebrew culture; and Betar identified with Zionist revisionism. Further, there was a non-Zionist youth section of the Bund. The Zionist youth movements, with the exception of Betar, were linked within the framework of Hehalutz to kibbutz movements in Palestine. From Eastern Europe those movements spread to Austria, Romania, Hungary, Slovakia, and Yugoslavia.

Although some of these groups were modeled on the German youth movements and the Scouts system, others on socialistic ideas and Russian populism, there were significant differences between the Western and Eastern European movements and between them and Hehalutz. Jewish youth in Eastern Europe had never moved as far away from the spiritual and intellectual sources of Judaism as did young Jews in Western Europe; therefore they did not need as much time or reeducation to arrive at the stage of *hagshamah*—commitment to and realization of Zionist and socialist aims. Jewish youth in the Western and Eastern Euro-

Friends and relatives waving goodbye to a departing Youth Aliyah group bound for Palestine from Berlin. 1936

pean movements also differed in social origin, perception of Zionism and socialism, attitude toward the idea of vocation and toward vocational training. Yet they shared many common features. Both rejected the surrounding non-Jewish society and longed for an intimate, true community; and they held fast to self-governance by their members, rejecting organizational methods or ideological lines imposed from above if those did not express their own "inner truth."

On the eve of the Holocaust both Zionist and non-Zionist organized youth had well-defined ideologies and fully developed institutions. Most activities common to the Jewish youth movement and Hehalutz—communes and training centers, administrative offices, arrangements for immigration to Palestine (aliyah), liaisons with the Labor movement and the various streams of the kibbutz movement—had already been established before 1933. Indeed, the success with which the Jewish youth movement in Germany was able to absorb great numbers of young people in 1933 and thereafter, as well as to train them and to encourage them to emigrate to Palestine, is due to this broad preparation. In Eastern and Central Europe, similarly, the fact that the youth movement had formed the attitudes and behavior patterns of its members and developed its organizational institutions enabled it to take the place of a leadership missing after the German conquest.

By the time the Nazis came to power in Germany, all Jewish youth organizations—whether Zionist or non-Zionist, independent or affiliated with a political party—were compelled by the authorities to belong to the Reichsausschuss der Jüdischen Jugendverbände (Reich Commission of Jewish Youth Associations). The Reichsausschuss had been established in 1924 to encourage Jewish youth organizations to do social work within the Jewish community. In time this committee became an umbrella organization for all Jewish youth groups, offering such services as access to youth hostels and reduced fares on railways.

The Reichsausschuss was recognized by the office of the Reichsjugendführer (Reich youth leader) as the sole legitimate negotiator for Jewish youth organizations and hence became the channel of communication for all orders. The Nazis made use of the Reichsausschuss to implement their policies toward Jewish youth, just as they would later create the Reichsvertretung der Deutschen Juden (Reich Representative Council of German Jews) to act as an executive arm for German Jews generally. Nazi policy sought to maintain strict control over the Jewish youth groups and their activities, and to segregate the Jewish youth movement from the German one. It also tended to favor those Jewish youth organizations that promoted emigration (such as by supporting vocational training) and discouraged those that called on Jews to remain in Germany.

The great range of activities of the Jewish youth movement fell into two major categories, internal work and external work. Internal work comprised most of the traditional activities of the youth movement—hiking trips, camping, singing, rituals and ceremonies, celebration of holidays, sports, study of the Hebrew language, and lectures and seminars on topics of Jewish life. External work included community service, social work, political education on behalf of various parties, vocational retraining, promotion of Youth Aliyah (immigration to Palestine), and above all the activities that the Zionist youth movement carried out together with Hehalutz.

As young Jews increasingly were ostracized by their non-Jewish German peers, into whose culture they had been born and with whose values they identified, the Jewish youth movement offered them a feeling of belonging, warmth, courage, and the spirit of action in a shattered and ruined world. Symbolic rituals were practiced when the time came for the group to part: a piece of a torn flag or a broken chain was given for safekeeping to members as a symbol of the continuity of the fellowship.

At the beginning of the German occupation, Jewish youth movements began to reorganize themselves. Many movement leaders were among the stream of escapees from the Nazi-occupied areas. However, unlike the party leaders who fled to Palestine or to the interior of the Soviet Union, the executive of the youth movements in the Soviet-occupied zone sent its most prominent leaders back to the German-occupied areas in order to restore the organizational structure and to revive branches throughout Poland and Lithuania.

Even under the worsening conditions for Jews in occupied Europe as they were herded into ghettos, Jewish youth movements tried at first to maintain their traditional educational activities. But gradually the reality of labor conscription, systematic starvation, and deportation to death camps turned the youth movements into underground resistance movements.

Under Nazi rule in the ghetto, the structures promoting a normal adolescence—stable homes, schools, and adult authority—were eroded and ultimately destroyed. The clandestine and intimate cells of the youth movements created an island of refuge from the harsh reality of ghetto life. Young people attempted to protest against the evil that had befallen them and to find solutions to daily problems. Secret clubs sponsored study groups, underground schools, and lending libraries.

Young Jews were sent by their youth movements and Hehalutz from the ghettos to work farms as long as they were tolerated by the German authorities. The youth movements exploited this opportunity and attempted to continue their preparation for eventual settlement in Palestine. Pioneering farms were set up near Warsaw and in more distant locales. When such groups could no longer function, "urban kibbutzim" were organized. Soup kitchens were opened, and seminars and symposiums were arranged to allow young people to continue their education after the Germans closed the schools. The youth movements also tried to reach the most unfortunate children in the ghetto, who had no family and roamed about in gangs.

The many illegal newspapers published by the youth movements were at first written only for the members of each particular movement. Eventually, however, material aimed at a broader audience was included— news of the war gathered from illegal radio broadcasts, reports of events in the ghettos, and calls for active resistance.

The youth movements set up networks of cells throughout Poland and Lithuania. These underground networks relied on couriers—most of them young women—to maintain contact between the widely dispersed Jewish groups and to transmit news. Later, when fighting units were formed, the couriers went on secret missions to purchase weapons and smuggle them into the ghettos, and to make contact with partisans.

This shift in the youth movements' aims and methods must be regarded not only as a reaction to the Jews' deteriorating situation under the German occupation, but also as a result of immanent mental processes. The youth movements had always maintained that consciousness of inner truth, not external reality, and the mental attitude that derived from that consciousness were decisive in shaping a person's existence. As the alternatives of immigrating to Eretz Yisrael, the Land of Israel, or assimilating to the European national cultures became increasingly unachievable and unrealistic, they retained and perhaps even intensified their hold on the

imagination. The Zionist movements continued to devote much space in their newspapers to affairs in Palestine and to promote their Zionist programs. "As a blind musician plucks the strings of his harp, so do we pluck the strings of our dream," declared one writer in the Warsaw Jewish underground press. "Since we are crushed by chains, we dream of flying. Since we are living as slaves, we dream of a life in freedom." Reading letters from Eretz Yisrael became "a moment of forgetting, of dissociation from reality."

Another astonishing phenomenon, related to this interaction of reality and imagination, within the youth movements during the Holocaust was their early, keen perception that wild stories of Nazi atrocities beyond the worst nightmares were quite true. Jewish youth groups, long before the Jewish Councils and the Jewish adult world, saw through the camouflaged activities of the Germans and recognized the bitter reality of the Nazi plan to annihilate all the Jews. News of the gassings at Chelmno and the mass murder at Ponary in 1942 was first carried in the youth movements' underground papers, which also published the first calls for resistance. The youth movements came to this brutal realization not on the basis of factual information but by intuition. Furthermore, the call to resistance that came from young persons not yet old enough for military service, who had never touched a weapon before, was based not on logic or any real prospect for victory, but on an inner decision in spite of reality.

The deeds of the youth movements are a substantial episode within the story of the Jewish resistance struggle in the ghettos. Members of the youth movements took an active part in the fighting in the ghettos of Warsaw, Vilna, Bialystok, Kraków, and Czestochowa. In Lithuania and elsewhere members of youth movements escaped into the forests and joined the partisans. They played a significant role in spontaneous uprisings and escapes from small towns in Belorussia and Ukraine. In the Slovakian national uprising of 1944 they were part of a separate Jewish unit. The Jewish resistance movement recruited fighters among the members of the youth movement. A Jewish underground headed by members of Makkabi Hatzair remained active in Bratislava.

The youth department in the Theresienstadt ghetto was operated mainly by members of Makkabi Hatzair, which organized kindergartens, children's homes, classes, medical care, and food distribution. After the deportation of the Theresienstadt inmates to Ausch-

Members of Youth Aliyah from Germany in tent camp Meshek Yagur. 1936

witz-Birkenau, former members of the Jewish movements took care of the children's block in the Birkenau family camp.

In France several Jewish youth movements—Eclaireurs Israélites de France, the Orthodox Yeshurun, and Hashomer Hatzair—as well as the Joint Distribution Committee were active in education and conducted seminars. In Romania—particularly Transnistria—Hanoar Hatzioni and other youth movements took care of the educational and social welfare of the orphans and other youths. Slovakian Jewish youth movements, such as Hashomer Kadimah, Hashomer Hatzair, Betar, Bnei Akiva, and Makkabi Hatzair, provided Jewish youth with educational opportunities (in place of the schools from which they had been expelled), ran summer and winter camps, and offered vocational training. In the Belgian cities of Brussels and Antwerp, Hashomer Hatzair, Bnei Akiva, and Makkabi Hatzair concentrated on education, cultural work, and mutual help. They also obtained food and ran an agricultural training farm in Mossal.

Jewish youth movements throughout occupied Europe were also involved in underground resistance and rescue operations. The French movements were active in forging and distributing identity papers to help bring thousands of Jews across the borders to safety in neutral Spain and Switzerland. In Hungary, Hashomer Hatzair, Dror, Habonim, Makkabi Hatzair, Hanoar Hatzioni, Bnei Akiva, and Betar were similarly engaged in forging documents and smuggling refugees out of the country—mainly to Romania, where those movements and others, including Gordonia and Brit Haknarnim, were in contact with the rescue committee of the Jewish Agency office in Geneva. In Slovakia the Jewish youth movements organized escape routes to Hungary and illegal immigration to Palestine. Members of the Zionist youth movements in Belgium organized rescue operations to Switzerland and Spain through southern France.

At the end of the war, surviving members of the youth movements worked to find Jewish children who had been in hiding from the Nazis in monasteries and Christian families, gathered wandering Jewish orphans, and brought them together in Jewish children's homes. They saved thousands of orphans and children separated from their parents, provided them with shelter and education in the children's homes, and helped prepare them for resettlement in Palestine within the framework of Youth Aliyah.

Chaim Schatzker

Joint Distribution Committee   The American Jewish Joint Distribution Committee, known as the JDC or the Joint, was founded in November 1914 to coordinate relief shipments to the Jews of Europe and Palestine after the outbreak of World War I. During the 1920s it continued to sponsor programs of relief and rehabilitation primarily in Jewish communities in Eastern Europe and the Middle East.

From the rise of Hitler to the end of World War II, the JDC was the major source of aid to the Jews of German-occupied Europe. It financed emigration, supported refugees in transit, sent relief to impoverished Jewish communities, and, during the war years, subsidized rescue activities.

The JDC provided almost $5 million in help for German Jewry after 1933, including funds for medical care, Jewish schools, and vocational training. After the Anschluss (the annexation of Austria) in March 1938, it supported the Jewish community of Vienna and, after the German takeover of Czechoslovakia in 1939, aided the Jewish communities of Bohemia, Moravia, and Slovakia. In 1939 JDC expenditures in Central Europe amounted to $2 million.

The JDC's primary efforts were directed toward promoting emigration. Out of a total budget of $8 million in 1939, $3 million was spent on emigration, and $600,000 was used to help settle refugees in Latin America. To avoid sending dollars into Nazi-occupied countries, the Joint asked prospective emigrants to deposit their funds with local Jewish communities; the Joint then paid the costs of the emigrants' journey from its overseas headquarters. By the outbreak of World War II, the JDC had helped more than 100,000 Jews emigrate from Germany.

By 1940 refugees in more than 40 countries in Eastern and Western Europe, Asia, and Latin America were receiving aid from the JDC; many who were in transit were being helped to continue their journeys to safety. In Lithuania alone the Joint supported more than 10,000 refugees in 1940, and when 2,000 of those people received visas for Japan in 1941, the JDC paid a substantial part of their transportation costs.

The JDC also gave help to shipwrecked or stranded "illegal" immigrants bound for Palestine without immigration certificates. When 1,200 such immigrants were left marooned in the Yugoslav town of Kladovo in 1940, the JDC supported them for an entire year, even contributing toward the purchase of a ship to take them to Palestine. Before the group could be rescued, however, they were murdered by the Nazis.

In addition, the JDC tried actively to find safe havens for refugees in Latin America. In 1938, in response to an offer by President Rafael Trujillo of the Dominican Republic to accept 100,000 Jewish refugees into his country, the JDC founded the Dominican Republic Settlement Association (DORSA), which brought several hundred refugees to the experimental farm of Sosua. In other Latin American countries the JDC paid landing money (bribes) to allow refugees to disembark and provided subsidies to the local Jewish communities to encourage them to absorb the newcomers. In 1939, when 907 passengers on the ship *St. Louis* were denied permission to land in Cuba despite the JDC's efforts, the JDC arranged for the passengers to be accepted by England, Holland, Belgium, and France so that they would not be returned to Germany.

After the outbreak of World War II, the JDC tried to continue its assistance to the Jews of Europe while adhering to U.S. State Department guidelines that required a U.S. Treasury Department license to transfer funds abroad. While the JDC's leadership, headed by Edward M. M. Warburg and Paul Baerwald, advocated strict adherence to these guidelines, its professional staff, including Morris Troper, director of European affairs, and his deputy and successor, Dr. Joseph Schwartz, pressed for a more flexible policy.

In June 1940 Troper and Schwartz left Paris shortly before the Germans entered the city and transferred the JDC's European headquarters to Lisbon. There, Schwartz leased every available passenger berth, often reserving entire ships, so that refugees arriving in Lisbon with visas for the United States or Latin American countries could proceed to their destinations. Schwartz also sent aid to refugees in Casablanca, Tangiers, and Barcelona. Between 1939 and 1941 some 80,000 refugees passed through Lisbon, and an additional 40,000 passed through in 1942.

Throughout the war the Lisbon office supported major relief and rescue activities in France. Prior to the German occupation of southern France in November 1942, Schwartz sent relief parcels to Jews in French internment camps via the Quakers and even tried to intercede with the Vichy government to prevent deportations. Between 1940 and 1944 he channeled funds to both legal and illegal Jewish organizations in France, including the UGIF (Union Générale des Israélites de France), the umbrella Jewish organization recognized by the Nazis; the OSE (Oeuvre de Secours aux Enfants), which operated children's homes; the FSJ

(Fédération des Sociétés Juives), headed by the Zionist Marc Jarblum; and the illegal Armée Juive, whose treasurer, Jules Jefroykin, became the JDC representative in France in 1941. Schwartz authorized the use of funds smuggled into France by couriers or raised by means of loans après—loans to be repaid by the JDC after the war—to support more than 7,000 children in hiding and to smuggle hundreds of children and adults to Switzerland and Spain. The JDC helped house, clothe, and feed the refugees who reached those countries and in 1944 arranged for more than 1,000 refugees in Spain to sail to Palestine. The JDC spent more than $1 million on rescue activities in France in 1944 alone, and more than $2 million on aid to refugees in Spain, Switzerland, and Portugal.

In 1941 the JDC sent Laura Margolis and Manuel Siegel to Shanghai, where 8,000 Jewish refugees were being fed daily in a JDC-supported soup kitchen. After the attack on Pearl Harbor, Margolis persuaded the Japanese, who had occupied Shanghai, to allow her to operate the soup kitchen by means of loans. She installed modern equipment and appointed a local committee to administer the program before both she and Siegel were interned as enemy aliens in early 1943. By 1944 the soup kitchen was providing daily meals to 10,000 impoverished refugees.

From the outbreak of World War II in September 1939 until the U.S. entry into the war in December 1941, the JDC functioned legally in German-occupied countries. After December 1941 its contact with the Jewish communities of Nazi Europe was maintained through Saly Mayer, the JDC representative in Switzerland, a retired businessman and former head of the Swiss Jewish community. Mayer converted JDC dollars into Swiss francs and, by means of couriers or the International Red Cross, channeled this money to Jewish communities in German-occupied Europe who had turned to "Uncle Saly" for assistance. Some of these funds were also used to support the thousands of Jewish refugees in Switzerland.

The JDC's greatest challenge was in Poland, where its Warsaw-based committee (headed by David Guzik and including Isaac Giterman, Leib Neustadt, Isaac Borenstein, and the historian Emmanuel Ringelblum) struggled to provide relief to Poland's 3 million Jews. After the German invasion of Poland in September 1939, the committee established temporary shelters for refugees, operated public kitchens, supported Jewish hospitals, and sent parcels to prisoners in labor

Part of a consignment of matzo and matzo meal weighing more than 1 million kilograms that the JDC shipped to Polish refugees in Asiatic Russia. 27 January 1943

camps. In spring 1940 the committee distributed tons of matzos and other foodstuffs provided by the JDC for Passover. By 1941 some 600,000 Jews in Poland were receiving assistance from the JDC.

After the establishment of the Warsaw ghetto in November 1940, the JDC opened soup kitchens, supported the "house committees" that provided food and educational programs to children, and subsidized underground schools and newspapers. In 1943 it helped finance the purchase of arms for the Warsaw ghetto rebellion.

Outside Warsaw, in the area of the Generalgouvernement, the JDC supported the Jüdische Soziale Selbsthilfe (JSS) and its successor the Jüdische Unterstützungstelle (JUS), which were headed by Dr. Michael Weichert and recognized by the Nazis as official Jewish welfare agencies. Food, clothing, and medication received from the Warsaw committee or from Saly Mayer were distributed by Weichert to ghettos

and labor camps within the area of the Generalgouvernement.

After December 1941 the JDC continued to operate in Poland, using loans après and funds sent by Saly Mayer. In 1943–44 the JDC transferred $600,000 to Poland via the London-based Polish government-in-exile; part of this money was parachuted into Poland by the Royal Air Force. After the Warsaw ghetto uprising David Guzik escaped to the Aryan side of the city, where he continued his activities, helping Jews obtain Latin American visas. The other members of the JDC committee were killed by the Nazis. Although the JDC could not rescue the vast majority of Polish Jews and could alleviate suffering only temporarily, its assistance to Jews in Poland enabled tens of thousands to survive a little longer than they otherwise would have, and helped keep many Jews alive until the liberation.

During 1943 and 1944 the JDC intensified its rescue activities. It sent more than 200,000 relief parcels containing food, clothing, and medicines from Teheran to Polish Jewish refugees in the Soviet Union, as well as parcels to Transnistria and to the concentration camps of Theresienstadt and Bergen-Belsen.

In 1944, with the approval of the United States government's newly established War Refugee Board, the JDC, in conjunction with the Jewish Agency, spent $3 million in financing illegal immigration to Palestine from Romania via Istanbul. The JDC gave $100,000 to Swedish diplomat Raoul Wallenberg, who furnished tens of thousands of Jews in Budapest with protection papers. Additional funds sent by Saly Mayer supported similar rescue efforts by the Swiss consul, Carl Lutz, and by the Zionist youth movements in Hungary. In Belgium JDC funds supported 7,000 persons in hiding, including 2,900 children. The JDC spent nearly $10 million on rescue projects during 1944.

The JDC's efforts to help the Jews of Europe during World War II were severely hampered by the limited income it received from American Jewry. JDC expenditures declined from $8.4 million in 1939 to $5.7 million in 1941 and totaled only $52 million for the entire war period. During the crucial years 1940–42, when many more Jews could have been saved, the JDC did not have the funds to help them.

Lack of funds, together with the JDC's reluctance to violate U.S. State Department regulations, played a role in two controversial episodes: the Europa Plan, proposed by the JDC in Slovakia in 1942, and the negotiations between Saly Mayer and the German officer

Kurt Becher in 1944. In both cases local JDC representatives hoped that substantial bribes would help stop the deportations, but both attempts foundered. Saly Mayer's delaying tactics in 1944, however, resulted in the rescue of more than 1,600 Jews from Hungary, who were transported to Bergen-Belsen and from there to Switzerland.

After the war American Jews gave generously to the JDC. Its income soared from $25 million in 1945 to more than $70 million in 1948, and it was able to bring massive relief to the survivors of the Holocaust. The JDC provided daily meals for more than 200,000 people in the displaced persons camps of Europe, and supplied them with medical care, clothing, schools, and religious and cultural programs. Massive shipments of food to the Jewish communities of Hungary and Romania saved hundreds of thousands more from starvation. The JDC aided in the reconstruction of the Jewish communities of Poland, France, Belgium, and other countries, supported orphanages for Jewish children, helped survivors locate their relatives through an extensive Location Service, and subsidized schools, theaters, and newspapers. In 1947 some 700,000 Jews, or one-half of the Jewish survivors in Europe, received aid from the JDC.

Under the influence of Joseph Schwartz the JDC leadership agreed to support the Briha, an illegal movement that smuggled more than 150,000 Jews out of Eastern Europe and set them on the road to Palestine. It also provided funds for Aliyah B, the group that organized the illegal immigration voyages. The JDC helped finance the voyage of the ship *Exodus* in 1947 and, after the ship was intercepted by the British, sent supplies to the passengers during their internment on British prison ships off the coast of France.

JDC emigration offices in Europe helped surviving Jews emigrate to the countries of their choice. After the establishment of the state of Israel in May 1948, the JDC also subsidized the immigration of tens of thousands to the fledgling state. In 1949, in cooperation with the Jewish Agency and the Israeli government, the JDC founded Malben to provide institutional care in Israel for survivors in need of long-term treatment. To this day, the JDC continues to care for elderly Holocaust survivors in Eastern Europe.

With the limited resources at its disposal, the JDC made valiant efforts to provide relief and rescue to the Jews of Europe during the Holocaust period. From a welfare agency engaged in temporary relief and reconstruction primarily in Eastern Europe and Palestine, it emerged as the only Jewish organization involved in emigration, refugee aid, and rescue activities in virtually every part of the globe. The JDC was not able to save the overwhelming majority of Europe's Jews, and perhaps, with hindsight, it could have used its resources more effectively. But there is no doubt that hundreds of thousands of Jews who escaped from Nazi Europe, as well as survivors who remained in Europe after the liberation, owed their lives to the JDC.

Sara Kadosh

Joodsche Raad Jewish council in the Netherlands, established by the German military government in 1941 to help keep order. It was headed by Abraham Asscher and David Cohen and composed mostly of businessmen. The Joodsche Raad believed that cooperation, rather than resistance, offered Dutch Jews their best chance for survival. The council distributed Jewish badges and provided deportation lists to German authorities. It was dissolved by the Germans in September 1943. After the war some leading members of the council were accused of having collaborated with the Germans. See NETHERLANDS

Judenrat *Judenrat* (Jewish council, literally "council of Jews"; pl. *Judenräte*) is the term most commonly used to designate the executive committees imposed by the Nazi authorities on many Jewish communities in occupied Europe. These councils were sometimes known as *Ältestenräte* (councils of elders), headed by a *Judenälteste*. Other titles for council chairmen included *Oberjude* and *Obmann*.

The term *Judenrat* appears for the first time in the Third Reich in a government draft proposal of April 1933 to regulate Jewish life. This document foresaw the legal segregation of all Jews in Germany as well as their inclusion within a separate Jewish organizational framework, the Verband der Juden in Deutschland, having legal status. The Verband would be headed by a democratically elected Judenrat consisting of no more than 25 members. It would be supervised by a *Volkswart* (people's guard) appointed personally by and reporting directly to Adolf Hitler. As the members of the committee that worked on the proposal intended it in effect to revoke Jewish emancipation, they studied the organizational structure of medieval Jewish life within the Holy Roman Empire. In the Middle Ages the councils of several Jewish communities in the Ger-

Security Police and SD officials give instructions to the newly formed Judenrat at a Jewish community hall. November 1939

man sphere were called Judenräte (such as the one in Nuremberg), and that is most likely the source of the term in the April 1933 document.

The proposal to establish the Verband and Judenrat was vehemently opposed by several officials, including leaders of the SS. They claimed that an organization anchored in the legal system would stiffen the resolve of the Jewish community to remain on German soil rather than emigrate. So for the time being the pro-

posal faded from view, and indeed the Verband was never created.

In 1937, however, within the circle of experts on Jewish affairs in the SD (Sicherheitsdienst, the security service of the SS), new ideas began to emerge to hasten the implementation of anti-Jewish policies. The SS was interested in promoting Jewish emigration, and a clear means of exerting pressure on the Jews was needed. Thus the SD men recognized a demand for some sort of reorganization of the German machinery as well as of the Jewish community and its leadership. Following the annexation of Austria (the Anschluss) on 11–12 March 1938, in the short interval between the collapse of the Austrian government and the establishment of a German administration, Adolf Eichmann, at that time an official in the Jewish Department of the SD, hurried to Vienna to begin implementing department policies toward Jews. All Jewish organizations were either abolished or forced to become part of the only officially recognized Jewish community association (Israelitische Kultusgemeinde Wien), whose head, Joseph Löwenherz, was appointed by Eichmann and answered directly to him. Eichmann's policies, executed through a newly established Zentralstelle für Jüdische Auswanderung (Central Office for Jewish Emigration), were geared toward forcing the Jews to emigrate. Thus, under Eichmann's auspices in Vienna there emerged a prototype of the later Judenräte. In an interview after the war, while in hiding in Argentina, Eichmann even claimed that the idea for the Judenräte was his own.

After Kristallnacht in November 1938, Eichmann's achievements in Vienna in promoting Jewish emigration played a decisive role in the establishment of the SS as the dominant factor in Nazi-designed anti-Jewish policies. As a result Hermann Göring ordered Reinhard Heydrich on 24 January 1939 to establish a Reichszentrale für Jüdische Auswanderung (Reich Central Office for Jewish Emigration) charged with preparing uniform applications for emigration. Two weeks later, the Reichsvereinigung der Juden in Deutschland (Reich Association of Jews in Germany) was created, including all Jews in Germany and under constant supervision by the Reichszentrale. In July 1939 a formal regulation was published establishing the Reichsvereinigung in law. But the shape and legal basis of the Reichsvereinigung were different from the Viennese prototype: it was countrywide and not local, and apart from furthering emigration it was officially also made responsible for the Jewish school and welfare systems. Apparently, this form of association was a compromise between the original views of the Jewish policy experts in the SS and those of other powerful Reich institutions.

Thus on the eve of World War II two models of Nazi-imposed Jewish organizations had evolved: a local model dependent mainly on authorities linked to the SS and police, and a nationwide model with a formal legal basis created especially for this purpose. Both systems were applied in occupied countries. Prevalence of the local model reflects the strength of SS-linked authorities in a particular area, whereas the nationwide model dominated when there was some need for compromise between the SS and various other authorities.

Within a week after the invasion of Poland on 1 September 1939 the *Einsatzgruppen*—special killing squads of the SD—began to appoint Jews to local councils in several places within the newly occupied Polish territories. A general order to do so was given after the fact, on 21 September, at a meeting of Heydrich and the Einsatzgruppen commanders in Berlin. The *Schnellbrief* (telegram) issued that same day confirming Heydrich's orders in several issues included also the establishment of a council of elders (*Ältestenrat*) in each Jewish community. The council was to be formed "from among the remaining rabbis and other persons of authority" and to be composed of up to 24 Jewish men. Furthermore, the council was "to be made *fully responsible,* in the literal sense of the term, for the exact and prompt implementation of directives already issued or to be issued in the future." In another place in the same document the word *Judenrat* is used instead of *Ältestenrat*, so the two terms were apparently already interchangeable.

This document is generally accepted as the basic formulation of the Judenrat system, even though its instructions were not precisely applied everywhere. However, the system outlined in the telegram was developed specifically for the Polish situation. It was modified in other occupied countries to fit local conditions, and it was not applied everywhere.

As a result of Heydrich's order, more than half the Jewish population of German-occupied Poland (including major communities such as Warsaw, Lodz, and Kraków) was living under Judenrat regimes by the middle of November 1939. Hans Frank, head of the Generalgouvernement (the part of Poland under German military administration), issued another official regulation, dated 28 November 1939, for the establishment of Judenräte in his territory. Paragraphs 2 and 3 of the regulation stipulated: "The Judenrat shall consist of 12 Jews in communities with up to 10,000 inhabitants, and 24 Jews in communities with more than 10,000 inhabitants. These are to be drawn from the local population. The Judenrat shall be elected by the Jews of the community. If a member of the Judenrat leaves, a new member is to be elected immediately . . . . The Judenrat shall elect a chairman and a deputy from among its members." The Judenrat was to be subordinated to a subdistrict commander or city commander, who could "order changes in the membership."

This regulation is usually regarded as the second basic document of the Judenrat system. A close examination, however, shows that the regulation, which in many respects resembled the 1933 proposal, was part of Frank's effort to appropriate control over the Jews to himself, thereby removing it from the various security agencies. In fact, Frank's regulation was never really implemented, and his intention to gain control was only partially successful. Hence, the main document concerning establishment of the Judenräte remains the Heydrich Schnellbrief.

As a local concern, the Judenrat had authority over Jews in one city, town, or village. But as a result of the interaction between Jews of one location and their coreligionists in the surrounding area, as well as decisions of local German commanders, the authority of several Judenräte extended more widely. For instance, a regional central council for East Upper Silesia, the Zentrale der Ältestenräte der Jüdischen Kultusgemeinden, was established in January 1940 on orders by the Germans. This council was organized and headed by Moshe Merin, chairman of the Sosnowiec Judenrat. By March 1941 this parent council encompassed 32 communities with a total Jewish population of about 100,000. Another central council was established at the end of 1939 in the Radom region, with authority over more than 282,000 Jews. Its chairman, Joseph Diamant, was less competent than Merin, and the council dissolved in April 1942, when Diamant was arrested together with three other council members and deported to Auschwitz. Another example is the Amsterdam Jewish Council (Joodsche Raad voor Amsterdam), formed 12 February 1941 in the wake of violent clashes between Dutch National Socialists and Jews in the Jewish quarter of Amsterdam. The council's authority was at first limited to the Jews of Amsterdam, who made up about 60 percent of all Dutch Jews, but gradually extended beyond the confines of the city. From the second half of 1941 the German authorities recognized in practice the council's influence throughout the Netherlands.

The second model—of a nationwide *Judenvereinigung* (Jewish association) designed along the pattern of the German *Reichsvereinigung*—was applied in several other countries. On 25 November 1941 the Association des Juifs en Belgique was established, chaired by Rabbi Salomon Ullman and headquartered in Brussels. Four days later, the Union Générale des Israélites de France was organized. The French union's council consisted of 18 members divided into two groups of nine persons. These two groups functioned almost as separate bodies, so that there were actually two subcouncils: one for the German-occupied area in the north and the other for the area of southern France administered by the government in Vichy. In several satellite states of Germany, similar nationwide bodies were established, apparently under the influence of the German example. In independent Slovakia in September 1940 a Jewish center (Ustredna Zidov) was established, and in December 1941 a similarly named Jewish center (Centrala Evreilor) was established in Romania. Algeria, ruled by Vichy France, had its own Union Générale des Israélites d'Algérie.

Functioning of the Judenräte

Although Germans originally established the councils as a means of controlling the Jews while they carried out German orders, the councils also took a leading role in many aspects of Jewish society. The councils' organizational structure reflected their multiple tasks: serving German goals, continuing Jewish communal services formerly carried out by the *kehilla* (Jewish community), resolving new problems as they arose, and, in ghettos, acting as a Jewish city council. Councils typically included departments dealing with administration and registration, finances (including taxation), labor (including forced labor and sometimes vocational retraining), security, health and sanitation, construction and housing, food supply and industry, welfare, education, culture, and sometimes religious affairs.

In the 1940s the councils received demands from the Germans to recruit people for forced labor, hold censuses, evacuate Jews from specified houses and neighborhoods, pay contributions, and regulate the concentration of local Jews and those from the surrounding areas in the ghetto. Initially some councils were also involved in promoting emigration. Later, during the deportation period, many but not all councils served the Germans in arresting, selecting, and concentrating the deportees. As part of these functions, a police force was needed, and in many places an *Ordnungsdienst* (Public Order Service) was established.

Smugglers of weapons in Kovno ghetto who were caught by the Jewish police and later joined the underground. 1941–42

In some instances the Ordnungsdienst was under the auspices of the Judenrat and independent of the German security forces; in others it was subordinated to them.

On the other hand, many tasks not required by the Germans were carried out by the councils on their own initiative. For instance, the councils' main task was to arrange for the regular supply and rationing of food. This could not be accomplished without German approval and local non-Jewish cooperation. The food always had to be paid for, either through confiscation and taxation or through barter for products manufactured inside the ghetto. In several areas the councils tried to organize the growing of vegetables in open spaces. In order to counter idleness and crime and to show that the Jewish community was productive, many councils initiated and developed industries. Health and sanitation services were of the utmost importance, because the degradation of living circumstances caused epidemics and high death rates. Accordingly,

hospitals and clinics were established, in many cases with the intensive help of other public organizations and volunteers.

Behavior and Leadership

It is impossible to generalize about the behavior of the many hundreds of Jewish councils. The common view—also to be found in most of the scholarly literature—is that the Judenräte represented the "Jewish leadership" of the period. This perception is inaccurate. First, the very fact that the councils were appointed by the German occupation forces for their own ends meant that the people serving on them could never fully carry out leadership functions of Jewish society, even if they wanted to do so. Second, Jewish society was very much divided on the eve of the Nazi period as a result of many decades of secularization, emancipation, and politicization. Hence there was no accepted central leadership of any Jewish community. Heydrich's notion that Judenräte should be composed of the remnant of leading personalities and rabbis thus did not mean that they would be really representative of local Jewish society (even when this policy was strictly applied). Third, alongside the councils other types of Jewish leadership continued to exist: rabbis, youth movements, and welfare organizations (such as the Yiddishe Sotziale Aleinhilf in Poland). In France and the Netherlands, the former community organizations—the Consistoire and the Nederlandsch-Israelitisch Kerkgenoot-schap—also continued to exist alongside the imposed body. Last, the German authorities had a major influence on the composition of the councils. Sometimes they would select a person to serve as chairman merely because he spoke German, as happened in 1941 in occupied areas of the Soviet Union. The Germans also intervened in the composition of councils, sometimes changing them entirely, as happened many times during the deportation period. In Lodz, for instance, the first Ältestenrat was removed at the end of 1939, except for the Judenälteste Mordechai Chaim Rumkowski. Thus it is clear that Jewish councils were never able to fulfill leadership roles completely, particularly if "leadership" is taken to mean the promotion of the group's internal integration and the pursuit and furthering of common goals of existence. Such leadership was impossible, especially when the Final Solution was being implemented, for the lethal ends pursued by the German occupiers were diametrically opposed to the Jews' aim to survive.

Nevertheless, the authority and position of the Judenräte, together with their efforts to continue Jewish life and society, allowed them to assume certain leading roles. In many cases, genuine Jewish leaders from before the German occupation joined the councils. Their participation is an important factor in examining the councils' policies and behavior.

Because they carried out German orders, the councils aroused sharp antagonism from within Jewish society, and this reaction grew as the measures against the Jews escalated. Sometimes Jewish councils took harsh measures against the Jews under their jurisdiction, either on their own initiative or with the aid of the Ordnungsdienst. This too engendered opposition, even if the measures served the proper regulation of daily life. The dependence on the councils and their administration, as well as the enormous power of the chairmen, gave way to bribery and corruption, especially in the large, overpopulated ghettos in Poland. In addition, several council chairmen perceived themselves as Jewish prime ministers (such as David Cohen in the Netherlands) or saviors of the Jewish people (such as Rumkowski in Lodz and Jacob Gens in Vilna), at times losing touch with the reality of their position.

But this is not the general picture. In many places the Jewish population supported the policies of the local council, which, insofar as they concerned the German authorities and their demands, were not uniform. According to Isaiah Trunk and Aharon Weiss, the principal scholars of the Judenräte in Eastern Europe, the attitudes of the Jewish councils ranged from strong reservations about any cooperation with the Germans, to readiness to carry out German orders in the economic sphere only, to a willingness to sacrifice parts of the Jewish community in order to save the majority or "the most important," and even to full compliance with German orders without regard for Jewish communal interests. Positions also changed when the deportations began: according to Weiss, compliance grew in the deportation period, plainly a result of terror and intimidation, and after many council members had resigned or had been removed from office, shot, or deported. Trunk, who collected data on 720 council members in Poland, found that 25.3 percent were murdered before the deportations began, and 53.2 percent died during the deportation period. Some committed suicide (1.2 percent), and only 12 percent survived the war.

A major policy line of Jewish councils in Eastern Europe was aimed at proving to the Germans the productivity of the Jews, with the goal of ensuring that at least a nucleus of the community would survive this dreadful period. It was hoped that the Third Reich's enormous need for all kinds of products and labor would give the German pragmatists priority over the fanatical ideological antisemites. This policy of "rescue through labor" was promoted by Rumkowski, Merin, and Gens, as well as by Efraim Barash of Bialystok and others. (As Jews in Western Europe were not ghettoized and were only partially recruited for forced labor, "rescue through labor" policies did not arise there.)

A central facet of the deportation period in Eastern Europe was the relationship between the councils and Jewish underground groups, especially the resistance organizations. (Again, in Western Europe this problem was almost nonexistent, because the Jews were not confined to ghettos.) As the Germans imposed collective responsibility on the Jews, some councils opposed the resistance groups by all means available—either because they feared that the Germans would liquidate the ghettos immediately upon discovering the existence of such groups, or as a result of the power struggle over influence in the ghettos (or for both reasons, as in Warsaw). Occasionally there was some cooperation between the Judenräte and the resistance fighters. Arguments focused on the interpretation of German intentions and, consequently, on the proper moment for armed resistance or mass escape to the forests (as in Bialystok). In several ghettos, including Kovno (Kaunas), there was full cooperation between the council and the resistance organization, and in some cases, such as Tuczyn, the underground activities were even headed by council members or chairmen.

Popular Attitudes after the Holocaust

Immediately after the war a clear-cut distinction was made throughout Europe between those who had been "good" during the Nazi period and those who had been "bad." The good were identified as members of the resistance, the bad as collaborators. In the Jewish world such terminology underwent a translation: "resistance" meant "ghetto fighters" and "partisans," whereas "collaborators" meant "Judenräte." This view deeply affected the ways in which the Holocaust was commemorated in Jewish circles for several decades and the manner in which surviving council members were accepted in postwar Jewish society. Indeed, many of council members tried to hide the fact of their involvement. The most extreme treatment of Judenrat members occurred in the Netherlands. A Jewish "Council of Honor" was established in February 1946, which "tried" five members of the former Joodsche Raad, including council leaders David Cohen and Abraham Asscher. The Council of Honor finally decided in December 1947 to ban both chairmen from any future position within the Jewish community. Asscher, a longtime leader of the prewar Jewish community, left the community entirely; Cohen fought for rehabilitation. In 1948 the Central Committee of the Ashkenazi Community umbrella organization resolved to annul the Council of Honor's decision, but without giving Cohen an opportunity to vindicate himself. Until recently, the generally negative attitude toward the Jewish councils prevailed in Jewish communities outside Israel, mainly under the influence of Holocaust survivors.

In Israel, resistance against nazism could easily be integrated into the national saga in the years following its establishment. The Judenrat phenomenon was more problematic; resentment felt by Holocaust survivors toward this issue only contributed to the entrenchment of a stigma. The wartime activities of the Hungarian Jewish leader Rudolf (Israel) Kasztner, whose efforts on behalf of Jews were tainted by his negotiations with Nazis, were perceived as representing typical Judenrat behavior, even though he was never a member of the Hungarian Jewish council. The Israeli judge Binyamin Halevi, in delivering his verdict in a libel suit brought on Kasztner's behalf, called Kasztner a man who had "sold his soul to the devil," and this phrase came to be applied to the surviving members of the Judenräte. Consequently in Jewish circles, especially in Israel, *Judenrat* became a synonym for traitor. Even today the term still appears in public discourse: in the 1990s the government of Israeli prime minister Yitzhak Rabin, for instance, was called a Judenrat by some rightists.

Even in the 1950s, however, some dissenting voices were heard. The poet Nathan Alterman, for example, in his "Between Two Roads," sought to justify the policies of the Judenräte. Later, some resistance fighters, such as Yitzhak (Antek) Zukermann, stated that their activities had stemmed mainly from their youthful status and mentality, and that other policies—such as those older people who had to care for families and the community—should not therefore automatically be considered "bad." Holocaust curricula in Israel, both at the high school and the university levels, since the end of the 1970s have helped change the general public attitude. The Israeli playwright Joshua Sobol based his 1980s play *Ghetto* on the life of Jacob Gens, head of the Vilna ghetto, thereby attempting to detach the Judenrat phenomenon from existing stereotypes and to provoke public discussion.

The main body of scholarly research on the Judenräte emerged after the trial of Adolf Eichmann in 1961, mainly as a result of a fierce controversy that arose in the wake of the statements made by the philosopher Hannah Arendt. During her coverage of the trial as a reporter for the *New Yorker* magazine, she referred to the chairmen and members of the Judenräte as the leaders of the Jews (according to her, Rabbi Leo Baeck, who chaired the German Reichsvereinigung, was "the Jewish *Führer*") and blamed the councils for the extent of the murder of the Jews. In Arendt's opinion, had the councils not existed, or had their members resigned, the number of victims would have been significantly lower.

Arendt's accusations spurred extensive research on the activities of the Judenräte and culminated in such pathbreaking works as Isaiah Trunk's *Judenrat* (1972) and the Yad Vashem volume *Patterns of Jewish Leadership in Nazi Europe* (1979). These studies revealed that the behavior and composition of the Jewish councils varied greatly from place to place, that several stages in the development of the councils are needed to be taken into account, and that this phenomenon has to be integrated into a more general picture of evolving Nazi anti-Jewish attitudes. Nevertheless, the view that Judenräte first appeared only after 21 September 1939 and that they were the "leaders" of the Jews still prevails, and the major issue in common scholarly literature remains the personal behavior of council members. Only recently have dissenting views on these questions been raised, particularly by Dan Michman (*Dutch Jewish History* 3, 1993; *Zeitschrift für Geschichtswissenschaft* 1993–94).   *Dan Michman*

K

Kaiserwald Concentration and labor camp in a suburb of Riga, Latvia, established in 1943. Most of the Jews expelled from Riga were detained at Kaiserwald, and most of the surviving Latvian Jews were sent there as well. The prisoners were forced to work in factories while contending with terrible overcrowding and hunger. Those unable to work were executed. In 1944 the Germans evacuated the camp by murdering some inmates and sending the remainder to other camps.

Kaltenbrunner, Ernst (1903–46) Senior SS commander, head of the RSHA (Reich Security Main Office) after Reinhard Heydrich. Kaltenbrunner worked on the so-called euthanasia program and was involved in the 1943 deportations to Theresienstadt and the murder of Hungarian Jews. Convicted of war crimes and crimes against humanity at the Nuremberg trials, Kaltenbrunner was hanged.

Kapo Head of a unit in a concentration camp. The term was also used to refer to any Nazi collaborator, although some kapos were not collaborators and behaved honorably. The kapos were inmates appointed by the camp authorities to insure that their fellow prisoners maintained order and adequately fulfilled work quotas. Many kapos were common criminals, but some were political prisoners who tried to obtain limited relief for the people under their nominal control. Kapos had better food and warmer clothing than other prisoners and lived in special barracks. Some were brought to justice after the war for the crimes they committed while in the camps.

Kappler, Herbert (1907–78) Senior SS commander, chief of the Nazi political police in Italy after the 1943 German occupation. Kappler played a key role in the liquidation of Italian Jews and the murder of other Italians. He was sentenced to life imprisonment after the war. He escaped from a hospital in Rome in 1977 but died soon afterward.

Karski, Jan (1914–2000) Courier to London for the Polish underground. Prior to his mission to the West in 1942 he visited ghettos and met with Jewish leaders in Poland. He wrote of his experiences in major American publications and met with American and British leaders, including President Roosevelt and British Foreign Secretary Anthony Eden. In his reports to Polish and Western leaders he provided detailed information about the treatment of the Jews. See POLES AND JEWS IN WORLD WAR II

Kasztner, Rudolf (Israel) (1906–57) Zionist activist and leader who negotiated with the Nazis for the rescue of Hungarian Jewry during the German occupation of Hungary. Israel (Reszo) Rudolf Kasztner was born in Cluj, Transylvania. During the 1920s he was one of the leaders of Barisia, a Zionist youth movement in Transylvania, and in the 1930s he became a prominent member of Haichud Haolami, the Diaspora branch of the Labor party in Palestine (Mapai). He was also a talented journalist and one of the editors of *Uj Kelet*, the organ of Transylvania's Zionist movement. Furthermore, he acted as secretary of the Jewish faction in the Romanian parliament. In 1937 he married Elizabeth (Bodio), the daughter of Yosef (Yoshko) Fisher, a member of the Romanian parliament, leader of the Zionist movement in Transylvania, and one of the richest and most prominent personalities in Cluj. Kasztner was quite well known in Transylvania and especially in Cluj; he was noted for his good relations with high-ranking officials both in Transylvania and in the Romanian government.

After Transylvania was annexed to Hungary in 1940, Kasztner moved to Budapest, where he worked for Keren Hayesod, the agency that raised funds for

Kapos (in white and black armbands) oversee prisoners at forced labor. 1941–42

building the Jewish community in Palestine. In 1942 Kasztner was one of the founders of Havaada Le'ezra Velehatzala (Relief and Rescue Committee), whose president was Otto Komoly, leader of the Zionist Organization of Hungary. The committee members (apart from Kasztner) were Joel Brand and Shmuel (Samo) Shpringman, both members of Haichud Haolami and refugees in Budapest. The chief task of the committee was to assist Jewish refugees who had fled to Hungary, mainly from Poland and nearby Slovakia. It provided them with money, food, false certificates, and places to live. Its assistance was vital, since most Hungarian Jews refused to break the law, and it was impossible to help the refugees without doing so.

On 19 March 1944 Germany invaded Hungary and began the last phase of the Final Solution. Until then Hungary had been a relatively safe place for Jews. They suffered persecution, but the Hungarian regime, including the regent, Adm. Miklós Horthy, refused to deport them to the death camps in the East. After the invasion the Germans executed their policy rapidly—

the first train to Auschwitz left Hungary on 15 May. Between then and 9 July, 437,402 Jews were deported to Birkenau. At that point, under orders from Horthy, deportations ceased. From the beginning of July until Ferenc Szalasi's coup d'état of 15 October, surviving Hungarian Jews lived in comparative security.

While the deportations were proceeding, Kasztner and his committee made one of the most important efforts to rescue Hungarian Jews. Kasztner and Dieter Wisliceny, one of Adolf Eichmann's closest aides, first met on 5 April 1944. This was the beginning of long and complicated negotiations between the committee and representatives of the SS in Budapest. The main point of the negotiations was the SS proposal to halt the extermination in exchange for 10,000 trucks from the Western powers, to be used only against the Soviet Union and not on the western front. The SS officers, who knew that Germany was on the verge of total defeat, wished to use their connection with Kasztner and the committee as a means of reaching the centers of power in London and Washington. Although the committee was virtually powerless, the Nazis, misled by their own antisemitic stereotypes, considered it part of omnipotent "international Jewry."

In order to further the deal with the West, the SS sent Joel Brand to Istanbul on 19 May with Bundy Grosz. Grosz was a marginal figure and a minor agent of both the Abwehr (German army intelligence) and the Hungarian secret service. The SS considered Grosz's mission, the attempt to negotiate a separate peace with the West, the main purpose of the trip. Brand's mission was designed to cover up the real purpose of Grosz's journey.

Brand was supposed to return to Budapest in two weeks, but he never did so. Kasztner, who had remained in the city, tried to convince the Germans that they had to demonstrate their goodwill to prove that their offer was serious. As a result of his persuasion, they agreed to send a train with 600 Jews on it to a neutral country. In the course of June 1944 they agreed to increase the number from 600 to 1,685, and on 30 June the "Rescue Train" left Budapest. Initially the passengers arrived in Bergen-Belsen, and only later (some in August and the rest in December) did they reach Switzerland. The train carried representatives of all the main sections of Hungarian Jewry, including Joel Teitelbaum, the Satmar rebbe, and members of the right-wing Betar movement, including Jacob Weiss, who later joined the Irgun and was executed by the British.

The Rescue Train was Kasztner's most outstanding rescue attempt, but it was not the only one. He also saved 15,000 Jews who were deported to Strasshof in Austria instead of Auschwitz, and during the last weeks of the war he was involved in efforts to save Jewish survivors in the camps.

After the war Kasztner lived in Geneva and then emigrated to Israel in December 1947. He became a close adviser of Dov Joseph, Mapai's senior leader and cabinet member, and appeared in the Mapai list for election to the First (1949) and Second Knesset (1951).

In the summer of 1952 Malkiel Grunwald, an old eccentric living in Jerusalem, produced a mimeographed leaflet in which he accused Kasztner of col-

Jews from the "Kasztner train" arrive in Switzerland after being in Bergen-Belsen concentration camp. August 1944

laborating with the Nazis in exterminating the Hungarian Jews. Haim Cohn, the Israeli attorney general, decided to prosecute Grunwald for libel, and because Kasztner was a public servant (in 1952 he was the spokesperson for the Ministry of Industry and Commerce), the case was brought by the state attorney's office. The trial of Malkiel Grunwald opened in the district court of Jerusalem on 1 January 1954. The presiding judge was Binyamin Halevi, the prosecuting attorney was Amnon Tel, from the Jerusalem district attorney's office, and Grunwald's lawyer was Shmuel Tamir (Katzenelson). At 31 years of age Tamir, a founder of the opposition right-wing Herut movement, harbored extreme animosity toward the Labor government of David Ben-Gurion.

The Grunwald hearing lasted 10 months. During this time it turned from a minor trial into the most dramatic and sensational court case in Israel in the 1950s. In what became known as the "Kasztner trial," the real accused were Rudolf Kasztner and the leadership of Mapai, including David Ben-Gurion and Moshe Sharett.

Tamir succeeded in turning the proceedings into an inquest on the behavior of the leadership of the Jewish community in Palestine (the Yishuv) in the war years. While accusing Kasztner of abandoning Hungarian Jewry and collaborating with the Nazis, Tamir accused the Yishuv leadership of abandoning the European Jews and collaborating with the British. The affair became a political trial and an embarrassment to the political system. In June 1954, in the middle of the trial, Haim Cohn took over the prosecution.

Judge Halevi delivered his verdict on 22 June 1955, after a delay of eight months. He accepted most of Tamir's arguments, agreeing that Kasztner's behavior had assisted the Nazis in their efforts to exterminate as many Jews as possible in the shortest possible time. Halevi saw the Rescue Train as the Nazi's bait to trap Kasztner: the 1,685 Jewish lives were a "gift" to him, including 388 from his home town of Cluj, and in return he was ready to collaborate in exterminating the rest. The judge declared that by agreeing to the deal, "Kasztner sold his soul to the devil." This one phrase, out of a verdict covering 300 pages, has stuck in the public mind to this day.

The verdict was announced just five weeks before the elections to the Third Knesset and became the main issue of the election campaign. Mapai, the ruling party, was severely attacked by both the right-wing Herut and the left-wing Maki (the non-Zionist Communist party), as well as Ahdut Haavoda (the radical left-wing Zionist party). "Mapai is Kasztner and Kasztner is Mapai," declared a Herut election slogan.

On 21 August 1955 the state attorney's office lodged an appeal to the Supreme Court, which in January 1958 overturned Halevi's verdict. The main judgment was delivered by Justice Shimon Agranat, who in 1965 became the third president of the Supreme Court. Agranat ruled that there had not been any real option to save most Hungarian Jews, so the Rescue Train was not a gift the Nazis made to Kasztner in return for his collaboration. Had he not succeeded in arranging the train, its passengers' fate would have been no different from that of millions of other Jews.

Kasztner did not live to hear this verdict. He had been murdered in Tel Aviv in March 1957 by three members of an extreme-right organization. The assassins were sentenced to life imprisonment but were pardoned after six years following Ben-Gurion's intervention. *Yechiam Weitz*

Katzenelson, Itzhak (1886–1944) Yiddish writer and poet who lived during the war in the Vittel camp in

Itzhak Katzenelson. 1939–44

France, in Lodz, and in Warsaw, before being murdered in Auschwitz. Katzenelson was one of the most important literary figures of the period, a prolific writer of Yiddish and Hebrew poetry and plays, including plays for children, and of textbooks. He wrote the famous poem "Song of the Murdered Jewish People" in Warsaw in 1942. Beit Lohamei Haghetaot (Ghetto Fighters' House) holds most of his surviving manuscripts. See LITERATURE

Kaunas See KOVNO

Kishinev (Chisinau) Capital of Bessarabia, part of Romania until 1940 and again occupied by Romanian troops after the German invasion of the Soviet Union. The Jews of Kishinev, approximately 60,000 in 1941, were either deported to Transnistria or killed on the spot.

Knochen, Helmut (1910–) Senior SS official in charge of internment and deportation of Jews in Belgium and all of occupied northern France. Knochen was also responsible for the murder of many French

and of British prisoners of war. Although he was sentenced to death by a British military court, a French court commuted the sentence to life imprisonment. He was released in 1962.

Koch, Karl Otto (1897–1945) Senior SS officer, commander of Buchenwald in 1937 and of Majdanek in 1941. Both Koch and his wife, Ilse, were known for their extreme cruelty and the practice of collecting the tattooed skin of their victims. Karl Otto Koch was arrested in 1945 by the Gestapo for forgery, embezzlement, mismanagement, and insubordination. He was sentenced to death by a Nazi court and executed in April 1945.

Königsberg Death March See PALMNICKEN MASSACRE

Korczak, Janusz (b. Henryk Goldszmit; 1879–1942) Physician and educator. As head of the Warsaw orphanage on Krochmalna Street, he refused to desert the children and go into hiding when the Germans were preparing to deport them. He was sent to Tre-

An elderly Jewish man sells shoes at the open market in the Kishinev ghetto. 19 August 1941

blinka with 200 orphans and killed there in August 1942. See CHILDREN

Korherr, Richard (1903–) Chief SS statistician, author of the Korherr Report, which estimated the number of Jews in various European countries at the beginning of World War II and the number that remained after deportations and killings had begun. Begun in 1942, the report was updated every three months in 1943 and 1944. Adolf Eichmann, at his own trial in 1961, testified to the importance of this report for the implementation of the Final Solution.

Kovner, Abba (1918–88) Local leader of the Hashomer Hatzair youth movement, commander of a partisan unit in the Vilna ghetto, and poet. Kovner was among the first to recognize that the Nazis were planning the complete destruction of European Jewry and call for resistance. After the liberation he emigrated to Palestine and joined Kibbutz Ein Hahoresh. Kovner was active in Israeli political and cultural life. See VILNA

Kovno (Kaunas) Capital of independent Lithuania between 1920 and 1939 and home to approximately 40,000 Jews in 1939. The vast majority of the Kovno Jews were killed in pogroms led by both the Germans and the Lithuanians and in the camps. A small number of Jews succeeded in hiding, and some escaped to the forests to join the partisans. See BALTIC COUNTRIES

Kraków City in southern Poland with a Jewish population of 60,000 in 1939, seat of the German administration of Poland (Generalgouvernement) during the occupation.

Kramer, Josef (1906–45) SS officer who held successive positions at several concentration camps. After

Jews are loaded onto trucks with their luggage during a deportation action from the Kovno ghetto. They will be transported to the Estonian concentration camp of Koramei. Among those on the back of the truck are members of the Miszelski family: Moishe Fishel, Chana, Jankel, Esther, and Chaim. 26 October 1942

Josef Kramer. April 1945

postings at Dachau, Sachsenhausen, and Mauthausen, Kramer became aide-de-camp to Rudolf Höss at Auschwitz. In April 1941 he was named commandant of Natzweiler-Struthof. In May 1944 he returned to Auschwitz to oversee the gas chambers at Birkenau. In the last months of the war he served as commandant of Bergen-Belsen. Kramer was tried by a British military court and executed in 1945.

Kristallnacht The unprecedented pogrom of 9–10 November 1938 in Germany has passed into history as Kristallnacht (Night of Broken Glass). The phrase, which spread among Berliners, does not appear in the German press or official documents, and some historians regard it with disfavor. The term *party pogrom* has sometimes been used, because the initiative, the organization, and the execution was the work of the whole Nazi party and its affiliated groups, the SA and SS, with the help of the national police.

Violent attacks on Jews and Judaism throughout the Reich and in the recently annexed Sudetenland began on 8 November and continued until 11 November in Hannover and the free city of Danzig, which had not then been incorporated into the Reich. There followed associated operations: arrests, detention in concentration camps, and a wave of so-called aryanization orders, which completely eliminated Jews from German economic life. The November pogrom, carried out with the help of the most up-to-date communications technology, was the most modern pogrom in the history of anti-Jewish persecution and an overture to the step-by-step extirpation of the Jewish people in Europe.

Hitler's diplomatic success with the Munich Pact of 29–30 September 1938, the behavior of his British, French, and Italian counterparts, and above all the support of the German people for official Reich policies swept aside all obstructions on the road to an intensification of anti-Jewish measures.

After Hitler's seizure of power, even as Germans were being divided into "Aryans" and "non-Aryans," the number of Jews steadily decreased through emigration to neighboring countries or overseas. This movement was promoted by the Central Office for Jewish Emigration (Zentralstelle für Jüdische Auswanderung) established by Reinhard Heydrich in 1938. In 1925 there were 564,378 Jews in Germany; in May 1939 the number had fallen to 213,390. The flood of emigration after the November pogrom was one of the largest ever, and by the time emigration was halted in October 1941, only 164,000 Jews were left within the Third Reich, including Austria. By September 1944, after the deportations to the concentration camps, the number of Jews still living in Germany had dwindled to 14,574.

The illusion that the legal repression enacted in the civil service law of 1 April 1933, which excluded non-Aryans from public service, would be temporary was laid to rest in September 1935 by the Nuremberg Laws—the Reich Citizenship Law and the Law for the Protection of German Blood and Honor. The Reich Citizenship Law heralded the political compartmentalization of Jewish and Aryan Germans. The complementary ordinances to the Reich Citizenship Law, dated 14 and 28 November 1935, sought to define who was a Jew; it also created a basis for measures limiting the scope of Jewish occupations and the opportunities for young Jews to get an education. Following the March 1938 annexation (Anschluss) of Austria, which brought 200,000 Austrian Jews under German domination, exclusion of Jews from the economy be-

The synagogue in Baden-Baden burning the morning after Kristallnacht. 10 November 1938

gan, first through the removal of Jewish manufacturers and business chiefs and their replacement by "commissars" in charge of "aryanization," the expropriation of Jewish businesses. Within a short time, from January to October 1938, the Nazis aryanized 340 middle-sized and small industrial enterprises, 370 wholesale firms, and 22 private banks owned by Jews.

The November pogrom was the peak of a series of events intended to expel the Jews from economic life and to force a hurried emigration. These included legally based procedures against Jews in the Altreich (Germany without Austria); actions in annexed Austria, at first unsanctioned, later incorporated into the legal system and modeled on those of Nazi Germany; and the unprecedented expulsion from Germany to Poland of 15,000–17,000 Jewish Polish citizens.

A sequence of normative legislation in 1938 heralded economic despoliation. Under the Law Concerning the Legal Position of the Jewish Religious Community (28 March 1938), the state subsidy for the Jewish community was withdrawn. Under the decree of 22 April 1938 against "continuing concealment of

Jewish business activity," Jews were obliged to declare their assets—an indication that their possessions might be seized. The Fourth Decree (25 July 1938) under the Reich Citizenship Law deprived Jewish doctors, as of 30 September, of their practices among Jewish patients. An edict by the police president of Breslau dated 21 July ordered that shops and businesses belonging to Jews should bear a notice: "Jewish Firm." Air Ministry political-economic guidelines of 14 October 1938 were accompanied by a recommendation, summed up by Hermann Göring (then head of the ministry): "The Jewish question must now be grasped in every way possible, for they [Jews] must be removed from the economy." Göring also said that he was in favor of the creation of Jewish ghettos in German towns. His words gave notice of a general anti-Jewish offensive in the coming weeks. The most favorable opportunity for unleashing the attack was afforded by the fatal wounding of the German diplomat Ernst vom Rath on 7 November 1938 in Paris by the 16-year-old Polish Jew Herschel Grynszpan.

On 16 March 1938 the head of the Sicherheitsdienst

(SD, security service), Reinhard Heydrich, commissioned Section II-112 under Adolf Eichmann to carry out a plan to drive the Jews out of Austria. A Jewish card index was set up, the spoliation of the Jews was ordered and carried out, and the political, cultural, and economic life of the Jewish people was completely paralyzed. As of 20 May 1938 the racial laws valid in the Altreich were extended to annexed Austria. About 16,000 children of Jewish origin were taken out of school; by the end of the school year 1938–39 it was virtually forbidden for Jews to pursue an education. In the first few weeks after the racial laws came into force, "wild" instances of confiscation were carried out in commissar-style authority. Göring's decree of 26 April 1938 created a legal basis for forced aryanization and for the registration of Jewish assets. Under the eyes of the Nazi gauleiter Joseph Bürckel and the Reich governor Arthur Seyss-Inquart, Nazi combat teams organized local pogroms in Vienna on the night of 4–5 October; and on 7 October, as the rioting turned also against Catholic authorities, not even the palace of Cardinal Theodor Innitzer was spared, even though he favored the Nazis. The arrest of about 2,000 Jews prompted an immediate retreat across Austrian borders.

On 24 October 1938 German foreign minister Joachim von Ribbentrop suggested to Josef Lipski, the Polish ambassador in Berlin, a "global" settlement of German-Polish disputes. The proposed settlement was to include the return of Danzig to the Reich, the building of an extraterritorial motorway through the Polish Corridor (between the German provinces of Pomerania and East Prussia), and Poland's entry into the Anti-Comintern Pact. Ribbentrop hinted at German-Polish collaboration in colonial questions and even a common path regarding the emigration of Polish Jews. Yet the Polish government was not ready to take these steps. A policy of intimidation toward Poland began, similar to that which had been used against Czechoslovakia and Austria. On 16 October the German Foreign Office, through Ambassador Helmuth von Moltke in Warsaw, presented an aide-mémoire strongly resembling an ultimatum regarding the transfer of Polish Jews from Reich territory. Without waiting for an answer from the Polish government, on the very same day Heydrich published a decree banning Jews who were Polish citizens from remaining within the Reich. Heydrich ordered a "Jew operation": this meant that the police should bundle the Polish Jews over the border. About 15,000–17,000 of these people, unless they had valid passports, were deprived of the right to stay in Germany and were swiftly removed to border areas, some of them by train to Neu-Bentschen (Zbaszynek), but mostly on foot to Bentschen, Beuthen (Upper Silesia), Fraustadt, Konitz, and Dworski Mlyn-Gdynia, and there driven over the frontier. A wave of indignation in the European press and retributive actions begun by the Polish authorities induced Heydrich to break off the operation. Jews not yet thrust into Poland were taken back to their former homes or in some cases sent to concentration camps. Despite an agreement of 26 January 1939 between the Germans and Poles, on 9 May 1939 Heydrich ordered a second deportation of Polish Jews from the Reich, which was carried out in part.

Among the 484 Polish Jews taken from Hannover to the German-Polish border at Neu-Bentschen and then driven over the border into Poland was the family of the tailor Sendel Grynszpan. The tragic fate of the Grynszpan family was spread over the European press when on 7 November 1938 their son Herschel (also called Hersch or Herman) Feibel, who was living in Paris with an uncle, as a gesture of revenge and protest shot the German diplomat Ernst vom Rath at the German embassy at 78 rue de Lille. Rath succumbed to his injuries on 9 November. Exhaustive inquiries in the Jewish quarter by the investigating magistrate and the famous defense lawyer Vincent Moro-Giafferi revealed that Grynszpan had had no accomplices, was not acting in the name of "world Jewry," and was not a German agent-provocateur, and that the attack originated in personal motives, specifically to avenge his family and other Jews for the grave injustices that had been heaped on them in Germany. Up until the outbreak of war there were no legal proceedings against Grynszpan in Paris. After the collapse of France in June 1940, Grynszpan fell into the hands of the Germans and was interrogated by the Gestapo, but despite advanced preparations for a trial by the People's Court in Berlin, Hitler waived the implementation of proceedings until the huge-scale deportation of Jews began after the Wannsee Conference (January 1942).

Ernst vom Rath's death gave the signal to the Reich propaganda minister, Joseph Goebbels, to unleash the pogrom against the Jews. The news of the death was received by Adolf Hitler during the traditional dinner for the "old fighters" of the Nazi movement, held in the assembly room of the Old Town Hall in Munich on the anniversary of the bloody march on the Feldherrn-halle and the unsuccessful putsch of 9 November 1923. This solemn anniversary was also the principal date for promotions in the Nazi party and the affiliated SS and SA (Sturmabteilung, or storm troopers). The atmosphere for announcements of victory or incitements to hate and revenge was optimal, not only in Munich but also among Nazi organizations throughout the country, where Germans awaited the radio transmission of the customary memorial celebration and Hitler's speech. The signal for retaliation had already been given by Goebbels (with Hitler's agreement) in an unusually aggressive speech, which Hitler did not attend. The political propaganda initiative and management of the pogrom was in Goebbels's hands, though he held no written authority from Hitler.

While the Führer went to his Munich apartment, the propaganda minister told the Nazi notables and old fighters present that there had already been acts of revenge on 8 November in Kurhessen and Magdeburg against State Enemy No. 1—the Jew. Synagogues and shops belonging to Jews had, he said, been destroyed. His words were understood by his audience to signify "that while the party would not openly appear as the originator of the demonstrations, in reality it would organize them and carry them through" (secret report of supreme party judge Hans Buch to Hermann Göring, 13 February 1939). These intimations were immediately passed on by telephone to the headquarters of the various districts and were followed by telegrams from the Gestapo. Heydrich's secret order, sent by teleprinter to all Gestapo offices and senior SD sections, was transmitted at 1:20 a.m. on 10 November. It concerned "measures against the Jews "in the course of tonight" and made the connection with the crime against Rath. Heydrich ordered the national police offices to "make contact" with the heads of local groups of the Nazi party to work together with them "in carrying out the demonstrations" and to behave accordingly when synagogues were set on fire.

Once Goebbels had given the Nazi district leaders the impetus to unleash a massive pogrom, the further initiative lay in their hands. Heydrich's directives stipulated that the national agencies and Gestapo should work together with party authorities and other police. At the same time these orders mobilized the criminal police, members of the SD, the reserve units, and the regular SS in a "police and security service action." Heinrich Himmler's directions gave instructions for the proper attitude of the Gestapo offices "towards the wishes of the propaganda offices" and the "protective task" of the Gestapo. The Ministry of Justice advised state lawyers not to open any sort of investigation or pursue crimes committed against Jews during the operation. That night Heinrich Müller, head of the Gestapo, gave clear orders concerning the duties of the security policy in the course of the pogrom and ordered the immediate arrest of 20,000–30,000 Jews.

The execution of the pogrom, under direction of the highest Nazi party leaders, was entrusted to police and state agencies, to units of the SS, and in part to SA members. By means of the latest communications technology—telephone, teleprinters, police transmitters, and radio—within a few hours the pogrom had reached almost every part of the Reich without meeting any resistance. (Danzig was affected the following night.)

A decision of the supreme party judge of the Nazi party, dated 20 January 1939 but not published at the time, concerned the activities of the SA group Nord-

Jewish shop owners clean up glass from store windows broken during Kristallnacht. 10 November 1938

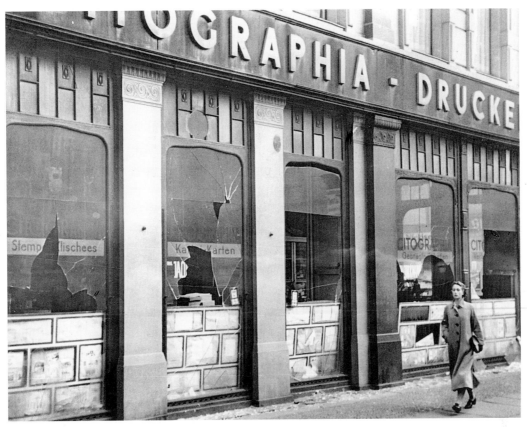

Storefront damaged by anti-Jewish raiders during Kristallnacht. November 1938

see, centered in Bremen. By telephone SA Gruppen-führer Hans Böhmcker ordered his men to wreck all Jewish shops and to set the synagogue of Bremen on fire. Lists of Jewish shops, warehouses, and depots were to be discussed and confirmed with local mayors. Böhmcker ordered that Jews who offered resistance should be shot on the spot, and that Jews should be evacuated from their homes so that non-Jews could be installed there.

During the night of 9–10 November 1938 Jewish shops, dwellings, schools, and above all synagogues and other religious establishments symbolic of Judaism were set alight. Tens of thousands of Jews were terrorized in their homes, sometimes beaten to death, and in a few cases raped. In Cologne, a town with a rich Jewish tradition dating from the first century C.E., four synagogues were desecrated and torched, shops were destroyed and looted, and male Jews were arrested and thrown into concentration camps. Brutal events were recorded in the hitherto peaceful town-

ships of the Upper Palatinate, Lower Franconia, Swabia, and others. In Hannover, Herschel Grynszpan's home town, the well-known Jewish neurologist Joseph Loewenstein escaped the pogrom when he heeded an anonymous warning the previous day; his home, however, with all its valuables, was seized by the Nazis.

In Berlin, where 140,000 Jews still resided, SA men devastated nine of the 12 synagogues and set fire to them. Children from the Jewish orphanages were thrown out on the street. About 1,200 men were sent to Oranienburg-Sachsenhausen concentration camp under "protective custody." Many of the wrecked Jewish shops did not open again. Following the Berlin pogrom the police president demanded the removal of all Jews from the northern parts of the city and declared this area "free of Jews." His order of 5 December 1938—known as the Ghetto Decree—meant that Jews could no longer live near government buildings.

In Silesia the highest SS and police leader, Erich

Male Jews are arrested during Kristallnacht and forced to march through the town under SS guard to watch the desecration of a synagogue, before they are deported. 10 November 1938

von dem Bach-Zelewski, ordered his subordinate policy agencies not to interfere in the excesses. He reported to Hitler that in the area under his command 80 synagogues had gone up in flames. The Silesian Nazi press reported the pogrom as "an expression of the people's anger," "a just measure of indignation," an indication that "our patience is exhausted."

Foreign diplomats in Vienna noted substantial material damage, numerous cases of physical injury, nervous breakdowns, and even fatalities. The theft of Jewish possessions rose to such a pitch that Gauleiter Josef Bürckel threatened to shoot looters.

The vast November pogrom had considerable economic consequences. On 11 November 1938 Heydrich, the head of the security police, still could not estimate the material destruction. The supreme party court later established that 91 persons had been killed during the pogrom and that 36 had sustained serious injuries or committed suicide. Several instances of rape were punished by the state courts as *Rassenschande* (social defilement) in accordance with the Nuremberg racial laws of 1935. At least 267 synagogues were burned down or destroyed, and in many cases the ruins were blown up and cleared away. Approximately 7,500 Jewish businesses were plundered or wrecked, and nearly all Jewish cemeteries were desecrated or laid waste. At least 177 apartment blocks or houses were destroyed by arson or otherwise. Damage to property amounted to several hundred million Reichsmarks (RM). The replacement of glass alone was estimated to cost 6 million RM. About 30,000 Jews were subjected to police arrest; a similar number were held in concentration camps—nearly 10,000 in Buchenwald, 11,000 in Dachau, and 5,000–10,000 in Sachsenhausen. Following the pogrom all Jewish activity in the German economy was prohibited and Jews were forced to make good the damages they suffered through the organized vandalism of SA and SS units.

On 12 November 1938 Göring called a conference in the Air Ministry at which decisions were taken regarding the complete exclusion of the Jews from the social and economic life of Germany. No objection was raised by Reich Justice Minister Franz Gürtner, thereby sanctioning the discrimination against the Jews and the decisions already made affecting their property, namely, that they should be robbed of their possessions, burdened with "contributions" (forced payments), squeezed out of businesses. Goebbels's assurances in the *Völkischer Beobachter* that "the pistol shots in Paris will be answered by the German government legally but harshly" were fulfilled by a wave of ordinances: the Decree Concerning the Reconstruction of Roads, the Decree Concerning the Compensatory Payment by the Jews of German Nationality, and the Decree Concerning the Expulsion of Jews from German Economic Life. On 26 July 1946 the chief British prosecutor, Sir Hartley Shawcross, in the Nuremberg war crimes trials described the attitude of Göring and the others at the conference: "The cynicism of these men and the ruthless character of their policy toward the Jews is apparent from Göring's conference on 12 November 1939, as they competed among themselves to suggest methods of degradation and persecution of their helpless victims."

The provisions of the Decree Concerning the Reconstruction of Roads (12 November 1938) legalized a system of plunder that brought in for the Reich 1.127 billion RM, a figure increased in October 1939 to 1.750 billion RM. This sum, paid by the Jews as "reparation" (*Judenbusse*) for the damage caused by the Nazis, threw thousands of Jewish families into extreme poverty. The decree, as well as the Finance Ministry's obses-

sively detailed rules, shows that aryanization had already been prepared before Grynszpan's assassination of Rath had presented a favorable opportunity to put economic persecution into practice. The Decree Concerning the Expulsion of Jews from German Economic Life prohibited Jews from carrying on any kind of independent trading enterprise, be it real estate transactions, retail sales, or the practice of a craft. It was followed by the exclusion of Jews from occupations (such as dentistry) involving contacts with the Aryan community under the Eighth Supplementary Decree to the Reich Citizenship Law (17 January 1939). The most brutal of all decrees, the Decree Concerning the Use of Jewish Wealth (3 December 1938), provided for forcible aryanization of any remaining Jewish businesses (or alternatively their closure), real estate, securities, land or forest enterprises, and the like. This expropriation was further intensified by a decree of 6 February 1939. The Nazi slogan "The Jews must get out of economic life" became a fact, for the decrees completed the legalized dispossession and exclusion of the Jews from the so-called German folk community (*deutsche Volksgemeinschaft*). In 1939 there followed decrees and ordinances that robbed the German Jews of the very basis of existence. It has rightly been said that with the November pogrom, radical violence had reached the point of murder and so had paved the road to Auschwitz.

Karol Jonca

L

Latvia See BALTIC COUNTRIES

Laval, Pierre (1885–1945) French premier, 1931–32, 1935–36. Premier of the Vichy government in 1940 and from 1942 till its abolition in September 1944. Laval collaborated with German authorities in the deportation of Jews from France. After the war he was tried for treason by the French government, convicted, and executed in October 1945.

Lemberg See LVOV

Lichtheim, Richard (1885–1963) Zionist leader in Germany and Palestine. During World War II Lichtheim was stationed in Geneva. He reported his findings about the situation and mass extermination of European Jewry to the Zionist Organization, but the information he disseminated was at first not fully believed. See FINAL SOLUTION: PUBLIC KNOWLEDGE

Literature Holocaust literature consists of all the literary responses to the destruction of European Jewry and other peoples by the Nazi German state and its collaborators during World War II. It includes the diaries of victims and memoirs of survivors; chronicles and documents compiled collectively by community groups, assembled in the forms of archives and "memorial books"; novels and short stories on Holocaust-related themes by those who witnessed the destruction, as well as by those removed from it; poetry and drama written in the concentration camps and ghettos, as well as works composed after the war with aspects of the Holocaust as subject; ballads and songs written both to inspire fighters in the ghettos during the war and to commemorate the Holocaust afterward; and religious responses that relate events of the Holocaust in the form of traditional Jewish legends and parables. It is an international literature, with works in all the European languages (including Yiddish and English), as well as in Hebrew. In the 1980s the children of Holocaust survivors began to add their own unique voices, in "comix" (comic books) and rock lyrics, to the more traditional literary genres.

Because Jewish religious tradition is an essentially literary one, with a 2,500-year-old history of responses to catastrophe, remembering the Holocaust in writing became something approaching a religious obligation. Both because they were the principal racial victims of the Nazis and because their tradition mandated it, Jewish writers have accounted for the great majority of the thousands of Holocaust literary works. By contrast, the primarily oral tradition of the Sinti and Roma (commonly known as Gypsies) practically guaranteed a frightful literary silence on their part. Because their story depended on the voices of the tellers themselves, the history of the Gypsies' deportations and mass murder died in the throats of the victims— and so remains largely unwritten.

Indeed, the very languages in which these works are written determine their shape, content, and preoccupying themes. The ghetto diarists Chaim A. Kaplan and Zelig Kalmanovitch, by choosing to write in Hebrew, located events within different linguistic realms from Emanuel Ringelblum, who kept his diary in Yiddish. Whereas Hebrew, essentially a liturgical language until the twentieth century, tends to recall events in the sanctified context of scripture, rabbinical disputation, and covenant, Yiddish, the vernacular language of the Central and Eastern European Jews, is well suited to emphasizing the details and hardships of daily life.

At some point nearly all who write about the Holocaust, be they diarists like Kaplan or memoirists like Elie Wiesel and Primo Levi, lament the sheer impossibility of their task. How to describe what seems indescribable? How to make believable what seemed incredible even to the eyewitnesses? Moreover, many writers were plagued by the fear that the narrative act itself, which imposed a sense of order and purpose on human actions, would betray what seemed to be the completely inchoate experience of the ghettos and camps. For writers attempting to leave behind a literature of testimony, questions of how to describe events without distorting them were nearly paralyzing. How was it possible, Kaplan asked, to describe a disorderly thing in an orderly fashion? In most cases, however, the writers concluded that as difficult as their literary conundrum seemed, silence was not an alternative. They recognized that without a literature, the Holocaust would have been a self-consuming catastrophe, and that failure to commemorate the life and death of Jews under the Nazis would give the killers a posthumous victory.

Every literary form represents the Holocaust in a slightly different way, conveying particular shades of meaning and its own understanding of events. Ghetto and camp diaries, because they were written from within the whirlwind, suggest themselves rhetorically as literal remnants of events. At the same time, the diarists are dependent on readers to complete their stories, since they wrote from day to day without knowing their ending. For a picture of the chaotic realities facing inmates of the camps and ghettos, the details of daily life under Nazi siege, and a sense of how the victims grasped their circumstances at the time, the diaries of writers like Ringelblum, Kaplan, Kalmanovitch, Moshe Flinker, Anne Frank, Eva Heyman, and others remain invaluable.

By contrast, the hundreds of Holocaust survivor-memoirists necessarily write with the advantage of hindsight, which allows them to know from the beginning of their recollections how it all turned out. Though they, like the diarists, have been inspired by the powerful urges to testify to the Nazi crimes and to bring order to the chaos they experienced, the memoirists also have had time to meditate on their survival and to reflect on their current lives in light of the destruction of their families and communities. Survivors like Levi and Wiesel were thus able to find significance in early events and relate them to later ones. The shape of a Holocaust memoirist's work may thus depend as much on the writer's current preoccupations as it does on the events themselves. The incoherence of events as experienced at the time can be relieved by the much more complete understanding a survivor brings to this past many years later. As a result the memory we find in memoirs is often darkened by the knowledge that the worst was indeed possible. At the same time, the memoirs can suggest a sense of coherence and sequence to events that is often missing in the diaries.

Novels and Short Stories

Literary historians agree that it is crucial to distinguish categorically between eyewitness literature, such as the diary and memoir, and the more imaginative realm of novels and short stories. Yet the lines between factual and fictional literature of the Holocaust are not always clear. A memoir like Wiesel's *Night* (1958), though based on the author's actual experiences during the war, also contains both formal elements of the parable and profoundly symbolic imagery. By opening *Night* with the story of Moshe the Beadle, who survived an early mass execution of Jews only to have his report of the atrocity disbelieved by the other inhabitants of the narrator's Hungarian shtetl, Wiesel warns his readers against disbelieving the harrowing tale he is about to tell.

Similarly, Holocaust fiction often borrows heavily from the nonfictional discourse of diaries and memoirs. In particular, what has come to be called documentary fiction of the Holocaust continues to raise some of the most troubling critical issues surrounding the incorporation of eyewitness accounts. To what extent, does a documentary novel of the Holocaust like Anatoly Kuznetsov's *Babi Yar* (1970) or John Hersey's *The Wall* (1950) accurately chronicle real events, and to what extent does it fictionalize them? Because the novel has traditionally blurred the line between fact and fiction, both writers and readers have asked whether it is an appropriate form for the representation of true but nearly unbelievable events.

As a result, some Holocaust novelists, like Jean-François Steiner in *Treblinka* (1967), have gone to great lengths to assert an absolute link between their fiction and the historical facts of the Holocaust. Others, like D. M. Thomas in *The White Hotel* (1981), have claimed on ethical grounds that they had no right to imagine such suffering and therefore have had to rely on the voices of actual witnesses. It is difficult to know whether such claims are generated by the needs of history or of literature, fabricated as part of these novels' essential fiction. The problem with these and other documentary novels of the Holocaust is that by mixing actual incidents with completely fictional characters, these works relieve themselves of an obligation to historical fact even as they imbue their fiction with the historical authority and pathos of real events.

Other issues in Holocaust fiction emerge from the

national, religious, and gender identifications of the authors. Both Sara Nomberg-Przytyk and Tadeusz Borowski wrote about internment at Auschwitz, but one is struck by the stark differences between their preoccupations, themes, and voices. In *Auschwitz: True Tales from a Grotesque Land* (1985) Nomberg-Przytyk brings into relief the unique experiences of women in the camps. A lifetime of subjugation to men in the world at large provided her with a ready-made literary lexicon for the humiliation and degradation she suffered at the hands of the Nazis, and her mixed identity as a Jewish woman and a Polish socialist allowed her to understand a variety of perspectives. Borowski, a non-Jewish Pole interned at Auschwitz as a socialist, was regarded after the war as one of Poland's finest young writers. Though his personal conduct in the camp was by all accounts beyond reproach, even at times heroic, the fictional narrator in *This Way for the Gas, Ladies and Gentlemen* (1967) relates stories through the self-incriminating eye of someone inured to the suffering and death surrounding him. Moreover, because nothing before or after the war seemed to compare to the atrocities he witnessed in Auschwitz, Borowski limited his language and metaphors to those of the camp's realities, thus sealing both his and the readers' minds into the concentration camp universe—from which he allowed no literary escape.

Unlike Borowski, whose direct depictions of horror in Auschwitz are merciless, other writers, such as the Czernovitz-born Israeli novelist and Holocaust survivor Aharon Appelfeld, eschew any pretense of documentation for the larger, more universally humane truths of despair, alienation, and hope that are revealed in his lyrically spare tales. In novels such as *Badenheim 1939* (1980), *The Age of Wonders* (1981), *Tzili* (1983), and *The Immortal Mr. Bartfuss* (1988), Appelfeld hews closely to the details of a war-ravaged childhood even as he explores the souls of those trapped in that time. Appelfeld's stories of a Jewish community oblivious to its impending annihilation, or of children wandering between Carpathian villages, or of the perpetually displaced survivor at home only in a criminal netherworld between the camps and refuge in Israel have been translated into more than a dozen languages and continue to find a universal resonance among the world's readers.

In the 1960s and early 1970s other Israeli novelists (some of them poets as well), such as Yehuda Amichai, Hanoch Bartov, Yoram Kaniuk, and Chaim Gouri, were more apt to explore the gap between their identities as Israeli Jews in their own land and their memory of a time when Jews were destroyed in exile. In Amichai's *Not of This Time, Not of This Place* (1963) and Gouri's *The Chocolate Deal* (1965) national preoccupations with reparations, archaeology, and newly found Jewish self-sufficiency in Israel provided thematic backdrops for trying to come to terms with the unimaginable loss the Jews had suffered in Europe. In *The Brigade* (1965) Bartov probed Israelis' conflicting impulses toward revenge and rescue by telling the story of the Jewish Brigade stationed in Italy and Holland after the war as part of the Allied occupation forces. Perhaps the richest and most intricate novel of this period is Kaniuk's *Adam Resurrected* (1969). Set in an Israeli psychiatric institution, it is a psychologically and spiritually devastating tale of a survivor's struggle with memory and sanity as he labors to conflate his past and his present.

In the 1980s in Israel the survivor-novelist Ida Fink and the second-generation novelist and essayist David Grossman (the so-called second generation includes the daughters and sons of survivors) added wondrously complicating strains to the Holocaust literary canon. In her collection of short stories, *A Scrap of Time* (1985), Fink conveyed the terror and madness of day-to-day life for ordinary, unheroic Jews trying to get by in Poland during the war. Full of quotidian details, Fink's stories restored the fabric of Jewish life that the Nazis had pulled apart one strand at a time. But rather than attempting to find meaning and reassurance in isolated moments of sanity during the war, the narrator is always on the verge of unremembering them altogether. From a completely different vantage point, Grossman made his inability to remember events he never experienced directly the subtext of his ambitious novel *See Under: Love* (1985). Regarded by many as the greatest single work of second-generation literature of the Holocaust, Grossman's novel is told through the wildly imaginative eyes of a child desperate to penetrate his parents' stories from "the land of there"—Europe and the Holocaust.

Indeed, the range of possible literary responses to the Holocaust by the descendants of survivors continues to grow. In an age dominated by popular culture, survivors' children and grandchildren are as likely to express themselves in the words of rock songs as they are in classical verse. The Israeli musicians Yehuda Poliker and Yakov Gilad pair lyrics responding to the Holocaust with haunting instrumentals in their recording *Ashes and Dust* (1988). Like Poliker and Gilad,

Cover of *Maus: A Survivor's Tale,* by Art Spiegelman.

the second-generation American novelists Melvin Bukiet and Thane Rosenbaum have made their relationship to Holocaust memory—not the Holocaust as such—the subject of their art.

The treatment of the Holocaust as a vicarious past may find its most remarkable expression in Art Spiegelman's Pulitzer Prize–winning "Holocaust comix," *Maus: A Survivor's Tale.* Though some early reviewers were taken aback by the audacity of representing the Holocaust in cartoons, that Spiegelman chose to render his father's tale of survival in a comix is neither surprising nor controversial. After all, as a comix-artist and founder of *Raw* magazine, Spiegelman had turned to what had always been his working artistic medium. As for possible objections to folding the deadly high-seriousness into what some regard as the trivial low-seriousness of comics, Spiegelman points to the ways in which the medium itself has raised—and dismissed—issues of decorum as part of its raison d'être. He has even recalled that the distinction between the high art of the masters and the low art of cartoonists was challenged by the manner in which mod-

ern masters like Lyonel Feininger, George Grosz, Käthe Kollwitz, and Juan Gris divided their time between painting and cartooning.

Written over a 13-year period between 1972 and 1985, the first volume of *Maus* thus integrated both the narrative and anti-narrative elements of the comics, weaving the father's coherent story into a garment ever threatening to fly apart at the seams. The result is a continuous narrative rife with the discontinuities of its reception and production, the absolutely authentic voice of Spiegelman's father counterposed with the fabular images of cartoon animals.

Poetry

In his famous admonition against poetry after Auschwitz, the Frankfurt School critic Theodor Adorno suggested that not only is poetry after Auschwitz barbaric, but it is immoral to derive the slightest bit of aesthetic pleasure from the suffering of Holocaust victims. Though Adorno later retracted this dictum—after having read Paul Celan's masterpiece, "Todesfuge" (Death Fugue)—critical questions about the poetic appropriation of Holocaust imagery persist. To what extent do lineation, rhyme, and meter distract from and domesticate the brutal facts of the Holocaust? Or, on the contrary, to what extent can the aesthetic qualities of poetry and figurative language reveal poetic truths unavailable to documentary narrative? Through the verse of Celan, Nelly Sachs, Jakov Glatstein, Abraham Sutzkever, Itzhak Katzenelson, and Dan Pagis (among many others), readers glean insights into the Holocaust and its devastating effect on the poet's inner life—a kind of knowledge that falls somewhere between public and private memory, between communal and personal history.

Had Adorno been aware of the poets writing in Yiddish in the ghettos and camps, he might never have issued his proscription of poetry after Auschwitz. For in poems like Katzenelson's "Song of the Murdered Jewish People" (composed largely in Vittel, a transit camp on the way to Auschwitz) or Sutzkever's shattering responses to the deaths of his mother and child in the Vilna ghetto, there is no redemption, no consoling beauty to be found. The poets' Yiddish allows them to invoke biblical precedents but always points to their inadequacy. The language enables the poets to argue with God eye-to-eye over the meaning of events, as Jakov Glatstein did in poems such as "Dead Men Don't Praise God," "Without Jews," and "My

Brother Refugee," which Glatstein wrote from safe haven in the United States during the war.

Widely regarded as the greatest postwar poem in the German language, Celan's "Todesfuge" continues to shock readers with the imagery and sounds of events irreconcilable with life, unassimilable to memory, and drawn elliptically from the death camps. Born Paul Antschel in Czernovitz in 1920, Celan first published the poem in a Romanian translation (as "Death Tango") in 1947 and prefaced it with a note suggesting that the poem was "built on the evocation of a real fact [that] the condemned were forced to sing nostalgic songs while others dug graves." Its opening lines are repeated in a mind-staggering refrain: "Black milk of daybreak we drink it at evening / we drink it at midday and morning we drink it at night / we drink and we drink" (trans. John Felstiner). Within ten years of its 1948 publication in its original German version, the poem became widely known and frequently quoted in Germany, it was included in anthologies and almost assumed a life of its own.

The other great German-language poet of the Holocaust, Nelly Sachs, won the Nobel Prize in Literature (shared with S. Y. Agnon) in 1966 at least partly for her collection of Holocaust poetry, *O the Chimneys* (1961). Born in 1891 in Berlin to an assimilated middle-class Jewish family, Sachs escaped to Sweden in 1940, where she spent the rest of her life. Unlike Celan's allusive images of the camps and his implied challenge to a religious understanding of the Holocaust, Sachs's literal fragments of destruction are embedded in biblical contexts while also drawing on the Zohar and its kabbalistic images of exile. Her poem "O the Chimneys" is prefaced by a quotation from Job: "And though after my skin worms destroy this body, yet in my flesh shall I see God" (19:26). The poem (trans. Michael Roloff) itself begins:

> O the chimneys
> On the ingeniously devised habitations of death
> When Israel's body drifted as smoke
> Through the air—
> Was welcomed by a star, a chimney sweep,
> A star that turned black
> Or was it a ray of sun?

Other poems, such as "Chorus of the Rescued" (trans. Michael Roloff), meditate on the survivors' difficulty in reentering a normal world:

> Lest the song of a bird,
> or a pail being filled at the well,

> Let our badly sealed pain burst forth again
> and carry us away

In addition to giving voice to the survivors' return to life, poetry can articulate the terrible void left in the wake of the victims. In six slim lines of Hebrew verse, "Written in Pencil in the Sealed Railway-Car" (trans. Stephen Mitchell), the Israeli poet Dan Pagis—who, like Celan, was born in Czernovitz—prepares the reader for the desolate feeling of unredeemed loss brought on by a sudden silence:

> here in this carload
> i am eve
> with abel my son
> if you see my other son
> cain son of man
> tell him that i

Criticism

As Holocaust literature has developed in various directions over the decades since the end of World War II, critical approaches to that literature have evolved along with it. Early commentators like A. Alvarez questioned the traditional critic's role as arbiter of good and bad literature, or even as definer of a Holocaust literary canon that would exclude too many voices needing to be heard. Others, like Lawrence Langer in his pathbreaking study *The Holocaust and the Literary Imagination* (1976), demonstrated how Adorno's early dictum against Holocaust literature was laid bare by the literature itself. Langer concentrated on formulating what he called an "aesthetics of atrocity." Through a series of close readings of writers as diverse as Charlotte Delbo, Ladislav Fuks, Anthony Hecht, Jerzy Kosinski, Jakov Lind, André Schwarz-Bart, and Jorge Semprun, Langer offered keen insights into how writers sought to express the inexpressible.

In 1980 Alvin Rosenfeld and Sidra DeKoven Ezrahi published two critical studies, also based in close readings, in which they reflected on the "problematics of Holocaust literature," as well as on the ethical and literary implications of appropriating the Holocaust through metaphor. Four years later, in two further studies, David Roskies and Alan Mintz located the literary responses to the Holocaust in the longer continuum of Jewish responses to catastrophe over the ages, beginning with biblical texts lamenting the destruction of the Temple and continuing through the Hebrew chronicles of the Crusaders' massacres and the early twentieth-century pogrom poetry of Hayyim

Nahman Bialik and Moshe Leyb Halpern. By restoring Yiddish and Hebrew Holocaust literature to a longer Jewish cultural and religious tradition, Roskies and Mintz showed how Jewish writers simultaneously invoke and challenge the tradition, rely upon it, and expand it with their own new responses to destruction.

In the 1990s critics began to ask not whether such destruction can be represented but how it has been represented—for better or worse, and toward what ethical, historical, and political ends. Rather than weighing "authentic" against "inauthentic" responses, this generation of critics tended to locate literary responses to the Holocaust within the national communities that spawned them and to compare Holocaust literature with other kinds of Holocaust memorialization, such as public sculpture and Holocaust museums. In this view neither the Holocaust nor its literature can be reduced to anything approaching an essential truth, work, or canon. The exercise of aesthetic judgment remains part of the critic's work, but the exploration of how readers interpret and evaluate this literature is now also an aim of Holocaust literary criticism.   *James E. Young*

Lithuania   See BALTIC COUNTRIES

Lodz   At the outbreak of World War II Lodz was the second most populous city in Poland. More than a third of the city's 665,000 inhabitants were Jewish. Forty-three percent of the Jews of Lodz worked in manufacturing, especially textiles.

The Jewish community of Lodz had developed a dynamic public and cultural life. Jewish schools, youth movements, sports clubs, theaters, and daily newspapers flourished. Renowned Jewish poets, authors, and creative artists, among them Artur Rubinstein, Julian Tuwim, Itzhak Katznelson, Moshe Broderson, and Artur Szyk, lived in Lodz.

When German forces occupied Lodz on 8 September 1939, they immediately embarked on a campaign of persecuting Jews, many of whom were arrested or conscripted for forced labor. These acts were usually accompanied by humiliation and physical abuse. The

The wedding ceremony of Henryk and Stefania Ross in the Lodz ghetto. Henryk was a photographer. After 1940

Germans issued a series of ordinances designed to destroy the Jews' economic, social, and religious foundations.

Initially Lodz was not included in the Wartheland, the section of Poland that the German Reich annexed in October 1939. However, owing to its industrial importance and after pressure from the German minority (about 60,000 persons) in Lodz, the Reich governor of the Warthegau, Artur Greiser, intervened, and Lodz was annexed to the Reich on 8 November. This move exacerbated the plight of the Jews. On 14 November Friedrich Übelhör, president of the Lodz district, ordered the Jews to wear a yellow arm band, and later a yellow star. On 15–17 November the Germans torched the city's main synagogues. German trustees were appointed to manage Jewish businesses, and Jews were dispossessed of all their property. This move was intended to compel the Jews to leave the city, as Lodz was now part of the Reich and had to be made *Judenrein*—free of Jews.

Simultaneously the Germans planned to deport thousands of Poles and Jews to the Generalgouvernement. The deportations started in mid-December 1939 but were soon halted, because Hans Frank, the governor of the Generalgouvernement, opposed such a large influx of refugees into his jurisdiction. Nevertheless, tens of thousands of Jews left the city. By the time the Jewish ghetto was sealed on 1 May 1940, about a third of the Jews of Lodz—mainly the economic and political elites, many of the intelligentsia, and most members of the community council—had left.

In accordance with the German policy of appointing Jewish councils as mediators between the authorities and the Jewish population, on 13 October 1939 the Germans nominated Mordechai Chaim Rumkowski as *Der Älteste der Juden* (lit., "eldest of the Jews"). Rumkowski was one of the few members of the Jewish community council who had remained in the city. It was his duty to carry out German orders and to assume personal responsibility for the total obedience of the Lodz Jews.

Rumkowski was born in 1877 in Ilino, Russia. He came to Lodz around 1900 and opened a textile factory. Later he went bankrupt and had to accept a position as an insurance agent. Meanwhile he became active in the political and public life of the Jewish community of Lodz. He was elected to the community council as the General Zionist party's representative and became director of an orphanage in Helenowek, a suburb of Lodz. (Rumkowski himself was childless.)

The Jews of Lodz were ambivalent about Rumkowski's appointment. They scorned his lack of education, his impatient, aggressive, domineering personality, and his lust for power. But at the same time they respected his dynamism and organizational skills. By order of the Germans, Rumkowski appointed a 31-member Council of Elders (*Ältestenrat*) composed of the remaining community leaders. The council did not last long: on 11 November 1939, three days after the annexation, the council members were imprisoned, and most of them were murdered. The Germans ordered Rumkowski to appoint a new council. This council proved to be ineffective, partly because its members were of lesser stature in the community and partly because Rumkowski preferred to act alone, without consulting anyone. He followed this path throughout his tenure in the ghetto, relying on several loyal assistants to carry out his orders.

District President Übelhör decided to quarantine the Jews until their final deportation. On 10 December 1939 he issued a secret order to create a ghetto in the Baluty neighborhood and the Old City, the most rundown section of the town. At the end of the document Übelhör made the following clarification: "The creation of the ghetto is obviously nothing but a provisional measure. . . . The final goal must be the total elimination of this pestilence."

On 8 February 1940 the official order establishing the ghetto was made public and the transfer of the Jews began. In order to speed up the process, the Germans launched a campaign of terror and violence that resulted in the killing of several hundred Jews.

The Lodz ghetto was officially sealed on 1 May 1940. It was enclosed by a fence and tightly guarded by the Schupo (German Guard Police), who were ordered to fire on anyone who approached. Throughout the existence of the ghetto hundreds of the Jewish residents were shot by the Schupo; the murders created an atmosphere of fear and terror aimed at preventing people from smuggling in food or attempting to escape from the ghetto. The suppression of smuggling made the Jews totally dependent on the Germans for their subsistence, unlike in other ghettos, where smuggled foodstuffs supplemented the paltry German rations. And because the Lodz ghetto was hermetically sealed, the Jews were completely isolated from the rest of the city and from other Jewish communities, and hence received no news from the outside world.

All ghetto affairs were handled by four German au-

A Jewish policeman and a German soldier direct pedestrian traffic across the main street dividing the two parts of the Lodz ghetto. Later a wooden footbridge was built over the street to allow the streetcar route to remain in the Aryan sector. The German sign at the entrance to the ghetto reads, "Jewish residential area, entrance is forbidden." 1940–41

thorities. A special ghetto administration (*Ghettoverwaltung*) was established in May 1940, headed by Hans Biebow (1902–47), a wealthy Bremen businessman, who played a crucial role in shaping German policy toward the ghetto. This administration was responsible for organizing ghetto life—food supplies, work allocation, and despoliation of the Jews. The Gestapo oversaw the political aspects of ghetto life. At a later stage it was the Gestapo's task to implement the Final Solution. The Kripo (Criminal Police) dealt with criminal acts by Jews against Germans but mainly organized the looting of Jewish property. The Schupo was responsible for patrolling the ghetto fence, preventing smuggling, and foiling escapes.

Because of Hans Frank's firm refusal to accept any more Jews into the Generalgouvernement, by the fall of 1940 the local German authorities realized that it was impossible to deport all the Jews from Lodz and that they would have to maintain the ghetto. At a meeting on 18 October it was decided to expand existing

factories inside the ghetto and to open new ones. The initial reason for these actions was to shift the burden of financing ghetto expenses from the Germans to the Jews themselves. The factories, called *ressorts* by the ghetto Jews (from the German word *Arbeitsressorte*), mainly produced materials for the benefit of the Reich war economy. At the same meeting it was also decided to send Jews to forced labor camps outside the ghetto. During the period of the ghetto's existence more than 13,000 people were sent to labor camps, where most of them perished.

For the back-breaking toil, performed under unbearably difficult conditions in the ressorts, Jews were to receive a small amount of food—half a prisoner's rations, costing 23–27 pennies a day for each Jew. The main meal was a foul, watery soup, occasionally enriched with a slice of bread and horsemeat sausage. Thus the Germans sustained the ghetto at minimum expense and maximum profit.

In the ghetto's first two years Rumkowski was given

relatively broad powers in the organization of its internal life. He understood early on that all the Jews had left to offer the Germans in exchange for their keep was their labor. Already in April 1940, before the ghetto was sealed, he proposed that thousands of Jews be put to work. His plan was accepted only in the fall of 1940, when it was also seen to be in the German interest. Throughout the German occupation he preached to the ghetto inhabitants the importance of participating in the labor force—initially to pay for their maintenance but later—from early 1942, when the Final Solution began to be implemented in the ghetto—as a means of salvation: those who could not work were sent to their deaths.

Much effort and resourcefulness was invested in arranging work, and more than 100 factories were open throughout the ghetto period. The number of persons employed rose constantly, especially when deportation to extermination camps began in 1942. Many elderly people, women, and children above the age of 10 joined the work force in order to avoid deportation. In 1943–44 more than 90 percent of the ghetto inhabitants were working.

Living conditions in Lodz, the second-largest ghetto in Poland (after Warsaw), were horrible. About 164,000 people were crammed into an area of four square kilometers, sometimes eight to 10 people per room. Many houses were built of wood, and most of them were dilapidated and lacked adequate sanitation. The winter cold brought great suffering because the Germans supplied no heating fuel. The Jews used anything made of wood for heating and cooking.

Worst of all was the gnawing hunger. By design the Germans supplied the ghetto with minimal quantities of food. Malnutrition and the terrible living conditions contributed to a high incidence of tuberculosis, pneumonia, and heart disease. The mortality rate rose steadily, to a peak of 18,000 deaths in 1942, when starvation was particularly acute. Throughout the ghetto's existence about 43,500 people died, in most cases from starvation and disease.

In order to organize internal life in the ghetto, Rum-

Jewish youth working in the Lodz ghetto.

kowski had to start from scratch. With organizational adroitness he and his team of assistants managed to create, under the harsh conditions of the ghetto, a reasonable system of services: housing, food supply, and health care. Thousands of pupils (63 percent of school-age children) studied in elementary and high schools. Kindergartens and orphanages were founded. To keep order, the ghetto had its own police. A social welfare department was opened to care for the needy, who composed the majority of the ghetto inhabitants. Soup kitchens and other services were provided.

Despite the tremendous hardships and high mortality, the ghetto Jews maintained an active political, cultural, and religious life. Political parties opened soup kitchens that also served as meeting places. During the summer and autumn of 1940 leftist parties organized large demonstrations blaming Rumkowski for the woeful ghetto conditions and demanding jobs and a fair distribution of food. Rumkowski persecuted the organizers, transferring some of them to labor camps and harassing others in various ways. Consequently, party activists had much less involvement and influence on ghetto life in the subsequent years, although Rumkowski never severed relations with them altogether.

Alongside the political parties, youth movements with thousands of members, ranging from Zionist and religious groups to the Bund and the Communists, were active. In the ghetto's first six months more than 1,000 members of some of these groups lived in collectives in Marysin, a semi-rural neighborhood of the ghetto, where they worked the land and held cultural events. These farms were disbanded in January 1941. The young people returned to the ghetto proper, where they clandestinely continued their activity, focusing on mutual assistance and cultural and social activities. The leftist youth movements, particularly the Communists, struggled to improve working conditions in the factories. Through such activities young people briefly managed to forget their hunger and hardships and to find meaning and purpose in their lives.

Although radios had been banned, several groups of activists managed to listen to broadcasts clandestinely and passed on news to others. For the isolated ghetto, it was the only contact with the outside world and had a considerable impact on public morale. On 7 June 1944, after the Allied invasion of Normandy, the Gestapo

uncovered one such group and executed most of its members.

Religious Jews continued to practice Judaism, especially in the first two years of the ghetto. Several kosher soup kitchens, *minyanim* (prayer quorums), and study groups were established. Organized religious activity diminished sharply after the deportations of 1942. Nevertheless, throughout the ghetto's existence, and despite acute starvation, some Jews refrained from eating meat because most of the meat the Germans supplied was from horses and therefore not kosher. They also engaged in group study and prayer.

Cultural activities in the ghetto took place at first at soup kitchens; later they became institutionalized. A cultural center was officially opened in March 1941, and concerts, plays, and other cultural events were held there. The center was shut down in 1943, but limited cultural activity continued. A group of Jewish authors and poets held cultural meetings as long as the ghetto existed. Music was created and performed, albeit on a small scale and in private locations, and quite a few painters continued their work.

The preparations for the implementation of the Final Solution in the Lodz ghetto started in the fall of 1941. Since the first areas to be "cleansed" of Jews were the Reich and the annexed territories, 20,000 Jews and 5,000 Gypsies from the Reich were deported to the Lodz ghetto in October and November 1941. This was to be an interim stage before their extermination in the death camps. At the same time the ghettos in the Warthegau were liquidated (a process that started in late September 1941 and lasted until the summer of 1942), and more than 17,000 "productive elements" were transferred to the Lodz ghetto. On 8 December 1941 the first Nazi death camp for carrying out the Final Solution became operational in Chelmno, 60 kilometers from Lodz.

A long shadow was cast over the lives of the Jews in the ghetto when deportation to Chelmno started in 1942. In the first phase, from 16 January until May 1942, 55,000 Jews were taken away, mainly the weak, the vulnerable, and the "unproductive elements." The second phase, starting on 1 September, was particularly cruel. First, hospital patients were taken from their sickbeds. Then, between 5 and 12 September, a merciless operation which the Jews called *Sperre* (from the German *Gehsperre*, meaning curfew) took place. The Germans, accompanied by Jewish police, went

Ruins of a destroyed synagogue in Lodz.

from house to house and dragged away all those who were elderly or ill and all children under 10 years old, deporting more than 15,000 people to Chelmno. Life in the ghetto was turned upside down and almost every home lost a family member. The brutality of this action would never be forgotten by those who survived. During 1942 over 70,000 Jews and all the Gypsies were deported from the Lodz ghetto and murdered in Chelmno.

Did the Jews of Lodz know the meaning of the deportations? Unlike in some other ghettos, conclusive information about the fate of the Jews did not reach the tightly sealed Lodz ghetto. Rumors abounded, but there was no definite knowledge. Did Rumkowski and his assistants know? It appears that during the first phase of the deportations Rumkowski learned of the fate of the deportees. Nevertheless, he assumed responsibility for compiling deportation lists in the belief that in this way he could at least save part of the ghetto community. His activities had been criticized from the very beginning, but with the deportations the criticism reached a high pitch. His critics felt that he had crossed the Rubicon in deciding who was to live and who to die. Rumkowski was essentially a tragic fig-

ure who evoked controversy then and continues to do so now. Many regard him as a megalomaniacal Nazi collaborator who sent his own people to their deaths. Some justify his policies as having been the only way to save at least some Lodz Jews.

From mid-September 1942 until the liquidation of the Lodz ghetto there were few deportations to the death camps. The entire nature of life in the ghetto changed. The ghetto became a massive labor camp, with more than 90 percent of its inhabitants participating in the labor force, and it lost the semblance of autonomy it had enjoyed up to 1942. Schools and hospitals were shut down, and work became virtually the only focus of life. Rumkowski's influence waned, and German intervention in the internal life of the ghetto became more dominant.

In the course of 1943 different German authorities began discussing the fate of the Lodz ghetto. Whereas the SS demanded its liquidation, the local German authorities—headed by the governor, Arthur Greiser, and by Hans Biebow—did what they could to maintain the ghetto because of the enormous profits reaped by both the Reich and the various echelons of the German authorities. This was the primary reason for maintaining the Lodz ghetto after all the other ghettos in Poland had been liquidated.

In February 1944, however, Himmler decided to begin gradual liquidation. To make this possible, the Chelmno camp, which had been closed in March 1943, was reopened in June 1944. During a period of three weeks, between 23 June and 14 July 1944, more than 7,000 Jews were murdered in Chelmno. Owing to the approach of the Red Army and the limited extermination capacity at Chelmno, in early August the Germans redirected deportations to Auschwitz, where more than 65,000 Jews were sent. Approximately 1,000 Jews were left in the ghetto by the Germans to clean up. These Jews were liberated by the Red Army on 19 January 1945.

Surprised by the rapid advance of the Soviet forces, the Germans did not have time to destroy evidence of their actions and left behind a full and well-documented record of the history of the Lodz ghetto. The materials, from both German and Jewish sources, include photographs, personal and official documents, and artifacts.

Of the 204,800 Jews who had lived in the Lodz ghetto over the years, only 7,000–10,000 survived.

Michal Unger

Lubetkin, Zivia (1914–76) Commander of ZOB, the Jewish resistance movement in the Warsaw ghetto. Lubetkin lived underground in Warsaw after the collapse of the ghetto uprising. After the war she emigrated to Palestine and helped found Kibbutz Lohamei Haghetaot, the Ghetto Fighters' kibbutz.

Lublin City in southeastern Poland. At the time of the German invasion of Poland on 1 September 1939 approximately 40,000 of its 125,000 inhabitants were Jewish. In the first two weeks of the war thousands of Jews fleeing the advancing German forces took refuge in Lublin. The Germans occupied the city on 18 September. Nazi leaders planned for a short while a Jewish reservation in the Lublin region (the so-called Nisko

German police discover an underground warehouse in Lublin. November 1940

Operation). In 1941 the Germans interned the Jews in a ghetto and in 1942 deported the majority of them to the Belzec and Majdanek extermination camps in a valley just outside the city; many others were shot to death in the forests surrounding the city. The remaining Jews (approximately 4,000) were moved to a small camp in the suburb Majdan Tatarski, where between 1942 and 1944 almost all were killed or selected for deportation to Majdanek for extermination. When liberated in 1944, Lublin became the temporary capital of Poland and the central gathering place for surviving Polish Jews.

Lvov (Lviv, Lwow, Lemberg) City in western Ukraine (Galicia). At the time of the outbreak of World War II Lvov was under Polish rule and had a Jewish population of approximately 110,000. The city was occupied by the Soviet Union in September 1939 and captured by the German army in June 1941. A Jewish ghetto was established there in November and December 1941. In 1942 and 1943 the Germans deported the Jews of Lvov to labor camps throughout Poland and to the Janowska, Belzec, and Auschwitz camps for extermination. The ghetto was liquidated in June 1943. See UKRAINE

M

Madagascar Plan The island of Madagascar, off the eastern coast of Africa, long exercised a fascination among antisemites as the ideal dumping ground for the European Jews. In the period between the two world wars, notorious antisemitic agitators like Henry Hamilton Beamish and Arnold Leese in England, the shadowy Georg de Pottere (often using the pseudonym Egon van Winghene), and Ulrich Fleischhauer in Germany advocated the complete segregation of all Jews by forcibly removing them to Madagascar. As Nazi persecution and the flow of refugees from Germany intensified, the idea became attractive to European leaders as well as some Jewish organizations. In 1938 the French government agreed to send the Lepecki commission from Poland to Madagascar, at the time a French colony, to explore the feasibility of a large-scale emigration of Polish Jews to the island. Even the most optimistic estimate of Mieczyslaw Lepecki himself put feasible Jewish immigration at 5,000–7,000 families. The estimate of the Jewish members of the commission was 500 families. In Nazi Germany, where the regime sought to make the country "free of Jews" (*Judenrein*) through forced emigration but felt increasingly frustrated by the barriers to immigration raised by other countries, various Nazi luminaries—Julius Streicher, Hermann Göring, Alfred Rosenberg, Joachim von Ribbentrop, Hans Frank, and Hjalmar Schacht—also mentioned Madagascar in the late 1930s as a potential home for German Jews.

Only in May 1940, however, did Madagascar become the focus of Nazi Jewish policy. The previous fall Heinrich Himmler had successfully proposed to Hitler a vast scheme of ethnic cleansing in German-occupied Poland. The western third of Poland was annexed to the Third Reich as the "incorporated territories." All Poles and Jews were to be deported from there to central Poland (organized as a German colony known as the Generalgouvernement) and replaced by ethnic Germans repatriated from the territories ceded to Stalin under the Nazi-Soviet Nonaggression Pact. The Jews expelled from the incorporated territories, and eventually also those of the Third Reich and the Generalgouvernement, were to be concentrated in a Jewish reservation in the district of Lublin. Implementation of Himmler's plan, however, was opposed by Hermann Göring, who was more interested in the economic exploitation of the incorporated territories than in "racial experimentation," and by Hans Frank, head of the Generalgouvernement, who wanted to turn his bailiwick into a model colony rather than a receiving station for the Third Reich's racially undesired. The combination of their opposition and logistical difficulties was effective. By the spring of 1940 Himmler's ambitious schemes for demographic engineering had been drastically scaled back and the plan for the Lublin reservation abandoned altogether.

Imminent victory over France provided Himmler with the opportunity to revive his proposals in a meeting with Hitler on 25 May 1940. Once again all Poles were to be expelled from the incorporated territories into the Generalgouvernement, where they would be reduced to the status of a denationalized reserve of slave labor. With the French empire soon to be at Germany's disposal, Himmler now suggested sending all the Jews within the expanding German sphere "to a colony in Africa or elsewhere." According to Himmler, Hitler found his proposals "very good and correct" and authorized Himmler to tell his Nazi rivals that the scheme was in line with the Führer's way of thinking.

Meanwhile the new so-called Jewish expert of the German Foreign Office, Franz Rademacher, was also pondering the possibilities opened by the looming collapse of France. Concerning preparations for the peace treaty, he wrote: "One question must be clarified: whereto with the Jews?" One answer was to send "all Jews out of Europe." Another was to keep the East European Jews in the Lublin region as hostages and to send the Western European Jews overseas, "to Madagascar," for example.

Foreign Minister Ribbentrop conveyed the suggestion to Hitler, who embraced the idea of sending to the island not just Western but all European Jews within the Nazi sphere. At a summit meeting in Munich on 18 June, Hitler and Ribbentrop mentioned Madagascar as an area for Jewish resettlement to the Italian dictator Benito Mussolini and to Italy's foreign minister, Galeazzo Ciano. Himmler's deputy, Reinhard Heydrich, quickly invoked his jurisdiction over Jewish emigration and staked his claim to a central role in planning for "a territorial Final Solution." As a result, Heydrich's own "Jewish expert," Adolf Eichmann, and Franz Rademacher of the Foreign Office simultaneously worked on versions of the so-called Madagascar Plan throughout the summer of 1940.

Rademacher feverishly churned out memorandums and commissioned studies. He noted that victory imposed on Germany the "obligation to solve the Jewish question in Europe." The solution was to send all the Jews of Europe to Madagascar, which would be transformed into a "superghetto." In Rademacher's plan, responsibilities were to be divided. The Foreign Office was to negotiate the peace treaty with France. Göring's Office of the Four Year Plan was to be in charge of confiscating Jewish property. The SS (security police) would collect the Jews in Europe and administer the island ghetto. Viktor Brack of the Führer Chancellery, already in charge of the transport of the mentally and physically disabled to the so-called euthanasia centers, was to coordinate the transport of the Jews. On Madagascar the Jews would be permitted a certain autonomy; they would have their own mayors, police, and postal service, so that for propaganda purposes Germany could exploit its great generosity in creating a homeland for the Jews.

Eichmann, in charge of planning within the SS, dispatched subordinates to conduct research in the French colonial archives and the Hamburg Tropical Institute. By mid-August he and his associates had produced a neatly printed brochure entitled "Reich Security Main Office: Madagascar Project." Its authors noted that "with the addition of the masses of the East, a settlement of the Jewish question through emigration has become impossible." In order to avoid lasting contact of other peoples with the Jews, "an overseas solution of insular character must be preferred above all others." Thus 4 million Jews—1 million per year—would be transported from the German sphere in Europe to Madagascar, which as a German mandate would be administered by the SS as a police state.

Word of the plan spread quickly. On 1 July 1940 Adam Czerniakow, head of the Warsaw *Judenrat* (Jewish council), was told by an SS officer "that the war would be over in a month and that we would all leave for Madagascar." Local German administrators in the Generalgouvernement received orders from Frank's colonial capital in Kraków "to stop all work on ghetto construction in view of the fact that, according to the plan of the Führer, the Jews of Europe were to be sent to Madagascar at the end of the war and thus ghetto building was for all practical purposes illusory." And in late July, Frank refused to permit the previously planned deportation of Jews from the Lodz ghetto into the Generalgouvernement because they were soon to be sent overseas instead.

The Madagascar Plan, which many Germans on trial after the war invoked in their defense but which few historians have taken seriously, was in fact very real to Nazi planners in the summer of 1940. It was, however, quite short-lived, for it was predicated on early victory over Great Britain, whose merchant marine was essential for transporting 4 million Jews overseas. German failure to win control of the skies in the Battle of Britain not only ended German plans for a cross-Channel invasion but also meant an end to the Madagascar Plan.

In the fall of 1940, therefore, Hitler faced a stalemate both militarily and in his search for a solution to his self-imposed "Jewish problem." After Hitler chose the military option of attacking the Soviet Union (Operation Barbarossa) in December 1940, German documents began to speak of an "evacuation" of the Jews, no longer to Madagascar, but to "a country yet to be determined." For reasons of security the Soviet target could not be named. It was on Soviet territory, not in Madagascar, that Hitler later began to implement the Final Solution—"in a way," as he put it, "that was not exactly more friendly."

Before September 1939 Nazi policy aimed at creating a Germany free of Jews through forced emigration. In 1941 Hitler decided on the Final Solution—the systematic mass murder of all European Jewry within the Nazi grasp. In the interim period between these two policies, the Nazi regime envisaged a German sphere in Europe made free of Jews through mass expulsion—what the Nazis euphemistically called "resettlement" before that term became a code word for deportation to the killing centers. The Madagascar Plan was the most spectacular and bizarre of the various resettlement schemes the Nazis pursued during this period. Given the total incapacity of the island to sustain an additional population of 4 million impoverished deportees, one of the consequences of the Madagascar Plan would surely have been a terrible decimation of the Jewish population from starvation and disease. Thus the scheme was clearly genocidal in intent. This "territorial final solution" was not yet the Final Solution, but it was a major step in that direction. *Christopher R. Browning*

Majdanek Prisoner-of-war and extermination camp outside Lublin in southern Poland. Majdanek began operation in October 1941 as one of the largest camps in Eastern Europe, with seven gas chambers. Its inmates included Soviet prisoners of war, imprisoned and deported Belorussians and Poles, and Jews from throughout Europe. Approximately 360,000 inmates died there: about 215,000 from starvation, abuse, exhaustion, and disease and about 145,000 from gassing or shooting. Most of the installations, but not the gas chambers, were destroyed before the Red Army reached the camp in July 1944. See EXTERMINATION CAMPS

Mauthausen Concentration camp in Austria, established in 1938 and liberated in May 1945. Although Mauthausen was not, strictly speaking, an extermination camp, about two-thirds of the 200,000 inmates perished as the result of executions, forced labor, inhuman squalor, starvation, and disease. In the early years of the war few Jews were sent there. The inmates were mostly German political prisoners, Spanish republicans, Soviet soldiers, and prisoners of war from various European countries. In 1944 the Germans trans-

The rear side of a gas chamber in Majdanek. The furnace to the right was used to create carbon monoxide for gassing prisoners. After 1944

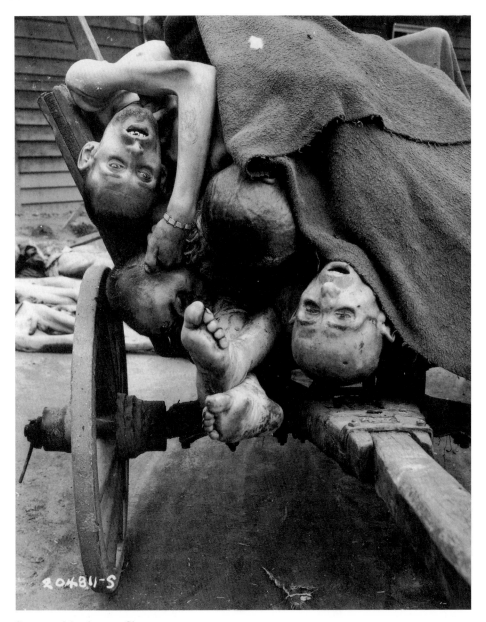

Corpses at Mauthausen. Circa 1945

ported many Jewish prisoners to Mauthausen from the Auschwitz, Plaszow, and Gross-Rosen camps and in 1945 from the Bergen–Belsen, Buchenwald, and Dora-Mittelbau camps, which were being evacuated.

Mayer, Saly (1882–1950) President of the Swiss Israelite Community Association (SIG) and representative of the American Jewish Joint Distribution Committee in Switzerland. Mayer was prominently involved in negotiations with the Swiss authorities concerning Jewish refugees, and he took part in talks with SS officials, including Kurt Becher, aimed at the release of Jews from Nazi-occupied Europe. See JOINT DISTRIBUTION COMMITTEE; SWITZERLAND

Medical Experimentation The Nuremberg war crimes trials in October 1946 revealed to the world that the Nazis had conducted cruel medical experiments

A survivor at Mauthausen carries a loaf of bread after the camp's liberation. May 1945

on human beings against their will and under horrifying conditions. The doctors who performed these experiments ignored widely accepted rules of human conduct and consciously violated the code of medical ethics, which requires physicians to act only to improve their patients' condition and never to do harm. Furthermore, they disregarded basic principles concerning experimentation on human beings, especially that test subjects must have volunteered and have been fully informed of any health risks from the experiment. The Nazi doctors consciously violated these principles, which conflicted directly with main points of Nazi ideology: antisemitism, mystical racism, modern scientific racism, and eugenics. The field of medicine in Nazi Germany was a tool used by the ruling system to implement the party doctrine and hence enjoyed institutional prestige. The experiments, under

the patronage of the SS chief, Heinrich Himmler, were advanced by support from universities and research institutions in Germany and Austria, and were even allocated plentiful resources and a work force to carry them out. Programs were designed to address certain needs of the armed forces and enjoyed the cooperation of various branches of the military establishment.

Nazi medical experiments fall into two main categories. The first group encompasses experiments that serve no conceivable medical objective but were intended to advance Nazi political, military, and ideological goals. The second includes experiments that, despite the abominable and unethical way in which they were conducted, sought to expand medical knowledge.

The first Nazi medical experiments took place not in the concentration camps during the war but much earlier, during the Nazi party's first year in power in Germany. The Law for the Prevention of Offspring with Hereditary Diseases, proclaimed on 14 July 1933, brought about the surgical sterilization of some 200,000 Germans who supposedly suffered from congenital disorders, including mentally retarded and mentally disturbed persons as well as alcoholics during the years 1933–39. (Many were later put to death in the so-called euthanasia program.) The sterilization program aroused much interest among government officials, particularly after the military victories in Poland and the East, as a way of allowing them to take advantage of local populations as a labor force without fear that the purity of the German ("Aryan") race would be compromised by intermixing of the nationalities. Experiments were conducted, often by the doctors from the euthanasia program, to develop cheaper and quicker methods of sterilization and castration that could then be widely implemented among the "inferior" races. The two main methods were exposure to radiation and the injection of chemicals. (A third method, promoted by Adolf Pokorny and involving an extract of the *Caladium segunium* plant, was not implemented owing to technical problems.) In fact, most of these experiments took place in the concentration and death camps of Auschwitz-Birkenau.

The first method, developed by Viktor Brack and Horst Schumann, was designed to achieve mass sterilization by means of X-rays in the "counter program." Candidates for sterilization would be summoned to a government office. While they stood in front of a counter to fill out a form, the X-ray apparatus would be operated behind the counter. Exposure to X-rays for two to three minutes was sufficient to cause sterilization. This program never went past the experimental stage.

However, experiments in sterilization by X-rays began at the end of 1942 in Block 30 at Birkenau, the Auschwitz death camp, and later at the women's concentration camp at Ravensbrück. They were carried out on young men and women, even children, under circumstances of poor hygiene and gross neglect on the part of the doctors performing the experiments. First, several large doses of X-rays were administered to the prisoners' genitals for five to seven minutes. About two weeks later, the prisoners' reproductive organs were surgically removed for examination of the effects of the radiation. The surgery was performed crudely, and many of the subjects died as a result. Those who managed to survive the terrible radiation burns and surgery were sent to die in the gas chambers, as their medical condition prevented them from working. This outcome demonstrates the utter absurdity of the experiment, for Viktor Brack had represented to Himmler that by the X-ray method he could sterilize 3 million Jews who would be fit for work and would otherwise have to be killed.

The second method, developed by Professor Carl Clauberg, aimed at mass sterilization by a single injection of chemicals into the womb. It was tested on thousands of women prisoners in Ravensbrück and in Block 10 at Auschwitz. Iodoform, a common antiseptic, was injected into the women's uteruses during a routine gynecological examination. Its effect was to destroy the uterine membrane and the ovaries. The women later underwent hysterectomies and ovariectomies, and the reproductive organs were sent to a research institute in Berlin for inspection. The injections and operations caused irreversible damage to the women's bodies and led to the death of scores of Jewish and Gypsy prisoners. Not long after these experiments were completed, Clauberg announced to Himmler that by this method one doctor and 10 assistants could sterilize 1,000 people in a single day.

Another type of experimentation, in line with Nazi racial policy, aimed at exploring the genetic differences between the races and promoting the advancement of the "Aryan" race. The first of three sets of such experiments was carried out primarily on twins and dwarfs. It took place at Auschwitz under the direction of Josef Mengele. The purpose was to discover a method that would enable German women to bear more than one fetus in every pregnancy. Twins beginning from the age of two were subjected to anthropological measurements and a variety of clinical tests, including ones comparing their reactions to various substances, such as chemicals placed in the eyes to induce a change of color. Although twins in Mengele's project were protected from the excesses of the SS officers in the camp, they paid the price of suffering a long and painful line of testing. In the end Mengele and his assistants would kill each pair of twins by injecting chloroform into their hearts and then would conduct comparative pathological examinations of their internal organs. Mengele's research on dwarfs, carried out in a similar manner, was meant to explore the hereditary and other causes of dwarfism in order to prevent their occurrence among German offspring. These experiments had an additional goal: to test the resistance of people of different races to infectious diseases and thus provide further proof of the superiority of the Aryan race.

The second kind of experiment involved anthropological research into the anatomy of Jews. The ostensible purpose of the project, directed by Professor August Hirt of the University of Strasbourg, was "to promote the science of anthropology" and to preserve knowledge of and exhibits from the "extinct" race. In fact it aimed to prove the inferiority of Jews and other peoples by examination of their skeletal structure. The experiments were performed on Jewish Soviet prisoners of war in Block 10 at Auschwitz. First, a long series of physical tests, experiments, measurements, and photographs of every one of their body organs, especially of their skeletal structures, were carried out on the prisoners. Next, the prisoners were sent to their deaths in the gas chambers in Natzweiler concentration camp. In the second stage, once they were dead, the bodies were sent to the Institute of Anatomical Research in the University Hospital in Strasbourg. There, Hirt examined the corpses to detect peculiarities in the skeletal structure of the Jewish "Bolsheviks," thereby proving their inferiority to other races.

The third type involved the scientific study of the blood serum. The Nazi doctrine of racial hygiene aimed to identify blood groups and types according to race, in an attempt to place the separation of Aryans and non-Aryans on a scientific foundation. These experiments, directed by Professor Eugen Fischer and Dr. Horneck, compared the serum of white-skinned people with that of dark-skinned people, using for this purpose prisoners of war and Gypsies in Sachsen-hausen concentration camp.

The second category of experiments—those whose objectives (but not methods) were medically and scientifically sound and ethical—includes experiments concerning the treatment and healing of war wounds and experiments relating to the rescue and recovery of military personnel.

Experiments on the treatment of common war wounds took place mainly in the concentration camps of Ravensbrück, Buchenwald, Dachau, and Auschwitz. Doctors examined the effectiveness of sulfanilamide in preventing infection and mortification of the limbs of prisoners who had been injected with the bacterium that produces gas gangrene, the cause of Reinhard Heydrich's death. Karl Gebhardt, Himmler's personal physician and the head surgeon of the SS and the police, was responsible for this series of experiments. Gebhardt had treated Heydrich's injury with sulfanil-amide; and since it had been suggested that had he used a higher dosage Heydrich could have been saved, he was highly motivated to prove the ineffectiveness of the drug at any price. Gebhardt caused prisoners to acquire particularly severe infections, and he redoubled his efforts when Ernst Grawitz, the SS chief physician, learned that during the course of the experiment there had been no deaths. Grawitz's "distorted impression" was indeed corrected after five of the women prisoners died and all the other women prisoners were severely burned as a result of the critical infections caused by the treatment with high doses of sulfanilamide.

Biochemical treatments of purulent wounds were also examined in a series of experiments conducted in the hospital of the Dachau concentration camp, where pus was injected into the prisoners' soft tissues. In this case, most of the victims were Catholic clergymen of various nationalities. Similar experiments were performed on prisoners at Buchenwald concentration

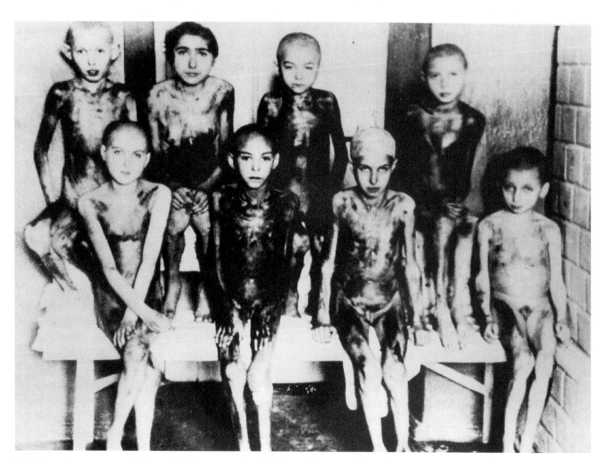

Children who were severely burned in the course of medical experiments at Auschwitz.

camp in order to determine the most effective treatment for phosphorus burns from incendiary bombs.

Similar cruel methods were used at Auschwitz in experiments to determine new treatments of second- and third-degree burns and to examine the factors that cause the blood to clot. At Dachau, Sigmund Rascher investigated the effectiveness of polygal-10 in stopping bleeding by administering the chemical to prisoners and then shooting them in various parts of the body. The prisoners died from their injuries within a few minutes.

Experiments to test treatments for injuries resulting from chemical warfare were conducted in the Sachsenhausen and Natzweiler camps, where prisoners were exposed to mustard gas and phosgene. At Neuengamme prisoners were made to drink water polluted by various chemicals in order to find means of purifying drinking water in the case of a chemical attack on the German water supply.

Vaccines and drug treatments for infectious diseases such as swamp fever and typhus were carried out mainly at Dachau, Natzweiler, Sachsenhausen, and Buchenwald. These tests required infecting some prisoners with the target diseases.

Another group of experiments at Dachau was conducted at the behest of the German military. They were designed to test a person's ability to survive harsh environmental conditions and to determine the most effective means of treatment after rescue. To discover the effects of extreme high altitudes that fighter pilots might have to endure, prisoners were placed in chambers that simulated atmospheric pressure and oxygen levels at an altitude of 21 kilometers, and their physical reactions to these extremes were monitored. Siegfried Ruff and Hans Romberg, who conducted these experiments, were both civilians from the German Experimental Institute for Aviation in Berlin, and had volunteered to participate together with Rascher, an air force physician and SS officer.

To test treatments for injuries caused by extreme cold—dry and wet—prisoners were kept in ice baths for hours or left naked in the yard of the experiment block throughout winter nights. These experiments were conducted by Professor Ernst Holzlöhner and A. Pinka from Kiel University, who were recruited for the project by the Luftwaffe and who worked on it with Rascher. About 60 prisoners were made to withstand air temperatures as low as −6 degrees Celsius (21 degrees Fahrenheit). The outdoor experiments were dis-

continued out of fear that the victims' screams would reach the nearby civilian population.

To increase downed airmen's chances of survival in the sea, prisoners were made to drink 500–1,000 cc of berkatit water (treated sea water) for 15 days in succession. After several series of experiments, Wilhelm Beiglboeck, a medical consultant for the Luftwaffe who conducted the experiments, reached a conclusion that was already known: in their effect on human dehydration, there is no difference between sea water and berkatit.

Nazi experiments on human beings were conducted on the personal initiative of Nazi medical staff, who were given complete freedom to act without regard for basic medical ethics. According to partial records, experiments were carried out on at least 7,000 people. Most of the men, women, and children who served as test subjects were tormented and killed by doctors seeking prestige and status in the Nazi system.

In the so-called Doctors' Trial, in Nuremberg in October 1946, 23 medical professionals (including 20 physicians) and one medical administrator were tried for crimes against humanity stemming from the quasi-scientific experiments on human beings. Sixteen doctors were found guilty under international law of having planned, directed, and conducted experiments on people without their agreement and of having knowingly caused the torture and murder of some of the victims. Seven of those convicted—Karl Brandt, Rudolf Brandt, Karl Gebhardt, Joachim Mugrowsky, Viktor Brack, Wolfram Sievers, and Waldemar Hoven—received the death penalty and were executed on 2 June 1948. Nine were sentenced to various terms of imprisonment. Seven of the defendants were acquitted. Some persons who had masterminded the experiments and held high positions in the Nazi hierarchy, such as Ernst Grawitz (who committed suicide), Carl Clauberg, Josef Mengele (who escaped from Europe, perhaps with Allied assistance), Horst Schumann, and Sigmund Rascher, were never brought to trial.

Ronit Fisher

Memorials Memorials provide fixed places in a chaotic and shifting landscape, where groups can project shared symbols to consolidate notions of pride, heritage, power, and self. Holocaust and other memorials are not built in a political or geographic vacuum and therefore reflect national myths and ideals as well as the changing demands of diverse political constituen-

A memorial obelisk erected in memory of persons killed in Bergen-Belsen.

cies and public tastes. The diversity of styles and content in the several hundred Holocaust memorials in North America, Europe, Asia, Australia, and the Middle East reflect local cultural differences in postwar politics and history. And yet they share certain common features apart from subject.

The remnants of former concentration camps form the core of many memorials. These disquieting ruins usually included barbed wire, guard towers, the bare stone foundations of wooden barracks, crematoriums, jail cells, rusty railroad tracks, broken cemetery headstones, and mass graves. Despite the ravages of time, neglect, and even deliberate destruction, these sites still serve as fragile and tenuous reminders of the past. As events fade into memory and turn into myth, the terrain and landscape have inevitably changed: roads have been built, the surrounding land designated for commercial use (as at Neuengamme), and historic structures destroyed. It is frequently impossible for

visitors to isolate the sites of former concentration camps from nearby modern obtrusions. Indeed, the preservation of these sites as such, even without additional monuments or public sculpture, is an act of memorialization. Since there are thousands of former concentration camps dotting the European countryside, the selection of former camps for preservation is often filled with conflict. The French have built a memorial and museum at Natzweiler-Struthof because it was the only concentration camp built by the Germans on French soil, whereas they have ignored the internment and transit camps built and run by the French at Les Milles, Gurs, and Rivesaltes, which raise uncomfortable questions about French collaboration and xenophobia.

Further, the environmental power of the surviving original structures at Auschwitz and Mauthausen contrasts dramatically with the empty, bucolic landscapes at Bergen-Belsen, Chelmno, and Gurs. These pastoral surroundings make the Nazi past seem remote, inaccessible, and elusive. At locations where no substantial ruins remain, such as the Warsaw ghetto or the Treblinka killing center, the role of the sculptor or landscape architect is essential for the symbolic representation of mass murder. The Warsaw ghetto memorial built in the late 1940s and the Treblinka memorial in the 1960s show different architectural solutions to the absence of archeological remains.

The absence of commonly accepted definitions of the Holocaust and the lack of consensus about appropriate rituals and symbols for its victims have also provided fertile ground for volatile political confrontations between survivors and governments. Thus, in Israel the Holocaust is seen as part of a continuum of antisemitic persecution and affords moral justification for the creation of the state. Despite certain common elements, most sites do not reflect the fate of *all* victims of the Holocaust at a particular locality, nor do their public monuments show sensitivity to all aspects of the subject.

After World War I most European nations failed to develop styles or conventions to mourn the mass dead. Furthermore, traditional funerary art in most war cemeteries used predominantly Christian iconography and symbols to communicate the heroism and patriotism usually associated with military casualties. These symbols were inappropriate and even offensive to the victims of Nazi mass murder—Jews, Gypsies, the disabled, and others—who frequently neither had specific grave sites to visit nor knew the dates of death of family members and friends. The traditional portrayal of death as an individual or familial event did not fit the Holocaust, which required new styles of memorialization. Nevertheless, sculptors, architects, and designers had to find individual and collective symbols that would facilitate an understanding of the past in order to represent it for the present and the future. Memorials for the Holocaust thus had to be designed as special places separated from the flow of everyday life while communicating didactic information and emotion.

Many East European memorials erected after the war do not mention Jews explicitly, thereby reflecting the ideological views of Communist regimes that emphasized political resistance. But similar problems arose in Western, non-Communist countries. The national memorials in the West are often self-serving, attributing a national identity to the victims that was not granted to them in their lifetimes. Thus, such posthumous acknowledgment transforms Polish Jews into Poles and French Jews into French (Ile de la Cité memorial, Paris). This obfuscation of Jewish victims stands in sharp contrast to American and Israeli memorials, where the reverse exclusion applies. Because the major impetus and financing for memorials in Israel and the United States has come from Jewish survivors, it is uncommon to find explicit acknowledgment of Gypsies, the disabled, or political victims.

After 50 years we should at least be able to articulate our expectations of what memorials might look like at European sites where the Holocaust once occurred and at distant localities that were not directly involved. Ought monuments built in Australia, Israel, Japan, South Africa, or the United States look different from those built in Europe? Are there appropriate iconographic traditions applicable to such memorials? There are still no definitive answers to these questions, although the existing patterns of memorials and monuments offer some options.

From 1945 through the 1950s general conditions in Europe as well as the enormity of recent events did not permit elaborate commemorations attended by a broad public. Initially many former concentration camps housed survivors and displaced persons. Nevertheless, during those years nascent memorials were established at selected concentration camps, often using only a portion of the camp terrain. At the same time survivors built the first museums and public monuments in Israel.

The first European memorials fell into one of two broad organizational patterns. In Eastern Europe, memorials were forms of symbolic politics under the direction and financial patronage of the central government. In Western Europe, memorials were usually left to private and local initiative and thus developed ad hoc and piecemeal. The ambivalences and inadequacies that marked this initial phase in the institutionalization and memorialization of the Holocaust were irreversible and provided the context for all subsequent developments. Thus, when the city of West Berlin decided to remove all surface vestiges of the former Gestapo headquarters on Prinz Albrechtstrasse in the mid-1950s, it created the physical constraints of an empty, rubble-filled lot on prime real estate that hampered the design of a memorial in the 1990s.

The situation of the Neuengamme concentration camp in suburban Hamburg is typical. It was not protected as a landmark, and the historic terrain was not preserved intact. In 1948 the city of Hamburg built a maximum security prison adjacent to the first memorial, and in the 1970s it added a juvenile correction facility adjacent to the prison. The two jails incorporated the former camp guard towers, barracks, *Appellplatz* (assembly grounds), and SS garage inside their walls. Other parcels of Neuengamme's real estate were leased for commercial purposes. The *Klinkerwerke,* a brick factory where prisoners had once labored, was leased to a builder of luxury yachts. The site remains problematical and underfinanced even today.

Elsewhere in Germany disquieting reminders of the past have been recycled as prisons, police or army barracks, and even municipal or commercial offices. Esterwegen is used for military maneuvers, and former prisoner barracks serve as storage facilities for the German army. The former SS barracks at the satellite camp at Herbrück houses a municipal finance office. The former canteen and laundry at Flossenburg are used by a local woodcutting concern, and the site of the Kemna camp in Wuppertal is now a factory. These pragmatic decisions *not* to remember the past in its most local and intimate associations make the events of the Holocaust seem remote, inaccessible, and elusive in many localities.

Similar patterns also applied in the East. Thus, in the former German Democratic Republic, at Buchenwald the Soviet army occupied the Gustloff factory area where prisoners once labored, and at Sachsenhausen, East German police used the adjacent former headquarters of the camp inspectorate. Similarly, in Lodz, where some buildings of the former ghetto have survived, few commemorative or historical markers indicate for the visitor where the ghetto once stood.

From the late 1950s to the 1970s a number of factors led to the resurgence of interest in the Holocaust. These convergent trends were also apparent in the new concentration camp memorials that opened. The three major East German memorials opened within a few years of one another: Buchenwald in 1958, Ravensbrück in 1959, and Sachsenhausen in 1961. Similarly in France the memorial at Natzweiler-Struthof opened in 1960, and in West Germany the Dachau and Neuengamme memorials were opened in 1965. In Italy the site of the former San Sabba camp in Trieste was also dedicated in 1965, and Mauthausen opened near Linz in Austria in 1970.

Despite local hostility to these tangible reminders of an uncomfortable past, an informal coalition of survivors and a younger generation favored confronting the traumas of the Nazi era. The student protest movement of the 1960s in Europe promoted open discussion and direct political action. In this same period monuments and public sculpture were built in Israel, South Africa, and the United States. Several of the artists who executed these commissions showed more civic fervor than artistic judgment. At the same time survivors and other artists began to incorporate the Holocaust in their work, thus giving the concept and event more flexible meaning than the strictly historical definition. In 1964 Louise Nevelson completed a painted, wooden wall sculpture entitled *Homage to Six Million* (1964), and Jozef Szajna in Warsaw finished large environmental installations combining concentration camp artifacts with other media. This was the beginning of a socially critical modern art that turned away from purely abstract and minimalist forms of expression.

The diversity of European public sculpture relating to the Holocaust represents the response of three different postwar generations since 1945. Holocaust monuments created immediately after the war served primarily as memorials to the dead. Initially they were few in number and relatively inconspicuous. Exemplified by the starkly functional gravestone for the Jewish dead at Bergen-Belsen (October 1945–April 1946), the first European and Israeli monuments modified the traditional secular tomb of the unknown soldier and extended it to the Jewish victims of Nazi mass murder.

By the 1960s the focus on such memorial sculpture was transformed and extended. In this period, memorials were designed for the living and as signposts for the future. Increasing chronological and geographical distance from the actual events yielded both innovative solutions and kitsch. The former was exemplified by the memorial at Treblinka, the latter by Nathan Rapoport's florid Philadelphia *Monument to the Six Million Jewish Martyrs* (1964). At Mauthausen, tradition and experiment blended in Mirko Baseldella's Italian memorial with the imposition of a symbolic barbedwire cage adjacent to a wailing wall containing cameo photographs provided by the families of the deceased. Perhaps the most provocative work incorporated a blackened and leafless tree outside the former Paviak prison in Warsaw. The tree was one of the few objects to survive the razing of the Warsaw ghetto in April

Memorial sculpture to the Hungarian victims of Mauthausen erected on the site of the former concentration camp.

1943, and by its mere existence it symbolized death and resurrection simultaneously.

By the 1980s Holocaust sculpture, although still primarily commemorative, was designed to communicate with a broader public. Changing public tastes allowed artists to choose their own styles. But the didactic needs of transmitting distant events to a new generation necessitated varying degrees of realism, as in George Segal's *The Holocaust* (1983). Although no narrow range of styles dominated these new memorials, a broad range of artistic and iconographic solutions posed greater risks and new challenges to sculptors, architects, and landscape designers. The inability to define appropriate styles and symbols for public art about the Holocaust often resulted in pointless debates in the American media about whether art and the Holocaust could coexist.

The resurgence of this subject and the proliferation of new memorials and educational centers in the 1980s is part of an international phenomenon. In Germany students used the tools of historical archeology at the Fort Obere Kuhberg and placed markers at Neuengamme to show their social responsibility and awareness. This restoration of sites as memorials provided a new generation with a sense of authenticity as well as catharsis. In the Netherlands, apart from the Gypsy and Ravensbrück memorials installed at Museumplein in Amsterdam, a museum was belatedly opened for part of the year at Westerbork in 1983, and a controversial public monument, *Homomonument*, was installed in Amsterdam in 1986. Similarly, two memorials at Lackenbach and Maxglan, both sites of former Gypsy camps, were erected in 1985. In Poland and Czechoslovakia many existing sites were repaired and restored for a new international tourist public.

Despite circumstances differing from those in continental Europe, the United States responded with parallel developments. Conditions in the immediate postwar period were not propitious for a broader reception of the Holocaust. Overshadowed by European reconstruction and the Cold War, the Holocaust was initially regarded by Americans as an uncomfortable foreign experience whose primary impact was felt abroad. Furthermore, those survivors and displaced persons who came to the United States were preoccupied with building new lives, and the timing was not auspicious for reflection about the war years.

The resurgence of American interest in the Holocaust reflected changes of the 1960s and 1970s. The civil rights and desegregation movements of the 1960s, the growing opposition to the Vietnam War, and the student rebellion of 1968 destroyed an earlier uncritical complacency and historical consensus. Moreover, the issues of civic ethics raised by the Watergate scandal created a climate of opinion favorable to questioning governmental policies, thereby increasing possible reception of the Holocaust as a subject. The rediscovery of ethnicity and genealogy in the 1970s also contributed to the growing needs of a younger generation of Jews, who demanded information about the Holocaust. These factors led in the 1980s to the growth in the United States of publications, exhibitions, conferences, and institutions concerned with the Holocaust.

Despite the installation of hundreds of Holocaust-based public sculptures in European and American cities since the 1960s, most works have at best evoked sporadic public interest. In part this can be attributed to their unobtrusiveness, inadequate design, or stereotyped iconography. Standardized visual symbols have been used to depict the Holocaust: the Star of David, prisoner triangles, symbolic urns, the Hebrew word *chai* symbolizing life, the shofar, and stylized barbed-wire fences. Although all these symbols are appropriate, they are inadequate as commemorative invocations in public sculpture.

The common denominator of all Holocaust memorials—irrespective of location—is a universal willingness to commemorate suffering experienced rather than suffering caused. As chronological and geographical distance from the Holocaust increases, the problems of memory are magnified, perhaps more so through growing public familiarity with literal images of the Holocaust distributed through photography, film, and television. The haunting sense of pastoral beauty at many European Holocaust sites in the 1980s seems inappropriate to the tragic historical setting and genocidal history. Nevertheless, this contrast was already inherent in the actual landscapes and physical layout of virtually every concentration camp in Europe. Only

San Sabba in Trieste was situated inside the confines of an urban site.

The political changes of 1989, which altered the configurations of power in the Soviet bloc, are still incomplete, and their implications for Holocaust memorials are still uncertain. Nevertheless, it is clear that these changes will at best transform and at worst diminish the status of most Holocaust and anti-Nazi memorials. The newly installed governments in Central and Eastern Europe have already dismissed the directors of many memorials and cut professional staffs and budgets. They have, moreover, insisted that so-called anti-Stalinist monuments and exhibits be erected in many memorials alongside those commemorating the Holocaust. At Buchenwald a member of the West German cabinet demanded that in the future the Buchenwald memorial should also commemorate German victims of the Soviet occupation authorities. These examples can be multiplied throughout Eastern Europe, where growing popular resentment against Jews and Gypsies, hatred of outsiders, and the reemergence of local fascist groups bode ill for the future of Holocaust memorials. European memorials to the Holocaust in the last decade of the twentieth century reflect the changing balance of local politics mingled with historical memory or amnesia.

Sybil Milton

Mengele, Josef (1911–79) SS official and physician who conducted inhumane medical experiments at Auschwitz. Mengele subjected prisoners to X-rays, mutilations, virulent diseases, and toxic injections. His special interest was in identical twins, whom he routinely selected for testing from among the new arrivals to the camp. When the Germans evacuated Auschwitz, Mengele was transferred to Mauthausen and then disappeared after the war. He resurfaced in Argentina in 1949 and moved to Uruguay (1958), Paraguay (1959), and Brazil (1961). In July 1985 forensic experts exhumed the body of a man who died in 1979 in a drowning accident in Brazil, and they identified him as Mengele. See MEDICAL EXPERIMENTATION

Merin, Moshe (1906–43) Head of the *Judenrat* (Jewish council) in eastern Upper Silesia (Zaglebie). Merin believed that if he collaborated with the German authorities, he could persuade them that Jewish workers were essential to the Nazi war effort. He strenuously fulfilled German labor requirements and often called for volunteers for the forced labor camps. The Jewish underground sentenced Merin to death, but the Germans deported him to Auschwitz and killed him there before the sentence could be carried out.

Mischlinge With the Nuremberg racial laws of 15 September 1935 and the subsequent decrees and commentaries, the Nazis introduced *Mischling* as a legal term to categorize German citizens of ethnically mixed parentage. The word was used in botany and zoology, in the sense of "hybrid" or "mongrel," before being applied to human beings by Anglo-European anthropologists and eugenicists about the mid-nineteenth century under the influence of Darwinism and colonialism. From the beginning, the term had definite racist and derogatory connotations of inferiority, abnormality, and degeneration.

The exclusion of persons without "German blood" from citizenship and the German national community had been a central objective of national socialism practically since its inception. The 1920 Nazi party platform declared that such persons should at best be tolerated as foreign guests and be subject to special legislation. Further immigration of non-Germans was to be prohibited, and those who had immigrated since 2 August 1914 were to be expelled. These proposals were primarily aimed at Jews but also included other alien "races" such as "Gypsies" (Sinti and Roma), "Negroes," and "Mongols." These ideas were not a Nazi invention; the myth of national unity and "purity of the blood" had long been two central themes of German national thought. As early as 1815 the nationalist writer Ernst Moritz Arndt alleged that "mishmash and bastardization are the main source of degeneration and decline of a people." Opposition to miscegenation and "intermarriage with non-Aryans" had been voiced in imperial Germany by the Pan-German League, one of the many *völkisch* (populist) groups that championed pan-Germanism, colonial claims, and racial doctrines. These forerunners of the Nazi völkisch ideology were the first to classify not only members of the Jewish religious community as aliens but also the baptized descendants of Judeo-Christian marriages as *Judenstämmlinge* (ethnic Jews).

Despite the ideas of equality proclaimed in the American and French revolutions, belief in the superiority of the white race remained dominant in the nineteenth and early twentieth centuries. "Scientific" theories of the day were used to back up popular prejudice. With the rediscovery of Gregor Mendel's principles of heredity in 1900, early geneticists were convinced that human beings followed the same laws. Almost unanimously, despite the lack of scientific data, they viewed physical and mental differences as hereditary and unalterable, and condemned racial interbreeding as dangerous to the survival of the "superior race." Mischlinge were believed to suffer from infertility, feeble-mindedness, and physical degeneracy.

Colonialism played a central part in the development of scientific racism. Biological theories provided a supposedly rational justification for the claim of cultural superiority of the European "Aryan race" over non-European races. The colonies also served as a laboratory for a number of German anthropological researchers, who later not only applauded the Nazi program of purging the German gene pool but willingly served as scientific experts and advisers on the racist population policy.

Eugen Fischer, professor at the University of Freiburg and from 1927 to 1942 director of the Kaiser Wilhelm Institute for Anthropology, Human Heredity, and Eugenics in Berlin-Dahlem, was the most influential German researcher on race-crossing and Mischlinge. His field study, *The Rehoboth Bastards and the Problem of Miscegenation among Humans*, published in 1913, influenced not only German colonial racial legislation but also all subsequent racial debates, and later provided scientific support for the Nuremberg racial laws.

In 1908 Fischer had conducted anthropological research in German South West Africa (Namibia) on members of the so-called Rehoboth Bastards, offspring of white Boer or German fathers and "colored" mothers. His study concluded with a call for strict prohibition of mixed marriages to prevent a "mixed race." He recommended that Mischlinge in the German colonies be granted protection only so long as they were of use but that finally they were to be eradicated. By 1912 interracial marriages were prohibited throughout the German colonies, and the Colonial Home Rule enshrined draconian regulations for the "protection of German blood and honor" long before the Nuremberg racial laws of 1935. Similarly, definitions used by the Nazis, such as Mischlinge of the first and second degrees (persons with two Jewish grandparents and persons with one Jewish grandparent), bastard, mixed marriage, and race defilement, and the measures taken against Mischlinge and mixed marriages had their antecedents in German colonial administration.

Immediately after the establishment of the dictator-

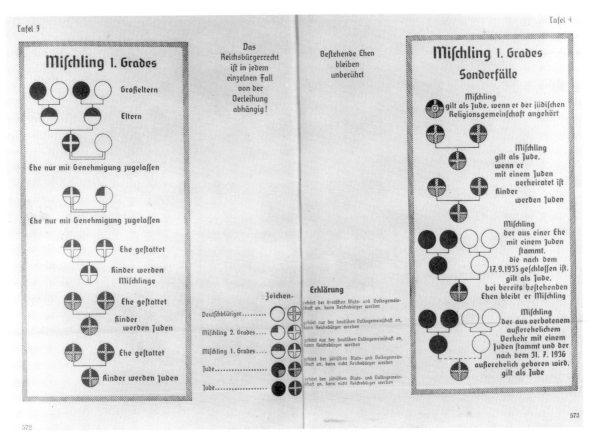

National Socialist Racial Teaching. Models for determining race.

ship in 1933, the Nazis began to implement their policy of excluding "racially undesirable aliens" from the German national community—primarily Jews but also Gypsies as well as their "mixed descendants." In addition, a small group of "colored" Mischlinge, the so-called Rhineland Bastards, illegitimate children of German mothers and African or Asian soldiers of occupying allied troops after World War I, was labeled racially undesirable.

Precise statistics regarding Mischlinge during the Nazi period cannot be obtained. The census of 1933 recorded only members of Jewish communities. Early estimates of the number of Jewish first- and second-degree Mischlinge run from 300,000 to 750,000, the latter figure from the Ministry of the Interior in April 1935. The census of 17 May 1939 showed 71,126 Jewish first-degree Mischlinge and 41,456 Jewish second-degree Mischlinge for the Greater German Reich (including Austria and Sudetenland). The much higher figures of the Ministry of the Interior were esti-

mates based on intermarriage rates dating as far back as before emancipation. In addition, 90 percent of the 30,000–35,000 German Gypsies were classified as Mischlinge. The registered Rhineland Bastards (estimates were higher) numbered 385 children between 7 and 17 years of age.

In April 1933 the Reich Interior Ministry, responsible for public health and racial legislation, opened a special office to conduct the genealogical registration of Mischlinge and mixed marriages and to compile official rosters. Achim Gercke from the Nazi party information service in Munich was appointed "expert for racial investigation." Since 1926 he had privately been collecting a card index about Germans of "Jewish" descent. His index, containing by then 500,000 entries, was transferred to the Ministry of the Interior and constituted the data base for the dismissal of "non-Aryans" under the April 1933 Law for the Restoration of the Professional Civil Service, which affected Jews and Mischlinge alike. Gercke issued certificates of

Aryan or non-Aryan descent, while his assistant from Munich, Wilfried Euler, concentrated on statistics and genealogical research about non-Aryans and Mischlinge, searching for Jewish ancestors even back into the seventeenth century. The office made use of numerous genealogies, parish registers, and statistics. The most important sources were parish registers. After Gercke was dismissed in spring 1935, his successor, the historian and SS colonel Kurt Mayer, intensified the collecting of personal data, extending the registration of non-Aryans to the annexed and occupied territories. Euler joined Walter Frank's Institute for Research into the Jewish Question, where he was commissioned to compile "global statistics on Jewish baptism and mixed marriages." He devoted special attention to the question of the reemergence of pure-blooded types after many generations (*Rückkreuzung*) and the "penetration of Jewish blood into the nobility and into the ranks of leading scientists, businessmen, and politicians." After 1940 Euler included Italy, France, and England in his research. After the enactment of the Nuremberg Laws, the Protestant Church of Berlin supported the compilation of a card index from all Berlin parish registers. Using entries of baptisms for Jews, Gypsies, Turks, and "Moors" or "Negroes," church employees extracted a special index of persons of "alien race" (*Fremdstämmigenkartei*), supplying a duplicate to the SS-dominated Reich Office for Genealogical Research (Reichsstelle für Sippenforschung). Without the close cooperation of parish registrars, the implementation of racial policies would have been far more difficult, because most Mischlinge and converts could not be identified by name, religion, or physical traits.

The main problem was that of definition. Racist legislation and propaganda prior to the Nuremberg Laws of September 1935 was based on the imprecise distinction between Aryans and non-Aryans. Most important for the Mischlinge was the so-called Aryan Paragraph of the first supplementary decree to the Law for the Restoration of the Professional Civil Service, April 1933, which excluded from the civil service—and subsequently from most professions—all descendants of one non-Aryan (particularly Jewish) parent or grandparent. Gypsy Mischlinge and others of mixed blood were equally subjected to the Aryan Paragraph.

The new racist propaganda and legislation led not only to discrimination against foreigners from Asian and South American states but also to negative effects

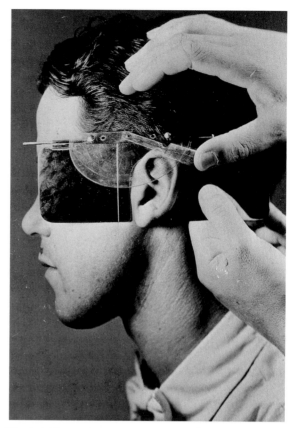

The facial features of a young German are measured during a racial examination at the Kaiser Wilhelm Institute for Anthropology. After 1933

on foreign relations. Several non-European governments reacted with complaints and boycotts. The German Foreign Office, therefore, called for more precise legal definitions focusing on Jewish descent. As a result, the terms *Aryan* and *non-Aryan* were replaced with the Reich Citizenship Law and the Law for the Protection of German Blood and Honor, enacted in September 1935 and known as the Nuremberg Laws. The laws distinguished between Jews and citizens of German or related (*artverwandt*) blood, yet the old terms continued to be used in many subsequent regulations and hence caused numerous bureaucratic problems of interpretation.

The position of Mischlinge changed with the Nuremberg racial laws. While applying the term *racial Jew* (*Rassejude*) to persons with at least three grandparents belonging to the Jewish religious community, government experts put Mischlinge into a separate category.

Persons with two Jewish grandparents were classified as half-Jews or Mischlinge of the first degree, and those with one Jewish grandparent were classified as quarter-Jews or Mischlinge of the second degree. Despite the Nazi principle that race or blood rather than religion was the basis for definition, affiliation to the Jewish religious community remained the primary criterion for identifying Jews. Paradoxically, a Mischlinge of the first degree was defined as a Jew (*Geltungsjude*) if he or she belonged to the Jewish community. Equally, a Christian convert to Judaism was treated as a Jew. The assessment of Aryan or non-Aryan descent was, in the case of the Jewish Mischlinge, primarily based on genealogical sources. Only in cases of doubt—for example, illegitimate birth or lack of documents—was physical examination carried out by the staff of university institutes of racial anthropology. Mischlinge of both degrees qualified for Reich citizenship, with the reservation that it could be rescinded. This classification, which also applied to Gypsies, "Negroes," and others, henceforth governed their legal status.

The Rhineland Bastards were the first Mischlinge to be precisely registered and anthropologically examined. Between 1933 and 1937 a commission of experts on population and race policy discussed various plans for the "solution of the bastard question." The options they considered were deportation to Africa or sterilization. In a secret operation of the Gestapo and Interior Ministry, these children were subjected to sterilization in the summer of 1937, bypassing the sterilization law of 1933, after their parents had been forced to consent.

A large but not precisely determinable number of Gypsy hybrids were involuntarily sterilized on the basis of the Law for the Prevention of Offspring with Hereditary Diseases. In contrast to the situation with the colored children, no foreign or internal complications were expected. Gypsy Mischlinge were not afforded the same exceptions as Jewish Mischlinge. In 1935 the police began to confine Gypsies in special municipal camps resembling ghettos, and under Himmler's decree of 16 December 1942 the Gypsy Mischlinge were deported to Auschwitz.

Between 1936 and 1941 German and Austrian Gypsy Mischlinge became the targets of racial research conducted by Robert Ritter and his staff at the Eugenic and Population Biological Research Station of the Reich Health Office. Ritter cooperated with the Criminal Police and Security Police, and his research was funded by the German Research Foundation.

Gypsy Mischlinge were classified by Ritter as "asocial" and even more dangerous than pure Gypsies.

The deportation of one group of Württemberg Gypsy Mischlinge children was postponed. Eva Justin, Ritter's assistant, was conducting anthropological research on the children for her doctoral thesis at the University of Berlin. At the time her thesis was published, in May 1944, 39 of the children—20 boys and 19 girls—arrived in Auschwitz. Only four of them escaped death in the gas chamber.

The policy toward German-Jewish Mischlinge remained an unsettled dispute between the ministerial bureaucracy, the party, and SS hard-liners until the end of the Nazi regime. The process of persecution was characterized by ideological consistency combined with tactical opportunism on the side of the party. The bureaucratic desk officers pursued a more pragmatic or rational policy, although not because of ethical objections to the Final Solution.

Between 1933 and 1935 the Jewish Mischlinge were, with few exceptions, subject to the same discrimination as full Jews in their working and private lives. They were excluded from party organizations and could not inherit a farm. They were admitted to military service but only in the lowest ranks. They were allowed membership in the German Labor Front (Deutsche Arbeitsfront) and Welfare League (Nationalsozialistische Volkswohlfahrt) but not entitled to any benefits. Mischlinge constituted a sizable potential labor force, yet party officials tended to avoid any concessions that might invite claims for further exemptions and jeopardize their final aim of equating Mischlinge with Jews. Only in education were Mischlinge treated as Aryans until 1942, provided the parents' marriage had been contracted before the Law against the Overcrowding of German Schools and Colleges was declared, in April 1933. In practice the treatment of Jewish Mischlinge varied and was often arbitrary. Many Mischlinge felt that they suffered more than the Jews, who could rely on a supportive community, whereas the Mischlinge were excluded from the society (Christian and German) with which they identified. As a reaction to this situation, a group of some thousand so-called Christian non-Aryans organized an association in July 1933, which, following several changes of name, became known as the Paulus-Bund. It existed until 1939 primarily as a body representing the interests of members to the authorities and to provide mutual aid and social services. This conservative association was not, however, truly representative of the Jewish Mischlinge, of whom the overwhelming majority remained unorganized and exposed to growing social isolation.

After the Nuremberg Laws the legal situation of the Mischlinge changed for the better in some aspects of daily life, but most of the possible exceptions from anti-Jewish regulations could be obtained only by petitioning, which met with varying success. For example, exemptions from the marriage restrictions were almost never granted. Although Mischlinge were not supposed to be economically disadvantaged, so that they should not become a burden on the state, they did face growing job discrimination. Exemption from adopting a Jewish name and from wearing the yellow star (which also applied to their Jewish parent) were the most important dispensations. Moreover, extramarital relations between Mischlinge of the first degree and Germans were not officially banned until 1941.

With the beginning of the war the situation of all Mischlinge rapidly deteriorated. Many volunteered for military service in the hope of improving their status by being equated with Aryans on the basis of the Reich Citizenship Law or by obtaining privileges for their Jewish parent. Hitler's attitude toward Mischlinge was unreliable and dictated by his moods. For example, he believed that on Mendelian principles, even after generations of interbreeding, pure Jews would appear (*herausmendeln*). As a result of the great number of requests for equalization, which had been granted in some hundred cases, on 8 April 1940 he suddenly determined that Mischlinge of the first degree and those married to Jews and half-Jews should be excluded from the army. Because of the campaign in the West, however, this decision did not take effect until May 1942.

From summer 1941 onward, with the beginning of the mass extermination of Jews in the Soviet Union, Mischlinge were in danger of losing their privileged status. The party chancellery and SD officials pressed for a revision of the Nuremberg regulations. Dissatisfied with the current definition of a Jew, the SS had given instructions to include Mischlinge, partners in mixed marriages, and Jewish elderly and war veterans in the Polish deportation and ghettoization programs. In August 1941 a new, extremely vague definition of a Jew was issued by the Reich Main Security Office (Reichssicherheitshauptamt) as a guideline for the occupied territories of the Soviet Union. The Min-

istry for the Four Year Plan also supported different regulations for the eastern territories, arguing that lack of documents would not allow clear racial classification and that there was no reason to save Jewish Mischlinge who were partly descendants of "inferior aliens" (*Fremdvölkische*).

At the same time, a new definition (intended for the Netherlands) of half-Jews as Jews was discussed. Plans to include Jewish Mischlinge and Jewish partners in mixed marriages in the Final Solution, as presented by Reinhard Heydrich at the Wannsee Conference of 20 January 1942, met with opposition. Instead, Wilhelm Stuckart from the Ministry of the Interior proposed the sterilization of German-Jewish Mischlinge of the first degree. Sterilization was discussed at two later conferences, in March and October 1942, but no action was taken. Nevertheless, the fate of one group of children, Jewish Mischlinge of the first degree maintained in welfare homes as wards of the state, bears witness to the undiminished intention to solve the so-called Mischlinge question. Between the spring of 1943 and the summer of 1944, the Ministry of the Interior transferred 42 Jewish Mischling children from various German and Austrian regions to the Hadamar State Hospital, a notorious "euthanasia" center, where 39 of them were murdered.

On 20 February 1944 a Führer decree directed that henceforth the Nazi party chancellery was to be involved in all Mischlinge affairs to guarantee uniformity of action. In October 1944 all male Mischlinge of the first degree were sent to the labor camps of Organisation Todt. In November 1944 a directive ordered the removal from the civil service of all remaining Mischlinge and persons related to Jews by marriage. The justification given was that following the attempted assassination of Hitler on 20 July 1944, no trust could be put in any civil servant whose blood and heritage clashed with the Nazi worldview.

Deportations are reported of Mischlinge of the first degree and those of illegitimate birth from Greece and Hungary, as well as of some Christian-Jewish partners and Mischlinge children from Italy under German rule. Italian Fascists, however, never recognized the category of Mischlinge; a person was either a Jew or an "Italian Aryan." In Holland the registration of all Mischlinge with Jewish or mixed blood (from Dutch colonies) was under way. Exemption from deportation was proposed for those in mixed marriages if the Jewish partner consented to sterilization; a few such cases occurred before protests by the churches halted the practice. And in February 1945 Jewish partners of existent mixed marriages were deported from some German regions to Theresienstadt despite the approaching end of the war.

Allied victory saved the majority of German Jewish Mischlinge and Jews in mixed marriages, but it was a narrow escape. For the German bureaucracy Mischlinge posed a problem because of their social and legal integration into German middle-class society. For pragmatic reasons the regime was unwilling to provoke thousands of Aryan Germans related to Jews and even retreated. One such event occurred in Berlin when, during the so-called factory operation of February 1943 the Gestapo arrested Jewish spouses for deportation to Auschwitz. Their non-Jewish wives, husbands, children, and relatives—some of them in army uniform—protested openly in the Rosenstrasse in front of Joseph Goebbels's office window. The Gestapo finally released their relatives.

The hierarchy imposed on different groups of Mischlinge followed the inner logic of Nazi racial ideology, with Jewish Mischlinge ranking above part-Gypsies and the Rhineland Bastards. Gypsy and colored Mischlinge, as well as the part-Jewish children murdered in Hadamar, were sufficiently socially isolated and helpless to require no special consideration. Had the Nazis won the war, the Mischlinge would have shared the fate of the Jews.   *Annegret Ehmann*

Morocco See NORTH AFRICA

Mueller, Heinrich (1900–1945?) Bavarian police officer, appointed to the SD (security police) in 1936 and named chief of the Gestapo in September 1939. Mueller's rise to power was spurred by his brutal suppression of the 1934 Röhm Putsch. A top aid to Reinhard Heydrich, he was instrumental in the Nazi reign of terror and in the implementation of the Final Solution. He caught and ruthlessly punished those involved in the 1944 plot against the dictator. Mueller disappeared in Berlin during the last weeks of the war.

Mussolini, Benito (1883–1945) Italian Fascist leader and prime minister (1922–43) who assumed dictatorial powers. Executed by partisans. See ITALY

N

Nazi Policy The anti-Jewish policies of the Nazi regime from Hitler's accession to power on 30 January 1933 to the beginning of World War II on 1 September 1939 evolved in two distinct phases. The first phase (1933–36) corresponded to the political and economic stabilization of the new regime; the second (1936–39) was influenced by the regime's internal radicalization and by its aggressive steps on the international scene. During each of these phases the policies directed against the Jews were determined both by the internal dynamics of a movement that had set antisemitism at the core of its ideological program and by the circumstances deriving from a changing political context. Moreover, whereas later Hitler granted a large measure of autonomy to his acolytes in the concrete implementation of the extermination of European Jewry, during the prewar years his intervention regarding the anti-Jewish measures was constant and relentless. Throughout, it was decisive.

Phase One: 1933–36

When Hitler came to power, the Nazis had no overall plan regarding the measures to be taken against the approximately 525,000 Jews living in Germany (less than 0.9 percent of the population). Yet notwithstanding the absence of any master plan, the steps decided upon during the years 1933–36 aimed at a series of concrete goals: the exclusion of the Jews from German public life, the gradual severance of their professional and social ties with surrounding society, the annulment of their political rights, their biological segregation from "Aryan" Germans, and—although not an overriding goal at this stage—their emigration from the Reich. These aims corresponded in essence to the anti-Jewish tenets included in the Nazi party (NSDAP) program of 24 February 1920, and they tallied with some of the more extreme anti-Jewish demands of the German

conservatives, at least as defined in the 1892 Tivoli program of the Conservative party.

The pace of these anti-Jewish policies was determined by the interaction of contrary elements. The "party radicals" agitated for an accelerated and uncompromising implementation of anti-Jewish measures, whereas the conservative allies of the NSDAP preached caution in order to avoid disturbances, protect the still difficult economic recovery of the Reich, and avoid hostile foreign reactions, particularly in the economic domain. During this first phase the de facto compromise decided on by Hitler and bolstered by the conservative Hjalmar Schacht's appointment as minister of the economy in July 1934 led to the stepwise political exclusion and social, then biological segregation of the Jews, while the economic basis of Jewish life in Germany was, in principle at least, partly preserved.

Sporadic anti-Jewish violence spread throughout the Reich after Hitler's accession to the chancellorship and mainly after the elections of 5 March 1933, which resulted in the victory of the coalition of Nazis and German Nationals. Foreign protests grew. They in turn became the pretext for an anti-Jewish economic boycott. But the boycott of 1 April itself illustrates the contrary trends that influenced these early decisions. It was demanded by party extremists led by Joseph Goebbels, the new propaganda chief and gauleiter of Berlin, and by the gauleiter of Franconia, Julius Streicher, the editor of the party's most rabidly antisemitic paper, *Der Stürmer.* This economic onslaught against the Jews could have been particularly harmful in a situation of deep crisis, with millions of unemployed. The compromise decided on by Hitler was indicative of his tactical pragmatism: the boycott was not called off, despite the readiness of the British and the American governments to make official declarations condemning the anti-Nazi demonstrations in their

An SA man stands guard outside a Jewish shop during the boycott of 1 April 1933.

countries; yet it was limited to one day only, and all threats to resume it within a short time were mainly face-saving devices.

The population did not show any enthusiasm. In a number of places German customers insisted on buying in Jewish shops, disregarding the massive propaganda campaign and ubiquitous SA (storm trooper) pickets in front of Jewish stores. Over the following years sporadic boycotting of Jewish businesses flared up in various regions of Germany as a result of incitement by party extremists. Boycotting and ongoing aryanization (the acquisition of Jewish businesses by Germans, usually at considerably reduced prices) kept pressure on Jewish economic activity in the Reich and led to its reduction. But it was only at the beginning of 1938 that the direct and massive assault against the economic basis of Jewish life in Germany started.

The boycott of 1 April 1933 had been preceded by measures aimed at stopping the immigration of Jews from Eastern Europe into Germany, to cancel their recent naturalizations, and eventually to facilitate their expulsion from the country. A few days after the boycott the first laws aiming at the exclusion of German Jews from the nation's public life were passed by the Reich government. (Following the Enabling Act of 24 March the government remained the only legislative and executive body; soon it too would cease to function regularly, and Hitler would be the sole authority to approve any new legislation.) The first and most important of these laws, the Law for the Restoration of the Professional Civil Service, was passed on 7 April 1933. In general terms, it aimed at excluding potentially hostile elements from service to the state. Paragraph 3 of the law prohibited Jews from entering the civil service unless they were World War I front-line veterans, had lost a father or a son during the war, or had already been in the civil service on 1 August 1914. These exemptions were a sop to the conservatives—mainly for President Paul von Hindenburg, who had demanded them from Hitler. The major importance of the civil service law was that its first supplementary decree of 11 April introduced a definition of who was a Jew (defined as "non-Aryan" in the decree). According to the decree a non-Aryan was "anyone descended from non-Aryan, particularly Jewish, parents or grandparents. It suffices if one parent or grandparent is non-Aryan." This definition was applied until the formulation of a final definition in the first supplementary decree to the Nuremberg racial laws of 1935.

Also on 7 April 1933 the Reich government decreed the disbarring of Jewish lawyers; two weeks later, on 22 April, it called for the exclusion of Jewish physicians from National Health Insurance Institutions. Yet the application of the exemptions from the civil service law to lawyers and the restrictive application of the decree regarding physicians ensured that in June 1933 Jews still made up more than 16 percent of all practicing lawyers in Germany and 11 percent of all practicing physicians. Once again, although the Nazi lawyers' and physicians' associations had demanded a radical application of the decrees, Hitler chose a compromise path, as he was well aware that a massive expulsion of Jews from these two professions meant the severance of their ties with tens of thousands of "Aryan" clients and patients as well as potential discontent among significant sectors of the population.

Jewish newspapers sold in Berlin. June 1935

On 25 April the law against the overcrowding of German schools and universities limited the registration of new Jewish pupils and students to 1.5 percent of the total number of registrations in any institution; as for their overall number, it was not to exceed 5 percent of the German pupils or students. In October 1933 Jews were excluded from journalism (except in the Jewish press); at the end of September they had been forbidden to own farms.

Beyond the practical consequences of the 1933 laws on the fate of thousands of Jews in Germany, they were a historical turning point: in a major European country the dismantling of Jewish emancipation had started. The process thus initiated was open-ended, its ultimate results unforeseeable. In any event, the message of these early anti-Jewish laws was well understood in the Nazi party and beyond. Within weeks, many local anti-Jewish measures, usually decided on by the new Nazi appointees to local government positions or by the heads of any number of institutions or associations, excluded Jews from the most diverse social frameworks and impinged on their daily life. No dissent was expressed by the traditional elites, neither the churches nor the academic world, nor for that matter by anyone else.

Compared to 1933, the year that followed was a year of apparent crisis. The first wave of Nazi "revolutionary" ardor had spent itself. Internal party tensions led to the liquidation of the SA leadership and simultaneously of prominent members of the conservative elite on 30 June 1934. This action was followed within weeks of President Hindenburg's death and Hitler's immediate self-appointment as Führer in addition to his position as Reich chancellor: he had become the unique source of authority and of legitimacy. Such momentous events deflected the attention from other internal issues. Moreover, the economy had not improved significantly, and the international scene appeared threatening following the failed Nazi putsch in Austria and the assassination of the Austrian chancellor, Engelbert Dollfuss. Notwithstanding the absence of major new anti-Jewish initiatives, however, local segregation went on. Public places were increasingly out of bounds for Jews, and signs forbidding Jews access to small towns and villages or to Aryan stores and public facilities (particularly bathhouses and swimming pools) sprouted all over the Reich. Some local initiatives preempted major steps yet to be taken by state agencies. Thus courts and registrars increasingly refused to sanction marriages between Jews and Aryans. This in turn led Wilhelm Frick, the interior minister, to announce on 26 July 1935 that mixed marriages would not be sanctioned any more and that new marriage laws were being prepared.

In early 1935 the situation took a marked turn for the worse. On 21 May, after general conscription had been reestablished and the new Wehrmacht replaced the small professional Reichswehr, military service was forbidden to Jews. A new wave of anti-Jewish incitement and violence spread throughout the Reich. Fanned by Goebbels's press, the anti-Jewish disturbances were mainly the work of disgruntled party members who had not benefited from the spoils expected from the change of regime and were often hard hit by the slow pace of economic recovery. Major anti-Jewish outbreaks took place in Munich in May and in Berlin (particularly on the Kurfürstendamm) in July. Repeated orders from the deputy Führer's office forbidding any unauthorized anti-Jewish initiatives did not suffice to calm the situation.

Such uncontrolled violence was unacceptable to the party leadership and to its conservative allies. In July 1935 Hitler concurred with Schacht about the negative impact of further anti-Jewish disturbances on the international economic situation of Germany. A few weeks later, on 20 August, the detrimental effect of the anti-Jewish initiatives on internal stability and economic recovery was stressed and agreed upon at a high-ranking meeting convened by the minister of the economy. Although one of the participants, Gauleiter and Interior Minister of Bavaria Adolf Wagner, stated that there were differences of opinion on the Jewish issue between the party and the state, he also agreed that the ongoing anti-Jewish incidents could not be further tolerated. Interior Minister Frick, Justice Minister Gürtner, and obviously Schacht himself all stressed the imperative need to restore order in all that pertained to anti-Jewish measures. Reinhard Heydrich, at the time chief of the Gestapa (the central office of the Gestapo) and the SD (the security service of the SS) underscored the need for further legislation that would set the Jews under alien status and lead to their biological segregation. Heydrich also mentioned accelerated emigration, but it was not yet stressed as a primary goal.

The annual party congress, the Reich Party Congress of Freedom, convened in Nuremberg on 11 September 1935. On 15 September, the last day of the con-

A class of schoolgirls and their teachers give the Nazi salute at a rally in Coburg, Germany. A column of Reich Labor Service men stands in the background. 1934

gress, Hitler proclaimed three new laws in his closing speech: the Flag Law, according to which the swastika flag became the national flag, and two laws that redefined the status of Jews in Germany, the Reich Citizenship Law and the Law for the Protection of German Blood and Honor.

Were the Nuremberg Laws the outcome of an unplanned initiative taken by Hitler during the congress itself, or were they systematically prepared? The sudden summoning to Nuremberg of the two main Interior Ministry specialists on Jewish matters, Bernhard Lösener and Albert Medicus, on 13 September and the seemingly improvised aspect of Hitler's demand that a racial segregation law and a citizenship law applicable to the Jews of Germany be prepared within two days is puzzling at first. We know, however, that both laws had been discussed at various levels of the party and the state administration, at least since the end of 1933.

Thus Hitler's initiative appears rather as one more surprise move aimed at overcoming the potential doubts and hesitations of the conservative allies and the legalistic objections of the state bureaucracy.

The laws were proclaimed in the presence of the Reichstag, which was specially convened at Nuremberg. The entire congress, in particular Hitler's speeches and the three laws, was meant as an homage to the party and as a clear message that the role of the party, the carrier of the anti-Jewish ideological orthodoxy, was as important as ever. In the atmosphere of resentment that pervaded the lower party ranks in 1935, and in the face of the sporadic anti-Jewish violence that it engendered, the Nuremberg Laws and the solemn salute to the party not only represented a further implementation of the ideological anti-Jewish program of the NSDAP but also fulfilled a clear internal political function.

During the days and weeks following Nuremberg, an intense debate about the scope of the laws, mainly in regard to definition of the mixed breeds (*Mischlinge*), developed between party radicals—such as the leader of the Reich Association of Physicians, Gerhard Wagner, the head of the party's Racial Policy Office, Walter Gross, and the kinship research specialist of the Interior Ministry, Artur Gütt—and Interior Ministry specialists such as State Secretary Wilhelm Stuckart and the Jewish affairs expert Bernhard Lösener. Hitler's opinion was sought several times by both sides.

Early in the debate it was agreed that three-quarter Jews (persons with three Jewish grandparents) were to be considered Jews, and that one-quarter Jews (persons with one Jewish grandparent) were Mischlinge. The confrontation focused on the status of the half-Jews (two Jewish grandparents). Whereas the party wanted to include the half-Jews in the category of Jews, or at least have a public agency decide who among them was a Jew and who a Mischling, the ministry insisted on integrating them into the Mischling category (together with the one-quarter Jews). The final decision, made by Hitler, was much closer to the demands of the ministry than to those of the party. Half-Jews were Mischlinge; only as a result of their personal choice (not as the result of the decision of a public agency), either by marrying a Jew or by joining the Jewish religious community, did they become Jews.

The supplementary decrees were finally published on 14 November. The first supplementary decree to the Reich Citizenship Law defined as Jewish all persons who had at least three full Jewish grandparents, or who had two Jewish grandparents and were married to a Jewish spouse or belonged to the Jewish religion at the time of the law's publication, or who entered into such commitments at a later date. From 14 November on, the civic rights of Jews were canceled and their voting rights abolished; Jewish civil servants who had kept their positions owing to their status as veterans were forced into retirement. On 21 December a second supplementary decree ordered the dismissal of Jewish professors, teachers, physicians, lawyers, and notaries who were state employees and had been granted exemptions.

The various categories of forbidden marriages were spelled out in the first supplementary decree to the Law for the Protection of German Blood and Honor: between a Jew and a Mischling with one Jewish grandparent; between two Mischlinge, each with one Jewish grandparent; and between a Mischling with two Jewish grandparents and a German (the last of these might be waived by a special exemption from the minister of the interior or the deputy Führer). Mischlinge of the first degree (two Jewish grandparents) could marry Jews and thereby become Jews—or marry one another, on the assumption that such couples usually chose to remain childless, as indicated by the empirical material collected by Hans F. K. Günther, professor of racial anthropology at the University of Jena. Finally, female citizens of German blood employed in a Jewish household at the time of the law's publication could continue their work only if they had turned 45 years of age by 31 December 1935.

The great majority of the German population seems to have acquiesced to the early anti-Jewish exclusion measures, to growing social segregation, and to the disenfranchisement and biological segregation imposed by the Nuremberg racial legislation. Whereas party activists called for further steps, the ordinary German appears to have accepted the fact that henceforth the Jews in Germany would become a distinct, alien, and separated minority with a measure of autonomy. Many Jews also perceived their own situation in the same way. Economic interests, moreover, maintained links between Germans and Jews, mainly in rural areas, where the Jews continued to play a major role in, for example, the cattle trade. In many cities the population and even party members (some of them in uniform) continued to patronize Jewish stores. Thus, at the end of the first phase, the segregation of the Jews from German society had been implemented, but continuing economic relations between Germans and Jews introduced sufficient ambiguity into the situation to convince part of the Jewish community at least that the storm would be weathered.

Shortly after the Nuremberg Congress on 25 September 1935, in a meeting with Walter Gross, Hitler defined the goals that now lay ahead: further exclusion of the Jews from the economy (yet without turning them into a public burden), accelerated Jewish emigration from Germany, and the integration of the Mischlinge into the German population. However, in the case of a war on two fronts (as in 1914–18) Hitler ominously declared that, regarding the Jews, he would be ready "for all the consequences."

Phase Two: 1936–39

When the Wehrmacht marched into the Rhineland on 7 March 1936, a new phase of European history began.

This flagrant breach of the Versailles and Locarno treaties was followed by the Anschluss (annexation) of Austria in March 1938, by the crisis over the Sudetenland, and in October 1938, after the Munich agreement, by the German occupation of the Sudeten area of Czechoslovakia. In March 1939 the Germans marched into Bohemia and Moravia; Czechoslovakia disappeared from the map. Hitler's next goal was Poland, and his attack unleashed World War II.

In France the 1936 elections brought the center-left Popular Front to power, and for a large segment of French society the threat of revolution and a Communist takeover became an obsessive nightmare. A few months earlier the Spanish electorate had brought a left-wing government to power, but its victory was short-lived. In July 1936 units of the Spanish army in North Africa, led by Gen. Francisco Franco, rebelled against the new Republican government and crossed over to Spain. The Spanish civil war—which was to become a murderous struggle of two political mystiques, backed on both sides by a massive supply of foreign weapons and regular troops as well as volunteers—had started. Between the summer of 1936 and the spring of 1939, the battle lines drawn in Spain were the points of reference for current ideological confrontations.

The year 1936 also clearly marks the beginning of a new phase on the internal German scene. During the first years of Nazi rule, the need to stabilize the regime, to ward off preemptive foreign initiatives, and to sustain economic growth and the return to full employment had demanded relative moderation in some domains. By 1936, full employment had been achieved and the weakness of the anti-German front sized up. Further political radicalization and the mobilization of internal resources were now possible. Himmler was named chief of all German police forces, and Hermann Göring was made overlord of a new four-year economic plan, whose secret objective was to prepare the country for war. The impetus for and the timing of both external and internal radicalization may also have been linked to unresolved tensions within German society itself or may have resulted from the fundamental needs of a regime that could only thrive on ever more hectic action and spectacular success.

It was in this atmosphere of global ideological confrontation and accelerated mobilization that the Jewish issue took on a new dimension. Now Jewry was again being presented as a worldwide threat, and anti-Jewish action could be used as justification for the ineluctable confrontation. In the regime's terms, in a time of crisis the Jews had to be expelled and their assets impounded for the benefit of German rearmament; and so long as some of the Jews remained in German hands, their fate could be used to influence the attitude toward Nazi Germany of world Jewry and of the foreign powers under its control. Most immediately, three main lines of action dominated the new phase of the anti-Jewish drive: accelerated aryanization, increasingly coordinated efforts to compel the Jews to leave Germany, and furious propaganda activity to project on a world scale the theme of Jewish conspiracy and threat.

Accelerated aryanization resulted in part from the new economic situation and from increasing confidence in German business and industrial circles that the risks of Jewish retaliation no longer had to be taken into account. Economic growth thus put an end to the contradictory measures that had earlier hindered the courses of anti-Jewish policy: by 1936 ideology and policy could progress along a single track. The appointment of Himmler and Göring to their new positions created two power bases essential for the effective implementation of the new anti-Jewish drive. And yet, although the framework of the new phase was clearly perceptible, the economic expropriation of the Jews of Germany could not be radically enforced before the beginning of 1938, after the conservative ministers had been expelled from the government in February 1938: most action, too, took place after Schacht had been compelled to leave the Ministry of the Economy in late 1937. During 1938 worse was to follow: economic harassment and even violence would henceforth be used to force the Jews to flee the Reich and the newly annexed Austria. Within the second phase, the year 1938 was a fateful divide.

The party congresses of September 1936 and especially September 1937 stood under the sign of the new anti-Jewish ideological fury. In his closing speech to the 1937 congress, Hitler abandoned all restraint. Never since the fall of the ancient world, he declared, never since the rise of Christianity, the spread of Islam, and the Reformation had the world been in such turmoil. This was no ordinary war but a fight for the very essence of human culture and civilization. "What the others profess not to see, because they simply do not want to see it, is something we must unfortunately state as a bitter truth: the world is presently in the midst of an increasing upheaval, whose spiritual and

Nazi officials and police question a busload of arrested Jews in Berlin. 11 April 1933

factual preparation and whose leadership undoubtedly proceed from the rulers of Jewish Bolshevism in Moscow. When I quite intentionally present this problem as Jewish, then you, my party comrades, know that this is not an unverified assumption, but a fact proven by irrefutable evidence." Identical themes were endlessly repeated at all levels of the system.

During the first half of 1936 any concrete anti-Jewish moves were avoided because of the preparation and staging of the Olympic Games in Berlin. Even the assassination on 6 February of the Nazi party representative in Switzerland, Wilhelm Gustloff, by the Jewish medical student David Frankfurter did not trigger any immediate retribution. Nazi officials, however, were not idle.

On 29 September 1936 Secretary Stuckart convened a conference of high officials from his own Interior Ministry, the Ministry of the Economy, and the Office of the Deputy Führer in order to prepare recommen-

dations for a meeting of ministers concerning further steps to be taken in regard to the Jews. The Office of the Deputy Führer represented the party line, the Ministry of the Interior (though headed by the Nazi Wilhelm Frick) often advocated middle-of-the-road positions between the party and the conservative state bureaucracy, and the Ministry of the Economy (still headed by Schacht) was decidedly conservative. It is remarkable, therefore, that at this conference the highest officials of the three agencies were entirely in agreement.

All those present recognized that the fundamental aim was now the "complete emigration" of the Jews and that all other measures had to be taken with such an end in view. After restating this position, Stuckart added a sentence that was soon to find its dramatic implementation: "Ultimately one would have to consider carrying out compulsory emigration."

The September 1936 conference was the first high-level meeting devoted to the regime's future anti-Jewish measures in which the priority of total emigration—if need be, expulsion—was clearly formulated. Before the passage of the Nuremberg Laws segregation had been the main goal, and it was only in September 1935 that Hitler, in his declaration to Walter Gross, mentioned "more vigorous emigration" of the Jews from Germany as one of his new objectives. Thus, sometime at the end of 1935 or in 1936, Hitler's tentative formulations became a firm guideline for all related state and party agencies.

Throughout 1937, preparations were made for a complete halt to the activities of Jewish physicians and lawyers. Meanwhile, further pressure and harassment made Jewish everyday life in Germany increasingly difficult. Yet only after most conservative ministers were compelled to leave the government, at the beginning of 1938, did Nazi policies in general and anti-Jewish measures in particular take a sharp turn for the worse. The radicalization of the anti-Jewish drive in 1938 found its main expression in the measures taken in the newly annexed Austria, in the destruction of all Jewish economic activity in the Greater Reich, in the forcible expulsion of Jews, and in the pogrom of November 1938.

The Anschluss was the result of a chain of unexpected circumstances that played into Hitler's hands. It was followed by an outburst of violence against the Jews of Austria, particularly those of Vienna, as yet unequaled in the Altreich (Germany within the pre-Anschluss borders). The pogrom-like atmosphere, the theft of Jewish property, and the public degradation and even murder of Jews took place on such a scale that on 17 March Heydrich had to threaten punitive action against the perpetrators. Nevertheless, it took several weeks for the anti-Jewish rampage to cease. During that time, systematic state-organized expropriation started. In Austria, now renamed Ostmark, the forced aryanization of Jewish businesses, mainly organized under the direction of Göring's Four Year Plan administration, was by far more rapid than in the Altreich, and within approximately 18 months of the annexation practically all Jewish economic activity in Austria had been either dismantled or taken over by German owners under the supervision of party and state authorities.

The second major characteristic of Nazi anti-Jewish action in Austria, its hallmark in many ways, was the organization of Jewish forced emigration by the SD office in Vienna under the direct command of Adolf Eichmann. The Central Agency for Jewish Emigration applied a conveyor-belt system, whereby the entire administrative and financial aspects of the emigration were centralized and standardized. The method was efficient: between the Anschluss and the beginning of the war more than half the Jews of Austria were forced to leave their country and to abandon almost all their property. Among the 100,000 Jews who left, by November some 5,000 (both from former Austria and from the Altreich) had been pushed into neighboring countries. At the end of October, in response to new Polish legislation aimed at preventing the return of Polish Jews who lived outside the country, and also to preempt a move by Poland to close its border to Jews, the Germans rounded up thousands of Polish Jewish families living in the Reich—some of whom had resided there for decades or more—and expelled them by force into Poland near the town of Zbaszyn. The plight of these Polish Jews incited the 17-year-old Herschel Grynzpan, then living in Paris, to buy a gun, go to the German embassy, and fatally shoot the first secretary, Ernst vom Rath.

In the meantime the full-scale economic campaign against the Jews of Germany had begun. Between 1933 and early 1938 Jewish assets in Germany had already been reduced from 12 billion Reichsmarks (RM) to approximately 6 billion RM, notwithstanding the measure of freedom still left to Jewish economic activity until the beginning of 1938. The numbers show that growing aryanization was already taking a heavy toll before 1938. On 26 April 1938 all Jews were ordered to register their property. On 14 June the problem that had defeated the boycott committee on 1 April 1933 was solved. According to the third supplementary decree to the Reich Citizenship Law, a business was Jewish if the proprietor was a Jew, if a partner was a Jew, or if, on 1 January 1938, a member of the board of directors was a Jew. Also considered Jewish was a business in which Jews owned more than a quarter of the shares or more than half the votes, or which was under predominantly Jewish influence. A branch of a Jewish business was considered Jewish if the manager of the branch was a Jew. A law issued on 6 July 1938 established a detailed list of commercial services henceforth forbidden to Jews, including credit information and real estate brokerage.

On 25 July the fourth supplementary decree to the Reich Citizenship Law put an end to Jewish medical practice in Germany. The licenses of Jewish physicians were withdrawn as of 30 September 1938. Those physicians who were authorized to provide medical services to Jewish patients were no longer allowed to call themselves physicians but only "carers for the sick." On 27 September 1938, the eve of the Munich conference, Hitler signed the fifth supplementary decree, forbidding Jews to practice law. The decree was not immediately made public because of the international tension, but on 13 October Hitler decided that the announcement should be made the following day. The decree was to take effect in the Altreich on 30 November and in the former Austria (with a partial and temporary exception in Vienna) on 31 December. The final blow that destroyed all Jewish economic life in Germany came on 12 November, when, just after the Kristallnacht pogrom, Göring issued a ban on all Jewish business activity in the Reich.

More than any major anti-Jewish event of the 1930s, the pogrom of 9–10 November 1938 was both planned and improvised. The improvisation derived from Grynzpan's unforeseeable attack on Rath and the diplomat's death on the afternoon of 9 November. But major violence against the Jews of Germany had been contemplated by the Nazis throughout the first months of 1938, and new disturbances had been fanned in Berlin, under Goebbels's orders, in June of that year. Reports about the probability of further violence reached foreign diplomats in Germany and Jewish leaders in Palestine.

On 7–8 November sporadic assaults on Jewish property and synagogues took place in some parts of the Reich, and on 8 November the Nazi press published threatening articles. According to Goebbels's diaries, on the evening of 9 November, after Rath's death had been officially announced to Hitler during the annual "Alte Kämpfer" (Old Fighters) dinner in Munich, Hitler told the propaganda minister what the next steps should be. He gave further instructions to Goebbels on the following day, but throughout he appeared personally uninvolved in the events. The violence was presented as a spontaneous outbreak of "popular anger."

After the pogrom of November 1938 the Nazis were confronted even more starkly than before by the dilemma that their own policies had created. Their main goal was the accelerated emigration or expulsion of all Jews from the Reich and the territories under its control, but the economic expropriation of the Jews, resulting in their drastic impoverishment, presented a major obstacle to emigration and made them a growing public burden. The German policies that developed during the last months before the war followed three related tracks:

1. Acceleration of Jewish emigration by the creation on 24 January 1939 of a Central Office for Jewish Emigration in Berlin under Heydrich's authority and the direct command of the Gestapo chief, Heinrich Müller, then the establishment of another such office in Prague in July 1939, under Eichmann. At the same time, negotiations with representatives of the Intergovernmental Committee for Refugees (set up at the July 1938 Evian Conference on refugees) were in progress for the transfer of hundreds of thousands of Jews from the Reich, possibly to colonies in Africa or Latin America with the direct help of Western countries. The resettlement was to be financed by a loan raised by Jewish organizations and guaranteed by the Jewish assets still remaining in Germany. The negotiations, however, were fruitless.

2. Cancellation of any German welfare assistance to Jews and the shift of the rapidly growing burden onto Jewish welfare organizations. Once it became clear that Jewish welfare could not cope with the new situation, destitute, able-bodied Jews, some of them professionals barred from practice by the decrees, were recruited for compulsory labor at such jobs as picking crops and sweeping streets.

3. Concentration of Jews in "Jew-houses" (*Judenhäuser*), the curtailment of their movements by a whole array of decrees left to the inventiveness of local authorities, and the imposition of tighter control over Jewish public life by the replacement on 4 July 1939 of the Reichsvertretung der Juden in Deutschland by the Reichsvereinigung der Juden in Deutschland, a totally centralized organization directly supervised by the Gestapo.

In 1939, as in every year since 1933, the Reichstag was convened in festive session on 30 January to mark the anniversary of Hitler's accession to power. The first part of the Führer's speech dealt with the history of the Nazi movement and the development of the Reich. He then castigated some of the main British critics of appeasement, whom he accused of calling for a war against Germany. Alleging that "Jewish and non-Jewish instigators" stood behind British opponents of Munich, Hitler promised that when National Socialist propaganda went on the offensive, it would be as successful as it had been within Germany, where "we knocked down the Jewish world enemy . . . with the compelling strength of our propaganda."

After referring to the "capitalistic-motivated" American intervention against Germany during World War I, Hitler—probably infuriated by the American reactions to the November pogrom and other Nazi measures against the Jews—thundered that nobody would be able to influence Germany in its solution of the Jewish problem. He sarcastically stressed the pity expressed for the Jews of Germany by the democracies but also the refusal of those same countries to help by taking the Jews in. And he issued a warning: "I believe that this [Jewish] problem will be solved—and the sooner the better. Europe cannot find peace before the Jewish question is out of the way. . . . The world has enough space for settlement, but one must once and for all put an end to the idea that the Jewish people have been chosen by the good Lord to exploit a certain percentage of the body and the productive work of other nations. Jewry will have to adapt itself to productive work like any other nation or it will sooner or later succumb to a crisis of unimaginable dimensions."

Up to that point Hitler was merely rehashing an array of anti-Jewish themes that had become part of his repertory. Then, however, he moved on to new threats never yet heard in the public pronouncements of a head of state: "One thing I would like to express on this day, which is perhaps memorable not only for us Germans: in my life I have often been a prophet, and I have mostly been laughed at. At the time of my struggle for power, it was mostly the Jewish people who laughed at the prophecy that one day I would attain in Germany the leadership of the state and therewith of the entire nation, and that among other problems I would also solve the Jewish one. I think that the uproarious laughter of that time has in the meantime remained stuck in German Jewry's throat." Then came the explicit menace: "Today I want to be a prophet again: if international-finance Jewry inside and outside Europe again succeeds in precipitating the nations into a world war, the result will not be the bolshevization of the earth and with it the victory of Jewry, but the annihilation of the Jewish race in Europe."

On its face Hitler's speech seems to have had a twofold context. First, British opposition to the appeasement policy, and the strong American reactions to Kristallnacht, would have sufficed to explain the Führer's multiple references to Jewish-capitalist warmongering. Second, it is highly probable that in view

of his project of dismembering what remained of Czechoslovakia, and of the demands he was now making on Poland, Hitler was aware that the new international crisis might lead to war. (He had mentioned this possibility in a speech given a few weeks earlier, in Saarbrücken.) Thus these threats of extermination, accompanied by the argument that his past record proved that his prophecies were not to be slighted, may have been intended to weaken anti-Nazi reactions at a time when he was preparing for his most risky military-diplomatic gamble. More precisely, Hitler may have expected that these menaces would impress Jews in European and American public life, so that they would reduce their "warmongering propaganda."

It would be a mistake, however, to consider Hitler's speech of 30 January merely in its short-term tactical context. The wider vistas may have been part calculated pressure, part uncontrolled fury, but they also may well have reflected a process consistent with his other projects for the Jews, such as their transfer to some remote African territory. This was in fact tantamount to a search for radical solutions, a scanning of extreme possibilities. Perceived in such a framework, the prophecy about extermination becomes one possibility among others, neither more nor less real than others. There were no plans and there was no decision; there probably would not be any until the summer or fall of 1941. Yet the possibility of annihilation, in case of war, had been expressed. It was in the air.

Saul Friedländer

Nebe, Arthur (1894–1945) German police official who advanced rapidly under the Nazis. Head of the Kripo (criminal police). After the invasion of the Soviet Union, Nebe became commander of Einsatzgruppe B, which killed more than 40,000 Jews in Belorussia. He maintained contact with anti-Hitler plotters, was arrested after the failure of the July 1944 coup, and was executed by the Nazis during the last months of the war.

Netherlands In 1941 approximately 140,000 Jews (as defined by the Nuremberg racial laws) resided in the Netherlands. More than half (80,000) lived in Amsterdam; another 29,000 resided in the two other large cities of Holland, The Hague and Rotterdam; and the remainder were spread throughout the country. Most Dutch Jews were of Eastern European origin (Ashkenazi), except for a small Sephardic community of about 4,000 persons located primarily in Amsterdam.

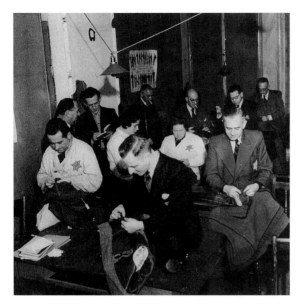

Jews employed in a sewing workshop established by the Jewish council on Oude Schansstraat in the Jewish quarter of Amsterdam. May 1942

In the 1930s, after the Nazi seizure of power, some 10,000 German Jews settled in the Netherlands. A relatively small number of them managed to emigrate overseas after the outbreak of war in 1939.

The Dutch Jewish population was characterized by rather extreme economic and social cleavages. Particularly in Amsterdam, many Jews were petty traders or vendors living on the edge of poverty. However, a Jewish middle class and a very wealthy bourgeoisie also had developed in the Netherlands. A deep economic and social division therefore existed within the Jewish community between wealthy Jews, who tended to provide the leadership in civic and religious associations, and the bulk of the Jewish proletariat, who mistrusted the Jewish bourgeoisie and favored the left of the political spectrum.

Dutch Jews had not developed strong religious allegiances in the early twentieth century. Only 12 percent of Jewish draftees asked for a military rabbi in 1939. The two existing religious congregations (Ashkenazi and Sephardic) were viewed by the majority of poorer Jews as being in league with the wealthy bourgeoisie. No prominent religious or civic leaders emerged during this period. Nor did Zionism make heavy inroads, in part because it too was viewed as a bourgeois movement; but even the socialist Zionist group Poale Zion

had only a few hundred members. In contrast to the working-class Jews of Belgium, who had immigrated more recently from Eastern Europe, poorer Dutch Jews had not retained a religious or proletarian sense of solidarity.

The Jews of the Netherlands at the start of the German occupation in May 1940 were a divided people, with pronounced social and economic distinctions, relatively weak ideological or religious bonds, and no strong leadership. These conditions and the lack of a common ethos made it difficult to develop attitudes of solidarity and common purpose in the face of persecution.

At the beginning of the occupation the Germans claimed that they did not plan any special measures against the Jews. In October 1940, however, a series of discriminatory decrees began to appear on orders from Berlin: first a prohibition of ritual slaughter; next the removal of Jewish government employees, including teachers and professors. Radio sets owned by Jews were confiscated, and Jews were excluded from recreational facilities, hotels, and restaurants. Most important, the Germans ordered all Jews to register with local Dutch authorities by January 1941. These files became the basis of future persecution and deportation. Hardly anyone at the time realized the crucial significance of this step.

The relative calm of the first occupation months was broken in February 1941 by the arrest and deportation to the Mauthausen concentration camp of a group of 389 young Jewish men in Amsterdam, in response to the alleged attack on German police by a Jewish self-defense group. In June the Germans arrested and sent to Mauthausen another group of approximately 300 young Jewish men in retribution for a bomb attack. In the fall of 1941 an additional convoy of 170 Jewish men from the provinces arrived in Mauthausen. Death notifications soon began to be received in Amsterdam in large numbers, and Mauthausen became known as a death camp in the Jewish community. Subsequently the German police used the threat of deportation to Mauthausen in the efforts to secure compliance.

In the midst of the February unrest in Amsterdam, the Germans established a Jewish council (*Joodsche Raad*) for Amsterdam headed by Abraham Asscher, a prominent Amsterdam businessman, and David Cohen, professor of ancient history at the Municipal University of Amsterdam. Cohen was destined to become

Employees of the Amsterdam Jewish council at work in the typing pool of the council offices at Nieuwe Keizersgracht 58. May 1942–43

the dominant spirit in the council. In Amsterdam, as elsewhere, the Jewish council was designed to implement German regulations and to take charge of all aspects of Jewish community life, such as educational and charitable organizations, excluding only religious congregations. As it turned out, it became a key instrument in the hands of the German police for the implementation of their designs.

The second stage of the destruction of Dutch Jewry was designed to isolate Jews completely and to ready them for deportation. In September 1941 the Zentralstelle für Jüdische Auswanderung (Central Agency for Jewish Emigration) established branches in Amsterdam and The Hague. In order to isolate the Jews further, Jewish students were excluded from regular schools, and Jews were ordered to resign from non-Jewish organizations. In April 1942, three months before the start of the deportations, Jews were required to wear the Star of David when in public.

In order to lay hands on Jewish property and assets, the Germans forced Jews to deposit their funds in blocked accounts in a designated bank under German control. The depositors were allowed to withdraw only small monthly allowances. Jews were also required to register and subsequently to dispose of their real property. In order to restrict the opportunities to earn a living even further, the Germans authorized employers

to discharge Jews at their discretion, and they prohibited Jews from engaging in certain professions. Unemployed (and later also employed) Jews were sent to labor camps, from which they could conveniently be seized for deportation later on. By June 1942 Jews living in Holland were isolated from the rest of the population, deprived of their livelihoods, and identified by special insignia. The Germans had prepared them for deportation.

The third stage of the persecution came with a letter from the Zentralstelle to the Jewish council dated 26 June stating that the Germans had decided to put Jews to work in the East "under police supervision" (*polizeilicher Arbeitseinsatz*). As a means to increase isolation and facilitate deportation, Jews were required to hand in their bicycles, and they were forbidden to use telephones or public transport. They had to remain at their registered residence from 8:00 p.m. to 6:00 a.m.

The first deportation train was scheduled for 14 July 1942. The German police, working from lists provided by the Dutch Population Records offices (Bevolkingsregisters), called up an initial group for removal, but only a fraction of those designated appeared, partly because of an especially threatening speech by a high German official, Commissioner General Fritz Schmidt, painting the fate of deported Jews in somber colors. In order to meet their quota, the German police therefore arrested approximately 750 persons in mass raids as hostages to ensure the compliance of the first group assigned to deportation. This strategy worked quite well at first, with more than 6,000 Jews in German hands by the end of July. In August, however, compliance dropped off again after another threatening peroration by Schmidt. In response the Germans enlisted the Jewish council in their effort to induce intended victims to report. They threatened deportation to Mauthausen for anyone who failed to comply with the summons, and they conducted raids in Amsterdam that netted thousands of persons.

Despite these threats, the turnout proved to be so unsatisfactory that the Germans had to give up their primary reliance on deportation notices delivered to prospective victims. Instead they staged a series of night raids in Amsterdam, starting in September, that captured between 300 and 500 persons each night.

Soon a routine became established for deportation from Amsterdam. First, intended deportees had to report to the office of the Zentralstelle or to the Holland-

A moving van owned by the Puls company, which collaborated with the German authorities in confiscating Jewish property. The sight of Puls vans became so common in the ghetto that a new term, *pulsen*, was coined to denote stealing. 1942–43

sche Schouwburg (Jewish Theater), which was designated as the Amsterdam collection center. (A courageous member of the Jewish council staff, Walter Süsskind, managed to smuggle approximately 1,000 infants and children out of the nursery in the Hollandsche Schouwburg.) Jews who reported "voluntarily" were able to take especially scheduled streetcars to their point of departure. The majority of Amsterdam Jews were sent to the transit camp Westerbork in the eastern part of the Netherlands. There families were housed together, and life was not totally intolerable, as the internal administration of the camp was in Jewish hands (mostly those of German Jews). Still, inmates lived in perpetual terror of publication of the list of people slated for the next train to the East.

Some Jews, particularly those living outside Amsterdam, were taken to the Vught concentration camp in southern Holland and deported to the East from there. Some persons, including those accused of an infraction of German regulations, were sent directly to the East.

In October 1942 the Germans shifted their attention from Amsterdam to the other big cities and the provinces. They also deported the Jews in work camps. These contained between 7,000 and 8,000 men who had complied with the summonses in the hope of avoiding deportation. In November previously exempted individuals who had worked in factories with German contracts were taken away with their families.

After a relatively short respite around Christmas, raids and call-ups were resumed in Amsterdam and elsewhere. Now the Germans made a special effort to deport institutionalized persons such as orphans, the aged, and the sick. In March and April 1943 the Germans again focused on Jews living outside Amsterdam.

In May 1943 the Germans decided to clean up. All Jews in Amsterdam who did not have valid exemptions were ordered to report. When only one-fourth of the persons called up complied, the Jewish council was ordered to nominate 7,000 of its exempted employees for deportation (or rather to name the employees it needed to retain). When that blackmail also turned out to be largely unsuccessful, the Germans conducted a large raid on 26 May; this yielded 3,000 Jews. On 20 June the German police seized another 5,700 people in raids in the eastern and southern districts of Amsterdam. The final blow came on 29 September, the Jewish New Year, when the German police managed to capture a total of 10,000 Jews, including the leaders of the Jewish council. This was the last of the mass raids on Jews under the occupation.

During the fourth stage of the persecution, from September 1943 to the end of the occupation, the German police continued to round up individual Jews whom they identified in the streets, in public places, or in private homes. Only Jews with special exemptions, primarily Jewish partners in mixed marriages, remained at large legally.

The German police employed a system of exemptions in order to divide the Jewish community and to obtain Jewish compliance and assistance with deportation. Temporary exemptions were granted, for example, to such categories as Protestant Jews, Jews in factories working for the Germans, diamond workers, and the staff of the Jewish council and their families. In order to secure the acquiescence and collaboration of the Dutch secretary general of the interior, K. J. Frederiks, the Germans allowed him to draw up a list of protected prominent Jews, who were at first interned in a castle in the east of the country but who eventually were deported to Theresienstadt. Most members of this group returned after the war. Other temporary exemptions included the Sephardic Jews, who claimed Mediterranean rather than Jewish descent. In the end this group, too, was deported to Auschwitz and exterminated.

It was also possible for individuals to claim that they had been listed as Jews in error and that they could prove at least partial Aryan ancestry. Such claims were examined by the office of H. G. Calmeyer, a German lawyer, who did his best to render favorable responses or to delay a decision in the face of the suspicious attitude of the German police. Individuals on the "Calmeyer list" were also given temporary exemption until a final disposition was made.

From the German point of view, these temporary exemptions were very useful. In the case of Jewish council staff, it meant that the police could count on the services, clerical and otherwise, of thousands of Jews trying to protect themselves and the lives of their families. In the case of other exempted groups and individuals, the exemption created the illusion of security, which in most cases kept the people concerned from trying as hard as they might have to escape or to go underground.

Paradoxically, the "normal" life of the Jewish population appeared to continue on through the years of isolation and deportation, from 1941 to September 1943. Under the auspices of the Jewish council, children attended schools even as their ranks thinned out after June 1942. Jewish cultural organizations presented concerts and plays, and there was a renewed interest in religious traditions. The pages of the *Joodsche Weekblad* (Jewish Weekly), published by the Jewish council, give the impression of an almost normal community life, except for announcements inserted on behalf of the German authorities or other, usually disguised instructions dealing with a reality of persecution that was in fact on everybody's mind.

The persecution of the Jews elicited a mixed response from the Dutch population and the government authorities. Some groups resisted: students at the University of Leiden and at the Technical University of Delft went on strike in November 1940 to protest the dismissal of Jewish faculty members. Some student associations dissolved themselves rather than exclude Jewish members, as required by the Germans.

In February 1941 shipbuilding workers and municipal employees struck in Amsterdam in reaction to the arrest of hundreds of young Jewish men. This was the most spectacular protest against persecution during the occupation, and the one occasion that primarily involved members of the working class.

The most consistent opposition to persecution of the Jews, however, came from the Dutch churches and from members of their congregations. In November 1940 the churches lodged a number of protests with the occupation authorities, beginning with a statement

Jewish performers onstage at the Eik en Linde café in the Plantage section of Amsterdam.

opposing the dismissal of Jewish government employees. In 1942 the Catholic church and most of the Protestant churches protested against the impending deportations, and the Catholic church had the letter read from the pulpit as a Sunday episcopal message in defiance of German instructions. As a punishment, the Germans deported racially Jewish Catholics. In 1943 the churches objected to the forced sterilization of Jewish partners in mixed marriages, and this time Reichskommissar Arthur Seyss-Inquart pulled back and ordered discontinuation of the sterilization program. In 1943 the Catholic church prohibited any participation in the persecution of the Jews.

From 1942 on, the churches, and particularly the Catholic church, took up special Sunday collections for assistance to the Jews and other victims of German persecution. The churches also encouraged their communicants to aid Jews whenever possible, and many Dutch people who helped the victims go underground or remain in hiding did so from religious motives. The underground press, particularly papers edited by Socialists and Communists, described and indicted the persecution and called for assistance to the Jews. But such articles did not appear very frequently, and on the whole the underground press did not pay a great deal of attention to the topic.

It is difficult to assess the attitudes and actions of the Dutch people at large. On the one hand, there was little or no sympathy (apart from among members of the Dutch Nazi movement) for the persecution of the Jews, but most Dutch people, preoccupied with the business of surviving in the midst of the occupation, paid little attention to what was going on. The general population, while viewing the German measures with distaste, saw them as one more inescapable aspect of the occupation regime. On the other hand, it is also true that thousands of Dutch people, acting from religious, political, and simply humanistic impulses, risked their freedom, their property, and their lives in attempts to assist their persecuted fellow human beings. It was easier to place Jewish children in families or institutions than it was to shelter adults.

Unfortunately, this determination to protect Jews was not shared by Dutch administrative officials, despite some ineffectual private protests lodged with the Germans. Instead the secretaries general, the highest administrative authorities left in the country after the departure of the government, chose a course of cooperation, instructing their subordinates to carry out German regulations. Therefore they implemented the dismissal of Jewish government employees in November 1940 and the registration of the Jewish population in January 1941, and they permitted the use of Dutch police in the rounding up of Jews, albeit in auxiliary functions. This willingness of the Dutch administration to assist in the implementation of German policies contributed significantly to the deplorable outcome.

In addition to government services, members of the Dutch Nazi party and of Dutch SS also performed auxiliary services. Dutch Nazis and collaborators figured largely among the denouncers of Jews in hiding. But in the end it was the collaboration of Dutch government agencies and the corresponding activities of the Jewish council that count most heavily in an explanation of the outcome.

Regrettably, the German drive to deport Jews living in Holland turned out to be extremely successful compared to German results in other occupied territories in the West. Of the approximately 140,000 people registered in 1940–41 as "full Jews" (*Volljuden*), approximately 12,000 were permanently exempted because they lived in mixed marriages. It has been estimated that approximately 2,000 managed to leave the occupied territory, while another 8,000, most of them children, managed to survive in hiding. Another 300 remained in Westerbork. All in all, the Germans deported approximately 107,000 Jews to the East, of whom only 5,450 returned after the war; thus they succeeded in killing almost 80 percent of the Jews in the Netherlands targeted for extermination. This was the highest percentage of Jews in any territory in the West, with the exception of the very small group of Norwegian Jews, and gives rise to the question of why the Germans were so successful in the Netherlands in their anti-Jewish campaign.

First, the geographical location of the Netherlands made escape from the occupied territory difficult. Escape to England via the North Sea was a virtual impossibility for most people. Escape to Spain or Switzerland meant crossing three or four borders guarded by German police and travel on trains or along roads where control of identity papers was common. A relatively small number of Jews managed to save themselves along these routes, but it was extremely difficult for families to escape in this manner.

Many other factors conspired to produce the disastrous outcome. Perhaps most important was the character of the German administration—the "Austrian Mafia," as it was called in some quarters. Apart from Norway, it was the only "civilian" administration in the West headed by a party functionary, Arthur Seyss-Inquart, an Austrian antisemite who fully supported the extermination policies planned in Berlin. The SS had a free hand in the Netherlands, with the appointment of a fanatical and energetic Higher SS and Police Leader, Hanns Albin Rauter, who was also a fierce antisemite. Despite Rauter's postwar denials, it is clear that he took a personal interest in Jewish affairs and that he inspired his subordinates in the Zentralstelle with appropriate zeal. By contrast, elsewhere in the West (except in Norway) the German police had to operate under the formal authority of military administrations, which did not assign the same priority to the persecution of the Jews as party and SS agencies did.

Second, the German police displayed considerable skill in manipulating the Jewish council and the Jewish population through a mixture of threats (deportation to Mauthausen), promises (exemptions), and deception (messages mailed back from Auschwitz). The staff of the Zentralstelle, though numerically very small, was relatively stable, serving throughout the critical period from 1941 to 1944, and their long tenure allowed them to take the full measure of the Jewish leadership and their followers.

Third, the cooperation of Dutch government agencies, especially the Population Records offices and the police, contributed substantially to the effectiveness of German policies. The pattern of this cooperation was forged by the Secretaries General and reaffirmed by a decision of the Dutch Supreme Court (Hoge Raad) to consider the dismissal of Jewish civil servants as lawful.

Finally, the reaction of the Jewish community itself played a part in the catastrophe. The Jewish council and its two leaders, Asscher and Cohen, significantly facilitated the deportation of their people, despite the best of intentions. The council unceasingly urged submission to German orders, published German threats, and provided personnel for the transactions involved in the deportations, including Jewish police at the rail heads and in Westerbork. The council's cooperation, within the context of a well-ordered and well-administered society, substantially facilitated the German project of removing the Jews from the occupied territory.

This assessment, rendered with the wisdom of hindsight, is not intended to condemn the council and its leaders without qualification. Asscher and Cohen believed that they were working in the interests of their people and that they were trying to save the "most valuable" part of the Jewish community. The assessment of history would indeed have been different if the war had ended in 1942, as many people on the Continent hoped and believed it would, or if the Germans had permitted a significant segment of the Jewish community to remain in Holland or to survive in the East. Yet it must also be noted that the council continued to function until September 1943, when information about the extermination camps in the East was available to those who wanted to know.

The character of the Jewish population also contributed to the outcome. The divisions in the Jewish community discussed above and the absence of a common ethos apart from lightly held religious beliefs, to-gether with a middle-class leadership bent on submission to the Germans in the hope of saving the lives of their primary constituency, weakened the potential for purposeful resistance. Even so, in the Netherlands as elsewhere the reality of genocide remained unimaginable even after information about Auschwitz had filtered back by 1943. But in the end the ruthlessness and effectiveness of German policies, limited by few restraints, the attitudes and policies of the Dutch government bureaucracy and of the Jewish leadership, and the absence of a common ethos among the Jewish population must be judged responsible for the extent of the disaster that befell the Jews in the Netherlands.

Werner Warmbrunn

Neuengamme Concentration camp near Hamburg, established in 1938 as a labor camp. Approximately half of the 100,000 inmates that the camp held during the war died there. Inmates, primarily Soviet nationals and Hungarian and Polish Jews, were forced to work in brick and weapons factories. Neuengamme was evacuated in April 1945.

A survivor who thinks U.S. soldiers forgot to evacuate him from Wöbbelin (a subcamp of Neuengamme) breaks into tears in the compound. 4 May 1945

German civilians are forced by American soldiers to inspect the Wöbbelin concentration camp, a subcamp of Neuengamme. 6 May 1945

Nisko Operation Abortive German plan, administered by Adolf Eichmann, to settle Jews and Gypsies of the Third Reich in southeastern Poland (1939–40). See FINAL SOLUTION: PREPARATION AND IMPLEMENTATION

North Africa The main factor that affected North African Jewry during World War II was the history of French colonial domination in Algeria (from 1830), Tunisia (from 1881), and Morocco (from 1912). Algeria was annexed to France; Tunisia and Morocco were French protectorates. As a result of French colonialism Jewish life improved in all domains, including the economy and education. The Jews of Algeria (150,000 in 1950) were made French citizens by the Crémieux decree in 1870. The legal status of the Moroccan Jews (200,000 in 1940) never changed; they were *dhimmis* ("protected people" under Moslem rule), but their living conditions and security improved as a result of the abolition of discriminatory statutes concerning the

clothing that Jews were required to wear. The legal status of the Tunisian Jews (100,000 in 1945) was complicated by differences between the three ethnic groups: Italian Jews, French Jews, and the majority, who were Tunisian subjects. French domination, the legal status, and the assimilation of the Jews into French culture gradually changed Moslem-Jewish relations. More and more, the Jews resembled the French and became detached from the Moslem culture and milieu.

The years before the outbreak of World War II were marked by an increasing deterioration of Jewish relations with the other ethnic groups. There were four factors that influenced the situation of the Jews: extreme right-wing French antisemitism, with its unique form of colonial antisemitism; German propaganda; Arab nationalism and its connection with the Palestinian conflict; and the Fascist Italian attitude toward Tunisian Jews. Expressions of this deterioration were antisemitic newspapers, journals, and special publications such as *La Flamme, Libre Parole,* and *L'Eclair,* and the establishment of antisemitic parties or organizations such as Amitiés Latines, Amitiés Françaises, and Action Française, some of which were affiliated with the parties of the same name in France.

The impact of the Palestinian conflict on the Arab nationalist movements was felt in 1929 after a violent outbreak at the Wailing Wall, which focused the Arab world's interest on events in Palestine. The commitment of North African nationalist movements to the Palestinians varied from country to country. Occasionally there were demonstrations against Jews, Jewish goods were boycotted, and there were even incidents of violence such as the one in Constantine, Algeria, in August 1934. Algerian Jewry, more than the Jews in Tunisia and Morocco, experienced this wave of antisemitism mainly in the form of an unpleasant and uncomfortable atmosphere. The 1938 Italian anti-Jewish legislation promulgated in Rome was applied in Tunisia and influenced, economically and morally, only the elite of Italian Jews. There was no real reaction on the part of Jews to the antisemitic atmosphere, and the Jewish communal institutions' reactions were particularly muted. Jewish protests were limited to a few newspaper articles, occasional letters of protest to the French authorities, and small demonstrations.

Germany conquered France in June 1940 and divided the country into two zones: the occupied zone, including the capital, Paris, which was under German military and administrative control; and the free zone, which was not occupied and was left to a pro-German and antisemitic French self-administration headed by Marshal Philippe Pétain in the small town of Vichy. The French possessions, including those in North Africa, were under Vichy government rule and all the anti-Jewish legislation was applied there.

The laws and decrees published by the Vichy government concerned three main areas: the legal status of the Jews, the *numerus clausus* (quota) in education, and the measures that were taken against the Jews' economic influence. In Algeria the abrogation of the Crémieux decree (7 October 1940) was the first stage of anti-Jewish legislation. Consequently all Algerian Jews lost their French citizenship. About two weeks later, the authorities published the Jewish Statute, which was identical to the statute in France and more severe than the Nuremberg Laws. The application of the Jewish Statute in Tunisia and Morocco was different. As most of the Jews in Morocco were not French citizens, their legal status did not change. The Jewish

Statute was published in Tunisia on 30 November 1940, but its implementation was only partial: the relatively few French Jews in Tunisia made an inordinately large contribution to the economy; the French *résident général*, Adm. Jean-Pierre Estéva, was sympathetic toward Tunisian Jews; and the Italian government representative in Tunisia, Giacomo Silimbani, carefully looked after the interests of Italian citizens there, including Italian Jews.

As a result of the Jewish Statute, Jews lost economic position and influence. Almost all public offices and liberal professions in the three countries were forbidden to Jews. Only 2 percent of Jewish lawyers were allowed to continue their work (decree of 5 November 1941), and similar restrictions were placed on Jewish midwives (decree of 29 November 1941). There is no doubt that Algerian Jewry suffered more than Jews in the other two countries because they were more assimilated into the French milieu. For example, the laws of November 1942 concerning the rights to real estate and movable goods were most rigorously applied to Algerian Jews in an attempt to aryanize Jewish property. The nomination of temporary managers of Jewish businesses was a part of that aryanization process. In Tunisia the Italian representative strongly opposed all French attempts to aryanize Jewish property as part of a policy of protecting the Italian colony in Tunisia.

Restrictions on the number of Jews allowed in schools and universities were applied in all three countries, but Algerian Jews, most of whom were educated at French schools, were affected more than Jews in the other countries. When the French educational system (including the Université d'Alger) was closed to them, they were left with no alternative but to create a Jewish self-education system for all ages. The Jews of Morocco and Tunisia had their own system of schools and were permitted to continue studying there.

The difficult situation of Algerian Jewry under the Vichy government was the reason that about 800 young Jews organized as an underground group and, with the help of French officers, took over the city of Algiers on 8 November 1942 and held it for more than 24 hours until the American army, in Operation Torch, liberated the city. Nonetheless, Algerian Jews had to wait approximately two years until they regained their citizenship. Operation Torch also freed Moroccan Jews, but the liberation was accompanied by sporadic violence in several towns.

From November 1942 to May 1943 the situation of

Tunisian Jewry steadily deteriorated as a result of the German occupation as well as Operation Torch and the British military campaign in Libya. The Jews suffered from the aerial bombardment by both sides in war. It appears that most of the Jews who died during the German occupation were killed in the bombings. The Germans created a new Jewish community committee, which in most of its functions was similar to the *Judenräte* (Jewish councils) established in Europe. The most important task of the committee was to supply forced labor for military purposes. Approximately 5,000 young Jews were conscripted to do forced labor. Their recruitment was carried out by the Comité de Recrutement de la Main d'Oeuvre (Committee for the Recruitment of Jewish Labor) headed by the lawyer Paul Ghez. The Jewish workers were housed at some 30 military camps near the front. The Comité de Recrutement was responsible for providing workers with food, clothes, transportation, and means of communication with their families; shortages and lapses led to widespread dissatisfaction on the part of the workers. The Germans confiscated Jewish property, including houses, cars, blankets, radios, and public buildings, such as the Alliance school. They imposed a fine of 23 million francs on the Jewish community, whereas in fact the estimate of damages to the community caused by German conscription is 63 million francs. Admiral Estéva did not, and probably could not, help Jewish leaders to dispute or at least to mitigate the Germans' demands. Thus Jews of Tunisia came to feel isolated from and abandoned by France. In contrast, many Tunisian Muslims offered shelter to Jews in their villages until the German threat passed, and no incidents of Arab violence against Jews during the German occupation appear to have occurred. On 7 July 1943 Tunisia was liberated from the Germans by the Allied Forces, and the threat that the Jews of North Africa would be annihilated, as was happening to the Jews of Europe, was lifted.

Nonetheless, the period of Vichy government in Algeria and Morocco and the Nazi occupation of Tunisia marked the beginning of the end of Jewish life in North Africa. The effect of the war was to unify and accelerate three historic developments: the waning of French power in North Africa, the national struggles for independence in the colonies, and the call from World Zionist organizations to the Jews of Arab countries to emigrate and help build the new state of Israel in the wake of the destruction of European Jewry.

Haim Saadoun

Norway Of the 1,700 Norwegian and foreign Jews in Norway when the Germans invaded the country on 9 April 1940, 736 died in gas chambers in Poland. The Jews who were saved were helped by non-Jewish Norwegians, who hid them and later secreted them across the border into Sweden. The many women helpers had gained much of their experience from Nansen Aid (Nansenhjelpen), a support organization of the 1930s named after the polar explorer Fridtjof Nansen. This organization served refugees and displaced persons, and one of its priorities was assisting Jewish orphans from Eastern Europe. Some of these helpers were policemen who ostensibly played the Germans' game but actually risked their lives in rescue operations. In contrast, the authoritarian police leaders who had maintained close contact with the German police since the early 1930s were all too eager to assist in German anti-Jewish actions.

Norway was a neutral in World War I, but 2,000 Norwegian sailors were killed when their ships were sunk by German submarines and ships harbored in Norwegian ports were blown up by German agents. Spy hysteria spread, as did suspicion of foreigners and immigrants. Official distrust of foreigners was directed just as much against Jews as against non-Jewish Germans. "Watch out for itinerant Jewish peddlers," warned a police official, J. Andersen, in a letter to the Norwegian Ministry of Justice during the summer of 1917. "These Jews support themselves largely through illegal trade (especially in clocks) and in part through card games. They are a people without patriotic sentiment, even if they have resided in Norway for many years; they think only of business deals and making money, regardless of the degree of respectability or even legality involved. Most of them are cunning, as well as good at languages. In my opinion, these Jews should be watched carefully as they travel around Trondheim and throughout Norway, and they should be deported without exception in all cases when permissible by law. No account should be taken of how long they have lived here in this country; the more at home they are in Norway, the more dangerous they are."

In 1917 the Norwegian immigration law was amended to impose some severe restrictions on Jews, in particular to prevent Jewish refugees from establishing themselves in Norway. The Oslo police chief of detectives, J. Sohr, warned "against this band of Jews who

Immigrant family from North Africa in Haifa. 1953

currently roam around Scandinavia" and the "not insignificant and undesirable invasion of Jews." The minister of justice, Lars Abrahamsen, echoed that sentiment. "When the rest of Europe has enacted strict regulations to prevent the scum of society from crossing their borders, it should not be us who are Europe's sewer, so that thieves, robbers, and murderers should unobtrusively push their way into our country."

In the early 1920s Norway's strict immigration law carried provisions to turn away "unwanted foreigners." The Aliens Act of 1927 made it even more difficult for foreigners to establish themselves in Norway: they had to have a work permit even before entering the country, and permits were available only for jobs that Norwegians did not want. Bureaucrats enjoyed discretionary authority in regard to acceptance or denial of applications. Preliminary work on the law left no doubt that it was especially directed toward Eastern European Jews. "It would, without question, be very unfortunate if immigration of this foreign type of race were allowed to any significant degree."

The Norwegian Foreign Affairs Department realized that Hitler's accession to power in Germany marked the beginning of a difficult time for German Jews. Reports from the Norwegian embassy in Berlin provided details about the April 1933 boycott of Jewish businesses and other anti-Jewish actions. During the summer of 1933, however, the Foreign Affairs Department instructed the embassy to turn away Germans who wanted to immigrate to Norway. "Our widespread unemployment and the pressing economic conditions make it much less possible to provide room for those Germans who, because of the current climate, wish to leave Germany." The Department of Justice concurred, saying that "an invasion of Jews must be repelled, even if in our hearts we have every possible sympathy for them." The immigration police in Oslo warned against the danger of a larger "Jewish colony." The refugee policy was softened for German Social Democrats and Communists after pressure from the Norwegian labor movement, but Jews were not defined as political refugees and therefore received no refugee status.

Jewish children were similarly treated. "They might establish themselves in the country," warned Deputy Secretary Carl Platou at the Department of Justice. "Like everyone else in an official position who has been confronted with the question, I am quite skeptical about the idea of awarding residence permits to Jewish children. . . . What has led me to take such a position is, of course, that the chance of never being rid of these children is overwhelming. . . . With all certainty, we must count on the great majority remaining in Norway and the formation of a Jewish element in the population and in the business sector. That in itself I do not look upon as a bad prospect, but I am afraid of the new impulse that this will give to the revival of antisemitism and that will not be to the benefit of our society."

Parliamentary debates about the restrictive refugee policy were brief, and opinion was unanimous in its favor. The Citizens Law was enforced in such a way as to discriminate against Jews. Department of Justice lawyers deliberately disregarded the citizenship guidelines provided by the law, and Jews who met the stated requirements, but were denied citizenship, were not given reasons for the refusal of their applications.

Journalists and members of volunteer organizations, such as Ragnar Vold of the newspaper *Dagbladet* and Sigrid Helliesen Lund in Nansen Aid, understood early on what nazism could bring about. In 1939 Lund traveled to Czechoslovakia to take 35 Jewish children back to Norway. In Berlin they had to change trains at different stations, and taxi drivers refused to drive the children. On the way they were spat on and jeered at by the German public—an experience exactly repeated when trains carrying Jews passed through Berlin in November 1942 on the way to the gas chambers at Auschwitz. In all, only 400 German and Eastern European Jews were ever admitted into Norway, on the condition that each was guaranteed private financial support to ensure that they would not become dependent on the state.

The German invasion of Norway on 19 April 1940 took Norwegians by surprise. The sinking of the German heavy cruiser *Blücher*, outside Drobak in the Oslo fjord at dawn, was also a surprise—to the Germans. Sailing on the *Blücher* was a large staff that was supposed to govern "the new Norway." But the Germans and the Norwegians quickly recovered and did their best to adjust to the new situation, each in their own way. The Germans' goal was to win the war and eliminate the Jews. It was not to nazify Norway, to the annoyance of Norwegian Nazis. The Germans saw themselves better served by having the Norwegian social machinery running as usual, with industry producing, police constables patrolling, and farmers delivering bacon and eggs to German soldiers. They did, however, establish a new police department and a state police with Norwegian bureaucrats and police leaders, who were closely but discreetly followed. "As far as possible, the Norwegian police should be allowed to carry out the measures we want implemented," the Gestapo instructed in the fall of 1940.

"It is the lot of the police to stay in their place, to receive German troops, and to take care of the general public's interests in the best possible way," said the minister of justice, Terje Wold, when the government fled Oslo to escape invading troops. The government and the monarchy went into exile in England, together with an elite group of officials and politicians. Other civil servants and politicians stayed behind to defend Norwegian interests as best they could. When the outcome of the war turned in favor of the Allies, the government-in-exile made plans to free Norway. To do so would require the assistance of the Norwegian police and experienced administrators, most of whom had protected their livelihoods by staying in their jobs during the occupation. The police department had been professionalized between the two world wars, and they did not intend to squander this achievement by yielding to foreign policemen or to uniformed fanatics and amateurs of the Norwegian Nazi party (Nasjonal Samling). Both the German and the Norwegian authorities saw their interests better served by relying on the existing police force. Norwegian civil servants and police were willing to collaborate with the Germans at the expense of the Norwegian Jews in order to shield non-Jewish Norwegians from German interest.

On 10 May 1940 Criminal Commissioner Wilhelm Esser instructed the Oslo police to confiscate radio sets from Norwegian Jews, and the order met with immediate compliance. The Germans brought with them a "Jew list"; the police, on seeing that it was incomplete, filled the gaps by conducting their own "research" in cooperation with the telegraph service. On 10 and 11 May they entered Jewish homes and seized radios. The Oslo police downplayed the action. The Germans found that only a few police chiefs refused to obey the order.

During the spring and summer of 1940 the German security police worked on registering Jewish groups and filing information on Jewish organizations (such as the Women's Union), businesses, kindergartens, and doctors. The membership list of the Mosaic Religious Community (Mosaike Trossamfunn) was passed to the Germans on 15 May 1940 by a representative of

the congregation. During the fall of 1940 and the spring of 1941, Norwegian Nazis arrested some Jews and closed Jewish shops and companies, while the Germans still hesitated on the question of how quickly they should proceed against the Jews. Adolf Eichmann, head of the Gestapo's Jewish section, determined that transporting Norwegian Jews by train through neutral Sweden was not possible. In any event, since there were very few Norwegian Jews, it would be obvious to the Norwegian public that action had been taken against them.

On 18 June 1941 Jewish men in Tromsö and Narvik were arrested, and five days later 64 stateless Jews in the eastern part of the country were taken into custody. Then on 2 October the minister of justice, Sverre Riisnaes, sent instructions to the regional commissioners about the registration of Jewish property, adding that "it is requested that any investigations in this case should be as discreet as possible." Riisnaes, who clearly disliked Jews, had been a district attorney and a member of Tysklandsvenn (Germany's Friend) in the 1930s but did not become a member of the Nazi party until July 1940. As district attorney in the 1930s he objected to Nazis who did not respect law and order and had prosecuted them at times. Yet he was quick to serve the Germans, who were then presented with a discreet escalation of Jewish persecution under Norwegian police. No protests were made by civil servants concerning the instructions to register Jewish property, and many sent in the information as a matter of duty. Others went even further: "It is not certain that the person mentioned is Jewish, but that is what is said," wrote one official. But some deliberately hampered the operation.

On 10 October 1941 the police department was instructed by the commander of the security police to stamp Jewish passports with a large "J." Details given to local police chiefs confirmed that there was no charge for the stamp and that if possible it should be made in red ink. The police department was headed by Jonas Lie, a well-known politician. He had previously been a police attorney, writer of crime novels, and vice-president of the State Police Force, which was used against striking workers in the interwar period. In 1937 the State Police Force was put under stricter civil control, to the annoyance of Lie, who saw the German occupation as an opportunity for revenge. He quickly built up a new State Police Force with a core of veterans from the 1930s. On 6 February 1942 the Ministry of Justice notified chiefs of police of a more extensive registration of Norwegian Jews and distributed a questionnaire (said to be drawn up by the Norwegian Nazi party) that required personal information on local Jews—their addresses, relations, assets, and organizational memberships—and on "Jewish crimes" (for example, white-collar crimes allegedly committed by Jews), a special interest of the Ministry of Justice. "Even if there are no Jews in the district, a report should be sent."

On 12 March 1942 the Ministry of Justice reinstated the "Jewish paragraph" of 1814 by revoking an 1851 decision that had deleted the provision "Jews are denied admission into the Kingdom." This move was initiated by, among others, Sverre Riisnaes. Vidkun Quisling, head of the Nasjonal Samling and minister president of the puppet government in Oslo, was another signatory to the revocation.

During the fall of 1942 the persecution of Jews in Norway was stepped up. On 24 October a law passed legalizing the arrests of Jewish men and the surveillance of Jewish women and children. The same day the chief of the State Police Force, Karl Martinsen, sent a coded order to the Norwegian police to arrest male Jews 15 years of age and older: "Property will be seized. Give priority to securities, jewelry, cash; then homes must be searched. Bank accounts and deposit boxes will be emptied. The confiscated property will remain with you until further orders. Registration documents will be dispatched from here as soon as possible. Managers must be appointed to run the business of the persons arrested."

On 25 October the State Police circulated this notice to Jewish homes: "By authority of the law of 24 October 1942 you are hereby informed that (1) all assets belonging to you and your family are being confiscated; (2) the eldest remaining family member is instructed to report daily to the police station in the district in which the family resides." On 26 October, the same day that Jewish men were arrested, another law was passed enabling the seizure of Jewish property. This was executed by the State Police, the criminal investigation police, and ordinary police throughout the country. The Norwegian branch of the German SS also participated, but the best method found was to use the well-mannered regular Norwegian police; it led to fewer disturbances and was more discreet. The order came from the Germans, but it is still uncertain who gave it. On 20 November 1942 the first large group of

Vidkun Quisling, prime minister of Norway, 1941–45, was a key instigator of the persecution of Norwegian Jews. 1943

Jews was shipped on the *Monte Rosa*, on their way to Auschwitz. On 25 and 26 November, Jewish women and children were arrested in a new countrywide action carried out by police and some Norwegian Nazi volunteers. The police inspector Knut Rod, who was responsible for Oslo and the eastern part of the country, was in charge of the operation of 26 November, when 532 Jews were put on board the *Donau* in Oslo harbor for the start of their journey to Auschwitz, where only a few survived. At the gangplank the Germans took over, putting an end to the courtesy that the Norwegian police had shown toward the Jews. They even beat up a Norwegian Nazi who was carrying an elderly Jewish woman's suitcase. On the same day the *Monte Rosa* left with 25 more Jews. On 25 February 1943 the *Gotenland* sailed with 158 Jews, who had been arrested after a mopping-up action carried out by the State Police and the local police.

The Germans killed 736 Norwegian Jews with the

help of Norwegian Nazis, officials, and police. Resistance groups and Nansen Aid veterans helped approximately 900 Jews to cross the border into neutral Sweden. Sigrid Helliesen Lund received early warnings from the Norwegian police on 25 October and 25 November 1942 and was able to alert probably more than 100 Norwegian Jews in Oslo. J. F. Myklebust, a policeman in Oslo, realized that the actions toward the Jews were a prelude to dreadful crimes. He accordingly warned Jews, as did colleagues throughout the country. "I just want you to know that we have orders from Oslo to arrest you," whispered Police Sergeant Anders Grut to Robert Savosnisk. Several people who helped Norwegian Jews paid with their lives, including the attorney Erling Malm, the physician Haakon Saethre, and Rolf Syvertsen, a gardener.

"Personally, I am absolutely opposed to violence and brutality," stated Police Inspector Rod when he was confronted with his responsibility for the Jewish persecution, and other policemen similarly attempted to defend themselves. The German view, however, was that the Norwegian police were to act as the velvet glove for the occupiers' iron fist. Even the plea of ignorance about the gas chambers exemplified a state of self-deception. Most Norwegians knew about German persecution of Jews after 1933, and they were aware of antisemitism on the part of Norwegian Nazis. Experienced civil servants and police officers understood that the seizure of the Jews' radios and property, the stamping of passports, and the arrests followed by confiscation of bank books and passports were all leading to something unthinkable. That is why some took pains to warn Jews of forthcoming arrests. Norway was a small country, and the police community and the civil service were even smaller. Jewish persecution could not be kept secret even from those who had no direct involvement.

A handful of Jews returned to their apartments and businesses after the war, only to find them taken over by other Norwegians. In a scandalous trial in 1947 Police Inspector Rod was acquitted of responsibility in deporting the Jews. The defense had pointed to his collaboration with the resistance movement at the end of the war. His "virtuous acts" in 1944 (when the Germans were about to be defeated) were made to counterbalance the evil done in 1942. Rod even obtained the court's backing for his application to return to his position as police attorney in Oslo, which he had held in the 1930s. Sverre Riisnaes escaped the death penalty by claiming insanity. Norwegian Jewish concentration camp survivors were physically and mentally debilitated, perhaps even too humble to speak out. After the war there were a great many stories about the heroic exploits of the resistance, but the true account of the Holocaust in Norway came out only much later.

Per Ole Johansen

Nuremberg Laws The so-called Nuremberg Laws of 15 September 1935 derive their name from the annual Nuremberg rally of the Nazi party. The legislation was initiated by Adolf Hitler on that occasion and unanimously promulgated by a specially convened session of the Reichstag. The two explicitly racist laws—the

Even before the Nuremberg Laws, the Nazis tried to eliminate Jewish businesses. Here an SA man enforces a boycott of Jewish businesses.

A woman forced to wear a sign reading, "I am a German girl, and I have let myself be defiled by a Jew!" Germany, 1935

Reich Citizenship Law and the Law for the Protection of German Blood and Honor—soon became the chief legal instruments in Nazi Germany for defining and segregating the Jews.

The "Party Rally of Freedom"—the Orwellian twist of language is comparable only to that of the "Party Rally of Peace" of September 1939—took place in Nuremberg 10–16 September 1935. It was the third annual party rally since Hitler's accession to power and even more spectacular than its predecessor, the 1934 rally filmed in Leni Riefenstahl's *Triumph of the Will*. Hundreds of thousands of party members and sympathizers from throughout Germany poured into the Franconian capital to listen to the Führer's speeches and to admire the mass parades and military drills on the Zeppelin field and in the newly renovated Luitpold arena. The highlight of the rally was the first public demonstration of the Third Reich's new tanks and planes, products of the recent rearmament effort.

Ever since the brutal removal of Ernst Röhm and his "fellow-conspirators" from the SA on the so-called Night of the Long Knives, 30 June 1934, Hitler had been strengthening his grip on power. On the death of President Paul von Hindenburg on 30 August, he became Reich chancellor and Führer, sole ruler of the country. The results of the January 1935 plebiscite in the Saar, in which the overwhelming majority of the inhabitants (including 9,000 Jews) voted for a return of the region to the German homeland, was a resounding confirmation of his foreign policy. The restoration of universal military conscription (Jews excepted) on 16 March 1935, in blatant violation of Germany's international commitments, passed with impunity. A naval agreement with Britain in May marked the de facto legitimation of German rearmament.

Emboldened by these successes, Hitler was ready

for a decisive blow against the emotional and ideological obsession of his adult life: the Jews. To crown the achievements of the young Nazi regime he had the Reichstag promulgate new antisemitic legislation. On the night of Sunday, 15 September 1935, emancipation and civic equality ended for the Jews of Germany, and they became legal pariahs in the land of their birth.

In their wide scope and clear racist terminology, the provisions of the Nuremberg Laws went beyond earlier discriminatory legislation in Nazi Germany, which had excluded Jews from the civil service and certain other professions but made exceptions for "special cases" such as front-line veterans and civil servants who had been in office before 1914. Henceforth the terms *German blood* and *Jewish blood* were to replace the earlier *Aryan* and *non-Aryan* in Nazi legislative language. The Reich Citizenship Law drew a distinction between two kinds of subjects of the state (*Staatsangehöriger*). Only those of German or related blood were entitled to be Reich citizens (*Reichsbürger*) with full political rights. Jews were considered mere Reich subjects, devoid of the right to vote or to be elected to office. The acquisition of Reich citizenship was to be formally recognized by the granting of a Reich citizenship certificate, but in fact such certificates were never granted during the Third Reich. The more detailed Law for the Protection of German Blood and Honor stated in its preamble that the purity of German blood was an essential condition for the continued existence of the German people (*Volk*). It prohibited marriages and extramarital relations between Jews and Reich subjects of German and related blood, prescribing severe punishments for the violation. The underlying obscenity was reflected in a further clause prohibiting the employment in Jewish households of German maidservants under 45 years of age.

The clause relating to the protection of German honor forbade Jews to fly the German national flag (though it conceded the right for them to display their own national flag). This provision harked back to the first of the three laws promulgated by the Reichstag on the night of 15 September 1935, which provided for the adoption of black, white, and red as the German national colors and the swastika as the official emblem of the state. The connection of the ceremonial Flag Law to the two specifically racial laws was expounded by the president of the Reichstag, Hermann Göring, in his address to its members: "By the same token that it

[the swastika] symbolized the struggle for our own race, so did it become a symbol of our fight against the Jews as race destroyers. It is therefore self-evident that no Jew should be allowed to display this flag in the future when it flies over Germany."

None of the hastily formulated laws offered any definition of the terms *Jew* and *Jewish blood*. The gap was filled only two months later, in the First Regulation to the Reich Citizenship Law of 14 November 1935. Failing to produce any credible racial criteria, the Nazi legal experts solved their problem, or rather sidestepped it, by defining a Jew essentially by the religion of his or her forebears. This resulted in a kind of circular definition. Thus, a Jew was defined as a person descended from at least three grandparents who were full Jews by race. The proof of the racial Jewishness of the grandparents, however, hinged on their affiliation to the Jewish religious community. On the other hand, a *Mischling* (mixed breed) was defined as a person descended from two full Jewish grandparents. However, a Mischling would be considered a Jew (1) if he or she belonged to the Jewish religious community at the time of the promulgation of the law, or subsequently was admitted to it; (2) if married to a Jew at the time of the promulgation of the law, or if subsequently married to one; (3) if born from a marriage between a Jew and a non-Jew contracted after 15 September 1935; or (4) if born after 31 July 1936 as the result of extramarital intercourse between a Jew and a non-Jew.

This concept of Jewishness reflected the tug-of-war between two contrasting approaches: that of the race fanatics of the Nazi party, led by Hitler's intimate associate, the chief Nazi doctor Gerhard Wagner; and the ministerial bureaucracy, represented by State Secretaries Hans Pfundtner and Wilhelm Stuckart and the race expert of the Interior Ministry, Bernhard Lösener. Whereas the Nazi party radicals would have stretched the definition to encompass anybody "tinged" with Jewish blood, however remotely, the more cautious and pragmatic bureaucrats strove to limit the law to exclude all but "full Jews" from its discriminatory provisions. The bureaucrats, most notably Lösener (who was entrusted with the actual drafting of the regulation), had their way in the end and succeeded in shielding most Mischlinge in the Third Reich from sharing the fate of the Jews. (Estimates of the number of half-Jews in Germany and Austria varied between 78,000 and 100,000.) Lösener's retrospective version of the genesis of the laws, as a surprise coup launched by Hitler and the party radicals against the unsuspecting and recalcitrant professional bureaucracy, carries little conviction. Not only did the German bureaucrats—not least Lösener himself—prove to be fully accommodating fellow travelers of the regime, but they could hardly have been taken by surprise when Hitler demanded legislation for which they themselves had been preparing various drafts since 1933. Furthermore, the timing of the antisemitic laws, preceded by a prolonged wave of anti-Jewish agitation and "spontaneous" violence throughout the summer of 1935, fitted into a well-established pattern from the early years of the Third Reich. The likelihood of an anti-Jewish law had even been discussed in the foreign press in August 1935.

The Nuremberg Laws provided a framework that acquired practical, operative force through supplementary decrees. The vaguely formulated Reich Citizenship Law, in particular, was conveniently seized upon by the Nazi legal experts as an all-purpose peg on which to hang no less than 13 measures relating to the Jewish *Sonderrecht* (the special legal position of the Jews) in Nazi Germany. The so-called Thirteenth Regulation to the Reich Citizenship Law (it was in fact the 12th) was published on 25 April 1943, after the deportation of the German Jews to the ghettos and death camps in the East had already been completed. It declared that no Jew, Mischling of the first degree, or Gypsy could become a Reich subject—a superfluous and anachronistic precaution considering the ongoing campaign of extermination.

Viewed retrospectively, the legal definition of the racial victim contained in the Nuremberg Laws—although flawed and self-contradictory—was an essential and logical step in the process of destruction unleashed against the European Jews. Historically, however, it would be a mistake to construe the enactment of the 15 September laws as a direct prologue to the Final Solution. Their real historical significance lies within the realm of the prewar Nazi drive against the Jews of Germany. They represented an act of public and symbolic humiliation of German Jews, rather than a frontal assault on the physical foundations of Jewish existence. It is indeed arguable that, in the context of the Jewish situation in Germany in the third year of Hitler's rule, the enactment of the laws, which spelled an official end to the "wild" antisemitic agitation that had been associated with uncontrolled street violence

Rudolf Höss, the former commandant of Auschwitz, testifies as a witness for defendant Ernst Kaltenbrunner at the International Military Tribunal trial of war criminals at Nuremberg. 15 April 1946

and physical assaults on Jewish life and property, was perceived by the Jewish victims as some kind of stabilization and hence a relief. But there can be no doubt that Hitler, anxious to avoid any interference with Germany's hosting of the forthcoming Olympic games, in his public utterances deliberately soft-pedaled the potential threat to the Jews. "The German government," he declared in presenting the racial legislation to the Reichstag, "is guided by the thought that through a single secular solution it may still be possible to create a basis for a tolerable relation between the German people and the Jewish people." Speaking shortly after the Reichstag session to a large gathering of Nazi party notables from all over Germany—as prominently reported on the front page of the *Völkischer Beobachter* (16 September 1935)—he sounded even more conciliatory, claiming "that after these laws the Jews in Germany have been given the possibility, unparalleled in any other land, of leading their own national [*völkisch*] life in all spheres." Thus was nurtured the fatal delusion that the Nuremberg Laws, although they put the final seal on the era of German Jewish emancipation, still left some room for a marginalized Jewish existence within the Third Reich.   *Daniel Fraenkel*

Nuremberg Trial   First of a series of trials against major German war criminals held in Nuremberg in southern Germany. The trial opened in October 1945 and concluded one year later. The International Military Tribunal (created by the Soviet Union, the United States, Great Britain, and France) indicted and tried 22 high Nazi officials for crimes against peace, crimes against humanity, war crimes, and conspiracy to commit those crimes. The tribunal acquitted three, imprisoned seven, and sentenced 12 to death (though only 10 of the death sentences were carried out). In addition, it condemned the Nazi party, the SS, and the Gestapo as criminal organizations. See WAR CRIMES

Odessa Port city on the Black Sea coast in Ukraine. Approximately 180,000 Jews lived in Odessa at the time of the German invasion of the Soviet Union in 1941. Fewer than half of the Odessa Jews managed to escape; the majority were killed by German and Romanian police and army units or perished in the camps of Transnistria.

Ohlendorf, Otto (1907–51) Senior SS official and commander of Einsatzgruppe D, which killed approximately 100,000 Jews in the southern districts of the eastern front. Ohlendorf was sentenced to death in "case 9," one of the post-Nuremberg trials, and hanged in Landsberg in June 1951.

Oneg Shabbos [Enjoyment of the Sabbath] (Ringelblum Archive) Code name for the secret archive in the Warsaw ghetto that preserved information about the persecution of the Jews. Many individuals worked with Emanuel Ringelblum, the historian who founded and administered the archive, to chronicle events in the Warsaw ghetto and occupied Poland, to collect newspapers, underground publications, letters, diaries, and German documents relating to Jewish deportations and murders, and to record the testimony of the Jews coming to Warsaw from other ghettos and labor camps. Ringelblum and his assistants perished when the ghetto was destroyed, but part of the archive, hidden in metal containers, was found after the war. The Jewish Historical Institute (Zydowski Instytut Historyczny) in Warsaw now houses the greater part of the archive. See WARSAW.

Operation Reinhard See REINHARD, AKTION

Orthodox Religious Thought From the late 1930s to immediate postwar years the persecution and destruction of European Jewry elicited a vigorous response from Orthodox Jewish thinkers. The development of Orthodox religious thought in response to the Holocaust may be divided into prewar, wartime, and postwar stages.

Before the War

Reflecting on the rise of nazism in the years 1936–38, the Lodz religious educator and writer Yehuda Leib Gerst placed anti-Jewish activities in the framework of cultural history. He defined Judaism in terms of the prophetic legacy of divinely rooted morality, which found expression in the Land of Israel and the Hebrew language. By its very existence Judaism became a target for those who despised the God of morality. Unable to assault God directly, they pursued the people who maintained His law. The hatred of Israel began with Amalek at Refidim, soon after the flight from Egypt, then passed to Haman, whose defeat is celebrated in the Purim festival, and continued from Apion in the first century C.E. all the way to Houston Stewart Chamberlain and Adolf von Harnack in the nineteenth and twentieth centuries. It initially assumed the form of idolatry and ended by asserting human autonomy, egoism, and instinct over divine morality. Its proponents ranged from the philosophers Immanuel Kant and Arthur Schopenhauer to Adolf Hitler and nazism, with their unbridled contempt for God and moral absolutes. What could Israel do but seek to preserve its existence by drawing from the source of its being? This was Torah, Hebrew scripture as explicated over time, which crystallized its absolute morality.

A leading rabbinical figure of Eastern European Orthodoxy, Elchanan Wasserman, who was killed outside the Kovno ghetto in 1941, took as his point of departure not history and its moral struggle but the metaphysical reality of Torah. History was a function of that reality, and the events surrounding Israel were

generated solely by its Torah-related behavior. Writing during the period between the March 1936 Polish legislation prohibiting ritual slaughter (*shehitah*) and Kristallnacht pogroms in Germany in November 1938, Wasserman explained that the absence of Torah in the life of Zionist nationalists, Enlightenment assimilationists (Orthodoxy identified Enlightenment with assimilation), socialists, and Communists cast them into the same anti-realm of being (*sitra ahra*) as the seed of Amalek. God thereupon entered history to reverse the loss of Torah and force Jews back to it. Thus, God provided national socialism in Germany to rebut Jewish nationalism and socialism. Wasserman predicted that the assaults on Jews would be unprecedented in intensity and speed and would include global mass expulsion and starvation. He was equally certain that they would end in redemption. The tribulations were intended to go beyond returning Israel to Torah and extend to lifting Israel out of history to the messianic realm. Israel's tribulations would prove to be the Messiah's birth pains. In 1937 Eliahu Botschko, founder and head of the Montreux yeshiva who was trained in the Musar (moralistic) movement founded by Israel Salanter, drew a path of interpretation between the cultural history of Gerst and the metaphysical reality of Wasserman. Botschko focused on the Land of Israel. For more than a century, he wrote, the Messiah had been searching for Israel. But Israel had turned its back on him, instead seeking redemption in Western lands or looking to the Holy Land in merely secular terms. The Messiah could not come, Botschko reasoned, for there was no one to receive him. By cruel coincidence Hitler did arrive, to stir up the long-latent hatred in a series of violent outbursts that culminated in systematic mass murder. The people of Israel, however, could endure, for God was with them. Moreover, the fact that Israel was returning to the very brink of the pre-Creation void, the lowest point of darkness, implied the bursting forth of messianic redemption amid the most intense light. Israel was to contribute to the process, which included restoration in the messianic Holy Land, rejecting false messiahs, turning to Torah, and returning in penitence. If Gerst saw the suffering as generated from without and Wasserman regarded it as coming from within, for Botschko it was a result both of Israel's failure to receive the Messiah in time and the advent of nazism. Whereas Gerst's

Professor Ismar Elbogen teaches Talmud class in Berlin. 1934

historicism did not address redemption and Wasserman's metahistory united suffering and redemption, Botschko's intermediate position provided a messianic resolution through the actual land of Israel.

By the time the move from persecution to mass murder had taken place, the process of religious reflection was under way. The themes included the parallel dimensions of history and metahistory and their interaction, Israel's behavior in transforming metahistory, Israel's responsibility for its troubles, and the correlations between disaster and salvation.

During the War

Mizrahi. Wartime thinkers who supported the religious national movement (*Mizrahi*) related to the Holocaust in terms of the Land of Israel's centrality to Jewish identity and security. The Bronx rabbi Aharon Halevi Petshenik, who trained at the Tahkemoni Rabbinical Seminary in Warsaw, lost most of his family in the July 1942 Dombrovitch pogrom in Poland. His wartime context for comprehending the tragedy was apocalyptic: the process of redemption had already begun and the Holocaust was its by-product. He cited the medieval biblical interpreter Abraham Ibn Ezra's commentary to Exodus 14:13, that God let the generation of the desert exodus die because the slavish mentality incubated by the sojourn in Egypt made it unable to assert itself and take Canaan. Similarly, the Holocaust resulted from the divine intention to remove the generation that had failed for the 40 years (since the founding of the Mizrahi World Organization) to move aggressively toward the Land of Israel. After the war Petshenik in effect set a metahistorical ceiling over the failed generation. The suffering was inevitable and messianic, and according to rabbinic tradition it necessarily preceded redemption. He spoke of self-generated persecution of Israel from without, so that its own territory was the only refuge from antisemitism and further tragedy. Restoration of the Holy Land constituted a mending (*tikkun*) of the victims' souls: those whose deaths were required for redemption would share in the results of their sacrifice. In part responsible for not moving to the Land of Israel in time, in part passive participants in the suffering necessary for redemption, these souls would also be reconciled upon completion of the redemptive process.

For Zalman Shraggai of Jerusalem and Gedaliah Bublick of New York the relationship between the Holocaust and the Land of Israel was primarily historical rather than apocalyptic. According to Shraggai, Israel's landlessness, decreed by God to educate the people against the assimilatory tendency of the Second Temple era, was liable to exacerbate the existing metaphysical antagonism between Jacob (Israel) and Esau (the other nations). Israel was a natural source of irritation for other peoples who could not swallow it into their midst and would not expel it. Antagonism generated by landlessness was aggravated by assimilation; European Jews sought redemption not through restoration of the Holy Land but through the French Revolution. Instead of recoiling from exile, Israel at first embraced it, but then stepped back from it, and the Zionist movement began. But it was too late: by then the nations felt threatened by the prospect of Israel's redemption and attacked it. The Holocaust, according to Shraggai's wartime considerations, was the collective consequence of the wrongheaded geographical and cultural assimilation generated by landlessness.

Two years after the war, at the end of 1947, Shraggai added an apocalyptic element. Given the fact that the people of Israel never really learned to resist assimilation, they did not merit the Holy Land. But the suffering brought on by their misdirected behavior reached such terrible proportions that it evoked divine compassion. Upon the void of the Holocaust, God acted to begin creation anew. He did so by establishing the Jewish state. Shraggai's wartime historical interpretation of the tragedy now yielded to a metahistorical drama of divine intervention, and God's initiative dissolved the point of tension that assimilation had generated between Himself and Israel, which, having failed once, could begin anew in the Holy Land. The very Holocaust which reflected the failure would become the basis for a second history.

Gedaliah Bublick shared the traditional premise of Esau-Jacob enmity. He wrote that the line of Esau eventually included nazism, with its rejection of religion in favor of the glorification of all-powerful man, instinct, and amorality—as espoused, for example, by Friedrich Nietzsche. The enmity now expanded into a bifurcated universe, with the realm of Esau-become-nazism on one side and civilization on the other. Israel was the heart of civilization, which included Scripture-based Christianity and was represented by Britain and the United States. Since the people of Israel were rooted in the eternity provided by God, they and their civilization would survive. Whereas Shraggai blamed Israel's suffering on its thrust into non-Jewish culture instead of isolating itself in its land, Bublick exonerated Israel and blamed anti-civilization for the nation's woes. Bublick agreed that the disastrous conflict could have been avoided had Israel returned to the land in time.

Like Shraggai and Bublick, Moshe Avigdor Amiel, the chief rabbi of Tel Aviv, looked to history for the explanation of the Holocaust and the meaning of the Land of Israel, although he shared Petshenik's transcendental inclination. Amiel's central reality was the divine as expressed immediately in Torah. In turn the people of Israel were rooted in Torah, and the land was Torah's vessel. The concentric spheres of God, Torah, and Israel constituted a spiritual and sacred reality, leaving the rest of the world to the material and secular. Amiel's land did not coincide with Israel's identity (as it had for Petshenik), nor did it assure refuge from distress (as it had for Shraggai). With his thought centered on God's Torah, Amiel looked on the Land of Israel as the best vessel—a vessel, as Yishuv secularists proved, that was all too frail. To the extent that the people of Israel anywhere remained rooted in Torah, their life was secure. If they diluted Torah and assimilated into foreign cultures—although to do so completely was impossible from the perspective of their ultimate being—their life would become disrupted, defined in terms of divine punishment, which was intended to push Israel back to its own territory. Enlightenment and secular Zionism, both aggravated forms of assimilation, brought on the worst imaginable consequences—the Holocaust, at once a reflection of chaos, divine punishment, and the return of Israel to its sacred self. The disruption this time was so severe, in fact, that Israel could no longer be entrusted by God to history. Like Shraggai after the war, Amiel believed that the consequences of Israel's failure in history were to be resolved by removing it from history. Only redemption, centered in the Land of Israel, would remain. Again like Shraggai and Bublick, he viewed Israel's plight in terms of historical interactions with other nations, but for him the plight was purely self-generated. At the same time he was inclined to acknowledge God's oversight of history, the metaphysical centrality of Torah, and the redemptive resolution to Israel's crisis. The land, located in the outermost range of Israel's sacred reality, was a posthistorical vessel, not a secure platform for Israel's second history but rather an opening for Israel to fill with Torah.

Eastern European Agudat Israel. In Eastern Europe,

Wasserman's anticipatory interpretation of the Holocaust as a function of metaphysical Torah was brought forward through the war by leaders of Agudat Israel, the rabbinical political organization that promoted Jewish life based on halakhah (rabbinic law). Yitzhak Meir Levin was a former member of the Jewish council in the Warsaw ghetto who escaped to Palestine in the winter of 1939–40 and served on the Jewish Agency's Rescue Committee. He shared the view that hatred for Israel was implanted into history at Mount Sinai and thereafter intensified. The proper response was for Israel to maintain its distance, since intimacy aggravated the hatred. Instead the assimilationist Enlightenment (Haskalah) eradicated the division. The reaction—the Holocaust—was virulent but in Israel's religious terms justified; the Nuremberg racial laws, for example, reflected divine judgment and mercy. Simultaneously, however, the reaction led to the ultimate level of separation and safety, namely redemption itself. Levin thought in terms of a metaphysical tension between the Torah of Mount Sinai Torah (thesis) and the hatred of nations (antithesis). Israel was obliged to maintain the separation in history but failed to do so. Divine intervention was required, and it took the form of Holocaust. But the outcome would be redemption, insofar as consolation followed calamity (Deuteronomy 32). For Levin the land played no special role in the process—if anything, he held Yishuv Jews in contempt for violating the metaphysical distance. Moshe Blau, the head of Agudat Israel's Jerusalem office, who died during a rescue mission to Italy, echoed the theme of separated Torah and blamed assimilationist German Jews and Zionists who incited Hitler with boycotts. He focused on an urgent need for repentance to restore the separation.

Wasserman's interpretation was also modified. The chief rabbi of Petah Tikvah, Reuven Katz, who was a student of Hayyim Ozer Grodzinski of Vilna (whose 1939 response to the troubles echoed his brother-in-law Wasserman's principle that disaster was a function of Torah-loss), introduced the land into the drama. Israel's survival as a national entity, he wrote, was never threatened by physical assault. But as its very life was drawn from Torah, assimilation was a threat. Involvement with the nations had to be limited to self-sacrifice (*mesirat nefesh*)—religious self-assertion in terms of physical self-destruction in the tradition of the Akedah (the binding of Isaac, Genesis 22). For Katz, the Holocaust was a complex of internally opposed elements, the greatest act of mesirat nefesh, the diminished life of the nation following Torah-loss, and divine punishment. Since for God all history was concentrated into a single moment, the punishment applied to past and future generations as well as to trespasses in the present.

Katz also considered the Holocaust to be an *olah* (sacrificial offering) in atonement for past sin. Its ashes would surely evoke God's mercy, to be manifested in the restoration of the Land of Israel. The Jews of the land, it followed, were responsible for assuring that the Holocaust's atonement-by-death would not be in vain, and that could be accomplished only by filling the land with Torah. Torah and the land became mutually indispensable, so that while Torah life after catastrophe could have meaning only in the land, there could be no land unless it was of Torah. Levin carried forward Wasserman's metaphysical Torah through the war and found consolation in the prospect of transhistorical redemption. For Katz the suffering went beyond punishment for violating Torah's separateness to include self-sacrifice and sacrificial offering. They could be resolved only by God's mercy, which involved the land. Perhaps confounded by the suffering of the pious, Katz blended the Torah with land to find empirical meaning in their death.

Western European Agudat Israel. The religious thought of Samson Raphael Hirsch, the founder of neo-Orthodoxy in the mid-nineteenth century, made its way into wartime interpretation of the Holocaust through his grandson Isaac Breuer of Frankfurt am Main, who moved to Jerusalem in 1936, and his student Jakob Rosenheim, also of Frankfurt, who escaped to London in 1937 and moved to New York in 1941. Breuer applied Hirsch's worldview, in which eternal Torah was created by God along with nature itself, to Israel's relation to the world. Sacred Israel, rooted in the dual creation, was located beyond the ravages of history. Anchored in its metahistorical station, however, Israel also entered exile and world history to draw the rest of the nations into its realm. But the nations were caught up in the pursuit of sovereignty and resisted. Then, by tragic coincidence, just when sovereignty combined with racism to assume its most vicious form, with Emancipation many Jews in the West abandoned the metahistorical refuge and made themselves completely vulnerable to assault. Chastened by the consequences, Breuer turned from the world's history to Israel's. The only safe place in history after the

Holocaust was the land, the only territory receptive to the nation of metahistory. Once secure there, Israel could once again take up its role in world history. Whereas for Eastern European thinkers the Holocaust forced Israel outside history, for Breuer it meant relocating Israel's history in the land.

Rosenheim described a world organism intended to concentrate around the God-center as crystallized in Torah. Israel, whose very soul was Torah, was closest to the center and was also called upon to bring about the concentration of all humanity. The nations had become obsessed with the pursuit of sovereignty—an obsession that culminated in the Holocaust. But the extremity of sovereignty was also its catharsis, leaving the world to a redemption that would be centered in the Land of Israel in history, as imbued with Torah. For Breuer the Holocaust made the metahistorical Israel's direct involvement with world history impossible, and now the world could become holy only indirectly, through the restored land. For Rosenheim the Holocaust was the universal end to sovereignty and the onset of hope for a God and Torah-centered universe. Whereas Breuer found great meaning in Zionist achievements, Rosenheim did not. But both, in contrast to Eastern European Agudat Israel's exclusive focus on Israel's plight, remained concerned with Israel's role in world history as it opened up to redemption.

Musar. Musar thinkers responded to the Holocaust in terms of penitence (*teshuvah*). In a December 1944 address Yehezkel Sarna, the movement's leading figure in Palestine, asserted that God's face was not hidden at all. God had remained near to His people in catastrophe ever since the first destruction of the Temple, and He was near still. He offered consolation and enabled Jews to weep because He Himself wept. The divine presence also made understanding of the catastrophe possible. The metahistorical realities of redemption (*geulah*), penitence, and disaster (*hurban*) were of one piece. As they manifested themselves across the temporal spectrum and became humanly comprehensible, they remained interrelated. The current disaster would bring redemption by acts of penitence. Insofar as the triad's reality was drawn simultaneously from above and below, God supported the Jews in their efforts to participate in and contribute to the process. He entered history to help each Jew make penance. Whereas Mizrahi thinkers understood the cataclysm in terms of land and Agudat Israel in terms of Torah, Musar transferred the focus to the existential reality of teshuvah and its divine parallel.

In Gateshead, England, Eliahu Dessler understood the Holocaust as the absence of God's presence and morality from the subjective or historical dimension of the universe, leaving only the sitra ahra, or anti-realm. The disaster was launched by Israel's turning from teshuvah and toward the values of the nations of the world. But just as abandoning penitence had caused historical life to break away from what was objectively real, penitence could reconnect the two and restore the flow of divine morality into history. Indeed, penitence would fill the world with God's loving-kindness. Sarna neutralized the issue of responsibility for the Holocaust by describing it as an indispensable manifestation of higher being, which would inevitably be succeeded by redemption following teshuvah. For Dessler the Holocaust was not cosmically inevitable and resulted rather from Israel's failure. The two Musar thinkers shared the perception that the inner change of penitence would reverberate through the empirical world and lead to redemption. This did not require territorial consideration (Mizrahi), realignment of Israel's position toward the nations (Eastern Agudat Israel), or universal change in world history (Western Agudat Israel).

Hasidism. Hasidic responses to the Holocaust shifted attention to aggressive religious-historical action. The Piaseczner rebbe, Kalonymous Kalman Shapira, who was murdered in 1943 during deportation from Warsaw, spoke from within the valley of slaughter. No difference existed for him between subject and object, between reflection and suffering. In his Sabbath and festival discourses in the Warsaw ghetto he sought to transform religious consciousness, alleviate suffering, and effect a mending (tikkun) of the relationship between victim, God, and universe. Shapira related how in the second century Rabbi Yose entered the ruins of the Temple to pray; lessening his own self, he expanded his consciousness to comprehend God's own suffering and heard God weeping over His people. Now too, Shapira asserted, by diminishing the ego one could comprehend God's infinite suffering. He suffered for the terrible events in Europe but had to withdraw from the world to weep alone, lest His unbounded sorrow destroy the world. Shapira urged his listeners to transcend finite suffering, to reach God in His hidden, infinite suffering. If they could immerse themselves in God's presence (shekhinah) they would know that God filled all, and that even the separation between finite and infinite belonged to His infinite presence. Then it would be possible to submerge one's suffering in God's and to transcend the physical pain that came with finitude.

The reflections of the rebbe of Belz, Aharon Rokeah, were expressed in a statement by his brother, Mordechai Rokeah of Bilgoraj, as they were about to escape to Palestine from Budapest in November 1943. God's hiddenness, Aharon Rokeah believed, was being abandoned with the miraculous phenomenon of his own imminent rescue. In his very person history from below met with divine intervention from above. Through their devotion to and trust in him and their support for his escape, Rokeah's hasidim could share in the miracle. Once in the Land of Israel, the heavenly spheres (*sefirot*) could bond with earthly reality in his personal presence and proclaim the onset of redemption. This would mean recession of the Holocaust—specifically relief to his followers in Hungary. At the edge between doom and escape, Rokeah's personal incarnation of miracle became the foundation for the salvation of his entire community.

In the first months of 1943 in Budapest, Issakhar Taykhtahl of Munkacs, who was later murdered during transport to Bergen-Belsen, reversed his earlier anti-Zionist position to identify the catastrophe as a call for massive emigration to the Land of Israel (aliyah). The hidden divine intention of exile and the punishment it included were always to awaken the people to go to the Land of Israel. The Holocaust—distinct because Israel had no place of refuge—was the ultimate forceful expression of this intent. It was the unambiguous statement that Israel's life in the Diaspora, where it could not defend itself, was over. Taykhtahl blamed opponents of Zionism for necessitating the use of ultimate force, and he revered the secular Jew who built the land more than the pious Jew who did not. He realized now that the Jews should not have relied on miracles but ought to have taken all possible action to reclaim the Land of Israel. Return to the Holy Land would mean national consolation. The reestablishment of Israel in the land would enable the divine sphere of kingdom (*malkhut*) to unite with Israel in redemption. Taykhtahl rejected Rokeah's personalized, miraculous means of redemption. He looked to collective action on the part of Jews, the realities notwithstanding.

Yosef Yitshak Schneersohn, who escaped Nazi-conquered Warsaw and arrived in New York in the early fall of 1940, focused on forming a religious army, Mahane Israel (Camp of Israel), to evoke teshuvah on the part of all Israel and thereby bring a halt to the dis-

aster and evoke transterritorial redemption. From the outset exile, by its harshness, was intended to bring about penitence, but instead sin increased, along with God's punishment. The tension finally brought Israel to the choice between penitence and death—that is, the Holocaust. Although certain that Israel would never die and that teshuvah therefore had to occur, Schneersohn was also convinced that it was up to Mahane Israel to open Israel's history to the higher process of penitence and to channel the metahistorical transition from exile to teshuvah into daily life. Once this happened, redemption would take place.

Kabbalah. The reality of redemption loomed over Orthodox wartime religious responses to the Holocaust. Yaakov Moshe Harlap (1883–1951) of Jerusalem, successor to Rabbi Abraham Isaac Kook (Rav Kook, d. 1935), the first chief rabbi of Palestine, was head of the Rav's educational institution, Merkaz Harav, and based his interpretation of the Holocaust on the actuality of redemption's onset. For Harlap, redemption preceded catastrophe. Drawing from sixteenth-century Lurianic Kabbalah, he wrote that the sacred was concentrated in Israel and available through it to the nations of the world. But the nations did not draw from Israel, fearful lest their identity be denied. Now it was too late, and without Israel's sacred life they were going to be destroyed as redemption was completed. So they attempted to stop the process by destroying its vessel, namely Israel. Aware of their imminent annihilation, they sought to destroy everything around them, especially the national symbol of their demise. This destruction was mirrored within Israel. Because redemption held only Israel's holy spirit, its body had to be diminished, even shattered—as were the bodies of Aaron's sons as they neared God's holiness (Leviticus 10:1–3). Some Jews, anxious to belong to the light, erred in their zealous attempts at perfect piety and collapsed into sin. And those who held on to the sins of exile would be destroyed once the sacred core of the nation hastened toward the light. Harlap's Holocaust did not belong to history, and in this sense it resembled that of Sarna and Schneersohn. But he went further. Because redemption had already begun, there was no action to change surrounding realities that Israel might take.

Silence. Two Orthodox thinkers within war-torn Europe, Shlomo Zalman Ehrenreich of Simleul-Silvaniei, Transylvania and Shlomo Zalman Unsdorfer of Bratislava, who were leaders of their respective communities amidst persecution, ghetto and transport to

Auschwitz, yielded their attempts to explain the events to silence. Ehrenreich sough to interpret the impending catastrophe according to rabbinic sources: God used the nations which stemmed from Esau to make Jews recoil from assimilation and Zionism. Then, He would have the attackers destroyed so that His name and power would be recognized by Israel and the world. The nations always hated Israel, but they were able to attack it only after God transferred His indignation over Israel's transgressions to them. Then they assaulted at will. But Ehrenreich was unable to explain why the righteous suffered, and this led him to denounce attempts to probe God's intentions and to advocate the silent suffering exemplified by Aaron after the death of his sons (Leviticus 10:3). Answers would be provided only from within redemption, drawn from divine wisdom and not defined in terms of historical time or geographical space. In the meantime, silence was to be filled with a life of piety: specifically, the study of Torah, which displaced suffering and which precipitated the ingathering of exiles, and penitent return, which elicited divine compassion. Self-deprivation and meeting death in terms of Torah and penitent return brought the pious life to fulfillment. It is reported that on the train to Auschwitz Ehrenreich prepared his family and students to carry out Torah's ultimate mitzvah (divine commandment), that of sanctification of the divine name, with joy and love for God.

For Unsdorfer as well, Esau's long-range hatred for Israel was activated by God alone. This happened when Jews surrendered Torah in the form of emulating the nations. Unsdorfer blamed assimilationist Jews of Germany in particular for evoking the current decrees against Jews—which were carried out in measure-for-measure detail under divine aegis. He ventured to explain the suffering of the pious in terms of a fire which had gone out of control (Exodus 22:6). But ultimately he drew a categorical distinction between the thoughts of man and the thoughts of God, and rejected attempts to explain in favor of silence. At that point, Unsdorfer turned his attention to a metahistorical process under way, from catastrophe to redemption. This higher drama was reflected and enhanced by a parallel process below, whereby the pious Jew silently endured the current darkness in faith and without trying to probe God's intentions. Such a Jew believed that upon redemption it would become clear that the suffering was for the good of Israel. Whereas for Ehrenreich silence was replaced by the pious life, for Unsdorfer silence was at its core. As with Abraham and the *Akedah*, silence belonged to trust in God despite rational comprehension. Five months after Ehrenreich, Unsdorfer sought to instill this piety into those with him, as he too was transported to his death at Auschwitz.

After the War

Simha Elberg (1908–95) of Warsaw escaped to Shanghai in the fall of 1941 and immigrated to New York in 1947. In early 1946, he wrote in *Akedat Treblinka* (The Akedah of Treblinka) that the Holocaust amounted to the destruction of the world and its history, leaving the pre-Creation void. But Torah and God remained, and if the light of Torah were taken up again, history could be renewed. For Elberg, the Akedah was the internal character of Israel's being. Mount Moriah, he wrote, remained with Israel throughout its exile, culminating in the Akedah of Treblinka; the binding of Isaac and the slaughter in the death camps belonged together. Treblinka required the holiest portion of Israel, namely the Jews of Poland and Lithuania. The victims fulfilled their role, sanctifying God's name by cries of the Shema ("Hear, O Israel"), which split the heavens. The Akedah survived even the destruction of world history, along with God and Torah. Elberg lifted the Akedah to the juncture between the void and history, where it remained the source for Israel's renewal in Torah, indeed for the re-creation of the world in the context of redemption. For Elberg, the blood of Israel's sacrifice would redeem the entire universe.

A year later, in Tel Aviv, in *Tamim Paalo* (His Ways Are Perfect) the Kotsk-Sokolover hasidic rebbe Chaim Tsimerman, who had emigrated to Palestine from Warsaw well before the war, dwelled on the suffering of the righteous. Redemption, he believed, was imminent. Because the people of Israel did not repent in time, as the sages of the Talmud had explained, God forced them to do so. But why were the righteous included in the punishment? Tsimerman offered a complex of reasons. Whenever tragedy came to the world, it began with the righteous. God judged each generation comprehensively, and if trespasses outweighed good deeds, everyone, including the righteous, suffered. The pious were also responsible for making every effort to put a stop to the trespasses of others but had not done so. Tsimerman also drew from Lurianic Kabbalah to assert that if sinners were not punished in their own time, their souls transmigrated for later punishment. This explained the increase in Jewish population in the early twentieth century. Altogether, under the pressure of imminent redemption and purification, the righteous were included in the rectification of Israel in terms of its totality and entire history.

In *Tamim Paalo* and *Akedat Treblinka* the issues of land, return to Torah, penitence, religiously inspired action, and apocalyptic concerns receded into the background. The immediate need was to explain the suffering of the righteous. The answers lay in Israel's very being, as the Akedah or the object of divine righteousness considered comprehensively.

Most Orthodox thinkers preceded their deliberations on the Holocaust by acknowledging the impossibility of natural or rational interpretation and the need to look to revealed sources to understand the tragedy. Exceptional ones concluded with the impossibility. They drew from common values. Religious thought belonged simultaneously to history and metahistory; God's absence was a subjective reality but not an objective one; midrash (allegorical interpretation of Scripture) offered a language to express unprece-dented events. Further, history itself may have been destroyed, but Torah remained; Israel's sacrifice was a positive expression of Torah; history could no longer be trusted, and Israel had to look to redemption. Finally, human responsibility (whether Israel's or the nations') for the cataclysm was undeniable; God was indirectly involved in the historical events; ancient events in Israel's relationship with God provided ontological precedents for contemporary ones; the catastrophe was simultaneously Israel's return to its authentic self and the onset of redemption. The Orthodox thinkers lived and died according to these values and sought to relieve all Israel by enunciating them publicly. Many issues were unresolved: How could man bring God to act? How did transcendental realities intermingle with historical ones? Why did redemption necessarily follow catastrophe? But the thinkers were able to move their communities ahead in religious terms, notwithstanding the apparent contradictions and paradoxes. By raising events into religious consciousness, they provided meaning and direction through catastrophe and produced a legacy for their successors in the next generation.

Gershon Greenberg

P

Palmnicken Massacre Perhaps 7,000 people, almost 90 percent of them Jewish women, perished in late January 1945 during a forced march from the city of Königsberg to the Baltic Sea town of Palmnicken and in a subsequent massacre on the beach there. Thirteen are known to have survived the killings, which occurred in what is now the Russian province of Kaliningrad. According to survivors and others, 20,000 inmates of so-called satellite camps, prisons which ringed the larger Stutthof concentration camp in Poland, were evacuated by German soldiers and forced to march north as Soviet troops advanced on the camps in the final months of World War II. Most were Hungarians or Lithuanians. At least 7,000 were taken to Königsberg and imprisoned there. On 26 January 1945, during one of the most bitter winters in memory, the 7,000 were ordered to march 40 kilometers to Palmnicken, an amber-mining center. During the march, some 3,000 inmates were said to have died of exposure or were shot while trying to flee. The remainder were briefly imprisoned in a vacant lock factory in Palmnicken and on the evening of 29 January were marched five abreast to the town mine. Some were shot execution-style there; many were forced to run onto Baltic Sea ice, where they were cut down by automatic weapons. The fate of the remaining 13,000 evacuees from the Polish camps is not known, although there are reports of a similar massacre in a Kaliningrad seaport now called Baltisk. The Red Army later seized the territory and deported its Germans; Königsberg is now the city of Kaliningrad, and Palmnicken has been renamed Yantarny. So thoroughly did the Soviets erase traces of the massacre that even Kaliningrad residents were unaware of the killings until 1998. *Michael Wines*

Parachutists' Mission One of the most extraordinary rescue and assistance missions initiated by the Yishuv (Jewish community in Palestine) during World War II was that of the Jewish parachutists dropped behind enemy lines throughout 1943 and 1944 to assist both the British forces and the Jews in occupied Europe. At its height the operation involved 250 candidates, most of whom were members of the kibbutz movements, soldiers in the British army, and members of the Palmach, the Jewish defense forces. Of this group, 42 were eventually chosen to be used in active missions, but only 32 men and women were actually sent to destinations in Yugoslavia, Romania, Hungary, Slovakia, Austria, Bulgaria, or Italy, either during the war or shortly afterward; 27 of them eventually reached their goal. Seven of the parachutists—Zvi Ben-Yaakov, Abba Berdichev, Peretz Goldstein, Haviva Reik, Rafael Reiss, Hannah Szenes, and Enzo Sereni—lost their lives at the hands of the Nazis or their collaborators during the last few months of the war.

The parachutists' mission was the culmination of a long-standing tradition of intelligence cooperation between the Yishuv and the British that had begun during the early 1930s and continued throughout the entire decade. Between 1936 and 1939 this relationship had its ups and downs. Reaching a zenith during the Arab revolt in Palestine, contacts declined after the British white paper of 1939, which set out the government's policy of limiting Jewish immigration to the Palestine mandate area. With the outbreak of war Yishuv leaders proposed to the British a number of cooperative missions involving volunteer commandos. Discussions took place between the leaders of the Jewish Agency and the department of British military intelligence known as the Special Operations Executive (SOE). Originally, joint plans were made for sabotage missions in Romania, intelligence missions in Palestine and Vichy-controlled Syria, and invasive missions into Italy. But at the end of 1940, when it appeared that none of these plans was near fruition, contacts between the British and the Jewish Agency for Palestine leveled off, and they were only renewed six months later.

In the spring of 1941 Axis forces began an intensive attack on the Balkan countries and the Middle East. British military losses, in particular the fall of Greece, meant a willingness to look for military assistance in new areas. Consequently, cooperative intelligence plans between the Yishuv leaders and the British military were once again on the agenda. When SOE headquarters were transferred to the Middle East, volunteers from Palestine became involved in a plethora of missions, almost none of which had any direct bearing on the fate of European Jewry. These included the unsuccessful sabotage in the Tripoli oil refineries, wireless propaganda transmissions from Palestine, and the preparation of an intelligence and communication unit that would begin operations should the area fall into enemy hands.

With the German defeat of North Africa in late 1942 and the start of new initiatives in the Balkans in early 1943, the Yishuv leaders realized that future suggestions for cooperative missions could no longer have a Middle Eastern orientation. In view of the fact that the British High Command appeared to be receptive to suggestions concerning European-based operations, several possibilities were resurrected from among the pre-1941 options. Another factor affecting changes in the Yishuv leaders' proposals was the growing amount of information regarding the so-called Final Solution, which was spreading throughout the free world from mid-1942 onward. The Yishuv leaders were particularly affected by firsthand testimony received in November 1942. During that month 78 Palestinian citizens caught in Europe at the outbreak of the war were exchanged with Reich citizens in Palestine: they came to the Yishuv with horror stories about the fate of European Jewry. Their testimony appears to have had an effect on the leaders of the Jewish Agency and their major proposals on military intelligence operations.

The British too appeared to be altering their originally negative attitude toward cooperative European-based intelligence operations including members of the Yishuv. As a result of the changing military situation, they now realized that the Yishuv was offering a desirable solution to their intelligence problems: highly motivated volunteers who were fluent in several foreign languages, familiar with the areas involved, and well versed in local customs. The Yishuv leaders, for their part, considered their initiative as having a twofold purpose: not only would they be assisting the Allies in their war against nazism, but their actions would also be a means of reaching the Jews still in occupied Europe and assisting them in escaping the Nazis or reorganizing local Zionist movements following liberation.

The first cooperative mission was planned during the spring of 1943, after the representatives of the Jewish Agency in Palestine came to an agreement with the "A Force"—a military body engaged in counterintelligence and in the rescue of prisoners of war—regarding a joint mission in the Balkans. Simultaneously the Jewish Agency reached a corresponding agreement with the Inter-Service Liaison Department (ISLD), a division of British military intelligence that had been training wireless operators from the Yishuv. The division of labor involved not only spheres of operation but also target populations: while the Yishuv volunteers working with the ISLD would primarily assist the British forces, those working with A Force would be permitted to concentrate on offering assistance to Jews found in occupied Europe. In May 1943 the first wireless operator from the Yishuv parachuted into Yugoslavia, where he served the local British forces as a communications officer. He was later joined by two more wireless specialists who trained other soldiers in communications.

Missions of this kind required extensive preparation. In early March 1943 a first group of 14 ISLD volunteers were chosen to participate in a training exercise held in Cairo as preparation for their European mission. The group returned to Palestine after two months of training but for various reasons were not sent on missions for more than a year. It appears that in Cairo tensions had developed between the volunteers, who were supposed to serve as parachutists, and their British officers regarding the level of importance given to the "Jewish" facet of their mission. Furthermore, the volunteers refused to be officially inducted into the British army, a condition which the British considered essential in case of capture by the enemy and over which there was general disagreement between various groups in the Yishuv and the British government.

In addition to these difficulties, internal Yishuv logistics of the bureaucracy surrounding the volunteers threatened to destroy their mission even before they left Palestinian soil. It seems that official responsibility for the group passed through several hands before coming to rest in those of the Chet committee, a special group established by the Jewish Agency to deal with the volunteer parachutists. The liaison officer between the British and this group was Enzo Sereni, an Italian Jew with a doctorate in philosophy who had immigrated to Palestine and was a founding member of a well-established kibbutz. A pivotal member of the Labor Movement in Palestine, the energetic Sereni had already participated in both official and clandestine missions abroad and was eventually to join one of the later groups on its mission to parachute into occupied northern Italy. Caught by the Germans, Sereni was held in camps in Italy and Germany and was executed in Dachau in November 1944.

Yet another group that played a major role in recruiting the parachutists and dealing with them prior to their mission was the Palmach, a military group that had begun as local defense units with British blessing. Many of the parachutists were originally members of the Palmach, which also maintained the responsibility of training the volunteers. In addition to their military instruction, the volunteer parachutists underwent ideological indoctrination during a seminar of several weeks held in Kibbutz Hazorea during the summer of 1943.

In spite of the plethora of Palestinian groups involved in the operation, Yishuv-based logistics played only a secondary role in the decision to drop parachutists from Palestine in occupied Europe. A major factor affecting the feasibility of the missions was the Allied advances in Sicily and southern Italy. With the capture of air bases close to occupied Europe, it became possible to fly parachutists over enemy territory and drop them on target. Thus Bari became a major base of parachutist operations and the last stop for all such missions before parachutists were dropped into enemy country.

The next pair of parachutists landed in Romanian territory in October 1943 and was immediately captured by the Romanian authorities. A later pair, also sent to Romania, was also taken shortly after arrival. In view of the problems of parachuting directly into occupied territory, it was suggested that parachutists should be dropped in the liberated areas of Yugoslavia, whence they would make their way to the target area. This procedure was adopted from early 1944 onward.

During the spring of 1944 several parachutists began their mission almost simultaneously in northern Yugoslavia. One group attempted to make their way to Romania, another to Hungary, and a third to Austria. Simultaneously other parachutists, destined for Slovakia, began their final training in Palestine in preparation for their mission.

The Nazi invasion of Hungary in March 1944 caused an abrupt change of plans in the group attempting to cross the border to Budapest. A quick border crossing was no longer feasible; instead the parachutists were destined to remain with the Yugoslav partisans for several months until one of them, Hannah Szenes, demanded to be allowed to carry out the original mission. Having crossed the border in the company of a local partisan, the 22-year-old Szenes was captured. She spent the next five months in various Hungarian and German prisons until her execution in November 1944. Refusing a pardon offered by the Hungarian authorities if she admitted her guilt as a spy, Szenes went valiantly to her death, becoming the Israeli symbol of the entire parachutist mission.

The other two members of Szenes's mission, Joel Palgi and Peretz Goldstein, the youngest of the parachutists, were imprisoned within days of reaching Budapest. The former had been arrested by the authorities, and the latter was persuaded by local Jewish leaders to surrender himself in order to protect his friend. During late summer 1944 the two men were moved to the prison where Szenes was being held, and the three managed to achieve sporadic contact. Following Szenes's execution the other two were transported to Germany. Palgi escaped from the cattle car en route to the Reich and managed to return to Budapest, where he assisted in reorganizing the Zionist movement after Hungary's liberation. Goldstein did not succeed in jumping from the train and was last seen in Oranienburg concentration camp in January 1945.

As the Hungarian drama unfolded, yet another mission was taking form. Following the Slovakian uprising in August 1944, an additional group of parachutists was sent to the area in order to assist downed British pilots in escaping through the newly liberated territory. Three of the parachutists were dropped; the fourth, Haviva Reik, was forbidden to participate in an unmarked drop on grounds of her sex but was later sent to the area in an American transport plane. This quartet was then joined by another parachutist, Abba Berdichev, who later attempted to travel overland to his native Romania. During early fall 1944 the five worked to-

A group of Jewish parachutists from Palestine, who were dropped behind enemy lines, with women from the Yugoslav underground. 1944

gether to carry out both their British military mission and their Zionist-related tasks. In addition to assisting the British pilots who had escaped into Slovakia, they joined local Zionist leaders in organizing Jews who had found refuge in the liberated enclave of Banska Bystrica.

In mid-October Berdichev left the Slovakian group, joining a British transport that was attempting to reach the Hungarian border. He and the British transport were captured by the Germans and transferred to the Mauthausen concentration camp in Austria, where they were murdered by the Nazis in January 1945. The rest of the Slovakian group did not fare much better than their hapless compatriot. Retreating from the advancing German forces, the parachutists had set up a temporary camp in the mountains in which about 40 local Jews of all ages had found refuge. In November 1944 the camp was overrun by the enemy and three of the parachutists—Haviva Reik, Rafael Reiss, and Zvi

Ben-Yaakov—were captured, imprisoned, and eventually executed.

Although both the Yishuv and the British military authorities were as yet unaware of what had happened to most of the parachutists, the direction that the overall mission had taken was obvious. By early 1945 it was decided to cancel the mission and order those parachutists still on European soil back to Palestine. By the beginning of 1946 the fate of nearly all the missing parachutists had been confirmed. With one exception all the surviving members of the parachutists' mission had returned home.

The possibility of success and the ultimate results of the parachutists' mission are a hotly debated theme in the historiography of the Yishuv during the Holocaust. Some claim that despite its lack of feasibility the parachutists' mission was proposed by the Yishuv leadership in order to counter the accusation that it was doing little to assist European Jewry during the

Holocaust. In response, others note that the idea of parachuting former Europeans behind enemy lines did not originate in Palestine but was put into action by British military intelligence in all parts of Europe. Furthermore, in the face of criticism regarding the parachutists' lack of success in their Zionist rescue mission, there are those who note their achievements in their original task of acting as wireless operators and assisting the Allied forces by helping escaped pilots to reach safety. Finally, both those who consider the parachutists' mission a success and those who portray it as too little and too late admit its achievement as a morale booster. Even when the parachutists were caught and executed, word of the mission reached hundreds if not thousands of Jews in occupied Europe, who thus received tangible proof that the Jewish leadership in Palestine had not abandoned them.

Judith Tydor Baumel

Paris On the eve of World War II two-thirds of the 330,000 Jews of France lived in Paris and its suburbs.

This was a result of an uninterrupted influx of Jews to the capital since the time of the French Revolution. The migration—first of Sephardic Jews after Emancipation, later of Ashkenazi Jews from Alsace, whose numbers increased even more after 1871—had brought to Paris the vast majority of the country's Jewish community, whose urbanization rate far exceeded that of other sectors of the population. Successive waves of immigration from Central and Eastern Europe, until the outbreak of the war, confirmed the capital's primacy.

This concentration was reflected in an extreme dynamism of organizations with which the many immigrant Jews in the Paris region were affiliated, particularly the central Jewish subsection of the Immigrant Workers Organization (MOI)—the union of Jewish Communists—which flourished almost exclusively in Paris. French-born Jews, on the other hand, weakly involved with Jewish organizations, blended into the general population; their social integration was on an individual basis.

Four young Jews walk through the Jewish Quarter of Paris. Circa May 1942

On 14 June 1940 Paris, having been declared an open city, was taken without resistance by the Germans, whose offensive had begun just a month earlier. On 17 June Marshal Philippe Pétain, the hero of Verdun and premier since the previous day, ordered the French army to lay down its arms; the armistice came into force on 25 June. Thereafter France was partitioned into zones, each with its own status. Paris became the German capital of France and the headquarters of the German occupation authorities, notably the Militärbefehlshaber in Frankreich (MBF, military command in France), the Abwehr (military intelligence), and the Judenreferat (the special department for Jewish affairs of the RSHA, the Reich Security Main Office), headed by Theodor Dannecker.

Conditions under the occupation—the organized looting by the Germans, annexation of coal-rich districts of northern France to the military government in Belgium—made the already difficult living conditions still worse. In Paris, more than any other place, poverty was endemic. Wintertime was particularly hard. The capital's population was constantly beset by problems of food supply.

While the French government relocated to the resort town of Vichy, the French fascist movements, which advocated unremitting collaboration and reproached the Vichy government for its softness in this respect, were developing in Paris, encouraged and financed by the Germans. Given the German presence, antisemitic propaganda in its most virulent form was prominent in the press. It justified the measures taken against the Jews and sometimes prepared public opinion in advance of an intensification of those measures. It was in Paris too that French antisemites, under German supervision, established the French Institute on Jewish Questions, which in the autumn of 1941 organized a widely publicized antisemitic exhibition entitled "The Jew and France." On the night of 2–3 October 1941 seven bombs exploded, causing damage to seven synagogues in the capital. Although this was an isolated incident, the attack nevertheless indicated the lengths to which the French collaborators were prepared to go.

The exodus that followed the defeat of the French armed forces, and then the German military government's ban on Jews' returning to the occupied zone (27 September 1940), were the first steps in a redistribution of the Jewish population, whose number in Paris kept dropping. The census ordered by the German authorities, carried out in the fall of 1940, recorded almost 150,000 Jews in Paris. A year later, another census found only 133,000.

Initially it was French-born Jews who predominated among those fleeing the capital. From the spring of 1941, however, immigrant Jews, the prime targets of the round-ups, also looked for every possible way out. This trend intensified in the summer of 1942, after the decree that all Jews six years of age and older in the occupied zone wear the yellow star and after the Vel d'Hiv round-up. A final census of foreign Jews in the Département of the Seine (Paris and its environs), conducted during the first week of December 1943, located only 6,472, less than 10 percent of those registered in the fall 1940 census.

Until May 1941 the Jews of Paris seemed to be menaced first and foremost by social marginalization and pauperization, accelerated by both French and German legislation. There had been four successive German orders concerning the Parisian Jews (27 September and 18 October 1940 and 26 April and 28 May 1941). They were required to report to police stations for the census, and they left carrying identity papers on which the word *Juif* (Jew) appeared in red ink. They had to affix a yellow sign to their shops and offices: *Jüdisches Geschäft, Entreprise Juive* (Jewish business). This was the first step toward the aryanization of their property. Next, temporary "Aryan" stewards were appointed, first by the Germans and then by the French. They were responsible for "definitively eliminating the Jewish influence on the French economy" by selling or liquidating the business. Deprived of their property, the Jews then witnessed the blocking of their bank accounts and found themselves banned from professions that brought them into contact with the public. At the same time Vichy legislation, which also applied to the occupied zone, excluded them from a large number of professions. In the summer of 1940 lawyers and doctors of foreign parentage had to abandon their professions. The Status of Jews law (3 October 1940) excluded Jews from a whole series of functions: the military, most civil service jobs (for example, 426 Jews working in the national education system were dismissed), and all occupations connected with the press, media, and cinema were henceforth off limits to Jews. Moreover, the combination of censorship and self-censorship had put an end to the professional activities of writers and journalists who had no outlets in which to publish their work, of artists who were no longer in demand, and of painters who were not allowed to exhibit their works. In the summer of 1941 half the Jewish population of Paris had no means of earning a living.

The indigent turned to Jewish institutions, which gradually resumed their operations in the capital. The most important Jewish leaders had taken refuge in the southern zone; hence the first groups to resurface were the Jewish immigrant organizations, associated since September 1939 in a social welfare bureau for immigrant Jews, part of a coordination committee sponsored by the Federation of the Jewish Societies in France. On 15 June 1940 they coordinated their efforts by setting up the Amelot Committee. There was also a welfare committee run by the representatives of French-born Jews under the aegis of the Jewish Consistory of Paris (ACIP). In addition to distributing financial assistance and running a used-clothing depot, they expanded their activities substantially with four soup kitchens serving an average of 1,500 meals a day and providing a meeting place for Jews eager for information. The Germans encouraged the development of welfare activities. They saw them as the nucleus of an organization that they wanted to set up to strengthen their control over the Jews. By exerting extreme pressure on the Paris Jewish leaders, they managed to create a coordinating agency and a newspaper, *Informations Juives*, the only authorized Jewish publication at the time. Its columns detailed the obligations to which Jews were subject and the penalties for disobedience. Under cover of a call for Jewish unity, Jews were invited to sign up at the coordination committee. The paper emphasized that no Jew, even if nonpracticing, could hope to escape his or her condition. Cultural trimmings and historical analysis—such as articles on episodes in the history of French Jewry, in which periods of Jewish decline were explained by internal divisions—appeared side by side with practical information, times of worship in the synagogues, and various welfare services for the needy.

Starting in the spring of 1941, however, the threat became more acute. On 14 May 3,710 Jews, most of them Polish, who had answered a summons to an "identity check," were arrested and sent to camps in Pithiviers and Beaune-la-Rolande in the Loiret. Between 20 and 23 August 4,232 Jews were picked up by the French police in the streets of the 11th Arrondissement or at home and sent to the Drancy camp outside Paris. In these and later cases the list of victims was drafted on the basis of a file compiled by the French authorities after the fall 1940 census.

The Drancy camp—a long, horseshoe-shaped building surrounded by barbed wire, which had previously housed British prisoners of war—was totally unequipped for its new occupants. Stripped of their identity papers and packed 50 to 60 to a barracks room, the inmates often had to sleep on the cement floor. Starvation swiftly became the norm. Visits were not allowed: only from the start of November 1941 were the Jewish welfare organizations able to send food parcels, via the Red Cross. Despite several improvements—mattresses, parcels, a semblance of heating, and the like—in this camp, under French administration, death from malnutrition was rampant. The desperate situation triggered a wave of releases—750 walking skeletons—which the Germans soon halted.

Late 1941 was marked by the shooting of hostages by the occupiers in revenge for attacks on German soldiers in Paris. There were 51 Jews among the 95 victims at Mont-Valerien (15 December 1941); Jews selected from the inmates of Drancy served as prime victims in this hostage system.

A new wave of arrests began on 12 December 1941. This time the Germans ran the show and aimed straight for the head: 743 affluent, mostly French-born Jews were arrested at home in a dawn raid. Menaced by machine guns, they were transferred that same evening in the most brutal fashion to the German-administered camp of Compiègne-Royallieu, where the conditions were particularly harsh and grew worse over the ensuing weeks.

On 27 March 1942, 565 inmates of Drancy, joined by 547 inmates of the Royallieu camp, were escorted by French gendarmes to the only deportation train ever composed of third-class compartments, and they left French soil forever. In June four more trainloads of Jewish inmates of Drancy were deported from France—this time in boxcars. Thereafter Drancy became a transit camp, an antechamber of Auschwitz.

At the same time ever more stringent restrictions were gnawing at the daily life of Parisian Jews. On 13 August 1941 they were required to deposit their radio sets at a police station. A decree issued by the Paris police headquarters on 10 December 1941 (reinforced by the sixth German order on 7 February 1942), forbade them to change their domicile. Their bicycles were confiscated at a time when identity checks at the exits of metro stations were increasing. In 1942 the theaters of Paris were packed with citizens seeking diversion from their daily travails, but the same edict instituted a curfew for Jews only, making it out of the question for them to go to an evening show.

On 1 June 1942 a new German measure was announced that radically altered the situation of the Jews of Paris. Henceforth they were required to sew onto their clothes, at chest height, a yellow star with the word *Juif* written in black. At first the decree applied only to French Jews, stateless Jews, and Jews from countries where the same measure was in force. Soon, however, the yellow star became mandatory for all Jews in the occupied zone. There followed a series of laws aimed at segregating Jews from the rest of the population. Jews were relegated to the last car of the metro, then barred from most public places, including parks, restaurants, cafes, theaters, swimming pools, beaches, museums, and libraries. The ninth German decree (8 July 1942) forbade them the use of public telephones just when their private telephones were shut off. Thereafter they were allotted only one hour a day to do their shopping.

The yellow star was in effect a preparatory measure heralding mass round-ups of Jews to keep the transports full. At dawn on 16 July 1942 some 4,500 French policemen were dispatched to arrest 27,361 stateless Jews aged two to 55. This round-up, which has gone down in history as the Vel d'Hiv round-up—the Vélodrome d'Hiver was the bicycle racetrack to which the arrested families were initially taken—netted 13,152 Jews. The proportion of women and children was particularly high, as rumors of an impending raid had circulated in the preceding days and many men had gone into hiding, never imagining that women and children would also be targeted. A few days after the round-up all the adults who had no children were transferred to Drancy and from there deported to Auschwitz. The transports, also supplied by round-ups in the southern zone, left Drancy at a rate of three a week (about 1,000 Jews on each train) until the end of September 1942. Children and their families were at first interned in the camps of Pithiviers and Beaune-la-Rolande. There the parents and the children were separated. The children were left by themselves in these camps, and the parents were deported to Auschwitz. Hence their parents were the first to travel the road to Auschwitz. At the behest of the French police, who did not want to be burdened with the unsupervised children left behind, the Germans later authorized their

inclusion in the convoys. The children were sent to the gas chambers two weeks after their parents.

In subsequent months Paris was the scene of numerous round-ups and no less numerous arrests of individual Jews, who were then interned in Drancy and in most cases deported. Baltic, Bulgarian, Dutch, and Yugoslav Jews were arrested on 14 September 1942, Romanian Jews on 23 September, and Greek Jews on the night of 4–5 November. These round-ups, carried out on German orders but by French policemen, who used lists compiled by police headquarters on the basis of census data, continued until February 1944. Neither hospitals nor old-age homes were spared. The lulls between round-ups did not put a damper on individual arrests. The crackdown on Parisian Jews continued until the city was liberated.

From the summer of 1942 on, Paris was being depleted of its Jewish population. In addition to the thousands who had been arrested and deported, many had fled to the south of France in search of refuge. By the summer of 1943 there were only about 60,000 Jews left in Paris and its inner suburbs. This number was to decrease further.

The General Union of French Jews (Union Général des Israélites de France, UGIF) was the official liaison group between the Jews and the French authorities. Established by a Vichy law of 29 November 1941 and replacing all previous organizations except the central Consistoire, the UGIF distributed aid and managed to liberate hundreds of children from Drancy—using every legal dodge—but on condition that they were

The arrest and round-up of Jews in the 11th Arrondissement of Paris. 20 August 1941

securely ensconced in the UGIF's own children's homes. The Amelot Committee, for its part, moved further into clandestine activity. It helped those who wanted to sneak across into the unoccupied zone and extended discreet assistance to those who could not turn to the UGIF—those needing false papers and looking for Aryan families to shelter children at risk. At the same time the committee continued to run the soup kitchens, which were financed mainly by the UGIF. The dual nature (legal and clandestine) of the committee's work compromised its leaders, who as Jews were a priori suspect and under surveillance. The arrest of its head, David Rapoport, on 1 June 1943, and then of Eugène Minkowski, director of the children's aid organization (the OSE, part of the Amelot Committee), on 23 August 1943, caused the organization to abandon any semblance of legality in the fall of 1943. Active rescue work was at an end; thereafter the Amelot Committee continued only its clandestine support for those children and adults who were already under its protection. More and more Jews were going underground and living under false identities.

While many went into hiding, some opted to join the resistance. The Jewish Communist resistance, in particular, first coalesced in Paris, where there were many immigrants. The cadres of the prewar organizations still existed, even though, as known Communists, they had had to go underground.

The Parisian districts that were home to the immigrant Jews were lively centers of Communist propaganda. When the Communists turned to armed struggle, Jews figured prominently in the FTP-MOI, Communist armed resistance groups, established in the spring of 1942. They constituted 90 percent of the first, "Romanian and Hungarian" detachment and all of the second detachment (there were four detachments) called the "Jewish detachment." There was also a group of Jewish women who carried weapons to the various units. After the Vel d'Hiv round-up, many young Jews whose parents or close friends had been brutally rounded up by the French police joined the Jewish partisans of the MOI. Until mid-1943 the FTP-MOI carried out many military operations in the capital, with Jews directly responsible for approximately two-thirds of the raids staged in Paris between July 1942 and July 1943. The only armed Communist party group in Paris had been neutralized after the arrest of the entire staff of the Paris-region FTP in January 1943. As liberation approached, the Communist leadership was eager to claim responsibility for military action in the capital. Hence when the Jewish fighters, aware that they had been targeted by the police, asked to be transferred to the southern zone in late April 1943, arguing that the Jewish masses had already taken refuge there, the leadership refused. The partisans continued their activities in the capital until the arrest of the Manouchian group in November 1943 put an end to the FTP-MOI in the Paris region.

For the Jews who had remained in the capital, the start of 1944 saw an escalation of the crackdown. The cruelest episode was the seizure by Alois Brunner, an SS lieutenant on Adolf Eichmann's staff, of 250 Jewish children from UGIF homes between 21 and 25 July 1944. As the hour of liberation drew near, the Jewish movements, copying the example of the general resistance, returned to Paris after a period of organizing in the south.

On 15 August 1944 the Paris police—the same police who had arrested the Jews—went on strike and gave the signal for an uprising against the occupying forces. The surviving members of the Zionist Jewish Fighters Organization (the OJC, whose Paris branch had been dismantled in mid-July) mobilized, as did the Communist-backed Jewish patriotic militias, which numbered some 200 men. Alois Brunner left the Drancy camp with the Germans and a last transport of 51 deportees on 17 August. The last 1,386 Jewish inmates there were liberated a few days later; their place was taken by collaborators arrested by the resistance.

On 26 August, Gen. Charles de Gaulle paraded triumphantly with his Free French troops down the Champs Elysées. On 2 September the provisional government of the French Republic was set up in liberated France. The period of reconstruction began. Of the 75,721 Jews deported from France, 97 percent had died in the gas chambers of Auschwitz. The handful of deportees who returned, as well as those who had found refuge in the southern zone, now attempted to recover their rights and property.

Renée Poznanski

Patria Ship on which the British Mandatory officials planned in November 1940 to deport to Mauritius Jewish refugees who had entered Palestine illegally. To prevent the deportation, the Haganah (Jewish underground defense force) sabotaged the ship while it was in Haifa harbor by detonating explosives in the engine room. The *Patria* sank within minutes; 267 refugees perished. See ILLEGAL IMMIGRATION

Pavelić, Ante (1889–1959) Leader of the radical Croat independent movement, later head of the Croat state established by the Germans and Italians after their conquest of Yugoslavia in 1941. Pavelić preached a fascist doctrine and became the founder of the Ustasha, a nationalist and terrorist organization. As head of state, Pavelić added antisemitism to the Ustasha ideology and brought about the deaths of many thousands of Serbs and Jews. His regime was distinguished by extreme brutality. Pavelić escaped to Argentina after the war and died in Spain. See YUGOSLAVIA

Pellepoix, Louis Darquier de (1897–1980) Commissar for Jewish affairs under the French government at Vichy, 1942–44. Pellepoix collaborated with German authorities and helped to organize the deportation of Jews from France. He escaped to Spain at the end of the war. See FRANCE

Pétain, (Henri) Philippe (1856–1951) Marshal of France, hero of World War I, head of the French government at Vichy after German conquest of France in June 1940. Pétain implemented French persecution of Jews. After the war the French government convicted Pétain of treason and condemned him to death, but his sentence was commuted to life imprisonment.

Pius XII (Eugenio Pacelli; 1876–1958) Head of the Roman Catholic church during part of World War II. Pius's refusal to publicly condemn the Nazis' treatment of Jews and Catholics, despite pleas from within and outside the church, was sharply criticized after the war. See CATHOLIC CHURCH, ROMAN

Plaszow Forced labor and concentration camp in a suburb of Kraków. Established in 1942, by 1944 Plaszow held 25,000 prisoners, about 10,000 of them Polish. Death from the exhausting slave labor and at the hand of the commandant Amon Goeth was common in the first two years of the camp. After the SS took over Plaszow in 1944, firing squads murdered 8,000 prisoners outright; the rest were deported to labor and death camps by January 1945.

Pohl, Oswald (1892–1951) Senior SS official, head of the SS business empire that included major building projects. Pohl was in charge of the forced labor units recruited from concentration camp inmates, a work force of more than 500,000 prisoners who were leased to private factories. He was responsible for selling Jewish possessions—jewelry, gold fillings, hair, and clothing—to provide funds for the German government. Captured in 1946, Pohl was sentenced to death in the Landsberg trial and was executed in June 1951.

Poles and Jews in World War II The question of the attitude of the non-Jewish Polish population (hereafter "Poles") toward the Jews during World War II is highly controversial, if not explosive. It is impossible to reduce the relationship of the Poles to the Jews to a one-sided assertion. All broad generalizations are bound to be not only false but also unjust.

Even before the war, Polish-Jewish relations had for many years been steadily deteriorating. The 1930s were marked by an unprecedented outburst of antisemitism. A dramatic rise of violence took the form either of pogroms or of fights in the universities, where Jewish students were forced to sit separately in what were known as the "ghetto benches." The *numerus clausus*—a "closed number" or racial quota—as applied to Jews in universities and the public service sometimes became in effect a *numerus nullus*. The liberal professions increasingly introduced the so-called Aryan Paragraph in their statutes. Rapidly growing nationalist groups pushed for the suppression of civil rights for Jews and fought for a radical exclusion of Jews from the rest of Polish society. The majority of the political elite considered the so-called Jewish question a foremost priority that implied the voluntary or forced emigration of Jews. (One proposal, to send Jews to the French colony of Madagascar, was actively explored by emissaries of France and Poland in 1938.) The civic culture, particularly weak in Poland owing to the late institutionalization of the state, was unable to transcend ethno-religious differences. Although formally citizens, Jews were nonetheless considered foreigners in Polish society without the same rights and legitimacy as other citizens. From a nationalist perspective, their simple presence in Poland constituted a threat to national identity. As a result, the social and political integration of Jewish citizens in Poland remained weak.

Solidarity of ethnic Poles with Jews during the occupation was in large part determined by the nature of the ties and social networks established before the war. The greater the density of these family ties, mutual friendships, and political links, the higher the chances of survival were for Jews. In the regions where antisemitism was rampant, the risk of being denounced

POLAND

■ Concentration camps
▬ National borders, 1929
⋯ National borders, 2000

0   50   100   200 Km

BALTIC
SEA

Memel

LITHUANIA

Kovno

Vilna

Königsberg (Kaliningrad)

Danzig
■ Stutthof

EAST PRUSSIA
(GERMANY)

Grodno

Minsk

BELORUSSIA

Bialystok

Warta

Schokken ■
Poznan

GERMANY

Vistula   Bug

■ Treblinka

Brest-Litovsk
(Brzesc nad Bugiem)

Pripet
Marshes

Pripet

Pinsk

Chelmno (Kulhof) ■

Warsaw ■ Pawiak

POLAND

Oder

Radogosz ■
Lodz (Litzmannstadt)

Sobibor ■

Radom

Lublin
Majdanek ■ ■

Poniatowa ■

Schmolz

Gross-Rosen (Rogoznica) ■

■ Breslau

Dzierzazna ■

SILESIA

Skarzysko-Kamienna

Trawniki ■

Huta-Komarowska
Chelm

UKRAINE

○ Kielce

Sandomierz ○

Belzec ■
Zamosc ○

VOLHYNIA

Biesiadka ■

Katowice

Kraków

Auschwitz-Birkenau ■

Prague

Mielec ○
Plaszow ■ ■ Pustkow
Wieliczka ■ Tarnow

Janowska ■

Lvov

Ostrova ○

■ Zakopane

GALICIA

Vinnitsa ○

Dniester

Brno ○

CZECHOSLOVAKIA

N

A Jewish-owned shop in Danzig (Gdansk), with "Jude" scrawled on the walls.

was great. But in some small villages, where Jews had coexisted for centuries with the local Christian population, they had a greater chance of finding refuge with their Polish neighbors.

Antisemitism was sufficiently established in Poland at the time of the German invasion that it did not become associated with collaboration with the Nazis, as the sociologist Aleksander Smolar has noted. The indifference, malevolence, and hostility already present in the 1930s may actually have gained ground during the war. For instance, during bombing raids in Warsaw, Jews were refused entry to some air-raid shelters. After the initial shock of the defeat, the period between October 1939 and November 1940 (when the Warsaw ghetto was sealed) was marked by incessant acts of popular anti-Jewish violence, such as random attacks on the streets. Polish delinquents often led Germans to Jewish apartments or shops and together plundered and humiliated Jews. The anti-Jewish vio-lence progressively increased in scale to turn into full-blown pogroms, during which could be heard such slo-gans as "We want Warsaw without the Jews." In March 1940, during the celebration of Passover, the violence in the capital lasted the full eight days of the holiday. The pogrom extended to several neighborhoods, where rumors spread of ritual murders committed by Jews. Groups of several hundred persons armed with clubs smashed windows and beat any Jews they en-countered.

These manifestations of popular antisemitism, some-times encouraged and always tolerated by the Ger-mans, were not ignored by the Polish authorities, as the report by Jan Karski sent in February 1940 to the gov-ernment-in-exile reveals. In the official version trans-mitted to the Allies, the report was falsified to temper the rampant antisemitism. The original version, how-ever, recognized the danger for the moral and political unity of the nation: the resolution of the Jewish ques-tion was creating "something akin to a narrow bridge upon which the Germans and a large portion of Polish society are finding agreement." According to the re-port, the creation of a Jewish-Polish front against the common enemy would "encounter serious resistance within the large segments of Polish society whose anti-semitism has not diminished."

Before the beginning of the extermination, neither the resistance movement nor the government-in-exile reacted with energy to denounce the violence and hos-tility against Jews. The absence of a forceful and ex-plicit condemnation undoubtedly lent the *szmalcown-icy*, or extortionists, a sense of impunity and probably contributed to the development of groups of black-mailers and informers, who had Jews at their mercy. In Warsaw the first execution of an individual by the re-sistance for the denunciation of Jews was not until August 1943. Two other informers were executed in December 1944.

As a result, Jews hiding in the so-called Aryan zone feared not only the Germans or the Gestapo. They also had to worry about the "navy-blue police" (the official Polish police) and, above all, the blackmailers. Rare are the survivors who did not encounter them at least once. Streets in large cities became hunting grounds. On the lookout for Jews in the Aryan zone, they robbed them of all their possessions by threatening to take them to the police. The danger could come from any-where—neighbors, caretakers, managing agents of buildings, and even, as numerous examples demonstrate, Polish children educated in the antisemitic tradition. Even those who had escaped from the camps or who had jumped off the transport trains were robbed. Consequently, Jews in hiding lived in constant fear that their lives were endangered not only by the Germans but also by Poles. One informer was enough to cause the death of hundreds or even thousands of Jews. The ghetto wall was crossed in both directions: most of those who escaped to the Aryan zone and managed to hide for a time became victims of blackmail and returned to the ghetto stripped of their possessions and psychologically defeated.

Young Jewish men conducting a business transaction over the Warsaw ghetto wall.

This general hostility is described in a telegram sent to London on 25 September 1941 by Stefan Grot-Rowecki, leader of the Polish underground Home Army (Armia Krajowa): "I report that all statements and policies of the government and the National Council concerning the Jews in Poland create the worst possible impression in the country and facilitate propaganda directed against the government. . . . Please accept it as a fact that the overwhelming majority of the country is antisemitic. Even socialists are not an exception in this respect. The only differences concern how to deal with the Jews. Almost nobody advocates the adoption of German methods. Even secret organizations remaining under the influence of the prewar activists in the Democratic Club of the Socialist party adopt the postulate of emigration as a solution to the Jewish problem. This has become as much of a truism as, for instance, the necessity to eliminate Germans."

To understand the complexity of Jewish-Polish relations, we must also consider the myth of the *zydoko-muna,* or Jewish commune. This myth had emerged at the beginning of the twentieth century and retained all its force at the moment of the sovietization of Eastern Europe. By combining the political adversary with the ethnic foe, it questioned the loyalty of Jews, who, along with other minorities in Eastern Europe, were often accused of plotting with the enemy. During World War II the Jews were accused of betraying Poland by welcoming with open arms the Red Army, which had occupied the eastern half of Poland in 1939, and of collaborating actively with the Soviets. In fact, the Communist influence was minimal among the Polish Jews. According to the 1944 data 30 percent of Polish citizens deported to the Soviet Union were Jews. Whether or not true, beliefs have a strong effect on society, and the myth of the Jewish commune, which fueled the accusation of Jewish sympathy for Russian communism, was widely diffused in the civilian population as well as the political elite. Moreover, it was reinforced by the opposition between the resistance directed by London and the Communist resistance groups backed by the Soviet Union. During the Warsaw ghetto uprising, for example, Yitzhak Zuckerman (known as Antek), a leader of the Jewish Fighting Organization (ZOB), asked a representative of the Home Army to prepare to evacuate the resistance fighters. The representative replied, "We simply don't trust you. According to us, the ghetto is simply a base of Soviet Russia. . . . The Russians have prepared the defense of the Warsaw ghetto, and you have more arms than you let on. I am convinced that on May 1 the Russians will liberate the ghetto."

Was it the fear of a loss of popular support, especially during the first two years of the German occupation, that explains the weak reaction of the Polish government-in-exile to the immediate sufferings of millions of Polish Jews? Whatever may be the causes, the underground resistance in Poland furnished no moral, material, or military aid to the Warsaw ghetto before August 1942. It behaved as though the destiny of the Jewish citizens did not concern them, as if the Jewish and Polish experience of the occupation belonged to two different social realities. This perception is reflected by Grot-Rowecki in an order dated 10 November 1942: "Regarding the extermination of the Jews by the occupier, a general feeling of anxiety is developing in Polish society, which fears that after the Jews, the Germans will begin to liquidate Poles in the same manner. . . . If the Germans ever attempted such an operation, they would meet with active resistance on our part. Even if the moment of the uprising has not yet arrived, the divisions under my orders will take up active combat to defend the existence of the nation."

In the eyes of the immense majority of Poles, it appeared natural that the resistance should be more concerned with the non-Jewish Poles than with the Jewish ones. For a society without a tradition of citizenship but with a history of strong ethnic nationalism, it seemed only normal that solidarity should depend on ethnic-religious proximity. The divergence of the destinies of Jews and Poles deepened old cleavages between the communities. Crushed by economic hardship, food shortages, and a German terror that had not spared the Polish elite, many Poles seemed to come to terms with the existence of the ghettos and the violence against the Jews by considering that they were not implicated in the "Judeo-German war." Writers such as Czeslaw Milosz, Jerzy Andrzejewski, and Szymon Rudnicki depict an increasing indifference toward the fate of the Jews in much the same way as historians describe the apparent anesthesia of the populations living in close proximity to the death camps.

Anti-Jewish acts, ranging from segregation and exclusion to expulsion, which were already widespread before the war, were broadly supported by public opinion. In the winter of 1940 certain Polish leaders, such as Roman Knoll, the former Polish ambassador to Berlin and a delegate of the government-in-exile to the

underground, considered that the only choice was between Zionism or extermination; he advocated resettling the Jews to the area around Odessa. With the exception of the Communist press and the major publications of the Home Army, the majority of the 1,500 underground publications remained more or less anti-Jewish. In particular the opinion of the press of the National Democrats and Christian Democrats, the dominant political force since the late nineteenth century, was that as long as there were Jews in Poland, there would also be a Jewish question, and thus postwar Poland should be free of Jews. Even if the German methods were rejected, the results of the initial policy of separation and isolation of the Jews were widely accepted and even applauded. In a report sent to London in the fall of 1941 a government delegate wrote, "The inhuman terror to which the Jews are subjected is universally condemned and evokes much pity. But the social and particularly the economic isolation are generally approved of. A certain fear, especially in merchant circles, goes with it—namely that the Jews might eventually return to their dominant position in the economy."

After the deportation and extermination of the Jews of Warsaw had begun, the attitude of certain sectors of Polish society seemed to change. In general, Poles had been well informed via the underground press since the beginning of the war about German atrocities regarding the Jews. Nevertheless, information transmitted to London by a member of the Home Army working at the railway station of Treblinka concerning the first deportations to the death camps was made public by the government-in-exile with much delay. But this was not a specifically Polish response. Even the BBC in London disregarded the reports on the deportations and seemed in no more of a hurry to broadcast the information to the public than the government-in-exile was.

The start of the exterminations provoked a reaction from the intelligentsia, but not necessarily deep reflection about Jewish-Polish relations. *Protest*, a pamphlet written in August 1942 by the Catholic writer Zofia Kasak-Szczucka, one of the founders of the Relief Council for Jews (RPZ) in the fall of 1942, is typical of the realization of the horror of the extermination. The pamphlet did not, however, go so far as to question traditional antisemitism. Condemning the silence of the world when confronted with the genocide, the pamphlet proclaims: "Those who remain silent in the face of crime become its accomplices. . . . As Polish Catholics, we speak out. Our feelings toward Jews have not changed. We continue to regard them as the economic, political, and ideological enemies of Poland. . . . One is not forced to like the Jews; one can hope for their emigration after the war, but as long as they are persecuted, as long as they are murdered, we must help them." The sudden surge of solidarity caused by the discovery of the horror resulted in a call to save the Jews not because of the feeling of proximity based on a common citizenship or humanity, but rather despite the fact that they fundamentally remained enemies. Anti-Jewish prejudice, therefore, did not necessarily result in anti-Jewish action: confronted with the visible effects of the prejudices and ideology to which they had contributed before the war, some notorious antisemites helped the Jews during the German occupation.

The question of aid is much debated. Beginning in November 1941, helping a Jew was punishable by death. Indeed, it is estimated that some 1,000 Poles were executed for that reason. Furthermore, the Relief Council for Jews, representing all the major Polish and Jewish political parties, was unique in all of Europe. It helped Jews find hiding places, issued them false identity papers, and provided medical assistance to Jewish children. As many as 3,000 to 4,000 Jews may have benefited from the council's financial relief in the middle of 1944. Its role was materially modest but symbolically important.

Despite the strength of antisemitism from the beginning of the war, some Poles—usually but not always leftists—helped Jews. Emanuel Ringelblum, who was saved on two occasions by the Polish and Jewish resistance before being captured and shot by the Nazis in 1944, left this testimony in his diary: "I am living proof that the declarations by certain Jews, who undoubtedly suffered from the tragedy of the Jewish nation in Poland, claiming that the entire Polish population rejoiced at the extermination of the Polish Jews, and that on the Aryan side there was not one person with a heart, is far from the truth." He noted that "there are thousands of idealists like these in Warsaw and throughout the country, both in the intelligentsia and the working class, who help Jews very devotedly at the risk of their lives." The actions of the underground courier Jan Karski, a non-Jewish Pole who first brought details of the Nazi persecution of the Jews to the attention of the government-in-exile, confirm Ringelblum's assertion.

It remains very difficult to estimate the number of Jews saved by the Poles during the war. The latest scholarship puts the number of Jews who survived the occupation hidden by Poles at between 30,000 and 60,000. A further 10,000–15,000 Jews survived in the resistance and in the forests.

In a report dated 12 February 1943, Henryk Wolinski, head of the Jewish department in the directory of the Home Army, stated just before the battle for the Warsaw ghetto that "the only real way to save a large number of people is to organize resistance groups in the forests," where they could find a haven. Nonetheless, integrating the Jews in the resistance organizations was far from easy. Just as the officials of Warsaw refused to integrate Jews in the civil militias to defend the city in 1939, the Home Army, unlike the Communist groups, rarely accepted Jews in their midst; it sometimes even verified the "Aryanness" of its members. The calls for cooperation emanating from the different ghettos often fell on the deaf ears of the officers of the Home Army. Increasingly, toward the end of the war, the resistance groups directed by London and the Communist formations came to violent exchanges. The Jews who had managed to escape from the ghettos risked being assassinated by the extreme right military groups or discovered by peasants who participated in the German measures to liquidate hidden Jews. They also felt threatened by military organizations linked to the Home Army, certain reports of which described the Jewish partisans as criminal gangs. For example, the ZOB group operating in the region of Czestochowa was decimated by a unit of the Home Army in a forest in September 1943 (although the commander of the unit was executed following the massacre). Order No. 116, issued on 15 September 1943 by Tadeusz Bor-Komorowski, the Home Army's deputy commander, which sought to repress criminal bands operating in forests, was sometimes used, independently of its initial intention, as a pretext to liquidate groups of Communists and Jews. This explains why perhaps some historians, such as Shmuel Krakowski, consider that Polish civilians were more likely than the resistance to help Jews.

Opportunities to aid Jews during the war were quite limited, but did the desire to assist them exceed the capacity? In which way was the help, so often emphasized by postwar Polish historians, represented in the social imagination? Public support was incomparably greater for the resistance than it was for the Jews. In the heroic mythology of the war, the deeds of the

Home Army were widely circulated, while the rescue of Jews was rarely, if ever, included in the patriotic accounts of the war.

Nevertheless, it is well known that the Home Army aided ZOB in logistics by providing maps of the Warsaw sewer system and instructions for making Molotov cocktails. During the Warsaw ghetto uprising the resistance created diversions, but it supplied relatively few arms: 10 revolvers by January 1943; 90 revolvers, 600 grenades, and 15 kilograms of explosives before the uprising. Other arms were supplied by Communist resistance groups. None of these actions was publicized by the leaders of the Home Army. The aid provided to the insurgents in the ghetto was also kept secret by the military and civilian underground press both before and after the uprising. Antoni Chrusciel, leader of the Home Army for the Warsaw district, asserted that the secrecy was necessary to avoid alienating the antisemitic elements in the resistance, who were hostile to all aid to Jews. The fact that many Poles who had hidden Jews from the Germans did not wish to see their names published after the war for fear of reprisals by neighbors seems to underscore this explanation. *Paul Zawadzki*

Polish Government-in-Exile The Polish government-in-exile gave legal expression to Polish sovereignty throughout World War II, when Poland was under German and Soviet occupation. It was recognized by Great Britain and the United States as the legitimate government of Poland from its formation on 2 October 1939 until 5 July 1945. Established in Paris and based initially in the French provincial town of Angers, it moved to London following the fall of France in June 1940.

The government-in-exile was formed at the behest of Wladyslaw Raczkiewicz, a former interior minister and Speaker of the Senate, who had been appointed president of the Polish republic on 30 September 1939 in accordance with established emergency constitutional procedures. Raczkiewicz assigned the premiership to Gen. Wladyslaw Sikorski, who had served briefly as prime minister in 1922–23 and had been living in France for much of the previous decade. Sikorski in turn assembled a coalition cabinet consisting mainly of members of the prewar opposition parties—the right-wing National Democrats (Endecja), the right-of-center Labor party, the centrist Peasant party, and the left-wing Polish Socialist party. This cabinet

was advised by the Polish National Council, a broadly based parliament-in-exile, but it was responsible to this body to a limited extent only. A short time later Sikorski was also named commander-in-chief of the Polish armed forces in Poland and abroad.

On 8 November 1939 the government established a Committee for Home Affairs, which undertook to supervise all Polish resistance activities, civilian and military, in the occupied homeland. Civilian resistance was coordinated through the office of the government delegate, which administered a highly ramified network of clandestine social, political, informational, financial, and judicial institutions aimed at strengthening Polish morale in opposition to the occupying regime, impairing the ability of the occupiers to govern, enforcing national discipline, and promoting the material welfare of the beleaguered Polish population. Military resistance was conducted initially by the underground Union for Armed Struggle (Zwiazek Walki Zbrojnej) and, from February 1942, by the Home Army (Armia Krajowa), which numbered more than 200,000 troops by 1944.

The government underwent a number of reorganizations during the war. Three cabinet members resigned following the conclusion of the Polish-Soviet agreement of 31 July 1941. This crisis precipitated the dissolution of the National Council; a second National Council was not summoned until February 1942. Following Sikorski's death in an airplane crash in July 1943, Stanislaw Mikolajczyk, who had been the interior minister and deputy premier, assumed the premiership, and Sikorski's place as commander-in-chief was taken by Gen. Kazimierz Sosnkowski. Mikolajczyk served until November 1944, when he was replaced by Tomasz Arciszewski.

Involvement in Jewish Affairs

Because the Nazi war against the Jews was carried out primarily in Poland, the Polish government-in-exile occupied a unique position among bystanders in the free world. Much of the news about the Final Solution emanated from sources inside Poland, making the Polish government a vital link in transmitting information about the fate of the Jews to the governments and peoples of the West. In addition, operations aimed at rescuing or assisting Jews threatened with death—hiding them, providing them with false papers, smuggling them across borders, or interfering with transports to the death camps—would have to be carried out largely

Polish civilians and resistance fighters stand atop a barricade built to hinder German tanks. 1 August 1944

by Poles, mainly through their government-directed underground apparatus.

The nature of the actions that the government-in-exile eventually took in this regard was influenced by existing attitudes of various government ministers and their parties toward Jews and the Jewish question, by considerations of general wartime political and diplomatic strategy, and by the tenor of government contacts with Jewish representatives throughout the war. Most Jews appear to have regarded at least some of the members of the government and National Council as generally not hostile or even favorably disposed toward their interests, and they were pleased that the National Council included Jewish representatives— Ignacy Schwarzbart and Herman Lieberman on the first council, Schwarzbart and Samuel (Szmul) Zygielbojm (replaced after his death in May 1943 by Emanuel Szerer) on the second. On the other hand, they expressed skepticism about other government and council members. Of the four parties that formed

the backbone of the government coalition, three had previously endorsed to some degree the notion that Poland would be better off if large numbers of Jews were to emigrate, and similar sentiments had begun to surface within the remaining party (the Socialists) on the eve of the war. There was considerable difference among the parties, however, on the urgency of achieving this goal, with only the National Democrats urging active measures to reduce the Jewish population and the Peasants and Socialists opposing them.

Few government figures regarded Polish Jewry as an integral part of the Polish community—a term that was generally defined in an ethnic sense. To be sure, in this attitude they did not differ substantially from many Jewish leaders. But whereas Jewish spokesmen maintained that the government was obliged to provide for the needs and interests of all Polish citizens equally, whether or not they identified as ethnic Poles, government members do not seem to have been of one mind on this issue. On the one hand, the government officially declared in July 1941 that it was "an instrument in the service of all Polish citizens." There is evidence, however, that many ministers tended to view themselves primarily as representatives of a narrowly construed Polish community. There is also disagreement among scholars concerning the extent to which this self-conception affected government responses to the Holocaust. Some hold that no matter how repulsed government ministers may have been by the brutality of the Nazi murder campaign, many viewed the outcome of a substantially smaller Polish Jewry as ultimately beneficial to Poland and were thus disinclined to pursue rescue possibilities in earnest. Others deny this suggestion entirely, arguing that once the gravity of the Jewish situation under Nazi rule was properly understood, humanitarian concerns displaced all previous attitudes toward the Jews. Still others suggest that practical politics and diplomatic strategy at times limited the degree to which the government could be guided by any considerations of principle.

The most important practical political problem that faced the government-in-exile was its desire to ensure its return to power in a liberated Poland within its prewar boundaries. Germany did not represent the sole obstacle to achieving this aim; the Soviet Union, which had occupied more than 50 percent of Polish territory between 17 September 1939 and 22 June 1941, had formally annexed the conquered lands and was determined to reclaim them at war's end. The Polish government hoped that Great Britain and the United States would support the Polish claim to the disputed territories. As the war continued, however, it became progressively less sanguine about the prospects for such support and more fearful of losing massive amounts of territory to the Soviets. Some members of the government expressed the opinion that Jews in the West might be able to sway British and American leaders to the Polish diplomatic cause. They believed that British and American Jews exercised considerable influence over public opinion in their countries, and as a result they sought to cultivate Jewish favor whenever possible. Thus on 3 November 1940 the government issued a proclamation pledging that "the Jews, as Polish citizens, shall in liberated Poland be equal with the Polish community, in duties and in rights." It did so, however, over much internal resistance.

Such overtures toward Western Jewish opinion generally did not result in widespread Jewish support for Polish territorial demands. On the contrary, Jews consistently complained about the government-in-exile's behavior in Jewish affairs, especially in the areas of welfare assistance for refugees of Polish citizenship and service in the Polish armed forces in exile. Following the conclusion of the Polish-Soviet agreement in July 1941, Western Jewish spokesmen charged that Polish Jewish refugees in the Soviet Union were deliberately being denied a share of the relief funds administered by the Polish government and were being barred from enlistment in the Polish army established on Soviet soil under the command of Gen. Wladyslaw Anders. These accusations can be substantiated only in part. Beginning in mid-October 1941 Jews were indeed permitted to comprise no more than 10 percent of enlistees into General Anders's forces, but before that time Jewish enlistments had amounted to perhaps as much as 40 percent. Moreover, more than 100,000 Jews received support in one form or another from a Polish relief institution in the Soviet Union; they amounted to almost 40 percent of the total number of Polish citizens served. However, the percentage of Jews among Polish soldiers and civilians evacuated from the Soviet Union in mid-1942 (between 4 and 6 percent) was far below their percentage among the Polish refugees as a whole (30–40 percent). Polish authorities in the Soviet Union were only partly responsible for this fact (Soviet and British actions also played a role), but most appear to have believed that the relatively low number of Jews was justified and proper.

Whatever the case, Jewish allegations of discrimination by the government-in-exile intensified throughout 1942, with the result that during the second half of that year the relations between the two sides reached their tensest level since the start of the war. It was precisely at this juncture that news of the systematic murder of Polish Jewry by the German occupiers began to be transmitted from sources inside Poland to the Polish government in London.

News of the Holocaust

The first comprehensive report describing a systematic German plan to kill all Polish Jewry was sent to London in May 1942 by the underground leadership of the Jewish socialist Bund in Warsaw and directed to the Bund's representative on the Polish National Council, Samuel Zygielbojm. Some but not all of the major details of this report were broadcast by Sikorski over the BBC on 9 June. Zygielbojm published an article in the London *Daily Telegraph* of 25 June containing the report's essential features, and Schwarzbart read from the text of the report on 29 June. On 9 July, Zygielbojm, Schwarzbart, Mikolajczyk, and interior minister Stanislaw Stronski held another press conference, together with British information minister Brendan Bracken, at which even more information about the Final Solution was made public.

Some scholars have argued that the government sought initially to downplay the information in the Bund report. They note that although the report had indicated that the Germans had already murdered 700,000 Jews, Sikorski's broadcast of 9 June spoke of only "tens of thousands" of Jewish deaths. They also observe that government statements about the killing of Jews were generally made in the context of broader declarations about the plight of the Poles under German occupation and took up only a small portion of the government's attention. Other scholars point out, however, that the Bund report was initially uncorroborated; therefore, they maintain, the government had necessarily to treat it with a certain reserve, especially because systematic mass murder on the scale described was unprecedented and thus extremely difficult to believe.

Similar controversy surrounds the government's handling of news of the mass deportations from the Warsaw ghetto between 22 July and 12 September 1942. Notices of the initial deportation appeared in Polish, Jewish, British, and American newspapers on 28–29 July; another round of short articles appeared in mid-August describing the suicide of the head of the Warsaw Jewish council (*Judenrat*), Adam Czerniakow, on 23 July. These articles, however, fell far short of conveying the full extent of the deportations or the fate of the deportees. In particular, no mention was made of the gassing of deportees at Treblinka. The question has been raised whether this situation was the result of the government's own lack of information or whether the government possessed additional information that it chose to suppress. What is clear is that, unlike in the case of the Bund letter, no government official made any formal statement about the Warsaw deportations until the end of November. At that time the National Council adopted a resolution protesting "the German crimes directed against the Polish nation, and with particular bestiality against the Jewish population of Poland."

This resolution coincided with the arrival in London of Jan Karski, a courier in the service of the underground government delegacy. Although he had been dispatched primarily to convey information about an internal Polish political problem, he also carried eyewitness testimony about the liquidation of the Warsaw ghetto and the mass murders of Jews. In London, Karski met Raczkiewicz, Sikorski, Mikolajczyk, Schwarzbart, Zygielbojm, and a host of British political, press, and intellectual leaders, conveying, among other things, pleas from Polish Jews for the Western Allies to "adjust [the strategy of war] to include the rescue of a fraction of the unhappy Jewish people." The government-in-exile appears to have given full support to Karski's endeavor to spread this message. On 10 December 1942 the acting Polish foreign minister, Eduard Raczynski, presented a lengthy memorandum to the Allied governments devoted exclusively to the German slaughter of Polish Jewry. The memorandum stated that "the German plans for the extermination of the Jews of Europe were being fulfilled by wholesale massacres of Jews in the Polish ghetto area"; it described the deportations from the Warsaw ghetto and the operations of the death camps at Chelmno, Belzec, Treblinka, and Sobibor, estimating that more than 1 million Jews had "perished during the last three years." This official Polish statement proved to be the essential catalyst for the publication on 17 December of a declaration by the three principal Allies and nine additional exile governments, in which the Germans' "bestial policy of cold-blooded extermination" was strongly condemned.

Participation in Rescue Activities

As news of the systematic killing of European Jewry began to be assimilated by bystanders outside the Nazi orbit, especially after December 1942, Jewish organizations in Great Britain, the United States, and Palestine began to exert pressure on the Polish government-in-exile to support activities aimed at rescuing Polish Jews as well as Jews from other countries who had been deported to Poland. They demanded that the government-in-exile issue an explicit instruction to the underground and to the Polish population to render all possible assistance to threatened Jews and to resist German anti-Jewish actions to the fullest. They also called on the government to establish a special cabinet-level agency to coordinate rescue work and to secure sufficient funds for it.

Initially the government was disinclined to issue an instruction for the homeland. This reluctance was acutely felt by Jewish leaders in contact with the government, including Schwarzbart, who repeatedly raised the demand throughout the early months of 1943 and complained regularly of an evasive Polish response. On 4 May 1943, however, in a radio broadcast to Poland, Sikorski thanked his countrymen for all that they had already done on behalf of their Jewish fellow citizens and asked them "to offer all succor and protection to the threatened [Jewish] victims." This action was undoubtedly influenced not only by the news then reaching the West about the Warsaw ghetto uprising but also by the political crisis faced by the government-in-exile following the severing of diplomatic relations with the Soviet Union, on 25 April 1943, in the wake of Polish allegations that the Soviets had murdered the Polish officers whose mass grave had recently been uncovered by retreating German forces at Katyn. Indeed, the ghetto uprising and the instruction to assist the Jews took up only a very small portion of Sikorski's broadcast of 4 May; the remainder underscored the general anti-Nazi credentials of the Polish government and people, which had been publicly impugned by the Soviets during the Katyn affair.

The government-in-exile was similarly reluctant at first to establish a rescue agency as demanded by Jewish spokesmen. As in the matter of the instruction to the Polish population, however, the government eventually reversed its position. On 20 April 1944 the Polish cabinet voted to create a Council for Matters Relating to the Rescue of the Jewish Population in Poland, which was charged with "providing food for the Jewish population . . . [and] arms to that portion of the Jewish population that is suited to do battle with the Germans, hiding the Jewish population in the cities and villages, providing the Jewish population with documents that might shield it from deportation and murder, transmitting funds to the homeland for the purpose of covering expenditures connected with on-site action, organizing the passage of a certain portion of the Jewish population to neighboring countries, ensuring the maintenance of those Polish Jews who make it across the border . . . , [and] undertaking any other steps aimed at improving the situation of the Jewish population in Poland." The government also pledged to allocate £80,000 to finance the Rescue Council's activities. This sum was considerably less than the council believed necessary for it to pursue its mandate; moreover, the government remitted only about one-sixth of this amount during the entire year of the council's existence. As a result much of the council's time was taken up in negotiations with the government over funding, and its members (who included leading Polish and Jewish political figures) eventually came to believe that the government had forsaken it.

Nevertheless, the government did involve itself in a number of rescue schemes outside the Rescue Council's purview. Some of these involved promoting Allied-German negotiations over ransoming Jews, exchanging them for German civilians interned in Allied countries, or evacuating Jewish children to neutral countries. In others the government served as a conduit for funds raised by Jewish organizations in the free world. From April through December 1944, for example, Jewish bodies in the United States and Palestine used the services of Polish government couriers to transmit more than $1.7 million to underground Jewish groups in Poland. Not all these funds reached their destinations, however, and this fact served as yet another point of friction between the government-in-exile and Jewish representatives.

In addition, the government continued to serve as a principal source of information about the fate of European Jewry. Through its offices, the underground Jewish National Committee and the Jewish socialist Bund were able to maintain regular contact with Schwarzbart, Zygielbojm, and Szerer from early 1943 until the end of the war. Several Polish underground couriers beside Karski—including Jerzy Lerski, Jerzy Salski, Jan Nowak, and Tadeusz Chciuk—also brought reports about the further development of the Nazi murder campaign during 1943–44. Karski himself spoke widely about the Jewish plight during two tours of the United States in 1943 and 1944; on the first occasion he met leading American political figures, including President Franklin Roosevelt.

In short, it was largely through the Polish government-in-exile that the free world received news of the mass murder of European Jewry, and it was toward the government-in-exile that much effort by free-world Jews to assist their brothers and sisters under Nazi rule was directed.   *David Engel*

Polish Jewry On the eve of World War II Poland contained the largest Jewish community in Europe. With its population of nearly 3.5 million, Polish Jewry still retained its position as one of the two main centers of the Jewish world. Western and Central Europe had seen the transformation of the Jews from a community

Jews selling off their possessions in the streets of the Kraków ghetto. Circa 1940

linked by a common religious tradition and way of life and transcending national boundaries into citizens of their respective countries—English, French, even Germans "of the Hebrew faith"—the lands making up the Polish Lithuanian Commonwealth had not followed this pattern. Because of the size of the Jewish population, its resistance to the proposed transformation, and the growth of anti-Jewish sentiment, the "assimilationists," whether Polish or Jewish, who had sought to make the Jews into "Poles of the Mosaic faith" had, by the late nineteenth century, largely failed in their efforts. A minority of Polish Jews, in Galicia (Austrian Poland) and in the Kingdom of Poland, had accepted the assimilationist dream and were fairly well integrated into Polish society. But in the parts of Poland that had been directly absorbed into the Russian em-

pire (the Pale of Settlement), where the majority of Jews from the former Polish Republic lived, the Jewish elite (*maskilim*) favored russification rather than polonization. In the late nineteenth century Zionism, Jewish autonomist socialism (Bundism), and other movements of Jewish self-identification rose to prominence. Modernized versions of traditional Orthodoxy also developed a following. A significant minority within the Jewish community was attracted to revolutionary socialism, with its vision of a new world in which the old diversions of Jew and Gentile would be subsumed by the creation of a new socialist humanity. The new ideologies went along with the emergence of Yiddish as a literary language and the development of modern Hebrew.

In the new Polish state, which inherited territory from Prussia, Russia, and Austria after World War I, regional differences developed in Jewish cultural and political patterns. But the general weakness of trends toward assimilation and integration persisted, as did the threefold division of political life into Zionist, Bundist, and Orthodox camps. In spite of the economic and political difficulties that the community faced, particularly after the death of the Polish statesman Jozef Pilsudski in 1935, it remained a vital source of Jewish secular and religious creativity in Yiddish, in Hebrew, and increasingly in Polish.

The Final Solution

The bulk of the Polish Jews lost their lives in the Nazi genocide. According to the records of the Central Committee of Jews in Poland (Centralny Komitet Zydow w Polsce, CKZP), the principal Jewish organization in postwar Poland, 74,000 people had registered by June 1945. Of these, 5,500 had returned from concentration camps in Germany and 10,000 from camps in Poland; 13,000 had served in the pro-Communist Polish army and about 30,000 had made their way back from the Soviet Union. These statistics suggest that fewer than 20,000 had survived on the "Aryan" side. This figure is certainly too low, since it does not include those who did not register with the CKZP, whether because they wished to stay away from Jewish organizations or because they had assimilated or converted to Christianity. But even if the figure is doubled, no more than 40,000 Jews survived in hiding. In the next two years 137,000 Polish Jews returned from the Soviet Union, mostly people who had been deported or evacuated to the interior of that country. In

1956 several thousand more returned to Poland, although between 100,000 and 150,000 remained in the Soviet Union. Thus, more than 90 percent of Polish Jewry perished in the Holocaust. Only in the Baltic states was the percentage of Jewish deaths higher.

Genocide was carried out in three stages. The first phase began with the radicalization of Nazi policy that accompanied Operation Barbarossa (the invasion of the Soviet Union) in June 1941. Mobile killing squads, the *Einsatzgruppen,* advanced behind the Wehrmacht (German army), executing Soviet officials and Jewish adult men first and Jewish women and children later. At least 1 million Jews were killed—most of them shot—between July and December 1941. This method of murder was abandoned because of its deleterious effect on the morale of those who had to carry it out. In the second stage it was replaced by death camps, where assembly-line techniques of mass murder were developed, first using carbon monoxide gas and then Zyklon B. During this period of genocide, which came to an end in late 1942, the Germans were operating in areas where there was no limitation on their freedom of action, when their power was at its height, and where the ability of the Allies or the subject populations to influence their behavior was minimal. At least 2.7 million Jews were killed in this phase; most of the actual killing was carried out by Germans. By the end of 1942 very few Jews from within the pre-1939 borders of Poland survived. In the third phase, which lasted until the end of the war, the Nazis found themselves obliged to persuade or coerce their allies, satellite states, and puppet regimes in Europe to hand over their Jews. By that time not only those governments but also the Western Allies and most people in leadership positions in Nazi-occupied Europe knew that Nazi policy toward the Jews involved genocide, and they were obliged to articulate some sort of response.

The central question in any discussion of the Jewish fate in Poland during World War II is why so few Polish Jews survived. The primary responsibility for this outcome clearly lies with the Nazis. Yet the question of Polish responsibility for the scale of the tragedy remains. The sociologist Helen Fein has argued that Jewish victimization can be accounted for only by relating it to the success of prewar antisemitism among European nations. Many Jewish diarists and historians have taken a harsh view of Polish conduct. Mordechai Tenenbaum, commander of the Jewish Fighting Organization in the Bialystok ghetto, wrote in his memoirs:

"If it had not been for the Poles, for their aid—passive and active—in the 'solution' of the Jewish problem in Poland, the Germans would never have dared to do what they did. It was they, the Poles, who called out 'Yid' at every Jew who escaped from the train transporting him, it was they who caught the unfortunate wretches, who rejoiced at every Jewish misfortune—they were vile and contemptible."

How accurate are these accusations? A fair assessment must rest on an understanding of specific features of the social landscape in Poland and of the Nazi occupation. First, the great majority of Polish Jews defined themselves, and were regarded by ethnic Poles, as a separate national group. Perhaps under happier political and social conditions a way could have been found to reconcile Polish national interests with those of the large, impoverished, diverse, and nationally conscious Jewish community. The conditions of the 1930s were not, however, conducive either to political pluralism or to interethnic toleration; the decade before the outbreak of the war saw a serious deterioration in the situation of Polish Jewry and a widening gulf between the two societies. As a result most Poles did not regard Jews as within what Fein calls their "universe of obligation."

Second, Poles saw themselves as faced by two enemies, the Nazis and the Soviets. Polish diplomacy and underground political strategy were dominated by the desire to ensure the reemergence of the country as an independent state within the frontiers of 1939, which could only be achieved at least by taking a firm line with the Soviets and probably by entering into conflict with them. The Soviets had already acted brutally in 1939 to secure the incorporation into the USSR of the areas they described as western Belorussia and western Ukraine. The Germans did not seek Polish collaborators against the Soviet Union until it was apparent that they were losing the war, by which time their own actions had created an almost impenetrable wall of hatred between them and the Poles. The fact that the Jews, by and large, did not accept Polish strategic thinking and took a favorable view of the Soviets, particularly after June 1941, greatly complicated Polish-Jewish relations.

The Nazis, for their part, were not interested in political collaboration in Poland. They kept the prewar Polish police in operation as a matter of convenience, but their long-term goal was to incorporate and colonize their Polish conquests, as they began to do almost immediately in the areas directly annexed to the Third Reich (Danzig, Warthegau, and Upper Silesia). Their harsh policies aroused violent opposition and caused great suffering, devastation, and loss of life. During the war Poland lost 19.6 percent of its population—including 3 million Jews but also 2 million other Poles. Of Polish doctors, 45 percent did not survive the occupation; neither did 40 percent of Polish professors, 45 percent of lawyers, 30 percent of engineers, 20 percent of priests, and most journalists. In the last years of the war more than 100,000 Poles were incarcerated in German concentration camps and prisons.

The Nazis embarked on a policy of genocide in the summer of 1941. Before that time they were not sure how to proceed in relation to the Jews—whether the Jews should be concentrated in some sort of reservation in Eastern Europe or expelled to an African penal colony such as Madagascar. Even then Nazi policy was brutal. The September campaign had been accompanied by sporadic anti-Jewish violence in which about 5,000 Jews lost their lives and a number of Jewish institutions were destroyed. Once the occupation regime had been established, Jewish property was expropriated and the Jews were confined to ghettos and deprived of the means of subsistence. In Warsaw alone, in the first 18 months of the occupation, nearly 85,000 Jews died from starvation or from diseases resulting from malnutrition and overcrowding. Yet it was in this period that the Polish-Jewish divide grew even wider, so that there was virtually no chance that Polish society could provide significant aid to the Jews once the policy of mass murder had begun.

The occupying authorities were determined to exacerbate Polish-Jewish relations. The numerous gratuitous acts of violence carried out against Jews, the confiscation of Jewish property by German soldiers, the seizure of Jews for forced labor, their subjection to humiliating physical punishments, and the plucking off or cutting of the beards (and often the hair) of Orthodox Jews were all intended, at least in part, to show that Jews had no rights and could be assaulted with impunity. The Jews were further isolated by the obligation to wear an arm band with a Star of David, which was introduced by Hans Frank on 1 December 1939. Jewish shops were also to be marked with a large Star of David, and Jews were to be barred from certain streets, public parks, and trains. Reinforcement of these measures came from the propaganda in the extensive Nazi-established Polish-language "reptile" press

and from the German-controlled radio, the public loudspeaker system, and antisemitic exhibitions, brochures, leaflets, and posters. The constant stigmatization of the Jews as dirty scum and as carriers of disease also had its effect. Once the ghetto walls had been erected, they were plastered with warning notices: "Jews, lice, typhoid."

With the outlawing of the Jews, anti-Jewish violence became widespread. Sometimes it was spontaneous, the work of antisemites or thugs, but generally it was inspired by the occupation authorities, who cynically explained that they were not responsible for the hatred aroused among the Poles by Jewish exploitation.

Another factor widening the Polish-Jewish divide was the belief by Poles that they were in fact more persecuted than the Jews. They were certainly subject to savage repression, intended both to make permanent the incorporation of the Polish lands into the Third Reich and to deter resistance. By February 1940 more than 200,000 Poles, as well as 100,000 Jews, had been expelled from the Warthegau. In accordance with Nazi policies of germanization more than 50,000 Poles were executed in the areas annexed by the Third Reich in the first months of the occupation. As early as 6 September, nearly 200 academics from the Jagiellonian University and the Mining Academy were arrested in Warsaw; 20 were executed. At the end of April 1940 Himmler ordered the incarceration of 20,000 Poles in concentration camps. To many Poles the fact the Jews were allowed a degree of (spurious) autonomy, and that Jewish political activity was not actively repressed, seemed confirmation that at this stage the Jewish fate was not significantly worse than that of the Poles and might even be somewhat better.

The aim of the Germans was clear—the rapid removal of the Jews from all significant participation in the economy of occupied Poland. They thus accomplished, however mercilessly, what much of prewar Polish society had seen as a desirable objective. They also created a large group of Poles who had benefited from Jewish dispossession and who would fight to retain what they had received at Nazi hands.

In addition, Polish antisemitic attitudes and policies were not seriously compromised by the establishment of Nazi rule. The Germans had no desire for genuine collaboration in Poland. The Polish elite was to be destroyed, and the remaining population forced to work for the Third Reich. In the long run the Polish lands were to be colonized on the analogy of the policy being

A Polish family says goodbye to a child held at the central prison, Zentralgefängnis. September 1942

pursued in Upper Silesia, the Warthegau, and the area around Danzig. This scheme had important consequences for the character of the Polish underground. It meant that while socialist and democratic organizations continued to advocate full equality for the Jews in a future liberated Poland, the patriotic credentials of the prewar antisemitic parties allowed them to maintain their previous hostility to the Jews.

Polish-Jewish relations were also adversely affected by Polish resentment at Jewish "collaboration" with the Soviet authorities after the Soviet occupation of eastern Poland in September 1939. It is true that a fair number of Jews—like the overwhelming majority of Belorussians, many Ukrainians, and even some Poles—welcomed the establishment of Soviet rule. For Jews, this attitude was natural, as it sprang from the wish for an end to the insecurity caused by the collapse of Polish rule in those areas, fear of the consequences of Nazi rule, the belief that the Soviets were a lesser evil, re-

sentment at Polish anti-Jewish policies in the interwar period, and support for the Communist system. Although the Soviets did offer new opportunities to individual Jews, they also suppressed organized Jewish religious and political life, dissolving community organizations (kehillot), banning virtually all Jewish parties, and arresting their leaders. Jews made up just under one-third of the nearly 1 million people deported (and in many cases thereby saved) by the Soviets from the areas they annexed. Under these conditions most of them quickly lost whatever illusions they had about the Soviet system. Most Poles, however, saw the situation differently. They were affronted by Jewish behavior in 1939; they probably exaggerated Jewish participation in the new system, since a Jewish presence in the Polish government was quite unprecedented; and they accused the Jews of disloyalty in a moment of national crisis.

The numbing effect of the brutality of Nazi occupation also inhibited the ability of ordinary people to think altruistically. So too did the shock of the defeat and of the effects of the Nazi onslaught. In the battle and siege of Warsaw, about one-quarter of the city's buildings were totally destroyed or badly damaged, and some 50,000 people were killed or seriously injured. The sense of betrayal and outrage led both to deep hostility toward the prewar government and to a search for scapegoats; and although this caused some Poles to rethink their views on Jews, in others it intensified their antisemitism. It is true that some prewar antisemites did attempt to aid Jews, sometimes even while retaining their antisemitic beliefs. But the increase in the gulf between the two societies and the growth in hostility toward the Jews seem to be beyond question and were widely commented on by political figures and taken into account in their calculations.

These attitudes inevitably affected political policies, in particular those of the Polish government-in-exile established first in Angers and then in London. Although it did issue a declaration on 5 November 1940 guaranteeing the full equality of Jews in liberated Poland, this action did not achieve the goal of a genuine improvement in Polish-Jewish relations. Neither side was able to rise to the very difficult moment, and there was no propaganda effort by the Polish government in occupied Poland to stress "the common suf-

A boy sits amid the ruins of his family's home, which was destroyed during the German invasion of Poland. September 1939

ferings in this most tragic time of affliction" alluded to in the declaration. Nor was any pressure put on the underground structures, whether political or military, to include Jewish groups in their activities. Very little was done to educate Polish public opinion on the dangers of Nazi antisemitism. Indeed, the reaction to the declaration in occupied Poland was such that it disinclined the government to take bold steps to change attitudes toward the Jews.

This was the situation when the Nazis embarked on genocide. Virtually all the links between Polish and Jewish society had been broken, and the moral authorities claiming to speak on behalf of Polish society either felt themselves too weak to protest strongly against this process or did not believe that to do so would necessarily be in the Polish interest. Moreover, by the time the genocide was begun, the Polish strategic position had deteriorated significantly and the London government was preoccupied with its bitter conflict with the Soviets, which also dictated the strategy of the underground it controlled. The Home Army wanted to avoid a major confrontation, partly to spare the civilian population but above all because it wanted to harbor its strength until the decisive moment when German power was collapsing.

What was the reaction to genocide by the government-in-exile in London? Its leaders were aware that Poles were divided on the Jewish question: they were also preoccupied with regaining Polish independence and with the increasing complexities of their diplomatic position. On 24 February 1942 the government reaffirmed its commitment to Jewish equality. In the summer it began to receive information about the genocide. By October its leaders well understood what was taking place, and on 29 October they made the news public at a protest meeting at the Albert Hall. Polish, Jewish, and British figures all spoke at the meeting, which was chaired by the archbishop of Canterbury. Gen. Wladyslaw Sikorski assured Polish Jews that, on an equal footing with all Polish citizens, they would benefit fully from the victory of the Allies. Yet although the government did protest strongly against the Germans' actions, it also stressed its powerlessness. Moreover, it may have been unwilling to press the underground authorities on a matter on which it knew there were divided counsels in Poland.

Under these circumstances the initiative for responding to the genocide fell to the underground authorities in Poland, both civilian and military. The Government

Delegation and its head, the government delegate, were basically sympathetic to the Jews but were aware that they lacked the power to impose their will on the various groupings that made up the underground. However, among the political parties comprising the underground state, there was no fundamental revision of attitudes toward the Jewish question. Those parties sympathetic to the Jews remained so, while the antisemitic group saw no reason to modify its stance. Alongside statements of solidarity with the Jews in their tragic situation there were many expressions of hostility and relief that the Germans were "solving" a difficult problem for the Poles.

As a result it was only in April 1943 that the government delegate issued an appeal calling on Poles to hide Jews. A few months earlier, at the end of 1942, the Council for Aid to the Jews (Rada Pomocy Zydom, code name Zegota) was set up by representatives of the Front for the Rebirth of Poland and some underground socialist and left-wing groups. Zegota obtained a degree of support from the London government. Between 1942 and the end of the war it was granted a total of nearly 29 million zloty (more than $5 million), which it used to provide monthly relief payments for a few thousand Jewish families in Warsaw, Lwow (Lvov), and Kraków. By the middle of 1944 between 3,000 and 4,000 families were benefiting from this financial support. In addition, Zegota provided Jews with the false documents they needed to survive on the Aryan side and established a network of safe houses where those of "unfavorable appearance" could be concealed.

One of the main problems facing Jews attempting to hide were the blackmailers, the *szmalcownicy* who battened on their misery. The Government Delegation ordered the trial and execution of a fair number of collaborators, yet it was only in April 1943 that it issued a condemnation of the blackmail of Jews—a threat that, as Ringelblum wrote, "remained on paper." Beginning in September 1943 death sentences began to be meted out to szmalcownicy. In 1943–44 five blackmailers were put to death in Warsaw and a few in Kraków and its environs.

The attitude of the military underground to the killing is both complex and more controversial. Throughout the period when genocide was carried out, the Home Army was preoccupied with preparing for Plan Storm (Burza), the strategy of confronting the Soviets, at the moment of the collapse of Nazi rule, with a political authority linked with the London govern-

ment. It was determined to avoid premature military action and to conserve strength (and weapons) for the crucial confrontation that would determine the fate of Poland. To the Home Army, however, the Jews were not a part of "our nation," and action to defend them was not to be taken if it endangered other objectives. Certainly the Home Army was not willing to absorb the Jewish partisan groups formed in the forests by ghetto fugitives, which it regarded as unreliable and potentially Communist in sympathy. There was one exception: in Volhynia, which was racked by a brutal ethnic conflict between Poles and Ukrainians, the Home Army eagerly cooperated with Jewish partisans to defend Polish villages. By and large, however, it was not willing to accept Jews as persons independent of their Jewish identity—though here too there were exceptions, such as the Propaganda and Information Bureau of the High Command. The Home Army, like the civilian underground, was composed of people of different political orientations, some sympathetic and others hostile to the Jews. But as an organization it was not sympathetic to the plight of individual Jewish fugitives, seeing them as security risks that were likely to endanger its own position. Local commanders and the High Command often referred to Jewish fugitives (and also to Communist partisans) as "bandits," an echo of the language used by the Nazis themselves. These attitudes—the desire to avoid a premature uprising, suspicions about the Jewish sympathy for communism, and a belief that the weapons provided would not be used efficaciously—largely explain the meager supply of arms to the Warsaw ghetto and to other ghettos. In the case of Warsaw, more weapons were supplied after the confrontation with the Nazis in mid-January 1943 had demonstrated the willingness of the Jewish Fighting Organization to undertake armed action. The smaller Jewish Military Union (Zydowski Zwiazek Wojskowy), controlled by the revisionist Zionists, who had some prewar links with the Polish military and were impeccably anti-Communist, had more initial success in obtaining weapons.

The small military formations linked with the various fascist groups—the National Armed Forces (Narodowe Sily Zbrojne, or NSZ) and the Rampart Group (Grupa Szanca)—were openly hostile to the Jews and frequently committed murders of Jewish partisans and of Jews hiding in the villages. This situation continued even when the NSZ became more closely linked with the Home Army toward the end of the war.

The pro-Communist resistance, the People's Guard, and its successor, the People's Army, were much more willing to absorb Jews, both because, in their isolation, they needed any support they could obtain and because their ideology stressed the importance of transcending national divisions. This was a mixed blessing, because the more Jews supported these groups, the more they seemed to confirm the belief within the Home Army (and elsewhere in Poland) that they were essentially siding with the Communists.

Discussions about the role of the Polish resistance and its attitude to the mass murder of the Jews take place in a sort of time warp. Elsewhere in Europe, the myth of the powerful resistance has been subjected to harsh and largely convincing criticism. It is probably unrealistic to expect the Home Army, which was neither as well armed nor as well organized as its propaganda claimed, to have been able to do much to aid the Jews. But the fact remains that its leadership probably did not want to do so.

The Polish literary critic Jan Blonski, in an article written in 1987, called on Poles to "stop haggling, trying to defend and justify ourselves. To stop arguing about the things that were beyond our power to do, during the occupation and beforehand. Not to place blame on political, social and economic conditions. But to say first of all, 'Yes, we are guilty.'" Blonski does not believe that Poles are culpable of direct involvement in the mass murder of the Jews, but they bear a burden of guilt in two respects. First, they are accountable for an "insufficient effort to resist." This "'holding back' from offering help to the Jews" was the consequence of the second fault, that in the nineteenth and early twentieth centuries the Poles had not created conditions in which the Jews could be integrated into the national community. "If only we had behaved more humanely in the past," Blonski writes, "had been wiser, more generous, then genocide would perhaps have been 'less imaginable,' would probably have been considerably more difficult to carry out, and almost certainly would have met with much greater resistance than it did. To put it differently, it would not have met with the indifference and moral turpitude of the society in whose full view it took place."

The destruction of the Jewish community of Poland was a blow from which world Jewry has not recovered. The diarist Abraham Lewin, who perished in Treblinka in January 1943, wrote at the end of 1942, after the deportation of most of the Jews of the Polish capi-

View of a major street in Kraków strewn with the bundles of deported Jews, after the liquidation of the ghetto. March 1943

tal: "Warsaw was in fact the backbone of Polish Jewry, its heart, one could say. The destruction of Warsaw would have meant the destruction of the whole of Polish Jewry, even if the provinces had been spared this evil. Now that the enemy's sword of destruction has run amok through the small towns and villages and is cutting them down with murderous blows—with the death-agony of the metropolis, the entire body is dying and plunging into the abyss. One can say that with the setting of the sun of Polish Jewry, the splendor and the glory of world Jewry has vanished. We, the Polish Jews, were after all the most vibrant nerve of our people. . . . Hitler has murdered an entire people."

Antony Polonsky

Ponary   Site, near Vilna, of the massacre and burial of tens of thousands of Lithuanian Jews. The killings at Ponary date from the beginning of the German invasion of the Soviet Union. Thousands of Soviet prisoners of war are also believed to have been killed there. Tens of thousands perished at Ponary. See VILNA

Portugal   Neutral country during World War II. In May 1940 the Portuguese government ordered its officials to stop issuing transit visas to Jews. Refugees trying to escape France were initially denied the visas needed to reach Portugal via Spain. The Portuguese

The Portuguese liner *Serpa Pinto* arrives in New York carrying 56 refugee children from France, Belgium, Czechoslovakia, Germany, and Hungary, under the sponsorship of the U.S. Committee for Care of European Children. 24 September 1941

consul in Bordeaux, Aristides de Sousa Mendes, disobeyed the mandate and issued some 10,000 visas to help the refugees to escape. See SOUSA MENDES, ARISTIDES DE

Prague Capital of Czechoslovakia and a major center of Jewish culture and learning. Some 46,000 Jews were deported from Prague between 1941 and 1945, mainly to the Lodz, Minsk, and Theresienstadt ghettos. Thousands of religious artifacts and prayer books from throughout the German-occupied territories were sent to Prague in an effort to collect and save them; the Nazis meant to use the collection as a mocking display of the extinguished race after the war. The objects now belong to the Jewish Museum of Prague.

Protectorate of Bohemia and Moravia See BOHEMIA AND MORAVIA, PROTECTORATE OF

Protestant Churches In the first half of the twentieth century the Protestant churches of Europe were deeply divided along denominational or national lines. They shared, however, a long history of animosity and antagonism toward Judaism and the Jewish people. It is true that Protestant leaders had put behind them, as evidence of medieval Catholic backwardness, the anti-Judaic theological polemics and practices of earlier centuries. For the most part Protestants welcomed the political emancipation of the Jews in Western Europe as a sign of liberal progress. Assimilation and eventual conversion to Christianity were widely expected. Most Protestants had conveniently forgotten or suppressed Luther's virulent outbursts against the Jews and instead adopted the view propagated by such leading scholars as Adolf von Harnack that Christianity, as the more modern and enlightened faith, had superseded Judaism in the covenantal relationship with God. For many, such as the noted British scholar Arnold Toyn-

Ancient Jewish cemetery, Prague.

bee, Judaism was a "fossilized relic." When assimilation did not take place, some leading Protestants like Heinrich von Treitschke or Adolf Stoecker expressed strong resentment, but more on social and political than on theological grounds. Almost all Protestant theologians saw ancient Israel only as a precursor for modern Christianity; lacking all contact with Jewish thinkers or scholarship, they experienced no antidote to feelings of indifference or disdain.

The rise of Adolf Hitler to power in 1933 was acclaimed by the majority of German Protestants. The evidence suggests that the Nazi victory was due more to nationalist fervor and a desire to return to authoritarian leadership than to the Nazi party's outright antisemitism. Nevertheless, the skillful manner in which Hitler and his propagandists took over and manipulated much of the religious vocabulary in the service of their racist ideology was an important factor in preventing the growth of any opposition. Prominent Protestant theologians in Germany, such as Paul Althaus, Emanuel Hirsch, and Wilhelm Stapel, had a significant influence in the development of a nationalist and racist theology that attacked Jews, liberals, and internationalists as the sinister bearers of secularism. None of them was sympathetic to the Jews or voiced opposition to antisemitism. German Protestants never possessed an arsenal of arguments against the more severe forms of Jew-hatred and were thus ill-equipped to combat the more menacing forms of antisemitic persecution that the Nazis quickly adopted.

In April 1933, when the first anti-Jewish measures were promulgated, some prominent Protestants, including Baron von Pechmann and Professor Siegmund-Schultze, called for the church to protest those actions on humanitarian grounds. They were overruled. Their leaders, for tactical and opportunistic reasons, were unwilling to take any action that might throw doubt on their support for the Nazis' nationalist revival or might give rise to suspicions that they were less than loyal to the new regime. At the same time, a small but vociferous group of pastors, calling themselves the Deutsche Christen (German Christians), were actively propagating their enthusiastic support for the Nazi cause. Their platform called for sweeping reforms within the church, especially through the removal of any Jewish-born pastors or church workers, the elimination of Jewish influences such as the Old Testament, the portrayal of Jesus as a "heroic Aryan," the prohibition of all missions to the Jews, and the institution of Nazi practices throughout the system of church government. In their crusade against Judaism the Deutsche Christen were proclaiming in a more exaggerated form theological tendencies already apparent in German Protestantism, and they received significant support from such well-known professors as Adolf Schlatter and Gerhard Kittel. Their efforts culminated in 1939 with the creation of the Institute for the Study and Eradication of Jewish Influence in German Church Life, which called for a church free of Jews (*Judenfrei*) in a Germany cleansed of them (*Judenrein*).

These activities, however, led to a strong reaction from more doctrinally conservative Protestants. Already in the summer of 1933 Pastor Martin Niemöller had established the Pastors' Emergency League to combat the imposition of Nazi practices in the church, particularly the demand for the removal of pastors of Jewish descent. A year later, the Pastors' Emergency League became the nucleus of the Confessing Church, which strongly defended church interests against anti-Christian tendencies, especially the deliberate inculcation of antisemitism with its idolatrous claim to German racial superiority. But this opposition was primarily designed to protect the autonomy of the church's institutions rather than the humanitarian interests of the persecuted Jews. Despite the fact that their attacks on the Nazi racist idolatry led to harsh Gestapo repression for many Confessing Church pastors and lay members, politically they remained staunchly nationalistic and hence welcomed Hitler's aggressive foreign policies. Theologically Niemöller and other Confessing Church leaders, such as Otto Dibelius, upheld the traditional pejorative views of the Jews, but they rejected the Nazi claim that conversion to Christianity made no difference. Their concern was therefore voiced only for the converted Jews.

Protestant prejudice against Judaism in Germany in the pre-Nazi years was widespread and virtually unopposed. The Nazis' rabid antisemitic campaigns only reinforced this intolerance and led many pro-Nazi Protestants to flaunt their anti-Judaic sentiments as proof of their devotion to the new regime. Even in the Confessing Church, which early on recognized the threat of Nazi totalitarian ambitions, there was a consistent hesitation to challenge Nazi ideology on the central points of its antisemitic program. Only a few Protestant theologians, exemplified by Karl Barth and Dietrich Bonhoeffer, in opposing the attempt of the Deutsche Christen to claim a purely Germanic nature for the church, stressed the Jewish origins of Christianity, maintained the vitality of both the Old and New Testament revelations, and acknowledged their debt to Judaism. But their views were isolated and ineffective. As a result there was little inclination to rethink the nature of the relationship between Christians and Jews or to accept the duty of the church to support Jewish victims of injustice or oppose the misuse of state power.

The same attitudes prevailed among minor Protestant sects in Germany. Only the Jehovah's Witnesses maintained their own special and positive theological relation to Judaism, which was one reason why this tiny group was persecuted by the Nazis more severely than any other.

It would be a mistake to attribute this Christian legacy of hostility toward Judaism and Jews as a sufficient cause for Nazi genocide. But it cannot be doubted that for many Germans these traditional Christian sentiments created a climate in which Nazi persecutions would be condoned without opposition. No adequate prophylactic existed, on either theological or humanitarian grounds, that could have led the church to recognize a sense of obligation among Christians toward the increasingly outcast Jews.

Many Protestants, to be sure, even when they shared the regime's evaluation of the so-called Jewish problem, had reservations about the ferocious methods employed against the Jews. This ambivalence could be seen as the anti-Jewish persecutions became more striking. Following the notorious November 1938 pogrom (Kristallnacht), Protestants shared the widespread public revulsion against the Nazis' acts of violence and vandalism. Yet no protest was raised by any of the church leaders. Spontaneous acts of charity, or the dangerous and heroic efforts of individuals to give refuge and shelter to the threatened Jews, were isolated examples of sympathy that made the silence of the church the more shameful.

In contrast to the indifference displayed by their German colleagues, the other Protestant churches of Europe and North America expressed vocal opposition to nazism and in particular to the mistreatment by Germany of its Jewish citizens from 1933 onward. Some foreign church observers mistakenly believed that the Confessing Church was engaged in a struggle for freedom against absolutism and for democracy against dictatorship. The limited extent of these churchmen's opposition to nazism came to them as disillu-

sionment. In April 1933 Dutch, British, and American church leaders called on their German counterparts to protest the Nazis' initial discriminatory measures against the Jews, which were held to be "altogether in contradiction to the teaching and spirit of the Gospel and of Jesus Christ." These churchmen were, however, aware that protests from abroad, without local encouragement, might well antagonize the persecutors and add to the sufferings of the Jews. But silence would suggest indifference or acquiescence. From 1933 to 1938 foreign Protestant leaders, including the archbishop of Canterbury, Cosmo Lang, and Bishop George Bell of Chichester, sought to make clear their repugnance to nazism without aggravating the situation of the Jews. It was a fine balancing act that had only limited success.

The infamous events of the November 1938 pogrom finally convinced the majority of foreign Protestants that nazi antisemitism was incompatible with their theology or moral teachings. But practical measures to assist even converted Jews were thwarted by the lack of any efficient structures and by the near-absence of support from within Germany. Attempts to help German Jews to emigrate were hampered by the restrictive immigration policies in many countries, and church pleas for a more open stance were ineffective. The Nazi invasion of Poland brought these efforts to a halt.

As in 1914, the outbreak of war in 1939 proved that national loyalties outweighed Christian solidarity. In Germany the majority of Protestants welcomed their nation's initial victories. They accepted the Nazi propaganda that Germany had been drawn into war by foreign, especially Jewish "intrigues" and that it was fighting a justified defensive struggle. The brutalities and atrocities inflicted on the occupied countries were explained away as the regrettable consequences of war. And the ever-increasing power of the Gestapo was excused as a wartime necessity. As a result the escalating persecution of the Jews, both in Germany and the in newly conquered territories, was not loudly denounced by the churches. The majority turned a blind eye on events, retreated into apathetic indifference, and even adopted a measure of sympathetic acquiescence.

The increasingly manifest discrimination against the Jews, both by word and by practice, implicated the German churches at one of their weakest and most vulnerable points. The absence of any pro-Jewish theological stance resulted in little or no remonstrance against the measures taken to isolate the Jews and to impose the wearing of the yellow Star of David. Any organized endeavor to alleviate the plight of the Jews was considered impossible.

Not until 1941, with the forcible deportation of the entire Jewish population to unknown destinations in the East, did the leaders of the Protestant churches realize that the Nazi attacks on the Jews went far beyond the requirements of wartime circumstances. The Deutsche Christen attempted to justify their antisemitic stance, along with their support for Hitler's attack on the Soviet Union, by claiming that this "crusade" was indispensable for safeguarding German life against the "Jewish-Bolshevik conspiracy." But, as increasing reports of atrocities and even mass murder of Jews in occupied Eastern Europe filtered back to Germany, the Christian conscience of a considerable portion of the Protestant population was aroused. In 1943 Bishop Theophil Wurm of Württemberg made himself the spokesman for this feeling of outrage and wrote a series of letters to the Nazi leaders in protest against measures that contradicted the God-given right to human existence and human dignity. But in order to avoid the charge of defeatism, or the possible exploitation of any public protest by enemy countries, these letters were not published. Not until the end of 1943 did the Prussian Synod of the Confessing Church address a letter to all its congregations, setting out its opposition to state-organized mass murder as contravening the Fifth Commandment.

But such protests had only a limited impact. It is clear that the majority of German Protestants were unaware of, or unwilling to recognize, the enormity of their government's crimes against the Jewish people. Even after the Nazi regime was defeated and the grisly details of the concentration camps revealed, most Germans were reluctant to believe the evidence. Virtually no Protestant theologians realized the implications for their Christian faith of their previous indifference toward the Jewish sufferings. In October 1945, when the surviving leaders of the Confessing Church issued the famous Stuttgart "Declaration of Guilt," in which they admitted their lack of faithful resistance to the evils of nazism and called for repentance and a new beginning, no specific reference was made to the fate of the Jews. This failure to take a stronger stand on behalf of the Jewish people became the basis of self-accusation among German Protestants in subsequent years

and led to new, if belated, attempts to reconsider the fateful relations between Christians and Jews.

In the Protestant countries occupied by the Nazis, such as Holland, Denmark, and Norway, reactions to the Holocaust were prompted by nationalist as well as humanitarian sympathies. In Denmark the well-organized escape of the Danish Jews to Sweden was backed by a clear church protest. In Holland the Calvinist tradition sponsored active support of the victimized Jews, which led to widespread efforts to hide and protect individuals and families, though the national synod's protests were limited to appeals for mercy rather than outright opposition. In Norway, in 1942, churchmen spoke out publicly, though only half the threatened Jews were able to escape. Similarly in France, where the small Protestant minority was very conscious of its own heritage as the victims of state oppression, numerous efforts were made to assist Jewish refugees, both by youth groups such as CIMADE (Commission Inter-mouvements auprès des Evacués) and by local parishes such as the village of Chambon-sur-Lignon. But protests made by the official Federation of French Protestant Churches to the Vichy authorities, seeking to mitigate the plight of Jews, especially of French nationals, were largely ineffective.

In the mainly Orthodox countries of Romania and Bulgaria church leaders protested vigorously, with considerable success. But in Greece and Hungary similar remonstrances did little to restrain the deportation of the majority of Jews within their borders.

In all these countries, fears concerning the repressive measures of the Germans and the secret police were too strong, and sympathy for the persecuted Jews too weak, for the churches to mobilize more significant challenges to the Nazis' systematic execution of their racist and genocidal plans. Despite numerous heroic actions by individual Protestants, the overall verdict must be that the reactions of the churches were too mild, vague, and belated.

Protestants in the countries at war with Germany— Great Britain and the United States—had no difficulty in expressing their revulsion for Nazi antisemitism as part of the moral justification for opposing German aggression. Public protests from the churches continued throughout the war. The leadership given by the bishops of the Church of England, the Church of Scotland, and the Federal Council of Churches in the United States, largely on humanitarian grounds, was notable. William Temple, archbishop of Canterbury from 1942 to 1944, resolutely expressed his horror at the persecution of the Jews and issued radio appeals to his fellow Protestants, for example in Hungary, to do all they could to assist the victims of Nazi atrocities. By 1942, when the newspapers carried numerous reports on the extent of the Nazis' extermination policies, pressure from the churches contributed to the declaration issued by the Allied governments in December 1942, which reaffirmed their solemn resolution to ensure that those responsible for those crimes should not escape retribution. In the same year a notable step forward was taken by Protestants, Catholics, and Jews in the formation of the British Council of Christians and Jews, specifically to arouse support for the victims of the Holocaust and to combat antisemitism at home.

The dilemma faced by these churchmen lay elsewhere. Despite the genuine and heartfelt protests against German atrocities, they were unable to mobilize sufficient pressure to compel their governments to take practical measures to rescue more Jews or to allow increased immigration to their countries. In April 1943 the Inter-Governmental Committee on Refugees met in Bermuda but signally failed to propose new policies, largely because of anti-immigrant and antisemitic sentiments opposed to allowing more help to Jewish refugees. The Bermuda Conference was a striking example of moral callousness and inertia, but it also marked the limits of the churches' influence in such highly sensitive political affairs.

Another factor in the response of the Protestant churches was the combined impact of skepticism and incredulity about the details and extent of the Nazis' extermination plans. In the early years of the war there was obvious difficulty in ascertaining the truth about reports and rumors of atrocities occurring in unverifiable circumstances and in inaccessible parts of Eastern Europe. From 1941 onward, however, the accumulation of information became impressive and overwhelming. Still, many churchmen reacted to this evidence of mass murder with disbelief. The information was ineffective because it seemed too improbable. Many Protestants, even those best equipped to know, could find no place in their consciousness for such an unimaginable horror, nor did they have the imagination or the courage to face it. The limited efforts made to rescue individual Jews, or to persuade the Allied governments to give sanctuary and temporary asylum to Jewish refugees in areas under Allied control, met with widespread apathy.

On the other hand, it should be remembered that these churchmen, as purveyors of moral passion, often had an insufficient awareness of the political realities and military factors involved. Many Protestant postwar commentators, with the advantage of hindsight and feelings of guilt, believe that the churches could and should have done far more to assist the Jewish victims of Nazi persecution. But the historical record shows that the political influence of the nationally and theologically divided Protestant churches, both in Germany and elsewhere, was too limited to be more than marginal, especially in the circumstances of all-out war.

The extent to which Protestant anti-Judaic theological traditions contributed to the churches' unwillingness to adopt more vigorous measures during the Holocaust has been the subject of intensive debate. Particularly in the 1960s and 1970s churches both in Germany and elsewhere undertook substantial initiatives to come to terms with this sad legacy, to prepare new teaching materials, and to promote a more ecumenical and fruitful theological approach, which included a readiness to renounce the long-held tradition of Christian mission to the Jews. The revision or abandonment of such pejorative attitudes and practices in many Protestant churches marks a significant step forward in the development of Christian-Jewish relations. *John S. Conway*

Protocols of the Elders of Zion *Protocols of the Elders of Zion* is a fictitious document that purports to offer conclusive evidence of the existence of a Jewish conspiracy to achieve world domination. The forgery, based largely on a compilation of literary materials from the second half of the nineteenth century, was probably concocted at the beginning of the twentieth century, when it first appeared in Russia. Since the 1920s it has spread throughout the globe and is used for antisemitic propaganda.

The most widely distributed editions of the *Protocols* consist of 60–80 pages subdivided into 24 sections, or "protocols." These are presented as a verbatim transcript of a speech by an unnamed Jewish leader at 24 consecutive meetings of the Elders of Zion; the dates and places at which these meetings were held are not indicated. In the speech, and thus apparently in open confession, the methods and goals of the alleged centuries-old Jewish conspiracy to destroy the Christian communities and to erect in their

Cover of *Le Péril Juif: Les Protocoles des Sages de Sion.*

place a Jewish world government are laid out in detail. In the struggle against church and state the worldwide conspiracy is said to make use of secret Masonic lodges. The Elders operate according to the slogan "The end justifies the means." Their most important instruments are the power of gold, the wholesale manipulation of public opinion through control of the press, and the propagation of discord and confusion among Gentiles. Toward this goal they incite partisan conflict and labor unrest, spread liberal ideas, corrupt morals, and undermine religious faith and respect for law and authority with the help of the dogmas of Darwin, Marx, and Nietzsche. Ultimately they unleash terror and incite nations to war. Upon the ruins of the old order the Elders are then supposed to establish a centralized, patriarchal government with a king from the House of David; as a benevolent despot, he will rule over a united, well-ordered world, perfectly con-

trolled thanks to a comprehensive system of spying, full employment, and social services designed to allay discontent.

The basic idea of the *Protocols* is twofold: the belief that the Jews are the opponents of Christianity's divine plan for salvation and the vanguard of the Antichrist, a concept reaching back to the Middle Ages; and a conspiracy theory, dating from the late eighteenth century, which interpreted the French Revolution and all subsequent movements against the old order as the work of secret transnational organizations. Freemasons, Illuminati, Jacobins, and anarchists (so it is claimed), using the motto of freedom and equality, sought to apply their satanic conspiracy toward the destruction of the monarchy and papacy. Here the real proponents of these activities were "revealed" to be the international community of Jews, the oldest enemies of the Christians and at the same time the obvious beneficiaries of Enlightenment and Emancipation. Predominantly Catholic circles were responsible for the notion of Jewish identification with Freemasonry, since the Catholics vilified it as "Satan's synagogue," an antichurch ruled by Jews and opposed to the "true church of Christ."

The earliest edition of the *Protocols* that is still extant was serialized by Pavel (Pavolakii) Krushevan, a Bessarabian writer and antisemite, in August and September 1903 in his St. Petersburg newspaper *Znamia* under the title "Program for World Conquest by the Jews." According to this publication, the text is a translation of an original French transcription of the meetings of the "World Union of Freemasons and Elders of Zion." In late 1905 or early 1906 Krushevan's Bessarabian ally Georgii Butmi published the first of several variants of the *Protocols* in book form in St. Petersburg. Between 1905 and 1907 about a dozen other editions—sometimes widely divergent versions—were printed in St. Petersburg, in Moscow, and in the provinces. The *Protocols* were attributed variously to the "World Union of Freemasons" or the Elders of Zion or both. Sometimes a relationship to Zionism was posited, although in one version this connection was explicitly rejected. France was typically named as the country of origin.

The version of the *Protocols* that eventually came to be known worldwide is linked with the name of Sergei Nilus (1862–1929). Nilus, a former landowner and lawyer of Baltic origin who at times lived in Russian monasteries and became known as a prolific religious author, first published his version of the *Protocols* in the second edition (1905) of his devotional book *The Great in the Small and the Antichrist as an Imminent Political Possibility: Notes of an Orthodox Believer*. Other editions of this book containing the *Protocols* appeared under various titles in 1911, 1912, and 1917. In his commentary Nilus interpreted the *Protocols* within the framework of his own deeply apocalyptic worldview as a foreboding of an imminent eschatological catastrophe and of the coming of the Antichrist. The last edition of his book, published in January 1917 by the famous Holy Trinity Monastery near Moscow, bore the threatening title *It Is Near, Even at the Doors: Concerning That Which We Choose Not to Believe and What Is So Near*.

Contrary to common belief, in prerevolutionary Russia the *Protocols* attracted little notice even among contemporary reactionary circles, and scarcely any traces of its influence can be found in the journalism of the day. There is no evidence, moreover, of a causal link with the pogroms. The *Protocols* were discovered only in the wake of the Bolshevik revolution of 1917. Among the possessions of the assassinated Tsaritsa Alexandra was a copy of Nilus's *Protocols*, and the White Russians interpreted this find as an indication that the Jews were responsible for the murder of the imperial family and that the Bolshevik revolution represented the victory of the Antichrist in Russia. During the civil war (1918–21) the White Russians published several new editions of the *Protocols* and used them in their propaganda against "Jewish Bolshevism."

Shortly after the revolution Russian émigrés brought the *Protocols*—hitherto unknown outside Russia—to Western Europe and North America, where they strove to promulgate the message of the Jewish Bolshevik danger. In Germany the *Protocols* appeared in the winter of 1918–19 among *völkisch* nationalistic and antisemitic circles in Berlin and Munich. In the spring of 1919 Nilus's version of the *Protocols* was translated into German, and in January 1920 the first German edition appeared with the title *The Secrets of the Elders of Zion*. Already toward the end of 1920 six editions of this work had been sold out, and by the end of the decade hundreds of thousands of copies appear to have been circulating in Germany. The editor of the *Protocols*, Gottfried zur Beek (a pen name of Ludwig Müller von Hausen), had extensive contacts with anti-Bolshevik Russian émigrés in Germany, among them Nilus's son and niece. Both collaborated later with the Nazis.

By the end of 1920 the *Protocols* had also been translated and published in Great Britain, France, Italy, Poland, and the United States, and in the years to come numerous other translations and publications followed. This was the age of the so-called Red Scare, the fear of the specter of Bolshevism as a conspiratorial anti-Christian movement led by the Jews. Even a number of the reputable newspapers in England initially supported the authenticity of the *Protocols*. A much-noted article in the *Times* of London, "The Jewish Peril" (8 May 1920), reflected the deep impression made by the "uncanny note of prophesy" in this "disturbing pamphlet" (although in August 1921 the newspaper declared them to be a forgery). Victor Marsden's English translation of the *Protocols*, based on the 1905 Russian edition in the British Museum, had sold more than half a million copies by the 1950s. Nilus's version of the *Protocols* made its way to the United States in 1918. Henry Ford published a series of antisemitic articles drawing on the *Protocols* in his newspaper, the *Dearborn Independent*, from 1920 to 1922. Many of the articles were reprinted in book form under the title *The International Jew: The World's Foremost Problem*, which sold more than half a million copies in the United States and was translated into 16 languages. Ford distanced himself from the book in 1927, but this had little influence on its popularity.

Thus began the triumphal march of the *Protocols*. In the precarious atmosphere between the two world wars, the *Protocols* "revealed" the Jews to be the secret masters of the globe and "exposed" their hidden motives and intrigues, which were interpreted as the ultimate cause of the Great War, the revolution in Russia, the fall of monarchies, the economic crisis, and social unrest. The key to the understanding of these global events lay in the Jews' alleged struggle to rule the world. The exegetical paradigm of the *Protocols* managed to resolve even the manifest contradictions between Bolshevism and international capital: both were represented as the foils of a Jewish conspiracy. The question of the authenticity of the *Protocols* and their origin ultimately proved irrelevant for those believing in the conspiracy. The path of contemporary history and its concurrence with the predictions of the *Protocols* alone was decisive and appeared to verify their inner truth.

The National Socialists took note of the *Protocols* at the beginning of the 1920s. Their foremost proponent was Alfred Rosenberg, the party's theoretician and

Russian affairs expert. In 1923 Rosenberg published an elaborate commentary on the *Protocols*, and in 1927 he composed a short work in which Theodor Herzl appeared as the crown witness for the authenticity of their contents. The impact of the *Protocols* (and the concomitant ideology of the radical right-wing émigrés from Russia, which Rosenberg also fostered) on the development of the antisemitic and anti-Bolshevik convictions of Hitler and the Nazi party has long been a subject of debate. Hitler himself occasionally mentioned the Elders of Zion in his speeches in the early 1920s, and in 1924 he made reference to the *Protocols* in *Mein Kampf.* Though he undoubtedly made use of the established myth of a Jewish conspiracy as a propaganda weapon, he seldom referred explicitly to the *Protocols.* The same holds good for other members of the Nazi leadership. Joseph Goebbels preached war against Jewish world domination and used the imagery of the Jew as the "Antichrist of world history," but he mentioned the *Protocols* in his voluminous diaries only once (13 May 1943), leaving open the question of whether they were genuine or "invented by an ingenious critic of contemporary society."

Although the *Protocols* were used as Nazi propaganda and had appeared in numerous editions in Germany by the end of the 1930s, party officials seem to have avoided the debate on their authenticity. This task was left to the privately organized antisemitic propaganda and publishing organization Weltdienst, founded as early as 1919 in Erfurt and headed by Ulrich Fleischhauer, who testified as an "expert" in the notorious Bern trial. Between 1933 and 1935 action was taken against the distributors of the *Protocols* in Bern. The legal procedure was initiated by the Jewish community of Switzerland and came to serve as an internationally recognized tribunal directed against the *Protocols.* With the aid of numerous witnesses and massive evidence, the plaintiffs sought to clarify the origin of the *Protocols* and to offer proof of their spuriousness. In the verdict of May 1935 the *Protocols* were indeed judged a case of falsification and plagiarism. Their distributors were convicted. The fact that this verdict was overruled by a superior court in Bern in November 1937 on purely formal legal grounds has since been celebrated by defenders of the *Protocols* as an admission of their authenticity.

The publishers and their advocates offered widely diverging and self-contradictory testimony concerning the origin, character, and age of the *Protocols.* The work was variously associated with the First Zionist Congress (held in 1897 in Basel), the French Freemasons, the B'nai B'rith lodges, the Alliance Israélite Universelle, the Illuminati, and the mysterious "Central Chancellery of Zion"; authorship was ascribed to Theodor Herzl, Ascher Ginzberg (Achad Ha'am), Adam Weishaupt, or the 12, 13, 33, or 300-odd secret "Elders of Zion" who purportedly composed the original document in Hebrew or French. One piece of testimony (quickly abandoned) maintained that the *Protocols* were composed in 929 B.C.E. during King Solomon's reign. As recently as the 1980s the authors of an international best-seller claimed that the *Protocols* emanate from a century-old conspiracy to reestablish the dynasty of the Merovingians. And a leading Russian conspiracy theorist, Aleksandr Dugin, added that at least in their "positive" part, where they speak of establishing a monarchy and a caste system, the *Protocols* bear "the imprint of traditional Aryan mentality."

The authorship of the *Protocols* is not yet clear. Most experts have asserted or assumed that members of the tsarist secret police, the Okhrana, in France—among them Piotr Rachkovskii (1853–1910), chief of the foreign affairs department in Paris, and his collaborator Matvei Golovinskii (1865–1920)—were involved in their creation around the turn of the century, but the manner and extent of their contribution has never been clarified or proven. Even the motives and intentions of the forgers are a subject of speculation. In the 1990s the Italian Slavist Cesare G. De Michelis compiled all early Russian editions of the *Protocols* and subjected them to a thorough philological and historical analysis. He established that the *Protocols* as we know them are the result of many revisions of a text that must have been written in Russia between April 1902 and August 1903. The Ukrainian elements in the earliest versions of the *Protocols* allow the assumption that Krushevan and Butmi may have been involved in their creation. It was only in later editions, De Michelis shows, that the *Protocols* were crudely frenchified in order to make them look more authentic as a foreign document. De Michelis thereby refutes the assertion of a French archetype as well as any involvement of Rachkovskii and the Paris counterfeit offices of the Okhrana.

Whoever the author or authors might have been, and to what ends the *Protocols* were composed, it is clear that they are a forgery, a plagiarized collation of various texts, some of which were identified years ago.

As early as 1921 Philip Graves, the Constantinople correspondent for the *Times,* discovered the major source of the *Protocols:* a brilliant political satire, *Dialogue aux Enfers entre Machiavel et Montesquieu, ou La Politique de Machiavel au XIXème Siècle* (Dialogue in Hell between Machiavelli and Montesquieu, or The Politics of Machiavelli in the Nineteenth Century), written by Maurice Joly in defense of liberalism during the Second Empire and published anonymously in Brussels in 1864. In Joly's book, which does not contain the slightest allusion to Jews, Machiavelli (read: Napoleon III) is depicted at work on a blueprint for a modern dictatorship. The forgers of the *Protocols* attributed not only Machiavelli's maxims but also those of Montesquieu (representing the proto-liberal position) to the Jews and developed them into an elaborate plan to conquer the world. In his *Warrant for Genocide,* a classic study of the *Protocols,* Norman Cohn demonstrated that in total more than 160 passages in the *Protocols*—two-fifths of the entire work—are based on Joly's book. In some chapters the plagiarized passages make up more than half the text; even the division into chapters is based on Joly's satire. Yet, as Umberto Eco has shown, Joly himself made use of the popular fiction of his age, adopting passages from Eugène Sue's novel *Les Mystères du Peuple* (including the classic formula "the end justifies the means") in his *Dialogue aux Enfers.*

Both the content and the setting of the *Protocols* are rooted in the popular literature of the day. In his novel *Biarritz* (published 1868) the German pulp-fiction author Hermann Goedsche, writing under the pen name Sir John Retcliffe, portrayed a secret midnight meeting in the Jewish graveyard in Prague, at which the representatives of the Twelve Tribes of Israel reported to the Devil their success in infiltrating and subverting the Christian world and discussed their future course of action. For that purpose Goedsche had plagiarized the prologue to the novel *Joseph Balsamo* by Alexandre Dumas père, which describes a plot of the Illuminati in alliance with Cagliostro. The chapter "In the Jewish Cemetery in Prague" from Goedsche's novel was subsequently published separately; it was later revised as a pamphlet, *The Rabbi's Speech,* and marketed as authentic evidence of a Jewish conspiracy. Therein the authors of the *Protocols* found the plot line for their forgery.

Conspiracy theories are founded on a dualist view of the world (good and evil, Christ and Antichrist, oppressors and oppressed, the free world and communism) and on the belief that the course of history is governed by hidden powers who act according to a secret plan toward an ultimate goal. Once one gains insight into the ways of these powers, the historical process can be interpreted as coherent and consistent. By transforming obscure conditions and anonymous structures into personified carriers of salvation or ruin, conspiracy theories reduce the complexity and contingency of reality and offer simple points of orientation (Who is to blame?) and paths of action (Whom must we fight?). This is the basis of their dangerous attraction.

Today the *Protocols* are still being published and distributed throughout the world—by white supremacists and black nationalists in the United States, by Russian chauvinists and Islamic fundamentalists, by Christian millenarians, who identify the Jews as allies of the Antichrist, and by those Communists who have replaced their "class enemy" with the proverbial "world conspirators." A forgery culled from obscure sources, the *Protocols* has proved a work whose infamy is exceeded only by its success.

Michael Hagemeister

Q

Quisling, Vidkun (1887–1945) Norwegian officer and politician. Quisling established a political movement along Nazi lines in the 1930s. He met with Hitler in December 1939 to plan the German occupation of Norway and proclaimed himself prime minister of the puppet government in April 1940. Within a week Quisling was removed from office by the Germans because of his inability to assuage the outrage of the Norwegian people, but he was reinstated with German support in 1942. Quisling allowed nearly 1,000 Jews to be deported to extermination camps. After the liberation he was arrested by the Norwegian government, convicted of treason, and executed in 1945. His name became a synonym for collaboration with the enemy. See NORWAY

Vidkan Quisling (left) with the Norwegian interior minister, Albert Hagelin, and Adolf Hitler in the Chancellory, Berlin. February 1942

R

Racism The distinguishing characteristic of Nazi Germany was its obsession with race. This assertion does not exclude the fact that nazism drew on pathologies and trends also common in free societies, such as Great Britain or the United States, or that it can be usefully compared with both Italian fascism and that other hubristic attempt to refashion humanity, Soviet communism. In the last decade or so, historians have dramatically increased our understanding of Nazi racism, which had been regarded as effectively identical with racial antisemitism. Attention is now being paid to the Nazis' treatment of the so-called asocial, Arab- or Afro-Germans ("Rhineland bastards"), foreign forced labor, homosexuals and lesbians, the mentally and physically disabled, Sinti and Roma (Gypsies), and Soviet prisoners of war. Their fate does not detract from the singularity of the Nazi murder of 6 million European Jews, nor is their suffering lessened by it. An understanding of the process of persecution now includes greater awareness of the culpable involvement of various sections of the professional intelligentsia, such as anthropologists, doctors, economists, historians, lawyers, and psychiatrists, in the formation and implementation of Nazi policies. Valuable, too, are some innovative studies of the interaction between the populace as a whole and the police agencies that enforced racial policy in both Germany and Austria by, for example, David Bankier, Robert Gellately, and David J. Horwitz.

Nazi racism had both long-term and international origins, even though its most heinous manifestation was the Nazi murder of the Jews between 1941 and 1945, an outcome that was neither entirely the product of circumstance nor absolutely predetermined. In line with other racists elsewhere and in other times, Hitler and the National Socialists believed that intellectual and physical differences between people were indica-

tive of their relative value in the human scale. This ideology had complex origins, frequently drawing upon venerable pathologies and prejudices. From the eighteenth century onward, racial anthropologists used external physical criteria, often the starting point for further gross generalizations, to legitimize their claim to superiority over other peoples. Within Germany an open, cosmopolitan rejection of French pretensions to cultural hegemony in favor of a relativistic appreciation of all world cultures gradually degenerated into an aggressive, chauvinistic form of nationalistic nativism that emphasized German cultural superiority over, for example, the Slavs. It also led to the need to "purify" the German "race" of Jews and Gypsies, who were frequently subsumed in nineteenth-century racist discourse as being criminal, foreign, dark-skinned, short of stature, and inclined to such activities as kidnapping children.

The first comprehensive theoretical expression of racial ideology was penned by the French restoration aristocrat Joseph Arthur Comte de Gobineau (1816–82) in his *L'Essai sur l'Inégalité des Races Humaines* (Paris, 1853–55). Supposed inherent racial inequalities became the motive force of historical development. High cultures were the work of an "Aryan" master race whose decline accompanied interbreeding with "lesser races," while the French Revolution was construed as the revolt of the "Gallic" plebs against the "Frankish" elite, whence Gobineau, groundlessly, traced his own ancestry. Ongoing miscegenation would end in a Europe in which the population would "be overcome by a dark desire to sleep, living insensitively in their nothingness, like the buffaloes ruminating in the stagnant puddles of the Pontine marshes."

In contrast to this rather marginal reactionary figure, the British naturalist Charles Darwin enjoyed enormous international prestige. Darwin's work on natural selection appealed to diverse political constituencies, who were united in the belief that his findings had prescriptive applicability to the society of man. His cousin Francis Galton (1822–1911), for whom a chair was established at University College, London (a bastion of anti-establishment educational progressivism), coined the term *eugenics* to denote the science of fine breeding. Social Darwinists, an unsatisfactory umbrella term covering a multitude of persuasions, shared the view that human beings should take charge of their own evolutionary process. Some believed that this should be achieved by doing nothing, so that the denizens of East End London slums would die through processes of auto-extermination. Others recommended various combinations of measures to encourage enhanced reproduction among the "fit," with negative procedures, such as sterilization (either voluntary or compulsory), that would curb the fertility of the "unfit" parts of the population. Modern, progressive, and scientific, these ideas appealed across the political spectrum, including English Fabian Socialists like Sydney and Beatrice Webb, cofounders of the London School of Economics, and the German Socialist doctor Alfred Grotjahn, for whom they became a means of eradicating the marginal *Lumpenproletariat*. In Germany one of their most influential exponents was the zoologist Ernst Haeckel (1834–1919), originator of a philosophy known as monism. Enthusing over what he probably wrongly took to be ancient Spartan practice, Haeckel recommended the killing of the mentally and physically defective in the interests of strengthening the culturally and physically superior "central type of people," whose most valuable part was the "Indo-Germanic" race. Even then, these questions became intertwined with health and emotional costings, a conflation which would be intensified by the financial problems caused by World War I.

A further aspect of these developments is most strikingly represented by the racial hygienist Alfred Ploetz (1860–1940), namely the idea that the health of a society, construed as a genetic collective, should be literally patrolled by medical experts, who would determine who should marry or reproduce—in other words, what type of people should be born. Scope for this interventionist power-seeking by the medical profession and others was dramatically enhanced as the early nineteenth-century small state, with its more modest concerns, was replaced by the big governments of the twentieth century reaching into most areas of life.

While these various ideas frequently transcended political differences, discontinuities and contradictions were often apparent. Not all those who advocated eugenic solutions to social problems countenanced sterilization; some in the pro-sterilization group were totally opposed to "mercy killing" of the terminally ill, let alone the mentally or physically disabled, and by no means all these people would have subscribed to other forms of racism, such as antisemitism or extreme nordicism. These differences matter. The first country in the world to give eugenics legislative expression was the United States, whose eugenic enthusiasts, such as Charles Davenport or Harry Laughlin, were also engaged in a "gene race" with their German equivalents.

Adolf Hitler's racism drew upon many of these various strands of racism. There was no one man from whom he took his notions; the process whereby his ideas were mediated was extremely complicated. Broadly speaking, Hitler—whose cardinal obsession was his hatred of the Jews—drew upon anthropological and racial-hygienic discourses, including the elective German Englishman, Houston Stewart Chamberlain, and American exemplars. According to Otto Wagener, head of the Nazi party's Economic Office, Hitler said: "I have studied with great interest the laws of several American states concerning prevention of reproduction by people whose progeny would, in all probability, be of no value or be injurious to the racial stock." Hitler believed in the existence of "higher" and "lesser" races, the former being Aryans, and in the deleterious biological and cultural consequences of racial interbreeding. The future *völkisch* state should pursue active pro-natalist policies based upon selective breeding and selective welfare benefits, coupled with the eugenic elimination of the unfit in order to maintain racial purity and the "victory of the better and stronger."

However, these prescriptions paled into insignificance beside Hitler's pathological hatred of the Jews, who stood behind such diverse modern phenomena as capitalism and Bolshevism. The Jew was a force of almost cosmic malevolence, the chief obstruction to racial redemption, who was responsible not only for Germany's capitulation in 1918 and ensuing socioeconomic miseries, but also for the subversion of the biological substance of the German "race" through such activities as domestic prostitution and the planting of black servicemen in the occupied Rhineland. All measures to promote racial purity would be worthless without a solution to the so-called Jewish question. None of these notions was especially new, although the specific synthesis undoubtedly was, and implementation would obviously depend upon a variety of external contingencies, such as domestic political considerations and foreign opinion. But however irrational and resentment-laden his ideas may seem, these views were held with unswerving conviction and expressed with tremendous emotional force by a man whose inner violence was poorly concealed. They were no ideological smokescreen for more material interests, nor simply reducible to antisemitism, but rather a broadly conceived vision—a mission statement—which, regardless of tactical shifts, the Nazis largely brought into being after attaining power.

One of the main instruments for achieving the goal of a racially pure national community was legislation, most of which took the form of decrees. Jews bore the brunt of an incremental assault involving thousands of individual decrees and enactments. Aryan clauses contained in the 7 April 1933 Law for the Restoration of the Professional Civil Service, a measure supposedly designed to depoliticize the Weimar civil service, opened the way for a host of similar initiatives throughout other trades and professions. The emancipatory measures of the previous century were finally reversed by the complex known as the Nuremberg Laws of 15 September 1935, which denied Jewish people citizenship and prohibited marriage or sexual relations between Jews and Aryans. Subsequent amendments and commentaries on these laws extended their scope to include Sinti and Roma, as well as "Negroes and their bastards." In addition to being subject to progressive formal and informal social ostracism, Jews were also victims of systematic attempts to deny them a livelihood (economic aryanization), whose effects were the gradual impoverishment of this part of the population. Those who remained in Germany became a stigmatized group, excluded from certain park benches, public transport, swimming baths, art galleries, concert halls, and libraries. Legislation and propaganda, which had regularly and semi-pornographically insinuated in such racist publications as *Der Stürmer* that Jews preyed on German women, gradually built up the imputation that Jews were the enemy within, a trend reflected in such measures as the wartime ban on Jewish ownership of carrier pigeons and radios. This culmi

A teacher points out the salient features of a student's profile during a lesson in racial instruction, which became mandatory in 1934.

nated in their physical labeling as something identifiably "other" with the introduction on 1 September 1941 of the compulsory wearing of the Star of David.

Like the Jews, Sinti and Roma were also deemed to be racially alien, although they were often also persecuted on the grounds of antisocial behavior. Like antisemitism, discrimination against Sinti and Roma has a long history, partly stemming from the clash between sedentary and peripatetic cultures, and like antisemitism it is a prejudice by no means local to Germany. Inheriting regional legislation whose effect was perpetual harassment, the Nazis centralized the apparatus of persecution in the Reich Central Office for the Combating of the Gypsy Nuisance, established in 1936. Sinti and Roma were also effectively subjected to the Nuremberg racial laws by commentaries such as those of Hans Globke and Wilhelm Stuckart, which prohibited marriages between racial aliens and Germans. While race experts such as Robert Ritter registered Germany's Sinti and Roma, local authorities fre quently took the initiative by corralling them in ad-hoc camps, often as a means of shedding obligations of health care, schooling, or basic utilities. Such imprisonment was frequently a response to popular complaints about the behavior of Sinti and Roma, which sometimes grated on their neighbors. Although final formal convergence of laws regarding the Jews and the Sinti and Roma did not take place until 1942, long before then wagons containing Sinti and Roma were regularly appended to trains deporting Jews to Poland. From 1941 onward, the *Einsatzgruppen*, SS and police killing units in the occupied Soviet Union, repeatedly referred in their reports to massacres of "Gypsies" (and also the mentally ill) as well as Jews.

Racial hygienic legislation began with the Law for the Prevention of Offspring with Hereditary Diseases, issued on 14 July 1933, which drew upon both Weimar and North American models. Passed in the same Cabinet session that concluded the Concordat with the Vatican, this law sanctioned the compulsory sterilization (by surgery or X-rays) of persons suffering from a range of supposedly hereditary illnesses, including congenital feeblemindedness, schizophrenia, manic depression, epilepsy, Huntington's chorea, blindness, deafness, severe physical deformity, and chronic alcoholism. At the time the hereditary character of many of these conditions was a matter of faith rather than scientific certitude. Asylum psychiatrists, midwives, and public health officials were obliged to report (and were paid for doing so) cases that fell within this law. Many of the psychiatrists needed little encouragement, since they had been enthusiastically advocating such measures throughout the Weimar Republic. The decision to sterilize individuals was then made by the new Hereditary Health Courts, which from 1933 to 1945 were responsible for the sterilization of between 320,000 and 350,000 people, of whom some hundreds died as a result of surgical or postoperative complications. On 26 June 1935 the law was amended to include eugenic abortion up to the sixth month of pregnancy for hereditarily diseased women. Although not all advocates of compulsory sterilization saw the need for "euthanasia" of the mentally ill, Nazi propaganda nonetheless tended that way, with its constant references to the costs of institutional care and to understanding for those who took the law into their own hands by killing their sick relatives. Crude graphics and progressively more sophisticated films, such as *Das Erbe* (Inheritance) or *Opfer der Vergangenheit* (Victim of the Past), depicted a nation apparently menaced by hordes of mental defectives, necessitating a cost of caring that was swallowing up funds that should have been spent on public housing for the racially deserving German poor.

Being tough on crime while making a fetish of work and "healthy popular morality," the Nazis also struck at those they regarded as sexual or social deviants— that is, the antisocial, homosexuals, and Sinti and Roma. Many of these people were sterilized simply through an extension of the notion of feeblemindedness from its medical meanings to encompass moral judgments about lifestyle or socioeconomic effectiveness. People living on the margins of society, where petty criminality was often part of the way of life, were highly vulnerable to these measures. The Law against Dangerous Habitual Criminals, issued on 24 November 1933, drastically enhanced police powers of preventive detention and sanctioned castration of sexual offenders. The range of offenses involving capital punishment was radically extended, from three in 1933 to 25 in 1939, with Hitler personally insisting on the death penalty for highway robbery on the new Autobahnen. Hitler also had the habit of ordering the shooting of criminals whose sentences he considered too lenient. The courts, as the police could effectively bypass them, became correspondingly accommodating to Nazi political and racial imperatives. In addition to the Hereditary Health Courts, the regime created an eventual total of 74 Special Courts and a peripatetic People's Court to deal with the massively increased workload.

In 1938 the SS, having once briefly rounded up beggars and vagrants without having adequate facilities in which to incarcerate them, swept into concentration camps the denizens of flophouses, hostels, and overnight shelters—in other words, the homeless. These people became part of the labor force in the second generation of SS concentration camps, such as Flossenburg, Mauthausen, and Gross-Rosen, established near stone quarries designed to supply the megalomaniac building plans of Hitler and Albert Speer, his chief architect. These measures were augmented locally by various initiatives, including ad-hoc and semicoercive camps for Sinti and Roma; demolition in Hamburg of slum areas with high incidence of crime; or the construction at Hashude, near Bremen, of a corrective housing project for entire "asocial" families. Although the idea was certainly regularly mooted, plans for a comprehensive law against "community aliens" never went beyond the drafting stage.

For much of the nineteenth century, homophobia was the preserve of the political left, who used it as a weapon against the allegedly effete upper classes, just as German Communists sometimes resorted to antisemitism to attack capitalism and pick up nationalist support during the Weimar Republic. Although the Nazis' political opponents sometimes drew attention to highly placed homosexuals within the movement, notably the SA (storm troopers) leader Ernst Röhm, and while nazism had its own share of homoerotic attitudes, nonetheless the Nazis could be described as virulently homophobic. Although they were not above using charges of homosexuality to discredit and destroy opponents, the primary reason for the assault on homosexuals was because the latter were self-evidently failing in their duty to contribute to the expansion of the "Aryan Germanic race" at a time when millions of young men of the previous generation had perished in world war. Existing legislation—notably Paragraph 175 of the Reich Criminal Code, which criminalized male homosexuality—was extended to include a wider variety of homosexual behavior, and the number of prosecutions dramatically increased. In 1934, 766 men were convicted and imprisoned; in 1936 the figure exceeded 4,000, and it rose to 8,000 in 1938. Men sentenced for homosexual offenses were regularly transferred to concentration camps after having served the statutory prison sentence. Lacking the group solidarities of, for example, professional criminals or political prisoners, and exposed to the sadism both of their guards and of other inmates, many homosexual camp prisoners perished.

Running parallel with efforts to exclude and ultimately exterminate people deemed racially alien, unfit, or criminal were various philogenerative measures designed to foster the Aryan Germanic race. Following the example set by Chancellor Heinrich Brüning, the Law for the Reduction of Unemployment (1 June 1933), part of whose agenda was to put men back to work by excluding married women from the work force, introduced marriage loans—in the form of vouchers for consumer durables—for families in which the man alone worked, the debt being reduced with every successful childbirth and canceled on the birth of a fourth child. Racial "aliens" and the "hereditarily diseased" were ineligible.

The results of these policies were disappointing, largely because of the long-term drift toward two-child families, but also because there was no commensurate housing policy. Prolific Aryan mothers were also encouraged by the awarding of decorations for outstanding service in this area, although the regime distinguished sharply between families deemed to be "rich in children" and what were disparagingly dubbed "large families," that is fecund Lumpenproletarians. After 1935 couples who wished to marry were obliged to supply fitness certificates, which involved interviews and tests with public health doctors and could result in an appearance before a Hereditary Health Court if any untoward facts surfaced. The Aryan birthrate was also promoted by the establishment of *Lebensborn,* or "Well of Life," institutions, in 1935, with maternity homes in Germany and later in occupied northern Europe. There both married and single mothers could give birth in relative comfort, availing themselves of an adoption service for unwanted babies. Lebensborn also mirrored SS chief Heinrich Himmler's aversion to conventional bourgeois morality, in the sense that for racial reasons he wished to destigmatize illegitimacy and, indeed, at least countenanced polygamy. There is no evidence that these homes contributed to an increased birth rate; on the contrary, SS officers were conspicuous for the below-average number of children they fathered.

Any discussion of Nazi racism must also include the individuals and organizations that implemented these policies and some tentative observations on the responses of the German population as a whole—tentative because crude and quasi-racist claims have been made about German subscription to eliminationist antisemitism. Of course, racist legislation did not arise in a societal vacuum. Some of it—notably the Nuremberg Laws—was undoubtedly the product of a complex dialectic involving pressure from grass-roots and Nazi party activists to take radical action on the Jewish question. Other measures, such as the Law for the Prevention of Offspring with Hereditary Diseases, clearly came about through the prompting of professional experts within and outside the party, who had been lobbying for such measures throughout the Weimar Republic. Nazi Germany brought boom conditions for "scientific" experts, that strange species of modern scholar for whom mere intrinsic intellectual curiosity is not enough. Invariably providing a scientific gloss for irrational and pertinacious prejudices, these men and women threw themselves in a Gadarene rush at the feet of a regime that probably despised them. The payoff took the familiar form of enhanced research funding, extra facilities, new posts, and promotions, as well as income supplements for writing reports on individuals for the courts or, in the case of natural scientists, a refashioned ethical climate that permitted horrible experiments on human subjects. Robert Ritter, as director of the new Criminal-Biological Institute of the Security Police, was responsible for categorizing all 30,000 of Germany's Sinti and Roma according to degrees of racial "purity," a pursuit that was a life-and-death affair for the persons involved. Selection on the ramps of Auschwitz complemented selection by card indexes and reports.

The pretensions of racial science recognized no limits. That no one was potentially safe from these attentions can be demonstrated by the case of Karl Astel's *Landesamt für Rassewesen* (Regional Office for Racial Issues), which by 1938 had gathered data on a quarter of Thuringia's population, so that "henceforth the less valuable, the asocial, and criminals could more easily be excluded than before." In Giessen, Astel's colleague Heinrich Wilhelm Kranz envisaged permanent racial selection, remarking that "not only the hereditarily diseased and asocial but also the hereditarily healthy and the socially valuable should be continually registered, genetically investigated and put on card indexes." No less an authority than Bishop Clemens August von Galen, in his sermon on euthanasia in 1941, recognized the unlimited potentialities in the program when he warned his flock that soon the elderly, the terminally ill, and wounded soldiers would join the insane in the gas chambers. During the war the ranks of these race experts were augmented by a small army of *Ostforscher,* or experts on the "German" Slavic East, who volunteered their expertise in the service of rearranging the ethnic composition of occupied Eastern Europe. Medical scientists availed themselves of the brains of victims of the euthanasia program (the Posen anatomist Hermann Voss acquired corpses supplied by the local Gestapo), carried out experiments involving immersion in freezing water or unbearable atmospheric pressures, subjected concentration camp inmates to tropical diseases and toxic substances, and took part in euthanasia killings as well as selection and gassing in extermination camps.

Control of racial policy was a congested arena. The first abortive attempt to establish a central clearinghouse in this area was the Committee of Experts for Population and Racial Policy, established by the minister of the interior, Wilhelm Frick, on 28 June 1933. This came to naught, although one of its three steering groups was heavily involved in drafting the Law for the Prevention of Offspring with Hereditary Diseases. The Law for the Consolidation of the Health System (3 July 1934) opened the way for would-be centralizers of health-care provision. However, the role of Reich medical chief was a contested one, the main candidates being Artur Gütt, Leonardo Conti, Gerhard Wagner, and the emergency surgeon attached to Hitler's retinue, Karl Brandt. Nor were either the German Labor Front leader Robert Ley nor the Reich SS doctor Ernst Grawitz prepared to withdraw from this terrain without a fight. Increasingly the implementation of racial policy was assigned to ad-hoc teams, such as the T4 apparatus attached to the Führer Chancellery, which carried out the euthanasia program beyond the control of the ordinary state bureaucracy.

One agency—or rather one continent-wide police empire—is rightly associated with the implementation of Nazi racial policy more than any other, namely the SS. Technically subordinate to Röhm's SA, Heinrich Himmler emerged from the Nazi seizure of power in 1933 with the comparatively modest office of commissary president of the Munich Police. In 1934 he became inspector of the Prussian Secret State Police (Gestapo). He rapidly shook off the tutelage of Hermann Göring, arranged the murder of Röhm in June 1934, and merged the Prussian Gestapo with the political police in other states. By 1936 he had secured control of all police activity with the conjoint title Reichsführer SS and chief of the German Police. SS control of the police was personified by Himmler's henchman Reinhard Heydrich, who also commanded the SS internal and external security service or Sicherheitsdienst (SD), which was responsible for monitoring domestic opinion, surveillance of ideological opponents, and espionage abroad. Its mood-monitoring activities were made possible by a network of approximately 30,000 "honorary" agents. Unlike the Gestapo and Kripo (criminal police), it had no powers of arrest, detention, or interrogation. Although rivalries within the SS polyocracy remained intense, control was nominally consolidated in 1939 with the creation of the Reich Main Security Office in Berlin. In 1939 Himmler further extended his powers with the title "Reich Commissar for the strengthening of ethnic Germandom," responsible for deportations and repatriations, while the original militarized units of the Armed or Waffen SS became a formidable military force in their own right.

Inspired by Himmler's eccentric and ahistorical understanding of a number of elite organizations, the sole task of the SS—whose creed was mindless obedience—was to destroy the regime's opponents, understood to include those who threatened the integrity or security of the master race. To that end it controlled the burgeoning concentration camp empire, which—beginning with Dachau in 1933—eventually resulted in about 10,000 core and satellite camps spread across occupied Europe. Reliable estimates suggest that, following a fall to 7,500 in 1936–37, there were some 25,000 prisoners in 1939 and approximately 100,000 by early 1942. During the 1930s increased SS involvement in racially motivated persecution was reflected in its control of Robert Ritter's Reich Central Office for the Combating of the Gypsy Nuisance and Josef Meisinger's Reich Central Office for the Combating of Abortion and Homosexuality, both located within Kripo headquarters.

With the outbreak of war the SS was primarily, if by no means exclusively, responsible for racial extermination. Special units were assigned to the killing of psychiatric patients, Jews, Sinti and Roma, and the elite in occupied Poland. The invasion of the Soviet Union, preconceived as a war of racial extermination, brought a gradual but massive expansion of the units involved, including the Einsatzgruppen, SS troops attached to the Higher SS and Police Leaders, sundry police formations, and indigenous collaborators. The German military frequently colluded with these agencies and was itself responsible for the deaths of approximately 3 million Soviet soldiers in captivity. Finally, many of the experts from the so-called euthanasia program, who had earlier provided mass gassing facilities for the concentration camps under Aktion 14f13, were now redeployed in the newly established extermination camps of Chelmno (Kulmhof), Belzec, Sobibor, and Treblinka, themselves dwarfed by the massive complex at Auschwitz-Birkenau, the apogee of industrialized mass murder.

Summaries of these institutional forms used to implement racial policy are inadequate unless accompanied by an appreciation of the broader societal dimension. Like fish, these policemen needed a sea in which to swim. For, contrary to the impression conveyed by the unreflective use of such terms as *police state,* we are actually considering what were often numerically quite small agencies. For example, the Gestapo regional headquarters based in Düsseldorf consisted of just 281 agents responsible for policing 4 million people. These desk-bound policemen were dependent upon denunciations and information supplied "from below" and by other agencies or the general public. Thus, of the cases of "racial pollution" dealt with by the Gestapo in Würzburg, 57 percent originated in denunciation by ordinary citizens, with only one case being a result of the Gestapo's own initiatives. The Saarbrücken housewife who denounced her own ex-Communist husband for listening to "enemy radio" in order to make room for her new lover, telling her son, "Your dad will go away and you will get a much better one," was unfortunately hardly atypical. The motives of such people were as heterogenous and idiosyncratic as the example suggests. Similarly, the impression that Nazi racial policy was something "done to" Germany, as if it were the first Nazi-occupied country, is further undermined by the obvious glee with which neighbors and local authorities regarded the removal of Sinti and Roma from their streets and neighborhoods; by the obvious dependency of the Gestapo upon informants to penetrate such discrete subcultures as that of homosexuals, whose elimination was actively welcomed by wide swathes of the working class; by the ease with which people adjusted to the presence of an army of coerced foreign labor in their midst; and by the all too evident willingness of many ordinary families to disburden themselves of sick members through the wartime euthanasia program. If they failed, as many did, to protest against these policies, what chance had such actively stigmatized groups as foreign forced laborers, prisoners of war, the Jews, or Sinti and Roma? Despite the minority who actively tried to thwart these policies through acts of individual courage, the majority response ranged from silent disapproval (mostly, as the November 1938 pogrom known as Kristallnacht suggests, of the manner of persecution rather than its nominal objective), through indifference—understood as a lack of emotional concern or moral awareness rather than self-preoccupation with one's own problems—down to baser forms of active endorsement such as denunciations. Yet the variety of responses, and the fact of various degrees of resistance, naturally militates against the simpleminded view that all Germans subscribed to an eliminationist mind-set exclusively directed against Jews, a view more redolent

Truck with SA "speaking choir" and characteristic drawings in the streets of Stuttgart. The inscription over the truck says, "We don't tolerate any sabotage of the constructive work of the Führer!" Sketches of Nazi "enemies" are shown below. The man on the left is saying, "Please don't sterilize"; above the nun is written, "Entrance fee to heaven." 16 August 1935

of wartime propaganda than of serious historical scholarship.

Regardless of any inconsistencies or inefficiencies of conception or implementation, which were not apparent to its victims at the time and which historical research sometimes exaggerates, the most salient historical characteristic of the Third Reich was the attempt to realize a unique racial state. This drew upon long-term historical pathologies and prejudices (notably toward the Jews and the Sinti and Roma) as well as more short-term, but equally complex, international intellectual trends mostly generated by industrial society and expressed in Germany, as elsewhere, in the unquestioning language of scientific certitude. Germany's experiences in the wake of World War I gave these tendencies a particularly radical political expression, resulting in the accession to power of a movement whose animating principle was the quest for racial purity, construed in quasi-religious terms, an atavistic

aim to be achieved with all available modern technologies and administrative structures. The effect was to plunge Europe into a nightmare involving the deaths of millions of people, a nightmare from which it is only just emerging. Modern genetic science has since revealed that the animating principle was a mirage, there being no substantive genetic differences between the races of people, but rather overwhelming similarity and shared characteristics. *Michael Burleigh*

Rademacher, Franz (1906–73) Head of the *Juden-referat*, the so-called Jewish desk, in the German Foreign Ministry, 1940–43. Rademacher promoted the abortive Madagascar Plan of 1940 to relocate the Jews of Europe and was instrumental in the murder of thousands of Serbian Jews in late 1941. After the Wannsee Conference in January 1942 he brought pressure on the governments of neighboring states under German occupation to deport the Jews residing there to the extermination camps. Rademacher received a short prison sentence in 1952 but fled to Syria in 1953 while free on bond to await appeal. He returned to Germany in 1966 and was sentenced to prison but died before his appeal could be heard. See MADAGASCAR PLAN

Rasch, Emil Otto (1891–1946) Commander of Einsatzgruppe C, which carried out the mass murder of Jews at Babi Yar and elsewhere in the first months following the German invasion of the Soviet Union. Rasch was recalled to Berlin in September 1941 and spent the rest of the war in administrative posts. He died in prison in Nuremberg during the war crimes trial.

Rath, Ernst vom (d. 1938) Third secretary at the German embassy in Paris. Rath was shot by the Polish Jewish student Herszel Grynszpan on 7 November 1938 and died two days later. The Nazis used the murder to incite anti-Jewish rioting and violence in German cities. See KRISTALLNACHT

Ravensbrück Major concentration camp north of Berlin. Ravensbrück was founded in 1939 as a camp for women, although in April 1941 a small camp for men, technically a satellite camp of Sachsenhausen, was established nearby, through which approximately 20,000 inmates passed during the war. In 1942 Ravensbrück had 11,000 inmates, and by 1944 the number swelled to 70,000. A total of 106,000 women passed through the camp, most of them non-Jews (Poles, Russians, Gypsies, and others). Thousands of women died from overwork, overcrowding, squalor, and starvation. Many others were shot or gassed (after the construction of gas chambers in early 1945) or died as the result of so-called medical experiments that involved surgery, amputation, infection with gangrene, and sterilization. In March 1945 the camp was partially evacuated, and 24,500 prisoners were sent to Mecklenburg. Three thousand women were turned over to the Red Cross or freed during the evacuation. The camp was liberated on 30 April 1945.

Red Cross, International Committee of the The International Committee of the Red Cross (ICRC) is among the most highly esteemed humanitarian organizations in the world. It traces its origin to the battle of Solferino (1859), where a Swiss businessman, Henri Dunant, witnessed the horrible suffering of wounded Austrian and French soldiers, many of whom were left on the battlefield without the slightest help or comfort. Dunant decided to create an organization to provide care for the wounded of all belligerents in wartime. His intention was realized in 1863, when the ICRC was founded in Geneva as a private association. The following year it convened a conference of 12 nations that ratified the first Geneva Convention, which established rules for the treatment of the wounded and the protection of doctors and nurses. The treaty was modified in 1929, in the wake of World War I, to include guidelines for the treatment of prisoners of war. At the Tokyo Conference of 1934 the ICRC extended its protection to civilians, prohibiting reprisals, deportations, and the execution of hostages.

According to its statutes, the members of the ICRC (25 at most) consist exclusively of Swiss citizens. Their responsibility is to oversee the national Red Cross societies of other countries and to promote contact between those societies. Until 1923 ICRC members were drawn from venerable Geneva families who exercised considerable influence in Swiss economy, science, and politics. This circumstance gave rise during World War II to criticism (at first internal) that allocating a seat to a member of the Swiss government would endanger the committee's neutrality—a fear that turned out to be justified.

From the early 1920s, and especially after the outbreak of war in September 1939, the ICRC had to face totalitarian regimes that had set out to liquidate liberalism and conquer the world. Neither the Soviet Union nor Fascist Italy worried about a humanitarian association from Geneva; and neither did the National Socialists in Germany. When Carl Burckhardt obtained permission in 1935 to visit the German concentration camps (including Dachau), he had to pledge to keep all information he uncovered strictly confidential. Because of this condition his official report was extraordinarily empty of content, though even in this emasculated form it was not published. Many passages betraying helplessness and even outright naivete are to be found in the report of Guillaume Favre, a high-ranking official and ICRC member who visited Dachau in 1938. The first thing that struck Favre was the order and discipline of the camp. He also remarked on the bright dormitories and the prisoners' opportunities for leisure, before acknowledging that to his surprise he could discover no trace of abuse. When he made inquiries—after all, newspapers were carrying articles on the terrors of the camps, and escaped prisoners were describing the most dreadful mistreatment—he was told "that it was forbidden to make any attack on the prisoners. Should a soldier on duty strike a prisoner, he would be severely punished and dismissed from the SS." By this time the German Red Cross had long been *gleichgeschaltet*—coordinated with the Nazi regime. Since 1 January 1938 it had been headed by an SS doctor, Ernst Grawitz.

After the war the questions that the ICRC and others have continually asked are, What was known in Geneva about the systematic destruction of the Jews in Europe? And if much was known, why did those in charge react hesitantly? The standard work on this issue is *Das Internationale Rote Kreuz und das Dritte Reich: War der Holocaust Aufzuhalten?* (The International Red Cross and the Third Reich: Could the Holocaust Have Been Stopped?), by the Swiss historian Jean-Claude Favez, who described Switzerland during the war years as "the hub of all kinds of international traffic." What was true of Switzerland in general was even more appropriate to Geneva, the seat of numerous international organizations. World-renowned and highly esteemed members of the ICRC, such as its president, Max Huber, or the diplomat and historian Carl Burckhardt, enjoyed far-reaching and influential relationships abroad. Burckhardt kept up a friendship with Ernst von Weizsäcker, secretary of state in the German Foreign Office, but also maintained links with Jewish and Christian aid organizations.

Since the Nazi seizure of power in Germany in 1933, the ICRC had been receiving news of the most appalling breaches of international law. Beginning in the fall of 1941, the Geneva headquarters received increasingly disturbing news about the plight of Jews in German-occupied areas. In a "Memorandum on the Situation in Poland" dated 29 October 1941, Pastor Visser't Hooft of the Ecumenical Church Council described to Huber and Burckhardt the deplorable conditions and demanded ICRC action:

> In the large cities, particularly in Warsaw, famine reigns among the Polish population and in all probability to a more severe degree among the Jews. Within and outside the Warsaw ghetto typhus rages. . . . The mortality rate of children under three is thought to have reached 26 percent. . . . Mid-October saw the start of what has so far been the most intense wave of deportations to Poland of German Jews and baptized Jews. Thus, on each of two nights, 18–19 and 19–20 October, 7,000 Berlin Jews were transferred, first to Litzmannstadt. Twenty thousand Rhineland Jews found themselves on the same path or were already in Litzmannstadt. . . . The Jewish question touches on the center of the Christian message: a failure of the church to raise its voice here in protection and warning or to give help to the best of its ability would be an act of disobedience toward its Lord. . . . Accordingly the Provisional Ecumenical Council of Churches turns to the appropriate authorities of the Red Cross, requesting that it should give particular attention to conditions in the Warthegau and in the Generalgouvernement in Poland. Our suggestion is that the Red Cross might arrange for the early dispatch of a delegate, if possible a doctor, to the areas mentioned.

Although the reports from Poland were acknowledged by the ICRC offices, nothing happened. Responding to a call for help from the Hungarian Red Cross, the Geneva headquarters wrote on 5 December 1941: "We fully understand the seriousness of the situation of the people deported under such appalling conditions. . . . Unfortunately, despite the great sympathy which we feel for all these unfortunate people, at the moment it is absolutely impossible for us to undertake anything." From the political and legal point of view, this was indeed the case, since the ICRC was concerned only with prisoners of war and civilian internees. Because the Jews did not form a nation, they fell under no category within international law. Legally speaking, persons persecuted "for reasons of race" simply did not exist. In other words, the tools that the ICRC had forged were largely ineffective under the circumstances.

The deportations continued unabated in 1942, and in the summer of that year, in full view of world public opinion, the Germans carried out their raids against the Jews in France. Although the number of horror stories mounted, and evidence of the systematic murder of European Jews by the Nazis hardened, the ICRC saw itself as unable even to mention the fate of the Jews. Why did the ICRC, until shortly before the end of the war, undertake so little to alleviate the fate of the persecuted Jews? Why did it not parade its information before the public? Why did it not pluck up courage to deliver a verdict on Nazi policies, particularly the racial laws and their consequences?

A key to answering these questions is the unsuccessful appeal of October 1942. In the Swiss parliament (the Bundeshaus) there had always been concern for the strict neutrality of the ICRC. An absolute division between the state and relief work was the rule. The guarantor of this policy was ICRC president Max Huber, a lawyer and expert on questions of neutrality and foreign policy. Huber, however, had health problems and often missed committee meetings. When

Federal Counselor Philipp Etter took his seat on the Geneva Committee in 1940 the neutrality of the committee was at an end. The Swiss government now possessed a means of directly influencing ICRC policy—and it intended to take advantage of it.

With the intensification of warfare in 1942, the ICRC was repeatedly asked to break its silence and to speak out publicly against breaches of international law. Should it disregard its fears and approach the German government? What effect might this kind of intervention have? In August 1942 the Coordination Council decided to send the ICRC members a draft appeal, attempting to define the attitude of the ICRC toward infringements of international law and calling for restraint on the part of the combatant nations. Members were asked to give their opinion of the draft in writing.

The Swiss Bundesrat received intelligence of ICRC intentions through Edouard de Haller, who in early 1942 was named the Swiss Federal Council delegate for international relief and had been an honorary member of the ICRC since 1941. De Haller immediately passed on information to his brother-in-law, Pierre Bonna, head of the Foreign Section in the Eidgenössisches Politisches Departement (Federal Political Department) and second-in-command at the Foreign Affairs Ministry. The reaction was quite clear: such an appeal, however toothless and inoffensive its text, would harm rather than help the committee. The ministry was also nervous about possible German protests, which could very well be followed by actual sanctions.

In the fall of 1942, when reliable information about the annihilation of the Jews had already reached Geneva, 21 out of 23 committee members expressed themselves in favor of a general appeal condemning the treatment of "certain categories of civilians of various nationalities who, for reasons of war, are being deprived of their nationality, deported or seized as hostages, and even threatened with death." Jews were not specifically mentioned in the text. Alarm at this clear majority led to the calling of a full meeting on 14 October 1942 in the Hôtel Métropole. The proposed appeal was on the agenda for a vote. This occasion marked Federal Councillor Etter's first appearance at an ICRC meeting in two years.

Although most committee members still favored an appeal, Burckhardt and Etter managed to turn the debate against it. Burckhardt questioned the efficacy of a general appeal and argued (according to the minutes of the meeting) that "action must be restricted to concrete instances. . . . Accordingly, intervention should be directly and discreetly addressed to the individual government or governments responsible for the incidents in question." Etter also objected to the appeal, but on opposite grounds. He was concerned that even in its present form the Germans would "interpret the appeal as a judgment, and if it aroused their annoyance, its effect would already have missed the mark." He appealed to the committee to preserve the ICRC's traditional role of "the Good Samaritan, who breaks his silence only by his deeds."

The appeal was defeated, and the ICRC continued to maintain extreme discretion in the following months, although Burckhardt, for one, knew of the existence of a plan to destroy European Jewry. The American consul-general in Geneva, Paul C. Squire, mentioned the dire plight of the Jews in a memorandum of 9 November 1942. Later Squire contacted Burckhardt and spoke to him of the matter. Burckhardt replied that he had not seen the order that Hitler was supposed to have signed early in 1941 directing that by the end of 1942 Germany must be *Judenrein*, free of Jews. According to Burckhardt, the source of this information was two "very well briefed Germans" who enjoyed his full confidence. In his memorandum Squire noted that the men involved were from the German Foreign Office and the War Ministry in Berlin. In order to be certain, Squire arranged for Professor Paul Guggenheim to make a sworn statement. Guggenheim testified to the existence of "an order given by Hitler concerning the eradication of all Jews in Germany and the occupied countries by 31 December 1942."

Leland Harrison, the U.S. envoy in Bern, took two days to gather more evidence. Then he acted, sending his information to Undersecretary of State Sumner Welles in Washington. On 24 November, Welles called Rabbi Stephen Wise, president of the World Jewish Congress, to his office, where he imparted his information, adding, "I have reason to believe that everything in these documents is correct. . . . There is no exaggeration."

The question of whether and how much Burckhardt knew of the annihilation of the Jews even before the 14 October meeting of the ICRC cannot yet be determined. What the ICRC wrote to the Americans, however, is well known. A letter from the ICRC dated 2

November 1942 contains this statement: "The International Committee has at the moment no reliable information about the fate of the Jews taken away to Poland. For the rest, the committee would deliberate very seriously before furnishing information to a government about the fate of persons who are not citizens of the country making the inquiry. The committee has already occupied itself with the fate of those deported and taken steps to obtain news of them and to be able to be allowed to come to their help; but in this respect it has as yet received no answer."

Burckhardt was the central figure of the flow of information between the ICRC and Jewish aid organizations in Switzerland. Among his interlocutors was Adolf Silberschein, who was a member of the Polish Jewish parliament and had taken part in the 21st Zionist Congress, held in Geneva in 1939. Taken unawares by the outbreak of war, Silberschein could not return to Poland but was able to remain in Geneva, where he founded the relief organization Relico (Comité pour l'Assistance à la Population Juive Frappée par la Guerre). In early December 1942 Silberschein showed Burckhardt telegrams from Tel Aviv pleading for help for the threatened Jews in Poland. The ICRC made copies of these telegrams. The minutes of the conversation record that among arrested refugees held in a Swiss prison Silberschein had recognized the son of a friend. The young man had escaped from Poland and carried with him a letter, which Silberschein had evidently read to Burckhardt. The letter stated that in August 1942 deportations from this particular refugee's hometown had begun: those able to work were transported from the town, while the unfit and the sick, as well as women and children, had been shot in the forest. In Lvov the population had shrunk from 140,000 to 40,000. In Warsaw only 30,000 Jews remained alive.

It also emerges from the minutes that Silberschein had urgently begged the ICRC for help for the beleaguered population. Later, Burckhardt suggested a possible exchange of Jews against the release of German prisoners of war interned abroad—a promise he could not keep.

At the beginning of 1943 the ICRC received a report about the extermination camps in Poland which was remarkable for its extraordinary exactness. "In Treblinka," the report noted, "prisoners are killed by gas or electrocution, or they are shot. Two special machines for the preparation of mass graves have been sent to Treblinka. The enormous number of corpses and the minimal depth of the graves has poisoned the area surrounding Treblinka with a sickening smell, which has driven the local inhabitants out of their houses. In these camps, Lithuanians, Letts, and Ukrainians are used as executioners: they are likewise destined beforehand to be killed after they have fulfilled their infamous task."

Now the Red Cross in Geneva apparently wished to react. The ICRC delegate in Romania, Vladimir de Steiger, was instructed to make clear how far assistance to the Jewish population was practicable. "We beg you," the committee wrote in the directive, "to proceed carefully and very discreetly. At all costs, we want to avoid alerting the authorities or the public, arousing an idea that the ICRC wants to undertake a major operation in favor of the Jews. Such a conjecture would have extremely undesirable consequences and could endanger our intention, which is merely not to exclude the Jews from the operations that the United Relief Work carries out within the bounds of possibility and with the agreement of the respective governments on behalf of the civilian population in the occupied countries."

How hesitantly the ICRC acted, despite the wealth of reports on the crimes in Eastern Europe, is demonstrated by its proceedings in the spring of 1944. On 7 April two Jewish prisoners escaped from Auschwitz and reported that all preparations had been made there for the murder of about 1 million Hungarian Jews. At the end of May two more escapees declared that each day, from the middle of that month, 12,000 Hungarian Jews were being sent to the gas chambers. This news was also brought to Geneva, but it was not until 5 July that ICRC president Huber sent a letter by special delegate to the Hungarian regent, Miklós Horthy. Huber acknowledged that the ICRC had been inundated with reports of "alleged" violence against the Hungarian Jews. "We are not in a position to counter this onslaught, since we are not in possession of any verifiable facts whatsoever in the matter. What has been brought to our notice seems so markedly to contradict the chivalrous tradition of the great Hungarian people that it appears to us almost impossible to credit even the smallest part of the information passed to us. In the name of the International Committee of the Red Cross, I should like to beg Your Highness to furnish guidelines which will put us in a position to counter rumors and accusations." The ICRC had finally, even though timidly, broken its silence, but it had done so too late. When the letter was delivered on 23 July 1944 in Budapest, the deportations had already been halted under the pressure of international protests—from the Vatican and the Swedish Red Cross, among others.

The ICRC could and should have intervened in Hungary much earlier, but in April 1944 it had recalled its delegate, Jean de Bavier, from Budapest—supposedly because his German was inadequate. In fact as early as the fall of 1943, and particularly in February 1944, de Bavier had been sending the Geneva headquarters urgent demands for action to rescue the Hungarian Jews. To this end he had even suggested a personal meeting between Hitler and Huber.

When Friedrich Born arrived in Budapest in May 1944, the deportation trains organized by Adolf Eichmann were already on their way to Auschwitz. Official ICRC policy at this time was the same as ever: no interference in the internal affairs of foreign states. For Born, however, the fundamental purpose of the Red Cross—to bring relief wherever possible—was more important than legal debates and bureaucratic directives. Guided by his own conscience and the example of his friend, the consul Carl Lutz, Born protected 25,000–30,000 human beings from certain destruction in Auschwitz, weeks before the ICRC deviated from its previous policy by approaching Horthy. After the war, Born was forbidden to speak to anyone, not even his family, about his time in Budapest. His and Lutz's heroism is now recognized, at the Holocaust memorial institute Yad Vashem in Jerusalem, where the two men have been included in the Righteous Among the Nations, a distinction accorded to only five other Swiss citizens.

Only toward the end of the war did the procedures of the ICRC undergo a marked alteration—too late for hundreds of thousands of Jewish civilians. Jean-Claude Favez comes to a clear conclusion: "As a nonpolitical institution, confronted with a totalitarian state, for it a new phenomenon, despite Soviet and Italian precedents, the ICRC, no more than its contemporaries, did not grasp the essence of the changes which the Third Reich had made to international relations, even in the humanitarian field, and to the role of law in the national and international community. It attempted to counter the assault on liberal values by reinforcing its own neutrality. . . . With its appeal to international law when confronted with victims who, though without legal status, called upon it for help, in the event the ICRC often did not seek out the possibilities for dealing with the situation, but rather looked for a justification of its inactivity. The aim was not to disturb or unsettle the mission, handed on through compromises and agreements, which at that time the ICRC saw as fundamental to its existence."

Gaston Haas

Refugees In 1933 approximately 1 million Jews lived in the area that came under Nazi rule prior to World War II—Germany, Austria, and Czechoslovakia. Of these, about 360,000 had emigrated by 1 September 1939, the day of the German invasion of Poland. The exodus took place in five phases, each of which followed specific measures against the Jews, as they were gradually expelled from all spheres of life.

1. Seizure of Power and Boycott. The first phase of emigration began when Adolf Hitler was sworn in as chancellor of Germany on 30 January 1933. The pace of emigration increased markedly after the nationwide boycott of Jewish businesses on 1 April and, a week later, the barring of Jews from the civil service and public employment at all levels of government. The number of refugees was relatively small, and many of them considered their departure to be temporary, expecting conditions in Germany to change for the better. And indeed, in the summer of 1933 the emigration rate began to decline—a trend that continued for about two years. Some émigrés returned to Germany, although the Gestapo tried to stop this reflux by interning returnees in concentration camps. During the first wave some refugees were able to take a substantial portion of their property with them.

2. The Nuremberg Laws. In September 1935, following the promulgation of the Nuremberg racial laws, which deprived the Jews of German citizenship and prompted extensive new exclusions of Jews from economic and public life, the number of refugees grew steadily. At the same time their economic resources dwindled, as the German government enacted measures to confiscate Jewish assets.

3. The Anschluss. Following the annexation (Anschluss) of Austria to the Reich in March 1938, the Jews of Austria experienced in a few weeks what the Jews of Germany had suffered over five years. Between April and November 1938 about 50,000 Jews left Austria, and another 30,000 left Germany. Whereas in the first two waves of emigration some family members had often stayed behind, from 1938 on entire families

Three refugee girls wearing tags come ashore at Harwich, England. They were among the 502 refugee children to come to Great Britain as a part of the first *Kindertransport*. 12 December 1938

left, and the migration turned into a massive flight of panic-stricken refugees stripped of almost all their property. Furthermore, the Germans decided to speed up emigration by initiating forced expulsion. This was carried out by the Gestapo, and in Austria it was organized by Adolf Eichmann. At the end of October 1938 about 17,000 Jews of Polish origin who had lived in Germany for many years were forcibly expelled to Poland.

4. The November Pogrom. Following the organized pogrom of 9–10 November 1938 known as Kristallnacht, penniless and demoralized Jews fled in chaos, not only from Germany and Austria but also from those parts of Czechoslovakia that had been handed to the Reich under the provisions of the September 1938 Munich Pact.

5. The Invasion of Czechoslovakia. Following the Nazi invasion of Czechoslovakia in March 1939, refugees hastily escaped as best they could from all territories governed by Nazi Germany.

At each stage the number of Jews seeking asylum in-

creased, their economic means diminished, and the destinations available to them became fewer as immigration laws abroad were made more strict. The first wave of refugees enjoyed a sympathetic reception on the part of many governments, the second group encountered at best indifference, and at the third stage refugees were confronted by a hasty tightening of immigration regulations by countries all over the world. Throughout the 1930s the United States made no change in its immigration laws or quota system to take in more refugees from Nazi Germany, nor was any distinction made between them and other immigrants. During the fourth wave most countries closed their doors to both permanent settlers and transmigrants, but when the fifth phase erupted some of them erected temporary camps to harbor the refugees until their further migration. When war broke out in September 1939, more than 100,000 Jewish refugees were scattered over Europe.

All in all, 87 countries in Europe and overseas received Jewish refugees from Greater Germany. The first wave of refugees went mostly to neighboring countries—primarily Belgium, the Netherlands, and France, but also Great Britain, Luxembourg, Switzerland, Czechoslovakia, Yugoslavia, Spain, Portugal, Sweden, Norway, and Denmark. Few of them crossed the Atlantic; the number of German Jews entering the United States in 1933 fell short of the annual immigration quota allocated to Germany. The place receiving the largest number of German Jews at this point was the British Mandate in Palestine.

In the second and third stages, departures to European countries declined in favor of overseas destinations. This change was partly due to family ties. In some cases, people who had recently emigrated arranged for close relatives to join them; in others, prospective émigrés revived old family ties with those who had emigrated in the past. At the same time the numbers of refugees who found a haven in Palestine decreased. Owing to economic difficulties and changes in the immigration policy of the British administration, the number of visas issued for Jews to enter Palestine was drastically reduced. Official records do not, however, provide full information on immigration to Palestine, as large numbers of Jews entered illegally. Illegal passage by ship was organized by private entrepreneurs in Europe, by various organizations in Palestine, and even by the Nazis as part of their efforts to encourage the migration of Jews. With the fourth wave

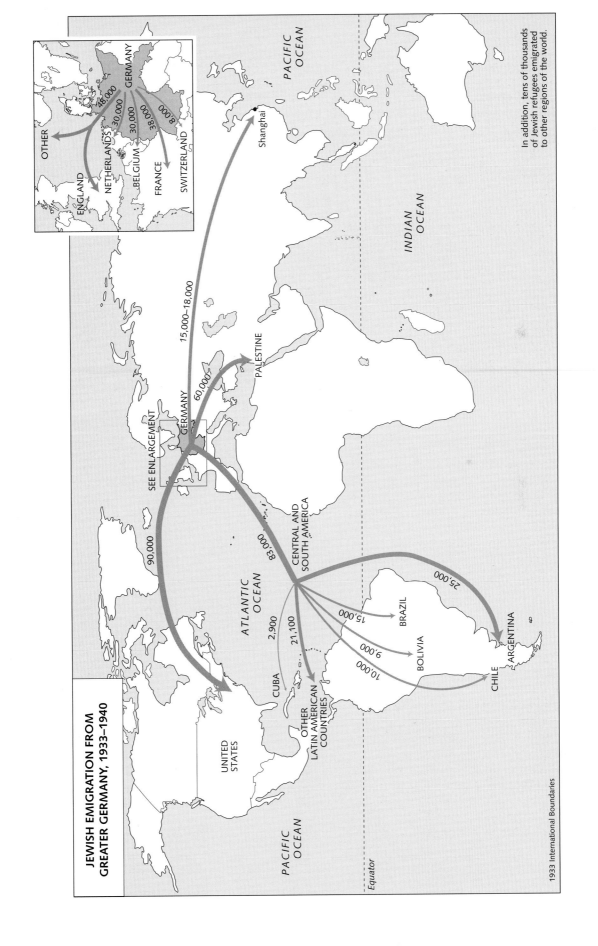

JEWISH EMIGRATION FROM GREATER GERMANY, 1933–1940

In addition, tens of thousands of Jewish refugees emigrated to other regions of the world.

1933 International Boundaries

Enlargement labels:
OTHER — 48,000
ENGLAND — 30,000
NETHERLANDS
BELGIUM — 30,000
FRANCE — 38,000
SWITZERLAND — 8,000
GERMANY

Main map labels:
UNITED STATES
GERMANY
SEE ENLARGEMENT
PALESTINE
Shanghai
CENTRAL AND SOUTH AMERICA
CUBA — 2,900
OTHER LATIN AMERICAN COUNTRIES — 21,100
BRAZIL — 15,000
BOLIVIA — 9,000
CHILE — 10,000
ARGENTINA — 25,000

90,000
60,000
15,000–18,000
83,000

PACIFIC OCEAN
ATLANTIC OCEAN
INDIAN OCEAN
Equator

The German Jewish emigrant Otto Richter with his wife at Ellis Island protesting the U.S. government's decision to deport him along with three other refugees because of invalid entry permits to the United States. Following a public outcry the government granted a temporary stay, permitting the refugees to depart to another county. However, no residency permit was issued for the United States. 12 June 1936

Jewish children cleaning up after a meal at a refugee camp in Dovercourt, England. 28 December 1938

of departure from German-ruled territories, the flow of refugees again turned mostly to Western Europe, and the fifth wave amounted to a frantic run to any and every possible destination.

Of approximately 360,000 Jews who left Greater Germany before the war, some 150,000 remained in continental Europe and Great Britain (50,000 permanently and 100,000 awaiting opportunities to go overseas), 40,000 in France, 30,000 in the Netherlands, 25,000 in Belgium, and 10,000 in Switzerland. Great Britain received about 50,000 Jews from Germany and Austria and another 6,000 from Czechoslovakia.

As to overseas countries, Palestine received the greatest number of Jewish immigrants from Greater Germany—more than 46,000 (36,000 from Germany, 5,500 from Austria, and 4,700 from Czechoslovakia). Toward the end of the 1930s the United States took the

lead, accepting close to 20,000 Jews in 1938 and more than 43,000 in 1939—over half the total number of immigrants to the United States in that year. The international settlement in Shanghai received 17,000 Jews from Greater Germany, 75 percent of them in 1939. Only a few hundred Jews entered Canada annually between 1933 and 1939; a few thousand went to South America and some hundreds to South Africa. Many overseas countries opened their doors only to close relatives of existing residents.

Several Jewish organizations, both in Germany and in other countries, were involved in efforts to ease the fate of the refugees fleeing the Reich. Most of the work was done by the Hilfsverein der Deutschen Juden (Aid Society of German Jews), which helped those desiring to travel overseas or seeking shelter in Great Britain and continental European countries, and the Palestine Office of the Jewish Agency, which was in charge of immigration to Palestine.

Outside Germany HICEM, from its main office in Paris, acted as a central agency for relocating refugees

French Jewish refugee children at Marseilles harbor.

from one country to another. The acronym HICEM derived from the names of the three parent organizations: the Hebrew Sheltering and Immigrant Aid Society (HIAS, New York), the Jewish Colonization Association (ICA, Paris), and Emigdirect (Berlin). Its activities were financed by the American Jewish Joint Distribution Committee (JDC), ICA, and the Central British Fund for German Jewry. The absorption of Jews from Germany into Palestine was made possible in part by special funds raised by Jews the world over and by the Haavara arrangement signed by the Jewish Agency and the German government for the transfer of Jewish property from Germany to Palestine.

Special programs were planned and carried out for rescuing children. By August 1939, 9,354 children had been transported from Germany to Great Britain, 7,482 of them Jewish. Some 1,500 children found refuge in the Netherlands, 1,000 in Belgium, 600 in France, 300 in Switzerland, 250 in Sweden, and 240 in the United States.

The Zionist Organization carried out a special program for sending young Jews, mainly from Nazi-ruled territories, to Palestine. Under this arrangement, called Youth Aliyah, 4,885 boys and girls were transferred during the years 1933–39 to Palestine from Germany, Austria, Czechoslovakia, Poland, Romania, and Hungary.

In October 1933 the League of Nations established a High Commission for Refugees Coming from Germany, headed by James G. McDonald of the United States. Because of German objections the commission was not directly affiliated with the League of Nations and was actually powerless. On 31 December 1935, when the situation had deteriorated after the proclamation of the Nuremberg Laws, McDonald resigned his post in protest of the priority given to diplomatic correctness over common humanity in dealing with German refugees. He asserted that no effective work could be accomplished without the authority of the League of Nations.

As the refugee problem entered a more critical stage with the Anschluss in 1938, U.S. president Franklin D. Roosevelt invited European and South American countries to participate in an international conference on German refugees, assuring the participants that "no country would be expected or asked to receive a greater number of immigrants than is permitted by its existing legislation." The conference, which took place 6–15 June 1938 at the French-Swiss border town

Jewish refugees from Europe, Upper West Side, New York City. 1942

of Evian, established an Intergovernmental Committee on Refugees, which in turn created a Refugee Aid Bureau in London headed by an American director. These bodies did not, however, develop any practical plan for the resettlement of homeless refugees. In February 1939 the bureau merged with the office of the High Commission for Refugees.

Up to the invasion of the Soviet Union in June 1941, the Nazi authorities put no obstacles in the way of Jews leaving the Reich; on the contrary, they were interested in making the Reich *Judenrein,* free of Jews. In his trial in Jerusalem, Adolf Eichmann claimed that the Final Solution had been made possible by the resistance throughout the world to Jewish immigration.

Aviva Halamish

Reichsvertretung der Deutschen Juden The Reichsvertretung der Deutschen Juden (Reich Representative Council of the German Jews) represented the interests of the beleaguered German Jewish minority during the early years of the National Socialist regime. Founded in 1933, the organization underwent a subtle but telling change of name in September 1935, after the declaration of the Nuremberg racial laws, to Reichsvertretung der Juden in Deutschland (Reich Representative Council of the Jews in Germany). Unlike the *Judenräte* (Jewish councils) set up in occupied Eastern Europe during World War II, and the Reichsvereinigung (Reich Union) der Juden in Deutschland, which replaced the Reichsvertretung in

1939, the Reichsvertretung did not owe its existence to a Nazi decree. It came into being through an independent Jewish initiative and of the Jews' own free will. The ambitious goal that the three founders—the president of the Essen Jewish community, Georg S. Hirschland; Hirschland's deputy, Ernst Herzfeld; and Rabbi Hugo Hahn—had set themselves was to draw together, under a single umbrella, all the major constitutive forces of German Jewry.

The magnitude of this historic task can only be appreciated in the light of the deep inner divisiveness of the German Jewish community in the pre-Nazi era. At the time of the Nazi takeover, the German Jewish public scene presented a bewildering spectrum of ideological and political organizations, religious institutions, charity and welfare associations, women's groups, and youth and sports movements. The most comprehensive system of organization was that of the 1,600 local communities (*Gemeinden* or *kehillot*). The Gemeinden were public corporations recognized by law and granted the power to tax their members, who included practically everyone who had not left the Jewish faith. The most important Gemeinde by far was that of Berlin, where some 175,000 Jews, out of an estimated total German Jewish population of 525,000, lived at the beginning of 1933. The Gemeinden in turn were organized in most of the German states in loose federations known as *Landesverbände,* or state associations. The most significant were the Bavarian and the Prussian Landesverbände; the latter had the largest membership and was dominated by the Berlin community. In the past all attempts to forge an effective umbrella organization out of the separate Landesverbände had been frustrated by the insurmountable rivalries among them. One notable attempt resulted in the establishment in early 1932 of the Reichsvertretung der Jüdischen Landesverbände, which was still in existence at the time of Hitler's accession to power. The "old" Reichsvertretung, as it came to be known, failed to function as a truly representative body of the whole of German Jewry and was monopolized by the powerful Berlin community, chaired by the liberal politician Julius Stahl and his Revisionist-Zionist deputy, the controversial Georg Kareski. Berlin's claim to hegemony over public Jewish life in Germany—which was rooted in the overweening ambitions of Stahl and Kareski—was destined to remain an unresolved issue of internal Jewish politics in Nazi Germany right to the very end.

To avoid the looming impasse, the initiators of the new Reichsvertretung had to reach out beyond the Gemeinden to other constituents of German Jewish life. Such were the so-called *Weltanschauungsorganisationen* (worldview organizations), which were based on voluntary membership. The most important were the Centralverein Deutscher Staatsbürger Jüdischen Glaubens (Central Association of German Citizens of the Jewish Faith), which stood for the irrevocable rootedness of the Jews in Germany, and the Zionistische Vereinigung für Deutschland (ZVfD, or German Zionist Federation), the ideological opponent of the Centralverein. Until the rise of the Nazis to power, the ZVfD was in a distinct minority position. A third organization, the Reichsbund Jüdischer Frontsoldaten (National League of Jewish Front-Line Soldiers), represented a special-interest group, Jewish veterans of the world war. The cooperation of the Zionists proved difficult to secure at first. Their leaders argued that the new turn of events in Germany and what they considered to be the historic defeat of the assimilationist thesis, coupled with the emerging importance of Palestine as a destination for Jewish emigrants, entitled them to more than the minority position that was offered to them on the executive board of the Reichsvertretung. The Zionists' strident insistence on parity of representation—the so-called 50-50 principle—remained a bone of contention marring their relationship with the non-Zionist majority in the Reichsvertretung. "We Zionists," ran the Zionist declaration of 5 May 1935, "demand a personal and organizational transformation of the local and central bodies of the Jews in Germany, which will secure us the influence . . . to which we are entitled." The Zionists finally achieved their goal in an organizational reshuffle of the Reichsvertretung in August 1936. On the same occasion, the steering committee of the Reichsvertretung was expanded to include representatives of significant local Gemeinden and Landesverbände hitherto excluded from taking part in its deliberations. The harmonious personality and diplomatic skill of Siegfried Moses, the Zionist representative on the steering committee, mitigated somewhat (until his emigration to Palestine in 1936) the bitterness of the differences arising between Zionists and non-Zionists.

The final agreement on the establishment of the Reichsvertretung was taken by all the parties concerned in a founding conference in Berlin on 17 September 1933. Leo Baeck, the Berlin rabbi and co-president of the old Reichsvertretung, was unanimously chosen to head the new organization as its president. Baeck, who had served on the governing body of practically every important German Jewish organization, was highly regarded by Zionists and non-Zionists alike and had valued connections among non-Jewish Germans. He was an admirable choice as a figurehead, but for the practical, day-to-day running of the affairs one had to turn elsewhere. The choice fell on Otto Hirsch, a prominent member of the Württemberg Jewish community. Hirsch, who had had a distinguished career as a public servant in the Weimar Republic, combined the organizational talent of a German civil servant with a deep-rooted Judaism. He was appointed executive director of the Reichsvertretung—a task he was to fulfill selflessly, working side by side with Baeck, until his deportation and murder at the Mauthausen concentration camp in 1941. The following anecdote gives a sense of the relationship between the two men. As Baeck approached the authorities after the Kristallnacht pogrom in November 1938 to intercede for the release of his deputy, he was badgered by a Gestapo official: "Why? Is Hirsch your right hand?" To which Baeck reportedly replied, "No, but I am Hirsch's left hand."

The Reichsvertretung, the supreme political representation of the Jews of Germany at the time of the Third Reich, was never recognized as such by the Nazi regime. The absence of formal recognition did not, however, prevent the authorities from negotiating with the Reichsvertretung on a strictly ad-hoc basis or from keeping close tabs on its activities. Gestapo officials attended some board meetings and demanded to be kept informed of what took place in others. Not infrequently the leaders of the Reichsvertretung were summoned to the Gestapo and at times arrested for some alleged misconduct. In October 1935 Baeck and Hirsch were taken into custody on account of a special prayer that Baeck had composed for the Kol Nidrei service of Yom Kippur, which fell shortly after the publication of the Nuremberg Laws. The prayer, which was sent by the Reichsvertretung to all synagogues in Germany—contrary to an express prohibition of the Gestapo—defiantly rejected the antisemitic defamation conducted by the Nazi propaganda machine. Both Jewish leaders were released after a short time, and no charges were filed. In another incident the Gestapo attempted in the spring of 1937 to force the appointment of Georg Kareski onto the executive council of the Reichsvertretung. In face of the resolute and unanimous opposition of the Reichsvertretung, led by Baeck, the Gestapo backed off. "You can force me to appoint Kareski as a member of the executive council of the Reichsvertretung," Baeck reportedly told Gestapo officials, "but you cannot force me to continue as its president."

One may well wonder how was it possible for a Jewish organization to undertake to represent Jewish interests to a totalitarian regime committed to the extirpation of Jews and Judaism. The Reichsvertretung's narrow maneuvering room was conditioned by the paradoxical phenomenon of Jewish autonomy within the Third Reich. Unlike the Jews of Eastern and Central Europe, who in the 1940s were engulfed by the Nazi maelstrom of destruction without so much as breathing space, the German Jews had an extended respite, a span of almost six years between Hitler's rise to power and the Kristallnacht pogrom of November 1938, before the Nazis finally suppressed their autonomy. During this grace period the Nazi regime, while persecuting the Jews as individuals and systematically displacing them from German society and economy, refrained from intervening directly in Jewish communal affairs. Jews were allowed both to emigrate and to cultivate an intensive cultural and educational program on German soil. It was within these strait limits of prewar Nazi policy that the Reichsvertretung had to configure its goals and formulate its responses to the antisemitic blows.

As a careful reading of the Reichsvertretung's pronouncements makes plain, the accommodation of the Jewish community to its forced alienation from German civilization was a slow and agonizing process that perhaps was never quite completed. Only gradually did the recognition gain hold that Jews had no future in Nazi Germany and that emigration was the only viable solution. During the first years of the Nazi regime, however, the emphasis was on holding out in Germany, not on emigrating from the country. Emigration, in Hirsch's epigrammatic formulation in an article that appeared in the newspaper *Der Morgen* (February 1934), was to be regarded as only one of the ways out (*einen Ausweg*), not *the* way (*den Weg*). The strategy was essentially that of defending to the utmost the existing Jewish position in Germany, in the hope that somehow the Nazi regime could be brought by reason to moderate its antisemitic policy. The first sentence of the memorandum that the Reichsvertretung

A man in the waiting room of the Reichsvertretung der Deutschen Juden. Berlin, 1936

submitted in January 1934 to Hitler's Chancellery and to all other Reich ministries read: "While the entire German people is called upon by the Reich government to [participate in] the renovation of the fatherland, the German Jews—who are rooted in Germany and in German culture—are subjected to spiritual and material repression." The first and second sections of the memorandum appealed for suspension of the anti-Jewish exclusion laws and the discriminatory economic practices of the German professions, arguing that the pauperization of the German Jews was against the best interests of Germany itself. In the third section the German government was called upon to assist in the vocational retraining program of those German Jews who would nevertheless be forced to emigrate. In the concluding section racial vilification was denounced, not only as an insult to the German Jewish

community, but also as a foreign policy threat to the German Reich itself, inasmuch as antisemitic slander would affect its standing abroad.

Less than two years later, in the Reichsvertretung's published response to the Nuremberg Laws of 15 September 1935, one can already discern a marked shift from the earlier insistence on the rootedness of the Jews in Germany to a new perception of the uniqueness of Jewish identity and the importance of the Jewish homeland in Palestine. In the preamble to the declaration, the official Nazi interpretation of the Nuremberg Laws as providing a basis for a "tolerable relationship" between the German and the Jewish peoples was declared to be irreconcilable with the ongoing campaign of antisemitic vilification. But the Jewish leaders were not really deceived by the Nazi propaganda to believe in a new future for the Jews in Germany. The programmatic part of the Reichsvertretung's statement addressed emigration, "particularly to Palestine," as the central and most urgent issue on the ideological, organizational, and educational agenda of German Jewry. To signal the shift to the Zionist point of view, the Reichsvertretung decided formally to join the Palestine Foundation Fund (Keren Hayesod), "warmly" advising all Jewish communities and organizations in Germany to follow suit.

On the practical, nonpolitical level, the Reichsvertretung, with a minimal operational staff (fewer than 100 workers), was dependent on the services of its executive arm: the Zentralausschuss der Deutschen Juden für Hilfe und Aufbau (Central Committee of the German Jews for Help and Reconstruction). Set up in April 1933 by Zionist and non-Zionist experts in the field of social welfare, the Zentralausschuss was the first German Jewish body to establish contacts with the great philanthropic organizations of Western Jewry—the Central British Fund (later Council for German Jewry) and the American Joint Distribution Committee—providing a channel for the considerable stream of money funneled from abroad. Quartered in the same building as the Reichsvertretung—158 Kant Street, Berlin—the Zentralausschuss launched and supervised a variety of rehabilitation, vocational retraining, and Jewish education programs. In addition, it coordinated the services of the three principal emigration agencies, which functioned as its affiliates: the Palästina-Amt (Palestine Office), which was responsible for emigration to Palestine; the Hilfsverein (Aid Association), which facilitated emigration overseas, and the Hauptstelle für Jüdische Wanderfürsorge (Main Department for Jewish Migration Welfare), which chiefly repatriated Jews to Eastern Europe. All in all, about half of the 150,000 Jews who were able to leave before the Kristallnacht pogrom were assisted by one of these agencies.

The German Jewish leadership has been criticized by some—mainly ex-Zionist activists—for its policy of maintaining, even intensifying, Jewish communal life under the gauntlet of the swastika. Georg Lubinski-Lotan, the Zionist welfare expert and one of the co-founders of the Zentralausschuss, has severely castigated the architects of this policy (himself included): "We still believed at that time that in Hitlerite Germany it would be possible to work for a renaissance of Jewish culture and to achieve orderly organization of Jewish life. A joint historic guilt here lies upon the shoulders of all those who were responsible for this form of our communal life in Germany." This self-reproach notwithstanding, the historical evaluation of the Reichsvertretung and its role in the prewar years has by and large been decidedly positive. Few would quarrel with Herbert A. Strauss's conclusion that, given the circumstances of the first five years of Hitler's rule, the totalitarian nature of the Nazi regime, and Jewish powerlessness, the Reichsvertretung's policies and programs "must be considered proper and adequate responses to Nazi policies." Strauss also points out that a whole segment of the Reichsvertretung's activity—its contacts with Nazi officials and confidential interventions on behalf of Jewish detainees—is not reflected in the extant archival material, probably having never been documented, and is thus difficult to evaluate.

In the course of the last few months of 1938 and the first half of 1939, the voluntary, loosely federative Reichsvertretung was transformed into the centralized and Nazi-sponsored Reichsvereinigung der Juden in Deutschland. The study of the central organization of German Jewry during the final phase of its history has been significantly advanced by the discovery—first published and utilized by Otto Dov Kulka—of the original archives of the Reichsvereinigung in the cellar of the destroyed synagogue building in Oranienburger Street in East Berlin. In their research based on this material, Kulka and Esriel Hildesheimer have strongly challenged the prevalent notion of a sharp break in the history of the Reichsvertretung, arguing for a revision of the still widely held view of the Reichsvereinigung—most forcefully propounded by Raul Hilberg—as an obsequious, compliant tool of the Nazi exterminators. It would appear, however, that the thesis of the seamless continuity between the two central Jewish organizations is oversimplified and has been greatly (and needlessly) overstated. It is not so much that the nature or the policy of the Jewish leadership as such suddenly changed after 1938 as that the different historical situation in which it operated created a new institutional dependence on the Nazi overlords.

There can be no doubt that the move toward a centralist, all-encompassing Jewish organization was not initiated by the Nazis but originated in the Jews themselves. Not only did the deliberations within the Jewish camp precede by many months the official legislative act formally constituting the Reichsvereinigung, but a Jewish-constituted body of the same name was clearly already in existence by the beginning of February 1939, four months before its formal promulgation in the so-called Tenth Regulation to the Reich Citizenship Law of 4 July 1939. The decisive argument from the Jewish point of view for restructuring the relationship between the central Jewish organization and the individual communities was the law of 28 March 1938, which rescinded the status of the Jewish Gemeinden as public bodies recognized by law. This undermined the authority of the local Jewish communities over individual members, turning the communities de facto into voluntary private associations devoid of legal powers or the right to levy taxes. To offset the legal vacuum thus created, the Reichsvertretung, in consultation with representatives of the local Gemeinden, had already resolved on 27 July 1938 to reconstitute itself as a unitary, centralist Reichsverband der Juden in Deutschland legally empowered to represent all Jews in Germany, whether or not they were registered members of the Gemeinden. The Jewish proposals failed, however, to win the approval of the authorities. Only in the wake of the Kristallnacht pogrom and the temporary closure of all Jewish institutions did the Jewish initiative coalesce with—or rather it was taken over by—a parallel Nazi initiative resulting in the formation of the Reichsvereinigung der Juden in Deutschland.

The Nazi authorities for their part were interested in the new organization primarily as a tool for the liquidation of the Jewish community, at that time by facilitating mass emigration from Germany. This was clearly reflected in the second paragraph of Article I of the Tenth Regulation, which stated: "The purpose of the Reichsvereinigung is to further the emigration of the Jews." Two other areas of responsibility that were outlined for the Reichsvereinigung—though in second place after emigration—were the maintenance of Jewish schools and of the Jewish welfare system.

The new, Nazi-sponsored organization differed from its predecessor, the Reichsvertretung, in three important respects. First, it was centralist in structure, incorporating all other Jewish institutions and the local Jewish communities as its branches. Second, it was a compulsory body, embracing all Jews according to the racial criteria of the Nuremberg Laws. Third, and most ominously for the future, it was subordinated to the Reich minister of the interior. As the German police force under Reinhard Heydrich, including the Gestapo, was formally part of the Interior Ministry, this meant in effect direct subordination to the Jewish department of the Gestapo under Adolf Eichmann. Already in early 1939 the Zentralstelle für Jüdische Auswanderung (Central Authority for Jewish Emigration), modeled on the similar institution set up by Eichmann in Vienna, was established on the top floor of the building of the Berlin Jewish Community in Oranienburger Street. In this way the Reichsvereinigung was structurally integrated into the Nazi bureaucracy of destruction. Despite these differences there was a large measure of organizational and personal continuity between the Reichsvertretung and the Reichsvereinigung. The members of the new government board were practically the same, with one important distinction: they all had to be formally approved by the Reich minister of the interior. One member who was to gain new prominence after 1939 was the liaison with the Gestapo, Paul Eppstein. It remained to be seen whether, and how far, these authentic Jewish leaders, none of whom was imposed by the Gestapo, would agree to toe the Nazi line.

In weighing up the evidence, one has to bear in mind that until the official ban on Jewish emigration in October 1941—and to a certain extent even later—the liquidation of the Jewish presence in Germany was effected in two principal ways: first, by the disbandment of existing Jewish associations and community organizations and their absorption, together with their assets, by the Reichsvereinigung; and second, by the promotion of large-scale Jewish emigration. The Reichsvereinigung proved fully accommodating in carrying out both these tasks, especially the latter. It helped finance the emigration of the poorer members of the community by imposing a special tax on the wealthier emigrants, and after the outbreak of the war it assisted in organizing illegal emigration to Palestine. At the same time the Reichsvereinigung continued to maintain a system of Jewish education and devoted an increasing share of its dwindling resources to catering to the welfare needs of those unable to emigrate. Two women social workers who distinguished themselves by their communal service at that time were Cora Berliner and Hannah Karminski. Both were deported by the Nazis to the death camps in the East.

The new evidence published by Kulka and Hildesheimer shows that the Reichsvereinigung put up stiff opposition to the first mass deportations from Stettin and Schneidemühl to Poland (February 1940) and from Baden and the Palatinate to France (October 1940). In the latter case the Jewish leadership reacted by declaring a fast day, discontinuing the activity of the Kulturbund (the Jewish cultural association), and threatening to tender its collective resignation. At least one prominent member of the governing board, Julius Seligsohn, paid with his life for this daring defiance of the Nazis. The final agonizing hour for German Jewry struck in the autumn of 1941 with the beginning of the deportations to the ghettos and death camps in the East. In Germany there were no ghettos as in Eastern Europe, but the Jews were concentrated in special Jewish apartments (*Judenhäuser*). The tragic dilemmas with which the German Jewish leadership was confronted were not unlike those faced by the Judenräte in Eastern Europe. Although there is no evidence that the central leadership in Berlin ever received direct orders from the Gestapo concerning the carrying out of deportations, there is no doubt that the Gemeinden, which functioned as local branches of the Reichsvereinigung, were deeply involved in preparations for the deportations. Yet it remains a moot question how far the Nazi authorities, who were extremely well informed on the numbers and whereabouts of the Jewish population in Germany, were dependent on the lists drawn up by the Jewish bureaucrats. With the deportation of Baeck and Eppstein to Theresienstadt in the early months of 1943, the central organization of German Jewry effectively ceased to function. The Nazis apparently never bothered to dissolve it officially, and it continued a spectral existence as the so-called Rest-Reichsvereinigung (Remnant Reichsvereinigung), which was located in the Jewish Hospital in Iranische Street in Berlin.

Two facts stand out clearly in the retrospective appraisal of the last tragic years of German Jewry. First, some 150,000 Jews were able to leave Germany between the pogrom of November 1938 and Heydrich's ban on emigration in October 1941. Their rescue was facilitated by the efforts of the Reichsvereinigung. Second, most of the German Jewish leaders (the Zionists had already left by 1939) could have saved themselves by emigrating abroad in time: they chose instead to remain at their posts. All but a few paid for their loyalty with their lives.

Daniel Fraenkel

Reik, Haviva (1914–44) Commando in the Jewish parachutists unit of the British army. Born in Slovakia, Reik emigrated in 1939 to Palestine, where she joined Kibbutz Ma'anit. She parachuted into Slovakia in September 1944 on a mission to contact the Jewish underground in Bratislava but was captured after several weeks and killed by the Germans in late November. See PARACHUTISTS' MISSION

Reinhard, Aktion German code name (adopted in commemoration of Reinhard Heydrich after his assassination in May 1942) for the systematic mass killing of Polish Jews that began in March 1942 and concluded in November 1943. The operation was created by Heinrich Himmler and run mainly by Odilo Globocnik. The extermination camps Belzec, Sobibor, and Treblinka were established under Aktion Reinhard, which led to the murder by gassing of 1.7 million Jews. See EXTERMINATION CAMPS

Reparations, German A central issue in the aftermath of the collapse of the Nazi regime in 1945 was how Germany would make amends to Holocaust survivors for their pain and suffering, the murder of their families, and the confiscation or destruction of their property and other assets. In the immediate postwar years individual and communal assets were restituted to survivors or heirs and to a Jewish charitable organization in cases where even heirs had not survived. By the early 1950s West Germany undertook to pay global reparations to these same organizations and to the state of Israel, to cover the costs of resettling 500,000 Jewish refugees from the Nazis, and agreed to pay indemnification to the survivors for the pain and suffering they had been exposed to, for their years of slave labor, and for their loss of health.

Almost immediately after Adolf Hitler rose to power in Germany, the Nazis took steps to isolate and expel the Jews from German economic life. As they gained experience in using the means of government, these measures were expanded from boycott, fines, special taxes, and disadvantageous exchange rates (for those emigrating) to outright expropriation and enforced liquidation of Jewish assets. Although originally intended as a way of excluding the Jews from German society, the spoliation of their assets became a profitable and significant factor in the development of the Nazi policy. Stripping citizens of their cash, their property, and their valuables provided many opportunities for corrupt officials and was so popular among the general public that it helped fuel antisemitism in Germany and elsewhere. As more and more Jewish communities in Europe fell under German control, the wealth available to the Reich through expropriation of public and private assets became almost unimaginable. And as German antisemitic policy became increasingly radical and murderous, all restraint in lucrative asset-stripping operations was thrown off.

Immediately on the outbreak of war in September 1939, Jewish organizations requested that the recovery of assets be made one of the war aims of the Allies. Although no reference was made to the loss of Jewish property, in January 1943 the United States, Great Britain, and the Soviet Union, together with 15 allied nations, issued the Inter-Allied Declaration against Acts of Dispossession Committed in Territory under Enemy Occupation or Control. The declaration marked the beginning of serious planning at the governmental level for the restitution of despoiled possessions. As the war drew to a close, property issues figured in the agendas of the Jewish Agency, the World Jewish Congress, and the American Jewish Committee. Each of these organizations looked to restored Jewish communal assets and the heirless Jewish estates (the property of those families that had been murdered) as the major source for financing the rehabilitation of the survivors of the Holocaust.

In April 1945 Gen. Dwight Eisenhower, commander in chief of the U.S. occupation forces in Germany, was instructed to ensure the "prompt" restitution of "property which has been the subject of transfer under duress or wrongful acts of confiscation, disposition or spoliation." These instructions were the first step in a long process of returning stolen physical assets to their owners or their successors. Much of the property, however, was heirless or belonged to communities that had been largely or entirely destroyed. German Jewry had been reduced from a population of 525,000 in 1933 to 15,000 resident German Jews in 1945, and there were no precedents for returning the schools, synagogues, community centers, hospitals, orphanages, rest homes, and cemeteries of communities that had perished.

In November 1947 the U.S. military government in Germany enacted Military Law No. 59 for the Restitution of Identifiable Property, which invited potential heirs to submit claims. Six months later all unclaimed Jewish property was assumed to be heirless, and an umbrella agency, the Jewish Restitution Successor Organization (JRSO), was empowered to assert rights to the property on the behalf of world Jewry. The JRSO began operations in the American zone of occupation in August 1948, and by 31 December 1948 (the official deadline) 163,000 claims had been submitted. In the years that followed, these claims were defended before German courts (with American military courts serving as courts of appeal). Similar legislation was promulgated in the British and French zones in 1949 and 1952, respectively. The Jewish Trust Corporation was appointed as the successor organization in these zones. The burden of defending so many cases in court encouraged the amicable settlement of many claims. The entire process, however, created widespread resentment among Germans, many of whom had no wish to pay proper compensation for ill-gotten Jewish real estate, and in a number of instances the JRSO preferred to accept an omnibus cash settlement from the governments of the German states (*Länder*) in lieu of actual repossession of property.

The restitution of assets did not touch on the broader question of reparations. In December 1945 the Allied claims against conquered Germany were discussed at the Inter-Allied Paris Conference on Reparations. Although the Jews were not considered an "allied nation," it was recognized that the stateless victims of Nazi persecution (largely Jews) also had grounds for a claim against Germany. Article 8 of the Final Act of the conference awarded all nonmonetary gold (gold not plundered from a reserve bank) found in Germany and a further $25 million derived from German assets in Switzerland, Sweden, Portugal, and Spain (estimated to be 6 percent of the total) to the victims of Nazi persecution. These funds were paid to the Inter-Governmental Committee for Refugees, with the Jewish

Agency and the American Jewish Joint Distribution Committee acting as agents. This first cautious payment of reparations was used to help the 200,000 Jewish displaced persons in camps in Germany and Austria from 1945 to 1948.

None of the initial restitution or compensation programs was on a scale commensurate with the full extent of the Jewish claims against Germany and its allies. Original estimates of Jewish losses, made in 1944–45, ranged between $8 billion and $14 billion, and these were for material losses of spoliated assets. They made no provisions for the indemnification of Jewish suffering at the hands of the Nazis.

This fact became increasingly clear to both the government of Israel and the various organizations that represented Jewish interests in international forums. The Jewish Agency (closely linked with the Israeli government), the World Jewish Congress, the American Jewish Committee, and the American Jewish Conference collaborated with unprecedented harmony in the formulation of a general Jewish claim for reparations and indemnification from Germany. In January 1951 Israel approached the Allied governments with the claim. The urgency to act came from the fear that as the Allied military occupation of Germany ended and sovereignty was increasingly vested in the new Federal Republic of Germany, the Jewish world would be forced to deal directly with Germans—something that Israel and the Jewish organizations wished to avoid so soon after the Holocaust. But the Western Allies insisted that Israel negotiate directly with the Federal Republic, and Jewish leaders in the United States and Great Britain received similar directions from their respective governments.

For various reasons the German chancellor, Konrad Adenauer, was interested in a resolution of the reparations claims. During the course of 1951 cautious contacts were established, and these allowed Israel and the Jewish organizations to test the sincerity of Germany's intentions. There was considerable anxiety that the Germans would assert that a settlement for material claims exonerated them from the burden of moral responsibility for the Holocaust, or that they would not negotiate in good faith. The initial indications, however, were positive. In September 1951 Adenauer delivered to the Bundestag (the West German parliament) a statement that had been approved in advance by the Jewish organizations, all German political parties, and the West German president (Theodor Heuss), inviting the government of Israel and a representative body of Jewish organizations in the Diaspora to negotiate the material claims against Germany. The chancellor also acknowledged in the statement that "unspeakable crimes have been committed in the name of the German people." This was the first official admission of German responsibility for the terrible crimes of the Nazi regime.

One month after Adenauer's statement 23 Diaspora Jewish organizations met in New York to consider the creation of a representative body to conduct negotiations with Germany. After four days of intense debate it was resolved that world Jewry was willing to negotiate the settlement of its material claims. The Conference for Jewish Material Claims against Germany was formed to conduct the necessary talks to ensure a reparations payment. A similar debate followed in Israel, where public discussion was accompanied by violent demonstrations against the Israeli government for its willingness to negotiate. The government won a narrow victory when the matter was voted on in the Knesset (the Israeli parliament) in January 1952.

When the negotiations opened in Wassenaar, the Netherlands, in March 1952, Israel and the Claims Conference (on behalf of the Jewish organizations) presented separate global claims for reparations. The Claims Conference also presented a claim for indemnification payments to individual victims of Nazi persecution. Israel's original claim of $1.5 billion was based on the cost of rehabilitating the 500,000 victims of nazism who had settled in Mandatory Palestine and Israel since 1933. The amount of the global claim of the Jewish organizations was $500 million, an estimate of the cost to Diaspora communities for the resettlement of Jewish refugees outside Israel. The talks between the various delegations were conducted in parallel, although the Claims Conference gave precedence to the Israeli claim. After one major breakdown, and following the direct intervention of Chancellor Adenauer (on the German side) and Nahum Goldman (representing the Jewish side), the talks were successfully concluded in August. A reparations agreement between Israel, the Claims Conference, and the Federal Republic of Germany was signed in Luxembourg on 10 September 1952. Goldman played a central role in creating the Claims Conference, in facilitating the pre-negotiation contracts with Germany, and in the successful administration of the reparations process throughout the life of the Luxembourg Agreement.

In the agreement the Federal Republic consented to manufacture and deliver to Israel goods valued at 3 billion Deutschmarks (DM), roughly $720 million—West Germany's share of a reduced Israeli claim—over a 12-year period from 1954 to 1966. The agreement was scrupulously honored, and German-made ships, trains, and industrial equipment contributed to the growth of Israel in the state's formative years. In two separate protocols with the Claims Conference, the Federal Republic undertook to introduce a Federal Indemnification Law for compensating victims of Nazi persecution. The law was passed in 1953, and improvements were introduced in 1956 and 1965. In addition, under the second protocol the Federal Republic agreed to pay DM 450 million for the reconstruction of Jewish communal and cultural life in Europe. This sum was remitted to the Claims Conference by means of the transfer of goods to Israel.

The global settlement with the Claims Conference and with Israel was the smallest part of the ongoing reparations process. Property and other assets worth an estimated DM 3.5 billion have been recovered from Germany. Indemnification payments to individuals, however, have dwarfed both the global payments to Israel and the Claims Conference and the restitution program. Additional payments were made to slave laborers and, before 1989 (i.e., the fall of the Communist regimes), for the benefit of Jews in the Communist countries. In all, it is estimated that through the restitution, reparations, and indemnification programs Germany has returned more than DM 110 billion to the Jewish world since the end of World War II.

Recently, continuing international public interest in the Holocaust has encouraged Swiss banks and various European insurance companies to address previously unresolved or overlooked problems relating to victims' assets. Restitution and indemnification programs deriving from these assets are currently under discussion. Limited settlements that were reached in the 1970s for slave labor claims have been reopened. Encouraged by the German government, many more German industries have offered to pay compensation for Jewish slave labor and non-Jewish forced labor imposed on the populations of occupied Europe during the war years. Settlements derived from the Swiss banking, insurance, and slave labor claims will be allocated to Jewish and non-Jewish survivors and to general humanitarian causes. See also RESTITUTION

Ronald Zweig

Rescue Zionist rescue refers to efforts made by the Executive of the Jewish Agency and the formal institutions of the Yishuv (the Jewish community of Palestine) to save the Jews of Europe from mass murder at the hands of Nazi Germany.

David Ben-Gurion, head of the political department of the Jewish Agency (a branch of the World Zionist Organization charged with facilitating immigration to Palestine) since 1933 and the agency's chairman since 1935, became aware of the Nazi threat to European Jewry in 1933. In Memel (Klaipeda, Lithuania) on 26 April of that year he expressed the fear that Hitler's Germany might bring about a world war and, under cover of the conflict, butcher the Jewish people. On 29 August he bought *Mein Kampf,* and his somber premonition turned into bleak certainty. On 13 January 1934, at a conference of the labor organization Histadrut, he predicted: "Hitler's rule places in danger the entire Jewish people. Hitlerism is at war not only with the Jews of Germany but with Jews the world over. Hitler's rule cannot last for long without war, without a war of vengeance against France, Poland, Czechoslovakia and other neighboring countries . . . or against vast Soviet Russia. . . . Perhaps only four or five years (if not less) stand between us and that day of wrath." Ben-Gurion had therefore realized that Hitler intended to annihilate the Jewish people and even foresaw how he would achieve his aim by starting a general war in Europe and then conquering Poland and vast areas of the Soviet Union—the two countries that contained the largest number of Jews in the world. Ben-Gurion repeated these warnings year after year, until the war broke out.

The plans based on his foresight varied with the changing circumstances, but the goal remained one and the same: to minimize the inevitable catastrophe by increasing immigration to Palestine—the only country then open to Jews—while there was still time. An early plan proposed doubling the Yishuv population between 1933 and 1938. Exploiting British prime minister Ramsay MacDonald's 1932 repeal of the 1930 white paper, the Jewish Agency helped nearly 450,000 Jews immigrate from Eastern and Central Europe to Palestine. No other rescue operation achieved such success.

Another proposal, put forward in Geneva in September 1934 to aides of the mufti of Jerusalem, was to create a "federal Palestine." It involved establishing an Arab federation, of which a Jewish Palestine would be a member state, on the condition that it could admit 6–8 million Jews without Arab objection. A third idea, developed in consequence of the Nuremberg racial laws of 1935, envisaged the transfer of 1 million Jews and their settlement in Palestine. A fourth plan, based on the Palestine Partition Scheme of 1937, saw the small Jewish state as a haven to millions of Jews escaping Hitler. Instead, the British government withdrew the partition scheme and slammed shut the gates of Palestine. In reaction to the British action and to the Munich Pact of 1938, Ben-Gurion proposed an "immigration revolt." According to this plan, masses of illegal immigrants would flee Europe by sea and fight for their right to land in Palestine; Haifa and its environs would be conquered and declared a Jewish state, and the port would open to mass immigration. In all these proposals the Jewish Agency demonstrated that in order to save the Jews while there was still time, it was ready to put aside sacred Zionist principles—by accepting less than complete Jewish sovereignty (in the federation plan put to the mufti) and by accepting a division of the Land of Israel (in the partition scheme).

However, none of these plans came to fruition. They were defeated by the Arab Revolt of 1936–39 and by the British response to it in the form of the white paper of May 1939, which allowed only 75,000 Jews to enter Palestine between 1939 and 1944. Instead of the Jewish state it proposed in 1937, the British government offered the millions of Jews bound for the extermination camps in 1942–44 a total of 29,000 certificates (entry permits). Ben-Gurion, musing on this show of inhumanity, suggested at the 1944 Mapai party conference that had there been a Jewish state in 1937, millions of European Jews would have been saved. His recognition that very little could be done to rescue the Jews once the war in Europe had started was completely borne out.

The war brought a significant change in the Zionist concept of rescue. Originally the Zionists held that the ingathering of exiles in Palestine was the only permanent solution to the Jews' precarious situation in Europe. All other solutions, such as settling Jews in other countries, were regarded as stopgap measure that would only displace the problem temporarily and would prompt further attacks on the Jews' existence. Immigration to Palestine was therefore the only true means of rescue. This was also the official position of the Zionist Congress. The congress instructed

the Jewish Agency to distinguish between Jews applying for "redemption"—settlement in Palestine—and Jews who wanted to go there only briefly for "rescue" and then move on to settle elsewhere. By its mandate the Jewish Agency was responsible for immigrants, whereas the welfare, shelter, and support of refugees was the task of philanthropic organizations (such as the Hebrew Immigrant Aid Society and the American Jewish Joint Distribution Committee) and individual Jewish communities the world over. These two categories of assistance were referred to respectively as the "Zionist agenda" and the "Jewish agenda" (or "individual agenda"). The terms expressed the difference between the concern for a radical, collective change in the status of the nation that only independence in Palestine could guarantee and the concern for the physical safety and civic equality of individual Jews or local Jewish communities in all countries.

Yet already before the war, events made it plain that the refugees had nowhere else to go except Palestine. The Jewish Agency came to recognize that the distinction between immigrants and refugees was no longer valid. It therefore would have wholeheartedly supported refugees' search for safe haven in any country, but none was available. As early as April 1936 Ben-Gurion, describing the worsening plight of Poland's Jews, had told the high commissioner for Palestine, Sir Arthur Wauchope: "Had there been the possibility of bringing Poland's Jews to the United States or Argentina, we would have done so regardless of our Zionist beliefs. But the world was closed to us. And had there not been room for us in Palestine, our people would have had only one way out: to commit suicide."

Proof that no country was ready to open wide its doors to the Jews was provided in July 1938 when the Evian Conference, which was convened to find countries willing to receive a large influx of immigrants, came up with not a single one. As Jewish refugees had no place of immigration but Palestine, the Zionist agenda and the Jewish agenda had become one.

Four months later the Kristallnacht pogroms reawakened world opinion to the plight of the Jews in Greater Germany. The British moved to grant 10,000 Austrian and German Jewish children, whose parents had been killed or expelled, temporary asylum in Great Britain—but not to let them enter Palestine. At

A boy says a prayer of thanks on board a train taking a group of Youth Aliyah to Italy and from there to Palestine. 1934

a meeting of the Histadrut central committee, Ben-Gurion reacted to the British offer, saying: "Were I to know that all German Jewish children could be rescued by transferring them to England and only half by transfer to Palestine, I would opt for the latter, because our concern is not only the personal interest of these children, but the historic interest of the Jewish people." In later years Ben-Gurion's foes willfully ignored the fact that he made this comment nine months before the war broke out and hence before rescue had become the only alternative to death. Rescue in 1938 still meant rescue from deprivation, humiliation, and despair. Moreover, as the stenographic record demonstrates, all committee members understood the remark in the spirit in which it was intended. Yitzhak Ben-Zvi, a future president of Israel, put the comment in context: "Ten thousand children are a small part of Germany's [Jewish] children. . . . They [the British] don't intend to save Germany's Jews, and certainly not all of them. The moment the Jewish State Plan [the Peel plan] was shelved, the possibility of complete rescue of Germany's Jews was shelved with it." The British pretext for refusing to allow the children into Palestine was that the Arabs would boycott the talks on Palestine's future, which were due to open in January 1939 at St. James's Palace in London. Ben-Gurion argued that this was not the only reason for the refusal. Chaim Weizmann, president of the World Zionist Organization, also regarded it as the harbinger of a change in British policy, a first step toward introducing restrictions on Jewish immigration to Palestine; he warned Malcolm MacDonald, the colonial secretary, against this "tendency," which was to find its full expression in the May 1939 white paper.

After extensive deliberations many of the 10,000 children were admitted into Britain between December 1938 and September 1939. But with the outbreak of the war the British government imposed an absolute ban on immigration from Germany and its occupied territories into all parts of the British Empire. The ban was not lifted until the war ended, so that only 10,000 more Jews were fortunate enough to find shelter in Britain throughout the war years.

The change in the Jewish Agency's strategy did not go unnoticed or uncriticized. In November 1941 the head of the British Zionists argued that the "fundamental object of Zionism" was "nation-building," not rescue. This was in answer to Ben-Gurion's statement that rescue was "the supremely important thing" and that under the present circumstances nation-building was "incidental." In December 1942 Ben-Gurion termed the rescue of all Jews, regardless of their orientation toward settlement in Palestine, the "new Zionism." In 1943 he elaborated: "Is Zionism the solution to the refugee problem, referred to in political jargon as 'rescue,' or is it the solution of a historic problem, called 'redemption'? . . . Can anyone really imagine that there is any justification for the Zionist movement . . . if this movement does not look after the burning needs of millions of Jews?" In his thinking, and in that of the Jewish Agency, "the Zionist agenda" and "the Jewish agenda" had become one: rescue of all Jews, by all means and wherever possible.

Such rescue, however, could be attempted only after Palestine itself was no longer in danger of Nazi occupation. In 1941 and 1942 the Yishuv was being threatened by Vichy French and German armies in Syria and the western desert. Toward the end of June 1942 Rommel's army reached the Egyptian border, and the threat that the entire Middle East would fall into German hands was very real. Only after Rommel's defeat at El Alamein in November could preparations to rescue the Jewish people in Europe become the concern and focus of all the Jewish Agency's and the Yishuv's rescue efforts. It was therefore only after the threat to the Yishuv's existence had faded that Ben-Gurion demanded a study of "any proposal that offers even the slightest hope" for rescue in Europe.

Rommel's defeat coincided with the Yishuv's move to organize for mass rescue in Europe during November 1942. Up until then British censorship had played a large part in maintaining public ignorance of Nazi slaughter of Jews in Eastern Europe. Ilya Ehrenburg's report of 8 February 1942 on the atrocities perpetrated by the Nazis against the Jews in the Soviet Union, which was covered prominently in the Soviet press, was completely censored. On 29 July news about pogroms against Jews in Bukovina and Bessarabia met the same fate. Therefore the first reports that gassing was among the methods used by the Nazis to murder Jews en masse were met with skepticism and disbelief.

Information passed through several hands before reaching the Jewish Agency. Jewish sources in Poland sent reports out of the country through the Polish underground to Jewish leaders in London, New York, and Geneva, but they did not always reach Jerusalem. In July 1942 doubt was thrown on Eduard Schulte's intimation that Hitler was conducting a planned, sys-

tematic genocide of the Jews of Europe, although it was the source of Gerhart Riegner's telegram to Rabbi Stephen Wise in New York and Richard Lichtheim's telegram to the Jewish Agency, which reached Jerusalem in August.

A change of attitude was brought about by a group of 69 Palestinian Jews who had been trapped in Europe and were exchanged for German residents of Palestine. They arrived in Palestine on 18–19 November 1942, providing the first eyewitness reports of the atrocities to reach the Yishuv. Of the gas chambers and crematoriums they had heard only rumors, yet the impact of their accounts of the ghettos and the mass murders was a tremendous.

On 30 November 1942 an emergency session of the National Assembly called for a day of fasting, a general strike, and 30 days of mourning, meant not only as an expression of the Yishuv's reaction to the news of the destruction of European Jewry but as a tactic to gain rescue operations. Ben-Gurion's keynote speech was an appeal to the conscience of the free world. He asked for work to prevent the destruction so that "when the victory of democracy, liberty, and justice" arrived, Europe would not be "one large Jewish cemetery." Directly addressing the leaders of the three Allied Powers—Winston Churchill, Franklin Roosevelt, and Josef Stalin—he asked them "to stand in the breach, with everything you have, and not permit the destruction" of the Jewish people. He entreated them to exchange German nationals in their own countries for Jews held in Europe. He urged the U.S. government to issue a warning to the governments of Hungary, Romania, and Bulgaria that whoever assisted Germany in the destruction of Jews would be judged a war criminal and held accountable. The responsibility for the destruction, he added, "should be also on the heads of all those who are able to rescue but do not do so, all those who are able to prevent the destruction and will not, and all those who are able to save and will not do so." Ben-Gurion called on all countries to rescue Jews, while at the same time he entreated the British government to open Palestine: "As long as the gates of our country are shut to Jewish refugees—your hands too are red with the Jewish blood that is shed in the Nazi hell."

The plea had no effect. Ben-Gurion's speech was severely censored by the Mandatory government in Palestine, and the press in Great Britain, the United States, and other countries did not print it. Thus the chances for the Jewish Agency and the Yishuv to arouse world public opinion were reduced almost to nil.

Early in November 1942 Stanislaw Kot, the representative of the Polish government-in-exile's minister to the Middle East, came to Palestine. In meetings with leaders of the Jewish Agency and the Yishuv, Kot provided much more complete and up-to-date information, from sources in occupied Poland, on Nazi atrocities against Jews than the Jews of Palestine had previously had. He directly told the leaders, including Ben-Gurion, that the "biological destruction of the Jews is taking place in Poland."

The Jewish Agency submitted four requests to Kot: "(1) That the government and national council of Poland should proclaim that all who take part in the persecution and murder of Polish Jews will be held responsible for their acts. (2) That the Polish government should try to exert influence on the Allies to take all necessary measures against the Germans; and that the Polish government should bring pressure to bear on the neutral countries to admit all those Jews who are able to escape German occupation and on the Germans to let them go. And perhaps the Polish government could do something through urging the Vatican to intervene. (3) That in its broadcasts to Poland the Polish government should instruct the Polish people not to be influenced by the anti-Jewish provocations and to resist the barbarous acts of the Germans. Reports arriving in Palestine from Poland make it clear that such educational work is needed. (4) That the Polish government should persuade the Polish clergy that it must raise its voice in protest against what is going on exactly as was done by the clergy in France."

On 3 December 1942 Ben-Gurion received Kot in Jerusalem. He asked the diplomat whether the Polish government-in-exile could infiltrate into Poland a number of "secret agents" and "commandos" of the Jewish Agency and enable them to transmit to Jerusalem accurate information about the situation of the Jews and to help in their rescue. (The sending of commandos to Poland had been discussed at a Jewish Agency meeting in November.) Kot emphasized that these agents would have no chance of returning. Nevertheless he promised that he would communicate the message and did in fact put the request for "secret agents" on his government's agenda. The Polish government-in-exile discussed it several times before rejecting it in June 1943.

Following Kot's report of the annihilation of Po-

land's Jews, Ben-Gurion cabled U.S. Supreme Court justice Felix Frankfurter on 8 December 1942 in an attempt to arouse American Jewish public opinion and so spur the Allied governments to undertake rescue actions. Jewish Agency officials in New York and London, as well as Moshe Sharett—co-director with Ben-Gurion of the agency's political department—assisted in this plan. In Britain, Jewish Agency representatives were instructed "to demand that PGE [the Polish government-in-exile] drop leaflets from RAF [Royal Air Force] planes addressed especially to Poland's Jews, and that the RAF, in cooperation with PGE, drop leaflets addressed to the Polish populace in general, to come to the Jews' defense, to defend them and rescue as best they can all who can be rescued; and that PGE should make it known, by leaflets, that the Jewish people in Palestine, in England and the U.S. are doing all they can for their rescue. We have further proposed that our English friends demand that His Majesty's Government scatter leaflets all over Germany, addressed to the German people, telling them about the massacre and atrocities committed by their government, for we have reason to believe that these are hidden from the German people . . . , and to ask the people to stay the murderer's hand. We have also asked them to demand that the English Government address an appeal to the governments of Bulgaria, Romania and Hungary . . . charging them with the responsibility if they allow the Nazis to conduct in their lands the massacre they are conducting in Poland."

On 17 December 1942, in response to a request from the Poles, British foreign secretary Anthony Eden, in the name of the Allied governments, condemned Nazi atrocities and promised retribution. But this proclamation contained no firm demand to stop the massacre and nothing in relation to rescue. Indeed, it turned out that the United States and Great Britain intended to do nothing in this respect. They argued that the destruction would end when the Allies achieved total victory, and that toward that goal all efforts must be directed. They further asserted that punishing the Nazis for crimes against the Jews in particular would not only provoke the Soviet Union, which did not recognize "national" distinctions, but would also confirm the impression in Britain and America that the war in Poland was a Jewish war and thereby would erode public support for the war effort.

With the German invasion of Poland in September 1939, the Jewish Agency had set up a committee on the affairs of Polish Jewry, composed of Yitzhak Gruen-baum, Moshe Shapira, Eliahu Dobkin, and Emil Schmorak (all Jewish Agency members) and known as the Committee of Four. Their main work had been collecting information, sending out parcels of food, clothing, and medicine, and searching for possibilities of further assistance. When news of the concentration of Jews in ghettos and of mass killings was first published—even though it was greeted by considerable public skepticism—the Jewish Agency was criticized for inaction, and a consensus that a more energetic and effective committee was needed quickly developed. In November 1942, when there was no longer any doubt that European Jewry was being systematically wiped out, the Jewish Agency decided to add a fifth member to the committee: Dov (Bernard) Joseph, secretary of the political department. It was hoped that with this addition the committee—whose name changed to Action Committee for the Jews of Europe or, of course, the Committee of Five—would become more effective in rallying governments and international organizations to the rescue attempt.

But other parties and public organizations in the Yishuv argued that this one change was not enough. They demanded a committee that would represent the entire Yishuv, arouse public opinion worldwide, and be far more active. Negotiations began with representatives of the National Council, Agudat Israel (an ultra-Orthodox, non-Zionist party), the Revisionists, the Landsmannschaft federations, and various other parties and associations. After tedious bargaining that lasted two months, in January 1943 the Jewish Agency for Palestine Committee for the Rescue of European Jewry was born.

Two months more were needed to set up all the rescue committee's constituents: the chairman (Gruenbaum); a 12-member presidency, whose majority was secured to the representatives of the Jewish Agency and the National Council; a secretariat of three (political, technical, and financial); a plenum of 30; and a public council of 60. Nothing short of this elaborate structure would have satisfied the many claimants. The resulting top-heavy, clumsy panel invited pressure from all sides and rendered it ineffective. There is therefore some truth in the argument that the Jewish Agency, which created the committee under both external and internal pressure, regarded it as unimportant, a mere lightning rod to attract public anger. From the outset the committee did not live up to its name.

In practice, all rescue operations, whether operational or in the planning stages, were directed by the senior Jewish Agency leadership—Ben-Gurion, Sharett, and Eliezer Kaplan, head of the agency's financial department—and not by the rescue committee. The Jewish Agency's offices in London, New York, and Geneva played a vital role in the rescue effort, as did the Palestine offices, wherever and whenever they could function in occupied Europe. But it was the Intelligence Section and the Agency for Illegal Immigration (Mossad le-Aliyah Bet) of the Haganah and the Jewish Agency's political department that bore the major responsibility for rescue and constituted the machinery of its execution. Under the political department's guidance, between the end of 1942 and 1 February 1943, an operational arm was created in Istanbul, close to the theater of destruction. It was known under a variety of names and references, the most common being the Yishuv's Rescue Committee or simply the Rescue Mission in Istanbul. This mission had impressive success in gathering intelligence, in establishing contact with Jewish organizations and individual Jews in occupied Europe, and in extending aid by parcels containing food and medicine. But it could do nothing to organize mass rescue.

Financing and implementing practicable rescue schemes was bone of contention between the Jewish Agency and its Istanbul mission. Whereas the mission held that the more money it had at its disposal, the more rescue work it could accomplish, the agency argued that plans came first and that workable plans would help to raise more money to put them into action. The agency's budget alone could not provide enough money for rescue, and a resort to public appeal was inevitable. Indeed, following the formation of the agency's Rescue Committee in 1943, a Rescue Fund was instituted; it was later amalgamated with the Mobilization Fund to become the Yishuv's Mobilization and Rescue Fund.

According to the official Jewish Agency statistical yearbook, Mobilization and Rescue Fund receipts in Palestinian pounds for the period from January 1940 to May 1944 amounted to £827,000, out of which only £234,000 was spent on rescue. The large balance, £593,000, indicates that money was more available then were practicable plans; it went mostly to mobilization needs, support for soldiers' families, and Yishuv defense (£106,000)—in other words, to the Haganah, the Yishuv's underground militia. Other

Jewish Agency resources, however, in addition to the Rescue and Mobilization Fund, were expended in areas related to rescue. The immigration budget, for example—£3,167,000 in the five-year war period, as well as a direct expenditure of £1,336,000 on "Rescue and help to refugees"—formed a pot of £4,503,000 ($18,012,000 in 1945 dollars). Rescue in the broader sense did not stop there. Upon their arrival in Palestine, refugees from Europe were in need of housing, medical services, jobs, and schools. A good part of the Jewish National Fund and the Foundation Fund budgets was allocated to meet the emergency.

Nothing better exemplifies the helplessness of the Jewish Agency and the Yishuv than the attempt at rescuing children. At first, expectations that such rescues would be successful were high. The Germans, it was believed, would be glad to be rid of Jews who were too young to work but not too young to eat; at the same time the Arabs could not regard them as an immediate threat to the balance of power in Palestine. The British government would not be able to object, as it usually did, that an influx of refugees would provide cover for "Nazi agents," therefore it would find it difficult to resist a public demand that the children be allowed entry into Palestine on humanitarian grounds.

On 7 December 1942 the Mandatory government notified the Jewish Agency, off the record, that "it allows the entry of 4,000 children, to be accompanied by 500 women from Bulgaria, into Palestine." On 9 December a report from Dobkin gave the Jewish Agency good reason to believe that it might be possible to bring 5,000 children who already had their certificates (the so-called 5,000 Plan). Within a day or two there seemed to be clear signals from the Mandatory government that the immigration of children might be doubled or even tripled.

Overnight a subcommittee was formed—Ben-Gurion, Kaplan, Gruenbaum, Dobkin, Shapira, and Joseph—and given responsibility both for the absorption of the children and for their welfare. On 14 December it discussed the immigration of children from the Balkan countries, the plan for accommodating them, and the necessary financing. It also discussed the "Teheran children"—some 1,000 Jewish children, mostly orphans, belonging to families who had escaped from Poland to the Soviet Union after the German invasion. They and some 800 adults accompanying the Polish army of Gen. Wladyslaw Anders had arrived in Iran between April and August 1942.

The British announcement had led Ben-Gurion and the other Jewish Agency members to believe—mistakenly, as it turned out—that the number of immigration certificates for children would be dependent on the agency's capacity for bringing them over and absorbing them, and that the British government would help the Jewish Agency in doing this. It was also believed that the British would not consider the children as part of the white paper quota of 29,000—a figure that was rounded up to form a "30,000 Plan." Thus the plan involving the 5,000 children from Bulgaria became part of the larger framework of bringing 30,000 children from the Balkans and Hungary. Toward the end of 1942 there emerged a general, undefined plan for the immigration of children—one that proved, however, only an illusion.

On 3 February 1943 the British colonial secretary, Oliver Stanley, stated in Parliament: "Some weeks ago the Government of Palestine agreed to admit from Bulgaria 4,000 Jewish children, with 500 adults to accompany them on the journey.... Steps are being taken immediately to organize the necessary transport, but I must point out that the practical difficulties involved are likely to be considerable." Stanley then said that the British would admit into Palestine "Jewish children, with a proportion of adults," up to the "29,000 still available under the white paper." He added that "it is essential, from the point of view of stability in the Middle East at the present time," that the white paper's regulations "should be strictly adhered to." In other words, the British government had restricted the rescue from Nazi Europe to Palestine to a total of 29,000 Jews, whatever their ages. Sharett, then in London, was quick to discern the deception. Pointing in advance to "the practical difficulties," he predicted that the immigration of children would be subjected to delays and bureaucratic obstacles that would prevent it from happening.

Three major problems hampered the 5,000 Plan from the start: exit permits, transit permits, and means of transport. All lay outside the control of the Jewish Agency. Although Turkey was the only land link between Europe and the Middle East and therefore was considered the safest and quickest route, Ben-Gurion held that sea transport was preferable. He feared that transporting 5,000 children by rail would take several months or longer, that the Nazis might overrun Bulgaria and cut off the route to Turkey, and that Churchill might persuade Turkey to give up its neutrality and join the Allies in declaring war against Germany. He urged the Jewish Agency to acquire ships, expecting that the agency would be able to run them more efficiently than anyone else could. In any event, the strategic and logistical circumstances in the midst of world war were so changeable that no time could be lost in executing a rescue plan while it was still feasible.

Jewish Agency pleas to governments and international organizations for help in rescuing the children were to no avail. Churchill turned down Ben-Gurion's request for an interview, but the largest obstacles to implementing the plan were placed by the Turks, who acted in part at the behest of the British. The cumbersome procedure for issuing immigration certificates to Palestine was under British control, and without certificates the Turks would not issue transit permits. The prospective immigrant had to send an application for an immigration certificate to Bern, the capital of neutral Switzerland, which represented British interests to the Axis Powers. There each application was minutely scrutinized—in order, the British claimed, to prevent Nazi secret agents from entering Palestine. Once the applications were approved, the certificates were dispatched to the capitals of Bulgaria, Romania, and Hungary by a diplomatic courier, who made the round once a month. While this process was taking place, at the end of 1943 and the beginning of 1944, the Nazis were exterminating 2,800 Jews a day. Between mid-May and mid-July the rate rose to 10,000 a day.

Negotiations over the details of transporting each group of refugee children took a further two months. It was determined that the children would travel by rail on the Taurus Express, a Turkish train, from Bulgaria through Turkey to the Syrian border. Using as a pretext the small number of passenger cars at their disposal, the Turks limited each group to 75 persons, including adults accompanying the children. Only after the Syrian border post had reported to Ankara, the Turkish capital, that one group had exited Turkey was a transit permit issued to the next group, which could set out only after the Turkish consulate in Sofia had received the permit. The delays created a six-week interval between groups. At that rate bringing 2,500 children from Bulgaria to Palestine would take the better part of a year. And this estimate did not take into account the time needed to bring the children from Romania, and later from Hungary, to Bulgaria.

At the end of February 1943 the Jewish Agency discussed ways to accelerate the children's immigration.

Ben-Gurion proposed asking the British and American governments for a ship. He expressed his concerns about the children's rescue mission at the Jewish Agency meeting on 7 March: "To our great sorrow the authorization [by the British] of certificates [to Palestine] is only theoretical, for there is no assurance that we can use the certificates and bring out of occupied Europe such a number of Jews." This problem put into question any sizable rescue by immigration to Palestine. Given the proportions and pace of the systematic extermination, Stanley's announcement of British steps to save a few thousand Jewish children—even if the "practical difficulties" could be overcome—was a cruel joke.

Yet hope of rescue died hard. Returning to Palestine from Istanbul in March, Eliezer Kaplan reported to the Jewish Agency that faith in Germany's victory was deteriorating among its satellites, whose policies regarding Jews had become less rigid. Romania's government was ready to allow the exit of 5,000 Jewish orphans if the Jewish Agency pledged itself to bear all the costs. Kaplan had committed the agency to allocate 2,000 immigration certificates to the Romanian children and to add to them as many more as required.

Securing transportation was mainly the responsibility of Sharett and Weizmann. They met in Washington with the British ambassador, Lord Halifax, and members of the British embassy, with Jewish members of Congress, and with President Roosevelt. The president promised a group of congressmen that he was ready to demand that Hitler release all children and to inform the dictator that if the Germans were butchering people to save food, he would take it upon himself to feed them. Roosevelt also promised to help the Jewish Agency get the shipping it needed. The argument that no ships were available for passengers was nonsense, he said, for American ships sailed to Europe loaded and came back empty. But after all their fine words, the Americans made their support conditional on British consent; and it was soon clear how very unlikely it was that such consent would be granted.

Meanwhile, Turkey was still "one big traffic jam," as Kaplan remarked, with its government putting a tangle of red tape in the way of the children's transit. It rejected the Jewish Agency's request to allow the passage of 300–500 children a week, as well as a reduced request for 200. The only fast route—by sea—was nearly impossible to implement. Ship owners showed interest, the International Red Cross agreed to let the refugee ships sail under its aegis, and the Soviets promised safe passage in the Black Sea. But the Turks, like the Americans, decided that British consent was necessary for ships' movement from Turkish to Palestinian ports, and the consent was never given. It now became clear beyond any doubt that the British were disrupting rescue efforts, both by sea and by land. Their behind-the-scenes diplomacy encouraged the Turks to slow down the children's transit.

Only the Germans constituted a greater hindrance to rescue operations, a fact that did not come to light until after the war. When Adolf Eichmann learned of the passage of the first groups of children through Turkey to Palestine, he made the exit of the 5,000 conditional on an exchange of 20,000 young, able-bodied Germans detained as enemy aliens in Allied countries. This condition—unknown to Ben-Gurion and his Jewish Agency colleagues at the time—completely paralyzed the plan. The Allies refused the exchange, the negotiations lingered on, and no one knew better than Eichmann how rapidly the number of Jewish children was dwindling in Europe.

In May 1943 there seemed to be a change, in all probability the result of public opinion. Kaplan was invited to Cairo to discuss sea transport for the children with Richard Casey, the British minister of state resident in the Middle East. Casey told Kaplan that the British government could only ask the Turkish government to expedite the children's passage and was completely unable to procure them a quicker exit from the Balkans. Also, his government could not undertake to make British and American ships available to the Jewish Agency, but he was ready "to take upon himself the responsibility for transferring the immigrants from Alexandretta [a port city in Turkey] to Palestine." Finally, he informed Kaplan that the British embassy in Ankara had received authority to simplify the administrative procedures and had appointed one of its members to assist the children in getting to Palestine.

Within days the Turkish government instructed its diplomats in the Balkans that any refugee who arrived in Turkey, by sea or by land, would be issued a visa to Palestine by the British. On the strength of this assurance the Turkish consul in Sofia began issuing transit permits to Jewish refugees. Permits were also given to Jews who had managed to escape from German-occupied territories and make it to Turkey by their wits. In Istanbul the British consulate issued them entry permits to Palestine as members of the contingent of 500 adults who were to accompany the children. When some of them arrived in Palestine, however, the Mandatory government sent an envoy to Turkey to remind the embassy, and through it London, that adults were supposed to enter Palestine only as escorts of children. As the transfer of children had not yet started, it was not legal to send adults ahead of them.

London stopped issuing visas, but the refugees kept coming to Bulgaria, and the Turkish consul there went on issuing them transit permits on the grounds that the Mandatory government was authorized to deport them "to Mauritius or somewhere else." Finally the British government officially requested that the Turkish government in Ankara instruct its consul in Sofia to stop issuing transit permits to Jewish refugees without consulting Ankara first. The Turks complied.

On his return from the United States in April 1943, Sharett joined the struggle against the British authorities in Palestine, shuttling between Egypt, the seat of the British high command and the minister of state resident in the Middle East, and Turkey, the only link with occupied Europe. He too believed that the 5,000 Plan was off to a good start. The British promised to grant any Jewish refugee who managed to reach Turkey an immigration certificate to Palestine, and Bulgaria announced that it would allow the exit of 1,000 Jews.

But then the British authorities in Palestine prevailed over Casey's policy, so that the government in London would not agree that Turkey should allow into Istanbul ships from Balkan ports with Jewish children aboard. Meanwhile Bulgaria, caving in to Nazi pressure, closed its borders. Casey's assurances evaporated, and with them the 5,000 Plan. Through June 1943 only 184 Jewish refugees from Bulgaria had arrived in Turkey, and in 1943 and 1944 only 3,600 refugees, adults and children, immigrated via Turkey to Palestine.

A senior adviser in the Jewish Agency's political department remarked in July 1943 in a note to Sharett, "It is an absurdity that for half a year it was not possible to get even one ship for refugees. It is an absurdity that out of 30,000 children certified for immigration, it was not possible to bring into Palestine even one." It is an even greater absurdity that all the Jewish Agency could do was to call it an absurdity. And so it was. The plan for the children's immigration came to naught.

Yet even though this outcome seemed to put an end to any further rescue, Ben-Gurion and his colleagues

Jewish refugees from Transnistria arrive in Palestine. They traveled by train from Istanbul. July 1944

at the Jewish Agency worked as hard as they could to bring off four further rescues: the Transnistria plan, the Slovakia plan, the Europa Plan, and "blood for trucks." Except for the last, which was initiated by the Nazis as a cover for exploring a separate peace between Germany and the Western Allies, their results equaled those of the rescue plans for children.

A good part of the rescue money—that allotted out of the Jewish Agency budgets and that raised by the Yishuv's Mobilization and Rescue Fund—was channeled directly by the Rescue Mission in Istanbul and the Jewish Agency office in Geneva to bring about the "ransom plans" (Slovakia and Europa). The remainder was spent on other efforts—principally on packages of food and medicine, the smuggling of Jewish refugees out of various countries in occupied Europe, and the maintenance of refugees in camps in Switzerland, Bulgaria, and Yugoslavia. Nathan Schwalb (Dror) of the Jewish Agency's Hehalutz Department, who operated out of the office in Geneva, was instru-

mental in updating addresses of groups and individuals in occupied Europe and in establishing a network of couriers that, together with similar endeavors by the Istanbul mission, helped save tens of thousands of lives by carrying vital information and supplies. Schwalb's archive of his correspondence with the rapidly diminishing European Jewry is a testament to a singular rescue effort as well as an invaluable documentary source.

In sum, Zionist rescue operations were constrained by the size of the Yishuv, British restrictions on Jewish immigration to Palestine, and Allied war policies. At the outbreak of World War II in September 1939, the Jewish population in Palestine was 474,600. By the end of 1944 it had grown to 565,500. The Yishuv had no army, no navy, and no air force. Any nonmilitary rescue efforts, had the Yishuv been granted a free hand in mounting them, would have been limited by the paltry resources at its disposal.

The only effective rescue open to Zionism and the

Yishuv was to bring Jews out of Nazi Europe into Palestine, where they could be cared for. But as the British proved adamant in enforcing the 1939 white paper quota, the scope of Zionist rescue was severely delimited. At the end of 1942, when Hitler's death machinery moved into high gear, the quota left room in Palestine for only 29,000 more Jewish refugees of all ages.

All other plans for rescue were constricted by Allied bans on contracts with the enemy and on transferring funds to them, as well as by Allied insistence on an unconditional German surrender. Pleas by Jewish Agency to the Allies for massive rescue invariably met with the answer given in the House of Commons by British deputy prime minister Clement Attlee on 19 January 1943, that "the only real remedy for the consistent Nazi policy of racial and religious persecution lies in an Allied victory; every resource must be bent towards this supreme object." This meant in practice the relegation of Jewish rescue, by direct or indirect Allied action, to a very low priority. And on the few occasions when public pressure for direct action required some sort of response, the insistence by London and Washington on the need for the cooperation of all Allies, including the Soviet Union, served to quash any initiative. In the race between V-E Day and Auschwitz, Auschwitz won.   *Shabtai Teveth*

Nathan Rapoport, monument to the Warsaw ghetto fighters (1948).

Resistance in Eastern Europe Most discussions about Jewish resistance during World War II raise the same questions: Why did the Jews go like sheep to the slaughter? Why did they refuse to fight? The assumptions behind the questions are that European Jews went to their deaths passively, and that the conditions for resisting existed but the Jews failed to take advantage of them. If opportunities existed to thwart Nazi aims but the Jews chose not to act on them, then they must bear some responsibility for their fate during the Holocaust. Even a cursory glance at the historical record shows, however, that these arguments rest on false assumptions. Favorable conditions for Jewish resistance were virtually nonexistent. Nonetheless, Jews actively resisted their Nazi oppressors.

Resistance in the Ghettos

In most countries under German occupation, Jewish mass murder was preceded by a carefully orchestrated sequence of abuses. In the first phase, laws were introduced defining who was a Jew. Then, Jewish property was confiscated, and Jews were denied gainful employment. Next, Jews were removed from their homes to special areas, usually sealed ghettos, out of sight of the gentile population.

For Jews in Poland and the surrounding countries, the last quarter of 1941 marked the beginning of the end. In contrast, not until 1943 did the Nazis decide to move against the Danish Jews by ordering their deportation.

Most historians agree that the Nazi plan to annihilate the Jews—the so-called Final Solution—crystallized after the Germans invaded the Soviet Union in June 1941. As they moved east, the Nazis began to search for more efficient ways of implementing their plan. The capture of Russian territory in the first months of war in the East coincided with the mass murder of Jews, particularly by the SS mobile killing units, the *Einsatzgruppen*.

Ghettos were first established by the Germans in late 1939 following the conquest of Poland. The practice of ghetto-building was extended in Belorussia in the second half of 1941 after the Germans occupied that territory. All ghettos were designed as temporary communities in which to concentrate a region's Jewish population in order to facilitate their immediate mass murder by Einsatzgruppen or their transfer to concentration and extermination camps.

Ghettos were always located in run-down urban areas. Overcrowding, disease, and starvation were endemic. The Germans continually issued new and ever-stricter directives; noncompliance by the Jews in the ghettos was severely punished. For example, a 1941 law in Poland decreed death for any Jew caught leaving a ghetto without authorization. Moreover, an individual's breach of the law entailed a collective punishment as well—the execution of an unspecified number of other ghetto inmates unconnected with the trespass. Rigid enforcement of such orders brought the Germans closer to their main goal of annihilating European Jewry and a secondary goal of humiliating the Jews before they died. The Nazis introduced various kinds of physical, social, and psychological degradation, and they excelled in inventing diabolical tortures.

Among such humiliating measures were orders that led to divisiveness within the ghettos, such as the forced influx of Jews from the surrounding communities. Gypsies and Jews who had converted to Roman Catholicism were often antisemitic, and their arrival in the ghettos caused conflict. Some ghettos mixed Jews from Western Europe with the native Eastern European Jews, despite the sharp cultural differences between the two groups. In addition, higher-class Jewish men were singled out for special treatment. The entire system of social status and privilege was inverted: factory owners and intellectuals were forced to clean toilets, and rabbis became road workers.

Faced with these assaults on Jewish life, the leaders of the *Judenrat* (Jewish council) and other Jews in the ghettos refused to submit. They organized fund-raising events, lectures, plays, and competitions. They established soup kitchens for the destitute and bought medicines. In the larger ghettos special committees set up theaters, libraries, and schools. Illegal schools flourished in the ghettos of Estonia, Poland, Lithuania, and Latvia. Thus the Jews resisted not only the physical deterioration that ghetto conditions caused but especially the spiritual degradation and humiliation that the Nazis counted on to break their will.

A teenage boy, Yitzhak Rudashevski, underscored the value of these efforts in his diary: "Finally I have lived to see the day. Today we go to school. The day passed quite differently. Lessons, subjects, both of the sixth classes were combined. There is a happy spirit in class. Finally the club too was opened. My own life is shaping in quite a different way. We waste less time. The day is divided and flies by very quickly . . . yes, that is how it should be in the ghetto, the day should fly by, and we should not waste time." Rudashevski, an inmate of the Vilna ghetto, was murdered by the Germans in 1943 at Ponary.

Zionist and non-Zionist youth movements alike were particularly active in the ghettos. At the beginning of the German occupation, young Jews saw the war as a passing phase and so concentrated on their own education, hoping to lessen the demoralizing effects of their environment and prepare for a future after the defeat of Germany. As conditions worsened, however, young activists broadened their cultural activities—teaching children, presenting lectures, staging plays, and promoting social welfare. Those involved seemed at once more daring and more realistic than their older leaders, for they recognized quite early that the Germans aimed at the total destruction of the Jewish people. In the second half of 1942 the heads of these youth movements began to prepare for armed resistance. They were under no illusion that with their limited resources they could prevail against the German army, but they were determined to stand against the enemy and so defend Jewish honor. In many ghettos political groups that were ideological opponents cooperated with one another in the preparations for armed resistance.

In 1942 rumors about forest partisans began to circulate, suggesting the possibility of fighting either inside the ghetto or with the partisans outside the cities. Most of the young underground activists were reluctant to leave the ghettos, as they felt responsible for the entire imprisoned community. At times the attitudes of the ghetto inmates toward the young resisters tipped the scale in favor of staying or leaving. Some of the older Jews, including members of the Judenrat, were suspicious of the young; others thought that only Jewish contributions to the German war economy could save a part of their people. To them, fighting in the ghetto or mass escape into the forests translated into the destruction of an entire community.

Plans about the place, form, and timing of resistance frequently changed. Some underground leaders compromised and went along with the vacillating Judenrat leaders. In the Bialystok ghetto, for example, after much discussion with Efraim Barash, head of the Judenrat, the resistance group decided to attack the Germans during the liquidation of the ghetto and to effect a mass escape into the forest. But the German assault on the ghetto came too suddenly, and a desperate, uneven battle ensued. In the end only a few fighters managed to escape the ghetto and reach the so-called Aryan side of town or the forest.

Like most resistance organizations, the Jewish underground in Kraków consisted of a coalition of youth movements. An important partner was Akiva, a politically moderate, non-violent Zionist group. The Kraków underground was first involved in cultural and welfare activities but soon turned to collecting and spreading information, printing newspapers, and forging documents. By 1942 its young leaders were convinced that all Jews were destined for annihilation. They therefore obtained weapons and established closer ties with the Polish underground, particularly the more accessible Polish Communist Party (PPR). Among the group's leaders were Shimshon and Gusta Draegner (Marek and Justyna) and Aharon Liebeskind (Dolek), all members of Akiva. Gusta Draegner, after her capture by the Germans in 1943, recorded the history of the Kraków ghetto underground on pieces of toilet paper, which were then smuggled out of the prison.

The history of the Jewish underground in Kraków was partly shaped by its failure to gain acceptance from the rest of the ghetto population. The young resistance fighters showed great courage, but success was hampered by inexperience. Through cooperation with the PPR they obtained two pistols and ammunition, but they failed to establish contact with forest partisans. Out of six men who in 1942 left for the forest, only one returned, and this tipped the scale in favor of urban anti-German operations. On 22 December 1942 they launched a grenade attack on Cyganeria, a Kraków coffee shop outside the ghetto, killing and wounding several Germans. Many Jewish resisters were arrested after the attack: Liebeskind was executed, but on 29 April 1943 the Draegners and other resisters escaped.

The group resumed urban sabotage activities and published a journal, *Hehalutz Halohem* (The Fighting Pioneer). In the fall of 1943 the Draegners were again captured (their specific fate is unknown), and by November 1943 the Kraków Jewish underground had ceased to exist. Among the few survivors was the courier Hela Szyper-Rufeisen, who later emigrated

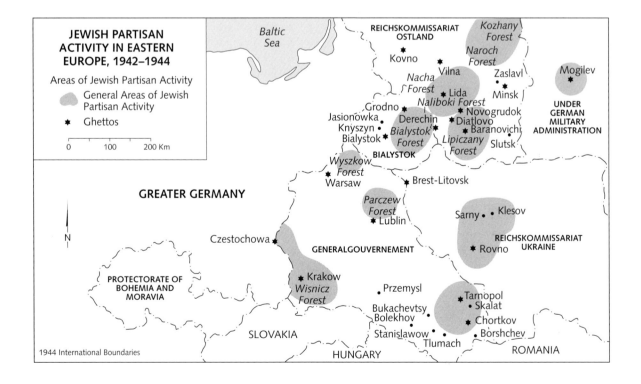

to Israel. In Eastern Europe, Jewish armed resistance organizations were set up in seven major ghettos—Bialystok, Czestochowa, Kovno, Kraków, Minsk, Vilna, and Warsaw—and 45 smaller ghettos.

Although the establishment of ghettos enabled the Germans to isolate the Jews both from the local populations and from each other, Jewish resistance groups, particularly those in large ghettos, set up illegal communications networks that eventually reached some smaller ghettos, labor camps, and people in the forests. Information, money, supplies, and weapons were transferred through these lines of communication. These clandestine transfers were accomplished by special couriers, most of them young women whose appearance did not betray their Jewishness. Many couriers disappeared without a trace; others were caught and executed or sent to concentration or extermination camps. After the liquidation of ghettos, most surviving couriers continued covert work on the "outside," some helping Jews in hiding, others maintaining links between labor camps and the remaining ghettos. The dedication of these couriers allowed ghetto underground organizations to develop into new forms and to continue resistance while living illegally on the Aryan side and in the forests.

Resistance in the Forest

Estimates of Jewish participation in the Soviet partisan movement range from 20,000–30,000 persons. Of Jews who fought as partisans, about 80 percent perished. The densely forested area of western Belorussia was the main center of the Soviet partisan movement and therefore also of Jewish partisan activity.

Following Hitler's massive attack on the Soviet Union on 22 June 1941, the rapid retreat of the Red Army left many soldiers without proper routes of retreat, and some of these men fled into the forests. Later some Soviet prisoners of war succeeded in escaping from captivity, and they too hid in the Belorussian forests. In addition, by 1942 young Belorussian civilians, trying to avoid forcible deportation to Germany as slave laborers, were joining the soldiers and escaped prisoners in hiding. They were followed by Poles, Ukrainians, and Lithuanians fleeing similar pressure from the Germans. Calling themselves partisans, these men formed small groups who roamed the countryside—undisciplined, leaderless, and lacking weapons. Competition among them for the meager resources available led to conflict, violence, and even killings.

In 1942 ghetto fugitives also reached the forests. Most of them were city dwellers unused to outdoor life, and they included many older people, women, and children. They were confronted by the early partisans, who often harbored strong antisemitic feelings. These rough bands saw the Jews as a threat to their own existence; they robbed them, chased them away, and beat and killed them. Only a minority of partisans were ready to give them assistance. Usually it was young Jewish men with guns, or doctors and nurses, who had any chance of being accepted into non-Jewish partisan groups. It was not until about the end of 1943, after the arrival of special partisan organizers from the Soviet Union, that the forest anarchy diminished.

Although some Jews managed to cooperate with non-Jewish partisans, others formed their own units, which were sometimes transformed into family camps. One such group was the Bielski unit. In the summer of 1941 the brothers Asael, Tuvia, and Zus Bielski, Jewish peasants from an isolated village in Belorussia, escaped to the countryside. After obtaining a few weapons, in the summer of 1942 they and more than 30 followers formed a partisan unit with Tuvia Bielski as commander. From the start Tuvia, a strong leader, insisted that all Jews, whatever their age, sex, or state of health, would be accepted into the unit. Some members of the opposition saw this policy as a threat to the group's existence. Tuvia argued that size meant safety. Indeed, as the Germans stepped up their program of annihilation, he became more determined and inventive in devising new means of rescuing Jews.

The Bielski partisans even sent scouts into the ghettos to help Jews escape and join them. They also collected Jews who were wandering in the forest. Jewish partisans suffering from the antisemitism of their Soviet groups knew that they could find shelter with the Bielski unit. Bielski partisans punished collaborators who denounced fugitive Jews. Tuvia Bielski obtained protection by working together with the Soviet partisans on such matters as obtaining food and launching anti-German military ventures; later on, the two groups engaged in economic cooperation.

In 1942 and 1943 the Bielski partisans led a nomadic existence. Toward the end of 1943, having grown to about 400 individuals, they established a more permanent home in the huge, swampy Naliboki Forest. The camp came to resemble a shtetl, a small town with many factories and workshops. One of its functions, therefore, was to supply services to the Soviet partisan movement and thus neutralize antisemitic complaints that the Jews contributed nothing. Moreover, the economic situation in the Bielski unit was improved so that fewer dangerous food-gathering expeditions were required.

Other Jewish partisans concentrated on waging war. Yeheskel Atlas, Alter Dworecki, and Hirsz Kaplinski distinguished themselves as Jewish partisan leaders, though by the end of 1942 they had all been killed in action. They operated in and around the huge Lipiczany Forest of western Belorussia, where the dense undergrowth, bogs, and rough country roads promised safety. Although Atlas, Dworecki, and Kaplinski identified strongly with the plight of their fellow Jews, the help they offered to the Jewish fugitives was sporadic, disorganized, and ineffective. Their commitment to battle hampered their desire to curtail the Nazi destruction of the Jews. They may have thought that fighting would ultimately save more lives. The Bielski Unit and the three partisan leaders represented two distinct modes of Jewish resistance: a fight for biological survival and a fight for revenge.

Data about Jewish participation in urban non-Jewish resistance movements are elusive. Some Jews joined such groups without revealing their origins, as in the main Polish resistance movement, the Home Army (Armia Krajowa). The official military arm of the Polish government-in-exile, the Home Army had many subgroups representing the various political parties in the government. Depending on the political affiliation (often unpublicized) of a subgroup, a Jew wishing to join its ranks might be accepted, rejected, or murdered; hence the need for Jewish candidates to conceal their identity. If accepted into the Polish underground as Jews, they often faced discrimination.

Some Jews also cooperated with the smaller Polish underground, the Communist PPR. Similarly, some Czech Jews belonged to the Czech underground, which operated in urban centers. Many of them were fully assimilated but never denied their ethnic origin.

Resistance in the Camps

Nazi concentration camps, more so than the ghettos, were places of degradation, coercion, economic exploitation, and murder. Some, like Treblinka, Sobibor, and Belzec, were built exclusively to put Jews to death. Where slave labor was combined with killing, as at Auschwitz, Jews were singled out for inhumane treatment. Nevertheless, Jews did organize several armed revolts—in Auschwitz, Chelmno, Janowska Road, Sobibor, and Treblinka, as well as in 18 labor camps.

The main camp at Auschwitz was originally intended to house political prisoners. It had an underground in which Polish and other political prisoners had some power and which maintained contact with the Home Army and the Polish government-in-exile. By 1944 this underground had begun to plan a revolt, to be coordinated with an outside uprising and to include the men of the Jewish *Sonderkommando*, a special detail assigned to work at the gas chambers. Every few months the members of the Sonderkommando were themselves sent to die in the gas chambers, and new prisoners were selected to take their place.

One Sonderkommando group, aware of their ultimate fate, was eager to participate in the uprising. It soon became clear, however, that the non-Jewish underground leaders were stalling. The delay was based on several factors: couriers had been caught with plans, which had to be revised; the Nazis had therefore increased their vigilance; massive deportation of Poles to other concentration camps followed. In mid-August 1944 it became clear that the Polish uprising in Warsaw had been unsuccessful. Other underground failures had followed, and the idea of coordinating the concentration camp uprising with outside resistance had been unrealistic. Finally, the Home Army and the Polish government-in-exile urged that no revolt should take place unless the prisoners faced total annihilation. Unlike the Sonderkommando, non-Jewish prisoners were not confronted by imminent death, and they waited.

But time was running out for the Sonderkommando. On 7 October 1944 the Jewish Sonderkommando, with some help from Soviet prisoners, staged an armed revolt at Auschwitz II (Birkenau). The dynamiting of Crematorium IV started the uprising. Prisoners who put up a fight nearby were massacred, and the SS forces assigned to the camp were swiftly mobilized against the rebels. SS men hunted down Jewish insurgents with dogs. Many fell trying to escape. Others sought refuge in a nearby forest but, realizing they had no chance of survival, set it on fire. At nightfall Auschwitz was surrounded by guards and fires; the crematorium burned, as did woodlands on each side of the camp. The ground was covered with the corpses of the Sonderkommando: 250 inmates were killed, and the SS later shot another 200 Sonderkommando men in reprisal. No prisoners managed to escape. German losses were two dead and about a dozen wounded.

JEWISH ARMED RESISTANCE
IN GHETTOS AND CAMPS
1941–1944
* Selected Ghettos
□ Selected Labor Camps
⊠ Extermination Camps

0   100   200   300 Km

1944 International Boundaries

The Auschwitz uprising benefited from cooperation between men and women. Explosives for the final confrontation had been smuggled by Jewish women, some of whom worked in a nearby munitions factory. On 6 January 1945, less than three weeks before Soviet troops arrived at Auschwitz-Birkenau, four young Jewish women accused of supplying the dynamite—Roza Robota, Ella Gaertner, Esther Wajcblum, and Regina Safirsztain—were publicly hanged. As the trap door opened, Robota shouted in defiance, "Be strong, have courage!" Despite brutal interrogation, any evidence these women possessed died with them.

Conditions and Forms of Resistance

For resistance to emerge and function, it must have a strategic base in the local population, among whom the partisans can move about and blend in. This base helps to compensate for small numbers of fighters and for lack of arms. All non-Jewish underground groups could count on local help for supplies and protection. Jewish resisters, however, had no such advantages. Confinement in scattered ghettos automatically deprived them of a strategic base, and only couriers could move between the ghettos. Neither they nor other Jews could rely on support from the local population. Only a handful of Gentiles risked their lives to save Jews, and some collaborated with the Germans to discover Jews in hiding.

National underground organizations could obtain advice and arms from political leaders in exile, while other resistance groups, like Josip Tito's partisans in Yugoslavia, received supplies through the Allies. Eastern European Jews had no such resources. Jewish leaders who had left Eastern Europe in 1939 failed to organize a unified front, and others had been murdered early in the occupation. Some prewar leaders were co-opted by the Germans to form the Judenräte. Few of them wholeheartedly supported the Jewish underground, though there were exceptions—the Judenrat leaders from Minsk, Kovno, Ivje, Pruzany, and Lachva.

The leadership gap was partly filled by the youth movements. Most of the young underground commanders were idealistic and eager to fight to protect the Jewish people. A few charismatic leaders, like Tuvia Bielski, emerged. But all these leaders suffered from inexperience. The Allies had no interest in the Jews, rejecting their pleas and desperate requests for weapons. Jewish political diversity and independence further reduced the ability to organize. In short, for Jews all doors leading to resistance seemed shut.

All countries in German-occupied Europe offered some kind of resistance, and each developed its own movement, whose organization and success varied in accordance with the attitude of the occupying forces, the local geography, and the national culture. Allied assistance, another crucial factor, depended on the country's strategic importance. The French historian Henri Michel argues that "the best recruiting agents for resistance were the savagery of the SS, the ineptitude of the occupying regime and the severity of the economic exploitation."

The diversity and secrecy of the national resistance movements prevented integration, so that there was no unified European resistance. Oppression by the German occupation varied from country to country, partly on racial grounds. In this respect Eastern Europe fared badly. The Nazis defined all Slavs and Balts as subhuman, only slightly above the Jews. In Poland the Germans set out at once to destroy the nation's culture, closing universities and schools and prohibiting all political expression. They targeted male Polish elites (intellectuals, professionals, clergy, and officers), murdering many and sending others to concentration camps. The Polish underground established illegal schools and organized clandestine literature and lectures, while the Home Army was deeply involved in distributing illegal information and accumulating weapons. Almost up to the time of the Warsaw uprising in the summer of 1944, Home Army operations resembled other urban underground activities in Eastern Europe. Only a few armed rebellions took place—

The public hanging of three members of the Communist underground on Karl Marx Street in Minsk. One man's body is draped with a placard that reads, "We are partisans and have shot at German soldiers." The execution was one of four carried out in Minsk on 26 October 1941 by German troops with the 707th Infantry Division.

in 1944, when Germany had already been weakened. The weapons so assiduously collected lay for a long time unused.

In contrast to the urban underground, various partisan groups in the forests and countryside used arms as early as 1941. Coordinated anti-German military assaults occurred in the latter part of 1943. The Soviet partisan movement claimed responsibility for 3,000 cases of sabotage against railroads and boasted of having immobilized 16 German army battalions. Not all these claims can be verified. By the end of 1943 the Soviet resistance was at least partly controlled by the Communist party, the secret police, and the Red Army.

Following the German military losses, resistance to the Nazi occupiers became more acceptable, and there were many more European volunteers, including former Nazi sympathizers and collaborators. The Allies only occasionally relied on underground organizations; indeed, the role of the resistance movements in winning the war has often been exaggerated.

Some have argued that for the Jews, a people targeted for annihilation, efforts merely to stay alive and maintain their moral traditions fall within the definition of resistance. In their daily activities in the ghettos many Jews ignored German prohibitions, such as the ban on educating Jewish children. All efforts at preserving oneself and others represented a form of opposition that undermined Nazi aims and were thus as much acts of resistance as were derailing trains or killing German soldiers.

Indeed, altruism in the ghetto required extraordinary spiritual strength while contributing to the perpetuation of Jewish life; it undermined Nazi policies. Even if it does not quite fit into the concept of resistance, such behavior can be viewed as unarmed humanitarian resistance.

The Jewish and non-Jewish resistance had two different chronologies. By the time non-Jewish undergrounds had become organized, most Eastern European Jews were dead or in the camps. Beyond their different chronologies and the fact that Jews were more likely to engage in armed resistance, both Jewish and non-Jewish underground movements collected information, printed and distributed news, forged documents, and gathered weapons.

Significant resistance groups were established by non-Jews in Buchenwald, Dachau, and Auschwitz. According to Hermann Langbein, an underground

political leader in Auschwitz, their illegal activities involved the destruction of incriminating materials, the transfer of prisoners (usually Communists) to better jobs, and occasional help in the escapes of prisoners.

Henri Michel has noted that although Jews had less opportunity than other oppressed groups—non-Jewish slave laborers in Germany, Soviet prisoners of war, and non-Jewish concentration camp inmates—to mount underground resistance, they were the most active in openly fighting Nazi oppression. Neither non-Jewish slave laborers nor Soviet prisoners of war engaged in organized armed resistance, and except for a few attempts to escape they generally complied with Nazi orders. In Michel's words, "Jews were placed by Nazis in conditions in which it was difficult for them not to succumb and not be rent to pieces. Nevertheless, one can honestly conclude that the Jewish resistance movement played an honorable role in European resistance and that in some respects its role was exemplary." *Nechama Tec*

Resistance in Western Europe Resistance, as a social phenomenon, emerges from the larger issue of the total war. With its attributes of mass mobilization and cancellation of the division between the military front and the civilian rear, the total war caused the irregular military activities of civilians to be unavoidable, necessary, and effective. The antecedents of the resistance movement—the Spanish *guerrillas* and the Russian *partizany*—appeared during the Napoleonic Wars, the first mass wars. Despite these origins the term *resistance* entered into general political usage in France only in 1943. Its usage was limited to Western and Northern Europe, whereas parallel phenomena in the East preferred the terms *underground* and *partisans*.

Nationalist Resistance

The development of the underground movement was a function of several factors: the changes in the war, the activities of the German occupying forces, and the processes taking place among the subjugated populations. Northern and Western Europe were conquered by the German army in 10 weeks. The speed of the German advance and the collapse of the defending armies left the conquered populations paralyzed and numb, apprehensive of their future and looking for the "real" culprits of their debacle.

This national mood led the political and cultural elite in two opposite directions—collaboration and resistance. Both movements expressed disillusion with the prewar national establishment, the political system, and the national spirit and declared a desire for national renovation. Collaborators emulated the Fascists in Italy or the Nazi regime in Germany, whereas members of the resistance rejected these models, preferring a democratic, socialist, or Communist style. Another difference between the collaborators and the resistance members was the mechanism of the ideological processes. The collaborators had a ready-made model, as the total negation of democratic ideas was the basis for the legitimation of their own rule. The resisters moved slowly from unspecified sentiments to a well-defined set of values based mainly on democratic and collectivist tenets. This transformation was not uniform. In countries where Nazi ideology denied the very status of nationhood (such as in Poland), the underground movement tended to adhere to simple nationalism. But in states where the military defeat elevated authoritarian groups to power that were alienated from democratic processes, the resistance had to combat not only foreign conquerors but their native admirers as well. Not surprisingly, the slogan of Combat, one of the major resistance groups in France, was "From resistance to revolution." In countries where the extreme right accepted the German domination and hoped to transform their own states into minor partners of the German empire, the resistance was mobilized by the left and gravitated toward it.

Another aspect of the resistance activities was their growing militancy. In the first stage after the German conquest, the primary task of potential resisters was a personal revolt of refusing to accept the inevitability of defeat. The next stage involved creating informal, close-knit groups, which struggled against the national mood and against German and police harassment. One of the leaders of the liberation movement summarized his experience: "That is the only period in my life when I lived in a truly classless society."

The only way for these groups to escape their isolation was to convince their fellow citizens that the picture of reality presented by the Germans and the collaborators was false and that conditions were even harsher than they seemed to be. The dissemination of anti-German views was required by the character of the total war, as only by negating the German presentation of truth and their "New Order" could the conqueror's hold on people's minds be broken. This battle was carried on in street graffiti, leaflets, and broad-sheets. Street propaganda was usually the domain of teenagers, for whom this activity served as apprenticeship for more daring tasks. The importance of broadsheets, which published news from the British radio (the BBC), Swiss radio, and (in the case of Communists) Radio Moscow, grew as the tide of war turned. The situation at the fronts caused the German authorities to prohibit the use of radios (in the Netherlands in 1943); the effect of the ban was to increase the circulation of the underground press.

Printing anti-German propaganda required a mass and sophisticated organization. Because the Germans controlled the publishing resources, many people were needed to obtain the requisite materials, not to speak of printing and distributing the newspapers. Toward the end of the war the resistance groups in Denmark published more than 300 newspapers and in France more than 1,000. The resistance propaganda gave the conquered nations back their sense of pride and created hope of a German defeat.

Simultaneously the German authorities pushed the local populations toward the resistance. Soon after the conquest the seemingly benevolent Germans overreacted to every breach of order. Any assault on their personnel was followed by random arrests and executions. After September 1941 the German army decided to avenge every assassinated German soldier by executing about 50 hostages. This method of punishment was systematized and legalized in December 1941 by the *Nacht und Nebel* (Night and Fog) order, which specified two penalties: execution and secret transfer to concentration camps in the East. This decree, promulgated in order to create mass terror, convinced many that resisting the Germans was a question of survival.

Apart from distributing resistance newspapers, there were other nonviolent activities of resistance: symbolic and moral resistance, such as the wearing of garments in the colors of the national flag and the resignation of the Norwegian bishops; economic resistance, including minor sabotage and strikes; spying for the Allies; rescuing Allied personnel from occupied Europe; and nonviolent interference in German plans. The most famous example of this last was the rescue of Danish Jewry on the eve of the planned deportation by the Germans.

Violent acts of resistance became more frequent as the scales of war turned against Germany. Although acts of personal terror against the German soldiers started immediately after the occupation (and caused savage German retribution), the first large-scale armed actions against the Germans began toward the end of 1942. The most famous single act of economic sabotage was the destruction of a heavy-water plant in 1943 by Norwegian resisters. In France the resistance cut German lines of communication and attacked isolated German units on the eve of the Allied invasion. The culmination of the French resistance activity was the Paris uprising in August 1944. At the same time, battles with the German army usually ended in defeat of those resisters who organized themselves into field guerrilla units, called Maquis, as shown by the battle of Vergers. Generally speaking, with the exception of certain areas in central France, the landscape of Western Europe was not suitable for partisan warfare, and fighting units operated mainly as urban guerrillas.

Organizationally the resistance movements developed only in the spring of 1941. From that point the resistance had two expressions: as quasi-military units and as political-ideological formations. Besides being a fighting unit, each resistance cell was an ideologically cohesive body, usually organized by a certain political party. This duality was immanent to the movement after the French Communist party joined the resistance following the German invasion of the Soviet Union (Operation Barbarossa) in June 1941. In the eyes of the Communists, the Nazi attack transformed the "imperialist war" into a people's war against inhuman tyranny. No doubt Barbarossa liberated the French Communist party from its quandary, enabling it to join the anti-Vichy forces while bringing a large, disciplined, and conspiratorial organization into the resistance. Both the Communists and other political entities tried to set up nationwide fighting organizations. In January 1943 three non-Communist movements in southern France established the MUR (Mouvements Unis de la Résistance). In May 1944 all national and local units of resistance united in the CNR (Conseil National de la Résistance). Similar trends of unification were observed in other resistance movements throughout Western Europe.

Two major features characterized the members of CNR: that of fighting the Germans and their collaborators and that of accepting the overall leadership of Gen. Charles de Gaulle in London. Acceptance of de Gaulle's government was paralleled in other resistance movements by allegiance to their governments-in-exile. Legally the government-in-exile was the source of authority for the resistance activity, which presented

itself as the local representative of that government. But the only link between the government-in-exile and the resisters was in the hands of the clandestine services of the Allies. Even the radio broadcasts of the leaders to their occupied countries took place courtesy of the BBC. All couriers to and from the Continent, as well as weaponry and instructors, were transferred by the British SOE (Special Operations Executive) and the American OSS (Office of Strategic Services). The SOE, organized in July 1940 following Churchill's orders "to set Europe ablaze," trained thousands of radio operators, saboteurs, and intelligence specialists and sent them to Europe.

From the British point of view, at least until the Allied invasion, the primary task of the resistance was to damage the German army. Consequently the SOE aided every organization without regard to its political hue. The OSS, richer than the SOE, declared the resistance movement's acceptance of free and general elections after the war as a condition for its support. Eventually the OSS supplied the same organizations as the SOE. Constant bickering about the tasks and the control of the resistance movements developed between the secret services and the governments-in-exile, frictions that had a negative impact on the performance of the resistance in the field. In eyes of the regular army the agents of the SOE and the OSS were "gentlemen-adventurers," and the resistance members were seen as a notch above average criminals. In the plans for the Normandy landing the resistance units did not play an important role, but they contributed in various ways to the German defeat. In Norway the Milord resistance movement accepted the capitulation of the German forces; in Belgium resistance units captured the Antwerp harbor intact; in France they paralyzed German retreat lines; and in Italy, after liberating Milan, they hung Mussolini upside down.

The Jewish Resistance

Most people in occupied Europe had two options: to adapt to German rule and so survive until the liberation; or to fight, often dying in the process. Resisters were those who had decided to fight. This choice did not exist for the Jews. At the beginning of the German occupation, when the Jews, even if persecuted, did not perceive the danger of total extermination, some Jews joined the resistance out of political convictions. In this sense they were similar to non-Jewish resisters. After 1942, when the Nazis started to implement their extermination policy, the only choice (if any) given to

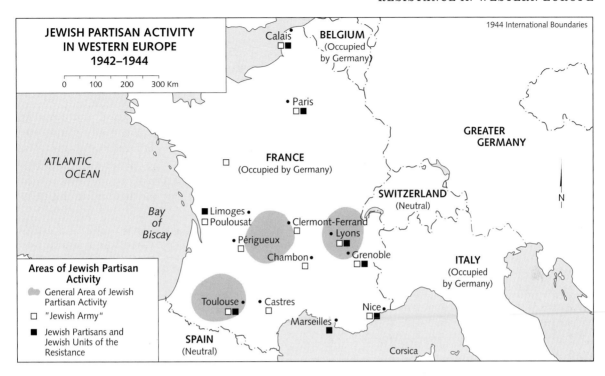

JEWISH PARTISAN ACTIVITY
IN WESTERN EUROPE
1942–1944

0   100   200   300 Km

1944 International Boundaries

Calais

BELGIUM
(Occupied
by Germany)

Paris

FRANCE
(Occupied by Germany)

GREATER
GERMANY

ATLANTIC
OCEAN

SWITZERLAND
(Neutral)

Bay
of
Biscay

■ Limoges
□ Poulousat

Clermont-Ferrand

Lyons

Périgueux

Grenoble

Chambon

ITALY
(Occupied
by Germany)

N

Areas of Jewish Partisan
Activity

General Area of Jewish
Partisan Activity

□ "Jewish Army"

■ Jewish Partisans and
Jewish Units of the
Resistance

Toulouse

Castres

Nice

Marseilles

SPAIN
(Neutral)

Corsica

Jews was the mode of death. Consequently the term *resistance* loses its usual sense in the Jewish context and becomes broader, including all possible modes of defying German decisions regarding the fate of the Jews. This definition, as suggested by Yehuda Bauer, takes in a spectrum of activities from armed resistance to steps to preserve one's dignity in spite of the German intentions. Most activities covered by this definition were sporadic, personal, and unchronicled. There is substantial evidence, however, of the resistance activities of Jews in Jewish and general organizations.

The general resistance in Western Europe was not tainted with antisemitism and readily accepted Jews into its ranks. The German authorities in the West tailored their policies to serve their particular needs in various areas, including different tactics in regard to the Final Solution. This versatility elicited different Jewish responses and various means of Jewish resistance. In the main, the Jewish resisters either concentrated on anti-German activities, both within general movements and within ethnically Jewish organizations, or dedicated themselves to rescue operations. A Jewish resister's choice of movement was a reflection of his or her ideology, the availability of organizations, and local conditions. The mode of operation was usually a response to the local German policy.

Denmark. Jewish participation in the Danish resistance is an excellent example of the fluidity of accepted terms dealing with Jewish resistance—*active resistance,* describing armed actions, and *passive resistance,* denoting the struggle for survival and rescue operations. Denmark, in addition to having a native Jewish community, became a shelter in the prewar years for German Jewish refugees, including young people organized in the Zionist Hehalutz movement. In 1941 one group of Zionist youth decided to find escape routes to Palestine, an endeavor that failed except in a few instances. In 1942 the remainder of the group started to look for contacts with Danish resistance. The only organization they encountered was a minor and marginal Communist resistance movement that had been organized in the summer of 1942. The Communists, including the Jewish resisters, performed acts of sabotage, attacked weapon storage sites, and shot at German officers and soldiers.

The Danish mass resistance movement appeared only after August 1943, when the Germans had dismissed the Danish government, and it included large segments of official Denmark. The German decision to round up the Danish Jews for transfer to the East spurred the resistance to bring about their rescue. The Jewish resisters, having learned about the rescue operation, joined the general resistance in its efforts. At that time they were the only link between the general and the Communist resistance movements, and the Communists turned to the Jewish resisters to help smuggle some of their members out of Denmark and into Sweden camouflaged as Jews. The history of this Jewish resistance group shows that the mode of resistance was influenced by the organization to which it belonged and, more important, to shifts in German policies. Although the great majority of the 7,000 Danish Jews were rescued to Sweden, many Jewish resistants ended up in German concentration camps.

Netherlands. As in Denmark, on the eve of the war the Jewish population of the Netherlands was augmented by a large influx of German Jewish refugees (including many Hehalutz groups). After the German conquest of the country, the two segments of the Jewish population chose different paths in response to the Nazi plans for implementing the Final Solution. The refugees, who regarded the Netherlands as temporary shelter, tried to save themselves by escaping or hiding. The Hehalutz rescue operations, which concentrated on efforts to map routes of communication from the Netherlands through German-occupied Europe to Switzerland or Spain, should be seen in the context.

The Dutch Jews found it almost impossible to organize themselves outside the boundaries of Dutch society, into which they had been integrated. The German-appointed *Joodsche Raad* (Jewish council) was perceived by many Dutch Jews as an artificial institution; in spite of its role in the deportations to the East, Jewish resisters took no steps against its policies. Following the Dutch Jewish tradition, these Jews preferred to join the Dutch rather than the Jewish resistance. Because of the predominance of the proletarian elements in Jewish society and their long involvement in workers' parties, the Jewish resisters joined mainly left-wing resistance groups. Another factor in this choice were anti-Jewish activities of the Dutch fascists (Mussert). The relative strength of collaborators and the lack of a coherent Jewish resistance policy figured in the enormous Jewish losses in the Netherlands—the highest attrition rate in Western Europe.

Belgium. The Jewish community in Belgium and its response to the Nazi persecutions were molded by a number of special circumstances. More than 90 percent of the Jews in Belgium at the time of the German invasion had arrived there after World War I, mainly from Eastern Europe. They had brought with them Eastern European habits, attitudes, and political affiliations. Their character as immigrants was illustrated by the mass escape of the Jewish community to France in May 1940. After the war about half of the community returned to Belgium. The Germans did not understand the structure of the Belgian Jewish community, and when in November 1941 they nominated the Judenrat (Association des Juifs en Belgique, AJB), it was composed of local Jews who were estranged from the immigrants. The AJB had almost no influence on decisions taken by the Jews and was perceived by them as a tool of the Germans. The traditional distrust among Eastern European Jews of any official state institutions also eased the passage into illegal, clandestine organizations, which evolved into resistance.

Jewish resistance in Belgium was rooted in the less assimilated character of Belgian Jewry; it was based in the main on two Jewish parties transplanted from the East: the Jewish Communists and the leftist Poale Zion. Toward the end of 1941 these two parties affiliated themselves with the National Front of Belgian Independence (Front d'Indépendance, FI) and established the National Committee for the Defense of the Jews. Although the FI was a broad coalition of Communists, Catholics, and everyone in between, in its attitude toward the Jewish resisters it followed the Communists' tactics of organizing emigrants into national units while accepting local Jews into Belgian units. From the beginning the National Committee pursued two parallel goals: armed anti-German activity and rescue of the Jewish community. Often a single action served both goals. Following a policy more prevalent among the resistance in the East, the National Committee fought directly against the AJB. In July 1942 it destroyed the AJB offices, where the lists of deportees to the East were prepared. The raid did not stop the German plans, and in September 1942 deportations to the extermination camps began. In April 1943 a small team of Jewish resisters stopped a transport bound for Auschwitz and liberated its inmates. This armed rescue by the National Committee was among the most publicized operations of the FI.

In addition to armed activities, the National Committee supported nonviolent rescue operations. Following the Eastern European Jewish pattern, those operations were carried out by two social organizations connected with the aforementioned parties. The separate bodies later united within the framework of the

National Committee. Its social workers, mainly women acting under the auspices of the Belgian National Committee for the Child (ONE), rescued children—often on the verge of deportation—from various institutions and arranged hideouts with Belgian families. More than 3,000 Jewish children were saved in this way. The activity of Jewish resistance in Belgium contributed to the astonishing fact that about half of the Jewish community survived the war.

France. The diversification of the modes and goals of Jewish resistance in France reflected the borders of the July 1940 armistice that divided the country. The north was under German occupation; the south was ruled from Vichy by a French government beholden to Berlin; the region around Nice was annexed to Italy; and North Africa was nominally ruled from Vichy. Another factor that molded the Jewish resistance was the structure of French Jewry, which was composed of three almost equal parts: Jews born in France, naturalized Eastern European Jews, and stateless Jews from the East. The first victims of the German persecution were the stateless Jews, and therefore the Jewish response to the German policy started within that group.

In occupied France the turning point in the history of the Jewish resistance was the establishment of the detention camps for the young, stateless Jews and the subsequent internment of many left-wing activists, Communists, and Zionists. The Communist trade union of the foreign workers (Main d'Oeuvre Immigrée, or MOI), demanding a response from their party, was the first group on French soil to develop the ideology of resistance. After the German invasion of the Soviet Union, the French Communist party, obliged to fight the Germans but unable at this stage to organize its French members, turned to MOI to be its first fighting organization. MOI subdivided itself along linguistic lines, and its Yiddish section was one of the largest and most active units. MOI-Yiddish was composed not only of Communists but also of left-wing Zionists and anti-Zionist Bundists, a mix that shows the fluidity of political divisions. The ideology of MOI emphasized two points: that the Jews were paving the way to resistance for the French people and that the Jewish resistance was fighting for an "independent national existence." MOI opposed any cooperation with German-appointed institutions—especially the Union Générale des Israélites de France (UGIF),

the French Judenrat—and the wait-and-see policies of other Jewish parties. In the midst of massive deportations to Auschwitz in August 1942 the MOI began armed operations, which continued until the fall of 1943, when its leadership was captured by the Gestapo. The MOI activities paved the way for Jewish activities in general Communist units in occupied France. At the same time it opposed the formation of special Jewish units, not on an instrumental basis (such as language), but because Jewish units would answer particular Jewish needs. Therefore MOI opposed the Communist party policy of forming Jewish units in the south within the Communist FTP (Francs-Tireurs Partisans), similar to the Communist Jewish units organized nationally in the Union des Juifs pour la Résistance et l'Entraide (UJRE). Of all Jewish units, the UJRE had the largest military impact, including the liberation of several towns in the south.

In Vichy France the evolution of the Jewish resistance passed through three stages: legal social help for the stateless Jews and inmates of concentration camps for displaced Jews (until the summer of 1942); the establishment of underground sections within the legal framework (until the fall of 1943); and a full underground movement including acts of armed resistance (until the liberation of France). This process suggests a general model of the growth of the Jewish resistance movement within the womb of nonviolent conspiratorial organizations, a model linking nonviolent resistance to armed activity. The first stage centered on improving the conditions in the detention camps and arranging orphanages and schools for the children in those camps. Certain social-aid agencies preferred to act through the UGIF, especially the Oeuvre de Secours aux Enfants (Children's Aid, or OSE) and the Scouts. On the other hand the social aid agencies, La Colonie Scolaire (La Amelot) and the Communist Solidarity refused to have any contact with the UGIF. With the mass deportations of the summer of 1942 the legal activities turned into illegal ones. Since the removal of the children from the camps was decreed illegal, the OSE developed clandestine sections that took charge of this removal, finding hideouts for the children. At this stage a secret department of the Scouts took part in reduced missions. Some groups within the OSE and the Scouts were skeptical of the chances to hide large numbers of children in France, especially after the German occupation of the south, and started to smuggle them into Switzerland and Spain.

In their smuggling activities the leaders of the youth movements cooperated with a number of Zionist movements from Belgium, the Netherlands, and Luxembourg as well as with members of the Jewish Army (Armeé Juive, AJ) who were carrying out similar activities. The AJ, an organization with Zionist-Revisionist leanings, was established in 1940 and aimed to smuggle young Jews out of Europe through Spain in order to establish an armed force in Palestine. The shifting conditions in the south after the German occupation, together with new membership, changed the AJ's attitudes, if not its ideology. In 1943 the AJ united with the Scouts, and in 1944 it changed its name to Jewish Fighters Organization (OJC). The armed activities of the AJ were a natural outgrowth of the border-crossing and rescue operations, and its first steps were against German spies and informers, especially in the Nice region. Later the OJC enlisted its members into two formations: the Blue-White Battalion and the Marc Haguenau Company, under the command of the Gaullist Free French forces. The Blue-White Battalion fought in the ranks of Black Mountain Commando, while the Marc Haguenau Company participated in the capture of German armored trains and the liberation of the town of Castres.

In 1944 all Jewish resistance movements, Communist and non-Communist, established a united organization, the Comité Général de Défense (CGD). But old divisions remained; the Communists wanted to keep a leading role and the non-Communists tried to prevent money sent to the Jewish resistance in France by the American Joint Distribution Committee from falling into Communist hands. The internal relations, cooperation, and rifts in the CGD molded the Jewish community after the war and affected its relations with French society.

Algiers. If November 1942 was a starting point of large-scale Jewish resistance in France (except MOI), the same is true with regard to North Africa. In Algeria the operations of the Jewish resistance were an integral part of Allied war plans. After the German defeat at El Alamein the Allies planned to trap retreating German units by an attack from the south. As it was the first American action against the German army, success was essential. The Allied landing forces needed a harbor for supplies, and the only port in the war zone was Algiers, which had to be captured in one stroke, before the Germans could destroy the port. As many French

Algerians supported Vichy, the resistance turned to Jews, who provided 75 percent of the resisters. The Jewish resistance organization in Algiers disguised itself as a sports club attached to a Jewish high school. On 7 November, a day before the Allied assault on Algiers, small groups of insurgents attacked and occupied strategic points in the town. In spite of their numerical weakness, the insurgents, by capturing telephone exchanges and radio broadcast stations, impeded the Vichy forces and gained the Allies time. Isolated from the outside world, the Vichy commanders started negotiations with the Americans and surrendered Algiers on the evening of 7 November. The Algiers insurrection was a unique achievement of Jewish resisters.

As a social phenomenon the Jewish resistance was an expression of divisions between various waves of immigration and also of ideological rifts. The Jewish resistance in Western Europe differed from its counterpart in the East, where rescue operations were indistinguishable from armed activity, in that it developed gradually from social work to rescue operations and eventually to armed combat. After the war participation in the Jewish resistance became the mark of legitimacy for the new Jewish leadership. From the distance of 50 years the internal splits and discussions became blurred, and what stands in the foreground of the historical canvas is the united effort to save Jewish lives and to preserve human values.

Eli Tzur

Restitution   The battle for the return of Jewish property misappropriated during the Holocaust was prompted by the collapse of the Soviet Union and the fall of communism in Europe. But gradually, for a variety of reasons, the focus of public attention moved to Western Europe. From 1995 to 1998 the world media was flooded with information on stolen Jewish property in Western European countries that had been occupied by Nazi Germany and also in countries that had been neutral during World War II. Many European leaders and observers had thought that the year 1995, with ceremonies marking the 50th anniversary of the Allied victory, would lower the curtain on the war's horrors; but instead it reopened the issue of the fate of Jewish property and exposed the war record of many countries to intense scrutiny.

The World Jewish Restitution Organization (WJRO) was established in 1992 in order to coordinate action directed toward the restitution of Jewish property. Members of the WJRO include the World Jewish Congress, the Jewish Agency, B'nai B'rith, the American Jewish Joint Distribution Committee, the American Gathering of Jewish Holocaust Survivors, the Center of Organizations of Holocaust Survivors in Israel, the Conference of Jewish Material Claims Against Germany, the World Zionist Organization, Agudat Israel, and the European Jewish Congress. In the Communist countries, satellites of Moscow in Europe, Jewish property that had been confiscated by the Nazis was turned over to the state authorities and nationalized, in accordance with Communist doctrine. The collapse of communism signaled a change in the Eastern European countries to a capitalist market economy. Governments began to pass legislation that would clear the path for a gradual transfer of the means of production as well as ownership of capital and property into private hands. In this historic period the WJRO took on the mission of clarifying to heads of state and parliaments in Eastern Europe that the Jewish people had claims to some of the property that was now designated for privatization.

According to the WJRO charter, the World Jewish Congress (WJC) was given the responsibility for maintaining contact with the Jewish communities in Eastern Europe as well as for conducting negotiations with the governments. In November 1992 Edgar M. Bronfman, president of the WJC and chairman of the WJRO, signed a memorandum of understanding on behalf of the WJRO with the Israeli minister of finance, Avraham Shochat, recognizing the role of Israel as "a natural heir to Jewish communal and heirless property, together with the Jewish world." The cooperation and coordination with the Israeli government was reinforced in successive letters by Israeli prime ministers Yitzhak Rabin, Shimon Peres, and Binyamin Netanyahu.

Negotiations on Jewish property in Eastern Europe were difficult and complex. The economic troubles of the former Communist countries as well as their political instability were a burden to the process. In Poland, for example, frequent changes of government have forced the WJRO to restart negotiations with each new prime minister from scratch. In addition to the objective problems, governments exploit the natural opposition of the populace to the return of property, which sometimes takes on antisemitic overtones.

From the outset the WJRO's leadership was con-

cerned with securing international support for its activities in Eastern Europe. In Washington and in the European capitals diplomatic efforts laid the groundwork for including the issue of restitution of Jewish property in discussions aimed at integrating Eastern European countries into the European Union and the North Atlantic Treaty Organization (NATO). On 10 April 1995 U.S. congressional leaders sent a letter to Secretary of State Warren Christopher in support of the claims made by the WJRO. They complained about discriminatory laws in Eastern European countries pertaining to Jewish property and insisted that the United States make it clear to such countries that their actions on this issue would "be seen as a test of their respect for basic human rights and the rule of law and could have practical consequences on their relations with our country." Earlier that year President Bill Clinton had publicly expressed his support for the WJRO and had appointed Stuart Eizenstat, then U.S. representative to the European Union, as special envoy on property restitution in Central and Eastern Europe.

Legislative progress on restitution in most Eastern European countries was painfully slow and disappointing. Officials of the WJRO made it clear that because of the poor economic situation in the former Communist countries they did not expect the immediate return of Jewish assets and did not intend to evict present tenants from their apartments. They did insist, however, on legal recognition of Jewish ownership.

In Hungary a breakthrough was achieved through legislation that acknowledges the obligation according to the Paris peace treaty of 1947 to provide reasonable compensation to property owners dispossessed during the Holocaust period. In July 1996 the Hungarian government reached an agreement with the WJRO to establish a joint foundation, together with the Jewish community, to oversee the distribution of $26.5 million in compensation and restitution of property. This is a limited agreement at present, but the recognition of the principle of commitment to restitution of property was gained. Two years later, in October 1998, the Hungarian government established a fund that will provide an annual allocation of about $3 million in perpetuity.

In Poland a vast chasm exists between the declarations and pledges of the heads of government and their actual deeds. The legislative process is very slow and has been far from satisfactory. The value of the communal property that belonged to the more than 3 million Polish Jews who were murdered by the Nazis is estimated at hundreds of millions of dollars, not to mention private property worth several billions which only in very rare cases was returned to its owners or their heirs. In February 1997 the Polish parliament approved a bill on the restitution of property to religious communities. The law, however, refers only to active religious communities—the remnant of Polish Jewry numbers only a few thousand persons—and does not deal with private and heirless property.

The case of Bulgaria is somewhat unusual, since most Jewish property was given back immediately after the war but was then sequestered; it was returned again after 1989. There are, however, more than 100 buildings in Sofia that were not restored to their Jewish owners. Through the efforts of the WJRO, assets have been returned to the local communities, and these have improved communal life in the areas of education, social services, culture, and religion.

In Romania in September 1997 the government, together with the WJRO and the Jewish community, established a foundation to restitute Jewish communal property. By the end of 1998 more than 20 properties (out of thousands) were in the process of being transferred to the foundation. In the Czech Republic and in Slovakia the governments agreed to restitute properties to the Jewish communities, including the cemetery and the buildings housing the Jewish Museum in Prague, but many claims still await adjudication. In the rest of Eastern Europe very little progress has been made.

In the free societies of Western Europe the new revelations about Jewish property confiscation during the war touched a raw nerve. It had been clear that Nazi Germany could not have carried out its crimes without the enthusiastic collaboration of many persons of other nationalities, as well as the opportunism of greedy bystanders who took advantage of the distress of their Jewish neighbors.

About 30 national commissions were established between 1996 and 1998 to investigate how each country behaved during the war and how stolen Jewish property was dealt with after liberation. These commissions include government officials, historians, financial experts, and sometimes representatives of the local Jewish communities. Commissions were installed in the following countries: Argentina (commissions on Nazi gold, bank transfers, and refuge for war criminals), Austria, Belgium, Brazil, France (commissions on Jewish property, stolen art, and for Paris and Lyons), Italy, the Netherlands (commissions on Dutch gold, Jewish property, and stolen paintings), Norway, Portugal, Spain, Sweden, Switzerland (a Foreign Ministry inquiry, the Volcker Committee on dormant accounts in Swiss banks, and the international historic and legal research commission), the United Kingdom, and the United States. An international commission on insurance claims from the Holocaust period was established in September 1998 under the chairmanship of former U.S. secretary of state Lawrence Eagleburger.

These matters of property ownership and financial claims have forced nations to confront their responsibility for the exploitation and extortion of Jews as they were led to their deaths. As long as the issues at hand were war crimes committed in the camps—the selections, the medical experiments, the gas chambers—many Europeans reacted with shock, distress, and contempt for the German perpetrators and wrapped themselves in a cloak of reverence for human rights. It was convenient to focus the discussion about guilt on Nazi Germany, on Hitler and his accomplices, who brought destruction on most of the nations of Europe. Each nation created for itself a collective memory in which historical facts were mingled with myths, half-truths, and denials. The Austrians, for example, cultivated the myth of having been the first unwilling victim of Germany, which annexed Austria in 1938; the French invented an artificial distinction between the French regime at Vichy, which collaborated with the Germans, and the "authentic" French people and republic; and the Swiss succeeded in convincing themselves and others of their honorable model of neutrality.

The public auction in Austria in November 1996 of 8,000 artworks stolen from their Jewish owners by the Nazis has exposed once more the active role that the Austrian people played in the Nazi machinery of destruction. These treasures were returned to Austria by the U.S. Army in 1955 with explicit instructions to give them back to their rightful owners and heirs. The Austrians, however, hastened to store the spoils in the Mauerbach monastery in order to avoid confronting the terrible truth. Deep in the cellars of the monastery near Vienna, the city in which half a million citizens cheered Hitler in 1938, Austria attempted to bury its national memory and foster the myth of the victim. The auction followed the first public admissions from

Austrian chancellors early in the 1990s of Austria's guilt and responsibility, and by the end of 1998 Austria established a commission on property confiscated in the course of the Holocaust.

In France turmoil erupted in 1996 following revelations in Paris concerning property that had belonged to Jews transported to the death camps with the willing aid of the French collaborationist authorities. These and later disclosures that France still holds many artworks seized by the Nazi occupation forces and returned after the war raised further questions about the French people's behavior during the occupation. François Mitterrand, president of France from 1981 to 1995, found historical truth too hard to take and developed his own theory—that the Vichy government, which had collaborated with the Nazis, had not been representative of the "real" France, and that it was thus an injustice to attribute Vichy crimes to the French nation. In January 1997 the French prime minister, Alain Juppé, announced the appointment of a commission to examine the seizure of Jewish property by the Nazis and their Vichy French collaborators. In its February 1999 report the Matteoli Commission determined that $1 billion worth of Jewish property had been seized in France during the Holocaust and emphasized that the financial institutions had been eager to implement the antisemitic decrees even before they were asked to do so. According to the report, an estimated two-thirds of the confiscated property had been reclaimed, but many bank accounts, much real estate, and thousands of seized paintings had not been restituted.

Norway had also to face the ugly record of its pro-Nazi regime under Vidkun Quisling. While hundreds of Norwegian Jews were led to their deaths, and about 1,000 were helped to escape to neighboring Sweden, a "Liquidation Committee" headed by a supreme court judge took over Jewish property and businesses. After the war some of the appropriators "forgot" to return the property to the survivors and heirs. After calls by the public and a few members of parliament for the removal of this "black stain" on Norway's past, a committee of experts, including nominees of the Jewish community, was established in March 1996. Norway was the first country to appoint a commission of inquiry of this kind and the first to submit a report. The way its government, parliament, and public dealt with the issue emphasized the sense of historic responsibility as well as the declared decision to reach a moral settlement with the Jewish community. In June 1998 the Norwegian government published a white paper on the subject and explained why it rejected the commission's majority report, which did not take into consideration the moral responsibility for the collective suffering of the Jews because of their race and religion. The moral approach of the Norwegian government was reflected in its decision to grant a $60 million package of economic compensation to Holocaust survivors in Norway, to the Jewish community (for its social and educational budget), and to various projects promoting tolerance and preserving the Jewish heritage. Because Norway has a small Jewish community of 1,200 people, this compensation arrangement established a high standard of moral and material restitution.

More than any other restitution issue, the case of the Swiss banks dominated the international media beginning in 1995. Switzerland's reputation as a neutral safe-haven during World War II was badly tarnished by reports on its wartime transactions with Germany. What began as an examination of the dormant bank accounts of Jewish Holocaust victims expanded to include the gamut of Swiss financial dealings with the Nazis.

Switzerland served as a repository for capital that Jews transferred or smuggled out of Nazi Germany and the states threatened by it, and also for vast quantities of gold and other valuables later plundered from Jews and others all over Europe. Right up until the end of the war Switzerland laundered hundreds of millions of dollars in stolen assets, including gold taken from the central banks of German-occupied Europe. After the war Switzerland resisted Allied calls to restore these funds, and in the Washington Agreement of 1946 the Allies contented themselves with restoration of a mere 12 percent of the stolen gold. Holocaust survivors and the heirs of those who perished met a wall of bureaucracy, and only a handful managed to reclaim their assets. As it turns out, some of the dormant accounts were taken by the Swiss authorities to satisfy claims of Swiss nationals whose property was seized by Communist regimes in Eastern and Central Europe.

In the mid-1990s international pressure steadily mounted on the Swiss to allow a transparent audit and investigation. Alfonse D'Amato, chairman of the U.S. Senate Banking Committee, spearheaded efforts to force the Swiss to restitute property and called for the

Washington Agreement to be renegotiated. In May 1996 the Swiss Bankers' Association signed an agreement with the WJC and the WJRO to establish the Independent Committee of Eminent Persons, under chairman Paul Volcker, former head of the U.S. Federal Reserve, to carry out a thorough audit in order to identify and recover dormant accounts. Switzerland and the United States have also established special committees to investigate the fate of plundered Jewish and other property that was secreted in Switzerland.

In December 1996 Swiss president Pascal Delamurez used an antisemitic stereotype when he accused the WJRO of "Jewish extortion"; he later apologized for the remark. The Swiss ambassador to Washington had to resign early in 1997 after the revelation of a cable to Bern in which he suggested that the Swiss "declare war" on Jewish organizations. Under the heat of international criticism the Swiss political and judicial system blundered again in its treatment of the security guard, Christopher Meili, who found that the Union Bank of Switzerland in Zurich was shredding documents on aryanized property, a practice which violated the Swiss Federal Act of December 1996. Meili, who was promptly dismissed and sent for police investigation, received threats to his life and finally received asylum as a refugee in the United States.

After additional public pressure the Swiss government, with the cooperation of the banks, announced in February 1997 the establishment of a $180 million humanitarian fund for Holocaust survivors. In March 1997 the president of Switzerland, Arnold Koller, announced in parliament the establishment of a "solidarity fund" to help victims of "poverty and catastrophes, genocide and other severe breaches of human rights, such as of course victims of the Holocaust." The money will come from the central bank, which will invest $5–$7 billion to create interest of several hundred million dollars a year for the fund. The fate of this fund is unclear, and it seems that the main purpose of the announcement was to preempt sharp criticism in the American report on Swiss wartime behavior. The Swiss government and press were outraged when the American special envoy, Stuart Eizenstat, suggested in his May 1997 report that the role of the Swiss in buying and laundering Nazi looted gold made them guilty of having prolonged the war.

A careful reading of documents published at the end of the 1990s from war archives of the Allies shows the justice in the belated outrage against Switzerland. As early as 1943 such leaders as U.S. president Franklin Roosevelt, British foreign secretary Anthony Eden, and Gen. Dwight Eisenhower, commander of the Allied Forces in Europe, had accused Switzerland of obstructing the Allied war effort by supplying the Germans with matériel and hard currency. Sanctions against Switzerland were considered in 1944–45 in series of working meetings, letters, and memorandums exchanged by the American and British governments. The Swiss continued to supply war matériel to the Nazis even when the defeat of Germany was a foregone conclusion.

From 1944 to 1947 the Swiss succeeded in misleading Allied negotiators and exploiting their internal differences in postwar negotiations. They disregarded their own commitments in the negotiations, and, as stated in the Eizenstat report, because of policy failure and the changing priorities of the Cold War, Washington failed to impose implementation of the agreements with neutrals.

In the late 1990s the Swiss were reluctant to accept responsibility for the behavior of their government and banks during and after the war. The $1.25 billion settlement reached in August 1998 between the Swiss banks, lawyers representing Holocaust survivors, and the WJRO was not welcomed in Switzerland, and even leading government officials called it a search for money and not a search for the truth.

Nazi gold found its way, mostly through Switzerland, to other neutral countries such as Sweden, Portugal, and Spain. In Sweden the issue received extensive coverage early in 1997. In addition to revelations about dealings with Nazi Germany, it included information on the Wallenberg family, which is still in control of a significant share of the Swedish economy. Raoul Wallenberg, a Swedish Christian who saved thousands of Hungarian Jews in the Holocaust, had two uncles, Jacob and Marcus Wallenberg, who according to U.S. intelligence reports had financial relations with the Nazis during the war and violated the economic boycott of Germany. In March 1997 the government of Sweden, together with the Jewish community and the WJRO, established a committee of experts to examine the issue. Swedish prime minister Goeran Persson launched a major education project on Holocaust studies in Swedish schools, which was extended in 1998 to an international experiment together with other governments.

There are several reasons for the 50-year delay in the pressing of Jewish property claims. The immediate postwar period was characterized by Jewish power-lessness, particularly in Europe. Jewish diplomacy concentrated on rescue efforts and on lobbying for the establishment of the state of Israel. In some places in Eastern Europe, where Holocaust survivors returned to their homes, they were met with violence and even pogroms as they attempted to reclaim their rightful property.

Perhaps the most significant factor in the conspiracy of silence surrounding the issue of Jewish property, bank accounts, and Nazi gold transfers is related to the Cold War atmosphere that dominated Western strategy and foreign policy after World War II. The United States sought to foster the political stability and economic rehabilitation of democracies in Europe. Hence it had little interest in promoting Jewish claims that might deprive Western nations of financial resources and expose them to accusations of improprieties. In some measure this development explains American acquiescence to the failure of some European countries to comply with economic commitments laid out in the peace agreements.

During the Cold War the West had a clear enemy, and it did not engage in self-examination. The United States, which was engaged in a major effort to strengthen its allies, did not want to articulate the serious accusations documented in its war archives on stolen Jewish property and plundered Nazi gold. Operation Safe Haven, initiated at the end of the war by American intelligence in order to recover assets seized by Germany and sent to Switzerland and other neutral states, was never implemented. Among the most shocking revelations of the post–Cold War era is that more than 50 years after the war both the United States and the United Kingdom still retained looted gold that had been recovered in Germany. The Tripartite Gold Commission, which was established in September 1946 to disburse the gold, was dissolved only in September 1998, an anachronistic reminder of the failure to act on restitution.

The collapse of communism in the late 1980s coincided with the opening of state archives, the readiness of some people to confess wrongdoing, and growing public awareness of the crimes committed by non-Germans in the Holocaust. This trend was reflected in media coverage of Holocaust-related issues, interest in movies and television programs on the Holocaust, and the opening of new museums, particularly the United States Holocaust Memorial Museum in Washington, D.C.

Aside from government-appointed commissions there were few landmarks in this unusual process of reevaluating history. In September 1996, following public pressure, the British Foreign Office published an official report on Nazi gold and Allied dealings with Nazi loot after the war. Although it did not admit to a British conspiracy, it pointed out Britain's responsibility for the delays and obstacles "that stood between the Nazis victims or their representatives and the money plundered from them to fund Hitler's war machine." The British report, released by Foreign Secretary Malcolm Rifkind, highlighted the refusal of Switzerland to return more than a fraction of the booty hidden in its banks. The report's revelation that the Swiss had also appropriated "nonmonetary" gold—that is, gold yanked from victims' fingers and teeth—amplified international pressure on Switzerland to act.

In the United States the Clinton administration took upon itself a far-reaching examination of American behavior with respect to stolen assets from World War II, as well as that of other countries. Eleven federal agencies combed through millions of archival documents in search of new evidence. Their findings were released by the special envoy, Stuart Eizenstat, in May 1997 in a report prepared by a team of State Department historians led by William Slany. The Eizenstat report mentions the lack of American leadership to enforce the implementation of restitution agreements and criticizes the Truman administration for unfreezing Swiss assets in the United States before Switzerland had met its obligations. In addition, it emphasized the damaging role of Switzerland and other neutrals

"Nonmonetary gold"—wedding bands.

that profited from their trading links with Nazi Germany. In June 1998 the Slany team published its second report, which focused on the postwar negotiations regarding looted gold and other assets.

In December 1997 the British Foreign Office invited more than 40 governments to the London Conference on Nazi Gold. The aim of the conference was to gather information on gold taken by the Nazis from the occupied countries and from individuals and to review what had already been done and what else should be done to compensate the victims. In December 1998 the Americans hosted a follow-up conference involving 50 countries and, as in London, several Jewish delegations. The meeting, opened by Secretary of State Madeleine Albright, addressed a broadened agenda, which included reports on the implementation of the restitution process in various countries. Special sessions and resolutions were devoted to art looted by the Nazis and to insurance claims. Just before the conference the White House announced the formation of the Presidential Advisory Commission on Holocaust Assets, chaired by Edgar M. Bronfman, president of the World Jewish Congress. The commission's mandate was to investigate the fate of Holocaust assets that found their way to the United States between 1933 and 1945. In October 1999 the commission published an interim report, which dealt with the seizure of painting and other valuables in Hungary by U.S. Army troops in May 1945. The report raised "troubling findings" concerning the way that recovered property that had been stolen from Jews by the Nazis was handled and the lack of response to Jewish groups immediately after the war.

The reevaluation of the historical record on restitution in much of Europe and the Americas, involving government officials, intellectuals, journalists, and historians, created shock waves in international public opinion. In many nations the disclosures concerning property theft triggered a broad reappraisal of their behavior during World War II and encouraged soul-searching with respect to their response to the Holocaust. See also REPARATIONS, GERMAN   *Avi Beker*

Revisionism See HOLOCAUST DENIAL

Rhineland Bastards See MISCHLINGE

Riegner Telegram In the last days of July 1942 the first authentic news report from German sources regarding the Nazi plans for the complete annihilation of European Jewry reached Switzerland. A major German industrialist having access to the highest Nazi authorities came to Zurich and reported that a plan was being discussed in the headquarters of Adolf Hitler to deport all the Jews of Europe—between 3.5 million and 4 million—to the East and to murder them there. The plan for the physical elimination of the Jews was to be executed by the end of 1942. The method of killing was still being debated. There was talk of using prussic acid. (Indeed, prussic or hydrocyanic acid is the poison in Zyklon B, the agent eventually chosen for use in the gas chambers.) Mention also had been made of gigantic crematoriums, in which all the European Jews, after transfer to camps in the East, would go up in flames.

The German industrialist recounted his story to a business friend in Zurich whom he visited from time to time, and asked him to warn the Jews and the Allies. This friend, Isidor Koppelmann, who worked for the Rosenstein banking and real estate concern, knew the press secretary of the Swiss Federation of Jewish Communities, Benjamin Sagalowitz, and informed him immediately. Sagalowitz, aware that the news had implications far beyond Switzerland, immediately telephoned Gerhart M. Riegner, the director of the Geneva office of the World Jewish Congress (WJC), with whom he was in constant touch, and suggested an early meeting.

The industrialist in question, whose identity was kept secret for several decades, was Eduard Schulte. He was the managing director of one of the largest German mining companies, the Bergwerksgesellschaft Georg von Giesche's Erben, with headquarters in Breslau, which employed about 30,000 workers for the war effort.

Sagalowitz met Riegner in Lausanne on 1 August and told him in detail the story he had heard from Koppelmann. They discussed the report for several hours. It seemed incredible: Was it possible to kill millions of people in cold blood? How reliable was the German source? Was the report perhaps a provocation? In spy-ridden Switzerland, such a possibility could not be excluded. But the more they talked, the more probable the report appeared to them. It was not the first news they had received of the terrible fate of the Jews in Eastern Europe. The Geneva office of the WJC, which systematically followed the developments of Nazi policy concerning the Jews, was aware of the terrible massacres of Jews that had taken place on the

Eastern front since the Nazi attack on the Soviet Union in June 1941. Riegner had already reported to the New York headquarters in October 1941 the details of those massacres and had stated that if the Nazi policy continued, not many Jews would survive the war. Together with Richard Lichtheim, the Geneva representative of the Jewish Agency, Riegner had described in great detail to the apostolic nuncio in Bern in March 1942 the terrible persecutions of Jews throughout Europe and had appealed to the Vatican to exercise its influence, at least in the Catholic countries, to put a stop to that process.

What distinguished the Schulte report from all other reports they had seen was that it had originated not with the Jewish victims but from a German who had access to the highest authorities. Moreover, it revealed that behind the various aspects of the persecutions—arrests, deportations, ghettoization, reduced food rations, imprisonment, forced labor, summary executions—was a scheme of total annihilation decided on at the highest levels of the state.

Three factors convinced Riegner and Sagalowitz of the truth of the report. First, on several occasions Hitler had publicly threatened to destroy the Jews. In his speeches made on the anniversary of the Nazi seizure of power (30 January) in 1939, 1941, and 1942 he had warned: "This war will terminate in the destruction of the Jewish people in Europe." The warnings in Hitler's *Mein Kampf* (1925) had not been taken seriously. Did that mistake need to be repeated?

Second, only two weeks before Schulte had confided in his Zurich friend, a sudden wave of arrests had taken place on 14–15 July 1942 throughout Western Europe. In Amsterdam, Brussels, Antwerp, Paris, Lyons, and Marseilles tens of thousands of Jews had been arrested and prepared for deportation to the East. News about deportations from Berlin, Vienna, Prague, and other localities in Eastern and Central Europe had been known for a long time. But the swift and massive round-up of Jews in Western Europe had taken observers in Switzerland by surprise. Schulte's report made sense of it.

Third, Riegner's own experience in Germany before he left that country persuaded him that the Nazis were capable of such deeds. Their brutality and fanaticism were well known to him. He had seen them on the streets, on the day they seized power in January 1933, on the day in April 1933 when the boycott of Jewish businesses went into effect, and on other occasions. He

had been involved in the student elections in Freiburg and Heidelberg in which the republican students had confronted the terror tactics of the Nazi students.

Riegner was fully aware of the enormous responsibility that rested on him. Should he transmit the report to his superiors? He decided to have another meeting with Koppelmann. Riegner wanted to hear the report directly from Koppelmann's lips and to ask some questions about the source. He would then consult Paul Guggenheim, a professor of law at the Graduate Institute of International Studies and a legal adviser of the WJC in Geneva.

Two days later Riegner and Sagalowitz met Koppelmann in his office in Zurich. Koppelmann repeated the story, and although he did not disclose the name of the source, he gave some details about the German industrialist's position, their relationship, and their previous encounters. The source, he stated, was a firm anti-Nazi. His information had been correct in the past. He had predicted, several weeks in advance, the exact date of the German aggression against the Soviet Union. There was no doubt that he had access to very high-ranking figures in the Nazi regime.

Upon his return to Geneva, Riegner wrote Guggenheim a detailed report on the Schulte message and on the conversation with Koppelmann. He indicated that he intended to inform the American and British consuls in Geneva of the news. Guggenheim agreed in principle with Riegner's plan of action. He advised him, however, to moderate certain expressions and to introduce certain reservations in the draft telegram Riegner intended to send to the WJC in New York and London. Referring to these reservations, certain historians have later stated that Riegner himself did not believe the German industrialist's story. This is not correct, as is shown by the testimony of the American vice-consul, Howard Elting, Jr. The prudent formulation suggested by Guggenheim did not alter the sense of the telegram.

On 8 August, Riegner went to the American consulate in Geneva. The consul, Paul C. Squire, whom Riegner had met socially once or twice at Guggenheim's home, was on vacation, so he was received by Vice-Consul Elting. Riegner had a long conversation with Elting and asked him to inform his government of the German industrialist's report. He also asked that the U.S. Secret Service check the information and that the consulate transmit a telegram outlining the report through official channels to the president of the

World Jewish Congress, Rabbi Stephen S. Wise, in New York. In their long conversation Riegner gave the reasons why he felt that the German's information was sound. Elting agreed. In his report to the American legation in Bern accompanying the proposed telegram to Wise, Elting stated: "My personal opinion is that Riegner is a serious and balanced individual and that he would never have come to the Consulate if he had not had confidence in his informant's reliability and if he did not seriously consider that the report may well contain an element of truth. Again, it is my opinion that the report should be passed on to the Department of State."

The draft telegram was accepted by the American legation in Bern and transmitted to the State Department in Washington, although the American minister in Bern had grave doubts about its content.

The text of Riegner's telegram read as follows:

RECEIVED ALARMING REPORT THAT IN FUHRER'S HEADQUARTERS PLAN DISCUSSED AND UNDER CONSIDERATION ACCORDING TO WHICH ALL JEWS IN COUNTRIES OCCUPIED OR CONTROLLED BY GERMANY NUMBERING THREE AND A HALF FOUR MILLION SHOULD AFTER DEPORTATION AND CONCENTRATION IN EAST BE EXTERMINATED AT ONE BLOW TO RESOLVE ONCE AND FOR ALL THE JEWISH QUESTION IN EUROPE STOP ACTION REPORTED PLANNED FOR AUTUMN METHODS UNDER DISCUSSION INCLUDING PRUSSIC ACID STOP WE TRANSMIT INFORMATION WITH ALL NECESSARY RESERVATION AS EXACTITUDE CANNOT BE CONFIRMED STOP INFORMANT STATED TO HAVE CLOSE CONNECTIONS WITH HIGHEST GERMAN AUTHORITIES AND HIS REPORTS GENERALLY SPEAKING RELIABLE.

On the same day Riegner went to the British consulate in Geneva. As at the American consulate, the consul, H. B. Livingston, whom Riegner knew quite well, was on vacation, and he was received by Vice-Consul Armstrong. The draft telegram he submitted to the vice-consul for transmission was addressed to Sidney (Samuel) Silverman, a well-known member of Parliament and chairman of the British section of the WJC. The text was identical to that addressed to Wise, but it ended with these words: "Please inform and consult New York." This indicates that Riegner was not sure that his message would reach Wise through the Americans and that he had more confidence that the British parliamentary system would deliver the cable to one of its members. The message was transmitted through the British legation in Bern to the Foreign Office in London on 10 August.

No one in Washington or London believed the news. The State Department refused to deliver the message to Wise, owing to "the apparently unsubstantiated character of the information which forms its main theme." Consul Squire informed Riegner of the refusal in a letter dated 24 August. He added, however, that if corroboratory information came to Riegner's attention, he should advise the consul and further consideration would be accorded the matter immediately.

The officials of the British Foreign Office were as skeptical and disinclined to act as their Washington colleagues. In the first 10 days after having received the message from Bern they did not undertake any serious investigation. One of the officials wrote as a comment, "Wild rumors born out of Jewish fears." The undersecretary of state for foreign affairs asked for background information on Riegner, but the Refugee Department knew nothing. Finally, unlike the U.S. State Department, the Foreign Office transmitted the message to its addressee. Immediately upon receiving it, Silverman wanted to telephone Wise, but permission was not granted. He was, however, allowed to send the message to Wise through the War Department.

Wise received the telegram on 28 August, and on 2 September he got in touch with the undersecretary of state, Sumner Welles. In their conversation Welles asked Wise not to publicize the Riegner telegram until it could be confirmed by the Vatican or the International Red Cross. Wise agreed.

Wise was deeply troubled by the Geneva report. He wrote a short letter to Supreme Court justice Felix Frankfurter, who had long been active in the American Jewish community, in which he described the report and asked that Frankfurter inform the "chief," meaning the president, not the chief justice. He also wrote a long, desperate letter to his close friend, the Unitarian pastor John Haynes Holmes, with whom he shared the terrible news. At the same time he contacted the Protestant clergyman Samuel McCrea Cavert, general secretary of the North American Council of Churches, on the eve of Cavert's trip to the provisional headquarters of the World Council of Churches in Geneva, and asked him to find out whether deportation really meant extermination. The reports that had reached the State Department had apparently stated that deported Jews would, like Poles and Russian prisoners, be put to work on behalf of the German war machine. Upon his arrival in Geneva, Cavert got in touch with Guggenheim and Riegner and learned that on the basis of the information available to them, there was no doubt that the Jews were to be murdered. Wise was immediately informed.

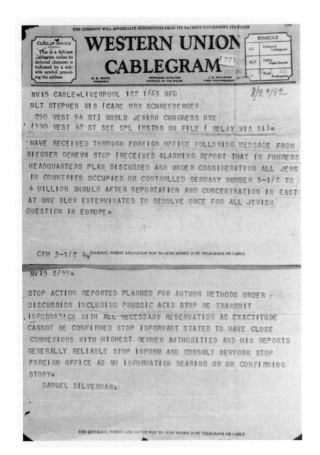

THE COMPANY WILL APPRECIATE SUGGESTIONS FROM ITS PATRONS CONCERNING ITS SERVICE

WESTERN UNION
CABLEGRAM

This is a full-rate Cablegram unless its deferred character is indicated by a suitable symbol preceding the address.

SYMBOLS

R. B. WHITE PRESIDENT   NEWCOMB CARLTON CHAIRMAN OF THE BOARD   J. C. WILLEVER FIRST VICE-PRESIDENT

NV15 CABLE=LIVERPOOL 122 1/63 NFD   8/2 9/92
NLT STEPHEN WIS (CARE MRS SCHNEEBERGER
250 WEST 94 ST) WORLD JEWISH CONGRESS NYK
(330 WEST 42 ST SEE SPL INSTNS ON FILE (RELAY VIA SI)=

HAVE RECEIVED THROUGH FOREIGN OFFICE FOLLOWING MESSAGE FROM
RIEGNER GENEVA STOP (RECEIVED ALARMING REPORT THAT IN FUHRERS
HEADQUARTERS PLAN DISCUSSED AND UNDER CONSIDERATION ALL JEWS
IN COUNTRIES OCCUPIED OR CONTROLLED GERMANY NUMBER 3-1/2 TO
4 MILLION SHOULD AFTER DEPORTATION AND CONCENTRATION IN EAST
AT ONE BLOW EXTERMINATED TO RESOLVE ONCE FOR ALL JEWISH
QUESTION IN EUROPE =

CFM 3-1/2 4   QUICKEST, SUREST AND SAFEST WAY TO SEND MONEY IS BY TELEGRAPH OR CABLE

NV15 2/59=

STOP ACTION REPORTED PLANNED FOR AUTUMN METHODS UNDER
DISCUSSION INCLUDING PRUSSIC ACID STOP WE TRANSMIT
INFORMATION WITH ALL NECESSARY RESERVATION AS EXACTITUDE
CANNOT BE CONFIRMED STOP INFORMANT STATED TO HAVE CLOSE
CONNEXIONS WITH HIGHEST GERMEN AUTHORITIES AND HIS REPORTS
GENERALLY RELIABLE STOP INFORM AND CONSULT NEWYORK STOP
FOREIGN OFFICE AS NO INFORMATION BEARING ON OR CONFIRMING
STORY=
        SAMUEL SILVERMAN.

THE QUICKEST, SUREST AND SAFEST WAY TO SEND MONEY IS BY TELEGRAPH OR CABLE

Cablegram from Sidney (Samuel) Silverman to Rabbi Stephen Wise of the World Jewish Congress on behalf of Gerhart Riegner. August 1942

On 5 September Wise convened a confidential meeting of representatives of some of the major Jewish organizations in New York. They discussed the news from Geneva and an Agudat Israel report stating that already 10,000 Jews in Poland had been killed.

The replies from the Vatican and the International Red Cross did not shed light on the situation. The Vatican's note said that reports of severe measures against the Jews had also reached them but that it had not been possible to verify their accuracy. The reply from the International Red Cross was along similar lines.

In the meantime, more information was reaching Switzerland. Koppelmann had informed Sagalowitz and Riegner that he had received a further report according to which the order to exterminate European Jews had been proposed by Herbert Backe, the Nazi commissar for food, and that his plan had been opposed by Hans Frank, head of the Generalgouvernement in Poland, who needed the Jews as laborers for the German war effort. It seems that this doubtful report did not originate with Schulte. But one aspect of Koppelmann's new report convinced Riegner and Sagalowitz that at least this part of his information came from Schulte. On his first visit to Switzerland the German industrialist had spoken of a plan of total extermination that was still under discussion; he now reported, six weeks later, that he was sure that the plan had been put into action. This confirmed the reports that had reached Geneva from many other sources.

Riegner was glad to learn during the second half of August that his report had been received in London and was now at the disposal of the Allied governments. The London leaders of the WJC had indeed informed all the governments to which they had access of the German report. Riegner waited with great impatience for some Allied reaction. He felt more and more that there was no doubt about the veracity of the report, and he doubled his efforts to obtain confirmation of the report by other testimonies. He was quite successful in receiving additional information from various sources during the months of August and September, and he made some of this new information available to the American consul in Geneva.

First, Riegner obtained copies of two letters from Warsaw, written from outside the ghetto to E. Sternbuch, head of an Orthodox Jewish relief organization in St. Gallen, Switzerland, reporting in somewhat veiled language the daily deportation of 6,000 Jews from Warsaw to the Treblinka camp, where there was absolute certainty that Jews were being murdered.

He then received a report from a young Jew, Gabriel Zivian, who had fled from Riga, Latvia, and eventually made his way to relatives in Switzerland. He vividly described the fate of the approximately 30,000 Riga Jews, who on 30 November and 7–9 December 1941 had been taken out of the city, shot, and buried in ditches. Among them was the famous historian of the Jewish people Simon Dubnow.

Next he produced an amazing report from a young Polish mechanic by the name of Isaac Lieber, who had been arrested in Antwerp in the middle of July and deported to the East. There Lieber became a chauffeur to a young German officer stationed near Stalingrad. The officer, who was tired of the war and had already lost two brothers, decided to save this Jew, and he hid him in a train transport all the way from the Russian front to the Gare de l'Est in Paris, whence the young man escaped to Switzerland. In his report Lieber described his conversations with the German officer, whom he questioned thoroughly about the fate of those who had been deported with him. The officer summed up the entire plan for extermination in three sentences: "Those who can be used for work—mainly building fortifications on the eastern front—will be employed. Those who are not fit for work will be murdered. Those who prove no longer fit for work will also be murdered."

The most important confirmation, however, came from the vice-president of the International Committee of the Red Cross, Carl J. Burckhardt, a colleague of Guggenheim's at the Graduate Institute in Geneva. Riegner also knew him, having studied at the institute for several years. After having received the news of the Final Solution, Guggenheim and Riegner decided at the beginning of September to ask Burckhardt whether the Red Cross had any information about these tragic events. Guggenheim put the question to Burckhardt in a private conversation at the institute. Burckhardt stated that he had confirmation of Hitler's order "to make Germany *Judenfrei* [free of Jews]" from two different sources, officials at the German Ministries of Foreign Affairs and of War. Moreover, he also stated that having made a number of personal interventions in individual cases with the German consulate general in Geneva, he had been advised in the beginning of September by a consular official to intervene no longer in such cases, as such pleas were futile.

In the meantime Washington had received other reports on the situation, and after a new conversation between Welles and Wise, the State Department asked Riegner and Lichtheim to submit their whole file to the U.S. minister in Bern, Leland Harrison. The two Jewish representatives came to the Bern legation on 22 October and presented Harrison with about 30 pages of documents. These included a short memorandum; a note on the German policy of deliberate annihilation of European Jewry country by country; the letters from Warsaw; and the Zivian and Lieber reports. Harrison read the documents twice in their presence and asked a number of questions. In the course of the conversation Riegner gave Harrison a closed envelope containing the name of the German industrialist, which he had received from Sagalowitz. (It was the only time that he ever revealed Schulte's identity.) He also conveyed to Harrison the confidential information that Guggenheim had received from Burckhardt. Harrison

gave Paul Squire at the Geneva consulate the task of obtaining sworn statements from those persons who had supplied the information to Riegner and Lichtheim. He also asked Squire to approach Burckhardt directly and to check Riegner's report to the legation. Squire met Burckhardt on 7 November and reported on their conversation in a letter and memorandum to Harrison. Burckhardt's statements were indeed identical with those he had made to Guggenheim. It is all the more astonishing that Burckhardt never shared this knowledge with his colleagues on the International Committee of the Red Cross.

When all this material reached Washington, Sumner Welles cabled Stephen Wise and asked him to come at once to the State Department. "I hold in my hands," he said, "documents which have come to me from our Legation in Bern. I regret to tell you, Dr. Wise, that these confirm and justify your deepest fears." The press embargo was lifted at the same time.

On 17 December 1942, more than four months after Riegner had first brought Schulte's report to American and British officials in Geneva, the Allied governments published simultaneously in Washington, London, and Moscow a statement regarding the implementation of the Final Solution. It said that the Allies had been presented with "reports which left no room for doubt that the German authorities . . . are carrying into effect Hitler's oft-repeated intention to exterminate the Jewish people in Europe."

> From all the occupied countries, Jews are being transported in conditions of appalling horror and brutality to Eastern Europe.
> In Poland, which has been made the principal Nazi slaughterhouse, the ghettos established by the German invaders are being systematically emptied of all Jews. . . .
> None of those taken away are ever heard of again. The able-bodied are slowly worked to death in labor camps. The infirm are left to die of exposure and starvation or are deliberately massacred in mass executions. . . .
> The number of victims of these bloody cruelties is reckoned in many hundreds of thousands of entirely innocent men, women and children.
> The [Allied] Governments condemn in the strongest possible terms this bestial policy of cold-blooded extermination. . . .
> They reaffirm their solemn resolution to ensure that those responsible for the crimes shall not escape retribution and to press on with the necessary practical measures to this end.

With the publication of this statement, any further pretense in the West to ignorance about the mass murder of Jews was untenable. The declaration spoke of hundreds of thousands of victims. In fact, about 2 million people had already been put to death. It would take another 13 months until the first Allied efforts were undertaken, by the creation of the War Refugee Board, to try to stop the process of annihilation and to attempt to assist and to rescue those European Jews who were still alive. *Gerhart M. Riegner*

Riga Jews settled in Riga, the capital of Latvia, in significant numbers only during the second half of the nineteenth century, when Latvia was part of the Russian empire. In 1867 there were 5,254 Jews in Riga, representing 5.1 percent of the population. During the next 30 years the Jewish population of the city grew to 22,000, 8.4 percent of the population. In 1935 there were almost 44,000 Jews in Riga, and their share of the population had risen to 11.3 percent.

In the late nineteenth century the Jewish community of Riga became one of the most prosperous in Eastern Europe. A number of magnificent synagogues were erected, such as the Old-New Synagogue and the Great Choral Synagogue. Various Jewish educational centers were established, such as the First Jewish Secular School and the Jewish Workmen's School. A Jewish hospital, Jewish social welfare institutions, and Jewish sport clubs were organized. In 1881 Jewish magazines and newspapers began to appear.

In November 1918, in the aftermath of the Russian revolution and World War I, Latvia declared independence. By the end of 1919 the Red Army as well as German troops had been cleared from Latvian territory, and a sovereign Latvian republic was established. In the first decade of Latvian independence the Jewish community of Riga continued to flourish. Various Jewish political parties were active. Prominent Jewish intellectuals and public figures included the brothers Minz—the surgeon Wladimir Minz and the lawyer Paul Minz. One of the foremost Jewish historians of his time, Simon Dubnow, lived in Riga after 1933.

The situation of Jews in Riga began to deteriorate after the revolt of Karlis Ulmanis in 1934 and the establishment of a semi-fascist regime in Latvia. On 7 July 1934 a law was passed limiting the rights of national minorities, including Jews. Jewish autonomy was abolished, and all Jewish political organizations, with the exception of Agudat Israel, were outlawed.

The Soviet Union had long had designs on Latvia, and the secret German-Soviet Nonaggression Pact of 1939 cleared the way for Soviet action. On 17 June 1940 the Red Army entered Riga. Jewish political parties and national institutions were dissolved. Most of the Jewish community suffered serious economic restrictions, as well as limits on their freedom and on religious activities. Jewish newspapers were closed, including the pro-Communist Yiddish-language *Kampf* (Struggle). Jewish cultural activity was totally suppressed. There were also, however, some positive changes. Jews were represented in the municipal government, and young people could easily enter institutes of higher education.

Those who were considered opponents of the Communist regime were deported to concentration camps within the Soviet Union. Among those deported were several thousand Jews, many of whom died under the harsh conditions of the Soviet camps. Paradoxically, for those who survived, deportation was their salvation: had they remained in Latvia, they most likely would have been murdered by the German and Latvian Nazis.

In June 1941 the Germans broke their pact with the Soviets and invaded the Soviet Union. The German army captured Riga on 1 July and immediately began the total physical destruction of the Jewish population. A few thousand Jews succeeded in escaping before the Germans entered the city, but thousands of Jewish refugees from other cities were trapped in Riga and fell victim to the German's plans for mass murder.

From the first day of the German occupation pogroms were launched against the Jewish population. Synagogues were burned, and Jewish property was looted. Jews were arrested by the hundreds, rounded up for forced labor, and driven to nearby Bikiernieki Forest, where several thousand were shot. Units of the German Einsatzgruppe A and units of Latvian fascist formations commanded by Voldemars Veiss, Victors Arajs, and Herberts Cukurs took part in these mass murder operations. In July 1941 alone, more than 5,000 Riga Jews were killed.

In Riga, as in all German-occupied cities, anti-Jewish legislation was enforced regarding the confiscation of public and private property, the prohibition on using public transportation, conscription for forced labor, and the obligation to wear the yellow star. A *Judenrat*—in Riga called the *Ältestenrat*, or Council of Elders—and an Order Service (*Ordnungsdienst*), popularly known as the Jewish police, were formed. The lawyer Michael Elyashov was appointed chairman of the Ältestenrat, and Michael Rosenthal was named head of the Order Service. Both Elyashov and Rosen-

A sign in German and Latvian forbidding unauthorized entrance into the Riga ghetto.

thal had distinguished themselves in the fight for Latvian independence during World War I.

In August 1941 a ghetto called the Moscow Quarter was set up in a northern suburb of the city. More than 30,000 Jews were interned there when German and Latvian police sealed the ghetto on 25 August. On 19 November the ghetto was divided into the so-called Small Ghetto, holding about 5,000 men and women listed as workers, and the Big Ghetto, for the rest of the Jews. The sections were separated from one another, and any contact between them was prohibited.

On 30 November, before the dawn hours, strong German and Latvian police forces entered the Big Ghetto. The ghetto inmates were ordered to leave their homes immediately. Hundreds who hesitated were shot on the spot. Most of the others—some 15,000 Riga Jews—were driven to the Rumbula Forest, about eight kilometers outside the city, and shot there that morning. A transport of about 1,000 Jews from Germany, deported to Riga, was also transferred to the Rumbula Forest, where all were murdered.

On 7–9 December the Nazis rounded up the remaining inmates of the Big Ghetto and drove them to the forest. Another 10,000 Jews were murdered, among them Simon Dubnow and the chief rabbi of Riga, M. M. Zak.

In December 1941 and during the first months of 1942, about 16,000 Jews deported from various cities in Germany and from Vienna and Prague were settled in the empty Big Ghetto, which became known as the German Ghetto. Several thousand of these Jews were driven out in February and March and murdered in the nearby forests. Also in February about 380 Jews from Kovno (Kaunas), in Lithuania, were deported to Riga and settled in the Small Ghetto. There they were joined by another 300 Kovno Jews in October 1942.

On 1 November 1942 the Nazi commander of the Riga ghetto, the SS Obersturmführer Kurt Krause, ordered the closing of the Small Ghetto, which then held about 3,000 inmates, and its incorporation into the German Ghetto. The latter was divided into two

Interior of one of the barracks in the Kaiserwald (Meza Park) concentration camp in Riga, soon after its evacuation in September 1944.

parts: Section R for German Jews and Section L for Latvian Jews. In the course of 1943 the ghetto was gradually emptied. Thousands died owing to starvation and rampant disease fostered by appalling living conditions and poor sanitation. Deportations continued; the largest took place during the summer of 1943, when most of the ghetto inmates were sent to concentration camps, particularly Kaiserwald and its satellite camps. Very few in those camps survived to the end of war. On 2 November 1943 those Jews still remaining in the Riga ghetto were rounded up. Most were taken to the nearby forests and shot. Many of the children were sent to Auschwitz, where they were gassed.

Despite the cruel conditions in the ghetto, the Jewish inmates succeeded in organizing social, cultural, and religious activities. An armed underground organization came into being and managed to smuggle in a small number of weapons, but attempts at launching active resistance or joining the partisans failed.

On 13 October 1944 the Red Army entered Riga. Some 150 Jews who had remained in hiding were thus liberated. About 40 were saved by the Latvian couple Janis and Johanna Lipke, who in 1987 were awarded the title of Righteous Among the Nations by Yad Vashem in Jerusalem.   *Shmuel Krakowski*

Righteous Among the Nations The designation Righteous Among the Nations (Hebrew *hasidei umot haolam*) was created by the Israeli Holocaust museum and memorial Yad Vashem as a tribute to non-Jews who endangered their lives during World War II in order to save Jews. Since 1963 a commission at Yad Vashem has been charged with awarding this distinction. For a person to qualify, actions on behalf of the Jews had to involve "extending help in saving a life; endangering one's own life; absence of reward, monetary and otherwise; and similar considerations which make the rescuers' deeds stand out above and beyond what can be termed ordinary help." More than 16,000 non-Jewish rescuers have been recognized as Righteous Among the Nations, and many other cases are pending before the Yad Vashem commission.

These figures, however, represent but a fraction of those non-Jews who risked their lives to save Jews from the Nazis. Only persons who were rescued can apply to the commission on behalf of their rescuers. Many Jewish survivors have died in the decades since the war; some have lost touch with their protectors; still others refuse to apply or are not aware that such a distinction exists.

As for the Christian rescuers, many of them died before they were recognized. Some lost their lives during the war precisely because they were protecting Jews. The names of many of these helpers have never been identified. Yet others, for a variety of reasons, refuse to be acknowledged as saviors of Jews.

Almost all publications about those who endangered their lives to save Jews concentrate on non-Jews who extended protection selflessly, without consideration of financial gain. This emphasis is partly justified. Existing evidence suggests that the overwhelming majority of rescuers protected Jews for reasons other than money. Nevertheless, by focusing only on altruistic Christians, researchers overlook other kinds of rescuers, such as persons whose primary motivation for saving Jews was profit and Jews who, while struggling for their own survival, devoted themselves to rescuing other Jews. Thus any discussion of the Righteous Among the Nations necessarily cannot cover the full range of persons who helped save Jews from the Nazis.

Under the German occupation all efforts to save Jews signaled an opposition to the Nazi policy of Jewish annihilation. Although such efforts were illegal and endangered the lives of the rescuers, in each country under German rule there were people who risked their lives to save Jews.

The most formidable obstacle to Jewish rescue was the extent to which Nazi occupying forces dominated the governmental machinery. Where the Germans were in virtual control, as in Poland, they were prepared to do whatever was necessary to annihilate the Jewish populations and would brook no interference from any individual or group. One influence on the Nazis' decision about how much direct power to exert was their attitude toward the occupied country's Christian population. In the world of Nazi-occupied Europe, policies and controls depended on racial affinities. For example, the Nazis defined the Slavs as subhuman, only slightly above the racial value of the Jews. In contrast, the highest social rank was reserved for the Scandinavians, who bore a close physical resemblance to the "Aryan" prototype valued by the Nazis. The rest of the European nationalities fell somewhere between these two extremes. The Germans, however, were not always consistent in translating these racial principles into action.

Another condition affecting Jewish rescue was the level of antisemitism within a given country. In a society with a strong antisemitic tradition, denunciations of Jews and their protectors were more common. Jewish rescue by Christians was likely to invite disapproval, if not outright censure, from local people. Indeed, even non-Jewish helpers themselves might have been imbued with long-taught anti-Jewish images and values. Such rescuers, though engaged in saving Jews, had to cope with their own antisemitic attitudes.

The sheer number of Jews within a particular country and the degree to which they were assimilated also affected the possibilities of rescue. It is easier to hide and protect fewer people. Moreover, the easier it was for Jews to blend in, the less dangerous it was for others to shield them. Finally, potential rescuers were more likely to try to save those with whom they could readily identify and with whom they had much in common. In terms of these various factors, Denmark and Poland represent opposite cases.

In Denmark, conditions for the rescue of Jews were favorable in virtually every respect, and the Danes took full advantage of them. Danish Jews numbered only 8,000, a mere 0.2 percent of Denmark's population, and they were highly assimilated. Danes regarded the Jews of Denmark as fellow Danes. Partly because the Nazis defined the Danes as an Aryan race, they left the Danes in charge of their own political destiny, retaining the prewar government. Of all European countries under German domination, Denmark enjoyed the most favored position, becoming Hitler's model protectorate, which functioned relatively undisturbed until 1943. Because of Denmark's local autonomy, the Jews were left alone. The minimal interference of the Nazis in the internal affairs of the country, together with the relative safety that the Danish Jews experienced in the first years of the occupation, made the idea of a righteous Christian superfluous.

The situation changed in 1943, when the Germans insisted on applying the Nazi policies of annihilation to the Danish Jews. The Danes refused to obey. The Germans reacted by taking over the Danish government and then trying to implement their anti-Jewish policies. Only at that point did the idea of righteous Christians become a reality in Denmark. When word spread in October 1943 that the Germans were about to round up the Jews for deportation, the Danish underground joined with ordinary Danish citizens to help ferry more than 7,000 Jews across the sea to safety in Sweden. Danish opposition to the Nazi measures saved even the 472 Jews who were seized by the Germans before they could be evacuated and who were sent to the Theresienstadt concentration camp. The Danes insisted on visiting them, and the Germans acceded to their demands. In comparison to the treatment of other Europeans, the Germans were lenient toward the Danes, even after rescue attempts started. Reprisals took the form of arrests and usually were directed only against the organizers of the Jewish exodus.

In contrast, Poland presented the most formidable obstacles to Jewish rescue. Quite early the Nazis had designated Poland as the center for Jewish destruction. Many European Jews were sent to Poland to die—some in ghettos, some in concentration and extermination camps. German control in Poland was direct, strong, and ruthless. The Nazis' contemptuous attitude toward the Slavs helped remove all potential constraints on their actions against Poles as well as Jews. Among the many measures aimed at annihilating the Jews of Poland was a 1941 decree that made any unauthorized exiting of the ghetto a crime punishable by death. The same punishment applied to Poles who were helping to smuggle Jews into the so-called Aryan side of the Polish cities. This law was tightly enforced, and executions of Christians and Jews caught violating it were swift.

In addition, the virulent Polish antisemitism provided fertile ground for the process of Jewish annihilation and served as a serious barrier to Jewish rescue. In 1939, of all the European countries, Poland had the highest concentration of Jews. About 10 percent of the country's population, more than 3 million out of 33 million people, was Jewish. The largest community of Jews in Europe, Polish Jews were also the least assimilated into Polish culture and society. The prevalence of hasidic sects, with their distinctive dress and ritual, made many Jews in towns and cities look conspicuously different from the Christian Poles and hence an easy object of ridicule and scorn.

Those Poles who wished to help Jews had to overcome several layers of obstacles. The Nazis had made helping Jews a crime punishable by death. Explicit anti-Jewish ideologies and the pervasive antisemitism put Poles who aided Jews at risk of being denounced to the authorities by their neighbors. And to some extent Polish rescuers had to overcome their own, often unacknowledged antisemitism. Nevertheless, despite all these barriers, in Poland the year 1941 marked the appearance of righteous Gentiles.

Unlike in Denmark, where Jewish rescue was undertaken en masse and nationwide, in Poland aid was extended by a single individual or by a group. It could be a part of an underground organizational activity or an activity initiated and carried out by a single person or a few individuals—members of a family or a group of friends. Some individual rescuers seem to have protected Jews even without the knowledge of their families, with whom they shared their homes. Given the German determination to destroy the Jews, secrecy was of the utmost importance.

Many offers of help were short-lived, but those who have qualified as Righteous Among the Nations most frequently extended aid over a prolonged period. Once a potential rescuer was faced with an individual Jew's extreme need and dependence and was moved by them, he could not easily abandon him. In some way, too, by becoming rescuers people invested their own safety in these relationships.

The rescuing of Jews took many forms. The least dangerous was to warn a Jewish acquaintance of impending arrests and deportations. A further step involved supplying Jews with false documents to help them survive outside the ghetto by passing as Christian Poles. Some rescuers offered shelter and food. Those who lived close to forests could limit their aid to feeding Jews who hid in the woods.

Who among the non-Jews was likely to try to overcome the many barriers and rescue Jews? Who was most likely to stand up for the persecuted Jews, traditionally viewed as "Christ killers" and blamed for every conceivable ill? What characteristics did they share in common?

When large numbers of Christian protectors are compared in terms of social class, education, political involvement, degree of antisemitism, extent of religious commitment, and friendship with Jews, they are very heterogeneous. Some of the rescuers came from higher, some from lower classes. Some were well edu-

Father Bruno with Jewish children he hid. From the left: Henrik Zwierszewski, George Michaelson, Father Bruno, Willy Michaelson, Henri Fuks, and Willy Sandorminski (Sandomirski). Father Bruno was recognized by Yad Vashem as a Righteous Among the Nations.

cated, while others were illiterate. Comparisons in terms of religious and political affiliations also show a great deal of diversity. In fact, most conventional categories according to which people are usually classified yield inconclusive results. A few examples will suffice to illustrate the diversity in rescuers' backgrounds.

Eduard Schulte was one of Germany's top industrialists. An independent, nonpracticing Christian, Schulte became convinced quite early that Nazi rule would lead to war and a disastrous end for Germany. Schulte's prominent position and impeccable reputation gave him access to important secrets about Nazi plans for the Jews. Hitler's growing power only increased the industrialist's apprehension about the future. Schulte decided to speed up the conclusion of the war by supplying sensitive information to the Allies. The actual transfer of secrets happened in Switzerland, where Schulte traveled frequently. There he delivered his illegally obtained evidence to Polish and

Swiss contacts, who sent it on through secret channels. Via Schulte and Gerhart Riegner in Switzerland, the Allies received the news about German troop movements and about the V-2 rocket program. Among Schulte's outstanding contributions was a special report in July 1942 alerting the British and American governments about the Nazi plan for the total annihilation of the Jews. Aware that some of the information was ignored and not acted upon, he nevertheless continued his mission. In 1943 Schulte received a warning that the Gestapo was investigating his case. He escaped to Switzerland, where he continued to reside until his death in 1966. For his wartime contributions Schulte sought no recognition or honors. In fact, no honors were bestowed on him.

Marion van Binsbergen (later Pritchard) was 20 years old when the Germans occupied her native Holland. She was the daughter of a prominent judge and an English mother, both of whom instilled in her tolerant values, a keen sense of justice, and a fierce independence. During the war, from 1942 until 1945, van Binsbergen devoted all her energies to anti-Nazi activities, which involved the saving of Jews, most of whom were young children. She would locate hiding places, help them move, and provide them with food, clothing, and ration cards. She also lent tremendous moral support to the Jewish fugitives as well as the families who hosted them. One extraordinary way in which she saved Jewish lives was by registering newborn Jewish babies as her own. She managed to register several of these children within a span of five months.

At one point van Binsbergen was asked by Michael Rutgers van der Loeff, a Dutch resistance leader, to find a hiding place for a Jewish friend with three young children. When she could not find one, she moved with the fugitives into a small house in the country. There she was soon confronted by a Nazi collaborator, who was about to discover the hidden Jews. To prevent this from happening, van Binsbergen shot the intruder, though she had never fired a gun before. She continued to take care of this family for two years, until the end of the war.

After the war van Binsbergen emigrated to the United States, married, and became a psychoanalyst and faculty member at the Boston Graduate School of Psychoanalysis. Marion van Binsbergen Pritchard has received the Yad Vashem Medal for the highest distinction of the Righteous Among the Nations, honorary citizenship of the state of Israel, and in 1996 the Raoul Wallenberg Award, bestowed by the University of Michigan.

In 1943 Stanislawa Dawidziuk (Szymkiewicz), a young factory worker in Warsaw, shared a one-room apartment with her husband, a waiter, and a teenaged brother. At the husband's request she agreed to add to her cramped quarters a Jewish woman whose looks betrayed her Jewish background. The woman, Irena, was brought by one Ryszard Kaminski, who begged Stanislawa's husband to keep her just for one night. But the next day Kaminski could not find a new home for Irena. When this one single day stretched into weeks, Stanislawa's husband became adamant and demanded that his wife dismiss Irena. Stanislawa objected. She knew that Irena's appearance in the street would lead to her death. Eventually, in protest, Stanislawa's husband left, never to return.

In his absence Stanislawa gave birth to a boy. She arranged a special place behind a movable closet for Irena. Kaminski continued to visit them, supplying them with modest provisions of food. Despite continuous threats and several close calls, Stanislawa Dawidziuk insisted that Irena stay on. When after the Warsaw uprising in 1944 the Germans were evacuating the Polish population, it was rumored that mothers of small children could stay on. Because Stanislawa worried about Irena's "Jewish looks," she wanted Irena to claim the baby as her own. She felt that by staying in the apartment with the baby, Irena would be safer. In the end both were given permission to remain in the apartment.

After the war Irena emigrated to Israel, where she died in 1975. Stanislawa Dawidziuk remained in Poland, where she remarried, had another son, and worked at the same factory until her retirement. In 1981 she was recognized by Yad Vashem as a Righteous Among the Nations. She died in 1991.

Sempo Sugihara, the Japanese consul in Kovno (Kaunas), had been ordered by the Soviets to leave Lithuania by 31 August 1940. Confronted with the plight of Jewish refugees, Sugihara decided on 10 August to spend his remaining time in Kovno issuing Japanese transit visas to Jewish refugees for purely humanitarian reasons. This he did without checking whether the refugees had the necessary supporting documents. When the Japanese Foreign Ministry heard about his actions, he was ordered to stop. Assuming full responsibility, and aware that the Foreign Ministry would dismiss him, Sugihara continued to issue visas. Indeed, in order to finish the necessary paperwork, he labored without stop for 12 consecutive days and enlisted the help of several Jewish refugees in stamping the documents. According to some sources, he continued to process these transit visas even after he had boarded a train for Berlin on 31 August. Years later Sugihara estimated that he had distributed 3,500 transit visas to Japan. The holders of these documents were permitted to pass through the Soviet Union, if they could pay the fare in dollars for the trip across Siberia.

When Sugihara reached Berlin, he was temporarily attached to a Japanese consulate in Königsberg. Later, in Tokyo, the Foreign Ministry dismissed him from office without explanation. For the rest of his life Sugihara had a hard time finding work and moved from job to job. Only when he was old and bedridden did his wartime help to Jews receive publicity in the West. In 1985 he was officially designated by Yad Vashem as a

Righteous Among the Nations, and the Japanese press finally gave Sugihara's story extensive coverage.

Only at close range does a cluster of characteristics and conditions shared by these rescuers come into focus. One of these characteristics, sometimes referred to as individuality, separateness, or marginality, shows that the rescuers did not quite fit into their social environments. Not all of them were aware of this tendency; but whether they were conscious of it or not, the individuality of these rescuers appeared under different guises and was related to other shared characteristics and conditions. Being on the periphery of a community means being less affected by the community's expectations and controls. Therefore, with individuality come freedom from social constraints and a higher level of independence, offering an opportunity to act in accordance with personal values and moral precepts even when these are in opposition to societal demands.

Rescuers seem to have had no trouble talking about their self-reliance and their need to follow personal inclinations and values. Nearly all defined themselves as independent. They were motivated by moral values that do not depend on the support and approval of others but on their own self-approval. They are usually at peace with themselves and with their own ideas of what is right or wrong. One of their central values seems to have involved a long-standing commitment to protect the needy. This commitment was often expressed in a wide range of charitable acts extending over a long period of time. Risking their lives for Jews during World War II fit into a system of values and behaviors that had to do with helping the weak and the dependent.

This analogy, however, has its own limitations. Most disinterested actions on behalf of others might have involved extreme inconvenience, but only rarely would such acts suggest that the givers had to make the ultimate sacrifice of their own lives. For righteous Gentile rescuers, the war provided a convergence between historical events demanding complete selflessness and their predisposition to help. People tend to take their repetitive actions for granted. What they take for granted they accept, and what they accept they rarely analyze or question. Therefore the constant pressure of, or familiarity with, ideas and actions does not necessarily translate into knowledge or understanding. On the contrary, easy acceptance of customary patterns often impedes understanding.

A related tendency is to view the actions that one habitually repeats as ordinary, regardless of how exceptional they may appear to others. And so the rescuers' history of helping the needy may have been in part responsible for their modest appraisal of their life-threatening actions. Rescuers seem to have seen in their protection of Jews a natural reaction to human suffering. Many insisted that saving lives was not remarkable and was unworthy of special notice.

Given such matter-of-fact perceptions of rescue, it is not surprising that aid to Jews often began spontaneously and without planning. The unpremeditated start underscores the rescuers' need to stand up for the poor and helpless. This need to assist those in distress overshadowed all considerations of their personal safety and that of their families. Most protectors, when asked why they had saved Jews, emphasized that they had responded to the persecution and the suffering of other human beings and said that the fact that the sufferers were Jews was entirely incidental to their impulse to act. A minority of rescuers claimed to have helped out of a sense of Christian duty and or in protest against the German occupation.

This ability to disregard all attributes of the needy except their helplessness and dependency point to universalistic perceptions. Practically all rescuers thought that in helping Jews, they were prompted by the needs of the Jews themselves.

As a group, rescuers who tried to save Jews without expectation of concrete rewards were engaged in altruistic behavior. Comparisons of such rescuers from several European countries underline six shared characteristics: individuality or separateness from their social environment; independence or self-reliance; a commitment to helping the needy; a modest self-appraisal of their extraordinary actions; unplanned initial engagement in Jewish rescue; and universalistic perceptions of Jews as human beings in dire need of assistance. The close interdependence of these six characteristics and conditions offers a preliminary explanation for the altruistic rescue of Jews.

Nechama Tec

Ringelblum, Emanuel (1900–1944) Polish Jewish historian and founder of Oneg Shabbos, an archive of materials that document the persecution of the Jews. Before the war Ringelblum worked for the American Jewish Joint Distribution Committee. He and his family were shot during the liquidation of the Warsaw ghetto. See ONEG SHABBOS; WARSAW

Roma See GYPSIES

Romania Unlike Germany, Poland, Russia, and Spain, Romania did not have a centuries-old history of antisemitism. Before the nineteenth century, antisemitic outbreaks occasionally occurred in Romania, but its territory actually served as a refuge for savagely persecuted Jews from Poland and Russia. Arising in the early nineteenth century, Romanian antisemitism spread with increasing violence, first among the political classes and intelligentsia and then to the lower and middle classes.

In 1878 Article 44 of the Congress of Berlin stipulated that, in exchange for recognition of Romanian independence, the state must recognize the rights of ethnic and religious minorities, including the Jews. In 1879, in contravention of this condition, the Romanian parliament enacted a law virtually blocking the naturalization of the Jews.

After World War I the condition of Jews in Romania changed. Once again under pressure from Western powers, the parliament abolished parts of the nineteenth-century antisemitic legislation, while the Constitution of 1923 granted civil rights to Jews. Meanwhile, antisemitism developed in the Romanian masses in the context of economic crises. Mainstream political parties and fascist organizations blamed the Jews for the problems confronting Romanian society. Rightwing ideologues of the National Christian Defense League and the Iron Guard portrayed the Jews as the ruling economic class in Romania, as spies, Communists, and agents of Soviet Russia. They proposed a *numerus clausus* or *numerus nullus*—limitations or prohibitions of Jewish entry into universities and professions—highly restrictive legislation expelling Jews from the bar and the medical profession, forced labor, and deportation from Romania.

During the December 1937 elections the Iron Guard and the National Christian party (the new name of the former National Christian Defense League) won 25 percent of the vote. In January and February 1938 King Carol II and Prime Minister Octavian Goga signed several decrees establishing "the proclamation of the law of the blood" and a "revision" of granting citizenship to Jews. During the 44 days of the National Christian government under Goga and A. C. Cuza, more than 100,000 Jews who had become Romanian citizens after World War I were deprived of citizenship. Soon after the Goga-Cuza government ended in 1938, the royal dictatorship of Carol II was established. At first the king organized a harsh campaign of repression against the Iron Guard. During the spring of 1940, when he saw clearly that Nazi influence was set to last in Eastern Europe, King Carol released the imprisoned Iron Guard members and included several of its leaders in the government. During the summer of 1940 Romania was forced by Germany and the Soviet Union to give up Bessarabia and northern Bukovina to the Soviet Union, northern Transylvania to Hungary, and two small counties, Caliacra and Durostor, to Bulgaria. At the end of King Carol's reign in August 1940, one month before Gen. Ion Antonescu took power in alliance with the Iron Guard, the government of Ion Gigurtu introduced severe antisemitic legislation openly inspired by the Nuremberg Laws promulgated by Nazi Germany in 1935. This legislation remained in force after the fall of Carol and the succession of Mihai to the throne on 6 September 1940 and was further developed by the Antonescu-Sima and Antonescu governments.

According to the 1930 census, Romania had a Jewish population of 756,930, the third-largest Jewish community in Europe. Approximately 300,000 Jews lived in Bessarabia and Bukovina and 150,000 in northern Transylvania; the remainder lived in the Old Kingdom (Wallachia and Moldavia) and southern Transylvania.

When in July 1940 Bessarabia and Bukovina were lost to the Soviet Union, the Jews were immediately accused of treachery by Romanian propaganda, and many of them were killed in Moldavia by the Romanian units retreating from Bukovina. Hundreds of Jewish refugees were massacred by Romanian soldiers in the Galati railway station, and at least 50 more were killed, again by Romanian soldiers, in a pogrom in the town of Dorohoi. Dozens of Jews, mainly soldiers trying to join their units but also civilians, were pushed out from moving trains in Bessarabia and Bukovina. Their graves still line the railway tracks.

During the summer of 1940 Romania also lost northern Transylvania to Hungary. The Jews of that region shared the fate of the Hungarian Jews and were deported in 1944 to the Nazi death camps by Hungarian police. Some 135,000 of them—nine out of 10 northern Transylvanian Jews—perished in the gas chambers.

On 6 September 1940 the fascist Iron Guard came to power in alliance with General Antonescu. Severe

Civilians walk along what is probably Cuza Voda Street in central Jassy, past the bodies of Jews killed by Romanian soldiers and civilians during the Jassy pogrom. 29–30 June 1941

antisemitic legislation was enacted, and the Iron Guard government organized a nationwide confiscation of Jewish properties and the dismissal of Jews from their occupations. At the end of January 1941 the alliance disintegrated; General Antonescu crushed a rebellion by the Iron Guard, who thereupon turned on the Jews, killing at least 120 in a massive pogrom in Bucharest. Dozens were butchered and their bodies hung on hooks in the slaughterhouse of Bucharest. One month later, at the Burdujeni crossing point, Romanian border guards killed more than 50 Jews who were trying to escape to the Soviet Union.

In June 1941 Romania, now allied with Germany, entered the war against the Soviet Union. During the first days of the war approximately 13,000 Jews were killed by Romanian army units, police, and gendarmerie in the town of Jassy (Iasi) and in two death trains. German units also participated in the Jassy massacre.

The survivors of the death trains were set free after two months of camp detention in Calarasi and Podul Iloaei.

Between 2,430 and 2,590 Jews, guarded by Romanian and German troops, were deported on the first death train to Calarasi. During the five-day journey more than 1,400 of them perished from dehydration, beatings, and heat in the overcrowded cattle cars. The journey of the second train, from Jassy to Podul Iloaei, lasted only 16 hours during which 1,194 Jews out of 2,500 died.

On 17 June in Galati and 18 June in Roman, Gen. C. Z. Vasiliu, deputy minister of the interior and commander of the gendarmerie, gave an order concerning the treatment of Jews to the legions of gendarmes who were scheduled to enter Bessarabia within a few days. He thereby established the principle of land-cleansing (*curatarea terenului*), which meant the extermination forthwith of all Jews found in rural areas and the confinement of urban Jews to ghettos. An additional order by General Vasiliu declared that the Jewish minority should be pursued with energy and vigilance so that none of them would escape their deserved fate. On 3 July, Mihai Antonescu, vice-president of the government and the regime's second-in-command, announced in a conference with heads of the military and civilian administration in Bessarabia and Bukovina that the Jews in those areas would be submitted to an "action of ethnic purification" and to a "forced migration" over the borders. He encouraged those officials not to show any humanitarian feelings and to use machine guns if necessary.

Five days later, on 8 July 1941, in a meeting of the Council of Ministers, Mihai Antonescu repeated the order to deport Jews from Bessarabia and Bukovina and emphasized that he did not care if history considered his administration barbaric. On the same day Gen. Constantin Voiculescu, the governor of Bessarabia, gave the order for the "elimination of Judaic elements" from the province. The next day General Voiculescu received the first reports that the gendarmes had indeed begun the land-cleansing operation. On 17 July, Gen. Ion Topor, commander of the military gendarmerie, promulgated an order requiring the deportation of Jews from Bessarabia and Bukovina and stating that "the country does not need Jews and must be cleansed of Jews." On 19 July, General Popescu, undersecretary of state at the Ministry of the Interior, gave an order in the name of Ion Antonescu concerning internment of Jews from Moldavia in forced-labor camps. This order also established a system of hostages and executions in the case of escape attempts.

Out of 300,000 Jews living in Bessarabia and Bukovina before 1940, about 100,000 retreated with the Red Army in July 1941 or were evacuated or deported by the Soviet authorities. In July and August 1941 at least 30,000 Jews in those regions were killed by the Romanian and German armies. At the very end of July and the beginning of August the Romanian military authorities attempted a massive deportation of the Bessarabian and Bukovinian Jews over the Dniester River, so that they would be located in the area that in three weeks would officially become Transnistria. This plan was aborted by the Germans, who mentioned in their reports that 27,500 Jews had been driven back over the Dniester into Bessarabia at the beginning of

August 1941. As a result the Romanian military administration immediately interned all the Jews from Bessarabia and Bukovina in transit camps and ghettos, where, according to a report by the Romanian gendarmerie, 30,000 Jews from Bessarabia died during the summer and fall of 1941.

These transit camps and ghettos were short-lived. Except for 20,000 Jews from Cernauti (Czernowitz) and a few hundred Jews from Bessarabia, the whole Jewish population of both provinces was deported to Transnistria during the fall of 1941. Another gendarmerie report, dated January 1942, states that 118,847 Jews from Bessarabia and Bukovina were deported there at that time, while a further 5,500 Jews from the same regions (most of them from the Cernauti ghetto), were deported there during the summer of 1942. A handwritten note from Ion Antonescu's cabinet secretariat responsible for the administration of Bessarabia, Bukovina, and Transnistria mentions that 90,334 Jews from Bukovina and 56,089 from Bessarabia had been deported to Transnistria.

The Romanian military authorities planned the fall 1941 deportations to the letter. Most of the deportees were pushed toward the Dniester in forced marches averaging 30 kilometers a day. Strict orders were given to execute any stragglers. Communal graves were prepared every five kilometers well before the columns of Jews had set out.

Another 2,000 Jews—mostly political prisoners and those who had tried to escape from forced labor—from the Old Kingdom were also deported to Transnistria by the Romanian authorities. About 25,000 Gypsies (Roma) followed the same route. The pretext for the Gypsies' deportation was the stereotype that they were robbers and nomads. Deported between the spring and the fall of 1942, most died from typhus or were executed in the Berezovka area by Ukrainians of German origin who had established German colonies in Ukraine and had enrolled in the SS. Some of these Gypsies had close relatives fighting in the Romanian army on the eastern front. In that summer, too, about 2,000 Baptists and members of other Protestant churches were interned in various camps in Bessarabia for refusing to renounce their faith.

In September 1944, out of more than 120,000 Romanian Jews who had been deported in 1941 and 1942 to Transnistria, 50,741 were still alive. In Transnistria Romanian authorities were also responsible for the killing of approximately 150,000 indigenous Jews in

Romanian Jews are transported across the Dniester River during a deportation action to Transnistria.

the Odessa and Golta districts. At the end of October 1941 about 25,000 Jews, mostly local people, were executed in Odessa by Romanian army units as a reprisal for an explosion that had killed 50 Romanian officers in the army headquarters. Between December 1941 and February 1942, 70,000 Jews were executed by Romanian gendarmes and Ukrainian militia in the camps of Bogdanovka, Domanievka, and Acmicetka in the Golta district. Also during the spring of 1942 the Romanian gendarmerie handed over for execution 31,000 Jews to SS units from the Mostovoi area of Berezovka. In the Bar area across the Bug River, thousands more Jews were given over to the Germans. Very few returned, the overwhelming majority having been executed. In 1942 the SS undertook other massive executions of the Jews of Transnistria in Balaiciuc (2,000 Jews killed), Cihrini (2,000), Zaharovka (1,500), and Rastadt (600). Tens of thousands of Jews were moved from one locality to another within Transnistria by the

Romanian authorities. The best-known examples include the deportation at the beginning of 1942 of at least 30,000 Ukrainian Jews from Odessa to Berezovka and the abortive attempt of the Romanian authorities for a massive deportation of the Jews from Transnistria over the Bug in the spring of 1942. A report by Gheorghe Alexianu, the governor of Transnistria, mentions that by 9 March 65,252 Jews, mainly from Odessa, Rabnita, and Tulcin, had been deported internally within Transnistria toward the Bug. At least 250,000 Jews perished under Romanian administration during World War II.

The Jews of Moldavia, Wallachia, and southern Transylvania also suffered greatly during the war, but they were spared the wholesale destruction that befell the Jews of Bessarabia, Bukovina, and Transnistria. Approximately 20,000 Jews, mainly from Jassy, Dorohoi, and the Old Kingdom, were killed. Tens of thousands of Jews from small communities in the Old

Kingdom were taken from their homes during the first days of the war and concentrated in larger towns; thousands of others were moved to camps in the south of the country. Until the beginning of 1942 thousands of the Jews from the Old Kingdom were held as hostages. On 12 November 1941, 47,345 Jews were conscripted into the Romanian military system of forced labor. Some were put to work in their home areas, and the rest were enrolled far away in what were called "exterior detachments of labor." During 1942 and 1943 more than 17,000 Jews worked in exterior detachments. Romanian military reports often emphasized the hard labor and the lack of food, clothes, and shoes that beset these workers.

From the perspective of solving the "Jewish problem" German-Romanian relations were never smooth. During the summer of 1941 the Germans protested several times because the Romanian military and police units did not bury their Jewish victims, thereby creating a danger of epidemics and damaging the image of both armies. Other conflicts arose in August 1941 and the spring of 1942, when the Romanians attempted large-scale deportations over the Dniester and the Bug. If at the beginning of the war the German authorities voiced dissatisfaction at the ad hoc nature of the Romanian killing of the Jewish population, and at the haste with which the Romanians tried to push huge numbers of Jews into German-controlled areas, in 1942 they were expressing strong displeasure at the Romanian refusal to deport Jews to the Nazi death camps in occupied Poland.

In the summer of 1942 the Antonescu regime decided that it would no longer shield those Romanian Jews residing outside Romania in Nazi-occupied Europe. This withdrawal of protection allowed the Germans to proceed with the deportation and murder of Romanian Jews living in France, Germany, Austria, the Netherlands, and Bohemia and Moravia. About 3,300 of the 7,000 Romanian Jews living in France, and all those living in Germany and Austria—about 1,600—were deported. At the end of 1943 the Romanian authorities, irritated that the Germans were not repatriating to Romania the Jewish property they had confiscated, once again began to protect Romanian Jews in occupied Europe.

The summer and fall of 1942 represented a critical time for the Jews from the Old Kingdom and southern Transylvania. The Romanian authorities decided to deport Romanian Jews to the Nazi death camps,

mainly Belzec and Auschwitz. The timetable for the train transports had already been established when, following international pressure by the Red Cross, the papal nuncio, and the Swiss legation (which also represented U.S. interests in Romania)—as well as intervention by the leaders of the Romanian Jewish community, several Romanian politicians and clergymen, and King Mihai and his mother, Queen Elena—Ion Antonescu postponed the deportation to the spring of 1943. During November and December 1942, despite strong German pressure, the Romanian authorities became more and more elusive in this matter, as they had begun to realize that the Germans might lose the war.

In early 1943, after the German and Romanian defeat at Stalingrad, the Romanian Jews became a bargaining chip for the Antonescu administration, which now began to consider the repatriation of certain categories of Jews from Transnistria. As of January 1943 it was clear to SS chief Heinrich Himmler that he would receive no cooperation from Ion and Mihai Antonescu regarding the deportation of the Romanian Jews, and accordingly he withdrew Gustav Richter, his expert in Jewish affairs, from Bucharest. During 1943 Ion Antonescu in principle approved the repatriation from Transnistria to Romania of several categories of Jews, mainly orphans (on condition that they emigrated to Palestine) and the deportees from Dorohoi, whom it was acknowledged had been deported by mistake. The government established several commissions to select Jews for repatriation. Contradictory orders were issued, but no Jews were repatriated until 20 December 1943, when 1,500 Jews from Dorohoi left Transnistria. Thanks mainly to the activities of Ira Hirschman, the representative of the War Refugee Board in Turkey, 1,846 Jewish orphans from Transnistria were transported through Romania for resettlement in Palestine in 1944.

Ion Antonescu's responsibility in the destruction of Romanian and Ukrainian Jewry is well established in many historical documents. In 1941, at the very opening of the eastern front, he ordered strict surveillance, ghettoization of the Jews from Moldavia, and exploitation of Romanian Jewry as forced laborers. On 30 June 1941, during the Jassy pogrom, it was Ion Antonescu who ordered the execution of all "Jewish Communists from Jassy and those found with red flags and firearms." On 18 July he directed that all Jews interned in labor camps be employed in hard labor, with one in

10 being shot in reprisal for any attempt to escape. In a letter to Mihai Antonescu on 5 September he equated the Jew with Satan and said that the war was not against the Slavs but against the Jews. He also expressed his intention to deport all Jews from Bessarabia to Transnistria as soon as possible. Indeed, the orders given by Ion Antonescu in mid-October 1941 began the massive deportation of practically all Jews from Bessarabia and Bukovina. The massacre of the Jews in Odessa on 24–25 October was carried out on specific orders from Ion Antonescu. Afterward he personally checked with Governor Alexianu to ensure that repression in Odessa was sufficiently harsh. The deportation to Berezovka of the remaining Odessan Jews followed orders given by Ion Antonescu in a meeting of the Council of Ministers in December 1941, and the deportation of the Gypsies also took place on his personal directive. On the other hand, in 1942 Ion Antonescu had a direct role in canceling the deportations of the majority of the Jews from the Old Kingdom to the Nazi death camps in Poland.

One of the main features of genocidal policies in Romania during World War II was the swift physical destruction of Romanian Jewry on the basis of selective geographical criteria. Similar policies were implemented by Hungary in 1941 in (Banat) Yugoslavia and (Kamenets-Podolsk) Ukraine and by Bulgaria in 1943 in Thrace and Macedonia. All these countries decided first of all to settle the fate of the Jews in the territories whose possession had historically been contested by their neighbors. Policies of destruction of the Romanian Jews were implemented severely and rapidly by the Romanian government at the beginning of the war but ended in 1943. It was not the rabidly antisemitic Iron Guard but the Romanian army and gendarmerie that carried out the massive destruction of Romanian and Ukrainian Jewry. Most of the time there was no coordination of Romanian and German policies in this matter.

On 23 August 1944 the Antonescu regime was overthrown by King Mihai and a coalition of political parties. Romania joined the Allies, and its armies started to fight against Nazi Germany. The Red Army entered Bucharest a few days after the coup. The antisemitic legislation was abolished by the king and the new Romanian administration. Several trials of Romanian war criminals followed, and hundreds were condemned to harsh prison sentences or forced labor. Only four Romanian war criminals were executed: Ion Antonescu,

Mihai Antonescu, C. Z. Vasiliu, and Gheorghe Alexianu. During World War II no country except Germany was involved on such a scale in the massacre of its Jews as was Romania. Yet it must also be said that no other country switched so dramatically and in such a short time from a system of mass murder and grave discrimination to a policy that allowed a substantial portion of its Jews—375,000, or roughly half the prewar Jewish population in Romania—to survive.   *Radu Ioanid*

Roosevelt, Franklin Delano (1881–1945) President of the United States, 1933–45. See AMERICAN POLICY

Rosenberg, Alfred (1893–1946) Ideologist of the Nazi movement. Born in Reval (Tallinn), Rosenberg moved to Munich after World War I. In 1930 he wrote *Myth of the Twentieth Century,* a book that propagated racist theories of art and culture. After the invasion of the Soviet Union Rosenberg was appointed minister for the occupied territories. His influence in the Nazi party declined throughout the era of the Third Reich. After his conviction on war crimes charges in the Nuremberg trial, Rosenberg was sentenced to death and executed.

RSHA (Reichssicherheitshauptamt) Reich Security Main Office, responsible for internal security and the execution of the Final Solution. The RSHA incorporated the police, the secret service (SD) of the SS, the Gestapo, and other departments. Heinrich Himmler controlled the RSHA, but its immediate chief was first Reinhard Heydrich and then, after Heydrich's assassination, Ernst Kaltenbrunner. See FINAL SOLUTION: PREPARATION AND IMPLEMENTATION

Rumkowski, Mordechai Chaim (1877–1944) Head of the Lodz *Judenrat* (Jewish council). Rumkowski believed that if Jews made an economic contribution to the German war effort, the Nazis would spare at least some of the ghetto inmates. He negotiated with the Germans to improve conditions in the Lodz ghetto but also helped to organize the deportations. Rumkowski died in Auschwitz, where he had been deported when the Lodz ghetto was liquidated between April and August 1944. See LODZ

Russia and the Soviet Union At the dawn of the twentieth century the country that appeared most ready and willing to initiate a genocide against Jews was not Germany but tsarist Russia. True, it had been a German journalist who coined the term *antisemitism* in the late 1870s as shorthand for a new post-Christian, racist hatred of Jews; but 25 years later this neologism aroused little more than bluster and threatening pamphlets from a fringe group of his compatriots and their admirers in France, Austria, and elsewhere in Europe. In Russia, however, following the assassination of Tsar Alexander II in 1881 by revolutionaries, the government encouraged bands of hooligans to carry out pogroms against their Jewish neighbors over the same quarter century. Even if Russia did not have a word for it, anti-Jewish sentiment had found open expression there.

In Germany what is now called "eliminationist antisemitic discourse" remained latent, but in Russia it had already been made manifest as state policy long before Hitler and the Nazis appeared on the European stage. The deaths of 49 Jews during the notorious 1903 pogrom at Kishinev (now in Moldova) brought both antisemitism and anti-Jewish violence to the attention of people throughout the world. Undismayed by universal condemnation, the Russian government continued to support a rising tide of pogroms in 1905–7, as Jews became the scapegoats for Russia's humiliating defeat at the hands of the Japanese, for industrial strikes, and for Tsar Nicholas II's frustrated anger at having to yield some political power at home to the Duma, a proto-parliament.

Members of the Black Hundreds, the Union of the Archangel Michael, and other perpetrators of countless pogroms became the fanatical but inefficient forefathers to Hitler's Brown Shirts and the jack-booted SS. What is more, tsarist Russia anticipated Nazi Germany by issuing a draconian series of laws and decrees that targeted Jews. From 1881 to 1905 the Russian government passed more than 1,000 pieces of anti-Jewish legislation, long before the Nuremberg racial laws of 1935 in Nazi Germany. Jews found life in Russia so intolerable that they emigrated in vast numbers. The tsarist government went so far as to negotiate the emigration of its Jewish subjects with Western officials and even private citizens, most notably the Belgian banker Baron Maurice de Hirsch. The parallel with Nazi policy is again clear. Before planning the Final Solution, Hitler sought to force German Jews to emigrate and indeed tried to press foreign governments to accept them.

German antisemitism had its source in centuries of Christian, particularly Roman Catholic and Lutheran, hatred for Jews. The Jews were routinely accused of being Christ-killers, poisoners of wells, ritual murderers of Christian children to bake matzo with their blood (the infamous "blood libel"), and desecrators of the Host. They were treated as scapegoats for any and all natural disasters or human failures that befell a German community.

Russian antisemitism also drew on religious intolerance. Eastern Orthodoxy was as dogmatically anti-Jewish as Roman Catholicism. Jews had been forbidden to enter, let alone settle in, Muscovite Russia, which regarded itself as the Third Rome after the fall of Constantinople to the Muslim Turks in 1453. But antisemitism became a prominent feature of Russian society only in the late eighteenth century, when the military conquests of Catherine the Great and the partitioning of Polish-controlled territory brought large numbers of Jews under direct Russian rule and permitted the more wealthy among them to join merchant guilds. Although the great majority of Jews in the Russian empire were restricted to the Pale of Settlement (a broad swath of land running from the Baltic to the Black Sea), a few were permitted to visit and even to live in Russia proper—particularly after the liberal reforms of Alexander II in the late 1850s and the 1860s.

The increased hostility toward Jews in both Germany and Russia in the latter half of the nineteenth century derived from envy and a sense of inferiority. German Jews took full advantage of the limited reforms, imposed by Napoleon, that permitted them a hitherto forbidden role in the social, cultural, and economic life of their country. In Russia, Alexander II not only emancipated the serfs in 1861 but also decreed a series of reforms which, though modest by Western (or even German) standards, greatly improved the status of the small minority of middle-class and wealthy Jews, chiefly in the merchant guilds.

A brief golden age for middle- and upper-class Russian Jews ended suddenly in 1881 with the murder of Alexander II. Only one Jew (a woman) was among the six members of the People's Will organization who were officially put on trial, but Jews were made the scapegoats for an assassination that in fact ran counter to their interests. It removed a unique supporter of Jewish rights and ended hopes for further social progress—for Jews in particular and for reform in general. Government repression led to more assassinations of tsarist officials, which in turn led to more repression and then to a rapid increase in revolutionary activity. Naturally, Jews played their part in these revo-

A Jewish old-age home in Kiev, administered by KEBO—Society for Relief of the Poor and the Sick. (Yiddishe Hilfs-Geselschaft). Before 1915

lutionary movements but were unjustly singled out by the authorities for blame and punishment.

As in Germany, an extreme and vicious nationalism played a central part in the rise of antisemitism in Russia, but it was more closely linked with religious intolerance. The Russian Orthodox church had remained almost untouched by the social, scientific, and philosophical turmoil that had challenged the exclusive authority of the Roman Catholic church and its various Protestant rivals. Russian Orthodoxy was the state religion, and Russians, who often called themselves simply "believers," viewed foreigners as *inovertsy,* "those of another belief."

Secularization of daily life in tsarist Russia never approached the levels achieved in Western Europe. The Russian authorities were, however, attracted to the new ideological basis for hostility toward Jews developed in Germany—that is, post-Christian antisemitism. Just like right-wing Germans, Russian right extremists saw antisemitism as a useful weapon against the challenge embodied in the liberal ideas and legal reforms emanating from Great Britain and France. Thus in 1905 the Russian government lent its authority to the *Protocols of the Elders of Zion,* a document adapted from a French model by Russian right-wing groups and published in small editions in various versions beginning in the 1890s. The turning point came when Russian agents in the Paris office of the Okhrana (secret police) declared that they had uncovered the document and that it provided conclusive evidence of a vast Jewish conspiracy to take over Russia and the world. They linked it with the radical activities of a large number of Russian students, many of them Jewish, attending French and Swiss universities. Even though this virulent tract was known to be a forgery almost at once in France and in Russia, the tsarist authorities had the document printed by official government typographers and Russian Orthodox church presses for broad distribution to the general public.

In this hate-filled atmosphere it is hardly surprising that many Russian Jews, particularly those educated in Western Europe, joined one of several revolutionary or radical groups that began to appear in the last two decades of the nineteenth century. Opposition to Russian chauvinism and antisemitism was an article of faith among these groups and parties, from the moderate Constitutional Democrats (Cadets) to the extreme left-wing Bolsheviks, and among non-Jews as well as Jews. In April 1917, following the collapse of the tsarist regime and the discrediting of the Russian Orthodox church that had supported it, the Provisional Government (which included no Jews) was quick to pass a law outlawing antisemitism of all kinds.

The Jews in Soviet Russia, 1917–41

From the ashes of tsarism arose a new multiethnic, atheistic state that proclaimed a secular faith in Marxist-Leninist internationalism, wherein all narrow national and ethnic interests were to be submerged. Lenin consistently inveighed against Russian chauvinism and was instrumental in reinforcing the Provisional Government's ban on antisemitism in 1918. The Bolshevik leader was, however, only interested in protecting the rights of secularized or assimilated Jews. Religious Jews lost the only right permitted to them grudgingly under the tsarist regime—the right to practice Judaism and observe Jewish customs. The teaching of Hebrew was forbidden, synagogues were closed (as were churches and mosques), and Yiddish schools were opened, but only as a means toward socializing Jewish children more efficiently. In addition, the Communist party established "Jewish sections" (*yevsektsii*), staffed by devoted Jewish Marxists, to root out Judaism and all "bourgeois survivals" among the shtetls that European-educated, secular Jews had long despised.

Nonreligious Jews were welcomed by the new Soviet regime. These well-educated and highly skilled Jews—many had degrees from prestigious European universities in such fields as medicine and engineering—were in great demand because most members of the tsarist empire's professional class had been arrested or had fled into exile. For the first time Jews were able to enter Russian universities and institutes without prejudice and on the basis of their abilities—a sharp contrast to the harsh discrimination in the tsarist period. Many Jews dreamed of turning the new Russia into a modern, enlightened state founded on the essential principles of European liberal and humanist thought.

Throughout the Soviet period, even in the worst times under Josef Stalin before and after World War II, some secular Jews were able to rise high in their chosen fields and to enjoy successful careers. Many adopted Russian names to conceal their Jewish origin (and perhaps to show their patriotism) and wisely avoided any connection with Yiddish, taking care to send their children to Russian, not Yiddish, schools. The process of russification was rapid. Statistics show that by 1939 a total of 54.6 percent of Soviet Jews listed Russian as their native language, more than double the figure of 25 percent obtained in the census of 1926. The 1939 census also revealed a massive migration of Jews from Ukraine and Belorussia to the Russian Republic, and from rural areas to towns and cities. As of 1939 nearly 1 million Jews inhabited the Russian Republic. Of this number about 400,000 lived in Moscow and 275,000 in Leningrad.

Nevertheless, even those Jews willing to submerge their cultural and religious background in order to enjoy equal rights and opportunities as Soviet citizens in an atheistic state found it increasingly difficult to escape the undertow of Russian nationalism and antisemitism. Although officially antisemitism was illegal, in the real world discrimination against Jews increasingly became the order of the day, blocking access to politically sensitive positions and restricting places at the top universities and institutes through a *numerus clausus* (quota). Jews became the targets of occasional purges and vicious media campaigns, of petty acts of prejudice in the workplace and at school, and of jokes that remained a part of the average Russian's repertoire.

The Union of Soviet Socialist Republics, ostensibly a voluntary federation of equal and independent states, was in fact dominated by Russians (or russified people of other nationalities), the Russian language, and the Russian Republic itself, which far exceeded in size and economic resources all the other Soviet republics. Lip service continued to be paid to Soviet internationalism, but during the 1930s Russian national interests came to the fore, sometimes at the expense of other nationalities or ethnic groups in the union.

In 1934, Stalin—a Georgian who became an extreme Russian nationalist—introduced the emotionally charged Russian word *rodina* (motherland) into public discourse to signal an officially sponsored focus on Russian history, Russian heroes, and Russian culture. The next three years were marked by an intense campaign against religion, including Judaism, which culminated in the mass arrests and executions of 1937–38. All minorities were at risk as a result of increasing official Russian intolerance of "nationalist deviations" and other real or imagined sins against the state. In Soviet Russia, however, Jews were a special case—as they had always been in tsarist Russia—from the high-profile victims in Stalin's show trials and the endless hounding of so-called Trotskyites to attacks on the old Jewish Bund, the Mensheviks, and the Zionists.

As so often in the Soviet period, laws on the books were ignored in favor of what was called "telephone law," or the unwritten laws that emanated from the Kremlin. Stalin, cautious as ever, did not reveal his dislike of Jews publicly (a tribute to Soviet hypocrisy), but during the 1930s he was behind a consistent effort to remove Jews from important party and state posts, replacing them as often as not with Russian peasants and workers. Such men presented no intellectual threat to Stalin, whose actions against Lenin's Jewish comrades appear to have been motivated by his own sense of inferiority and his profound paranoia, as well as by a streak of antisemitism that grew over the years of his rule until it threatened to erupt into a major pogrom shortly before his death in 1953.

Stalin's actions against Jews formed part of his attempts to russify his own image and to link himself with the towering heroes of Russian history, particularly with Peter the Great. In addition to Hitler's own personality cult (Stalin kept a close eye on Hitler's successes), the talented and sycophantic writer Aleksei Tolstoi may have helped inspire this self-aggrandizement by producing *Peter the First* (1929), an admiring novel about the conquering, ruthless tsar who forced modernization onto a reluctant, obscurantist populace. A major film version of Aleksei Tolstoi's novel appeared in 1936, making quite obvious the parallel between Peter and the "red tsar," Josef Stalin.

The steady marginalizing of Jews was linked most obviously to Stalin's russification policy at home. But it also had a specific foreign policy dimension. The removal of Jews from many important government positions appears to have been a cautious but unmistakable signal to Hitler of Stalin's willingness to cater to Nazi antisemitism. At the same time Stalin was building up his own image as a strong leader in the Russian tradition, ready to defend Mother Russia against all foes, foreign and domestic. Moreover, as the leader of the world Communist movement, Stalin did not hesitate to support anti-fascist forces in the Spanish civil war. To balance overtures toward the Nazis, Stalin ordered Sergei Eisenstein (one of several Jews who enjoyed success in Soviet cultural life) to produce a major feature film about Alexander Nevsky, the grand prince of Novgorod and a Russian Orthodox saint. Nevsky's main achievement was his defeat in 1242 of the Teutonic knights, crusaders sent by the pope to force the Eastern Orthodox Slavs into the Roman Catholic fold. Eisenstein's *Alexander Nevsky* had its premiere in November 1938. It was designed to appeal to Russian nationalism, not Soviet internationalism, and to serve as a warning to the Nazis that the Russians had defeated their crusading forebears and were ready to do it again.

But less than a year after *Alexander Nevsky* first appeared to rapturous reviews, it was suddenly withdrawn, and all negative references to Nazi Germany were forbidden. In the intervening months negotiations with Germany toward a mutual nonaggression pact had gathered momentum. Stalin was determined that nothing should spoil the chances of reaching an agreement. To this end he intensified removal of prominent Jews from their posts and ordered far more brutal measures against other prominent Jews, including arrest, torture, exile, and murder. By the spring of 1939 Soviet policy began to appear as antisemitic as that of the tsars. Stalin made sure that Hitler could not misunderstand his signals. In April the central government newspaper *Izvestiia* ceased publishing articles from the celebrated Jewish ex-patriot Ilya Ehrenburg, who frequently assailed Nazi racism and intolerance. The following month Stalin fired his Jewish foreign minister. Maksim Litvinov was replaced by the non-Jewish Russian Vyacheslav Molotov, whose abject obedience to his boss did not waver, even when Stalin had the new foreign minister's Jewish wife arrested and sent to the Gulag. Molotov was no doubt more concerned about his own fate. Stalin had recently ordered his secret police chief, Nikolai Yezhov, to have his own Jewish wife murdered; then he arrested Yezhov and executed him.

On 23 August 1939 Molotov and the German foreign minister, Joachim von Ribbentrop, signed a nonaggression pact on behalf of their respective governments. Shocking though the German-Soviet Nonaggression Pact might have been to outside observers, the agreement had been under discussion for some time. It resulted from Stalin's consistent courting of Hitler and his readiness to make a public show of assuaging Nazi sensitivities. In making at first indirect, and later direct, overtures to Hitler, Stalin also indicated his readiness to sacrifice fundamental Marxist-Leninist principles in order to secure friendly relations with the German dictator, who had referred repeatedly to "Jewish Bolshevism" as his main target. Perhaps Stalin felt more at home with another nationalistic, totalitarian state than with the liberal, bourgeois, capitalist states like Britain and France, which had long been the traditional ideological foes of Marxism-Leninism. In any case, the weak response to Hitler from Britain and France (including the Munich Agreement of September 1938) could do little to inspire Stalin's confidence.

The German-Soviet Nonaggression Pact sealed the beginning of World War II. In accordance with the secret protocols, Germany invaded Poland on 1 September, prompting Britain and France to honor their treaty obligations to Poland (at least nominally) by declaring war on Germany. The Soviet Union followed the script laid out in the secret protocols by invading Poland on 17 September. Very soon thereafter, the two armies moved to the agreed borders and celebrated their partition of Poland by arranging a joint parade in Brest (now in Belarus). The salute on the German side was taken by the famous tank commander, Gen. Heinz Guderian. Freed of concerns about his eastern flank, in May 1940 Hitler launched a successful blitzkrieg invasion against his Western European neighbors, leaving Britain the only country at war with Nazi Germany.

Over the next few months the adjustments on spheres of influence between Nazi Germany and Soviet Russia carved up Eastern Europe, permitting Stalin to reclaim most of the territory that had been part of the tsarist empire. The peoples of eastern Poland, the Baltic states, and occupied Romania suffered loss of life and liberty, as the Soviet authorities moved with characteristic speed and ruthlessness to arrest, execute, or deport many thousands of local and national leaders in all fields, particularly those with any history of "bourgeois-nationalist" or anti-Soviet activities.

As for the huge numbers of Jews caught unaware by this sudden seizure of territory, some may have thought that there was little difference between the two occupying powers. Jews were unable to practice their religion or celebrate their cultural traditions in territories occupied by either Nazi Germany or Soviet Russia. At this stage it was still Nazi policy to expel Jews, not kill them. Some Jews were shunted back and forth between Nazi and Soviet territory—neither side wanted them. But many Jews surely must have understood that they had much more to fear from Nazi racism than from Soviet communism. As a result, for several months until borders were finally sealed, large numbers of Jews fled to Soviet-occupied territory, sometimes in the hope of moving on to Palestine, where the Jewish community (the Yishuv) was encouraging European Jews to immigrate.

It is impossible to obtain accurate figures, but historians estimate that the number of Jews living in Soviet territory after 1939, either as a result of the initial Soviet occupation or of later migration by refugees, may have increased by close to 2 million. That brought the total number of Jews living in Soviet territory to around 5 million. Thus the Nonaggression Pact gave Nazi Germany and Soviet Russia a common border; the Soviet Union gained territory but lost the benefit of having buffer states between itself and Germany. Hitler had spoken and written of *Lebensraum*, "living space," in the East ever since his memoir-manifesto *Mein Kampf* (1925–27). The vast number of Jews living in Soviet territory made it a natural target for Hitler's Final Solution. Hence he could achieve two major policy goals with a single action—the decision to invade the "Jewish-Bolshevik" state.

The German Invasion and the Beginning of the Holocaust

The invasion of the Soviet Union on 22 June 1941 gave Hitler the opportunity to carry out the annihilation of the Jews of Europe. Implementing the Final Solution required wartime conditions, large concentrations of Jews, indifferent or hostile neighbors, and vast spaces far away from the prying eyes of the world media to serve as a killing ground. Although random brutalization and murder of Jews had taken place throughout

Russian women make their way through the ruins of Smolensk, which was destroyed by German forces. 13 August 1941

occupied Europe and in Germany itself, and had taken on a particularly savage character in western Poland since 1939, it was only after the Germans had invaded the Soviet Union that the systematic genocide of all Jewish men, women, and children began. Hitler had ordered a war not only against the Soviet Union but against the Jews as well.

The first unmistakable signal of the impending Holocaust came in the spring of 1941, when SS chief Heinrich Himmler directed the recruitment and training of special task forces, known as *Einsatzgruppen*. Four Einsatzgruppen were created (A, B, C, and D), consisting of about 700 men each. They were led for the most part by civilian professionals—people with advanced degrees in various fields and included academics, lawyers, and even a pastor of the Lutheran church. Their "special task" was in fact to follow behind the advancing German army (Wehrmacht) and round up and kill all Soviet Jews. Einsatzgruppe A was responsible for the Baltic states and the Leningrad area; Einsatzgruppe B for Belorussia, Russia, and the

Moscow region; Einsatzgruppe C for northern Ukraine and Kiev; and Einsatzgruppe D for southern Ukraine and the Caucasus. Hitler wanted his Lebensraum to be *Judenrein*, that is, totally free or "clean" of Jews, and he succeeded largely in this aim because of Stalin's incompetence and his indifference to the fate of Jews and because of the broad collaboration of the Soviet population with the Nazis.

The German advance during the summer and fall of 1941 was spectacularly successful. The invasion came as a complete surprise to the Soviet defense forces, which had been left totally unprepared. Several top commanders were in fact enjoying vacations at resorts on the Black Sea when the assault came. Stalin had stubbornly refused to pay attention to numerous and specific warnings about Hitler's plans from a variety of sources, including British prime minister Winston Churchill (who had access to Germany military codes), the Soviet spy Richard Sorge in Tokyo, and German defectors. Even as German troops advanced and German planes strafed and bombed Soviet troops, Stalin ordered his officers not to respond, thinking that the German actions might be some kind of provocation. Stalin's dreadful miscalculation and paralysis gave rise to a Russian joke: Stalin only ever trusted one man in his life, and that was Hitler.

Even after he recovered his nerve and delivered a radio address to the Soviet people on 3 July, Stalin persisted in making bad decisions that cost the lives of countless men and women at the front and enabled the Germans to roll ever faster into Soviet territory. Because Stalin ordered troops not to retreat under any circumstances, the German invaders were able to take literally millions of prisoners of war within just a few months in vast encirclement maneuvers against immobile military formations. Apparently incensed at their surrender, Stalin declared all Soviet soldiers captured by the Germans to be officially "enemies of the Motherland."

The civilian population had almost no time to recognize the danger from the Germans' lightning advance and to take steps to flee. In some cases, it must be said, civilians had no particular desire to escape the Germans. On the contrary, many people in the Baltic states and in Ukraine welcomed the German invaders as deliverers. Ideologically based hatred of the Soviet regime was intensified by long-standing national hatred of the Russians as imperialists and still vivid memories of the ruthless cruelty of the Soviet secret police, the NKVD (later renamed the KGB). The invasion opened up old wounds and soon cut through the facade of internationalism fostered by Stalin, even as he promoted Russian patriotism and had himself portrayed as a new Peter the Great. Understandably, the Germans made every effort to exacerbate political and ethnic hostility between Russians and Ukrainians, and between Russians and most other subject nationalities.

At the same time the Germans played on the established reputation of both Russians and Ukrainians for antisemitism. A telling example of German efforts to link Jews with Bolshevism is the leaflet that was dropped from aircraft over Red Army concentrations. Its message, illustrated with vivid drawings, urged soldiers to "get rid of your yid commissars; their ugly mugs deserve a brick." Most political commissars were not Jewish, but all were at risk as a result of Hitler's *Komissarbefehl* (commissar order), which declared that all Soviet political officers were to be shot on sight. In fact this order was often ignored as the war

dragged on, since the German military learned that a surprising number of non-Jewish Soviet political officers were willing and capable allies in the task of administering vast areas of occupied territory.

Whatever their hostility toward Russians and Bolshevik ideology, the German SS always viewed Jews as their primary target. It seems that most Wehrmacht officers and soldiers also hated Jews, as a result of long indoctrination. Hitler had correctly foreseen that the invasion of the Soviet Union would offer him the best opportunity to execute the Final Solution. And so the first stage of the Holocaust began, before the Wannsee Conference of January 1942 and before Himmler's July 1942 order that the ghettos be "liquidated" and Jews be sent to newly built death camps in Poland.

There were two particularly striking aspects of the Holocaust in Nazi-occupied Soviet territories: its blatantly public nature and the documented widespread collaboration of non-Jewish Soviet citizens in the murder of their neighbors and the staffing of the death camps. Before the establishment of the camps the chosen method of murder was by shooting, with the bodies dumped into large pits previously dug by Soviet prisoners of war or, in some cases, blasted open with explosives. The pits were usually located outside urban areas and near railroad tracks, since the victims were often transported by the thousands in cattle cars. The executions, which often lasted whole days at a time, could be seen and heard by neighbors in the vicinity, and frequently by regular German troops, who sometimes took photos (even though this was officially forbidden). The Nazi authorities would have preferred more privacy, but there was little they could do to prevent local inhabitants and German military personnel in the vicinity, often on leave, from witnessing these terrible crimes.

Hundreds of thousands of Jews were killed in this manner on Soviet territory, but anything like an exact figure for the total number of victims is very hard to obtain. To conceal evidence of their crimes, the SS destroyed all the records they could lay their hands on; but some records did survive. They also adopted a method in the Soviet Union that was used in the death camps in Poland: they turned their victims into ashes. As the Wehrmacht retreated after the decisive Soviet victories at Stalingrad and Kursk in 1943, the SS assigned special units to have the victims' bodies exhumed from the pits and burned. But the Soviet counteroffensive was so rapid that the SS did not always

An unidentified unit executes a group of Soviet civilians kneeling by the side of a mass grave. 22 June–September 1941

have time to destroy the evidence. In an as yet undetermined number of places, the pits within the Soviet Union still contain the remains of victims of the Holocaust. Only recently, and chiefly since the collapse of the Soviet regime in 1989, have some of these pits been marked as grave sites, although it often happens that the victims of the massacres are not identified as Jews.

Two contradictory issues have been raised with regard to the fate of Soviet Jewry. First, why did so many Jews fall victim to the Einsatzgruppen and so few escape? Second, why is it that such a large percentage of Soviet citizens evacuated away from the German advance were in fact Jews? Echoes of antisemitism can be detected in both questions, particularly the second, but they do reflect valid historical issues that deserve attention.

As to the first issue, it has been argued that Soviet Jews might not have known about Nazi actions against Jews in Germany and elsewhere. That seems unlikely. Before the signing of the German-Soviet Nonaggression Pact, the Soviet press contained articles about Nazi mistreatment of Jews, including reports from Ilya

Ehrenburg, who was still living in Paris. What is more, Soviet citizens, whether Jewish or not, relied on word-of-mouth accounts, which often spread faster than official news and were trusted more readily. After the pact many Eastern European Jews fled to Soviet-occupied territory and explained why they had done so to people they met. Soviet soldiers returning on leave from the new German-Soviet border region would also have told their families and friends stories of what they had witnessed. Finally, correspondence by letter with persons abroad was still possible, in spite of random NKVD censorship.

Of course, some Soviet Jews might have doubted both official news and rumors. Older people would have recalled the German occupation of their towns and cities during and after World War I and may well have found it hard to believe that the cultivated German people would behave in such a barbarous fashion. There were still Jews living in the Soviet Union who had visited Germany in pre-Soviet times; some had attended German universities and trained there as doctors, engineers, and scientists. It would have been difficult for such people to give up their admiration for German education, scientific advances, and cultural life.

The main reason, however, that so many Soviet Jews fell victim to the Einsatzgruppen was the sheer speed of the German advance. For example, by 7 July 1941, just over two weeks after the German attack on the Soviet Union, Army Group South had captured two important rail junctions, Berdichev and Zhitomir, only 160 kilometers west of Kiev, which itself lies more than 560 kilometers east of the border established by the 1939 pact. German armored columns often traveled more than 32 kilometers a day, although they often had to wait for the following infantry columns to catch up. Even before taking Kiev, the Germans succeeded in cutting off huge numbers of Soviet soldiers and civilians in various pockets. Those who were surrounded, particularly the unarmed civilians, had little option but to wait until the German infantry arrived to secure the areas. Then the German armored columns continued their advance. In spite of growing Soviet resistance, the Germans took Kiev before the end of September, capturing some 600,000 Soviet troops and killing another 400,000, in the greatest single Soviet military disaster of the war.

Only a very small percentage, probably less than 10 percent, of the Jews living in the areas of Soviet territory captured by the Germans in the first months of the war managed to escape. The failure of the Soviet authorities to give adequate warning to all citizens in the early weeks and months of the war was also a factor. Evidence suggests that party and government officials, as might be expected, had up-to-date information about the German advance. Under explicit orders not to cause a panic by making "defeatist" public statements, these highly placed officials avoided reporting the terrible news from the approaching front lines. Instead they took quiet and effective measures to save themselves and their families.

Some of these officials were Jewish, but this fact hardly affected their behavior as Soviet officials or indeed as human beings determined to focus on their own welfare. Their failure to warn other citizens, who happened to be Jewish, of the impending tragedy did not save them from the charge of favoritism by anti-semites or those who did not have the advantage of official connections and privileges. Quite early in the war, Russians—most notoriously the novelist Mikhail Sholokhov, a favorite of Stalin's—began charging that

Jews did not make good soldiers, that they were cowards, and that far too many of them had received preferential treatment in getting evacuated to Central Asia. This talk in its turn gave rise to the denigrating phrase "Tashkent partisans," used throughout the war to ridicule Jews.

In fact, about a half-million Jews served in the Soviet military during the war. Nearly 200,000 Jewish soldiers were killed or went missing in action. The extraordinary casualty rate among Jews (40 percent) was much higher than that of the Soviet population as a whole (25 percent). As for honors, Jews won more than their share, in spite of occasional hostility from superiors. In all, 123 Jews (including one woman, a pilot) were named Hero of the Soviet Union. Of these, 45 decorations were awarded posthumously; eight other honorees died in action before the war ended.

Jewish representation in partisan groups was much smaller than it was in the Soviet military. Of an estimated 1 million partisans, at most 50,000 were Jewish. But the reasons for this lower level of participation have nothing to do with Jewish willingness to fight. Jews were rejected by Russian and particularly Ukrainian partisan groups; some of the Ukrainian groups were in fact anti-Soviet and anti-Russian as well as anti-Jewish. Jewish civilians had a great deal of difficulty in escaping from German encirclement or occupation, as they were marked targets for isolation in ghettos and deportation to camps—not only by Germans. Moreover, Jews often faced war on two fronts: from the foreign invader and from their non-Jewish neighbors and Soviet compatriots.

Only one-third of all Jewish partisans operated in Ukraine, whereas one-half fought in Belorussia, which has a much smaller population base. Not only was Ukraine a more hostile environment for Jews, because of widespread antisemitism and collaboration with the Nazis, but it also lacked the forest cover that Belorussia provided for partisans and their families. The Jewish partisans in Belorussia and Lithuania performed heroic service for the Soviet cause against the German invaders and their local collaborators. Many Jewish partisan units came to specialize in constructing and laying explosives. They blew up so many railways, supply trains, and bridges that the Germans were obliged to divert an entire division to prevent crippling losses in men and matériel on the Belorussian railway linking Warsaw and Smolensk. These efforts failed, even though the German division was reinforced by allied Lithuanian and Cossack units. One of the most celebrated bombings was conducted by a woman partisan, Yelena Mazanik, who planted the device that blew up Wilhelm Kube, gauleiter of Belorussia, in Minsk on 22 September 1943.

Thus the Jews, both in regular military units and in partisan groups, played a valuable part in the Soviet war effort. Nevertheless, in the postwar period the Soviet authorities discounted their contributions. During the war itself, Jews who managed to attain positions of command in mixed-ethnic partisan groups were quietly ordered to drop their Jewish-sounding names. Only when Red Army units retook territory that had been occupied by the Nazis did the Jewish partisans receive a token of respect: Jews were sent immediately to join front-line units because they were trusted completely, whereas non-Jewish partisans were thoroughly interrogated because their loyalty to the Soviet Union was considered suspect.

Jews indeed were well represented among those whom the Soviet government evacuated to the rear, but for reasons unrelated to their fighting spirit. In spite of Stalin's purge of highly placed Jews during the Great Terror of the late 1930s and the period leading up to the Nazi invasion, in 1941 Jews still made up a significant proportion of the country's professionals and skilled workers. As such, they naturally acquired high-priority status for the Soviet war effort, and their names landed on lists of people to be evacuated. What is more, such people enjoyed much better connections within the party and the government than ordinary unskilled industrial workers or collective farm workers. As a result, most urban Jews with needed skills and talents managed to avoid the fate of hundreds of thousands of other Jews living in the immediate path of the invading German troops and the Einsatzgruppen that followed them. Even so, Jews remained a small minority of the evacuees.

Postwar Soviet Policy

Only one country after World War II made Holocaust denial state policy. That country was the Soviet Union, which had done by far the most to defeat Nazi Germany, inflicting over 80 percent of German losses in men and matériel, and had suffered more than any other country from German aggression and occupation. In a macabre irony, the Soviet Union became an accomplice of Nazi Germany in concealing evidence of a genocide committed against its own citizens and on its own soil. The fact that the Einsatzgruppen and SD targeted Jewish civilians did not fit with the party line that all nationalities suffered equally in the "Great Patriotic War."

The Soviet position on the death camps in Poland, which the Red Army had liberated, paralleled the official attitude toward the beginnings of the Holocaust on Soviet territory. It tried to blur any distinctions between Jews and other victims, and between the extermination camps (reserved for Jews) and the slave labor camps (reserved for non-Jews) that constituted the total camp system. Of course, large numbers of people from almost every country in occupied Europe were brutalized and died in Nazi slave labor camps, but no nationality or ethnic group besides Jews and Gypsies was targeted for extermination in gas chambers, whether immediately on arrival or after they had been used as slave labor.

Soviet policy can be summed up in the scripted phrase "Do not divide the dead." The phrase and the policy it represents began to be used even before the war ended. Both continued after Stalin's death, until the collapse of the Soviet regime itself. Their link to Russian nationalism and antisemitism is clear, if only from the fact that official statements and histories always stressed the leading part that Russians had played in the victory and in the sacrifice that victory demanded. The pattern began as early as May 1945, when, in a celebrated speech given at a banquet in the Kremlin for senior military officers and for guests from allied nations, Stalin toasted the dominant Russian role in the triumph over Nazi Germany. There is much justification for this praise of the remarkable effort by ordinary Russian people.

The Soviet denial had its distant origins in Russian history, but it also followed naturally enough from the actions taken by Stalin during the war. The Nazis' surprise attack on the Soviet Union and the devastating military successes of the Wehrmacht obliged Stalin to make a quick adjustment in his prewar policy of dismissing Jews from prominent positions in an effort to cater to Hitler's antisemitism. But Stalin was nothing if not flexible. He quickly reversed course and symbolically awarded Sergei Eisenstein a State Prize (First Class) for *Alexander Nevsky*, which had been banned since the signing of Nonaggression Pact. And in August 1941 Stalin orchestrated a large public meeting of prominent Soviet Jews in Moscow (Ilya Ehrenburg was not among their number). The meeting, broadcast over Moscow radio, was devoted to a series of speeches condemning Nazi racism and calling on Jews throughout the world to assist the Soviet Union in its struggle against unprovoked aggression.

In his scramble for allies Stalin even released two Polish-Jewish leaders of the socialist Bund, Henryk Erlich and Victor Alter, from an NKVD jail. His agents encouraged the two men to come up with ideas that would enlist broad Jewish support from all parts of the political spectrum and to work together with the Polish government-in-exile in London. Nothing substantial came of the latter initiative (Polish-Jewish relations were always very strained), but Erlich and Alter did make one fruitful suggestion: the creation of an international Jewish Anti-Hitler Committee to mobilize worldwide opinion against the Nazis.

The German advance on Moscow stalled in the deep freeze of an early winter. Alerted by his spy Richard Sorge that he had nothing to fear from the Japanese because they were planning to attack Pearl Harbor and not the Soviet Union (on this occasion the Soviet dictator wisely trusted Sorge's reports), Stalin had several armies of fresh Siberian troops transported by train in high secrecy to Moscow. On 5 December 1941 these troops mounted a surprise counterattack on the German forces that had come so close to capturing Moscow earlier in the fall.

Stalin seems to have been confident of success, and indeed the Wehrmacht was driven back and never fully recovered from this shattering blow. A day before the counterattack he had Erlich and Alter arrested again. (Erlich later committed suicide, and Alter was shot.) He had never wanted to deal with them because they belonged to the Bund (which had been condemned by Lenin). Now he did not need them any more, although he did remember their proposal. It was adopted in April 1942, with the name changed to the Jewish Antifascist Committee (JAC). It remained under strict Soviet control, without the foreign membership that Erlich and Alter had suggested. Stalin had to make an accommodation with his suspect capitalist allies, but he was determined to keep them at arm's length until they had served their purpose.

Stalin's handling of the JAC illustrates his dual approach to dealing with Jews during the war. For foreign consumption he supported the committee but restricted its domestic activities because he did not want Soviet and particularly Russian troops to think that they were fighting merely to protect Jews from the German invaders. It was vital that the struggle against Hitler be viewed as a national—that is, Russian—war, not a Soviet war for internationalism or Marxism-Leninism. That is why the war was called from the outset the Great Patriotic War—a deliberate echo of the Patriotic War, the name given to the struggle against Napoleon in 1812–13. For the same reason the Russian Orthodox church was permitted to revive, although under strict government control; the object was to intensity the effort to turn the war into yet another episode in the long history of conflict between Teuton and Slav, between (from the Russian point of view) the heretical Western church and the true faith.

The same careful distinction between foreign and domestic concerns marked Stalin's handling of *The Black Book*, a volume of testimony about Nazi atrocities against Jews, produced under the aegis of the JAC. *The Black Book* was to be aimed at the foreign market, and some draft copies did reach the West. But it was never published in the Soviet Union, not even during the glasnost period of relaxed censorship in the late 1980s.

A similar fate awaited a concerted official effort to document all the atrocities committed during the Nazi occupation, chiefly against the civilian population. In 1943, as Red Army troops began their advance toward Berlin, the Soviet authorities established the Extraordinary State Commission for the Investigation of Atrocities Committed on Soviet Territory by the German Fascists and Their Accomplices. Staffed chiefly by NKVD and party officials, this commission produced a massive amount of data based on interviews with perpetrators, eyewitnesses, and survivors. Some of the evidence was presented at the Nuremberg war crimes trials, but then the archives were sealed.

What had happened? It appears that the commission documented the Holocaust on Soviet soil by accident. When it became clear that Nazi atrocities were committed chiefly against Jewish civilians and Russian prisoners of war, the authorities stepped in. Like *The Black Book*, the archives of the commission were never made public during the Soviet period. What is more, known sites of massacres of tens of thousands of Jews were left unmarked in any manner that would truthfully acknowledge the Jewish victims.

Another reason that the Soviet authorities treated the commission archives with great circumspection is that they revealed extensive collaboration by Soviet citizens, most notably in Ukraine, in identifying, bru-

Jewish prisoners ordered to disrobe by German police and Ukrainian auxiliaries before being shot.

talizing, and assembling Jews for the massacres committed by the German SS members of the Einsatzgruppen. Once the cautious authorities read their own reports, they locked them away in the NKVD closed archives. Only after the dissolution of the Soviet Union were energetic researchers from Yad Vashem able to photocopy portions of the massive archives. Even this partial record confirms that in many cases the SS could hardly have carried out the massacres

quickly and effectively without assistance from collaborators, chiefly the Hilfspolizei (auxiliary police) or *politsai*, as they were commonly called.

A recently discovered Wehrmacht document in the German National Archives reveals where most of the Ukrainian Polizei came from and why they were so adept at using arms and brute force. The document, entitled "Situation Regarding POWs in Operational Area and Romania" (Kriegsgefangenenlager im Operationsgebiet und Rumänien) and dated 20 February 1942, states that by 31 January 1942 a total of 280,108 Soviet prisoners of war had already been released. Of this number fully 270,095 were Ukrainians. Not a single released prisoner was Russian. Indeed, the document notes specifically that Russians "do not qualify" for release. The document confirms that Russian POWs were treated far more harshly than Soviet POWs of all other Soviet nationalities, and that Ukrainian POWs were treated with particular favor.

In the case of Ukrainian collaboration, Soviet and Russian policy considerations coalesced. It was as important for a Soviet leader as it would have been for a tsarist leader to keep Ukraine within the fold. After World War II it took a long time for the ethnic fault lines revealed by the German invasion to be patched. The case of Ukraine was uniquely important for Russian leaders in Moscow. Western Ukraine (Galicia), which had become part of the Soviet Union as a result of the German-Soviet Nonaggression Pact, continued to resist sovietization at the end of the war. A decision was made in the Kremlin that it would be wise to paper over collaboration in other parts of Ukraine so as to enlist Ukrainian support for complete reunification.

Such issues of state policy became moot with the collapse of the Soviet Union in 1991, when Ukraine started a new phase in its history as an independent state. The new Russian Federation had other more immediate problems to wrestle with in the 1990s and could spare little time to consider the injustice done to its Jewish citizens. For 50 years their suffering was ignored and their contribution to the war effort denigrated. The revival of Russian nationalism in its anti-Western form may well delay even further the publication in Russia of a truthful account of the German occupation, most specifically the Holocaust, which began on Soviet territory. See also UKRAINE.

John Garrard

S

SA (Sturmabteilung) Storm troopers, the uniformed section of the Nazi party, founded in 1923. The SA played a role in the street fighting of the last years of the Weimar Republic. After the purge of its leadership in the Night of the Long Knives (30 June 1934), its importance greatly declined. The 9–10 November 1938 pogrom known as Kristallnacht was one of the few occasions on which the SA was mobilized to manifest the "people's rage." After 1939 the SA trained men for Home Guard units.

Sachsenhausen Concentration camp north of Berlin, established in 1936. Some 200,000 inmates passed through Sachsenhausen. Most were Poles and Russian prisoners of war, but some were Germans. The maximum population of the camp was 47,000. According to estimates, about half of those registered in the camp, and most of those brought to Sachsenhausen but not registered, perished. After the war political internees of the German Democratic Republic (East Germany) were imprisoned at Sachsenhausen.

Salonika (Thessaloníki) Second-largest Greek city, with the largest prewar Jewish community in Greece, numbering about 50,000 at the time of the German invasion and occupation in April 1941. The great majority of the city's Jews were deported to Auschwitz in 1943. Several hundred survived forced labor in Germany or escaped to the mountains of northern Greece. See GREECE

Schulte, Eduard (1891–1966) German industrialist who first informed the Jewish institutions in Switzerland in July 1942 that the Nazi regime had decided to destroy European Jewry. Schulte also provided information to Jewish and Allied organizations on other topics and helped individual Jews. He escaped to Switzerland in December 1943 and lived the rest of his life there. See RIEGNER TELEGRAM

Schwarzbart, Ignacy (1888–1961) Polish Jewish leader who represented the Zionists in the Polish parliament prior to the outbreak of the war and subsequently in the Polish government-in-exile in London. Before the war he was a leader of the Jewish community in Kraków. See POLISH GOVERNMENT-IN-EXILE

SD (Sicherheitsdienst) Security Service. Part of the RHSA, the Nazi security apparatus. In contrast to the Gestapo, the SD was primarily engaged in espionage and the collection of information both inside and outside Germany. The SD took part in the preparation and implementation of the Final Solution. Its members often served in the *Einsatzgruppen*, or mobile killing squads, that followed the German army into conquered Soviet territory in 1941 and murdered hundreds of thousands of Jews.

Serbia See YUGOSLAVIA

Sinti See GYPSIES

Slovakia Slovakia, a province of Hungary until 1918, was part of the Czechoslovak Republic during the years between the two world wars. On 6 October 1938 it became an autonomous region within federal Czechoslovakia. Andrej Hlinka's Slovak People's party (Hlinkova Slovenska Ludova Strana, or HSLS) came to power and outlawed all other parties—the Communist and Social Democratic parties as well as the Jewish party. Only the German and Hungarian minorities were granted the right to form parties on ethnic grounds. Almost simultaneously the paramilitary Hlinka Guard (HG) was established. The Germans too formed their own armed volunteer squadron, the Freiwillige Schutzstaffel (FS). During a conference with Hermann Göring on 16–17 October the Slovak leaders declared that they considered their primary task to be the solution of the Jewish problem in a way

A German corporal (Obergefreiter) leads three Jewish men in forced calisthenics on Eleftheria (Freedom) Square in Salonika. 11 July 1942

similar to that adopted by Germany. Street attacks on Jews and looting of property became the order of the day. Under the terms of the Vienna Award (2 November 1938) Adolf Eichmann visited Bratislava to advise the Slovak authorities on the forced removal of "stateless" persons. Jews born in territories ceded to Hungary were dragged from their beds, put on trucks, and driven to the no-man's-land between the Slovakian and Hungarian borders.

Upon the instigation of Adolf Hitler an independent Slovak state was proclaimed by the parliament in Bratislava on 14 March 1939. The new government was headed by the leader of the HSLS, the Catholic priest Jozef Tiso; his deputy, Vojtech Tuka; and Ferdinand Durcansky, minister of foreign affairs and the interior. The next day Tiso appealed to Hitler for the "protection" of the Reich. On 23 March the Slovak leaders and the Reich foreign minister, Joachim von Ribbentrop, signed a treaty that provided that in foreign policy Slovakia would follow the lead of Germany. On 26 October 1939 Tiso was elected president of the

Slovak state. The 1930 census counted 135,918 Jews in Slovakia, about 4.5 percent of the inhabitants of the region. Three-quarters of the population was Roman Catholic, and the rest of the citizens were Eastern Catholic (Uniate) and Protestant. The greater part of the Jewish populace had been nationally conscious: eastern Slovakia was the stronghold of the strictly observant Orthodox Jews, whereas the more well-to-do and educated strata of Jews in Bratislava and other western cities prided themselves on a small but vibrant Zionist organization and a growing youth movement. There was, however, a Neolog and a small Status Quo Ante community, a residue of the Hungarian community pattern.

Antisemitism in Slovakia had a long tradition; accusations of corruption, "magyarization," and (later) "czechization" were rampant. The first restrictions, sporadically inflicted on the Jewish population, were intended to oust them from economic life and to limit their activity in the free professions; those affected were mainly lawyers and physicians. The process of eviction was intensified in the second half of 1939, when land in Jewish possession was confiscated and Aryan trustees were appointed to run large Jewish businesses. Jews were expelled from the government and the army and obliged to perform forced labor. A watershed was the Salzburg Conference (28 July 1940), attended by Hitler and Ribbentrop, during which the Slovak leaders Tiso, Tuka (who had become prime minister and foreign affairs minister), and Alexander (Sano) Mach (nominated as the new minister of the interior) consented to introduce a National Socialist regime.

By the end of August 1940 Dieter Wisliceny, Eichmann's delegate from the Reich Security Main Office (RSHA), had arrived in Bratislava as "adviser for Jewish affairs," along with a score of specialists to be attached to the various ministries and the Hlinka Guard, which soon became modeled on the SS. Henceforth Jewish males, instead of being conscripted into the armed forces, were drafted into special auxiliary labor units in labor centers erected throughout the country. According to the census of 15 December 1940, the number of Jews who remained in truncated Slovakia (following the cession of territories to Hungary and the emigration of a few thousand Jews) had dropped to 88,951, or 3.35 percent of the population (2,655,964). An estimate of the value of Jewish property showed that collective Jewish assets amounted to more than 3 billion Slovak crowns (approximately 105 million 1938 U.S. dollars); 44 percent was in real estate, 23 percent in businesses, and 33 percent in Jewish community property (mostly immovables).

As an outcome of the Salzburg Conference two institutes were set up in September 1940, both based on special decrees whose objective was the solution of the so-called Jewish problem in Slovakia: the Central Economic Office (Ustredny Hospodarsky Urad, or UHU), which reported to the prime minister and was headed by Augustin Moravek, an expert on aryanization of property; and the Jewish Center (Ustredna Zidov), under the UHU. The Jewish Center was the only body authorized to represent the Jews of Slovakia and to regulate their lives. Funding for these organizations came from the confiscation of property belonging to 175 liquidated Jewish organizations and welfare societies, as well as from taxes imposed on all Jews. The Jewish Center, headquartered in Bratislava, had local branches in towns in every district. Beginning 7 March 1941 a community gazette, *Vestnik*, issued by the Jew-

ish Center, served to transmit the orders and regulations of the authorities. Augustin Moravek appointed Heinrich Schwartz, a lawyer and former chairman of the Orthodox community, as the first Jewish elder (*starosta*), and he also named the 10 members of the presidium. In April 1941, however, Schwartz was arrested on charges of obstructing the relocation of the Jews of Bratislava and was replaced by Arpad Sebestyen, a school principal who lacked any experience in community affairs. Sebestyen, closely cooperating with Karol Hochberg, who was in charge of the Department for Special Tasks and whose unrestrained ambition brought him to collaborate with Wisliceny, cast a deep shadow on the reputation of the Jewish Center during the crucial period 1942–43.

Upon the German invasion of the Soviet Union, Slovakia, as a joint member of the Axis powers, dispatched a division to the eastern front. It was through the chaplain of the Slovak army, Michal Buzalka, that the apostolic delegate in Bratislava, Monsignor Giuseppe Burzio, first learned in late summer 1941 about the massacre of the Jews on Soviet territory. Burzio promptly informed the Vatican.

The fall of 1941 brought a number of radical innovations. On 9 September 1941 the so-called Jewish code (*zidovsky kodex*) was promulgated by the government. Its complex set of 270 articles introduced the requirement that Jews wear the yellow badge as well as forced labor for Jews aged 16–60. The code defined a Jew no longer on the basis of religion but according to race, with criteria (regarding mixed marriages and half-Jews) more severe than those established in the Nuremberg Laws of 1935. However, a certain category of Jews "vital" for the Slovak economy—such as technicians, financial experts, and physicians—was exempted from the law. The president of Slovakia was authorized to grant certificates of exemption to converts and to some privileged individuals, in exchange for payment. Ten thousand Bratislava Jews were evicted from their homes and deported, mainly to the eastern district of Saris-Zemplin. To accelerate the removal, Department 14, headed first by Gejza Konka and later by Anton Vasek, was set up within the interior ministry. In the spring of 1942 its principal task became that of organizing deportations to the death camps with the assistance of the Hlinka Guard and the FS.

The aryanization process had been carried out swiftly. Within a year 10,025 Jewish enterprises and businesses had been liquidated and 2,223 had been transferred to non-Jewish ownership. Once the Jewish population had been totally impoverished, the authorities decided to act swiftly to get rid of this new burden on public relief. The initial step was taken in May 1941, when Moravek proposed to Wisliceny and Erich Gebert of the German embassy that part of the Slovak Jewish population be dumped in the Generalgouvernement, the military district of Poland. The matter was discussed in concrete terms on 23–24 October 1941 during the official visit of the Slovak leaders to Hitler's headquarters in the East, when Ribbentrop and SS chief Heinrich Himmler held negotiations with Tuka. As a result, at the beginning of 1942 a German demand was received in Bratislava to supply 20,000 workers to German factories. The Slovak leaders complied eagerly. Thus without any legal basis, merely in accordance with an agreement reached in February 1942 between Prime Minister Tuka and the German ambassador in Bratislava, Hans Ludin, it was decided to deport 20,000 strong, able-bodied Slovak Jews. Slovakia was to pay 500 Reichsmarks to Germany for every deported Jew to cover such expenses as clothing, food, housing, and "vocational training." Tuka for his part demanded a guarantee that the Jews would not be returned and that the Reich would not present further claims as far as Jewish property was concerned. Not until 23 May 1942, after 40,000 Jews had been deported, did the Slovak parliament pass Law 68/1942, which provided that "Jews may be expelled from the territory of the Slovak republic." Only one member of parliament, the Hungarian minority delegate Count Janos Eszterhazy, abstained; none voted against the measure.

Even before the passage of Law 68/1942, pleas for mercy addressed to the Slovak president by the Jewish communities (5 March) and the rabbis of Slovakia (6 March), on the grounds that the deportation of 80,000 Jews would mean their physical annihilation, were denied. Moreover, efforts by the vicar of Bratislava, Augustin Pozdech, and a letter of protest from the bishop of Trnava, Pavol Jantausch, were to no avail. Even a note sent by the Secretariat of the Holy See on 14 March 1942 and a protest by Monsignor Burzio appealing to President Tiso's feelings as a Catholic priest were left unanswered. The government's self-righteous response addressed to the Holy See concerning the "resettlement" and "humane treatment" accorded to deportees "under protection of the Reich" (*Schutzbefohlene*) had to wait until 23 May.

The first transports of young men and women were dispatched as of 26 March 1942 to Auschwitz, Majdanek, and the camps in the Lublin region. After the Slovak government had persuaded Eichmann that "in the Christian spirit" families should not be separated, whole families were deported. By October 1942 around 60,000 Jews had been shipped out of Slovakia; only 250 survived the war. Some daring individuals made their escape from the camps and returned to Slovakia as early as the end of April. Also several clandestine letters, conveying coded messages of death and horror, were received by relatives of the deported as well as at Jewish Center headquarters. Rumors spread and thousands of young Jews fled to neighboring Hungary in search of refuge. (Many of these young people became the nucleus of the only resistance group active in Budapest after the occupation of Hungary by the Wehrmacht in March 1944.) Others avoided deportation by acquiring certificates of labor or baptismal papers, issued mainly by the more lenient and sympathetic Evangelical clergy. Both the Protestant and the Roman Catholic churches made attempts to obtain privileges for baptized Jews. Any Slovak Christian assisting Jews was mockingly labeled a "white Jew" (*bily zid*). The cruel methods employed by the Hlinka Guard and the FS, who crammed elderly and sick persons as well as babies into cattle cars, evoked mute horror and compassion among the religious Slovak villagers.

The transports came to a standstill between July and mid-September 1942, owing to renewed German attacks on the eastern front and "other technical obstacles," as indicated by the Slovak Railway Administration. On 25 June Ambassador Ludin informed Berlin that "deportations had become widely unpopular." President Tiso himself, however, on 15 August declared in a speech at Holic that "it was a Christian deed to expel the Jews, since it was for the benefit of the Slovak nation that it should free itself of its pest."

During the halt in the deportations the clandestine Working Group (Pracovna Skupina) came into being, headed by Gisi Fleischmann, the only Jewish woman acting as the leader of a community under siege. This shadow government was composed of Zionists, rabbis, and assimilated Jews: Rabbi Michael Dov Ber Weissmandel, Tibor Kovacs, Rabbi Armin Frieder, Andrej Steiner, Oscar Neumann, Vojtech Winterstein, and Vilem Furst. Most of them were associated with the Jewish Center. They had the support of some highly placed Slovak officials such as the minister of educa-

Slovak members of the "Guarda Maria" police cut the beard of Liper Baum during a deportation action in Stropkov. 23 May 1942

tion, Josef Sivak; the governor of the National Bank of Slovakia, Imrich Karvas; and the lawyer Ivan Pietor, who kept them informed and were assisting them in various ways out of humanitarian motives. The Working Group staked its hopes on getting financial assistance from Jewish organizations abroad and maintaining regular contact with the Jewish Defense Committee, the Jewish Agency, and the World Jewish Congress through the good offices of the representative of the Hehalutz movement in Geneva, Nathan Schwalb. The main objective was to stop further deportations by bribing Wisliceny and some of the Slovak officials. Within the framework of the Jewish Center the Working Group sought to increase productivity in the labor camps Sered Vyhne and Novaky by launching new projects and workshops, thus producing goods and material vital to the Slovak economy.

In an attempt to ransom the lives of the remaining Jews in German-occupied Europe, Rabbi Weissmandel initiated the so-called Europa Plan. Wisliceny was to act as mediator between the Working Group and the SS chiefs. Although the plan never materialized, it opened the way to various rescue schemes in 1944–45. After the defeats suffered by Germany and with the turning of the tide in 1943, the strife between the two rival groups, the "moderate" Tiso and the radical Tuka-Mach clique, sharpened. The latter called for a resumption of deportations of the remaining 20,000 Jews in Slovakia. Owing to the alertness of the Working Group, the new threat, sounded in February 1943 by Sano Mach, was thwarted.

In this chain of interventions the apostolic nuncio of Istanbul, Monsignor Angelo Roncalli (who in 1958 became Pope John XXIII), was instrumental. A pastoral letter condemning totalitarianism and antisemitism was issued on 8 March 1943 by the Roman Catholic episcopate. The so-called quiet years were fruitfully used by the Working Group for the consolidation of the remnant community and for rescue work. Arpad Sebestyen had been ousted as Jewish elder and replaced by the Jewish Center's own trusted member, Oscar Neumann. The Working Group was instrumental in helping to smuggle Jewish orphans and survivors from the neighboring Generalgouvernement in coal carts and hay wagons, first back to Slovakia, then via Hungary to safety in Palestine. It also kept transmitting information to the free world about the ongoing mass murder in Poland, including accounts and testimonies written by fugitives from the extermination camps at Sobibor, Majdanek, and Treblinka.

On 21 April 1944 the first two Slovak Jewish escapees from Auschwitz, Alfred Wetzler and Walter Rosenberg (Rudolf Vrba), who had been deported in 1942, reached Slovakia. Through the assistance of the Working Group their eyewitness account—the famous Auschwitz Protocol—of the structure and methods of annihilation in the extermination camp was dispatched to Budapest and via Switzerland to the free world. Rabbi Weissmandel's letter accompanying the protocol contained an urgent appeal for the immediate bombing of the murder installations and the rail lines leading to Auschwitz in an attempt to save Hungarian Jewry.

With the approach of the Red Army, the Slovak underground was reinforced by Russian partisans, who parachuted into the area. Sporadic fighting began in the mountains and culminated in a prematurely proclaimed Slovak national uprising (29 August 1944) at Banska Bystrica. The Slovak National Council (established in December 1943) called for the restoration of the Czechoslovak Republic. Jewish inmates liberated from the Novaky labor camp formed an independent fighting unit. Altogether the Jewish partisans numbered approximately 2,000, of whom around 15 percent fell in the fighting. In the middle of September they were joined by four parachutists from the Yishuv (the Jewish community in Palestine)—Haviva Reik, Zvi Ben-Yaakov, Raphael Reiss, and Haim Hermesh—who formed a British unit whose aim was to organize armed resistance among European Jews and to boost their morale. After the collapse of the insurgence, during the withdrawal to the mountains, three of the parachutists were captured in a German surprise attack, jailed, and later executed at Kremnicka on 20 November 1944, together with some 100 local Jews. With the suppression of the uprising, the fate of the remaining Jews was sealed. Under the pretext of reprisal for their participation, of the 4,653 Jews caught in the combat zones, 2,257 were shot on the spot by an SS squadron under Oskar Dirlewanger and by attached special squadrons of the Hlinka Guard. The rest were sent to concentration camps.

In spite of intervention by the president of the International Red Cross, by the Swiss consulate, and by the archbishop of Uppsala (Sweden), President Tiso remained adamant to the end. On 8 November 1944 he wrote to Pope Pius XII: "The deportations were undertaken in order to defend the nation before its foe. . . . We owe this as [an expression] of gratitude and loyalty to the Germans for our national sovereignty. . . . This debt is in our Catholic eyes the highest honor." Following the arrival of the new RSHA emissary, Alois Brunner, about 13,500 Jews were deported between October 1944 and March 1945. The first five transports were sent to Auschwitz and the rest to Ravensbrück, Bergen-Belsen, and Theresienstadt. On the eve of liberation in April 1945 there remained around 4,000–5,000 Jews in hiding with non-Jews or in bunkers and mountain huts; others survived by carrying false "Aryan" identification papers.

After the war, in the reestablished Czechoslovakia, People's Courts were set up to try persons accused of war crimes. Members of the Slovak puppet government, including President Tiso, were convicted of treason and crimes against humanity, sentenced to death, and executed in Bratislava in 1947. The losses suffered by Slovak Jewry during the two deportation waves (in 1942 and 1944–45) are estimated at 68,000–71,000 persons. Together with the Jews who were deported in May 1944 to Auschwitz from the territory annexed to Hungary in 1938, the number of deaths comes to more than 100,000. Only about 25,000 Slovak Jews—less than 20 percent of the prewar community—survived the war. Half of that remnant emigrated to Israel during the mass exodus of 1948–49. More than 50 years after the Holocaust merely 3,000 Jews were registered with the Jewish community in the Slovak Republic. *Livia Rothkirchen*

Sobibor Extermination camp established in 1942 near Lublin in the south of Poland. The gas chambers of Sobibor claimed the lives of a quarter-million Jews and other prisoners deported from Poland, Austria, Czechoslovakia, France, Germany, the Netherlands, and Slovakia. The Red Army liberated the camp in the summer of 1944. By that time all the inmates had been killed, the guards evacuated, and most traces of the mass murder obliterated. See EXTERMINATION CAMPS

Aristides de Sousa Mendes and family in Portugal. Circa 1940

Sousa Mendes, Aristides de (1885–1954) Portuguese consul general in Bordeaux, France. In 1940 Sousa Mendes issued Portuguese entry visas to many Jewish refugees, ignoring instructions from Lisbon not to do so. Upon learning of his insubordination, the Portuguese government recalled him to Portugal and dismissed him from the foreign service. Various Jewish organizations honored Sousa Mendes after the war, including Israel's Yad Vashem, which named him one of the Righteous Among the Nations. The Portuguese parliament rehabilitated him in 1988.

Spain In 1933, when antisemitism became the official policy in Germany, Spain was ruled by a republican government, which had replaced the monarchy in 1931. Jewish refugees began to arrive in Madrid and Barcelona, where they were assisted by a local committee sponsored by the HICEM, an umbrella organiza-

tion for groups assisting European Jews to emigrate to new countries, except Palestine (to which the World Zionist Organization and the Jewish Agency for Palestine were responsible). The acronym HICEM derives from the names of three agencies: HIAS, which stands for Hebrew Sheltering and Immigrant Aid Society of America; ICA, a Yiddish version of the Jewish Colonization Association; and Emigdirekt. In 1935 the HICEM explored the possibilities of a larger Jewish immigration and settlement in Spain, but soon after the Spanish civil war broke out in July 1936 it was forced to support the evacuation of refugees to other destinations. The total number of Jews at that time in Spain was believed to be 6,000, of whom some 3,000 were refugees. By 1 April 1939, when Gen. Francisco Franco, leader of the fascist Nationalist forces, declared victory over the Republicans and an end to the civil war, almost all the refugees and many of the native Jews had left Spain. Those who remained were deprived, as non-Catholics, of any legal means of maintaining an organized Jewish community life.

Fifteen months later, when France collapsed, Spain became the only territorial escape line for a flood of refugees. Its borders were not closed to those who held Portuguese visas or who were booked to sail from one of the Spanish ports. French exit permits were also required, and men could only leave if they were outside the age of military service. Although traditionally antisemitic and heavily influenced by Germany, the Spanish authorities did not establish sweeping discriminatory rules that might have blocked Jewish refugees from escaping the German net. Nevertheless, Spanish officials were reluctant to grant transit permits to Jews. The number of Jews who were allowed to cross Spain between June 1940 and July 1942 is unknown, but it may have reached tens of thousands. Refugees who were caught after having illegally crossed the Spanish border were expelled or imprisoned, mainly in the Miranda de Ebro concentration camp. No systematic discrimination against Jews was established even in this case, yet no Jewish organization was allowed into Spain to work on their behalf. By July 1942 it was estimated that 300–500 refugee Jews were to be found in Spain, most of them imprisoned and among them many who had entered legally but had missed their ships.

The Nazi persecution of the Jews in the occupied countries did not extend to nationals of neutral countries. There were some 4,000 Jews in Europe who, because of their Sephardic origin, had been under Spanish protection in the Turkish empire until its collapse during World War I and who possessed Spanish documents to this effect even after they had emigrated to other parts of Europe. Some 3,000 of them lived in France, 640 in Greece, and the others in Bulgaria, Hungary, Romania, Belgium, and the Netherlands. A small number of Moroccan Jews from Spanish Morocco lived in French Morocco. The local antisemitic laws in France, Romania, and Bulgaria, and the physical violence and systematic robbery of Jewish property in occupied northern Greece, constituted the first challenges for the Spanish consuls with whom these Jews were registered. Many of the Spanish protégés owned large properties, and none of them was hostile to the Nationalists' cause during the civil war. The order transmitted to the consuls by the Spanish Foreign Office was that they should try to protect the rights of their Jewish nationals, especially the Spanish patrimony of their properties, but nevertheless not oppose the application of general racial laws to the Spanish nationals. Aryanization of Jewish property would thus have been carried out under their aegis. Petitions to be allowed to settle in Spain, presented by some of the Jewish Spanish nationals, were systematically denied. In the case of the Spanish-Moroccan Jews, where Spanish sovereignty was put in jeopardy by the Vichy French authorities, the Spanish ambassador to Vichy, José Felix Lequerica, even suggested that Spain should retaliate by persecuting Jews of French Morocco who lived in Spanish Morocco.

In spite of the very limited support and encouragement from Madrid, the consul generals Bernardo Rolland in Paris, José Rojas y Moreno Conde de Casa Rojas in Bucharest, Julio Palencia y Alvarez in Sofia, and later Sebastian Romero Radigales in Athens did their best on behalf of their protégés.

In August 1942, following the initiation of the mass deportations from the occupied and unoccupied zones of France, the Spanish border resumed its vital importance as an escape line. By October several hundred Jewish refugees, of all ages and on their own initiative, had crossed the border. The Spanish authorities soon realized that these newcomers were almost exclusively Jewish and began to expel them back to France. The American embassy protested, but by then the whole situation had changed as a result of the successful landing of the Allies in Algiers on the night of 8–9 November and the invasion of southern France by the Germans on 11 November. Many French now began

to enter Spain on their way to the Free French Forces in North Africa, and the fate of the refugees became an issue of vital and conflicting interest between the Germans, who pressured Spain to close its border, and the Allies, who urged that the frontiers should remain open. On 25 March 1943 Spain yielded to the German pressure; on 7 April the British prime minister, Winston Churchill, warned the Spanish ambassador that this act might cause the "destruction of good relations" between Spain and Great Britain. Spain annulled its decision.

Refugees continued to arrive in the country until September 1944, when the south of France was liberated. During that period no systematic discrimination against Jewish refugees took place. Having crossed the Pyrenees, Jews and non-Jews were interned in the provincial prisons or the camp at Miranda de Ebro. They were initially released only when the arrangements for their evacuation from Spain were completed, but they were later allowed to wait in assigned residences for their departure. In order to secure the financial maintenance and the evacuation of Jewish refugees, Spain tolerated the presence of an unofficial representative of the American Jewish Joint Distribution Committee (JDC) in Barcelona, under a transparent disguise of representing the Portuguese Red Cross. It also authorized the establishment in Madrid of an official representation of the American charities, under the auspices of the American embassy, most of whose budget was covered by the JDC. It is roughly estimated that from July 1942 to September 1944 as many as 7,500 Jews, stateless and of all nations and armies, crossed into Spain.

According to German decisions, Jews of neutral nationality could be spared destruction by evacuation to their respective countries. This decree applied to all those who had possessed their status prior to the date on which their governments were requested to repatriate them. Spain was officially informed in January, February, and April 1943 that it could remove its Jews from Western Europe, Eastern Europe, and Greece, respectively, until the end of June 1943. Fearing complications with a friendly country, Germany actually prolonged the term. After internal deliberations Spain informed its representatives in Germany and the occupied countries of the rules regarding those who would be allowed to enter its territory: only those who could "prove with complete and satisfactory documents their own [Spanish] nationality and the nationality of each member of their family accompanying them." This determination excluded the majority of the 4,000 Jews who, according to the German criteria, could have been saved. Nevertheless, it did not annul Spain's claim to "administer" the assets of Jews who were "sent to work in the Eastern territories," thus demanding the right to inherit from the very people it had decided not to save.

Another rule went even further in limiting the number of those who were actually rescued. It stated that each group of Jewish Spanish nationals would be admitted only after the group that had preceded them had left Spain. Consequently 365 Spanish nationals from Salonika had to wait in the Bergen-Belsen concentration camp from 13 August 1943 until 3 February 1944 because 79 Spanish Jewish nationals from France, who had arrived in Spain on 11 August 1943, were not evacuated to North Africa until December 1943. Another group of 155 Jewish Spanish nationals from Athens, who were waiting in Bergen-Belsen for their turn, never arrived in Spain, because the Salonikans could not leave Spain until the liberation of southern France. The number of Spanish Jewish nationals—almost all of the Sephardic Jews—who were saved by repatriation did not exceed 800. Nevertheless, through successful postwar propaganda Spain managed to persuade many people that it had acted as a magnificent protector not only of its nationals but also of all the Sephardic Jews in the occupied countries. It should be said, however, that in the summer and fall of 1944 Spain, with other neutral countries, participated in the rescue of Hungarian Jews by issuing several thousand documents of protection to non-Spanish nationals.

Haim Avni

SS and the Police   The Schutzstaffel, or SS, was the embodiment of terror and repression during the Nazi era. The origins of the SS go back to the year 1923, when Adolf Hitler created a bodyguard, the 50-man Stosstrupp Adolf Hitler (Assault Platoon Adolf

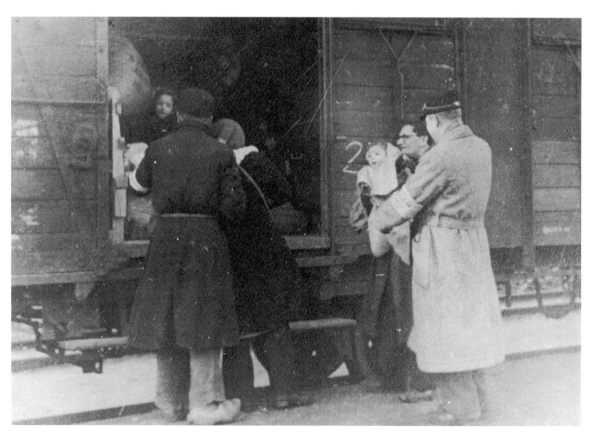

Members of the Dutch Ordedienst (Jewish police) give assistance to prisoners boarding a train to Westerbork. 1943–44

Hitler). This unit was banned following the failed November 1923 putsch, but in spring 1925, when the Nazi party (NSDAP) was reconstituted, Hitler established a similar group, the Stabswache (Headquarters Guard) headed by his chauffeur, Julius Schreck, and comprising mainly ex-members of the Stosstrupp. Other local Nazi party groups created similar organizations of activists to protect their leaders, to make propaganda, and primarily to act as crack troops in violent conflicts with political opponents. Beginning in the summer of 1925 these groups were known as *Schutzstaffeln* (defense squadrons) and were under the direct authority of Hitler as party leader; at that time he could not be sure whether the recently reorganized Sturmabteilung (SA, storm troopers), the party's paramilitary mass organization, would remain loyal to him. Henceforth an atmosphere of rivalry developed between the brown-uniformed SA and the men of the SS, who saw themselves as members of an exclusive elite and were distinguished by their black caps and Death's Head insignia. After 1926, however, when Hitler had come to terms with the SA leaders and had given them permission to establish a central command within the Nazi movement, the SS was also put under that authority.

The SS as an independent organization was set up in January 1929, when Heinrich Himmler, the new Reichsführer-SS, took over the leadership of what was still a small unit. Himmler, born in 1900, had received a strongly Catholic upbringing in a bourgeois family with monarchist leanings. In 1917 he volunteered for the army but was not sent to the front. After the war he completed his studies in agriculture and was active in several nationalist and paramilitary organizations. He began his NSDAP career in 1925 as a full-time party functionary and became head of the Reich propaganda section. As SS chief he increased the number of SS members from some hundreds to more than 50,000 by the end of 1932. In particular, Himmler endeavored to reinforce SS elitism. He laid special stress on the disciplined appearance of SS men and set specific "racial" criteria for acceptance; he forbade participation in inner-party conflicts and ensured that the SS poached the SA's most capable members. Because of its exclusive image the organization attracted people of a higher social status than those who joined the SA; among its leaders were found many former officers of the *Freikorps* (private volunteer units) who had failed to find a place in civilian life and were hoping for a second military career.

Himmler's notion of the SS as an elite was inseparable from a peculiar agrarian-romantic "blood-and-soil" ideology. An agricultural graduate, he intended that over several generations a new, pure, "Aryan" aristocracy would arise out of the SS; a return to the simple life of their Germanic forefathers would mean that as warriors, farmers, and fathers of large families, they would be part of a new wave of colonization of the East. As early as 1931 he set up a Race and Settlement Office (RuSHA), which was intended to prepare for these tasks and to stand guard over SS purity.

In particular, however, the SS progressively took over the function of a party police within the Nazi movement. In the fall of 1931 it began to build up a military-style intelligence service, headed by the former naval officer Reinhard Heydrich; this later became the Sicherheitsdienst (SD, security service) and was chiefly responsible for twice putting down inner-party rebellions headed by the SA—the revolts led by Walter Stennes in 1930 and 1931.

The SS was divided into groups on the military model: *Trupps* (platoons), *Stürme* (companies), *Sturmbanne* (battalions), and *Standarten* (regiments). At the end of 1932 further regional divisions were created: *Abschnitte* (sections) and *Oberabschnitte* (main sections). The black uniform for all SS members was introduced in 1932.

Development after 1933

After Hitler was named chancellor of Germany in January 1933, the SS not only substantially increased in numbers (from 50,000 at the end of 1932 to 200,000 a year later) but was also soon able to take over important executive functions. Himmler, having been appointed commander of the Bavarian political police on 1 April 1933, was able to install himself as the head of political police in almost all German states during the winter of 1933–34. Finally, in the spring of 1934 he succeeded in taking over the secret political police in Prussia, the largest German state; this was the Geheime Staatspolizei, or Gestapo. At the same time Heydrich became chief of Gestapo headquarters, the Geheime Staatspolizeiamt (Gestapa). The Gestapo, founded in April 1933, was by that time completely separated from the police organization and domestic administration and had become an independent branch of the state apparatus. This fact was all-important to the expansion of SS power.

In addition to taking over the political police, the organization was able to develop independent armed units in the first few months of the Third Reich. In March 1933 the Stabswache of 120 men was established, at first for the personal protection of Hitler—the third Führer's bodyguard since 1923, later named the Leibstandarte Adolf Hitler. Other armed units, the *politische Bereitschaften* (political alarm units), were founded in various places.

After the SS had taken an active part in the murder of the SA ruling clique around Ernst Röhm on 30 June 1934, its status within the party was raised. After 20 July 1934 it was relieved of its subordinate position under the SA and became an independent organization within the NSDAP.

Three developments were crucial for the history of the SS between 1934 and 1939: the SS takeover and incorporation of the general police apparatus, its development of the concentration camp system, and the creation of armed units in significant numbers, including provision of concentration camp guards.

Beginning in 1934 Himmler systematically unified the different political police forces under his command, until in June 1936 he became head of the entire German police in the Interior Ministry, with the official title Reichsführer-SS und Chef der Deutschen Polizei im Ministerium des Innern. In his new position he formed two new leadership organizations. The Hauptamt Ordnungspolizei (under Kurt Daluege), was responsible in particular for the regular police—the Schutzpolizei (active in the larger cities), the Gemeindepolizei (in smaller towns), and the Gendarmerie (in the countryside). The Gestapo and the criminal police, meanwhile, were placed under the Hauptamt Sicherheitspolizei (Security Police Main Office).

By making a division between Ordnungspolizei (order police) and Sicherheitspolizei (security police), Himmler pursued a policy of setting up a special political police elite intimately bound up with the SS and differentiated from the ordinary uniformed police. Heydrich headed both the security police and the SO-Hauptamt (Main Office). With his 1936 reforms Himmler was successful in centralizing the entire police and making it completely independent of the rest of the administration; it was now to become ever closer to the SS. He considered it essential that as many police officers as possible be members of the SS, and for that purpose he was prepared to relax the strict conditions of entry and to grant police officers who joined the SS a rank equivalent to that which they already held. By introducing *Höhere SS- und Polizeiführer* (Higher SS and Police Leader/Leaders, HSSPF) in

1937, Himmler was able to establish an institution at the regional level that represented the entire police and SS/police apparatus and was also designed to reinforce their integration.

Under the direction of Himmler and Heydrich, the police changed more and more from a state organization to an unequivocal instrument of the Führer executive. Among the Gestapo's initial responsibilities was that of police enforcement of the regime's measures against the Jews. In contrast, the SD, as a party organization, had no executive power; its Department for Jewish Affairs nevertheless developed long-term independent strategies. To a greater extent than the Gestapo, it emphasized that the step-by-step discrimination and isolation of the Jewish minority was serving a specific political aim which it characterized as early as May 1934: "The goal of Jewish policy must be the complete emigration of the Jews." The crux of this policy, as the SD quickly recognized, had to be the destruction of the economic position of German Jews; at the same time, however, the Jews had to be allowed sufficient means to finance their emigration. It also recognized that this policy would only be workable in the long term if the persecution—until then pursued separately by the state bureaucracy, the various party organizations, and the Gestapo—were coordinated and efficiently managed.

In the years 1936–37 a group of ambitious younger SD men from the Department for Jewish Affairs—among them Dieter Wisliceny, Herbert Hagen, and Adolf Eichmann—began to develop a series of initiatives designed to claim for themselves a major role in the state persecution of the Jews. The SD's claim to leadership as against the Gestapo was to some extent acknowledged in Himmler's decree of 1 July 1937, which stated that "all basic issues in regard to the Jews" should be dealt with by the SD, although "special executive measures" would be carried out by the Gestapo. In the next eighteen months, as the Nazi anti-Jewish policy became ever more thorough, the SD continually intensified its role as a persecutor. Thus in the summer of 1937 it took an active part for the first time by implementing antisemitic laws in the eastern part of Upper Silesia, where Jews had previously been protected by the region's unique status under the Versailles Treaty. Most significantly, after the Austrian Anschluss (annexation) of March 1938 Eichmann was granted an official commission to set up the Zentralstelle für Jüdische Auswanderung (Central Office for Jewish Emigration) in Vienna. This agency was

Raid by Berlin police to gather Jews for a document check. 1933

able to force the emigration of almost 35,000 Austrian Jews between August 1938 and the end of the year. Since Third Reich emigration policy was deadlocked at the time, Eichmann's "success" was highly regarded by his superiors in the SS empire.

When the Reichszentrale für Jüdische Auswanderung was established in January 1939 on the model of the Vienna office to promote the forced emigration of Jews from the entire Reich, the SD was able to appropriate a central role in the process of persecution. The solution to the "Jewish problem" by means of organized removal of Jews became its specialty.

Further to taking over the police organization, the SS was able to improve its power position by setting up more armed bands. In fall 1934 the Leibstandarte and the Bereitschaften were amalgamated as the *SS-Verfügungstruppe* (disposition troops), that is, an armed force directly under the orders of Himmler and Hitler. At the same time three *Junkerschulen* (Junker

schools) were created to educate the next generation of leaders for the entire SS as well as the police; they were to provide military instruction, as well as political and ideological indoctrination. Special emphasis was laid on personality training—in the National Socialist sense—for future SS leaders: this was considered far more important than an education in the "theory" of the Nazi worldview. The Junkerschulen communicated a sense of superiority, ruthlessness, and toughness as well as complete identification with the value system set by the SS; in addition, they fostered a self-confident instinct in exercising leadership and reliance on a community of like-minded and dependable men. The fact that a significant number of order-police officers emerged from the SS Junkerschulen is also a major factor in explaining the merging of the police and the SS.

Concentration camp guard units provided a second source for the buildup of armed sections. After having been given responsibility for the Prussian Gestapo in

April 1934, Himmler appointed Theodor Eicke inspector of concentration camps and head of the camp guard units. Since June 1933 Eicke had been commandant of Dachau, where he developed a system that became the model for all concentration camps. His reorganization included the introduction of forced labor for prisoners and revised regulations for the SS guards, who now came under the direct orders of camp commandants. Within a few months of his appointment Eicke had collected the numerous smaller camps into seven larger ones and had organized the guards into five integrated battalions. In March 1936 the guard units were styled *Totenkopfverbände* (Death's Head units). These notoriously brutal units also provided training for SS men who were intended to be used in a future war as auxiliaries for the armed SS units. By the outbreak of war the SS had altogether about 40,000 trained men under arms. After 1939 older members of the rank-and-file SS were similarly set up as *Totenkopfsturmbanne* (Death's Head battalions) to guard concentration camps, while the earlier Death's Head units were used in combat. This move clearly indicated the function of the ordinary SS as a reservoir of personnel for the armed SS units.

By virtue of its authority over the secret service, the police, and the concentration camps, as well as its armed units, the SS constituted a highly integrated complex of various forms of organized violence. It was, and recognized itself to be, the Third Reich's protective corps. It did not, however, regard its task as simply protecting the dictatorship; rather, it understood the huge potential for violence, which it had itself organized, as a decisive instrument of power that guaranteed implementation of its claim to form a new elite. In addition to functioning as an instrument of repression, the SS considered itself the guardian of an ideology, a center for the breeding of the Aryan race, and the coordinator of preparation for extensive conquests and the creation of a *völkisch* New Order in Eastern Europe. In short, the SS set out to be the nucleus of the future master race of the Third Reich.

These sweeping SS pretensions were underscored by the assumption of ever more responsibility and the establishment of an increasing number of institutions. With the founding of Lebensborn (Well of Life), Himmler created a system of maternity homes for the wives of SS men and for single mothers. The society Ahnenerbe (Ancestral Heritage) carried out pseudoscientific research into "Germanic prehistory," in order to document the superiority of the race. During the war the SS empire expanded further when Hitler entrusted Himmler with "the reinforcement of Germandom," and when a system of special SS and police courts was set up.

In sum, the different functions and ambitions of the SS within the Nazi dictatorship should be seen as an attempt to create a qualitatively new form of comprehensive control—a peculiar combination of violence, bureaucracy, ideology, and enforced racial biology. These ever more heterogeneous organizations were held together by Himmler's own personality and by the SS ideology he had single-handedly developed. His attempt to use the SS as an elite, a new political order, was modeled on historical examples such as the Jesuits (whom he admired, although he treated them as enemies) and the medieval Order of the Teutonic Knights.

Himmler tried to lay down a compulsory catalog of virtues for the SS man—a special SS ethic. He continually advocated particular values—faithfulness, honor, comradeship, honesty, decency—and meticulously tried to discover how far these rules were being kept within the SS. The high value placed on such moral qualities within an organization responsible for millions of murders might at first glance appear surprising. In fact, these central SS values were little more than synonyms for the complete subordination of men to the organization. Himmler bestowed on the SS man the role of a "political soldier": he was under strict military discipline, but—unlike a normal soldier, whose duty is to obey the orders of his country—he must rather be prepared to fight for goals formulated by the SS itself. The political-soldier slogan consciously located the SS within the tradition of the Freikorps and the paramilitary units formed from the remnants of the Imperial Army at the end of World War I; they too had pursued their own political goals and refused to bow to state authority. The SS leadership justified its demand for complete obedience by the notion that the organization was pursuing a "historic mission" that would lead to a "heroic and fateful struggle" (in a Social Darwinist sense) to promote the preeminence of the superior Aryan race.

All the rationalizations invoked by the SS to justify its role as the executor of a metaphysical world plan boil down to one point: the justification of the absolute dominance of the inner circle of the SS elite. Their mentality demanded a morality-free space. The extraordinary brutality and lack of scruple with which the SS dealt with its victims and adversaries is a direct consequence of this superman ideology. To validate such a worldview, Himmler developed a specific SS myth, a cult conjuring up the world of the Germanic forefathers. For this purpose he constructed a whole system of pseudo-religious rites and symbols, invented idiosyncratic insignia and badges, organized a precise schedule for a system of ceremonies, constructed monuments and places of worship, and built up a hero cult around the medieval kaiser Heinrich I, whose successor he fancied himself to be. Anti-Jewish stereotypes played a central role in the SS ideology; in a black-and-white schema the Jew was portrayed as a figure of evil and was contrasted with the idealized image of the pure Aryan.

The SS/Police Complex during World War II

Security Police. On 1 October 1939, one month after the outbreak of war, the headquarters of the SD and the security police were united in the Reichssicherheitshauptamt (Reich Security Main Office, RSHA). The SD, the Gestapo, and the criminal police (Kripo) were thus brought together in one body. Heydrich was director of RSHA and head of the security police and SD until his death in June 1942, when Ernst Kaltenbrunner was appointed his successor.

Following the Anschluss of Austria, the security police organized special units to penetrate almost all conquered territories, with the aim of disposing of all the enemies of the Third Reich and preparing the basis of a repressive system. It was during the occupation of the Sudetenland that these special troops were first referred to as *Einsatzgruppen* (assault squads).

The Einsatzgruppen, in which all branches of the security police—SD, Gestapo, Kripo—were represented and whose organizational structure mirrored that of RSHA, were themselves divided into *Einsatzkommandos* (assault commando units) and *Sonderkommandos* (special commando units). Once occupation was complete, the mobile Einsatzgruppe was transformed into a permanent regional organization of the security police. In each of the occupied territories a commander in chief (*Befehlshaber*) was appointed, who was superior to the commanders of the security police and the SD. Within the area of the Reich the RSHA oversaw the security police inspectorate, whose primary task was to unify the various branches of the security police and to further their independence from the other police and administrative bodies.

Ordnungspolizei. Units of the *Ordnungspolizei* (order police) had been employed in the process of annexing foreign states as early as 1938. Seventeen battalions were engaged in the war against Poland. Many of these men were middle-aged reservists, who since 1937 had received short-term training within the Ordnungspolizei structure. Following the outbreak of war this police section was also allowed to recruit a limited number of younger volunteers.

In August 1940 the total strength of the security police amounted to 245,000 men, of whom 59,000 formed 101 police battalions. Almost half of these units were stationed in the occupied territories. In 1944 the numbers had reached about 3.5 million, including members of all the subordinate units (such as the fire department, air raid protection, and auxiliary foreign units). Altogether there were 40 police regiments (SS/police regiments in 1943), about 110 police battalions, and more than 200 auxiliary police battalions made up of men from the occupied territories, where, apart from the mobile units, the headquarters and stationary units constituted the second arm of the Ordnungspolizei. This body had authority over the Schutzpolizei, which was responsible for policing the larger cities, and the Gendarmerie, which manned rural police stations.

The Waffen-SS. After the Polish campaign the SS-Verfügungstruppen were transformed into a division (Das Reich), and the Death's Head units became the Totenkopf-Division. Added to these was a police division originating from the Ordnungspolizei, so that Himmler now controlled a considerable armed force, but one that as yet lacked a central organizational structure. In the winter of 1939–40 the term *Waffen-SS* was introduced as the label for all armed SS units, including concentration camp guards. It was only in August 1940 that a central headquarters (SS-Führungshauptamt) was established for the leadership of the Waffen-SS and the military training of the regular SS.

Since the Wehrmacht regarded the Waffen-SS as a rival and therefore sought to limit its intake of men, the function of the Führungshauptamt more and more became the search for new recruits outside Reich borders. At the end of the war between 250,000 and 300,000 *Volksdeutsche* (ethnic Germans) and "Germanic" volunteers from western and northern Europe had joined the SS, whereas the number of eastern and southeastern European recruits continued to grow (reaching about 200,000). After 1942 the volunteer principle was abandoned and Waffen-SS members were increasingly found within the Reich. Hence the original concept of the Waffen-SS as an elite corps faded away; by the end of 1942 it comprised more than 900,000 men.

The Role of the SS/Police Complex in Persecution and Murder

As Reichskommissar für die Festigung des Deutschen Volkstums—Reich commissar for the consolidation of Germandom—Himmler took on the task of creating an extensive ethnic renewal program for eastern and southeastern Europe, involving the racial selection and mass relocation of human beings. The projects he decreed as Reichskommissar, which resulted in different versions of the General Plan for the East, envisaged the removal of the Jews as a condition for the further relocation of other peoples. The fact that the HSSPF, who played a central role in the implementation of the Holocaust, were at the same time the representatives of the Reichskommissar makes clear the connection between mass murder and the idea of an ethnic New Order.

As mass killing of the European Jews began, the various branches of the SS/police system took over differing functions within the process of wholesale murder. The interaction of three operations was essential: the system of annihilation in the camps, the concentration of Jews and their deportation to the extermination camps, and the mass execution of Eastern European Jews by mobile units of police, Einsatzgruppen, and Waffen-SS. The HSSPF, who were appointed in the occupied lands as Himmler's plenipotentiaries, played an important part in coordinating the different functions. At the regional level, smooth relations between the different branches was ensured by the SS and police leaders (SSPF). During the war millions of people in the occupied countries were imprisoned in the SS camp system, which grew to enormous proportions. Twenty-two main camps and more than 1,200 branch camps were set up. The task of guarding the camps was progressively taken over by Volksdeutsche and Eastern Europeans. All camps, except the camps of the Aktion Reinhard, were subordinated to the authority of the concentration camp inspectorate, whose duties were allocated in March 1942 to the SS Wirtschafts- und Verwaltungshauptamt, the Economic and Administrative Main Office (WVHA), under Oswald Pohl.

More or less simultaneously with this organizational change, the "economization" of the prison system began. This step in no way led, however, to a dimi-

nution of mass murder. On the contrary, because of poor food and accommodation, and also through the killing of people incapable of further work, the SS achieved a system of "extermination through toil," in which prisoners were literally worked to death. Meanwhile even their most meager possessions were ruthlessly exploited for the benefit of the state. Numerous other types of camps existed within the SS empire. In the Generalgouvernement (i.e., occupied Poland), for example, were the extermination camps of Aktion Reinhard, run by Odilo Globocnik, the SSPF in Lublin. More than a thousand forced labor camps for Jews were governed by the security police or the HSSPF.

Planning and coordination of deportations to the extermination camps was the responsibility of Section IVb within the RSHA. The head of that office was Eichmann, who had dealt with plans for a "Jewish reservation" in eastern Poland in 1939 and had already organized the evacuation of Jews from the Polish lands seized by the Reich.

The Gestapo was responsible for deportations from the territory of the greater German Reich, which included annexed Austrian, Czech, and Polish areas. In most occupied lands, security police officers were in charge of special departments for Jewish affairs; they organized the deportation in close collaboration with Eichmann's office and with the support of the appropriate HSSPF. The same function was fulfilled by the SS "Jewish advisers," who were attached to diplomatic missions in the Axis-allied countries. In 1944, for the deportations from Hungary, Eichmann created a Sonderkommando in Budapest under his personal direction. In the Generalgouvernement the organization of deportations fell to the SSPF, although in Lublin Globocnik took over personally.

A significant number of Jews in the Generalgouvernement, the Baltic states, and the Soviet Union were murdered by firing squads drawn from the various branches of the SS/police system. The best-known of these squads are the Einsatzgruppen, which were employed as early as the Polish campaign, in conjunction with the Selbstschutz (Self-Defense), a group manned by Volksdeutsche and under SS command. They shot several thousand Poles, mostly leading figures, and large numbers of Jews. The SS leadership fell back on this murderous experience when in spring 1941 they introduced four Einsatzgruppen into the police school at Pretzsch, near Leipzig. Einsatzgruppen A, B, and C were each assigned to an army group. Ein-

Corpses and survivors in the "quarantine camp" section of Mauthausen. May 1945

satzgruppe D was attached to the 11th Army, which together with Romanian troops was to push forward on the southern edge of the eastern front. Men of the Einsatzgruppen came from the Gestapo, the Kripo, and Ordnungspolizei, the SD, and the Waffen-SS. In addition, technical personnel—usually not SS members—were seconded to the squads for emergency duties. Each Einsatzgruppe was made up of between 600 and 1,000 men, the total force being approximately 3,000. The top leadership of these units for the most part came from the SD. Most high-ranking members of Einsatzgruppe A were committed Nazis and university graduates; more than half of them held a doctorate in law.

The main task of the Einsatzgruppen was to help set up the occupation regime and to secure German rule through unbridled terrorism. From the very beginning, this included wholesale executions of the leading classes of the Soviet empire, who, according to the Nazis, were usually Jews. In a letter to the HSSPF dated 2 July 1941 Heydrich named the types of per-

sons to be executed according to his previous verbal orders: "All Comintern functionaries (similarly all professional Communist politicians), higher and mid-ranking party officials (and low-ranking officials, if extremist), . . . Jews in party and state positions, other extremist elements (saboteurs, propagandists, snipers, assassins, malicious agitators, etc.)." In addition to this general list, the order required the local populace to be incited to organize pogroms against the Jews. In fact Einsatzgruppen reports, from the start of the military campaign, make it clear that such orders were understood to give carte blanche for full-scale massacres, especially of the Jews.

At an early stage the Einsatzgruppen were able to encourage some of the local people to start pogroms (especially in the Baltic states and in Ukraine) while themselves shooting hundreds and thousands of civilians, mostly Jewish men, in myriads of mass liquidations. Since the groups offered various, almost random justifications for the killings (revenge, punishment, clean-up operations, antilooting measures, prophylaxis against epidemics), it is plain that their goal was the systematic destruction of the Jewish population.

Furthermore, three Ordnungspolizei regiments (each comprising three battalions) were founded at the time of the attack on the Soviet Union. Each was put under one of three HSSPF, who in turn were subordinate to the military commanders of the rearguard of the three German army groups that had invaded the Soviet Union. In addition, more battalions were gradually added, so that by the end of 1941 26 battalions operated in the East.

The Ordnungspolizei played an essential role in the murder of the Jews in the Soviet Union. Battalion 309, for example, killed at least 2,000 Jews at the end of June 1941 in Bialystok; Battalion 332 two weeks later also was assigned to Bialystok and murdered approximately 3,000 Jews. Battalion 307 carried out a massacre in Brest-Litovsk in July 1941, and in the same month Battalion 316 killed hundreds of Jews in Baranovichi. In the fall of 1941 the Reserve Police Battalion 12 executed thousands of Jews in Minsk, Smilowiche, Slutsk, and other localities in Belorussia. From 1942 onward, police battalions also carried out mass executions in the Generalgouvernement. The Ordnungspolizei provided guards on the deportation trains in other European countries.

As early as 21 May 1941 an edict by Himmler had made it clear that Waffen-SS troops would be given "tasks similar to those of the Ordnungspolizei" as well as "special tasks, which will be directly communicated by me."

At the end of July 1941 Himmler and Daluege, head of the Ordnungspolizei, began an attempt to unify the various pro-German partisan units and auxiliary police forces that the invaders were setting up in the newly occupied areas and to bring them together as *Schutzmannschaften* (auxiliary police, abbreviated to *Schuma*). In the next few months Lithuanian, Estonian, Latvian, Ukrainian, and Belorussian Schuma came into being. A distinction was made between independent Schuma, who were auxiliaries of the German Gendarmerie, and the Schuma battalions subordinated to the Ordnungspolizei commanders. These units, in principle made up of volunteers, were often used outside their homelands for mass executions of Jews and Communists as well as for "clean-up" and antipartisan operations. Jews were killed under the pretext that they were supporting anti-German partisans.

Throughout 1942 Schuma battalions increasingly

German soldiers of the Waffen-SS and the Reich Labor Service look on as a member of Einsatzgruppe D prepares to shoot a Ukrainian Jew kneeling on the edge of a mass grave filled with corpses. 1942

replaced German police in mass shootings. In October 1942, for example, in the Reichskommissariat Ostland there were 4,428 German police, compared with 31,094 Schuma in independent service and 23,758 in Schuma battalions.

In April 1941 Himmler had begun to set up a special commando staff directly responsible to himself. Until the beginning of the Russian campaign SS Death's Head units of more than 20,000 men were seconded to this staff; they included two motorized brigades and a cavalry brigade. Their task was primarily to "calm" those areas before they came under political administration.

The cavalry brigade first took part in an important

murder operation between 29 July and 1 August 1941 in the Pripet marshes, where it had murdered more than 15,000 Jews whom it depicted as "looters and partisans." In Ukraine 44,000 Jews were killed in the month of August alone by the 1st Brigade, assisted by police units.

The scheme for execution commandos in the first months of the Russian campaign was as follows: in the furthest eastern areas Sonderkommandos were to operate in the rear of the German armies; behind them came the Einsatzkommandos, reinforced by police battalions, while in the western areas designated for political administration the Waffen-SS were active.

Total responsibility for the use of all these units remained with Himmler, who, according to Hitler's decree of 17 July 1941, was responsible for "police security of the newly conquered territories." The HSSPF in the occupied areas were assigned the task of enforcing these policies, as well as coordinating the activities of the various detachments. They were put in charge of certain major operations and also controlled the Einsatzgruppen, police units, and Waffen-SS, so that ultimately Himmler was in a position personally to direct the mass murder of the Jews in the Soviet Union by his orders to the HSSPF and his headquarters staff.

About six weeks after the attack on the Soviet Union, at the end of July 1941 and in particular in August and September, there was a perceptible change in operational methods. Now the units were ordered to include women and children in the executions. Orders to this effect were often given when troops were inspected by high-ranking SS officers, including Himmler, who at this crucial period was making extensive tours of "the new eastern territories." During this period the number of executions (including those of men) was significantly increased. The precondition for this change was the fact that, quite apart from the Einsatzgruppen, an armed force of SS and police units comprising tens of thousands of men had now been organized within the Soviet Union; its chief task was to murder Jews. The prolongation and brutalizing effect of the war, which the Germans initially expected to last only some ten to twelve weeks, gave SS leaders the opportunity to begin the so-called Final Solution of the Jewish question *during* the Russian campaign, although hitherto it had been scheduled to take place *after* the war. This original plan was for mass deportations to the areas in the East lacking in the basic necessities of life.

The perpetrators, even after the spread of executions to Jews of all ages and both sexes, do not appear to have expected at this stage to exterminate Soviet Jewry completely by these means. Apparently the SS, like the Wehrmacht and the civil administration, did not begin to concentrate at least some of the Jews in ghettos and to use them for forced labor until late summer 1941. Thus a report of 12 September 1941 made by Einsatzkommando 6 declared that if 70–90 percent—or sometimes even 100 percent—of the Jews had fled from a given area, this fact "may be considered as an indirect success for the work of the security police." Other reports from September and October make it clear that the Jews were considered indispensable as a work force, especially as artisans. Einsatzkommando 5 reported on 12 September that there was only one possibility: "the solution of the Jewish problem by all-out utilization of the Jews for labor. This will result in their gradual elimination."

After the initial phase of the invasion, at the end of 1941 and beginning of 1942, the SS began a second wave of murdering Jews in the Soviet Union, at the same time making a fundamental change of method. Under the leadership of the HSSPF and the direction of the Einsatzgruppen (which had meanwhile been transformed into local security police offices), it was now primarily the Ordnungspolizei, consisting of police battalions and local Gendarmerie (often aided by Schuma) who committed the majority of murders. The killings took place in the course of real or imaginary battles with partisans or of ghetto actions, in which some or all inhabitants of a ghetto were liquidated, sometimes in gas vans. The police battalions of Gendarmerie and Schuma operated similarly in the Generalgouvernement; the inhabitants of smaller ghettos were usually shot on the spot instead of being deported to extermination camps. From the fall of 1941 the Gendarmerie in the Generalgouvernement and the Soviet Union systematically shot Jews found outside the ghettos or camps.

The motivation of the men in the killing units is still not clear. The majority of the men in the Einsatzgruppen and in the Death's Head companies were prepared for the inhuman task by long careers within the SS or police. The members of the Ordnungspolizei were largely professional policemen, trained primarily to crush an eventual revolt within Germany, but a significant number of ordinary German citizens, who became criminals only during the war, also served in these units as reservists.

Among the members of the execution squads, two minorities can be distinguished: men who had repeatedly asked to take part in the shootings and who had become notorious for especially cruel actions, and men who refused the order to carry out executions or tried to avoid participation in the massacres. The objectors could not be pursued by military courts, since the murders took place outside the law, and on the whole suffered no severe personal difficulties. Their behavior, however, was atypical for the world of the Third Reich; it argues for a strongly nonconformist mentality.

The background of most members of the police units was characterized by authoritarian education, ideological indoctrination, and extreme nationalism, which also included varying degrees of antisemitism, to say nothing of prejudices against other minorities. It is still not clear what role such a mentality, growing and hardening over many years, played in the transformation of normal citizens and fathers of families into mass murderers. Nevertheless, the history of these ordinary men does reflect individual viewpoints and attitudes to be found in the areas of interwar German society from which the Nazi party emerged.

Peter Longerich

Stahlecker, Franz (1900–1942) Senior SS official. As head of Einsatzgruppe A, which operated in the northern sector of occupied Soviet territory, Stahlecker was responsible for the mass murder of Jews and other nationals, particularly in the Baltic region. He was killed in a clash with Soviet partisans.

Stalin, Josef (1879–1953) Soviet dictator and supreme commander of the Red Army during World War II. See RUSSIA AND THE SOVIET UNION

Stangl, Franz (1908–71) Senior SS official, Austrian by birth. Stangl took part in the execution of the so-called euthanasia program and was commander of the Sobibor and Treblinka extermination camps. Detained after the war, he escaped first to Italy, then to Syria and Brazil. Deported to Germany in 1967, he was condemned to life imprisonment in 1970.

Streicher, Julius (1885–1946) Early Nazi leader, friend of Adolf Hitler, head of the region of Franconia. Streicher founded and edited *Der Stürmer*, the most rabidly antisemitic of Nazi publications. Involved in

Local office of the anti-Jewish newspaper *Der Stürmer* in Danzig. 1939

various corrupt dealings and personal scandals, he was stripped of his rank and functions by a Nazi court in 1940 but continued to edit *Der Stürmer*. He was convicted of crimes against humanity at the Nuremberg war crimes trial and executed in October 1946.

Stürmer, Der [The Attacker] Nazi antisemitic weekly newspaper founded by Julius Streicher in 1923 with the slogan, "The Jews are our misfortune." Its circulation was approximately 2,500 in 1923; 65,000 in 1935; and 500,000 in 1937. *Der Stürmer* specialized in tabloid-like stories, lurid sexuality, and vicious antisemitic cartoons. Its language was crude and it continually alleged Jewish conspiracies and perversions of every sort. At times the Nazi party felt it necessary to distance itself from the publication. *Der Stürmer* was widely displayed in public places in Nazi Germany and circulated until 1 February 1945.

Stutthof Major concentration camp near Danzig, established in January 1942. Inmates were mostly Poles until 1944, when large numbers of Jewish women arrived from Auschwitz. Of the 115,000 detainees who were brought to Stutthof, at least 65,000 died there. Almost none of the 50,000 Jewish inmates survived. The camp was largely evacuated in January 1945, and many of its inmates perished in a death march westward. A few hundred prisoners remained alive in the camp at the time of its liberation on 9 May 1945.

Sugihara, Sempo (1900–1986) Japanese consul general in Kovno, Lithuania, in 1939–40. Disregarding the instructions of his government, Sugihara issued many hundreds of Japanese transit visas, which enabled Jewish applicants to escape from Soviet-occupied Lithuania. The Soviets had agreed to allow the applicants travel visas only if they could first obtain such visas from Japan. Sugihara issued at least 1,600 such visas. He was dismissed from the diplomatic service after the war because of his insubordination and shunned in his own country. Sugihara's rescue actions received attention in the United States and elsewhere, and he gained posthumous recognition in Japan. He was made one of the Righteous Among the Nations by Israel's Yad Vashem in 1984.

Sweden Sweden maintained a nonbelligerent status throughout World War II. Its proximity to Germany, as well as the intimate cultural and business relations between the two countries, made Sweden a significant factor in the history of the Holocaust. Information about the increasingly violent spiral of Nazi treatment of the Jews reached Sweden steadily, but the Swedish public and government did not share full understanding of the extent of the deportations and killings in the 1940s. The presumed outcome of the war in favor of the Allies, overtures to the Western powers, concerns about fellow Scandinavians, and broader humanitarian commitments were the central factors in the evolution of official government responses.

Swedish channels for gathering information about developments in Germany and German-controlled territories were multiple and surprisingly open. Diplomats, the press, the clergy, and academics faced few formal restrictions on travel. Many Swedes had studied in German universities and maintained a myriad of personal ties with Germans. In addition, Sweden broke the codes both of the Polish underground, which transmitted messages to the Polish government-in-exile in London via Stockholm, and of the German military, which sent messages to and from Norway.

There were also, however, obstacles to the dissemi-

In Malmö, Sweden, a Red Cross officer gives assistance to a woman who was liberated from a concentration camp. April 1945

nation of accurate reports on the Nazis' treatment of Jews. The pervasive fear in Germany and the occupied countries tempered some persons' willingness to share information and to risk attention from German security agencies. Strict Swedish censorship of the press meant that articles deemed anti-German might not be published. Information gathered did not necessarily mean information shared or understood. Still, an impressive amount of accurate information about German actions found its way into government records and the public media.

The Swedish consul general in Stettin, for example, forwarded the following description of the destruction of the Jews on 20 August 1942 as part of his regular, well-circulated reports: "The picture which my informant gave me concerning the treatment of Jews in Poland is such that it can hardly be expressed in writing. . . . The intention is to exterminate them eventually. . . . In a city, all the Jews were assembled for what was officially announced as 'delousing.' At the entrance they were forced to take off their clothes . . . ; the delousing procedure, however, consisted of gassing and, afterward, all of them could be stuffed into a mass grave. . . . The source from whom I obtained all this information on the conditions in the Generalgouvernement is such that not the slightest shade of disbelief exists concerning the truthfulness of my informant's descriptions."

The next day a young Swedish consular official in Berlin, Goran von Otter, shared an overnight train carriage from Warsaw to Berlin with a German SS officer, Kurt Gerstein, whose job was to transport poison gas from northern Germany to the killing centers in Poland. Gerstein, a member of a Protestant resistance group, gave von Otter detailed information about the entire killing process, including references in Berlin that von Otter could check. Although von Otter confirmed the information and testified after the war that it was brought to the attention of the government in Stockholm, no Swedish wartime evidence has been found for such a meeting. Given the fullness of this information, as well as its reliability, the absence of any written documentation is both curious and suggestive. Clearly, principal Swedish Foreign Office members eventually learned of the Gerstein information, but when and under what circumstances has not yet been determined.

By late August or early September 1942 the Foreign Office appreciated the enormity of the German persecution of the Jews. The immediate threat to the Jews in Norway in October and November would lead Sweden into a more active policy to impede the progress of the Final Solution.

Sweden's initial policy responses to German persecution of the Jews began almost from the beginning of the Nazi regime. King Gustav V and other prominent and traditionally pro-German Swedes warned Hitler in late spring of 1933 that continued persecution of the Jews would erode sympathy for Germany. Between 1934 and 1938 Sweden actively participated in extensive discussions within the League of Nations to address the problem of a flood of Jewish refugees from Nazi persecution.

Sweden did not, however, envision itself as an appropriate destination for significant Jewish emigration, and when war loomed in 1938 Sweden's emigration policies became even more restrictive. Sweden was among those border states that encouraged Germany to develop the so-called J-pass. The passports of German citizens identified as Jews were stamped with a large "J." Such individuals were viewed as refugees by Germany's neighbors and often were not allowed to enter the country. The Soviet invasion of Finland in 1939 and the German invasions of Denmark and Norway in 1940 left Sweden isolated from the West and at the mercy of Germany. The coalition government of all parliamentary parties except the Communists sought to avoid hostilities and opted for policies that would give Germany little reason to be interested in occupying the country. Trade, especially in iron ore and ball bearings, remained the staple of German-Swedish relations. Knowledge of German "sensitivity" on the Jewish question encouraged Sweden to remain passive.

In November 1942 attempts by the Germans to round up and deport the 1,500 Jews living in Norway raised an outcry among the Norwegian public and clergy. Although some Swedish church officials openly supported their Norwegian brothers and sisters, the general Swedish church response was more muted than that in occupied Norway. Still, the Swedish government sought to provide refuge for Jews who could escape across the long Norwegian-Swedish border. In addition, Swedish diplomats in Oslo tried to protect Jews with any Swedish connections. Other diplomatic efforts were directed toward protecting 20–30 such Jews in Germany. The Germans showed little interest in Sweden's willingness to take in Jews and treated

Sweden's diplomatic efforts patiently and properly. Approximately half (750) of the Jews in Norway reached Sweden safely; most of the remainder perished in Auschwitz.

During the spring of 1943 Sweden became the focus of a major diplomatic effort to rescue 20,000 Jewish children in Belgium and France. Initiated by the Jewish Agency of Palestine, the scheme called for Sweden to negotiate with Germany over the fate of the children. Sweden's interest and willingness in participating had more to do with its attempts to build goodwill in the West, particularly the United States, than with the government's humanitarian concerns. Swedish policymakers wanted to shift toward the West but resisted Western demands to cut Swedish trade with Germany. The enthusiastic but fruitless efforts on behalf of these thousands of children stand in contrast to a much more deliberate but largely successful response to the plight of less than 200 Jews from Finland, who eventually reached Sweden.

The most dramatic success in rescue came on the heels of the declaration of martial law in Denmark in late August 1943. Warned by a German diplomat of imminent deportations, Danish Jews went underground on the eve of Rosh Hashanah as the German SS sought to round them up. Christian Danes guided the Jews to boats and ferried them across the sound to Sweden and safety. Convoys were deliberately ignored by German naval vessels patrolling the waters between the two countries. Of 8,000 Danish Jews, 7,200 were rescued.

The Swedish haven for Denmark's Jews was accepted in Berlin. By this time nearly 180,000 refugees had found their way to Sweden; only a small fraction of them were Jewish. Sweden sought primarily to aid fellow Scandinavians, being both mindful of and sensitive to the suffering of its immediate neighbors. Broader humanitarian concerns also contributed to Sweden's policies. Greece, among other nations, received Swedish aid, in the form of ships and food.

The success of the Danish rescue gave Sweden much positive publicity in the United States. A large rally at Madison Square Garden in New York City hailed Sweden as a leader in efforts to help the Jews of Europe. When the administration of President Franklin Roosevelt established the War Refugee Board (WRB) in late 1943, it looked to Sweden for help in its new initiatives to aid Jews. Sweden was ready to comply.

Iver Olson, the WRB representative in Stockholm, showed interest in many schemes to rescue trapped Jews throughout German-controlled territory. Most efforts never got off the ground or failed miserably. The one major success occurred in Hungary. By March 1944 the 800,000 Jews of Hungary represented the largest Jewish population remaining in Nazi-occupied Europe. Adolf Eichmann, the Gestapo chief in charge of implementing the Final Solution, was sent to Budapest to organize the extermination of Hungarian Jewry.

Sweden reacted immediately. It sought to protect any Jew in Hungary who had a remote connection with Sweden. This policy, which had been tested in Germany and Norway, was extended in Hungary by developing the idea of a "protective pass"—a document that attempted to protect its holder from German predation by suggesting an official relation to the Swedish embassy. The embassy carefully limited the number of protective passes it issued, hoping thereby to safeguard their effectiveness but also curtailing their general impact. A Swedish citizen, Valdemar Langlet, using the Swedish Red Cross as an institutional cover, also issued protective passes. In addition, the Swedish government made official representations to Adm. Miklós Horthy, head of the Hungarian government, on behalf of the Jews. Yet although these Swedish initiatives saved thousands of Jews, they left thousands more at the mercy of the Germans. By July 1944 nearly 75 percent of Hungary's Jews were caught in the killing process or had perished.

As early as March 1944 the idea of sending a special envoy to Budapest had been a lively topic of discussion in Stockholm and New York among Jewish groups looking for any way to help protect the Hungarian Jews. Folke Bernadotte, head of the Swedish Red Cross and a member of the Swedish royal family, was the most prominent person named. Bernadotte was willing to serve but was otherwise engaged. In his place a little-known member of Sweden's leading business family, the Wallenbergs, was selected. The choice of Raoul Wallenberg as Sweden's envoy to Hungary appears to have been the result of discussions among leading Jewish figures in Stockholm and Iver Olson. The Swedish Foreign Office approved the appointment, and Wallenberg arrived in Budapest in early July.

Raoul Wallenberg brought energy, imagination, organization, and a disregard for traditional bureaucratic concerns to his task. For the next six months, with the full support of the Swedish legation, he demonstrated a remarkable ability to protect Jews and to befuddle German authorities. The techniques he used—protective passes and safe houses—were similar to ones already employed by Swedish diplomats and others; but Wallenberg put no limit on the number of Jews he would try to save. Estimates differ as to the full effectiveness of Wallenberg's efforts, but certainly 20,000 and maybe as many as 100,000 Jews were saved. In January 1945 Soviet troops liberating Hungary arrested Wallenberg, presumably as a spy, and he disappeared into the Gulag. His postwar fate became a major symbolic issue in the Cold War.

The last major Swedish effort to aid Jews occurred at the end of the war. Playing on the desire of SS chief Heinrich Himmler to appease the Western powers, Sweden negotiated a Swedish Red Cross rescue mission led by Folke Bernadotte to liberate nearly 7,000 Jews from concentration camps within Germany. Using white buses, a caravan of Swedes drove into war-ravaged Germany and brought the refugees to Sweden. These efforts continued immediately after the war as well.

Because all residents of Sweden were required to be registered as members of state-approved religious congregations, the more than 10,000 registered Jews in Sweden represented an extraordinarily diverse population. Orthodox Jews and professed atheists; assimilated professionals and recent immigrants; conservatives, liberals, socialists, and Communists—all coexisted in an environment that was unsympathetic toward Jews or any people different from the Lutheran norm. The official spokesman for the community was the chief rabbi, Marcus Ehrenpreis, and the leading congregation was in Stockholm.

The Jewish community in Sweden remained highly divided on the issue of helping Jews from Germany and occupied nations both in the 1930s and once implementation of the Final Solution had begun. The official leaders, who were assimilated Jews, tended toward caution. They feared that extensive immigration would cause an increase in Swedish antisemitism, and they worried about how the refugees would be cared for. Before the war the government expected the Jewish community to maintain recent immigrants until they were self-supporting. The leaders also wanted to be loyal to a government that saw itself threatened by the war.

Jewish immigrants, meanwhile, tended to be outspoken in their support of a more active rescue policy.

Former prisoners of a Nazi concentration camp at a Red Cross transit point in Switzerland. These are some of 300 women rescued at the end of the war by the efforts of Count Folke Bernadotte. 9 April 1945

They showed less concern about the possibility of increased Swedish hostility toward Jews or the economic ramifications of immigration for Sweden. Their sense of the immediate need to rescue Jews from German persecution overwhelmed all other considerations. Hillel Storch, a Baltic Jewish refugee, deserves special mention as a source of consistent efforts to help Jews in German-controlled areas. Groups representing recent immigrants became very frustrated with the official policies of the Stockholm congregation as the war proceeded. Existing deep divisions within the broader Jewish community were exacerbated. The government was relieved to work with the more politically sensitive groups.

European countries did not act forcefully to help Jews faced with persecution and death at the hands of Nazi Germany. Sweden was no exception. There was much Sweden could have done that it did not attempt or even contemplate. Antisemitism, fear of foreigners, and apprehension over possible economic reprisals by Germany all contributed to Swedish resistance to work as actively as possible on behalf of the endangered Jews. Once the war began and Sweden became isolated, fear of Germany played a major part in Sweden's temerity. Yet by the end of 1942 the combination of shifts in war prospects, a vigorous policy to help Scandinavians, humanitarian interests, and a desire to demonstrate the value of Swedish neutrality to the Western powers led Sweden into more energetic efforts to save Jews. Swedish successes were impressive but would not have been possible without the willingness of certain elements of the German government to negotiate, look the other way, or even cooperate in the rescue efforts.   *Steven Koblik*

Switzerland   After World War II Swiss officials sought to portray Switzerland during the years when most of Europe was under German domination as an oasis of freedom, a refuge for the persecuted, and a rock of humanity amid the surging tides of war. But the Swiss playwright and essayist Friedrich Dürrenmatt, in the late 1960s, corrected that picture. "It's not so much that we didn't take in refugees," Dürrenmatt wrote, "but that greatness only shows itself in standing by a refusal. The guilt comes from our wriggling out of it: this is where Switzerland shows herself small, even smaller than on the atlas. She sees herself as heroic and humane, and aims to get clear away, without a stain on her character." The "profiteer," as Dürrenmatt called Switzerland, perceived herself as a victim, although the country, which remained a neutral during the conflict and was never invaded by Germany, had been largely shielded from the effects of war.

This carefully nurtured image has sustained more than a few blemishes over the past five decades. At the beginning of the 1950s the *Schweizerische Beobachter*, a newspaper traditionally espousing the rights of the disadvantaged and oppressed, revealed that the "J" stamped in the passports of German Jews had been introduced following a Swiss request and was not an invention of the Gestapo, as was commonly believed. The details of the Swiss role in this action caused major reverberations in Switzerland—not least because they differed totally from what Swiss citizens had previously been told by their own government. Federal Councillor Eduard von Steiger, for many years director of the Confederal Justice and Police Department (Eidgenössisches Justiz- und Polizeidepartement, or EJPD) and accordingly the person mainly responsible for Swiss policy on refugees, professed after the war that the Swiss government had been ignorant of the mass destruction of European Jewry, intimating that "had we known what was happening over there in the Reich, we might have widened the bounds of what was possible."

But the Swiss public learned just the opposite from the *Schweizerische Beobachter*. In March 1938, shortly after the entry of German troops into Austria, the Swiss government stepped up its anti-refugee policy. When the National Socialists declared all Austrian passports invalid and replaced them with German documents, Switzerland unexpectedly found itself in a difficult situation: How would it be possible in the future to distinguish Jewish refugees from "Aryan" holders of German passports? There could be no question of insisting on visas for German travelers. The solution was an indication on the passports that the holder was non-Aryan. Contacts between the Swiss embassy in Berlin and the German Foreign Office finally opened the way for Jewish passports to be marked "J." In the fall of 1938 Heinrich Rothmund traveled to Berlin for the conclusion of negotiations. Rothmund, as head of the Police Department in the EJPD, was directly subordinate to Councillor Steiger. The minutes of the discussion, held on 27–29 September 1938, included a statement that the German authorities were obliged to detain "Jews of the German Reich" wishing to travel to Switzerland without a visa; in addition, the passports "should be furnished as quickly as possible with an indication marking out the holder as a Jew." On 4 October the Swiss people were informed that "German passport holders of German nationality and who, according to German law, are not Aryan" required a visa to enter Switzerland. Utter silence prevailed concerning the active involvement of the Swiss government.

Following this revelation further reports appeared. Investigations were carried out which, almost without exception, portrayed a dismal picture of Switzerland's role in World War II. Particularly worthy of mention are the "Ludwig Report" and the "Bonjour Report," both the result of federal commissions, as well as *Das Boot Ist Voll: Die Schweiz und die Flüchtlinge, 1933–1945* (The lifeboat is full: Switzerland and the refugees) (1967), by the journalist Alfred A. Häsler.

Despite these and other reports, deep reflection and serious thought regarding Swiss behavior during the war remained at best sporadic. Did the responsible officials really have nothing with which to reproach themselves, as they repeatedly asserted? Could it be true that people in Switzerland did not know what was happening to the Jews? Had the relevant information been available to them but ignored and forgotten? Or had it been held back from them by the government? If so, for what reason and in whose interest? Out of fear of antagonizing the Germans and thereby risking invasion? Or had sympathy for antisemitism penetrated the government, the diplomatic service, and the army more deeply than anyone cared to admit?

Carl Lutz (1895–1975), one of the Righteous Among the Nations. Arriving in Budapest in 1942, Lutz, a Swiss diplomat, represented the United States, Britain, and other countries. In 1942 he issued British certificates allowing 200 children to reach Palestine. In June 1944 he pressured the Horthy regime to stop deportations of Hungarian Jews and issued collective passports and certificates that saved 50,000 Jews by placing them under Swiss protection in safe houses. Finally, Lutz saved many Jews in the November 1944 death march by distributing Salvadoran certificates.

Heinrich Rothmund of the EJPD provides a regrettable example of the official attitude. On 15 July 1942 the Germans, in combination with the French militia, had hunted down the Jews of Paris. Anyone managing to avoid capture fled to the unoccupied zone in southern France or attempted to find safety in Switzerland. On 18 July the Social Democratic newspaper *Volksrecht* printed a report from Stockholm stating that "80,000 Jews from the French metropolis have been deported to Poland and Russia." It said that the captive Jews had been concentrated in transit camps in France whence deportation trains conveyed them to the East. Early in August a newspaper in western Switzerland, the *Sentinelle*, told of 28,000 Jews having already been deported from Paris and of Jews being detained even in unoccupied France. As well as giving detailed descriptions of the deportations, many publications called for a reassessment of Swiss policy on refugees.

The situation must have horrified Rothmund, who for 20 years had made it his duty to protect Switzerland from, in his words, "Jewish domination." At the French frontier—especially in the Jura area, which in places was difficult to supervise—the overworked border police registered innumerable illegal crossings. The papers printed reports of professional "passeurs," who daily smuggled dozens of escapees from France into Switzerland.

The Swiss government in Bern felt itself caught in a crisis. On 4 August 1942 Steiger informed the other six federal councillors of the plans concerning refugees. It had been decided to take a hard line. Civilians, a resolution records, would in the future be sent back, even if they were "foreigners for whom serious detriment (danger to life and limb) may arise." As more and more people risked flight to Switzerland, on 13 August, Rothmund arranged for the borders to be closed. "Refugees on racial grounds only, for example Jews," did not qualify as political refugees and were refused entry. Some fugitives already in Switzerland illegally were handed over to the German border police. The government took this action even though since late July 1942 the Police Department had been in possession of an internal report that unequivocally described the dreadful situation of the Jews within the German sphere of influence. The author of the report had come to the conclusion that sending back Jewish fugitives was no longer defensible: "The consistent and reliable reports about the manner in which the deportations are carried out, and about conditions in Jewish districts in the East, are so revolting that the desperate attempts of the refugees to escape such a fate are only too understandable." Thus the Swiss government cast out Jewish fugitives and shut the door in the full knowledge that Jews under German sovereignty would be murdered.

After the war Steiger, who in 1942 had coined the notorious phrase "the boat is full," made every effort to play down his own responsibility for the refugee policy and tried to shift blame to subordinates, as an admission of guilt would have damaged his own image as well as that of Switzerland. A report concerning the refugee policy prepared in Steiger's own department, the EJPD, has never been published. At a governmental session in 1951 Steiger remarked with astounding arrogance, "We did not intend to publish the report. . . . Publication would in all likelihood have been followed by a discussion, which would certainly have been of no help on the subject but would once again have aroused disquiet concerning a question that now might in essence be regarded as settled."

Nevertheless, at a very early stage the Swiss authorities had received intelligence that could have left no doubt in their minds as to German intentions. One of the first Swiss diplomats to report comprehensively on Nazi crimes in Germany was Franz Rudolph von Weiss, the consul in Cologne. As early as the end of 1940 he had sent a report to his superiors in the Confederal Political Department (Eidgenössisches Politisches Departement, or EPD)—the equivalent of a foreign ministry—about the so-called euthanasia program in the Reich. Consul Weiss wrote: "A few months ago, a rumor was circulating here that the inmates of homes for epileptics, asylums, and hospitals were being done away with in secret. . . . Again, not long ago, a surgeon with whom I had become friendly told me the same thing, although he could not give more detailed information. . . . I feel it to be my duty to bring to your attention these new, pragmatic, ominous methods for radical removal of the mentally ill by order of competent German authority—in case these measures are not already known to you." Although the relevant offices in the EPD did not react, Weiss continued to send intelligence. He collected evidence substantiating the deportation of the Jewish population of Cologne, described how Jews had to report to the Gestapo, and, as the deportation trains removed Jews from the German Reich to the East in 1941, reported regularly and fully. Panic reigned among the Jews of Cologne, Weiss wrote, and he attached a clipping from a German newspaper, which declared that the Führer's words were "even now being fulfilled: at the end of this war stands a Jew-free Europe."

Normally Weiss sent his reports to the Swiss embassy in Berlin, which forwarded them to the EPD in Bern. But he received news, probably early in May 1942, that impelled him to depart from his usual practice and approach the head of the Military Information Service, Roger Masson. He addressed to Masson the following handwritten lines in French: "Colonel, I venture to send you, enclosed herewith, in strict confidentiality, some photographs taken on the Russian front. One represents the execution of Poles; the oth-

ers show the removal from German trains of asphyxiated Jewish corpses."

What prompted Weiss to contact the army intelligence rather than the political authorities remains uncertain. It is known, however, that his attitude toward the EPD, in particular his chief, Marcel Pilet-Golaz, was far from happy. The photographer is not identified, but the diplomat appears to have relied on his informant. These grave accusations against the Germans, had they been made public, might have forced the government to modify its position. Swiss intelligence could no longer dismiss German deserters' accounts of conditions in Eastern Europe as anti-German propaganda.

The German attack on the Soviet Union in June 1941 brought a flood of information about German atrocities against Jews in the newly conquered territories. Shortly before the outbreak of war, however, the Swiss ambassador in Romania, René de Weck, had begun to keep a political diary, which together with his regular political reports to Bern forms a unique chronology of crimes in occupied Eastern Europe. About October 1941 de Weck quoted an Italian officer returning from Odessa, who reported that the Germans had murdered all the Jews of that city. Later a Swiss businessman who had been staying in Odessa told the diplomat that of the 200,000 Jews once residing there he had come across just two who remained among the living. The others had been shot, burned alive in warehouses near the harbor, or dragged to unknown locations. From the Brazilian ambassador came the news that the "antisemitic crusade" had claimed 280,000 victims. The acts of cruelty, wrote de Weck, far outstripped those of the Turkish massacre of Armenians which had horrified Europe some 30 years earlier. When in late 1942 the news from Bucharest at last gradually dried up, there was one simple reason: in the areas observed by de Weck there were no more Jews.

But information poured into Switzerland from other sources, too. The Swiss army obtained high-quality intelligence as to the progress of the Final Solution. Deserters from the German army were closely questioned by Swiss officers, and the detailed interrogation records were carefully preserved. Although the Swiss army was primarily interested in military information, virtually every transcript carried some indication of German war crimes. Some of the reports were corroborated by other sources. Others were so detailed that they could not have been invented, particularly as the interrogating officers usually were satisfied with credibility of other information, mostly military, provided by the informants.

At the end of 1943 the Swiss military attaché in Helsinki, Major Lüthi, sent Bern a report by a Balt who on his own admission had been involved in the murder of about 16,000 people. He had decided to inform the Swiss army command because, according to Lüthi, he wanted to "show up a bit of the truth." The man described the systematic mass shootings but noted that with the passage of time "the execution procedure had got humane." By "humane" the informant meant that the Germans had switched the murder method from shooting to asphyxiation with carbon monoxide gas from engine exhaust. In the same report Lüthi mentioned a high-ranking German officer who confirmed the mass executions and put the number of victims in Lodz at 450,000 and in Warsaw at 380,000.

The Swiss authorities, however, were not interested in the fate of the Jews. On the contrary, some highly placed officials made remarks that, in the choice of words, could scarcely be distinguished from German spokesmen. For example, when Eugen von Hasler, a colonel in the army and a federal judge, wrote to the head of the first Swiss Medical Mission, Eugen Bircher, he gave free rein to his enthusiasm for German-Swiss cooperation. Hasler asserted that the Swiss must at last recognize that "it is also in our own interest that the greatest thing of all is coming to pass, and our hearts beat as one with the young white men who, dog-tired, forge onward to the East as bringers of European culture." And the leading doctor in the Swiss Red Cross, Hugo Remund, spoke about Jewry in terms with which Nazi racial theorists would have agreed heartily: "From the moment when the Jews increased their number to became a mass whose dimensions could not be justified, antisemitism began to flourish."

Anyone bold enough to criticize the German government publicly had to pay a price. Consul Weiss was denigrated by his superiors in the Berlin embassy as a "defeatist." Peter Surava, editor of the journal *Nation,* having intervened unsuccessfully on behalf of Jewish children on holiday in Switzerland (they were sent back to France), found his career systematically destroyed. Rudolf Bucher, a physician who gave public lectures describing what he had seen and heard on the eastern front, was described as "not normal . . . in his exhibitionism and his hatred for the German race"

and as a "dangerous fantasist" whose conduct suggested a need for psychiatric assessment. The source of those remarks was Albert von Erlach, a founding member of the Committee for Assistance Operations, which had initiated activities by the Swiss Medical Mission on behalf of the Germans.

And yet Bucher had told only of what he had personally seen or, at least, had himself heard. As a member of the Swiss Medical Mission, which had treated the Germans on the Russian front, he had obtained access to extraordinary information:

> In January 1942, in the North Field Hospital, Smolensk, the chief doctor (Captain Wagner) assured me that from year to year things were getting worse and more critical, in that more and more Jews were being killed in the most brutal manner, and moreover not so much by mass shooting (as in the Minsk Ghetto, where 7,000 Jews died by machine-gun fire) but by gassing in gas chambers and the burning of masses of corpses in giant crematoria. He knew in any case that the establishment of this kind of extermination camp, if not yet completed in various places, had nevertheless been tried out in Auschwitz.
>
> In Smolensk I saw on the outskirts of town about 10 Jewish women digging their own grave. I did not attend the execution but the next day saw the pit earthed over. In Warsaw I saw, watched by some SS men, a deportation train of Warsaw Jews, from old people to infants, crammed into third-class coaches. An SS man told me that these "Jewish swine" naturally had no idea that after twice 48 hours they would be buried. . . . When I was returning in February 1942, a young blonde woman on the train between Breslau and Berlin . . . explained to me the collection of people's belongings and the washing procedures in the extermination chambers in Auschwitz. She also spoke about the arrangements for executions and burning, and mentioned the "blue cross gas," usually brought there in bomb-shaped iron containers. For the first time I heard about the cynical "delousing" operation.

Franz Blättler, a driver attached to the second Swiss Medical Mission on the eastern front between 28 January and 19 April 1942, on his return to Switzerland produced a report of his experiences, but it was not published until after the war had ended. Despite the strictest prohibition Blättler had managed to enter the Warsaw ghetto, where he talked with Jewish police aides. He also took photographs of the corpses of people who had died from disease and hunger. After returning to Switzerland, Blättler began to give public lectures on what he had seen and heard, but he was quickly stopped by the Swiss authorities.

Other wartime documents similarly detailing German atrocities against Jews are plentiful in the Swiss Federal Archive. They, too, testify to the Swiss government's surrender of its humanitarian ideals by turning back Jews at the Swiss borders.

Yet there existed also a Switzerland that courageously opposed official restrictions. In 1938, for example, a police captain from Saint Gall, Paul Grüninger, allowed thousands of Jewish refugees to enter the country illegally. In consequence he was dismissed from the police force and stripped of his pension. Grüninger died in 1972 in straitened circumstances. Not until 1995 was he granted a full, posthumous reinstatement. The Swiss consul in Budapest, Carl Lutz, saved tens of thousands of Hungarian Jews from deportation and certain death in Auschwitz by issuing "collective protection passports." His reward was to be packed off after the war to an insignificant provincial post. And there were many other men and women—some known and others whose identities remain unknown—who quietly achieved impressive results on behalf of Jewish refugees. In a 1948 report summing up the situation during the war, J. Bosch Ridder van Rosenthal, the Dutch envoy in Switzerland, severely criticized the Swiss authorities but praised the citizenry: "Help for the Netherlands arose spontaneously, in consequence of the great sympathy in Switzerland for the Netherlands. . . . The higher authorities showed goodwill to Germans and were in some respects afraid of them. Subordinate officials stuck strictly to their instructions. They were disagreeable and dilatory. The people themselves were charming. 'Non-official' citizens looked after refugees, in a way that Swiss authorities could not have imagined. Over and over again, people took in fugitives."

Antisemitism, "adjustment," admiration, and fear marked Swiss policy toward the Third Reich. The behavior of the Swiss authorities changed only when the defeat of Nazi Germany became a certainty. On 3 November 1944 Switzerland intervened in Berlin against the deportations and declared itself ready to accept Jewish escapees. There followed various rescue operations—for example Aktion Musy, in which 1,200 Jews from the Theresienstadt camp were released and brought to Switzerland when the former federal councillor Jean-Marie Musy, having made contact with the head of the SS Foreign Communications Service, Walter Schellenberg, managed to ransom their freedom. Even the Jewish establishment in Switzerland—particularly Saly Mayer, president of the Swiss Israelite Community Association (Schweizerischer Israelitischer Gemeindebund, or SIG), the umbrella organi-

Saly Mayer, president of the Swiss Israelite Community Association.

zation for Jews in Switzerland—had to face the reproach that he had sometimes shown too great forbearance concerning official refugee policy. But toward the end of the war he too, in his capacity as representative of the Joint Distribution Committee, had contacted the SS and managed to organize two operations leading to the release of nearly 1,700 Hungarian Jews.

On 8 May 1945, the day that U.S. president Harry S Truman announced the unconditional surrender of Germany and declared the war in Europe over, refugees in Switzerland numbered 115,000, the great majority of them non-Jews. Official records showed that during the closure of the frontiers 9,751 fugitives were refused entry, almost all of them Jews. The actual number who would have taken refuge in Switzerland may be several times higher, for many people, convinced of the impossibility of entering Switzerland, simply did not make the attempt.

In 1995, when the 50th anniversary of the end of the war in Europe was celebrated, Switzerland, in the person of President Kaspar Villiger, officially apologized to the Jewish people for its disastrous refugee policy.

Gaston Haas

Szenes, Hannah (1921–44) Gifted poet and parachutist in Jewish commando unit of the British army. Born in Budapest, Szenes moved to Palestine in 1939 and joined Kibbutz Sdot Yam. In 1943 she volunteered to join the parachutists who planned to infiltrate occupied Europe. She parachuted into Yugoslavia, spent several months with the partisans there, and crossed the Hungarian border in June 1944. The Hungarian police caught her, and a court appointed by the fascist Arrow Cross regime sentenced her to death. She was executed in November 1944. See PARACHUTISTS' MISSION

T

Tenenbaum, Mordechai (1916–43) Leading member of the Zionist youth movement in Poland and a student at the University of Warsaw. Tenenbaum took a prominent role in organizing Jewish resistance first in Vilna, later in Warsaw, and eventually in Bialystok, where he led an uprising in March 1943 and was killed.

Terezin See THERESIENSTADT

Thadden, Eberhard von (1909–64) Member of the SS, official of the German foreign ministry. From April 1943 to the end of the war Thadden succeeded Franz Rademacher as liaison officer between the foreign ministry and the authorities in charge of the Final Solution. He organized the deportation of Jews from Europe, especially those from Hungary in 1944, to their destruction in the extermination camps. He was accused of war crimes after the war; the charges against him were dropped for lack of evidence but later were resumed. Thadden died in a traffic accident before proceedings against him could be renewed.

Theological and Philosophical Responses In the beginning was silence, silence because what use were words. There was so much to say, so little that could be said. Ludwig Wittgenstein concluded the *Tractatus Logico-Philosophicus* with the words, "Whereof one cannot speak, thereon one must remain silent."

It was not the word but the deed that first articulated the response. In the displaced persons camps the survivors felt lonely and isolated, anguished and pained—and they attempted to overcome loneliness and isolation by marrying and having children. The unspoken response to death was life. As a rule, only the young and able-bodied had survived. With their past annihilated, all they had was the future.

There was also a political response. In the aftermath of World War I Jews had sought their rights as a minority culture within dominant majorities. After World War II the Jewish future was secured by sovereignty and a state, an army and a flag. Zionism overshadowed its ideological alternatives because it alone had a plan for the future.

For survivors who emigrated to Israel, the task was state-building. Those who went to the United States had adjustments to make, a new language to learn, new lives to build.

The first religious response was traditional. As the liturgy on the Jewish festivals proclaims, "Because of our sins, we were exiled from the land." The only debate was the nature of the sin—and the proportionality of the punishment. The Satmar rebbe maintained that the sin was secularization. Followers of the Zionist leader Vladimir Jabotinsky argued that it was the sin of remaining in exile and not heeding the Zionist call. The philosopher Martin Buber presented the compelling image of the "eclipse of God." False gods, Buber argued, were placed by humanity between God and the human community, and thus the presence of God was obliterated by idolatry. The absence of God was not of God's doing but was effected through the overwhelming presence of falsehood and evil. But Buber wrote soon after the Holocaust, and his anti-idolatry response did not generate new thinking in others.

The boldest restatement of traditional theology was written by Ignatz Maybaum, a Viennese-born, London-based Reform rabbi, who described the Holocaust as the third *hurban*—the first two were the destruction of Jerusalem by the Babylonians in 586 B.C.E. and by the Romans in 70 C.E.—the sacrificial offering of the Jewish people in order to bring the world fully into the new way. The murder of the Jews, by this account, was a form of creative destruction serving the divine purpose. Maybaum invoked the language of Isaiah: God forsook Israel for a moment but will gather Israel again with great compassion.

But Maybaum's framework collapsed. For in the words of theologian Irving Greenberg, "no statement—theological or otherwise—should be made that cannot be said in the presence of burning children." Indeed, how can one speak of God's love and God's justice when we are in the presence of such memories? How can one speak of the Holocaust as punishment? What sin would merit such a punishment? Thus, there were early attempts at lamentation, statements of woe, and protest against God and humanity.

Perhaps Emil Fackenheim's response was most typical of the early silence. A survivor of the Sachsenhausen concentration camp who found refuge in Canada, for the first 25 years after the Holocaust this distinguished Jewish philosopher endeavored to prove that no event between Sinai and the final redemption can change the content of Jewish faith. Like Franz Rosenzweig, Fackenheim situated Jewish faith apart from history and regarded it as inviolable by human events.

Enter Richard Rubenstein, an American-born ordained rabbi, who in 1966 published a collection of essays entitled *After Auschwitz: Radical Theology and Contemporary Judaism*. Rubenstein argued that after the Holocaust the belief in a redeeming God who is active in history and who will redeem humankind from its vicissitudes was no longer tenable. Belief in such a God and an allegiance to the rabbinic theodicy that attempted to justify God would imply that Hitler was part of a divine plan and that Israel was being punished for its sins. "To see any purpose in the death camps," Rubenstein wrote, "the traditional believer is forced to regard the most demonic, antihuman explosion in all history as a meaningful expression of God's purposes. The idea is simply too obscene for me to accept." Rubenstein called for a new, vital theology based on acknowledgment of the absence of God. Such a theology would be "rooted in the fact that it has faced more openly . . . the truth of the divine-human encounter in our times. The truth is that it is totally nonexistent. Those theologies which attempt to find the reality of God's presence in the contemporary world manifest a deep insensitivity to the art, literature, and technology of our times."

For Rubenstein, Jewish consciousness of the death of God did not entail a triumphant exultation or a glorious

Boy from Poland on board ship for Israel. 1949

freedom but rather a sober acceptance of the impossibility of affirming God's presence after Auschwitz. Nor were Jews exempt from rethinking their own theology. He even challenged the notion of the Jews as a chosen people. Rubenstein wrote:

> Can we really blame the Christian community for viewing us through the prism of a mythology of history when we were the first to assert this history of ourselves? As long as we continue to hold to the doctrine of the election of Israel, we will leave ourselves open to the theology . . . that because the Jews are God's Chosen People, God wanted Hitler to punish them.
>
> . . . Religious uniqueness does not necessarily place us at the center of the divine drama of perdition, redemption, and salvation for mankind. All we need for a sane religious life is to recognize that we are, when given normal opportunities, neither more nor less than other men, sharing the pain, the joy, and the fated destiny which Earth alone has meted out to all her children.

The widespread reception accorded to Rubenstein's work demanded a response, and Emil Fackenheim, who had struggled in vain to situate Judaism outside history, was the first to answer. He declared his enterprise of the quarter-century after the Holocaust a failure. For the March 1967 symposium "On Jewish Values in the Post-Holocaust Future," sponsored by the magazine *Judaism*, Fackenheim wrote his most famous dictum on the "614th commandment":

> Jews are forbidden to hand Hitler posthumous victories. They are commanded to survive as Jews, lest the Jewish people perish. They are commanded to remember the victims of Auschwitz, lest their memory perish. They are forbidden to despair of man and his world, and to escape into either cynicism or otherworldliness, lest they cooperate in delivering the world over to the forces of Auschwitz. Finally, they are forbidden to despair of the God of Israel, lest Judaism perish. A secularist Jew cannot make himself believe by a mere act of will, nor can he be commanded to do so. . . . And a religious Jew who has stayed with his God may be forced into new, possibly revolutionary relationships with Him. One possibility, however, is wholly unthinkable. A Jew may not respond to Hitler's attempt to destroy Judaism by himself cooperating in its destruction. In ancient times, the unthinkable Jewish sin was idolatry. Today, it is to respond to Hitler by doing his work.

Fackenheim touched a raw nerve of anger among Jews, and the cry of no posthumous victories echoed deeply within the Jewish community. Yet his theological response was less an act of religious belief than it was a demonstration of his fear of consequences—the key word in his argument is "lest." Since the consequences of a failure to believe were so drastic, we dare not follow the thought to its logical conclusion. Fackenheim himself later rejected these views.

The events surrounding the Six Day War in June 1967 pushed esoteric theological debate to the center of Jewish consciousness. If before the war Rubenstein's conclusions were the lone views of a prominent theologian, afterward the issues he raised came to dominate the Jewish agenda. Rubenstein had argued that no theology could be created that did not relate to the two revolutions of contemporary Jewish life, the Holocaust and the rebirth of the state of Israel. For a time, after the Six Day War, these were the only issues of theological concern.

In the 1960s the writer Elie Wiesel became the embodiment of the Jewish response to the Holocaust—the de facto high priest (in the words of Steven Schwarzschild) of that generation. Wiesel's works center on the image of the void and the theology of protest. At the same symposium where Fackenheim first spoke of the 614th commandment, Wiesel said: "In a world of absurdity, we must invent reason, we must create beauty out of nothingness. And because there is murder in the world—and we are the first ones to know it—and we know how hopeless our battle may appear, we have to fight murder and absurdity and give meaning to the battle, if not to our hope." For Wiesel, the response to the void is revolt. In *Souls on Fire* (1972), he wrote that "Jewish tradition allows man to say anything to God, provided it be on behalf of man. Man's inner liberation is God's justification. It all depends on where the rebel chooses to stand. From inside the community, he may say everything. Let him step outside it, and he will be denied the right. The revolt of the believer is not that of the renegade."

Just as traditional Jewish theology resorted to midrash (biblical legends) to speak most profoundly of God, Wiesel adopted storytelling as his means of articulating the divine-human relationship after the Holocaust. In his first dozen books he searched for searing images to speak of God and Israel. In *Night,* for example, he recalls a rabbi who compared God unfavorably to Hitler: at least Hitler kept his promises to the Jewish people. In a memorable scene he describes the hanging of a young boy too light to die quickly and too brave to implicate others in the conspiracy: "Behind me I heard the same man asking: 'Where is God now?' And I heard a voice within me answer him: 'Where is He? Here he is, hanging on the gallows.'" In his novel *Day* the protagonist speaks of God with deep anger: "Man prefers to blame himself for all possible sins and crimes rather than come to the conclusion that God is capable of the most flagrant injustice. I still blush every time I think of the way God makes fun of human beings, his favorite toys." Wiesel writes of God's dependence on man in equally livid tones: "Yes, God needs man. Condemned to eternal solitude he made man only to use him as a toy, to amuse himself. . . . In the beginning there was neither the Word, nor Love, but laughter, the roaring eternal laughter whose echoes are more deceitful than the mirages of the desert."

In his later work Wiesel mutes his critique of God, preferring to write and speak of men who believe in God, who challenge God. But he does not speak of God directly. David R. Blumenthal, in *Facing the Abusing God* (1993), extracts from Wiesel's early works an articulate theology, complete with prayers and commentary that confront the God of the Holocaust and the God who permits other abuses. His bold work does not back away or seek easy solace.

A more Orthodox approach is offered by Eliezer Berkovits, who in *Faith after the Holocaust* (1973) attempted to shift the debate from history to cosmology. Berkovits argues that the issue is miscast. God's presence in history must be reunderstood; so, too, must God's power. Humanity exists only because God has renounced power and given room for humanity to function in history. God is not present in manifest material power. History is the result of human, not divine, actions.

Thus for Berkovits humanity, not God, is responsible for the Holocaust. By withdrawing from the world, God permitted history to be the domain of human responsibility. Still, Berkovits does not solve the problem of God. He merely delays the moment of responsibility:

> Yet all this does not exonerate God for all the suffering of the innocent in history. God is responsible for having created a world in which man is free to make history. There must be a dimension beyond history in which all suffering finds its redemption through God. This is essential to the faith of a Jew. The Jew does not doubt God's presence, though he is unable to set limits to the duration and intensity of his absence. This is no justification for the ways of providence, but its acceptance. It is not a willingness to forgive the unheard cries of millions, but a trust that in God the tragedy of man may find its transformation.

Irving Greenberg is one of the few systematic theologians among contemporary Jewish thinkers. At the core of Greenberg's work is a genuine, deep, and authentic confrontation with the Holocaust. Greenberg attempts to deal with the implications of this critical event in human history. He does not shy away from the task even when it challenges the core of his Orthodox faith and puts him at odds with the more facile solutions of his community.

Greenberg argues that the Holocaust and the rise of the state of Israel have initiated the third great era of Jewish history. The very nature of the divine-human relationship, according to Greenberg, is being transformed before our eyes. Even though the content of that covenant has been altered, and the circumstances and interrelations between God and the Jewish people have been changed, continuity is to be found in the covenant that binds Israel and God and that moves history toward redemption. Unlike most of his Orthodox colleagues, who speak of the simultaneity of the biblical (written) and rabbinic (oral) teachings, Greenberg daringly writes of transformations and discontinuities, of the shifting role of power, initiative, and responsibility between Israel and God, and of the revolutionary impact of history.

Greenberg also writes of the shattering of the covenant in the Holocaust. Following Elie Wiesel and Jacob Gladstein ("The Torah was given at Sinai and returned at Lublin"), Greenberg recognizes that the Holocaust has altered perceptions of God and humanity. He offers a powerful verification principle, which must become the test of religious integrity after the Holocaust. The divine authority of the covenant was broken in the Holocaust, says Greenberg, but the Jewish people, released from their obligations, chose to renew it again: "God is no longer in a position to command, but the Jewish people are so in love with the dream of redemption that [they] volunteered to carry out the mission." The choice to remain Jews is thus a response to the covenant with God and between generations of Jews, a communal utterance of the response to Sinai, "We will do and we will hear."

Even a theologian such as Arthur A. Cohen could not escape the problem of the Holocaust. Borrowing from Rudolph Otto's concept of God as the "tremendum," Cohen uses that word (in his book *The Tremendum*, 1981) to denote "the human tremendum, the enormity of an infinitized man who no longer seems to fear death, or perhaps, more to the point, fears it so completely, denies death so mightily, that the only parent of his refutation and denial is to build a mountain of corpses to the divinity of the death, to placate death by the magic of endless murder." Cohen's God, unlike the early Fackenheim's, is active not in history but in

the future of history, which is inaccessible to contemporary empirical confirmation. But God's people, the Jewish people, are undeniably the chosen ones after the Holocaust.

A year after *The Tremendum* appeared, Emil Fackenheim reentered the lists with the publication of *To Mend the World* (1982). There Fackenheim defines the Holocaust as a nearly total rupture—philosophical, political, and spiritual—in the fabric of civilization. In the aftermath of the rupture, the human task is to mend. The great hasidic master Rabbi Nahman of Bratzlav (Breslov) once said that "nothing is as whole as a heart that has been broken." Similarly, the strongest part of a garment, Fackenheim would remind us, is the part that has been mended.

The philosopher-theologian Eliezer Schweid was born in the Yishuv, shaped by the institutions of pre-state Palestine, not prewar Europe. He is most persuasive when he speaks of a religious Zionism that sees the state of Israel, not merely as a consolation, but as a manifestation of the divine presence in the aftermath of the Holocaust. This condition requires a new and more active understanding of the Jewish people's role in the encounter between God and Israel. Schweid restates the Zionist critique of exile—namely that after the Holocaust, exile is no longer a significant option. Jews must return home, where they will discover their roots and stand firm. Schweid concludes, as does Eliezer Berkovits, with an assertion of faith in the loneliness of the believer before a hiding God. He rejects the most powerful but unarticulated response to the Holocaust in contemporary Orthodox circles: messianism.

Two movements in contemporary Jewry have faced messianic crises in the 1990s: Chabad-Lubavitch hasidism and Gush Emunim. Some followers of the Lubavitcher rebbe Menachem Mendel Schneerson, who died in 1994, have proclaimed their teacher *melekh ha-mashiah*, the Messiah king. For some of the Lubavitchers, messianic enthusiasm was cooled by the rebbe's death, but for others the ardor was intensified by his death, in which they read the promise of his imminent return.

There are many factions within Gush Emunim (Hebrew, "block of the faithful"), the religious settlement movement in Israel. One major faction comprises those who view the Jewish return to the land of Israel as the "dawn of redemption" and who see the efforts at settlement, especially after the Six Day War, as moving toward the imminent messianic moment of return. The withdrawal of Israeli forces from Judea and Samaria (the West Bank) and the relinquishing of those lands to the Palestinian authority have provoked a crisis among the messianists, who view the actions of the Labor governments not as the deeds of a secular state, but as antimessianic assaults by those who would maintain Israel in exile.

Common to both Chabad-Lubavitch and Gush Emunim is an often unspoken premise that the Holocaust was the final battle between Gog and Magog and constituted *hevlei mashiah*, the birth pangs of the Messiah. Theologically, this account would place the Holocaust in the realm of the divine, and all challenges to the covenant would be mistaken. The Holocaust, in this view, is justified as the prelude to redemption.

Some theologians, such as David Hartman, are so enamored of the Jewish state's redemptive role that they refuse to focus on the problem of evil. Others protest against the prominence of the Holocaust in contemporary Jewish theology. In a 1971 review in *Judaism* of Fackenheim's work, Michael Wyschogrod wrote: "Israel's faith has always centered about the saving acts of God: the election, the Exodus, the Temple and the Messiah. However, more prevalent destruction was in the history of Israel; the acts of destruction were enshrined in minor fast days while those of redemption became the joyous proclamation of the Passover and Tabernacles, of Hanukkah and Purim. The God of Israel is a redeeming God; this is the only message we are authorized to proclaim."

In *Death and Birth of Judaism: The Impact of Christianity, Secularism and the Holocaust on Jewish Faith* (1987), Jacob Neusner takes both a theological and a historical approach. Neusner characterizes American Judaism after the Six Day War as the Judaism of Holocaust and Redemption; the stories that Jews tell about their Jewishness have less to do with their own circumstances than with what happened to another Jewish community more than a half-century ago or with what Americans have chosen not to become—Israelis. Who is Israel (i.e., the Jewish people) according to this view? Those who could have been victims of the Holocaust (all Jews) and those who are willing to work against its recurrence. What does Israel do? It engages in philanthropy, politics, and organizational life.

Neusner offers four critiques. First, "the Judaic system of Holocaust and Redemption leaves unaffected the larger dimensions of human existence of Jewish Americans—and that is part of that system's power." But as people look for answers to questions in their private lives—in issues of life and death, suffering and celebration—the vicariousness of American Jewry's new theology does not serve them well. Second, the American Judaism of Holocaust and Redemption works only with what is near at hand, "the raw materials made available by contemporary experience— emotions on the one side, and politics on the other. Access to realms beyond require learning in literature, the only resource beyond the immediate." Third, American Jews today, unlike their ancestors, no longer regard being Jewish as a matter of intellect. Unlike all other Judaisms of the nineteenth and twentieth centuries, the Judaism of Holocaust and Redemption is not the product of intellectuals but of bureaucrats, fund raisers, administrators, and public relations experts. In Neusner's eyes, this Judaism lacks spirit and charismatic leadership. "The correlation between mass murder and a culture of organizations proves exact: the war against the Jews called forth from the Jews people capable of building institutions to protect the collectivity of Israel, so far as anyone could be saved. Consequently, much was saved. But much was lost." Finally, the consummate historian-empiricist becomes a theologian: "The first century found its enduring memory in one man on a hill, on a cross; the twentieth, in 6 million men, women, and children making up a Golgotha, a hill of skulls of their own. No wonder that the Judaism of the age struggled heroically to frame a Judaic system appropriate to the issue of the age. No wonder they failed. Who would want to succeed in framing a world view congruent to such an age, a way of life to be lived in an age of death."

The most creative work in Christian responses to the Holocaust has required the recognition of the role of antisemitism in the Holocaust and the contribution of Christianity to that antisemitism. Where the rupture has been recognized, mending has taken place. Unrepentant Christianity has had no mending.

The pronouncements on the Jews made at the Second Vatican Council in the early 1960s provide a typical example of this sense of rupture and mending. The council was called by Pope John XXIII, who during the time of the Holocaust, as Archbishop Angelo Roncalli, participated in rescue operations in Turkey. When Roncalli became pope, he continued this mending work by leading the effort to reevaluate the role of the Jews in the crucifixion of Jesus and in the ongoing religious life of humanity, changing liturgical and scriptural readings for the Good Friday service. This mending has been continued by Pope John Paul II, whose recent pronouncements against antisemitism, in such popular publications as the Sunday newspaper supplement *Parade* magazine, have been unprecedented. As the young priest Karol Wojtyla, John Paul II helped rescue Jews in Poland during the occupation and did not insist on their conversion to Christianity.

In 1994 the Lutheran American church renounced Martin Luther's antisemitic teachings about the Jews. The writings of such Protestant theologians as Paul van Buren, A. Roy and Alice Eckhart, Franklin Little, and John Roth, and such Catholic theologians as John Pawlikowski, Rosemary Ruether, Eugene Fisher, and Gregory Baum, have gone a long way toward transforming Christian doctrine with respect to the Jews by ending the inculcation of contempt for Jews and by deemphasizing, if not canceling, the theology of supersessionism, which teaches that Christianity has taken the place of Judaism and that there is no ongoing role for the Jewish people in history. Furthermore, there has been an effort to rediscover the Jewish roots of Christianity and recover an understanding of Jesus the Jew, to comprehend sympathetically and respectfully the impact of the mother religion, Judaism, on the daughter faith.   *Michael Berenbaum*

Theresienstadt   The Jewish ghetto established by the Nazis in the winter of 1941–42 in the Czech town of Terezin—known to the Germans as Theresienstadt—differed from other ghettos in Eastern Europe, for it had many of the attributes of a concentration camp and was designed to meet unique objectives. In October 1941 Reinhard Heydrich, in his new capacity as acting protector in Prague, announced that, in accordance with the wishes of Adolf Hitler, the Protectorate of Bohemia and Moravia would be cleared of Jews by the end of the year. The Lodz ghetto, where the first 5,000 Jews from Prague and Brno were deported between 26 November and 3 December, refused to absorb more transports, so an interim transit camp was needed. The small garrison town of Terezin, about 56 kilometers north of Prague, was chosen as the site. Built at the end of the eighteenth century by the Habsburg emperor Joseph II and surrounded by moats and walls, Terezin suited the purpose: access to the town could easily be controlled through a few gates, and 11 army barracks were available for mass occupation.

The Jewish community in Prague assumed that the move to Terezin would be permanent and drew up a detailed plan for a self-supporting city. On 26 November and 1 December 1941 the first two labor units of engineers, artisans, and construction workers left Prague to prepare Terezin to receive and house tens of thousands of Jews. They did not know that the Nazis' ultimate intention was to deport the Czech Jews to the East and make Theresienstadt a modern German settlement.

A second objective, announced by Heydrich at the Wannsee Conference (January 1942) on the Final Solution, was for Theresienstadt to serve as a ghetto for German Jews over 65 years of age who would not be transported to the East, for Jewish invalid veterans of World War I, and for Jews who had been awarded high military honors, in order to stop once and for all unwanted interference on their behalf. This was the seed of the third objective behind Theresienstadt—in Adolf Eichmann's phrase, "to save face." Theresienstadt was designed as a means of disinformation, a "model" ghetto that would persuade the free world that the Jews under German sovereignty were not being mistreated.

For the Jewish leadership, especially the Jewish elder (*Judenälteste*) Jakob Edelstein, the former head of the Palestine Office in Prague, there was only one aim: to hold out until the end of the war and the defeat of Hitler's Germany, and meanwhile to save the Jews of Bohemia and Moravia from transport to the East by integrating them into war industry. As early as 9 January 1942 the first 1,000 deportees left the ghetto for Riga. By the end of the deportations in October 1944, out of the approximately 140,000 brought to Theresienstadt from the Protectorate, Germany, Austria, Denmark, and the Netherlands, some 87,000 had been sent eastward to concentration and extermination camps—at first mainly to Izbica, Maly Trostinets (near Minsk), Sobibor, and Treblinka, later (beginning in the fall of 1942) primarily to Auschwitz. Only about 3,300 of them survived the war. Generally, instructions were received from SS headquarters through the Berlin-Prague chain of command as to the date of transports, the number of deportees, the country of origin, the age group, and special penalties for violations of SS orders. The actual list of names, where parents and children under 16 years of age were kept together, was compiled by a transport commission, on which the Council of Elders (*Ältestenrat*) and the various ghetto departments were represented. These administrative bodies were subject to much pressure for exemptions.

Women and men—with the exception of a few privileged families—were housed in separate guarded barracks. Only beginning in July 1942, after the complete evacuation of the local population, could most families meet after working hours. As in concentration camps, food was distributed daily to all occupants; the rations, even though meager, prevented starvation.

In the first months of the Theresienstadt ghetto's existence, groups of laborers were sent to work mining coal and foresting. Inside the ghetto, workshops were established, mainly for making clothes. The aim of Theresienstadt to become economically self-sufficient seemed near fulfillment. But in June 1942 the first transports of the elderly from Germany and Austria began to arrive, and in the summer they flooded in— more than 37,000 in three months. This was the time of the worst overcrowding and the highest mortality. There were up to 58,000 people in an area where 3,500 civilians and about the same number of soldiers had resided. For lack of living space, many of the elderly were crowded into attics and cellars, where at first they had to sleep on the floor. In Germany they had been promised a place of safety, and many of them had signed a contract in exchange for their property, believing that they were being sent to a rest home with proper amenities. Their spirits broken, they died in the thousands from disease and exhaustion.

Partly because those over 65 years of age were exempted from work and from transports to the East, a labor shortage—primarily in supplying the needs of the ghetto—developed and soon became acute. In the fall of 1942 Berlin changed its policy: out of 18,000 persons sent to Treblinka in September and October, 85 percent were elderly. This improved the labor balance, but only 10 percent of the work force produced goods or services for "export" outside the ghetto. Besides workshops for repairing uniforms and manufacturing supplies for army personnel, only two war industries materialized. In July 1943, in a huge tent in the city square, an assembly line was established for making crates and packing them with winter equipment for army vehicles on the eastern front; it closed five months later. And in June 1943 several hundred women began to work at splitting mica, which was needed for insulation in the aircraft industry.

The ghetto bureaucracy was huge but well organized, so it worked more or less efficiently. Living conditions slowly improved: the supply of water and electricity grew, the sewage system was enlarged, kitchen boilers were installed, hospitals opened, children were inoculated against infectious diseases, and three-tiered bunks were put up in the dormitories. These improvements were accomplished by resourcefulness and determination and with the approval of German authorities, who furnished the necessary materials. Fifty truckloads of pipes were brought into the ghetto. Theresienstadt was on the border of the Reich, and epidemics could easily spread.

Food parcels could be received beginning in October 1942, but after July 1943 a special permit stamp was needed. Few ghetto inhabitants still had relatives and friends outside the ghetto walls who could send parcels.

Theresienstadt reflected the character of its inmates—Central European Jews, most of them assimilated to Western society and deeply rooted in Western culture. They were a people accustomed to keeping law and order. Despite overcrowding and the other nerve-racking living conditions in the ghetto, there was no violence between Jews—no murder, no rape, no physical assaults. The only significant crime was theft, especially of food from common property. Thieves, if caught, were dealt with by Jewish courts. Several underground movements—Czech, Communist, and Zionist—existed in the ghetto, but there was never any real preparation for armed uprising. Many worked outside the ghetto walls, but for escape and survival there, help was needed. Ties to the family inside the ghetto were usually stronger than the urge to save oneself. Only 700 people escaped.

Women arriving in the ghetto pregnant were allowed to give birth, but beginning in July 1943 all new pregnancies were terminated by abortion. As official policy concerning births changed, so too did policy concerning the dead. At first the dead were buried; but in 1942 a crematorium was built outside the walls. Thenceforth the dead were cremated after a short prayer service and their ashes were put in separate cardboard urns. In November 1944, when eventual Allied victory became apparent, the German command sought to erase the traces of their crimes at Theresienstadt and so ordered that the contents of all 33,000 urns be thrown into the nearby Eger River.

The three Judenältester of Theresienstadt differed in personality. Jakob Edelstein, born in Galicia in 1905,

Wagon loaded with corpses in front of the crematoriums at Theresienstadt. May 1945

had no illusions as to the Nazi aim of crushing the Jewish people but tried his utmost to save lives, especially of the young, even at personal risk. In January 1943 he was replaced by Paul Eppstein. Born in Mannheim in 1906, Eppstein, a brilliant sociologist, was one of the heads of Reichsvereinigung, the Jewish central organization. Neither Edelstein nor Eppstein survived the war. After discrepancies in the ghetto registry to cover up for escapees had been discovered, Edelstein was arrested in November 1943, brought to the punishment block in Auschwitz, and executed on 20 June 1944 after having witnessed the shooting of his wife and his only son. Eppstein was arrested on 27 September 1944, at the beginning of the last mass deportations, on the pretense of a technical offense; he was shot the same day at the Small Fortress, the Gestapo prison near the ghetto. The last Jewish elder, Benjamin Murmelstein, a rabbi and a scholar from Vienna who was born in 1905, was arrested after the liberation by the Czechoslovak authorities on charges of collaboration but released in 1946 for lack of evidence. He died in Rome in 1989.

Theresienstadt was under control of the Office for the Solution of the Jewish Question in Prague, which was responsible to the Zentralverein (Central Office) in Berlin, headed by Adolf Eichmann. All three SS commanders of the ghetto, like Eichmann, were Austrian-born: Siegfried Seidl (November 1941–July 1943), who was captured after the war, sentenced in Vienna, and hanged there in February 1947; Anton Burger (July 1943–February 1944), who managed to escape from arrest after the war and died under an assumed name in Essen in 1991; and Karl Rahm, who left the ghetto on 5 May 1945, was caught in Austria, handed over to Czechoslovakia, sentenced to death by a people's court, and hanged in April 1947.

The SS command was small, and routine guarding was carried out by Czech gendarmes. In the first months 16 inmates were hanged in the ghetto for breaches of SS orders, but later offenders were sent to the Small Fortress on the next transport with a *Weisung*, a special order meaning death on arrival. Though dreading the transports to the unknown East, only a few of the ghetto inhabitants knew about the mass extermination. One of these was Leo Baeck, the spiritual authority of German Jewry. But even those with information were unable to grasp its full meaning and mostly kept the knowledge to themselves, hoping that the war would end soon. Two groups were exempted from the transports: the "prominents"—former ministers of state, world-famous scientists and scholars, people connected with the German nobility—and 464 Danish Jews who had not managed to escape to Sweden (as did most of the Jews of Denmark) in the first days of October 1943 and were under the patronage of the Danish Red Cross and the Danish government.

Heinrich Himmler, chief of the SS, in an attempt to silence "horror propaganda" about the fate of Jews and to use Theresienstadt as a cover, gave his consent to a visit to Theresienstadt by delegates of the International Committee of the Red Cross and the Danish Red Cross. The place had therefore to be prepared for the occasion. In May 1943 it ceased to be called a ghetto and became a Jewish settlement (*Siedlungsgebiet*); money bearing the portrait of Moses and the signature of Edelstein was introduced; a bank was established; streets previously only numbered were given poetical names; dummy shops and cafes were opened; a concert hall and a playground were built. To ease the overcrowding, transports started after a lull of seven months, this time to a new destination—a family camp in Auschwitz presented as "Arbeitslager Birkenau bei Neu-Berun," in case the Red Cross delegation should wish to see the camp in the East also. But Maurice Rossel of the Red Cross, after a half-day visit carefully prepared by the Nazis in June 1944, had only praise for the conditions in the Jewish town. In his report he asserted that Theresienstadt was "a final destination." The family camp in Birkenau, where 17,500 Theresienstadt inmates were sent between September 1943 and May 1944, was liquidated in July 1944; most of its inmates were gassed.

According to an agreement reached in Prague in 1941, the Czech Jews and the Zionists were equally represented in the 12-member Theresienstadt Judenrat in its first year. Some of its basic attributes, however, were influenced by Zionist beliefs: the importance of making the Jews more productive, the effort to save the lives of the children and young people as the biological kernel of the Jewish people, and their education within the framework of the Youth Care Department (*Jugendfürsorge*). Most of the children between

Money of Theresienstadt.

the ages of 10 and 16 lived in homes, separate from their parents. Their living conditions were better than those of the adult inmates; they received a little more food and a clandestine education. They painted, wrote newspapers, played football, and acted in theater. (The children's opera *Brundibar* was a special favorite.) They were hungry, they longed for home, they suffered from many diseases, but they knew happy hours too. Out of 10,000 children sent to the East, some 220 survived. In the ghetto itself 1,569 were liberated, including children of mixed marriages and those transported from Hungary and Slovakia who had arrived after deportation ceased.

Out of a deep need for culture, from the first days of its existence the ghetto inmates organized recitals of poetry and improvised performances in the closely guarded barracks. After July 1942, when the whole town became a ghetto, cultural activity grew considerably. Most of the best Jewish artists of Central Europe took part. Victor Ullman, Pavel Haas, Gideon Klein, Hans Krasa, and others composed musical works. Leo Haas, Petr Kien, Fritta (Fritz Taussig), Otto Ungar, Ferdinand Bloch, and others painted the reality around them; some of them paid with their lives for an attempt to smuggle their works out of the ghetto. There were hundreds of lectures, satirical cabarets in Czech and German, theatrical performances, operas in concert form (including *The Bartered Bride, The Marriage of Figaro,* and *Carmen*). But the greatest achievement was the performance of Giuseppe Verdi's

Requiem, directed by Rafael Schachter, including the call from the depths "Libera me Domine." Almost all the artists, actors, singers, and musicians were sent to their deaths in Auschwitz with the last wave of transports in September and October 1944, a few days before the gas chambers there ceased to function.

After nearly all the able-bodied men had been deported—officially to another labor camp but evidently out of fear of the possibility of an uprising—only 11,000 remained, mostly women and elderly people. In February 1945, as part of Himmler's negotiations with the West, the unbelievable happened: 1,200 Jews left Theresienstadt for Switzerland.

If there were plans for liquidation (installations that could be used as gas chambers had been built into the ghetto wall and called storerooms), they did not materialize. On 20 April the survivors of the death marches from other concentration camps started to arrive, living skeletons crazed by hunger and bringing with them lice and typhoid. On 3 May Theresienstadt was taken over by the International Red Cross, and five days later the Soviet Army took charge. After Russian, Czech, and Jewish doctors and nurses succeeded in stopping the typhoid outbreak, repatriation to the countries of origin began. On 15 August 1945 the Theresienstadt ghetto ceased to exist.

Ruth Bondy

Thessaloníki See SALONIKA

Thomas, Max (1891–1945) Commander of Einsatzgruppe C in 1942, which was active in Ukraine. Thomas's unit organized pogroms, mass murders, and massacres of Jews and other persons deemed dangerous by the Reich. He was responsible, inter alia, for the mass murders at Kharkov. Thomas attempted to hide after the war but was apprehended and committed suicide in December 1945.

Tiso, Jozef (1887–1947) Slovak nationalist politician and priest, head of the nominally independent Slovak state from 1939 on. Tiso was the first leader of a satellite nation to collaborate fully with the Nazis in regard to the deportation of Jews, even though the Vatican had informed him of the fate of the Jews in Poland. Tiso was apprehended after the war in Germany. He was sentenced to death and executed in 1947. See SLOVAKIA

Transnistria Transnistria was the temporary designation assigned to the artificially created region annexed to Romania during World War II. Before the war

the region, situated between the Dniester and the Bug rivers, was part of southwestern Soviet Ukraine. Mainly an agricultural area, its population consisted of a Ukrainian majority and comparatively large minorities of Russians, Jews, Romanians, and Germans. The Jewish population, estimated at 300,000, was concentrated in the cities, particularly the port city of Odessa. The existing national and socioeconomic structure of the surrounding local population had a decisive effect on the fate of the Jews in the region, as did Romanian antisemitic proclivities and opportunism. The latter, coupled with the forces of Nazi ideology and efficient implementation of the Final Solution, led to 90,000 deaths among the 150,000 Jews deported to Transnistria from Romania, and to the deaths of 185,000 Ukrainian Jews in this region.

Deep-seated Romanian antisemitism received new impetus in 1919, when the country was forced to guarantee the rights of its minorities. From that point on, nationalist organizations, the extremist Iron Guard in particular, disseminated the slogan "Save Romania from the Jews." The Jews were portrayed as foreigners who had flooded the nation, taking over its economic resources. With the spread of German influence in Romania after the Nazi rise to power, a new dimension was added to this anti-Jewish agitation. In August 1940 the promulgation of anti-Jewish regulations stripped most Romanian Jews of their citizenship. Concurrently the dictator Ion Antonescu embarked on a program aimed at "Romanizing" the economy, effectively driving the Jews out of commerce and industry. His partners in government, the Iron Guard, demanded even more stringent measures. Initially they embarked on an anti-Jewish wave of terror; their dissension eventually culminated in an anti-government revolt. Antonescu, having received German backing in suppressing the revolt, was ultimately left even more dependent on German goodwill. Shortly thereafter a new German ambassador was posted to Bucharest along with a "special adviser," with an eye to impelling Romania to exercise the spirit of the German solution to the "Jewish problem." Immediate plans were made to ghettoize the Jewish population and to expel the Jews to Polish areas.

These measures applied to the Jews of the Regat—Romania in its pre-1914 borders. Significantly harsher and more extreme measures were exercised against the Jews of Bessarabia and Bukovina, regions that had been annexed to Romania immediately after World

War I. These border areas, with their large, unassimilated Ukrainian and Jewish populations, aroused feelings of disquiet among the Romanians. Romanian bitterness was further fueled by the return of those regions to the Soviet Union in June 1940, along with the ceding of additional land to Hungary and Bulgaria at the German behest. Moreover, the joyful reception afforded the Red Army by a handful of Jewish youths, who perceived the Russians as liberators in light of reported pogroms perpetrated by the retreating Romanian army, further reinforced the Romanian attribution of questionable loyalty to Jews in the border areas. Jewish participation in local Soviet councils also afforded the Romanians an opportunity to denounce Jews as Communist agents. Generally speaking, Jews were denigrated as a nation of enemies, spies, and traitors, a conviction that had a direct bearing on subsequent events.

Shortly before the June 1941 invasion of the Soviet Union Hitler succeeded in dragging Romania into the war in return for the promised reannexation of Bessarabia and Bukovina and eventual hegemony over Transnistria. Antonescu and other Romanian nationalists found this offer attractive, and in August 1941 a Romanian-German agreement was signed at Tighina (Bessarabia). This pact granted Romania administrative jurisdiction in security and economic matters over Transnistria and the region between the Bug and the Dnieper. Nonetheless, the Tighina agreement also firmly anchored German influence in Transnistria, granting the Germans the right to station their own units there for security and intelligence-gathering purposes; to establish naval and air bases; and to operate liaison units. These units served as advisers to the Romanian military and civil authorities and, like their senior colleagues in Bucharest, concerned themselves with the Jewish question, admonishing the Romanian government, for example, that its appointees in the Transnistria region lagged behind in their implementation of the Final Solution.

In Odessa the Final Solution was swiftly and cruelly initiated. The Romanian occupation of the city in October 1941 was accompanied by brutality against Jews and the singling out of Jewish doctors for execution. The situation took a turn for the worse following a partisan attack on the Romanian general military headquarters in Odessa. The Germans and the Romanians embarked on a widespread campaign of anti-Jewish reprisals and mass murder. Thousands of Jews, ostensibly held responsible for the war, were shot outside the city. Thousands more were assembled in a large warehouse, which was then dynamited. In addition, thousands were hanged while other Jews were forced to witness their execution.

The survivors of the Odessa actions had the unenviable fate of being crowded into the ghetto of Slobodka, where living conditions were intolerable. Slobodka became an inescapable trap, an embarkation point for deportations to a chain of death camps from the Black Sea to the Bug—Domanievka, Bogdanovka, and others. The deportation process itself acted as a form of "natural selection." Many Jews died en route, whether they were made to travel on foot, by forced march in freezing conditions, or were transported in sealed, overcrowded, and airless freight cars. Those who managed to survive the journey subsequently perished in the camps from starvation, the bitter cold, and disease. Since the ground was frozen, they could not even be buried, and the corpses were devoured by the camp dogs. Death by so-called natural causes was deemed insufficient, so the Romanian camp administrators instituted additional measures: burning, drowning, clearing of minefields, or execution by firing squad near an open pit. Jewish children were killed by having their skulls crushed, as they were not considered worth the waste of ammunition. Women were raped and mutilated. The German method of execution was more systematic. In Gradovka, a village in the Odessa region, the Germans used lime pits to incinerate some 7,000 corpses of Jews who had been shot nearby.

The Jews of Bessarabia and Bukovina fared little better. Antonescu and his cohorts perceived the reconquest of these areas, with their large Jewish centers of Czernauti (Czernowitz) and Kishinev, as an unparalleled historic opportunity to make Romania *Judenrein*, free of Jews. The combined Romanian-German forces that invaded these areas, accompanied by the German killing units of Einsatzgruppe D, translated the prevailing anti-Jewish atmosphere into deeds. As these troops traversed the local villages, towns, and cities, they attacked and murdered Jews and stole or burned Jewish property. The survivors were either herded into centralized ghettos or deported to unspecified locations. The transfer process itself claimed many victims, who died of exhaustion or beatings. The success of these operations encouraged the Romanian regime to initiate deportations across the Dniester River even before the conclusion of the military operations there.

Romanian Jews en route to Transnistria assemble on the west bank of the Dniester River during a deportation action.

The Germans, who had not yet succeeded in exterminating the local Ukrainian Jewish population, temporarily halted these deportations and sent the first groups back to Bessarabia.

Organized deportations across the Dniester were carried out in three phases. The first and largest, which began in September 1941, comprised some 120,000 Jews who had survived the mass killings in Bessarabia, Bukovina, and Dorohoi (which originally was part of the Regat; its Jews were deported to Transnistria by administrative error). The second wave, which began in the summer of 1942, consisted of 5,000 Jews, mostly from the Bukovinian city of Czernauti. Also deported were thousands of Jews from "Old Romania" who were accused of being Communist sympathizers or having made requests to emigrate to the Soviet Union, or who were charged with economic crimes or evasion of forced labor. This third and final wave began in the fall of 1942. The deportees were transported either in overcrowded, carbide-contaminated freight cars or were forced to march on foot. The Dniester, whose bridges had been destroyed, was a major obstacle in their path. At the river the victims boarded barges; during the crossing some were thrown overboard or forced to swim under a hail of bullets.

Following this difficult and protracted journey, the remaining deportees were concentrated in ghettos situated in permanent settlements or in camps located outside the cities, particularly in northern and central Transnistria. Jurisdiction over the ghettos and camps was in the hands of the gendarmerie headquarters and the Romanian administrative authorities in Transnistria headed by Gheorghe Alexianu. In actual fact, however, the Jews were also at the mercy of German forces and of local *Volksdeutsche* (ethnic Germans) and Ukrainian militia. Conditions in the ghettos were appalling; people lived in bombed-out houses, in stables, barns, and pigsties. Denied freedom of movement, the deportees were drafted into forced labor virtually without pay. Under these conditions tens of thousands died of starvation, cold, and disease in the course of the winter of 1941–42.

These harsh circumstances notwithstanding, the Jews in the ghettos were somewhat better off than those sent to the camps, particularly those camps across the Bug River, which were under German control. In the work camps the Jewish internees were made to cut trees, pave roads, and dig peat under inhuman conditions. Political prisoners, Communists in particular, were incarcerated in separate camps. In one of these, Vapniarka, the prisoners were fed peas normally used as horse fodder but toxic to humans. Consequently hundreds of them developed paralysis. At the Akhmetchetka and Peciora extermination camps those Jews whom the Romanians considered unfit for labor—the sick, the disabled, the elderly, women, and children—were starved to death.

Physical condition was not the sole factor determining a deportee's chances of survival. The circumstances of deportation also played a significant role. The Jews of Bessarabia and northern Bukovina are a case in point. As they were initially concentrated in Bessarabian camps, where they were robbed of their belongings, they were destitute on reaching Transnistria. Moreover, as most of their leaders had been exiled to Siberia under the Soviet occupation in 1940–41, they were also deprived of this important human resource, thus adding to their vulnerability. The Jews from southern Bukovina and Czernauti were more fortunate on both counts; they arrived in Transnistria directly from their homes, bringing with them cash and valuables. Furthermore, they were accompanied by their leaders, who were imbued with a strong sense of mutual responsibility and the ability to take the initiative. This handful of exceptionally capable and courageous leaders succeeded in uniting the masses of up-rooted, impoverished, desperate, and persecuted individuals, in effect creating a state within a state.

One such exemplary leader was Mayer Teich. By bribing and interceding with the authorities, he and other members of the Suceava Jewish council succeeded in ameliorating the conditions of the deportation. They extracted permission to hire wagons and automobiles as needed and to transport whatever goods possible. Their success in smuggling out cash and valuables comprised the basis for continued public activity. In the Shargorod ghetto, for example, these resources financed the establishment of three public institutions—a bakery, a soup kitchen, and a cooperative store. Moreover, the money was also utilized to exploit internal rivalries among the governing authorities, as when the Romanian appointee was persuaded to allow the formation of a Jewish police force in the ghetto over the objections of his Ukrainian colleague. This carefully chosen Jewish police force succeeded in freeing the city from the depredations of the Ukrainian militia.

In actuality, however, in Shargorod, as in other ghettos, the most pressing problems were overcrowding and poor sanitary conditions. In the absence of uncontaminated water, soap, or latrines, an outbreak of typhus soon affected nearly the entire population. The ghetto administration, which represented the various communities in its midst, took practical steps to fight the epidemic. It acted to found advanced disinfection plants and a soap factory, repair the power station and water system, and clean streets and wells. A burial society was established, in addition to a pharmacy and a hospital. By the spring of 1942 these measures had stemmed the typhus epidemic.

Other noteworthy public institutions in the ghettos were the soup kitchens and the orphanages. In Mogilev alone the soup kitchen founded by workers' organizations distributed 37,000 portions daily. A second kitchen, organized by one of the communal leaders, sold a daily meal to community members at reduced prices. The destitute received this meal free. Nonetheless in many of the ghettos and smaller camps the establishment of soup kitchens was delayed either until the deportees recovered from the initial shock or, in some places, until assistance arrived from the Bucharest-based Autonomous Committee for Assistance (Comisia Autonoma de Asistenta) in early 1943.

Worst off among the deportees were the orphans, whose numbers reached 6,000 in the first winter after the deportations. Although seven orphanages were founded in the Transnistrian ghettos beginning in April 1942, they did little to ameliorate the young people's lot. Housed in overcrowded, unventilated halls, the orphans were often forced to remain in bed owing to lack of clothing. At times corpses were left in the halls so that their rations could be collected and distributed among the living—a practice that resulted in epidemics. This in turn contributed to the high mortality rate. Despite their limited means, some orphanages, like the ones in Shargorod and Bershad, managed to cultivate a lively social and cultural atmosphere.

Shaken by news of the harsh fate that had overtaken the deportees to Transnistria, Romanian Jewry was galvanized into action on their behalf. The president of the Union of Romanian Jews (Uniunca Evreilor Romani), Wilhelm Filderman, took immediate steps to obtain permission to send aid to Transnistria. The Autonomous Committee for Assistance began fundraising efforts, coordinating its humanitarian assistance with the Jewish Center (Centrala Evreilor—the newly created representative body for Romanian Jewry), Jewish organizations worldwide, and the International Red Cross. In early 1942 the governor of Transnistria gave permission for shipments of funds and medical supplies to be sent to the deportees. Nonetheless, this aid encountered fiscal and administrative obstacles—funds were held up or appropriated; exorbitant exchange rates were charged for the Romanian lei; and high customs duties were imposed, among other measures.

Conditions remained substantially unchanged even after the shift in Romanian policy in late 1942, which had been precipitated by news of German reversals at the front. In early 1943 Romanian authorities approved a visit to Transnistria by a delegation of the Autonomous Committee, headed by Fred Saraga; by late 1943, 80 million lei in cash, medical supplies, clothing, food, coal, and salt, as well as tools and raw materials for construction and industry, had reached Transnistria. Nevertheless, the deportees received only a fraction of this aid.

A more significant turning point took place only when the Autonomous Committee was officially recognized in October 1943 and Filderman was drafted to its ranks. During this period aid began to arrive from additional sources—the American Jewish Joint Distribution Committee, the World Jewish Congress, and the Oeuvre de Secours aux Enfants (OSE, Children's Aid). The aid forwarded separately by the Jewish Agency's Rescue Committee based in Turkey was channeled mainly to members of the Zionist youth movement Hehalutz. The various committees took steps to ensure the safe transfer of funds and employed more trustworthy emissaries. Nonetheless, obstacles remained: for example, the committee representing the deportees in the Mogilev ghetto, strategically located near a crossroads, detained the aid intended for distribution to other ghettos and misappropriated those funds. This was an exception, however. The majority of the Transnistrian ghetto and camp committees faithfully disbursed such funds for the public good.

The Transnistrian Plan

In late November 1942, following extremely heavy Romanian losses on the eastern front, Romanian circles broached a secret plan. In return for 200,000 lei per person for transport and lodging in Bucharest, and the assumption of responsibility by international Jewish agencies for their emigration (mainly to Palestine), the Romanian government would release the 70,000 Jews still remaining in Transnistria.

The Romanian-Jewish leadership, the Jewish Agency heads, and the leaders of other Jewish organizations to whom the clandestine offer was made were hard put to assess whether it was serious. Several points were clear. First, the Romanian attitude toward emigration had always been a positive one. Second, a policy shift had occurred in the fall of 1942 as a result of several factors—the heavy losses incurred by the Romanian army on the eastern front; warnings issued by the Allies to German satellites; the growth of internal opposition; and Jewish intercession. Nonetheless, doubts remained regarding the plan's feasibility. Could the change in policy be considered wholehearted at a time when certain Romanian circles still backed German policy and remained strongly opposed to emigration? Could Romania realistically abandon Germany in late 1942 and join the Allied Forces at a time when 600,000 of its troops were still fighting on the eastern front and when Romania itself was surrounded by German allies? Did Romania exercise enough sovereign power to enable the Transnistrian deportees to emigrate while Germany, which strongly opposed emigration, had a stronghold there?

While the Romanian offer was still under consideration by the Jewish organizations, the American Jewish

playwright Ben Hecht decided to leak the details of the plan to the American press. By publicizing the plan in a full-page advertisement in the *New York Times*, Hecht intended to promote fundraising for the project as well as to mold public opinion in favor of lifting the prohibition on sending donations to enemy territory. The American Jewish and Zionist organizations, fearful of the potentially adverse effects of this publicity, openly denied the plan's existence. Nonetheless, they did not abandon their clandestine efforts to realize it through diplomatic channels, despite the difficulty of dismissing the Allied contention that the plan was a trap, an attempt at blackmail. By the time the State Department finally approved transfer of funds to Europe in late 1943, the Romanian emigration plan was no longer feasible. Hecht, who was connected with the Irgun Zvai Leumi (IZL) delegation in the United States, and others held the Jewish organizations responsible for the plan's failure. Still, it seems that the lack of success can better be attributed both to German opposition and to the Romanian realization, with the approaching end of the war, that it would not retain control of Transnistria.

With the failure of the large-scale plan, a less ambitious scheme to transfer 5,000 orphans from Transnistria to Palestine was broached in the course of 1943. This more limited idea, which had British approval, sparked a burst of activity on the part of Zionist, Jewish, and international bodies, which organized aliyah certificates (for emigration to Palestine), raised money, and made efforts to solve transport problems. Ultimately, however, they were unable to entirely overcome problems posed by Romania's lack of goodwill. It was not until February 1944 that Romania agreed to the repatriation of a limited number of Transnistrian orphans. Acquiring permission to pass through territory within the German sphere of influence was yet another obstacle. Romanian restrictions, which specified that the orphans must have no surviving parent, further reduced the number repatriated to 2,000. Romanian Jewry invested great efforts in their assembly, transfer, and support. Several hundred immediately boarded small ships bound for Palestine. Yet misfortune continued to dog their steps: 61 died when the *Mefkure* sank, and 520 orphans from Bessarabia and Bukovina were sent back to the Soviet Union following the liberation of Romania.

While these more circumscribed efforts to repatriate orphans were being undertaken, the Romanian

Jewish leadership demanded the repatriation of all Jews deported to Transnistria. When it became obvious that this goal was unattainable, the leadership concentrated on specific categories, such as individuals cleared of political crimes and disabled war veterans. The repatriation of 1,500 prisoners from Dorohoi in December 1943 encouraged the Jewish leadership to intensify its efforts. Nonetheless, only 2,500 deportees were repatriated prior to the liberation of Romania by the Red Army.

Testimony provided by survivors of the Transnistrian experience falls short of conveying their terrible suffering. Yet the picture is not totally black. The efforts invested by the Jews of the Regat on behalf of the deportees and later for their repatriation, as well as self-help measures undertaken by the victims themselves, were partially rewarded. This joint struggle, which was unique in the annals of Nazi Europe, ultimately resulted in the survival of 60,000 of the 150,000 Jews deported to Transnistria.

Hava Eshkoli-Wagman

Treblinka Extermination camp located northeast of Warsaw. Treblinka was established in 1942 mainly to kill the Jews of Warsaw and other Polish districts. Approximately 870,000 Jews from Poland, Greece, and Yugoslavia died there, as well as at least 2,000 Gypsies. Originally the camp was designed with three gas chambers but no crematoriums; corpses were buried by slave laborers in mass graves behind the chambers. By October 1942 the number of gas chambers had increased to 13, and those too weak to walk were taken to a secluded ditch disguised as an infirmary and killed there. In 1943 the bodies of the dead were exhumed

Treblinka Extermination Center

This map is taken from a model shown at the Treblinka trial in Düsseldorf, which was recognized as accurate by all defendents and witnesses. It is not drawn to scale.

Administration and Staff-Accommodation Camp

1. Entrance gate and beginning of Seidel Street.
2. Sentry post.
3. SS living quarters.
4. Ammunitions storeroom.
5 and 6. Gasoline pumps and garage.
7. Entrance to station square.
8. Offices and housing of the camp administration.
9. SS service building—barber, sick bay, dentist.
10. Living quarters of the female Polish and Ukrainian staff.

11 and 12. Bakery and food stores.
13. Barrack used as workshop for *Goldjuden* (Jews given the task of recovering gold.
14. Living quarters of Ukrainian auxiliaries (Max Bialas barracks).
15. "Zoo."
16. Stables, pigpen, henhouse.
17–19. Living quarters of Jewish prisoners who belonged to the work details.
20. Locksmiths and blacksmiths.
21. Latrines.
22. Roll-call square.

Reception Camp

23. Railroad ramp and square.
24. Storeroom for clothing and baggage.
25. Assembly area.
26. Women's undressing barrack.
27. Barrack where the women's hair was cut.

28. Men's undressing barrack.
29. "Selection square" (area where the selections were made).
30. "Hospital."
31. "The Tube."

Extermination Sector

32. New gas chambers (ten).
33. Old gas chambers (three).
34. Mass graves.
35. Place where the bodies were burned.

36. Living quarters of the members of the Jewish special work details (*Sonderkommandos*).

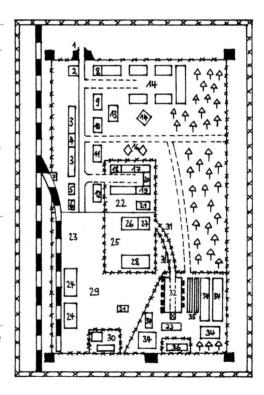

and burned to eliminate evidence of the murders. In August 1943, days before the camp's scheduled liquidation, 750 prisoners rebelled, perhaps 70 of whom managed to escape. The camp was then burned to the ground, plowed under, and turned into a farm. The site is now a Polish national monument. See EXTERMINATION CAMPS

Turkey Turkey's location at the edge of German-occupied Europe and its neutrality until the final days of World War II determined the country's special role during the Holocaust. It offered an escape route for Jews fleeing Nazi persecution and became a base for covert rescue operations, mostly by Zionist groups. Turkey was more open to both efforts than were Switzerland, Sweden, and Spain, the other neutral countries in a position to help Jews.

Although the Turkish leadership was partly inspired by the example of the Ottoman empire's openness to Jews expelled from Spain in 1492, its actions were always limited and defined by Turkey's interests. Turkish authorities considered that a small number of Jews having professional skills and financial means was very useful in the country's drive toward modernization. The great majority of the refugees, however, were allowed to enter the country only if they had visas ensuring they would move on to other places fairly quickly.

Thus Turkey's main virtue was its willingness to provide a safe haven for refugees and to let others do the work of rescue from its soil. This aspect of Turkish policy came into play in the 1930s, when Turkey was one of the few countries that welcomed Jews seeking to leave Germany. Perhaps 1,000 people who needed to flee the Nazi regime—not all of them Jews—were hired by Turkish institutions. They included 120 doctors, lawyers, scientists, and laboratory workers, along with their families, at Istanbul University and a small number at Ankara University. At the Istanbul University Medical School these emigrants directed nine of the 12 institutes and six of the 17 clinics.

Other Jewish refugees set up the government's social security system, designed public buildings, and organized theatrical troupes, ballet and opera companies, and symphony orchestras. A few were active in the anti-Nazi struggle, but most lived quietly. Their passports were revoked by Germany only in 1940. This revocation had no effect on their permission to stay in Turkey. Hundreds, perhaps several thousand, refugees also found other ways to stay in Turkey—in some case by bribing officials.

In contrast to this highly selective immigration, however, those fleeing for their lives could enter Turkey only if they had documents allowing them to travel on to British-ruled Palestine or elsewhere. One of the best-known examples of this policy is the case of a Romanian ship, the *Struma,* which arrived in Istanbul with 769 Jewish refugees on 16 December 1941. The Turkish authorities would not let the passengers disembark and demanded that all repairs be paid for in hard currency. On 23 February 1942 they forced the *Struma* to lift anchor and sail out of Turkish waters into the Black Sea, despite the vessel's poor condition and the desperate overcrowding on board. The *Struma* was sunk by a Soviet submarine on the same day.

The Turkish decision to send the ship away was in response to British pressure on Turkey to help curb Jewish emigration to Palestine. Britain had already asked Turkey to prevent ships sailing under its flag from carrying Jewish refugees. Following London's orders, the British ambassador Hughe Knatchbull-Hugessen explained that the passengers would not be admitted to Palestine but added on his own initiative that instead of forcing the ship back to German-held territory, "If [the refugees] reached Palestine, they might, despite their illegality, receive human treatment." This enraged the Colonial Office. The ambassador, an official wrote, "on absurdly misjudged humanitarian grounds" was undermining Turkey's refusal to let more Jews enter. Colonial Secretary Lord Moyne complained that if passengers on the *Struma* were to land, it would have the "deplorable effect [of] encouraging further Jews to embark."

Although relatively few Jews escaped to or through Turkey in the early years of war, Istanbul was a key location for gathering information on the implementation of genocide. One of the first reports on the Nazi death camps was brought through Istanbul by an escapee from Auschwitz in early 1943 and passed on to the Allied and Zionist intelligence services.

The presence of representatives of the Jewish community in Palestine (the Yishuv) was due to David Ben-Gurion's initiative in 1941 to send a team to Istanbul under the leadership of Jewish Agency representative Chaim Barlas to investigate conditions in occupied Europe and to rescue as many people as possible.

Istanbul, said Teddy Kollek, one of the Jewish Agency members, provided "a narrow crack in an otherwise impenetrable wall." This group, numbering about 20 people—many of whom operated under the pretext of being businessmen—was one of the first bases for promoting illegal immigration to Palestine.

Despite their own lack of official standing and the clashes of interest between Jews and the British, Barlas's group cooperated closely with British intelligence. They bribed officials to let in Jewish refugees, who were housed and fed for weeks or months by the delegation. To finance this operation, diamonds were smuggled into Istanbul inside toothpaste tubes and other common objects, then turned into currency on the black market. New arrivals were interviewed to gain information on conditions in Europe, and the intelligence collected was used as leverage to try to get the British to grant entry permits into Palestine.

Beginning in September 1942 the Zionist delegation sent thousands of letters by post and courier into the occupied countries in the hope of establishing contacts with Jews there, both to show them they were not forgotten and to prepare the ground for rescue. Thousands of responses were received using simple codes, like transliterating Hebrew words into the Latin alphabet. Barlas wrote to Jerusalem with detailed accounts of the massacres, deportations, and mistreatment, especially in Romania, with its "cruelty and torture" that was unequalled in history.

Once these links were made, attempts to send aid followed. Couriers smuggled funds in the form of diamonds, gold coins, or local currency. Some diplomats helped in exchange for payments. Material was forwarded to Greece via small boats that the British were sending to aid the partisans there.

Starting in April 1943 the British asked the Turks to give transit visas to nine families a week. Between April and December 1,350 people were saved from Hungary, Bulgaria, and Romania. Another 312 escaped from Greece on British boats. About 2,100 more people already in Turkey were sent on to Palestine. Barlas noted that "the results . . . in numbers are in no comparison with the tragic situation . . . but taking into consideration the almost unsurmountable difficulties, I may say that it is a miracle that even this small number has escaped from the hell."

Barlas also sought help in January 1943 from Angelo Roncalli, the papal emissary in Istanbul who later (in 1958) became Pope John XXIII. He requested that the Vatican ask neutral states to grant temporary asylum to escaping Jews, declare that helping Jews "is considered by the Church to be a good deed," and indicate to the Germans that the British would give immigration certificates to 5,000 Jews if they were released. The Vatican refused to do anything.

Barlas tried every possible channel. Through the Polish ambassador in Turkey he gained entry for 542 Polish Jewish refugees stranded in Tehran. In 1944 the U.S. government's War Refugee Board also opened in Turkey, warning the envoys of Hungary, Romania, and Bulgaria that their leaders would be considered war criminals unless they ended the persecution of Jews on their soil. But, wrote Kalman Rozenblat of the Jewish delegation in November 1943, "the key rests with Great Britain. It is in her power to increase the number of transit visas through Turkey a hundredfold."

Frustrated by bureaucratic barriers, the delegation organized its own shipping fleet. Officials in Romania were bribed to accept the idea that Jews were tourists taking excursions to neutral Istanbul. The first ship, the *Milka*, brought 240 Jews, who were admitted into Turkey when the British promised them admission into Palestine. Only on 19 May 1944 did London at last allow Barlas a free hand in granting visas. Thereafter the delegation's two ships brought hundreds of Jews to Istanbul.

Still, practically all the Jews rescued were brought out by the Zionist delegation. After one of its ships sank while returning empty back to Romania and the other was detained by the Germans in Bulgaria, the delegation bought one Greek and four Turkish boats. Between January and August 1944, 2,672 refugees were brought by sea and 408 by land to Turkey, though one ship was sunk by a Soviet patrol boat just outside Istanbul's harbor and almost all the passengers, including 96 children, were drowned.

The pace of rescue accelerated. During a three-week period near the end of 1944, 1,200 Romanian and Bulgarian Jews were granted visas and moved across Turkey by railroad. Eight hundred more were saved from Greece. There was no doubt, however, that only a tiny portion of those who might have been saved were rescued.

Dani Shind, one of the delegation's members, wrote the best summary of its effort, referring to the day the *Milka* arrived in Istanbul with its first load of refugees:

"Our feelings were mixed: we were overjoyed by the arrival of the ship, yet . . . thoroughly disgusted with our 'well-wishers' who had left the remnant of our people to fend for themselves. . . . Let the *Milka* bear witness to the sin of neglect on the part of the enlightened world. We have often met with setbacks, but our work has not been in vain after all."

Barry Rubin

U

Ukraine An independent country since 1991, Ukraine spreads across a vast territory (approximately 595,000 square kilometers) east of Poland and southwest of Russia. Its position between those two historic states earned it its name—the borderland—and its past destiny as a buffer zone. The ambiguous borders (except in the south, where they extend to the Black and Azov seas) are the result of ethnic divisions and historical developments. Its ethnic majority, the Ukrainians, speak a language akin to Russian, although the eastern parts are heavily russified. The dominant religion is Eastern Orthodox Christianity, although there are many Eastern Catholic (Uniate) communities in the western provinces.

With the Bolshevik revolution and the fall of the tsarist regime in Russia in 1917, a group of Ukrainian nationalists in Kiev convoked an autonomous Central Council, which declared the establishment of the Ukrainian People's Republic. In March 1918 the German army, under the terms of the Brest-Litovsk peace agreement, occupied Ukraine and nominated the hetman Pavlo Skoropadsky as chief of a puppet state. The advent of the Bolsheviks in the winter of 1918–19 and the arrival of Gen. Anton Denikin's anti-Bolshevik White Army in 1919 spelled the end of repeated efforts to establish an independent Ukrainian state. Until the conclusion of the Russian civil war in 1921, the fate of Ukraine hinged on the power struggle between the Reds and the Whites. The victory of the Bolsheviks resulted in the creation of the Ukrainian Soviet Republic as part of the Soviet Union. The Ukrainian nationalists were pushed into the western Ukrainian territory of Galicia, which had been part of the Habsburg Empire. There they encountered the Poles, who, under the leadership of Marshal Josef Pilsudski, hoped to resurrect Poland within its historical boundaries, including Ukraine. In 1920 Pilsudski's forces expelled the Ukrainian nationalists from Galicia and tried to capture eastern Ukraine, but the Red Army drove them back into Poland. In the Peace of Riga (March 1921) Ukraine was divided between Soviet Russia and Poland.

The Jews in Ukraine

The war years, from 1914 to 1921, had their worst effect on the Jews. Each new conqueror during the civil war seemed to consider it a duty to murder a certain number of Jews and to terrorize the rest. In addition to many cases of petty brutality, pogroms broke out in some towns and cities, including Lvov and Pinsk. The Hebrew term *shoah*, denoting a terrible and unforeseen disaster, was revived to describe the events taking place in Ukraine.

The horrors of the civil war came in the wake of World War I, during which many Jewish communities in the battle zone cutting across western Ukraine and Galicia were uprooted or evacuated, their property destroyed and looted. Therefore the traditional Jewish township, the shtetl, could not reconstruct itself socially and economically, especially in the adverse conditions on each side of the border. In Soviet Ukraine, after the relatively quiet years of the New Economic Policy in the mid-1920s, collectivization and industrialization plunged traditional Jewish society into deep crisis, which the state tried to ease by resettlement campaigns, like the famous Birobidjan project to found a Jewish autonomous region in Central Asia. On the other hand, the Soviet regime and its needs enabled Jewish youth to acquire an education sufficient for them to join the bureaucracy and become part of the ruling elite. This process, which originally had looked so tempting, later became a source of danger to its participants; they fell victim in the late 1930s to the Great Purge, which concentrated on members of the elite.

WESTERN SOVIET UNION

■ Concentration camps
▬ National borders, 1930
⋯ National borders, 2000
╌ Extreme limit of German
  advance, 1941–1942

0 100 200 300 400 500 Km

BALTIC SEA

Tallinn
Klooga Lagedi
ESTONIA Vaivara
Dundaga
Lenta Pskov
Riga
LATVIA
Eleje- Kaiserwald (Meza Park)
Meitenes
LITHUANIA
Daugavpils
Königsberg (Kaliningrad)
Ponary Vilna
Kielbasin
Grodno Lida Minsk
Koldichevo
BELORUSSIA
Brest-Litovsk
(Brzesc nad
Bugiem)
Pripet
POLAND
Trawniki
VOLHYNIA
Janowska Lvov Zhitomir Kiev
Babi
Yar Khorol
Bar Vinnitsa
Cernauti Balanowka
(Czernowitz)
Vertugen TRANSNISTRIA
Edineti UKRAINE
BUKOVINA Southern Bug
MOLDAVIA Domanievka
Acmicetka Nikolayev
Kishinev Bogdanovka
(Chisinau) Odessa
ROMANIA

Leningrad
Novgorod

SOVIET UNION

Vitebsk
Smolensk
Tula
Dnieper
Gomel Orel Tambov
Kursk Lipeck
Voronezh
Pripet
Poltava Kharkov
Donets
Dnepropetrovsk
Doneck Vorozhilovgrad
Zaporozje Gorlovka
Rostov-on-Don

Moscow
Gorky
Ulianovsk
Penza
Saratov
Don
Volga
Stalingrad
Astrakhan

N

CRIMEA
Sevastopol
Krasnodar
Grozny
CASPIAN
SEA

Danube

BULGARIA

BLACK SEA

GEORGIA
Tbilisi
Baku

TURKEY

Young mother with her two children, sitting among a large group of Jews from Lubny who have been assembled for mass execution by the Germans. 16 October 1941

In Polish Ukraine the Jews were trapped between their political image, the economic situation, and national tensions. Jews were suspected both by the authorities and by ordinary people of being pro-Communist and sympathetic to the nationalist cause. Public opinion and the Polish government agreed that the only solution to the Jewish problem was mass emigration. This attitude resulted in widespread exacerbation of antisemitism, which found its most rabid expression at Lvov University. The Jewish communities, having barely survived the war years, deteriorated even more in the 1930s. If Polish Jewry in general suffered heavily in the 1929 economic crisis, the Jews of western Ukraine suffered more. The economic crisis deepened the social deterioration of a community in the grip of prolonged stagnation. In spite of these obstacles the Galician Jews shared in a period of manifold

cultural activity, which psychologically compensated for social and economic hardships.

In September 1939 the two parts of Ukraine, and the Jews living therein, came under the rule of the Ukrainian Soviet Republic. The way for this unification was paved on 23 August, when Nazi Germany and the Soviet Union signed a mutual nonaggression pact, which included secret protocols dividing Poland between the two great powers. On 1 September 1939 the Wehrmacht attacked Poland, scattering the Polish army, part of which retreated to the east of Poland, where it hoped to reorganize. But in accordance with the protocols, the Red Army entered Poland from the east on 17 September and pushed the Polish forces back. Both the Polish authorities and the civilian population accepted the Soviet invasion with mixed feelings. Poles harbored deep and long-standing national and ideological fear and hatred toward the Soviets, but they also recognized a deliverance from the Nazis. The Polish high command, just before escaping to Romania, ordered its forces not to oppose the Red Army. Nevertheless, some Polish units fought the invaders. On 27 September, after negotiations with the Germans, whose units withdrew to the west, the Soviets annexed eastern Poland, uniting western Ukraine with the Ukrainian Soviet Republic.

Throughout the period from the annexation of eastern Galicia (part of Poland) by the Soviet Union until the German invasion of the Soviet Union, almost the entire Ukrainian Jewish population came under one rule. Nevertheless, the gap remained between the peoples in the old and new Soviet territories. Whereas those Jews living in the new territories had learned of the German practices in Poland through stories told by refugees, those in the central and eastern Ukraine remained unaware of the danger. Living conditions in the former Soviet territory generally improved with the cessation of the purges, whereas in the annexed parts the inhabitants lived in a state of social and economic upheaval. In general, the Jewish population accepted the Red Army with gratitude as a deliverer from the Germans and from the Ukrainian peasant revolt, which endangered both the Poles and the Jews. But the underdevelopment of the area, aggravated by the masses of refugees and coupled with mismanagement by the Soviet military authorities, created an economic crisis that resulted in food shortages.

One sign of the crisis was a movement of refugees

back to German-occupied Poland. The Soviet government decided on a new legal status for western Ukraine which would allow them to move part of the refugees into the pre-1939 Soviet Union, in order to improve the food situation. After rigged balloting, the newly elected "people's assembly" voted on 22 October 1939 to be united with Soviet Ukraine. In the wake of this vote the Supreme Soviet decided on 1 November that everyone in the annexed area was entitled to Soviet citizenship. Delivery of the new passports began in April 1940. This move started a wave of panic among the refugees, who suspected that their new citizenship would prevent any future reunion with their families, and many of them applied for permission to return to Poland. Consequently, first in Lvov and later in the provinces, the Soviets arrested thousands of refugees who had applied to return and exiled them within the Soviet Union. Those who accepted Soviet passports were divided by their social status, and those citizens defined as "bourgeois" were also marked out for deportation. In October 1939 the Soviets began to nationalize private property, starting with banks, large estates, and factories. In the spring of 1940 private ownership of rental property was annulled, followed by the outlawing of wholesale commerce. Small traders suffered because of regulations preserving unrealistic prices from the past. The new policy caused acute deterioration in the well-being of all the population, but many of the changes struck mainly at the Jewish community because of its socioeconomic structure. The legal and economic innovations in the annexed regions demanded a tightening of political control, and in the summer of 1940 the Soviets initiated and enforced a transition from the local officials to cadres brought in mainly from Soviet Ukraine.

The legal and economic changes were paralleled by the disintegration of Jewish political life and communal framework. Before the war the Jewish political community in Galicia and Volhynia was characterized by its conservatism and backwardness. The smaller communities were ruled by an oligarchy of rabbis and local potentates concentrated around synagogues. Among secular Jews the Zionist party, which had conservative tendencies, was dominant; the socialist Bund, the radical Zionists, and the Communists (belonging to the Communist Party of Western Ukraine) were rather weak. The Zionist influence on education was apparent in the abundance of Hebrew schools in the region. These schools were early victims of the new regime, which transformed them into Yiddish schools with Soviet curricula in the fall of 1939. About the same time all parties except the Communists were banned, and some of their leaders, especially the Bundists, were arrested. The main wave of political arrests and deportation to the Soviet interior came in the wake of the passport imposition in April 1940 and included almost all non-Communist political figures. These arrests paralyzed the Jewish parties, which ceased activities; some of their rank-and-file members supported the new regime. At the same time Jewish youth movements, well entrenched among local young people, continued their activities clandestinely. At first these movements were not persecuted, as the Soviets hoped that their members would automatically join the Communist youth movement, the Komsomol. But when their hope did not materialize, in the summer of 1940 Zionist youth movement activists were arrested, brought to trial, and sentenced to long prison terms. Even this harsh treatment did not stop their activity, although it was now performed in deeper secrecy. The continued existence of youth movements and the conspiratorial methods they adopted enabled them to continue functioning later, after the Nazi conquest of Soviet Ukraine. The disruption of Jewish political and communal life, and the economic changes detrimental to many Jews, passed unobserved by their Polish and Ukrainian neighbors, who regarded the changes of ethnic status brought by the Soviet occupation as benefiting only the Jews, whom they viewed as pro-Soviet collaborators.

On 22 June 1941 the German army invaded the Soviet Union. According to the plan of Operation Barbarossa, the German Southern Command was to conquer Ukraine by moving swiftly toward Kiev while encircling the Red Army. As the battles continued, the German forces advanced north of Ukraine and along the Black Sea coast, and the Russian forces, which had previously slowed down the German advance in Ukraine, found themselves isolated. In order to speed up the conquest of Ukraine, the Germans attacked the region from the north, corralling all the Russian armies in the area. Kiev was conquered on 19 September 1941; the Soviet units, who had only belatedly received permission to retreat, either surrendered or were annihilated. After the Kiev debacle, which resulted in the surrender of half a million Soviet soldiers, the Red Army was reorganized. This step did not prevent the Germans from crossing the Dnieper and Donets rivers, conquering Kharkov on 24 October. The only Ukrainian territory left in Soviet control was the Odessa region, defended by the Separate Coastal Army until November 1941. By the end of 1941 the whole of Ukraine was in German hands.

In addition to the usual wartime uprooting of civilians, the Soviet-German war featured an organized evacuation as part of the Soviet grand strategy. On 24 June a Supreme Evacuation Council, chaired by Lazar Kaganovitch, was appointed, and on 3 July Stalin called on the nation to leave behind in evacuated areas no strategic industry or matériel. Even so, it took several months to establish the means of large-scale evacuation; meanwhile the Germans were advancing rapidly. When the evacuation finally was organized, all the annexed territories and most of pre-1939 Ukraine (home to the majority of Soviet Jews) had already been overrun by the German army. Although both Stalin and the Supreme Evacuation Council concentrated on the removal of matériel, the council also set up evacuation points where Ukrainians could board trains bound for the east to escape the invading German army. Only on 26 September 1941 did the Supreme Council establish a Population Evacuation Administration to take charge of refugees' movements; it remained in operation until January 1942. Yet throughout the summer months, before the evacuation mechanism was in place, refugees continued to flee the western Soviet provinces ahead of the rapidly advancing German forces. Among Jews the decision to leave or to stay was affected by the extent of one's connection with the Soviet regime and the impact of the rumors of German atrocities in Poland. Some of the Jews who chose to stay were influenced by memories of a benign German occupation in 1918, firsthand impressions of the refugees' hard lot, and animosity toward the Soviet system.

In the first days of the invasion only those Jews who were directly linked with the Soviets (such as party members, soviet officials, and military families) escaped, even where flight was possible, such as in Lvov, where the Germans entered several days after it had been abandoned by Soviet troops. In western Volhynia fewer than 3 percent of the Jewish population got away. In July, particularly in areas with rail connections, the proportion of the Jews that fled rose steadily; in Rokitna 25 percent left before German troops arrived. Some fugitives, unfortunately, were later overtaken by the advancing Germans and compelled to return to their towns. Generally speaking, about 8 percent of the Jews in the Soviet-annexed territories escaped.

The situation was somewhat better in pre-1939 Ukraine, where, in the regions conquered by the end of July, about one-third of the Jewish population managed to get away. By that time the first impetus of the German onslaught was exhausted. Both Soviet and German data show the growing scale of Jewish evacuation after 1 August. Except in the areas of major German encirclement, such as Kiev (taken in September) or the Crimea (occupied in November), evacuation now included the majority of local Jews. About 70 percent of Jews in the region of Ukraine overrun by the Germans after July were evacuated to the East. The number of Jews among the millions of evacuees from Ukraine was disproportionately high, owing to personal initiative, the proximity of many Jews to urban centers, and the readiness of local civilian and military officials in many cases to help the endangered Jews, despite lack of instructions to that effect from the central authorities.

The so-called Commissar Order, issued by Hitler at the start of Operation Barbarossa, assigned the task of murdering Soviet officials, disrupting Communist activities, and annihilating the Jews in Ukraine to SS *Einsatzgruppen* (special duty squads) C and D. As these task forces were limited in size, their success depended on securing the cooperation of Ukrainian nationalists. The illegal Organization of Ukrainian Nationalists, the OUN, led by Stepan Bandera, had developed close links with the Nazis before the outbreak of the war. With the connivance of the OUN, German military intelligence (the Abwehr) mobilized young Ukrainians into two battalions, whose task was to encourage Ukrainians serving in the Red Army to defect to the Germans. The SS directed these forces to take an auxiliary role in executing the Commissar Order and also nominated them to incite pogroms against the Jews. Although the OUN did not oppose the German objectives, it saw the main purpose of the battalions as being both a symbol and a tool in establishing an independent Ukraine.

The first stage of the destruction of western Ukrainian Jewry (22 June–1 August 1941) was defined by a mixture of these three purposes. This becomes obvious from the events that occurred in Lvov, the capital of Galicia. As the Red Army prepared to abandon the city at the end of July, the Soviet secret police, the NKVD, executed the inmates of the local prison so as

The round-up of the Jews of Kiev. 29 September 1941

til then had comprised only central Poland. Although this was the end of the independent Ukrainian state, the nationalists remained in intermediate and low-level bureaucratic posts.

The Ukrainian population perpetrated similar anti-Jewish actions, although on a smaller scale, in other localities of western Ukraine—sometimes even before the Red Army retreated and the Wehrmacht arrived. In these new pogroms, mobs looted Jewish houses, raped Jewish women, and, as the situation escalated, murdered Jews. The pogroms signaled the disappearance of all authority and were therefore more common in small townships and villages rather than in large cities. The arrival of the German army and, in its wake, the Einsatzgruppen turned this mob into an extermination tool, especially when the local populace was inflamed by the sight of the corpses of prisoners executed in Soviet jails. As a result of this wave of violence, the Jewish population disappeared from large areas of western Ukraine.

The transition from pogroms to planned acts of extermination by the SS occurred without any geographic or chronological interval. During the first period of German occupation, when the Soviet territory was governed by military authorities, the activity of the Einsatzgruppen was unrestricted and a legal framework aimed at harming Jews and damaging Jewish property was created. It ended in eastern Galicia on 1 August with the transfer to the Generalgouvernement and in Volhynia on 1 September, when the Reichskommissariat Ukraine was organized.

Einsatzgruppe C, composed of 700–800 SS men, began its activity in the area by organizing pogroms in the major cities of western Ukraine. Divided into subunits and assisted by other SS formations and police forces (German and Ukrainian), it operated in all major cities: Lvov (Einsatzkommandos 5 and 6), Tarnopol (Sonderkommando 4b), and Rovno in Volhynia (Sonderkommando 4a). Einsatzgruppe D (about 600 SS men) followed the invading forces from Romania to southern Ukraine and acted along the Black Sea coast. Direct executions by Einsatzgruppe C began with the "anti-Soviet functionaries" action; aided by police and army volunteers, Einsatzgruppe C arrested and killed Jews who had been denounced by their non-Jewish neighbors in an operation that ended during the last days of August. During this action, under the pretext of searching for hidden functionaries, the regular police decimated the local Jewish elite. As the majority of

not to leave anti-Soviet elements in the area—a practice repeated in many other places in Ukraine. Although many Jews were among those executed, the Germans used the execution to incite the Ukrainians against the Jewish population by associating Jews with Communists. Thousands of Jews were murdered outright; the remainder were brought to the prison yard to bury the NKVD's victims and then were shot on the spot. The total number of Jews killed in the "prison action" was around 4,000. Simultaneously a group of OUN leaders declared the establishment of the Ukrainian state, nominated a government, and staffed the main offices. This declaration was sanctioned by the head of the Ukrainian Uniate church, Andrey Sheptytsky. Acting under orders from Berlin, the German military authorities arrested the most vociferous OUN leaders, and on 1 August 1941 eastern Galicia was annexed to the Generalgouvernement, which un-

Jews are forced to crawl on the ground in front of the fence of the Lvov ghetto.

victims and community leaders were men, the surviving Jewish population of western Ukraine, consisting mainly of women, children, and the elderly, was left quite vulnerable in the new situation.

Soon after their conquest the military authorities published a set of regulations aimed at isolating and persecuting the Jewish population. Aryanization decrees transferred Jewish property to non-Jews; other laws differentiated between the Jews and the general population and conscripted Jews for forced labor. These measures were seen by the Germans as temporary and were identical to the 1939 orders in Poland, in spite of the fact that conditions of Jewish life in Ukraine were different from those in the Generalgouvernement. The regulations, although causing the Jews great hardship, sometimes prevented the instant annihilation of entire communities by the SS. When local German military commanders required Jewish manpower, they directed Hungarian officers to stop the Ukrainian pogroms. Whereas in western Ukraine these edicts were used to establish ghettos, in eastern Ukraine they were a prelude to the total extermination of the Jewish population.

After the wave of executions in western Ukraine, Einsatzgruppe C (apart from sections of Einsatzkommando 5, which remained in Volhynia) moved to the east, following the front-line units. After the massacre in Zhitomir, Einsatzkommando 4a carried out the annihilation of the Jewish population in Kiev. On 29–30 September this subunit, led by Paul Blobel and assisted by auxiliary German and Ukrainian forces, shot and killed 33,771 Jews in 36 hours, the largest operation of this sort. In January 1942 it murdered the Jewish inhabitants of Kharkov. Einsatzkommando 6 operated mainly around the lower reaches of the Dnieper River and in the Donets Basin (Donbas). After a major action in which refugees from Ruthenia were murdered, Einsatzgruppe D operated in the coastal area of Ukraine, executing the Jewish communities of Kherson and Nikolayev. It was also active in Transnistria, a part of Ukraine occupied by the Romanians, where it assisted the Romanians in destroying the large Jewish community of Odessa. Between October 1941 and May 1942, this community, which numbered about 185,000 people before the war, was completely wiped out.

Though all this activity was organized and usually performed by the Einsatzgruppen, it would not have been possible without the cooperation of the German army and sometimes demands by its generals, who wished to have the rear of their units cleared of Jews and others believed to be pro-Soviet. The scope of the mass executions and the speed with which they were carried out not only prevented any resistance on the part of the Jews but also hampered any outside help. They also make it nearly impossible to determine with accuracy the number of victims, but a reliable estimate is that about 700,000 Jews were murdered, almost all before the spring of 1942, out of 1.5 million who lived within the pre-1939 borders of the Ukrainian Soviet Republic.

During the summer of 1942 the only remaining Jews in western Ukrainian ethnic regions were to be found in Volhynia, eastern Galicia, and Transnistria. For the Volhynian Jews the period of civil administration was marked by the mass execution on 7–8 November 1941 of the Jews of Rovno, the capital of Reichskommissariat Ukraine. Twenty-three thousand were shot, probably in order to free up quarters for the staff of the new administration. The surviving Jews were crowded into a ghetto, one of those created in the region between October 1941 and the summer of 1942. The timing of ghettoization in the various towns and cities depended on the extent of SS control over the local administration and the power relationships in each locality. Sometimes a bribe postponed the building of the fence separating the ghetto from the outside world. This degree of flexibility ended after the period of relative calm in May 1942. Up to 10 August the murder victims were mainly limited to "nonproductive elements," and the executions were random, except for the total annihilation of the Rovno ghetto (13 July) and of some minor ghettos. By October, in parallel with Aktion Reinhard, the operation to annihilate the Polish Jews in the Generalgouvernement, almost all the Jews of western Ukraine had been killed.

The extermination methods used in western Ukraine differed from those adopted in Poland. Despite the proximity of the death camps, the victims were not transferred there but were shot by the SS. A remnant of the Jews—specialized workers of use to the German economy—survived the massacres but were then killed during the first half of 1943. As the executions took place in front of open pits in the forests, many Jews were able to escape into the woods, where the Germans, often assisted by the local populace, hunted them down.

The annexation of eastern Galicia to the General-gouvernement was followed by the German authorities' decision to separate the Jews from the rest of the population. This step was viewed favorably by most Jews, who hoped for a cessation of Ukrainian pogroms, but the new system did not bring any lull in the killings. In this respect conditions in Galician ghettos differed from those in Poland, where life in the ghettos continued without direct German intervention. In Galicia the extermination process went forward, although on a limited scale, and the Jewish men were seized for labor camps. Full-scale extermination, an offshoot of Aktion Reinhard in the Generalgouvernement, began with the first transport to the Belzec death camp in March 1942, reached a peak in August, and curtailed in December. At the beginning of 1943 the survivors of the action were concentrated into a few ghettos, which, as the annihilation continued, were transformed into labor camps. Eventually these camps too were liquidated. In November 1943 the Germans declared Galicia, which had been inhabited by 620,000 Jews before the German invasion in 1941, *Judenrein*, free of Jews. With the liquidation of the labor camps, the last Galician Jews were tracked down by the Germans and their local assistants as well as by the Ukrainian Insurgent Army (UPA)—Ukrainian nationalists affiliated with Bandera.

Jewish resistance in Ukraine was of three types: passive opposition, unorganized armed resistance, and partisan warfare. In eastern Ukraine, within the pre-1939 Soviet border, the immediacy and scope of the German extermination actions left no young men and hence prevented any sort of organized resistance. In western Ukraine, where the mass of the Jewish population survived into 1942, no ideological nucleus of resistance organizations developed, because of Soviet policy after annexation in September 1939 and owing to uninterrupted German terror after the invasion of June 1941. Historians, therefore, are not aware of any sort of underground publications in the ghettos—a necessary step toward this type of organization. On the other hand, on the eve of liberation armed groups of the Jewish underground resistance operated in 40 ghettos, hoping to fight the Germans on the streets or to escape to the forests. In 50 ghettos and also in the labor camps there were attempts to break out at the last moment.

In western Ukraine three opposing armed resistance forces operated: the UPA, whose goals included the total liquidation of the Jews; the generally antisemitic Polish Home Army (Armia Krajowa); and the Soviet partisans. Although many cases of callousness toward the Jewish plight may be found in the Soviet partisan movement, there was no official antisemitic policy, and it was only there that Jewish fighters were accepted. The Soviet partisans were not formed until the fall of 1941, and the movement's centralized structure was built up in the spring of 1942, by which time the Jewish communities in pre-1939 Ukraine had been decimated. Only individual survivors and Jewish escapees from camps were left in the area to join the Soviet partisans. The partisan brigades arrived in western Ukraine in 1943, too late to prevent murder (even if their commanders had wished to do so) but still available to take in survivors. It is almost impossible to estimate the numbers of Jews in the partisan units. According to unpublished official statistics from 1946, Jews amounted to 1.2 percent of the partisans in Ukraine, but recent data from former Soviet archives suggest that the real proportion was at least four times as great.

The rescue of the Jews, like other aspects of the Holocaust, reflected the major differences between the pre-1939 Soviet republic and western Ukraine. Owing to the speed with which the exterminations took place in eastern Ukraine, opportunities for rescue attempts in that area were practically nil. The Soviet underground preferred to disregard the unique predicament of the Jews and instead followed political expediency: it rescued Communists, many of whom happened also to be Jews. Those cases where Jews were rescued as Jews were not publicized after the war because of the Soviet policy of playing down the Holocaust while emphasizing the sufferings of the "Soviet people."

In western Ukraine acts of rescue were molded by the multiracial ethnic conflict. In parallel with the Soviet-German war, an armed struggle was taking place between Ukrainian nationalists, the Polish minority, and Soviet partisans. The Home Army and most urban groups harbored pronounced antisemitic attitudes.

Nevertheless, Zegota, the official Polish rescue organization, and individual Poles saved Jews in urban centers, while in rural areas, especially in Volhynia, the Poles rescued their Jewish neighbors and cooperated with them against UPA units. The small Czech minority also acted courageously in saving some Jews.

The Ukrainian majority, led by the nationalists and influenced by the Eastern Catholic (Uniate) church, was persistent in its antisemitic activities, although there were Ukrainians who endangered themselves in saving Jews. The most contradictory attitude was evinced by the head of the Uniate church, Andrey Sheptytsky, who gave spiritual support to cooperation with the German army and sponsored mobilization in the SS Galicia division, which specialized in hunting down Jewish fugitives. At the same time, however, Sheptytsky protested to the Vatican against the extermination of the Jews and in November 1941 published a special missive, "Thou Shalt Not Murder," to the Uniate church and made personal efforts to save Jews.

The Red Army entered Ukraine in the fall of 1943 and finished liberating the area in the summer of 1944. It encountered only pitiful remnants of the Jewish population. In the pre-1939 territory there were almost no survivors; in Volhynia 1.5 percent of the prewar population lived to see the liberation. Moreover, whereas large portions of the Jewish population in eastern Ukraine survived through escape and evacuation in 1941, there were almost no Volhynian Jews to be found outside Volhynia. Those Ukrainian Jews returning from Soviet Russia encountered a strong antisemitic trend, which culminated in a pogrom in Kiev. These tendencies were combined, however, with fierce anti-Soviet sentiments, and after a few years of Soviet police activity the Jews were able to return to Ukraine. In western Ukraine the term "liberation" was meaningless for the survivors, who were too few to revive Jewish communities and instead opted to accept Polish citizenship in order to be "repatriated" to Poland. Most of them eventually decided to emigrate to the West, mainly to Israel, where they were joined by their compatriots from eastern Ukraine during the massive Jewish emigration from the Soviet Union in the late 1970s and 1980s. *Eli Tzur*

Union Générale des Israélites de France The Union Générale des Israélites de France (General Union of French Jews, UGIF) was the official organization created by the French government at Vichy by law on 29 November 1941. The initiative came from the German occupation authorities, who intended it only for the northern part of the country. The UGIF was supposed to unite all previous Jewish organizations in one single structure in order to facilitate the implementation of the Nazis' "Jewish policy."

On the eve of World War II the French Jewish community was noted for its diversity. There were French Jews—some with long Gallic pedigrees, others recently naturalized—and foreign Jews who had immigrated from the Levant and from Central or Eastern Europe. They represented a wide range of religious and cultural forms of Judaism, as well as a variety of political tendencies. All these were reflected in a plethora of dynamic Jewish organizations to which most French Jews did not belong.

The process of creating an organization that would include, as a matter of law, all the Jews of France and replace all the previous structures involved three actors: the German occupation authorities, the Jewish leaders, and the first commissioner-general for Jewish affairs of the Vichy government, Xavier Vallat. The project was initiated by Theodor Dannecker, head of the Judenreferat (Jewish Bureau) in the Paris office of the Gestapo. His policy fit in with "the solution to the Jewish question in Europe" that was being hatched in Adolf Eichmann's offices in Berlin. Taking as his model the Reichsvereinigung der Juden in Deutschland (Reich Union of the Jews in Germany), which had embraced all German Jews since 1939, Dannecker set about forcing the Jews of Paris to organize themselves into a community.

Brandishing the threat of a ban on all philanthropic activities at a time when German edicts were leading to the extreme impoverishment of the Jewish population of the occupied zone (northern France), he managed to force the Jewish leaders to create on 30 January 1941 a Committee for Coordinating Jewish Charitable Works in Paris. He also imposed a newspaper on them—the *Informations Juives,* which first appeared on 19 April 1941—by importing two Jews from Vienna. But passive resistance by the Jewish leaders kept him from transforming into a unified institution what essentially remained a committee coordinating between preexisting organizations.

Dannecker then approached his French counterparts. On 29 August 1941 he instructed Xavier Vallat to set up forthwith a *Zwangsorganisation* (compulsory organization) of the Jews in the occupied zone. Vallat,

motivated by the dual aim of replacing German jurisdiction with French and of harmonizing the policy toward Jews in both zones, took up the cause. Starting in the fall of 1941, he conducted negotiations with Jewish leaders in both the occupied zone and Vichy-controlled France to set up a Jewish umbrella organization that would incorporate all preexisting structures throughout French territory. In the occupied zone the leaders were persuaded by the futility of previous resistance to the pressure exerted by the Germans, the threat of massive round-ups if they refused to comply, and the idea of a French authority mediating between themselves and the German occupier.

In the south the situation was different. The central Consistoire and its president, Jacques Helbronner, represented the entire Jewish community to the Vichy authorities. Chief Rabbi Isaïe Schwartz had already created on 31 October 1940 a coordinating committee for the major Jewish philanthropies—the Central Commission of Jewish Welfare Organizations (Commission Centrale des Organisations Juives d'Assistance, CCOJA). The Refugee Aid Committee (Comité d'Aide aux Réfugiés, CAR), under the leadership of Raymond-Raoul Lambert, was its main constituent organization; the Federation of Jewish Societies of France (Fédération des Sociétés Juives de France, FSJF) represented immigrant Jews.

Vallat first approached Helbronner, but in the wake of the latter's reservations he turned to Lambert. The negotiations between the Jewish leaders and the commissioner-general lasted until the decree of 8 January 1942, which named the 18 members of the administrative council of the new organization, created by the law of 29 November 1941. These were indeed negotiations, if not between equal parties. On the one hand, it was clear that Xavier Vallat, who preferred to obtain the cooperation of the recognized leaders of the Jewish organizations, would do without them if their support was not forthcoming. On the other hand, all the Jewish leaders were opposed in theory to this new measure, albeit in different degrees.

The Consistoire at first rebelled against the idea of a ghetto organization that would embrace French and foreign Jews, implicitly replace the religious definition of Jewishness by a racial one, and further deepen the divide between French Jews and their Gentile compatriots. There was also concern about the moral repercussions of the permission granted the new organization to use the so-called Solidarity Fund, which derived from stolen Jewish property, for welfare purposes. There was resistance to the idea of an organization that would be invested with tasks that exceeded the traditional competence of a religious association. Finally, the Consistoire believed it could influence the final decision by applying political pressure on the head of the Vichy government, Philippe Pétain.

The CCOJA's opposition was based on the same reasoning. In its case, though, philanthropy was the clear priority, and it feared that the social welfare projects on which the foreign Jews were so dependent might be sacrificed on the altar of the Consistoire's ideological opposition. For their part, the leaders of the FSJF, in particular its president Marc Jarblum, were totally opposed to any contact with Vallat's office, fearing the takeover of all Jewish organizations by the antisemitic collaborationist regime. Several strategies were adopted with the aim of hindering Vallat's plan. These included submission of a counterproposal by Helbronner, an appeal for arbitration by the Council of State, and a common front of all the existing organizations in the form of a memorandum describing the scope of the welfare activity endangered by the proposed new organization. A series of consultations between Vallat and Lambert convinced the former that this was his man; for his part, Lambert thought that he had no choice but to trust the commissioner-general and that this was the price to be paid to ensure the future of all welfare activity.

The result of these negotiations was the creation of the Union Générale des Israélites de France, whose purpose was to "represent Jews to the authorities, particularly in matters of welfare, relief, and rehabilitation." Article 2 of the law that established the new organization stated that all Jews "who were domiciled or resident in France were automatically members" and that "all existing Jewish associations were dissolved, with the exception of the legally constituted Jewish religious associations." Thus the central Consistoire and the local synagogues maintained an autonomous existence. The word "particularly" allowed all sorts of interpretations as to the role of the UGIF, but the Consistoire could, at least in theory, maintain its role as the political representative of the Jews of France to the authorities.

The new organization, whose leaders were directly answerable to the commissioner-general's office, drew some of its operating monies from the Solidarity Fund—but only in part and without this being an im-

perative. In practice the new law effectively created two organizations, each with its own administrative council, one in the occupied zone and the other in Vichy-ruled France.

The UGIF-North, headed by André Baur, frequently had to deal directly with the Germans. Its structure was more centralized than that of its southern counterpart, but the entire council participated in the decision-making process. In the southern zone, on the other hand, Raymond-Raoul Lambert dealt with the French authorities. In addition, the transfer of various organizations and their leaders to the southern zone allowed him to create a flexible structure in which, under cover of a unified organization, they actually continued to function almost autonomously. Nonetheless, decisions affecting the UGIF-South as an organization tended to be made by Lambert alone.

In both the north and the south priority was given to the welfare activities (soup kitchens, subsidies, clothing distribution centers, children's homes, medical and legal aid) that allowed thousands of Jews to survive. In the north, however, given the rapid impoverishment of an increasingly drained population, financial difficulties forced the leaders to draw on the Solidarity Fund to continue to pay for welfare projects.

Various crises marked the history of the dual organization: the German imposition of a fine of 1 billion francs in retaliation for the attacks on German soldiers in the streets of the capital (December 1941); the order to the leaders of the UGIF-North to provide food and blankets for Jews interned in the Drancy transit camp awaiting deportation (from 1 July 1942); the order to the UGIF to dismiss all its foreign employees (fall 1942), thereby exposing them to arrest and deportation (UGIF employees carried cards that protected them against deportation); and the round-up of Jews from UGIF-run institutions, at first in the northern zone (February 1943). Throughout this period, and despite the mass round-ups and deportations, the UGIF leaders opted for legal behavior alongside passive resistance, playing for time in order to contain the damage. Thanks to the diligence of the French police and authorities, who collaborated with the Germans, the UGIF was never involved in drafting lists of deportees or in assisting in police operations.

Beginning in the summer of 1942, however, clandestine activities developed apace behind the law-abiding facade of the UGIF. In the northern zone these activities were managed by the Amelot Committee, a welfare organization created by immigrant Jewish leaders in June 1940. The committee soon began helping Jews who wanted to escape to the Vichy-controlled zone, finding places for children they managed to rescue from the Poitiers concentration camp, sending away children at risk, producing false papers, and quietly distributing aid to those who could not turn to the legal organizations. At the same time the committee ran legitimate soup kitchens and clinics—such as the one in Paris on rue Amelot, from which it took its name—so that it occupied the shifting ground between legal and illegal activity. The leaders of the committee, while condemning the UGIF and refusing any responsibility within it, did not hesitate to shelter behind the legal screen it offered.

In the south the raids of the summer of 1942, the German entry into the Vichy zone (November 1942), and the German occupation of the Italian zone (September 1943) and gradual transformation of that zone into a fascist state, which was followed by a series of arrests at the local offices of the UGIF, marked the stages through which certain UGIF-provided services went underground. This was the case with the Children's Aid (Oeuvre de Secours aux Enfants, OSE) and the French-Jewish Scouts (Eclaireurs Israélites de France, EIF), which operated within the UGIF while gradually evolving a clandestine branch, playing a double game that lasted until the mass arrests in February 1944.

Nevertheless, the official organization continued to exist in both north and south. In the summer of 1943, when it became increasingly obvious that the Germans would lose the war and that the end of the occupation was approaching, and the rift between the Vichy regime and French society was deepening, the Vichy-controlled organizations rapidly lost their legitimacy. The resistance became an organized counterforce in France. In parallel the Jewish organizations that were active underground joined forces in the General Defense Committee (Comité Générale de Défense, CGD, founded in Grenoble in late July 1943); together with the central Consistoire, they subsequently formed the Representative Council of French Jews (Conseil Représentatif des Israélites de France, CRIF), whose charter was signed in May 1944), which portrayed itself as an outgrowth of the Jewish resistance.

In any case, as the German noose tightened around the Jews of France, whose very existence was imperiled from mid-1942 on; as the Vichy regime's collusion with the occupier became increasingly evident; and as the resistance gained strength, an all-embracing welfare organization lost its long-term viability. Beginning in July 1943 German pressure on the UGIF-North was increasingly harsh. After the arrival in Paris of Alois Brunner, a lieutenant of Eichmann's who had organized the mass deportations in Vienna and Salonika, the Drancy camp, previously run by the French authorities, was transferred to German control, and the UGIF was ordered to assume the management of daily life there. This was one more level of collaboration with the Germans, and it was roundly condemned by most Jews. Baur, aware of this opprobrium, tried to steer a safe course; but his delaying tactics led to his arrest, along with his family (they were deported to Auschwitz on 17 December 1943) and dozens of UGIF employees. One month later Raymond-Raoul Lambert suffered the same fate. The delegitimization of the UGIF in the eyes of those who still held it in some esteem was not long in coming.

In the southern zone, on 20 October 1943, the Gestapo surrounded the UGIF's La Rosecenter in La Verdière and took away 10 mothers, 29 children, and the center's director, Alice Salomon, who refused to abandon her wards. Gaston Kahn, who replaced Lambert, had been warned about the raid the previous day but would not allow members of the resistance to hide the children, because the Gestapo had threatened a massive round-up of the Jews in Marseilles if the children vanished from the center. From that point on, the paths of clandestine operations and shilly-shallying with the German authorities diverged radically. During the subsequent months UGIF offices and centers were systematically raided by the Gestapo and their personnel arrested, along with any members of the public who happened to be there at the time. By the spring of 1944 almost all the constituent organizations of the UGIF-South had gone underground. In Paris, meanwhile, the UGIF-North continued to run soup kitchens and children's homes. The closure of the northern branch, demanded by Jewish resistance organizations, seemed more and more necessary. It did not come, however, and the 250 Jewish children rounded up from the UGIF homes in the Paris area between 21 and 25 July, on Brunner's orders, paid the price for this delay.

The balance sheet of UGIF activity is mixed. Those

who accepted posts with the UGIF opted for technical collaboration in order not to endanger the welfare activities that kept many Jews alive. None of them had any truck with the German designs or the aims of the Vichy regime. Their purpose was damage control to steer between the rocks and save whomever they could. They always acted within the law but did not oppose—even if they did not encourage—the use of other methods by other organizations, for whom they covered passively or provided a front. They took no heed of their personal safety, given that they all had the option of escaping across the border or melting into French society and chose not to do so. The senior leaders of the UGIF paid for their commitment to social welfare over political considerations with their lives and those of their families. By accepting these functions, however, they became caught in a system from which they could not extricate themselves. In the summer of 1943, as Brunner tightened his hold and demonstrated by a series of arrests that there was no longer any room for the slightest maneuvering, political logic should have dictated dissolution of the organization. Honor would have been intact, but at the price of how many lives?

Confronted by an enemy ruled by an ideology of annihilation, only a political reply is truly effective—though only in the long term. The UGIF was neither an extension of the Gestapo nor a resistance organization. It was the Germans' whipping boy in the occupied zone, a liaison with the French authorities, and a provider of philanthropy to numerous Jews. It generated an illusion of normality but afforded a cover for rescue operations. Some of its directors were notable for their acts of bravery, whereas others stood out for their cowardice. But it was also a death trap for those who were rounded up from its offices and centers—the children deported by Brunner come particularly to mind. Any attempt at a fair appraisal of the UGIF must take all these elements into account.

Renée Poznanski

United States Holocaust Memorial Museum

Located in the heart of Washington, D.C., within sight of the Washington Monument and the Jefferson Memorial, the United States Holocaust Memorial Museum opened to the public on 26 April 1993. The museum was the culmination of a 15-year effort to create a national memorial to the victims of the Holocaust.

The museum originated in a unique combination of initiatives by the president and White House staff. President Jimmy Carter saw the creation of the museum as a way to emphasize his concern for human rights. Three Jewish White House officials—Stuart Eizenstat, Mark Siegel, and Ellen Goldstein—understood the immediate importance of the Holocaust to American Jews and its potential significance to the American people as a whole. By the late 1970s courses on the Holocaust were being taught in colleges as never before, new scholarly works of significance were appearing, and with the airing of the NBC docudrama *The Holocaust*, the event had entered the mainstream of American culture as a defining moment of twentieth-century history.

President Carter chose a political occasion, the 30th anniversary of the establishment of the state of Israel, to announce in May 1978, in the presence of Israeli prime minister Menachem Begin and 1,000 American rabbis, the formation of the President's Commission on the Holocaust. The White House was not unaware of the fact that the president had alienated much Jewish support by pressing for the sale of F-15 fighters to an Arab country. This new effort of remembrance was considered a gesture to the American Jewish community.

The commission, with Elie Wiesel as its chairman, began its work on 15 January 1979. Three simple questions—what, where, and how?—resulted in three decisions that shaped the entire museum: to make the museum a living memorial that would tell visitors the story of the Holocaust; to locate the museum in Washington rather than New York; and to build the museum on public lands with private funds. The museum was envisioned as an American creation relating to a Jewish catastrophe to stand as the national memorial to victims of the Holocaust.

By 1980 the commission was superseded by the United States Holocaust Memorial Council, a 55-member body appointed by the president. Five senators appointed by the Senate Majority Leader and five representatives named by the Speaker of the House served on the council. Once the museum opened in 1993, the council was responsible for its operation.

The museum building was designed by James Ingo Freed of Pei, Cobb, Freed and Partners. It was erected under the leadership of Harvey M. Meyerhoff, who succeeded Wiesel as chairman of the council in February 1987.

Freed's work on the museum brought back painful

memories of his childhood in Germany and a sense of disquiet that found expression in his evocative design. Unsatisfied with his first plans for the building, Freed went to the sites of Nazi death camps in Poland. There he sketched a new design. Instead of creating a shell to house the exhibition, he designed a monumental building that would itself speak of the Holocaust. "The container and that which is contained would be one," the architecture critic Herbert Muschamp wrote. The permanent exhibition had to be shaped to fit within the building, which served as both a memorial and a museum engaging the intellect and emotions of visitors.

The museum building could not, however, re-create the emblematic architecture of the Holocaust: the death camps and their crematoriums. The architect had to work within other constraints as well, including the museum's location near the National Mall and the process by which a public building in Washington must be approved by the National Capital Planning Commission and the Fine Arts Commission. The 23,250-

square-meters building was constructed of limestone and brick to harmonize with the buildings adjacent to it. Still, intense pressure for a traditional design was resisted.

Four brick towers, evoking the watch towers and crematorium chimneys of Auschwitz, comprise the museum's north side. The materials of the interior are all industrial: rough granite, brick, concrete, and glass. In the Hall of Witness the brick is framed in steel, as the crematoriums of Auschwitz were lined with steel. The atrium is dominated by angled twisted steel; the effect is one of dissonance, making the visitor uneasy. The floor is canted at an angle that permits the concourse to be flooded with natural light, but it also fragments the hall, intensifying the raw emotion that the building summons. Triangular shapes are used throughout the building, a reminder that prisoners in the camps were marked with a variety of triangles to denote their status. Beams are exposed. Metal gates mark entry points into special exhibition spaces.

The core of the museum is its permanent exhibi-

The Fifteenth Street / Eisenhower Plaza entrance of the U.S. Holocaust Memorial Museum, Washington, D.C.

tion. Collections of artifacts, photographs, films, and documents are used to relate the events of the Holocaust from the rise of nazism and its reign of terror to the Final Solution and its instrumentalities: ghettos, mobile killing units, railways, concentration camps, and death camps. The permanent exhibition portrays resistance and rescue as well as the aftermath of the Holocaust, from liberation and displaced persons camps to the emergence of Israel and resettlement of survivors in the United States. The exhibition concludes with a 78-minute film entitled *Testimony* that links fragments of survivors' memories to tell of their experience throughout the ordeal, adding a human and contemporary voice to the historical narrative.

The creation of the permanent exhibition as a conceptual story-telling display was shaped by a design team consisting of Jeshajah Weinberg, who developed Israel's Museum of the Diaspora; a Holocaust scholar, Michael Berenbaum; a filmmaker, first Martin Smith and later Raye Farr; and a designer, Ralph Appelbaum; and their staffs. Among the more remarkable artifacts they assembled are a barracks from Birkenau, a railway car of the type used to transport Jews from Warsaw to Treblinka, and a Danish boat that ferried Jews to freedom in Sweden.

Many of the artifacts were obtained as gifts or permanent loans from Communist governments in Eastern Europe during the late 1980s, when the Soviet Union was in decline and the Warsaw Pact nations were anxious to establish American connections. Miles Lerman, who was to succeed Meyerhoff as council chairman in May 1993, negotiated many of these agreements.

In addition to its permanent exhibition of more than 3,350 square meters and two special exhibition halls, the museum serves as the central repository in North America for the documents and artifacts of the Holocaust period. An educational center at the museum teaches American teenagers—mainly from groups visiting the nation's capital—about the Holocaust. It includes an interactive computer facility—the Wexner Learning Center—so that a visitor to the museum is able to study about the Holocaust in texts, graphics, maps, films, documentaries, oral histories, music, and self-paced interactive programs that provide an opportunity for individualized learning. An exhibition designed for elementary school children called "Remember the Children" is featured on the main floor of the museum. This exhibition was the result of the leadership of Addie Yates, who chaired the Committee to Remember the Children and whose husband, Rep. Sidney R. Yates, led congressional efforts to develop and support the museum.

The museum is the home of the Center for Advanced Holocaust Studies, a working institute for scholars and a site of conferences and lectures that enable the public to learn more about what happened to Jews and other peoples targeted for extermination by the Nazis. The museum's library and six archives—a registry of survivors—form the backbone of the research facilities. The museum also has a large theater and an auditorium.

Education is a primary mission of the museum. In its early years it developed a wide range of outreach programs to the inner-city schools of the District of Columbia. Its efforts have been rewarded with visits by hundreds of thousands of children. Because of its location in Washington, the museum also became a magnet for government officials—both domestic and foreign—as well as for government agencies, which use its facilities to further their training programs in ethics and government.

The museum's hexagonal Hall of Remembrance is the National Memorial to the Holocaust, a site for state visits by American presidents and foreign dignitaries, a solemn place to commune with memory. The names of the six death camps and the major concentration camps are etched into its walls, memorial candles are lit, and ashes from the camps and other sites of mass murder rest in a bier. The walls are engraved with quotations from the Genesis story of Cain and Abel and from Deuteronomy—the admonition not to forget "the things that you saw with your own eyes" and the positive commandment to tell of them "to your children and to your children's children."

In the first six years of its existence more than 12 million people visited the museum. Four out of five visitors were non-Jews. One-fourth were school-age children, many with their classes on field trips to Washington. According to exit surveys, visitors spend on average more than three hours at the museum—much longer than they do at other Washington museums.

The task of the permanent exhibition is to take visitors off the National Mall, move them back in time, transport them a continent away, and bring them into intimate contact with a people in the throes of an unprecedented physical and moral catastrophe. The imaginative work required for Americans to gain emotional access to the lives and deaths of millions of Jews during the Holocaust is extremely difficult; it is the museum's mission to aid and guide them in that work.

It has been said that the death of millions of people is a statistic, but one person's death is a tragedy. If individuals are reduced to statistics, it is easier to eradicate them. Hence the museum's permanent exhibition strives to convey the personal dimension of the catastrophe. Every visitor is given an identification card that describes an actual person of his or her sex who went through the Holocaust. Each of the three floors of the permanent exhibition represents a separate period of the Holocaust: 1933–39 (from Hitler's rise to power to the beginning of World War II, a time of escalating persecution of Jews in Germany), 1939–44 (the war years, when the so-called Final Solution was implemented and European Jewry was destroyed), and 1945 and after (the fate of Jewish survivors after the liberation of the camps). Visitors take an elevator to the top floor and then descend on foot through the three periods. At each station the card the visitor was handed reveals the fate of the personal companion.

The middle floor of the museum depicts the core of the process of the Holocaust: transit camps and persecution in the West, ghettoization in the East, the *Einsatzgruppen* (mobile killing units), the Wannsee Conference, the Warsaw ghetto uprising, deportation, hiding, and the death camps. Artifacts of the period enhance the museum displays. In the ghetto exhibition area the visitor walks on cobblestones brought from Chlodna Street in the Warsaw ghetto. On an adjacent wooden bridge the visitor encounters one of the two milk cans, discovered after the war, that contained part of the Oneg Shabbos archive of documents that Emanuel Ringelblum gathered in the Warsaw ghetto and hid from the Germans. Other artifacts include sewing machines and work utensils from various ghettos, the gate to the Jewish cemetery in Tarnow, and fragments of a stained glass window from Kraków. Elsewhere on the bridge are video displays of life in the ghettos of Warsaw, Lodz, and Kovno as well as smaller towns.

The ghetto experience is followed by scenes of massacres by the mobile killing units, the Einsatzgruppen. Photographs and film footage of round-ups, forced marches, mass murder, and disposal of bodies are displayed on monitors behind privacy walls, which permit visiting parents to shield their children.

Rubble from the Warsaw ghetto, strewn across the bridge, creates the environment in which the Warsaw ghetto uprising is displayed. A false-bottomed table that served as a hiding place, a sewer cover from Warsaw, and a death cart from Terezin (Theresienstadt) surround the entrance to the railway car that symbolizes the transition from mobile killing units who murdered their stationary victims one by one, bullet by bullet, to mobile victims who were transported to stationary killing centers—the death camps.

The depiction of the death camp experience is situated in an actual barracks from Auschwitz-Birkenau. Inside the barracks the visitor sees the bunks in which inmates slept and the bowls from which they ate. A model of Crematorium II by Polish sculptor Mieczyslaw Stobierski is used to depict the killing process at Birkenau. Adjacent to the barracks visitors hear the voices of former inmates as they describe the details of the struggle to survive in Auschwitz. Visitors also see the letter by Assistant Secretary of War John J. McCloy denying the request of American Jewish leaders that Auschwitz be bombed.

The visitor then walks across a bridge whose glass wall is engraved from floor to ceiling with the first names of those who were murdered in the camps. In a sequence of four spaces the visitor sees thousands of shoes from the Majdanek death camp, photographs of the left forearms of Auschwitz inmates tattooed with their prisoner numbers, bales of hair prepared for shipment to manufacturers to stuff mattresses and line submarines, and the implements of cremation—large forceps and a sliding slab on which the corpses were placed.

The visitor enters a tower room 19.5 meters high and 8.5 meters wide containing hundreds of photographs of Jews from the village of Ejszyszki in Lithuania. Jews had been living in Ejszyszki for 900 years, but the Germans managed to wipe out almost the entire population of 3,500 in two days, immediately after Rosh Hashanah in September 1941. The photographs, many from wallets and albums, show not victims but people—often at celebrations such as weddings, bar mitzvahs, and graduations. These portrait treasures capture the glory of life and convey to visitors the magnitude of loss—not only of the people in the pictures but also of their children and grandchildren who will never be born. Through the efforts of the Holocaust scholar Yaffa Eliach, who as a young girl was one of the handful of survivors of the Ejszyszki massacre, to gather photographs after the war, the village of Ejszyszki not only lives on but also commemorates the thousands of Jewish communities in towns and cities throughout Eastern Europe that were annihilated.

When the Holocaust Memorial Museum was first proposed in 1979, a problem arose that threatened to scuttle the project before it could get under way. Who were the victims of the Holocaust? Does that term refer to the destruction of the Jews alone, or does it encompass Nazi mass murder of other groups of people as well?

Within the Holocaust Memorial Museum a simple practice is honored. All victims of the Nazis' crimes are represented and their memory respected. At the center of the tragedy of the Holocaust are the European Jews—who were murdered not because of the identity they proclaimed or the religion they practiced but on account of the blood of their grandparents. Near that center is the murder of the Gypsies (Sinti and Roma), though historians are still uncertain whether there was a single decision by the German authorities to undertake their complete annihilation. Nevertheless, historians have recognized—both in the museum and elsewhere—the plight of the Gypsies, who were killed in great numbers, and of the mentally incompetent and emotionally disturbed Germans killed in the T4 "euthanasia" operation. The persecution, incarceration, and murder of homosexuals, political prisoners, Soviet prisoners of war, and slave laborers of various nationalities are also presented in museum exhibits. The evolution of both the concept of genocide and the technology that made it possible cannot be understood without addressing the victimization of people other than Jews. Because a museum is not a proper place to resolve ideological and historiographical issues, the Holocaust Memorial Museum strives to include all groups targeted for persecution and murder by the Nazis, while at the same time maintaining a proper focus on the fate of the European Jews.

In the United States Holocaust Memorial Museum, Auschwitz and Treblinka are recalled differently from the way they are at memorials in Jerusalem, Berlin, or Warsaw. In the act of recollection, the past is projected onto the screen of the present with which it interacts. The museum is seen differently because of Bosnia and Rwanda. And it tells the story differently because it is in Washington. Interactive monitors describe American responses to the emerging Nazi menace between 1933 and 1939 and to the Holocaust between 1940 and 1945.

Since it was created primarily by American Jews, the museum represents a milestone in American Jewish history. It was conceived at a time when there were few obstacles for Jews participating as Jews in American culture and politics. The museum can be viewed as the most significant and bold public expression of American Jews as Jews in the United States. In the early days of the President's Commission there had been a lively debate concerning where the national Holocaust memorial should be located—in New York or in Washington. Indeed, there arose the question of whether an American memorial to European Jews who were murdered by European Christians was appropriate at all— perhaps memorials in Jerusalem and Berlin should suffice. But the commission had the foresight and daring to take what might otherwise have remained the parochial memories of a bereaved community and transport them to the center of American national life, thereby asserting that the Holocaust has a place in the American national memory and the American future. Controversial during its creation, the museum opened to both critical and public acclaim. Those who were apprehensive came to respect its faithfulness to history.

Still, the subject of the American memorial to victims of the Holocaust cuts against the grain of the American ethos. The United States is a nation of new beginnings, of eternal hope. Americans believe that tomorrow will be better than yesterday. The founding fathers proclaimed that human equality was a self-evident truth. In the Holocaust Memorial Museum visitors learn of unredeemed evil, of death and destruction. The Holocaust offers no happy ending, no transcendent meaning, no easy moralism. And even if the museum also tells visitors about isolated acts of courage and valor, heroism and decency, that punctuated the Holocaust, the overriding theme is evil perpetrated by individuals, organizations, and governments.

Michael Berenbaum

Ustasha Croatian nationalist terrorist organization that came to power after the German invasion of Yugoslavia in 1941. The Ustasha deported and murdered hundreds of thousands of Serbs and tens of thousands of Jews and Gypsies. See YUGOSLAVIA

V

Vaad Hatzala The Rescue Committee, founded in the United States in 1939 by the Union of Orthodox Rabbis of the United States and Canada to help rabbis and yeshiva students escape from Poland and Lithuania. Branches existed in Hungary, Palestine, Slovakia, Sweden, Switzerland, and Turkey. The committee was criticized for limiting its rescue activities to Orthodox Jews.

Vallat, Xavier (1891–1972) Head of the "Jewish department" of the Vichy government in France until May 1942, when he was dismissed because of German pressure. Vallat's antisemitism was indisputable, but he was also a militant nationalist who was hesitant to follow policies that would materially assist the German government. After the war Vallat was convicted of collaboration and sentenced to 10 years in prison; he served two and was then released. See FRANCE

Vichy After the German conquest of France in June 1940, the country was divided into two parts. The occupied zone in the north remained under direct German control, whereas the unoccupied zone in the south of France maintained some autonomy and was run by a French government established in the town of Vichy. Headed by Philippe Pétain, the Vichy government was nationalist, antisemitic, and friendly to Roman Catholic interests. It courted Nazi goodwill and acquiesced to round-ups of Jews for forced labor and deportation. Resistance among the French to the Vichy regime grew in 1941 and 1942, especially after the German invasion of the Soviet Union. In November 1942 German and Italian troops occupied Vichy France. Most high Vichy officials fled as Allied armies approached the town in the summer of 1944; some were later arrested and tried for treason. See FRANCE

Vilna Vilnius, the capital of Lithuania since the fourteenth century, has been known to the Jews as Vilna since they first came to the city in the sixteenth century. Yet it was in the second half of the eighteenth century that the famous gaon of Vilna, Rabbi Eliyahu, turned it into a world center of *halakha* (rabbinic law). Vilna was called Yerushalayim de Lita, the Jerusalem of Lithuania, as a token of its stature in the Jewish world. During the nineteenth and twentieth centuries the city continued to be a center of Jewish life, second in importance in Europe only to the Warsaw community. It was home to a diversity of newspapers and publishing houses, famous writers, important libraries, and a variety of educational, political, and religious institutes and organizations. During almost 20 years of Polish rule, from 1920 to 1939, the economic and social status of the Jewish community in Vilna (Polish "Wilno") deteriorated and antisemitism was on the rise. On the eve of World War II, Jews in Vilna numbered about 57,000, a quarter of the city's population.

Lithuania retained a temporary independence from 28 October 1939 until the Soviet Union forcibly annexed the country on 15 June 1940. Consequently, on the outbreak of war, about 15,000 Jewish refugees from German-occupied Poland, mostly representing the cream of Polish Jewry, were able to reach Vilna, where they enriched local Jewish life. In June 1940 the Jews welcomed the new Soviet regime as a barrier against Nazi Germany. The Soviets, however, outlawed all forms of Jewish public and cultural life and nationalized all property, individual as well as public. The Jewish population diminished as about 6,000 of the refugees managed to leave for Palestine, the Far East, and other destinations; several thousand more were expelled to Siberia; and 3,000 fled to the Soviet interior ahead of the invading German army in the first days of Operation Barbarossa. Thus when the Germans occupied Vilna on 24 June 1941, the community again numbered 57,000 Jews.

The German and Lithuanian authorities waited only a few days before enforcing the anti-Jewish measures that had already been tested in the ghettos of Poland: confinement of movement within certain city limits; restriction of shopping to designated stores at fixed hours; a nighttime curfew; the requirement that Jews wear yellow Stars of David on their clothing; banning from the sidewalks; arbitrary hard labor; and, most important, the establishment of a Jewish council (*Judenrat*), chosen by Jewish notables. Shaul Trotzki was appointed council chairman, with Anatol Fried as his deputy.

Unlike in the ghettos of Poland, where a minimum of stability was reached during 1940–41 before the beginning of the deportations to the death camps, killing operations around Vilna started immediately after the invasion. The Lithuanian Jewish community was the first on whom the Final Solution was implemented, and it was the worst affected. By the end of 1941, 80 percent of Lithuanian Jews had been killed not far from their homes; the death toll reached 96 percent by the end of the war. This large-scale massacre was made possible by Lithuanian volunteers, who collaborated with the German *Einsatzgruppen* (mobile killing units) to an almost unparalleled extent, hastening the pace and scope of indiscriminate mass murder.

Mass killing began even before the ghetto was established. Five thousand men were rounded up and killed in Ponary, a wooded resort about 11 kilometers outside Vilna. Ponary later became the killing site for Jews from Vilna and elsewhere in Lithuania. Under the German civil administration, which was established in August 1941, the pace of murder accelerated: at the end of August 8,000 more Jews were killed, including the recently appointed Jewish council. After 6,000 additional Jews had been killed and a third of the Jewish population was dead, Ghetto I and Ghetto II, housing 30,000 and 10,000 people, respectively, were fenced off and established on 6 September 1941.

It soon became clear that Ghetto I contained those families without *Scheine*—working permits issued by German and Lithuanian employers—whereas inmates of Ghetto II did possess such certificates. In a series of *Aktionen*—German round-ups for killing—Ghetto I was liquidated by the end of October 1941. The Germans then planned to reduce the ghetto population to no more than 12,000; accordingly they issued 3,000 "yellow certificates" for families of two adults and two children. Another series of round-ups followed during November and December. By the end of 1941 almost two-thirds of prewar Vilna Jews had been murdered. The ghetto remained, holding the 15,000 members of the families who had proper certificates and about 5,000 who stayed illegally. A few thousand fled the ghetto to hide in nearby villages, or to neighboring Belorussia, where the mass killings had not yet started.

From the beginning of 1942 to the spring of 1943 the population of the Vilna ghetto remained relatively stable, as the deportations and murders stopped. During that period a Jewish underground emerged which preached self-defense, and the Judenrat developed its policy of life-saving labor.

During the five months of intensive murders the leadership of each of the youth movements attempted to maintain contacts with the remnants of its members and with one another. In 1939 an umbrella organization of youth movements had already been formed in independent Lithuania and was strengthened by the arrival of Polish refugees. During Soviet rule in 1940–41, they acquired some experience in clandestine activity. Following the German occupation and the communities' constant elimination, youth movement leaders and members, whether in the ghetto or in hiding outside, tried to comprehend the significance of the unprecedented events taking place before their eyes. At first they were misled by the fact that Lithuanians, claiming that the Jews had welcomed the Soviet regime that had robbed Lithuania of its independence, carried out most of the killing. Furthermore, information about the murders in nearby Kovno (Kaunas) and in the countryside was not received in Vilna for a few months. And the Germans continued their ongoing deception regarding the fate of the tens of thousands of Jews who had been removed from the ghetto. Their false promises strengthened the natural self-delusion that the Jews were working somewhere and would eventually return, that this or the next "action" was bound to be the last, that the report about shots being heard from Ponary was exaggerated.

But as time passed and more information was gathered, particularly at youth movement meetings (notably those held in the Pioneers' public kitchen on Strashun Street), an overall German plan to kill the Jews came into clear view. If the same fate awaited all Jews as had already befallen tens of thousands, the only remaining choice was self-defense. These two major

Abba Kovner in Vilna after the fall of the city to the Red Army. Circa July 1944

formed in the ghetto, in which all Zionist youth movements, as well as the Communists and the Bund, were represented: hence the name United Partisans Organization (Fareynegte Partizaner Organizatsye, FPO). Yitzhak Wittenberg, a veteran of the Communist party, was chosen as commander, headquarters were established, and an internal clandestine division began operations. The first goals were acquisition and production of armaments and ammunition, training of the members, sabotage of German workshops and supply lines, rescue of the activists from deportation to Ponary, and establishment of contacts outside the ghetto. In the summer of 1943 the underground was about 400 members strong. Still, it was a long process before the two basic ideas of the Vilna underground were internalized, even in Vilna itself, let alone in other ghettos, such as Warsaw and Bialystok, where the period of relative stability was still in effect.

The underground did not clash with the Judenrat while working to achieve its primary goals, despite their opposing opinions. It waited for the proper moment to rise up, whereas the Judenrat did its utmost to postpone any clash with the Germans until the longed-for moment when the Red Army would march in. Accordingly the Judenrat—headed by Anatol Fried from September 1941 to July 1942 and then by Jacob Gens, formerly the Jewish police commander—organized life in the ghetto. It established departments of health, welfare, education, religion and culture, and employment, among others. A theater, choir, soup kitchen, health care system, newspaper, and schools all operated. The ghetto was clean, and its inmates did not perish of disease and starvation. Its population maintained its size until the final days. In the summer of 1943 two-thirds of the ghetto inmates were employed either within or outside the ghetto. A Jewish police force maintained order, relying both on a court of law and a prison.

Under the given conditions these were formidable achievements. Yet they were accomplished at the price of a gloomy public atmosphere, in which Jewish police were feared and held in contempt. This atmosphere was different from that which prevailed in the other two major ghettos of Lithuania, Kovno and Shavli (Siauliai). In those ghettos there was a stronger sense of one common Jewish fate shared by all, and the Judenrat chairmen and police leaders were admired. In Shavli the chairman and his deputy volunteered to ac-

realizations were first formulated in writing by the poet and leader of the leftist Hashomer Hatzair youth movement, Abba Kovner. On the eve of the new year 1942, at a gathering of about 150 youth movement members, Kovner read out a proclamation entitled "Jews! Let Us Not Go Like Sheep to the Slaughter!" in which he forcefully claimed that Hitler was plotting "to kill all the Jews of Europe"—an assessment based at that time more on intuition than on known facts. Then followed his plea: "Jews! Let us defend ourselves, to our last breath!" Thus the Vilna ghetto became the first place in occupied Europe where a Jewish populace faced reality and drew the proper conclusions to guide future action.

Three weeks later an underground organization was

company the ghetto's children to Auschwitz, and most of the policemen in Kovno were tortured to death for refusing to disclose children's hiding places. Gens in Vilna, on the other hand, ordered his policemen to collect old people in a nearby town and turn them over to the Germans to be killed—though only after a long bargaining effort to reduce their number.

Gens, the strongman of the Vilna ghetto, was married to a non-Jewish Lithuanian woman. His comrades from the Lithuanian army, where he had served as an officer, offered him shelter. Yet he chose to be a leader in a hopeless situation. There were also important public figures still alive in the ghetto—political and cultural activists, a remnant of the glory of Vilna— but they did not openly oppose Gens's policy, even when he gathered them to report the handing over of the old Jews to the Germans, because they had no alternatives to offer. Even the underground waited and did not act overtly during the period of relative stability, so as not to bring an untimely disaster on the ghetto. The key to the Jewish tragedy in the Holocaust was that even a Jewish leadership that did its best to protect the interests of its fellow Jews did not alter their fate.

The end came in the summer of 1943. Small towns and labor camps around Vilna had been liquidated in the spring. The question of when Vilna's turn would come brought about the inevitable clash between the underground, ready for action in the ghetto's last days, and Gens, who still tried to delay that action. Weapons in the ghetto and contacts with partisans and Communists on the outside were obstacles to his policy. In Gens's attempts to get rid of the underground commanders, he managed to remove Josef Glazman, formerly his deputy in the police command, and later a Betar (a Revisionist-Zionist right-wing youth movement) deputy commander of the underground. Gens also exploited the German search for Yitzhak Wittenberg—not as the FPO's commander but as a Communist—in order to manipulate the ghetto population against the underground; he threatened that the Germans would put an end to the ghetto if Wittenberg were not handed over to them. Following a dramatic night of clashes and deliberations, Wittenberg gave himself up as a result of a decision taken by his comrades, the Communist members in the ghetto, which the other members of the underground headquarters reluctantly accepted. The underground realized that

Ruins of Vilna's Gaon Synagogue. 1944

night that the ghetto population would not join in the fighting they proposed to initiate when the final moment came.

German deceit again had the upper hand. When the Germans entered the ghetto in August and the beginning of September 1943 in order to carry out a series of Aktionen, the underground called for resistance, claiming that Ponary was the destination. Nevertheless, in accordance with Himmler's orders to send the work force to camps and to kill the rest of the population of the ghettos, about 7,000 people were indeed taken to labor camps in Estonia, as promised by the Germans. Gens managed to stop the battle that had erupted between the underground and the German forces—in which Yechiel Scheinbaum, commander of an underground group, was killed—but was executed himself ten days later. On 23 and 29 September the ghetto collapsed. The remaining 12,000 were deported—some to labor camps, some to the Sobibor death camp, and the rest to Ponary. About 1,000 Jews hid in the ghetto but were gradually caught. The underground group, in a process that began after Wittenberg's arrest in mid-July, left for the forests, joined the Soviet partisans, and outdid itself in fighting the Germans. When the partisans, including Jewish units, and the Red Army entered Vilna on 13 July 1944, the ghetto was practically empty. Of this unique community only about 2,500 scattered Jews survived.

Dina Porat

Wallenberg, Raoul (1912–?) Raoul Wallenberg was the most inventive, daring, and successful rescuer of Jews from the Nazis during the period of the Final Solution. He was a driven man, but as a Christian and a Swede he had little in common with the people whose lives he saved, and he knew little about them.

Born on 4 August 1912 in his maternal grandparents' summer home on an island near Stockholm, Wallenberg came into a world of wealth and privilege. Tragedy stalked him from the beginning: his father had died of cancer shortly before his birth, and he was raised by his mother and her mother, who had also just lost her husband. His surrogate father was his paternal grandfather, Gustaf Wallenberg, a man of iron will and Sweden's ambassador to such countries as China and Japan. Gustaf placed great expectations on his one grandson. It was his idea to send Raoul to the United States for college; he was determined that his grandson acquire American-style self-reliance and an indomitable will, and become a great internationalist rather than an insular Swede.

Though young Raoul traveled throughout Europe in the 1930s and spent six months in Haifa during the Arab riots, the Jewish question did not absorb him; nor did the struggle against nazism. Influenced by his grandfather, he kept his focus on a business career. But when looking for a job, he was rebuffed by Jacob Wallenberg, the head of his father's prestigious family. Jacob thought Raoul was impulsive and too independent, much like his grandfather Gustaf. Those close to Jacob say that he considered Raoul a distant relative and believed that each branch of the family should look after its own. After Gustaf died in 1937, the only thing Wallenbergs would do for Raoul was refer him to a Hungarian Jew, Kalman Lauer, owner of a small export-import firm in Stockholm. With his bachelor's degree in architecture from the University of Michi-

gan, Wallenberg went to work processing invoices for paprika and goose liver paté.

In June 1944 Lauer fell into a casual conversation in an elevator with Iver Olson of the U.S. legation, which rented offices in the same building in downtown Stockholm. When Lauer mentioned his birthplace, Olson asked if he knew anyone who would have the courage to travel to Hungary to help its Jews, by then the only remaining large Jewish community in Nazi-occupied Europe. Lauer suggested Wallenberg.

As the representative of the U.S. War Refugee Board (WRB), established by President Franklin Roosevelt to help the remaining Jews of Europe, Olson offered a tough assignment to Wallenberg, then 31 years old and without experience in diplomacy or clandestine operations, to work out of the Swedish legation and dispense American funds to keep Jews from being sent to what the Allies had known since 1942 were extermination camps. Wallenberg saw his chance to prove himself. Olson cabled Washington that Wallenberg "left in a hell of a hurry with no instructions and no funds."

From his arrival on 9 July 1944 until his arrest by the Red Army on 16 January 1945, Wallenberg devoted himself to saving as many as possible of the more than 300,000 Jews and Christians of Jewish origin who hung on to life in Hungary's capital, most of them in ghettos but some in hiding.

Shortly before Wallenberg's arrival in Budapest, Regent Miklós Horthy, the head of state, stopped the deportations to Germany that had begun after the Wehrmacht occupied Hungary, a nominal ally, on 19 March. Under the supervision of Adolf Eichmann, trains bound for the Third Reich had emptied the provinces of all 476,000 Jews living there. Though President Roosevelt threatened Horthy that following the Nazi model in treating Jews would dim Hungary's prospects in a postwar settlement, it was probably a sharply worded protest from neutral Sweden's King Gustaf that swayed the weak, indecisive Horthy, an old-fashioned antisemite. A gentleman of Old Europe, Horthy deferred to another member of that club, who also happened to be a king.

Sensing that the respite was temporary, Wallenberg proceeded with his plan. He upgraded the protection papers that his partner, First Secretary Per Anger, had been handing out to a few hundred Jews who could prove some link with Sweden, however tenuous. The document, which would soon become known as "the Wallenberg passport," was impressive, bearing the emblem of the Swedish crown. Wallenberg talked Hungarian officials into accepting his contention that a Budapest Jew equipped with a *Schutz-Pass,* or "protective passport," was a quasi-citizen of Sweden waiting to emigrate as soon as transportation became available. These were absurd claims without precedent, which could work only in that time of absurdity—and when promoted aggressively by someone like Wallenberg. Concerned about public opinion in Sweden and elsewhere, the Hungarian government promised that those who held such passports would be allowed to live unmolested in apartment buildings that Wallenberg had bought or rented for them. The blue-and-yellow Swedish flag fluttered over them; signs at the main entrance declared them Swedish state property.

But the number of Swedish protégés had to be very small, the Hungarians insisted. Wallenberg drove a

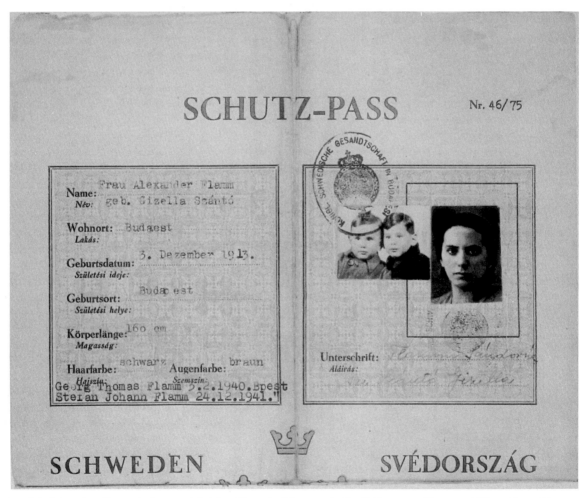

Swedish *Schutz-Pass* (Protective Passport) for Frau Alexander Flamm, née Gizella Szanto, and her two children, Georg Thomas and Stefan Johann. 27 August 1944

hard bargain, and they agreed on 4,500. Worried about depreciating the value of the passports, Wallenberg's office initially issued only a few thousand extra. But soon Wallenberg let the number go past 10,000, and eventually, to 20,000, which is the low figure used by historians seeking to determine how many lives he saved. That figure—first used by Jeno Levai, a Hungarian Jew who wrote several books on the Holocaust shortly after the war's end—rose after the German-engineered putsch of the extreme-right Arrow Cross movement on 15 October 1944 and the removal of Regent Horthy, who had failed in his attempt to cancel Hungary's Axis membership. The deportations resumed under the Arrow Cross regime, which was subservient to Germany. Wallenberg responded by organizing neutral diplomats, such as the Swiss consul, Carl Lutz, to set up "an international ghetto," which sheltered some 33,000 Jews, 7,000 of them holding Swedish papers. Jokingly, people referred to him as Budapest's "number-one landlord."

Wallenberg became reckless as Arrow Cross units combed the city, even entering the Swedish houses, to round up Jews, whom they either shot or crowded into boxcars bound for the death camps. He drove to train stations, brickyards, the ghetto, and other collection points, and he ordered the officer in charge to release the people whose names he had on his list as holding Swedish documents. The list was usually bogus, which quick wits among the detainees understood when they reacted as if their own names had been called. The ruse worked amazingly well.

When Soviet forces surrounded the capital and trains could no longer get through to Germany, Arrow Cross thugs ordered many thousands of Jews of all ages to march westward on foot. Those who from sickness or exhaustion could not keep pace were shot or beaten and left by the side of the road to die. Wallenberg raced after the Jews, and he procured trucks to bring them back to Budapest. His "flying squadrons" spared thousands during the marches.

By November, with the Red Army approaching the capital, the Nazis speeded up their campaign to make the city of Jews *Judenrein*. Wallenberg no longer observed agreements he himself had negotiated with Hungarian officials. He shrugged when they charged that Jews forged thousands of copies of his documents. Most of the day he had his car driven from one location to another to hand out more documents and to save Jews with a relentless energy that matched that of the

Hungarian Nazis. On occasion the Nazis were quicker, and they told him, mockingly, that the Jews he was looking for were already "fish swimming in the Danube." Wallenberg knew that the phrase meant they had been shot at the river's edge so that their bodies fell into the water.

Hungarian and German officials warned Wallenberg to stop his rescue activities. On orders from Eichmann the SS attempted to assassinate him by blowing up his car. Wallenberg happened not to be in the vehicle when it exploded. Eichmann threatened to try again. At a Swedish dinner party arranged to bring the two antagonists together, Eichmann rejected Wallenberg's suggestion that he should stop the deportations and thus save himself from a postwar death sentence. Eichmann replied that he was prepared to be shot by the Russians. But by Christmas the engineer of the Final Solution in Hungary had escaped by plane to Vienna; eventually he made his way to Argentina.

Challenging the Nazis to let go of their Jewish prisoners was an objective commensurate with Wallenberg's ambitions. In Budapest he found his calling, which had nothing to do with the Wallenberg tradition of making a fortune. He volunteered for a unique, perilous international assignment that not even his worldly wise grandfather could have foreseen. A Lutheran, he was saving Jews. A neutral Swede, he was dispensing American money to thwart Germany. He was applying his will to saving lives.

Wallenberg's example inspired others from neutral embassies, such as those of Switzerland, Spain, Portugal, and the Vatican, to issue hundreds of protective papers of their own. But theirs were the acts of traditional diplomats trained to avoid creating a public spectacle and reluctant to offend their host government. None of them dared to go as far as Wallenberg went by brazenly issuing as many documents as he did and by fearlessly confronting officers at collection points for the transports. Moreover, nobody had Wallenberg's temerity to invent bogus lists of protégés.

Wallenberg threatened some Nazis and bribed others. He was adept at inspiring converts, such as the disillusioned Arrow Cross official Pal Szalai, who in the last days of the Nazi occupation of Pest (one of the two historic cities that comprise Budapest) helped him convince the ranking German officer, the SS general August Schmidthuber, to stop the massacre of some 70,000 Jews in the central ghetto.

Although Wallenberg's funds came from the WRB,

Raoul Wallenberg in the office of the Swedish legation. 26 November 1944

declassified documents of the U.S. Office of Strategic Services (OSS) suggest that Wallenberg had an additional assignment. The American he reported to, the WRB's Olsen at the U.S. legation in Stockholm, also worked for the OSS, the wartime precursor to the Central Intelligence Agency. The OSS ran the WRB's communications, and the two clandestine agencies often had joint ventures, such as their efforts to assist the resistance in Norway. Though on several occasions the OSS tried to penetrate Hungary, its men were quickly discovered. Nor did the OSS have a network of agents in that country. It does appear that Wallenberg was the one person whom U.S. intelligence could rely on in Budapest. It seems reasonable to suppose that he was responsible for strategic information cabled to Stock-

holm by the Swedish legation in Budapest or sent by courier to Olson as often as every second day.

Wallenberg's diary showed that he kept in touch with the underground and with others whom he thought might turn against the Nazis. His aim seemed to be in line with the OSS director William Donovan's directive to his people dealing with Central Europe: set up contacts with members of the ruling class who were not in sympathy with the Nazis. The goal, as described in a declassified document in the U.S. National Archives, was "to immobilize and isolate the 18 German divisions in the Balkans." Wallenberg's role as an American intelligence emissary is the probable explanation for his access to a tête-à-tête with Horthy. A stickler for protocol, the former admiral of the Austro-

Hungarian navy would not normally have agreed to grant the privilege of such an audience to the most junior member of the Swedish legation.

One tantalizing question has to do with Wallenberg's purpose in crossing the Danube River to Pest in early January and his intention to contact Soviet authorities as soon as the first Red Army soldiers burst into the cellar where he had taken shelter. (His ambassador had ordered him back to the legation in Buda.) Eventually the soldiers agreed to escort him to headquarters, where he spent the night. The next day, 14 January 1945, three Soviet soldiers escorted him to the international ghetto he had helped to set up. Wallenberg saw a few of his protégés, still wearing yellow stars, venturing outside. He explained to a friend he ran into that he was on his way to Debrecen, the provincial Hungarian city then used by the Red Army as a regional headquarters. He said he would ask for food and medicine for the ghetto and return in a week.

Nothing is known about what happened to Wallenberg in Debrecen. But by the end of January 1945 he was a prisoner in Moscow's Lubyanka Prison. His two cellmates were Germans. One was Gustav Richter, Eichmann's representative in Bucharest, who was eventually freed and gave testimony on Wallenberg's fate.

Since the end of the war U.S. intelligence officials have kept silent about Wallenberg lest they confirm the Soviet charge, never pressed in court, that he had been an American spy. President Truman offered the Swedish government his help in talking the Soviets into releasing him, but the Swedes thought they could do a better job. They did not.

Over the years the Soviet line on Wallenberg zigzagged. After Sweden first inquired about him in 1945, the Soviet ambassador in Stockholm assured Wallenberg's mother that he would be home soon. Then the Soviets denied that he had ever been in their country. Following General Secretary Nikita Khrushchev's historic denunciation of Stalin in front of a shocked Communist party congress in 1956, Deputy Foreign Minister Andrei Gromyko surprised Sweden by announcing that Wallenberg had died of a heart attack in a Soviet jail in 1947.

From the late 1940s to the late 1980s there were persistent sightings of Wallenberg in the Gulag, the Soviet netherworld of prisons, work camps, and psychiatric hospitals. Though the Swedish foreign office, which has investigated scores of sightings, believes that up to 15, including some from the 1970s, are "serious," the post-Communist regime in Russia continues to maintain that Wallenberg died in 1947. Nevertheless, not even under Boris Yeltsin's presidency has the state been able to produce a death certificate, and no one has been able to point to a grave. Close observers, such as Wallenberg's one-time colleague Per Anger, believe that he was alive as late as 1989.

At first Wallenberg's fame was limited to Hungary and Sweden. In the Communist era he quickly became a nonperson in Hungary, though a street named for him immediately after the war was permitted to retain his name, and a marble plaque cited his heroism in saving Jews. In the mid-1950s the CIA began asking Soviet defectors questions about him. In the 1960s there was talk within the CIA of exchanging him for a Soviet spy, but the idea did not crystallize into a recommendation. In the 1970s the first in-depth articles about Wallenberg appeared in the world press. His life inspired several biographies and television specials, and he soon became a legend of World War II. In 1981 Tom Lantos, a Budapest-born U.S. congressman from California and one of his erstwhile protégés, achieved the rare feat of having him declared an honorary U.S. citizen, a distinction accorded previously only to the marquis de Lafayette and Winston Churchill.

Charles Fenyvesi

Wannsee Conference Official gathering held in Wannsee, a lakeside neighborhood of Berlin, on 20 January 1942. The meeting was called by Heinrich Himmler to coordinate between various German ministries the preparation and execution of the so-called Final Solution of the Jewish question. Reinhard Heydrich chaired the meeting, and Adolf Eichmann was in attendance. The state secretaries present were officially informed about their part in the impending deportations, the mass murder of Jews, and the economic and legal consequences of those actions. The site of the meeting is now a center for research on the history of the Holocaust. See FINAL SOLUTION: PREPARATION AND IMPLEMENTATION

War Crimes Midway through World War II it was not certain that the Nazi leadership would be called to answer for its criminal acts, even if Germany was defeated. The British Foreign Office was skeptical about news of atrocities emanating from within German-occupied Europe. It was also haunted by the fiasco after World War I, when it had proven impossible to enforce

The defendants listen as the prosecution begins introducing documents at the International Military Tribunal trial of war criminals at Nuremberg. 22 November 1945

the clauses of the Versailles Treaty requiring the trial of the kaiser and alleged German war criminals. Prime Minister Winston Churchill, however, was more sensitive to the issue of war crimes. In a speech to Parliament on 25 October 1941, and in a statement he issued with U.S. president Franklin Roosevelt, he condemned the massacres in Russia and he described retribution as one of "the major purposes of the war."

The governments-in-exile in London also received horrifying data about Nazi conduct in the occupied countries. On 13 January 1942 they issued the St. James's Palace Declaration pledging retribution against German war criminals. The major Allied Powers were eventually driven to adopt a war crimes policy by the confirmation during mid-1942 that the Germans were engaged in the systematic extermination of the Jews in occupied Europe. In July 1942 the British War Cabinet approved a Foreign Office memorandum setting out general policy on war crimes. This was the basis for the creation of the United Nations War Crimes Commission. On 17 December 1942 the foreign secretary, Anthony Eden, read to the House of Commons a joint Allied statement condemning the extermination of the Jews and affirming the Allies' determination to bring the perpetrators to justice.

Little substance was given to these declarations. Allied officials were wary of any step that might provoke German reprisals against Allied prisoners of war. The Foreign Office resisted proposals to violate the principle of national sovereignty by putting Germans on trial for crimes committed against their own citizens. In the Moscow Declaration of 1 November 1943 the Allied leaders announced that most Germans who committed war crimes would be tried where their crimes were committed, but that the "major war criminals" whose crimes were international would be tried together by the Allies. There were intense debates about how this would be achieved.

In Washington the war crimes issue became entangled with the conflict between Treasury Secretary

Henry Morgenthau, Jr., and Secretary of War Henry L. Stimson over the fate of Germany. Morgenthau wanted a draconian peace imposed on a defeated Germany and the summary execution of leading war criminals, but Stimson favored a more tempered settlement. By October 1944 Stimson had prevailed, although to do so he had been obliged to incorporate a more moderate version of his rival's policy on war crimes. He convinced Roosevelt that an international tribunal should be established to try the Nazi leaders for planning and waging a war of aggression and for war crimes. Roosevelt carried these plans to the Yalta Conference in February 1945, where they were accepted by Churchill and Josef Stalin. The Soviet dictator acceded because he wanted to don the mantle of legalism and use trials to demonstrate the expansionist nature of capitalism. Churchill and Eden, who preferred the summary trial and execution of 50 leading Nazis, bowed to the majority. Britain remained uneasy with the concept of charging officials with conducting a war of aggression and never approved the principle of putting Germans on trial for crimes against their own people.

Scant attention was given to the practicalities until an inter-Allied conference of experts met in London from 26 June to 8 August 1945. It hammered out the London Agreement, which embodied the Charter of the International Military Tribunal (IMT). The charter established the tribunal's membership, the principles governing its procedures, and the categories of crimes. To reach agreement between British, American, French, and Russian jurists, a number of compromises were necessary, some with serious consequences.

Anglo-American jurisprudence clashed with continental theory. The U.S. team, led by Supreme Court justice Robert Jackson, was intent on trying Nazi leaders for conspiring against peace and planning a war of aggression. The culpability of such organizations as the Gestapo and of subordinates who executed the wishes of the Nazi hierarchy was central to American thinking. The idea of conspiracy was anathema to the French, and the Soviets balked at trying organizations. The British, mindful of the 1938 Munich Agreement, by which they facilitated German expansionism at the expense of Czechoslovakia, questioned the wisdom of accusing the Germans of conspiring against peace. The Soviets, worried about setting a precedent for crimes against humanity in peacetime, preferred to restrict this charge to the war years.

Ambiguity was built into Article 6 of the charter, which empowered the IMT to try persons "whether as individuals or as members of organizations" who committed "crimes against peace" or participated in a conspiracy to perpetrate "war crimes" or "crimes against humanity: namely, murder, extermination, enslavement, [or] deportation" of civilians "before or during the war, or persecutions on political, racial or religious grounds." The charter also held that the "leaders, organizers, instigators and accomplices participating in the formulation or execution of a common plan or conspiracy to commit any of the foregoing crimes are responsible for all acts performed by any person in execution of such a plan."

The charter thereby blurred the line between war crimes and crimes against humanity, restricting the latter to German acts in wartime. Because the authors were wary of creating new crimes of which the defendants could claim not to have known, they grounded the charges on the 1899 and 1907 Hague Conventions and the 1929 Geneva Convention. But those conventions delineated crimes under wartime conditions. The tension between war crimes and crimes against humanity would recur in all later war crimes trials.

Crimes committed specifically against the Jews disappeared among the other charges and, when treated, were limited to wartime. Largely at the behest of the Russians, the charter did not utilize the concept of genocide framed in 1944 by the Polish-born Jewish jurist Raphael Lemkin. Although under Article 6(c) the charter enabled the indictment of defendants for crimes perpetrated against the Jews before 1939, Article 6(a) tied conspiracy to commit such crimes to the war. Even though the "conspiracy" to persecute the Jews predated 1939 and the evidence for it was stronger than that for planning aggression, no attempt was made to establish it. By focusing on the Axis Powers, the tribunal ignored the role of Germany's allies and collaborators.

The proceedings of the IMT lasted from 18 October 1945 to 1 October 1946. Twenty-two defendants including Hans Frank, Wilhelm Frick, Hermann Göring, Rudolf Hess, Ernst Kaltenbrunner, Joachim von Ribbentrop, Alfred Rosenberg, Fritz Sauckel, Baldur von Schirach, Arthur Seyss-Inquart, Albert Speer, and Julius Streicher stood trial on four counts: crimes against peace; war crimes; crimes against humanity; and conspiracy to commit such crimes. The selection of defendants reflected the American determination to construct a case of conspiracy and to represent culpable sections of German society. Frank, Frick, Göring, Kaltenbrunner, Ribbentrop, Rosenberg, Sauckel, Seyss-Inquart, and Streicher were sentenced to death by hanging. Schirach and Speer were sentenced to serve 20 years, and Hess was sentenced to life imprisonment. The Nazi party leadership, the SS, and the Gestapo were condemned as criminal organizations, but not the SA, the Reich Cabinet, the High Command, or the Army General Staff.

The Nuremberg tribunal established a model for the future. It generated a detailed record of the Nazi regime and accumulated a mass of material which ensured that the history of the Nazi era would not be forgotten easily and would make political distortions more difficult. The tribunal focused the judicial process and satisfied the popular desire for retribution. It made, for the first time, the political echelon accountable in a court of international law for the planning and conduct of war. The defense of obedience to superior orders was definitively undermined. Despite the confusion between war crimes and crimes committed during war, the concept of crimes against humanity was firmly established, and it fed the development of human rights legislation such as the 1948 Genocide Convention and the 1948 Declaration on Human Rights.

However, the IMT was highly controversial, and its impact has been exaggerated. The tribunal stood on shaky constitutional ground. Many jurists held that the charges of conspiracy to wage war and crimes against humanity were retrospective. The Soviet Union was equally guilty of aggression against Poland in 1939, Finland in 1939–40, and the Baltic states in 1940. Britain and France launched a preemptive invasion of Norway in 1940. All had concluded international agreements with the "criminal" Nazi regime before September 1939. Critics protested that all parties to the war had committed war crimes. The area bombing of German cities by the British Royal Air Force was contestable in such terms. It struck many observers as dubious that Soviet jurists should sit in judgment over anyone, a sentiment undiminished by the Soviets' insistence that the massacre of Polish officers in the Katyn Forest in 1941 be attributed falsely to the Germans during the trial.

To most Germans the trial smacked of victors' justice, and it had little impact on their perceptions of the Nazi era. The selection of defendants and the assignment of penalties reinforced the appearance of arbitrariness, and most Germans were absorbed by the problems of daily life in their ruined cities. The British public was preoccupied with postwar reconstruction and overtaken by guilt about Dresden and the atomic bomb. In Britain and the United States the IMT was poorly reported. The public tired of the long, intricate proceedings. A substantial minority considered the trials juridically unsound—they lacked an appeals mechanism, for example—and virtually invalidated by the Soviet presence. For these reasons the Americans abandoned plans to continue using the IMT for further trials and operated their own judicial program to deal with captured Nazis awaiting justice.

These "subsequent trials" were conducted by the U.S. Office of the Military Government for Germany (OMGUS) under the authority of Allied Control Commission Law 10, dated 20 December 1945. Law 10 was based on the principles set out in the IMT charter, but it decoupled crimes against humanity from the waging of war. Even so, the persecution and attempted extermination of the Jews was subsumed as before under crimes committed in connection with the war. Twelve major trials, involving 185 defendants, were held at Nuremberg by OMGUS between December 1946 and April 1949. The defendants included the doctors responsible for the medical experiments in the camps, the Interior Ministry officials who drafted the race laws, the foreign personnel who helped to implement the Final Solution, industrialists who had stolen Jewish property and used slave labor, senior army officers responsible for the taking and shooting of Jewish and non-Jewish hostages, the SS central administration of the concentration camp system, the SS personnel responsible for the resettlement and *Lebensborn* (Well of Life) programs, and the commanders of the *Einsatzgruppen* (mobile killing units).

These trials also faced criticism in Germany and abroad. The jurisdiction of the United States was challenged and the lack of an appeals procedure condemned. Of the accused, 24 were sentenced to death (14 in the Einsatzgruppen case, 7 in the doctors case, and 3 in the case of the WVHA, the Economic and Administrative Main Office of the SS), 20 to life imprisonment, and 98 to terms of imprisonment ranging from one and a half years to 20 years. Thirty-five were acquitted. Only 12 death sentences were actually carried out. In a host of lesser trials, in which the defendants included guards at a number of concentration camps, 1,672 persons were tried, of whom 1,416 were convicted; there were 324 death sentences.

Before these trials were over, the political climate

The defendants in the I. G. Farben trial hear the indictments against them at the Palace of Justice, Nuremberg. 5 May 1947

changed. The revelation that investigators interrogating suspects in connection with the massacre of American soldiers at Malmedy during the Battle of the Bulge had used physical violence caused a backlash in the United States and Germany. John J. McCloy, appointed U.S. high commissioner in 1949, tried to placate critics by equalizing sentences and reviewing certain cases. An advisory board set up in March 1950 moderated 87 percent of the sentences. Trials, and the fate of those sentenced to death, became an embarrassment following the establishment of the Federal Republic of Germany and the development of the Cold War. In order to smooth relations with West German chancellor Konrad Adenauer and to meet the demands of German lobby groups, including the nascent Bundeswehr (parliament), death sentences were commuted and sentences reduced. This generated the impression that the trials had been unfair in the first place and stoked demands for the release of prisoners. By 1958 the U.S. authorities had discharged all those convicted by its courts between 1945 and 1955.

War crimes trials in the British zone of occupation in Germany, and in Italy, were carried out under a Royal Warrant, issued on 14 June 1945, which limited the charges to traditionally defined war crimes committed only against British subjects or Allied nationals in the British zone. Military courts tried more than 1,000 persons, including SS personnel from Bergen-Belsen, Auschwitz, and other camps. The British also tried Field Marshals Albert Kesselring and Ernst von Manstein and the manufacturers of Zyklon B poison gas. The systematic persecution and extermination of Jews was never made a charge. The British public, impatient with continuing trials, by mid-1946 demanded an end to them. In June 1948 the British military government announced that trials would cease in the British zone of Germany at the end of 1948. By the time Manstein, the last defendant, was tried in late 1949, the public mood had so changed that even Winston Churchill contributed to his defense fund.

In September 1949 the British authorities began reviewing sentences, with an eye to equalization, and immediately reduced by one-third the prison sentences in 66 out of 372 cases. Successive reviews in 1950, 1951, and 1955 responded to pressure from the Foreign Office to end the burden represented by these prisoners and remove obstacles to harmonious relations with an independent Germany. Between 1953 and 1956 the number of prisoners in British custody was reduced from 81 to 10. The last Nazi war criminal serving a custodial sentence under British jurisdiction was released in 1958.

French war crimes trials mainly centered on crimes committed in concentration camps on French soil. It is estimated that 2,107 persons were convicted, of whom 104 were sentenced to death. Some French trials were also conducted in North Africa and marginally concerned the maltreatment of North African Jews and European Jews. French nationals were also culpable of war crimes and crimes against humanity, but there were grave political and legal problems in dealing with these cases.

Following the liberation of France thousands of French men and women faced trial in kangaroo courts. About 9,000 were summarily executed, most before the liberation of Paris in August 1944 and the establishment of the provisional government. Subsequent trials were conducted under the 1939 penal code, in which crimes against humanity did not figure. From 1945 to 1954 the French high court, courts of justice, civil courts, and military courts heard tens of thousands of cases mainly in connection with crimes against national security and with collaboration. They pronounced 1,500 death sentences. But the complicity of the Vichy regime in the persecution and deportation of Jews in France was never addressed. In order to restore national unity, and in view of the Cold War, several amnesties were implemented in 1951 and 1953. By 1954 fewer than 1,000 persons were still held in prison. This judicial amnesia was not challenged until the late 1970s.

War crimes trials were conducted throughout Europe in areas that had been occupied by the Germans. In July 1943 the Soviet Union had mounted a trial against Soviet citizens who had collaborated with Einsatzkommando SK10a in Krasnodar. After the war thousands of Germans were tried by Soviet courts, often for massacres of Jews. In 1950, 10,000–13,000 Germans were serving prison sentences under Soviet jurisdiction for the commission of war crimes.

War crimes trials in Poland commenced in August 1945 under the auspices of the Polish National Liberation Committee. From 1944 to 1949 thousands of rudi-

mentary trials were conducted by special courts. In 1946 a national tribunal was established to try major cases. Between 7 June 1946 and 5 June 1948 it heard the cases of, among others, Arthur Greiser, head of the Warthegau (the German administration in western Poland); Amon Goeth, commandant of Plaszow; and Rudolf Höss, commandant of Auschwitz. The charges drew on the IMT principles and embraced crimes against humanity. The Polish authorities also attempted somewhat erratically to extradite suspects held in the custody of the Western Allies. More than 1,800 were extradited before impatience with poor legal procedure and the Cold War caused the West to desist from cooperation. Later war crimes trials were conducted by normal courts under the restored Polish penal code. Defendants included local Nazi officials and SS personnel, such as Erich Koch, Reich commissar of Ukraine; Jürgen Stroop, whose SS troops suppressed the Warsaw ghetto uprising; and Hans Biebow, who supervised the Lodz ghetto. The Polish courts enlarged the number of criminal organizations to include the administration of the Generalgouvernement (central Poland) and the ethnic-German self-defense militia. By 1977, 5,450 war criminals (5,358 German nationals) had been tried, including guards at Auschwitz, Majdanek, and Stutthof.

In the Netherlands after the liberation 450,000 Dutch citizens—5 percent of the population—were arrested. Expediency demanded, however, that most be released. By 1946 the number of detainees was below 100,000, of whom fewer than 15,000 were eventually convicted and sentenced for collaboration or war crimes. There were 109 death sentences, of which 39 resulted in execution. As a result of hearings by review boards, which typically reduced sentences, and amnesties, fewer than 60 prisoners were still held by 1960. War crimes trials in Holland were complicated by the charges leveled against Jewish members of the *Joodsche Raad* (Jewish council). More than 200 Germans were tried for war crimes against Dutch nationals; 19 of them were sentenced to death.

German nationals and collaborators were also tried in Denmark (80), Norway (80), Belgium (75), and Luxembourg (68). Collaborators in those countries also faced punishment for crimes that included the deportation and murder of Jews. Hungary mounted a series of trials of wartime leaders, some of whom faced charges connected with the persecution of the Jews in Hungary before 1939 and the massacre, despoliation, and deportation of Jews under Hungarian control during the war. Several Hungarians implicated in mas-

This picture was among several introduced at the war crimes trials in Nuremberg showing destruction in Warsaw in the spring of 1943.

sacres on Yugoslav soil were extradited, tried, and sentenced to death in Yugoslavia. War criminals were punished there and in Greece and Czechoslovakia, but there is little material on those proceedings. In the case of Yugoslavia, retribution was often meted out informally, brutally, and arbitrarily.

From 1945 to 1950 the resurrected courts in Allied-occupied Western Germany were prevented from trying Germans for offenses committed against all but German nationals and stateless persons. Despite the lack of resources, records, or expertise, these courts responded to denunciations and evidence connected mainly with the Röhm purge (June 1934), Kristallnacht (November 1938), the so-called euthanasia operation, and the reign of terror during the death throes of the Third Reich.

After independence the full jurisdiction of German courts was restored, but there were still obstacles to trying Germans for Nazi crimes. The IMT charges could not be applied because they were considered retrospective, an anathema after 13 years of Nazi ex post facto laws. Germans could be tried only for such common crimes as murder, homicide, manslaughter, grievous bodily harm with malice, and unlawful detention. To prove murder, however, it was also necessary to prove *blutdürstig* (thirst for blood)—base motives, malice, or cruelty. This was not usually possible in the case of *Schreibtischtäter* (desk murderers)—the men who ordered and organized the deportation of Jews. To convict, proof of a defendant's "interest" in a fatal outcome was required. This too was hard to establish because many defendants could point to the secrecy surrounding the Final Solution and claim ignorance about the precise destination of transports to the East.

Many prosecutors consequently settled for charges of manslaughter; but because the sentence for manslaughter was 15 years, and the statute of limitations was tied directly to the length of sentence prescribed by law for the particular crime, no trials on charges of manslaughter committed during the Nazi period would be possible after May 1960. From then on, German prosecutors had to seek the more demanding indictments for murder.

By 1951 the rate of prosecutions and convictions dropped as the number of denunciations tailed off and potential witnesses either emigrated (in the case of displaced persons) or lost the resolve to risk a court appearance. There was no proactive policy of searching for Nazi criminals, and no resources to do so. In May 1951 hundreds of policemen and jurists who had been barred from office owing to Nazi affiliations were allowed to return to government employment. This created a powerful blocking force within the legal system. Nevertheless, by 1955 some 5,866 Germans had been sentenced for Nazi crimes. In May 1955, however, the allies inadvertently introduced another barrier by decreeing that persons tried once by an Allied court could not be retried in a German one. This ruling enabled thousands of Germans who had been tried but acquitted for lack of evidence to escape any future trial once more evidence had been accumulated. Those who had received light sentences or had been released early could not be retried either, even if more seriously incriminating information was unearthed.

In 1958 a major trial of SS personnel active in Lithuania came about, by chance, in Ulm. The hearings exposed the multitude of crimes that had escaped proper investigation and the number of perpetrators who had never faced justice. The federal government ordered the establishment of the Zentrale Stelle der Landesjustizverwaltungen zur Aufklärung Nationalsozialistischer Gewaltverbrechen (ZS), Central Office for the Prosecution of National Socialist Crimes, at Ludwigsburg. The ZS, which commenced work on 1 December 1958, was charged with collecting material, launching investigations, and coordinating legal activity occurring at state and local levels. It explicitly eschewed war crimes in favor of crimes committed against civilians outside the sphere of military operations. Once a case was assembled, it was handed over to a public prosecutor. Although the ZS took time to gather staff, material, and experience, it was soon generating hundreds of cases annually.

In 1955, after strenuous debate, the statute of limitations in the case of Nazi crimes liable to a 10-year sentence was extended. In 1965, when the statute of limitations on crimes of murder dating from 1945 was due to come into effect, it was extended to 1969, again after heated discussion in the Bundestag. When in 1969 there was still a backlog of cases, limitation was interrupted until 1979. By now world opinion was more alert to Nazi war crimes, and there were demands for the statute of limitations to be abrogated in cases of war crime and crimes against humanity. In response to the upsurge of feeling after the screening of the television series *Holocaust* in Germany in January 1979, the Bundestag finally abolished the statute of limitations.

From 1945 to 1992 West German courts indicted more than 100,000 persons for Nazi crimes. More than 13,000 cases were tried, and 6,487 persons were convicted; 6,197 were sentenced to prison terms, including 163 to life imprisonment; 12 were sentenced to death. From 1958 to 1993 the ZS instigated 4,853 prosecutions. Although German courts never indicted on charges of crimes against humanity or genocide, the fate of the Jews was sharply exposed in a spate of trials. These included the Treblinka guards' case (1959–65), the Majdanek and Auschwitz SS personnel trials (1960–79 and 1963–64), the trial of Franz Stangl, commandant of Sobibor and later Treblinka (1974–75), and the trial of Josef Schwammberger, who ran and eventually liquidated the Przemysl ghetto (1991–92). In addition, from 1949 German courts arraigned with mixed success the Gestapo staffs responsible for the deportation of Jews from the major German cities and the members of several German police battalions implicated in mass murder in Poland and Russia. For all their failures, the German courts enabled a confrontation with the Nazi past, documented Nazi crimes, kept the plight of their victims from being forgotten, and sustained the principle of seeking justice.

The attitude of superiority toward Germany that was popular among the Western powers was proven less than justified when the spotlight was turned on the record of their own governments. Journalistic investigations in the mid-1970s exposed the Allied governments' policy of recruiting German scientists and technicians who had willingly served the Nazis. At the same time détente with the Soviet Union facilitated the flow of information about crimes committed on Soviet territory, and research showed that many thousands of East European collaborators had found refuge after the war in the United States, Canada, Australia, and Great Britain, some with the connivance of the authorities.

In 1977–78 Rep. Elizabeth Holtzman and Rep. Joshua Eilberg organized hearings in the U.S. House of Representatives that substantiated many of these claims. In 1978 Congress passed the Holtzman Amendment, which rendered aliens deportable if it were proven that they had been Nazi collaborators or accessories to Nazi crimes. In Canada in February 1985 an investigation into allegations that Nazi criminals had found refuge in that country was set up under Justice Jules Deschenes. The Deschenes Commission's report in March 1987 convinced the Canadian government that legislation was needed to deal with the presence of former Nazi auxiliaries in Canada. Canadian immigration and citizenship law was amended in September 1987 to facilitate proceedings against suspected war criminals. In Australia a government inquiry was mandated in June 1986, and a report was issued five months later. It confirmed the presence of a significant number of war crimes suspects in Australia and recommended that action be taken. In October 1987 the Australian federal legislature amended the 1945 War Crimes Act to enable Australian courts to try persons suspected of participation in crimes of genocide during World War II.

In August 1986 Greville Janner, a British Labour MP, raised the case of an East European collaborator who had entered postwar Britain. In March 1987 the Simon Wiesenthal Center in Los Angeles sent the British government a list of suspected war criminals living in Britain. An All-Party Parliamentary War Crimes Group was set up in November 1986 to lobby for an investigation, and an official inquiry was ordered in February 1988. Its report, released in July 1989, verified the presence of suspected war criminals in Britain and recommended that action be taken in more than 100 cases. Deportation or extradition to a Soviet-bloc country was unacceptable, but under current law it was not possible to try persons domiciled in the United Kingdom who were suspected of committing war crimes in areas not under British jurisdiction and at a time when they were not British citizens. The report recommended the introduction of legislation to remove this anomaly. After protracted debate a war crimes bill was introduced in Parliament in March 1990. It became law in May 1991, in the teeth of opposition from the House of Lords. Police war crimes units were then set up in Edinburgh and London.

In the United States, war crimes trials have taken the form of hearings to decide whether to denaturalize and deport suspected war criminals. A Special Litigation Unit was first established in 1978 under the Immigration and Naturalization Service. In 1980 the unit was renamed the Office of Special Investigations (OSI) and transferred to the Justice Department. The OSI solicits information from foreign governments, checks lists of known war criminals against U.S. immigration registers, and invites submissions from the public. From 1980 to 1992 it instigated proceedings against more than 100 persons, of whom 43 were denaturalized, 32 were deported, and 3 were extradited. Two of the best-known cases involved Karl Linnas, who was deported to face justice in Estonia in 1987, and John Demjanjuk, a Ukrainian accused of operating the gas chamber at Treblinka, who was deported to stand trial in Israel. Demjanjuk was found guilty in 1988, but in 1993 the verdict was overturned by the Israeli Supreme Court after it was shown he had been wrongly identified. This debacle was a serious setback to the work of the OSI.

In Canada, Australia, and Great Britain the law required full criminal trials. The first case brought to court by the Canadian Justice Department was that of a former Hungarian policeman, Imre Finta. The case was poorly prepared and resulted in an acquittal. In March 1992 the Justice Department dropped the case against a prime suspect, Michael Pawlowski, after procedural problems. A short time later it announced that after March 1994 no further investigations would take place. In Australia a special investigations unit mounted three cases in 1992–93. The first to come to court became mired in procedural wrangles and the defendant was eventually acquitted. The second rapidly collapsed. No progress was made with the third. This poor record is mainly attributable to the inexperience of the prosecution teams and to procedural difficulties.

In Britain the Scottish war crimes investigation centered on the case of Antanas Gecas, a former platoon commander in the 12th Lithuanian Police Battalion, who arrived in England in 1946 after defecting to the Allies in Italy in 1944 and joining the Polish army. In a libel case in 1992 the judge, Lord Milligan, ruled that he was "clearly satisfied" that Gecas had "participated in many operations involving the killing of innocent

Soviet citizens including Jews in particular" in Belorussia in the fall of 1941. Nevertheless, it proved impossible to marshal the eyewitnesses to mount a war crimes trial. In February 1994 Scotland's war crimes unit was disbanded. On 12 July 1995, the London-based Metropolitan Police War Crimes Unit charged Szymon Serafinowicz, aged 85, a former Belorussian district police chief, under the 1991 act. After committal proceedings in April 1996 he was sent for trial at the Central Criminal Court. However, on 17 January 1997, as a result of the defendant's ill health, the trial was suspended almost as soon as it had begun; Serafinowicz died the following year.

On 30 October 1997, Anthony Sawoniuk, aged 76, who had commanded a collaborationist police unit in Belorussia in 1942–43, was charged with murder under the War Crimes Act. His trial at the Central Criminal Court lasted from 8 February to 1 April 1999, when he was found guilty on two counts of murder. He was sentenced to life imprisonment.

Wherever war crimes legislation has been introduced, it has been contentious. Opponents of war crimes trials object that the legislation is retrospective and preordains a group of suspects who could not have known that their acts would subsequently be deemed illegal. Antagonists protest that after such a lapse of time trials cannot possibly be fair. Witnesses cannot make safe identifications, and documentary evidence, especially of East European provenance, cannot be trusted. The demand for trials has been characterized as an exercise in vengeance and linked to a supposed Jewish predilection for relentless justice in contradistinction to Christian notions of mercy and forgiveness.

Those who resist trials ask what they are supposed to achieve. The incidence of genocide and mass murder since 1945 shows, they assert, that such war crimes trials do not work as a deterrent. As it is hardly likely that aged war criminals will re-offend, a custodial sentence is not necessary to protect the public. Trials would indicate society's repugnance for these crimes, but sending elderly people to prison might cause an equally strong reaction. What sentence could match the alleged crimes? Trials would prove divisive by directing attention backward to a bloody past instead of toward international and interethnic harmony. Opponents suggest it would be better to leave ultimate judgment to the Almighty.

In response it is argued that war crimes committed during World War II were violations of existing international and national law. Time does not absolve the murderers of guilt, and it would be a betrayal of justice, as well as an offense against the victims, not to pursue the perpetrators. Although war crimes trials may not be an effective deterrent, proponents of war crimes trials say that failure to investigate and prosecute war criminals just because of the passage of time would serve to reassure potential mass murderers involved in current conflicts that they will evade retribution if they can escape detection for long enough. The failings of earlier trials should encourage efforts to perfect the law and the enforcement system rather than compound the situation by abandoning the hope of achieving justice. It is a scant deterrent to future perpetrators, or balm to survivors, to defer justice to the afterlife. And though in the short term trials may be divisive, history since 1945 has shown that such crimes cannot be forgotten or conveniently buried. They have erupted violently from time to time, not least because of the unfreezing of European history since the collapse of the Communist regimes and the revival of the nations and nationalisms characteristic of the 1940s.

Signs of such eruptions are apparent in France. In January 1983 Klaus Barbie, former head of the Gestapo in Lyons, was arrested in Bolivia, where he had found refuge after the war. It had taken more than a decade of work by Nazi hunters Serge and Beate Klarsfeld to achieve this result. French politicians preferred to avoid the issue since the trial risked opening questions about Vichy France. Barbie was eventually extradited, and he stood trial in Lyons from 11 May to 4 July 1987. His defense, conducted by Jacques Verges, did not contest the charges but did challenge the right of the court to try a man for acts that the French state had sanctioned in its colonial wars since 1945. The Barbie investigation had exposed postwar cooperation and deals between fleeing SS personnel and Allied intelligence services, which, Verges argued, further compromised the moral stance of the accusers. Resistance veterans saw Barbie's murder of the resistance leader Jean Moulin as his greatest crime, but Verges played on the rumors that Moulin was actually betrayed by a Frenchman to expose the ambiguities of Vichy history. He also exploited the contest of memory between resistance veterans and the Jews, who wanted attention focused on Barbie's role in the deportations. The trial widened the differences between Jews and non-Jews in France. Barbie was found guilty on 4 July 1987 and sentenced to life imprisonment, but the trial left a sour taste.

In May 1989 Paul Touvier, a former officer in the

collaborationist militia in Lyons, was imprisoned pending trial for crimes against humanity. Touvier had twice been tried in absentia for treason but had gone into hiding with the connivance of the Roman Catholic church. In 1967, after the statute of limitations came into force, he launched a campaign for his rehabilitation. This strategy backfired after French president Georges Pompidou attempted to pardon him in 1971. Resistance veterans and Jewish groups demanded that Touvier be retried. Legal wrangles delayed the profferment of charges until 1979, whereupon Touvier could not be found. He was finally located in 1989 at a monastery near Nice and charged. On 13 April 1992 the Court of Appeal acquitted him of crimes against humanity because he had been a servant of Vichy France, which, it asserted, was not culpable in such terms. This verdict provoked outrage, and in November 1992 Touvier's acquittal was overturned by the Criminal Chamber of the High Court of Appeals. On 20 April 1994 Touvier became the first French citizen to be convicted of crimes against humanity.

In October 1997 after 18 years of legal tussles, Maurice Papon, aged 86, went on trial for his role in the deportation of Jews from Bordeaux. He was found guilty in April 1998 but was allowed to appeal. He was imprisoned after attempting to flee France prior to his appeal hearing in September 1999. René Bousquet, former head of the Vichy police, was indicted for war crimes in 1992, but on 8 June 1993, before his case came to court, he was shot by a demented assassin.

The Barbie, Touvier, and Papon cases show the dangers inherent to war crimes trials. Court hearings may dramatize the past, but they can also oversimplify history. Judges are not historical experts. The law reduces complex processes and attitudes to raw polarities. Trials can be a way of not confronting the past, which is a patchwork of contradictions and ambiguities. A Barbie or Touvier can serve as an alibi for larger social groups or a whole nation. Because the trials of old people can never deliver a sentence commensurate to the offense, they appear futile when set against crimes of such magnitude. By putting history and memory in the dock, the Barbie and Touvier trials aggravated historic rivalries between deportees, "racial deportees," and resistance fighters. Even if they clarified the culpability of the Vichy government, one set of victims always felt resentful that another one was getting more attention in the trial process.

The value and limitations of war crimes trials may be seen also in the contrast between the trials of Adolf Eichmann and John Demjanjuk. The Eichmann trial in Jerusalem from 10 April to 15 December 1961 was the first in which crimes against the Jews were stipulated alongside crimes against humanity and other offenses. It reasserted the principles of Nuremberg and served to explain to the Israeli and world publics the genesis and implementation of Nazi anti-Jewish legislation, persecution, despoliation, deportation, and mass murder. Second to the application of justice, this assertion was perhaps its greatest accomplishment.

By contrast the Demjanjuk trial was supposed to instruct a new generation about the Holocaust; but Demjanjuk was misidentified, and the case against him collapsed on appeal before the Israeli Supreme Court. As a result, the process looked more like a show trial and placed all other pending war crimes trials in jeopardy.

Justice is ultimately at the heart of such trials. Regardless of any pedagogic side effects, their objective is to penalize violations of international peace, to establish the limits of warfare, and to assert human rights. They reiterate the responsibility of the political leadership of states at war and remove the defense of obedience to superior orders deployed by those executing their wishes. War crimes trials, in reality designating crimes committed against civilians, usually far from any front line or military engagements, assert the rule of law over and against lawlessness. Societies that claim to be based on the rule of law and on respect for human rights have an obligation to punish states and individuals who challenge that order; otherwise they open the way to anarchy. Even apparently local and small-scale crimes must be investigated and their perpetrators put on trial. Only in this way, it is argued, will people come to understand and accept their human and moral responsibility for the conduct of politics and war.

David Cesarani

Warsaw Warsaw has been the capital of the Polish state since 1596. Although Jews were living in Warsaw at least as early as the fifteenth century, there was no continuous Jewish presence. In 1527 Jews were forbidden to live in the city. The ban was gradually abolished beginning at the end of the eighteenth century. The Jewish community in Warsaw grew rapidly during the nineteenth and the first decades of the twentieth century.

Warsaw's Jews contributed greatly to the economic development of Poland. A few well-known Jewish families in Warsaw were pioneers in industry and banking. Some Jews became members of the Polish intelligentsia and others took part in the Polish national uprising of 1863.

Besides the small number of prosperous and thoroughly polonized Jews, the Jewish masses were concentrated in separate quarters and streets. They were preoccupied with trade, mostly as small dealers or as middlemen between the agricultural countryside and the town. Around 20 percent of the Jews were artisans.

Until the end of the nineteenth century the great majority of Warsaw's Jews lived among their own people, in the framework of the Jewish community and traditional religious rules. But at the dawn of the twentieth century a new awareness of open cultural and political life emerged, particularly among the Jewish youth.

The two interwar decades—the period of the independent Polish republic—were a time of hardship for Warsaw's Jews both because of economic crisis and owing to the growing incidence of antisemitism. At the same time Warsaw was becoming the largest and most influential Jewish center in Europe, largely as a result of the almost total disconnection of Jews in the Soviet Union from the rest of the Jewish world. Warsaw Jews were in the majority strong proponents of national self-identification and fostered dynamic creativity in Yiddish and Hebrew language and culture.

Just before World War II Warsaw's Jewish population was 375,000, almost 30 percent of the city's total population. Jews were found throughout the city, but the largest concentration was in the northern area, where many apartment houses and certain streets were inhabited exclusively by Jews. According to 1931 census data, 16.8 percent of gainfully employed Jews worked in crafts and industry and 32.7 percent in commerce and finance; 8 percent of all persons in the liberal professions were Jewish. Government offices and Polish firms were reluctant to employ Jews, and this was sometimes true also of Jewish-owned enterprises. The antisemitic tendency of the Polish administration added to the generally poor state of the economy and led to the pauperization of the Jews. During the years leading up to World War II, the Jews of Warsaw suffered increasing discrimination without any chance of emigration, owing to the closed-door policy of the target countries and the drastic limitations on immigration to Palestine put in force by the British in 1936.

Warsaw was the home of the head offices of the polit-

Group portrait of students and staff of the ORT (Institution for Vocational Guidance and Training). Circa 1934

ical parties, the trade unions, and a great many welfare, educational, and religious institutions. It was in Warsaw that most of the Jewish newspapers and periodicals were published and that the various educational trends received their central direction. Sports organizations and youth movements also made their headquarters in the city. The cultural drive emanating from Warsaw stood in stark contrast to the economic depression and abject poverty that plagued Warsaw's Jewish masses. The growing political tension in the months preceding the outbreak of war led to an understanding between Poles and Jews, both of whom were in a state of anxiety and insecurity. Although it had been expected, the war that began on 1 September 1939 found the state unprepared and helpless in the face of the German war machine that was about to engulf them.

By the end of the first week of war the German forces stood at the gates of Warsaw. On the night of 6–7 September a high-ranking Polish officer in Warsaw called on all men able to bear arms to leave the city and flee eastward. This call created a panic; throngs of people, mostly young and middle-aged men, crossed the bridges over the Vistula River to the east. Their exodus from the city was joined by government cadres and top officials, as well as by the leaders of political and public organizations. Also swept along were Jewish public figures, leaders, and activists of the different political movements, among them Maurycy Mayzel, the appointed head of the Jewish Community Council. No meaningful preparations had been made for an evacuation, and no individuals or organizations were assigned to replace those fleeing the city.

On 28 September Warsaw surrendered; the next day German forces entered the city. There is no evidence that the Germans deliberately trained their fire on Jewish streets, but the Jews felt that they had been a special target. Adam Czerniakow, who was to become head of the Warsaw *Judenrat* (Jewish council), stated on 22 September, "Today is the Day of Atonement, truly the day of judgment. All night long the guns were shelling the city."

From the very first days of occupation, Jews were subjected to attacks, driven away from food lines, and seized for forced labor. Religious Jews in traditional garb were assaulted, and Jewish shops and homes were plundered. The indiscriminate seizure of Jews for forced labor, regardless of age, sex, or health, paralyzed the community as Jews kept off the streets. Most of the business enterprises were not reopened, for the owners were afraid to display their wares. Teachers, ar-

tisans, professionals, journalists, and members of cultural and social-welfare institutions lost their positions, without severance pay and with no prospect of finding new work.

In November the first anti-Jewish decrees were issued, such as the introduction of a white arm band with a blue Star of David to be worn by all Jews, the requirement of signs identifying Jewish shops and enterprises, the order to hand in radios (which applied to the entire Polish population), and a ban on train travel. The hardest blows came from economic decrees and regulations. On 17 October the Warsaw district governor, Ludwig Fischer, prohibited non-Jews from buying or leasing Jewish enterprises without obtaining a special permit. In November regulations were issued requiring Jews to deposit all their funds in blocked bank accounts. These orders made it impossible for Jews to carry on economic activity in the open, especially outside Jewish circles. Another decree, concerning the pensions of widows, the disabled, the elderly, and retired civil servants, excluded Jews from all welfare assistance. The Germans also began to confiscate Jewish enterprises, except for small stores in the Jewish district. In general the custodians got rid of the Jewish owner and employees, retaining the owner as an adviser only in specific circumstances.

From the early stages of occupation, assets accumulated in the past served the Jews as their main source of sustenance. As time went on, and their property and resources dwindled, more and more penniless Jews faced a slow death from lack of food and elementary means of existence.

Tens of thousands of Jews left Warsaw in the exodus during the first few days of the war; on the other hand, until the establishment of the ghetto in November 1940 an estimated 90,000 Jews were added to the city's population, either as refugees or as deportees sent to Warsaw by the Germans. Many of the newcomers came from Lodz, Wloclawek, Kalisz, and towns in the area of Warsaw. They were housed in schools, public institutions, and even synagogues.

The Jews were not permitted to reopen their schools, and for awhile they were also barred from attending prayer services. Even in small groups Jews were not allowed to meet without a permit. In place of the many institutions of the past, only two Jewish institutions were allowed to function—the Judenrat and a welfare agency. The Judenrat was set up by the Germans in place of the traditional Jewish Community Council. Adam Czerniakow was ordered to head it. Although Czerniakow was a member of the old council, he was not a well-known public figure among the Jews of Warsaw. Other members of the Judenrat in its first stage included the Zionist leader Apolinary Hartglas, Moshe Kerner of the General Zionist party, the ultra-Orthodox Agudat Israel leader Rabbi Yitzhak Meir Levin, and the Bund leader Samuel Zygielbojm. It was therefore quite natural for the Jewish population to regard the Judenrat at the beginning as a continuation of the Jewish Community Council. Indeed, most referred to it as the Kehillah (Community), all the more so since it had its offices on Grzybowska Street, in the same building as the former Kehillah.

Among the first challenges the Judenrat faced was its helplessness to resolve the tragic dilemmas confronting it on issues such as forced labor, the collection of large contributions, confiscation, and the indiscriminate arrest and execution of groups of Jews as retaliatory measures. In the course of time it appeared that random seizures of Jews by the Germans to perform forced labor would be replaced by an orderly procedure. The Judenrat proposed to the Germans that it should provide them with a fixed quota of men in place of the haphazard kidnappings that had brought Jewish life to an almost total standstill. Under this arrangement every Jew was assigned a fixed number of days per month for forced labor. Consequently the Judenrat, lacking the financial resources to cover the wages of the forced laborers, was in financial straits at all times.

The other framework in which Jews were allowed to remain active throughout the ghetto's existence was that of welfare and mutual assistance. The financial base for such operations consisted of funds accumulated by the American Jewish Joint Distribution Committee (JDC). But before long it became evident that the number of needy cases was growing and that an organization had to be created and properly equipped to meet the requirements of the entire Jewish population. The JDC-sponsored Jewish Mutual Aid Society (Zydowski Towarzystwo Opieki Spolecznej, ZTOS) lent assistance to 250,000 Jews during Passover in 1940. Its most important means of mass aid were its soup kitchens, which doled out a bowl of soup and a piece of bread to all comers. When this operation was at its height, more than 100 such soup kitchens existed in Jewish Warsaw. In October 1939, 188,611 portions of soup were provided; the figure for March 1940 was 1,986,263. From the middle of 1940 and especially 1942 on, the JDC faced enormous problems. After the United States entered the war it became illegal to ship

food and transfer funds to an enemy state. Officially, the Jewish welfare organizations were included in the main welfare council recognized by the German administration in the Generalgouvernement. Non-Jewish American organizations also extended relief and even insisted that needy Jews should also benefit from their assistance. Important instruments created by Jewish self-help, under the direction of the JDC, were the House Committees (Komitety Domowe). Such committees had been set up on an emergency basis during the September 1939 fighting, but Emmanuel Ringelblum and his associates felt that they could become a permanent feature for mutual help. The committees were staffed by volunteer activists, who developed into an important local leadership group. Their first task was to take care of the penniless tenants in their buildings, but they also set up kindergartens and youth clubs and arranged cultural activities.

The Jewish and Polish populations of Warsaw had little public contact with each other. Although not the capital of the Generalgouvernement, Warsaw was the capital of underground Poland. It was there that the underground military organizations were formed, political parties were clandestinely active, and the delegacy representing the Polish government-in-exile had its main office. Warsaw's Jews had ties with Poles on an individual basis, and certain Jewish political groups were in contact with their Polish counterparts; but no links of any sort were created between the Polish underground forces, the military and political branches of the Polish government-in-exile, and Jewish public bodies. No Jewish element became a recognized part of a Polish-sponsored underground body established by official Polish underground organizations. Nevertheless, the Polish heads of the Main Welfare Council took the terrible situation of the Jews into account in their distribution of aid.

In mid-November 1940 the Jewish ghetto in Warsaw, surrounded by a high wall, was sealed off. It was situated in the heart of the Jewish quarter, in the northern section of the city, and encompassed the Jewish-inhabited streets. The first attempt to set up a ghetto had been made by the SS in November 1939, but at the time the military governor, Gen. Karl Ulrich von Neuman-Neurode, put a stop to the plan. In February 1940 the official in charge of evacuation and relocation in the German district administration was ordered to draw up plans for the establishment of a ghetto. On 12 October 1940, the Day of Atonement, the Jews were informed of the decree establishing a ghetto. A few days later a map was published indicating the streets assigned to the ghetto area.

The construction of the wall surrounding the ghetto took many months, with the Judenrat obliged to defray the costs. Up to the very last day, the Jews did not know whether the ghetto would be open or closed. On 16 November the ghetto was officially sealed off, and thousands of Jews who had left their belongings on the other side of the wall no longer had access to them. The Germans had planned for 113,000 Poles to be evacuated from their homes and settled elsewhere and for 138,000 Jews to take their place. As soon as the ghetto was set up, a flow of refugees converged on it. Some 30 percent of the population of Warsaw was being packed into 2.4 percent of the city's area. According to German statistics, the density of the population in the ghetto was six or seven people to a room. The apartment buildings in the ghetto area were in poor condition and lacked sanitary facilities, and there were no lawns or trees in sight. Of Warsaw's 1,800 streets, no more than 73 were assigned to the ghetto. The ghetto wall was 3.5 meters high and topped by a barbed wire. Two thousand Christian-Jewish converts were also sent into the ghetto. One church was left open, under a priest of Jewish parentage, who, with the rest of his flock, was regarded as Jewish under fascist laws. The Nazis did not use the term *ghetto*, referring to it as the "Jewish quarter." The ghetto cut the Jews off from the rest of the world and put an end to any remaining legal and direct business ties with the Poles.

The number of persons employed by the Judenrat increased rapidly, and a 1,000-man Jewish police force was formed, which eventually increased to 2,000 persons. At its maximum size the Judenrat staff consisted of 6,000 people, compared to the 530 employed by the Jewish Community Council before the war. The daily food ration for Warsaw Jews provided 181 calories, about 25 percent of the Polish allotment and 8 percent of the nutritional value of the German ration. Consequently, death from starvation in the ghetto was common. As a survival mechanism, an economic structure was gradually created which sustained a thin upper stratum made up of smugglers of food into the ghetto and of valuables out to the "Aryan" side, and of skilled artisans who made deals with German enterprises. Pauperization and starvation, however, proceeded at an ever-growing rate.

The ghetto's ties with the outside world were handled by the Transferstelle (Transfer Office), a German authority in charge of the traffic of goods into and out of the ghetto. Only official food shipments into the ghetto and the products manufactured in the ghetto for clients on the outside passed through the Transferstelle. Most economic activities in the ghetto were illegal, and the ghetto economy was essentially an illegal operation made up of two basic elements: the smuggling of food and the fabrication of illegal goods inside the ghetto.

German involvement in the ghetto took a number of forms. The German authorities' main interest was to plunder Jewish property and to make use of Jewish expertise in certain fields. From the earliest stage of the occupation some Jews were employed in collecting scrap metal, feathers, and textiles. Later, growing numbers were dispatched to labor camps, where they were made to do back-breaking jobs and suffered from hunger, poor sanitary conditions, and grueling discipline.

German manufacturers appeared in the ghetto in the summer of 1941, having obtained authorization to operate in the Warsaw area. The most important of them was a German named Walther Toebben, a manufacturer of textile goods, who began his activities in the fall of 1941. The Judenrat, seeking to play a role in these operations, encouraged Jews to accept employment in German factories and formed a special department for this purpose. But as a rule the Jews preferred to work in places that manufactured goods for "illegal export," where they were treated better and where the pay was much higher. Smuggling was carried out through those buildings that were connected with buildings on the Aryan side, through camouflaged openings in the walls, and along subterranean canals. Smuggling on a small scale was also engaged in by children and many women, who at the risk of their lives crossed over to the Polish side in order to bring food back to their families. Hardly a day passed without people being caught and losing their lives, but this did not deter the smuggling organization and did not bring it to even a temporary halt. Attempts by the Germans to stop the smuggling completely met with the desperate resistance of human beings fighting for their lives.

Among the prohibitions that the Germans did not enforce fully was the ban on gatherings, which applied even to the privacy of homes. For a while the ban also specifically included public prayer services. This did not prevent Jews from holding daily services in private dwellings, and on Jewish festivals thousands still attended prayer services. In the spring of 1941 the ban was abolished and the synagogues were permitted to reopen. The Great Synagogue on Tlomacki Street was reopened in June 1941 with a festive ceremony.

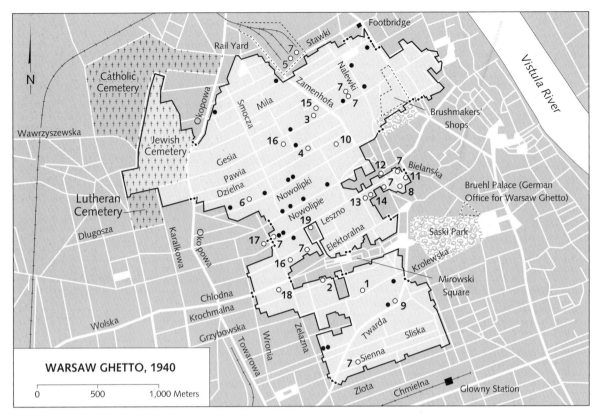

WARSAW GHETTO, 1940

0   500   1,000 Meters

— Ghetto Boundary, 15 November 1940:
   Wall with Barbed Wire on Top
⦂ Entrances, Gates to Ghetto
● Selected Ghetto Factories
○ Selected Features
1. Jewish Council (Judenrat)
2. Jewish Police
3. Gesiowka Prison
4. Pawiak Prison
5. Umschlagplatz

6. Hiding Place of Ringelblum Archive
7. Hospitals
8. The Great Synagogue
9. Nozjik Synagogue
10. Moriah Synagogue
11. ZTOS (Jewish Mutual Aid Society)
12. CENTOS (Federation of
    Associations in Poland for
    the Care of Orphans)
13. Office for Combatting Usury
    and Profiteering

14. ORT (Organization for
    Rehabilitation through Training)
15. Post Office
16. Center for Vocational Training
17. Labor Bureau (Arbeitsamt)
18. Korczak Orphanage
19. Courthouse (Tribunals)

From time to time the Judenrat chairman, Adam Czerniakow, asked the German authorities for permission to reopen the schools. In 1941 permission was granted to organize elementary school classes. The major educational effort, however, was an underground operation. Hundreds of clandestine classes at different levels were held in homes in the ghetto. Although regular schools were banned, the Judenrat was allowed to maintain the vocational training schools sponsored by the ORT (Institution for Vocational

Guidance and Training). In mid-1941, 2,454 students were attending such courses.

Cultural life in the ghetto was conducted by the underground organizations. The Idische Kultur Organizacje (Yiddish Culture Organization), a clandestine society for promoting Yiddish culture, sponsored literary evenings and special meetings to mark the anniversaries of noted Jewish writers. The members of Tekumah (Rebirth), another underground organization, studied the Hebrew language and Hebrew literature. The

A Passover Seder at 6 Leszno Street in the Warsaw ghetto. 22 April 1940

ghetto had clandestine libraries that circulated officially banned books. An 80-member symphony orchestra performed from a repertoire that included the works of the great German composers. Well-known writers and poets, including Itzhak Katzenelson, Israel Stern, Hillel Zeitlin, and Peretz Opoczynski, continued their work. Theatrical troupes gave performances before an audience consisting mostly of the ghetto's nouveaux riches, who wanted cheap entertainment that would help them forget the surrounding reality.

Underground activities by political circles and organizations had already begun around the time that the Germans entered Warsaw. Missing were the veteran and experienced Jewish leaders, who had left the city and the country. Nevertheless, after Warsaw was occupied, members of the youth movements and parties joined together and began to prepare plans of action. As time went on, the underground embarked on several courses of action, one of which was to provide assistance to persons who were in the most dire straits. The next step was to establish an underground press and to communicate with political elements outside the country.

German lack of interest in the underground activities and the secrecy observed by their Jewish agents in the ghetto enabled the underground, prior to the spring of 1942, to engage in a broad range of activities without the Germans' taking drastic steps to suppress them or to punish the participants. The underground press had two achievements: it provided the news-hungry ghetto population with reliable information on international issues and the war, and it raised issues that encouraged political awareness and an opposition to the Judenrat's policy. All parties from the prewar Jewish political scene were active in the ghetto underground. Especially prominent were the Bund, the Socialist Zionist party (Poale Zion), and the youth movements.

A unique and important enterprise created in the ghetto was the Ringelblum Archive, code-named Oneg Shabbos, which was initiated by the historian Emmanuel Ringelblum. The archive depended in large measure on the support of the public leaders and the underground organizations. The material collected by the Ringelblum Archive consisted of tens of thousands of pages—documents, notes, diaries, and a rich collection of underground newspapers. It is the most important documentary resource on the fate of the Jews under Nazi occupation in Warsaw and in Poland generally.

The Jewish youth movements and their leaders played a key role in the underground, particularly in the later stages—following the great deportation, during the months of preparation for the uprising, and during the Warsaw ghetto uprising itself. The Zionist and the pioneering movements constituted the driving force. In the ghetto the activities of the youth movements underwent a gradual change, as did their relative importance. Primarily they manifested a greater aptitude than other movements for adapting to the changing circumstances and for taking dynamic action when necessary. The leaders assembled in Warsaw, among them Mordechai Anielewicz, Yitzhak Zuckerman, Zivia Lubetkin, Josef Kaplan, and Israel Geller, through their keen political instincts and leadership qualities, had become more than heads of youth groups; they were acknowledged leaders of the underground.

The youth movements did not confine their activities to the local scene. The leadership extended its work to cover the undertakings of the different movements' branches and cells in all the ghettos and Jewish communities in occupied Poland. The maintenance of such a countrywide network was made possible by an organization of liaison officers, young men and women, using underground methods. These couriers, especially the women, used false identities, and they provided the link with isolated ghettos.

Prior to the stage in which mass killings of Jews were launched, no basic differences of activity existed among the political parties and youth movements in the underground. A drastic change in the relation between the component parts of the underground took place when the mass murders began. The first reports of mass murders were of the massacre at Ponary, near Vilna. At that point a new concept arose among the youth movements—that the Germans had embarked on the total destruction of the Jews and that therefore the Jews had no choice but to stand up and fight, even if this struggle offered no prospect of survival.

In March 1942, at a meeting of the Warsaw Jewish leaders, the youth movement sought to win agreement for the formation of an overall self-defense organization. The proposal was turned down. However, following the mass deportation from the Warsaw ghetto and the suicide of Judenrat chairman Czerniakow, the Judenrat's standing declined, as did its ability to function.

In the first few days of the great deportation, which began on 22 July 1942, the ghetto inhabitants streamed into the German factories ("shops") or into workshops that were under German protection; there, they thought, they would be safe from deportation. But during the first 10 days of the deportation alone, 65,000 Jews were taken from the ghetto. In the second phase, from 31 July to 14 August, the German forces and their accomplices took direct charge of the operation, with the Jewish police in the secondary role. The third phase of the deportation began on 15 August and ended on 6 September. At that point the deportation assumed the character of a total evacuation. The Germans and their accomplices conducted a manhunt, combing the streets and apartment houses, seizing everyone they found, looking into every corner, and taking little note of the papers and exemptions. All the victims caught were sent to the Treblinka death camp and killed in gas chambers. Simultaneously, from mid-August, individuals who had managed to escape from the Treblinka extermination camp (in the freight cars that carried out victims' clothing) succeeded in returning to the ghetto and reported on the fate in store for the deportees.

The final phase began on 6 September. The shops and the Judenrat were allotted a number of permits; 35,000 such permits were issued, meaning that the Germans intended to leave in the ghetto 10 percent of its pre-deportation population. The permit holders were assembled in a narrow street, where they had to pass through a final inspection and selection. In addition to the 35,000 with permits, another 25,000 or more managed to escape illegally by hiding in the ghetto. This was a new ghetto, consisting of three separate parts not contiguous with one another; the residents of one part could not enter another for social purposes, even after having worked there for hours. In effect, this was no longer a ghetto but a labor camp.

The Jews who were left, mostly women and young men, went through a great psychological trauma. As long as the deportations were going on, they had been in a constant state of tension, concentrating all their

A German soldier arrests an elderly Jewish man he discovered hiding in a bunker, presumably during the suppression of the Warsaw ghetto uprising. 19 April–16 May 1943

strength on one goal: survival. When the deportations came to a halt, they had time to take stock of their situation. It was clear from the experience of other ghettos that they had only a short time before another deportation would continue the physical liquidation of the remaining Jews. They were lonely and deeply troubled by a sense of guilt at having forsaken their dear ones and having failed to protect them. They were tormented by not having offered resistance, not having used force to defend themselves, and not having even raised a hand against the hated Jewish police. More and more of them said that they would not surrender to the Germans without a fight.

On 23 July, the day after the deportation was launched, a meeting was called of underground leaders and public figures close to the underground. There were those who argued that armed resistance would put the entire ghetto in jeopardy. Some put their faith in God; others pointed out that resistance offered no hope. On 28 July representatives of the Hashomer Hatzair, Dror, and Akiva Zionist youth movements held a meeting at which they decided to form the Jewish Fighting Organization (Zydowska Organizacja Bojowa, ZOB). A headquarters was set up, and it was decided to send a delegation to the Aryan side. Mordechai Anielewicz, who became the ZOB commander in its formative stage and the leader of the revolt, was absent from the meeting, having left Warsaw on a mission to the area of Zaglebie.

Although the organization was founded, it had no means at its disposal and had as yet to adopt a clear strategy on the way it would conduct the struggle. One of the ZOB's first steps was to publish and distribute leaflets informing the public of the fate of the deportees and what Treblinka stood for. The majority of the ghetto population did not seem to take kindly to the publication of these leaflets, regarding them as a provocative act that would give the Germans a pretext for the total liquidation of the ghetto.

The underground then tried to acquire weapons

and draw up a plan of action. Attempts to establish ties with the Armia Krajowa (Home Army), the main Polish military underground organization, did not succeed. During the month of September several leaders of the ZOB were caught and murdered, and a deep sense of frustration set in among the members. When the wave of deportations came to an end, the ZOB began operating under different conditions. Anielewicz returned to the ghetto and assumed a leading role in the organization's activities. Contacts were established with the Home Army and the Communist underground, which supplied the ZOB with a limited number of arms. Most of the ZOB's weapons, however, were purchased from middlemen who had bought or stolen them from the Germans.

In addition to the ZOB, the Jewish National Committee (Zydowski Komitet Narodowy) was formed, composed of prominent public figures who gave the ZOB its support. The Bund was not prepared to join a public body together with Zionists, but it agreed to establish a joint coordinating committee with the national committee. During that period another organization came into being in the ghetto under Revisionist Zionist auspices. The Zionist Betar movement and the Revisionist underground did not integrate into the ZOB, and their members set up their own fighting organization, the Jewish Military Union (Zydowski Zwiazek Wojskowy, ZZB).

On 18 January 1943 a second wave of deportations began. This time Jews who were ordered to assemble in the courtyards of their apartment buildings refused to comply and went into hiding. The first column that the Germans managed to round up in the early hours, consisting of some 1,000 people, offered up a different kind of resistance. A group of fighters, led by Anielewicz and armed with pistols, deliberately infiltrated the column, and when the signal was given, the fighters stepped out and engaged the German escorts in hand-to-hand fighting. The column dispersed, and news of the fight soon became common knowledge. The whole action lasted only a few days, by which time the Germans had rounded up about 5,000–6,000 Jews from all parts of the ghetto; after the events of the first day hardly any Jews responded to the German order to report.

The fact that the action was halted after a few days, and that the Germans had managed to seize no more than 10 percent of the ghetto population, was regarded by Jews and Poles alike as a German defeat. It is now known that the Germans had not intended to liquidate the entire ghetto at that time and were actually carrying out Himmler's order to remove 8,000 Jews from the ghetto to reduce its population. Nonetheless, these deportations had a decisive influence on the ghetto's last months. The Judenrat and the Jewish police lost whatever influence they still had; the fighting organizations were the groups that were obeyed by the population. The Jewish resistance also impressed the Poles, and they now provided more aid to the Jewish fighters. The ghetto as a whole was engaged in feverish preparations for the expected deportations. The general population concentrated on preparing bunkers. Many believed that resistance could save the remaining Jews. Much thought went into the planning of the sophisticated entries and exits of the subterranean hiding places. Bunkers and wooden bunks were installed in them, and air circulation was provided for, as well as electricity. Water, food, and medicines to last for months were stockpiled.

The final liquidation of the ghetto began on Monday, 19 April 1943, the eve of Passover. This time the deportation did not come as a surprise. The Jews had been warned, and they were ready. The Germans had a substantial military force on the alert, which entered the ghetto in two sections; it was met with armed resistance and was forced to retreat. On that first day the Germans became aware of the kind of uprising they were facing. The central ghetto, which had a population of more than 30,000, was completely empty; not a soul was to be seen on the streets or in the buildings, except for a small Jewish police unit and a handful of Judenrat members. No Jews could be rounded up for deportation, and the freight cars that had been brought in and were waiting in the Umschlagplatz had to remain empty. In the first three days street battles were fought, but the systematic burning of the ghetto, building by building, forced the fighters to abandon their positions, take refuge in the bunkers, and use a different method. The ghetto had now gone underground. The air temperature reached 38 degrees Celsius, and the food was spoiled by the heat; the water was warm, and it stank. The Jews inside took off their clothes; they could hardly breathe or talk and were on the verge of going mad. Even so, they would not surrender. Under cover of darkness they tried to move to bunkers where the conditions were slightly better, although those too were bound to suffer the same fate and become uninhabitable within a few days.

In the second week of the uprising the bunkers were the main arena of resistance. In this fight the Germans

Jews captured during the suppression of the Warsaw ghetto uprising are marched to the Umschlagplatz for deportation. The original German caption reads, "To the Umschlagplatz." The woman at the head of the column, on the left, is Yehudit Neyer (born Tolub). She is holding on to the right arm of her mother-in-law. The child is the daughter of Yehudit and Avraham Neyer, a member of the Bund, who can be seen just behind the little girl. Of the four, only Avraham survived the war. 19 April–16 May 1943

had to struggle for each bunker. By throwing hand grenades or by pumping tear gas into bunkers, in the end they compelled the Jews to emerge.

On 16 May, Gen. Jürgen Stroop, who had supervised the operation, announced that the *Grossaktion* had been completed. To celebrate the victory he ordered Warsaw's Great Synagogue, which was situated then outside the ghetto, to be burned. In his daily dispatch Stroop made it a point to brag that "the Jewish quarter of Warsaw no longer exists." The fact is, however, that even after 16 May some Jews were still hiding out in bunkers. There were also reports of armed clashes taking place amid the ruins of the ghetto. Even a year later, during the Polish uprising in Warsaw, launched in August 1944, individual Jews were still found in the labyrinth of the ghetto's bunkers.

In his final report on the military campaign against the ghetto revolt, Stroop provided the following data:

"Of the total of 56,065 Jews who were seized, 7,000 perished during the course of the *Grossaktion* inside the former Jewish quarter; in the deportation 6,929 were exterminated, which adds up to 13,929 Jews destroyed. In addition to the 56,065, another 5,000–6,000 lost their lives in explosions or fires." Stroop's figures are exaggerated. He also mentions that German casualties were 16 killed and 85 wounded; these figures do not tally with the daily casualty reports submitted during the fighting. Most other sources believed that the German losses were much higher.

In the last few months of its existence some 20,000 Jews left the ghetto to seek refuge on the Polish side. A special organization, the Council for Aid to the Jews, which used the code name Zegota, was created by the underground Polish political parties within the Polish underground movement, in conjunction with members of the Jewish underground in hiding. A few thousand Jews benefited from its assistance. In Poland it was more difficult to help Jews than in other countries; offering shelter to Jews was punishable by death. But the proliferation of extortionists was the main reason that Jews were not able to go into hiding. Extortionists were Poles who out of greed or for some other reason made it their business to turn Jews over to the Germans. Yet in addition to the heroic "righteous among the nations," who helped Jews out of humanitarian motives, quite a few Poles sheltered Jews for money. No exact data are available on the number of Jews who saved themselves by hiding or posing as Poles. Many fell in battle or were killed during the Polish uprising, in which Jews took an active part.

The revolt in the ghetto had a great reverberation among the remaining Jews of Poland, among the non-Jews in the country, and throughout Europe. Even while the war was still in progress, the story of the Warsaw ghetto uprising became a legend that was passed on, with awe and emotion, as an event of rare historical significance.

Warsaw Jews who were forced out of the bunkers or otherwise fell into German hands during the uprising were not all murdered on the spot. Nor were all the people transported from the Umschlagplatz in April and May 1943 taken straight to their deaths. Transports made up of Jews from the shops area, where resistance had not been so fierce, were sent to Poniatowa and Trawniki. Transports from the central ghetto had Majdanek or Budzyn as their destination. Most of those Jews were killed in early November 1943 in the so-called *Erntefest* (Harvest Festival) murder operation. Several thousand Jews taken to the Majdanek concentration camp were deported, after a short time, to Auschwitz and to labor camps in the western parts of occupied Poland. When all the selections, transfers, and evacuations were over, no more than 1,000–2,000 of the Warsaw Jews had survived.

Israel Gutman

Weissmandel, Michael Dov Ber (1903–56) Orthodox Jewish leader in Slovakia. Rabbi Weissmandel and Gisi Fleischmann negotiated with Adolf Eichmann's emissaries in the belief that the deportations of Jews would be stopped or at least slowed down if "world Jewry" paid the SS officials a large ransom. In the spring of 1944 Weissmandel participated in the dissemination to the Western Allies of the Vrba-Wetzler Report, which described in greater and more precise detail the operations, location, and structure of Auschwitz, and pleaded for its bombing. See EUROPA PLAN

Westerbork Dutch transit camp in the northeastern Netherlands, established in 1939 by the Dutch government to house Jewish refugees. In 1941, after the German invasion, Westerbork became a concentration camp. Although almost 100,000 Jews passed through Westerbork on their way to Auschwitz-Birkenau and other extermination camps in Poland, a more permanent group of around 2,000 remained in the camp. Anne Frank and her family, after their arrest in August 1944, were briefly interned at Westerbork before being deported to the East.

Wiesel, Elie (1928–) Novelist and educator. Born in the Romanian town of Sighet, which became part of Hungary prior to World War II, Wiesel and his family were sent to Auschwitz in 1944, where his mother and the youngest of his three sisters were gassed upon arrival. He and his father were then moved to Buchenwald, where his father died. His experiences of deportation and the camps are the material of his memoir *Night* (1958). Other books include *Town beyond the Wall* (1962), *Souls on Fire* (1972), and *The Fifth Son* (1983). His efforts to promote remembrance of the Holocaust led to the adoption of Holocaust materials in the curricula of many schools in the United States. Wiesel was awarded the Congressional Medal of Honor in 1985 and the Nobel Prize for Peace in 1986.

Wiesenthal, Simon (1908–) Collector of Holocaust documentation and hunter of Nazi war criminals. A Polish national, Wiesenthal spent most of the war in the concentration camps Plaszow, Gross-Rosen, Buchenwald, and Mauthausen, where he was liberated by American soldiers. Trained as an architect, he went to work for the war crimes unit of the U.S. army and in 1947 established and headed the Jewish Documentation Center in Linz, Austria, to trace Nazis suspected of war crimes. The Linz office closed in 1954, but the center reopened in Vienna in 1964 in response to renewed interest in hunting war criminals. Wiesenthal investigated and helped bring to justice many war criminals, including Franz Stangl, the commandant of the Treblinka and Sobibor death camps, and Karl Silberbauer, the police officer who arrested Anne Frank and her family. In 1977 the Simon Wiesenthal Center for Holocaust Studies in Los Angeles was established in his honor. Wiesenthal, who lives in Vienna, was

The so-called Boulevard of Misery in Westerbork, before the rail spur into the camp was laid in mid- to late 1942. 1941–June 1942

awarded the United States' Congressional Gold Medal (1980) and Presidential Medal of Freedom (2000) and France's Légion d'Honneur (1986).

Wirth, Christian (1895–1944) SS official who was instrumental in the development and administration of the so-called euthanasia program. Wirth was sent to Lublin in 1941 to set up the first euthanasia center outside Germany. He later supervised the killing of Jews at the Belzec, Sobibor, and Treblinka extermination camps. See EUTHANASIA

Wisliceny, Dieter (1911–48) SS official, close collaborator of Adolf Eichmann's, organizer of the deportation of the Slovak, Greek, and Hungarian Jews. Wisliceny accepted the first installment of the ransom in the Europa Plan and was involved in the "blood for trucks" proposal in Budapest. He was a witness for the prosecution at the 1945–46 Nuremberg war crimes trial. In 1948 Wisliceny was sentenced to death in Czechoslovakia for war crimes and was executed. His testimony was used posthumously in the 1961 trial of Adolf Eichmann. See EUROPA PLAN

Wittenberg, Yitzhak (1907–43) Head of the Jewish armed resistance in the Vilna ghetto. A Communist, Wittenberg was betrayed by a fellow party member and turned himself over to the Jewish police under pressure from the Judenrat and nonpartisan Jews in the ghetto. He committed suicide after his arrest.

World Jewish Congress (WJC) International Jewish defense organization, in operation since 1936. An early and vehement opponent of nazism, the congress organized anti-Nazi rallies in the United States and brought pressure to bear on the government to aid European Jews. Rabbi Stephen Wise and later Nahum Goldman chaired the organization. Gerhart Riegner, whose 1942 dispatch about the Final Solution attracted American attention to the plight of European Jews, was among the representatives of the WJC in Europe during the war. See RIEGNER TELEGRAM

Yad Vashem The Holocaust Martyrs' and Heroes' Remembrance Authority, or Yad Vashem, is the official Israeli national institution for commemoration of the Holocaust. It is situated on Har Hazikkaron (Memorial Hill) in Jerusalem. The law empowering this national authority defined its function as follows: "To gather into the homeland all commemorative material regarding members of the Jewish people who fell, fought, and rebelled against the Nazi enemy and German satellites; to establish a memorial for them and for the communities, organizations, and institutions that were destroyed because they were Jewish; and to perpetuate the memory of the righteous among the nations."

The name Yad Vashem derives from Isaiah 56:5, "And to them will I give in my house and within my walls a memorial [*yad vashem*, "monument and name"] . . . that shall not be cut off," which promises everlasting memory to those who attach themselves to God. Yad Vashem's activities proceed along two main tracks. First, the institution devotes itself to research and education—amassing documentary and oral evidence, fostering academic studies and publications, and infusing the theme of the Holocaust into educational and cultural settings. Second, it maintains on Memorial Hill a commemorative landscape sacred to Israeli society.

Students of the Holocaust and teachers of its history have at their disposal the Yad Vashem Archives, which house some 50 million pages of documents and testimonies in a variety of languages, over 100,000 photographs, and more than 600 documentary and feature films. Adjoining the archives is a library containing more than 80,000 titles, mainly studies of the Holocaust, World War II, fascism, nazism, and the rise of modern antisemitism. The Hall of Names is the repository for some 3 million "pages of testimony" (*dapei ed*), which commemorate the names and biographic details of Jews who perished in the Holocaust. The pages of testimony are filled out by family, friends, or neighbors and serve as symbolic "tombstones" (*mazevot*).

Since its founding in 1953 Yad Vashem has engaged in multifaceted research under the direction of an academic advisory board, whose members are drawn from the faculties of Israeli universities. Its publications include *Yad Vashem Studies*, which has appeared in Hebrew and English since 1957; conference papers; collected documents and personal memoirs; and the Dr. Janusz Korczak Book Series for Youth. Among the publication department's major projects are the bibliography of the Holocaust, published in conjunction with YIVO, New York; *Pinkas Hakehillot* (Record Books of Jewish Communities), a multivolume geographical and historical lexicon of the European Jewish communities from their founding to their destruction during the Holocaust; and the *Encyclopedia of the Holocaust* (1983), edited by Israel Gutman.

Since 1973 an education department at Yad Vashem has offered courses for Israeli and Diaspora educators and pupils, as well as Israeli soldiers. Presently operating as the Holocaust Teaching Department, it publishes the monthly *Bishvil Hazikkaron* (In Memoriam) in cooperation with the Hebrew University, the Vidal Sassoon International Center for the Study of Antisemitism, the Joint Authority for Jewish-Zionist Education, and the Jewish Agency. In addition, in 1993 the International Center for the Study of the Holocaust was launched at Yad Vashem. Among those who have served as directors of Yad Vashem are Ben-Zion Dinur (1953–59) and Yitzhak Arad (1972–94). Avner Shalev currently holds this post.

The idea of establishing a memorial in Palestine to Jewish Holocaust victims was first broached even before the end of World War II. The father of the idea, and the driving force behind the struggle to bring it to fruition, was Mordechai Shenhavi, an energetic public activist and a founding member of the Hashomer Hatzair youth movement. The Austrian-born Shenhavi emigrated to Palestine in 1919. He joined Kibbutz Mishmar Haemek and served as a representative to the National Institutions of the Yishuv (Jewish community in Palestine). He died in the kibbutz in 1983.

As early as September 1942 Shenhavi submitted to the directorate of the Jewish National Fund (JNF) a document titled "An Outline for a National Project," which set forth a detailed plan for the commemoration of the victims of the Nazi atrocities. The proposal did not confine itself to a general description of the idea; it also included estimated construction costs, as well as suggestions for potential sources of funding—the sale of tombstones and tree planting by persons wishing to honor the memory of relatives who perished in the Holocaust. Shenhavi envisioned a national park, at least 20 hectares in area, to be located in the heart of one of the Jewish agricultural centers, either in the Huleh Valley north of Lake Kinneret or in the Jezreel Valley near Haifa. The plan called for the site's focal point to be a monumental building—the Missing Persons' Pavilion—designated to house a complete registry of names, both of Jewish victims of the Nazi regime worldwide and of Jewish soldiers who had fought in the war. Shenhavi proposed in addition that the site incorporate pavilions devoted to the history of Jewish heroism throughout the ages; a symbolic cemetery for Holocaust victims and an ordinary cemetery for local and foreign Jews; hotel rooms and a conference center; and playing fields and sports centers to host the annual Jewish Youth Olympics. Despite the fact that news of the Nazi atrocities in the death camps, and of Jewish ghetto and camp uprisings, had already received extensive publicity worldwide during the course of 1943, the JNF directorate failed to adopt Shenhavi's plan. It was shelved for three years.

On 3 February 1945, three months after the International Committee of the World Jewish Congress met in New York to discuss the rescue and rehabilitation of Jewish displaced persons in Europe, Baruch Zuckerman, chairman of the governing council of the World Jewish Congress, and Dr. Jacob Helman, the congress's Latin American representative, submitted to the board of directors their plan for a memorial to the victims of the Nazis, to be erected on Mount Carmel in Palestine. The plan called for the memorial that would incorporate special rooms where the names of all the victims would be preserved on strips of parchment; a boxcar and a gas chamber; a monument to the unknown victim; and a room specifically dedicated to the ghettos. Helman and Zuckerman further suggested that "every person who counts himself as a member of the Jewish nation" be called upon to contribute a brick to the main memorial monument, and that 14 Nissan, the Hebrew date of the outbreak of the 1943 Warsaw ghetto uprising, be chosen as a day of commemoration, to be marked by special ceremonies. As chairmen for this project of "eternal commemoration," they put forward the names of Chaim Weizmann, a leader of the World Zionist Organization and later president of Israel; Rabbi Stephen S. Wise, a leader of the Zionist movement in the United States; Rabbi Isaac Herzog, chief rabbi of Palestine and later Israel; and Albert Einstein, the Nobel Prize–winning physicist.

The placing of the Helman-Zuckerman commemorative plan on the Jewish public agenda spurred Mordechai Shenhavi to present to the Jewish National Institutions in Palestine an updated plan of his own, which he made public under the title "Yad Vashem Foundation in Memory of the Lost Jewries of Europe—Outline of a Plan for the Commemoration of the Diaspora." Consequently the Jewish National Council adopted Shenhavi's idea and presented the plan at the first postwar meeting of the Zionist Actions Committee in London in August 1945.

A decision emerged from that meeting to delegate the responsibility for the commemoration of the Holocaust to the Jewish National Council, an assignment it fulfilled until the founding of the state. In 1946 a special committee headed by David Remez, a leading figure of the Second Aliyah (wave of immigration) and later Israel's first transportation minister, developed a proposal that included an impressive architectural plan. The committee's plan distinguishes for the first time between two focal points of commemoration—tragic destruction and heroic resistance. "In founding this monument here in Palestine," the committee declared, "we will base it on two pillars: the pillar of valor and the pillar of holy martyrdom."

Two pavilions were planned: a Hall of Remembrance, whose Holy Arks would house the names of the Jewish communities, towns, and people destroyed by the Nazis, and a Hall of Heroism, which would display the names of all the Jewish participants in military campaigns against the Nazis and their collaborators. The plan also called for the erection of a monument, an "eternal light," to commemorate the 6 million Jews killed by the Nazis and the acts of heroism, copies of which were to be placed in every Jewish cemetery. The approach to the Hall of Remembrance was envisioned as being through "the field of Europe," an enclosure shaped like the European continent and delineating its geographic and political features, on which each and every village or town that had had a Jewish community was to be indicated. The second pavilion, the Hall of Heroism, which was to be visible opposite the first, was intended to highlight the role of 1.5 million Jewish soldiers who served in any of the anti-Nazi military forces and Jewish volunteers from Palestine. The visitor would exit through the "field of the homeland," to be shaped like Palestine and to mark all its Jewish settlements as a manifestation of the Zionist achievement, in contrast to the destruction represented by the "field of Europe."

The founding meeting of Yad Vashem was held in Jerusalem on 1 June 1947. Seven weeks later, on 13–14 July, a conference on the theme "The Study of the Holocaust and Resistance in Our Time" was held at the Mount Scopus campus of the Hebrew University in Jerusalem, at the joint initiative of Yad Vashem and the university's Institute for Jewish Studies. By then, the JNF had already allocated the ridge of Har Haruhot near Neve Ilan, about 13 kilometers west of Jerusalem, as the designated commemorative site. Both the JNF and the Jewish Foundation Fund (Keren Hayesod) refrained, however, from undertaking fundraising activities on the project's behalf, for fear that a special campaign for Yad Vashem would jeopardize their current funding. Bureaucratic stumbling blocks and the outbreak of the War of Independence in November 1947, which made Har Haruhot a border point with Jordan, caused an indefinite delay in implementation of the plan.

In the summer of 1949, with the war's end and the signing of the cease-fire agreements, efforts to found Yad Vashem were renewed. In April 1951 the Knesset designated 27 Nissan as a memorial day for the Holocaust and named it Day of the Holocaust and the Ghettos' Revolt (Yom Hashoah Vemered Hagetaot). At the same time a special government-appointed committee, initially directed mainly at the passage of legislation conferring recognition on Jewish Holocaust victims as citizens of the state of Israel, was convened to

The Hall of Remembrance at Yad Vashem. 1960

investigate the issue; it was also raised at the 23rd Zionist Congress held in the summer of 1951. When consultations with jurists worldwide led to the conclusion that such a conferral of citizenship lacked any legal precedent or standing, the thrust of activity now shifted to the establishment of a national authority to oversee all Holocaust-related matters.

On 12 May 1953 the minister of education and culture, Ben-Zion Dinur, presented the proposed Holocaust and Heroism Remembrance (Yad Vashem) Law to the Knesset. It received final approval on 19 August, thereby establishing the Martyrs' and Heroes' Remembrance Authority. The authority's goals were to initiate and oversee commemorative projects; to collect, investigate, and publish all testimony concerning the Holocaust and resistance and to impart its conclusions to the public; to secure the observance of Martyrs' and Heroes' Remembrance Day in Israel and the Diaspora; and to confer honorary Israeli citizenship on the "righteous among the nations" (non-Jews who rescued Jews from the Nazis) in recognition of their merit.

A year later Memorial Hill in Jerusalem, located near Mount Herzl and the national military cemetery, was officially designated as the site of Yad Vashem. On 29 July 1954 the cornerstone was laid for the building that since its completion in 1957 has housed the administration, the library, and the archives of the memorial.

In the summer of 1956 the directors of Yad Vashem conferred with architects and intellectuals in an attempt to develop a concept for the landscape and building design of the proposed site. They did not succeed in coming up with a master plan but agreed that the site should consist of three elements: a symbolic tomb for the victims, a historical museum, and a synagogue. The first goal was the construction of the Ohel Yizkor (Hall of Remembrance), which was designated as the official site for commemorative ceremonies for Holocaust victims. Designed by Aryeh Elhanani, Aryeh Sharon, and Benjamin Idelson, it was dedicated in April 1961. From the outside the building appears to be a large cube with two heavy iron gates; it rests on huge basalt stones girded by a cement strip. Light barely penetrates through a small opening at the top of the pyramidal interior space; the opening also provides an outlet for the voices of prayer and the smoke emitted by the ritual *ner tamid,* or eternal flame. The floor is paved with black tiles engraved in white letters with the names of 22 concentration and extermination camps. The ashes of tens of thousands of Jews who perished in the camps are interred in the center.

Another focal site at Yad Vashem is the Historical Museum, which had its inception in 1956 as a small exhibit in the basement of the administration building and later moved to the ground floor of the Hall of Remembrance. In 1973 the museum doubled in size and a new chronological-thematic exhibition format was introduced. Visual and textual documentation combined with artifacts and brief explanatory notes to tell the story from the Nazis' rise to power through the first postwar years. The auditorium, synagogue, and art museum, built in 1982, are located nearby. The art museum displays works by survivors, composed both during and after the Holocaust, and works by other artists on themes related to the Holocaust.

The approach to the Historical Museum is via the Avenue of the Righteous Among the Nations, a monument to non-Jews who risked their lives to save Jews

during the Nazi period. The avenue, lined by carobs, was dedicated in 1962; Oskar Schindler, the German industrialist who saved 1,100 Jews, was among the first of the Righteous to plant a tree there. Some 2,000 have been planted, and the number of Righteous recognized by Yad Vashem has reached more than 16,000.

In 1968, to mark the 25th anniversary of the Warsaw ghetto uprising, the Pillar of Heroism, made by Buki Schwartz, was erected. The stainless-steel column soars to a height of 21 meters from the middle of a courtyard surrounded by images of fallen walls. In 1975 a replica of Nathan Rapoport's Warsaw Ghetto Monument, which was unveiled in Warsaw in 1948, was set at the entrance to the Historical Museum, opposite Warsaw Ghetto Square. It serves as the venue for the national commemoration ceremony on Martyrs' and Heroes' Remembrance Day.

Forty years after the end of World War II, in 1985, the Soldiers, Partisans, and Ghetto Fighters Monument, by Bernie Fink, was erected to mark the anniversary. The monument, nearly 6 meters tall and situated in a grove, is composed of six black granite blocks, each weighing more than 22 metric tons. The stones, whose faces are hexagonal, are laid in such a way that the internal angles between them form a Star of David through which the sky is visible; a steel blade bisects the space.

The Children's Memorial, designed by Moshe Safdie and dedicated to the memory of the estimated 1–1.5 million Jewish children who perished in the Holocaust, was unveiled in 1987. The memorial is divided into two sections. The upper section, located atop a hill, consists of four rows of 20 white limestone pillars with broken apexes arranged in descending order of height. The lower section, which is underground, is reached via a corridor that leads to a dark chamber lit by five candles, set in the center of the hall, whose light is reflected by mirrors on the walls, floors, and ceiling. In the background voices intone the names, ages, and birthplaces of the murdered children. The exit, situated opposite the entrance, leads out onto a hill overlooking the mountains and the forests. In the artist's conception this movement "symbolizes the return to life and a hopeful future."

The largest monument at Yad Vashem is the Valley of the Communities, by Lipa Yahalom and Dan Zur, a memorial to the thousands of European Jewish communities destroyed by the Nazis. Dedicated in 1992, the Valley of the Communities covers an area of more than 6,000 square meters and is situated between two hilltops. It is designed as a huge maze excavated from rock, and the names of annihilated towns and villages are engraved on its walls, which are modeled on the contours of the prewar map of Europe. The House of Communities (Beit Hakehillot), a center for the study of the history of the Jewish communities, is positioned in the heart of the valley.

In 1991 the Polish government presented Yad Vashem with a boxcar that had been used to transport Jews to the extermination camps. Three years later Moshe Safdie made the boxcar the centerpiece of his Memorial to the Deportees (1994) by mounting it on a suspension bridge near a train platform to symbolize the final journey in airless, overcrowded compartments that millions of Jews were forced to make before their deaths.

In 1996 the Holocaust Martyrs' and Heroes' Remembrance Authority embarked on a comprehensive plan to renovate the memorial and museum. The project, called Yad Vashem 2001, includes the construction of a new archives building; the computerization of Yad Vashem's documentation system; the establishment of an International School for Holocaust Studies; the construction of a new entrance plaza and Visitors' Center, designed by Moshe Safdie; and the expansion and refurbishment of the museum complex, also under Safdie's direction.

The idea behind the new entryway to Yad Vashem is to help visitors make the transition between the mundane and familiar outside world and the sanctified space within the memorial complex. The upper floor of the two-story Visitors' Center is meant to suggest a *sukkah*—an open shelter where Jews eat meals during the fall festival of Sukkot—and will afford a panoramic view from atop Memorial Hill. A series of hollow stone columns supporting a trellislike roof will be bathed in light penetrating from above.

Upon exiting the building, visitors will follow the Avenue of the Righteous Among the Nations to the new Historical Museum building. The elongated, linear structure, with more than 930 square meters of exhibition space, dramatically cuts into the hillside, thus symbolizing the chasm created by the Holocaust. The museum galleries are arrayed along the 175-meter spine of the building. The entrance and the exit cantilever from the hillside. Most of the interior is underground, and light filtering down lends an atmosphere of mystery and continuity. The central section is illuminated through an impressive atrium. From there visitors are led to the Hall of Names, the symbolic resting place of the millions of Jews who perished in the Holocaust. The design of the hall, crowned by a triangular roof, will create a sanctuary for quiet reflection and remembrance. The museum complex will also have a learning and information center, which will house, among other resources, the master tapes of interviews with tens of thousands of Holocaust survivors filmed by Steven Spielberg's Survivors of the Shoah Visual History Foundation.

Yad Vashem, by its location in Jerusalem, the capital of Israel, near the national military cemetery and at the foot of Mount Herzl, the burial site of Israeli statesmen, gives expression to the centrality of the Holocaust in Israeli collective consciousness. The symbolic burial of Holocaust victims in the Holy Land both ensured the future resurrection of the Jewish people and constructed the state of Israel as an antidote to the Nazi cabal to exterminate European Jewry. The themes of rebirth and heroism served as cornerstones in the construction of Yad Vashem's commemorative landscape. Since its founding Yad Vashem has established its role as a leading international authority on the Holocaust, and it has become a sacred space to which almost 2 million Israelis and foreign visitors make pilgrimage annually.

Mooli Brog

Yishuv   The pre-statehood Jewish community in Palestine, known as the Yishuv, played a unique role during the Holocaust years because of the historical status and the symbolic value of the land of Israel for the Jewish people. The Yishuv's elite regarded itself as the vanguard of the nation. A large portion of the Jews who had immigrated to Palestine in the 1930s had a personal involvement, through family and friends, in the events in occupied Europe during the war. Furthermore, as the only autonomous Jewish community, the Yishuv enjoyed a degree of political freedom of action and independent facilities. Its leaders, including Chaim Weizmann and David Ben-Gurion, were the only true Jewish leadership in the free world, in the sense that they were empowered to make decisions of state for a Jewish community.

Three factors—the foundation of the state of Israel three years after the war, Israel's central place in the Jewish world, and Israel's claim to be the collective heir of those who perished in the Holocaust—have turned the spotlight on the Yishuv's behavior at the time of the Nazi persecution and murder of the European Jews. The Yishuv may also be seen, however, as no more than an isolated community of 500,000 Jews, encircled by hostile Arabs, subordinate to and dependent on the British Mandatory regime for its security, and living on financial support from abroad. Under such circumstances the Yishuv could hardly have been expected to live up to its ambitions. Both approaches are valid. It is impossible to treat Palestinian Jewry merely as one of the many other communities in the free world. Yet it would be foolish and anachronistic to attribute to the Yishuv the capacities of its successor, the state of Israel, and to judge it accordingly.

Until 1933 the Zionist enterprise was primarily a social and political experiment unconnected with the problems of most Diaspora Jews. But the Nazis' rise to power in Germany changed its standing and transformed it into a place of mass refuge. Between 1933 and 1937 Palestine absorbed more Jewish refugees than any country, the United States included. Yet the growing distress in Europe, the outbreak of the Arab revolt in 1936, and the subsequent restrictions on immigration imposed by Britain hampered the Yishuv's ability to confront the crisis of European Jewry. In 1938–39 its contribution to alleviating the refugees' plight thus diminished both in absolute numbers and in comparison with that of other countries, particularly Great Britain and the United States.

The principal political goal of the Zionist leadership during those years was to preserve the linkage between the catastrophe in Europe and the Palestine question. The Jewish national home in Palestine, granted by the Balfour Declaration in 1917 and approved by the international community, should have been the solution to the breakdown of European Jewry. Under Arab pressures and the threat of a global war, British policy strove for the opposite: to separate the two problems and to find alternative areas for Jewish emigration. After the promulgation of the Nuremberg racial laws in the fall of 1935, the non-Zionist Jewish organizations in the West gradually gave priority to seeking other havens, rejecting the Zionist claim for the exclusiveness of Palestine. The split between Zionists and non-Zionists widened, to the detriment of all. Unless efforts were linked with Palestine, the Yishuv was indifferent to endeavors to defend emancipation and to ameliorate the Jews' lot. Meanwhile American and British Jews gave preference to the refugees' prob-

lems rather than the Zionist struggle. Both efforts failed.

David Ben-Gurion, who was largely responsible for creating this breach late in 1935, realized its consequences only when the American Zionists refused to sustain his concept of the struggle against the British white paper of May 1939, which severely restricted Jewish immigration and purchases of land in Palestine. At the 21st Zionist Congress in Geneva in August 1939, the American Zionist activist Abba Hillel Silver told Ben-Gurion that the Yishuv was incapable of battling the white paper alone, yet that American Jewry would not involve itself in an open clash with Britain, which was the only power ready to do something for the European Jews. Aware of his previous mistake, Ben-Gurion devoted his energies during the next three years to bridging this gap and securing the backing of American and British Jews for his political plans.

Members of the Yishuv wait on the beach in Tel Aviv for newly arrived immigrants to disembark from the *Tiger Hill*, an illegal refugee ship that sailed from Romania with 1,417 passengers. 1 September 1939

His efforts culminated in the adoption of the Biltmore program in May 1942.

The resolutions of the American Zionists' conference at the Biltmore Hotel in New York were a compromise between the Zionist and non-Zionist prewar stances. They provided both for reinstituting emancipation in Europe after the war and for creating a Jewish "commonwealth" (later "state") in Palestine for those Jews who would not or could not reconstruct their lives in the liberated countries. Yet the Biltmore resolutions were anachronistic. They offered an answer to the circumstances of the late 1930s but failed to respond to the profound change that had taken place since the Nazis had begun the execution of the Final Solution. For the majority of European Jews, the Biltmore declaration was already inapplicable when it was adopted.

The news about the systematic mass murders in Europe, which had been disseminated a few months after Biltmore, seemed to ruin the program and shatter the entire Zionist policy. The leadership's embarrassment was best (though naively) described by Bernard Joseph, the director of the Jewish Agency's political department. Following a meeting with journalists, who had urged him to arouse public opinion and told him of their efforts to mobilize their colleagues around the world, Joseph noted in his diary: "I warned them about publishing exaggerated figures of Jewish victims, for if we announce that millions of Jews have been slaughtered by the Nazis, we will justifiably be asked where the millions of Jews are for whom we claim Palestine should provide a home after the war ends."

During the first half of the war the Yishuv was preoccupied with its own survival in new circumstances: the political defeat imposed by the promulgation of the white paper in May 1939; the subsequent domestic controversies over the means to fight the new British policy; the unavoidable cessation of immigration; a severe economic crisis; the fear of a new Arab revolt; and the menace of an Axis invasion. This danger showed itself three times: following France's surrender to Germany in June–July 1940; in the wake of Britain's defeats in the Western Desert, Greece, and Crete in the spring of 1941; and after the fall of Tobruk and Rommel's advance on El Alamein in June–July 1942. These events distracted the Yishuv from anti-Jewish actions in occupied Europe; it regarded the occasional press reports about sporadic pogroms and massacres as by-

products of war that would be stanched by the ultimate victory.

The first news about the actions of the *Einsatzgruppen* (mobile killing units) in the rear of the advancing German army in the Soviet Union reached Palestine early in January 1942. After the Red Army's winter counteroffensive had regained territory in Ukraine, the Soviets found eyewitnesses to the mass murders as well as other evidence and released the information to the West. Although newspapers published the chilling details, the public tended to dismiss them as Bolshevik propaganda.

In the following months more news about the massacres in Lithuania, Latvia, Belorussia, and Ukraine leaked to the outside world. The Hebrew press in Palestine published these reports without arousing exceptional excitement. The public doubted their authenticity and denounced the journalists who irresponsibly spread terrible rumors without verification.

Contemporary Hebrew newspapers, from those reflecting the views of the Orthodox Agudat Israel to the extreme left-wing Zionist journals, differed little in their treatment of the subject. Exceptions were rare, although a few journalists demanded top priority for the publication of news about the Jewish plight in occupied Europe. Most conspicuous was a group of intellectuals called Al Domi (No Silence), who tried in vain to shake the prevailing indifference.

The response to the Bund Report on the annihilation of Polish Jewry, smuggled out of Poland in May 1942 and published in London in late June, illustrated the role played by the military situation in influencing reactions. Although headlines mentioned the figure of 700,000 Jewish victims, the report passed almost unnoticed in Palestine. In the same week Rommel had reached El Alamein and the Yishuv's concern focused on the situation in the Western Desert and possible repercussions in Palestine. Only when the desert front stabilized in August and September did the news of round-ups, deportations, mass executions, and the huge numbers of victims become prominent in the press.

In 1942 the course of the war and its accompanying agitation determined the slow pace of popular response in Palestine to early accounts of the mass murders in Europe. Public opinion was stimulated only later, by reports in the fall of that year, even though they contained little information that had not been released earlier. This transformation may be attributed to the victory at El Alamein in October and the Allies' landing in North Africa in November, which relieved the impact of earlier setbacks.

An official announcement by the Jewish Agency on 22 November 1942 followed the newspaper reports. It referred to the interrogation of exchangees—Jewish Palestinian citizens who had been released from occupied Poland and Germany in return for German citizens released by Britain—who had arrived in the country a few days earlier, after having just witnessed massacres and "actions" (*Aktionen*) in various ghettos and towns. By confirming many of the earlier rumors and reports, these witnesses transformed the general atmosphere in Palestine. The announcement, published concurrently with news of Rommel's defeat, and the release of similar reports from other sources in Washington and London created a comprehensive and shocking picture that shifted the attitude of the Yishuv toward the Holocaust and the war.

Although the Jewish Agency's statement added no new details, it caused a fundamental change in perception. Hitherto it had been customary to believe that the massacres were on a local scale, at the initiative of low-ranking authorities, and no more than an accompaniment to military conquest. For all who had thought in this way, the realization that these were components of an overall program of extermination, which was planned and carried out by machinery of the state, was unprecedented.

The turmoil that now swept the Yishuv was caused not only by the psychological shock but even more by fear concerning the fate of those Jews still alive. Thus far the Jewish aspect of the war had been regarded as subsidiary to the universal struggle against nazism. In late 1942 the Yishuv's leadership declared a week of mourning in the manner of traditional Jewish responses to calamities: collective fasting, praying, and marching. It summoned the Assembly of Deputies for a special session to express their feelings. Most parties, movements, and other organizations also held meetings as a means of identifying themselves with the surrounding anguish.

The Yishuv leadership under Ben-Gurion soon recovered from the emotional shock of the news and determined the organized and official reaction. For several months the feeling of impotence was paramount, and most people believed that after the war nothing would remain of European Jewry. This mood changed, however, in the fall of 1943, when news arrived from the mission in Istanbul that more than a million Jews still survived in Hungary, Romania, Slovakia, and Bulgaria. The reports revived the Yishuv's hopes and also convinced Ben-Gurion and several of his colleagues that the survivors' stance after liberation might be crucial for the accomplishment of Zionist goals in the postwar era. Though the remnant of living Jews was only a tiny fraction of the number mentioned before the adoption of the Biltmore program, the survivors might play a key role in its implementation if they were properly organized and indoctrinated.

The Zionist leadership resumed its instrumental and pragmatic approach. Henceforth its primary concern was to secure the survivors' participation in the struggle for a Jewish state after the war. The Yishuv's active involvement in rescue efforts was essential for the attainment of that goal through winning the goodwill of the survivors, particularly as the Zionist leaders expected strong Communist competition after the war because of both simple opportunism and popular gratitude to the liberating Red Army.

Ben-Gurion determined that the whole concept of links with Diaspora Jewry, as formulated since the end of 1942, should be reevaluated to take into account the survivors' future role in the postwar Zionist struggle. This conclusion, combined with developments in the course of the war and improving communications between the Zionist centers, increased the efforts to assist European Jewry. But the capability for independent action remained limited, and the Yishuv was still obliged to operate within a framework constructed by the Allies.

Official Zionist ideology with regard to immigration began to change. The Yishuv became increasingly aware that after the war it would have to absorb all the survivors, and expressions of guilt about its previous selectiveness were frequently heard. Gradually it became apparent that the Yishuv could no longer rely on its hinterland in the Diaspora; on the contrary, from now on the Diaspora would be relying on the Yishuv.

Ben-Gurion adopted this standpoint and broadened it to include not only Holocaust survivors but also the Jews of the Middle East. He regarded such a mass transfer of Jews to Palestine as the main Zionist political goal for the period up to the end of the war and as the essence of Zionist action afterward. His colleagues were still apprehensive, however, about the compass of his vision and the uncontrolled and unselective immigration that would ensue.

Apart from mere survival, the main goal of the Zionist movement and the Yishuv throughout the war was to achieve recognition as one of the Allies, at least in practice. This ambition ruled out any action not consonant with it, such as having independent contact with the enemy, infiltrating agents without the Allies' knowledge and consent, violating the economic blockade of Europe by sending parcels, or paying for rescue opportunities with hard currency. Furthermore, the Yishuv lacked facilities for independent action in Europe, and its only chance to extend help was by cooperating with the British and serving their aims and interests.

Most rescue plans were impractical in wartime, since they depended on the movement of masses of people across Europe. This assumption derives from examining German actions during the early exchanges of prisoners of war. Before each interchange the Germans plotted the exchangees' planned routes on a map of Europe, relinquishing any responsibility for their safety if Allied bombings persisted during the week preceding the exchange. It is easy to imagine how they would have exploited movements of Jews and what the Allied reaction would have been.

As early as the end of 1943 efforts within Palestine were stepped up to maintain and widen contacts with the underground and rescue committees in Europe. In particular, the German occupation of Hungary in March 1944 caused deep concern for the fate of the largest Jewish community still left in Europe.

At the beginning of April 1944 the Jewish Agency Executive again discussed the problems related to rescue operations. Yitzhak Gruenbaum, the chairman of the Yishuv's Rescue Committee, brought several proposals, including the revolutionary idea "to negotiate with the German representatives in Istanbul about halting the annihilation of the survivors." Ben-Gurion disagreed, pointing to the contradiction with the principle of unconditional surrender. In his opinion it was impossible to persuade the Allies to condone such contacts, and it was inconceivable to proceed without Allied agreement.

A month later the appearance in Istanbul of Joel Brand, an emissary of the Rescue Committee in Budapest, signaled a turning point. With his arrival the Yishuv's mission in Istanbul—and later the leadership in Palestine—was confronted with a new situation, which forced on them decisions more crucial than any since the outbreak of war. Brand brought Adolf Eichmann's famous offer of "blood for trucks," suggesting that deportations from Hungary to Auschwitz be suspended in return for a supply of trucks and other commodities for use on the eastern front. This proposition revived the question of negotiating with the enemy but left even less room for maneuver, as the Jewish Agency would have had to respond to a German initiative.

Ben-Gurion insisted on reporting the news immediately to the British authorities. Despite Gruenbaum's opposition the Executive decided to inform the high commissioner and to dispatch Moshe Sharett, the head of its political department, to Turkey. Meanwhile Brand turned himself over to the British, and Sharett met him in Aleppo under British supervision before returning to Jerusalem to discuss the Jewish Agency's next steps.

The Executive dispatched Sharett together with Weizmann, to London to impress on the Allies the need to gain time by pretending to negotiate with the Germans on Eichmann's proposition and other possibilities of saving the Jews of Hungary. At the same time the Yishuv's mission in Istanbul received another invitation to negotiate the fate of Hungarian Jewry, by sending its member Menachem Bader to Berlin under a safe conduct. Ben-Gurion ordered Bader not to go, pending reception of Sharett's report on developments in London.

The Zionist leaders met the foreign secretary, Anthony Eden, to discuss various ideas concerning rescue opportunities, including the bombing of Auschwitz and an appeal to Josef Stalin to promulgate a joint warning to Hungary. By now, however, the matter was far beyond the Zionists' control and had become a question of political warfare. The Russians had to be informed, and Churchill vetoed any contact with the Germans on this issue, even through mediation. He wrote to Eden: "I cannot feel that this is the kind of ordinary case which is put through the Protecting Power [Switzerland] as, for instance, the lack of feeding or sanitary conditions in some particular prisoners' camp. There should be . . . no negotiations of any kind on this subject." Churchill's decision put an end to Brand's errand. In late July the British leaked the story to the press. It appeared that high-level political efforts for a comprehensive campaign to save Hungarian Jewry had come to a halt.

The Jewish Agency, through its Istanbul and Geneva offices, persisted in smaller-scale efforts to distribute thousands of forged documents throughout Western Europe, thereby helping the holders to survive until the liberation. Moreover, the Istanbul mission was still active in transferring Jews by land and by sea from the Balkan countries to Turkey and thence to Palestine.

While the American Jewish Joint Distribution Committee and the World Jewish Congress were holding last-minute negotiations with the Germans—via various neutral channels—about the fate of the Jews within the remaining Nazi-controlled territories, the Yishuv's leadership turned most of its attention to the survivors. Its efforts had two directions: on the one hand, an attempt to reach the liberated countries, talk with their new rulers, and establish links with the remnants of the Jewish communities; and, on the other, a political, sometimes violent campaign for the opening of Palestine to the Holocaust survivors.

The political struggle was postponed until immediately after the final triumph over Germany. The endeavors to reach liberated Jews began in the fall of 1944. The first emissaries parachuted into the occupied countries during the war, and some of them remained to continue their task of locating survivors after the liberation. Members of the Istanbul mission sought ways to reach the Balkan countries in the wake of their occupation by the Red Army. The climax of this effort was Ben-Gurion's journey to the Balkans in November 1944. The Yishuv leader had actually intended to visit Romania, where he wanted to meet the largest community that had survived the war and to start a dialogue with the new Russian rulers. But he was refused entry into Romania and was obliged to make do with a short visit to Bulgaria.

The second and principal route to the survivors was through Italy. As in the fall of 1943, Palestinian Jewish units of the British army in Italy were instrumental in establishing an educational, organizational, and logistical infrastructure for helping Jews who had been liberated from Italian concentration camps as well as refugees from Yugoslavia and northern Italy. The arrival of the Jewish Brigade Group at the end of 1944 further strengthened this infrastructure. After the war the presence in Italy of more than 10,000 Jewish soldiers from Palestine became a springboard for penetration into liberated Europe and a precondition for consolidating and organizing the surviving remnant of European Jews to fulfill its role in the Zionist struggle for free immigration and the establishment of a Jewish state in Palestine.

Yoav Gelber

Yugoslavia On 6 April 1941 German and Italian troops, soon joined by Hungarian and Bulgarian units, opened the conquest of Yugoslavia. The Yugoslav army collapsed within 10 days, and the victors dissected the defeated state.

Serbia, ruled directly by Germany, and Greater Croatia, the so-called Independent State of Croatia, were the largest territories carved out of the defeated kingdom. Greater Croatia included Croatia proper, Slavonia, Bosnia, Herzegovina, Dalmatia, and parts of Srem and Slovenia. Over a wide region along the Dalmatian coast and in Herzegovina the Italians enjoyed primacy, in spite of nominal Croatian sovereignty. Italy incorporated areas of central Dalmatia and several adjoining islands, Istria, and about 40 percent of Slovenia. It also occupied Montenegro, most of Kosovo-Metohija, and parts of Macedonia. (Albania too became Italian.) The Bulgarians acquired most of Macedonia and some Serbian land. (Greek Thrace also became Bulgarian.) The Germans kept by far the major part of Serbia, the Banat area of Vojvodina, and portions of Macedonia and Srem. Hungary was given Backa (Bacska) and Baranija (Baranya) and the areas of Croatia and Slovenia known as Prekomurje (Muravidák) and Medjumurje (Muraköz).

At the time of the outbreak of World War II there were between 71,000 and 82,000 Jews in Yugoslavia. Of these, about 12,500 lived in Serbia, of whom some 11,000 perished. In Croatia and Slavonia there were about 25,000 Jews, about 20,000 of whom died during the war. Approximately 20,000 Jews were living in Vojvodina; their losses by the end of the war were about 17,000. The Jewish population in Slovenia amounted to some 1,500 persons, of whom at least 1,300 perished. Approximately 14,000 Jews lived in Bosnia-Herzegovina, and about 4,000 survived the war. In Macedonia 700 out of 7,700–8,000 Jews remained at the war's end.

Serbia and Banat

A considerable ethnic-German minority lived in Banat. The *Volksdeutsche* absorbed Nazi ideology and hatred for Jews, and their antisemitism increased as a result of economic competition. After the conquest the Volksdeutsche assembled the Jews and tortured them mercilessly; they later transferred them to Serbia, where almost all of them were killed. Local Germans, German soldiers, and inhabitants of the Reich looted Jewish property.

The Jews of Serbia were gradually concentrated. First, in April 1941, the Germans collected the Jewish men. When the Communist and non-Communist resistance began operations, the Germans shot 100 hostages for each German killed, and many of those executed were Jews. About 5,000 Jewish men remained alive, and they were shot between September and December 1941.

The Germans now had to decide the fate of 5,000–6,000 Jewish women and children. First they kept them under terrible conditions in Belgrade's Sajmiste fairground; they then loaded the Jews into vans and pumped in exhaust fumes from the engines. All the Jewish women and children were thus killed by carbon-monoxide poisoning. Except for several hundred Jews who had joined the resistance or escaped to Italian-ruled Albania, Dalmatia, Montenegro, and Slovenia (as well as to Bulgaria), Serbian Jewry was exterminated. The Germans also executed stateless Jews (Czech, Austrian, and German) stranded in Serbia in their attempt to reach Palestine. The Nazis expropriated Jewish property, leaving only a few morsels for the Volksdeutsche and Serbs.

Croatia

Germany and its Italian ally handed over Greater Croatia to the Ustashi movement, which proclaimed the Independent State of Croatia on 10 April 1941. This extreme-right terrorist group acted in coordination with Fascist Italy and others against the Yugoslav monarchy. Initially the Ustasha movement was anti-Serbian but not outspokenly racist, having Jews and Jewish converts within its ranks. Several of its leaders had Jewish relatives. Once the Ustashi had developed close relations with the Nazis in the mid-1930s, it emphasized local anti-Judaism and imported antisemitic and racist theories. Catholic antisemitism was accepted by part of the Croatian population and leadership, and some intellectuals cherished racist concepts about the origin of the Croatian people. Soon after becoming masters of their country, the Ustashi began anti-Jewish activity, which was enshrined in Croatian legislation. Several laws, including the Law Safeguarding Croatia's National Inheritance (established about a week after the seizure of power), the Law of Citizenship, the Law Concerning Racial Affiliation, and the Law Concerning Defense of the National and Aryan Culture of the Croatian Nation (the last three passed on 30 April 1941), were constructed along the lines of the Nazi Nuremberg racial laws of 1935. The Croatian laws were racist in spirit, aimed at Serbs, Jews, and to a lesser degree Roma (Gypsies). This battery of laws was intended to terrorize and isolate the persecuted minorities and the internal opposition and to popularize the Ustasha. The first months of Ustashi rule were a free-for-all during which mainly Serbs, as well as others, were imprisoned and butchered by the thousands. The Serbs soon rose up and took bloody revenge. During this period Jews were still a secondary target, although synagogues, cemeteries, and Jewish property were already being destroyed in many places. Motivated by the opportunity to acquire Jewish property, Croatians and Volksdeutsche entered into the first wave of unorganized looting of Jewish and Serbian goods soon after the occupation by German troops. In a short time organized "expropriation" of Jewish and Serbian property developed throughout the country, with the participation of merchants, artisans, peasants, workers, and professionals, both as individuals and within their guilds, trade unions, and associations.

Members of the Ustasha pose for a photograph during the torture and execution of a Serb. 1943

Members of the Ustasha staff in Jasenovac at work dividing property looted from prisoners killed in the camp.

In Zagreb the Ustashi led the anti-Jewish drive by arresting several wealthy Jews in May 1941 and forcing them to give 120 kilograms of gold and 50 million dinars to the state treasury. This sum was gathered from the entire Jewish population.

Gestapo and SS experts already active in Zagreb before the beginning of the war set out to instruct their Croatian comrades and, above all, to extract Jewish wealth for themselves and for the Reich. They requisitioned the assets of the Zagreb congregation and the Zionist organization and imprisoned several Jewish leaders. Although most of the leaders were later released, these were the first arrests of Jews in Zagreb. The first Ustashi arrests affected 80 lawyers detained on 28 April 1941 but also later released. On 18 June 1941 another 28 lawyers were arrested, all of whom perished. On 29 April 1941, 168 youths from 15 to 22 years of age were conscripted for labor; they were murdered in the fall of 1941 when the Jadovno camp was evacuated before the arrival of the Italians. According to some reports, the young men were thrown into a deep gorge, and hand grenades were hurled in after them. Dozens of other Jews were hunted down for various reasons. After several terrorist attacks by Com-

munist resistance groups, 259 Jewish hostages were shot for "intellectual instigation" of the raids. Murders of Jews occurred all over Greater Croatia.

The sporadic atrocities soon gave way to organized terrorizing of Jews. On 22 June 1941 a well-planned anti-Jewish action began in Zagreb. Jews were gathered either according to prepared lists, which were published in newspapers along with orders that those named report at designated assembly points, or by house-to-house searches following the closing of entire streets and quarters. Policemen received monetary rewards for each captured Jew. And the Jews, law-abiding and unsuspecting, appeared at the appointed places carrying food and clothes. After the Zagreb hunt came the rural Jews' turn. Finally the process reached Bosnia-Herzegovina, where it continued until November 1941. Of 40,000 Jews in Greater Croatia, only some 8,000–9,000 remained unmolested. Those captured were sent to camps in Croatia, the males mostly to the Jasenovac extermination camp, the women and children to other sites.

This undertaking was carried out with the utmost brutality. In Sarajevo the sadistic Ustashi commander Ivan Tolj dispatched trains without receiving permission to do so—in fact against the will of his German supervisors. Since the trains had no destination, they moved around the country aimlessly during the severe Balkan winter, the people locked in the cars without food or water. At least one train returned to Sarajevo, where the living were found mingled with corpses. Eventually all these Jews perished—first the men in Jasenovac, then the women and children.

In Jasenovac the Jews were beaten and starved to death, slashed with knives, shot, battered with hammers, and thrown into the Sava River. The defrocked Franciscan monk M. Filipović-Majstorović, nicknamed Satan, took special pleasure in knifing the inmates or gunning them down. The fate of the women and children was equally horrible. In the internment camps most of them starved to death, died of disease, or were executed; others were deported to Auschwitz. In many towns and villages, executioners prepared a variety of killings according to their tastes: Jews were shot on bridges and thrown into rivers, hanged, beaten, or tortured to death. Sadism and sexual perversions were the trademark of the Ustasha. (In October 1999 a Croatian court convicted Dinko Savić, commandant of Jasenovac in 1944, of responsibility in the killings of some 2,000 inmates of the camp.)

The second hunt was organized by the Germans themselves, since they did not trust Ustashi efficiency. In Croatia there was competition between the SS and the German Foreign Office, which was staffed partly by SA veterans. One manifestation of this rivalry was the deportation and liquidation of Jews. Representatives of the Foreign Office initiated the second wave of deportations. There was a certain synchronization with Slovakian practice: as in that country, the Jews were deprived of citizenship. The Croatian government paid 300 marks for each deportee, and transports rolled in August, when there was less activity in Slovakia. Unlike in Slovakia, however, in Croatia the Roman Catholic church made some efforts to prevent the deportations, although the clergy played a leading political role in both countries. In August 1942 about 5,500 Jews were sent to Auschwitz.

The ultimate effort to rid Croatia of its last Jews took place in May 1943. The targets of this action were Jews who had eluded the two previous waves of deportation, half-Jews, those who had intermarried, and "honorary Aryans" who previously had assisted the Ustashi movement. These final deportations met with Croatian opposition. Perhaps because of the touchy question of converted Jews and those related to the Ustashi, or because of the timing (after the German defeat at Stalingrad) or intervention by the local church and the Vatican, the Ustashi elite resisted participation. The Nazis had to go to great lengths to persuade the Ustashi to collaborate in the deportations. On 5 May 1943 Heinrich Himmler, chief of the SS, visited Zagreb and conferred with the Ustashi leader, Ante Pavelić. The Ustashi then helped the Germans round up some 1,400 Jews, who were sent in two transports to Auschwitz. By the time the Red Army liberated that camp, only 24 Croatian Jews remained alive there.

In April 1944 Pavelić abolished all racial legislation, and Jews were granted equality with the rest of the citizens. At that time, however, his power extended only over the city of Zagreb.

Several places in Greater Croatia served for concentration and extermination of Serbs, Jews, Gypsies, and antifascists. Jadovno and the island of Pag were the sites of atrocities. When the region was to be handed to the Italians, inmates were either murdered or shipped to the interior of Croatia. The victims included several groups of Jews from Zagreb. It is evident that, chronologically, Serbs were killed ahead of Jews, thus setting a precedent and establishing a modus operandi. How-

ever, the need for evacuating certain areas led to the extermination of the Jews there first.

The question as to whether the Ustashi intended from the outset to clear Croatia of all Jews—to adopt an ideological position similar to that of the Nazis to make Germany and the occupied territories *Judenrein*—remains open. Their primary target was the Serbs, whom they regarded as a national enemy. It appears that, at least in the initial actions against Jews, the Ustashi copied the methods that had already served them with respect to the Serbs. Only with the passage of time did Jews (and Gypsies) become independent targets of racial extermination.

Nazi instigation and initiatives should also be borne in mind. Once the Jews became the focus, the Croatians demonstrated ingenuity in slaughtering them. The horrors visited on Jews were on a par with the madness to which Serbs and Gypsies were exposed. The difference, to the Jewish disadvantage, was in the racial approach. Serbs, who were Eastern Orthodox Christians, could convert to Roman Catholicism and thus be saved. Many Orthodox Christian Gypsies living in Muslim regions embraced Islam and were sheltered by local Islamic authorities. But conversion was of little help to Jews. Therefore, the extermination of the Jews was more thorough than that of the Serbs and Gypsies.

Roman Catholic institutions cooperated closely with the state administration and with the Ustasha. Catholics regarded prewar Yugoslavia as an Eastern Orthodox state and the Serbs as schismatics. Clergy accepted the functions of the state, and young priests and friars participated in atrocities. The church hierarchy took an ambivalent position by disseminating anti-Serbian and anti-Jewish propaganda and by exploiting material and political advantages. Clergy carried out forced conversions of the Orthodox to Catholicism. But the church also tried to protect converted Jews, and to a lesser degree the unconverted, with some limited success. After the drive in the fall of 1941 the hierarchy took a negative view of further deportations, and the Nazis had to increase their efforts to overcome the opposition.

The Muslim public institutions were not pleased with the slaughter taking place in Bosnia and Herzegovina. Although Muslim soldiers (including those who enlisted in the two Bosnian SS divisions) excelled in cruelties against Jews, religious and civic bodies protested time and again against the anti-Serbian and

A Jewish prisoner at Jasenovac extermination camp takes off his ring before his execution.

anti-Jewish drives. Individual Muslims hid Jews, and converts to Islam enjoyed protection; after the war they returned to Judaism.

Expropriation of Jewish and Serbian property moved along two parallel tracks: "wild" robbery and organized robbery. Perpetrators of each claimed to be recovering the nation's wealth. Robbery was related to pogroms and included the looting of Jewish apartments and shops after the deportations. Croatians contended with the ethnic Germans in wild robbery, and the state had to compete with official Reich organizations. Organized robbery, combined with the embezzlement of Jewish wealth, was carried out through legal channels. The treasury hoped to cover at least a part of its budgetary expenses in this manner. Because of embezzlement and theft, however, these hopes proved false. Muslims complained that Catholics snatched the spoils and they were left empty-handed.

German competition was tough, particularly when major industry was involved. Regarded by the Croatians as their national inheritance, industry was the choice prize for the German elements—both SA and SS—never to be released to the Croatians. The SS and SA were also engaged in mutual competition, often using the ethnic Germans as stalking horses. Central German Reich institutions, such as the Treasury, took

an interest in Jewish property in Croatia. This was a contest of dirty tricks, and the Jewish owners paid the price. Thus Jewish property itself increased the tensions in Croatia.

Thousands of Jews in Greater Croatia were temporarily or permanently rescued by Italian efforts and goodwill. In the areas of Croatia under Italian rule Jews were protected from being hunted or transported to extermination camps. Other Jews who managed to make their way into the Italian region were also protected from deportation, both by military authorities and by civilian institutions.

Although in a few cases Jews were massacred, and on several occasions maltreated, particularly if they were involved in resistance, the Italians usually kept them interned in camps, prisons, even in private hotels and apartments. A tug of war developed between Croatian authorities, who, like the Germans, wished to deport all Jews within their sovereign territory, and the Italians, who refused to participate in deportations. The most the Italians were willing to do was to hand over Jewish property. The German Foreign Office intervened, and on 21 August 1942 the matter reached Benito Mussolini. The Italian dictator agreed to let the Croatian Jews go. Nevertheless, Italian institutions decided on procrastination since they were aware of the real meaning of such an act. On 21 November 1942 Mussolini changed his mind and decided to delay the transfer further.

The Italian surrender of 25 July 1943 brought about a major change. Mussolini was overthrown, and the German troops soon occupied the Italian-held territories in the Balkans. Jews were once again in danger. They kept fleeing to Italy proper. Those who could not get there tried to reach the regions already liberated by the partisans. The internees on the island of Rab, for instance, left in an organized fashion and included a Jewish military battalion. Thus the Germans caught only a relatively small fraction of the Jews, whom they delivered to Auschwitz.

Moreover, Jews living in Italian-occupied Slovenia, Montenegro, Kosovo, and Macedonia (as well as Albania) could enjoy relative protection. Serbian and Macedonian Jews who managed to reach Albania survived there even under German occupation, assisted by the local people.

The territory of Greater Croatia was liberated mostly by Josip Tito's partisan troops. The Holocaust dissolved the barriers between the Sephardic and

Ashkenazi congregations; the survivors created unified bodies and later had to adjust to the Communist regime.

The Hungarian Acquisitions

Hungary harvested the spoils of its participation in the German battle for Yugoslavia. In the two Mura districts the number of Jews was small (about 2,000); there were some 500 more in Baranija, and more than 16,000 Jews lived in Backa. The new territories were incorporated into the historic Hungarian districts but were ruled by the Hungarian military. All anti-Jewish legislation in force in Hungary was also valid in the acquired territories.

The military command chose to regard Serbs and Jews as potential enemies and to treat them accordingly. Among the population evicted to Serbia after the annexation were numerous Jews. The military recruited auxiliary troops, in which Jews were exposed to a severe and unending regime of cruel punishments, senseless toil, and degradation. Enlisted men were executed without cause. Even when the central authorities terminated the military regime in September 1941, Jews remained the victims of ceaseless harassment. Military and local authorities tried to seize their property under a variety of inimical activities. When the Hungarian army began to organize nationwide Jewish Labor Units (Munkaszolgalat), men recently released from the auxiliary units were again recruited to face the same soldiers and the same treatment they had just left. Their bitter fate was echoed in all Jewish Labor Units, and most of the members died.

An increase in resistance activity in the neighborhood served the authorities stationed in Novi Sad (Ujvidék) as an excuse for major organized pogroms against the local Jews and Serbs. By the beginning of January 1942 Sajkas, a swampy region in the south, was searched for guerrillas. On that occasion the army killed the entire Jewish population of the few townships there, as well as several hundred Serbs. In Backa courts-martial condemned scores of Jews to death for alleged illegal activities and conspiracy. These executions served to prepare the public for the pogrom of 21–23 January, when the army killed about 1,100 Jews and 900 Serbs. An attempt to investigate the pogrom failed, and some of the Hungarian perpetrators escaped to Germany. Hundreds of local Jews perished in the Bor copper mine and in the Backa-Toplja camp, both under Hungarian control. Hundreds more died

during the death marches already carried out by the Germans. Lastly, after the German occupation of Hungary on 19 March 1944 the Hungarian authorities and German forces deported Jews from the whole of Hungary, including Backa and Mura, to Auschwitz. Some 9,000 Jews never returned to their homes. Altogether only 1,800 Yugoslav Jews living in the territories occupied by Hungary survived the war.

Macedonia

On 6 April 1941 German forces attacked southern Yugoslavia from Bulgarian territory and seized Macedonia. Bulgarian armed forces took over the region on 18 April.

Bulgaria formally joined the Axis on 1 March 1941, but anti-Jewish feeling and deeds had begun earlier. On 21 January 1941 the Bulgarian parliament passed the Law for the Defense of the Nation, which imposed a number of restrictions on Jews. The next significant step was a law of 28 June 1942, which ordered the Council of Ministers to take "all necessary steps to solve the Jewish question and the problems involved." Numerous ordinances and lesser orders completed the anti-Jewish legislative system.

Although these laws were valid throughout Bulgaria, additional decrees applied to Macedonia only. The most important of them excluded Jews from Bulgarian citizenship, leaving them in the position of aliens. They were thus deprived of any legal defense within the Bulgarian state. Jewish property was sequestered, in numerous ways and on various pretexts. On 23 November 1942 the Macedonian representative of the Central Commissariat for the Jewish Problem promulgated an order obliging Jews to wear the yellow star. Personal liberty, freedom of employment, freedom of movement, and the possibility of purchasing goods were severely curtailed. In close cooperation with the Nazis, the Bulgarian government determined to exile all Bulgarian Jews to German-held Poland. The first to leave were 14,000 Macedonian and Thracian Jews, together with 6,000 Jews from Bulgaria proper. Heavy public pressure forced the authorities to cancel the plans to expel Bulgarian Jews, but Jews from Macedonia and Thrace were abandoned to their fate.

On 11 March 1943 Bulgarian army personnel, police, and other government agencies collected Jews from the whole of Macedonia and moved them to a tobacco factory in Skopje, the capital of Macedonia. More than 7,000 people were squeezed into the small factory, where there was minimal sanitation, little food, and almost no water. Even Bulgarian authorities described the conditions as "dreadful." The Jews remained there until 22 March, when the first transport left for the Treblinka extermination camp in Poland. The second transport left on 25 March and the last on 29 March. Altogether 7,144 Jews were sent to their death to Treblinka; not a single deportee survived. Jews from the German-held part of Macedonia were all killed, but those from the Italian area remained unmolested until the German occupation in September 1943, when the Nazis dispatched several groups of Jews to extermination camps.

After the deportations Jewish property in Macedonia was commandeered and divided between many institutions, organizations, and private persons. Bulgaria and the ethnic Bulgarians generally enjoy a favorable reputation for saving Bulgarian Jews from deportation and extermination; nevertheless, they did not hesitate to send the "foreign" Jews of Macedonia and Thrace, some 10,000 persons, to their death.

A few Jews lived in Slovenia. In the German area the fate of the Jews was the same as in the rest of the Reich. Jews in the Italian part were protected until September 1943, when German troops occupied the region. At that time and previously, Jews tried to reach Italy proper. The Ferramonti camp in southern Italy was used to intern Yugoslav Jews.

The Resistance

The massive resistance of the Yugoslav people began in the fall of 1941 and later grew. This was about the time when the Jews of Serbia and Croatia were already imprisoned, and many had been executed. Yet as telling as these facts may be, they do not answer the question as to why the Jews agreed to accept German and Croatian orders. The reasons are complicated; they involve terror, Nazi deception and perfidy, middle-class mentality, and loneliness. Nobody raised a voice in protest. The sporadic or tacit protests emanating from the Communist underground were of no value. In fact there was also a mixed reaction from the Communists. In Croatia and Macedonia they recognized that the Nazis and their collaborators were carrying out systematic mass murder, and they appealed to the Jews as an entity. In Serbia and Vojvodina the Communists refused to protest or to incorporate Zionist groups as a whole (such as the leftist Hashomer Hatzair and Blau-

Weiss). They accepted Jews on an individual basis only. Furthermore, when the Jews confined on the island of Rab banded together in 1943 to create a Jewish unit, the partisan command dispersed them among other units. The Communist ideology, which denied the existence of a separate Jewish ethnic group in Yugoslavia and was hostile to Zionism, prevailed even under conditions of war and the Holocaust.

According to Yugoslav sources, 4,572 Jews fought in the partisan ranks, some 3,000 on the front line. Of the fighters, 1,318 fell in battle; 11 (seven posthumously) were awarded the highest form of recognition, the title National Hero of Yugoslavia; and 150 were decorated as Partisan of the Year 1941. Jews probably constituted the single largest ethnic group within the partisan army, given their absolute number within the whole population. Jews were members of the Partisan High Command, commanders of crack units, and political commissars, and they engaged in all kinds of resistance activity. The partisan medical service relied on Jewish doctors (mostly from Croatia), who were sent by the Ustashi authorities to fight syphilis in Bosnia but preferred instead to join the armed struggle. Jews were among the earliest, and in some cases the very first, to oppose Germans and collaborators in various regions of Yugoslavia. An interesting feature was family participation in the struggle. Two, three, even five siblings might volunteer, and often most or all of them were killed in action.

Jews also enlisted in the monarchist Chetnik movement headed by Gen. Dragolub Mihailović, especially those who were members of the Zionist right movements, such as Betar. Eventually, however, they left the Chetniks—not because of antisemitism, although it also existed there, but because they were alienated by Serbian xenophobia. Chetnik cooperation with the Italians, and later even with the Germans, also created an incongruous environment for Jews.

Antisemitism, or at least religious antipathy toward Judaism, was not infrequent in the partisan ranks, although it was resisted by the High Command. Jews enlisted in Yugoslav units abroad, in the Soviet Union, in the West, and in the unit organized by the partisans in Italy. Some miraculously survived within the ranks of Yugoslav prisoners of war imprisoned in Germany.

Palestine paratroopers parachuted into Yugoslavia as regular members of the British military missions to Titoist and Chetnik partisans. Their attempts to meet

Jews failed because most Jews were already dead and because the few Jews in the mountains were afraid of arousing suspicions among their comrades by talking to Western mission members. The Zionist idea of sending emissaries to the Jews of Nazi Europe failed miserably, as those who conceived the idea were insufficiently familiar with conditions in the Nazi-ruled territories.   *Yeshayahu A. Jelinek*

Z

Zegota Code name of the Council for Aid to the Jews, established by Zofia Kossak-Grobelny in 1942. Operating inside Poland, Zegota assisted Jews financially, provided forged identity papers, and found hiding places, especially for children. It published pamphlets calling for Polish sympathy for the Jews, and urged sanctions against informers. Limited funds hampered the organization. See POLISH JEWRY

ZOB (Zydowska Organizacja Bojowa) Jewish Fighting Organization, founded by members of the left-wing Zionist youth movement in Warsaw in July 1942. An armed resistance group, the ZOB executed German sympathizers and informers in the Warsaw ghetto after the first wave of deportations in 1943. Mordechai Anielewicz commanded the ZOB in the April 1943 Warsaw ghetto uprising, in which most of its members were killed. See WARSAW

Zuckerman, Yitzhak (Antek; 1915–81) ZOB leader in Warsaw; also active in Kraków and other parts of Poland. Before learning of the mass murder of Jews, Zuckerman ran an underground press and prepared Jewish youth for immigration to Palestine. He engaged German troops in the January 1943 Warsaw ghetto resistance action and helped organize the April 1943 Warsaw ghetto uprising. He commanded a group of Jewish fighters in the August 1944 Polish uprising in Warsaw. He emigrated to Palestine after the war and joined Kibbutz Lohamei Haghetaot. In 1961 Zukerman was a witness in the trial of Adolf Eichmann in Jerusalem.

Zygielbojm, Samuel (Szmul) Artur (1895–1943) Official of the Bund in prewar Poland and its representative with the Polish government-in-exile in London. Zygielbojm escaped from German occupied territory upon the request of his party and went to Belgium, France, the United States, and ultimately

Yitzhak Zuckerman.

England. Reports of mass murders from the Polish underground reached him in May 1942. He attempted to draw public attention to German atrocities and made many public addresses on the BBC. On 12 May 1943 he learned of the final liquidation of the Warsaw ghetto and of the deaths of his wife and son. After writing letters to the Polish president and prime minister castigating the Allies for their passivity in the face of the extermination of Jews in Nazi-occupied Europe, he took his life. See POLISH GOVERNMENT-IN-EXILE

Zyklon B Zyklon B was the main cyanide compound that delivered poison gas into the killing rooms at Nazi extermination camps. It was composed of hydrocyanic acid (prussic acid, HCN) absorbed onto diatomaceous earth (diatomite) or a siliceous base diluted with a stabilizer, possibly including an irritant. The original purpose of the preparation with the irritant was as a fumigant to destroy insects; it was particularly effective in closed spaces because of its physical, chemical, and toxicological properties. Hydrocyanic acid boils at 26 degrees Celsius (79 degrees Farenheit) and in its gaseous state is lighter than air.

Hydrocyanic acid was discovered in 1786 by the Swedish pharmacist and chemist Carl W. Scheele. But preparations from plants containing cyanide had been administered as poisons since at least ancient Egypt, where some offenses were punishable by the "penalty of the peach." (Peach pits are cyanic.) The Greek physician Dioscorides employed bitter almonds to poison criminals in the first century C.E. The Roman emperor Nero disposed of his enemies with a brew of cherry laurel leaves.

Expansion of the German organic-chemical industry around the turn of the twentieth century led to many discoveries related to the chemistry, pharmacology, development, and use of nitriles, including hydrocyanic acid. Irving Langmuir's theory of gas absorption and release made possible the practical storage of gases. Early cyanide studies, including research on the rate of action and on detoxification, were reported in the scientific literature before World War I and between the two world wars. During World War I Fritz Haber, a Jewish scientist and Nobel laureate, directed German research into the use of hydrocyanic acid as a chemical weapon. In 1917 the Germans used cyanide as an inexpensive gas which would kill troops rapidly and en masse. In 1925 Otto Warburg proposed the mechanism of toxic action for cyanide as the inhibition of cytochrome oxidase. In 1930 William Wendell reported that hemoglobin oxidizes to form a stable, less toxic cyanide compound.

In the 1920s and 1930s hydrocyanic acid came to be used in fumigation, electroplating, and many other commercial applications. Because it was thought not to leave a persistent residue on crops, it was soon prized in agriculture as a pesticide. Still, American hobos traveling in freight cars that carried agricultural produce were accidentally gassed from time to time. Cases of suicide by cyanide were seen during the Depression in the 1930s in the United States (where a threefold or fourfold increase in incidents of cyanide poisoning was reported), South America, and Europe.

Zyklon was not the first means of genocide employed by the Nazis. In the first years of the war Jews were starved, shot, or burned to death; they were poisoned by carbon monoxide fumes from engine exhaust and by drugs such as Luminal (phenobarbital), other barbiturates, and a morphine and scopolamine combination. Highly toxic nerve gases—organophosphonates such as tabun, sarin and soman—were tested on humans to establish a lethal dosage. There is also documentary evidence that biological weapons were employed, including infection by the organisms that cause cholera, typhus, paratyphus A, and paratyphus B.

But all those methods of murder have serious drawbacks. Starvation is slow and inefficient and leaves a distinctive pathology. Carbon monoxide, although thought at the time to be untraceable, was difficult to ship after manufacture, and diesel fuel, by which the gas could be produced at the killing site, might well be in short supply as the war continued. Shooting, it was argued, was too costly and labor-intensive. Studies had suggested, however, that cyanide gas might be untraceable, since it dispersed into the atmosphere. Moreover, the use of cyanide in a poison gas in World War I furnished a historical precedent, and a steady supply could be counted on from the flourishing German chemical industry, represented by companies like I. G. Farben, which controlled the pesticide manufacturer Degesch, and Tesch & Stabenow (Testa), which made cyanide.

Another reason for the choice of hydrocyanic acid as the primary agent in killing millions of Jews quickly and efficiently may have been its association in the minds of the Nazi leaders with pesticides. From the beginning of the Third Reich Nazi propaganda had portrayed Jews as vermin and parasites, and there had been calls to dispose of them as such. A children's book published in 1940, *Die Pudelmopsdackelpinscher*, contained a series of animal fables that included "The Jew," who was put on the same footing as "The Drones," and "The Louse."

A family of Zyklons (also known as cyclones)—

Canisters containing Zyklon B found at Majdanek. 1944

Zyklon A, Zyklon B, and Zyklon C—were developed initially as fumigants. One formulation of Zyklon B was composed of hydrocyanic acid and bromoacetate ester (an irritant introduced as a warning gas) absorbed on a porous granulated diatomite. Bromoacetate ester causes considerable pain and was employed during World War I to affect the enemy's lungs: it may also act as a tear gas and gives rise to intense distress if it reaches the stomach, causing nausea, vomiting, colic, and diarrhea. Although death by cyanide poisoning appears painful, because of the distressing sight of the victims' aberrant movements and seizures, in fact the poison releases pain-inhibiting endorphins. It may be, then, that it was the bromoacetate ester, not the cyanide, in Zyklon B that caused the pain in victims that was apparent to those who witnessed the mass gassings at the Nazi extermination camps. It has been suggested that the bromoacetate ester was removed from the formulation, either because it decreased operational efficiency or because its function as a warning was unnecessary for use in murder.

Zyklon B was shipped in tin canisters heavy enough to withstand a pressure of five atmospheres, in sizes ranging from 20 to 1,200 grams (about three pounds). The substance, which continues to be produced for use as a fumigant, appears as dry or slightly moist particles of sandy clay, varying in color from pale reddish-yellow to orange-yellow. The large surfaces provided by the diatomite promote rapid discharge of hydrocyanic acid. Because of changes in the manufacturing processes in the past 60 years, the rate of toxicity of the gas and the quality and composition of the absorbing material today may differ from those of the 1940s. The Reich Institute also tested a new absorption material marketed by Degesch, the so-called Lambda Cubes, which consisted of a gypsum material mixed with starch (Erco), giving a whiter and bluer appearance than diatomite (also referred to as Diagriess). It was supplied by Dessauer Werke or Testa. Such factors could alter the characteristics of poisoning, and the product may well have varied during the war period.

In 1989 the pathologist Paul Brendel estimated that approximately 13–27 times the lethal dose of cyanide was used in the gas chambers in the Nazi camps.

Rudolf Höss, the Auschwitz commandant, estimated that 40 times the lethal dose produced a "flash" death—that is, a death in which the killing time is as brief as possible. The amount of cyanide as a sodium salt required to kill 50 percent of a group of humans is 1.8–2.2 mg/kg. A range of approximately 10–25 mg/kg (sometimes perhaps more) was used in the gas chambers.

Cyanide kills by interfering with the ability of cells to bind oxygen. The initial effects of hydrocyanic acid, however, suggest that cyanide may also directly inhibit the transmission of nerve impulses or regional blood flow. A typical exposure to hydrocyanic acid in gaseous form in concentrations greater than 250–270 parts per million (ppm) in air is fatal within minutes. The initial hyperpnea (rapid breathing) is soon followed by loss of consciousness, seizures, cardiac arrest, and death. Within 15 seconds high doses of cyanide stimulate the chemoreceptor bodies, sensors in the aorta that register the presence of the compound in the blood. The body then reacts by increasing the rate of breathing in an effort to increase the amount of usable oxygen in the blood. However, after a second and third breath of the cyanide-laden air the victim has inhaled enough poison to cause death. In a confined area, such as the Nazi gas chambers, hydrocyanic acid probably entered the victims not solely by inhalation but also by absorption through the skin and the cornea. A host of factors, such as a person's age, sex, diet, and metabolism may determine the rapidity of the poison's action and the lethal dosage. Exposure to the gas at concentrations lower than 120 ppm may result in slower and less severe effects. Not all people can detect the odor of cyanide, which resembles bitter almonds or burning rope. This odor may well have added to the anxiety and fear in the crowded gas chambers.

In addition to its lethal function in the gas chambers, Zyklon B was used in the delousing of concentration camp inmates. Long before World War II, investigations of possible antidotes to cyanide poisoning had been carried out. The use of antidotes was known and confirmed in the German scientific literature. By the mid-1930s a combination of methemoglobin formers (i.e., nitrites) and sulfane sulfur donors (i.e., thiosulfate) developed by Enrique Hug in Argentina and K. K. Chen and his colleagues in the United States had been found to be clinically effective. But there is no evidence, despite extensive searches in the documentary record, that any therapies for cyanide poisoning were made available for concentration camp inmates.

In 1946 two partners in Tesch & Stabenow were tried before a British military court on charges of genocide, and in 1949 the manager of Degesch was prosecuted in Frankfurt for his role in the mass murders by means of Zyklon B. The accused must, it was argued, have realized that the supply of tons of Zyklon B to the camps was far above the quantity required for delousing, and they therefore must have had constructive knowledge of the true purpose. Other lines of evidence were obtained that gave credence to their guilt. For example, the warning agent, bromoacetate ester, was removed to make the killing process more efficient. All three were convicted, and the Tesch & Stabenow partners were hanged.

The trial records and published documents clearly show that the Zyklon (primarily formulated as Zyklon B) sent to the camps had the warning odor removed. The quantities of Zyklon ordered by the camp authorities were enough to kill millions of people. Summaries of purchase and other trading records maintained by the camps were submitted in evidence at the trials and have been analyzed by year, amount, and camp, together with other statistics. Zyklon was used at a number of camps, but Auschwitz-Birkenau was the largest consumer.

Several forensic toxicology examinations of gas chamber walls at Auschwitz-Birkenau have been carried out to determine whether any cyanide residue was present. Although cyanide, particularly in the form of hydrocyanic acid, is unstable and breaks down over time, it leaves behind more stable forms that may persist for decades and can be detected. Following the publication of the notorious, unscientific report by self-proclaimed "expert" Fred Leuchter (1989) and the controversial and now scientifically repudiated report by Germar Rudolf (1992), the forensic toxicologist Jan Markiewicz and his associates made a new study based on core sections of the crematorium walls. The report in 1994 by Markiewicz and his associates found sufficient cyanide compounds present in the gas chamber ruins and absent in control areas to be consistent with its use as a weapon of mass destruction—clear evidence that portions of the Auschwitz-Birkenau complex functioned as an extermination camp.

Cyanide continues to be manufactured legally for a variety of benign purposes. Cyanide polymers are used to produce many consumer goods, from carpets to tennis rackets. Much of this technology may be exported to Third World countries. Cyanide as a weapon, however, also appears to have become an export commodity, in particular to the Middle East. In 1986 Amnesty International reported that 10,000 of the Muslim Brotherhood died from its effects in 1970 in Hama, Syria. The *United Nations Chronicle* reported in 1985 that cyanide, perhaps combined with other substances, killed Kurds in Halabiya and Iranians in other cities during the Iraq-Iran war. There have been unsubstantiated claims that cyanide has been used in terrorist attacks. See also HOLOCAUST DENIAL

Steven I. Baskin

Bibliographical Essay

The best estimate of the number of publications about the Holocaust and related subjects may be made from the holdings of the Yad Vashem Library (Israel), which contains more than 75,000 items, mainly books but also offprints of journal articles. The Wiener Library (London and Tel Aviv) specializes in collecting materials about the Holocaust in Central and Western Europe. Other large collections, containing some 35,000 items primarily about the Holocaust, are the Simon Wiesenthal Center Library (Los Angeles) and the Ghetto Fighters' House Library (Israel). The collection in the U.S. Holocaust Memorial Museum in Washington, D.C., is widely known. Books about the Holocaust and related subjects have been written in virtually every language in the world, although most of them have been published in German, English, Hebrew, French, Polish, Yiddish, and Russian.

The range of publications on the Holocaust is vast. Scholars have produced historical, sociological, and psychological studies of the Shoah. Many survivors and other persons touched by the Holocaust have written memoirs, biographies, works of fiction, poetry, and philosophical and theological essays.

There is no clear line between published material on the Holocaust and published material on related subjects. It may seem obvious that a book about the Warsaw ghetto uprising or extermination camps is about the Holocaust, but it is not nearly as clear whether a book about Vichy France or the Slovak Hlinka party should be considered part of the bibliography of the Shoah or should be considered as related background material. Even more problematic is whether the vast body of publications about nazism, the Nazi rise to power, the nature of Nazi Germany and Nazi rule, leading Nazi personalities, and the legacy of nazism should be considered publications about the Holocaust. These problems of classification notwithstanding, a core bibliography of books in English about the Holocaust and related topics has emerged over the years.

The focus of this article is books about the Holocaust that have been published in English. Nevertheless, it is important to recognize that many excellent scholars have published their research in other languages, especially German, French, and Hebrew. Scholarly studies in German that treat the Jews as subjects have been published by such researchers as Uwe Adam, Wolfgang Benz, Konrad Kwiet, Ladislav Lipscher, Arnold Paucker, Herbert Rosenkranz, Josef Walk, and others. In French, similar studies by Asher Cohen, Lucien Lazare, Alain Michel, Renée Poznanski, Adam Rayski, Lucien Steinberg, Maxime Steinberg, Georges Wellers, and others have contributed greatly to our understanding of the Holocaust. Much of the noteworthy research written in Hebrew has been translated into English. Among the exceptions are studies by Jean Ancel, Daniel Blatman, Gila Fatran, Avraham Margaliot, Yael Peled, Avihu Ronen, Menachem Shelah, and Yechiam Weitz.

Since the early 1960s a number of comprehensive histories of the Holocaust have been published in English. A pioneering work of this type is Raul Hilberg's *The Destruction of the European Jews* (1961). Hilberg's massive and meticulous treatise, based primarily on German documentation, analyzes the development of Nazi policies against the Jews from both a chronological and a geographical perspective. Although his discussion of Jewish responses to the unfolding events has been a point of contention over the years, his explanation of the Nazi machinery of murder and the role played by Nazi Germany's allies, client states, puppet regimes, and collaborators in the destruction of the Jews is a masterpiece of historical research. Other significant comprehensive works include the very early books based on the Nuremberg trial documentation by Gerald Reitlinger, *The Final Solution* (1953, rev. ed. 1968), and Léon Poliakov, *Harvest of Hate* (1954). Lucy Dawidowicz's *The War against the Jews, 1933–1945* (1975) was written in part as a response to Hilberg, relying more heavily on Jewish sources. Leni Yahil, in *The Holocaust: The Fate of European Jewry* (1990), has tried to integrate the scholarship of the 1970s and 1980s into a one-volume history of the Holocaust.

Two very different types of comprehensive histories were also written in the latter half of the 1980s, and they too reflect newer scholarship. Michael Marrus's *The Holocaust in History* (1987) is a discussion of the historiography of the Holocaust. The four-volume *Encyclopedia of the Holocaust* (1990), edited by Israel Gutman, presents the history of the Holocaust topically, with approximately 1,000 entries of diverse size and scope. The encyclopedia has emerged as a central reference work for students of the subject.

A book that presents a broad history of the Holocaust through the eyes of witnesses to the event, and thereby straddles the line between documentation and historical narrative, is Martin Gilbert's *The Holocaust: A History of the Jews in Europe during the Second World War* (1986). Two textbooks by noted scholars may also be considered comprehensive histories of the Shoah: Yehuda Bauer, *A History of the Holocaust* (1982), and Israel Gutman and Chaim Shatzker, *The Holocaust and Its Significance* (1984).

One cannot divorce discussion of the Holocaust from its roots in modern antisemitism and racism. Books such as those by Shmuel Ettinger (in Hebrew); Jacob Katz, *From Prejudice to Destruction: Anti-Semitism, 1700–1933* (1980); and Léon Poliakov, including *The History of Anti-Semitism* (4 vols., 1965–85); James Parkes, including *Antisemitism* (1963); Paul W. Massing, *Rehearsal for Destruction: A Study of Political Anti-Semitism in Imperial Germany* (1949); and Norman Cohn, *Warrant for Genocide: The Myth of the Jewish World-Conspiracy and the Protocols of the Elders of Zion* (1967), are basic texts for the study of modern antisemitism. Studies of the history of racism, by such authors as George Mosse, *The Crisis in German Ideology* (1964) and *Toward the Final Solution: A History of European Racism* (1978), and Fritz Stern, *The Politics of Cultural Despair: A Study in the Rise of the Germanic Ideology* (1961), along with studies of antisemitism, cast much light on the genesis and nature of Nazi ideology and the acquiescence of so many people in the Nazi murder of the Jews.

Any discussion of how the Holocaust was possible and any assessment of the uniqueness of the Nazi attempt to destroy the Jews must address the role of Nazi ideology. A great many authors have written monographs about Nazi ideology or have addressed the issue at length within books on prominent Nazis, the Nazi state, or the development and implementation of Nazi anti-Jewish policies. One of the first studies of Nazi ideology is still meaningful today: Franz Neumann, *Behemoth: The Structure and Practice of National Socialism* (1942). The works of Karl Dietrich Bracher in German and English, especially *The German Dictatorship: The Origins, Structure and Effects of National Socialism* (1970), have contributed to our understanding of the nature of nazism, as have the works of Martin Broszat, Jeremy Noakes, and Robert Wistrich. An early study of the Nazi rise to power, which provides much insight into popular German support of the Nazis and their anti-Jewish program, is William Sheridan Allen, *The Nazi Seizure of Power: The Experience of a Single German Town* (1965; rev. ed. 1984). The classic biographies of Hitler—Alan Bullock, *Hitler: A Study in Tyranny* (1962); Joachim Fest, *Hitler* (1974); Ian Kershaw, *Hitler, 1889–1936: Hubris* (1998), *Hitler* (1991), and *The Nazi Dictatorship* (1985); and Eberhard Jaeckel, *Hitler's Weltanschauung: A Blueprint for Power* (1972) and *Hitler in History* (1984)—contain a great deal of information about Hitler's attitude toward and plans concerning the Jews. A very readable summary of Nazi ideology, based on secondary sources, is John Weiss, *Ideology of Death: Why the Holocaust Happened in Germany* (1996). Biographies of other Nazi leaders can not only elucidate the role of Nazi ideology in the activities of specific leaders but also make a pivotal contribution to the discussion of other central issues concerning the Holocaust. Richard Breitman's *The Architect of Genocide: Himmler and the Final Solution* (1991) is one of the most important studies about the genesis of the Final Solution and the first to make a strong case, on the basis of archival documents, for Hitler's deep involvement in all its phases.

Until the end of the 1990s the academic discussion about the course of Nazi anti-Jewish policy has focused on what has come to be known as the "intentionalist-functionalist" debate. Scholars who saw the policy that culminated in the Final Solution as having been conceived in its essential outlines early on by Hitler were pitted against those who saw it as having evolved gradually, through the active involvement of Hitler's lieutenants and under the influence of broader political events. Among the most influential studies of Nazi anti-Jewish policy to appear in English are those of Karl Schleunes, *The Twisted Road to Auschwitz* (1970); Christopher Browning, *Fateful Months: Essays on the Emergence of the Final Solution* (1985) and *The Path to Genocide: Essays on Launching the Final Solution* (1992); and David Cesarani, ed., *The Final Solution: Origins and Implementation* (1994), Henry Friedlander, *The Origins of Nazi Genocide from Euthanasia to the Final Solution* (1995), as well as the previously mentioned books by Ian Kershaw and Eberhard Jaeckel. At the end of the 1990s the research of Christian Gerlach showed even more clearly that Hitler ordered the overall destruction of European Jewry. His article in *European History*, "The Wannsee Conference, the Fate of German Jews and Hitler's Decision in Principle to Exterminate All European Jews" (1999), seems to have capped the debate.

Books about the SS and the nature of the perpetrators also provide valuable insights regarding the development of Nazi anti-Jewish policy and the motivation of those who implemented it. One of the most debated books on the subject, an outcome of the trial of Adolf Eichmann in Israel in 1961, is Hannah Arendt's *Eichmann in Jerusalem: A Report on the Banality of Evil* (1963). The historical basis for Arendt's thesis, which suggests that Nazi criminality is prosaic and not nearly as unique as some would assert, has been sharply challenged by historians over the years. Two early works of lasting importance about the SS, which spearheaded the destruction of European Jewry, are Helmut Krausnick, Martin Broszat, et al., *The*

Anatomy of the SS State (1968), and Heinz Hoehne, *The Order of the Death's Head: The Story of Hitler's SS* (1969). Gitta Sereny's books about two prominent Nazis—*Into That Darkness: From Mercy Killing to Mass Murder* (1974), about Franz Stangl, and *Albert Speer: His Battle with Truth* (1995)—discuss very different kinds of perpetrators. Stangl at different times ran the Sobibor and Treblinka extermination camps, and Speer, Hitler's architect who became minister of armaments, was responsible for bureaucratic directives that led to the deaths of thousands of slave laborers. Studies of different groups involved in the murder, such as the psychiatrist Robert Lifton's massive tome *The Nazi Doctors: Medical Killing and the Psychology of Genocide* (1986) and Christopher Browning's provocative study *Ordinary Men: Reserve Police Battalion 101 and the Final Solution in Poland* (1992), have shed light on the smaller cogs in the machinery of death. Browning in particular has argued that factors other than ideology were crucial for making men of the lower echelon into mass murderers. Another book concerned primarily with men of the middle and lower ranks, Ernst Klee, Willi Dressen, and Volker Riess, *The Good Old Days: The Holocaust as Seen by Its Perpetrators and Bystanders* (1991), uses the words of perpetrators and bystanders themselves to illuminate their actions. Daniel Jonah Goldhagen's *Hitler's Unwilling Executioners: Ordinary Germans and the Holocaust* (1996) caused quite a stir when it appeared, which led to several publications that dealt less with Goldhagen's central thesis that Germany was imbued with a kind of murderous antisemitism than with why the book engendered such a lively debate.

Several significant studies about the extermination camps and concentration camps have explored the heart of Nazi barbarism and the camp inmates' response to it. Early seminal studies about life in the Nazi camps and its effect on inmates that were written by former prisoners are Eugen Kogon, *The Theory and Practice of Hell: The German Concentration Camps and the System behind Them* (1950), and Viktor Frankl, *From Death Camp to Existentialism: A Psychiatrist's Path to a New Therapy* (1959; revised and reissued as *Man's Search for Meaning,* 1968). The scholarly study by Yitzhak Arad, *Belzec, Sobibor, Treblinka: The Operation Reinhard Extermination Camps* (1987), explores the workings of three extermination camps from the points of view of the Nazi murder machinery and of the Jewish response to it. Israel Gutman and Michael Berenbaum, eds., *Anatomy of the Auschwitz Death Camp* (1994), is the first scholarly study of the Auschwitz camp complex to examine the symbol of Nazi inhumanity from the angles of perpetrators, victims, and bystanders. The fourth Yad Vashem International Historical Conference on the Nazi camps, held in January 1980, attempted a broad assessment of the Nazi camp system; the papers presented there were published in Israel Gutman and Avital Saf, eds., *The Nazi Concentration Camps: Structure and Aim, the Image of the Prisoner, the Jews in the Camps* (1984). Although lacking solid historical analysis, Konnilyn Feig, *Hitler's Death Camps: The Sanity of Madness* (1981), presents much useful information about most of the more prominent Nazi camps. In his book *The Survivor: An Anatomy of Life in the Death Camps* (1976), Terrence Des Pres examines life in the camps through the eyes of the inmates. Des Pres's study was one of the first to use memoirs by survivors to paint a picture of the horror suffered by camp inmates. Using the tools of the sociologist, Wolfgang Sofsky's study *The Order of Terror: The Concentration Camp* (1997) provides useful insights about the social structure in the camps. From a very different direction, that of urban and regional planning, Debórah Dwork and Robert Jan van Pelt analyzed the creation and development of the Auschwitz-Birkenau camp in their treatise *Auschwitz: 1270 to the Present* (1996).

Many historians have sought to describe and analyze the course of the Holocaust in specific countries. Comprehensive works of this kind have not been published for all the countries of Europe, and of those that have been published not all have appeared in English. In part these gaps reflect problems regarding access to archival materials, as was (and to an extent continues to be) the case in many of the states of the former Communist bloc. The lack of comprehensive histories of the Holocaust in Poland and Germany perhaps reflects the enormous challenge in writing a broad history of the murderous assault on the Jews, the Jewish response to it, and the response of the bystanders in nations where the scope and depth of available source material is immense and where the core events of the Holocaust occurred.

Still, certain aspects of the destruction of Polish Jewry have been examined extensively. Isaiah Trunk's groundbreaking study of some 400 Jewish councils, *Judenrat: The Jewish Councils in Eastern Europe under Nazi Occupation* (1972), has done much to help students of the Holocaust see the official Jewish leadership of the period not in shades of black and white but in full color. Trunk also provides information about the destruction of many Jewish communities throughout greater Poland.

The activities of the Polish government-in-exile regarding the destruction of Polish Jewry have also generated much argument. Two carefully researched and clearly articulated volumes by David Engel, *In the Shadow of Auschwitz: The Polish Government-in-Exile and the Jews, 1939–1942* (1987) and *Facing a Holocaust: The Polish Government-in-Exile and the Jews, 1943–1945* (1993), discuss the factors that shaped that government's response to the persecution and subsequent murder of most of the Jews of Poland.

Among the most significant monographs concerning Polish Jewry during the Holocaust is Israel Gutman, *The Jews of Warsaw, 1939–1943: Ghetto, Underground, Revolt* (1982). Gutman's authoritative study focuses on the lives of the Jews in Europe's largest ghetto. Relying on a large body of documentary material, especially that which was collected by the underground *Oneg Shabbos* and diaries and memoirs of Jews who were in the ghetto, Gutman examines the range of responses by individuals, political groups, and institutions to the squalid, inhuman conditions in the ghetto and describes the brutal deportation drive to the Treblinka extermination camp in the summer of 1942. In particular, he investigates the genesis of the Warsaw ghetto uprising, explaining its timing and goals in addition to describing the course of the uprising itself.

Shmuel Krakowski, *The War of the Doomed: Jewish Armed Resistance in Poland, 1942–1944* (1984), probes one type of Jewish response—armed resistance. Krakowski not only discusses the ghetto revolts in Warsaw, Bialystok, and other Polish cities but also presents much information about Jewish partisans and the difficulties they faced in the Polish forests. Krakowski demonstrates that flight to the forests was essentially an act of desperation and, like the ghetto revolts, held out little hope for survival. Other important historical treatises about Poland during the Holocaust years have been published in Hebrew, Polish, and German by Daniel Blatman, Sarah Bender, Dieter Pohl, Teresa Prekerowa, Czeslaw Luczak, Czeslaw Madajczyk, and Jerzy Tomaszewski, among others.

Comprehensive histories of the Holocaust in the Baltic states, Belorussia, and Ukraine have yet to be published in English. Yitzhak Arad, *Ghetto in Flames: The Struggle and Destruction of the Jews of Vilna in the Holocaust* (1980), is a scholarly study concerned with the destruction of Vilna and the Jewish response to it. Dov Levin, *Fighting Back: Lithuanian Jewry's Armed Resistance to the Nazis, 1941–1945* (1985), takes a broader look at the Lithuanian Jewish response, but solely from the standpoint of armed resistance. Shalom Cholawski, *Soldiers from the Ghetto* (1980), examines Jewish armed resistance in the town of Nieswiez, Belorussia. No similar English-language monographs exist for Latvia or Estonia, but several important articles in English, Hebrew, and German have been written about the Holocaust in various Latvian and Estonian towns. Moreover, several consequential books in German discuss the murder of the Jews in those countries from the standpoint of the perpetrators; chief among them is the study by Helmut Krausnick and Hans Heinrich Wilhelm.

Except for the treatise by Shmuel Spector, *The Holocaust of Volhynian Jews, 1941–1944* (1990), no scholarly monograph about the Holocaust in Ukraine has appeared. Anatoly Kuznetsov, *Babi Yar* (1967), did much to raise public consciousness of the murder of the Jews of Kiev but does not purport to be an academic work. Another principal source of information for Ukraine and other parts of the former Soviet Union is Ilya Ehrenburg and Vasily Grossman, *The Black Book* (1981), essentially a compendium of contemporary accounts of the murder of Jews throughout these areas. Howard Aster, ed., *Ukrainian-Jewish Relations in Historical Perspective* (1988), issued by the Canadian Institute of Ukrainian Studies, examines Ukrainian-Jewish relations and includes material about the destruction of Ukrainian Jewry.

Documentary materials on the Holocaust in Western Europe have generally been more available to scholars than have materials in the East for France. One of the first books published that sought to analyze the role of Marshal Pétain's regime in the destruction of French Jewry was Michael Marrus and Robert Paxton, *Vichy France and the Jews* (1981). Susan Zuccotti's *The Holocaust, the French and the Jews* (1993), probes the plight of French Jewry during World War II from the perspective of perpetrators, bystanders, and victims. Both Richard Cohen, *The Burden of Conscience: French Jewish Leadership during the Holocaust* (1987), and Jacques Adler, *The Jews of Paris and the Final Solution: Communal Response and Internal Conflicts, 1940–1944* (1987), scrutinize the response of the French Jewish leadership. From a somewhat different viewpoint, Renée Poznanski published an extensive examination in French of what it was like to be a Jew in France during the Holocaust years. For Belgium, the papers presented at a conference were published in a volume edited by Dan Michman, *Belgium and the Holocaust: Jews, Belgians, and Germans* (1998). (No scholarly books have been devoted to the Holocaust in Luxembourg.)

The first treatment of the fate of Dutch Jewry during the Holocaust was written by Jacob Presser, *The Destruction of the Dutch Jews* (1969). A more scholarly but less well-rounded publication is G. Jan Colijn, ed., *The Netherlands and Nazi Genocide: Papers of the 21st Annual Scholars' Conference* (1992). The most important body of work about the Netherlands during World War II is contained in the many volumes published, primarily in Dutch, by Louis de Jong. This compendium divulges a great deal of information about the persecution of Dutch Jewry. Among de Jong's writings that have appeared in English is *The Netherlands and Nazi Germany* (1990). The numerous articles by Josef Melkman discuss specific central aspects of the Holocaust in the Netherlands, such as the nature of the Joodsche Raad, the Dutch Jewish council.

A small body of research has been published in English about the fate of the Jews of Scandinavia during the Holocaust. The Jews of Denmark and Finland survived the war nearly unscathed, as is shown by Leni Yahil, *The Rescue of Danish Jewry: Test of a Democracy* (1969), and Hannu Rautkallio, *Finland and the*

Holocaust: The Rescue of Finland's Jews (1987). Yahil posits that the Danish democratic tradition contributed greatly to the rescue there, whereas Rautkallio suggests that the lack of Finnish antisemitism led to the protection of most of that nation's small Jewish community. Samuel Abrahamsen, *Norway's Response to the Holocaust: A Historical Perspective* (1990), demonstrates that in Norway a tradition of humanism was pitted against antisemitism and xenophobia. On the one hand, this led to compliance and even cooperation by some Norwegians in the deportation of roughly half the small Jewish community, and on the other hand, it led to attempts by other Norwegians to rescue Jews. A comparative study of the war years in Norway and Denmark by Richard Petrow also contains much information about the fate of the Jews in those nations.

The list of published scholarly works about various aspects of Italian fascism and Italy during World War II is very long. Nevertheless, only a handful of studies focusing on the fortunes of Italian Jewry during the Holocaust have been published in English. The most well-rounded study of this subject is Susan Zuccotti, *The Italians and the Holocaust: Persecution, Rescue and Survival* (1987). In *Mussolini and the Jews: German-Italian Relations and the Jewish Question in Italy, 1922–1945* (1978), Meir Michaelis concentrates on what was done to the Jews and not on their response to the evolving situation. The highly regarded monograph by Daniel Carpi, *Between Mussolini and Hitler: The Jews and the Italian Authorities in France and Tunisia* (1994), along with Carpi's many articles in English and Hebrew, have also contributed greatly to the discussion of the relation between fascist Italy and the Jews.

The body of scholarship regarding the Balkans is uneven. No historical treatise about the Jews in wartime Romania has yet appeared in English, although Jean Ancel has published widely on the subject in Hebrew. Mark Mazower, *Inside Hitler's Greece: The Experience of Occupation, 1941–1944* (1993), sheds much light on Greece during the war, but a monograph on Greek Jewry during the Holocaust has yet to be published. Three books have been published in English about the fate of Bulgarian Jewry; the most scholarly of these is Frederick Chary, *The Bulgarian Jews and the Final Solution, 1940–1944* (1972). Michael Bar Zohar's *Beyond Hitler's Grasp: The Heroic Rescue of Bulgaria's Jews* (1998) has engendered renewed controversy about the role of King Boru in the destruction of the Jews of Thrace and Macedonia, as well as the rescue of the Jews of Bulgaria proper. A great number of publications have appeared about wartime Yugoslavia, especially about partisan fighting and the Croatian massacre of Serbs, but no broad study has yet been published in English about the fate of the Jews in the states that made up that country. In Hebrew, Menachem Shelah wrote a treatise about the Holocaust in Yugoslavia, and in Serbo-Croatian and German several monographs have appeared. An article by Christopher Browning, "The Final Solution in Serbia: The Semlin Judenlager, a Case Study," *Yad Vashem Studies* 15 (1983), remains one of the most important English-language sources about the murder of the Jews of Serbia.

Despite the legion of books that have appeared about Nazi Germany, no single comprehensive history of the German Jews during the war has been written. Marion A. Kaplan's *Between Dignity and Despair: Jewish Life in Nazi Germany* (1998) is the most serious contribution to date about the fate of German Jews under the Nazi regime. Saul Friedländer, in *Nazi Germany and the Jews: The Years of Persecution* (1997), has woven together the history of the persecution through 1939 and its effect on the Jews in a masterful fashion. Read together, these two books approach a comprehensive picture of the situation of German Jewry until the outbreak of the war. Most of the available scholarly material in English is contained in journal articles. Perhaps the richest source is *The Leo Baeck Institute Year Book,* published since 1956. Among the more highly regarded books in English about German Jewry before the advent of the Nazi state are Peter Pulzer, *Jews and the German State: The Political History of a Minority, 1848–1933* (1992); Monika Richarz, ed., *Jewish Life in Germany: Memoirs from Three Centuries* (1991); Werner Eugene Mosse, *The German-Jewish Economic Elite, 1820–1935: A Socio-Cultural Profile* (1989) and *Jews in the German Economy: The German-Jewish Economic Elite, 1820–1935* (1987); the books by George Mosse, among them *German Jews beyond Judaism* (1985); the works of Jehuda Reinharz, *Fatherland or Promised Land: The Dilemma of the German Jew, 1893–1914* (1975) and, with Walter Schatzberg, ed., *The Jewish Response to German Culture: From the Enlightenment to the Second World War* (1985); Peter Gay, *Freud, Jews and Other Germans: Masters and Victims in Modernist Culture* (1978); Stephen Poppel, *Zionism in Germany, 1897–1933: The Shaping of Jewish Identity* (1977); Uriel Tal, *Christians and Jews in Germany* (1975); Ismar Schorsch, *Jewish Reactions to German Anti-Semitism, 1870–1914* (1972); and Donald Niewyk, *The Jews in Weimar Germany* (1980).

There are virtually no scholarly treatises in English about German Jewry during the Nazi era that are not concerned principally with the development and implementation of Nazi anti-Jewish policy. Among the few studies that view Jews primarily as subjects and not objects are: Avraham Barkai, *From Boycott to Annihilation: The Economic Struggle of German Jews, 1933–1943* (1989); Leonard Baker, *Days of Sorrow, Days of Pain: Leo Baeck and the Berlin Jews* (1978); and Werner Angress, *Between Fear and Hope: Jewish Youth in the Third Reich* (1988). The anthology by Otto Dov Kulka and Paul Mendes-Flohr, eds., *Judaism and Christianity under the Impact of National Socialism, 1919–1945* (1987), presents much material about the relationship between Jews and Christians throughout Nazi-dominated Europe, including Germany itself. The Jewish press in Nazi Germany is the subject of a dissertation by Jacob Boas (University of Michigan, 1977). The posthumous publication of the research of Avraham Margaliot in Hebrew is a singular examination of the response of German Jews to the unfolding events of the Holocaust. The many articles by Herbert Strauss in English and German are also an invaluable source for information on German Jewry under the Nazi regime.

Because the destruction of the Jews in Hungary took place in the last year of the war, it has been the focus of attention from scholars interested particularly in the Allied response to the Holocaust. Moreover, the story of the Swedish diplomat Raoul Wallenberg, who saved thousands of Hungarian Jews, has captured the imagination of many writers and led to examinations of the rescue activities of the neutral diplomats in Budapest. One of the most thorough studies of the Holocaust in a single country is Randolph Braham, *The Politics of Genocide: The Holocaust in Hungary* (1981; rev. ed. 1994). In two dense volumes Braham explores the events of the Holocaust in Hungary from the perspectives of internal Hungarian politics, Hungarian-German and Hungarian-Jewish relations, the Jewish response, and rescue activities. The monograph by Asher Cohen, *The Hehalutz Resistance in Hungary, 1942–1944* (1986), focuses on the Jewish response to the Holocaust in Hungary, supplementing Braham's original research in this area. Nathaniel Katzburg, *Hungary and the Jews, 1920–1943* (1981), is primarily concerned with Hungarian attitudes toward the Jewish community and the actions taken against Jews in the period before the destruction of Hungarian Jewry reached full force. Several conferences were held in 1994 to mark the fiftieth anniversary of the destruction of Hungarian Jews. Two significant publications which resulted from them were David Cesarani, ed., *Genocide and Rescue, the Holocaust and Hungary* (1997), and Randolph L. Braham, ed., *The Nazi's Last Victims: The Holocaust in Hungary* (1998). In addition to these books, significant articles have been published about the Holocaust in Hungary by Zvi Erez, Sari Reuveni, Livia Rothkirchen, Robert Rozett, Maria Schmidt, and Bela Vago.

The only comprehensive history of Slovak Jewry during the Holocaust was published in German by Ladislav Lipscher, *Die Juden im slowakischen Staat: 1939–1945* (1980). An abridged version of his research constitutes a chapter in *The Jews of Czechoslovakia: Historical Studies and Surveys* (3 vols., 1968–84), which also contains useful articles by Livia Rothkirchen, Erich Kulka, Avigdor Dagan, and others about the background and destruction of the Jews of former Czechoslovakia. A collection of articles about the destruction of Slovak Jewry, which presents a great deal of data about the subject, is Dezider Toth, ed., *Tragedia slovenskych zidov: materialy z medzinarodneho sympozia, Banska Bystrica, 25–27 marca 1992* (The Tragedy of Slovak Jews: Proceedings of the International Symposium, Banska Bystrica, 25–27 March 1992). Significant information about Jewish response in Slovakia, especially the semi-underground Working Group, can be found in the biographies of two of the de facto leaders of Slovak Jewry during the Holocaust, Rabbi Michael Dov Ber Weissmandel (Abraham Fuchs's *The Unheeded Cry* [1984]) and Rabbi Armin Frieder (Emanuel Frieder, *To Deliver Their Souls: The Struggle of a Young Rabbi during the Holocaust* [1987]). Several important background studies about Slovak Jewry were published in English and Hebrew by Yeshayahu Jelinek, and perhaps the best study to date about the Jewish response in Slovakia was published in Hebrew by Gila Fatran, concentrating on the Slovak Jewish leadership. The articles by Yehoshua Büchler, and especially his German-language booklet, *Kurze Übersicht der Jüdischen Geschichte in dem Gebiet Slowakei* (1982), also constitute a noteworthy source of information about Slovak Jewry.

Except for the three-volume *Jews of Czechoslovakia*, no scholarly study about the Jews of the present area of the Czech Republic has been published in English. Books about the Theresienstadt ghetto generally contain substantial material about Czech Jewry during the Holocaust, but most of the works about the ghetto have been published in German and Czech. Perhaps the best-known English-language study about the ghetto is Ruth Bondy, *"Elder of Jews": Jacob Edelstein of Theresienstadt* (1989). An important source for the Holocaust in the Czech Republic and Slovakia are the articles published by Livia Rothkirchen, including "Czech Attitudes toward the Jews during the Nazi Regime," *Yad Vashem Studies* (1979), and "The Situation of the Jews in Slovakia between 1939 and 1945," *Jahrbuch für Antisemitismusforschung* (1998).

Over the years, a number of broader historical issues regarding the Holocaust have come to the fore: the debate about the development of the Final Solution; the Jewish response to the Holocaust; and the responses of the Allies and various institutions to Nazi persecution of the Jews.

Among the earliest attempts to deal objectively with the Jewish response were the Yad Vashem conferences, the proceedings of which were subsequently published by Yad Vashem: *Jewish Resistance to the Holocaust* (1968), *Rescue Attempts during the Holocaust* (1977), and *Patterns of Jewish Leadership in Nazi Europe, 1939–1945* (1979). Also noteworthy are several books by Yehuda Bauer: *Jews For Sale? Nazi-Jewish Negotiations, 1933–1945* (1994); *The Jewish Emergence from Powerlessness* (1979); *The Holocaust in Historical Perspective* (1978); and *American Jewry and the Holocaust: The American Joint Distribution Committee,*

1939–1945 (1981). The phenomenon of family camps, partisan units that included children as well as non-combatant men and women, was a distinctly Jewish response to Nazi persecution. In *Defiance: The Bielski Partisans* (1993), Nechama Tec explores the history of the largest family camp.

The responses of the Allies and various institutions to Nazi persecution of the Jews have been examined from many angles. Henry Feingold, *The Politics of Rescue: The Roosevelt Administration and the Holocaust* (1970), and David Wyman, *Paper Walls: America and the Refugee Crisis, 1938–1941* (1968) and *The Abandonment of the Jews: America and the Holocaust* (1984), investigate the attitude and actions of the U.S. government in light of Nazi anti-Jewish measures. Both authors, basing their works on massive primary source material, try to explain the factors that colored the government's response and offer biting critiques of that response. In a similar vein, Judith Tydor Baumel, *Unfulfilled Promise: Rescue and Resettlement of Jewish Children in the United States, 1934–1945* (1990), focuses attention on an especially morally charged aspect of U.S. refugee policy. An analysis of the complex interplay between principal personalities, the workings of the American bureaucracy, and institutional priorities is set forth in Richard Breitman and Alan Kraut, *American Refugee Policy and European Jewry, 1933–1945* (1987).

The responses of the governments of Canada and Britain have also been the subject of research and intense criticism. The Canadian government is scrutinized by Irving Abella and Harold Troper, *None Is Too Many: Canada and the Jews of Europe, 1933–1948* (1982). The title of that book succinctly sums up the attitude of the Canadian government to the problem of Jewish refugees. Bernard Wasserstein, *Britain and the Jews of Europe, 1939–1945* (1979), probes the many factors that deterred the British government from providing greater refuge for the persecuted Jews of the Continent, whether in Great Britain or in its colonies, especially Palestine. In his monograph *The British Government and the Holocaust: The Failure of Anglo-Jewish Leadership* (1999), Meier Sompolinsky highlights the valiant yet mostly futile rescue efforts of the leaders of Great Britain's Jewish community. A less critical but still imporant early study of British refugee policy is A. J. Sherman, *Island Refuge: Britain and Refugees from the Third Reich, 1933–1939* (1973). Focusing more closely on Britain and Palestine are Michael Cohen, *Palestine, Retreat from the Mandate: the Making of British Policy, 1936–1945* (1978), and Ronald Zweig, *Britain and Palestine during the Second World War* (1986). Written from the point of view of those who sought to flee to Palestine, and from the standpoint of those who tried to facilitate that flight, is Dalia Ofer, *Escaping the Holocaust: Illegal Immigration to the Land of Israel, 1939–1944* (1990). Yet another perspective, that of Nazi Germany's attitude toward the creation of a Jewish homeland in Palestine, is clarified in Francis Nicosia, *The Third Reich and the Palestine Question* (1985). Tony Kushner, *The Holocaust and the Liberal Imagination: A Social and Cultural History* (1994), explores the impact of the unfolding Holocaust and its aftermath on Western society, especially in Britain, seeking not to condemn but to explain society's responses.

American and British responses, both from government and from the public, to growing evidence during the war that the Jews of Europe were being systematically murdered have been the subject of numerous books. Walter Laqueur, *The Terrible Secret: Suppression of the Truth about Hitler's "Final Solution"* (1980), Martin Gilbert, *Auschwitz and the Allies* (1981), and Deborah Lipstadt, *Beyond Belief: The American Press and the Coming of the Holocaust* (1986), explore from somewhat different viewpoints how information reached the Western world and how the Allied nations reacted to it.

Most of the literature about the response of the Jews of Palestine to the Holocaust is in Hebrew. The primary work in English is Dina Porat, *The Blue and the Yellow Stars of David: The Zionist Leadership in Palestine and the Holocaust, 1939–1945* (1990). Porat explains many of the conditions that made effective intervention on behalf of the European Jews difficult and hence compounded the Jewish tragedy of the war years.

Several scholars have examined the attitude of the neutral countries of Europe toward Jewish refugees before the outbreak of war and their role in the rescue of Jews during the war. Steven Koblik, *The Stones Cry Out: Sweden's Response to the Persecution of the Jews, 1933–1945* (1988), shows how Swedish policies changed from pro-Nazi to pro-Allies over the course of the war, and how Sweden gradually became more inclined to provide aid to Jews. The study of Swiss policy toward the persecuted Jews has accelerated in recent years, especially with the works of Jacques Picard, Dominique Ferrero, Stefan Keller, and Yaacov Tanner, which have not appeared in English. A highly critical account of Swiss policy toward Jewish refugees is Alfred A. Häsler, *The Lifeboat Is Full: Switzerland and the Refugees, 1933–1945* (1969), which contains no citations of primary source material. At the end of the 1990s the issue of the fate of Jewish property and money, especially that which reached Switzerland, was examined in many publications, mostly not by scholars. Among the more controversial publications is the book by Jean Ziegler, *The Swiss, the Gold and the Dead: How Swiss Bankers Helped Finance the Nazi War Machine* (1998). See also Jean-François Bergier, *Switzerland and Refugees in the Nazi Era* (1999).

Not only the governments of the West but also some of Western society's central institutions have been scrutinized by historians. The laden issue of the Vatican's response came to the fore in a play by Rolf Hochhuth, *The Deputy* (1964). The role of the Vatican subsequently received more scholarly treatment in Saul Friedländer, *Pius XII and the Third Reich: A Documentation* (1966), John Morley, *Vatican Diplomacy and the Jews during the Holocaust, 1939–1943* (1980), and John Cornwell, *Hitler's Pope* (1999).

The subject of the International Red Cross is touched upon in many books concerning the Allied response, but only two monographs about the organization's activities have been published, primarily owing to difficulty in obtaining documentary material from Red Cross archives. The single scholarly study of the Red Cross throughout Europe during the Holocaust years is in French: Jean-Claude Favez, *Une Mission Impossible? Le CICR, les Déportations et les Camps de Concentration Nazis* (1988). In English, a study of its activities in Budapest was written by Arieh Ben-Tov, *Facing a Holocaust in Budapest: The International Committee of the Red Cross and the Jews in Hungary, 1943–1945* (1988).

Rescue not only by institutions but also by individuals, including many people later awarded the title of Righteous Among the Nations by Yad Vashem, has also been considered by several scholars. This body of literature generally straddles the line between history, sociology, and psychology and includes the often-cited works of Nechama Tec, *When Light Pierced the Darkness: Christian Rescue of Jews in Nazi-Occupied Poland* (1986); Samuel Oliner, *The Altruistic Personality: Rescuers of Jews in Nazi Europe* (1988); Eva Fogelman, *Conscience and Courage: Rescuers of Jews during the Holocaust* (1994); and Mordecai Paldiel, *The Path of the Righteous: Gentile Rescuers of Jews during the Holocaust* (1993).

More than 300 diaries kept by Jews during the Holocaust had been published as of 1999, more than 80 of them in English. These diaries not only comprise a rich source of documentary evidence but also provide an unparalleled view of the state of mind of Jews in the ghettos and camps of Nazi-dominated Europe. The most widely read, unquestionably, is *The Diary of Anne Frank* (1947), which is often the first encounter young readers have with the Holocaust. Other lesser-known but no less potent diaries include *The Diary of Eva Heyman* (1974); *The Warsaw Diary of Adam Czerniakow* (1979); *Scroll of Agony: The Warsaw Diary of Chaim Kaplan* (1965); *Notes from the Warsaw Ghetto: The Journal of Emmanuel Ringelblum* (1958); *The Terezin Diary of Gonda Redlich* (1992); Avraham Tory, *Surviving the Holocaust: The Kovno Ghetto Diary* (1990); Etty Hillesum, *Etty: A Diary, 1941–1943* (1983); and Philip Mechanicus, *Waiting for Death: A Diary* (1968).

According to the Yad Vashem Library, some 3,000 memoirs in many languages have been published by Jews who either survived the camps or managed to escape from the Nazis. These works include some of the most eloquent and heartrending accounts of the Holocaust, among them Elie Wiesel, *Night* (1960); Primo Levi, *Survival in Auschwitz: The Nazi Assault on Humanity* (1961); Fania Fénélon, *The Musicians of Auschwitz* (1977); Saul Friedländer, *When Memory Comes* (1979); David Rousset, *The Other Kingdom* (1947); Yitzhak Zuckerman, *A Surplus of Memory: Chronicle of the Warsaw Ghetto Uprising* (1993); Thomas Geve, *Youth in Chains* (1958); Kitty Hart, *I Am Alive* (1961); Filip Müller, *Auschwitz Inferno: The Testimony of a Sonderkommando* (1979); and Miklos Nyiszli, *Auschwitz: A Doctor's Eyewitness Account* (1960). Both Charlotte Delbo and Olga Lengyel published fascinating memoirs of the camps from the point of view of Christian inmates.

Lawrence Langer has asserted that until the Holocaust, writers relied on their imagination to create a literature of atrocity, but after it, reality surpassed anything the human mind could invent. The body of fiction, poetry, and plays on the theme of the Holocaust is vast. It ranges from novels by Holocaust survivors such as Elie Wiesel, *The Accident* (1968), *Dawn* (1961), *The Gates of the Forest* (1966), and *The Fifth Son* (1985), and Primo Levi, *If Not Now, When?* (1985); to novels and short stories by non-Jewish former camp inmates like Tadeusz Borowski, *This Way to the Gas, Ladies and Gentlemen* (1967), and Jewish survivors like Ida Fink, *The Journey* (1992) and *A Scrap of Time and Other Stories* (1987); to poems by poets who did not go through the Holocaust but identified with it intensely, including Sylvia Plath, *Crossing the Water* (1971) and *Winter Trees* (1971). Distinguished authors including Aharon Appelfeld, *Unto the Soul* (1994), *The Age of Wonders* (1981), *The Immortal Bartfuss* (1988), and *Katerina* (1992); Louis Begley, *The Man Who Was Late* (1993) and *Wartime Lies* (1991); Saul Bellow, *Mr. Sammler's Planet* (1970); John Hersey, *The Wall* (1950); Ka-tzetnik, *House of Dolls* (1956); and George Steiner, *The Portage to San Cristobal of A. H.* (1981) have found among the Holocaust's victims, perpetrators, and bystanders the characters for their novels, and among the torments of the Shoah they have found their themes. Highly regarded poets like Paul Celan, Dan Pagis, Nelly Sachs, and Abraham Sutzkever have crafted compelling verse that emanates from reflection on the terrible events of the period.

The analysis of the arts steeped in the Holocaust has generated its own body of scholarship. Among the most thoughtful studies are Alvin Rosenfeld, *A Double Dying: Reflections on Holocaust Literature* (1980); David Roskies, *Against the Apocalypse: Responses to Catastrophe in Modern Jewish Culture* (1984), Sidra DeKoven Ezrahi, *By Words Alone: The Holocaust in Literature* (1980); George Steiner, *Language and Silence: Essays, 1958–1966* (1967); James E. Young, *Writing and Re-Writing the Holocaust: Narrative and the Consequences of Interpretation* (1988), and *The Texture of Memory: Holocaust Memorials and Their Meaning* (1993); Ziva Amishai-Maisels, *Depiction and Interpretation: The Influence of the Holocaust on the Visual Arts* (1993); Joza Karas, *Music in Terezin, 1941–1945* (1985); and Gila Flam, *Singing for Survival: Songs of the Lodz Ghetto* (1992).

Some of the best minds of the second half of the twentieth century have reflected on the philosophical reverberations of the Holocaust. Much of this discourse has found expression in historical studies, literature, and literary criticism, and many of the authors already cited have made incisive contributions to this discussion. Especially noteworthy are the books of Lawrence Langer, *The Holocaust and the Literary Imagination* (1975), *Versions of Survival: The Holocaust and the Human Spirit* (1982), *Holocaust Testimonies: The Ruins of Memory* (1991), *Admitting the Holocaust: Collected Essays* (1995), and *Preempting the Holocaust* (1998). Langer's investigation of the nature of memories of the Holocaust leads him to a profound articulation of the horror and blackness at the core of the tragedy. Saul Friedländer, *Memory, History and the Extermination of the Jews of Europe* (1993), reflects on the relationship between private memory, collective memory, and historiography of the Holocaust. On a somewhat different level of philosophical reflection, Steven Katz, *The Holocaust in Historical Context* (vol. 1, 1993), examines the historical basis for asserting the uniqueness of the Holocaust and makes a strong case for its singularity.

In the aftermath of the Holocaust, theologians of Western religions have probed religious literature and their own souls for insight into God's role in history, the nature of free will, the human capacity for evil, and divine punishment. From the point of view of Jewish civilization, Arthur A. Cohen, *The Tremendum: A Theological Interpretation of the Holocaust* (1981), seeks to create a new language with which to grapple with the cataclysmic break that he sees as the essence of the Holocaust. Emil Fackenheim, in his works *God's Presence in History: Jewish Affirmations and Philosophical Reflections* (1970), *The Jewish Return to History: Reflections in the Age of Auschwitz and the New Jerusalem* (1978), *The Jewish Thought of Emil Fackenheim, A Reader* (1987), and *To Mend the World: Foundations of Post-Holocaust Jewish Thought* (1989), asserts that Jews must not give Hitler a posthumous victory by disappearing as a people through assimilation. Eliezer Berkovits, *Faith after the Holocaust* (1973) and *With God in Hell: Judaism in the Ghettos and the Death Camps* (1979), looks for motifs in Jewish practice and belief that help resolve the dilemma posed by the existence of Auschwitz in a world created by God, including the tradition of *hester panim*, the hiding of God's face from humankind. Richard Rubenstein, especially in *After Auschwitz: Radical Theology and Contemporary Judaism* (1966), takes a revolutionary approach that is antithetical to the positions of Fackenheim and Berkovits. Rubenstein believes God was not present in Auschwitz, and thus it is up to all of us to imbue life with meaning and up to Jews to find a path to their renewal. Two substantial studies that attempt to analyze this evolving Jewish thought are Eliezer Schweid, *Wrestling until Daybreak: Searching for Meaning in the Thinking of the Holocaust* (1994), and Steven Katz, *Post-Holocaust Dialogues: Critical Studies in Modern Jewish Thought* (1983). Not only Jewish theologians and philosophers have grappled with the implications of the Holocaust. A number of Christian thinkers, including Franklin Littell, Harry James Cargas, A. Roy Eckardt, and Alice Eckardt, have contemplated the nature of Christianity in its wake.

Despite massive documentary evidence of the murder of millions of Jews by the Nazis, there continue to be people who vehemently deny that the Holocaust occurred. Several thoughtful books trace the history of Holocaust denial and refute the deniers' arguments: among the best are Deborah Lipstadt, *Denying the Holocaust: The Growing Assault on Truth and Memory* (1994), and Pierre Vidal-Naquet, *Assassins of Memory: Essays on the Denial of the Holocaust* (1992).

The postwar trials of Nazi war criminals and the search for Nazi perpetrators in hiding have led to studies of the victors' attitude toward war criminals and to memoirs by those who have hunted fugitives from justice. Among these fascinating accounts of the capture and trial of such fugitives are Telford Taylor, *The Anatomy of the Nuremberg Trials: A Personal Memoir* (1992); Gustave Mark Gilbert, *Nuremberg Diary* (1947); Simon Wiesenthal, *The Murderers among Us* (1967); Isser Harel, *The House on Garibaldi Street* (1976); Allan Ryan, *Quiet Neighbors: Prosecuting Nazi War Criminals in America* (1984); Alain Finkielkraut, *Remembering in Vain: The Klaus Barbie Trial and Crimes against Humanity* (1992); and Efraim Zuroff, *Occupation, Nazi-Hunter: The Continuing Search for the Perpetrators of the Holocaust* (1994).

It is virtually impossible to determine accurately the quantity of documents about the Holocaust that exist in the world. Yad Vashem, the largest archive on the subject, estimated that as of 1999 it held some 50 million documents, which represent about one-third of the material that will eventually reside there. Published document collections, although a mere drop in the bucket beside this ocean of material, are also extensive. Scholars such as Yitzhak Arad, Randolph Braham, John Conway, Lucy Dawidowicz, Tuvia Friedman, Israel Gutman, Raul Hilberg, Avraham Margaliot, John Mendelsohn, George Mosse, and David Wyman have edited significant collections in English, in addition to the published documents from the International Military Tribunal at Nuremberg and subsequent Allied trials, photo albums, and books of survivors' testimonies.

In addition to the books cited above, thousands of important articles have been written about the Holocaust. Often these articles are the only scholarly study of a particular aspect of Shoah history. Several academic journals are devoted to the study of the Holocaust, and many more frequently contain articles about the subject. The two most important ongoing journals in English are *Yad Vashem Studies* and *Holocaust and Genocide Studies.* Other current publications devoted primarily to the Holocaust are *The Journal of Holocaust Education* and *Dimensions.* Journals that have been discontinued but whose back issues still illuminate the subject of the Holocaust include *The Simon Wiesenthal Center Annual, Shoah, Yad Vashem Bulletin,* and *The Wiener Library Bulletin.* Other historical journals contain considerable information about the Holocaust in English, among them *Studies in Contemporary Jewry, The Leo Baeck Institute Year Book, Patterns of Prejudice, History and Memory, Polin, Jewish Social Studies,* the recently resurrected *YIVO Annual, German History,* and the major American Jewish periodicals *Midstream, Moment, Jewish Spectator, Commentary,* and *Tikkun.* Many significant articles related to the Holocaust have also been published in academic journals dealing with broader subjects, such as psychology, sociology, literature, regional or ethnic studies, and religion.

A number of Web sites have also been created to aid researchers in the Holocaust. Although some of these have been short-lived (About.com's excellent Holocaust page has disappeared), two of the best English-language sites are Yahoo's Holocaust directory (http://dir.yahoo.com/Arts/Humanities/History/By_Time_Period/20th_Century/Holocaust_The/), which links to more than 100 Web sites, and the ultimate Holocaust links site, Nizkor (http://www.nizkor.org/). Articles and documents on Jewish history, including many pages devoted to the Holocaust, can be found at the Jewish Student Online Research Center (http://www.us-israel.org/jsource/). Yahoo and other search engines will guide readers to sites on specific topics, such as sites devoted to particular camps and nationalities. Among the best of these sites is one (http://holocaustsurvivors.org/) that includes photo and audio galleries.

Many Holocaust museums and memorials maintain Web sites. In particular, the U.S. Holocaust Memorial Museum Web site (http://www.ushmm.org) allows access to thousands of photographs in the museum's collection and provides up-to-date material on restitution of assets. Yad Vashem's Web site (http://www.yad-vashem.org.il), which includes a bibliography, timeline, and FAQs page, is an excellent resource for basic information about the Holocaust. The online Museum of Tolerance and Multimedia Learning Center of the Simon Wiesenthal Center in Los Angeles (http://www.wiesenthal.com/) provides access to articles from *The Encyclopedia of the Holocaust* (ed. Gutman), Holocaust bibliographies, FAQs, "virtual exhibits," and teaching resources. One of the largest repositories of testimonies by Holocaust survivors is the Fortunoff Video Archive for Holocaust Testimonies at Yale University. Excerpts from its collection of more than 4,000 videotaped interviews with witnesses and survivors of the Holocaust are available online (http://www.library.yale.edu./testimonies/).

The Web Genocide Documentation Centre (http://www.ess.uwe.ac.uk/genocide.htm), compiled by Stuart Stein at the University of the West of England (Bristol), includes many useful pages devoted to the Holocaust, in particular "Appropriation of Assets and Labour by the Third Reich," profiles of major figures in the Third Reich, an "explanatory" timeline of the "Destruction of European Jewry," a glossary of terms relating to the Third Reich and World War II, and a page of links to primary Holocaust sources on the Web.

Despite this compendium of material, there are many aspects of the Holocaust that have yet to be researched, and significant works that have yet to be translated into English. It is clear that in much of the world the Holocaust has entered popular consciousness to such a degree that exploration of its history, discussion of its ramifications, and its expression through art will continue for some time to come. More books will undoubtedly be published that will merit addition to a core bibliography on the subject, and new authors will add insights that may increase our understanding of an event that most of the Western world has come to regard as a fearful, haunting milestone in human history.   *Robert Rozett*

Contributors

SHLOMO ARONSON is professor of political science at the Hebrew University of Jerusalem.

HAIM AVNI is head of the Division for Latin America, Spain, and Portugal of the Avraham Harman Institute of Contemporary Jewry at the Hebrew University of Jerusalem.

DAVID BANKIER is professor of contemporary Jewry at the Hebrew University of Jerusalem.

STEVEN I. BASKIN is team leader of biochemical toxicology, pharmacology division, and principal investigator with the U.S. Army Medical Research Institute of Chemical Defense.

JUDITH TYDOR BAUMEL teaches modern Jewish history at Bar-Ilan University, Ramat Gan, Israel.

AVI BEKER is executive director of the World Jewish Congress in Israel.

WOLFGANG BENZ is professor of modern history at the Technical University of Berlin and director of the Center for Research on Antisemitism.

MICHAEL BERENBAUM is adjunct professor of theology at the University of Judaism, Los Angeles, former director of the U.S. Holocaust Research Institute, and former president of the Survivors of the Shoah Visual History Foundation.

RUTH BONDY is a writer and historian of the Czech Jews during the Holocaust.

STEVEN B. BOWMAN is a professor of Judaic studies at the University of Cincinnati.

RICHARD BREITMAN is professor of history at American University, and editor-in-chief of *Holocaust and Genocide Studies* at the U.S. Holocaust Memorial Museum.

MICHAEL BRENNER is professor of Jewish history and culture at the University of Munich.

MOOLI BROG is a doctoral student at the Hebrew University in Jerusalem.

CHRISTOPHER R. BROWNING is Frank Porter Graham Professor of History at the University of North Carolina, Chapel Hill.

ABRAHAM BRUMBERG is a political scientist specializing in Russian, East European, and Jewish studies.

MICHAEL BURLEIGH is professor of history at Washington and Lee University.

DANIEL CARPI is professor emeritus of modern history at Tel Aviv University.

DAVID CESARANI is Parkes-Wiener Professor of Twentieth-Century European Jewish History and Culture at Southampton University and director of the Institute of Contemporary History and Wiener Library, London.

YEHOYAKIM COCHAVI is senior teacher and researcher at the Zivia and Yizhak Zuckerman Study Center, Ghetto Fighters' House, Western Galilee.

ASHER COHEN was before his death professor of history at the University of Haifa.

MICHAEL COHEN is a professor in the department of general history, Middle East studies, and American studies at Bar-Ilan University, Ramat Gan, Israel.

WILLIAM B. COHEN is professor of history at Indiana University.

JOHN S. CONWAY is professor emeritus of history at the University of British Columbia.

ANNEGRET EHMANN is executive director of RAA Brandenburg e.V. at Potsdam-Regional Centers for Intercultural Understanding, Education and Schools in the State of Brandenburg.

DAVID ENGEL is Skirball Professor of Modern Jewish History at New York University and a fellow of the Diaspora Research Institute at Tel Aviv University.

HAVA ESHKOLI-WAGMAN is a senior researcher and lecturer at the Finkler Institute for Holocaust Research at Bar-Ilan University, Ramat Gan, and at Levinsky College for Education, Tel Aviv.

HENRY L. FEINGOLD is professor emeritus of American Jewish history and Holocaust studies at Baruch College, City University of New York.

CHARLES FENYVESI is a senior writer with Radio Free Europe / Radio Liberty.

RONIT FISHER is a doctoral student at the University of Haifa and works in the education division of the Ghetto Fighters' House in Western Galilee.

JOHN P. FOX has taught in the department of Hebrew and Jewish studies at University College, London, and at the former Jews College, London.

DANIEL FRAENKEL is editor of the *Yad Vashem Encyclopaedia of the Jewish Communities* in Germany and fellow of the International School for Holocaust Studies at Yad Vashem.

HENRY FRIEDLANDER is professor of Judiac studies at Brooklyn College, City University of New York.

SAUL FRIEDLÄNDER is professor of history at the University of California, Los Angeles, and at Tel Aviv University.

JOHN GARRARD is professor of Russian literature at the University of Arizona.

DICK GEARY is professor of modern history at the University of Nottingham, England.

YOAV GELBER is professor of history and head of the Herzl Institute for Research and Studies of Zionism, University of Haifa.

GÜNTER GRAU is a historian at the Institute of the History of Medicine at Charité Hospital, Humboldt University, Berlin.

LAWRENCE GRAVER is J. H. Roberts Professor of English Emeritus at Williams College.

GERSHON GREENBERG is a research fellow for the Finkler Institute for Holocaust Research, Bar-Ilan University, Ramat Gan, Israel.

ROGER GREENSPUN has taught film history and criticism at Rutgers University and at Columbia University and written extensively on film for the *New York Times, Film Comment,* and other publications.

GIDEON GREIF is a researcher and lecturer at Yad Vashem, Jerusalem.

NAOMI GROSSMAN is a lecturer and researcher in Yad Vashem, Givatayim, Israel.

ISRAEL GUTMAN is professor emeritus at the Hebrew University of Jerusalem and chief historian of Yad Vashem, Jerusalem.

GASTON HAAS is a former editor at Swiss Radio.

MICHAEL HAGEMEISTER is a lecturer at the Lotman Institute for Russian and Soviet Culture at the University of Bochum, Germany.

AVIVA HALAMISH is on the staff of the department of history at the Open University of Israel.

RAUL HILBERG is professor emeritus of political science at the University of Vermont.

RADU IOANID is associate director, International Programs Division, U.S. Holocaust Memorial Museum.

YESHAYAHU A. JELINEK is associate professor of history (retired) at Ben-Gurion University of the Negev, Israel.

PER OLE JOHANSEN is professor in criminology at Oslo University.

KAROL JONCA is professor of law at Wroclaw University, chair of political and legal doctrines, and a corresponding member of the Polish Academy of Sciences.

SARA KADOSH is the director of the Archives of the American Jewish Joint Distribution Committee in Jerusalem.

NILI KEREN is chair of the history department and head of the Holocaust Resource Center at Kibbutzim College of Education in Tel Aviv.

HANS KIRCHHOFF is professor of contemporary history at the University of Copenhagen.

STEVEN KOBLIK is president of Reed College.

SHMUEL KRAKOWSKI is the former director of the Yad Vashem Archives and connected with the International School for Holocaust Studies, Yad Vashem, Jerusalem.

MATTHIAS KRÖN is a former researcher at the Leo Baeck Institute in New York.

DOV LEVIN is professor and head of the Oral History Division in the Institute of Contemporary Jewry at the Hebrew University, Jerusalem.

WALTER LAQUEUR is the co-chairman of the International Research Council of the Center for Strategic and International Studies, Washington, D.C., university professor emeritus at Georgetown University, director emeritus of the Wiener Library and the Institute of Contemporary History, London, and founder and co-editor of the *Journal of Contemporary History*.

PETER LONGERICH is reader at Royal Holloway College, University of London.

MICHAEL R. MARRUS is professor of history and the dean of the graduate school at the University of Toronto.

DAVID MELTSER holds a doctorate in history from Minsk University, Belarus, and is currently an independent scholar living in New York.

DAN MICHMAN is professor of Jewish history, Bar-Ilan University, Ramat Gan, Israel.

SYBIL MILTON is vice-president of the Independent Commission of Experts: Switzerland–World War II, and an independent historian and exhibition consultant.

DALIA OFER is affiliated with the Institute of Contemporary Jewry, the Hebrew University, Jerusalem.

STANLEY PAYNE is professor of history at the University of Wisconsin, Madison.

ANTONY POLONSKY is Albert Abramson Chair of Holocaust Studies at Brandeis University.

DINA PORAT is head of the Stephen Roth Institute for the Study of Contemporary Anti-Semitism and Racism and holds the Alfred P. Slaner Chair for the Study of Racism and Anti-Semitism at Tel Aviv University.

RENÉE POZNANSKI is professor of contemporary history at Ben-Gurion University of the Negev, Israel.

PETER PULZER is Gladstone Professor of Government Emeritus, All Souls College, University of Oxford.

GERHART M. RIEGNER is a representative of the World Jewish Congress in Switzerland.

RINAT-YA GORODNZIK ROBINSON is affiliated with the Institute of Contemporary Jewry at the Hebrew University of Jerusalem.

HERBERT ROSENKRANZ is senior researcher emeritus at Yad Vashem, Jerusalem.

LIVIA ROTHKIRCHEN is the former editor of *Yad Vashem Studies* (1967–1984).

ROBERT ROZETT is director of the Yad Vashem Library, Jerusalem.

JOSHUA RUBENSTEIN is the Northeast Regional Director of Amnesty International USA and an associate of the Davis Center for Russian Studies at Harvard University.

BARRY RUBIN is a professor at Bar-Ilan University, Ramat Gan, Israel.

HAIM SAADOUN is dean of students at the Open University of Israel.

CHAIM SCHATZKER is professor emeritus of Jewish history at the University of Haifa.

SHLOMO SHEALTIEL is director of the Yad Yaari Documentation and Research Center of Hashomer Hatzair, Givat Haviva, Israel.

JÜRGEN SVENSSON is professor of English at the University of Umeå.

NECHAMA TEC is professor of sociology at the University of Connecticut, Stamford.

SHABTAI TEVETH is senior fellow at the Moshe Dayan Center for Middle Eastern and African Studies, Tel Aviv University.

SAMUEL TOTTEN is professor of curriculum and instruction in the College of Education and Health Professions, University of Arkansas.

ELI TZUR teaches history at Seminar Hakibutzim Teaching College in Tel Aviv and heads the Youth Movements Research Institute at Givat Haviva.

MICHAL UNGER is a historian at Yad Vashem, Jerusalem, and teaches history at Ashkelon Regional College, Israel.

WERNER WARMBRUNN is professor emeritus of history at Pitzer College, Claremont, California.

DAVID WEINBERG is director of the Cohn-Haddow Center for Judaic Studies and professor of history at Wayne State University.

YECHIAM WEITZ is senior lecturer in the Eretz-Israel studies department at the University of Haifa.

MICHAEL WINES is a correspondent with the Moscow bureau of the *New York Times*.

ROBERT S. WISTRICH is the Erich and Foga Neuberger Professor of Modern Jewish History at the Hebrew University of Jerusalem.

HANNA YABLONKA is senior lecturer in the department of history at Ben Gurion University of the Negev, Israel.

JAMES E. YOUNG is professor and chairman of the Judaic studies department and professor of English at the University of Massachusetts, Amherst.

PAUL ZAWADZKI is professor of political philosophy and sociology at the Paris 1 (Pantheon), the Sorbonne.

RONALD ZWEIG is senior lecturer in Jewish history at Tel Aviv University.

Credits

Adam Kaczkowski's Photographs

In the early 1960s, Adam Kaczkowski, an independent Polish art photographer, was given the assignment to photograph "camps." But when he got in the staff car, instead of the children's summer camps he expected to visit, the chauffeur took him to the Museum of Auschwitz. Moved by the ruins of this most infamous of extermination camps, Kaczkowski began a 10-year photographic tour of first the major, and then all the extermination and concentration camps of Poland, eventually publishing a selection of his many thousands of negatives as *Bramy Tragedii* (The Gates of Tragedy, 3d ed. 1989). Kaczkowski's photographs that appear in this encyclopedia, drawn from that book and from his personal collection, testify to the perishable memorials but enduring memory of the Holocaust. Adam Kaczkowski passed away in 1995. We thank his son, Piotr Kaczkowski, for permission to reprint the pictures here.

Archival Photographs

Page

ii   Israeli worker with a camp number tatooed on his arm, 1956. Herbert Sonnenfeld, from the Herbert and Leni
       Sonnenfeld Archive

4   Courtesy of USHMM Photo Archives

12   AP / Wide World Photos

17   AP / Wide World Photos

21   AP / Wide World Photos

23   Musée Juif de Belgique, Brussels

24   AP / Wide World Photos

27   Courtesy of Jozef Szajna

28   Courtesy of the Leo Baeck Institute, New York

30   Courtesy of the Leo Baeck Institute, New York

32   Courtesy of the Leo Baeck Institute, New York

33   Copyright Ullstein Bilderdienst, photo courtesy of USHMM Photo Archives

34   Yad Vashem Photo Archives, courtesy of USHMM Photo Archives

35   Glowna Komisja Badania Zbrodni Przeciwko Narodowi Polskiemu, courtesy of USHMM Photo Archives

36   Yad Vashem Photo Archives, courtesy of USHMM Photo Archives

38   Bundesarchiv, Koblenz

40   Archiwum Panstwowego Muzeum w Oswiecimiu-Brzezince, courtesy of USHMM Photo Archives

41   National Museum of Auschwitz-Birkenau, courtesy of USHMM Photo Archives

42   (top) Yad Vashem Photo Archives, courtesy of USHMM Photo Archives

42   (bottom) Yad Vashem Photo Archives, courtesy of USHMM Photo Archives

45   Dokumentationsarchiv des Österreichischen Widerstandes, courtesy of USHMM Photo Archives

46   Österreichische Gesellschaft für Zeitgeschichte, courtesy of USHMM Photo Archives

47   AP / Wide World Photos

51   Leni Sonnenfeld, from the Herbert and Leni Sonnenfeld Archive

52   National Archives, courtesy of USHMM Photo Archives

53   Avraham Tory, courtesy of USHMM Photo Archives

54   Central State Archive of Film, Photo and Phonographic Documents, courtesy of USHMM Photo Archives

55   Avraham Tory, courtesy of USHMM Photo Archives

56   AP / Wide World Photos

57   Belgian Radio and TV

63   Bundesarchiv, Koblenz

65   Glowna Komisja Badania Zbrodni Przeciwko Narodowi Polskiemu, courtesy of USHMM Photo Archives

66   Alice Lev, courtesy of USHMM Photo Archives

67   AP / Wide World Photos

69   Herbert Sonnenfeld, from the Herbert and Leni Sonnenfeld Archive

73   The Jacob Rader Marcus Center of the American Jewish Archives, courtesy of USHMM Photo Archives

76   Bildarchiv Preussischer Kulturbesitz, Berlin

77   Jerzy Tomaszewski, courtesy of USHMM Photo Archives

79   AP / Wide World Photos

80   Bildarchiv Preussischer Kulturbesitz, Berlin

82   National Archives, courtesy of USHMM Photo Archives

83   Zydowski Instytut Historyczny Instytut Naukowo-Badawczy, courtesy of USHMM Photo Archives

85   (top) The Jacob Rader Marcus Center of the American Jewish Archives, courtesy of USHMM Photo Archives

222	Courtesy of the Simon Wiesenthal Center, Museum of Tolerance, Los Angeles
227	Glowna Komisja Badania Zbrodni Przeciwko Narodowi Polskiemu, courtesy of USHMM Photo Archives
237	Glowna Komisja Badania Zbrodni Przeciwko Narodowi Polskiemu, courtesy of USHMM Photo Archives
243	Herbert Sonnenfeld, from the Herbert and Leni Sonnenfeld Archive
244	Herbert Sonnenfeld, from the Herbert and Leni Sonnenfeld Archive
245	Gift of Ursula Eisner Nathan, Museum of Jewish Heritage, New York
248	Herbert Sonnenfeld, from the Herbert and Leni Sonnenfeld Archive
250	George Fogelson, courtesy of USHMM Photo Archives
251	YIVO Institute for Jewish Research, courtesy of USHMM Photo Archives
257	Michael Hofmekler, courtesy of USHMM Photo Archives
259	Courtesy of the Simon Wiesenthal Center, Museum of Tolerance, Los Angeles
263	Bundesarchiv, Koblenz
265	(top) AP / Wide World Photos
265	(bottom) AP / Wide World Photos
266	YIVO Institute for Jewish Research, courtesy of USHMM Photo Archives
271	(left) Yad Vashem Photo Archives, courtesy of USHMM Photo Archives
271	(right) Keystone / Paris
272	Hanna Meyer-Moses, courtesy of USHMM Photo Archives
273	Bundesarchiv, courtesy of USHMM Photo Archives
275	Photo courtesy of the Simon Wiesenthal Center, Museum of Tolerance, Los Angeles
280	Photo courtesy of the Simon Wiesenthal Center, Museum of Tolerance, Los Angeles
283	Lottie Kohler, courtesy of USHMM Photo Archives
286	Photo courtesy of the Simon Wiesenthal Center, Museum of Tolerance, Los Angeles
292	AP / Wide World Photos
302	(left) AP / Wide World Photos
302	(right) AP / Wide World Photos
313	Schwules Museum, courtesy of USHMM Photo Archives
316	Photo: Sandor Ek, courtesy of USHMM Photo Archives
319	Hans Kobi, Switzerland
320	Magyar Nemzeti Muzeum Torteneti Fenykeptar, courtesy of USHMM Photo Archives
323	Glowna Komisja Badania Zbrodni Przeciwko Narodowi Polskiemu, courtesy of USHMM Photo Archives
326	Dokumentationsarchiv des Österreichischen Widerstandes, courtesy of USHMM Photo Archives
329	Courtesy of USHMM Photo Archives
334	Courtesy of Publifoto, Rome
335	YIVO Institute for Jewish Research, courtesy of USHMM Photo Archives
344	Beth Hatefutsoth Photo Archive, courtesy of Yair Hendl, Israel
346	State Archives of the Russian Federation, courtesy of USHMM Photo Archives
347	Martin Tillmans, courtesy of USHMM Photo Archives
350	YIVO Institute for Jewish Research, courtesy of USHMM Photo Archives
352	YIVO Institute for Jewish Research, courtesy of USHMM Photo Archives
355	AP / Wide World Photos
357	Archives of the State Museum in Oswiecim, courtesy of the Simon Wiesenthal Center, Museum of Tolerance, Los Angeles
359	AP / Wide World Photos
360	Leni Sonnenfeld, from the Herbert and Leni Sonnenfeld Archive
362	Norman and Amalia Petranker Salsitz, courtesy of USHMM Photo Archives
363	Leni Sonnenfeld, from the Herbert and Leni Sonnenfeld Archive

366   Leni Sonnenfeld, from the Herbert and Leni Sonnenfeld Archive

369   American Jewish Joint Distribution Committee, courtesy of USHMM Photo Archives

371   Bildarchiv Preussischer Kulturbesitz, Berlin

374   Photo: Zvi Kadushin (Beth Hatefutsoth Photo Archive, Zvi Kadushin Collection)

380   K-Z Gedenkstätte Neuengamme, courtesy of USHMM Photo Archives

381   Yad Vashem Photo Archives, courtesy of USHMM Photo Archives

382   Hashomer Hatzair and Moreshet Archives, courtesy of USHMM Photo Archives

383   Werkarchiv Westermann

384   George Kadish, courtesy of USHMM Photo Archives

385   Hadassah Rosensaft, courtesy of USHMM Photo Archives

386   Stadtmuseum Baden-Baden, courtesy of USHMM Photo Archives

388   Nederlands Instituut voor Oorlogsdocumentatie, courtesy of USHMM Photo Archives

389   AP/Wide World Photos

390   Lydia Chagoll, courtesy of USHMM Photo Archives

396   Copyright ©1986 by Art Spiegelman. Reprinted by permission of Pantheon Books, a division of Random House, Inc.

398   Beit Lohamei Haghetaot, courtesy of USHMM Photo Archives

400   Zydowski Instytut Historyczny Instytut Naukowo-Badawczy, courtesy of USHMM Photo Archives

401   YIVO Institute for Jewish Research, courtesy of USHMM Photo Archives

403   Beit Lohamei Haghetaot, courtesy of USHMM Photo Archives

404   Photo: Hilmar Pabel, Ullstein Bilderdienst/YIVO Institute for Jewish Research

409   Archiwum Panstwowego Muzeum na Majdanku, courtesy of USHMM Photo Archives

410   Photo: Sam Gilbert, T4c, National Archives and Records Administration

411   Whitney Gardner, courtesy of USHMM Photo Archives

413   Yad Vashem Photo Archives, courtesy of USHMM Photo Archives

415   Hadassah Rosensaft, courtesy of USHMM Photo Archives

418   Robert Seibel, courtesy of USHMM Photo Archives

421   Bayerische Staatsbibliothek München

422   National Archives, courtesy of USHMM Photo Archives

428   Courtesy of the Simon Wiesenthal Center, Museum of Tolerance, Los Angeles

429   Herbert Sonnenfeld, from the Herbert and Leni Sonnenfeld Archive

431   Imperial War Museum Photograph Archive, London

434   AP/Wide World Photos

438   Nederlands Instituut voor Oorlogsdocumentatie, courtesy of USHMM Photo Archives

439   Nederlands Instituut voor Oorlogsdocumentatie, courtesy of USHMM Photo Archives

440   Nederlands Instituut voor Oorlogsdocumentatie, courtesy of USHMM Photo Archives

441   Verzetsmuseum Amsterdam

443   National Archives, courtesy of USHMM Photo Archives

444   Courtesy of USHMM Photo Archives

447   Leni Sonnenfeld, from the Herbert and Leni Sonnenfeld Archive

450   Photo: Walter Frenz/Odd V. Aspheim

451   AP/Wide World Photos

452   Niedersächsisches Staatsarchiv

454   Bilderdienst Süddeutscher Verlag, Munich

458   Herbert Sonnenfeld, from the Herbert and Leni Sonnenfeld Archive

470   Israel Government Press Office, courtesy of USHMM Photo Archives

471   Bibliothèque Historique de la Ville de Paris, courtesy of USHMM Photo Archives

626   Leni Sonnenfeld, from the Herbert and Leni Sonnenfeld Archive

633   Terezin Memorial Museum, courtesy of USHMM Photo Archives

634   Courtesy of the Simon Wiesenthal Center, Museum of Tolerance, Los Angeles

637   Yad Vashem Photo Archives, courtesy of USHMM Photo Archives

640   From Eugen Kogon, Hermann Langbein, and Adalbert Rückerl, *Nazi Mass Murder: A Documentary History of the Use of Poison Gas* (New Haven: Yale University Press, 1993), 240–41

647   Hessisches Hauptstaatsarchiv Wiesbaden, courtesy of USHMM Photo Archives

650   Hessisches Hauptstaatsarchiv Wiesbaden, courtesy of USHMM Photo Archives

651   Dokumentationsarchiv des Österreichischen Widerstandes, courtesy of USHMM Photo Archives

658   USHMM Photo Archives

665   Vitka Kempner Kovner, courtesy of USHMM Photo Archives

666   George Kadish, courtesy of USHMM Photo Archives

670   Ferenc Flamm, courtesy of USHMM Photo Archives

672   Thomas Veres, courtesy of USHMM Photo Archives

674   National Archives, courtesy of USHMM Photo Archives

677   National Archives, courtesy of USHMM Photo Archives

679   AP / Wide World Photos

684   YIVO Institute for Jewish Research, courtesy of USHMM Photo Archives

689   Yad Vashem Photo Archives, courtesy of USHMM Photo Archives

691   YIVO Institute for Jewish Research, courtesy of USHMM Photo Archives

693   National Archives, courtesy of USHMM Photo Archives

695   Yad Vashem Photo Archives, courtesy of USHMM Photo Archives

699   Yad Vashem Photo Archives, Jerusalem

702   Jabotinsky Institute, courtesy of USHMM Photo Archives

707   Muzej Revolucije Narodnosti Jugoslavije, courtesy of USHMM Photo Archives

708   Jewish Historical Museum of Yugoslavia, courtesy of USHMM Photo Archives

710   Jewish Historical Museum of Yugoslavia, courtesy of USHMM Photo Archives

715   Zydowski Instytut Historyczny Instytut Naukowo-Badawczy, courtesy of USHMM Photo Archives

717   Central Armed Forces Museum, courtesy of USHMM Photo Archives

720   Israeli veterans, 1956. Leni Sonnenfeld, from the Herbert and Leni Sonnenfeld Archive

Poems

On page 397, three lines from Paul Celan's "Death Tango [Deathfugue]," trans. John Felstiner, are reprinted from John Felstiner, *Paul Celan: Poet, Survivor, Jew* (New Haven: Yale University Press, 1995), 31, by permission of Yale University; seven lines from Nelly Sachs's "O the Chimneys" and four lines from her "Chorus of the Rescued," trans. Michael Roloff, are reprinted from Nelly Sachs, *O the Chimneys: Selected Poems, Including the Verse Play ELI*, trans. Michael Roloff and others, pp. 3 and 25, translation copyright © 1967, renewed 1995 by Farrar, Straus & Giroux, Inc., by permission of Farrar, Straus & Giroux LLC and Suhrkamp Verlag; and six lines from Dan Pagis's "Written in Pencil in a Sealed Railway Car," trans. Stephen Mitchell, from Dan Pagis, *Selected Poems*, trans. Stephen Mitchell (South Hinksey, Oxford: Carcanet Press, 1972), by permission of Carcanet Press Ltd.

Index